UNITED KINGDOM   Butterworth & Co (Publishers) Ltd,
                  88 Kingsway, **London** WC2B 6AB and
                  61A North Castle Street, **Edinburgh** EH2 3LJ

AUSTRALIA   Butterworths Pty Ltd, **Sydney, Melbourne,
                  Brisbane, Adelaide, Perth, Canberra**
                  and **Hobart**

CANADA   Butterworths. A division of Reed Inc, **Toronto** and **Vancouver**

NEW ZEALAND   Butterworths of New Zealand Ltd, **Wellington** and **Auckland**

SINGAPORE   Butterworth & Co (Asia) Pte Ltd, **Singapore**

SOUTH AFRICA   Butterworth Publishers (Pty) Ltd, **Durban** and **Pretoria**

USA   Butterworth Legal Publishers, **Seattle**, Washington,
                  Boston, Massachusetts, **Austin**, Texas and
                  St Paul, Minnesota
                  D & S Publishers, **Clearwater**, Florida

ISBN 0 406 85160 3

Typeset by CCC, printed and bound in Great Britain by William Clowes Limited, Beccles and London

THE
ALL ENGLAND
LAW REPORTS
1986

Volume 3

Editor
PETER HUTCHESSON LL M
Barrister, New Zealand

Assistant Editor
BROOK WATSON
of Lincoln's Inn, Barrister
and of the New South Wales Bar

Consulting Editor
WENDY SHOCKETT
of Gray's Inn, Barrister

London
BUTTERWORTHS

REPORTERS

House of Lords

Mary Rose Plummer Barrister

Privy Council

Mary Rose Plummer Barrister

Court of Appeal, Civil Division

Mary Rose Plummer Barrister
Frances Rustin Barrister
Diana Procter Barrister
Carolyn Toulmin Barrister

Wendy Shockett Barrister
Patricia Hargrove Barrister
Sophie Craven Barrister
Celia Fox Barrister

Court of Appeal, Criminal Division

N P Metcalfe Esq Barrister
June Meader Barrister
Raina Levy Barrister

Dilys Tausz Barrister
Marc Beaumont Esq Barrister
Michael Wall Esq Barrister

Chancery Division

Jacqueline Metcalfe Barrister
Evelyn M C Budd Barrister

Hazel Hartman Barrister
Vivian Horvath Barrister

Queen's Bench Division

M Denise Chorlton Barrister   J M Collins Esq Barrister
K Mydeen Esq Barrister

Family Division

Bebe Chua Barrister

Admiralty

N P Metcalfe Esq Barrister

Revenue Cases

Rengan Krishnan Esq Barrister

Courts-Martial Appeals

N P Metcalfe Esq Barrister

SUB-EDITORS

Radhika Edwards Barrister
Emma Majdalany

MANAGER

Eric W Spalding Esq

House of Lords

The Lord High Chancellor: Lord Hailsham of St Marylebone

Lords of Appeal in Ordinary

Lord Keith of Kinkel
Lord Bridge of Harwich
Lord Brandon of Oakbrook
Lord Brightman
Lord Templeman

Lord Griffiths
Lord Mackay of Clashfern
Lord Ackner
Lord Oliver of Aylmerton
Lord Goff of Chieveley

Court of Appeal

The Lord High Chancellor

The Lord Chief Justice of England: Lord Lane
(President of the Criminal Division)

The Master of the Rolls: Sir John Francis Donaldson
(President of the Civil Division)

The President of the Family Division: Sir John Lewis Arnold

The Vice-Chancellor: Sir Nicolas Christopher Henry Browne-Wilkinson

Lords Justices of Appeal

Sir Frederick Horace Lawton
    (retired 21 December 1986)
Sir Tasker Watkins VC
Sir Patrick McCarthy O'Connor
Sir Michael John Fox
Sir Michael Robert Emanuel Kerr
Sir John Douglas May
Sir Christopher John Slade
Sir Francis Brooks Purchas
Sir George Brian Hugh Dillon
Sir Stephen Brown
Sir Roger Jocelyn Parker
Sir David Powell Croom-Johnson

Sir Anthony John Leslie Lloyd
Sir Brian Thomas Neill
Sir Michael John Mustill
Sir Martin Charles Nourse
Sir Iain Derek Laing Glidewell
Sir Alfred John Balcombe
Sir Ralph Brian Gibson
Sir John Dexter Stocker
Sir Harry Kenneth Woolf
Sir Donald James Nicholls
Sir Thomas Henry Bingham
    (appointed 30 September 1986)

Chancery Division

The Lord High Chancellor

The Vice-Chancellor

Sir John Norman Keates Whitford
Sir Raymond Henry Walton
Sir John Evelyn Vinelott
Sir Douglas William Falconer
Sir Jean-Pierre Frank Eugene Warner
Sir Peter Leslie Gibson

Sir David Herbert Mervyn Davies
Sir Jeremiah LeRoy Harman
Sir Richard Rashleigh Folliott Scott
Sir Leonard Hubert Hoffmann
Sir John Leonard Knox
Sir Peter Julian Millett

Queen's Bench Division

The Lord Chief Justice of England

Sir Bernard Caulfield
Sir William Lloyd Mars-Jones
Sir Leslie Kenneth Edward Boreham
Sir Alfred William Michael Davies
Sir Kenneth George Illtyd Jones
Sir Haydn Tudor Evans
Sir Peter Richard Pain
Sir Kenneth Graham Jupp
Sir Walter Derek Thornley Hodgson
Sir Frederick Maurice Drake
Sir Barry Cross Sheen
Sir David Bruce McNeill
Sir Christopher James Saunders French
Sir Thomas Patrick Russell
Sir Peter Edlin Webster
Sir Thomas Henry Bingham
   (appointed Lord Justice of Appeal,
   30 September 1986)
Sir Peter Murray Taylor
Sir Murray Stuart-Smith
Sir Christopher Stephen Thomas Jonathan
   Thayer Staughton
Sir Donald Henry Farquharson
Sir Anthony James Denys McCowan
Sir Iain Charles Robert McCullough
Sir Hamilton John Leonard
Sir Alexander Roy Asplan Beldam
Sir David Cozens-Hardy Hirst
Sir John Stewart Hobhouse

Sir Michael Mann
Sir Andrew Peter Leggatt
Sir Michael Patrick Nolan
Sir Oliver Bury Popplewell
Sir William Alan Macpherson
Sir Philip Howard Otton
Sir Paul Joseph Morrow Kennedy
Sir Michael Hutchison
Sir Simon Denis Brown
Sir Anthony Howell Meurig Evans
Sir Mark Oliver Saville
Sir Johan Steyn
Sir Christopher Dudley Roger Rose
Sir Richard Howard Tucker
Sir Robert Alexander Gatehouse
Sir Patrick Neville Garland
Sir John Ormond Roch
Sir Michael John Turner
Sir Harry Henry Ognall
Sir John Downes Alliott
Sir Konrad Hermann Theodor Schiemann
Sir John Arthur Dalziel Owen
Sir Denis Robert Maurice Henry
Sir Francis Humphrey Potts
   (appointed 30 September 1986)
Sir Richard George Rougier
   (appointed 30 September 1986)
Sir Ian Alexander Kennedy
   (appointed 30 September 1986)

Family Division

The President of the Family Division

Sir John Brinsmead Latey
Sir Alfred Kenneth Hollings
Sir Charles Trevor Reeve
Dame Rose Heilbron
Sir Brian Drex Bush
Sir John Kember Wood
Sir Ronald Gough Waterhouse
Sir John Gervase Kensington Sheldon

Sir Thomas Michael Eastham
Dame Margaret Myfanwy Wood Booth
Sir Anthony Leslie Julian Lincoln
Dame Ann Elizabeth Oldfield Butler-Sloss
Sir Anthony Bruce Ewbank
Sir John Douglas Waite
Sir Anthony Barnard Hollis
Sir Swinton Barclay Thomas

CITATION

These reports are cited thus:

[1986] 2 All ER

REFERENCES

These reports contain references to the following major works of legal reference described in the manner indicated below.

Halsbury's Laws of England

The reference 26 Halsbury's Laws (4th edn) para 577 refers to paragraph 577 on page 296 of volume 26 of the fourth edition of Halsbury's Laws of England.

Halsbury's Statutes of England and Wales

The reference 4 Halsbury's Statutes (4th edn) 105 refers to page 105 of volume 4 of the fourth edition of Halsbury's Statutes of England and Wales, and the reference 39 Halsbury's Statutes (3rd edn) 895 refers to page 895 of volume 39 of the third edition of Halsbury's Statutes of England.

The Digest

References are to the green band reissue volumes of The Digest (formerly the English and Empire Digest).

The reference 36(2) Digest (Reissue) 764, *1398* refers to case number 1398 on page 764 of Digest Green Band Reissue Volume 36(2).

Halsbury's Statutory Instruments

The reference 17 Halsbury's Statutory Instruments (4th reissue) 256 refers to page 256 of the fourth reissue of volume 17 of Halsbury's Statutory Instruments; references to other reissues are similar.

Cases reported in volume 3

Digest of cases reported in volume 3

House of Lords petitions

This list, which covers the period 16 August to 10 December 1986, sets out all cases which have formed the subject of a report in the All England Law Reports in which an Appeal Committee of the House of Lords has, subsequent to the publication of that report, dismissed a petition for leave to appeal either on a perusal of the papers or after an oral hearing. Where the result of a petition for leave to appeal was known prior to the publication of the relevant report a note of that result appears at the end of the report.

Damon Cia Naviera SA v Hapag-Lloyd International SA, The Blankenstein, The Bartenstein, The Birkenstein [1985] 1 All ER 475, CA. Petition for leave to appeal dismissed for want of prosecution 9 October 1986 (Lord Keith, Lord Templeman and Lord Griffiths) (perusal of papers)

Muirhead v Industrial Tank Specialities Ltd [1985] 3 All ER 705, CA. Leave to appeal refused 6 November 1986 (Lord Keith, Lord Templeman and Lord Griffiths) (oral hearing)

R v Central Criminal Court, ex p Raymond [1986] 2 All ER 379, DC. Leave to appeal refused 25 November 1986 (Lord Bridge, Lord Griffiths and Lord Mackay) (oral hearing)

R v Waltham Forest Justices , ex p Solanke [1986] 2 All ER 981, CA. Petition for leave to appeal dismissed 2 December 1986 (Lord Bridge, Lord Brandon and Lord Griffiths) (perusal of papers)

CORRIGENDUM

[1986] 2 All ER

p 958. **Scottish Special Housing Association v Wimpey Construction UK Ltd.** Counsel for the appellants should read '*John Blackburn QC* and *M G Clarke* (of the Scottish Bar)'.

R v Nedrick

COURT OF APPEAL, CRIMINAL DIVISION
LORD LANE CJ, LEGGATT AND KENNEDY JJ
20 MAY, 10 JULY 1986

c *Criminal law – Murder – Intent – Intent proved by reference to foreseeability of consequences – Distinction between motive and intent – Intent inferred from foresight of consequences – Appropriate direction to jury.*

d The appellant, after threatening to burn out a woman against whom he bore a grudge, poured paraffin through the letter box of her house and set it alight. The woman's child died in the resulting fire and the appellant was charged with murder. He confessed to starting the fire but claimed that he had merely wanted to frighten the woman and did not want anyone to die. At his trial the judge directed the jury that if the accused knew that it was highly probable that his act would result in serious bodily injury to someone inside the house he was guilty of murder. The appellant was convicted. He appealed on the ground that the judge had misdirected the jury.

e **Held** – In regard to the mental element in murder a jury were merely required to determine whether, having regard to all the circumstances, including what he said and did, the defendant intended to kill or do serious bodily harm. It followed that the judge's direction was wrong because it equated foresight with intent, whereas foresight of consequences could only be evidence of intent to commit murder. The appeal would f therefore be allowed and a conviction of manslaughter substituted (see p 3 *a* to *c*, post).

R v Moloney [1985] 1 All ER 1025 and *R v Hancock* [1986] 1 All ER 641 applied.

Per curiam. Where a defendant does an act which is manifestly dangerous and which results in the death of someone else but the primary desire or motive of the defendant was not to harm that person or anyone else, the appropriate direction to the jury is, first, to explain that a man may intend to achieve a certain result while at the same time not g desiring it to come about, and then to suggest that the jury determine (a) how probable was the consequence which resulted from the defendant's act and (b) whether he foresaw that consequence. If he did not appreciate that death or serious harm was likely to result from his act, he cannot have intended to bring it about; if he did appreciate that death or serious injury might result but thought the risk was only slight the jury could easily conclude that he did not intend to bring about the result; if he recognised that death or h serious harm were virtually certain to result from his act, barring some unforeseen intervention, the jury could easily infer that he intended to kill or do serious bodily harm even though he may not have had any desire to do so. The jury should therefore be further directed that they are not entitled to infer the necessary intention unless they feel sure that death or serious bodily harm was a virtually certain result of the defendant's action (barring some unforeseen intervention) and that the defendant appreciated that j fact (see p 3 *e h* to p 4 *c*, post).

Notes

For the mental element in murder and other crimes of specific intent, see 11 Halsbury's Laws (4th edn) paras 15–16, 360, 1157, and for cases on the subject, see 15 Digest (Reissue) 1109–1111, 9313–9338.

Cases referred to in judgment
R v Hancock [1986] 1 All ER 641, [1986] AC 455, [1986] 2 WLR 357, HL.   *a*
R v Moloney [1985] 1 All ER 1025, [1985] AC 905, [1985] 2 WLR 648, HL.

Case also cited
Hyam v DPP [1974] 2 All ER 41, [1975] AC 55, HL.

Appeal against conviction   *b*
Ransford Delroy Nedrick appealed against his conviction of murder in the Crown Court
at Stafford before Otton J and a jury on 25 January 1985. The facts are set out in the
judgment of the court.

Lord Hooson QC and David Guishard (both assigned by the Registrar of Criminal Appeals)
    for the appellant.   *c*
Stephen Coward QC and Brian Leech for the Crown.

At the conclusion of the argument the court announced that the appeal against conviction
of murder would be allowed and a verdict of manslaughter substituted for reasons to be
given later.
          d
10 July. The following judgment of the court was delivered.

LORD LANE CJ. On 25 January 1985 in the Crown Court at Stafford the appellant,
was convicted by a majority verdict of murder and was sentenced to life imprisonment.
The jury were discharged from returning verdicts on two further counts, one of arson
with intent to endanger life and the other of arson being reckless as to life being   *e*
endangered.
    On 20 May 1986, having declined to apply the proviso, we substituted for the verdict
of murder a verdict of guilty of manslaughter and passed therefor a sentence of 15 years'
imprisonment under the provisions of s 3 of the Criminal Appeal Act 1968. We now
give our reasons.
    The case for the Crown was that the appellant had a grudge against a woman called   *f*
Viola Foreshaw, as a result of which, after threats that he would 'burn her out', he went
to her house in the early hours of 15 July 1984, poured paraffin through the letter box
and onto the front door and set it alight. He gave no warning. The house was burnt
down and one of Viola Foreshaw's children, a boy aged 12 called Lloyd, died of
asphyxiation and burns.
    After a number of interviews during which he denied any responsibility, the appellant   *g*
eventually confessed to the police that he had started the fire in the manner described,
adding, 'I didn't want anyone to die, I am not a murderer; please tell the judge; God
knows I am not a murderer.' When asked why he did it, he replied, 'Just to wake her up
and frighten her.'
    The appellant's defence, rejected by the jury, was that he had neither started the fire
nor made any admissions to that effect.   *h*
    The sole effective ground of appeal is that the judge misdirected the jury on the intent
necessary to establish a charge of murder. This is the direction which he gave:

        'It is not necessary to prove an intention to kill; the Crown's case is made out if
    they prove an intention to cause serious injury, that is sufficient ... There is,
    however, an alternative state of mind which you will have to consider. If, when the   *j*
    accused performed the act of setting fire to the house, he knew that it was highly
    probable that the act would result in serious bodily injury to somebody inside the
    house, even though he did not desire it, desire to bring that result about, he is guilty
    of murder. If you are sure that he did the unlawful and deliberate act, and if you are
    sure that that was his state of mind, then, again, the prosecution's case in the
    alternative of murder would be established.'

The direction was given before the publication of the speeches in the House of Lords
a in *R v Moloney* [1985] 1 All ER 1025, [1985] AC 905 and *R v Hancock* [1986] 1 All ER
641, [1986] AC 455. In the light of those speeches it was plainly wrong. The direction
was based on a passage in *Archbold's Pleading Evidence and Practice in Criminal Cases* (41st
edn, 1982) p 994, para 17-13 which has been repeated in the 42nd edn (1985) para 17-13.
That passage was expressly disapproved in *R v Moloney* [1985] 1 All ER 1025 at 1036,
[1985] AC 905 at 925–926, in that it equates foresight with intention, whereas 'foresight
b of consequences, as an element bearing on the issue of intention in murder . . . belongs
not to the substantive law but to the law of evidence' (see [1985] 1 All ER 1025 at 1038,
[1985] AC 905 at 928 per Lord Bridge). The judge was in no way to blame of course for
having directed the jury in this way.

What then do a jury have to decide so far as the mental element in murder is
concerned? They simply have to decide whether the defendant intended to kill or do
c serious bodily harm. In order to reach that decision the jury must pay regard to all the
relevant circumstances, including what the defendant himself said and did.

In the great majority of cases a direction to that effect will be enough, particularly
where the defendant's actions amounted to a direct attack on his victim, because in such
cases the evidence relating to the defendant's desire or motive will be clear and his intent
will have been the same as his desire or motive. But in some cases, of which this is one,
d the defendant does an act which is manifestly dangerous and as a result someone dies.
The primary desire or motive of the defendant may not have been to harm that person,
or indeed anyone. In that situation what further directions should a jury be given as to
the mental state which they must find to exist in the defendant if murder is to be proved?

We have endeavoured to crystallise the effect of their Lordships' speeches in *R v
Moloney* and *R v Hancock* in a way which we hope may be helpful to judges who have to
e handle this type of case.

It may be advisable first of all to explain to the jury that a man may intend to achieve
a certain result whilst at the same time not desiring it to come about. In *R v Moloney*
[1985] 1 All ER 1025 at 1037, [1985] AC 905 at 926 Lord Bridge gave an illustration of
the distinction:

f 'A man who, at London Airport, boards a plane which he knows to be bound for
Manchester, clearly intends to travel to Manchester, even though Manchester is the
last place he wants to be and his motive for boarding the plane is simply to escape
pursuit.'

The man who knowingly boards the Manchester aircraft wants to go there in the sense
that boarding it is a voluntary act. His desire to leave London predominates over his
g desire not to go to Manchester. When he decides to board the aircraft, if not before, he
forms the intention to travel to Manchester.

In *R v Hancock* the House decided that the *R v Moloney* guidelines require a reference
to probability. Lord Scarman said ([1986] 1 All ER 641 at 651, [1986] AC 455 at 473):

'They also require an explanation that the greater the probability of a consequence
the more likely it is that the consequence was foreseen and that if that consequence
h was foreseen the greater the probability is that that consequence was also intended.'

When determining whether the defendant had the necessary intent, it may therefore
be helpful for a jury to ask themselves two questions. (1) How probable was the
consequence which resulted from the defendant's voluntary act? (2) Did he foresee that
consequence?
j If he did not appreciate that death or serious harm was likely to result from his act, he
cannot have intended to bring it about. If he did, but thought that the risk to which he
was exposing the person killed was only slight, then it may be easy for the jury to
conclude that he did not intend to bring about that result. On the other hand, if the jury
are satisfied that at the material time the defendant recognised that death or serious harm
would be virtually certain (barring some unforeseen intervention) to result from his
voluntary act, then that is a fact from which they may find it easy to infer that he

intended to kill or do serious bodily harm, even though he may not have had any desire
to achieve that result.

    As Lord Bridge said in *R v Moloney* [1985] 1 All ER 1025 at 1036, [1985] AC 905 at
925:

> '... the probability of the consequence taken to have been foreseen must be little
> short of overwhelming before it will suffice to establish the necessary intent.'

Later he uses the expression 'moral certainty' (see [1985] 1 All ER 1025 at 1037, [1985]
AC 905 at 926) and says, 'will lead to a certain consequence unless something unexpected
supervenes to prevent it' (see [1985] 1 All ER 1025 at 1039, [1985] AC 905 at 929).

    Where the charge is murder and in the rare cases where the simple direction is not
enough, the jury should be directed that they are not entitled to infer the necessary
intention unless they feel sure that death or serious bodily harm was a virtual certainty
(barring some unforeseen intervention) as a result of the defendant's actions and that the
defendant appreciated that such was the case.

    Where a man realises that it is for all practical purposes inevitable that his actions will
result in death or serious harm, the inference may be irresistible that he intended that
result, however little he may have desired or wished it to happen. The decision is one for
the jury to be reached on a consideration of all the evidence.

Appeal allowed.

Solicitors: *Director of Public Prosecutions.*

N P Metcalfe Esq   Barrister.

R v Wells Street Metropolitan Stipendiary Magistrate and another, ex parte Westminster City Council

QUEEN'S BENCH DIVISION
WATKINS LJ AND SIR ROGER ORMROD
20 FEBRUARY, 21 MAY 1986

*Town and country planning – Building of special architectural or historic interest – Demolition,
alteration or extension – Offence – Offence of demolishing, altering or extending except as
authorised – Whether offence of strict liability – Town and Country Planning Act 1971, s 55(1).*

*Divisional Court – Jurisdiction – Supervisory jurisdiction – Committal proceedings – Whether
Divisional Court having jurisdiction to interfere with committal proceedings if magistrate declining
to exercise, or acting outside jurisdiction.*

On the true construction of s 55(1)[a] of the Town and Country Planning Act 1971 the
offence of executing or causing to be executed 'any works for the demolition of a listed
building or for its alteration or extension in any manner which would affect its character
as a building of special architectural or historic interest' otherwise than as authorised
under the 1971 Act is an offence of strict liability. It follows that the prosecution is not
required to prove mens rea in order to establish an offence under s 55(1) (see p 8 *a j*, post);
dictum of Lord Scarman in *Gammon (Hong Kong) Ltd v A-G of Hong Kong* [1984] 2 All ER
at 508 applied.

---

a   Section 55(1) is set out at p 6 b, post

a The Divisional Court has jurisdiction to interfere with committal proceedings if it is satisfied that the magistrate has declined to exercise, or has acted outside, his jurisdiction (see p 9 g h, post); *R v Roscommon Justices, ex p Blakeney* [1894] 2 IR 158 distinguished.

Notes
For the preservation of buildings of special architectural or historic interest, see 46 Halsbury's Laws (4th edn) para 380.

b For the Town and Country Planning Act 1971, s 55, see 41 Halsbury's Statutes (3rd edn) 1653.

Cases referred to in judgment
Chilvers v Rayner [1984] 1 All ER 843, [1984] 1 WLR 328, DC.
Gammon (Hong Kong) Ltd v A-G of Hong Kong [1984] 2 All ER 503, [1985] AC 1, [1984] 3
c   WLR 437, PC.
Maidstone BC v Mortimer [1980] 3 All ER 552, DC.
R v Adamson [1875] 1 QBD 201.
R v Coleshill Justices, ex p Davies [1971] 3 All ER 929, [1971] 1 WLR 1684, DC.
R v Horseferry Road Magistrates' Court, ex p Adams [1978] 1 All ER 373, [1977] 1 WLR
    1197, DC.
d *R v Ipswich Justices, ex p Edwards* (1979) 143 JP 679, DC.
R v Marsham [1892] 1 QB 371, CA.
R v Norfolk Quarter Sessions, ex p Brunson [1953] 1 All ER 346, [1953] 1 QB 503, [1953] 2
    WLR 294, DC.
R v Roscommon Justices, ex p Blakeney [1894] 2 IR 158.
R v Warner [1968] 2 All ER 356, [1969] 2 AC 256, [1968] 2 WLR 1303, HL.
e *R v Wells Street Stipendiary Magistrates, ex p Seillon* [1980] Crim LR 180, DC.
Sweet v Parsley [1969] 1 All ER 347, [1970] AC 132, [1969] 2 WLR 470, HL.

Case also cited
R v Wells Street Magistrates Court, ex p Deakin [1980] AC 477, [1979] 2 All ER 497, HL.

f **Application for judicial review**
Westminster City Council applied, with leave of Forbes J granted on 23 July 1985, for (i) a declaration that on the true construction of s 55(1) of the Town and Country Planning Act 1971 the offence created thereby was an offence of absolute liability, (ii) an order of certiorari to bring up and quash the decision of the first respondent, Mr Edward Branson, a metropolitan stipendiary magistrate sitting at Wells Street Magistrates' Court, dated 29
g April 1985, whereby he declined to commit the second respondent, Brian Martin, for trial by jury for the offence of altering a listed building known as 42 and 43 Wimpole Street, London W1, contrary to s 55(1) of the 1971 Act on the ground that there was insufficient evidence, and (iii) an order of mandamus requiring the magistrate to inquire into the offence, to consider the evidence and having properly directed himself as to the law to give his opinion whether there was sufficient evidence to put Martin on trial by
h jury for any indictable offence. The facts are set out in the judgment of the court.

Andrew Collins QC and *Helen Rogers* for the council.
Philip Engelman for Martin.
The first respondent did not appear.

j   *Cur adv vult*

21 May. The following judgment of the court was delivered.

WATKINS LJ. There is before us an application for judicial review of a decision of Mr Branson, a metropolitan stipendiary magistrate, sitting at Wells Street on 29 April 1985,

whereby he refused to commit for trial an offence under s 55(1) of the Town and Country
Planning Act 1971, holding that this is not an offence of absolute liability and that the   *a*
necessary mens rea had not been proved by the prosecutor, the Westminster City Council.
    Section 55, so far as material, provides:

> '(1) Subject to this Part of this Act, if a person executes or causes to be executed
> any works for the demolition of a listed building or for its alteration or extension in
> any manner which would affect its character as a building of special architectural or
> historic interest, and the works are not authorised under subsection (2) of this   *b*
> section, he shall be guilty of an offence . . .
> (4) Without prejudice to subsection (1) of this section, if a person executing or
> causing to be executed any works in relation to a listed building under a listed
> building consent fails to comply with any condition attached to the consent under
> section 56 of this Act, he shall be guilty of an offence.
> (5) A person guilty of an offence under this section shall be liable—(a) on   *c*
> summary conviction to imprisonment for a term not exceeding three months or a
> fine not exceeding [the prescribed sum under the Magistrates' Courts Act 1980,
> s 32(2)], or both; or (b) on conviction on indictment to imprisonment for a term not
> exceeding twelve months or a fine, or both; and, in determining the amount of any
> fine to be imposed on a person convicted on indictment, the court shall in particular   *d*
> have regard to any financial benefit which has accrued or appears likely to accrue to
> him in consequence of the offence.
> (6) In proceedings for an offence under this section it shall be a defence to prove
> that the works were urgently necessary in the interests of safety or health, or for the
> preservation of the building, and that notice in writing of the need for the works
> was given to the local planning authority as soon as reasonably practicable.'
>   *e*

    The council has for some time been concerned about the large number of thefts from
premises within its boundaries of valuable architectural features from listed buildings of
which there are approximately 9,000. On 30 March 1983 the city planning officer was
informed that such things were, without consent of the council, being removed from 42
and 43 Wimpole Street, which are Grade II listed buildings. On that day the council's
historic buildings officer, Philip Davies, visited the premises in company with a police   *f*
officer and found that Martin Hopkins and Brian Martin, of a firm known as Amazing
Grates, were assisted by other servants of this firm, taking away chimney pieces, panelled
doors and staircase balustrading from the premises.
    The freeholds of the premises belong to the Howard de Walden Estate. The headlease
belongs to the Wimpole Street Clinic Ltd, of which one S B S Livesey is a director.
Hopkins was said to be a kind of agent of Livesey.   *g*
    This company's solicitors, on 29 April 1983, wrote a letter to the council, in part of
which helpful information was provided about the state of the premises, the use to which
it was hoped to be made of them and the circumstances of the removal of the architectural
features. This part reads as follows:

> 'Our clients greatly regret the removal of architectural features from the above   *h*
> listed buidings. It has never been their wish or intention that any such items should
> be removed. Your records will show that our clients have had extensive
> correspondence with your Department concerning these buildings and we are
> confident that references to this correspondence will demonstrate that our clients
> are responsible people, who are anxious to comply with all statutory requirements.
> The facts of the matter are that, following our clients' acquisition of the headleases   *j*
> in 1978, they expended considerable time and money in obtaining possession from
> the various professional and business tenants, with a view to carrying out a complete
> restoration of these buildings. Unfortunately, owing to various problems our clients
> have been unable to implement their intentions, and for a considerable period No.
> 42 has been unoccupied, and No. 43 has been substantially unoccupied. There has

a
been great difficulty in keeping the properties secure, and there have been numerous break-ins and thefts, particularly since a fire at No. 42 when the Fire Brigade made the position worse by smashing virtually every door in No. 42. The thefts from the properties have included various fixtures and fittings, despite our clients' efforts to secure the properties against unauthorised entry. Our clients have used the premises for the storage of furniture, but in March other storage space became available, and they decided to remove the furniture from the premises. They therefore instructed

b
an independent contractor, Mr. Martin Hopkins, to carry out the removal. The instructions were given orally over the telephone to Mr. Hopkins and were confirmed when he called upon our clients, and it is believed that the instructions were that Mr. Hopkins was to 'remove everything of value'. Our clients' intention was of course that all the furniture of value should be removed, leaving items of little value which were not worth the trouble of moving. Unfortunately, Mr.

c
Hopkins interpreted his instructions as meaning that he was also to remove fixtures and fittings of value, and he proceeded accordingly, until he was prevented from doing so. We trust that in the light of the above explanation you will accept that our clients and Mr. Hopkins acted innocently, and that you will not proceed with your recommendation that there should be a prosecution.'

d
It did not persuade the council to refrain from laying informations, as was done on 5 July 1984, against Livesey, Hopkins and Martin, alleging a breach of s 55(1). Hopkins had, however, left the country to live in Australia. He has not therefore been further proceeded against.

The first hearing of the informations affecting Livesey and Martin took place on 27 August 1984. On that and subsequent days the hearing, for reasons which are not material, was adjourned. At one of the adjourned hearings Livesey and Martin elected

e
trial by jury and requested committal proceedings under s 6(2) of the Magistrates' Courts Act 1980. These took place on 15 January and 29 April 1985. During the course of the hearings the council called the historic buildings officer from whom a deposition was taken and their counsel read the statements of five other witnesses. At the close of the prosecution's case it was clear from submissions made on their behalf that Livesey and Martin challenged little of relevance in the evidence, but it was contended in respect of

f
Livesey that there was no evidence he had caused the alterations to the listed buildings and none that the alterations materially affected the character of the buildings.

The first of these contentions was accepted by the magistrate (he rejected the second) who thereupon discharged Livesey. There is no complaint, nor could there be, about the discharge of Livesey on that basis.

On behalf of Martin it was submitted that s 55(1) of the 1971 Act should be construed

g
as requiring mens rea and there was no evidence that Martin knew the buildings were listed. Despite the council's contention, inter alia, that the offence was an absolute one, the magistrate accepted the defence submission and discharged Martin.

The magistrate was asked to give reasons for his decision. He refused to do so, saying merely that with reluctance he accepted what defence counsel had said.

h
The relief sought by the council is (1) a declaration that on the true construction of s 55(1) of the 1971 Act the offence created thereby is an offence of absolute liability, (2) an order of certiorari, quashing the decision of the magistrate and (3) an order of mandamus directing the magistrate to inquire into the offence, having properly directed himself on the law.

The grounds relied on for relief are simply that the magistrate was wrong in law in

j
applying to the evidence the test that the offence under s 55(1) of the 1971 Act required the prosecution to prove mens rea and therefore wrong to refuse to commit Martin for trial.

There are two issues which concern us. They are whether s 55(1) of the 1971 Act creates an absolute offence, and, if it does, whether this court has jurisdiction to give the relief sought.

We turn first to consider s 55(1), the offence within which was first created by s 40 of the Town and Country Planning Act 1968.

Counsel for the applicant submits that on a plain reading of s 55(1) of the 1971 Act it is not possible to conclude other than that it creates an offence which is not truly criminal and is of strict liability. There is no indication of mens rea in it. He points to the context in which the section appears in the 1971 Act. It is within Pt IV, which is headed, 'Additional Control in Special Cases', and provides for control of buildings of special architectural or historic interest as well as trees and other things.

By s 102(1) of the 1971 Act it is an offence to cut down or wilfully destroy a tree, for which an offender is liable to a fine not exceeding level 4 on the standard scale, or twice the value of the tree, whichever is the greater. In *Maidstone BC v Mortimer* [1980] 3 All ER 552, it was held in this court that s 102(1) created an absolute offence. Reliance was also placed on *Chilvers v Rayner* [1984] 1 All ER 843, [1984] 1 WLR 328, in which it was held that s 1(1)(b) of the Hallmarking Act 1973 created an absolute offence. In the course of his judgment Robert Goff LJ referred to the well-known cases of *R v Warner* [1968] 2 All ER 356, [1969] 2 AC 256 and *Sweet v Parsley* [1969] 1 All ER 347, [1970] AC 132, and concluded that an offence under s 1(1) of the 1973 Act was of a quasi-criminal character.

From these cases it is clear that punishment by imprisonment is not an indication that thereby Parliament must inevitably be taken to have intended mens rea to be an essential ingredient of the offence.

Primarily counsel for the applicant seeks support from *Gammon (Hong Kong) Ltd v A-G of Hong Kong* [1984] 2 All ER 503, [1985] AC 1. Lord Scarman in giving the judgment of the Privy Council proposed the following test ([1984] 2 All ER 503 at 508, [1985] AC 1 at 14):

> 'In their Lordships' opinion, the law relevant to this appeal may be stated in the following propositions (the formulation of which follows closely the written submission of the appellants' counsel, which their Lordships gratefully acknowledge): (1) there is a presumption of law that mens rea is required before a person can be held guilty of a criminal offence; (2) the presumption is particularly strong where the offence is "truly criminal" in character; (3) the presumption applies to statutory offences, and can be displaced only if this is clearly or by necessary implication the effect of the statute; (4) the only situation in which the presumption can be displaced is where the statute is concerned with an issue of social concern, and public safety is such an issue; (5) even where a statute is concerned with such an issue, the presumption of mens rea stands unless it can also be shown that the creation of strict liability will be effective to promote the objects of the statute by encouraging greater vigilance to prevent the commission of the prohibited act.'

It is submitted that the circumstances of the present case clearly give rise to an issue of social concern and that the creation of strict liability will be effective to promote the objects of the statute by encouraging greater vigilance to prevent breaches of s 55(1) of the 1971 Act. It will be a deterrent to those tempted to breach it.

Counsel for Martin accepts the test in *Gammon (Hong Kong) Ltd v A-G of Kong Kong* as apt to the issue, but contends that the offence is truly criminal in character and what was said of relevance in *Maidstone BC v Mortimer* was obiter dicta. The punishment for the offence is a powerful indication that mens rea is involved in it. The defence in s 55(1) of the 1971 Act does not assist to say to the contrary. It would be wrong for third parties to be fixed with strict liability.

We see no injustice in holding, as we do, that this offence is an absolute one. The fears expressed by counsel for Martin are all capable of being allayed by the discretion used whether to prosecute or not, and in the power to refrain from punishment by either fine or imprisonment in appropriate cases.

We are drawn to the conclusion, for the reasons advanced by counsel for the applicant, that s 55(1) of the 1971 Act creates an absolute offence.

Do we have jurisdiction to grant relief?

a Counsel for Martin contends that we do not. There was, he said, no defect and no irregularity in the proceedings. This was a preliminary inquiry in which the magistrates had a discretion whether to commit or not. An error of law committed in that decision does not permit this court to intervene with it. He relies heavily on *R v Roscommon Justices, ex p Blakeney* [1894] 2 IR 158, which is an authority for the proposition, often down the years since successfully advanced, that the decision of justices of the peace committing a defendant for trial cannot be brought up for certiorari. As a matter of

b policy, it is suggested, this court should not interfere, even if the magistrate acted outside his jurisdiction.

The facts in *R v Roscommon Justices, ex p Blakeney* are very different from those in the present case, the issues likewise, as is clear from the following extract from the judgment of O'Brien J (at 176):

c 'The case of *Reg.* v. *Adamson* ((1875) 1 QBD 201) is altogether distinguishable from the present question. There the court granted the mandamus because they came to the conclusion from the facts that the magistrates, in refusing the summons, declined jurisdiction. This is not a case of declining jurisdiction. The jurisdiction is to receive or refuse informations for a criminal offence. They have received informations. The question whether the place was a dwelling house is not a matter

d of jurisdiction, but a fact to be determined on the evidence, like any other fact, as much as the identity of the person charged.'

We do not have to consider a finding of fact but an error of law in construing s 55(1) of the offence created by which Martin was charged with. It was an offence of strict liability which the magistrate had to inquire into. He did not do that because he ruled that mens rea was an ingredient of the offence.

e The circumstances in which this court has been invited to interfere with committal proceedings has been considered on a fairly large number of occasions in recent years. In most of them the complaint has been that the magistrates' court has been in error in assessing, rejecting or admitting evidence: see in this respect *R v Horseferry Road Magistrates' Court, ex p Adams* [1978] 1 All ER 373, [1977] 1 WLR 1197, *R v Coleshill Justices, ex p Davies* [1971] 3 All ER 929, [1971] 1 WLR 1684, *R v Norfolk Quarter Sessions,*

f *ex p Brunson* [1953] 1 All ER 346, [1953] 1 QB 503, *R v Ipswich Justices, ex p Edwards* (1979) 143 JP 679. In the first two of these cases the committal was quashed. In the last two this court refused to interfere.

All these cases and others indicate that in order to be moved to interfere with committal proceedings, this court has to be satisfied that the magistrates' court declined or acted outside its jurisdiction. This was the basis on which an order of mandamus was

g issued in *R v Marsham* [1892] 1 QB 371 to a magistrate who had refused to hear evidence of matters he was bound by statute to inquire into. He was said to have declined jurisdiction.

So we think in the present case the magistrate in refusing to inquire into an offence of strict liability declined jurisdiction to inquire into a case which by the proper construction of s 55(1) of the 1971 Act he was legally obliged to. Put in another way, his error of

h construction deprived him of jurisdiction: see Lord Widgery CJ in *R Wells Street Stipendiary Magistrates, ex p Seillon* [1980] Crim LR 180.

We would quash the decision of the magistrate not to commit Martin for that and order him to inquire further into existing evidence and other evidence, if any, to be given and then decide whether, on the basis that the offence created by s 55(1) of the 1971 Act is one of strict liability, this evidence is sufficient to commit Martin for trial.

j *Appeal allowed. Case remitted to magistrate.*

Solicitors: *G M Ives* (for the council); *Offenbach & Co* (for Martin).

Michael Wall Esq   Barrister.

Schiavo v Anderton   a

QUEEN'S BENCH DIVISION
WATKINS LJ AND NOLAN J
10, 11 FEBRUARY 1986

Criminal law – Bail – Absconding from bail – Magistrates' court's jurisdiction to deal with   b
absconder – Nature of offence of absconding – Whether magistrates having jurisdiction to commit
absconder to Crown Court for sentence – Bail Act 1976, s 6(1).

In May 1983 the defendant was charged with obtaining property by deception and was
bailed to appear before a magistrates' court on 9 June. He failed to appear on that date
and a warrant for his arrest was issued by the magistrates under s 7(1)[a] of the Bail Act
1976. However, the defendant absconded to Spain and the warrant was not executed   c
until May 1985, when he returned to England, was arrested and charged under s 6(1)[b] of
the 1976 Act with failing to surrender to custody. In July the defendant appeared before
the magistrates on that charge and pleaded guilty. He was committed to the Crown
Court for sentence, but when he appeared before the Crown Court he applied to change
his plea to not guilty, contending that the magistrates had no jurisdiction to try the
offence under s 6(1) because it was a summary offence and an information had not been   d
laid within six months from the date on which the offence was committed, as required
by s 127(1)[c] of the Magistrates' Courts Act 1980. The defendant was given leave to change
his plea and the matter was remitted to the magistrates' court, which held that failing to
surrender to bail contrary to s 6(1) was an indictable offence and therefore s 127 of the
1980 Act did not apply, and that even if s 127 did apply in effect an information had
been laid against the defendant on 9 June 1983 when the warrant was issued under s 7(1)   e
of the 1976 Act, because applying for the warrant and informing the magistrates of the
circumstances in which it was required were sufficient to constitute an 'information'.
The defendant appealed.

Held – The offence of failing to surrender to bail, contrary to s 6 of the 1976 Act, was an   f
exception to the general rule that proceedings in a magistrates' court must be preceded
by the laying of an information against the defendant, because the offence under s 6 was
not a conventional criminal offence but was akin to a contempt of court in that it
concerned an act committed in defiance of an essential condition of bail laid down by the
court. Accordingly, the proper way of dealing with such an offence was for the court to
deal with it of its own motion and not for proceedings to be initiated by formal charge.   g
The offence was not triable on indictment nor should proceedings be begun by
information. The offence was only triable in the court at which the proceedings in
respect of which bail had been granted were to be heard and trial of the offence under s 6
should take place immediately following the disposal of the offence in respect of which
bail had been granted. Although the defendant had appeared before the magistrates'
court for the wrong procedural reasons that had been the right court to deal with him   h
and since it was clear that he was guilty of an offence under s 6 the appeal would be
dismissed (see p 16 b to e j to p 17 c, post).

---

a   Section 7(1) provides: 'If a person who has been released on bail in criminal proceedings and is
     under a duty to surrender into the custody of a court fails to surrender to custody at the time
     appointed for him to do so the court may issue a warrant for his arrest.'   j
b   Section 6 is set out at p 13 j to p 14 c, post
c   Section 127(1), so far as material, provides: 'Except as othewise expressly provided . . . a magistrates'
     court shall not try an information or hear a complaint unless the information was laid, or the
     complaint made, within 6 months from the time when the offence was committed, or the matter
     of complaint arose.'

a *R v Harbax Singh* [1979] 1 All ER 524, *R v Tyson* (1979) 68 Cr App R 314, and *Hill v Anderton* [1982] 2 All ER 963 considered.

Per curiam. Applying to magistrates to issue a warrant under s 7 of the 1976 Act and informing them of the circumstances in which it is required does not amount to the laying of an oral information, since an information must be a deliberate act which commences, in the conventional sense, a prosecution which will ultimately have the effect of bringing an offence and offender before the court (see p 12 *f* to *j* and p 17 *c*, post).

b

Notes

For failure to surrender to bail, see 11 Halsbury's Laws (4th edn) para 155 and 29 ibid para 349, and for cases on the subject of bail generally, see 14(1) Digest (Reissue) 241–245, 1728–1765.

For the Bail Act 1976, ss 6, 7, see 12 Halsbury's Statutes (4th edn) 720, 722.

c   For the Magistrates' Courts Act 1980, s 127, see 50(2) Halsbury's Statutes (3rd edn) 1552.

Cases referred to in judgments

Hill v Anderton [1982] 2 All ER 963, [1983] 1 AC 328, [1982] 3 WLR 331, HL.

R v Brentford Justices, ex p Catlin [1975] 2 All ER 201, [1975] QB 455, [1975] 2 WLR 506,

d   DC.

R v Harbax Singh [1979] 1 All ER 524, [1979] QB 319, [1979] 2 WLR 100, CA.

R v Hughes (1879) 4 QBD 614, CCR.

R v Tyson (1979) 68 Cr App R 314, CA.

Cases also cited

e *Morris v Crown Office* [1970] 1 All ER 1079, [1970] 2 QB 114, CA.

R v Parke [1903] 2 KB 432, [1900–3] All ER Rep 721, DC.

R v Tibbits [1902] 1 KB 77, [1900–3] All ER Rep 896, CCR.

Appeal

The defendant, Vincent Anthony Schiavo, appealed by way of case stated by C T Latham

f Esq, a stipendiary magistrate for the county of Greater Manchester, acting in and for the petty sessional division of Salford, in respect of his adjudication when sitting at the Salford Magistrates' Court on 23 September 1985 whereby he committed the defendant for sentence to the Crown Court for failing to surrender to custody, contrary to s 6(1) of the Bail Act 1976. The respondent was Cyril James Anderton, the Chief Constable of Greater Manchester (the prosecutor). The facts are set out in the judgment of Watkins

g LJ.

Christopher Limb for the defendant.

John Bailey for the prosecutor.

WATKINS LJ. This is an appeal by case stated from a decision of Mr C T Latham, a

h stipendiary magistrate for the county of Greater Manchester acting in and for the petty sessional division of Salford in respect of a decision he made when sitting at the Salford Magistrates' Court.

On 23 September 1985 the defendant appeared before that court charged that having been released on bail on 12 May 1983 he failed without reasonable cause to surrender to custody on 9 June 1983, contrary to s 6(1) of the Bail Act 1976. This so-called charge was

j heard on 23 September 1985 when the magistrate found these facts. On 12 May 1983 the defendant appeared before the court charged with obtaining property by means of deception, contrary to s 15 of the Theft Act 1968. That charge was not dealt with on that day, so he was bailed to reappear on 9 June 1983. He failed to appear. These circumstances were brought to the notice of the court and the justices were invited to issue a warrant for the arrest of the defendant under s 7(1) of the 1976 Act. Unbeknown to the justices

at that time, the defendant had absconded to Spain. The warrant for his arrest could not
therefore then be executed.

The defendant returned to England on 9 May 1985. He was arrested on the following
day under the warrant. He appeared yet again at the Salford Magistrates' Court on 3 July
1985, this time charged with the offence contrary to s 6(1). He pleaded guilty to that
charge. The justices thereupon committed him to the Crown Court for sentence under
other provisions of s 6 to which I shall return. On 14 August he appeared at the Crown
Court at Manchester in order that he should be dealt with for the offence under s 6(1).
He applied to the judge to change his plea from guilty to not guilty on the ground that
the magistrates' court on 3 July 1985 had no jursidiction to try that offence. It was, so it
was contended, a summary offence and an information had not been laid within six
months from the time when the offence was committed as required by s 127 of the
Magistrates' Courts Act 1980. The judge, unwisely I think, allowed the defendant to
change his plea to not guilty to determine the issue of jurisdiction and, if appropriate, to
try the defendant.

It was contended by the defendant before the stipendiary magistrate that the offence
of failing to surrender contrary to s 6(1) was a summary offence and an information had
not been laid within six months from 9 June 1983 when the offence was committed, as
required by s 127 of the 1980 Act. A number of other arguments were addressed to the
magistrate, amongst which were an assertion on behalf of the defendant that the offence
was not one which was triable on indictment, nor was it one which was triable either
way. Accordingly, it being a summary offence the only way in which justices could have
jurisdiction was as though an information had been laid and, moreover, an information
laid within the requisite period of six months.

There is no doubt that an information was not in fact laid within that period of six
months. The magistrate was invited to say that he was dealing with a summary matter
and he was not entitled to proceed with it because there was no information in proper
form and nothing which could be regarded as an information in substitution therefore.

Among the matters which were contended to the contrary by counsel on behalf of the
prosecution were that the offence under s 6(1) of the 1976 Act was an indictable one and
therefore s 127 of the 1980 Act did not require an information to be laid within six
months of the offence. Alternatively, if s 127 did apply an information was laid against
the defendant on 9 June 1983. The way in which it was asserted that an information was
laid was somewhat ingenious. The contention was (it was repeated in this court) that
when justices are asked to issue a warrant (commonly called a bench warrant) under s 7
of the 1976 Act and informed of the circumstances in which a defendant has failed to
comply with the essential condition of bail, namely to surrender at a time and place laid
down, that may suffice as an information. The prosecution is therefore called on to do no
more in order to lay an information. It need take no further action, safe in the feeling
that merely applying for a bench warrant and telling the justices of the circumstances in
which it is required can be taken to be an information. I profoundly disagree. An
information, it is true, may be made orally or, as is more often, in writing and laid in
that form.

For present purposes what is important is that it must actually be what it seems to be,
namely an information designed for the purpose of initiating criminal proceedings. In
other words, a deliberate act which commences in the conventional sense a prosecution
which ultimately will have the effect of bringing an offence and offender before the
court. In this case it was a mere incident in the history of the affair that a warrant was
applied for and issued as long ago as two or three years before the defendant reappeared
in this country after his sojourn in southern Spain.

It was also contended by the prosecution that there had been no delay in bringing this
matter to the court. Section 6 of the 1976 Act is, it was said, anomalous in the sense that
it is not akin to other offences with which a magistrates' court is called on to deal up and
down the country day in, day out.

The magistrate heard these and many other submissions, as indeed did we. He had
referred to him a large number of cases, to some of which I shall myself be referring in a

moment or so and he came to these conclusions. He was of the opinion that the offence
a of failing to surrender to bail contrary to s 6(1) of the 1976 Act was an indictable offence
and therefore s 127 of the 1980 Act requiring that an information be laid within six
months did not apply. If he was wrong about that and s 127 did apply, an information
was laid within six months, namely on 9 June 1983. Then he sets out the reasons for
forming that last-mentioned opinion with which, as I have already indicated, I do not
agree and believe him to be wrong about. There is, he says, no provision in the 1976 Act
b referring to the mode of trial for an offence under s 6. He was referred to what Cantley J
said in *R v Tyson* (1979) 68 Cr App R 314 and to what Roskill LJ said in *R v Harbax Singh*
[1979] 1 All ER 524, [1979] QB 319.

He accepted the evidence as to the hearing on 9 June 1983. He accepted further that
all material necessary to inform the justices of the offence of failing to surrender to bail
was in fact presented to the court. No specific reference was made to s 6 of the 1976 Act,
c but this was a defect which could be cured. Further, that the prosecutor was not
specifically addressing his mind to the laying of an information in respect of the offence
under the 1976 Act. He then looked at, inter alia, *R v Brentford Justices, ex p Catlin* [1975]
2 All ER 201, [1975] QB 455 and *Hill v Anderton* [1982] 2 All ER 963, [1983] 1 AC 328
and formed this final conclusion: when the justices were considering whether to issue a
warrant under s 7(1) of the 1976 Act they were exercising a judicial discretion and
d accordingly had before them all the material necessary to found an information. They
acted judicially on it. In those circumstances an information was laid even though the
prosecutor did not give his mind to such a consequence.

Having come to those conclusions, among others, he convicted the defendant and
committed him yet again to the Crown Court for sentence.

The defendant has appeared at the Crown Court. He was dealt with there by another
e judge, his Honour Judge Henry Kershaw. He sentenced him to nine months'
imprisonment for the offence under the 1968 Act and a consecutive term of six months'
imprisonment for the offence under the 1976 Act. He is still in the midst of serving the
sentence under the 1968 Act. He still has to begin the sentence under the 1976 Act. So it
is obviously a matter of very considerable concern to him whether he should continue to
be liable to serve that.

f We have had the advantage in this court of two excellent submissions from counsel on
behalf of the prosecution and the defendant. The arguments which they addressed to the
magistrate were very carefully rehearsed here. As a general rule, the criminal process in
the magistrates' court is undoubtedly commenced by the laying of an information. By
rr 4 and 100 of the Magistrates' Courts Rules 1981, SI 1981/552, provision is made for
the laying of an information by the prosecutor orally or in writing. It is laid before a
g justice of the peace or the clerk to the justices or one of his clerks. The rules provide that
an information shall contain a statement of the offence charged. That offence is thereafter
dealt with as a summary offence in the magistrates' court or by committal for trial at the
Crown Court on indictment or, in the case of an offence triable either way, in one or
other of those courts.

In respect of the last-mentioned type of offence, the initial procedure for, inter alia,
h determining in which court the offence will be dealt with is contained in ss 17 to 28
inclusive of the Magistrates' Courts Act 1980. In Sch 1 to this Act there is to be found the
large body of offences declared to be triable either way. The offence created by s 6 of the
1976 Act is not declared to be one of them. That section provides:

'(1) If a person who has been released on bail in criminal proceedings fails without
j reasonable cause to surrender to custody he shall be guilty of an offence.

(2) If a person who—(a) has been released on bail in criminal proceedings, and (b)
having reasonable cause therefore, has failed to surrender to custody, fails to
surrender to custody at the appointed place as soon after the appointed time as is
reasonably practicable he shall be guilty of an offence.

(3) It shall be for the accused to prove that he had reasonable cause for his failure
to surrender to custody.

(4) A failure to give to a person granted bail in criminal proceedings a copy of the record of the decision shall not constitute a reasonable cause for that person's failure *a* to surrender to custody.

(5) An offence under subsection (1) or (2) above shall be punishable either on summary conviction or as if it were a criminal contempt of court.

(6) Where a magistrates' court convicts a person of an offence under subsection (1) or (2) above the court may, if it thinks—(*a*) that the circumstances of the offence are such that greater punishment should be inflicted for that offence than the court *b* has power to inflict, or (*b*) in a case where it commits that person for trial to the Crown Court for another offence, that it would be appropriate for him to be dealt with for the offence under subsection (1) or (2) above by the court before which he is tried for the other offence, commit him in custody or on bail to the Crown Court for sentence.

(7) A person who is convicted summarily of an offence under subsection (1) or *c* (2) above and is not committed to the Crown Court for sentence shall be liable to imprisonment for a term not exceeding 3 months or to a fine not exceeding [level 5 on the standard scale] or to both and a person who is so committed for sentence or is dealt with as for such a contempt shall be liable to imprisonment for a term not exceeding 12 months or to a fine or to both.'

Section 7, as I have earlier indicated, provides the power to the court to issue a warrant *d* for the arrest of a person who has absconded and thus broken the essential condition of bail. It also enables a constable in certain circumstances to arrest a person who is in that situation.

Prior to the 1976 Act absconding was not an offence known to the law. The only power which courts had which was in any way akin to punishment was to estreat the recognisances of an accused person when he was arrested and possibly that of his or her *e* sureties. The offence created by s 6 is therefore unique in the sense that it has no ancestor and unique for reasons which later I shall in this judgment explain in the sense that it is other than what might be called a conventional criminal offence. In the course of argument both here and in the court below the power of courts to punish for contempt of court has been to a limited extent examined.

Before referring to the context in which that was done, it is pertinent to observe that *f* prior to the Contempt of Court Act 1981 there was no power in the magistrates' court to punish for contempt. Section 12(1) of the 1981 Act provides:

'A magistrates' court has jurisdiction under this section to deal with any person who—(*a*) wilfully insults the justice or justices, any witness before or officer of the court or any solicitor or counsel having business in the court, during his or their *g* sitting or attendance in court or in going to or returning from the court; or (*b*) wilfully interrupts the proceedings of the court or otherwise misbehaves in court.'

It also provides power to inflict in the magistrates' court imprisonment for a period not exceeding one month or a fine not exceeding £1,000 or both. The Crown Court and its predecessors, the assizes and quarter sessions, by inherent jurisdiction has and had that *h* power. The 1981 Act affected that by s 14 only to the extent of providing for a maximum term of imprisonment and maximum fine whereas previously there was no maximum. Until the early part of this century, a criminal contempt was triable on indictment. In theory that mode of trial is still available, but its use is heavily discouraged and has been in recent times by the Court of Appeal on more than one occasion. An offence under s 6 of the 1976 Act is not a contempt of court, although it may be said to bear some relation *j* to it in the sense that a person who commits it has acted in defiance of an essential condition of his bail, namely that he surrender so as to appear before the court at a place and at a time appointed. The invariable procedure for dealing with a contempt of court in the Crown Court is for the judge of his own motion to do so at a time during or usually at the end of the trial of an accused, being careful to ensure in the interests of fairness that the contemnor has an opportunity either to purge his contempt or to

mitigate the consequences of it with the assistance, if fitting and desirable, of a solicitor
a and barrister.

There are a number of cases decided in the Court of Appeal in the last two or three
years in which observations on this process have been made. Seeing that it is an order in
the term of a condition of bail of the court which has been disobeyed to bring about a s 6
of the 1976 Act offence, why should the procedure for dealing with it differ from that
resorted to in the Crown Court for contempt? It is a simple, expeditious process of
b dealing with, inter alia, disobedience of court orders shorn of the time-consuming and in
some ways cumbersome processes of the laying of information, the issuing of warrants,
committal proceedings, trial on indictment and so forth. It is because, so it is argued, in
the magistrates' court the trial of an offence must be preceded by the laying of an
information within the time prescribed. The offence is subject to the general rule. It is
either triable summarily or on indictment or either way and accordingly is subject to the
c provisions of the 1980 Act.

Reference was made, as I have said already, to a number of cases. I propose to examine
them in just a little detail. In *R v Harbax Singh* [1979] 1 All ER 524 at 527, [1979] QB 319
at 325 Roskill LJ, in giving the judgment of the court, dealt in some detail with the
question of how s 6 of the 1976 Act should in some respects be construed. What he said
which is of relevance here was:

d
> 'This court finds itself unable to agree with the underlying premise of counsel's
> argument for the appellant that the omission of words such as "contempt committed
> in the face of the court" limits the powers accorded by s 6(5). On the contrary we
> think the omission is deliberate and is designed to give a court other than a
> magistrates' court, that is the Crown Court, power to deal with an offender as if he
> had committed a criminal contempt of court, leaving the Crown Court to deal with
e > him in whatever way as the Crown Court could do if he were guilty of criminal
> contempt of court. In some cases it may not be appropriate to deal with the offender
> summarily in this way. We are not deciding this question finally since it does not
> arise, but one can imagine circumstances in which there might be a dispute whether
> or not particular facts amounted to absconding; the judge might then think that
> that was not a suitable matter for determination by him summarily under the latter
f > part of sub-s (5). In such a case he might think it right to direct that summary
> proceedings should be begun before a magistrates' court, or he might think he could
> deal with the matter adequately himself. But the purpose of the provision seems to
> us to be to create swift and simple alternative remedies, either by way of proceedings
> for a summary offence or by way of committal for what is to be treated as a criminal
> contempt of court, without the necessity for more elaborate proceedings of a kind
g > which sometimes are necessary when questions of criminal contempt of court arise.'

Save to say that with respect I do not agree with Roskill LJ when he says that it might be
possible for a judge at the Crown Court to, so to speak, remit a matter to the magistrates
for summary proceedings to commence, I agree with what he says in those passages and,
of course, with his observations on the expeditious nature of the process contemplated
by Parliament for dealing with offences under s 6 of the 1976 Act.
h
In *Hill v Anderton* [1982] 2 All ER 963 at 973, [1983] 1 AC 328 at 344 Lord Roskill
quoted from *R v Hughes* (1879) 4 QBD 614 at 625:

j
> 'The information, which is in the nature of an indictment, of necessity precedes
> the process; and it is only after the information is laid, that the question as to the
> particular form and nature of the process can properly arise. Process is not essential
> to the jurisdiction of the justices to hear and adjudicate. It is but the proceeding
> adopted to compel the appearance of the accused to answer the information already
> duly laid, without which no hearing in the nature of a trial could take place [and
> these are the important words] (unless under special statutory enactment)'

Section 6 of the 1976 Act came under the scrutiny of the Court of Appeal in *R v Tyson*
(1979) 68 Cr App R 314. Cantley J, giving the judgment of the court, said (at 318):

'In the Bail Act the offence is defined in section 6(1). Subsections (5), (6) and (7) deal merely with procedure for punishing the offence. There are three available *a* procedures: (i) summary conviction and sentence by a magistrates' court, (ii) summary conviction by a magistrates' court followed by committal to the Crown Court for sentence and (iii) procedure as if the offence were a criminal contempt of court. A criminal contempt of court can be dealt with by indictment (although there is no reported instance of this since 1902), by information, by motion or summarily.' *b*

Save to say that I do not think it is open to anyone under the 1976 Act to be tried on indictment nor do I think proceedings should be begun by information, I agree broadly speaking with what the judge said on that occasion. I agree especially that the court may and, as I shall say in a moment or two, is under the terms of s 6 bound to regard the matter as for initiation of their own motion.

In my judgment, on a proper construction of s 6 of the 1976 Act in its setting, *c* Parliament intended effects of the provisions of the section other than those which are plainly obvious from the text of them. They are: (1) the magistrates' court and the Crown Court each require separately a power to punish for the offence of absconding; (2) the offence is not subject to the general rule that trial be commenced by information; (3) the initiation of the simple procedure for trial by the court's own motion and not by formal charge, as seems to have happened here, is the only proper way to proceed; (4) it is not *d* one of those offences triable on indictment or either way; (5) it is an offence only triable in the court at which proceedings are to be heard in respect of which bail has been granted; (6) it is expected that the trial of the offence will take place immediately following the disposal of the offence in respect of which bail was granted. There is nothing said save what I have already commented on in any of the cases to which we were referred and especially in those from which I have quoted which in any sense serves *e* to deny what I regard to be the plain intention of Parliament as I have just expressed it and which I have deduced from the language used in s 6, at any rate the first seven subsections of it.

So in this sense too it is unique. It is, of course, subject to the normal appellate procedures and possibly judicial review. It has, as has already been noted, built within it the power to justices to send somebody to the Crown Court for sentence if they are *f* satisfied that their powers are insufficient properly to punish the offender.

I now have to look therefore at the questions which have been asked of us by the magistrate. They are these:

'(i) Was I right in finding that the offence of failing to surrender to bail contrary to section 6(1) of the Bail Act 1976 was an indictable offence and that section 127 of *g* the Magistrates' Court Act 1980 requiring that an information be laid within 6 months did not apply?'

He was not right in finding that it was an indictable offence.

'(ii) Further, was I right in finding that, although an offence under section 6(1) of the Act of 1976 was triable either on indictment or summarily depending on the *h* circumstances of the case, the procedural provisions of sections 18 to 23 of the Magistrates' Courts Act 1980, did not apply?'

In my judgment the assumed basis for that is entirely erroneous.

'(iii) If I was wrong in my finding in (i) above, and an offence under section 6(1) of the Act of 1976 was a summary offence, was I right in finding that in this case an *j* information was laid on 9th June 1983, the day of the offence, thus complying with the provisions of section 127 of the 1980 Act?'

I think he was fundamentally wrong about that too.

How does the defendant now stand? He appeared before the magistrate. True it is that according to the way in which I look at it he was wrongly brought before him, because a he was brought on a charge when that was wholly unnecessary, the fact is that he did appear there to answer for his conduct in absconding. The magistrate, on ample evidence, came to a decision which in my judgment is unchallengable, namely that he was guilty of an offence under s 6 of the 1976 Act. Moreover, having found him guilty the magistrate was exercising a power given to him which I do not think we are in any position to interfere with, namely that in view of the seriousness of the offence he ought to send the matter to the Crown Court for sentence.

b Accordingly, although I have with very considerable regret to say that for wrong procedural reasons the magistrate had the defendant before him he came rightly to a conclusion that this defendant ought to be convicted and punished. The wrong reasons do not serve the defendant to have his conviction interfered with nor, for that matter, his sentence, seeing that this court is not a court of appeal for the purpose of sentence. For those reasons I would dismiss this appeal.

c **NOLAN J.** I agree.

Appeal dismissed.

d Solicitors: *Betesh & Co*, Manchester (for the defendant); *D S Gandy*, Manchester (for the prosecutor).

June Meader   Barrister.

R v Newham Juvenile Court, ex parte F (a minor)

e

QUEEN'S BENCH DIVISION
STEPHEN BROWN LJ AND McCULLOUGH J
13 MARCH 1986

f *Magistrates – Summary trial – Offence triable summarily or on indictment – Decision to proceed with summary trial of juvenile – Differently constituted bench refusing to proceed with summary trial and committing defendant for trial at Crown Court – Whether magistrates having power to review a properly considered decision as to mode of trial before summary or committal proceedings commence – Magistrates' Courts Act 1980, s 24(1)(a).*

g On 20 September 1985 the defendant, who was aged 16, appeared before magistrates charged with robbery and possessing a firearm, both of which were offences in respect of which the magistrates had power under s 24(1)(a)[a] of the Magistrates' Courts Act 1980 to commit the defendant to the Crown Court for trial on indictment. The magistrates decided not to commit the defendant for trial but to proceed summarily. No plea was taken and the hearing was adjourned. Subsequently, the defendant failed to surrender to

h bail and allegedly committed further offences while on bail. On 6 November the defendant appeared before a differently constituted bench of magistrates which, considering the charge of robbery to be unsuitable for summary trial, purported to reverse the decision made by the first bench on 20 September and committed the defendant for trial at the Crown Court. The defendant sought, inter alia, an order of certiorari to quash the second bench's decision, contending that magistrates had no power

j to review a properly considered decision of a differently constituted bench of magistrates.

Held – A decision by magistrates under s 24(1)(a) of the 1980 Act to commit for trial or proceed summarily could be reviewed by magistrates at any time up to the beginning of

---

a   Section 24(1), so far as material, is set out at p 19 c to e, post

summary trial or the committal proceedings if there had been a change of circumstances
since the original decision was made or if the court's attention was drawn to circumstances *a*
which the court had not been aware of when the original decision was made. However,
once magistrates had made a decision under s 24(1)(*a*) after proper inquiry and
consideration of all relevant factors that decision could not be reversed merely by re-
examining the case afresh on the same material. Since the second bench had merely
taken a different view of the facts from the first bench and had not taken into
consideration any new circumstances, such as the offences committed while on bail, they *b*
had exceeded their power. The application would therefore be granted and their decision
to commit the defendant for trial would be quashed (see p 22 *g h*, p 23 *b c f* to p 24 *c*,
post).

Notes
For offences triable either way in proceedings before a magistrates' court, see 29 Halsbury's *c*
Laws (4th edn) para 302.
   For the summary trial of young persons, see 24 ibid para 898:9.
   For the Magistrates' Courts Act 1980, s 24, see 50(2) Halsbury's Statutes (3rd edn) 1465.

Case referred to in judgments
Chief Constable of West Midlands Police v Gillard [1985] 3 All ER 634, sub nom *R v Dudley* *d*
   Justices, ex p Gillard [1986] AC 442, [1985] 3 WLR 936, HL.

Cases also cited
R v Birmingham Justices, ex p Hodgson [1985] 2 All ER 193, [1985] QB 1131, [1985] 2 WLR
   630, DC.
R v Highbury Corner Metropolitan Stipendiary Magistrate, ex p Weekes [1985] QB 1147,
   [1985] 2 WLR 643, DC.   *e*
R v Nottingham Justices, ex p Davies [1980] 2 All ER 775, [1981] QB 38, [1980] 3 WLR 15,
   DC.
R v South Hackney Juvenile Court, ex p R B (a minor) and C B (a minor) (1983) 77 Cr App R
   294, DC.

Applications for judicial review   *f*
F, a juvenile, applied by his next friend and father, with the leave of Nolan J granted on
21 January 1986, for (i) an order of certiorari to quash a decision of the respondents, the
Newham Juvenile Court (the magistrates), on 6 December 1985 whereby the court
declined to assume summary jurisdiction over the applicant on various charges brought
by the Metropolitan Police (the prosecutor) and on which he appeared before the court,
(ii) an order of mandamus compelling the magistrates to begin to try summarily the   *g*
charges against the applicant, and (iii) an order of prohibition to prohibit the magistrates
from committing the applicant for trial at the Crown Court. On 22 January the applicant
was committed for trial at the Crown Court at Snaresbrook. The applicant, by his next
friend and father further applied, with the leave of Simon Brown J granted on 11
February 1986, for orders of (i) certiorari to quash the decision of 22 January, (ii) certiorari
to quash the applicant's committal for trial on a charge of dishonest handling, and (iii) *h*
mandamus to compel the magistrates to try the dishonest handling charge summarily.
The facts are set out in the judgment of Stephen Brown LJ.

Richard Sutton for the applicant.
F A Philpott for the magistrates.
Barry Press for the prosecutor.   *j*

STEPHEN BROWN LJ. This is an application for judicial review by F, a juvenile, by
his next friend and father. He seeks to quash decisions of the Newham Juvenile Court,
firstly, of 6 November 1985 whereby the court purported to decline to entertain
summary trial of two offences, robbery and possessing a firearm, and, secondly, the

subsequent order of 22 January 1986 that he should be committed for trial on those
a charges to the Crown Court at Snaresbrook. He also seeks to quash an order of the same
bench of magistrates committing him to the Crown Court for trial on an offence of
dishonestly handling stolen goods.

The facts giving rise to these applications are somewhat unusual. The applicant, who
is 16 years of age, appeared before the magistrates at the Newham Juvenile Court on 9
August 1985 charged with an offence of robbery, it being alleged that on 6 August 1985
b at Barking Road, he robbed one Peter Uhl of a Trustee Savings Bank security bag
containing a quantity of foreign currency and correspondence valued at £200. He was
subsequently also charged with an offence of having with him an imitation firearm.

The matter was then adjourned. It appears that when interviewed he had made
'confessions' to those particular matters. He next came before the court on 20 September
1985 when the court considered, pursuant to s 24(1) of the Magistrates' Court Act 1980,
c the mode of trial of this juvenile offender. Section 24(1) provides:

> 'Where a person under the age of 17 appears or is brought before a magistrates'
> court on an information charging him with an indictable offence other than
> homicide, he shall be tried summarily unless—(*a*) he has attained the age of 14 and
> the offence is such as is mentioned in subsection (2) of section 53 of the Children
> and Young Persons Act 1933 (under which young persons convicted on indictment
d > of certain grave crimes may be sentenced to be detained for long periods) and the
> court considers that if he is found guilty of the offence it ought to be possible to
> sentence him in pursuance of that subsection . . . and accordingly in a case falling
> within paragraph (*a*) . . . of this subsection the court shall commit the accused for
> trial if either it is of opinion that there is sufficient evidence to put him on trial or it
> has power under section 6(2) above so to commit him without consideration of the
e > evidence.'

The charges of robbery and of carrying a firearm were offences falling within the
ambit of s 53(2) of the Children and Young Persons Act 1933, and accordingly the court
had to consider whether, if he were to be found guilty of those offences, it ought to be
possible to sentence him in pursuance of that subsection.

f On that occasion the affidavit of the applicant's solicitor shows, and this is confirmed
before this court by counsel who then appeared to prosecute on behalf of the Metropolitan
Police, that details of the prosecution evidence were served, that the prosecution indicated
that the case was ready to proceed, and that representations were then made by counsel
for the prosecution that the proceedings were suitable for summary trial. Prosecuting
counsel referred the court to the section which I have just read and drew the attention of
g the court to its powers under that section and suggested the approach which he submitted
it would be appropriate for the court to adopt. It so happened that at that stage the
solicitor for the applicant opposed summary trial and invited the magistrates to consider
committing the applicant for trial to the Crown Court.

In his affidavit before this court Mr Murphy, the solicitor acting for the applicant, says
very frankly:

h > 'At that stage, on behalf of [F], I invited the court to consider committing him for
> trial to the Crown Court. At that stage, I had in mind certain advantages to the
> defendant of a trial by judge and jury in view of the nature of his defence.'

However, the magistrates did not accept his representations; they acceded to the
submission of counsel for the prosecution and decided that the matter should proceed by
j way of summary trial.

It appears to be quite clear therefore that the magistrates listened to the competing
representations and made a considered decision and then announced it in open court. No
plea was taken: they remanded the applicant for further consideration of the evidence.

On 27 September the matter came before the court again. No pleas were taken to the
charges, but the solicitor acting for the applicant intimated to the court that all the

charges were to be contested. The magistrates then adjourned the proceedings to be tried
summarily by the Newham Juvenile Court on 21 October. They then also granted bail *a*
to the applicant subject to certain conditions.

On 27 September, both parties, that is to say the prosecution and the applicant, were
represented: the prosecution by counsel, and the applicant by his solicitor, Mr Murphy.

It would seem therefore that, had matters taken their ordinary course, on 21 October
summary trial of the charges would have commenced. However, on 21 October the
applicant failed to appear in answer to his bail. A warrant was issued and after arrest he *b*
appeared again on 30 October.

He was then charged with further additional offences. First of all with failing to
surrender to his bail on 21 October, and also with a number of offences contrary to the
Road Traffic Acts alleged to have been committed on 10 May 1985 and on 27 September
1985.

In addition to those matters he was also charged with an offence alleged to have been *c*
committed on 28 October 1985 of dishonestly handling stolen goods. It is also the fact
that he should have appeared at the Newham Juvenile Court on 25 October 1985 in
relation to charges of driving whilst disqualified, but he failed to appear on that occasion
as well as on 21 October so that it was on two separate occasions that he failed to answer
his bail.

On 30 October a differently constituted bench of magistrates was sitting from the *d*
bench which had sat on 20 September. In addition this bench were served by a different
clerk. It appears from the affidavit of Mr Murphy that on this occasion both the
magistrates and the clerk expressed surprise that on 20 September the bench had
considered the charge of robbery to be suitable for summary trial, and indicated that the
court would wish to review their decision. The matter was then adjourned and the court
sat next on 6 November 1985. *e*

On 6 November 1985 the justices purported to review the decision on their colleagues
on 20 September to try the robbery charge and the firearms charge summarily. This
court has the advantage of full affidavits from the magistrates sitting on this occasion.
The affidavit of Mr George Waldron reveals what occurred on 30 October and
6 November. He states:

> 'On the 30th day of October, 1985 the Applicant appeared before me and my *f*
> colleagues. We were bewildered and concerned with the decision of the 20th day of
> September, 1985 and we inquired of our clerk as to whether we had the power to
> reconsider the mode of trial after being apprised of the circumstances giving rise to
> the commission of the offences of the 6th day of August, 1985. In our view the
> circumstances were consistent with a robbery carried out in a professional and
> ruthless manner and our powers of sentencing would have been totally inadequate. *g*
> Our clerk advised that in order to be fair to both the prosecutor and the Applicant
> we should accede to a request from the Applicant for a short adjournment to enable
> both parties to research the issue and argue it out in court. We accordingly adjourned
> the hearing until the 6th day of November, 1985.'

On 6 November the affidavit shows that the magistrates inquired of the parties as to *h*
what material and circumstances were placed before the bench which had sat on 20
September and Mr Waldron's affidavit continues:

> 'In our view the bench on the 20th day of September, 1985 could not have had
> proper regard to all the material factors because they were never referred to them.
> We were of the opinion that our colleagues may well have been misled into thinking
> that whatever view they took of the circumstances in which the offences were *j*
> committed it was open to them at the end of the day to commit for sentence. That
> with respect is not the proper approach. With reference to the effect of section 25 of
> the Act of 1980 we appreciated that although the juvenile court (as with the adult
> court) may at any time before the conclusion of the evidence for the prosecution

a
discontinue the summary trial and proceed to inquire into the offence as examining justices such a power is limited to cases where there is a trial after a plea of not guilty (see *Chief Constable of West Midlands Police v Gillard* ([1985] 3 All ER 634, [1986] AC 442)). Effectively therefore any plea of guilty to the charges renders the section ineffective. All the more reason we thought that proper inquiry be made at the outset.'

b
Then Mr Waldron sums up the view which the magistrates came to on 6 November in the following sentences:

'To put it in a nutshell on the facts of this case the lack of an informed decision based upon all the criteria referred to in *extenso* was in truth no decision at all. We accordingly refused jurisdiction.'

c
Indeed, the magistrates then purported to reverse the decision of the bench of 20 September and they proceeded in due course to commit the applicant for trial to the Crown Court on those two charges.

In order to give a complete picture of the events which took place on 6 November it is necessary also to consider what took place in relation to the charge of dishonestly handling stolen goods. This was of course a new charge which had not been before the bench which had sat on 20 September. The offence had not then been committed, and so the

d
magistrates on 6 November were obliged to consider under s 24 of the Magistrates' Courts Act 1980 whether the offence of handling stolen property should be committed for trial or whether it should follow the prima facie normal procedure of being tried summarily under the provisions of s 24(1)(*a*) of the 1980 Act.

This is an offence which in fact falls within the ambit of s 53(2) of the Children and Young Persons Act 1933, and accordingly the court had to consider whether, if the

e
applicant were to be found guilty of that offence, it ought to be possible to sentence him in pursuance of that subsection. In fact the magistrates say that they then considered the further count of handling stolen goods, and I quote from the affidavit of Mr Waldron:

'We then considered the further count of handling stolen goods which was alleged to have been committed while the Applicant was on bail. We took a serious view of

f
this fact. We were told that the property in question had been stolen from a motor vehicle in the Hornchurch area which is some considerable distance away from where the Applicant was apprehended. Illegal use of such property [I interpolate, they were bank credit cards] could have caused loss to many innocent people with little or no prospect of compensation. Having regard to the nature of the offence and the circumstances in which it was committed we declined jurisdiction.'

g
That meant that they declined to try it summarily and in due course they committed that matter for trial at the Crown Court. That was a separate committal, for it is clear from the affidavit of Mr Waldron that the magistrates dealt quite separately with the robbery and firearms offences and the later offence of dishonestly handling stolen credit cards.

h
For the sake of completeness I should say that the road traffic offences of which there was a substantial number, driving whilst disqualified, taking a motor car without consent, and driving whilst not covered by a policy of insurance, were adjourned sine die.

The submission made by counsel on behalf of the applicant is that in relation to the committal of the robbery and firearms offences, the magistrates exceeded their powers.

j
He submits that the bench on 20 September having made their decision and announced it and given the necessary directions to proceed to a summary trial, it was not open to review by a differently constituted bench. It is submitted that the magistrates on 20 September considered all material matters. That this is so is established by the submission made by counsel who appears today for the prosecution and was himself present in court acting on behalf of the prosecution on 20 September. I accept from him that the

magistrates were told all the relevant facts and that he directed their attention to the relevant considerations arising under s 24 of the 1980 Act.

In those circumstances I am unable to accept the contention made in the affidavit of Mr Waldron that the full facts were not placed before the bench on 20 September.

The submission which counsel for the applicant makes therefore is that the magistrates on 6 November had no power to reverse a decision which had been taken after due and proper consideration on 20 September. It is of course the case, as appears from the evidence contained in the affidavits, that on 6 November, and indeed on 30 October, it was a differently constituted bench of justices with a different clerk from the bench and the clerk which had sat on 20 September.

It would appear that the draftsman of the 1980 Act drafted the provisions of s 24 and other related provisions of the Act on the basis that one bench of magistrates would be dealing with all the stages of proceedings envisaged in s 24 and the succeeding sections. However, it is inevitable in practice that a totally differently constituted bench of magistrates may deal with succeeding stages of a case. There seems little doubt that that is the reason why this matter has arisen in this form. For my part I am bound to say that I have very considerable sympathy with the magistrates sitting on 6 November. It seems to me to be somewhat surprising that a bench of magistrates should have taken the view that an armed robbery, for that is what the offence was, was appropriate for summary trial; but of course that is not a consideration which this court can act on. The magistrates have a discretion, and it does not appear from the evidence before us, and indeed from what counsel for the prosecution has told the court, that it can be said that the magistrates did not act within their powers on 20 September.

That decision having been taken, this court has to consider what is the status of the decision of 6 November. As I have already indicated, I have very considerable sympathy with the justices who sat on 6 November. It is unfortunate in my judgment that they did not then take into account the new circumstances which had undoubtedly arisen in relation to this defendant. He had committed a further serious offence on bail, indeed more than one offence, but one serious offence in particular. He had twice broken his bail, which had been granted originally following his appearance on the robbery and firearms charges. Unfortunately, the magistrates, as is clear from their affidavits, did not take into account any additional circumstances nor, it would seem, any additional facts beyond those which had been placed before the magistrates on 20 September. In those circumstances the question has to be asked: were they at liberty to review and reverse a decision which had been formally taken and announced by a properly constituted bench of magistrates having the power and duty to make the inquiry under s 24(1)? There is an apparent anomaly if they do not have such power, because s 25 provides that where a court has begun to try an information summarily it can, if it takes the view that it should not continue to try the case summarily, continue the hearing as examining magistrates with a view to committal for trial. It may therefore seem anomalous that they cannot change their minds before actually embarking on a summary trial.

Magistrates, like every other court, must of course exercise such discretion as they have judicially, but this is not merely a matter of discretion; it is a matter of power. Have they got power to reverse a decision taken by their colleagues at an earlier hearing? In my judgment the whole scheme of the 1980 Act suggests that they do not have that power before embarking on the hearing. Once a decision has been made after proper inquiry and consideration of all relevant factors, it cannot be reversed merely by re-examining the case afresh on the same material.

It seems to be that they may well have had the opportunity for taking a different view from that taken by their colleagues in the light of the new and additional factors which had emerged since 20 September. For example, not only was it alleged that a further serious offence had been committed whilst the applicant was on bail, and with which the bench had to deal quite separately, but in addition a great deal more information was before them as to the character of this defendant. They now knew that a number of other offences were alleged to have been committed by him from May onwards. Those a were matters which were not before the bench which had sat on 20 September, so there was in my judgment material on which it could be argued that it would be proper for the magistrates to review the question as to mode of trial.

As I have said, that was not in fact the way in which these magistrates proceeded. Their affidavits are very frank and clear about that matter. It seems to me that this was simply a different view formed on the same facts by a differently constituted bench. In my judgment in the result they did exceed their powers. Prima facie therefore that
b decision should be quashed and also the decision to commit for trial.

I have considered whether, in exercising the discretion which this court has, it might however be appropriate in this case to say: 'Well, no real harm has been done because although the magistrates did not in fact consider the new material available, nevertheless it was available, and if it had been taken into account it would have justified their decision to commit for trial.' However, I bear in mind that the applicant would be put at
c a disadvantage as a result. Accordingly, I take the view that it is inevitable, although unfortunate, that his committal for trial on those two charges should be quashed.

The position with regard to the handling offence is, however, quite different in my judgment. The magistrates had to exercise their discretion under the provisions of s 24(1)(a) in relation to that matter quite separately. The affidavit of Mr Waldron to which I have referred shows that they did in fact do so, and took into account, as they
d were entitled to take into account, the nature of the charge, the fact that the offence alleged was alleged to have been committed whilst the defendant was on bail for the very serious offence of robbery. In my judgment they were fully entitled within the exercise of their discretion to decide that summary trial was not appropriate and therefore to commit for trial.

Arguments have been addressed to us as to whether that was reasonable in view of the
e fact that prima facie dishonest handling is not so serious an offence as robbery. Would it, counsel for the applicant asks, really merit a punishment which exceeded the powers that the magistrates had under their summary jurisdiction? It is not for this court to decide the merits of the matter. We have to consider the exericise of their powers by the magistrates and to decide whether it is shown that they exceeded their powers or exercised their discretion so wrongly that we have to say that their decision was plainly
f wrong. That is not the case in my judgment in this instance. The magistrates were fully justified in committing the defendant for trial in relation to that matter. The application in relation to that decision fails.

The result will be that the court will have to say that the committal for trial in relation to the robbery and firearms offences must be quashed and these cases remitted to the justices for the summary trial of these offences. It will be open to the magistrates, having
g commenced the summary trial, to consider exercising their powers under s 25(6) of the 1980 Act.

McCULLOUGH J. I agree. In my opinion a decision under s 24(1)(a) of the Magistrates' Courts Act 1980 is not irrevocable. However, once such a decision has been taken and announced, it will in the great majority of case stand. But in a case where trial on
h indictment has been decided on, it is in my opinion open to the justices to review that decision at any stage up to the start of their inquiry as examining justices. Such a review will be permissible if a change of circumstances has occurred since the original decision was taken, and also if circumstances are brought to the attention of the court which, although existing when the original decision was taken, were not then drawn to the attention of the court. I am thinking, for example, of a case where justices are told on a
j later occasion that the facts of the charge were less serious than the court was originally led to believe; or where the court learns facts about the defendant's background, character, and antecedents, which indicate that if he is found guilty there will be no need after all for it to be possible to sentence him in pursuance of s 53(2) of the Children and Young Persons Act 1933.

Similarly, in a case where summary trial has been decided on, it is in my opinion open

to the justices to review that decision at any stage up to the beginning of the summary
trial. Such a review is permissible if a change of circumstances has occurred since the *a*
original decision was taken and also if circumstances are brought to the attention of the
court which, although existing when the original decision was taken, were not then
drawn to the attention of the court. I am thinking in this instance of a defendant who
commits further serious offences whilst on bail, or where the court perhaps is told that
the factual circumstances of the charge which it was considering were more serious than
was originally believed to be the case.   *b*

Put more shortly, at any stage before the tracks divide, the decision as to which track
is to be pursued is open to revision on the demonstration of what may shortly be called a
change of circumstances. I see nothing in s 24(1)(*a*) of the 1980 Act to prevent this. On
the contrary, I take it to have been the intention of Parliament that the decision should
be taken on the fullest information available to the court immediately before the tracks
divide. Any other construction might lead to injustice. I see no observation in *R v South* *c*
Hackney Juvenile Court, ex p R B (a minor) and C B (a minor) (1983) 77 Cr App R 294 as
tending to the contrary. That case was not concerned with a change of circumstances
occurring before the tracks divided. Nor in my view does the existence of s 25(5), (6) and
(7) of the 1980 Act prevent the construction which I believe to be right. Those subsections
deal with the situation after the division in the tracks has been passed.

In *Chief Constable of West Midlands Police v Gillard* [1985] 3 All ER 634, [1986] AC 442 *d*
that point had been passed: Gillard had already pleaded guilty. Therefore the process of
summary trial had already begun. The situation with which I have been dealing is that
which appertains before the tracks divide.

Application allowed.

                                                                              e
14 March. *The court refused leave to appeal to the House of Lords but certified, under s 1(2) of*
the Administration of Justice Act 1960, that the following point of law of general public importance
was involved in the decision: whether, in the absence of fresh material or any change in
circumstances, justices have power to review a decision previously made by justices for the same
petty sessional division under s 24(1)(a) of the Magistrates' Courts Act 1980 before the
commencement of the summary trial or the inquiry as examining justices.   *f*

Solicitors: *Duthie Hart & Duthie* (for the applicant); *Sharpe Pritchard & Co* (for the
magistrates); *D M O'Shea* (for the prosecutor).

                                            Marc Beaumont Esq   Barrister.

R v Martindale

a

COURT OF APPEAL, CRIMINAL DIVISION
LORD LANE CJ, TAYLOR AND SCHIEMANN JJ
24 JUNE 1986

b

Drugs – Controlled drugs – Unlawful possession – Defence – Presence of drug forgotten – Applicant obtaining cannabis in Canada, putting it in his wallet and forgetting about it – Whether applicant in possession of cannabis – Misuse of Drugs Act 1971, s 5(2).

The applicant was stopped and searched in the course of a police operation in connection with the possession of drugs. He had in his pocket a wallet containing a small quantity of cannabis resin and was charged with possession of a controlled drug, contrary to s 5(2)

c

of the Misuse of Drugs Act 1971. At his trial the applicant contended that the drug had been given to him two years previously in Canada and that he had forgotten about its presence in his wallet. The judge ruled that since the applicant knew what the substance was and had kept it in his possession, even though he had forgotten about its existence, he had no defence to the charge. The applicant changed his plea to guilty and was convicted. He applied for leave to appeal against the conviction on the ground that

d

because he had forgotten about the existence of the drug in his wallet there could be no 'possession' of the drug on his part.

Held – Possession did not depend on the alleged possessor's powers of memory nor did it come and go as memory revived or failed. Accordingly, although a person did not necessarily possess every article which he might have in his pocket, if he himself put an

e

article into his wallet knowing what it was and put the wallet into his pocket he remained in possession even though his memory of its presence faded or disappeared altogether. It followed that the judge had been correct in his ruling. The application for leave to appeal would therefore be dismissed (see p 26 *g* to *j* and p 27 *j*, post).

R v Buswell [1972] 1 All ER 75 followed.

R v Russell (1984) 81 Cr App R 315 not followed.

f

Notes

For the unauthorised possession of a controlled drug, see 11 Halsbury's Laws (4th edn) para 1092, and for cases on the subject, see 15 Digest (Reissue) 1068–1071, 9154–9169.

For the Misuse of Drugs Act 1971, s 5, see 41 Halsbury's Statutes (3rd edn) 884.

g

Cases referred to in judgment

R v Buswell [1972] 1 All ER 75, [1972] 1 WLR 64, CA.

R v Russell (1984) 81 Cr App R 315, CA.

Cases also cited

R v Bello (1978) 67 Cr App R 288, CA.

Warner v Metropolitan Police Comr [1968] 2 All ER 356, [1969] AC 256, HL.

h

Application for leave to appeal against conviction

Clive Martindale applied for an extension of time and for leave to appeal against his conviction in the Crown Court at Leeds before his Honour Judge Randolph on a charge of unlawful possession of a controlled drug, namely 366 mg of cannabis resin, contrary to s 5(2) of the Misuse of Drugs Act 1971. The applicant had pleaded not guilty to the

j

offence but, following a ruling by the judge, he changed his plea to guilty and was conditionally discharged for 12 months. The facts are set out in the judgment of the court.

Jeremy Hill-Baker (assigned by the Registrar of Criminal Appeals) for the applicant.
H A Richardson for the Crown.

LORD LANE CJ delivered the following judgment of the court. On 19 December 1985 in the Crown Court at Leeds the applicant pleaded not guilty to possessing a *a* controlled drug (cannabis resin).

Submissions were made to the judge at an early stage of the trial as to the proposed defence to be put forward by the applicant. After the judge had heard those submissions he came to the conclusion, and so ruled, that the proposed defence could not amount to a valid defence to the charge. The result was that the applicant then pleaded guilty and was conditionally discharged for 12 months for the offence. *b*

He now applies for an extension of time of one day, which we have granted, and he also applies for leave to appeal against his conviction.

The facts of the case are simple and are these. On 11 July 1985 the police in Bradford mounted an operation in connection with the possession of drugs. As a result of that operation the applicant was stopped, because the police suspected that he might be in possession of a controlled drug. He was consequently searched. In a leather wallet, which *c* was in his pocket, was found a small quantity, 366 mg to be precise, of cannabis resin. He was cautioned. He was asked what the substance was, and he replied, 'Blow, but I didn't know it was there.' He was then taken to the police station and interviewed. He said that the substance had been given to him in Canada some two years previously. He did not smoke cannabis and he did not know that it was in his wallet.

The submissions to which reference has already been made were these. Counsel for *d* the applicant said that that would be the defence, namely that the applicant had been given the cannabis some little while before whilst he was living in Canada. He then came to this country and that small quantity of cannabis stayed in his wallet. The submission was that he did not know he had it when he came back to this country. It had gone completely out of his mind.

Having heard argument, the judge ruled that it was immaterial when the applicant *e* acquired the drug, or indeed where he acquired it. The mere fact that he got it outside of the jurisdiction was neither here nor there. That part of the judge's ruling is now conceded to be correct. The ground based on its acquisition in Canada is abandoned. He knew, said the judge, what the substance was, he had kept it and he was in possession of it even if he had forgotten its existence.

Counsel for the applicant has repeated those submissions before this court. His *f* contention is this. Although the applicant had admittedly been given the cannabis in Canada and had put it in his wallet where it remained ever since, nevertheless, it is submitted, that was two years or more previous to the arrest. In the meantime the applicant had forgotten all about it. Therefore when it was found in his wallet in his pocket he was not in possession of it. Possession, goes on the argument, does not exist unless there is knowledge of the presence of the article and of its nature. There is no *g* knowledge if recollection of the presence of the article has failed. In other words there is no possession if the alleged possessor has forgotten that he has the article.

In the judgment of this court that argument is fallacious. It is true that a man does not necessarily possess every article which he may have in his pocket. If, for example, some evil-minded person secretly slips a portion of cannabis resin into the pocket of another without the other's knowledge, the other is not in law in possession of the cannabis. That *h* scarcely needs stating.

But the present situation is different. Here the applicant himself put the cannabis in his wallet knowing what it was and put the wallet into his pocket. In our judgment, subject to the authorities, to which reference will have to be made in a moment, he remained in possession, even though his memory of the presence of the drug had faded or disappeared altogether. Possession does not depend on the alleged possessor's powers *j* of memory. Nor does possession come and go as memory revives or fails. If it were to do so, a man with a poor memory would be acquitted, he with the good memory would be convicted.

We had our attention drawn to a recent decision of another division of this court, namely *R v Russell* (1984) 81 Cr App R 315. The facts of that case were these. Police officers stopped a car driven by the appellant. Inside was found a knife taped to the inside

of the compartment under the dashboard and a cosh, consisting of a piece of rubber hose
a   filled at one end with metal. The cosh was under the driver's seat. The appellant was
charged with possessing offensive weapons in a public place, the knife which was the
subject of count 1 and the cosh the subject of count 2. He was acquitted on count 1 and
convicted on count 2. His defence to count 2 was that although he had put the cosh
under the seat he had forgotten all about it. On appeal that the trial judge had failed to
direct the jury that the onus was on the prosecution to prove that the appellant had the
b   cosh with him 'knowingly', Jupp J, delivering the judgment of the court, said (at 319):

'It would in our judgment be wrong to hold that a man knowingly has a weapon
with him if his forgetfulness of its existence or presence in his car is so complete as
to amount to ignorance that it is there at all. This is not a defence which juries
would in the ordinary way be very likely to accept, but if it is raised it should be left
to them for their decision.'

c
Counsel on behalf of the Crown invites us to say that that decision in R v Russell is
distinguishable on its facts from the instant case.
We do not pause to consider the matter on that basis, because what was not drawn to
the attention of the court in R v Russell was an earlier decision of this court, namely R v
Buswell [1972] 1 All ER 75, [1972] 1 WLR 64. It is only necessary for me to read a passage
d   from R v Buswell to illustrate how, had the decision been brought to the attention of the
court in R v Russell, the decision in R v Russell would almost certainly have gone the other
way. The judgment was delivered by Phillimore LJ, the other two members of the court
being Park and Griffiths JJ, and the passage reads ([1972] 1 All ER 75 at 78, [1972] 1
WLR 64 at 67):

'Dealing with what seems to be the one real problem here, namely the question
e   whether drugs lawfully acquired by a prescription in some way pass out of your
possession if you forget you have got them, or if you think that they have been
destroyed, whereas in fact they are still sitting in your drawer, this court thinks that
it cannot be said that simply as a result of your mistaken belief or your failure to
appreciate that you have got them, thereby they in some way passed out of your
f   possession. Of course it is quite different if I hand something over to someone else
to destroy, so that it passes from my custody and they officiously put it back in my
house without telling me; or if I throw something into the dustbin for disposal by
the borough council and some officious person decides that I could not have meant
to throw it away and puts it back in my house, so that I have it without knowing.
In those sort of cases you are back on the problem which was dealt with in the cases
to which I have referred, ie whether something comes into your possession. But if
g   you have got it in your custody and you put it in some safe place, and then forget
that you have got it, and discover a year or two later, when you happen to look in
that particular receptacle that it is still there, it seems to this court idle to suggest
that during those two years it has not been in your possession. It has been there
under your hand and control. If it has not been in your possession, in whose
possession has it been? Presumably it has not been in a state of limbo.'

h
As I say, had that judgment been brought to the attention of the court in R v Russell,
the decision in that case would almost certainly have been different. In any event, so far
as the two cases are inconsistent, we follow the earlier case, namely R v Buswell. It is in
accordance with the views which we ourselves have formed. In our judgment the judge
in the present case was right to take the course which he did, and this application is
j   accordingly refused.

Application refused.

Solicitors: *Richard Otley*, Wakefield (for the Crown).

N P Metcalfe Esq   Barrister.

Kingdom of Spain v
Christie Manson & Woods Ltd and another

CHANCERY DIVISION

SIR NICOLAS BROWNE-WILKINSON V-C

13, 18, 19, 20, 21 MARCH 1986

Declaration – Right of action – Legal or equitable right enforceable by declaration – Injury to property or pecuniary damage – Foreign state alleging export documents relating to valuable work of art forged – State not claiming title to work of art or legal interest in documents – Whether forged export documents would cause injury to property of or pecuniary damage to foreign state and its subjects – Whether foreign state having legal or equitable right enforceable by declaration.

In 1983, following a series of sales, a valuable oil painting by Goya was removed from Spain to Zurich, where it was bought by art dealers (the owners) who offered the painting to an American museum. As a result of representations made by the Spanish government to the museum that the export documents obtained for the removal of the painting from Spain were forgeries, the museum refused to buy the painting and the owners announced that it would be offered for sale by auction in London in April 1986. By an originating summons issued in March 1986 the Spanish government sought declarations as against the auctioneers and the owners that the official export documents had been illegally forged. The auctioneers and the owners applied to strike out the summons, contending that the Spanish government had no legal or equitable rights as against them relating to the use of the allegedly forged documents and that therefore the summons disclosed no cause of action or should be struck out as an abuse of process because the ulterior purpose of the proceedings was to force down the price of the painting at the auction. The Spanish government did not make any claim to title to the painting or to ownership or interest in the export documents.

Held – Since the court had jurisdiction to restrain a deliberate act or threat to do an act on the part of a defendant which would injure the property of, or cause pecuniary damage to, a plaintiff who would not otherwise have a cause of action, such an act or threat could give rise to a legal or equitable right which the court would enforce by way of a declaration. Applying that principle, the continued use of forged export documents of the Spanish state purporting to allow the lawful export of works of art from Spain could debase the credibility of genuine export documents issued by the Spanish government and such debasement would cause damage to the property of, or pecuniary damage to, the Spanish state and its subjects. It was therefore arguable that the Spanish government had a legal or equitable right which it was entitled to have enforced by way of a declaration even though it did not have and did not claim title to the painting. Furthermore, since the Spanish government had a legitimate interest in preventing the continued use of forged documents of the Spanish state and since it had not been shown that its predominant objective was to force down the auction price, the summons would not be struck out as an abuse of process (see p 34 *c j*, p 36 *d* to *f j* to p 37 *e j* and p 38 *a c e f*, post).

Emperor of Austria v Day and Kossuth (1861) 3 De GF & J 217 applied.

Notes

For declaratory judgments, see 1 Halsbury's Laws (4th edn) paras 185–186 and 37 ibid paras 252–253.

Cases referred to in judgment

Emperor of Austria v Day and Kossuth (1861) 3 De GF & J 217, 45 ER 861, CA.

Gouriet v Union of Post Office Workers [1977] 3 All ER 70, [1978] AC 435, [1977] 3 WLR 300, HL.

a   *Lewis's Declaration of Trust, Re, Lewis v Lewis, Lewis v Ryder* [1953] 1 All ER 1005, sub nom
    Loudon v Ryder (No 2) [1953] Ch 423, [1953] 2 WLR 863.
    RCA Corp v Pollard [1982] 3 All ER 771, [1983] Ch 135, [1982] 3 WLR 1007, CA.
    Reuter (R J) Co Ltd v Ferd Mulhens [1953] 2 All ER 1160, [1954] Ch 50, [1953] 3 WLR
    789, CA.

Cases also cited

b   *A-G of New Zealand v Ortiz* [1983] 2 All ER 93, [1984] AC 1, HL.
    British Medical Association v Marsh (1931) 48 RPC 565.
    Dysart (Earl) v Hammerton & Co [1914] 1 Ch 822, CA.
    Erven Warnink BV v J Townend & Sons (Hull) Ltd [1979] 2 All ER 927, [1979] AC 731, HL.
    Goldsmith v Sperrings Ltd [1977] 2 All ER 566, [1977] 1 WLR 478, CA.
    Guaranty Trust Co of New York v Hannay & Co [1915] 2 KB 536, [1914–15] All ER Rep 24,
c   CA.
    Henderson v Radio Corp Pty Ltd [1969] RPC 218, NSW SC.
    Lonrho Ltd v Shell Petroleum Co Ltd (No 2) [1981] 2 All ER 456, [1982] AC 173, HL.
    Springhead Spinning Co v Riley (1868) LR 6 Eq 551.
    Thorne RDC v Bunting [1972] 1 All ER 439, [1972] Ch 470.
    Tolley v J & S Fry & Sons Ltd [1931] AC 383, [1931] All ER Rep 131, HL.
d   *Williams & Humbert Ltd v W & H Trade Marks (Jersey) Ltd* [1986] 1 All ER 129, [1986] 2
    WLR 24, HL.

Originating summons and summons

By an originating summons dated 5 March 1986, the Kingdom of Spain (the Spanish
government) sought as against the defendants, (i) Christie Manson & Woods Ltd
e   (Christie's) and (ii) Overseas Art Investments Ltd (OAI), declarations that documents
purporting to authorise the export of an oil painting from Spain were forgeries and that
the painting had been illegally exported. By a summons dated 11 March 1986, the
defendants sought orders (i) that the Spanish government's claim be struck out and
judgment be given for the defendants with costs on the grounds that the Spanish
government's claim disclosed no reasonable cause of action and/or was scandalous,
f   frivolous or vexatious and/or was otherwise an abuse of the process of the court pursuant
to RSC Ord 18 and 19 and/or pursuant to the inherent jurisdiction of the court, and (ii)
that if the Spanish government's claim was not struck out, for an order pursuant to RSC
Ord 28, r 8 that the proceedings continue as if begun by writ of summons. The facts are
set out in the judgment.

g   *Mark Littman QC* and *M G Tugendhat* for the Spanish government.
    Christopher S C S Clarke QC and *George Leggatt* for Christie's.
    Peter Scott QC and *Peter Goldsmith* for OAI.

SIR NICOLAS BROWNE-WILKINSON V-C. These proceedings relate to an oil
painting by Goya called 'La Marquesa de Santa Cruz'. By an originating summons dated
h   5 March 1986 the Kingdom of Spain claims certain declarations relating to three
documents; two of them are dated 30 March 1983 and the third is dated 5 April 1983.
Those three documents purport to be official documents of the State of Spain authorising
the export of the picture from Spain. The declarations are sought against the first
defendants, Christie Manson & Woods Ltd (which I will call 'Christie's'), who are offering
the picture for sale at auction in London on 11 April 1986 on the instructions of the
j   owners of the picture, the second defendants, Overseas Art Investments Ltd (which I will
call 'OAI').

The summons is headed up 'IN THE MATTER OF . . .' the three documents in question.
The declarations sought are these:

'1. That the first of the above mentioned instruments is false in that it purports to
have been altered on 30th March 1983 by the addition of stamps and seals purporting

to be of a department of the Government of Spain, namely the Ministerio de
Cultura, Direccion General del Patrimonio Artistico Archivos y Museos (which was *a*
in March 1983 called Direccion General de Bellas Artes y Archivos), and by the
addition of the signature of the Secretary General thereof, whereas no person had
authority to or did make the said alterations on behalf of the Government of Spain
and the signature is not that of the said Secretary General:

2. That the second of the above mentioned instruments is false in the same
respects as the first of the above mentioned documents: *b*

3. That the third of the above mentioned instruments is false in that it purports
to have been made signed and sealed on the authority of the Ministerio de Comercio
of the Government of Spain on 5th April 1983 whereas no person had authority to
or did make or sign the said document on behalf of the Government of Spain on the
said date or at all, the seal is not that of the Ministerio de Comercio (of which the
correct name was in March 1983 Ministerio de Economia y Hacienda Secretaria de *c*
Estado de Comercio) and the signature is not that of any signatory thereof:

4. That the export from Spain of the oil painting known as 'La Marquesa de Santa
Cruz' by Goya was in violation of the Laws of Spain.'

Shortly stated, the background to this case is as follows. Until 1983 the picture was in
Spain and was owned by a Senora Valdes. It is alleged in correspondence that she sold the *d*
picture while it was still in Spain to a gentleman, Mr Saorin Bosch (who I will call
'Saorin'), at a price of about $US180,000. Saorin in turn sold the picture to Khamsin Ltd
(Khamsin) at a price of approximately $US1m, or so it appears from the documents
impugned. The negotiations for the purchase of the picture on behalf of Khamsin were
conducted by a Mr Simpson, a member of a firm of London art dealers. The defendants
in correspondence allege that the sale by Saorin to Khamsin took place when the picture *e*
was in Zurich. The defendants further allege in correspondence that the picture was
exported from Spain by Mr Saorin with the export authorities and licences required
under Spanish law for objects of historic or artistic importance, such as this picture. The
Spanish government, on the other hand, allege that those authorities and licences (being
the documents as to which the declarations are sought) were forgeries, that the requisite
consents were not obtained and that the picture was illicitly exported from Spain. *f*
Certainly the picture was removed from Spain and arrived in Zurich in April 1983.

The ultimate beneficial owners of Khamsin are the trustees of certain trusts for the
benefit of Lord Wimborne's family. The evidence of the defendants is that for fiscal
reasons Khamsin in turn sold the picture on to OAI (the present owners of the picture) in
April 1983. According to the defendants' evidence, OAI were incorporated in Liberia in
1983 and are resident in the British Virgin Islands. The majority of the board of OAI are *g*
partners in Peat Marwick Mitchell & Co, who are resident in the British Virgin Islands.
The ultimate beneficial owners of OAI are again the trustees of the Wimborne family
trusts. Lord Wimborne is himself resident in Paris.

The picture, having come into the ownership of OAI in April 1983 in Zurich, was
immediately offered to the J Paul Getty Museum in California at a price of $US12m, and
the picture was flown to the United States for inspection. It was with the museum from *h*
12 May to 8 July 1983. In July 1983 the Spanish authorities, so they allege, became aware
of the export of the picture and made representations to the museum to the effect that it
had been illegally exported. As a result of those representations the museum refused to
purchase the picture from OAI. There is no evidence where the picture was between July
1983 and January 1986; the defendants refused to disclose its whereabouts to the Spanish
authorities.   *j*

From June 1984 onwards attempts were made to negotiate a sale of the picture to the
Spanish government. Those negotiations did not get under way until February 1985 and
continued sporadically throughout that year. In broad outline OAI were offering to sell
the picture to the Spanish government at its current open market value, which they
alleged was greater than the $US12m at which it had been offered to the Getty Museum,
but subject to a small discount; having negotiated on that basis, they put forward a figure

of $US12m. The Spanish government on the other hand were negotiating on the basis of recouping to OAI their costs of acquisition plus a moderate uplift. The Spanish government never put an exact figure on their offer. Finally, by letter dated 17 December 1985 OAI gave the Spanish government until noon on 17 January 1986 to make a satisfactory offer. No response was received to that ultimatum and on 26 January 1986 an article appeared in the Sunday Times (plainly based on information provided by OAI) announcing that the picture was to be sold at Christie's in London on 11 April 1986 and giving the defendants' account of the matter.

Thereafter both sides, through the media in this country and in Spain, have indulged in a verbal battle which, in retrospect, they may think to have been at least in part ill-advised. Representatives of the Government of Spain have been reported as making allegations against the bona fides of the defendants and saying that they would take every step to stop the sale. Representatives of the defendants on the other hand have accused the Spanish government of hyperbole, of covering up an administrative blunder by accusations of forgery and of trying to depress the price of the picture. On the view I take of this case it is not necessary for me to go further into these allegations in much greater detail.

Finally by way of background I must mention two documents: first, an international convention relating to the exporting of works of art and, second, a code of practice to which Christie's are a party. The convention is called 'Convention on the means of prohibiting and preventing the illicit import, export and transfer of ownership of cultural property' and it was adopted on 14 November 1970. The United Kingdom has not acceded to the convention; Spain has acceded but only as recently as 3 February 1986 and only with effect from 10 April 1986. That convention in no way forms any part of the law of the United Kingdom. The convention defines 'cultural property' in terms which plainly cover this picture. Article 2 provides:

'The States Parties to this Convention recognise that the illicit import, export and transfer of ownership of cultural property is one of the main causes of the impoverishment of the cultural heritage of the countries of origin of such property and that international co-operation constitutes one of the most efficient means of protecting each country's cultural property against all the dangers resulting therefrom. To this end, the States Parties undertake to oppose such practices with the means at their disposal, and particularly by removing their causes, putting a stop to current practices, and by helping to make the necessary reparations.'

Article 3 provides:

'The import, export or transfer of ownership of cultural property effected contrary to the provisions adopted under this Convention by the States Parties thereto, shall be illicit.'

Article 7 deals in 7(a) by undertaking to provide measures to prevent museums and similar institutions from acquiring property which has been illegally exported. Article 7(b)(i) provides:

'The States Parties to this Convention . . . shall prohibit the import of cultural property stolen from a museum or a religious or secular public monument or similar institution . . .'

Article 7(b)(ii) then provides:

'at the request of the State Party of origin, to take appropriate steps to recover and return any such cultural property imported after the entry into force of this Convention in both States concerned, provided, however, that the requesting State shall pay just compensation to an innocent purchaser or to a person who has valid title to that property.'

It is no part of my function to construe that convention. It is sufficient to say that it appears to me that it apparently only provides for the return of goods which have been stolen from museums and other public places. It does not seem to provide for the return of pictures which have been merely illicitly imported or exported. The general tenor, *a* however, of the convention is clear: it is against illicit import and export.

The dealers code of practice stands on a rather different footing. It is a document signed by a number of bodies and institutions concerned in this country in the marketing of works of art. Amongst the signatories are Christie's themselves, the Society of London Art Dealers, Sothebys, British Antique Dealers Association and others. The code provides:

'1. In view of the world-wide concern expressed over the traffic in stolen antiques *b* and works of art and the illegal export of such objects, the U.K. fine art and antiques trade wishes to codify its standard practice as follows:

2. Members of the U.K. fine art and antiques trade undertake, to the best of their ability, not to import, export or transfer the ownership of such objects where they have reasonable cause to believe . . . (b) That an imported object has been acquired in or exported from its country of export in violation of that country's laws . . .' *c*

'4. Where a member of the U.K. fine art and antiques trade comes into possession of an object that can be demonstrated beyond reasonable doubt to have been illegally exported from its country of export and the country of export seeks its return within a reasonable period, that member, if legally free to do so, will take responsible steps to co-operate in the return of that object to the country of export. Where the code has been breached unintentionally, satisfactory reimbursement should be agreed *d* between the parties . . .'

At first sight I thought that under para 2(b) of the code, if it were established that the picture had been exported from Spain with the use of forged documents, Christie's, giving effect to that clause, would not have been prepared to auction it. That certainly was the view of the Spanish government when they started these proceedings. However *e* in the course of argument counsel for Christie's made it clear that, even if it were to be declared by the court that the documents were forgeries, Christie's would feel free to continue with the sale. They take the view that para 2(b) does not apply where the vendor has acquired the picture innocently (ie is not implicated in the illegal export) and that such a case falls to be dealt with under para 4. Christie's also apparently take the view that the Spanish government have refused to agree 'satisfactory reimbursement' to OAI. *f*

Whether Christie's are right on either of those views is not for this court to say. The fact is that Christie's are prepared to and will go ahead with the sale, even if the documents are found by the court to be forgeries. In any event the code is not a document on which the Spanish government can directly rely: they are not a party to the code.

After the announcement of the sale there were meetings between the solicitors for the parties, and on 5 March 1986 the Spanish government issued these proceedings. As I *g* understand it, their original intention was to join only Christie's as defendants, but OAI were joined because they wished to be involved in any proceedings. OAI, although resident outside the United Kingdom, co-operated in every way to accept service of the proceedings as quickly as possible through their London solicitors, Messrs Freshfields. The Spanish government's summons was supported by evidence of two kinds. (1) Evidence from representatives of the Spanish authorities seeking to prove in the greatest *h* detail that the documents were forgeries in the way alleged in the originating summons, namely that they carried the wrong stamps, had forged signatures and were wrongly signed by the wrong parties. The evidence also deposes to the fact that there is no record of licences having been granted, or of the export of the picture. I shall say no more other than that the evidence, until tested by cross-examination and discovery, is strong. (2) The second type of evidence supporting the summons was that Christie's were going to sell *j* the picture and on a sale it would be customary to hand over to the buyer the export documents.

At this stage it is appropriate to say that although there is no direct evidence of the fact, the very existence of the dispute and the positions taken up by the parties suggests that if the picture were illicitly exported its open market value is likely to be less than if

it were legally exported. There was some indication of that at least from the fact that the
Getty Museum itself refused to go on with the purchase after learning that the picture
was alleged to be illicitly exported.

In response to the Kingdom of Spain's evidence, the defendants immediately issued
two summonses to strike out the originating summons on the grounds, first, that the
originating summons discloses no cause of action and, second, that it is in any event an
abuse of the process of the court. The evidence filed by the defendants to date does not
allege either generally or in detail that the documents are genuine. There is no reason on
a striking out application such as this why the defendants should go into the merits, the
factual merits, of the dispute. The evidence filed on behalf of the defendants is directed
to the history of the matter, and in particular to showing that the defendants acquired
the picture in good faith without in any way being involved in any dishonesty. The
evidence also sets out those points relied on as showing that the bringing of these
proceedings is an abuse of the process of the court.

During the hearing the evidence was supplemented by the production of Christie's
catalogue for the sale, which had just been produced, which contains the following. The
third condition of sale reads:

> 'The Seller will transfer to the Buyer only such title as the Seller may have in the
> Lot. The Seller is Overseas Art Investments Ltd., a company principally owned by
> one of Lord Wimborne's family trusts and in which there are other minority
> interests. Claims have been made by the Government of Spain concerning the
> circumstances in which the painting left Spain, and in particular they have alleged
> illegal export. Christie's give no independent warranties.'

Further on in the catalogue there appears this under the heading 'Terms of Sale':

> 'Purchasers should note that this Lot is not being sold on Christie's Standard
> Conditions of Sale and that the Seller is selling only such title as it has to the picture,
> as set out in clause 3 of the Conditions of Sale in this catalogue. The Purchasers
> should take their own advice. Further information as to the recent history of the
> picture is available from the Seller to whom Purchasers and their advisers are
> referred.'

It is therefore clear that on the sale the existence of the dispute is being disclosed perfectly
frankly to any purchaser. What has not become clear, and again there is no reason why it
should be come clear, is whether the defendants are still alleging that the documents, far
from being forged, are genuine. Their attitude, as it has emerged during the hearing, is
that they have taken note of the Spanish government's allegations, they have seen the
evidence, they wish to test that evidence to see whether it is true, and they are not
committing themselves one way or the other on the matter.

At this stage it is also right to say that although allegations have in the course of the
history of this matter been made against the good faith of OAI in this matter, those
allegations for the purpose of these proceedings have not been persisted in. There are
proceedings in the criminal courts in Spain against Mr Simpson, but in these proceedings
it is not alleged that OAI are in any way involved in the export itself.

There is also before me a summons by the Spanish government for directions as to
how the trial should take place, with a view to getting the final action determined before
11 April. I am not dealing with that application specifically in this judgment.

Before turning to the relevant law, there are certain points on which there is no dispute
and which should be made clear. First, the Spanish government have not and make no
claim to any title to the picture itself. There is nothing in this action which impugns the
title of OAI as owners of the picture. Second, the Spanish government have no claim to
any ownership or interest in the documents. As alleged forgeries, it must be clear that
they are not the documents of the government of Spain on their own case.

Against that background I turn to the law. This is an application to strike out the
proceedings before trial. That is an extreme step for a court to take and is only done

when it is obvious and clear beyond doubt that the plaintiff has no claim fit to go to trial. To shut out somebody from the judgment seat has been said many times to be an extreme step. Only in exceptional circumstances, therefore, is it right on such an application finally to determine any difficult point of law. Normally, if a case involves sustained argument, it is not a case for striking out but for a preliminary point of law to be set down.

In the present case, as will emerge, as the argument went on the basis of possible resistance to striking out changed, and what at one time might have been thought to have been a plain and obvious case may no longer be so.

For the purpose of considering whether a case should be struck out as disclosing no cause of action, it is necessary for the court to assume the truth of the facts alleged by the plaintiffs; but I must emphasise that that is an assumption.

The fundamental difficulty in this case is that the plaintiffs have chosen only to claim declarations. They have made no claim against the defendants by way of injunction or for damages. It is clearly established by the authorities that in proceedings for a declaration, other than for judicial review, the court will only make such a declaration in defence of a legal or equitable right on the plaintiff: see *Gouriet v Union of Post Office Workers* [1977] 3 All ER 70 at 100, [1978] AC 435 at 501, where Lord Diplock said:

'The only kinds of rights with which courts of justice are concerned are legal rights; and a court of civil jurisdiction is concerned with legal rights only when the aid of the court is invoked by one party claiming a right against another party to protect or enforce the right or to provide a remedy against that other party for infringement of it, or is invoked by either party to settle a dispute between them as to the existence or nature of the right claimed. So for the court to have jurisdiction to declare any legal right it must be one which is claimed by one of the parties as enforceable against an adverse party to the litigation, either as a subsisting right or as one which may come into existence in the future conditionally on the happening of an event.'

Obviously in that statement 'legal rights' include equitable rights.

The decision of Harman J in *Re Lewis's Declaration of Trust* [1953] 1 All ER 1005, [1953] Ch 423 is not entirely easy to fit in with that proposition. In that case the defendant honestly but wrongly maintained that the plaintiff was not entitled to certain property. The plaintiff sought an injunction to restrain the defendant from alleging that title. The judge dismissed the claim to the extent that it was based on a claim of slander of title, because the defendant's assertions although false were made without malice and in the honest belief that they were true. However, as the defendant persisted in his false assertions, the court made a declaration as to the plaintiff's title to the property in issue. As will be seen, there was no legal claim in that case against the defendant since the claim of malicious falsehood had failed, yet a declaration of right as to the title to the property was made.

That decision was approved by the Court of Appeal in *R J Reuter Co Ltd v Ferd Mulhens* [1954] Ch 50 at 74–75, where Lord Evershed MR, said:

'Nor do I doubt the power of the court to make a declaration as to the plaintiff's title in an action for slander of title or goods, even though such slander has not been proved, where the court may think it appropriate to state, in the form of a declaration, its conclusions upon the title of the plaintiff which the defendant has in good faith challenged and continues to challenge.'

It appears from those two cases, therefore, that if the plaintiff has legal or equitable rights which are challenged, it is an appropriate case for a declaration, even though there is no accrued cause of action giving the right to sue for damages or injunction.

The defendants in this case contend that the Spanish government have no rights as against them at all relating to the use of the allegedly forged documents. The central question therefore is what legal or equitable rights do the Spanish government have in relation to these documents and as against these defendants.

During the course of the argument my view has changed more than once. At the outset it seemed to me extraordinary if the law of England provided no civil remedy to a man whose signature or stamp has been forged on a document to prevent the continued circulation of that document as a genuine document. If the law provides no such remedy for a citizen of this country to prevent the continued circulation of a false representation in the form of a document, in my judgment the law is defective.

However, as the argument developed it seemed to me more and more likely that I was going to be forced to the conclusion that no such right did exist. Counsel for the Spanish government put his case in this way. He said he did not need to show an accrued cause of action to restrain the use of the documents: all he had to do was to isolate a right which, when other factors were added to it, would constitute a cause of action. He relied on three well-known forms of action: the right to restrain passing off, malicious falsehood and defamation. As I understand it, he did not claim that he had an accrued cause of action for any of those wrongs; and, indeed, in my judgment he plainly has not.

The requisite constituent elements of a claim in passing off are: first, that there has to be misrepresentation; second, that it is made by a trader in the course of trade; third, to a prospective customer of his, or to consumers of goods or services supplied by him; fourth, which is calculated to injure the business or goodwill of another trader; and fifth, which causes actual damage to the business or goodwill of the trader by whom the action is brought. It would be stretching concepts of trade and business in this case well beyond anything that has previously occurred to suggest either that the Spanish government are a trader or that OAI are a trader in business.

As to malicious falsehood, there has to be not only an untrue statement but that untrue statement must be made maliciously and said without any belief in its truth. The evidence here certainly does not suggest that that is the current position.

Finally, in relation to defamation, in addition to any untrue statement there has to be at least damage to the reputation of the plaintiff. At the moment I can see no way in which it can be said that the continued circulation of forged documents would be defamatory to the Spanish government.

However, counsel for the Spanish government submits that that is not the question. He says that the underlying right in each of those forms of action is the basic right of a citizen not to have untruths told about himself. Having identified that as the right, he says that the other elements necessary to bring an action successfully are mere appendages or conditions attached to the possession of a cause of action rather than being basic legal right protected. Therefore, says counsel, he is entitled in this case to a declaration of the falsity of the documents, there being a general right to restrain the circulation of untrue statements. He has shown a basic right and therefore is entitled to a declaration to the effect that the documents are untrue.

I was unpersuaded by that analysis. In the pragmatic way in which English law has developed, a man's legal rights are in fact those which are protected by a cause of action. It is not in accordance, as I understand it, with the principles of English law to analyse rights as being something separate from the remedy given to the individual. Of course in quia timet proceedings you do not have, for example, to show that damage has occurred even if damage is a necessary constitutent of the cause of action. It is enough to show that the defendant has an intention to do an act which, if done, will cause damage. But in my judgment in the ordinary case to establish a legal or equitable right you have to show that all the necessary elements of the cause of action are either present or threatened. I am fortified in that view by submissions made by counsel for OAI that, if there were any such general right as counsel for the Kingdom of Spain contends for, it is impossible to see why the specific constituent elements of passing off or malicious falsehood have ever developed. If every man can protect the false use of his name or reputation by having a basic right so to do, why is it that the courts have developed the very limited class of cases in which an action for passing off or malicious falsehood can be brought?

Therefore, I was very far from satisfied that counsel for the Spanish government had shown that the plaintiff had any legal or equitable right as against the defendants that

they were entitled to enforce by way of declaration. The case is just not one in which the
defendants have done or are threatening to do acts which constitute defamation, malicious   *a*
falsehood or passing off.

However, the case took a new turn when a number of cases were cited, one of which
at least was directly in point. *Emperor of Austria v Day and Kossuth* (1861) 3 De GF & J
217, 45 ER 861 is a decision of the Court of Appeal in Chancery. The headnote reads as
follows:

'The defendant Kossuth, a Hungarian refugee, caused to be manufactured in   *b*
England a large quantity of notes, which though not made in imitation of any notes
circulating in Hungary, purported to be receivable as money in every Hungarian
State and public pay office, and to be guaranteed by the State of Hungary. The
Plaintiff, as King of Hungary, sued to have these notes delivered up and to restrain
the manufacture of any such, alleging that the issue of such notes would injure the   *c*
rights of the Plaintiff by promoting revolution and disorder, would injure the State
by the introduction of a spurious circulation, and would thereby also injure the
Plaintiff's subjects. Held, that, although the Court has not any jurisdiction to restrain
the commission of acts which only violate the political privileges of a foreign
sovereign, the manufacture of these notes ought to be restrained.'

I find it very difficult to discover what was the cause of action of the Emperor of Austria   *d*
in that case. The judgments make it clear that the court was not enforcing the prerogative
rights of the emperor as sovereign of Hungary. The essential ingredient concentrated on
by the court was that the acts of the defendant in printing the notes were a threat to do
some act which would injure the property or cause pecuniary damage to the Emperor
and to his subjects. So far as I can see, the court proceeded on the basis that if the acts of
the defendant did threaten such damage, it was self-evident that there was a threat of an   *e*
equitable wrong which should be restrained by injunction (see 3 De GF & J 217 at 233,
240, 245, 45 ER 861 at 868, 870, 872 per Lord Campbell LC and Knight Bruce LJ). The
proposition being put forward by the Court of Appeal in that case appears to be that a
deliberate act of the defendant which will cause injury to the plaintiff's property or
pecuniary damage to him will be restrained by injunction in the courts of equity. Turner   *f*
LJ said (3 De GF & J 217 at 253–254, 45 ER 861 at 875–876):

'But it is said that the acts proposed to be done are not the subject of equitable
jurisdiction, or that if they are, the jurisdiction ought not to be exercised until a trial
at law shall have been had. To neither of these propositions can I give my assent. I
agree that the jurisdiction of this Court in a case of this nature rests upon injury to
property, actual or prospective, and that this Court has no jurisdiction to prevent   *g*
the commission of acts which are merely criminal or merely illegal, and do not
affect any rights of property, but I think there are here rights of property quite
sufficient to found jurisdiction in this Court. I do not agree to the proposition, that
there is no remedy in this Court if there be no remedy at law, and still less do I agree
to the proposition that this Court is bound to send a matter of this description to be
tried at law.'   *h*

The case also establishes that the head of a foreign state can sue in respect of injury to the
subjects of that state.

That decision has never been overruled by the House of Lords expressly. It has recently
been referred to, without disapproval, by the Court of Appeal in *RCA Corp v Pollard*
[1982] 3 All ER 771, [1983] Ch 135. For the purposes of deciding whether a case should   *j*
be struck out, it is unnecessary for me to decide what, if any, limits there are to the
principle applied in the *Emperor of Austria* case. But it does appear to me that at that date
at least there was assumed by the Court of Chancery a general jurisdiciton to restrain by
injunction deliberate acts which either did or were calculated to cause damage to the
plaintiff. It certainly is not plain and obvious to me at least that in this case the Kingdom

of Spain does not have an equitable right to restrain the doing of deliberate acts in this
country by the defendants if, but only if, those acts will cause damage to the property of
the State of Spain or its inhabitants, or cause them pecuniary damage. Is such damage
possible in this case? It is certainly not currently alleged in the originating summons as
such. However, in my judgment it is certainly arguable in the present case that the
continued use of forged documents of the Spanish state, purporting to show the lawful
export of works of art from Spain, is directly comparable to the false currency which was
under consideration in the *Emperor of Austria* case. The issue of false currency could
debase the lawful currency of Hungary; the use of forged documents of the government
of Spain could debase the credibility of genuine export documents issued by that
government. The question in this case will be whether such debasement would cause
damage to the property of the Kingdom of Spain or the property of its subjects.

It is plain that in the *Emperor of Austria* case 'property' in relation to a claim by a
foreign sovereign was used in rather a loose sense: see per Oliver LJ in the *RCA* case.
Counsel for the Spanish government suggested that such damage flowing from the
continued use of forged documents is in this case to be found in the diminution in the
value of pictures still in Spain for which genuine export licences could be obtained in the
future and the fact that, if illicitly exported pictures can continue to be sold with forged
documents, the expense to the Spanish state of buying them back for the benefit of Spain
will be pro tanto increased. To that I would add that possibly the ability to continue to
use forged documents after illicit export is a factor calculated to increase the attractions
of illicit export to wrongdoers, thereby depriving the inhabitants of Spain of public
works of art owned by the State of Spain and injury to the property in Spain.

Whether those arguments are well founded or not is not for me to determine finally
on this application. The *Emperor of Austria* case has satisfied me that there may be, and I
say no more than that, a legal right in this case which the Kingdom of Spain is entitled to
have declared by way of declaration in the way sought. It is not plain and obvious that
the action cannot succeed.

I turn then to consider the second ground on which the defendants seek to strike out
this claim, namely that the claim is an abuse of the process of the court.

It is submitted on behalf of the defendants that the purpose of these proceedings is to
denigrate the value of the picture at the forthcoming sale by a collateral attack so as to
secure the eventual return of the picture to Spain at a cheaper price. They point to what
they say is delay in the bringing of proceedings: that although the Government of Spain
had known of the illegal export since 1983, and indeed have known that OAI were the
owners since then, they have not thought fit to bring proceedings until just before the
forthcoming sale. The defendants say that there is no way in which this action can be
determined before the sale on 11 April, and the intention is to have it as a blight cast on
the sale. They point to the statements made in the Spanish press to the effect that the
government is going to do everything it can to stop the sale. They point also to the fact
that the Spanish government have not sought to proceed by way of an application for an
injunction which would require them to give a cross-undertaking in damages, but have
satisfied themselves with this unusual procedure of a simple declaration as to truth and
falsity.

In the light of all those circumstances, it is said that the court is being used by the
Spanish government for a collateral purpose and not bona fide for the purpose for which
the right of action, if any, exists.

I agree with the defendants that if they could make out that case it would be a case for
striking out. But I am not myself satisfied that the Spanish government are motivated
either exclusively or primarily by the collateral motive suggested. Firstly, as to delay, I
can see no grounds for criticising the Spanish government in not having taken
proceedings. For purposes which are no doubt good ones, the defendant OAI are a
cosmopolitan body of people spread over many jurisdictions, Liberia, British Virgin
Islands, Channel Islands and Paris. There is no obvious jurisdiction in which they could
be sued. What is more, the whereabouts of the picture have been unknown since it was

with the Getty Museum. There was no cause for proceedings when the picture was with
the Getty Museum because that museum declined to go on in any event. I ask rhetorically:
where could these proceedings have been brought, unless and until the Spanish
government knew that the picture was to be in this country and that there was to be a
sale of it? I can see no ground for criticism of the Spanish government on that head.

Secondly, as to the chances of the matter being tried before 11 April, although I have
not yet decided or indeed heard full argument I am bound to say that my present
impression coincides with that of the defendants, namely that there is really no hope of
this matter being tried before 11 April on the merits. The Spanish government are
advised by very reputable and skilled solicitors and counsel, and I am told that the legal
advisers took the view that the case could be determined before 11 April, and it was for
that purpose that the claim for relief was limited to a declaration. I am satisfied that that
was a view genuinely, if possibly mistakenly, held.

In my judgment the Spanish government have here, if I am right on there being a
possible cause of action, a legitimate interest which they are seeking to defend in this
action, namely in preventing the continued use of forged documents of the Spanish state.

As to the failure to apply for an interim injunction, it is not a necessity that a party
threatened with an injury is forced to apply for interlocutory relief. If they choose not to
do so, that is for them to decide. The Spanish government say that they will continue
with this action, even if the sale does take place on 11 April and is not postponed. It is
suggested that that is in some way indicative also of an abuse. I cannot see it that way.
Proceedings now having started in a jurisdiction in which OAI have consented to be
joined, it seems to me no hardship for the action to continue (if it is to go on) until
judgment, even if the defendants choose not to postpone the sale.

It may well be that the Spanish government will receive a collateral advantage by
pursuing this action in the form of a diminution in the price of the picture. They have
said that they are not intending to bid at the sale, but there is no suggestion that they are
no longer interested in buying under any circumstances. But I am not satisfied that their
sole or predominant objective in this case is to force down the price. It appears to be a
much wider concern, namely the concern not to permit false documents to continue to
circulate in support of a picture which they say has been illicitly exported. Often in
litigation parties hope to use the litigation as a weapon to achieve wider results. In my
judgment, in such cases the action cannot be struck out as an abuse of the process unless
it is shown that that is their predominant objective as opposed to a collateral benefit. I
therefore refuse also to strike out the whole summons as an abuse of the process of the
court.

Finally, in fairness to the defendants I should emphasise two points, because it is
important that the existence of these proceedings should not be either misconstrued or
misunderstood. The action does not in any way impugn the title of OAI to sell the
picture. The title to the picture of any buyer will not be affected by anything which
eventually happens in this action. The action only relates to the question whether the
picture was or was not lawfully exported from Spain.

Secondly, I must emphasise that for the purposes of this judgment I have had to
assume that the allegations as to forgery as made by the Spanish government are correct.
This judgment in no way constitutes a finding or any indication that those allegations
have been proved.

Declarations granted. Application to strike out dismissed.

Solicitors: *Farrer & Co* (for the Spanish government); *Stephenson Harwood* (for Christie's);
Freshfields (for OAI).

Vivian Horvath Barrister.

a
Masterson and another v Holden

QUEEN'S BENCH DIVISION
GLIDEWELL LJ AND SCHIEMANN J
18 APRIL 1986

b *Public order – Offensive conduct conducive to breaches of peace – Threatening, abusive or insulting words or behaviour – Insulting – Nature of insulting behaviour – Homosexual activity in public place – Defendants engaged in overt homosexual behaviour at bus stop – Defendants' behaviour observed by passing couples – Defendants unaware of other persons in vicinity – Whether defendants using 'insulting ... behaviour ... whereby a breach of peace may be occasioned' – Whether necessary for conduct to be directed at another person in order to be insulting – Whether overt homosexual behaviour in public place insulting to member of public witnessing it –*
c *Metropolitan Police Act 1839, s 54(13).*

In the early hours of the morning in a public street in London the defendants were seen by two passing couples to be engaging in overt homosexual behaviour. The defendants appeared to be unaware of other persons in the vicinity. They were arrested and charged
d with using insulting behaviour whereby a breach of the peace might have been occasioned, contrary to s 54(13)ᵃ of the Metropolitan Police Act 1839. The defendants were convicted. They appealed, contending (i) that in order to be insulting the conduct had to be directed at another person or persons and in the light of the justices' finding that the defendants appeared to be wholly unaware of other persons in the vicinity their conduct could not be said to be directed at another person, and (ii) that in the case of overt behaviour between two male persons that behaviour could only be said to be
e insulting if it amounted to a statement that the person who saw it was believed to be homosexual and therefore the behaviour could not have been insulting to the two couples.

f **Held** – In the circumstances it could properly be said that the defendants' conduct was insulting, even though it was not deliberately aimed at a particular person or persons, if in fact it could be insulting to any member of the public who might see it. Furthermore, the defendants' conduct was such that it could be said to be insulting within the ordinary meaning of the word, since overt homosexual or heterosexual conduct in a public street might well be considered by many to be objectionable, and although objectionable behaviour did not constitute an offence, the display of such conduct in a public street might well be regarded by another person as conduct which insulted him by suggesting
g that he was somebody who would find such conduct in public acceptable himself. It followed that the justices had been entitled to conclude that the defendants' conduct was insulting. The appeal would therefore be dismissed (see p 43 j to p 44 f, post).
Parkin v Norman [1982] 2 All ER 583 explained.

h **Notes**
For the offence of using insulting words or behaviour likely to cause a breach of the peace, see 11 Halsbury's Laws (4th edn) para 850, and for cases on the subject, see 15 Digest (Reissue) 908–910, 7797–7807.
For insulting behaviour in London, see 40 Halsbury's Laws (4th edn) para 452.
For the Metropolitan Police Act 1839, s 54, see 28 Halsbury's Statutes (3rd edn) 36.

j _____

a   Section 54, so far as material, provides: 'Every Person shall be liable to a Penalty not more than [level 2 on the standard scale], who, within the Limits of the Metropolitan Police District, shall, in any Thoroughfare or public Place, commit any of the following Offences ... 13. Every Person who shall use any threatening, abusive, or insulting Words or Behaviour with Intent to provoke a Breach of the Peace, or whereby a Breach of the Peace may be occasioned ...'

Cases referred to in judgments
Brutus v Cozens [1972] 2 All ER 1297, [1973] AC 854, [1972] 3 WLR 521, HL.   a
Parkin v Norman, Valentine v Lilley [1982] 2 All ER 583, [1983] QB 92, [1982] 3 WLR 523, DC.

Cases also cited
Jordan v Burgoyne [1963] 2 All ER 225, [1963] 2 QB 744, DC.
R v Ambrose (1973) Cr App R 538, CA.   b

Case stated
Simon Thomas Masterson and Robert Matthew Cooper appealed by way of case stated by the justices for the Inner London area for the petty sessional division of South Westminster in respect of their adjudication at Marlborough Street Magistrates' Court on 7 August 1984 whereby they found the appellants guilty of using insulting behaviour on 11 June   c
1984 in Oxford Street, London, whereby a breach of the peace might have been occasioned contrary to s 54(13) of the Metropolitan Police Act 1839. The justices ordered that the appellants be discharged absolutely and bound over to keep the peace in the sum of £100 for 12 months. The facts are set out in the judgment of Glidewell LJ.

Adrian Fulford for the appellants.   d
Victor B A Temple for the respondent.

GLIDEWELL LJ. This is an appeal by way of a case stated by justices for the Inner London area for the petty sessional division of South Westminster sitting as a magistrates' court at Marlborough Street. An information was preferred by the respondent, Pc Holden, against the two appellants, Simon Thomas Masterson and Robert Matthew   e
Cooper, that they on 11 June 1984 in Oxford Street had used insulting behaviour whereby a breach of the peace may have been occasioned, contrary to s 54(13) of the Metropolitan Police Act 1839. I note in passing that the wording of the offence under the 1839 Act uses the verb 'may' have been occasioned in relation to the question of breach of the peace. Grammatically perhaps it should be 'might', though nothing turns on that, but in that way the section is to be distinguished from the similar offence under   f
the Public Order Act 1936, where the wording is 'is likely to be occasioned'. However, in the circumstances of this case no point arises on the difference in wording.
    The justices set out the facts which they found at their hearing on 7 August 1984 shortly and with clarity. The alleged offence occurred at 1.55 am on 11 June 1984. Two couples were walking along the south footway of Oxford Street. First there were two young men about 21 years of age and second two young women of about 20. They were   g
all together in fact but the two young men were walking ahead followed by the two young women. The defendants who are both men were standing at a bus stop on the same south footway of Oxford Street and they were cuddling each other and kissing each other on the lips. Then, the justices find, Cooper rubbed the back of Masterson with his right hand and later Cooper moved his hand from Masterson's back and placed it on Masterson's bottom and squeezed his buttocks. Cooper then placed his hand on   h
Masterson's genital area and rubbed his hand round this area. The defendants continued kissing and cuddling. The two couples approached the defendants. The case finds that the two young men appeared not to notice them, but the two young women stopped opposite the defendants and one of them raised a hand to her mouth and both of them then ran up to the two young men. After a short conversation one of the girls pointed at the defendants who were still cuddling and 'the appellants appeared wholly unaware of   j
other persons in the vicinity'. Both the young men then walked towards the defendants and one of them shouted, 'You filthy sods. How dare you in front of our girls?'
    At that stage some police officers approached the group of four people and told them to wait and then approached the defendants and arrested them. When he was cautioned Masterson replied, 'We can cuddle can't we, what's up with you?' Cooper made no reply.

a The four young people, although asked to wait by the police, in fact did not, perhaps not wholly surprisingly, and when the police turned round to turn their attention to them they had gone.

The case says that it was contended on behalf of the appellants, referring to *Parkin v Norman, Valentine v Lilley* [1982] 2 All ER 583, [1983] QB 92, that the appellants' behaviour was not insulting and a reference is made to the judgment of McCullough J in that case to which I shall refer in a moment. It was further submitted that an insult is
b given by someone directing his words at someone else and in this case the defendants were not doing that. Those, to which I shall return, were the arguments addressed to us and I will deal with them in a little more detail.

The justices said this:

c
  'We were of the opinion that having found the facts as set out in para 2, and taking the word insulting to be a straightforward word in ordinary usage, and giving it its ordinary natural meaning, the defendants' behaviour was insulting. Particularly in view of the reaction of the female in the group and what was shouted by one of the males. We were also of the opinion that quite different criteria apply to behaviour at a bus stop in the street than apply to behaviour in a gentlemen's public lavatory and accordingly the narrow interpretation of insulting used in *Parkin v Norman* ([1982] 2 All ER 583 at 588, [1983] QB 92 at 100–101) did not apply to
d the facts of this case. We were further of the opinion that in view of the actions of the two male members of the group and of what was shouted by one of them at the defendants, that a breach of the peace may have been occasioned. We further ordered that the defendants should be discharged absolutely, and that each defendant should be bound over to keep the peace and be of good behaviour in the sum of £100 for 12 months. The question of law on which the opinion of the Divisional
e Court is sought is whether the actions of the defendants could, in the circumstances of the case, constitute insulting behaviour whereby a breach of the peace may have been occasioned.'

Counsel for the appellants, who, if I may say so, has put his arguments in a most attractive and moderate way, advances the same arguments as he did in the magistrates'
f court. He says that the conduct described in the facts found by the magistrates cannot have come within the meaning of the words 'insulting behaviour', particularly having regard to the decision of this court in *Parkin v Norman*. Before I come to that authority, I go back to what must remain the leading authority on this branch of the law, namely *Brutus v Cozens* [1972] 2 All ER 1297, [1973] AC 854, a decision of the House of Lords. That was a case in which the background facts were very different. The defendant, who
g was the appellant in the House of Lords, went to the All England Lawn Tennis Tournament at Wimbledon and during the course of a match, in order to make a demonstration, he went on to the court, blew a whistle and threw some leaflets about bearing slogans. Play was stopped. He was charged with using insulting behaviour whereby a breach of the peace was likely to be occasioned under s 5 of the Public Order Act 1936. The justices held that his behaviour had not been insulting and dismissed the
h information.

On appeal the Divisional Court allowed the appeal and the appellant appealed further to the House of Lords. In his speech, with which others of their Lordships agreed, Lord Reid said ([1972] 2 All ER 1297 at 1298–1299, [1973] AC 854 at 861):

j
  'It is not clear to me what precisely is the point of law which we have to decide. The question in the case stated for the opinion of the court is "Whether, on the above statement of facts, we came to a correct determination and decision in point of law". This seems to assume that the meaning of the word "insulting" in s 5 is a matter of law. And the Divisional Court appear to have proceeded on that footing. In my judgment that is not right. The meaning of an ordinary word of the English language is not a question of law. The proper construction of a statute is a question

of law. If the context shows that a word is used in an unusual sense the court will determine in other words what that unusual sense is. But here there is in my *a* opinion no question of the word "insulting" being used in any unusual sense. It appears to me, for reasons which I shall give later, to be intended to have its ordinary meaning. It is for the tribunal which decides the case to consider, not as law but as fact, whether in the whole circumstances the words of the statute do or do not as a matter of ordinary usage of the English language cover or apply to the facts which have been proved. If it is alleged that the tribunal has reached a wrong decision then *b* there can be a question of law but only of a limited character. The question would normally be whether their decision was unreasonable in the sense that no tribunal acquainted with the ordinary use of language could reasonably reach that decision. Were it otherwise we should reach an impossible position. When considering the meaning of a word one often goes to a dictionary. There one finds other words set out. And if one wants to pursue the matter and find the meaning of those other *c* words the dictionary will give the meaning of those other words in still further words which often include the word for whose meaning one is searching.'

The authority on which counsel for the appellants relies, as I said, is the decision of this court in *Parkin v Norman*. There were two appeals there, but they both concerned prosecutions arising out of events in public lavatories. The charges were both under s 5 of the 1936 Act. In *Parkin v Norman* a police officer in plain clothes entered a public *d* lavatory where I suppose it was suspected that those with homosexual tendencies might be present. The defendant was masturbating in a way which clearly indicated that he wanted his behaviour to be seen by the other man, that is the police officer. Of course, he did not appreciate that the other man was a police officer. He was convicted, as indeed the other appellant was convicted. The appeal to the Divisional Court in *Parkin v Norman* concerned both the questions whether on those brief facts the behaviour of the defendant *e* could be said to be insulting within the ordinary meaning of the word and, secondly, whether a breach of the peace was likely to be occasioned. The court on the second of those points found in favour of the appellant and allowed the appeal on that issue. That is not a question which arises before us, because counsel for the appellants has expressly accepted that he cannot properly challenge the justices' finding on that matter.

In relation to the first question McCullough J, sitting with Donaldson LJ, and giving *f* the judgment of the court said ([1982] 2 All ER 583 at 588–589, [1983] QB 92 at 100–101):

'The Act does not make it criminal to use offensive or disgusting behaviour whereby a breach of the peace is likely to be occasioned. It requires, in the circumstances material to this case, "insulting behaviour". What then is an insult? *g* We do not propose to attempt any sort of definition, particularly after the speeches in *Brutus v Cozens* [1972] 2 All ER 1297, [1973] AC 854, but some consideration of its characteristics are necessary in the light of counsel's submissions that behaviour of the type here is not insulting. One cannot insult nothing. The word presupposes a subject and an object and, in this day and age, a human object. An insult is perceived by someone who feels insulted. It is given by someone who is directing *h* his words or his behaviour to another person or persons. When A is insulting B, and is clearly directing his words and behaviour to B alone, if C hears and sees is he insulted? He may be disgusted, offended, annoyed, angered and no doubt a number of other things as well; and he may be provoked by what he sees and hears into breaking the peace. But will he be insulted? The appellant's conduct was aimed at one person and only one person. He obviously hoped, and after a little while would *j* presumably have believed, that the person to whom it was directed was another homosexual. Whatever he was trying to do, he was not trying to insult him. Whatever another homosexual would have felt, he would not, presumably, have felt insulted. In fact the second person was a police officer. Was he insulted? He had gone there in plain clothes to catch anyone whom he saw doing this sort of thing,

a
and he caught one. It seems to us quite unrealistic to say that he would have felt insulted. Suppose, as was possible, that the person to whom the behaviour was directed had been a heterosexual using the lavatory for its proper purpose. He would almost certainly have felt disgusted and perhaps angry, but would he have felt insulted? The argument that he would is that the behaviour was tantamount to a statement, "I believe you are another homosexual", which the average heterosexual would surely regard as insulting. We regard this as the only basis on which the

b
behaviour could fairly be characterised as "insulting" . . .'

It is on that basis that on that point the appeal failed.

On those passages from that judgment counsel for the appellants bases two arguments. The first is that in order to be insulting conduct must be directed at another person or persons and in the light of the finding here by the magistrates that 'the appellants appeared wholly unaware of other persons in the vicinity' that cannot be said to be the

c
case. Second, he submits that McCullough J's judgment is authority for the proposition that in the case of some sort of overt behaviour between two male persons that behaviour could only be said to be insulting if it amounts to a statement that they believe that the person who sees it is a homosexual and there is nothing in that here.

I will take the second of those points first. Every decision must be read in the light of the facts on which it is based. That is not to say that decisions of this court or of higher

d
courts do not deal with matters of principle. They do of course. But that was a case of conduct in a public lavatory at a time when only two persons were present, the defendant and the complainant. It was with facts of that kind that McCullough J was quite clearly dealing. What he was saying was that where you have two men in a public lavatory and one of them displays some homosexual activity, then the only way in which the other person can be said to be insulted is the implied suggestion that the other person is a

e
homosexual. That no doubt, if I may say so respectfully, is a correct appreciation of the situation in relation to that sort of factual situation, but that is not the factual situation here. The factual situation here was that there were four other people present, two of them male and two of them female, and it was not in an enclosed place, albeit public; it was in the open street, one of the busiest streets in the United Kingdom, although it was

f
1.55 am. The situation is quite different and in my view the justices were perfectly entitled to say, as they did say in effect, that that passage in the judgment really had nothing to do with the situation which arises in the present case.

The more persuasive argument is the first one that an insult must be directed at somebody and if the person or persons who are alleged to have used insulting behaviour are totally unaware that other people are present they cannot be said to be directing the insult at somebody. To come to that I have to go back to the judgment in *Parkin v*

g
Norman. McCullough J cited a passage from the speech of Viscount Dilhorne in *Brutus v Cozens* and immediately afterwards he said ([1982] 2 All ER 583 at 587, [1983] QB 92 at 99):

'The question of intent was not material to the decision in *Brutus v Cozens*. The decision was simply that, whatever annoyance, resentment and anger had been

h
occasioned by B's behaviour, no one, on any ordinary use of the word, had been insulted; nor was anyone likely to have been insulted. So there had been no "insulting behaviour". There was therefore no need to consider whether an intention to insult was required. Having regard to the tenor of the 1936 Act as a whole, we believe that no such intent need be proved. What is required is conduct of a threatening, abusive or insulting character which is likely in the circumstances to

j
occasion a breach of the peace.'

How does one reconcile the clear statement that an intention to insult somebody else is not a necessary part of the offence with the later passage that an insult is something which is directed by one person at another? Reading the two together, what the second passage must be understood to mean is that words or behaviour cannot be insulting if there is not a human target which they strike, whether they are intended to strike that target or not. In the present case, as I have said, Oxford Street, even at 1.55 in the *a* morning, is no doubt a street that is more likely to contain people than most other places and in fact there were four young people not merely in the street but actually on the same footpath walking past these two men.

The magistrates were perfectly entitled to infer that the two appellants must have known that other people would be likely to be present and if they had glanced up for a moment they would have seen that four people were present. Their conduct, therefore, *b* if in the ordinary sense it was capable of being insulting, would be likely to make some impact on anybody who was nearby in the vicinity. In that sense, while not disagreeing with the way McCullough J put it, in circumstances such as this it can properly be said that the conduct could be insulting, albeit it was not deliberately aimed at a particular person or persons if in fact it could be insulting to any member of the public who might be passing by. So one comes back to this. Was it conduct which within the ordinary *c* meaning of the word could be said to be insulting? The magistrates have found as a question of fact that it was. In my judgment, they were entitled so to find. Overt homosexual conduct in a public street, indeed overt heterosexual conduct in a public street, may well be considered by many persons to be objectionable, to be conduct which ought to be confined to a private place. The fact it is objectionable does not constitute an offence. But the display of such objectionable conduct in a public street may well be *d* regarded by another person, particularly by a young woman, as conduct which insults her by suggesting that she is somebody who would find such conduct in public acceptable herself. The magistrates do not say that that was the reason for their finding. We cannot say for certain that that was their reasoning. Certainly it may have been. I content myself with saying that in my view in the ordinary use of the word 'insulting' on the material in this case they were perfectly entitled to conclude that the conduct was insulting. I *e* have already said that no point is raised about the second limb of the offence. Accordingly, in my judgment the appeals of both these appellants should fail.

SCHIEMANN J. I agree. I only add this. *Parkin v Norman* [1982] 2 All ER 583, [1983] QB 92 identifies the nature of the insult in that case. It does not and could not lay down that this is the only possible type of insult and this type of case in my judgment is one *f* peculiarly suitable for decision by justices. They are the ones sitting at Marlborough Street who are most likely to know what is insulting behaviour at 1.55 am on a June morning. I agree with the order proposed by Glidewell LJ.

Appeal dismissed.

g

Solicitors: *Bindman & Partners* (for the appellants); *D M O'Shea* (for the respondent).

Michael Wall Esq   Barrister.

a
Re Drummond's Settlement
Foster and another v Foster and others

CHANCERY DIVISION
MERVYN DAVIES J
23, 30 APRIL 1986

b

Rule against perpetuities – Application of rule – Objects of trust capable of taking outside perpetuity period – Gift by way of remainder to 'issue' of beneficiary – Settlement – Class gift – Date on which class to be ascertained – Gift to issue on attaining 21 – Whether issue limited to children – Whether issue limited to those in being at date of death of beneficiary or date of death of child of beneficiary – Whether gift void for remoteness.

c

By a settlement made in 1924 the settlor declared that certain funds were to be held on trust for himself during his lifetime and after his death for such of his three daughters as were living at his death and attained the age of 21 or married under such age and the issue of any daughter who might have predeceased him, such issue to take their parent's share equally amongst themselves on their attaining the age of 21 or marrying under
d such age. The settlement further provided, by cl 3(c), that if a daughter died without any child living to take a vested interest in her share that share was to be divided equally 'amongst such of the Daughters as shall then be living and the issue of any of them who may be then dead such issue taking their parent's share only on attaining the age of 21 or marrying under such age'. All three daughters survived the settlor, and in 1984 one of the daughters, E, died without issue. The trustees of the settlement sought the
e determination of the court on the question whether E's share was to be held on trust for the surviving two daughters or whether the trust relating to E's share infringed the rule against perpetuities because potential beneficiaries would have included the issue of either of the other daughters if they had predeceased E.

Held – On the true construction of cl 3(c) of the settlement the word 'issue' meant issue
f through all degrees and not merely children. The issue intended to take on the death of a daughter who died without leaving a child were those issue living at the date of the daughter's death but the issue entitled to take on the failure of a child to attain the age of 21 were all issue alive at the death of that child and not merely such of those issue who were alive at the death of the child's mother (ie one of the daughters). Accordingly, looking at the settlement as it existed in 1924, there was the possibility of the issue
g limitation taking effect outside the perpetuity period, since the issue living at the death of a child who failed to attain 21, although necessarily identifiable within 21 years of the death of the daughter, would not necessarily take vested interests within that 21-year period because there could have been issue born after the death of the daughter who were included in the issue class when that class closed on the death of the child and the interest of such issue would not vest until they attained the age of 21. It followed that
h the limitation in cl 3(c) was void for remoteness, and accordingly there was a resulting trust in favour of the settlor's estate (see p 47 *j* to p 48 *a f g* and p 49 *e* to *h*, post).

Re Cockle's Will Trusts [1967] 1 All ER 391 and *Re Deeley's Settlement, Batchelor v Russell* [1973] 3 All ER 1127 applied.

Notes
j For the meaning of issue and for ascertaining the class of issue, see 50 Halsbury's Laws (4th edn) paras 518, 520, and for cases on the subject, see 51 Digest (Reissue) 150–154, 9490–9519.
For the rule against perpetuities, see 35 Halsbury's Laws (4th edn) paras 908, 912, and for cases on the subject, see 51 Digest (Reissue) 25–27, 8367–8385.

Cases referred to in judgment

Andrews v Partington (1791) 3 Bro CC 401, [1775–1802] All ER Rep 209, 29 ER 610, LC.   *a*
Cockle's Will Trusts, Re [1967] 1 All ER 391, [1967] Ch 690, [1967] 2 WLR 637.
Deeley's Settlement, Re, Batchelor v Russell [1973] 3 All ER 1127, [1974] Ch 454, [1974] 2
    WLR 41.
Hipwell, Re, Hipwell v Hewitt [1945] 2 All ER 476, CA.
Manly's Will Trusts, Re (No 2), Tickle v Manly [1976] 1 All ER 673.
Pruen v Osborne (1840) 11 Sim 132, 59 ER 824.   *b*
Sibley v Perry (1802) 7 Ves 522, 32 ER 211, LC.
Surridge v Clarkson (1866) 14 WR 979.

Cases also cited

IRC v Williams [1969] 3 All ER 614, [1969] 1 WLR 1197.
Manly's Will Trusts, Re, Burton v Williams [1969] 3 All ER 1011, [1969] 1 WLR 1818.   *c*
Pearks v Moseley (1880) 5 App Cas 714, HL.
Turney, Re, Turney v Turney [1899] 2 Ch 739, CA.

Adjourned summons

By an originating summons dated 25 October 1985 the plaintiffs, Alexander Neil Foster
and the Royal Bank of Scotland plc, two of the trustees of a settlement dated 26 August
1924 made between George Henry Drummond (the settlor) and others, sought the   *d*
determination of the court of the question whether, on the true construction of the
settlement, and in the events which had happened, the one-third share of the trust fund
comprised in the settlement in which the settlor's daughter, Edwina Gillian Miville,
deceased, was entitled to a life interest in possession was held (a) in trust for the first
defendant, Rosemary Lucia Foster (who was beneficially interested under the settlement
and the third trustee thereof), and the second defendant, Eve de Trafford (who was also   *e*
beneficially interested under the settlement), in equal shares, or (b) on a resulting trust in
favour of the estate of the settlor (by reason that the material trusts of the settlement had
failed for perpetuity), or (c) on some other and, if so, what trusts. The third defendant,
George Albert Harley Drummond, was one of the personal representatives of the settlor
and as such claimed to be interested under the trusts of the settlement. The facts are set   *f*
out in the judgment.

Mark Herbert for the plaintiffs.
Robert Walker QC for the first and second defendants.
Gavin Lightman QC for the third defendant.

Cur adv vult   *g*

30 April. The following judgment was delivered.

MERVYN DAVIES J. This is an originating summons concerning a settlement dated
26 August 1924 and made between George Henry Drummond (the settlor) of the one
part and the settlor, his wife Kathleen Helena and Charles Aikin Lawford of the other   *h*
part. The plaintiffs are two of the present trustees of the settlement, Mr Alexander Neil
Foster and the Royal Bank of Scotland. There is a third trustee, Mrs Rosemary Lucia
Foster, who is the first defendant. The second defendant is her sister, Mrs Eve de Trafford.
Those two defendants are interested as beneficiaries under the settlement. The third
defendant is Mr George Albert Harley Drummond. He is (with Mrs Foster) a personal
representative of the settlor. As such personal representative, he claims to be interested   *j*
under the trusts of the settlement.
    A family tree shows that the settlor died on 12 October 1963. He was twice married.
His first wife, Kathleen Helena, died on 15 December 1933. There were four children of
that marriage, all girls: (1) Mrs de Trafford, the second defendant, born 16 January 1918
and married but without issue; (2) Mrs Foster, the first defendant, born 21 January 1919
and married with two children: the plaintiff Alexander Neil and his sister Roseanne

Madeleine; (3) Edwina Gillian Miville born 21 April 1920. Mrs Miville died on 13
a October 1984 after having married but leaving no issue; (4) there is a fourth daughter of
this marriage, Diana Kathleen, but born after the date of the settlement; she is not
interested in the matter before me. The settlor's second wife was Honora Gladys Myrtle.
There are four children of this marriage, a son and three daughters, of whom I need
mention only the third defendant, George Albert Harley Drummond. He was born in
1943.

b   The settlement recites that the settlor had three daughters (ie daughters (1), (2) and (3)
above mentioned) who were referred to as 'the daughters' and that the settlor was desirous
of making such a settlement for their benefit as was thereinafter contained. The trusts of
the settlement that now fall to be considered are as follows:

> 'And the Trustees shall stand possessed of the said messuages lands and
> hereditaments or the investments for the time being representing the same
c > (hereinafter referred to as "the Settled Estate") Upon trust [1] to pay the rents profits
> and income arising or to arise therefrom to the Settlor during his life and [2] from
> and after his decease Upon trust to pay the income thereof to such of the Daughters
> as shall be living at the time of his decease and shall have attained or shall attain the
> age of Twenty one years or marry under such age and the issue of any of the
> Daughters who may have predeceased the Settlor such issue taking their parents
d > share only equally amongst them if more than one on their attaining the age of
> Twenty one or marrying under such age in equal shares and so that the Daughters
> shall not have power to anticipate charge or incumber the same and [3] after the
> decease of each of the Daughters [a] Upon trust to pay transfer and divide such share
> unto and amongst such one or more of the children or other issue of that said
> Daughter in such shares and proportions and subject to such conditions as she shall
e > by Will or Codicil direct and appoint [b] And in default of any such directions and
> appointments and subject thereto and so far as the same shall not extend Upon trust
> to pay transfer and divide such share unto and amongst all the children or any child
> of such Daughters who shall attain the age of Twenty one years or being a daughter
> marry under such age and if more than one in equal shares [c] And in case there
> shall be no such child who shall live to take a vested interest in such share Upon
f > trust to pay transfer and divide such share equally amongst such of the Daughters as
> shall then be living and the issue of any of them who may be then dead such issue
> taking their parents share only on attaining the age of twenty one years or marrying
> under such age'

The figures (1), (2) and (3) and the letters (a), (b) and (c) do not appear in the settlement. I
g have inserted them for easy reference in the future. The question arising under the
originating summons reads:

> '1. That it may be determined whether on the true construction of the said
> Settlement and in the events which have happened the one-third share of the trust
> fund comprised in the Settlement in which the said George Henry Drummond's
> daughter Edwina Gillian Miville deceased was entitled to a life interest in possession
h > is now held—(a) In trust for the first defendant Rosemary Lucia Foster and the
> second defendant Eve de Trafford in equal shares or (b) On a resulting trust in favour
> of the estate of the said George Henry Drummond deceased (by reason that the
> material trusts of the settlement have failed for perpetuity) or (c) On some other
> and, if so, what trusts.'

j It was common ground that the impact of the perpetuity rule (as operating on a deed
executed before the passing of the Perpetuities and Accumulations Act 1964) was to
make invalid the limitation in cl 3(c) of the settlement if 'issue' therein is construed as
issue and not as children, and, if the 'issue' will not be ascertained within the perpetuity
period.
   In these circumstances it was agreed that the first question for consideration is the true
meaning of the word 'issue' in the settlement and in particular in cl 3(c). Counsel for the

third defendant submitted that the settlement was professionally drawn and plainly in
its terms distinguishes between 'children' and 'issue'. Thus when the word 'issue' was   *a*
used its meaning was intended as embracing issue of all degrees. In the same way the
word children bore its ordinary meaning. It was thus unacceptable, he said, anywhere in
the settlement to read 'issue' as 'children'. He relied on *Re Hipwell, Hipwell v Hewitt* [1945]
2 All ER 476 including the words of Lord Greene MR where he said (at 478):

> '... I am disposed to assume, like other sensible people, that this testator when he
> drew a distinction between "children" and "issue" was intending to draw a real   *b*
> distinction.'

On the other hand, counsel for the first and second defendants, while accepting that
the word 'issue' in cl 3(a) meant 'issue' in that the word there appears in the context of
'children or other issue', submitted that elsewhere in cl 3, and in particular in cl 3(c), the
word 'issue' is to be read as 'children'. He drew attention to the phrase in cl (2) and in cl   *c*
3(c) which reads 'such issue taking their parents' share' coupled with the gift to children
in default of appointment in cl 3(b). Using those threads counsel for the first and second
defendants added the consideration that in cl 2 there is in effect a gift of capital, in that
the gift is of indefinite income, and in cl 3(b) there is again a gift of capital, and plainly to
children. So, it is said, it may reasonably be inferred that the settlor was referring to
'children' when he used the word 'issue'. I do not find this suggested inference all   *d*
compelling. It appears that nowadays *Sibley v Perry* (1802) 7 Ves 522, 32 ER 211 and
Pruen v Osborne (1840) 11 Sim 132, 59 ER 824 are not now held in the highest regard.

When the word issue is used in a deed or will it is a matter of looking at the particular
document as a whole and deciding what meaning the testator or settlor had in mind: see
the judgments of Lord Greene MR and Morton LJ in *Re Hipwell* [1945] 2 All ER 476 at
477, 480 and Walton J in *Re Manly's Will Trusts (No 2), Tickle v Manly* [1976] 1 All ER   *e*
673 at 678. Reading through the trusts one sees reference in cl (2) to 'issue' (twice), in
cl 3(a) to 'children or other issue', in cl 3(b) to 'children' and in cl 3(c) to 'child', 'issue' and
'issue taking their parents' share'. The settlor appears to choose his words and if one tests
his choice of words it appears that there is reason behind the choice. For example there is
a gift to children in default of appointment and if there is no child then the gift is to
issue. I do not think the phrase 'issue taking their parents share' is at all strong enough to   *f*
influence the meaning of 'issue' throughout the trusts: see *Re Hipwell* [1945] 2 All ER
476 at 477. My reading of the trusts is that in cl 3(c) the word issue means issue through
all degrees and not children. Counsel for the third defendant expressed the matter very
clearly.

I now proceed to consider the second question that is whether the limitation in cl 3(c)
is void for perpetuity, bearing in mind that 'issue' therein means issue of all degrees. If   *g*
there is no date for closing the class of issue within the perpetuity period then there is a
perpetuity. For example, looking at the matter from the standpoint of 1924, there was
the possibility that a daughter would die leaving a child of, say, two years. That child
might not attain 21 and so not take a vested interest. On the other hand such child might
leave a child (ie issue of the 'daughter') and such child would not take a vested interest
(on attaining 21) within 21 years of the death of its grandmother, or other life in being.   *h*

Two authorities afford guidance as respects the fixing of a date for closing a class when
the class is an 'issue' class such as in cl 3(c) in this case. In *Re Cockle's Will Trusts* [1967] 1
All ER 391, [1967] Ch 690 was a case of a will with (put briefly) a limitation to M for life
and then to her issue at 21. In *Re Deeley's Settlement, Batchelor v Russell* [1973] 3 All ER
1127, [1974] Ch 454 was a case of a settlement with (again put briefly) a limitation to JD
for life and then to his issue at 21. In both cases the question for consideration was, which   *j*
of the issue were intended to take after the life interest? For the answering of that
question Stamp J in *Cockle* and Goff J in *Deeley* regarded *Andrews v Partington* (1791) 3 Bro
CC 401, [1775–1802] All ER Rep 209 as inappropriate, for the reason that *Andrews v
Partington* applies as respects a limited or finite class, such as 'all my grandchildren', but
not to an open or infinite class such as 'issue': see *Deeley* [1973] 3 All ER 1127 at 1131,
[1974] Ch 454 at 461. There is, as I see it, the further reason that the class closing rule of

Andrews v Partington is a rule of convenience that is not, at any rate as respects pre-1964
a limitations, to be taken into account when considering, by reference to the time when a
limitation is created, whether or not there is the possibility that the interest or interests
then intended to be created will necessarily vest within the perpetuity period. However
that may be, Stamp J's conclusion was that as a matter of construction those issue took
who were in existence at the death of M the life tenant. Goff J said ([1973] 3 All ER 1127
at 1133–1134, [1974] Ch 454 at 464):

b   'The question in the *Re Cockle* type of case is one of construction, and in my
judgment the words are plainly ambiguous. One cannot take their literal legal
signification, because that is absurd, and one cannot read issue as children for want
of a sufficient context to give it that meaning and therefore ambiguity must result.
The question then is which of the issue did the testator or settlor intend should take:
see *Re Cockle*. I respectfully agree with the decision in that case and the reasoning on
c   which it was based. In any event, to put it at its lowest, not being persuaded that it
and the *Surridge* case [*Surridge v Clarkson* (1866) 14 WR 979] must be wrong I would
in comity follow two English decisions which are directly in point. Accordingly in
my judgment all issue born after the death of the tenant for life are excluded and
there is no perpetuity.'

d   I respectfully agree with the decisions in *Cockle* and *Deeley*; but it is to be noted that the
limitation in this case (unlike *Cockle* and *Deeley*) is not drawn so that issue necessarily
follow directly on after a life interest that is a life interest in being. The limitation here,
following the daughter's life interest, is (see cl 3(b)) to the daughter's child or children at
21. It is only if there is no child who lives to take a vested interest that the issue come
into share and such issue have to attain 21. So, in short, the limitation is to a child at 21,
e or, if there is no such child, to issue at 21. In line with *Cockle*, I feel able to construe the
settlement as meaning that the issue intended to take on the death of a daughter dying
without leaving a child are any issue living at the daughter's death. On the other hand I
do not feel able to construe the settlement as meaning that the issue intended to take on
the failure of a child to attain 21 are the issue who were alive at the death of the child's
mother.

f   Surely, in line with *Cockle*, one would say that the indicated issue are those alive at the
death of the child. If that be so then at the outset of the settlement there was the
possibility of the issue limitation taking effect outside the perpetuity period; since issue
living at the death of the child, although necessarily identifiable within 21 years of the
death of the daughter (a life in being) would not necessarily take vested interests within
that 21-year period in that issue interest vests at 21 and there may be issue born after the
g death of the daughter but included in the issue class on the occasion of the closing of the
class on the death of the child. I appreciate that in the events that have happened Mrs
Miville died without having a child. But, as I understand, that does not affect the position
since as to this pre-1964 settlement one has to have regard to possibilities as they existed
in 1924. It follows that the limitation in cl 3(c) is void for remoteness. The summons is
answered in the sense of para (b) in question 1, that is to say there is a resulting trust in
h favour of the estate of the settlor.

Declaration accordingly.

Solicitors: *Walters Fladgate* (for all parties).

Jacqueline Metcalfe   Barrister.

Austin Rover Group Ltd v Crouch Butler Savage Associates (a firm) and others

COURT OF APPEAL, CIVIL DIVISION

MAY, LLOYD LJJ AND SIR JOHN MEGAW

24, 25 MARCH 1986

Practice – Service – Service by post – Sending copy of writ by post – Send – Redirection by Post Office – Writ posted by plaintiff to defendant at old address – Writ redirected by Post Office to defendant's new address – Whether writ 'sent' to defendant – Whether writ validly served on defendant – RSC Ord 10, r 1(2).

Writ – Service on partnership – Service by post – Writ posted to old address but redirected by Post Office to new address – Whether writ 'sent' to partnership's 'principal place of business' – Whether writ validly served on partnership – RSC Ord 10, r 1(2), Ord 81, r 3(1).

Writ – Extension of validity – Cause of action statute-barred – Discretion to renew writ – Exceptional circumstances justifying exercise of discretion.

The plaintiffs wished to sue the defendants, a firm of architects. On 28 December 1983 they issued a writ of summons against the defendants and on 18 December 1984 they posted the writ by first-class post to the defendants at premises from which, unknown to the plaintiffs, they had recently moved. The writ was redirected by the Post Office to the defendants' new premises and was received there by a partner in the defendant firm. The defendants asserted that the writ had not been duly served, and so the plaintiffs sought and obtained renewal of the writ on the grounds that there were exceptional circumstances justifying renewal. The defendants applied for the renewal of the writ to be discharged and for a declaration that the writ had not been properly served on them in December 1984. The judge dismissed the application. The defendants appealed, contending (i) that the judge should not have extended the writ retrospectively if the effect was to deprive the defendants of a possible limitation defence and (ii) that the writ had not been served by 'sending' it to the 'principal place of business' of the defendants, as required by RSC Ord 81, r 3(1)(c)[a] and Ord 10, r 1(2)[b].

Held (Lloyd LJ dissenting) – The 'sending' of a writ by post for the purposes of service under RSC Ord 81, r 3(1)(c) did not refer merely to the initial dispatch of the writ but connoted the whole process of dispatch, transmission and delivery to the receiver. Accordingly, even though the address was not correct at the time of posting, service of the writ had been validly effected in December 1984 because it had in fact been delivered by the Post Office to the defendants' principal place of business. Accordingly (Lloyd LJ concurring on the facts), the appeal would be dismissed (see p 55 b h, p 56 e f, p 59 d to f and p 61 e to p 62 b e j, post).

Per May and Lloyd LJJ. Although RSC Ord 81, r 3(1)(c) is to be construed by reference to Ord 10, r 1(2), a firm's 'principal place of business' cannot be construed as being at its 'usual or last known address' although (per May LJ) if a firm moves its address a letter posted to the old address but redirected to the new address may be said to have been sent to its 'usual' address (see p 56 g and p 59 g, post).

Per May LJ and Sir John Megaw. The requirements of the Rules of the Supreme Court relating to service must be strictly complied with in the context of the operation of the Limitation Act 1980 and there must be exceptional circumstances to justify the exercise of the discretion to renew a writ, e g circumstances in which the plaintiff has been unable to serve the writ because the defendant has disappeared, gone abroad or cannot be traced

---

a   Rule 3, so far as material, is set out at p 53 e to j, post

b   Rule 1, so far as material, is set out at p 52 j to p 53 a, post a or circumstances in which the plaintiff has been led to believe that service was unnecessary, e g because negotiations were in progress (see p 58 *j* to p 59 *b* and p 62 *f* to *h*, post); dicta of Megaw J in *Heaven v Road and Rail Wagons Ltd* [1965] 2 All ER at 413, 415 applied.

Notes

b For methods of service of a writ of summons and renewal thereof, see 37 Halsbury's Laws (4th edn) paras 124, 149–151, and for cases on the subject, see 37(2) Digest (Reissue) 245–249, 257–258, 1602–1623, 1671–1683.

For service of a writ of summons on a partnership, see 35 Halsbury's Laws (4th edn) para 82 and 37 ibid para 161, and for cases on the subject, see 36(2) Digest (Reissue) 679–691, 709–803.

For the Limitation Act 1980, see 50(1) Halsbury's Statutes (3rd edn) 1253.

c **Cases referred to in judgments**

Afro Continental Nigeria Ltd v Meridian Shipping Co SA, The Vrontados [1982] 2 Lloyd's Rep 241, CA.

Baker v Bowketts Cakes Ltd [1966] 2 All ER 290, [1966] 1 WLR 861, CA.

Heaven v Road and Rail Wagons Ltd [1965] 2 All ER 409, [1965] 2 QB 355, [1965] 2 WLR 1249.

d *Leal v Dunlop Bio-Processes International Ltd* [1984] 2 All ER 207, [1984] 1 WLR 874, CA.

National Westminster Bank Ltd v Betchworth Investments Ltd (1975) 234 EG 675, CA.

Portico Housing Association Ltd v Brian Morehead & Partners (1985) 1 Const LJ 266, CA.

Western National Bank of the City of New York v Perez Triana & Co [1891] 1 QB 304, CA.

Case cited

e *Pirelli General Cable Works Ltd v Oscar Faber & Partners (a firm)* [1983] 1 All ER 65, [1983] 2 AC 1, HL.

Interlocutory appeal

The first defendants, Crouch Butler Savage Associates (a firm), appealed with the leave of the Court of Appeal against the order of his Honour Judge John Davies QC hearing
f official referees' business, dated 4 October 1985, whereby he (i) refused the first defendants' application for an order discharging the order of Master Topley made on 18 January 1985 extending until 26 March 1985 the validity of the writ of summons issued by the plaintiffs, Austin Rover Group Ltd (formerly British Leyland UK Ltd) against (1) the first defendants, (2) Turriff Ltd, (3) Joseph Price & Sons, (4) Specialist Plasterwork Ltd, (5) White Young Consulting Engineers (an unlimited company), (6) John Williams
g of Cardiff plc and (7) Jonwindows, (ii) refused to set aside service of the renewed writ of summons on the first defendants on 29 January 1985 and (iii) refused to grant the first defendants a declaration that the writ of summons had never been duly served on them. The facts are set out in the judgment of May LJ.

G Caws for the first defendants.
h *Timothy Elliott* for the plaintiffs.

MAY LJ. This is an appeal against an order of his Honour Judge John Davies QC dismissing a summons issued by the first defendants on 25 June 1985. That summons asked (1) that an order made by Master Topley on 18 January 1985, extending the validity of the writ in this action until 26 March 1985, should be discharged and that service of
j the renewed writ on 29 January 1985 should be set aside, and (2) for a declaration that the writ of summons had never been duly served on the first defendants on the grounds that the purported service in December 1984 did not comply with the Rules of the Supreme Court.

The judge held that the writ had been validly served in December 1984. He went on in the alternative to hold that if he had been wrong about the service in December 1984 the writ had been validly renewed and then properly served in January 1985.

Having been granted leave by this court, the first defendants now appeal against the order of the judge, asking that Master Topley's order be set aside and for a declaration that the writ in this action has never been validly served.

The facts of the matter I take quite shortly from the judgment of the judge below. The litigation concerns the construction of a block of offices in Birmingham. The plaintiffs (the respondents to this appeal) became lessees of that block of offices. They were built in 1974 through to 1976 and the architects concerned in their construction were the first defendants, the present appellants. In 1983 or thereabouts the plaintiffs became aware of defects in the floors and windows of the premises and on 28 December 1983 they issued writs against the builders and the architects, but did not serve them. It would seem that those writs are what are commonly described as 'protective' writs, guarding against the possibility that the limitation period might be running.

The plaintiffs had been in correspondence with the first defendants (the architects) in 1976, before they had entered into possession. They were in contact again in 1977 and 1978 and finally in April 1984, when there were further investigations into what was occurring at the premises. That is material, as the judge below pointed out, because letters from the first defendants bore the addresses of their places of business, the relevance of which will become apparent in a moment. The address which figured first, and was the material one at the time to which I have referred, was an address at 533 Coventry Road, Birmingham.

The writ having been issued in December 1983, by December 1984 the time was coming when that writ had to be served, and when purporting to do so the plaintiffs addressed it to 'The Secretary, Crouch Butler Savage and Associates' (being, with one minor error, the name of the architects) at the address 533 Coventry Road Birmingham, as the one they knew. As sometimes happens when time is allowed to pass, unknown to the plaintiffs the first defendants had in the three months or so before the attempted service of the writ moved their office from Coventry Road to another address in Birmingham and had asked the Post Office to forward their correspondence to that address. They moved, it seems, in about September 1984.

It is not disputed that the writ, having been put in the post addressed as I have indicated, was redirected through the good offices of the Post Office, and ultimately arrived at the new address, the proper place of business at that time of the first defendants, on 21 December 1984, that is to say some six days before it would have expired. Nor is it disputed that the envelope was opened either by a Mr Cliff, a partner in the firm, or alternatively by his secretary, who immediately handed the contents including the writ to him. The first defendants got in touch with their solicitors on 2 January 1985, which, it will be appreciated, was over a year after the original issue of the writ in December 1983. Their solicitors told the plaintiffs that, in their view, service had not been properly effected and that the writ was in consequence invalid. The plaintiffs then applied to Master Topley, as I have indicated, to renew the writ and he ordered that that should be done on 18 January 1985. That renewed writ was served on 29 January 1985.

It is against that background that the points which arise in this case have to be determined.

Two questions need consideration. Firstly, whether the service or purported service of the writ by post in December 1984 was valid. Secondly, if it was not, whether the judge properly exercised his discretion in dismissing the appeal against Master Topley's renewal of the validity of the writ so that the second service on 29 January 1985 was itself valid.

I deal with the first question initially, namely whether the service in December 1984 was or was not valid. The relevant parts of the Rules of the Supreme Court are, firstly, Ord 10, r 1(1), (2) and (3), which are as follows:

'(1) A writ must be served personally on each defendant by the plaintiff or his agent.

(2) A writ for service on a defendant within the jurisdiction may, instead of being served personally on him, be served—(a) by sending a copy of the writ by ordinary first-class post to the defendant at his usual or last known address, or (b) if there is a

a
letter box for that address, by inserting through the letter box a copy of the writ enclosed in a sealed envelope addressed to the defendant. In sub-paragraph (a) "first-class post" means first-class post which has been pre-paid or in respect of which prepayment is not required.

(3) Where a writ is served in accordance with paragraph (2)—(a) the date of service shall, unless the contrary is shown, be deemed to be the seventh day (ignoring Order 3, rule 2(5)) after the date on which the copy was sent to or, as the case may
b
be, inserted through the letter box for the address in question; (b) any affidavit proving due service of the writ must contain a statement to the effect that—(i) in the opinion of the deponent (or, if the deponent is the plaintiff's solicitor or an employee of that solicitor, in the opinion of the plaintiff) the copy of the writ, if sent to, or, as the case may be, inserted through the letter box for, the address in question, will have come to the knowledge of the defendant within 7 days thereafter;
c
and (ii) in the case of service by post, the copy of the writ has not been returned to the plaintiff through the post undelivered to the addressee.'

Then there is Ord 81, which deals with actions by and against firms of partners. By
r 1:

d
'Subject to the provisions of any enactment, any two or more persons claiming to be entitled, or alleged to be liable, as partners in respect of a cause of action and carrying on business within the jurisdiction may sue, or be sued, in the name of the firm (if any) of which they were partners at the time when the cause of action accrued.'

One can then turn to Ord 81, r 3, from which it is necessary to read paras (1), (2) and
e
(4):

'(1) Where by virtue of rule 1 partners are sued in the name of a firm, the writ may, except in the case mentioned in paragraph (3) [I interpolate that that is not relevant] be served—(a) on any one or more of the partners, or (b) at the principal place of business of the partnership within the jurisdiction, on any person having at the time of service the control or management of the partnership business there; or
f
(c) by sending a copy of the writ by ordinary first-class post (as defined in Order 10, rule 1(2)) to the firm at the principal place of business of the partnership within the jurisdiction and subject to paragraph (2) where service of the writ is effected in accordance with this paragraph, the writ shall be deemed to have been duly served on the firm, whether or not any member of the firm is out of the jurisdiction.

(2) Where a writ is served on a firm in accordance with sub-paragraph (1)(c)—(a)
g
the date of service shall, unless the contrary is shown, be deemed to be the seventh day (ignoring Order 3, rule 2(5)) after the date on which the copy was sent to the firm; and (b) any affidavit proving due service of the writ must contain a statement to the effect that—(i) in the opinion of the deponent (or, if the deponent is the plaintiff's solicitor or an employee of that solicitor, in the opinion of the plaintiff) the copy of the writ, if sent to the firm at the address in question, will have come to
h
the knowledge of one of the persons mentioned in paragraph (1)(a) or (b) within 7 days thereafter, and (ii) the copy of the writ has not been returned to the plaintiff through the post undelivered to the addressee . . .

(4) Every person on whom a writ is served under paragraph (1)(a) or (b) must at the time of service be given a written notice stating whether he is served as a partner or as a person having the control or management of the partnership business or both
j
as a partner and as such a person; and any person on whom a writ is so served but to whom no such notice is given shall be deemed to be served as a partner.'

The writ, when it was received by Mr Cliff, was not accompanied by any such written notice as is provided for by para (4) above and therefore he must be deemed to have been served as a partner.

The second comment that I make on those two orders and the relevant rule is that it

will be apparent that the third possible method of service contemplated by Ord 10,
namely by insertion through the letter box of the person whom it is intended to serve, is **a**
not open in the case of partners sued as a firm under Ord 81.

Counsel for the first defendants, in an attractive and cogent argument, submitted first
of all that, as a general approach, one must view the question of service, particularly of
writs, as a technical matter. It is something which one has to get right. In that context
she referred to *Baker v Bowketts Cakes Ltd* [1966] 2 All ER 290, [1966] 1 WLR 861 and in
particular to passages in the judgments of Lord Denning MR and Harman LJ respectively. **b**
Although now some 20 years old, they are passages which should be borne firmly in
mind by all who find themselves in situations similar to those which obtained in the
instant litigation. Lord Denning MR said ([1966] 2 All ER 290 at 293, [1966] 1 WLR
861 at 866):

> 'The one point that has troubled me in the case is the last minute effort of the
> plaintiff's solicitors to serve the defendants. They telephoned and tried to find the **c**
> address of the registered office and were given the wrong address. By reason of that
> mistake they failed to serve the writ on the last day or the last day but one. If they
> had been given the right address, they would have served the writ on May 26, 1965,
> and would have been in time. It seems to me that, if they leave it as late as that, it
> behoves them to make absolutely sure that they have it properly served. They left it
> until the very last day, or the last day but one or two, of the twelve months. They **d**
> should not have relied on the telephone message. They should have instructed
> London agents, or done whatever was necessary, to ensure that no mistake was
> made. Having failed to have it properly served, they must take the consequences.'

Harman LJ in his turn said ([1966] 2 All ER 290 at 293, [1966] 1 WLR 861 at 867):

> 'The only matter which has given me pause, as it did LORD DENNING, M.R., was **e**
> this matter of trying to serve the defendants by post in the last two days. Now it is
> true that you may wait until the 364th day of the third year before issuing your
> writ and until the 364th day of one year more before serving it and you will still be
> in time. If you choose, however, to wait until the last moment like that, you must
> be very careful to be right and there is no reason why you should be given any
> further indulgence. The nearer you are to the last moment, the stricter ought to be **f**
> the attitude of the court [and there is a reported case within the last five years which
> says this].'

Counsel for the first defendants submitted that there were three underlying general
considerations which one must bear in mind in relation to the question of service. Firstly,
there must necessarily be a positive act by the plaintiff or his agent. Secondly, that act **g**
must be directed at an identified or identifiable object. And, thirdly, the act referred to
in the previous criteria must be one which complies with the Rules of the Supreme
Court. Her submission continued that in the instant case, if the service in December
1984 was good, it had to have complied with Ord 81, r 3(1), which I have quoted. She
contended that it was not entirely clear whether the judge below had held the original
service in December 1984 to be good under sub-para (*a*) or sub-para (*c*) of r 3(1) of Ord **h**
81. I respectfully agree, but, in order fully to deal with the matter, counsel for the first
defendants went on to make submissions about both sub-paragraphs. Counsel for the
plaintiffs, I think, felt that his position was stronger on sub-para (*c*) rather than sub-para
(*a*), and counsel for the first defendants dealt with that paragraph first.

She submitted that one could not incorporate or make use of the provisions of Ord 10,
r 1(2)(*a*) when considering the position under Ord 81, r 3(1)(*c*) because of the immediate **j**
patent inconsistency between a reference to 'usual or last known address' in Ord 10 and
address 'at the principal place of business' in Ord 81. She relied on other grounds in
support of that submission, but it was accepted as correct by counsel for the plaintiffs. I
think that he was correct to accept that situation and therefore it is unnecessary for me to
deal further with the matter.

a   The submission of counsel for the first defendants then went on to deal with the
proper meaning of the word 'sending' in the rule. She suggested that there were two
possible interpretations to be put on the word, or the idea behind the word, in the context
of the order and service. Firstly, it is referring merely to the initial act of sending the writ
to be served on its journey towards its intended recipient, that is to say in the present
context the act of putting it in the hands of the Post Office, either by putting it through
a letter box or handing it across the counter of a post office. Alternatively, the word
b   contemplates not merely the initial act of dispatch, but also the whole process of the
transmission of the document from the sender to the recipient, from the moment the
sender puts it in the hands of the Post Office until its arrival at its destination. Counsel
for the first defendants submitted that, if the proper construction was the first to which I
have referred, namely the one relating to the initial act of dispatch, then the rule was not
complied with in the circumstances which I have outlined because the address on the
c   envelope was not that of the principal place of business: it was the address of the firm at
its old address, from which it had moved in April 1975. Alternatively, if the word
contemplated the whole of the transmission process, then counsel submitted that, even
so, that process must throughout be by the plaintiffs or their agents (namely, in this case,
the Post Office), and the redirection of the envelope containing the copy writ by the Post
Office from the old office to the new office address was at the request of, and, it was
d   submitted, as agents for, the appellant first defendants, and that fatally interrupted the
necessary continuous transmission process which counsel submitted had to exist. Thus,
to the extent that the judge relied on Ord 81, r 3(1)(c), on whatever construction one took
of the word 'sending', counsel for the first defendants submitted that the service could
not be shown to be valid; it was indeed invalid and the judge was in this respect in error.
     Counsel for the first defendants then turned to consider Ord 81, r 3(1)(a), if the judge
e   must be taken to have been proceeding under that sub-paragraph. She pointed out that
in the instant case there was no question of personal service on Mr Cliff, properly so
called. The court is restricted to considering whether or not there had been valid service
by post. In considering Ord 81, r 3(1)(a) one can read that rule with the provisions of Ord
10, r 1(2)(a), but, submitted counsel, if one was relying (as one was in this case) on the
validity of service on a particular partner, then the postal service must have been directed
f   at that partner personally. As will be seen, counsel's argument for the first defendants
was based on the three principles for which she contended at the start. Merely addressing
the envelope in the name of the firm (which in the event by accident reached Mr Cliff, a
partner) was not enough. Further, counsel for the first defendants submitted that the
words 'last known' in Ord 10 did not mean last known to the respondent plaintiffs, but
they mean known by way of general reputation: the last-known address to the general
g   public; and consequently, again, if the judge had relied on Ord 81, r 3(1)(a) and Ord 10,
r 1(2)(a), it was demonstrable that the service was not valid.
     In reply to those arguments counsel for the plaintiffs submitted that the word 'sending'
must be construed in the second of the two senses to which I have referred. The way in
which he put it was that the word must be construed along the lines of 'causing
something to be conveyed or transmitted by an intermediary to another person', that is
h   to say 'sending' is putting into operation a process. Thus, his submissions continued, it is
clear that the service in December 1984 was valid under Ord 81, r 3(1)(c): there was a
sending by first-class post of a copy of a writ to the firm at its principal place of business,
where it was there read by a partner.
     Alternatively, if his submission as to the proper construction of the word 'sending' was
wrong and it had to be read in the sense of the initial dispatch, then he submitted that
j   the writ was indeed dispatched to the first defendants at their principal place of business,
the new address, when the Post Office redirected the writ through the post with the new
address substituted on the envelope for the old address. He contended that Ord 81, r 3
does not require that the service or the sending was throughout to be carried out by the
plaintiff.
     Alternatively, turning to Ord 81, r 3(1)(a) and Ord 10, r 1(2)(a), he relied principally

on the reference to 'usual place of business', that is to say, at the material time, the new
address at which the firm was carrying on business, ie their usual place of business. *a*
Again there was a sending by first-class post to Mr Cliff at that usual address and
alternatively, even if the sending had to be construed again as the original dispatch, the
writ was sent to the partners of the firm at their last-known address, namely 533 Coventry
Road. He submitted that the phrase 'last known address' should be construed according
to its ordinary English usage. He referred in that connection to the decision in *National
Westminster Bank Ltd v Betchworth Investments Ltd* (1975) 234 EG 675. Thus counsel for the *b*
plaintiffs submitted that the judge was right in holding that the service in December
1984 had been valid, whether one approached the matter under sub-para (*c*) or sub-para
(*a*) of r 3(1) of Ord 81.

For my part I repeat the salutary warnings contained in the passages from Lord
Denning MR's and Harman LJ's judgments in *Baker v Bowketts Cakes Ltd* [1966] 2 All ER
290 at 293, [1966] 1 WLR 861 at 866–867, which I have already quoted. They are, as I *c*
have said, a salutary warning to plaintiffs and their solicitors holding ageing writs and
facing arguable Limitation Act defences. Further, the Rules of the Supreme Court have,
if I may so describe it, been honed by long experience and use. They have been drafted,
redrafted and edited by persons of vast knowledge of the practice and procedure of the
High Court. Consequently, unless I am forced to do so, I do not propose to imply into
them anything which is not there and, so far as possible (unless it produces an absurdity), *d*
I would wish to give the words of the Rules of the Supreme Court their simple, ordinary,
natural meaning.

In the context of the process of service of a writ, in my opinion the rules must be
construed as involving both a server and the recipient. Service, even by post, cannot be
complete until that which is being served, in this case the writ, is actually received or
deemed to have been received under the terms of the rules. I for my part do not accept *e*
that the word 'send' where it appears in the rules only comprehends the initial dispatch.
I think it must in the context mean the whole process of transmission from server to
recipient. On that approach and construction it is clear that there was valid service of the
writ in this case pursuant to the provisions of Ord 81, r 3(1)(*c*) and it is sufficient if I say
that I accept the way that counsel for the plaintiffs put it in relation to that particular sub-
paragraph in his submissions resisting this appeal. *f*

That makes it unnecessary for me to consider sub-para (*a*) of Ord 81, r 3(1) with Ord
10, r 1(2)(*a*). However, in my opinion, first the words 'last known' mean last known to
the plaintiffs (the respondents in the instant appeal) and the address in Coventry Road
was that on the facts of the present case. But in this case I do not think that one can rely
on that, because, as I have said, one must look to the whole process of transmission to Mr
Cliff, and, although it was originally addressed to him at Coventry Road, it was not in *g*
fact received by him there. However, moving on from 'last known', I would if it were
necessary be prepared to hold that the new address in Wheeleys Road, Birmingham was,
within the rule, Mr Cliff's usual address at that time. Further, that it was sent to him,
because the use of the firm's name on the envelope comprehends each of the partners. In
that connection I refer briefly to a dictum of Lindley LJ in *Western National Bank of the
City of New York v Perez Triana & Co* [1891] 1 QB 304. The facts are immaterial for *h*
present purposes. The dictum is in these terms (at 314):

'When a firm's name is used, it is only a convenient method for denoting those
persons who compose the firm at the time when that name is used, and a plaintiff
who sues partners in the name of their firm in truth sues them individually, just as
much as if he had set out all their names.'

Reference was made in the course of the argument (more from the bench rather than *j*
the bar) to s 7 of the Interpretation Act 1978. That is in these terms:

'Where an Act authorises or requires any document to be served by post (whether
the expression "serve" or the expression "give" or "send" or any other expression is
used) then, unless the contrary intention appears, the service is deemed to be effected

by properly addressing, pre-paying and posting a letter containing the document
a   and, unless the contrary is proved, to have been effected at the time at which the
letter would be delivered in the oridinary course of post.'

The 1978 Act is applied in general to the Rules of the Supreme Court by the provisions
of Ord 1, r 3, and the suggestion was that reliance might be placed on the words 'properly
addressed' in s 7 of the 1978 Act in support of the submission that there had been no
valid service here, as the address on the envelope was the address in Coventry Road and
b   the firm had already moved to the new address in Wheeleys Road. In my judgment,
however, in the context with which we are presently concerned, that is to say the context
delineated by RSC Ords 81 and 10, the contrary intention referred to in s 7 does appear.
The rules make reference to relevant addresses in relation to service as 'usual', 'last known'
and 'the principal place of business', and in my judgment, therefore, s 7 of the 1978 Act
is not to be taken to apply to the service provisions in Ord 81 combined with Ord 10.
c   Thus, I would come to the conclusion that the service in December 1984 was a valid
service and that the judge was correct in so holding.

In those cirucumstances it might be thought unnecessary to go on to deal with the
second point which arises in this appeal, namely the question of the exercise of discretion
in renewing the writ by Master Topley. Nevertheless I propose to add a few brief
d   comments on that point. It may be that in the event the service in January 1985 became
a nullity, there having been service the previous December, but it may be important to
be precise about when the service in this particular case took place. In my experience,
important points do arise on this question of renewal of writs, particularly in the presence
of impending expiry of limitation periods.

Any renewal of the validity of a writ is a matter of discretion for the court. That is
quite clear from the provisions of RSC Ord 6, r 8(2). In exercising that discretion, in my
e   opinion the court must take into account all *relevant* circumstances. For instance, when
the application for renewal is made is a relevant consideration to take into account. So
also is the question why the writ had not been served during its initial validity period.
That the defendant may have a defence under the provisions of the Limitation Act is also
quite clearly another relevant circumstance. The weight to be given to this last
f   consideration, as indeed with the others, must depend on the strength, as it appears, of
the Limitation Act defence in the given case.

The general principles relevant in these circumstances were set out by Megaw J in the
locus classicus on this particular point in *Heaven v Road and Rail Wagons Ltd* [1965] 2 All
ER 409 at 413, [1965] 2 QB 355 at 361, a decision which has frequently been approved
by this court. Megaw J set out the general principles in these terms:

g   '... the principle, or the general rule, to be applied is that leave will not be given
to extend the validity of a writ when application is made retrospectively after the
period of twelve months prescribed by the rules has expired, if the effect of so doing
would be to deprive the defendant of a defence which he would have had under the
relevant statute of limitation, supposing that leave to extend were not given and the
plaintiff were thus compelled to serve a fresh writ. To justify the exercise of the
h   discretion there must be exceptional circumstances.'

Megaw J then went on to discuss the grounds that were there put forward in support of
a proposition that the discretion should have been exercised (see [1965] 2 All ER 409 at
415, [1965] 2 QB 355 at 364–365). Having considered those grounds, he then continued
in a well-known passage in these terms ([1965] 2 All ER 409 at 415, [1965] 2 QB 355 at
j   365):

'Clearly, the fact that the plaintiff will be deprived of the possibility of successfully
pursuing his claim against the defendants, since the latter can plead the statute of
limitation to any fresh writ, cannot be a ground. It is not an exceptional circumstance,
it is the necessary consequence of applying the general rule; it is, indeed, the very
fact which gives rise to the existence of the rule. Nor can the fact that the defendants
knew of the existence of a claim, or knew that a writ had been issued, be a ground.

These are in no way exceptional circumstances. Nor can it be a ground that the
defendants are unable to show that, if the validity of the writ were to be extended, *a*
there would be any specific prejudice or detriment to them in conducting their
defence, compared with what their position would have been if the writ had been
duly served on them within the twelve months' period. It must be rare, indeed, that
a defendant would be able to show such specific detriment by reason of the lapse of
time between the end of the twelve months and the date when, after retrospective
extension of its validity, the writ is actually served. If that were a relevant factor, the *b*
exceptions to the general rule, requiring or justifying the exercise of the discretion,
would vastly exceed in number the cases where the general rule is to be applied. In
other words, the application of the general rule would be quite exceptional—a
contradiction in terms.'

One should note also that more recently 'exceptional circumstances' were not found to
exist in *Afro Continental Nigeria Ltd v Meridian Shipping Co SA, The Vrontados* [1982] 2 *c*
Lloyd's Rep 241, even though the existence of the claim and the issue of the writ had
come to the notice of the defendants before the expiry of the relevant limitation period.
A similar view was taken in *Leal v Dunlop Bio-Processes International Ltd* [1984] 2 All ER
207, [1984] 1 WLR 874, and in the more recent case of *Portico Housing Association Ltd v
Brian Morehead & Partners* (1985) 1 Const LJ 226.

The judge below, as I have said, in deciding that the master's order should not be *d*
disturbed, was exercising a discretion of his own and, as both counsel accepted, that can
only be disturbed in this court on the usual principles regarding appeals against the
exercise of discretion below. Counsel for the first defendants submitted that, when one
looks at the judge's judgment, although he started by taking into account the possibility
of Limitation Act defences, he does not seem to have carried it through to the end of his
judgment. In any event, the judge referred to two reasons which counsel for the first *e*
defendants submitted were not proper for him to take into account in and about the
exercise of discretion. The judge said this:

'Looking at all the circumstances here, the fact that the writ was in the hands of
the [first] defendants seven days before the expiry of its period of validity, the fact
that for understandable reasons the [first] defendants were not able to inform the *f*
plaintiffs that (as they thought) the writ was invalid until 2 January, the fact that the
plaintiffs then proceeded to apply for a renewal and obtained it by 18 January, seems
to me to indicate that, if there are exceptional cases where it is justifiable to renew a
writ, this is one of them.'

Counsel for the first defendants submitted that, although the first of those three *g*
considerations was one which the judge was entitled to take into account, the second and
third were not.

I respectfully agree, and consequently it is demonstrated, as I think, that the judge was
in error in approaching this particular point. Consequently the exercise of the discretion
can be a matter for this court.

Counsel for the plaintiffs in his submissions accepted that the judge had been wrong *h*
in taking those two matters into account and that the exercise of discretion was indeed
for this court. But he went on to submit that this was an exceptional case. Here the writ
was in the hands of a partner of the defendant firm before the expiry of its initial validity.
Rhetorically counsel for the plaintiffs invited the court to state the facts of this case in
that particular context to an informed and reasonable outsider and ask what he would
think if, notwithstanding the fact that the partner had already received the writ before *j*
the expiry of its initial validity, this court were to hold that it was a wrong exercise of the
discretion to extend its validity.

I appreciate the force of that argument, but I wish again to stress that the provisions of
the Rules of the Supreme Court, particularly in the context of service combined with the
operation of the Limitation Acts, must be strictly complied with. I respectfully disagree
with the dictum of Lord Denning MR in *The Vrontados* [1982] 2 Lloyd's Rep 241 at 246
that we are dealing here with mere technicalities. It is in the interests of both plaintiffs

and the public that litigation should proceed with all diligence. It is in the interest of
_a_ defendants that they should be able to know when claims against them are statute-barred.
This type of case, where a writ is held for too long and service is attempted in haste
within the last week of its validity, continues to arise far too frequently. As a matter of
discretion is involved I do not attempt any catalogue of exceptional circumstances which
might allow the exercise of discretion in these circumstances, but in the majority of such
cases I myself would be looking for circumstances showing that a plaintiff had indeed
_b_ been unable to serve the writ during the material time: for instance, where a defendant
had disappeared, gone abroad or could not be traced; or where a defendant, his insurers
or his other representatives had specifically led a plaintiff to think that it was unnecessary
to serve the writ because they were negotiating. This ground, based on these last
considerations, however, should be approached, as I think, with caution. In my
experience, too often unnecessary delay is sought to be excused by alleged negotiations.
_c_   In the instant case, if it were necessary to decide the point, I would hold that there
were no exceptional circumstances entitling the master to exercise his discretion to renew
the writ and in the exercise of my own discretion I would not renew the writ, as he did
in January 1985. Consequently, had I thought that the service in December 1984 had
been invalid, I would also have set aside the master's renewal and allowed the appeal.
However, for the reasons which I gave earlier in this judgment, I think that the service
_d_ in December 1984 was valid and, consequently, would dismiss the appeal.
     I would merely add this. As I have already indicated, there are many authorities other
than _Baker v Bowketts Cakes Ltd_ [1966] 2 All ER 290, [1966] 1 WLR 861 to the effect that
the nearer one gets to the end of the limitation period the greater is there the obligation
to proceed diligently and timeously on the parties concerned. Neither side in the instant
litigation seems to have done so, so far. Each side must realise that, now the litigation has
_e_ been started (and, as I think, started validly), they must both proceed with all due
expedition, and I trust that any court who in the future has to deal with the progress of
this particular litigation will keep each side up to the mark. Nevertheless, for the reasons
that I have sought to advance, I would dismiss the appeal and uphold the service in
December 1984.

_f_ **LLOYD LJ.** I agree that this appeal should be dismissed, but I reach that result by a
different route. The official referee held that the writ was properly served because it was
sent to the first defendants at their usual or last-known address. By this I take the official
referee to mean that there was valid service on the firm under RSC Ord 81, r 3(1)(c) by
dint of reading Ord 81, r (3)(1)(c) in conjunction with Ord 10, r 1(2)(a).
     I have every sympathy with the official referee in his desire to avoid technicalities, but
_g_ like May LJ I cannot see how 'usual' or 'last known' address can be read into Ord 81,
r 3(1)(c) when Ord 81, r 3(1)(c) refers expressly not to the usual or last-known address but
to the firm's principal place of business. Counsel for the plaintiffs did not seek to argue
the contrary.
     Instead counsel for the plaintiffs sought to support the official referee's decision on two
alternative grounds set out in the respondent's notice.
_h_   First he argued that, though the letter containing the copy writ was addressed to the
old place of business, nevertheless it was sent to the new place of business because the
word 'send' in Ord 81, r 3(1)(c) means putting into operation a process which results in
the arrival of the writ at the new place of business.
     I cannot accept that argument, ingenious though it is. It seems to me that 'sending' in
Ord 81, r 3(1)(c) bears what I would regard as its ordinary meaning, namely putting the
_j_ document in the post. The only question which then arises is whether the document was
sent to the firm at its principal place of business. The answer must be 'No, it was sent to
the firm at its previous place of business'. It was not sent to the firm at its new place of
business for the simple reason that it was never properly addressed to the firm at its new
place of business. By properly addressed, I do not mean that the address need be correctly
spelt. But it must designate the correct premises.
     Counsel for the plaintiffs conceded that the document was not correctly addressed
when posted. But he argued before us (though not, I think, before the official referee)

that the document *became* correctly addressed when it was readdressed by the Post Office acting, he said, as the plaintiffs' agent. In my judgment that does not suffice. I have never *a* heard it suggested that a document is properly addressed for the purposes of s 7 of the Interpretation Act 1978 if it is readdressed by the Post Office. To bring the deeming provision into operation, it must be properly addressed when posted. The same, in my view, applies to Ord 81, r 3(1)(c). The copy writ is not sent to the firm by post unless it is properly addressed to the firm at its principal place of business when posted, which, as is conceded, was not the case. The document was not sent to the firm at its principal place *b* of business when posted by the plaintiffs: it was sent *on* by the Post Office.

I can understand it being said, 'But here the writ arrived at the principal place of business and arrived in time, so what does it matter where it was sent?' I have much sympathy with that view. I dislike technicalities as much as anyone. But unfortunately the provisions relating to service by post have to be complied with. The fact that a writ has arrived does not mean that it has been properly sent. Suppose, for example, the *c* document had been accidentally dropped on the way to the post, picked up by a stranger and delivered by hand. Nobody suggests, or could suggest, that that would have been good service. For the document would not have been served personally and it would not have been sent by post.

Counsel's second argument for the plaintiffs was that there was valid service under Ord 81, r 3(1)(a), since it was sent to one of the partners of the firm, Mr Cliff, at his usual *d* or last-known address.

I agree that, so far as Ord 81, r 3(1)(a) is concerned (and in this respect it differs from Ord 81, r 3(1)(c)), we are entitled to read in the provisions of Ord 10, r 1(2)(a), as indeed counsel for the first defendants conceded. But the difficulty of counsel for the plaintiffs here is that the document was not sent to Mr Cliff: it was sent to the secretary. The fact that it reached Mr Cliff's hands is, I fear, irrelevant: it was not properly addressed by post *e* to Mr Cliff.

There was a second argument relied on by counsel for the first defendants under this head that, even if the letter had been addressed to Mr Cliff, it was not addressed to him at his usual or last-known address. 'Last known' address cannot, she submitted, mean simply last known to the plaintiff: it must mean last ascertainable address or last address known generally. Just as the 'usual address' involves an objective test, so also must the *f* last-known address.

In the absence of authority there would be much to be said for that argument. But in the light of the decision of this court in *National Westminster Bank Ltd v Betchworth Investments Ltd* (1975) 234 EG 675, to which counsel for the plaintiffs helpfully drew our attention, I say no more about it. So that argument fails. But the other arguments of counsel for the first defendants, however technical, are in my view well founded. I would *g* conclude, reluctantly, that this writ was never validly served.

That brings me to the second part of the case: was the official referee justified in renewing the writ? If not are we justified in interfering with his discretion in the matter?

Counsel for the first defendants submitted that the official referee misdirected himself, or acted on a wrong principle, since, having mentioned the argument that part or all of the claim might be time-barred, he did not carry the argument through to its conclusion. *h* What the official referee said on that point was this:

'It is true to say that the writ should not be extended retrospectively after the expiry of the 12-month period of its validity if the effect of so doing would be to deprive the defendant on a limitation defence. Indeed, it could be said that there is a heavy burden on a plaintiff to justify that course even where there is no more than a possibility of that being the case, but certainly, to justify the exercise of discretion *j* to extend in circumstances such as I have referred to, there must be something of an exceptional nature especially where there is a high probability that a defendant might lose the advantages of relying on a limitation point.'

In my view that was a correct direction. It cannot be necessary for the court to try the case in order to determine whether a limitation defence has accrued or not. Nor, as

counsel for the first defendants argued, could it be right for the court to assume a
a limitation defence in a defendant's favour. It is a factor to be taken into account, like
other relevant factors. The more likely it is that the defendant has an accrued limitation
defence, the greater the weight that should be attached to that factor. In cases where it is
plain that a defence has accrued, something really exceptional is needed to justify the
court exercising its discretion, as has been made clear in a number of recent cases. But
this was not such a case.

b   The second criticism of counsel for the first defendants turned on the three
considerations which led the official referee to reach the result he did. Those
considerations are set out in the passage from the official referee's judgment which May
LJ has already read. As to the second and third of those considerations, counsel for the
first defendants submitted that delay in applying for renewal would have been a relevant
circumstance if the official referee had been otherwise justified in renewing the writ; but
c promptitude in applying for renewal is not a positive factor in the plaintiff's favour. So
the second and third considerations, said counsel for the first defendants, were irrelevant.
That leaves the first consideration. The first consideration alone, she said, could not
amount to sufficiently exceptional circumstances to justify renewing the writ.

What is a sufficient ground for renewing a writ is, of course, a question of discretion
and degree. It might not be sufficient, Megaw J pointed out in *Heaven v Road and Rail*
d *Wagons Ltd* [1965] 2 All ER 409 at 415, [1965] 2 QB 355 at 365, that the defendant
merely knows of the existence of the claim, or knew that the writ had been issued. But
here the facts go further. The first defendants not only knew that the writ had been
issued: the writ was in their hands. Mr Cliff, one of the partners, must have known that
it was intended to be served on the firm. The argument that the writ was not validly
served (an argument which I have with reluctance accepted) is technical in the highest
e degree. The official referee was, in my view, entitled to rely on the circumstances as
sufficient ground for justifying the renewal of the writ, notwithstanding the possibility
of a limitation defence. At any rate the case falls within the area where different views
can reasonably and properly be held. I would therefore decline to interfere with the
official referee's discretion in the matter. If we are entitled or obliged to exercise our
discretion afresh, I would reach the same conclusion. On that ground I would dismiss
f this appeal.

SIR JOHN MEGAW. I agree that this appeal should be dismissed. In agreement with
May LJ, on the first point considered by him, I am of opinion that there was on the facts
a valid and effective service of the writ on 21 December 1984, ie within the period of a
year from the date of its issue. It was issued on 28 December 1983. The service was, in
g my view, effective in accordance with the requirements of RSC Ord 81, r 3(1)(*c*). Let it
be assumed that the word 'send' or 'sending' in sub-para (*c*), in the context of the words
'by ordinary first-class post', means 'put into the post'. Although the word 'deliver' or
'delivery' does not appear in the rule, it is in my view beyond dispute that the sending,
the posting, of the copy of the writ does not by itself effect service. It is an element. The
writ must be put in the post. But there is another, and an essential, requirement if service
h is to be effected: ie delivery of the writ through the post. If the writ is not delivered
through the post to the defendant firm at the principal place of business of the
partnership, service has not been effected under sub-para (*c*). True, there may be a
'deemed' service seven days from the date of posting or sending. That arises under Ord
81, 3(2)(*a*). But that 'deeming' is subject to evidence to the contrary in every instance. If
it should be relevant for any purpose in connection with the service of the writ, it is open
j to either party to prove the actual date of the delivery through the post so as to establish
the date of service. So also it is open to the defendant to prove that the copy of the writ
was not delivered at all at the address of the principal place of business of the partnership.
If the defendant does so prove, then there has been no valid effecting of service, however
accurately the envelope containing the copy of the writ may have been addressed at the
time when it was posted and however clearly it is proved that the envelope was duly
posted so addressed. Since delivery by post is thus an essential element of the service

under sub-para (*c*), there is no need to treat the words in the sub-paragraph 'to the firm at the principal place of business of the partnership' as indicating that the address of the current principal place of business at the time when it is posted must be accurately expressed in the writing on the envelope. It is the delivery which must be at the address of the principal place of business. Ordinarily, of course, it is to be expected that that address would be set out accurately on the envelope when it is posted. But that is not an essential requirement any defect of which invalidates the service. If the address is not correct at the time of posting, the plaintiff, of course, takes the risk of non-delivery or of a delay in delivery through the post at the correct address. But, if the envelope containing a copy of the writ is in fact delivered by post at the right address, service has been effected as at the date of that delivery.

To my mind that is not only the meaning of the words used in sub-para (*c*), it also conforms with common sense. It avoids a potential absurdity, or at best the highly unsatisfactory questions of degree which would arise if an envelope were to be posted with some possibly quite minor error in the address: for example, an error in the number of a building or in the spelling of the name of the street, which in fact did not prevent delivery through the postal service at the right address. It avoids the extreme absurdity which would arise, on the first defendants' construction of the sub-paragraph, if the principal place of business had been changed by the defendant firm on the day before the copy of the writ was posted by a plaintiff who did not know, and had no reason to know, of that change. It avoids many other absurdities which would do no credit to the law. Lloyd LJ's example of a letter being dropped and picked up by an officious stranger and delivered by hand appears to me, with respect, to be a relatively trivial anomaly compared with the anomalies which would arise from the construction of the sub-paragraph for which the first defendants contend. As the copy of the writ here was sent by the plaintiffs by ordinary first-class post and as it was thereafter in fact delivered by the Post Office to the firm at its principal place of business, which was its principal place of business at the time of the posting, the requirements of Ord 81, r 3(1)(*c*) were fulfilled. There is no justification, as a matter of construction or common sense, for construing sub-para (*c*) as though it contained before the words 'at the principal place of business of the partnership' the words 'correctly addressed to the firm at the time when the copy of the writ is posted'; yet that is what is necessarily involved in the construction put forward by the first defendants.

If that be right, the second point which has arisen on this appeal does not require to be decided. That is whether, if the service were not effected on 23 December 1984 because of the address on the envelope at the time of posting, it would be a proper exercise of discretion to grant an extension of the writ. But, as my brethren disagree on that issue, I find it necessary to express my view.

I have been persuaded by the cases cited by counsel for the first defendants and in particular by what was said in this court in *Afro Continental Nigeria Ltd v Meridian Shipping Co SA, The Vrontados* [1982] 2 Lloyd's Rep 241 and *Leal v Dunlop Bio-Processes International Ltd* [1984] 2 All ER 207, [1984] 1 WLR 874, that the principles laid down by this court must have the result of preventing the exercise of the discretion of the court in favour of the plaintiffs in a case such as this case would be if the service on 21 December 1984 were not a valid and effective service. In the result, if this point had arisen, I should agree with what May LJ has said as to the way in which that point would have had to be decided. But, on the first point, I am satisfied that the technicality relied on by the first defendants is not valid even as a technicality.

On that ground I agree that the appeal should be dismissed. I should like to express my gratitude to both counsel for their admirably clear and succinct arguments.

Appeal dismissed.

Solicitors: *Waltons & Morse*, agents for *Pinsent & Co*, Birmingham (for the first defendants); *H B Beake*, Uxbridge (for the plaintiffs).

Carolyn Toulmin   Barrister.

a

Practice Note

CHANCERY DIVISION (NORTHERN AREA)

Practice – Chancery Division – Northern Area – Lists – Fixed dates – Warned cases – Motion days – Papers for judge – Urgent matters

b

The following direction, issued by the Lord Chancellor's Department as a press notice, was given by his Honour Judge Blackett-Ord V-C on 31 July 1986 and is to apply from 1 October 1986. It replaces the memorandum of 3 December 1984 (*Practice Note* [1985] 1 All ER 190).

c 1. The Senior Chancery Clerk (the clerk) in the district registries at Leeds, Liverpool, Manchester, Newcastle upon Tyne and Preston will each maintain separate lists of cases in the Chancery Division of the High Court proceeding in that registry or intended to be tried at that centre, namely: (a) a *setting down list* comprising all cases for hearing by the judge except cases entered in the motion day lists. In this list cases will be identified as 'witness' cases (involving the oral examination of witnesses or deponents) or 'non-witness'
d cases (not involving oral evidence); (b) a list for each motion day at that centre, comprising motions, company petitions and all cases estimated to occupy the time of the court for two hours or less.

2. *The setting down list*
e   (a) Cases will be entered when they are set down, adjourned into court or otherwise ready for hearing or when transferred from a motion day list and will be deleted when disposed of.
       (b) Each case will be given an identifying number. The plaintiff's solicitor will be sent a letter enclosing a blank counsel's certificate of estimated hearing time and giving a date (which will normally be one month ahead) by which the certificate is required to be
f returned signed by all counsel in the case.
       (c) On receipt of counsel's certificate the setting down list will be marked accordingly and the clerk at each district registry (except Manchester) will send to the Chancery listing officer at Manchester a photocopy of counsel's certificate and a completed pro forma.
       (d) If counsel's certificate is not lodged within the period specified or if it appears to the clerk that through the default of any party the trial of the case may be delayed he will
g communicate with the party concerned. In the absence of a satisfactory reply the case will be referred to the district registrar (under RSC Ord 34, r 5 or Ord 28, r 10) or to the judge for directions.

3. *Fixed dates*
h   (a) The Chancery listing officer will maintain a list of cases from *all* the Chancery district registries (including Manchester) where counsel's certificate has been filed.
       (b) Fixed dates will be allotted for all cases expected to last three days or more, the Chancery listing officer keeping the judge's diaries and acting as co-ordinator. Applications for fixed dates at Leeds will continue to be made to the clerk at Leeds. Now that there are usually three judges sitting to hear Chancery cases in the Northern Area, more cases are
j required at short notice to fill the gaps caused by settlements and it is intended to use the gaps to expedite the hearing of shorter cases. The listing officer will have a discretion whether or not to give a fixed date for any case with an estimated length of hearing of less than three days but initially fixed dates for such cases will not be given.
       (c) A fixed date may be vacated by the listing officer if a revised certificate lengthening counsel's estimate of the length of hearing is lodged, otherwise his Honour Judge Blackett-Ord V-C's direction dated 14 July 1980 ([1980] 3 All ER 831) will apply with the

addition of the words 'or his Honour Judge O'Donoghue' after each reference to his Honour Judge FitzHugh QC.

4. *Warned cases*
(a) Cases not given a fixed date for trial (short cases) will be liable to be called on for trial at short notice.
(b) Parties or their solicitors in short cases will be notified as soon as practicable that their case is warned for a particular date (or dates).
(c) In the event of a short case not coming on for trial during the warned period the listing officer will then allocate a fixed date for trial.

5. *Motion day lists*
(a) Any case falling within para 1(b) above may be entered on the list for any motion day at any centre, but motions and petitions with a time estimate of over two hours may (at the discretion of the judge) be adjourned to another motion day or other date to be fixed as seems appropriate. In exercising his discretion the judge will take into account the state of the lists generally and the relative urgency of the case.
(b) Subject to the above, motions will continue to be heard on any motion day and at any centre named in the notice of motion and may be stood over or saved for hearing at any other centre.

6. *Papers for the judge*
(1) In additon to any documents in the court file legible copies must be provided as follows:
(a) *Writ actions* On setting down, copies of the pleadings and other documents specified in RSC Ord 34, r 3(1) and complying with Ord 66.
(b) *Originating summonses* and other cases involving affidavit evidence (other than simple creditors' winding-up petitions) when listed under para 2(a) above: (i) the originating summons or other originating process; (ii) the affidavits and exhibits, which must comply with the practice direction of the Lord Chief Justice dated 21 July 1983 (see *Practice Note* [1983] 3 All ER 33, [1983] 1 WLR 922). Copies of exhibits which do not lend themselves to photographic reproduction may be omitted; (iii) any orders of the district registrar which have been drawn up; (iv) any requisite legal aid documents.
(c) *Motions*: (i) the writ and any subsequent pleadings; (ii) the notice of motion; (iii) the affidavits and exhibits (see sub-para (b)(ii) above which applies); (iv) in the case of motions for judgment, the documents referred to in *The Supreme Court Practice 1985* vol 1, p 328, para 19/7/8 (with the exception of Form E26 praecipe).

(2) The provision of these documents is the responsibility of the solicitor for the plaintiff, the petitioner or the party moving the court (as the case may be) except that (a) the court will provide copies of writs and orders on request, (b) the solicitor for any defendant or respondent is responsible for copies of affidavits on which he relies and of their exhibits.

7. *Urgent matters*
On a certificate of urgency (oral or in writing) by a solicitor or (if possible) counsel, arrangements will be made to communicate with the judge without delay, by telephone if necessary.

8. In this memorandum the expression 'the judge' means and includes his Honour Judge Blackett-Ord V-C, his Honour Judge FitzHugh QC and his Honour Judge O'Donoghue.

a
Drake v Chief Adjudication Officer
(Case 150/85)

COURT OF JUSTICE OF THE EUROPEAN COMMUNITIES (FOURTH CHAMBER)
JUDGES BAHLMANN (PRESIDENT OF CHAMBER), KOOPMANS, BOSCO, O'HIGGINS AND SCHOCKWEILER
ADVOCATE GENERAL G F MANCINI

b 22 JANUARY, 22 APRIL, 24 JUNE 1986

European Economic Community – Equality of treatment of men and women – Social security –
Scope of schemes and conditions of access – Invalidity benefit – National legislation providing that
benefit not payable to married woman living with or maintained by husband – Benefit paid to
married man in corresponding circumstances – United Kingdom invalid care allowance –
c *Allowance not payable to married woman living with or maintained by husband or woman living*
with man as husband and wife – Whether fact that allowance paid to third party and not directly
to disabled person placing United Kingdom scheme outside statutory schemes referred to in
European Communities directive on equal treatment for men and woman in matters of social
security – Whether scheme contrary to principle of equal treatment – Whether conditions in
scheme constituting discrimination on grounds of sex – Social Security Act 1975, s 37(3)(a)(i) –
d *EC Council Directive 79/7, arts 1, 3(1)(a), 4.*

Social security – Invalid care allowance – Sex discrimination – Allowance not payable to married
woman living with or maintained by husband or woman living with man as husband and wife –
Allowance paid to man in corresponding circumstances – Whether United Kingdom scheme of
invalid care allowance outside statutory schemes referred to in European Communities directive
e *on equal treatment for men and women in matters of social security – Whether scheme contrary*
to principle of equal treatment – Whether conditions in scheme constituting discrimination on
grounds of sex – Social Security Act 1975, s 37(3)(a)(i) – EC Council Directive 79/7, arts 1,
3(1)(a), 4.

The applicant, a married woman who lived with her husband, had for a number of years
f held a variety of full-time and part-time jobs. In 1984 the applicant's mother, a severely
disabled person who received an attendance allowance under s 35(1) of the Social Security
Act 1975, came to live with her, whereupon the applicant gave up her work in order to
look after her mother. The applicant applied for an invalid care allowance under s 37[a] of
the 1975 Act but the adjudication officer stated that by virtue of s 37(3)(a)(i) the allowance
was not payable to a married woman residing with her husband. The adjudication officer
g referred the claim, however, to the Social Security Appeal Tribunal, which held that the
rule in s 37(3)(a)(i) constituted discrimination on grounds of sex contrary to EC Council
Directive 79/7. On an appeal by the adjudication officer, the Chief Social Security

---

h a   Section 37, so far as material, provides:
      '(1) Subject to the provisions of this section, a person shall be entitled to an invalid care
allowance for any day on which he is engaged in caring for a severely disabled person if— (a) he is
regularly and substantially engaged in caring for that person; and (b) he is not gainfully employed;
and (c) the severely disabled person is either such relative of his as may be prescribed or a person of
any such other description as may be prescribed.
      (2) In this section, "severely disabled person" means a person in respect of whom there is payable
j   either an attendance allowance of such other payment out of public funds on account of his need
for attendance as may be prescribed.
      (3) A person shall not be entitled to an allowance under this section if he is under the age of 16
or receiving full-time education; and a woman shall not be entitled to any such allowance if— (a)
she is married and either—(i) she is residing with her husband, or (ii) he is contributing to her
maintenance at a weekly rate not less than the weekly rate of such an allowance; or (b) she is
cohabiting with a man as his wife . . .'

Commissioner referred to the Court of Justice of the European Communities the questions whether the right to payment of a benefit to a person who cared for a disabled *a* person constituted part of a statutory scheme providing protection against the risk of invalidity to which Directive 79/7 applied under art 3(1)(*a*)*[b]* thereof and, if it did, whether a condition that benefit was not payable to a married woman who lived with or was maintained by her husband, although it was paid in corresponding circumstances to a married man, constituted discrimination on the grounds of sex contrary to art 4(1)*[c]* of that directive. *b*

Held – (1) In order to ensure that the progressive implementation of the principle of equal treatment referred to in art 1*[d]* of EC Council Directive 79/7 and defined in art 4 thereof was carried out in a harmonious manner throughout the European Community, art 3(1) was to be interpreted as including any benefit which in a broad sense formed part of one of the statutory schemes referred to in art 3(1)(*a*) or a social assistance provision *c* intended to supplement or replace such a scheme. Moreover, the payment of the benefit to a person who provided care still depended on the existence of a situation of invalidity inasmuch as such a situation was an indispensable condition for its payment, and there was a clear economic link between the benefit and the disabled person, since the disabled person derived an advantage from the fact that an allowance was paid to the person caring for him. It followed that the fact that a benefit which formed part of a statutory *d* invalidity scheme was paid to a third party and not directly to the disabled person did not place it outside the scope of Directive 79/7. A benefit provided by a member state and paid to a person caring for a disabled person therefore formed part of a statutory scheme providing protection against invalidity which was covered by Directive 79/7 pursuant to art 3(1)(*a*) thereof (see p 73 *j* to p 74 *c* and p 75 *b*, post).

(2) Since s 37(3) of the 1975 Act placed married women living with their husbands *e* and women who lived with a man as husband and wife at a disadvantage by precluding them from obtaining invalid care allowance and since art 4(1) of Directive 79/7 provided that the implementation of the principle of equal treatment, with regard in particular to the scope of schemes and the conditions of access to them, meant that there should be no discrimination whatsoever on grounds of sex, it followed that a national provision such as that made by s 37 of the 1975 Act was contrary to the aim of Directive 79/7, which *f* under art 189*[e]* of the EEC Treaty was binding on member states as to the result to be achieved. Accordingly, discrimination on grounds of sex contrary to art 4(1) of Directive 79/7 arose where national legislation provided that a benefit which formed part of one of the statutory schemes referred to in art 3(1) of that directive was not payable to a married woman who lived with or was maintained by her husband although it was paid in corresponding circumstances to a married man (see p 74 *f* to *j* and p 75 *b c*, post). *g*

Notes

For invalid care allowance, see 33 Halsbury's Laws (4th edn) para 449.

For the principle of equal treatment of men and women in matters of social security, see 52 ibid para 21·14.

For the Social Security Act 1975, ss 35, 37, see 45 Halsbury's Statutes (3rd edn) 1120, *h* 1123.

For the EEC Treaty, art 189, see 42A ibid 316.

b Article 3(1), so far as material, is set out at p 71 *j*, post
c Article 4(1) is set out at p 72 *a b*, post *j*
d Article 1, so far as material, is set out at p 71 *g h*, post
e Article 189, so far as material, provides: 'In order to carry out their task the Council and the Commission shall, in accordance with the provisions of this Treaty ... issue directives ... A directive shall be binding, as to the result to be achieved, upon each Member State to which it is addressed, but shall leave to the national authorities the choice of form and methods...'

Reference

a By order dated 15 May 1985 the Chief Social Security Commissioner referred to the Court of Justice of the European Communities for a preliminary ruling under art 177 of the EEC Treaty two questions (set out at p 72 c to e, post) regarding the interpretation of EC Council Directive 79/7 of 10 January 1979 on the progressive implementation of the principle of equal treatment for men and women in matters of social security, with a view to determining the compatibility with that directive of a provision of national law,

b viz s 37(3)(a)(i) of the Social Security Act 1975, laying down conditions for the granting of an invalid care allowance. The questions were raised in the course of proceedings before the commissioner between Mrs Jacqueline Drake and the Chief Adjudication Officer on an appeal by the latter from the decision of the Social Security Appeal Tribunal on 1 March 1985 whereby, on a reference to it by the adjudication officer of a claim by Mrs Drake for invalid care allowance in respect of care provided by her to her mother,

c the tribunal held that the rule in s 37(3)(a)(i) of the 1975 Act constituted discrimination on grounds of sex contrary to Directive 79/7. Mrs Drake, the adjudication officer and the Commission of the European Communities submitted observations to the court. The language of the case was English. The facts are set out in the opinion of the Advocate General.

d *Richard Drabble* for Mrs Drake.
Francis Jacobs QC for the adjudication officer.
J R Currall for the EC Commission.

22 April. **The Advocate General (G F Mancini)** delivered the following opinion[1]. Mr President, Members of the Court,

e   1. In the context of proceedings between Jacqueline Drake and the Chief Adjudication Officer, the Chief Social Security Commissioner of the United Kingdom has asked the court to interpret two provisions of EC Council Directive 79/7 of 19 December 1978 on the progressive implementation of the principle of equal treatment for men and women in matters of social security. In particular, the commissioner wishes to know: (a) whether a benefit such as the 'invalid care allowance' paid in Great Britain constitutes part of a

f statutory scheme providing protection against invalidity, covered by the directive; (b) whether the fact that a married woman who lives with her husband is excluded from that benefit constitutes discrimination on grounds of sex, contrary to the directive.

     2. Jacqueline Drake is married and lives with her husband; prior to the middle of 1984 she held a succession of full-time and part-time jobs. In June 1984 her mother, a severely disabled person entitled to an attendance allowance under s 35 of the Social

g Security Act 1975, came to live with her, and Mrs Drake gave up her job in order to look after her.

     On 5 February 1985 Mrs Drake applied for an invalid care allowance under s 37 of the 1975 Act. The adjudication officer pointed out that under s 37(3)(a)(i) married women who live with their husbands are not entitled to the allowance, but in order to expedite the procedure he referred the matter to the Social Security Appeal Tribunal. In a decision

h given on 1 March 1985 the tribunal held that that provision constituted discrimination on grounds of sex, contrary to Directive 79/7. The Chief Adjudication Officer appealed against that decision to the Chief Social Security Commissioner, who, by an order dated 15 May 1985, stayed the proceedings and referred to the court the following questions for a preliminary ruling under art 177 of the EEC Treaty:

j   '1. If a Member State provides a benefit payable (provided certain residence and other conditions are met) to a person who is not gainfully employed and is regularly and substantially engaged in caring for a person in respect of whom a benefit is payable as a severely disabled person by reason of that person requiring attention or

1 Translated from the Italian

supervision as prescribed (and provided that that person meets certain residence and other conditions), does the benefit payable to the first-mentioned person constitute *a* the whole or part of a statutory scheme which provides protection against invalidity to which Article 3(1)(*a*) of Directive 79/7/EEC applies?

2. If the answer to the first question is yes, does a condition that a married woman is not entitled to that benefit if she is residing with her husband or he is contributing to her maintenance above a certain level constitute discrimination contrary to Article 4(1) of that Directive in circumstances where married men do not have to *b* meet a corresponding condition?'

According to the order of the commissioner the sole point at issue between the parties is the scope of s 37(3)(*a*)(i) of the 1975 Act. The parties are agreed that the claimant fulfils the other conditions of entitlement to the invalid care allowance.

3. In the interests of a better understanding of the questions it may be helpful to summarise the British legislation on invalidity benefits and the relevant Community *c* provisions. The British rules are contained in the 1975 Act. Section 37 provides:

'(i) . . . a person shall be entitled to an invalid care allowance for any day on which he is engaged in caring for a severely disabled person if—(*a*) he is regularly and substantially engaged in caring for that person; and (*b*) he is not gainfully employed; and (*c*) the severely disabled person is either such relative of his as may be prescribed *d* or person of any such other description as may be prescribed. . .'

For the purposes of that rule s 37(2) defines 'severely disabled person' as a person entitled to an attendance allowance or other benefit of the same nature. An attendance allowance is paid to a disabled person who requires attention or supervision to the extent set out in the Act (s 35). Under s 37(3) the invalid care allowance is not paid (a) to any *e* person who is under the age of 16 or is engaged in full-time education, (b) to a married woman who lives with her husband or to whose maintenance her husband contributes a weekly sum not less than the weekly rate of the allowance, (c) to a woman who lives with a man as husband and wife.

The benefits in question are not contributory and are paid directly to the person who undertakes the care of a disabled person. *f*

The relevant Community provisions are those contained in Directive 79/7, whose purpose is to extend to the area of social security the principle of equal treatment for men and women laid down in art 119 of the EEC Treaty. That extension is viewed as a gradual process. For present purposes it is sufficient to recall that in the first stage equal treatment was to be implemented in statutory schemes providing protection against 'classic' risks (sickness, invalidity, old age, industrial accidents, occupational diseases and unemployment) and in the rules on social assistance in so far as they are intended to supplement or *g* replace such schemes; in subsequent stages the principle was to be applied to the rules concerning survivors' benefits or family benefits and occupational schemes.

The member states may however exclude a number of benefits from the scope of the directive. Among these I would mention the advantages granted in respect of old-age pension schemes to persons who have brought up children, the granting of old-age or *h* invalidity benefit entitlement by virtue of the derived entitlements of a wife and the granting of increases of long-term invalidity, old-age, industrial accident and occupational disease benefits for a dependent spouse.

The effect of the principle of equal treatment is laid down in art 4. The principle means that there should be no discrimination whatsoever on ground of sex either directly or indirectly by reference in particular to marital or family status with regard to the *j* scope of the schemes and the conditions of access thereto; the obligation to contribute and the calculation of contributions, the calculation of benefits including increases due in respect of a spouse and for dependants and the conditions governing the duration and retention of entitlement to benefits.

4. As I have already stated, the first question referred to the court seeks to determine whether a benefit such as the invalid care allowance paid in Great Britain constitutes part

of a statutory scheme providing protection against invalidity to which art 3(1)(a) of
a   Directive 79/7 applies. The Chief Adjudication Officer argues that the answer should be
in the negative, while the Commission of the European Communities and of course Mrs
Drake argue in favour of an affirmative reply.

In support of his contention the adjudication officer raises arguments based on the
wording and on the intent of the relevant provisions. The first of these may easily be
summarised. Under art 3(1)(a), says the adjudication officer, the directive applies to
b   'statutory schemes which provide protection against . . . [the risk of] invalidity . . .'. The
protection must be understood as being provided in respect of the risk *itself*, not risks to
third parties. That may be inferred from the provision defining the persons to whom the
directive applies; under art 2 the directive applies to workers whose activity is interrupted
by illness, accident or involuntary unemployment and to retired or invalided workers.
That is to say it envisages only persons *directly* affected by illness, accident or
c   unemployment and excludes from the scope of the directive benefits to which other
persons are entitled.

It is clear from art 2 and from the preamble that the benefits with which the directive
is concerned are all work related. Since it is intended for persons who do not work and
thus do not form part of the working population the benefit in question does not fall
within that class. Nor can it be said, adds the adjudication officer, that it supplements or
d   takes the place of an invalidity pension. Its sole object is to provide a benefit for persons
who look after severely disabled persons.

Finally, in regard to the intent of the directive, the adjudication officer argues that, far
from being a comprehensive code for the implementation of equal treatment in matters
of social security, the directive constitutes only a first step towards placing men and
women on an equal footing; that is why benefits such as that at issue in the main
e   proceedings do not come within its ambit.

5. That submission cannot be upheld. There are more persuasive arguments, I think,
for the view that the benefit in question lies within the scope of the social security
schemes which under the directive are to be immediately subject to the principle of
equal treatment, in particular the scheme regarding invalidity.

As is well known, invalidity is the physical and economic condition of the person
f   concerned resulting from a reduction in his working capacity which has repercussions
on his earning capacity. Sometimes it is so serious that the invalid needs assistance from
other people in his daily life. In such cases the social security schemes of the member
states generally grant the invalid a special benefit or increase the principal benefit so as to
make up all or part of the cost to him of such assistance. The British scheme is different.
The two benefits which it provides are paid to two separate persons: on the one hand, the
g   invalid, on the other, the person who furnishes him with care and assistance.

Having said that, let me return to art 3(1). According to that article Directive 79/7
applies to 'statutory schemes which provide protection against . . . [the risk of] invalidity
. . .' (sub-para (a)) and to 'social assistance, in so far as it is intended to supplement or
replace' the invalidity scheme (sub-para (b)). There can be no doubt that in that provision
the accent is placed on two points: the Community legislature's use of the word 'schemes'
h   (whereas, when it desires to exclude a measure, it has recourse to the much narrower
terms 'benefits', 'advantages' or 'entitlements') and the fact that it expressly mentions
social assistance provisions. It follows, in my view, that the directive applies to a coherent
and comprehensive system of protection against invalidity; it must therefore include *all*
the benefits, however defined and organised in the national legal systems, which make
up the relevant scheme.

j   All the benefits: that is to say even those which, like the benefit at issue here, are paid
to a person other than the invalid. There are at least two reasons for which that method
of payment should not have the effect of excluding this benefit from the invalidity
scheme. The first is that its payment logically depends on a situation of invalidity in the
sense that the existence of a person covered by the scheme is a condition sine qua non for
its payment, as counsel for the adjudication officer admitted at the hearing. The second
is the clear economic link between this benefit and the benefit paid to the invalid; that is

to say the invalid derives an advantage from the fact that a subsidy is paid to the person
who provides assistance. The essential point is that the mechanisms used in the United
Kingdom (allowance paid to the person who provides assistance) and in the other member
states (increase in the benefit paid to the invalid) may be different, but their objective is
in substance identical (cf Interim Report of the Commission of the European Communities
on the implementation of Directive 79/7, COM (83) 793 final, 6 January 1984).

It may also be remarked that the effectiveness of the directive would be seriously
compromised if the limits of its application were defined by the way in which a benefit
was paid. It is clear that if that were the case a member state would need only to make a
few slight amendments to its legislation in order to exclude numerous sectors of its social
security system from the application of the principle of equal treatment.

That solution is not affected by the adjudication officer's argument based on the fact
that the principle of equal treatment was to be implemented gradually; as I have pointed
out in section 3 of this opinion, the benefit in question is not one of those (occupational
schemes etc) which were to be brought into conformity with the principle in a second
stage. Nor is there any more merit in the argument that the directive applies only to
members of the working population, so that a benefit paid to a person who is not a
worker must be considered to be excluded. It seems obvious to me that in a case such as
this the persons in favour of whom it is intended that the principle of equal treatment
should apply are disabled workers. It is on the basis of the connection between the main
benefit paid to invalids and the benefit paid to persons caring for them (but intended to
assist them indirectly) that the conditions governing the payment of the second benefit
must also be the same for men and for women.

6. In the second question the Chief Social Security Commissioner asks whether the
fact that a benefit such as that at issue in this case is not paid to a married woman who
lives with her husband constitutes discrimination on grounds of sex contrary to Directive
79/7.

The answer to that question can only be in the affirmative. As counsel for the
adjudication officer acknowledged himself, the provisions governing that benefit place
certain categories of women (married women who live with their husbands, women
who live with a man as husband and wife) at a disadvantage and deprive them of
entitlement to the benefit. Furthermore, there are no reasons, nor was it argued that
there were any, justifying the resulting discrimination.

7. For all the foregoing considerations I propose that the court give the following
replies to the questions formulated by the Chief Social Security Commissioner in his
order of 15 May 1985 in the appeal proceedings between the Chief Adjudication Officer
and Mrs Drake: (1) the benefit paid to a person who is not gainfully employed and is
regularly and substantially engaged in caring for a person entitled to a social security
benefit as a severely disabled person because his disability requires continued supervision
constitutes part of a statutory scheme which provides protection against invalidity as
referred to in art 3(1)(a) of Directive 79/7 or qualifies for inclusion among the provisions
of social assistance intended to supplement that scheme; (2) the fact that certain categories
of women (married women who live with their husbands, married women whose
husbands contribute a specific amount for their maintenance and women who live with
a man as husband and wife) are excluded from that benefit constitutes discrimination on
grounds of sex contrary to art 4(1) of that directive, in so far as married men and men
who live with a woman as husband and wife are not excluded from the benefit in the
same manner.

24 June. **THE COURT OF JUSTICE** delivered its judgment which, having
summarised the facts, procedure and submissions of the parties, dealt with the law as
follows.

1. By an order of 15 May 1985, which was received at the court on 20 May 1985, the
Chief Social Security Commissioner referred to the court for a preliminary ruling under
art 177 of the EEC Treaty two questions regarding the interpretation of EC Council
Directive 79/7 of 19 December 1978 on the progressive implementation of the principle

of equal treatment for men and women in matters of social security, with a view of
a determining the compatibility with that directive of a provision of national law laying
down conditions for the granting of an invalid care allowance.

2. Those questions were raised in the course of proceedings before the commissioner
between Mrs Drake and the adjudication officer concerning the latter's refusal to grant
Mrs Drake the said invalid care allowance.

3. Mrs Drake is married and lives with her husband. Over a number of years, until
b the middle of 1984, she held a variety of full-time and part-time jobs. In June 1984 her
mother, a severely disabled person who receives an attendance allowance under s 35(1) of
the Social Security Act 1975, came to live with her. Mrs Drake thereupon gave up her
work in order to look after her mother.

4. The British legislation on invalidity benefits is laid down in the 1975 Act. Section
37(1) of that Act provides for the payment of an invalid care allowance where (a) the
c applicant is regularly and substantially engaged in caring for a severely disabled person,
(b) the applicant is not gainfully employed, (c) the severely disabled person is such relative
of his or such other person as may be prescribed by the law. For the purposes of the
application of that provision, s 37(2) defines 'severely disabled person' as a person entitled
to an attendance allowance under s 35 of that Act or to any other benefit of the same
nature. Under s 37(3) the invalid care allowance is not paid to any person who is under
d the age of 16 or is engaged in full-time education, to a married woman who lives with
her husband or to whose maintenance her husband contributes a weekly sum not less
than the weekly rate of the allowance, to a woman where she and a man to whom she is
not married are living together as husband and wife.

5. On 5 February 1985 Mrs Drake applied for the allowance in respect of the care
provided by her to her mother. The adjudication officer responsible for the award of the
e benefit stated that under s 37(3)(a)(i) the benefit was not payable to a married woman
residing with her husband. In order to accelerate the proceedings, however, he referred
the claim to the Social Security Appeal Tribunal.

6. By a decision of 1 March 1985 the tribunal held that that rule constituted
discrimination on grounds of sex contrary to Directive 79/7. The adjudication officer
appealed against that decision to the Chief Social Security Commissioner. In his order
f referring the matter to the Court of Justice, the Chief Social Security Commissioner states
that the sole point at issue between the parties concerns s 37(3)(a)(i) of the 1975 Act and
that the other conditions laid down in that Act for the grant of the invalid care allowance
are fulfilled.

7. The Chief Social Security Commissioner also states in his order that s 37(3) of the
Act has not been repealed or amended since the entry into force of Directive 79/7, the
g relevant provisions of which are set out below.

8. Article 1 states that the purpose of the directive is—

'progressive implementation, in the field of social security and other elements of
social protection provided for in Article 3, of the principle of equal treatment for
men and women in matters of social security, hereinafter referred to as the "principle
of equal treatment".'

h

According to art 2, the directive applies to:

'. . . the working population—including self-employed persons, workers and self-
employed persons whose activity is interrupted by illness, accident or involuntary
unemployment and persons seeking employment—and to retired or invalided
workers and self-employed persons.'

j

Under art 3(1), the directive applies to:

'(a) statutory schemes which provide protection against the following risks: —
sickness, —invalidity, —old age, —accidents at work and occupational diseases, —
unemployment; (b) social assistance, in so far as it is intended to supplement or
replace the schemes referred to in (a).'

Article 4(1) provides:

> 'The principle of equal treatment means that there shall be no discrimination *a*
> whatsoever on ground of sex either directly, or indirectly by reference in particular
> to marital or family status, in particular as concerns: —the scope of the schemes and
> the conditions of access thereto, —the obligation to contribute and the calculation
> of contributions, —the calculation of benefits including increases due in respect of
> a spouse and for dependants and the conditions governing the duration and retention
> of entitlement to benefits.' *b*

9.   The Chief Social Security Commissioner considered that a decision on the
interpretation of the directive was necessary for his decision in the case; he therefore
stayed the proceedings and referred the following questions to the court for a preliminary
ruling:

> '1. If a Member State provides a benefit payable (provided certain residence and *c*
> other conditions are met) to a person who is not gainfully employed and is regularly
> and substantially engaged in caring for a person in respect of whom a benefit is
> payable as a severely disabled person by reason of that person requiring attention or
> supervision as prescribed (and provided that that person meets certain residence and
> other conditions), does the benefit payable to the first-mentioned person constitute
> the whole or part of a statutory scheme which provides protection against invalidity *d*
> to which Article 3(1)(a) of Directive 79/7/EEC applies?
> 2. If the answer to the first question is yes, does a condition that a married woman
> is not entitled to that benefit if she is residing with her husband or he is contributing
> to her maintenance above a certain level constitute discrimination contrary to
> Article 4(1) of that Directive in circumstances where married men do not have to
> meet a corresponding condition?' *e*

10.   Observations were submitted by Mrs Drake, the adjudication officer and the
Commission.

Question 1   *f*
11.   By his first question the Chief Social Security Commissioner seeks to know
whether the right to the payment of a benefit to a person who cares for a disabled person
constitutes part of a statutory scheme providing protection against the risk of invalidity
to which Directive 79/7 applies under art 3(1)(a) of that directive.

12.   Mrs Drake and the Commission consider that the answer to question 1 should be
in the affirmative.   *g*
13.   Mrs Drake submits in the first place that the expression 'working population'
used in art 2 of the directive must be interpreted as including individuals who have
worked, who wish to return to work, who are of working age, but who are temporarily
unable to work because of some particular risk covered by the social security system,
which is precisely her situation. She considers that she is therefore a person to whom the
directive applies.   *h*
14.   Secondly, Mrs Drake argues that art 3(1)(a) of the directive must be interpreted
as applying to any benefit which forms part of a national statutory scheme providing
protection against the risks referred to in that provision. She argues that in the United
Kingdom the statutory scheme of protection against the risk of invalidity is provided by
two benefits: the attendance allowance payable to the disabled person and the invalid
care allowance payable to the person who cares for him. It would thus be impossible to *j*
describe the relevant statutory scheme without describing both benefits.
15.   The Commission argues first of all that a person belongs to the working
population for the purposes of art 2 of the directive if he is in fact working, is unemployed
and seeking work, is a former or retired worker, or is prevented from working by reason
of illness or invalidity, whether his own or that of a person for whom he is caring. The
Commission considers that Mrs Drake gave up work by reason of invalidity, albeit that

of her mother, and that she should therefore be regarded as a member of the working

a population for the purposes of the directive.

16.   The Commission argues that the fact that the benefit in question is paid to a third party and not directly to the disabled person does not put it outside the scope of the risk of invalidity, the scheme for which is covered by the directive. It points out that the effectiveness of the directive might be seriously compromised if it were to be held that the way in which the benefit is paid could determine whether or not the benefit was

b covered by the directive.

17.   The adjudication officer, on the other hand, considers that the invalid care allowance cannot in itself be regarded as providing protection against the risk of invalidity within the meaning of art 3(1)(a) of Directive 79/7. In his view, that provision is directed at schemes providing persons with protection against risks to them, not, as in the case of the invalid care allowance, against risks to third parties. He argues that art 2, which

c defines the persons to whom the directive applies, is concerned only with persons who are directly affected by one of those risks and thus excludes from the scope of the directive benefits made available to other persons.

18.   The Adjudication officer goes on to point out that it is clear from art 2 and from the preamble to the directive that the benefits to which the directive refers are all work-related. Since the allowance in question is intended for persons who do not work and

d therefore do not belong to the working population it cannot be regarded as one of those benefits.

19.   Finally, the adjudication officer states that far from being an all-embracing code for the implementation of the principle of equal treatment in matters of social security, Directive 79/7 is only a first step towards equal treatment for men and women in that area. He argues that the scope of the directive is restricted to the working population as

e defined in art 2. Allowances such as those at issue in the main proceedings therefore fall outside its scope.

20.   It must be pointed out first of all that, according to the first and second recitals in the preamble to Directive 79/7, the aim of that directive is the progressive implementation of the principle of equal treatment for men and women in matters of social security.

21.   According to art 3(1), Directive 79/7 applies to statutory schemes which provide

f protection against, inter alia, the risk of invalidity (sub-para (a)) and social assistance in so far as it is intended to supplement or replace the invalidity scheme (sub-para (b)). In order to fall within the scope of the directive, therefore, a benefit must constitute the whole or part of a statutory scheme providing protection against one of the specified risks or a form of social assistance having the same objective.

22.   Under art 2, the term 'working population', which determines the scope of the

g directive, is defined broadly to include 'self-employed persons, workers and self-employed persons whose activity is interrupted by illness, accident or involuntary employment and persons seeking employment . . . [and] retired or invalided workers and self-employed persons'. That provision is based on the idea that a person whose work has been interrupted by one of the risks referred to in art 3 belongs to the working population. That is the case of Mrs Drake, who has given up work solely because of one of the risks

h listed in art 3, namely the invalidity of her mother. She must therefore be regarded as a member of the working population for the purposes of the directive.

23.   Furthermore, it is possible for the member states to provide protection against the consequences of the risk of invalidity in various ways. For example, a member state may, as the United Kingdom has done, provide for two separate allowances, one payable to the disabled person himself and the other payable to a person who provides care, while

j another member state may arrive at the same result by paying an allowance to the disabled person at a rate equivalent to the sum of those two benefits. In order, therefore, to ensure that the progressive implementation of the principle of equal treatment referred to in art 1 of Directive 79/7 and defined in art 4 is carried out in a harmonious manner throughout the Community, art 3(1) must be interpreted as including any benefit which in a broad sense forms part of one of the statutory schemes referred to or a social assistance provision intended to supplement or replace such a scheme.

24.   Moreover, the payment of the benefit to a person who provides care still depends on the existence of a situation of invalidity inasmuch as such a situation is a condition sine qua non for its payment, as the adjudication officer admitted during the oral procedure. It must also be emphasised that there is a clear economic link between the benefit and the disabled person, since the disabled person derives an advantage from the fact that an allowance is paid to the person caring for him.

25.   It follows that the fact that a benefit which forms part of a statutory invalidity scheme is paid to a third party and not directly to the disabled person does not place it outside the scope of Directive 79/7. Otherwise, as the Commission emphasised in its observations, it would be possible, by making formal changes to existing benefits covered by the directive, to remove them from its scope.

26.   The answer to the first question referred by the Chief Social Security Commissioner must therefore be that a benefit provided by a member state and paid to a person caring for a disabled person forms part of a statutory scheme providing protection against invalidity which is covered by Directive 79/7 pursuant to art 3(1)(a) of that directive.

Question 2

27.   Since Question 1 has been answered in the affirmative, it is necessary to examine Question 2, which concerns the issue whether discrimination on grounds of sex contrary to art 4(1) of Directive 79/7 arises where legislation provides that a benefit which forms part of one of the statutory schemes referred to in art 3(1) of the directive is not payable to a married woman who lives with or is maintained by her husband, although it is paid in corresponding circumstances to a married man.

28.   Mrs Drake, the Commission and the adjudication officer all suggest that that question should be answered in the affirmative.

29.   Mrs Drake and the Commission argue that the exclusion of married women from such a benefit, where married men residing with their wives are not excluded, constitutes a clear example of direct discrimination on grounds of sex.

30.   The adjudication officer himself has recognised that the provision governing the benefit in question places certain categories of women (married women living with their husbands and women who live with a man as husband and wife) at a disadvantage by precluding them from obtaining that benefit.

31.   It should be noted that art 4(1) of Directive 79/7 provides that the implementation of the principle of equal treatment, with regard in particular to the scope of schemes and the conditions of access to them, means that there should be no discrimination whatsoever on grounds of sex.

32.   That provision embodies the aim of the directive, set out in art 1, that is to say the implementation, in the field of social security and between men and women, of the principle of equal treatment, a principle which the court has frequently described as fundamental.

33.   It follows from the foregoing that a national provision such as that at issue before the Chief Social Security Commissioner is contrary to the aim, as stated above, of the directive, which under art 189 of the EEC Treaty is binding on the member states as to the result to be achieved.

34.   The answer to question 2 must therefore be that discrimination on grounds of sex contrary to art 4(1) of Directive 79/7 arises where legislation provides that a benefit which forms part of one of the statutory schemes referred to in art 3(1) of that directive is not payable to a married woman who lives with or is maintained by her husband, although it is paid in corresponding circumstances to a married man.

Costs

35.   The costs incurred by the Commission of the European Communities, which submitted observations to the court, are not recoverable. As these proceedings are, in so far as the parties to the main proceedings are concerned, in the nature of a step in the

a action before the Chief Social Security Commissioner, the decision as to costs is a matter for him.

On those grounds, the court (Fourth Chamber), in answer to the questions referred to it by the Chief Social Security Commissioner by an order of 15 May 1985, hereby rules: (1) a benefit provided by a member state and paid to a person caring for a disabled person forms part of a statutory scheme providing protection against invalidity which is covered
b by EC Council Directive 79/7 pursuant to art 3(1)(a) of the directive; (2) discrimination on grounds of sex contrary to art 4(1) of Directive 79/7 arises where legislation provides that a benefit which forms part of one of the statutory schemes referred to in art 3(1) of that directive is not payable to a married woman who lives with or is maintained by her husband, although it is paid in corresponding circumstances to a married man.

c Agents: *Roger Smith* (for Mrs Drake); *Ann V Windsor*, Senior Legal Assistant, Solicitor's Office, Department of Health and Social Security (for the adjudication officer); *J R Currall*, Legal Department of the EC Commission (for the Commission).

Mary Rose Plummer   Barrister.

d Space Investments Ltd v Canadian Imperial Bank of Commerce Trust Co (Bahamas) Ltd and others

PRIVY COUNCIL
e LORD KEITH OF KINKEL, LORD TEMPLEMAN, LORD OLIVER OF AYLMERTON, LORD GOFF OF CHIEVELEY AND SIR ROBIN COOKE
23 JUNE, 7 JULY 1986

Trust and trustee – Corporate trustee – Bank – Winding up of bank – Bank appointed trustee of trust funds – Funds deposited with bank as banker – Bank becoming insolvent and going into
f *liquidation – Whether beneficiaries under trust ranking in priority to or pari passu with unsecured creditors.*

Where a bank trustee is insolvent, trust money wrongfully treated as being on deposit with the bank must be repaid in full so far as possible out of the assets of the bank in priority to any payment of customers' deposits and other unsecured debts. However,
g where a bank trustee lawfully deposits trust money with itself as banker pursuant to express authority in that behalf conferred by the trust instrument the beneficiaries under the trust do not become entitled to any interest in the assets of the bank but merely to a sum equal to the amount standing to the credit of the trust deposit account; it follows therefore that, if the bank becomes insolvent and goes into liquidation, the beneficiaries are entitled to prove in the winding up of the bank only for the amount standing to the
h credit of the trust with the bank in the trust deposit account at the date of the liquidation, and accordingly are unsecured creditors whose claims rank pari passu with, and not in priority to, the claims of customers of the bank and other unsecured creditors (see p 76 g to j and p 77 j to p 78 d, post).

Notes
j For the effect of bankruptcy of a trustee, see 48 Halsbury's Laws (4th edn) para 621, and for cases on the subject, see 48 Digest (Reissue) 639–640, 5848–5849.

Case referred to in judgment
Re Hallett's Estate, Knatchbull v Hallett (1880) 13 Ch D 696, [1874–80] All ER Rep 793, CA.

Appeal

Space Investments Ltd, representing the unsecured creditors of Mercantile Bank and *a*
Trust Co Ltd (in liq) (MBT), appealed with special leave to appeal granted on 11 April
1984 against the order of the Court of Appeal of the Commonwealth of the Bahamas
(Luckhoo P, Smith and Zacca JJA) dated 24 June 1983 whereby it dismissed an appeal by
the appellants against the decision of the Supreme Court of the Commonwealth of the
Bahamas (da Costa CJ) given on 20 July 1981 whereby he held that money deposited by
MBT as trustees in favour of MBT as bankers was still impressed with a trust in favour of *b*
the trust creditors and that the remedy of tracing was available to the trust creditors, who
were entitled to take priority over ordinary creditors of MBT. The first respondent,
Canadian Imperial Bank of Commerce Trust Co (Bahamas) Ltd, represented the trust
creditors. The second respondent, Dennis Cross, and the third respondent, Patrick
Hamilton, were the joint liquidators of MBT. The facts are set out in the judgment of
the Board.   *c*

Nicholas Stewart for the appellants.
Alan Sebestyen and *Orville A Turnquest* (of the Bahamian Bar) for the first respondents.
Charles Purle and *Colin Callender* (of the Bahamian Bar) for the second and third
    respondents.
                                                                                                    d
7 July. The following judgment of the Board was delivered.

LORD TEMPLEMAN. The question is whether in the winding up of an insolvent
bank trustee the liquidator must pay the trust deposit accounts lawfully maintained by
the bank trustee in priority to payment of the customers' deposit accounts and the debts
owed by the trustee bank to other unsecured creditors.   *e*
    A customer who deposits money with a bank authorises the bank to use that money
for the benefit of the bank in any manner the bank pleases. The customer does not
acquire any interest in or charge over any asset of the bank or over all the assets of the
bank. The deposit account is an acknowledgment and record by the bank of the amount
from time to time deposited and withdrawn and of the interest earned. The customer
acquires a chose in action, namely the right on request to payment by the bank of the *f*
whole or any part of the aggregate amount of principal and interest which has been
credited or ought to be credited to the account. If the bank becomes insolvent the
customer can only prove in the liquidation of the bank as unsecured creditor for the
amount which was, or ought to have been, credited to the account at the date when the
bank went into liquidation.
    On the other hand a trustee has no power to use trust money for his own benefit unless *g*
the trust instrument expressly authorises him so to do. A bank trustee, like any other
trustee, may only apply trust money in the manner authorised by the trust instrument,
or by law, for the sole benefit of the beneficiaries and to the exclusion of any benefit to
the bank trustee unless the trust instrument otherwise provides. A bank trustee
misappropriating trust money for its own use and benefit without authority commits a
breach of trust and cannot justify that breach of trust by maintaining a trust deposit *h*
account which records the amount which the bank has misappropriated and credits
interest which the bank considers appropriate. The beneficiaries have a chose in action,
namely an action against the trustee bank for damages for breach of trust and in addition
they possess the equitable remedy of tracing the trust money to any property into which
it has been converted directly or indirectly.
    A bank in fact uses all deposit moneys for the general purposes of the bank. Whether *j*
a bank trustee lawfully receives deposits or wrongly treats trust money as on deposit
from trusts, all the moneys are in fact dealt with and expended by the bank for the
general purposes of the bank. In these circumstances it is impossible for the beneficiaries
interested in trust money misappropriated from their trust to trace their money to any
particular asset belonging to the trustee bank. But equity allows the beneficiaries, or a
new trustee appointed in place of an insolvent bank trustee to protect the interests of the
beneficiaries, to trace the trust money to all the assets of the bank and to recover the trust

money by the exercise of an equitable charge over all the assets of the bank. Where an
a insolvent bank goes into liquidation that equitable charge secures for the beneficiaries
and the trust priority over the claims of the customers in respect of their deposits and
over the claims of all other unsecured creditors. This priority is conferred because the
customers and other unsecured creditors voluntarily accept the risk that the trustee bank
might become insolvent and unable to discharge its obligations in full. On the other
hand, the settlor of the trust and the beneficiaries interested under the trust never accept
b any risks involved in the possible insolvency of the trustee bank. On the contrary, the
settlor could be certain that if the trusts were lawfully administered the trustee bank
could never make use of trust money for its own purposes and would always be obliged
to segregate trust money and trust property in the manner authorised by law and by the
trust instrument free from any risks involved in the possible insolvency of the trustee
bank. It is therefore equitable that where the trustee bank has unlawfully misappropriated
c trust money by treating the trust money as though it belonged to the bank beneficially,
merely acknowledging and recording the amount in a trust deposit account with the
bank, then the claims of the beneficiaries should be paid in full out of the assets of the
trustee bank in priority to the claims of the customers and other unsecured creditors of
the bank: '". . . if a man mixes trust funds with his own, the whole will be treated as the
trust property". . . that is, that the trust property comes first' (per Jessel MR in *Re Hallett's*
d *Estate, Knatchbull v Hallett* (1880) 13 Ch D 696 at 719, [1874–80] All ER Rep 793 at 802,
adopting and explaining earlier pronouncements to the same effect). Where a bank
trustee is insolvent, trust money wrongfully treated as being on deposit with the bank
must be repaid in full so far as may be out of the assets of the bank in priority to any
payment of customers' deposits and other unsecured debts.

Equity thus protects beneficiaries against breaches of trust. But equity does not protect
e beneficiaries against the consequences of the exercise in good faith of powers conferred
by the trust instrument.

Although as a general rule a trustee is not allowed to derive a benefit from trust
property, that general rule may be altered by the express terms of the trust instrument.
One illustration is an express provision in a settlement which permits a trustee to charge
and deduct from trust money remuneration for the services of the trustee. A settlement
f may also confer on a trustee power to make use of trust money in other ways. Certain of
the settlements of which Mercantile Bank and Trust Co Ltd (MBT) was appointed trustee
conferred power on MBT—

> 'To open and maintain one or more . . . savings accounts or current accounts . . .
> with any bank . . . even if . . . such bank shall be acting as trustee . . . to deposit to
> the credit of such account or accounts all or any part of the funds belong to the Trust
g > Fund whether or not such funds shall earn interest from time to time . . . [and] to
> withdraw a portion or all of the funds so deposited . . .'

The trial judge, da Costa CJ sitting in the Supreme Court of the Commonwealth of the
Bahamas, held, the Court of Appeal (Luckhoo P, Smith and Zacca JJA) agreed and it is
not disputed that—

h > 'The effect of that clause was clearly to empower MBT as trustee to deposit with
> MBT as banker moneys which they received in trust.'

The effect of the clause was also to empower MBT to treat trust money so notionally
deposited as if MBT were beneficially entitled to the trust money, just as MBT was
entitled to treat customers' money deposited with MBT as if MBT were beneficially
j entitled to that money. Trust money deposited with MBT as banker and customers'
money deposited by customers with MBT as banker were alike lawfully available to MBT
for payment of MBT's expenses, for making investments for the benefit of MBT and in
any other manner for the benefit of MBT as money belonging absolutely and beneficially
to MBT, to be disposed of without regard to the interests of beneficiaries or customers.

When a customer deposited money with MBT and the amount of the customer's
money was credited to a customer's deposit account, the customer did not become
entitled to any interest in any asset or in all the assets of MBT. The sole right of the

customer was to be paid at his request a sum equal to the amount standing to the credit of his deposit account. There was nothing to trace.

When MBT as trustee lawfully deposited trust moneys with MBT as banker pursuant to the authority in that behalf conferred by the settlement and the amount of the trust fund so deposited was credited to a trust deposit account, the beneficiaries interested under the trust did not become entitled to any interest in any asset or in all the assets of MBT. The sole right of the beneficiaries was for a sum equal to the amount standing to the credit of the trust deposit account, to be applied by MBT in any manner authorised or required by the settlement or by law as and when MBT decided to make such application in the proper exercise and discharge of its discretionary powers and duties in the due course of administration of the trust. If MBT ceased to be trustee and a new trustee were appointed, then it would be for the new trustee to decide whether to close the trust deposit account with MBT and to require MBT to pay to the new trustee the amount standing to the credit of the trust in the MBT trust deposit account. There would be nothing to trace.

When MBT became insolvent and went into liquidation the beneficiaries were entitled to obtain and have obtained the appointment of a new trustee in the place of MBT. The new trustee can only prove in the winding up of MBT for the amount standing to the credit of the trust with MBT in the trust deposit account at the date of liquidation. The claim of the new trustee will be as an unsecured creditor ranking pari passu with the claims of a customer proving for the amount standing to his credit with MBT in the customer's deposit account.

There is no justification for the intervention of equity. The settlor has allowed trust money to be treated as if it were customers' money. The settlor has allowed MBT to appropriate trust money and to treat the trust money as belonging absolutely and beneficially to MBT. By depositing money with MBT a customer accepted the risk of MBT's insolvency. By allowing MBT to treat trust money as a deposit with MBT the settlor accepted the risk of MBT's insolvency. In these circumstances it would be inequitable if the trust were in a better position than the customer.

da Costa CJ, supported by the Court of Appeal, held that when MBT transferred trust money 'into its banking business that money does not cease to be impressed with a trust'. But the trust money did cease to be impressed with the trust. The trust money became the property of MBT in law and in equity and MBT was entitled to use that money for the purposes of MBT in any manner that MBT pleased. The trust fund did not continue to be the money transferred into the banking business of MBT. The trust fund became the obligation of MBT to treat the trust deposit account with MBT as banker in the same manner as MBT would have dealt with a deposit account credited with trust money lawfully transferred and deposited by MBT as trustee with another independent bank as banker. On the insolvency of that independent bank the trustee MBT could only rank as unsecured creditor for the amount of the deposit account. Similarly, on the insolvency of MBT which lawfully appropriated trust money to itself and credited the amount of the moneys so appropriated to a trust deposit account, the new trustee of the trust can only rank as an unsecured creditor on behalf of the trust.

Their Lordships will humbly advise Her Majesty that the appeal should be allowed, that the orders made by the courts below, save for the orders relating to costs, should be discharged and that it should be declared that the trust creditors of MBT claiming in respect of trust money lawfully treated as on deposit with MBT rank pari passu with the unsecured creditors of MBT in the distribution of the assets of MBT in liquidation. The costs of all parties of the hearing before the Board should be paid by the liquidators as expenses of the winding up.

Appeal allowed.

Solicitors: *Philip Conway Thomas & Co* (for the appellants); *Simmons & Simmons* (for the first respondents); *Lovell White & King* (for the second and third respondents).

Mary Rose Plummer   Barrister.

a   # Ross v Lord Advocate and others
   # Trustee Savings Banks Central Board and
                 # others v Vincent and others

b   HOUSE OF LORDS
   LORD KEITH OF KINKEL, LORD ROSKILL, LORD TEMPLEMAN, LORD OLIVER OF AYLMERTON AND
   LORD GOFF OF CHIEVELEY
   25, 26, 30 JUNE, 1, 2, 3, 31 JULY 1986

   *Trustee Savings Bank – Closure – Assets – Transfer of bank to private ownership – Effect of
   transfer – Whether depositors having proprietory interest in assets over and above their
c   contractual rights to principal and interest – Trustee Savings Banks Act 1981, ss 1(3)(a)(4), 32
   – Trustee Savings Banks Act 1985.*

   Prior to 1985 the property, rights, liabilities and obligations of trustee savings banks were
   regulated by the Trustee Savings Banks Act 1981 and rules made thereunder. The
   Trustees Savings Banks Act 1985 made provision for the abolition of trustee savings
d   banks in their existing statutory form and their replacement by limited liability
   companies established for that purpose. The shares in the successor companies were to be
   held by a holding company which in turn was to be floated on the Stock Exchange as the
   means of transferring the banks to private ownership. The abolition was to take effect on
   a vesting day to be appointed under the 1985 Act when the property, rights, liabilities
   and obligations of each bank was to vest in its successor company. The appellant R, who
e   was a depositor with the Trustee Savings Bank Scotland, brought proceedings in the
   Court of Session before the vesting day claiming an interest in the surplus assets of the
   bank on closure. The Lord Ordinary granted declarators that the bank was an
   unincorporated association whose assets belonged to its depositors and that any order
   appointing a vesting day would divest the depositors of their property, rights and
   entitlement without compensation. The Inner House of the Court of Session reversed his
f   decision and dismissed R's claim. The R appealed to the House of Lords. In order to settle
   the question raised by the Scottish proceedings whether the depositors of the bank had
   any proprietory interest in the assets of the bank generally the Trustee Savings Banks
   Central Board and the custodian trustees for the Trustee Savings Bank England and Wales
   issued proceedings in England against V, a depositor with the bank, and the Treasury
   Solicitor. The judge granted declarations in those proceedings to the effect that (i) the
g   depositors of the bank were only entitled, in accordance with the terms applicable to
   their respective accounts with the bank, to repayment of the principal amounts credited
   to such accounts and interest where appropriate and were not entitled to any other
   amounts, and (ii) the assets of the bank were held, subject to the statutory provisions and
   the rules for the time being in force, on trust to provide for payment to the depositors of
   the sums due to them. V appealed direct to the House of Lords against the first declaration
h   and the board and the bank, supported by the Treasury, cross-appealed against the second
   declaration. R and V contended in the House of Lords that s 1(3)(a)[a] and (4)[b] of the 1981
   Act, which, inter alia, empowered a trustee savings bank to 'accumulate the produce of
   the deposits . . . at compound interest, and . . . to return the deposits and produce to the
   depositors', gave them an interest in the assets of the bank over and above their contractual
j   rights.

   Held – (1) On the true construction of s 1(3)(a) and (4) of the 1981 Act the trustee savings
   banks' duty to accumulate the 'produce' of deposits at compound interest and to return
   the deposits and 'produce' to the depositors was a duty to return only the amount of the
   deposits and interest contractually due under the contracts of deposit and did not require

   ---
   a   Section 1(3), so far as material, is set out at p 82 *d e*, post
   b   Section 1(4) is set out at p 82 *f*, post

the banks to pay over any increase in the assets of the banks attributable to the
employment of the deposits in their business. Moreover, it was clear from s 32^c of the   *a*
1981 Act that on the closure of a bank its depositors were entitled only to sums owed by
way of principal and interest in respect of deposits and they had no residual interest in
the surplus assets of the bank. It followed therefore that the depositors of the banks had
no proprietory rights against the banks or their assets apart from those rights arising
from and under their respective contracts of deposit. Accordingly, the appeals of R and
V would be dismissed (see p 82 *g* to p 83 *d j* to p 84 *f h j*, p 91 *c d* and p 93 *d* to *f*, post).   *b*

(2) The rights which the depositors in the English action had under the bank's rules
to appoint and remove trustees, to examine the accounts of the bank and to obtain the
appointment of a commissioner to examine the affairs of the bank were not sufficient to
convert the depositors into trust beneficiaries and therefore the second declaration
granted by the judge in that action, namely that the bank's assets were to be held on trust
to provide payment to the depositors of the sums due to them, would be discharged and   *c*
the cross-appeal of the board and trustees allowed (see p 84 *f* to *j* and p 92 *j* to p 93 *f*, post).

Per curiam. Statutory trustee savings banks and their assets belong to the state subject
to the contractual rights of depositors to the return of their deposits and interest and
subject to the powers and duties from time to time conferred and imposed by Parliament
on the National Debt Commissioners and the Central Board, both of which are
institutions of the state. The effect of the 1985 Act is to privatise the statutory trustee   *d*
savings banks and to present their surplus assets to the successor companies established
in accordance with that Act (see p 84 *g* to *j*, p 92 *d* to *f* and p 93 *d* to *f*, post).

Notes
For the constitution of trustee savings banks, see 3 Halsbury's Laws (4th edn) paras 17–
24.   *e*
    For the Trustee Savings Banks Act 1981, ss 1, 32, see 51 Halsbury's Statutes (3rd edn)
1483, 1502.

Cases referred to in opinions
Farrell v Alexander [1976] 2 All ER 721, [1977] AC 59, [1976] 3 WLR 145, HL.   *f*
Space Investments Ltd v Canadian Imperial Bank of Commerce Co (Bahamas) Ltd [1986] 3 All
    ER 75, [1986] 1 WLR 1072, PC.

Appeals and cross-appeal

Ross v Lord Advocate and others   *g*
James Matthew Ross appealed against an interlocutor of the First Division of the Court
of Session (the Lord President (Lord Emslie), Lord Grieve and Lord Kincraig) dated 12
March 1986 (a) allowing the reclaiming motion of the respondents, (1) the Lord Advocate
(Lord Cameron of Lochbroom QC) as acting in terms of the Crown Suits (Scotland) Act
1857 on behalf of the Commissioners of Her Majesty's Treasury, (2) the trustees of the
Trustee Savings Bank Scotland and (3) the Trustee Savings Bank Central Board, against an   *h*
interlocutor of the Lord Ordinary (Lord Davidson) dated 12 November 1985 by which
the appellant, a depositor of the bank, had been granted declarators that (i) the Trustee
Savings Bank Scotland was an unincorporated association, (ii) without prejudice to any
claim that might be established by the Trustee Savings Bank Central Board in terms of
s 32 of the Trustee Savings Banks Act 1981, the assets of the association were the property
of the depositors, (iii) unless a vesting day was appointed in terms of the Trustee Savings   *j*
Banks Act 1985 the depositors would remain beneficially entitled to and owners of the
assets of the Trustee Savings Bank Scotland and (iv) any order made under the Trustee
Savings Banks Act 1985 by the Commissioners of Her Majesty's Treasury appointing a

---

c Section 32 is set out at p 83 *j*, post

vesting day in terms of s 1(1)(d) of that Act would, if made, divest the depositors of their
a property, rights and entitlement without compensation, (b) recalling the Lord Ordinary's
interlocutor and (c) dismissing the appellant's petition seeking certain declarators in
respect of the rights of the depositors in the bank. The facts are set out in the opinion of
Lord Templeman.

Trustee Savings Banks Central Board and others v Vincent and others
b By an originating summons dated 18 December 1985 the Trustee Savings Banks Central
Board and the custodian trustees for the Trustee Savings Bank England and Wales sought
as against the Rev John Vincent, a depositor of the bank, and Her Majesty's Treasury (i) a
declaration that the depositors of the bank were entitled to repayment of the principal
amounts credited to their accounts with the bank and to the periodic payment of interest
thereon applicable thereto, but had no present or future, actual or contingent right, title
c or interest to or in the assets of the bank and (ii) an order that the Rev Vincent be
appointed to represent all other depositors of the bank. On 28 April 1986 Scott J granted
declarations (i) that the depositors of the Trustee Savings Bank England and Wales were
entitled in accordance with the terms applicable to their respective accounts with the
bank to repayment of the principal amounts credited to such accounts and in the case of
interest bearing accounts to the periodic payment of interest thereon at the rates from
d time to time applicable thereto but to no other amount and (ii) that the assets of the bank
were held subject to the statutory provisions and the rules for the time being in force on
trust to provide for payment to depositors of the sums due to them respectively in
accordance with the foregoing declaration and ordered that the Rev John Vincent be
appointed to represent all other depositors of the bank. On 6 June 1986 the Appeal
Committee of the House of Lords granted the Rev Vincent leave to appeal direct to the
e House of Lords pursuant to s 13 of the Administration of Justice Act 1969 against the
first declaration and the respondents, the Trustee Savings Banks Central Board and
custodian trustees for the Trustee Savings Bank England and Wales, were granted leave
to cross-appeal against the second declaration. The cross-appeal was supported by Her
Majesty's Treasury. The facts are set out in the opinion of Lord Templeman.

f *W D Prosser QC* (Dean of Faculty) and *W S Gale* (of the Scottish Bar) for Mr Ross.
John Hicks QC, Anthony C Taussig and *David Sears* for the Rev Vincent.
The Lord Advocate (Rt Hon Lord Cameron of Lochbroom QC), Alan C M Johnston QC (of the
   Scottish Bar) with him, in his own behalf.
John Murray QC and *Donald J D Macfadyen QC* (both of the Scottish Bar) for the Trustees
   Savings Bank Central Board and the trustees of the Trustee Savings Bank Scotland.
g *Andrew Morritt QC* and *Christopher Symons* for the Trustee Savings Bank Central Board
   and the custodian trustees for the Trustee Savings Bank England and Wales.
Timothy Lloyd QC for Her Majesty's Treasury.

At the conclusion of the arguments their Lordships dismissed the appeals and allowed
the cross-appeal stating that they would give their reasons for judgment later.
h
31 July. The following opinions were delivered.

LORD KEITH OF KINKEL. My Lords, the fundamental questions at issue in these
appeals is whether the depositors in a trustee savings bank have any interest in the assets
of the bank other than the right to receive back their deposits together with the interest
j thereon contractually agreed, if any.
   Trustee savings banks are at present regulated by the Trustee Savings Banks Act 1981
and by their rules certified by the registrar in pursuance of s 2 of that Act. By virtue of
s 6(1) these rules are binding on the trustees and officers of the bank and on the depositors.
The depositors can have no other rights than such as are conferred on them by the Act
and the rules and such as they may have acquired by contract with the bank. As regards

the latter, there is nowhere to be found any indication of a contract extending further than the normal banker/customer relationship. In particular there is no trace of the type *a* of contract which mutually binds the members of a voluntary association.

To ascertain the nature and extent of the rights falling into the former category it is necessary to construe the relevant provisions of the Act and the rules. In my opinion, no assistance towards elucidation of the question at issue is to be gained from looking back at the long series of repealed Trustee Savings Banks Acts from 1817 onwards. We are concerned with the present state of affairs, not with any which may have existed in the *b* past and been of interest to former generations of depositors. While some present-day depositors may have first become so under legislation later repealed, they are now bound by the legislation and rules currently in force. I have been unable to find in any relevant provision of the 1981 Act (the latest in a series of consolidating enactments) such an ambiguity or obscurity as to require or warrant for its resolution resort to legislative antecedents. I refer to *Farrell v Alexander* [1976] 2 All ER 721, [1977] AC 59.   *c*

The provision of the 1981 Act on which the appellants principally relied as giving depositors an interest in the assets of the bank over and above their contractual rights is s 1(3), which is in these terms:

> 'In this section and sections 2 and 3—(*a*) "savings bank" means a society formed in the United Kingdom, the Isle of Man or any of the Channel Islands for the purpose of establishing and maintaining an institution in the nature of a bank—(i) *d* to accept deposits of money for the benefit of the persons making the deposits and deposits of money by a trustee, and (ii) to accumulate the produce of the deposits (so far as not withdrawn) at compound interest, and (iii) to return the deposits and produce to the depositors after deducting any necessary expenses of management but without deriving any benefit, from the deposits or produce . . .'

e

This provision is reproduced in r 3 of the rules of both the Scottish and the English bank.

It was argued for the appellants that the 'produce' in sub-paras (ii) and (iii) meant more than merely the interest on the deposit and embraced any increase or appreciation in the total assets of the bank which was attributable to employment of the deposit in its business. The argument sought reinforcement from s 1(4), which provides:

> 'Subsection (3)(*a*)(iii) shall not be construed as requiring the return to a depositor *f* of the produce of any deposit standing to the credit of an account in his name on which no interest is paid.'

This subsection, so it was contended, drew a clear distinction between 'produce' and 'interest', so as to indicate the intention that the former word should have a wider meaning than the latter.   *g*

The construction contended for presents serious difficulties. Sub-paragraph (ii) of s 1(3)(*a*) refers to accumulating the produce of the deposits at compound interest. The parenthetical words '(so far as not withdrawn)' must, I think, qualify 'produce' and not 'deposits'. If deposits are withdrawn they can no longer have produce, whereas if the produce is withdrawn the deposits will continue to earn further produce. The depositor might ordinarily be entitled only to simple interest, but this provision says that if and in *h* so far as the produce is not withdrawn it is to be accumulated at compound interest. What is withdrawn can only be interest, and likewise what is accumulated at compound interest can only be interest. There could not possibly be any question of accumulating at compound interest any increment in the assets of the bank which might come about through capital appreciation of investments in which it chose to invest its funds. Then sub-para (iii) refers to returning deposits and produce to depositors after deducting *j* expenses. Such return might, no doubt, take place when the bank closed, but it could also, and more regularly, take place when depositors chose to withdraw their deposits. It is inconceivable that in the latter event any depositor could demand to receive more than the amount of his deposit with interest, compounded so far as appropriate. He could not expect to receive some share, which it would be impossible to quantify in relation to the

amount of his deposit, in any appreciation in the value of the assets of the bank which
a might have taken place during the currency of his deposit. Trustee savings banks have
power, under s 18 of the 1981 Act, to carry on the ordinary business of banking, a power
first conferred on them by the Trustee Savings Banks Act 1976. They also have power to
borrow money under s 19 of the 1981 Act. These powers are apt to enable the banks to
earn revenue profits, and no doubt they do. To regard these profits as attributable in
ascertainable shares to individual deposits is plainly out of the question. The appellants
b disclaim any suggestion that the depositors might be entitled, on withdrawal of their
deposits while the bank is a going concern, to receive any share of the capital or revenue
profits of the bank earned during the currency of particular deposits. But they maintain
that such a right would arise on closure of the bank, and that the distribution would be
an equal one. The distribution of surplus assets on closure is dealt with by s 32 of the
1981 Act, which I shall consider later. But the notion of equal distribution is inconsistent
c with a depositor being entitled to the produce, whatever that may mean, of his own
deposit. On closure of a bank, it would be completely impossible to attribute any
particular proportion of surplus assets to current depositors on the one hand, and on the
other hand to past employment in the bank's business of deposits since withdrawn and
of money borrowed from other sources. These considerations lead invariably to the
irresistable conclusion that 'produce' in s 1(3)(*a*) and (4) of the 1981 Act can only mean
d interest.

Then s 20(1) of the 1981 Act provides:

e 'It shall be the duty of each trustee savings bank to secure that at any time—(*a*)
such proportion of the aggregate of the sums owed by it to its depositors as the
Treasury may from time to time determine is matched by assets of the trustee
savings bank of one or more of the classes referred to in Part I of Schedule 4; and (*b*)
the residue of that aggregate is matched by assets of the trustee savings bank of one
or more of the classes referred to in Part II of that Schedule.'

And s 21(1) provides;

f 'It is declared that a trustee savings bank has power, subject to the relevant
requirements, namely—(*a*) section 20, (*b*) any direction under section 7(3)(*d*) with
respect to the manner in which trustee savings banks are to invest their funds, and
(*c*) the rules of the bank, to invest its funds in assets of any description whatever
(including loans, whether temporary or otherwise and whether secured or
unsecured).'

These provisions contemplate that the aggregate of the sums owed by the bank to its
g depositors shall be ascertainable at any particular time, and also that the bank may have
assets of a value in excess of that aggregate amount. 'The sums owed by it to its depositors'
can only mean sums owed to them in respect of the amount of their deposits and interest
thereon to the extent contractually due. It cannot include anything over and above these
amounts in respect of a residual interest of the depositors in the assets of the bank,
otherwise there would be no surplus capable of investment under s 21(1). These
h provisions thus constitute further indications against the view that depositors have any
such residual interest.

Section 31 of the 1981 Act lays down the procedure for closing a trustee savings bank.
Section 32 provides:

j 'When a trustee savings bank is finally closed, the trustees shall pay over to the
Central Board any surplus moneys remaining in the hands of the trustees, after
providing for the sums due to depositors and for any expenses auhorised by the
bank's rules; and the Central Board may distribute the moneys among such other
trustee savings banks as the Board think fit.'

This provision, with the omission of the second sentence, is reproduced in r 16(4) of the
rules of the Scottish bank and r 17(4) of those of the English bank. It is, in my opinion,

completely destructive of the argument that the depositors have a residual interest in the
surplus assets of the bank. 'The sums due to depositors' must have the same meaning as
'sums owed by it to its depositors' in s 20, that is to say sums owed by way of principal
and interest in respect of deposits. If depositors were entitled to share in surplus assets
over and above such sums, there would be no surplus to be paid over to the Central
Board. It was sought to be maintained that the enactment was designed to sweep up
anything as regards which the legal entitlement could not be ascertained, such as deposits
the owners of which could not be traced or which were in accounts opened in false
names. Such deposits, however, would properly fall within those for which the trustees
are required to make provision. Counsel for the appellants drew attention to the
circumstance that s 32 made no provision for what the Central Board was to do with
surplus assets paid over to it on the closure of the last trustee savings bank, and suggested
that in such an event the depositors in that last bank to be closed would be entitled to
have the surplus assets distributed among them by the Central Board. If that result had
been contemplated by Parliament, one would have expected it to have been expressly
provided for. The likelihood is that Parliament did not make provision for any ultimate
destination of the surplus assets of the last bank to close because it did not consider that
such an event was in the realm of reasonable possibility. If the event did come about it
would be necessary for Parliament to legislate for the winding up of the Central Board,
which is nowhere provided for in the statute, and the legislation would require to contain
provision for the disposal of its assets in such manner as Parliament thought fit. The fact
remains that on closure of the last bank it would cease to have any right of property in its
surplus assets, and no legal basis would exist for any claim by its depositors against the
Central Board.

My Lords, in my opinion, the necessary conclusion is that the depositors in a trustee
savings bank have no proprietary rights against the bank or its assets, their only rights
being those arising from and under their respective contracts of deposit. It follows that
the petitioner in the Scottish proceedings is not entitled to the declarators which he seeks,
in so far as they are directed to establishing entitlement to proprietory rights, and that
the petition was rightly dismissed by the First Division. It also follows that in the English
proceedings the respondents are entitled to a declaration establishing that the appellant
has no other rights as against the bank than those arising from his contract of deposit.
For these reasons I would dismiss the appeals in both proceedings.

As regards the cross-appeal in the English proceedings, I have had the opportunity of
reading in draft the speech prepared by my noble and learned friend Lord Templeman.
I agree with him that, for the reasons he gives, Scott J fell into error in pronouncing the
second of the declarations contained in his order dated 28 April 1986, and that the cross-
appeal should be allowed to the effect of altering the order so as to omit that declaration
and modify the first declaration by adding to it the words 'but have no present or future,
actual or contingent right title or interest to or in the assets of the bank'.

I am also in complete agreement with my noble and learned friend Lord Templeman
in his analysis of the trustee savings banks legislation preceding the 1981 Act, and his
conclusion that the depositors in such a bank have historically never had any proprietory
interests in its surplus assets.

LORD ROSKILL. My Lords, I have had the advantage of reading in draft the speech
delivered by my noble and learned friend Lord Keith and the speech to be delivered by
my noble and learned friend Lord Templeman. I agree with both speeches and for the
reasons given by my noble and learned friends I would dismiss the appeal in the Scottish
case and I would allow the cross-appeal in the English case to the extent proposed by my
noble and learned friends.

LORD TEMPLEMAN. My Lords, the appellants claim that a depositor in a statutory
trustee savings bank has an interest in the surplus assets of the bank. The respondents
contend that a depositor is only entitled to repayment of his deposit together with any
interest payable in accordance with the terms of the deposit.

a   A clearing bank provides banking facilities for customers. A savings bank provides facilities for savings. As a general rule, money deposited in a bank is repayable on demand or on notice with or without interest in accordance with the bank's published terms. A depositor in a bank acquires no interest in the assets of the bank. The money deposited becomes the money of the bank. The depositor has no claim to or liability for any gains or losses which the bank may enjoy or suffer by investment or by any other application of the money received on deposit. The depositor requires and expects safety

b   for his principal, liquidity to enable him to obtain instant repayment and regularity in the amount and crediting of interest.

In the case of an unincorporated association which carries on a banking business it is possible, although unlikely, for its rules to provide that every depositor, on making a deposit and so long as he is a depositor, shall become and be a member of the association with rights expressed in the rules of the association and entitled together with the

c   agreement of all or a specified majority of members of the association to dissolve, wind up and share in the surplus assets of the association. The question is whether in the case of a statutory trustee savings bank a depositor was at any time accorded the rights of a member and, if so, whether those rights have survived the limitations imposed on statutory savings banks by Parliament.

In the first quarter of the nineteenth century the business of a bank, like any other

d   business, could be carried on by a sole proprietor, by a number of persons forming a partnership, by an unincorporated association or by a proprietor incorporated by charter or by special Act of Parliament. The enactment of a public Act of Parliament enabling the incorporation of a company with limited liability lay in the future. By the Act 57 Geo 3 c 130 (savings banks (1817)), Parliament sought to encourage unincorporated associations formed to establish savings banks for small savers. The benefits of the Act

e   were offered to savings banks which filed their rules with justices of the peace and complied with the conditions imposed by the Act. The main advantage offered by the Act to a statutory savings bank was the power granted to the bank to lend money to the National Debt Commissioners repayable on demand at a rate of interest fixed by the Act. Parliament provided for statutory savings banks, and thus for their depositors, safety, liquidity and regularity. Repayment of money lent to the commissioners by the banks

f   was certain, and available at any time and the fixed rate of interest payable by the commissioners enabled the banks to determine the rate of interest which could be provided for depositors after making provision for the costs incurred by the banks in collecting, lending and repaying deposits and in the expenses of administration. But Parliament was not prepared to make public money available to a savings bank if the proprietors were in a position to make personal profit out of the business of the savings

g   bank.

Section 1 of the 1817 Act provided:

h   '. . . if any Number of Persons who have formed or shall form any Society in any Part of *England*, for the Purpose of establishing and maintaining any Institution in the Nature of a Bank, to receive Deposits of Money for the Benefit of the Persons depositing the same, and to accumulate the Produce of so much thereof as shall not be required by the Depositors, their Executors or Administrators, to be paid in the Nature of Compound Interest, and to return the whole or any Part of such Deposit and the Produce thereof to the Depositors, their Executors or Administrators, deducting only out of such Produce so much as shall be required to be so retained for the Purpose of paying and discharging the Necessary expences attending the

j   Management of such Institution, according to such Rules . . . as shall have been or shall be established for that Purpose, but deriving no Benefit whatsoever from any such Deposit or the Produce thereof, shall be desirous of having the Benefit of the Provisions of this Act, such Persons shall cause the Rules . . . established or to be established for the Management of such Institution to be entered, deposited and filed in manner hereinafter directed, and thereupon shall be deemed to be entitled to and shall have the Benefit of the Provisions contained in this Act.'

The appellants contend that depositors entitled under the Act to 'produce' were thereby entitled to share in any assets of a statutory savings bank not required to pay all the deposits, interest and expenses. But produce not required to be repaid was directed to be accumulated at compound interest and no depositor closing his account with the bank would be in a position to claim, identify or quantify any 'produce' other than the accumulated interest to which he was entitled pursuant to the contractual terms of his deposit. The appellants seek to meet this difficulty by claiming that the Act conferred on those depositors fortunate enough to be depositors at the date when the bank ceased business a share by way of 'produce' in the assets of the bank not required to discharge all its obligations at that date. But Parliament was not concerned in 1817 with the fate of any statutory savings bank which ceased business and s 1 of the 1817 Act does not disclose any intention to deal with surplus assets not required to repay depositors their capital and interest. The appellants then seek to say that the effect of the Act was to make every depositor a member of the unincorporated association which constituted the savings bank and that by the common law of England every member of an unincorporated institution at the date of its dissolution is entitled to share in surplus assets. But there is nothing in the 1817 Act which confers on any depositor the rights of a member. Persons in control of the bank were deprived by Parliament of any benefit from the statutory savings bank and if any money of the bank was not required to pay deposits and interest to the depositors in accordance with the terms of the deposit and expenses it was for Parliament to direct the application and distribution of that money. As will appear, Parliament gave such directions from time to time whenever any question of a surplus became material.

Section 2 of the 1817 Act required every statutory savings bank to record its rules in a book available for the inspection of depositors and to deposit a copy of the rules with the local clerk of the peace. Section 3 required the rules to provide that—

'no Person or Persons being Treasurer, Trustee or Manager of such Institution, or having any Control in the Management thereof, shall derive any Benefit from any Deposit made in such Institution, but that the Persons depositing Money therein shall have the sole Benefit of such Deposits and the Produce thereof . . .'

This section was only concerned with the deposits and was enacted to ensure that no manager made a profit out of the administration of the bank.

Section 10 of the 1817 Act authorised the trustees of a statutory savings bank to pay into the Bank of England any sum or sums of money not being less than £50 to the account of the National Debt Commissioners to the credit of an account in the names of the commissioners to be called 'The Fund for the Banks for Savings'. By s 11 the commissioners were bound to pay back any sums deposited by a statutory savings bank on demand together with interest at the rate of 3d per cent per day. Section 19 debarred any depositor in a statutory savings bank from depositing more than £100 in the first year and £50 in every year thereafter.

The 1817 Act did not compel a statutory savings bank to lend all its money to the National Debt Commissioners. The bank might make income and capital profits from other investments and might also possess profits from activities prior to becoming a statutory savings bank. Section 13 of the Act 1 Geo 4 c 83 (savings banks (1820)) directed that—

'in all Cases where the Joint Stock or Property of the Depositors in any Savings Bank in *England* may have been or may be increased by any Change of Stock, or by any increased Rate of Interest . . . beyond the Rate of Interest payable to the Depositors by the original Rules . . . or by any other Means, it shall and may be lawful to and for the Trustees for the time being of any such Savings Bank, to make such Rules . . . for the Application and Disposal of any increased Stock or Property belonging to any such Saving Bank, to and amongst the Depositors therein, either by way of an Increase of Interest beyond the Rate of Interest originally stipulated to be paid to such Depositors, or by way of Bonus or Increase of Capital to the Sums deposited by them respectively, or by both such Means, as the Trustees and Managers of such Saving Bank . . . shall from time to time think fit and proper . . .'

This power to distribute income and capital profits in the form of additional interest or capital bonus to depositors was expressly conferred by the 1820 Act and was exercisable at the discretion of the trustees, and not at the behest of the depositors. Section 11 of the Act 5 Geo 4 c 62 (savings banks (1824)) directed that the rights conferred by s 13 of the 1820 Act to distribute profits in the form of additional interest or capital bonus should only be exercisable once in ten years and required one-half of any profits to be retained to meet future deficiencies. The express power of distributing profits conferred by the 1820 Act and amended by the 1824 Act is inconsistent with the theory that depositors possessed any interest in surplus assets or profits conferred by the 1817 Act or by common law.

The Savings Banks Act 1828 repealed and replaced the 1817, 1820 and 1824 Acts with amendments. The trustees of a statutory savings bank remained entitled to distribute income and capital profits which had been made before 20 November 1828 but s 23 of the Act provided:

'. . . in all Cases where the Joint Stock or Property of any Savings Bank, arising from Deposits made under this or any former Act, shall, from and after Twentieth Day of *November* One thousand eight hundred and twenty-eight, be increased by the Interest received beyond the Rate of Interest payable to the Depositors by the Rules and Regulations of such Savings Banks, or by any other Means, the said Trustees or Managers . . . shall, within Six Months after the Twentieth Day of *November* in each Year, ascertain, certify and pay over to the said Commissioners the Amount of such increased Stock and Property, reserving Such Portion as may appear necessary to meet current Expences; and the Amount of such Surplus . . . shall be discharged from the Account of Such Savings Bank standing in the Books of the said Commissioners; and the said Commissioners shall keep a separate and distinct Account of such Surplus so discharged from the Account of the said Savings Banks respectively as aforesaid, and apply the same in such Manner, and under such Regulations, from time to time, as any other Monies under the Provisions of this Act: Provided always, that it shall and may be lawful for the Trustees or Managers of the said respective Savings Banks to claim and receive of and from the said Commissioners . . . for the Purposes of the Institution, any Sum of Money equal to the Whole or any Part of the Principal Monies which may have been so discharged from the Account of such Savings Banks as aforesaid.'

Thus, no profits or surplus accruing after 20 November 1828 could lawfully be distributed to depositors. Profits were to be handed over to the commissioners to form a separate surplus fund available to ensure that every depositor from time to time received the full amount of principal and contractual interest due to him but no more. At that stage Parliament did not consider that it was necessary to provide for the ultimate destination of surpluses paid to the commissioners under s 23 of the 1828 Act and maintained by the commissioners in a separate surplus fund. The reasons which impelled Parliament to withdraw the limited power conferred by the 1820 Act on the trustees of a statutory savings bank to distribute profit in the form of additional interest or capital bonus sufficiently appear from other provisions of the 1828 Act. By s 11 of the 1828 Act the trustees of a statutory savings bank were compelled to invest all their moneys on loan to the commissioners and not in any other form of security. By s 16 the rate of interest payable by the commissioners to statutory savings banks was fixed at $2\frac{1}{2}$d per cent per day. By s 24 the maximum interest payable by a statutory savings banks to a depositor was fixed at $2\frac{1}{4}$d per cent per day. It follows that any surplus or profit made by a savings bank after 20 November 1828 was attributable to the use of public money and provision was therefore made by s 23 of the 1828 Act for any such surplus or profit to be returned to the commissioners. By the 1820 and 1824 Acts profits made prior to 20 November 1828 were distributable amongst depositors at the discretion of the trustees in the form of an addition to contractual interest or in the form of a capital bonus. By the 1828 Act profits made after 20 November 1828 could not be distributed save for the purpose of meeting deficiencies.

By the Savings Banks (Scotland) Act 1819 Parliament provided for the creation of statutory savings banks in Scotland. By the Savings Banks Act 1835 the provisions of the 1828 Act were applied to Scotland as well as England and Ireland.

The 1828 Act provided for current surpluses and profits from time to time to be paid over the the commissioners. If a statutory savings bank ceased business and was dissolved the separate surplus fund maintained by the commissioners remained with the commissioners and became the surplus fund of a closed savings bank. By 1863 it was realised that on the closure of a solvent savings bank further surpluses might arise on the sale by the savings bank of its property and equipment and other assets. The Post Office Savings Banks Act 1863 provided expressly for any such surplus. Section 2 of the 1863 Act directed that on the final closing of any statutory savings bank the trustees should, with the consent of the National Debt Commissioners, convert into money any property held on behalf of the bank and should pay over the net proceeds to the commissioners—

'to be by them carried to the Separate Surplus Fund standing in the Books of the said Commissioners . . . subject to any Claim that may thereafter be substantiated on account of any Depositor in the Savings Bank so closed.'

Section 3 directed that when the trustees of any savings bank determined to close the bank and paid off three-quarters of the amounts due to depositors, either in money or by transfer to a post office savings bank, the trustees could then deposit with the commissioners a list of outstanding deposits and pay over any savings bank moneys in the hands of the trustees to the commissioners, again to form part of the separate surplus fund. All unpaid depositors—

'shall thenceforth be considered to be Depositors in a Post Office Savings Bank; and such Depositors, on presenting their Deposit Books at any Post Office Savings Bank, shall be entitled to claim Payment of the Sums due to them respectively, with the Interest due to them thereon,'

and should be entitled to be paid out of the separate surplus fund held by the commissioners. These two sections are inconsistent with the suggested right of any depositor on the closure of a statutory savings bank to receive any part of any surplus of the bank. The depositor was entitled to the return of his principal and to his contractual interest and if he was not repaid by the savings bank he became a depositor in a post office savings bank. He was entitled to be paid his principal and interest but had no further claim on the separate surplus fund.

Since 1863 and down to the present day, Parliament has from time to time authorised expenditure out of or given directions for the application of surplus funds of closed trustee savings banks. In no instance has Parliament provided any benefit for any depositor in addition to the repayment of his principal and contractual interest.

The Trustees Savings Banks Act 1863 repealed and replaced the earlier Savings Banks Acts with amendments. Section 15 repeated the requirement that a statutory savings bank should invest only in loans to the National Debt Commissioners but subject to s 16, whereby the banks were authorised at the request of depositors to receive special deposits to be invested in special investments. Section 29 repeated the requirement that the trustees of a statutory savings bank should pay over every year their profits, if any, to the separate surplus fund maintained by the commissioners subject to the power of a savings bank to require repayment from the separate surplus fund for the purposes of the bank. By s 61 the commissioners were directed to publish annual accounts of the separate surplus fund. By s 6 of the Savings Banks Act 1880 the trustees were relieved of their obligation to pay over any surplus annually to the National Debt Commissioners except when required so to do by the commissioners. Any amount paid over to the surplus fund was directed to carry interest. The Savings Banks Act 1891 established an inspection committee to examine the books and report on the conduct of statutory savings banks,

a and by s 5(2):

> 'No application to the National Debt Commissioners for a payment from the separate surplus fund standing at the credit of any savings bank shall be entertained unless it have the previous sanction of the Inspection Committee.'

Section 4 of the Savings Banks Act 1904 authorised the trustees of a statutory savings

b bank with the consent of the commissioners to purchase land or erect buildings and for those purposes to apply money standing to the separate surplus funds account of their bank. On any sale of such land or buildings the net proceeds of sale were directed to be paid into the separate surplus fund. Section 5 of the 1904 Act authorised the trustees by special resolution to carry out an amalgamation with one or more other banks 'with or without any dissolution or division of the funds of such Banks'. The Trustee Savings

c Banks Act 1918 limited and defined the powers of trustees of a statutory savings bank to enter into special investment business. Section 2 provided that for the purpose of providing for any deficiency which might arise in respect of special investments made by trustee savings banks there should be established a guarantee fund under the control of the commissioners. By sub-s (2):

> *d* 'The guarantee fund shall consist of—(a) The reserves both in respect of general business and of special investments of all trustee savings banks which make special investments; and (b) Such part of the separate surplus fund as stands to the credit of closed trustee savings banks; and for the purpose aforesaid the reserves of every such trustee savings bank shall be at the disposal of the Commissioners . . .'

Thus Parliament authorised the disposition of the surplus funds of certain trustee

e savings banks and of all closed trustee savings banks to meet the deficiencies of other trustee savings banks incurred in carrying on special investment business.

The Savings Banks Act 1929 prohibited the closure of a solvent trustee savings bank without the consent of the commissioners, which was directed not to be given unless the commissioners satisfied themselves that there were no proper persons able and willing to act as trustees and managers of the bank. Section 7 of the 1929 Act authorised the

f commissioners when approving the formation of a new trustee savings bank to 'advance to the trustees of that bank out of such part of the separate surplus fund as stands to the credit of closed trustee savings banks such sums as they think fit . . .' Section 6 of the Trustee Savings Banks Act 1947 authorised the trustees of a trustee savings bank with the approval of the National Debt Commissioners to make advances to the trustees of other trustee savings banks out of any money standing to the credit of the bank in the separate

g surplus fund. The Savings Banks Act 1949 authorised the commissioners to maintain a mutual assistance account to which a trustee savings bank could contribute for the benefit of other trustee savings banks out of money standing to the credit of the donor bank in the separate surplus fund. Section 6 of the 1949 Act dealt with the discontinuance by a trustee savings bank of the business of making special investments. If on such discontinuance, after payment of the amount due to depositors there remained a surplus,

h then by s 6(4)—

> 'An amount equal to the surplus shall be carried to the separate surplus fund and be treated as an amount standing to the credit of a closed trustee savings bank, and the bank shall have no claim to the principal thereof or any interest thereon.'

The Trustee Savings Banks Act 1954 consolidated the enactments relating to trustee

j savings banks. The separate surplus funds and guarantee funds were maintained. Powers of amalgamation and powers to make advances and grants were repeated. Section 56 repeated the procedure to be followed on the closure of a bank. Trustees closing a bank were authorised to pay all money remaining in their hands to the commissioners together with a list of depositors who had not applied to receive their deposits and of the amounts due to them respectively. And it was provided:

'. . . (3) All the said moneys shall be held by the Commissioners, subject to the rights and claims of the depositors named in the list and those depositors shall *a* thereafter be considered to be depositors in a post office savings bank.

(4) The said depositors, on presenting their deposit books at any post office savings bank, shall be entitled to claim payment of the sums due to them respectively, with the interest due to them thereon, and on establishing their claim shall be paid out of the moneys so paid over by the trustees . . . and the moneys in the hands of the Commissioners . . . *b*

(5) The surplus of the said moneys, if any, after providing for the sums due to the said depositors, shall be carried to the separate surplus fund in the books of the Commissioners and shall be subject to any claim that may therefore be substantiated on account of any depositor in the bank . . .'

Consistently with earlier legislation s 56 makes it quite clear that on the closing of a bank a depositor is only entitled to his principal sum deposited and to his contractual *c* interest.

By s 3(5) of the Trustee Savings Banks Act 1958 the separate surplus fund of a continuing statutory savings bank was merged with and ceased to be separated and distinguished from other moneys standing to the credit of the bank in the books of the commissioners:

d

'. . . but the part of the separate surplus fund standing to the credit of closed banks shall continue to form a distinct account, to be called the "closed banks fund" . . .'

Section 56 of the 1954 Act was amended so that, on the closure of any bank after the coming into force of the 1958 Act, any surplus moneys remaining after paying or providing for depositors was directed to be carried to the 'closed banks fund'.

The Trustee Savings Banks Act 1969 consolidated the earlier Acts with amendments. *e* For present purposes it suffices that, by ss 64, 65 and 66, regulations were made for the closing or dissolution of a statutory trustee savings bank whereupon the trustees were directed to pay the bank's moneys to the commissioners and by s 66(5):

'The surplus of the said moneys, if any, after providing for the sums due to the said depositors, shall be carried to the closed banks fund in the books of the *f* Commissioners and shall be subject to any claim that may thereafter be substantiated on account of any depositor in the bank.'

The Trustee Savings Banks Act 1976 established the Trustee Savings Banks Central Board with power to give directions to and provide banking services for trustee savings banks. The Central Board was directed to secure that its revenues were sufficient to meet the total outgoings of the board and its subsidiaries and to enable the board to make such *g* allocations to reserve as the Central Board considered adequate. By s 2(2) the reserves of the Central Board were directed to be applied for such purposes as the Central Board might determine. To finance its expenditure the Central Board was authorised to levy contributions on trustee savings banks. The National Debt Commissioners were directed by s 16(5) to pay to each trustee savings bank the amount standing to its credit with the commissioners and— *h*

'(6) After paying each bank in accordance with subsection (5) above, the National Debt Commissioners shall pay any surplus amount remaining in the Fund into the Consolidated Fund.'

Section 22 of the 1976 Act amended s 65 of the 1969 Act so as to read: *j*

'When a trustee savings bank is finally closed, the trustees shall pay over to the Central Board any surplus moneys remaining in the hands of the trustees, after providing for the sums due to depositors and for any expenses authorised by the bank's rules; and the Central Board may distribute the money's among such other trustee savings banks as the Central Board think fit.'

As regards banks which were closed prior to the coming into force of the 1976 Act, it
a was provided by s 23 of that Act as follows:

'(1) The closed banks fund, within the meaning of section 65(3) of the Act of
1969 (which makes provision regarding the proceedings of the sale of property on
the closing of a bank), shall be closed and as soon as may be thereafter the National
Debt Commissioners shall pay over to the Central Board any moneys standing to
the credit of that fund.

b
(2) The moneys received by the Central Board by virtue of subsection (1) above
shall be subject to any claims that may thereafter be substantiated on account of any
depositor in a bank up to the amount of money (if any) carried in the fund on
account of the bank.'

The Trustee Savings Banks Act 1981 consolidated the earlier Savings Banks Acts with
c amendments. The analysis of the 1981 Act set forth in the speech of my noble and
learned friend Lord Keith leads him to the conclusion, with which I agree, that under
the 1981 Act no depositor in a statutory trustee savings bank is entitled to anything other
than the return of his principal and contractual interest. This result is consistent with the
legislation which in 1817 established statutory savings banks and with the legislation
which has since 1817 regulated the affairs of statutory savings banks.

d   No evidence was produced that, prior to this appeal, any complaint was made that in
making dispositions of the separate surplus funds of statutory trustee savings banks from
time to time Parliament was guilty of expropriation or unfairness towards depositors.
No evidence was produced that, prior to this appeal, any depositor of a closed statutory
savings bank laid claim to share in the surplus funds of the bank. Between 1862 and
1879 the closure of 201 statutory trustee savings banks was recorded and of these 92 had
e surplus assets. Between 1880 and 1891 a further 149 banks were closed. Thereafter 45
more were closed and by 1981 the number of statutory trustee savings banks had been
reduced by closures and amalgamations to four. Each depositor in a statutory trustee
savings bank must be deemed at least since the 1981 Act to have notice of the fact that he
had no interest in surplus assets. Rule 17(4) of the Rules of the Trustee Savings Bank
England and Wales and r 16(4) of the Rules of the Trustee Savings Bank Scotland
f provided:

'When the bank is finally closed, the trustees shall pay over to the Central Board
any surplus moneys remaining in their hands, after providing for the sums due to
depositors and for all expenses properly incurred in connection with or incidental
to the closure of the bank, or otherwise authorised by these rules.'

g   The Trustee Savings Banks Act 1985 abolished statutory savings banks and replaced
them by successor limited liability companies established for the purpose. Abolition took
effect on the vesting day, appointed under the Act to be 26 July 1986. By s 3 of the 1985
Act:

'... (3) ... on the vesting day, there shall, by virtue of this subsection, be
transferred from each of the existing banks to and vested in its successor all the
h property, rights, liabilities and obligations of the bank.

(4) The liabilities referable to a depositor's deposit with a bank which are
transferred by subsection (3) above to the bank's successor are liabilities to return his
deposit and to pay interest on it (if it was payable) at the rate prevailing immediately
before the vesting day, but, as from that day, the rights, liabilities and obligations
referable to the deposit shall become instead rights, liabilities and obligations
j incident to the relationship of customer and banker (and variable accordingly) ...'

The appellants disapprove, as they were entitled to disapprove, of the abolition of
statutory trustee savings banks. The appellants in the Scottish action brought proceedings
with the object of frustrating or postponing the abolition of the Scottish trustee savings
bank by claiming an interest in the surplus assets of the bank. The First Division

dismissed the claim of the appellants in the Scottish proceedings and I would dismiss this appeal from the order of the First Division.

The appellant in the English proceedings seeks the like object of frustrating or postponing the abolition of the Trustee Savings Bank England and Wales. Scott J declared that the depositors of the Trustee Savings Bank England and Wales were entitled, in accordance with the terms applicable to their respective accounts with the bank, to repayment of the principal amounts credited to such accounts and in the case of interest-bearing accounts to the periodical payment of interest thereon at the rate from time to time applicable thereto but to no other amounts. I agree and would dismiss the appeal of the appellant in the English action against the first declaration made by Scott J. Depositors who disapprove of the abolition of the statutory trustee savings banks by the 1985 Act are entitled to voice their disapproval and are entitled to mark their disapproval if they so wish by withdrawing their principal and interest from the limited liability successor companies to which their deposits have been transferred by the 1985 Act. No one doubts the ability of the successor companies to meet their obligations to the depositors who confided their savings to statutory trustee savings banks prior to the 1985 Act.

The appellants pressed the emotive arguments that if the statutory trustee savings banks and their surplus assets are not 'owned' by the depositors then the banks have no owners and the surplus assets are in 'limbo'. The arguments are false. The 1817 Act and its successors enable a savings bank to volunteer for and submit to nationalisation on filing their rules and claiming the benefits of the Act. Statutory trustee savings banks and their assets belong to the state subject to the contractual rights of depositors to the return of their deposits and interest and subject to the powers and duties from time to time conferred and imposed by Parliament on the National Debt Commissioners and the Central Board, both institutions of the state. The 1985 Act privatised the statutory trustees savings banks and Parliament decided to present their surplus assets amounting, it is said, to £800m to the successor companies established in accordance with the Act. Your Lordships are not concerned with the wisdom of this decision. The depositors at the date of the 1985 Act had no proprietary interest in the surplus assets of the statutory trustee savings banks and cannot therefore complain of the transfer of those assets to the successor companies.

Scott J declared, secondly, that the assets of the Trustee Savings Bank England and Wales were held subject to the statutory provisions and the rules for the time being in force on trust to provide for payment to depositors of the sums due to them respectively. Against this second declaration the respondents in the English action have appealed to this House by way of cross-appeal.

The theory that statutory savings banks held their assets on trust to provide for repayment of the deposits was founded on the erroneous assumption that prior to the 1828 Act a depositor possessed some kind of equitable interest in the assets of the savings bank. As I have indicated, a depositor after the 1820 Act and before the 1828 Act might hope to obtain, at the discretion of the trustees, additional interest or a capital bonus but that possibility did not confer any equitable interest in assets on a depositor and did not apply to profits made after 28 November 1828. Scott J discerned differences between a statutory trustee savings bank and a clearing bank but he accepted that a depositor in a savings bank was entitled to no more than a depositor in a clearing bank, namely to a payment of principal and contractual interest. It would be strange if the same contractual right produced different proprietory rights.

Scott J relied on the fact that under the 1981 Act the rules were made binding on all depositors who were entitled by the rules to appoint and remove the trustees, and were entitled to examine the accounts of the bank and to obtain the appointment of a commissioner to examine the affairs of the bank. These rights prevented the trustees of a savings bank from being a self-perpetuating oligarchy and enabled depositors to ensure that the affairs of the bank were properly conducted and that the solvency of the bank and the safety of deposits were not jeopardised by unlawful or improvident management. But these rights did not suffice to convert creditors into trust beneficiaries. The

proposition that a statutory trustee savings bank held its assets on trust to provide for
a repayment of the depositors is as heretical as the theory that a trustee bank holds its assets
on trust to provide for repayment of its authorised trust deposits: see *Space Investments
Ltd v Canadian Imperial Bank of Commerce Trust Co (Bahamas) Ltd* [1986] 3 All ER 75, [1986]
1 WLR 1072. The proposition that a statutory trustee savings bank held its assets on trust
to repay its depositors would create a new kind of floating charge hitherto unknown to
the law and possessing unexplored incidents and priorities. Alternatively, the theory
b would produce a new kind of equitable interest hitherto unknown to the law and
valueless and unnecessary. If a bank is solvent the depositors will be paid in full and no
equitable charge or interest is necessary. If a bank is insolvent there is nothing which will
enable the depositors to be paid in full. The transfer of the assets and liabilities of a trustee
savings bank to a successor company bank pursuant to the provisions which Parliament
has seen fit to include in the 1985 Act did not interfere with any of the rights of the
c depositors. The depositors prior to the 1985 Act were and now are entitled to principal
and interest and no more. If they dislike being depositors in a company bank as opposed
to being depositors in a statutory trustee savings bank they have had full opportunity
since the enactment of the 1985 Act to withdraw their deposits and they are at liberty to
withdraw their deposits now. I would accordingly allow the cross-appeal against the
decision of Scott J and discharge the second declaration made by him.

d
LORD OLIVER OF AYLMERTON. My Lords, I agree with the speeches delivered
by my noble and learned friends Lord Keith and Lord Templeman. For the reasons given
by my noble and learned friends, I too agree that both appeals should be dismissed and
that the cross-appeal in the English case should be allowed to the extent proposed by my
noble and learned friend Lord Keith.

e
LORD GOFF OF CHIEVELEY. My Lords, I have had the advantage of reading in
draft the speeches to be delivered by my noble and learned friends Lord Keith and Lord
Templeman. I agree with both speeches and for the reasons given by them I would
dismiss the appeal in the Scottish case and would allow the cross-appeal in the English
case to the extent proposed by my noble and learned friend Lord Keith.

f
Appeals dismissed ; cross-appeal allowed.

Solicitors: *Martin & Co*, parliamentary agents for *Drummond & Co WS*, Edinburgh (for
Mr Ross) and agents for *John Howell & Co*, Sheffield (for the Rev Vincent); *Treasury
Solicitor*, agent for *A A McMillan*, Solicitor in Scotland to HM Treasury, Edinburgh;
g *Theodore Goddard*, agents for *McClure Naismith Anderson & Gardiner*, Edinburgh (for the
trustees of the Trustee Savings Bank Scotland) and agents for *W & J Burness WS*,
Edinburgh (for the Trustee Savings Bank Central Board); *Theodore Goddard* (for the
Trustee Savings Bank Central Board and the custodian trustees for the Trustee Savings
Bank England and Wales); *Treasury Solicitor*.

Mary Rose Plummer   Barrister.

Gomba Holdings UK Ltd and others v Homan and another

CHANCERY DIVISION
HOFFMANN J
19, 20, 21, 24 MARCH 1986

Company – Receiver – Duty – Duty to company – Duty to provide information to debtor company – Company's right to information dependent on whether information necessary to enable directors to exercise powers or perform duties – Company's right to information subordinate to receiver's responsibility to debenture holder – Extent of receiver's duty to provide information to company – Companies Act 1985, ss 497(1), 499(1).

The plaintiffs, which were six companies forming part of a group, granted fixed and floating charges over their assets to a bank to secure the group's indebtedness to the bank. The bank appointed receivers under the charges, who in the exercise of their powers of sale realised various assets of the group. However, the plaintiffs still owed about £11m to the bank. The sole, and controlling, director of the plaintiffs claimed to have entered into an agreement with an undisclosed third party on undisclosed terms, which would provide funds to pay off the outstanding debt owed to the bank. The arrangements were said to involve the sale of all or some of the group's remaining assets to the undisclosed third party after redemption. In order that the negotiations with the third party could be concluded the plaintiffs claimed that they required certain information from the receivers about the current state of the receivership and accordingly issued a notice of motion against the receivers seeking an order that they disclose full details of all disposals of assets made or proposed to be made and in particular disclose contracts relating to various assets which were known to be sold or agreed to be sold. By a further notice of motion the plaintiffs sought an order restraining the receivers from disposing of any further assets unless they first gave the plaintiffs written notice five clear working days before any proposed commitment was entered into.

Held – (1) Since the charges gave the receivers an unrestricted right to sell at any time assets which were the subject of the charges, the court could not make an order requiring the receivers to give advance notice to the plaintiffs before entering into any commitments to dispose of the assets. In any event, the possibility that the plaintiffs would, as they claimed, soon be in a position to redeem the security did not restrict the powers of the receivers. The second motion would therefore be dismissed (see p 96 *j* and p 97 *b*, post).

(2) A receiver's duty to provide accounts or other information to a debtor company was not restricted to his statutory obligations under ss 497(1)*ᵃ* and 499(1)*ᵇ* of the Companies Act 1985. The extent of the receiver's obligation to provide additional information was to be deduced from the nature of the receivership and a company's right to such information depended on showing that the information was needed to enable the board of directors to exercise its residual powers or to perform its duties. Any right which a company had to obtain information from the receiver was qualified by the receiver's primary responsibility to the debenture holder, which entailed that the receiver was entitled to withhold information where he formed the opinion that disclosure would be contrary to the interests of the debenture holder in realising the security. Since the

---

a Section 497(1), so far as material, provides: '. . . the receiver shall [within the specified period] send the requisite accounts of his receipts and payments to the registrar of companies, to any trustees for the debenture holders on whose behalf he was appointed, to the company and . . . to all such debenture holders.'

b Section 499(1), so far as material, provides: 'If a receiver or manager of a company's property—(a) having made default in filing, delivering or making any return, account or other document . . . which a receiver or manager is by law required to file, deliver, make or give, fails to make good the default . . . the court may . . . make an order directing the receiver or manager . . . to make good the default within such time as may be specified in the order.'

a plaintiffs had not demonstrated a need to know the additional information which they sought and the receivers were not obliged to furnish the information until there was firmer evidence of a realistic prospect that the charge would be redeemed and since it was reasonable for the receivers to conclude that disclosure of prospective sales would not be in the interests of the debenture holder, their refusal to make the disclosure sought was justifiable. The first motion would accordingly be dismissed (see p 97 j, p 99 b c e g h, p 101 f g and p 102 a b, post).

b **Notes**
For an order against a receiver to give discovery of documents belonging to a company, see 7 Halsbury's Laws (4th edn) para 885, and for cases on the subject, see 10 Digest (Reissue) 887, 5143.
For a receiver's statutory obligations, see 7 Halsbury's Laws (4th edn) para 902.
c For the Companies Act 1985, ss 497, 499, see 8 Halsbury's Statutes (4th edn) 507, 509.
As from a day to be appointed s 497 of the Companies Act 1985 is to be replaced by s 54 of the Insolvency Act 1985.

Cases referred to in judgment
Filhol (J P) Ltd v Haigh (8 December 1977, unreported), Ch D.
Jeffreys v Dickson (1866) LR 1 Ch App 183, LC.
d *Johnson (B) & Co (Builders) Ltd, Re* [1955] 2 All ER 775, [1955] Ch 634, [1955] 3 WLR 269, CA.
Moss Steamship Co Ltd v Whinney [1912] AC 254, HL.
Newhart Developments Ltd v Co-op Commercial Bank [1978] 2 All ER 896, [1978] QB 814, [1978] 1 WLR 636, CA.
Smiths Ltd v Middleton [1979] 3 All ER 842.
e
Cases also cited
Bradford Metropolitan CC v Brown (18 March 1986, unreported), CA.
Gosling v Gaskell [1896] 1 QB 669, CA; *on appeal* [1897] AC 575, [1895–9] All ER Rep 300, HL.
Greenwood v Sutcliffe [1892] 1 Ch 1, CA.
f *Law v Glenn* (1867) LR 2 Ch App 634, LJJ.
NWL Ltd v Woods [1979] 3 All ER 614, [1979] 1 WLR 1294, HL.
R v Board of Trade, ex p St Martins Preserving Co Ltd [1964] 2 All ER 561, [1965] 1 QB 603, DC.
Redland Bricks Ltd v Morris [1969] 2 All ER 576, [1970] AC 652, HL.
Standard Chartered Bank Ltd v Walker [1982] 3 All ER 938, [1982] 1 WLR 1410, CA.
g
Motions
By a notice of motion dated 4 March 1986, the plaintiffs, Gomba Holdings UK Ltd, Gomba UK Group Ltd, Duchess Theatre Co Ltd, Garrick Theatre Co Ltd, Gomba Exim Ltd, and Routestone Ltd, sought, inter alia, an order that the defendants, Andrew Mark Homan and Colin Graham Bird, receivers appointed by Johnson Matthey Bankers Ltd h (the bank), disclose all disposals made or proposed to be made by the defendants as receivers and managers of the plaintiffs, and for disclosure of the terms of certain specified disposals. By a notice of motion dated 18 March 1986 the plaintiffs also applied for, inter alia, an order restraining the receivers from disposing of the assets. A third motion, in which the plaintiffs applied for an order against the bank, requiring the bank to provide the plaintiffs with a redemption statement, was granted by consent. The facts are set out j in the judgment.

Terence Cullen QC and *Anthony Trace* for the plaintiffs.
Richard Adkins for the receivers.

HOFFMANN J. There are before the court three motions in two actions brought by six companies in the Gomba Group, a conglomerate group of companies controlled by Mr Abdulhamid Shamji. The defendants to the first action are the receivers of the assets and undertakings of the first five plaintiffs and certain freehold land belonging to the sixth plaintiff. They were appointed in the last week of October and the first week of November 1985 by Johnson Matthey Bankers Ltd, the defendant in the second action, under fixed and floating charges securing a group indebtedness which at the time of the appointments amounted to about £22m. Since that date the receivers have in the exercise of their powers of sale realised various assets of the group and the current indebtedness stands at about £11m.

The immediate cause of these proceedings is that, according to the evidence, Mr Shamji as sole director of the plaintiff companies has entered into an agreement in undisclosed terms with an undisclosed third party which, it is said, will provide the funds needed to pay the whole outstanding indebtedness to the bank and redeem the remaining assets. The arrangements are said to involve the sale of some or all of the group's remaining assets to the undisclosed third party after redemption. For the purposes of concluding negotiations with the third party, the plaintiffs wanted certain information from the receivers about the current state of the receivership. The receivers have from time to time provided information, both before and after the commencement of these proceedings, but the plaintiffs consider that this falls short of their legal entitlement.

Accordingly, the plaintiffs on 4 March 1986 issued the writ in the first action against the receivers, claiming disclosure of full details of all disposals of assets made or proposed to be made and in particular for disclosure of the contracts relating to various assets which were known to have been sold or agreed to be sold. On the same date the plaintiffs issued their first notice of motion (motion 1) seeking the same relief as that claimed in the writ.

The second action was against the bank for redemption in the standard form commenced by originating summons dated 18 March 1986 and accompanied by the notice of the second motion (motion 2) which seeks an order for, so to speak, summary redemption, requiring the bank to provide the plaintiffs with a statement of the redemption price and ordering that on payment of that price within a stipulated period the bank should discharge the receivers and its security. The third motion (motion 3), also by notice dated 18 March, is in the action against the receivers and asks for an order restraining the receivers from disposing of any further assets until five days after they have given the plaintiffs notice of their intention to do so. I gave leave to serve both of these motions to come on with motion 1 on 19 March.

I need say little about motion 2 in the redemption action because the bank is and no doubt always has been willing to discharge its security on the receipt of payment in full. The receivers produced a redemption statement which I gather is acceptable to the plaintiffs and the bank has consented to an order in the terms of a minute to be signed by counsel by which on payment within 21 days in accordance with the redemption statement, suitably adjusted for the actual date of redemption, the bank will discharge its security.

I turn therefore to the action and motions 1 and 3 against the receivers and I shall consider first motion 3 to restrain the receivers from entering into any commitments to dispose of assets unless they have first given the plaintiffs five working days written notice of the details of any such proposed commitment. Counsel for the plaintiffs submitted that pending the proposed redemption, the balance of convenience favoured such an order because the sale of an asset without notice to the plaintiffs might upset the arrangements with the unknown third party. This may be true, although I think that there are other matters which also enter into the balance of convenience. But the primary difficulty is that I can see no arguable cause of action which could entitle the plaintiffs to such relief. The security documents give the receivers an unrestricted right to sell at any time. Until actual redemption or at least a valid tender of the redemption price, these powers continue to exist. The fact that the plaintiffs claim that they will shortly be able to redeem cannot give them a right in law to restrict the powers granted to the receivers.

Even if there were a cause of action, I do not think that the balance of convenience would favour an injunction. The receivers are entitled to take the view that they should continue with realisations on the assumption that redemption may not take place. The

circumstances of Mr Shamji's secret arrangements with the anonymous purchaser are to
a say the least unusual and the receivers, while no doubt hoping that he will come up with
the money, could hardly be blamed for retaining some scepticism. It is not the first
occasion on which Mr Shamji has assured them or the bank that repayment is imminent.
It does not follow that unless restrained in this way the receivers will take any opportunity
to sell. It is in the interests of the debenture holder as well as the plaintiffs that the
receivers should not unnecessarily jeopardise a bona fide and realistic proposal to
b discharge the indebtedness in full. No doubt the receivers will exercise a commercial
judgment in the matter. But an enforced delay of five working days or even the need to
reveal the proposed transaction to the plaintiffs may cause the loss of an advantageous
sale. As against this possibility of loss, the plaintiffs are unable to offer anything in
support of a cross-undertaking in damages. I therefore dismiss motion 3.

Most of the three-day hearing of these motions was taken up with discussion of motion
c 1 for information. The cases do not provide very much guidance on the extent of the
duty of a receiver and manager of the property of a company to provide information to
the directors during the currency of the receivership. A receiver is an agent of the
company and an agent ordinarily has a duty to be ready with his accounts and to provide
his principal with information relating to the conduct of his agency. But these
generalisations are of limited assistance because a receiver and manager is no ordinary
d agent. Although nominally the agent of the company, his primary duty is to realise the
assets in the interests of the debenture holder and his powers of management are really
ancillary to that duty: see *Re B Johnson & Co (Builders) Ltd* [1955] 2 All ER 775 at 779,
[1955] Ch 634 at 644–645.

Section 497 of the Companies Act 1985 requires a receiver or manager of the whole
(or substantially the whole) of a company's property appointed under a floating charge to
e send accounts of his receipts and payments in a prescribed form to the company, the
debenture holder (or trustee for debenture holders) and the registrar of companies. These
accounts have to be sent annually and within two months of the termination of the
receivership. If a receiver makes default in furnishing accounts and does not make good
his default within 14 days of service of a notice requiring him to do so, any member or
creditor of the company or the registrar of companies may apply under s 499 for a
f summary order requiring the receiver to supply the accounts. In the case of receivers
appointed solely under fixed charges or of less than the whole or substantially the whole
of the company's property, there is under s 498 a different statutory obligation to provide
accounts. Under that section accounts must be provided half-yearly but need be sent only
to the registrar of companies.

It has been suggested that these provisions are exhaustive of a receiver's obligations to
g provide accounts or other information but I do not think that this can be right. For one
thing, there can be no doubt that a receiver under a fixed charge is under an equitable
duty to account to the mortgagor: see *Jeffreys v Dickson* (1866) LR 1 Ch App 183 at 190.
Section 498 imposes no duty on a receiver of a company's property appointed under a
fixed charge to provide any account to the company and it seems unlikely that the
obligation to send accounts to the registrar of companies was intended to supplant the
h receiver's accountability to the mortgagor. If this is correct in the case of receivers under
fixed charges, it is hard to see why Parliament should have taken a different view of
receivers under floating charges. Furthermore, s 497(6) says in terms:

> 'This section does not prejudice a receiver's duty to render proper accounts of his
> receipts and payments to the persons to whom, and at the times at which, he may
> be required to do so apart from this section.'

j

This provision in my judgment is intended to leave unaffected any obligation on a
receiver to account or provide information which may exist in equity or by contract. An
obvious example is a receiver who under the terms of his appointment has agreed to
provide monthly returns to the debenture holder. In *J P Filhol Ltd v Haigh* (8 December
1977, unreported) Slade J was, on second thoughts, provisionally inclined to accept a
submission that s 497(1) was exhaustive and that s 497(6) preserved only the rights of

persons who are not given a right to accounts by s 497(1). I share the judge's original
view that this is not the natural meaning of s 497(6) and would add that it seems to give   *a*
no weight to the words 'and at the times at which'. I would therefore respectfully agree
with his Honour Judge Blackett-Ord V-C in *Smiths Ltd v Middleton* [1979] 3 All ER 842
that the statutory obligations are not exhaustive.

That does not, however, mean that the statutory obligations are irrelevant to the
questions at issue in this motion. I have already indicated that for the purpose of
determining the extent of a receiver's equitable obligation to provide accounts and   *b*
information to the company, his status as agent provides a starting point for the inquiry
rather than its solution. It cannot simply be assumed that his obligations are the same as
those of an ordinary agent who owes a duty of undivided loyalty to his principal. They
must depend on the express or implied terms of the bargain between the debenture
holder and the company under which he was appointed. In this case we are really
concerned with implied terms and the powers and duties of receivers under the   *c*
Companies Act 1985, which automatically take effect on appointment, are necessarily
part of the material to be taken into consideration in deciding what other duties should
be implied.

There are, I think, certain principles which can be deduced from what the parties may
be supposed to have contemplated as the commercial purpose of the power to appoint a
receiver and manager. The first is that the receiver and manager should have the power   *d*
to carry on the day-to-day process of realisation and management of the company's
property without interference from the board. As Lord Atkinson said in *Moss Steamship
Co Ltd v Whinney* [1912] AC 254 at 263 the appointment of a receiver—

'entirely supersedes the company in the conduct of its business, deprives it of all
power to enter into contracts in relation to that business, or to sell, pledge or
otherwise dispose of the property put into the possession or under the control of the   *e*
receiver and manager. Its powers in these respects are entirely in abeyance.'

This relationship between the receiver and the company would suggest that the board
may be entitled to periodic accounts but cannot, merely because it is the board and the
receiver is agent of the company, demand current information about the conduct of the
business. There seems to me an analogy in this respect with the ordinary relationship   *f*
between the board and the shareholders, even though the one is technically a relationship
of agency and the other is not.

Counsel for the plaintiffs relied strongly on the decision of the Court of Appeal in
Newhart Developments Ltd v Co-op Commercial Bank [1978] 2 All ER 896, [1978] 1 QB 814
which decided that the residual powers of the board in receivership enabled it to authorise
an action for damages against the debenture holder to be brought in the name of the   *g*
company without the consent of the receiver. This was an exceptional case in which the
receiver for obvious reasons did not consider that the debenture holder's interests would
be served by pursuing the action. The alleged chose in action was therefore not an asset
which, in Lord Atkinson's words, the receiver had 'taken into his possession or control'.
He wanted to have nothing to do with it. The court decided that the board was therefore
free to bring the action in the interests of unsecured creditors and shareholders. But   *h*
counsel for the plaintiffs relied in particular on the following passage in the judgment of
Shaw LJ ([1978] 2 All ER 896 at 900, [1978] 1 QB 814 at 820):

'The receiver is entitled to ignore the claims of anybody outside the debenture
holders. Not so the company; not so, therefore, the directors of the company. If
there is an asset which appears to be of value, although the directors cannot deal   *j*
with it in the sense of disposing of it, they are under a duty to exploit it so as to
bring it to a realisation which may be fruitful for all concerned.'

It is easy to see what Shaw LJ meant in the context of the case before him, but counsel for
the plaintiffs relies on the generality of this statement for a submission that the directors
have a continuing duty to exploit the assets of the company and that the receivers are
therefore obliged to provide whatever information is necessary to enable the directors to

carry out that duty. I cannot accept that the Court of Appeal contemplated some kind of
a diarchy over all the company's assets. This would be contrary to principle and wholly
impractical. In my judgment the board has during the currency of the receivership no
powers over assets in the possession or control of the receiver.

The second principle which can be deduced from the nature of receivership is that, in
the absence of express contrary provision made by statute or the terms of the debenture,
any right which the company may have to be supplied with information must be
b qualified by the receiver's primary duty to the debenture holder. If the receiver considers
that disclosure of information would be contrary to the interests of the debenture holder
in realising the security, I think he must be entitled to withhold it and probably owes a
duty to the debenture holder to do so. The company may be able to challenge the
receiver's decision on the grounds of bad faith or possibly that it was a decision which no
reasonable receiver could have made, but otherwise I think that the receiver is the best
c judge of the commercial consequences of disclosing information about his activities.

All these considerations, which in my view tend to negate a general obligation on a
receiver to provide information to the company, are valid only during the currency of
the receivership. Once the receivership has ended, the case is altered. There is no longer
any right to manage the property or duty to the debenture holder which can conflict
with a receiver's duty to account as agent to the company. It is not necessary for me to
d express a view on whether provision of the statutory accounts on the termination of the
receivership should be assumed prima facie to be a proper accounting or whether, even
in the absence of some challenge to the figures provided, the company can ask for
something more. I only wish to emphasise that *Smiths Ltd v Middleton* [1979] 3 All ER
842, in which Judge Blackett-Ord V-C decided that a company was entitled to a general
order for an account against a receiver, was a case in which the receivership had come to
e an end.

During the receivership, the company's right to information beyond the statutory
accounts must in my judgment depend on demonstrating a 'need to know' for the
purpose of enabling the board to exercise its residual rights or perform its duties. I do
not want to explore the question of what this might entail further than is necessary for
the purposes of this case. An instance given in some of the cases is that the board may
f need information from the receivers in order to comply with its statutory obligation to
render accounts. There has not yet been any suggestion in these proceedings that
information is required for this purpose. More relevant in this case is the fact that the
board may need information in order to exercise the company's right to redeem. It seems
to me at least arguable that the right to redeem gives rise to a right on the part of the
company to ask for sufficient information to make it effective. If the company has no
g way of finding out which assets have been sold and which remain to be redeemed, the
right may in practice be incapable of exercise.

For the purposes of this motion I therefore propose to assume that a board which
demonstrates a bona fide intention and ability to redeem is entitled not merely to a
redemption statement showing how much is still owing but also to reasonable
information about the nature of the assets remaining in the hands of the receivers. On
h the other hand, conformably with the principles I have discussed, I think that the
receiver's duty to provide such information must be subordinated to his primary duty
not to do anything which may prejudice the interests of the debenture holder.

I turn therefore to the facts of this case. Part of the background is that the relationship
between Mr Shamji's solicitors, Messrs Holman Fenwick & Willan (Holmans) on the one
hand and the receivers and their solicitors, Messrs Freshfields, on the other has not been
j easy. Few disposals of assets have not provoked threats of legal proceedings for breach of
duty in selling at an undervalue. Holmans have been free with accusations of bad faith
against the receivers and the bank. Letters of complaint dealing with every aspect of the
receivership have been written to the receivers' professional body. The first two and a
half months of the receivership were taken up with heavy litigation, fought to a finish,
in which the validity of the receivers' appointment was challenged. I am not suggesting
that the receivers are entitled to penalise Mr Shamji for being difficult. But I do not think
it is unreasonable for them to be wary about the disclosure of even apparently innocuous

information about their activities in case it should precipitate legal proceedings in which
they would have to disclose more confidential information in order to defend themselves.   a
    Shortly before the trial of the earlier proceedings to which I have referred, Mr Shamji
brought a motion for the disclosure of information rather similar to this one. The basis
of the motion was that a third party, which on that occasion he did identify, was ready
and willing to provide funds to pay the group's debts to the bank in full. The receivers
provided a redemption statement and offered to provide the third party with information.
On this basis, the plaintiffs consented to their motion being dismissed with costs. The   b
receivers did enter into negotiations with the third party but it appeared that he was not
willing to pay the indebtedness in full and no agreement was reached.
    Further requests for information began immediately after the failure of the action to
remove the receivers, when Holmans asked for another redemption statement. Freshfields
wrote on 28 January 1986 enclosing such a statement but saying:

> 'When you are in a position to demonstrate that the necessary funds are available   c
> for settlement and to identify a specific date for payment, we will arrange for new
> figures to be calculated to the agreed date.'

By a letter of the same date, Holmans asked for—

> 'full details . . . of the disposals made by the Receivers and the terms upon which
> those disposals have been made, or upon which the Receivers have contracted to   d
> make such disposals.'

This request was made on the ground that the receivers were agents of the companies
and that Mr Shamji as sole director was therefore entitled as of right to the information.
In my judgment the claim was misconceived. The legal argument was debated between
the solicitors for most of February. On 20 February Freshfields wrote giving some and   e
refusing some of the information which had been requested, but adding, 'If we were
convinced that repayment was imminent, the Receivers would of course provide more
details'.
    On 26 February Holmans sent a telex saying that the companies were now in a position
to discharge their liabilities and asking for an urgent meeting to arrange for agreements
bringing the receiverships to an end. They asked for Mr Shamji's accountants to be given   f
access to all files to verify the balance due. Freshfields replied on the same day saying a
minimum of £11·4m was needed to discharge the indebtedness and adding:

> 'As we have emphasised before our clients are not prepared to enter into detailed
> discussions about the sums needed to discharge the total amounts owing to JMB
> until you can provide us with firm evidence satisfactory to our clients that your
> client has sufficient monies held to his order to satisfy the debt in full . . . Our clients   g
> are not prepared to give access to the files to your accountant.'

This telex was met by an accusation of bad faith and a claim of legal right. On 28
February 1986 Holmans telexed saying:

> 'Mr. Shamji is a director of the companies in receivership and is entitled to
> information regarding their affairs and full access to their records including all   h
> contracts and correspondence.'

This assertion, as I have already said, was quite wrong. The telex did however add the
information that Mr Shamji was not in a position to redeem from his own resources but
that—

> 'The payment will be made by a third party who will have assigned to him the   j
> benefit of all sales not complete. A substantial deposit is immediately available to be
> paid on exchange of contracts.'

On 3 March 1986 Holmans followed this up with a telex saying that they held £500,000
on a joint account to be available as a deposit until completion and that the remaining
balance up to £12m was 'available'. They also asked for copies of all contracts to be

a   assigned to the third party at completion to be made available to a Mr G D Silver who
    was acting as his solicitor.
        On the same date Freshfields sent a telex asking for more information about the third
    party. Who was he and who was his banker? There were also questions about the
    proposed form of the transaction. Was the third party going to buy the assets (including
    the uncompleted contracts) from the receiver? Or was he going to pay off the debts and
    take over the bank's security? Or was he going to take over the plaintiff companies and
b   then redeem? The telex ended:

        'It is not our intention to frustrate a genuine offer by Mr. Shamji to settle in full
        all outstanding liabilities owed to JMB. As we have repeatedly told you, we are
        prepared to have a meeting but only if your client can show to our clients' satisfaction
        that the potential purchaser has the funds available to discharge the full indebtedness.
        In view of your telex we would also need to know the identity of the third party to
c   which you refer.'

        On the following day, 4 March, there was a further exchange of telexes. Freshfields
    asked for information about the joint account and added:

        'We anticipate that it is unlikely that our clients will be prepared to release [the
        requested contracts] at least until the points referred to above and in our yesterday's
d   telex have been met and it is apparent that bona fide and realistic negotiations are
        proceeding.'

    Holmans said that they confirmed that it was the intention to discharge the full
    indebtedness 'by means of a sale of assets to a third party'. No further details about the
    third party, his means or the nature of the transaction were supplied.
e   I have set out the correspondence leading up to 4 March in some detail because that
    was the date of issue of the writ and notice of motion claiming information which are
    now before me. The first question is whether the plaintiffs had at that date an arguable
    case for saying that they were entitled to more information than they had been given.
    All the relevant facts are in the correspondence between the solicitors. In my judgment
    the plaintiffs had not demonstrated any need to know more facts than they had already
f   been given. I am willing, as I have said, to assume that a company mortgagor is entitled
    for the purposes of exercising its right to redeem to be given particulars of the amount
    still due and the assets which would be returned on redemption. These would include
    particulars of the uncompleted contracts made by the receivers. But I do not think that
    for this purpose it is sufficient for the mortgagor merely to say that he wants to redeem
    or that he has some mysterious third party who will put up £12m. The history of this
g   case, both before and after the appointment of the receivers, is a chronicle of unfulfilled
    assurances by Mr Shamji that someone was just about to provide the money to pay his
    debts to the bank. In my judgment the receivers were under no obligation to provide
    any information until they had firmer evidence that there was a realistic prospect of
    redemption.
        That finding is sufficient to dispose of the motion but I should say something about
h   what has happened since the issue of the writ. The receivers have been told, as I said at
    the beginning of this judgment, that Mr Shamji has entered into an agreement with the
    anonymous third party. Neither the terms of the agreement nor the identity of the third
    party have yet been disclosed. Mr Shamji says that this is because the third party insists
    on secrecy and anonymity. Nevertheless, on the basis of assurances from Holmans that
    funds to redeem were available, Freshfields on 14 March 1986 sent copies of most of the
j   completed and uncompleted contracts into which the receivers had entered. One or two
    items were omitted in error but I understand that these have now been supplied. Counsel
    for the plaintiffs nevertheless asks for an order for the disclosure of all contracts in case
    there may be some which his clients have not seen. But there is no evidence that any are
    missing and therefore even if I thought that the plaintiffs were entitled in law to the
    contracts, I would not be willing to make an interlocutory mandatory order which
    appears to me quite unnecessary.

This means that the only live issue in the plaintiffs' motion is the request for details of
all contracts which the receivers may be proposing to make in the future. Counsel for   *a*
the receivers says that they are willing to disclose any future contracts if and when they
make them but not to give advance details of negotiations. Mr Homan (one of the
receivers) in his affidavit explains why he does not think that it would be in the interests
of the debenture holder for such details to be disclosed. I need not say more than that in
my judgment this is a view which on the evidence he is reasonably entitled to hold. Once
again it seems to me that an order for disclosure would involve risk of loss to the bank   *b*
for which the plaintiffs are in no position to provide any indemnity by way of cross-
undertaking. For these additional reasons motion 1 will be dismissed.

Order accordingly.

Solicitors: *Holman Fenwick & Willan* (for the plaintiffs); *Freshfields* (for the receivers).   *c*

Evelyn M C Budd   Barrister.

R v Navvabi   *d*

COURT OF APPEAL, CRIMINAL DIVISION
LORD LANE CJ, McCOWAN AND ROSE JJ
20 JUNE, 8 JULY, 1986

Criminal law – Theft – Appropriation – Assumption of rights of owner – Payment by cheque   *e*
using cheque card to guarantee payment – Cheque drawn on bank account in fictitious name –
Insufficient funds in bank account to meet cheque – Whether use of cheque card an assumption of
rights of bank – Whether an appropriation of bank's money by person delivering cheque and
tendering card – Theft Act 1968, s 3(1).

The appellant used various false names to open accounts with two banks and a building   *f*
society. Subsequently he obtained membership of a number of casinos in those false
names and drew 12 cheques in exchange for gaming chips in the casinos when there was
not sufficient money in the bank accounts to meet the cheques. Each cheque was
accompanied by a banker's card. The appellant was charged with, inter alia, 12 counts of
theft and at his trial the judge directed the jury that, if a person operating a fictitious
bank account drew a cheque on the account when there was no money in the account   *g*
and supported the cheque with a banker's card, that constituted appropriation for the
purposes of s 3(1)[a] of the Theft Act 1968 by the person delivering the cheque and
tendering the card. The appellant was convicted. He appealed.

Held – The use of a cheque card to guarantee payment of a cheque delivered to a payee
and drawn on an account with inadequate funds was not an assumption of the rights of   *h*
the bank and thus not an appropriation within s 3(1) of the 1968 Act because the use of
the cheque card and delivery of the cheque did no more than give the payee a contractual
right as against the bank to be paid a specified sum from the bank's funds on presentation
of the guaranteed cheque and that was not in itself an assumption of the rights of the
bank to that part of the bank's funds to which the sum specified in the cheque
corresponded. There was therefore no appropriation by the appellant either on delivery   *j*
of the cheque to the casino or when the funds were ultimately transferred to the casino
and his conviction on the charges of theft would accordingly be quashed. To that extent
the appeal would be allowed (see p 106 *e* to *h*, post).

---

a   Section 3(1), so far as material, is set out at p 105 *f*, post

a *R v Pitham and Hehl* (1977) 65 Cr App R 45 and *R v Kohn* (1979) 69 Cr App R 395 considered.

Notes
For appropriation as an element of theft, see 11 Halsbury's Laws (4th edn) para 1264, and for cases on the subject, see 15 Digest (Reissue) 1264, 10831–10832.
For the Theft Act 1968, s 3, see 12 Halsbury's Statutes (4th edn) 517.

b
Cases referred to in judgment
R v Kohn (1979) 69 Cr App R 395, CA.
R v Pitham and Hehl (1977) 65 Cr App R 45, CA.

Case also cited
c *Lacis v Cashmarts* [1969] 2 QB 400, [1969] 2 WLR 329, DC.

Appeal against conviction and sentence
On 22 November 1985 in the Crown Court at Newcastle upon Tyne before his Honour Judge Johnson and a jury the appellant, Hemasadin Navvabi, was convicted of one count of obtaining property by deception (count 1), four counts of attempting to obtain property by deception (counts 2, 4, 6 and 7), two counts of forgery (counts 5 and 9) and
d twelve counts of theft (counts 10 to 21) and was sentenced to twelve months' imprisonment on each count concurrent and was in addition ordered to pay compensation in the sum of £926 to an insurance company and sums of £850 to each of two banks. He appealed with leave of the judge against his conviction for theft and also against his sentence. The facts are set out in the judgment of the court.

e
J T Milford (assigned by the Registrar of Criminal Appeals) for the appellant.
Richard Lowden for the Crown.

Cur adv vult

f 8 July. The following judgment of the court was delivered.

LORD LANE CJ. At the Crown Court at Newcastle upon Tyne on 22 November 1985 the appellant was convicted before his Honour Judge Johnson and a jury on 19 of the 24 counts in the indictment. Counts 1, 2, 4, 5, 6 and 7 involved frauds on an insurance company, count 9 involved the forging of a reference and counts 10 to 21 involved theft from two banks. In relation to all the counts the appellant was sentenced to 12 months'
g imprisonment on each concurrent, and he was in addition ordered to pay compensation in the sum of £926 to the insurance company and sums of £850 to each of the two banks.

The appellant was an Iranian student undertaking a Ph D course in civil engineering at Newcastle University. It was the prosecution case that between July 1983 and January
h 1984, using the names Mobarac, Tabarok, Talghi and Nori Zadeh in addition to his own, the appellant took out five insurance policies for personal property cover with Endsleigh Insurance. During that period he made one successful claim in his own name for £926, having falsely represented that he had been burgled. That gave rise to count 1. In addition he made four further unsuccessful claims in false names for the loss of property worth almost £2,000 from various addresses and from his motor car. This gave rise to
j counts 2, 4, 5, 6 and 7.

During the latter part of the same period the prosecution alleged that the appellant was responsible for opening accounts with two banks and a building society in false names and providing false references, in particular a National Westminster bank account in the name of Nori Zadeh, a Lloyds account in the name of Mobarac and Halifax Building Society accounts in the names of Norani, Tabarok, Nori Zedeh and Olaki. In relation to the Lloyds account the appellant was said to have provided a reference in the name of Talghi for Mr Mobarac on paper indorsed with a Newcastle University Division of Transport Engineering stamp which had been stolen in August 1983. This gave rise to count 9.

In relation to counts 10 to 21, between November 1983 and January 1984 a number of casinos in Manchester and London received applications for membership in the names of Mobarac and Nori Zadeh. The bank accounts in each name had been very little used during this period. Suddenly over the weekend of 12–15 January 1984 £1,050 worth of cheques, all drawn in sums of either £50 or £100, were drawn on the two bank accounts in twelve transactions. In each case the cheque, accompanied by a banker's card, was drawn in the name of Mobarac or Nori Zadeh and delivered at a casino in exchange for gaming chips. At the time of drawing and delivery there were inadequate funds in the account on which it was drawn to meet the cheque. No arrangement had been made for an overdraft. The time at which these cheques were drawn and delivered showed that the activity started in Manchester, moved to London, moved back to Manchester and then ended in London: evidence in relation to inter-city train times showed that one person could have been in both places at the relevant times.

It was the prosecution case that the appellant was responsible for drawing the cheques and using false names. The prosecution relied on a variety of documents found at his flat and in his locker at the university, including a number of cash cards in different names and a piece of paper which contained what appeared to be practice signatures for Mobarac. He also had in his possession a British Rail rover ticket for travel between 12 and 18 January and over £1,100 worth of United States dollars.

A handwriting expert gave evidence that specimens of the appellant's handwriting suggested that he was the author of the insurance claim forms and cheques.

The appellant had told a Mr Kari that he had wanted to join some casinos to cash cheques and in the early hours of 15 January he was seen on the King's Cross to Newcastle train in possession of a Sony radio similar to one purchased from a London shop by someone using the Mobarac identity.

When interviewed the appellant denied that he was responsible for the offences and said that the documents found in his possession were not his. The appellant did not give evidence and no witnesses were called on his behalf. The defence case was that he had spent the whole weekend in Newcastle and that the incriminating documents had been planted on him by someone else.

The particulars of counts 10 to 21 each alleged that the appellant stole either £50 or £100 belonging to one of the banks (National Westminster or Lloyds) by drawing a cheque on an account in the name of Mobarac in the case of Lloyds or Nori Zadeh in the case of National Westminster.

At the close of the prosecution case counsel submitted that these counts (amongst others) should not be left to the jury, since the facts proved did not amount to theft. The judge did not accede to that submission and ruled that the counts should be left to the jury to consider, and in due course he directed the jury as follows:

> 'I direct you that if somebody operating a fictitious account draws a cheque on that account, an account in which there is no money to meet the cheque, and supports the cheque which he has drawn when he delivers it to the person to whom it is made out with a banker's card, as a matter of law that could constitute the appropriation by the person delivering the cheque and tendering the card. It could amount to an appropriation of the assets of the bank on which the cheque is drawn, assets of the bank to the value of the cheque which has been drawn on it.'

There was a further direction as to the meaning of appropriation and as to the intention of permanently depriving the owner.

The case was presented by the prosecution and left to the jury on the basis that the theft occurred at the moment that the cheque was handed over to the casino.

Before the trial judge and again in this court counsel for the appellant submitted that no identifiable property was appropriated, because the contractual obligation imposed on the bank was referable not to any asset which it had at the time the cheque was drawn

and delivered to the casino, but to those funds which it had at the time of presentation
a by the casino. It was further submitted that, if there was identifiable property, its
appropriation took place when the bank honoured the cheque and the funds were
transferred to the casino by the bank, and not at the time the cheque was drawn and
delivered to the casino. Furthermore, it was contended that theft in such a way was so
academic a concept that only an academically-minded person understanding such niceties
would be able to form the necessary intention permanently to deprive the owner.
b Counsel for the appellant conceded, although this court doubts the correctness of that
concession, that if the prosecution case had been presented on the basis that the
appropriation took place at the time the funds were transferred by the bank to the casino
the conviction would be unimpeachable.

On behalf of the Crown it was submitted that the sums of £50 and £100 were
sufficiently identifiable notwithstanding that they were only part of the bank's assets;
c that when a cheque backed by a guarantee card is drawn on an account without funds,
the drawer assumes the rights of the bank in their money by directing them to do
something with their property which they did not want to do, the property in question
being either money or other intangible property but not a chose in action; and the
elements necessary for theft being dishonesty, misappropriation of the property of
another and an intention permanently to deprive, the thief's knowledge of the identity
d of the owner and whether the drawer believed he was stealing from the bank or the
casino was immaterial.

In order to test the validity of these submissions one turns to the Theft Act 1968.
Section 1(1) provides:

> 'A person is guilty of theft if he dishonestly appropriates property belonging to
> another with the intention of permanently depriving the other of it.'

e

There are therefore four elements in the offence: (i) dishonesty; (ii) appropriation; (iii)
property of another; (iv) the intention permanently to deprive the owner. As to (i), it is
accepted in the present case there was ample evidence on which the jury could find
dishonesty. As to (ii), appropriation is defined in s 3(1) of the 1968 Act: 'Any assumption
by a person of the rights of an owner amounts to an appropriation . . .' As to (iii), property
f is defined in s 4(1) of the Act:

> '"Property" includes money and all other property, real or personal, including
> things in action and other intangible property.'

As to (iv), s 6(1) provides:

> 'A person appropriating property belonging to another without meaning the
> *g* other permanently to lose the thing itself is nevertheless to be regarded as having
> the intention of permanently depriving the other of it if his intention is to treat the
> thing as his own to dispose of regardless of the other's rights; and a borrowing or
> lending of it may amount to so treating it if, but only if, the borrowing or lending
> is for a period and in circumstances making it equivalent to an outright taking or
> disposal.'

h

It is common ground between counsel that no authority directly in point is to be
found in the several decisions of the courts which have been cited. No discourtesy is
intended to the diligence of counsel if we refer to only two of these decisions, namely *R
v Kohn* (1979) 69 Cr App R 395, on which the appellant relies, and *R v Pitham and Hehl*
(1977) 65 Cr App R 45, on which the prosecution rely.
j   *R v Kohn* was a decision of a differently constituted division of this court. The appellant,
a director of a limited company, had been convicted of theft from the company in
drawing cheques for his own purposes on the company's account in amounts (i) within
the credit standing to the account, (ii) within the overdraft limit on the account, and (iii)
in excess of the overdraft limit. The convictions in relation to situations (i) and (ii) were
upheld and in relation to (iii) quashed. In relation to (i) and (ii) it was held that the
company's thing in action was stolen, whereas in situation (iii) no thing in action existed.

The following is an extract from the judgment of the court referring to the debt owed
by the bank to the company (69 Cr App R 395 at 407)   *a*

'It is a right of property which can properly be described as a thing in action and
therefore potentially a subject of theft under the provisions of the 1968 Act. The
cheque is the means by which the theft of this property is achieved. The completion
of the theft does not take place until the transaction has gone through to completion.'

The last sentence of this passage did not affect the result in R v Kohn and was to that   *b*
extent obiter. It suggests (and has been taken by Professor Griew in 'Stealing and
Obtaining Bank Credits' [1986] Crim LR 356 at 362 to mean) that theft occurs at the
time when the bank transfers the funds. But Professor Smith has argued (see [1985] Crim
LR 367 at 370 and Smith The Law of Theft (5th edn, 1984) para 106), that the delivery of
the cheque to the payee is 'an assumption of the rights of an owner' and therefore the
appropriation. There may, however, as Professor Griew points out, be practical difficulties   *c*
with this approach, for the state of the account may be much more difficult to ascertain
when the cheque is delivered to the payee than when it is presented to the bank. Such
difficulties, however, do not arise or call for resolution in the present case.

In R v Pitham and Hehl another division of this court upheld the appellants' convictions
for handling on the basis that a third man, in purporting to sell to them someone else's
furniture, had assumed the rights of the owner to the furniture when he showed it to the   *d*
appellants and invited them to buy what they wanted: at that moment he appropriated
the goods to himself.

We note that R v Pitham and Hehl has also been criticised by both Professor Glanville
Williams (see Text Book of Criminal Law (2nd edn, 1983) p 764) and Professor Smith (see
The Law of Theft para 27). It is sufficient for the purposes of the present case to say that
despite the submissions of counsel before us, we see no incompatibility between the   *e*
decisions in R v Pitham and Hehl and R v Kohn.

Neither of these cases, however, helps us to resolve the present matter which, it seems
to this court, turns essentially on the construction of s 3(1): was use of the cheque card to
guarantee payment of a cheque delivered to the casino and drawn on an account with
inadequate funds an assumption of the rights of the bank and thus appropriation? In our
judgment it was not. That use of the cheque card and delivery of the cheque did no more   *f*
than give the casino a contractual right as against the bank to be paid a specified sum
from the bank's funds on presentation of the guaranteed cheque. That was not in itself
an assumption of the rights of the bank to that part of the bank's funds to which the sum
specified in the cheque corresponded: there was therefore no appropriation by the drawer
either on delivery of the cheque to the casino or when the funds were ultimately
transferred to the casino.   *g*

In our judgment it is not in these circumstances appropriate to apply the proviso and
accordingly the appellant's convictions on counts 10 to 21 of the indictment are quashed
as are the sentences of 12 months' imprisonment on each of these counts. Likewise the
orders for compensation in the sums of £850 in favour of National Westminster Bank
and Lloyds Bank are also quashed.

So far as sentence in respect of the remaining counts is concerned, it has been somewhat   *h*
faintly contended on behalf of the appellant that 12 months is an excessive sentence. The
matter is somewhat academic, as the appellant has already been released on parole. But
this court sees no reason to interfere with the sentences which were passed on the other
counts in this indictment, which were serious offences of fraud and forgery. Accordingly,
the appeal against sentence is dismissed, save to the extent already indicated.

j

Convictions and sentences for theft quashed. Appeal against sentence on other charges dismissed.

Solicitors: *David Dracup*, Newcastle upon Tyne (for the Crown).

N P Metcalfe Esq   Barrister.

Maharaj v Chand

PRIVY COUNCIL

LORD BRIDGE OF HARWICH, LORD TEMPLEMAN, LORD OLIVER OF AYLMERTON, LORD GOFF OF CHIEVELEY AND SIR ROBIN COOKE

19 JUNE, 7 JULY 1986

Estoppel – Promissory estoppel – Reliance on representation – Unmarried couple – Plaintiff acquiring house in sole name on representation that defendant was his wife and that house would be family home – Defendant leaving own flat to move into house with children – Plaintiff subsequently leaving house and allowing defendant to remain – Plaintiff then claiming vacant possession – Whether plaintiff entitled to vacant possession – Whether plaintiff estopped from denying defendant's right to remain in house – Native Land Trust Act (Fiji), s 12.

Fiji – Native land – Unlawful dealing – Land vested in Native Land Trust Board for benefit of Fijian owners – Plaintiff obtaining sublease of native land by representing that defendant was his wife and that property to be used for family home – Plaintiff subsequently leaving and allowing defendant to remain – Plaintiff later claiming vacant possession of property – Whether plaintiff estopped from denying defendant's right to remain – Whether defendant's right a 'dealing' in land requiring board's consent – Native Land Trust Act (Fiji), s 12.

The plaintiff was granted a sublease of native land vested in the Fiji Native Land Trust Board. The plaintiff stated in his application for the sublease that he was married to the defendant, who was in fact his de facto wife, and he gave an undertaking to use the land solely for the purpose of providing a house for himself and his family, which consisted of himself, the defendant, their child and her two children. The plaintiff told the defendant that the house would be a permanent home for her and the children. The defendant gave up her own flat, moved into the house and looked after the plaintiff and the children as wife and mother. The plaintiff financed the sublease and the building of the house while the defendant contributed to household expenses from her own earnings. In 1980 the relationship broke up and the plaintiff left the house telling the defendant that she could stay there. The plaintiff subsequently commenced proceedings in the Fiji Supreme Court seeking vacant possession of the property. The judge dismissed the action on the ground that the plaintiff was estopped from evicting the defendant. The Fiji Court of Appeal allowed an appeal by the plaintiff, holding that he had, on leaving the property, conferred a licence on the defendant to occupy the house without the consent of the board and that the licence was therefore an unlawful dealing with the land under s 12[a] of the Fiji Native Land Trust Act, which provided that it was 'not lawful for any lessee ... to ... deal with the land comprised in his lease ... without the consent of the board ...' The defendant appealed to the Privy Council.

Held – On the natural and ordinary meaning of s 12 of the Fiji Native Land Trust Act a purely personal right arising out of a promissory or equitable estoppel was not a 'dealing' with land for the purpose of s 12. Furthermore, the defendant had such a personal right as against the plaintiff because at the time of the acquisition of the land and the building of the house he had represented to her that it would be a permanent home for her and the children and that she would be treated as living there as his wife, she had acted to her detriment in reasonable reliance on that representation by giving up her flat, she had supported the application to the housing authority, she had used her earnings to pay for household needs and she had looked after the plaintiff and the children as wife and

---

a   Section 12 is set out at p 109 *e f*, post

mother. Accordingly, it would be inequitable for the plaintiff to evict her. The
defendant's appeal would therefore be allowed (see p 110 g to j and p 112 e to g j, post).   *a*
   Kulamma v Manadan [1968] AC 1062 applied.
   Chalmers v Pardoe [1963] 3 All ER 552 distinguished.

Notes
For promissory estoppel, see 16 Halsbury's Laws (4th edn) para 1514, and for cases on the
subject, see 21 Digest (Reissue) 8–16, 52–74.   *b*

Cases referred to in judgment
Chalmers v Pardoe [1963] 3 All ER 552, [1963] 1 WLR 677, PC.
Gissing v Gissing [1970] 2 All ER 780, [1971] AC 886, [1970] 3 WLR 255, HL.
Grant v Edwards [1986] 2 All ER 426, [1986] 3 WLR 114, CA.
Kulamma v Manadan [1968] AC 1062, [1968] 2 WLR 1074, PC.
Moses v Macferlan (1760) 2 Burr 1005, [1558–1774] All ER Rep 581, 97 ER 676.   *c*
Plimmer v Wellington Corp (1884) 9 App Cas 699, PC.

Cases also cited
Greasley v Cooke [1980] 3 All ER 710, [1980] 1 WLR 1306, CA.
Western Fish Products Ltd v Penwith DC [1981] 2 All ER 204, CA.   *d*

Appeal
The defendant, Sheila Maharaj, appealed with special leave in forma pauperis from the
decision of the Court of Appeal of Fiji (Speight V-P, Mishra and O'Regan JJA) dated 30
March 1984 whereby it allowed an appeal by the plaintiff, Jai Chand, against the decision
of Rooney J in the Supreme Court of Fiji dated 26 August 1983 dismissing the plaintiff's
action against the defendant for possession of a dwelling house and ordered that the   *e*
defendant give up to the plaintiff vacant possession of the house. The facts are set out in
the judgment of the Board.

Austin Allison for the defendant.
Bhupendra C Patel (of the Fijian Bar) for the plaintiff.   *f*

7 July. The following judgment of the Board was delivered.

SIR ROBIN COOKE. By special leave granted by Her Majesty in Council to her as a
poor person, the appellant, who was the defendant in an action in the Supreme Court of
Fiji, appeals from a judgment of the Fiji Court of Appeal (Speight V-P, Mishra and
O'Regan, JJA) delivered by O'Regan JA on 30 March 1984. The plaintiff in the action is   *g*
the former de facto husband of the defendant, the parties having lived together as man
and wife for 12 years from 1968 to 1980; they had one child of their own and she had
two children of a former union. In the action, commenced in October 1981, the plaintiff
claimed against her an order for possession of the house which had been their family
home.   *h*
   The trial judge, Rooney J, held in a judgment delivered on 26 August 1983 that the
plaintiff was estopped from turning the defendant out and that the defendant could raise
this estoppel inter partes notwithstanding the provisions of s 12 of the Native Land Trust
Act (cap 134) of Fiji, a section prohibiting dealings with certain land without the consent
of the Native Land Trust Board.
   The Court of Appeal reversed that decision and ordered that the defendant give the   *j*
plaintiff vacant possession of the house. They held that s 12 was decisive in favour of the
plaintiff. On that view it was unnecessary for the Court of Appeal to rule on whether
there would have been an estoppel apart from the section, but they said nothing to cast
doubt on Rooney J's conclusion on that point. Indeed, observations and citations in the
judgment delivered by O'Regan JA favour the approach that, as he put it—

'the malleable principles of which Lord Mansfield spoke are being shaped to
a   accommodate the needs of the day and to reflect the dictates of the social facts.'

He cited *Moses v Macferlan* (1760) 2 Burr 1005 at 1012, [1558–1774] All ER Rep 581 at
585, and Canadian, New Zealand and New South Wales cases to which it becomes
unnecessary for their Lordships to refer specifically.

Before their Lordships two points arise, namely the effect of the section and estoppel
apart from the section. The points are linked inasmuch as the estoppel has to be defined
b   to enable a decision to be reached on whether the section excludes it. There is some
advantage, however, in considering the statutory point first, as it is of some general
significance in Fiji and other countries where similar provisions are in force and on it
alone the courts below have differed. For this purpose it is enough to note that the effect
of the trial judge's decision and the express contention advanced for the defendant before
their Lordships is not that she has (or should be awarded) any legal or equitable interest
c   in the land on which the house stands. It is simply that the plaintiff is estopped against
her from denying that she has his permission or licence to live permanently in the house.
The right is not put forward as one of exclusive possession against the plaintiff himself;
nor is it claimed that the rights of third parties, such as the plaintiff's lessor and
mortgagee, are affected.

d
The scope of the statute
Section 12 of the Native Land Trust Act provides:

> '(1) Except as may be otherwise provided by regulations made hereunder, it shall
> not be lawful for any lessee under this Act to alienate or deal with the land comprised
> in his lease or any part thereof, whether by sale, transfer or sub-lease or in any other
e   > manner whatsoever without the consent of the Board as lessor or head lessor first
> had and obtained. The granting or withholding of consent shall be in the absolute
> discretion of the Board, and any sale, transfer, sub-lease or other unlawful alienation
> or dealing effected without such consent shall be null and void: Providing that
> nothing in this section shall make it unlawful for the lessee of a residential or
> commercial lease granted before the twenty-ninth day of September 1948, to
f   > mortgage such lease.
> (2) For the purposes of this section "lease" includes "a sub-lease" and "lessee"
> includes "a sub-lessee".'

The land in question in this case is native land within the meaning of the Act. As such,
by s 4 its control is vested in the Native Land Trust Board and it is to be administered by
g   the board for the benefit of the Fijian owners. The land is leased by the board to the Fiji
Housing Authority. The plaintiff holds the land under a registered sublease from the
housing authority, approved by the board, for a term of 94 years, 6 months, 9 days from
21 November 1973. To finance the construction of the house, he mortgaged the leased
land to the authority in return for an advance of $11,200 and was required to raise $1,242
against his Fiji National Provident Fund contributions. The footwear company by which
h   he was employed as a foreman also assisted him financially with the acquisition of the
lease and the building project.

It seems that the Native Land Trust Board has never expressly consented to the
defendant's living on the land, and her case has not been conducted on the footing of an
implied consent. Nevertheless their Lordships note that the contention that the limited
right relied on by her is rendered null and void by the statute appears technical and
somewhat lacking in merit. The evidence was that the housing authority made such land
j   available to married couples only. In the application to the authority, on which at some
stage the name of the defendant was inserted as a co-applicant, the plaintiff indicated that
they were married and had two young children living with them; and he undertook that
the land would be used solely for the erection of a house and appurtenances to be used by
him solely as a residence for himself and his family. What at least purports to be the

signature of the defendant appears on the application, as well as the signature of the plaintiff. It seems unlikely that the board would have been unaware of the authority's *a* policy of helping married people. While it is not certain what attitude the two public bodies would have taken if they had known that the defendant was only a de facto wife, there is nothing before their Lordships to suggest that the board has any objection to the defendant's continuing to live on the property as long as the rent and mortgage payments are kept up.

In terms s 12 is directed against alienating or dealing with *the land* without the consent *b* of the board. Manifestly the section is intended to ensure that the board's power of control and the beneficial interests of the Fijian owners are not to be prejudiced by unauthorised transactions. Neither the terms nor the spirit of the section are violated by an estoppel or equity operating solely inter partes.

According to the plaintiff's evidence, he left the property in 1980, terminating his relationship with the defendant and telling her to stay there without mentioning any *c* time limit. But by written notice in March 1981 he required her to quit. The Court of Appeal thought that when he left he conferred a licence on her, and that they were bound by *Chalmers v Pardoe* [1963] 3 All ER 552, [1963] 1 WLR 677 to hold that such a licence was caught by the section.

Their Lordships agree with Rooney J that *Chalmers v Pardoe* is distinguishable. That was a case between two former friends and business associates, one of whom as lessee of *d* native land had consented to the building by the other (the appellant) of a house and appurtenant buildings, which were in fact erected in accordance with that consent. The case proceeded on the assumption that the Native Land Trust Board's consent had not been obtained. The appeal to the Judicial Committee was concerned only with the appellant's claims to an equitable charge or lien, for which he relied on the kind of proprietary estoppel exemplified by *Plimmer v Wellington Corp* (1884) 9 App Cas 699. *e* There is a dictum in the judgment of the Privy Council, delivered by Sir Terence Donovan, that even treating the matter simply as one where a licence to occupy coupled with possession was given for the purpose of erecting a dwelling house, when this purpose was carried into effect an unlawful 'dealing' with the land took place. The decision that the appellant there was not entitled to an equitable charge or lien does not assist in determining whether the present dependant, who now makes no such claim, *f* can resist the present plaintiff's action for possession. *Chalmers v Pardoe* was not concerned with purely personal rights in a family context, nor even with whether it would be inequitable to grant an order for possession to the registered proprietor.

Counsel for the plaintiff properly drew the attention of their Lordships to *Kulamma v Manadan* [1968] AC 1062, a case apparently not cited to the Court of Appeal. Had that court enjoyed the advantage of considering that case, the result there might well have *g* been different. *Kulamma's* case concerned a share farming agreement which was claimed to be void under s 12. In a judgment delivered by Lord Wilberforce the Judicial Committee distinguished *Chalmers v Pardoe*, holding that merely because an agreement can in certain of its aspects be described as a licence, it is not necessarily to be described as a *dealing with* the land; rather the decision has to be based on an analysis of the particular agreement. Lord Wilberforce analysed the agreement there in issue as in its whole effect *h* 'one of a purely contractual and personal character, which, even in the most general sense, could not be said to amount to a dealing with the land'.

The present case likewise is concerned with a purely personal right. In the opinion of their Lordships such a right is outside the purview of s 12. The context of the section and the purpose of the Act contain nothing to suggest that the words of the section bear other than their natural and ordinary meaning. In the natural and ordinary sense a promissory *j* or equitable estoppel such as is set up in this case would not be described as a dealing with land.

Estoppel

The conclusion that the statutory point taken for the plaintiff fails makes it necessary to decide the question which did not arise on the view of the Act taken by the Court of

Appeal: whether the trial judge was justified in finding an estoppel. In this part of the
a case some further facts have to be taken into account.

The association of the parties began after the defendant obtained work in the footwear
factory where the plaintiff was employed. He was then living with his parents. The child
of the parties was born in 1970. For some time they lived in the house of the plaintiff's
brother. The trial judge found that in 1973 the defendant moved to a flat in Nabua.
Apparently she had their child and one or both of her other two children with her. She
b gave evidence that the plaintiff came to stay with her there. He denied that in his
evidence, saying that he used to visit her there but that they did not set up house together
until they moved to the house at Kinoya with which the case is concerned. Relying
partly on the evidence of a neighbour, Rooney J rejected the plaintiff's evidence, finding
that the parties had already lived as man and wife at Nabua. What is equally noteworthy,
however, is that the plaintiff maintained in evidence that the flat was the defendant's.
c Evidently the judge accepted that the defendant had at least an interest in the flat, for he
said in his judgment, when referring to the move to Kinoya:

> 'Her present situation, in which she stands in peril of being put out on the street
> might never have come about if the plaintiff had made it clear to her at the relevant
> time that she could never have any expectation of a permanent home with him.'

d In 1973 they also decided to apply to the housing authority for land. On 29 November
1973 the plaintiff completed a form of tender for residential allotments, declaring that
he was married, and his tender of $2,400 for the land in question was accepted. A cheque
of $30 for a deposit was drawn on a joint bank account which the parties had opened in
1970; at the request of the housing authority both parties indorsed the cheque.
Subsequently, as already mentioned, the plaintiff obtained the lease in his own name but
e on representations that the defendant was his wife and that the property was for a house
for them and their family. The defendant remembered going with the plaintiff to the
housing authority offices and signing a form. The plaintiff said in evidence: 'When I got
the property I got it for myself and the defendant, we talked on that line.' The judge
found:

f 'I have no doubt that when the plaintiff obtained the land and later set about
constructing a house he told the defendant that he was building it for what was in
fact his family at that time. It is possible that he was entirely sincere in this purpose.
I have no reason to disbelieve the defendant when she said that she was under the
impression the plaintiff was providing a home for her and her children. As she is
uneducated, she took no steps to protect her interest. Whether or not the housing
authority would have granted the sublease if they had known of the true relationship
g between the parties, I do not know. The fact remains that the plaintiff obtained the
sublease with the support of the defendant and on the premise that they and two of
the defendant's children constituted a family unit eligible to receive an allocation of
land.'

The house was completed in 1978 or 1979 and the family then moved in. It is not in
h dispute that the plaintiff financed the acquisition of the lease and the building of the
house from borrowed money and his own savings, and that the defendant made no direct
contribution to the cost. But the judge was satisfied that the defendant as a working
housewife used her modest earnings for the support of the family as a whole. In that way
there was an indirect but significant contribution by her to the instalments payable to
keep the property. She was also a contributor to the provident fund and that money was
j not drawn on for the house; but the suggestion made in argument that in some way this
should tell against her defence to the claim for possession is without substance.

Relations between the parties deteriorated, and in 1980 the plaintiff left the house,
leaving the defendant there with the three children. She has looked after them at all
material times. The plaintiff has since married and has a child of the marriage; but he
did not suggest in evidence that he wanted the house for the occupation of his new
family. Be that as it may, his prior obligations are to his first family.

As to the principles of law to be applied to those facts, references were made in argument to cases where constructive trusts, carrying beneficial interests in land, arise between parties who are man and wife, whether de jure or de facto, on or after the acquisition of their home. The authority now classic is the speech of Lord Diplock in *Gissing v Gissing* [1970] 2 All ER 780 at 789–795, [1971] AC 886 at 903–911, and later English cases are reviewed in the judgments of the Court of Appeal in *Grant v Edwards* [1986] 2 All ER 426, [1986] 3 WLR 114, which concerned an unmarried couple. In such cases a contract or an express trust as at the time of the acquisition may not be established, because of lack of certainty or consideration or non-compliance with statutory requirements of writing; but a constructive trust may be established by an inferred common intention subsequently acted on by the making of contributions or other action to the detriment of the claimant party. And it has been held that, in the absence of evidence to the contrary, the right inference is that the claimant acted in the belief that she (or he) would have an interest in the house and not merely out of love and affection: see for instance *Grant v Edwards* [1986] 2 All ER 426 at 439, [1986] 3 WLR 114 at 130 per Sir Nicolas Browne-Wilkinson V-C.

It is possible that, but for s 12 of the Native Land Trust Act, the defendant here could have made out an entitlement to an equitable interest in the land on the principles just mentioned. In the face of the section, however, no such interest is contended for and none was found at first instance. The finding and the contention are more limited, and justifiably so. No matter whether or not the facts of a given case go far enough to establish an equitable interest in land, they may satisfy the requirements for a promissory estoppel. The doctrine of promissory estoppel is now firmly established, although its frontiers are still being worked out. For present purposes it is enough to refer to the account in *Spencer Bower and Turner on Estoppel by Representation* (3rd edn, 1977) ch 14.

The present case fairly satisfies the requirements. On Rooney J's findings, at the time of the acquisition of the land and the building of the house the plaintiff represented to the defendant that it would be a permanent home for her and her children. Indeed, the representation was that she would be treated as living there as his wife. In reasonable reliance on the representation she acted to her detriment by giving up the flat. Moreover, she supported the application to the housing authority, she used her earnings to pay for household needs, and she looked after her de facto husband and the children as wife and mother. A sufficient relationship had previously existed between the parties. It is not possible to restore her to her former position.

In these circumstances it would plainly be inequitable for the plaintiff to evict her. It is right to hold that as against him she has in effect permission to reside permanently in the house, on the basis that the children may be with her for as long as they need a home. As has already been noted, it is a personal right not amounting to a property interest diminishing the rights of the plaintiff's lessor and mortgagee. It has not been contended for the defendant that the plaintiff is under any obligation to her to continue to pay the rent or the mortgage interest. The appeal raises no question regarding the plaintiff's ability to assign the sublease. In any event that is subject to the control of the Native Land Trust Board under s 12.

Their Lordships add the caveat that they are far from saying that whenever a union between an unmarried couple comes to an end, one who is the sole owner in law and equity of the property hitherto their home should not be able to obtain an order for possession against the other. It is the particular combination of facts which has led to the estoppel in the present case.

For these reasons their Lordships will humbly advise Her Majesty that the appeal should be allowed and the dismissal of the action by the trial judge restored. There should be no order for costs before their Lordships' Board or in the Fijian courts.

Appeal allowed. No order for costs.

Solicitors: *Philip Conway Thomas & Co* (for the defendant); *Charles Russell & Co* (for the plaintiff).

Mary Rose Plummer   Barrister.

a
R v Central Criminal Court, ex parte Adegbesan and others

QUEEN'S BENCH DIVISION
WATKINS LJ AND SCHIEMANN J
20 MAY 1986

b

Police – Powers – Practice – Special procedure material – Power of police to order production of material to be produced or discovered – Whether notice of application must contain details of precise documents to be produced or discovered – Police and Criminal Evidence Act 1984, s 9, Sch 1.

c For the purposes of an application by the police under s 9[a] of and Sch 1[b] to the Police and Criminal Evidence Act 1984 for an order for the production of material which the police wish to have produced or discovered, it is incumbent on the police to set out in the notice of application which is sent to the person whose assistance is required a description of all material which is sought to be produced or discovered, notwithstanding the risk that evidence might be destroyed (see p 117 h to p 118 a f, post).

d   Where the police are proceeding to obtain information from an unincorporated body they ought to name an officer of that body as the person against whom they are moving by way of application (see p 118 e f, post).

    Quaere. Whether an unincorporated body is a 'person' for the purposes of an application under Sch 1 to the 1984 Act (see p 118 b to f, post).

e **Notes**

For police access to excluded material and special procedure material, see Supplement to 11 Halsbury's Laws (4th edn) para 125B.

    For the Police and Criminal Evidence Act 1984, s 9, Sch 1, see 12 Halsbury's Statutes (4th edn) 957, 1029.

f **Cases cited**

Anton Piller KG v Manufacturing Processes Ltd [1976] 1 All ER 779, [1976] Ch 55, CA.
IRC v Rossminster [1980] 1 All ER 80, [1980] AC 952, HL.

Application for judicial review

Victor Adegbesan, Miss Lea Jack, Mrs M Osamore and Miss Y Hazelwood applied, with
g the leave of Kennedy J granted on 25 April 1986, for judicial review by way of an order of certiorari to quash the orders made on 18 April 1986 by the Common Serjeant at the Central Criminal Court under s 9 of and Sch 1 to the Police and Criminal Evidence Act 1984, on the application of Detective Chief Inspector Atkins of the Company Fraud Department at New Scotland Yard, requiring the applicants to produce certain documents to a constable within seven days. The facts are set out in the judgment of Watkins LJ.

h

Geoffrey Shaw for the applicants.
Susan Jackson for the police.

WATKINS LJ. This application raises important issues for the first time in this court on certain provisions of the Police and Criminal Evidence Act 1984. They assume
j importance not only because it is the first occasion on which this court has had the opportunity to consider them, but also because it is essential that on the one hand the police have guidance on what is properly to be expected of them according to the provisions to which I shall be referring in a moment or so, and also that persons who are

---

a   Section 9, so far as material, is set out at p 114 c d, post
b   Schedule 1, so far as material, is set out at p 115 e to p 116 c, post

called on to obey the orders of the court under the 1984 Act shall know what it is they are entitled to know before a hearing takes place, the object of which is to enable a circuit judge, if he thinks fit so to do, to make an order for the (to use a neutral term for the moment) discovery of documents in the course of an investigation into crime.

The 1984 Act by Pt II (ss 8–23, Sch 1) makes provisions for powers of entry, search and seizure. It specially makes provision for the issue of search warrants by justices and as to access, and further as to entry and search without search warrant in appropriate circumstances. It gives power in certain other circumstances to the police to seize material which is required for the purpose of the proper investigation into crime.

It is sufficient to say of those provisions for the moment that by s 8 of the 1984 Act the power of justices to authorise entry and search of premises is extensively deployed and that by s 9 it is provided:

'(1) A constable may obtain access to excluded material or special procedure material for the purposes of a criminal investigation by making an application under Schedule 1 below and in accordance with that Schedule.

(2) Any Act (including a local Act) passed before this Act under which a search of premises for the purposes of a criminal investigation could be authorised by the issue of a warrant to a constable shall cease to have effect so far as it relates to the authorisation of searches—(a) for items subject to legal privilege; or (b) for excluded material; or (c) for special procedure material consisting of documents or records other than documents.'

The material which is relevant to the case in hand is by the 1984 Act called special procedure material. That is defined by s 14 where, so far as it is necessary to recite the provisions of it, it is provided:

'(1) In this Act "special procedure material" means—(a) material to which subsection (2) below applies . . .

(2) Subject to the following provisions of this section, this subsection applies to material, other than items subject to legal privilege and excluded material, in the possession of a person who—(a) acquired or created it in the course of any trade, business, profession or other occupation or for the purpose of any paid or unpaid office; and (b) holds it subject—(i) to an express or implied undertaking to hold it in confidence . . .'

With that background of statutory provision I turn to the application before this court. It is made on behalf of four persons. The first of them is Mr Adegbesan, who trades as Victor Leo in Erith in Kent as an accountant; secondly, Miss Lea Jack, who is a secretary employed at the Broadwater Farm Youth Association, Broadwater Farm Estate, London N17; thirdly, Mrs Osamore, a secretary employed at a day care centre on the same estate; and, fourthly, Miss Hazelwood, a secretary employed at the mothers' project at the same address as the day care centre already referred to. If those ladies are not actually employed in the sense of having a contract of employment, they hold the position so described as duly appointed persons serving the association. Each of them was the recipient of notices served, as I shall describe them, under Sch 1 to the 1984 Act. They came to be served in these circumstances. There can hardly be anyone who has not heard of the tragic events of October 1985, when riots occurred in Tottenham; in fact on this very estate, the Broadwater Farm, a police officer was killed in the course of them.

Mr Leo, as I shall call him, has the responsibility of preparing the accounts for the youth association, and likewise the day care centre and mothers' project. Those two associations are part of the youth association, so Mr Leo was at all material times obviously in a position to assist the police about the state of the accounts of these three unincorporated bodies.

There are two other persons to whom it is necessary to refer at this stage. One is Mr Carr of Messrs Ellis Carr & Co, who were and are solicitors to the four applicants, and a Mrs Kiffin. Mrs Kiffin and Mr Carr are the trustees of the Broadwater Farm Youth Association. So far as I know, they play no active part in the association in any other

a
capacity, but whether all the facts as to the activities of Mrs Kiffin with regard to these bodies are known to this court, one cannot possibly tell. What is known is that she has sued the Daily Mail for libel. It was alleged in that newspaper some while ago that public moneys, which had been donated to the association for obviously its sole use and the use of the other unincorporated bodies associated with it, had been used by Mrs Kiffin for her own personal use by the purchase of property for herself somewhere in the erstwhile British West Indies. That of course was a very grave allegation. I do not pursue it in detail

b
any further save to observe that it is the cornerstone of the action for libel.

We have amongst our papers copies of the article which appeared in the Mail on Sunday newspaper for 27 October 1985. Consequently on the publication of that article the Fraud Squad at Scotland Yard became interested in the allegations which therein appeared, and investigations into the donation of funds to the association began, and likewise into the association, if any, which Mrs Kiffin has had with those funds and

c
further, if she has had anything to do with them, whether or not she has misused them in the manner, or some such manner, as suggested in the article in the Daily Mail. That is the background to this matter, factually speaking.

It was in the course of the investigations by the police thought necessary to examine the documents which supported the annual accounts of the bodies I have already mentioned. It would seem that the police were anxious, having regard to the sensitivity

d
of prevailing circumstances, bearing in mind what had happened in the so recent past, to avoid seeking search warrants and executing them so as to search premises on the Broadwater Farm Estate. I think that is perfectly understandable. They therefore decided that they would pursue another route, and perhaps the one least likely to cause trouble, by seeking to make an application under s 9 of the 1984 Act. Section 9 brings into play Sch 1 to the Act. There are in that schedule highly significant provisions. I begin by

e
reciting such parts of Sch 1 as I think it is necessary for the purposes of this judgment to refer to:

'1. If on an application made by a constable a circuit judge is satisfied that one or other of the sets of access conditions is fulfilled, he may make an order under paragraph 4 below.

f
2. The first set of access conditions is fulfilled if—(a) there are reasonable grounds for believing—(i) that a serious arrestable offence has been committed; (ii) that there is material which consists of special procedure material or includes special procedure material and does not also include excluded material on premises specified in the application; (iii) that the material is likely to be of substantial value (whether by itself or together with other material) to the investigation in connection with which the application is made; and (iv) that the material is likely to be relevant evidence;

g
(b) other methods of obtaining the material—(i) have been tried without success; or (ii) have not been tried because it appeared that they were bound to fail; and (c) it is in the public interest, having regard—(i) to the benefit likely to accrue to the investigation if the material is obtained; and (ii) to the circumstances under which the person in possession of the material holds it, that the material should be produced or that access to it should be given.'

h
I interject here to say that counsel who appears on behalf of the applicants does not submit that the police did not bring themselves within this mode of access. Paragraph 4 provides:

'An order under this paragraph is an order that the person who appears to the circuit judge to be in possession of the material to which the application relates

j
shall—(a) produce it to a constable for him to take away; or (b) give a constable access to it, not later than the end of the period of seven days from the date of the order or the end of such longer period as the order may specify.'

The other relevant provisions of Sch 1 are:

'7. An application for an order under paragraph 4 above shall be made inter partes.

8. Notice of an application for such an order may be served on a person either by delivering it to him or by leaving it at his proper address or by sending it by post to him in a registered letter or by the recorded delivery service.

9. Such a notice may be served—(a) on a body corporate, by serving it on the body's secretary or clerk or other similar officer; and (b) on a partnership, by serving it on one of the partners . . .

11. Where notice of an application for an order under paragraph 4 above has been served on a person, he shall not conceal, destroy, alter or dispose of the material to which the application relates except—(a) with the leave of a judge; or (b) with the written permission of a constable, until (i) the application is dismissed or abandoned; or (ii) he has complied with an order under paragraph 4 above made on the application . . .

15.—(1) If a person fails to comply with an order under paragraph 4 above, a circuit judge may deal with him as if he had committed a contempt of the Crown Court.

(2) Any enactment relating to contempt of the Crown Court shall have effect in relation to such a failure as if it were such a contempt.'

It is obvious that a person such as one referred to in Sch 1 to the 1984 Act who destroys material which by an order of a circuit judge he is called on to preserve will be in contempt of court. He may be in contempt of court if he has received notice of the application for that order and, between the receipt of the notice of the application and the inter partes hearing, he destroys any of the material which is the subject of the application. But we are not called on to decide here whether that is actually so or not on a proper construction of Sch 1.

The penal provision is of course of importance because the power of the court to sentence for contempt includes the power to imprison a contemnor.

I look back now to what in fact has happened here by the use of these provisions on the part of the police. What they did was to serve on each of the applicants a notice of the application that they sought to make for the discovery of a large number of documents likely to be supportive of accounts. The notice in each case was brevity itself. It read merely:

'An application will be made at the Central Criminal Court at 10 am on Friday, 18th April, 1986 for an order under Schedule 1, Special Procedure, Police and Criminal Evidence Act, 1984.'

I take as an example only for additional reference the notice which was sent to Mrs Jack, which described her as secretary of the Broadwater Farm Youth Association. The notice was sent to her by Det Chief Superintendent Macnamara. It referred to the Broadwater Farm Youth Association and the Willan Road Day Care Centre.

The solicitors for the applicants were understandably concerned that this notice told them almost nothing about the application. They therefore sought further and better particulars. They wrote to the superintendent. They received this reply:

'I am in receipt of your letter dated 16th April, 1986. Application for Production Orders will be made in respect of Special Procedure Material relying on the first set of Access Conditions. Information to support the application will be given at the Central Criminal Court by Detective Chief Inspector Atkins of this department.'

That told the applicants very little more than they already knew. It is true it referred them to 'special procedure material', but as to what material precisely the application was related to, the answer to the query, properly directed in my estimation by the solicitors, was unhelpful. What the applicants did not know was that there was in existence at that time what is called an information in support of application for a production order. This is a document specially prepared by the police (and, I might say, in my view properly prepared by them for help in this new procedure), which sets out the bases on which the application is to be made, and describes in detail the material to which it relates.

a The material in the present case is set out in considerable detail. It refers to cash books, ledgers, bank paying-in books, correspondence and various other papers, among other things. It does not make reference to any time save that the papers required will cover a period from 1 November 1981 to the date presumably of the application.

If the applicants had been served with this information they could not possibly have complained of being unaware before the inter partes hearing of the call in detail which was made on each one of them. Counsel for the applicants has submitted that not only *b* should all the information which is contained in the information in support have been given to the applicants before the inter partes hearing, but that they should have been informed in that document of the nature of the case which prompted the making of the application. I cannot accept that but, as will appear as I proceed, his submission to the effect that the applicants received almost no information, when they should have received a great deal in the circumstances, is one which I find no difficulty whatsoever in *c* accepting. To that I shall return in a moment or so.

It is necessary to pursue the history of the matter into the inter partes hearing, as will soon become obvious. When the applications came before the Common Serjeant at the Central Criminal Court, Inspector Atkins gave evidence. Miss Jackson, counsel who appeared for the police, and Mr Shaw, counsel who appeared for the applicants, both of whom appear before us today, had the opportunity, the one of examining Mr Atkins on *d* oath and the other of cross-examining him. They availed themselves of that opportunity to the full. There is disagreement between them as to precisely what happened in the course of this hearing which took up various parts of a day. I think it is unnecessary to refer to the disagreements in detail. They emerge from differences in recollection about what occurred.

If it had been necessary to say anything about how an inter partes hearing of that kind *e* should be conducted, what, for example, the police should give by way of information at the outset to the other side, it may have been necessary further to try to resolve the differences between counsel. All I think there is need to say about that inter partes hearing is that it terminated in orders which were made in three instances not against the applicants, but against the unincorporated bodies themselves. The exception is the accountant. He was applied against, and the order was made against him in name.

f So there is a plain irregularity, incurable in my judgment, which arises from the fact, as we are told it is, that the Common Serjeant, when announcing his decision, made the orders against the three applicants to whom I have referred; but when signing the written order, he signed an order which in each instance was made against the unincorporated body. That was a most unfortunate feature of these applications by itself. That alone, it seems to me, would bring about, inevitably, a decision to quash the three *g* orders in respect of those three applicants, for they were not the recipients of a notice of application. Indeed, no application was made in respect of them. That, however, would still leave the order untouched against the accountant, Mr Leo.

Unfortunately there is, I think, an impediment in the way of maintaining the orders in respect of all four of them. It springs from the failure of the police (whom I do not criticise, seeing that this is new procedure, and they obviously seek guidance about it) to *h* appreciate that it was incumbent on them, when notifying the applicants of the application which was being made under Sch 1 to the 1984 Act, to set out in the notice, or to accompany the notice with, the details of the material which the police wished to have produced or discovered, as the case may be. It would be impossible for a person who was a recipient of such a notice as was given here to know whether he was complying with the clear provisions of para 11 of Sch 1 unless he was informed precisely of what it *j* was he was called on to preserve, and so that a judge, if asked to make the order, could effectively make an order in respect of the material sought.

Unwittingly, if the notice was not to contain such information, the person who was the recipient of an application could destroy that which he was called on to preserve, or alter or conceal it, and so bring himself within the contempt provisions in para 15 of Sch 1 to the 1984 Act. That would be a ludicrous situation, especially seeing, as I have already said, that those provisions have penal consequences which could involve in certain circumstances a loss of liberty.

Thus for the future the police should know, that although they may think there is a risk in stating in some detail what it is they are looking for of destruction of evidence, *a* that is a risk which they must bear. Their duty within these provisions is to set out in the notice which goes to a person whose assistance is required a description of all that it is sought to be produced or to be discovered. The failure here to do that goes to the very root of the procedure properly to be applied for bringing effectively into being the power of the judge to make an order under Sch 1 to the 1984 Act, and for that reason I would quash these orders. I see no alternative to doing it. *b*

There is one further issue which, having regard to what I have said, does not need to be resolved, but which I think it is appropriate to refer to, seeing that I suppose the police hereafter will have to make fresh applications for what it is they seek. I have already read a reference to a body corporate and a partnership in para 9 of Sch 1. No reference is made in the schedule at that place or any other to an unincorporated body. What then is the position of an unincorporated body? Is an unincorporated body a person for the purpose *c* of Sch 1?

In s 5 of the Interpretation Act 1978 it is stated:

'In any Act, unless the contrary intention appears, words and expressions listed in Schedule 1 to this Act are to be construed according to that Schedule.'

In Sch 1 to the 1978 Act it is provided that '"Person" includes a body of persons corporate *d* or unincorporate'.

The question is: does a contrary intention appear in Sch 1 to the 1984 Act, seeing especially that a corporate body and a partnership have merited special mention? I do not think it is necessary to decide that point. It would need much further argument than we have invited from counsel in order adequately to reach a conclusion about it. I mention it only to illuminate the fact that it exists as a problem, and also to advise the *e* police that it would be wise of them, when proceeding to obtain information from an unincorporated body, to name as the person against whom they move by way of application an officer of that body: chairman, or secretary, as the case may be.

For those reasons I would allow these applications and quash the orders.

SCHIEMANN J. I agree with the order proposed. It seems also to me clear from para *f* 11 of Sch 1 to the Police and Criminal Evidence Act 1984 that the material to which the application relates must be specified.

So far as the danger is concerned of encouraging people by giving them ample opportunity to destroy the material concerned, Parliament seems to have taken care of that point by providing in paras 12 to 14 of Sch 1 to the Act that in circumstances where a circuit judge is satisfied that notice of application for an order under para 4 may *g* seriously prejudice the investigation in question, he can issue a warrant authorising a constable to enter and search the premises, and the constable may seize and retain anything for which the search has thus been authorised.

We are dealing ex hypothesi with a different situation, and there Parliament has provided that an application for an order under para 4 shall be made inter partes. For my part I would leave open precisely what has to be specified in a notice. I do see a substantial *h* argument for saying that, where there is an inter partes hearing envisaged by Parliament, that requirement is there for the purpose of helping the circuit judge to be satisfied in relation to all of the matters set out in Sch 1, and that each party is best placed to help the circuit judge in that task if ample warning is given to the respondent of the matters which the police allege, not merely the documents in question but also the other matters of which the circuit judge has to be satisfied. We do not need to decide that on this *j* occasion, and we have not heard full argument on it.

It is clear from para 15 of Sch 1 that if a person fails to comply with the order under para 4, then he can be committed for contempt. The schedule does not in terms spell out what is to happen if there is a breach under para 11, which inevitably will take place before the order is made. Again we have not heard precise argument as to how such a *a* breach of para 11 is going to be dealt with, but we do not need to hear such argument for the purpose of the present application.

Order of certiorari granted.

Solicitors: *Ellis Carr & Co* (for the applicants); *Director of Public Prosecutions.*

b   Marc Beaumont Esq   Barrister.

R v Miller

c COURT OF APPEAL, CRIMINAL DIVISION
WATKINS LJ, FARQUHARSON J AND SIR RALPH KILNER BROWN
30, 31 JANUARY, 1 MAY 1986

Criminal evidence – Admissions and confessions – Answers and statements to police – Oppression – Requirement that confession be made voluntarily – Accused confessing while in irrational state
d *of mind – Irrational state of mind caused by police questioning – Questioning not deliberately aimed at producing irrational state of mind – Judge exercising discretion to admit confession in evidence – Whether confession made as a result of oppression – Whether confession ought to have been admitted in evidence.*

The defendant was a paranoid schizophrenic. On 12 April 1984 he was charged with the
e murder of his girlfriend. During the evening of that day and the early hours of the following morning he was interviewed by various police officers and consistently denied the murder. The next day, during an interview with another police officer, he confessed to the murder in a statement which contained a mixture of reliable and unreliable matter. Two hours later the defendant tried to retract the confession, stating that he was not his 'full self' when he made it, and reverted to his original denial of the murder. At
f his trial his counsel contended that the confession ought to be ruled inadmissible because it had been obtained as a result of protracted and oppressive interviews by police officers which had caused the defendant to suffer an episode of schizophrenic terror. There was medical evidence that, having regard to the acute state of the defendant's mental illness, the length of time he was questioned and the style of questioning had produced a state of involuntary insanity in which the defendant's language reflected a set of delusions and
g hallucinations rather than reality. The judge found that the conduct of the police did not amount to oppressive conduct and refused to exclude the evidence. The defendant was found guilty of manslaughter and the judge made an indefinite hospital order in respect of him. The defendant appealed against his conviction contending, inter alia, (i) that 'oppression' meant conduct which in fact produced an effect of oppression, so that if a police officer was aware of a suspect's mental illness but by his questioning, however
h brief, inadvertently caused a delusionary state in the suspect, that conduct constituted oppression, irrespective of the police officer's state of mind, and (ii) that if there was any doubt whether a defendant could make a free choice or whether the content of a confession was rational the confession ought to be equated with a confession obtained as the result of oppression and ruled inadmissible.

j **Held** – (1) Although questions which were deliberately asked with the intention of producing a disordered state of mind would amount to oppression, the mere fact that questions addressed to the defendant triggered off hallucinations and flights of fancy was not indicative of oppression. Having regard to the ordinary meaning of the word 'oppression', the police officer's questions did not amount to oppression (see p 127 *e* to *g*, post); *R v Prager* [1972] 1 All ER 1114 applied; *R v Isequilla* [1975] 1 All ER 77 considered.

(2) Furthermore, where a statement was made by a person while in an irrational state of mind, ie when he was beset with delusions and hallucinations, the judge was not *a* bound to rule the statement inadmissible but, instead, had a discretion to decide whether to refuse or to admit such a statement. Having regard to the fact that the jury would have had no difficulty distinguishing between the rational and irrational parts of the defendant's confession, the judge had correctly exercised his discretion to admit it to evidence. The appeal would therefore be dismissed (see p 126 *j* to p 127 *c* and p 128 *a*, post); *Sinclair v R* (1946) 73 CLR 316 and *R v Williams* [1959] NZLR 502 not followed. *b*

Notes
For the admissibility of confessions, see 11 Halsbury's Laws (4th edn) paras 410–417, and for cases on the subject, see 14(2) Digest (Reissue) 582–586, 4662–4708.

Cases referred to in judgment *c*
DPP v Ping Lin [1975] 3 All ER 175, [1976] AC 574, [1975] 3 WLR 419, HL.
Ibrahim v R [1914] AC 599, [1914–15] All ER Rep 874, PC.
R v Isequilla [1975] 1 All ER 77, [1975] 1 WLR 716, CA.
R v Marchant (27 November 1981, unreported), CA.
R v Prager [1972] 1 All ER 1114, [1972] 1 WLR 260, CA.
R v Priestly [1965] 51 Cr App R 1. *d*
R v Starecki [1960] VR 141, Vic SC.
R v Williams [1959] NZLR 502, NZ CA.
Sinclair v R (1946) 73 CLR 316, Aust HC.

Cases also cited
R v Clarke (9 March 1982, unreported), CA. *e*
R v Stewart (1972) 56 Cr App R 272, CCC.

Appeal against conviction
On 19 October 1984 in the Crown Court at Chester before Leonard J and a jury the defendant, Alvin Miller, was found not guilty of murder (by direction of the court) but guilty of manslaughter. He was made the subject of a hospital order without limit of *f* time. He appealed against conviction. The facts are set out in the judgment of the court.

Martin Thomas QC and Michael Farmer (both assigned by the Registrar of Criminal
   Appeals) for the defendant.
Philip Owen QC and Huw Daniel for the Crown.

g
Cur adv vult

1 May. The following judgment of the court was delivered.

WATKINS LJ. Sir Ralph Kilner Brown is on holiday and cannot be present. He agrees with the judgment which is about to be read. *h*
   Between 4 and 4.45 pm on 12 April 1984 24-year-old Mrs Victoria Caroline Jones (Vicky) was stabbed to death in a flat which she shared with 30-year-old Alvin Robert Miller (the defendant) at 23 Butterton Road, Rhyl, North Wales. At about 4.45 pm the defendant walked into the police station at Rhyl and said to a constable, 'I've come to report a murder. I've just got back to my flat and my girlfriend's been killed.' One of his hands was bleeding freely from a wound caused, he said, when he took a knife from his *j* girlfriend. He also said that he had had a premonition something like that would happen. He had been out for only half an hour, and when he returned she was dead.
   Very soon it was verified that she had indeed died. Six deep stab wounds, one a double entry, were observed on the front of her body as she lay on her back on a bed. A kitchen knife lay alongside her. She had been stabbed with that. It appeared to have been washed.

Taps at a sink, a matchbox, a cigarette, a ring and some clothes were stained with blood,
a as was water in a bowl. There was no evidence of a struggle and no sign that Vicky had
tried to defend herself.

In the opinion of the pathologist who examined her she could not have stabbed herself.
By whose hand then did she die? If a written confession made by the defendant was true,
undoubtedly by him. Before that was made, the police suspected the defendant, and
eventually he was charged with her murder.

b After a trial lasting five days at the Crown Court at Chester, on 19 October 1984 a jury
found it was he who had killed her. They convicted him of manslaughter, having been
directed by the judge, at the invitation of the prosecution, not to find him guilty of
murder, because he was at the material time suffering from a disease of the mind which
substantially impaired his mental responsibility for his act in killing Vicky, if that was
what they found he did. He was, and is, a sufferer from paranoid schizophrenia. She too
c had been mentally ill. The judge made him the subject of a hospital order without limit
of time.

He appeals against his conviction with the leave of this court. His grounds of appeal
are that (i) the judge was wrong to rule that his confession was admissible in evidence,
(ii) he was wrong to reject submissions made on behalf of the defendant that the
confession and other admissions made by him were inadmissible, because they were
d obtained by oppression when the defendant's free will was overcome as a result of
protracted and oppressive interviews, and the deliberate exploitation of the defendant's
mental condition by a police officer in order to obtain the confession, so that the
defendant suffered an episode of schizophrenic terror, or delusion, or both, all of which
made the confession unreliable, as Dr Trevelyan by his evidence in the voire dire
demonstrated, (iii) the judge was wrong in holding that the jury were capable of
e distinguishing between apparently rational and irrational parts of the defendant's so-
called confession, and selecting which part or parts of the confession they could safely
rely and act on to convict the defendant, and (iv) the judge gave no warning to the jury
about the difficulty of distinguishing between the rational and the irrational, and none
of the danger of, in the circumstances, acting on the defendant's confession.

The defendant and Vicky had been living together for some time before her death.
f That very afternoon they were seen in a local cafe arguing. She stormed out of it, but he
managed to make her return, whereupon she apologised to the owners for the noise she
had been making. After they left the cafe they seem to have resumed their argument,
until eventually they were seen to embrace and walk off with their arms around one
another. They went to Woolworths and bought some electrical equipment and a kitchen
knife. They visited a library. One witness claimed to have seen them going into their flat
g at 4 pm. Others claimed to have seen Vicky walking on her own in the street near the
flat between 4.10 pm and 4.20 pm. Two witnesses called for the defence said they saw
the defendant at about 4.15 pm walking away from the flat towards the town. The story
of their movements obtained from witnesses was undoubtedly, but understandably,
somewhat confused.

According to the defendant himself, he left the flat after they had both returned to it
h in order to obtain some cigarettes. It was on his return from that errand that he found
her in the dreadful condition already described.

He was kept in custody at the police station. During the evening of that day and the
early hours of the following morning he was interviewed by police officers on a number
of occasions. During every one of those interviews he stoutly denied that he had killed
Vicky.

j In the afternoon of the following day however he was interviewed for the first time by
Det Insp Cooke, who was taking a hand in the investigation after being off duty for a
while. He knew about the defendant's mental condition before he questioned him. His
initial questions were, it was asserted by the defence, in objectionable and insensitive
terms. They enabled him to enter the defendant's closed and bizarre world and caused
the defendant to experience an episode of schizophrenic terror, during which he made a

statement which contained a mixture of obviously unreliable, questionably reliable and obviously reliable matter.

The statement reads as follows:

> 'I have been going with Vicky for three and a half years and have lived with her as man and wife, although we haven't actually got married. I have been having these voices in my head for the last year from a million people whom have told me to kill Vicky. They kept going on and on and on. The voices were a percentage of a planetary force which told me to do what I did to Vicky. The voices started getting bad lately and the voices were all in pain and crunching out. Vicky had this remorse thing about her and this is what started it all. I had decided that the only way to save these people was to kill. To start with I was strong enough to resist them, but it got so bad that I had to do what they said. Yesterday I went out to buy this knife because I knew I would need it. It's all ridiculous but it made sense at the time. I bought it in Woolworths for £1·90 together with two plugs. I took the knife back to the flat and Vicky was with me. She was with me when I bought the knife. When I got back to the flat about 4 or half four, Vicky sat down on settee in the living room. I had put the knife on a tray by the sink. The voices started badly again and I knew it was time to end her life to save the people. I picked the knife up and walked towards her. I touched her calmly with the knife in a playful way and this made her smile. I didn't want to frighten her and she smiled because she thought I was playing around. I did it quickly then—the knifing. I stuck it in her quickly and I think I stuck it in her about five times. She took it very well I thought and I picked her up and took her to the bedroom. As she moved her hand she knocked the knife and I cut my thumb. I laid her on the bed and stayed with her. She was white and she said she felt pain in her chest. After about five minutes she went very white and died. I got up and put the knife in the bowl to clean the blood away. I put the knife back on the bed alongside her nearest the door. I then came to the police station to confess. When I came in I changed my mind because I thought there was a chance. I have not had the voices since. They are satisfied now Vicky has gone. Everything else I've said is there.'

That is for the most part a repetition of what the defendant had told Det Insp Cooke, who was accompanied by Det Con Blythin, in answer to his questions shortly before this written statement was made.

The line of questioning objected to and which was said to have triggered off a schizophrenic episode, in order to be fully comprehended, has to be set out verbatim. It was, so far as material, as follows:

> '*Q.* Let us get rid of doubt: are you religious? *A.* Yes.
> *Q.* What religion? *A.* Methodist.
> *Q.* Did you go to church? *A.* No.
> *Q.* What happens when people die? *A.* They go home.
> *Q.* Where is that? *A.* Somewhere else.
> *Q.* Do you think Vicky is listening? *A.* Yes.
> *Q.* Do you think she would like the lies about her death? What would Vicky say? *A.* I Don't know.
> *Q.* Vicky would be able to tell us what happened; but you can't turn the clock back? *A.* No, I didn't murder her.
> *Q.* What do you call murder? *A.* I speculate, I hear voices and speculate.
> *Q.* When did you hear these voices? *A.* A few days ago. I don't want to talk about it. I didn't do it. I don't know how it happened.
> *Q.* You caused Vicky's death didn't you? *A.* No, I came back to the flat and found her.
> *Q.* Would you think Vicky would want you now? You only said maybe when we

a

just asked you; why only maybe? *A.* I had a paranoid symptom. I did do it. I just turned on her. I saw millions of people's lives in her hands. I saw a percentage number.

Q. Was she threatening the lives of these people? *A.* Yes, I saw people in front of me and she was responsible. She was on this planet and something stupid happened. I should have knocked the symptom out of my head.

b

Q. Let me stop you there for a moment. Somewhere around this stage, at what sort of speed was he speaking at? *A.* Normal pace.

Q. Normal pace. I see, very well, carry on.

Q. Are you saying that someone, through you, killed her, another force? *A.* Yes, she was a planetary risk. She was asking me to kill her in her subconscious brain. The screaming in my head had gone on for too long and she was responsible. It was the inter-planetary signs.

c

Q. How many times did you stab her? *A.* Seven times. I went to the police station and just said I found her dead. Arbitrised humans and small molecular people were screaming at me. My body has been breaking up for the last year. Our relationship was broken. People in my head were yelling out and telling me to kill her, she heard them as well. My birthday came and a little town was telling me for their sake to kill her, millions of lives depended on it. There was trouble in the town and I turned

d

and said I couldn't take it no longer. I pulled the knife out and killed her and lay her on the bed. I then went to the police station, I just wasn't strong.'

Of those questions and answers Dr Trevelyan, who had been treating the defendant for his illness, observed in the voire dire at the trial:

e

'Q. Another word that is sometimes used in this context is "voluntary", where a person makes voluntary admissions having regard to his character and his illness, do you have any comment to make about that type of questioning that was involved? *A.* I think it was inevitable that the length of time for which he was questioned and the style with which he was questioned, I say that with no criticism intended, given his, the acuteness of his, mental illness, would have produced a state of involuntary insanity in which words and phrases he said would reflect almost entirely the set of delusions and hallucinations that he was suffering from rather than ordinary reality.

f

Does that answer you?'

A couple of hours or so after making his written confession, the defendant at his request saw the two detectives again. He was in a very agitated state but, although his speech was somewhat difficult to understand, he made it plain to them that he wished to retract his confession. He said he was not his full self when he made it and that what he

g

had said in the beginning was the truth. He had gone out to buy cigarettes and had found Vicky dead on his return.

Counsel for the defendant in the voire dire strove to persuade the judge to exclude the confession made orally and in writing from becoming evidence, sensing that if he were successful in doing so the defendant would be altogether acquitted, seeing that counsel for the prosecution told the court that the confession was regarded by the Crown as

h

central to the case brought against the defendant. Counsel for the prosecution has never resiled from that position.

In a reasoned judgment rejecting the submissions of counsel for the defendant the judge observed finally:

j

'The statement again contains what, on the face of it, appear to be factual statements interspersed with what appears to be delusionary material. Counsel for the defendant has sought to persuade me that the whole of the evidence should be excluded because fundamentally there is no basis on which the jury could discriminate between what I regard as being the two kinds of material. It is true that the doctor said that that was so. He also said that there were the three

possibilities (to which I have referred to again) for those words which would appear
to be words of confession. I do not believe, as I have indicated previously, that a jury   *a*
properly directed and in possession of the necessary material would have difficulty
about sorting the one out from the other. It seems to me that one can almost tell
which is delusionary and which is factual. They will have to be very carefully
directed that even in relation to what appears to be factual material they must be
entirely sure that it is reliable before they can act on it. I can see no basis for saying
that the confession was obtained by oppression having regard to the definition of   *b*
"oppression" as it is contained in particular in the judgment of Lord Lane CJ in *R v
Isequilla* [1975] 1 All ER 77, [1975] 1 WLR 716. I cannot say that this is so extreme
a case that it would be proper to exclude the confession because of the mental
condition of the accused. I do not think it is that sort of case. I think that the jury
will have to make up their minds about it. I accordingly reject the submissions by
counsel for the defendant and I have come to the conclusion that I am satisfied   *c*
beyond reasonable doubt that this confession was not obtained by oppressive conduct
by the police and I am satisfied that the probative value is not so small in comparison
with the prejudicial value of the evidence as to make it necessary for me to withhold
the material from the jury. They are the proper tribunal in my judgment to resolve
these issues of fact.'

Earlier in his judgment the judge had referred to the basis on which counsel for the   *d*
defendant sought to exclude the evidence of confession. Firstly counsel relied on the
principle explained in *R v Prager* [1972] 1 All ER 1114, [1972] 1 WLR 260 that statements
obtained by oppression or oppressive conduct are inadmissible. The judge clearly ruled
against him on that. Secondly counsel for the defendant sought support from what was
said by Lord Widgery CJ in *R v Isequilla* [1975] 1 All ER 77 at 83–84, [1975] 1 WLR 716
at 722–723:   *e*

'That is not an end of the matter because he takes a second and related, though
independent point. He submits that if one forgets about the gun and the form of
the arrest, there is a wholly independent principle, namely that if the suspect's
mental state is such that he is deprived of the capacity to make a free choice whether
to confess or not, then any confession which he makes is necessarily not a voluntary   *f*
confession because it was not supported by the capacity to make a voluntary choice.
This is a relatively novel submission, although it is supported by certain
Commonwealth authorities and is hinted at, if no more than that, in Cross on
Evidence ((3rd edn, 1967) pp 450, 451) where the learned author says: "A good deal
of Commonwealth authority supports the view that a confession will be inadmissible
if obtained at a time when the accused's mind was so unbalanced as to render it   *g*
wholly unsafe to act upon it. There is no clear English authority on this point, but,
if one of the reasons for excluding confessions is the danger that they may be
untrustworthy, it would be in accordance with principle to exclude a confession
made by someone whose mental state was such as to render his utterances completely
unreliable. It is, however, difficult to formulate a governing principle, and it is
possible that, in England, the matter will be treated as one of judicial discretion."   *h*
We would accept that summary of the position as it stands at the present time, and
we would recognise that one must not regard Professor Cross's phrase in which he
describes the suspect as being in a condition where his utterances are completely
unreliable as being the sole and only test in these matters. It may be in time other
tests will be developed, but however one reads that and however one seeks to
anticipate further developments of this kind, we find it quite impossible to say on   *j*
the evidence in this case that the mental state of the appellant at the time of the
confession which amounted to no more than the fact he was sobbing and frightened
and later became hysterical was within any sort of range of the test Professor Cross
had in mind. Of course, in an extreme case where a man is a mental defective, it
would be no doubt absolutely right to rule out evidence of his confession as being

a   wholly unreliable. Not only does the appellant not come in that class, he does not come anywhere near that class. We do not need to consider developments on that aspect of counsel for the appellant's submission but content ourselves with saying this particular appellant could not come within this principle however widely it was applied.'

b   For a reason unknown to us, unless it was thought that ss 76 and 78 of the Police and Criminal Evidence Act 1984 rendered reference to it no longer necessary, the extract from *Cross on Evidence* referred to has been omitted from the latest edition of that work (6th edn, 1985). Be that as it may, the judge said of it:

c   'Those concluding words, I am bound to say, seem to me to embody what I understand to be the position, which is that where a court is of the view that so bad is the mental condition of a defendant that his confession really is wholly unreliable then the court excludes that confession not on any strict legal ground but as a matter of discretion.'

So directing himself he came to the conclusion as appears in the final paragraph of his judgment, that he could not say that this was so extreme a case that it would be proper to exclude the confession because of the appellant's mental condition. He did not think it was that sort of case.

d   Counsel for the defendant challenges the rulings of the judge which, he submits, originate in part from misconceptions of the law governing the admissibility of confessions. He says, rightly in our view, that the primary task of a judge in his conduct of a voire dire where admissibility is the issue is to decide whether a confession is inadmissible simply because it was not voluntary.

If, as a finding of fact, the conclusion is that the confession was not voluntary, the *e*   judge must exclude it. He has no discretion in the matter. If to the contrary, the confession becomes admissible, subject to the discretion of the judge to exclude it in, for example, the interests of a defendant having a fair trial.

In *DPP v Ping Lin* [1975] 3 All ER 175 [1976] AC 574 the House of Lords held that the question whether a statement was voluntary was basically one of fact and that in determining admissibility the trial judge should apply the test in *Ibrahim v R* [1914] AC *f*   599 at 609, [1914–15] All ER Rep 874 at 877, in a commonsense way, asking himself whether it has been proved that the statement was voluntary, in the sense that it was not obtained by fear of prejudice or hope of advantage excited or held out by a person in authority. Proof of impropriety in the conduct of that person is not necessary to render the statement inadmissible.

In *R v Isequilla* reference was made to *R v Prager* as establishing that interrogation by *g*   police officers carried on to the point of oppression may be held to have destroyed the will of a suspect and prevented a confession from being held to be voluntary.

In *R v Prager* [1972] 1 All ER 1114 at 1119, [1972] 1 WLR 260 at 266 this court adopted Lord MacDermott's definition of 'oppressive questioning' which was:

h   'questioning which by its nature, duration, or other attendant circumstances (including the fact of custody) excites hopes (such as the hope of release) or fears, or so affects the mind of the subject that his will crumbles and he speaks when otherwise he would have stayed silent'.

and the definition of 'oppression' provided by Sachs J in *R v Priestly* (1965) 51 Cr App R 1, in which he referred to the characteristics of the person who made the statement as one of the many elements on which depended whether or not there had been oppression.

j   The judge was shown the authorities on oppression. He was no doubt well aware of them anyway. But, so it is contended, he approached the factual issue in this case in the wrong way. He regarded it as though it had to be shown that the interrogating officer had improperly and consciously so questioned the defendant as to cause him to confess when otherwise he would not have done, and he instanced the previous interview as indicative of the defendant's capacity to maintain denials of guilt over fairly protracted periods of time. What he should have recognised and did not was that it can be oppressive for a police officer to excite a delusionary state in a suspect whom he knows is mentally ill, even if this is done inadvertently. What is in the mind of the police officer is irrelevant. It is sufficient if his questioning, no matter how brief, excites the delusionary state and is therefore in fact oppressive. The word oppression includes many forms of conduct which produce an effect of oppression. In this context s 76(8) of the 1984 Act, it is said, is worthy of note.

Before giving our response to this submission it is, we think, convenient to examine the other main error of law which is said to have wrongly guided the judge into admitting the confession. It is not the law, it is submitted, that although the delusionary state has arisen without oppression from anyone, it is a matter for the discretion of the judge whether a confession made by a person when in that state be admitted to evidence. The judge in this case clearly stated he had such a discretion. He was misguided, so it is said, in that. He should have asked himself whether the prosecution had proved that the defendant in his delusionary state had the capacity to make a sensible choice whether to confess, and whether it had been proved that the confession had been rational, springing from reason and not delusion. If there was doubt whether the defendant could make a free choice or whether the content of the confession was rational, the confession is involuntary, it is inadmissible and must, equating it with a confession obtained by oppression for example, be so ruled to be. Here the medical evidence was all one way, coming as it did from one source, namely the psychiatrist called on behalf of the defendant. There was no reason why it should not have been accepted, and consequently none for the refusal of the judge to rule the confession inadmissible.

In any event, so it is argued, even if the judge on proper grounds had ruled the confession admissible, he should, in his discretion, have excluded it, because its prejudicial effect outweighed its probative value. We found that a surprising argument in the circumstances of Vicky's death, and have no hesitation in saying we believe it to be ill founded.

We were referred to ss 77 and 78 of the 1984 Act, which relate to confessions by a mentally handicapped person and exclusion of unfair evidence, but derive no assistance from their provisions for our present purpose.

There is no English authority for the claim advanced by counsel for the defendant that in a case where the only consideration is that a person is in a disordered state of mind, i e one beset with delusions and hallucinations and makes a confession, the first task of the judge is to decide whether the confession was strictly speaking voluntary.

He referred us to R v Williams [1959] NZLR 502, in which it was held that before any admission or confession can be tendered in evidence in criminal cases the Crown must discharge the onus of satisfying the court that it was a free and voluntary one made by the accused in such a proper physical and mental state as is required at common law for its admissibility.

We were also asked to pay regard to two Australian cases, namely Sinclair v R (1946) 73 CLR 316 and R v Starecki [1960] VR 141, in which in some of the judgments are statements apparently supportive of counsel's argument for the defendant. That of Dixon J in Sinclair v R we have found particularly instructive, and we note that it was held by the whole court that a confession is not necessarily inadmissible as evidence on a criminal trial because it appears that the prisoner making it was at the time of unsound mind, and by reason of his mental condition exposed to the liability of confusing the products of his disordered imagination or fancy with fact (Sinclair was a schizophrenic).

Whether the true construction to be placed on these New Zealand and Australian cases is that in those countries a judge is bound to rule inadmissible a confession obtained when an accused's mind was so disordered as to render it wholly unsafe to act on it, thus equating it with an involuntary confession as explained in DPP v Ping Lin, is not entirely clear. But assuming that to be the effect of them, we are not persuaded that they represent the law in this country.

As recently as 27 November 1981 in R v Marchant (unreported) this court, of which *a* Kilner Brown J and I were members, acted on the basis which we believe is correct in law, that a judge here has a discretion whether to refuse or to admit to evidence a confession which came from a mind which at the time was possibly irrational and what the defendant said may have been the product of delusion and hallucinations. There may be cases (*R v Marchant* was ruled in this court to be one) where on the evidence discretion can only be exercised in one way, namely in favour of excluding the confession. There are others in which reaching a decision one way or the other will be far less simple.

b In the present case the judge had in this respect no easy task to perform. It is clear to us however that he brought his judgment to bear on it with very great care. We find it impossible to accept that he wrongly exercised his discretion to admit the confession. In saying that we reject the suggestion that the judge, possibly because, so it is further suggested, he had formed a mildly hostile view of him, erroneously evaluated the evidence of the psychiatrist. We see no justification for that criticism. Furthermore, we *c* cannot say, as we are invited to, that he was wrong in deciding that the jury was incapable of distinguishing between what was fact and fancy in the written confession.

So we return to the question of oppression. It seems to us to be implicit from the judge's finding on oppression, although he referred to *R v Isequilla* in this context when possibly he meant to refer to *R v Prager*, which earlier in his judgment he had quoted on the subject of oppression, that he declined to hold there had been a deliberate attempt in *d* interrogation to excite a delusionary state in the appellant. That is not, counsel for the defendant says, fatal to his argument on this point because, as I have said before, he contends that no matter what prompted the police officer to ask the offending questions, if the effect of them was to bring disorder into the mind when previously there was none, the defendant was by that oppressed. Only oppressive conduct could, it is argued, have produced that kind of oppressive state.

e It is an ingenious argument, but it fails to convince us that the police officer's questions amounted to a form of oppression within the ordinary meaning of that word, and as was contemplated as oppressive conduct rendering a confession inadmissible in the cases cited on this subject both here and to the judge. We know of no other cases of assistance on this point. We think the judge was right when he said there was no basis for saying that the confession had been obtained by oppression, he earlier in his judgment having *f* examined the whole process of interrogation in one interview after another.

It may well be, as the psychiatrist stated, that in all probability some of the questions triggered off hallucinations and flights of fancy, but that by itself is not, in our view, indicative of oppression. Whether questions skilfully and deliberately asked so as to produce that kind of disordered mind could amount to oppression is an altogether different matter. The judge did not find that such obviously wicked conduct had taken *g* place. Had he done so, and been satisfied that the questions had the effect sought, we fail to see how he could have avoided ruling out the confession, whether this had to be considered on the basis of no discretion to do otherwise or as an exercise of discretion.

Finally we examine the contention that the judge did not warn the jury of the difficulties involved in seeking to place any reliance on the confession. There is, we find, no substance in this complaint. Early in his summing up he said:

h

> 'The defendant in evidence maintains that it was an untrue confession, and the defence case with regard to this matter is that the form of the questions which were put to the accused at the interview on the Friday afternoon, were such as to have effect of triggering off, I quote the words that were used on more than one occasion, triggering off the defendant's undoubted state of paranoid schizophrenia, with the *j* result, say the defence, that what was said by way of a confession is wholly unreliable. That is the way the defence put it. You and I, members of the jury, will examine together this contention and you can consider it when you retire to consider your verdict. I shall go into some detail about it to try and help you, but will you bear in mind that you must not act on the confession unless you are sure that it is safe to do so, safe to do so because it is true or essentially true, at any rate, not necessarily true

in every detail but essentially true, and a confession on which you can safely rely. If
you are satisfied that that confession is a reliable and true confession then that really   *a*
may be the end of the matter and you will find the defendant guilty.'

Later he advised the jury to look at the confession very carefully in the light of what
had been said about it. Towards the end of his summing up the judge spent some time
reminding the jury of the evidence of the psychiatrist, which bore in a substantial way
on the reliability or otherwise of the confession. He ended the subject by saying:

b

'I think I am right in thinking I should take you through the evidence with
regard to that question of the confession. It is a matter for you and I have explained
the principles which you should apply and the assistance you will no doubt get from
your own common sense and knowledge of the world and of people and the way
they act and behave, supplemented, of course, by the specialist evidence you have
about this type of person, how they act and behave. I have not gone in any detail,   *c*
nor do I propose to, into the mental condition of Miss Jones.'

The warnings to the jury to use much care in their consideration of the confession
were, in our view, more than adequate. The jury must have been well aware of the need
for caution in this respect.

The appeal will be dismissed.

d

Appeal dismissed.

Solicitors: *Director of Public Prosecutions.*

                                                         Marc Beaumont Esq   Barrister.

R v Oxford Justices, ex parte D

QUEEN'S BENCH DIVISION (CROWN OFFICE LIST)
WAITE J
19 JUNE 1986

Child – Welfare – Child in care of local authority – Access by putative father – Right of putative father to access – Order regarding right of access to child – Jurisdiction to make order – Illegitimate child – Application by putative father to court for access – Whether court having jurisdiction to entertain application – Guardianship of Minors Act 1971, ss 9(1)(b), 14(1).

A putative father is entitled under ss 9(1)(b)[a] and 14(1)[b] of the Guardianship of Minors Act 1971 to apply for access to his illegitimate child notwithstanding that the child is in the care of a local authority, since ss 9 and 14 confer jurisdiction on the court to make custody and access orders regarding a child, whether illegitimate or not, on the application of a parent, whether lawful or not. It follows that the putative father is entitled to issue a summons for access in addition to a summons for custody of the child (see p 131 b c h j, post).

R v Oxford City Justices, ex p H [1974] 2 All ER 356 applied.
Re K (an infant) [1972] 3 All ER 769 explained.

Notes

For order regarding the right of access to illegitimate children, see 24 Halsbury's Laws (4th edn) paras 541–543.

For the Guardianship of Minors Act 1971, ss 9, 14, see 6 Halsbury's Statutes (4th edn) 310, 319.

Cases referred to in judgment

A v Liverpool City Council [1981] 2 All ER 385, [1982] AC 363, [1981] 2 WLR 948, HL.
K (an infant), Re, Re M (an infant), Hertfordshire CC v H [1972] 3 All ER 769, DC.
M (an infant), Re [1955] 2 All ER 911, [1955] 2 QB 479, [1955] 3 WLR 320, CA.
R v Oxford City Justices, ex p H [1974] 2 All ER 356, [1975] 1 QB 1, [1974] 3 WLR 1, DC.
W v Hertfordshire CC [1985] 2 All ER 301, [1985] AC 791, [1985] 2 WLR 892, HL.

Application for judicial review

D, the father of an illegitimate child, applied, with the leave of Mann J granted on 4 October 1985, for an order of mandamus directed to the clerk of the Oxford Justices requiring him to exercise his jurisdiction to issue a summons under s 9 of the Guardianship of Minors Act 1971 on the applicant's complaint seeking access to his illegitimate daughter and that the justices hear and determine the complaint. The facts are set out in the judgment.

Leo Curran for the father.
Simon Readhead for the clerk to the justices.
Peter Singer as amicus curiae.

---

a   Section 9(1), so far as material, provides: 'The court may, on the application of the mother or father of a minor . . . make such order regarding . . . (b) the right of access to the minor of his mother or father, as the court thinks fit having regard to the welfare of the minor and to the conduct and wishes of the mother and father.'

b   Section 14(1), so far as material, provides: 'Subject to the provisions of this section, subsection (1) of section 9 of this Act shall apply in relation to a minor who is illegitimate as it applies in relation to a minor who is legitimate, and references in that subsection . . . to the father or mother or parent of a minor shall be construed accordingly.'

WAITE J. This application for judicial review concerns the vexed topic, which has often troubled the courts, of the rights of the putative father of an illegitimate child regarding *a* custody and access when the child is in the care of a local authority. It is by coincidence exactly 14 years today since Latey J in *Re K (an infant)* [1972] 3 All ER 769 at 773 drew attention to the anomaly that whereas a putative father is given the right of application for custody of, or access to, his illegitimate child by s 9 of the Guardianship of Minors Act 1971 there is no matching provision in the statutory code of the Children Act legislation which recognises him as a person having any parental rights or duties at all. *b* The same judge there expressed the hope that when there was further legislation in this area the position might be made clear. There has since then been a whole tide of legislation in precisely this area, including the Children Act 1975 and the Child Care Act 1980, but none of it has reached high enough to come to the aid of a putative father, who is still left like a beached whale on the shore where the law first deposited him in 1971.

The facts are not in controversy and can be shortly stated. The applicant is aged 69 and *c* for a number of years had an association with a lady who bore him a child, born on 7 September 1977 and thus now nearly nine years of age, to whom I will refer as 'the minor'. The association between the parents has broken down. On 11 February 1981, the juvenile court made an order under s 1 of the Children and Young Persons Act 1969, committing the minor to the care of the local authority. The father was, for a time, allowed to enjoy access to the minor after she had been placed with foster parents, but a *d* time came in March 1982 when access was stopped. The local authority made it plain that the reason for this was not any personal objection to the character of the father but the fact that the access upset the child, perhaps because it brought back unhappy memories of the time when her parents were together. The father was, however, permitted at least to maintain contact with the minor by writing her letters and cards and so on to be delivered to her at the foster home. Matters continued on this basis until *e* August 1984, when the local authority told the father that they were intending to apply to free the minor for adoption and that the adoptive couple whom they had in mind were the same foster parents with whom she had been originally placed.

A formal application to free for adoption was made by the local authority on 13 November 1984, but its hearing was held over in view of the following events. On 14 November, the father took out wardship proceedings with a view to restoring him to *f* access to the minor and preventing the proposed adoption going any further. At an early stage of those proceedings the local authority applied to discharge them for want of jurisdiction. That objection prevailed (after a brief adjournment while the decision of the House of Lords was awaited in *W v Hertfordshire CC* [1985] 2 All ER 301, [1985] AC 791). That left the father with only one remaining remedy to pursue.

On 23 July 1985 he made a complaint to the magistrates' court seeking against the *g* mother of the child an order for custody and against both the mother and the local authority an order for access. The response of the clerk to the justices to the father's application for summonses to be issued in pursuance of those complaints was as follows. The summons was allowed to issue in relation to the claim for custody. A summons was, however, refused in relation to the claim for access on the ground that the magistrates had no jurisdiction to entertain it. *h*

In these proceedings the father moves by leave for judicial review of that refusal. In the course of the reasons which the justices' clerk has supplied in an affidavit resisting the claim, he states that his view (that the domestic court had no jurisdiction to make an order for access) had been reached after consideration of *Re K (an infant)*.

The statutory background to this application has been most helpfully and succinctly summarised by the father's counsel. It is common ground between him and counsel who *j* appeared as amicus curiae that apart from any rights the father may have under the 1971 Act, all doors to an access claim designed to enable him to see his daughter again are closed. He cannot invoke the wardship jurisdiction because that will not prevail against the statutory code of the 1969 Act (see *A v Liverpool City Council* [1981] 2 All ER 385,

[1982] AC 363). He cannot claim to be a 'parent' for the purposes of the 1969 Act when
a the reasoning of the Court of Appeal in *Re M (an infant)* [1955] 2 All ER 911, [1955] 2 QB
479, in the clearly analogous context of the adoption legislation, is applied to it. He is
expressly excluded from the definition of 'parent' in the 1980 Act; and when (in
attempted mitigation of the breadth of power left in local authorities' hands by the
decision in *A v Liverpool City Council*) that Act was amended in 1983 to introduce a
detailed procedure and code of practice for access by parents to children in care, this
b exclusion was maintained. He is similarly prevented by express definition from claiming
to be treated as a person with parental rights and duties under the 1975 Act.

The father's rights are accordingly limited entirely to those conferred by ss 9 and 14 of
the 1971 Act, under which the court, including a magistrates' court, has jurisdiction to
make an order regarding the legal custody of, or parental access to, a minor, whether
illegitimate or not, on the application of a parent, whether lawful or not.

c Precisely such an application was made by a putative father in *Re K (an infant)* [1972] 3
All ER 769. Magistrates had made a limited access order in his favour, against which the
local authority successfully appealed to the Divisional Court of the Family Division. The
grounds for upsetting the magistrates' order were stated by Payne J in terms with which
Latey J agreed as follows (at 772):

d 'Bearing in mind the existence of the order under s 2 of the Children Act 1948, it
seems to me that the justices in the circumstances of this case had no alternative but
to decline the application of the father and to leave the discretion with regard to
access to the local authority. It may be—argument has been addressed to us on this
basis—that one could go further and say that the justices had no power to make an
order on such an application in any event. For myself I would prefer to leave that
e second limb of the argument until some later occasion, should it arise, when full
argument on both sides may be addressed to the court.'

The first part of those remarks, without (unfortunately) the qualifying disclaimer in the
second part of any intention to pronounce on jurisdiction, was in due course reproduced
in the headnote when the case was reported. The phrase 'no alternative' is language
f which does, certainly, at least suggest strongly an absence of jurisdiction; and no doubt
that is how it was interpreted by the justices' clerk in the present case. I am satisfied,
however, that the remarks in *Re K (an infant)* were not intended to be interpreted in that
sense. Nor were they so interpreted when a similar point came before the court in *R v
Oxford City Justices, ex p H* [1974] 2 All ER 356, [1975] 1 QB 1, where it was held that
magistrates were wrong to have dismissed for want of jurisdiction a putative father's
g application for custody of an illegitimate child in local authority care.

With the utmost respect to the remarks of Bagnall J in *R v Oxford City Justices, ex p H*
[1974] 2 All ER 356 at 360–361, [1975] 1 QB 1 at 8, remarks doubtless made in the
course of a courteous endeavour to distinguish the difficulties to which the wording of
the judgment in *Re K (an infant)* had given rise, I do not see how any distinction of
principle can be drawn, so far as pure jurisdiction is concerned, between a putative
h father's application for custody of a child in care and the same person's application for
access.

Counsel appearing as amicus curiae, to whom I am indebted for a full and helpful
argument, has not felt able to defend the refusal of a summons to enforce the access
complaint for want of jurisdiction as a valid exercise of the clerk's discretion. For the
reasons already stated, I agree that the father is entitled to have such a summons issued in
j addition to his summons for custody. An order for mandamus will therefore issue as
prayed.

This is, of course, a decision of pure law on a bare question of jursidiction. It has not
involved any consideration of the merits of the father's access application at all. Those
merits will in due course have to be considered, for whatever strength or weakness they

may have, by the magistrates when they hear the evidence and investigate all the circumstances of the case in detail.

a

Order accordingly.

Solicitors: *Cole & Cole*, Oxford (for the father); *P J Floyd*, Oxford (for the clerk to the justices); *Official Solicitor.*

b

Bebe Chua   Barrister.

Re Briamore Manufacturing Ltd (in liq)

c

CHANCERY DIVISION (COMPANIES COURT)

HOFFMANN J

15 MAY 1986

Discovery – Production of documents – List of documents – Mistake in list – Privileged documents mistakenly included in list of documents for production – Privileged documents inspected and *d* *copied by other side – Whether too late to correct mistake – Whether production of documents should be ordered – RSC Ord 24, rr 5, 9.*

In proceedings to set aside an alleged fraudulent preference the liquidator's solicitor made a mistake in his list of documents for discovery prepared under RSC Ord 24, r 5 by including in the list of documents which he did not object to produce a number of letters *e* obtained from third parties for the purposes of the litigation and for which privilege could have been claimed and which should have been included in the list of documents which he objected to produce. The respondent's solicitor was shown copies of the privileged documents when carrying out inspection pursuant to Ord 24, r 9 at the offices of the liquidator's solicitor, and he read them, made notes of their contents and had a photocopy of at least one of them made for him. Although the liquidator's solicitor *f* informed the respondent the following day about the mistake, the respondent's solicitor nevertheless made a formal request for copies of the privileged documents. Ten days later the liquidator's solicitor served a revised list in which the documents in question had been transferred to the list of documents which he objected to produce. On an application by the respondent, the registrar refused to order delivery of copies of the privileged documents. The respondent appealed.

g

Held – Inspection in the sense of an examination of the privileged documents having already taken place, the respondent's solicitor had acquired knowledge of their contents and accordingly he could give secondary evidence of the contents of the documents and the liquidator could be examined on them. It would therefore be illogical to deny the court access to the best evidence, which was the documents themselves. Furthermore, *h* since it was clear from RSC Ord 24, r 9 that the right to take copies was ancillary to the right to inspect, it would be illogical that the respondent's solicitor, having carried out the inspection but not having gone through the physical process of making copies at the time, should be disentitled from obtaining the best evidence of the documents he had seen. It followed therefore that it was too late for the liquidator to correct the mistake in the list and consequently the respondent was entitled to the copies sought. The appeal *j* would therefore be allowed and production of the documents ordered (see p 134 *d* to *h*, post).

Semble. Until inspection has taken place, there must be a right to correct a list of documents for discovery even if only by notifying the other side that there are documents which the litigant objects to produce (see p 134 *b*, post).

Notes

a   For the list of documents for discovery, see 13 Halsbury's Laws (4th edn) para 40.
     For production for inspection of documents, see ibid paras 56–57, and for cases on the
     subject, see 18 Digest (Reissue) 70–72, 490–505.

Cases cited

     Calcraft v Guest [1898] 1 QB 759, [1895–9] All ER Rep 346, CA.
b   *Mutter v Eastern and Midlands Rly Co* (1888) 38 Ch D 92, CA.
     Ormerod Grierson & Co v St George's Ironworks Ltd [1905] 1 Ch 505, CA.

Motion

     By notice of motion dated 30 April 1986 the respondent, Moonbridge Shippers Ltd,
     sought an order (1) discharging so much of the order of Mr Registrar Bradburn made on
c   15 April 1986 as provided that no order should be made on para 2 of the respondent's
     summons dated 20 November 1985 for delivery of copies of certain documents listed by
     the applicant, Patrick Walter John Hartigan, the liquidator of Briamore Manufacturing
     Ltd, in his list of documents for discovery dated 3 October 1985 and (2) substituting
     therefor an order that the liquidator provide to the respondent under RSC Ord 29, r 9
     and/or Ord 66, r 3 copies of those documents. The facts are set out in the judgment.

d
     John Sessions for the respondent.
     Hazel Williamson for the liquidator.

     HOFFMANN J. The question which arises on this motion is whether the liquidator in
     proceedings to set aside what is alleged to be a fraudulent preference can correct a mistake
e   which his solicitor made in the preparation of his list of documents for discovery or
     whether it is now too late. The mistake was that the list included in Part 1 of Sch 1 of the
     list of documents a number of letters which were obtained from third parties for the
     purposes of the litigation and for which privilege could have been claimed. They ought
     properly to have been inserted in Part 2 of the schedule.
     The list was dated 3 October 1985, and on 17 October the respondent's solicitor came
f   to the offices of the liquidator's solicitors to carry out inspection pursuant to RSC Ord 24,
     r 9. He was shown these privileged documents, he read them and made some notes of
     their contents. One at least he found so interesting that he procured a copy to be made
     on the liquidator's solicitors' photocopier. There is some dispute about whether he told
     the partner in question that this was what he had done, but nothing presently arises on
     that matter. He went back to his office with his notes and his photocopy. On the
g   following day the liquidator's solicitor telephoned to tell him that a mistake had been
     made and to say that the documents in question were privileged. Notwithstanding this,
     the respondent's solicitors on 21 October made a formal request for copies of those
     documents. On 31 October the liquidator's solicitors served a revised list in which the
     documents had been transferred from Part 1 to Part 2 of Sch 1.
     This matter came before the court on a summons to the registrar for delivery of copies
h   of the privileged documents, on which the registrar made no order, and this motion is to
     set aside the registrar's order and for an order that copies be delivered. RSC Ord 24, r 5
     deals with the form of the list which a litigant is obliged to deliver and r 5(2) says that if
     it is desired to claim that any documents are privileged from production, the claim must
     be made in the list of documents with a sufficient statement of the grounds of privilege.
     No such claim was made in the list as first delivered. What the respondent's solicitor was
j   therefore doing on 17 October was exercising his right under r 9, which says that a party
     who has served a list of documents on any other party must allow the other party to
     inspect the documents referred to in the list, other than any which he objects to produce,
     and to take copies thereof.
     On the day when inspection took place no objection to production had been made
     either in accordance with r 5 or in any other way. Objection was made between the

inspection and the request for copies, and the question is whether by that time it was too late to correct the error.

It has been submitted on behalf of the respondent that, once the list had been delivered, it was the list for the purposes of r 9 and therefore inexorably there was a right to inspect and take copies. The rule makes no provision for an amendment to the list. I doubt whether the irrevocability of the list could be maintained in this extreme form. It seems to me that, at any rate until inspection has taken place, common sense would suggest that there must be a right to correct the list even if only by notifying the other side that there are documents which the litigant objects to produce. It is noticeable that the objection which is referred to in r 9 is confined neither to objections stated in the list nor indeed to objections on the ground of privilege. Under r 13 the court is not to make any order for the production of documents for inspection unless the court is of opinion that the order is necessary either for disposing fairly of the cause or matter or for saving costs. It is therefore quite conceivable that there may be an objection to production on the grounds that production would not be justifiable within that rule and not simply on the ground of privilege.

The problem in this case, however, is that inspection, in the sense of an examination of the documents, had already taken place. The solicitor had acquired knowledge of their contents and had made some notes of what they said. It is accepted that he could give secondary evidence of the contents of those documents, that he could produce the photocopy which he had made and that the liquidator could be cross-examined on them. That, on the face of it, suggests that unless an order for the production of copies is made the court will be in the position of receiving evidence about the contents of the documents and being able to act on that evidence but not have access to the best evidence, which is the documents themselves. That seems to me to be an illogical position. If the policy of the conduct of litigation requires that the privilege relating to those documents should be preserved, then it would seem that it should be right that nothing at all about the documents should be put before the court. On the other hand, if (as is conceded) secondary evidence is going to be admissible, there seems to me to be no logic in the court not seeing the documents themselves.

There is authority which states, as one can see from the reading of r 9, that the right to take copies is ancillary to the right to inspect. Originally, I imagine, the solicitor carrying out inspection or his clerk would himself have copied down at the same time the parts of the documents which he wished to refer to. Again, it is agreed that if the respondent's solicitor had copied the documents himself at the time of inspection, or made more extensive use of the photocopier belonging to the liquidator's solicitors, no objection could now be made. It would seem to me illogical that having carried out the inspection, but not gone through the physical process of making copies at the time, he should now be disentitled from obtaining the best evidence of the documents which he has seen.

Accordingly, on this very narrow point, namely whether the process can be put into reverse between the moment of inspection and the request for copies of the documents inspected, I would respectfully disagree with the registrar and hold that once inspection has taken place it is too late to correct the mistake and that the respondent is entitled to his copies.

Order accordingly.

Solicitors: *Jeffrey Green & Russell* (for the respondent); *Underwood & Co* (for the liquidator).

Evelyn M C Budd   Barrister.

a
Johnston v Chief Constable of the Royal Ulster Constabulary

(Case 222/84)

COURT OF JUSTICE OF THE EUROPEAN COMMUNITIES

b JUDGES LORD MACKENZIE STUART (PRESIDENT), KOOPMANS, EVERLING, BAHLMANN, JOLIET
(PRESIDENTS OF CHAMBERS), DUE, GALMOT, KAKOURIS AND O'HIGGINS

ADVOCATE GENERAL M DARMON

9 OCTOBER 1985, 28 JANUARY, 15 MAY 1986

c
European Economic Community – Equality of treatment of men and women – Judicial control –
Exclusion of power of review by courts – National authority issuing certificate stating that
conditions justifying derogation from principle of equal treatment satisfied – National legislation
providing that certificate conclusive evidence that conditions satisfied – Whether principle of
effective judicial control allowing certificate to be treated as conclusive evidence – Whether
individual who has been wronged by unlawful discrimination entitled to pursue effective judicial
remedy against member state notwithstanding issue of certificate – Whether individual entitled to
d *claim that national legislation be set aside so far as it exceeded permitted exceptions to principle of*
equal treatment – Sex Discrimination (Northern Ireland) Order 1976, art 53(1)(2) – EC Council
Directive 76/207, arts 2(1)(2), 3(1), 4, 6.

European Economic Community – Equality of treatment of men and women – Derogation from
principle of equal treatment – Concern for protection of women – Risks and dangers of occupation
e *– Employment in armed police force – Risks and dangers not specifically affecting women as such*
– Whether such risks and dangers justifying difference in treatment of men and women – Whether
internal situation characterised by frequent assassinations a factor to be considered in determining
whether requirements of public safety justifying restriction of general policing duties to men
equipped with firearms – EC Council Directive 76/207, art 2(2)(3).

f In the United Kingdom police officers did not as a general rule carry firearms in the
performance of their duties except for special operations, and no distinction was made in
that regard between men and women. Because of the high number of police officers
assassinated in Northern Ireland in the terrorist campaign which began in 1970, the
Chief Constable of the Royal Ulster Constabulary (the RUC) decided that in the RUC and
the RUC Reserve men would carry firearms in the regular course of their duties but that
g women would not be equipped with them and would not receive training in the
handling and use of firearms. Accordingly in 1980 the Chief Constable took the view
that general police duties, which frequently involved operations requiring the carrying
of firearms, would no longer be assigned to women and decided not to offer or renew
any more contracts for women in the RUC Reserve except where they had to perform
duties assigned only to women officers. The applicant was a member of the RUC Reserve
h from 1974 to 1980 and had during that time efficiently performed the general duties of
a uniformed police officer, but in 1980 the Chief Constable refused to renew her contract
because of his new policy with regard to female members of the RUC Reserve. The
applicant challenged the decision not to renew her contract and give her training in the
use of firearms, and complained to an industrial tribunal that she had suffered unlawful
discrimination contrary to the Sex Discrimination (Northern Ireland) Order 1976. Before
j the industrial tribunal the Chief Constable produced a certificate issued by the Secretary
of State under art 53(1)[a] of the 1976 order certifying that the act of refusing to offer the
applicant further employment in the RUC Reserve was done for the purpose of
safeguarding national security and protecting public safety and public order. By art 53(2)

---

a   Article 53, so far as material, is set out at p 153 g h, post

of the 1976 order a certificate that an act was done for that purpose was conclusive
evidence that it was so done. The applicant conceded that, by virtue of art 53(2), when   a
read in isolation, the issue of the certificate deprived her of any remedy, but she relied on
the provisions of EC Council Directive 76/207 on the implementation of the principle of
equal treatment for men and women with regard to access to employment, vocational
training and promotion, and to working conditions. The industrial tribunal referred to
the Court of Justice of the European Communities the questions, inter alia, whether a
member state could exclude from the directive's field of application acts of discrimination   b
done for the purpose of safeguarding national security or of protecting public safety or
public order, whether employment as an armed member of a police force was an activity
where the sex of the worker constituted a determining factor, whether the Chief
Constable's policy could be justified out of a concern to protect women within art 2(3)[b]
of the directive and whether the applicant was entitled to rely on the directive before the
national court.   c

Held – (1) A provision which, like art 53(2) of the 1976 order, required a certificate to be
treated as conclusive evidence that the conditions for derogating from the principle of
equal treatment for men and women laid down by art 2(1) of EC Council Directive
76/207 were fulfilled would allow the authority issuing the certificate to deprive an
individual of the possibility of asserting by judicial process the rights conferred by the   d
directive, and accordingly such a provision was contrary to the principle of effective
judicial control laid down in art 6[c] of the directive. It followed, therefore, that the
principle of effective judicial control laid down in art 6 did not allow a certificate issued
by a national authority which stated that the conditions for derogating from the principle
of equal treatment for the purposes of protecting public safety were satisfied to be treated
as conclusive evidence so as to exclude the exercise of any power of review by the courts,   e
and an individual who considered himself wronged by a failure to apply to him the
principle of equal treatment could rely on art 6 to pursue an effective judicial remedy as
against a member state which had not ensured that that principle was fully implemented
in its internal legal order. Moreover, an individual could claim, as against a state authority
charged with the maintenance of public order and safety but acting in its capacity as
employer, that the principle of equal treatment laid down in art 2(1) of the directive be   f
applied to the matters referred to in arts 3(1)[d] and 4[e] concerning the conditions for access

b   Article 2, so far as material, provides:
      '1. For the purposes of the following provisions, the principle of equal treatment shall mean
    that there shall be no discrimination whatsoever on grounds of sex either directly or indirectly by
    reference in particular to marital or family status.
      2. This Directive shall be without prejudice to the right of Member States to exclude from its   g
    field of application those occupational activities and, where appropriate, the training leading
    thereto, for which, by reason of their nature or the context in which they are carried out, the sex
    of the worker constitutes a determining factor.
      3. This Directive shall be without prejudice to provisions concerning the protection of women,
    particularly as regards pregnancy and maternity . . .'
c   Article 6 is set out at p 149 e f, post
d   Article 3(1) provides: 'Application of the principle of equal treatment means that there shall be no   h
    discrimination whatsoever on grounds of sex in the conditions, including selection criteria, for
    access to all jobs or posts, whatever the sector or branch of activity, and to all levels of the
    occupational hierarchy.'
e   Article 4 provides: 'Application of the principle of equal treatment with regard to access to all types
    and to all levels, of vocational guidance, vocational training, advanced vocational training and
    retraining, means that Member States shall take all necessary measures to ensure that: (a) any laws,   j
    regulations and administrative provisions contrary to the principle of equal treatment shall be
    abolished; (b) any provisions contrary to the principle of equal treatment which are included in
    collective agreements, individual contracts of employment, internal rules of undertakings or in
    rules governing the independent occupations and professions shall be, or may be declared, null
    and void or may be amended; (c) without prejudice to the freedom granted in certain Member
    States to certain private training establishments, vocational guidance, vocational training, advanced
    vocational training and retraining shall be accessible on the basis of the same criteria and at the
    same levels without any discrimination on grounds of sex.'

a to posts and to vocational training and advanced vocational training in order to have a derogation from that principle contained in national legislation set aside in so far as it exceeded the limits of the exceptions permitted by art 2(2) (see p 156 *g h*, p 161 *e h* and p 162 *c d g*, post).

b (2) Because of their limited character, the provisions of the EEC Treaty which allowed for derogations in situations involving public safety did not lend themselves to a wide interpretation and it was not possible to infer from them that there was a general proviso in the Treaty covering all measures taken for reasons of public safety. It followed that acts of sex discrimination done for reasons related to the protection of public safety had to be examined in the light of the derogations from the principle of equal treatment for men and women laid down in Directive 76/207 and accordingly, although a decision by the competent police authorities in Northern Ireland to depart from the principle of not arming the police in the ordinary course of their duties because of the requirements of

c public safety did not in itself involve any discrimination between men and women, a decision by the Chief Constable that women would not be armed or trained in the use of firearms, that general policing duties would in future be carried out only by armed male officers and that contracts of women who had previously been entrusted with general policing duties would not be renewed had to be appraised in the light of the derogations from the principle of equal treatment laid down in the directive. Article 2(2) of the

d directive, being a derogation from an individual right laid down in the directive, was to be interpreted strictly and as meaning that, in deciding whether, by reason of the context in which the activities of a police officer were carried out, the sex of the officer constituted a determining factor for that occupational activity, a member state could, in an internal situation characterised by frequent assassinations, take into consideration requirements of public safety in order to restrict general policing duties to men equipped with firearms.

e However, it was clear that the derogations allowed by art 2(3) were intended to protect a woman's biological condition and the special relationship which existed between a woman and her child, and accordingly the differences in treatment between men and women that art 2(3) allowed out of a concern to protect women did not include risks and dangers, such as those to which any armed police officer would be exposed in the performance of his duties, that did not specifically affect women as such (see p 157 *c* to *f*,

f p 158 *c* to *e h* to p 159 *e j* to p 160 *b* and p 162 *e f*, post).

Notes

For the application of Community law in national courts, see 51 Halsbury's Laws (4th
g edn) paras 3·01–3·85.

For the principle of equal treatment for men and women as regards access to employment, vocational training and promotion, see 52 ibid para 21·13.

Article 53 of the Sex Discrimination (Northern Ireland) Order 1976 corresponds to s 52 of the Sex Discrimination Act 1975. For s 52 of the 1975 Act, see 6 Halsbury's Statutes (4th edn) 732.

h For the EEC Treaty, see 42A Halsbury's Statutes (3rd edn) passim.

Cases cited

Amministrazione delle Finanze dello Stato v Simmenthal SpA Case 106/77 [1978] ECR 629.
j *Becker v Finanzamt Münster-Innenstadt* Case 8/81 [1982] ECR 53.
Harz v Deutsche Tradax GmbH Case 79/83 [1984] ECR 1921.
Hofmann v Barmer Ersatzkasse Case 184/83 [1984] ECR 3047.
Marshall v Southampton and South West Hampshire Area Health Authority (Teaching) Case 152/84, [1986] 2 All ER 584, [1986] QB 401, [1986] 2 WLR 780, CJEC.
Van Duyn v Home Office (No 2) Case 41/74 [1975] 3 All ER 190, [1975] Ch 358, [1975] 2 WLR 760, [1974] ECR 1337, CJEC.
von Colson and Kamann v Land Nordrhein-Westfalen Case 14/83 [1984] ECR 1891.

Reference

By a decision dated 8 August 1984 the Industrial Tribunal of Northern Ireland sitting in *a*
Belfast referred to the Court of Justice of the European Communities for a preliminary
ruling under art 177 of the EEC Treaty several questions (set out at p 154 *g* to 155 *e*, post)
on the interpretation of EC Council Directive 76/207 on the implementation of the
principle of equal treatment for men and women as regards access to employment,
vocational training and promotion, and working conditions and of art 224 of the EEC
Treaty. The questions were raised in a dispute betweeen Mrs Marguerite Johnston and *b*
the Chief Constable of the Royal Ulster Constabulary concerning the latter's refusal to
renew Mrs Johnston's contract as a member of the Royal Ulster Constabulary Reserve
and to allow her to be given training in the handling and use of firearms. The language
of the case was English. The following summary of the facts of the case, the course of the
procedure and the observations submitted pursuant to art 20 of the Protocol on the
Statute of the Court of Justice of the European Economic Community is taken from the *c*
judgment of the court.

I—Facts and written procedure
A   The facts of the case
   1. The Royal Ulster Constabulary (the RUC) is placed under the authority of its Chief
Constable. Under the Police Act (Northern Ireland) 1970 the Chief Constable has the *d*
power to appoint reserve constables to the Royal Ulster Constabulary Reserve (the RUC
Reserve). The appointment and conditions of service of members of the RUC Reserve
are governed by the Royal Ulster Constabulary Reserve (Appointment and Conditions of
Service) Regulations (Northern Ireland) 1973, SR & O 1973/83. Regulation 4 provides
that such appointments are limited to persons who are of good character, healthy and
physically fit. The Chief Constable may appoint reserve constables on a full-time basis; *e*
they form 'the RUC full-time Reserve'.
   The 1973 regulations and the conditions of service for RUC full-time reserve constables
make no distinction between men and women as regards duties that is relevant in the
present case. The first reserve constables were appointed to the RUC Reserve in 1970.
Women were first appointed to the RUC Reserve in 1973. The first appointments to the
RUC full-time Reserve were made in 1972; women were first appointed to it in 1974. *f*
   From 1972 appointments to the RUC full-time Reserve were made on the basis of
three-year contracts. Until 1977, as contracts of employment, whether of male or female
members, fell due for renewal, further three-year contracts of full-time employment
were offered to members if their service had been satisfactory and they remained suitable
for employment.
   2. Whereas in England and Wales police officers are not generally armed except for *g*
specific operations and there is no general policy against the training of women officers
in the handling and firing of firearms or against their deployment on duties requiring
the carrying of firearms, a different policy has been adopted in Northern Ireland by the
Chief Constable of the RUC owing to the terrorist campaign which has been carried on
there for a number of years. The assassination of a substantial number of police officers
has made it impossible in Northern Ireland to achieve the aim that police forces should *h*
carry out their duties as an unarmed force, as in the rest of the United Kingdom.
   Male officers carry firearms in the regular course of their duties. However, female
members of the RUC are not, save in exceptional cases, and female members of the RUC
Reserve are never issued with firearms and do not receive training in the handling and
firing of firearms. The reason for this policy of the Chief Constable that women officers
should not carry firearms is that he considers that, if female officers were armed, it would *j*
increase the risk that they might become targets for assassination. The Chief Constable
further considers that armed women officers would be less effective in certain areas for
which women are better suited, in particular welfare type work which involves dealing
with families and children. Finally, he considers that, if women as well as men were to
carry firearms in the regular course of their duties, it would be regarded by the public as
a much greater departure from the ideal of an unarmed police force.

a   The number of male officers of the RUC and RUC Reserve who have died as a result of terrorist activities since 1969 is 180, 59 of whom were individually picked out in advance as targets for assassination. During the same period two women officers were killed. However, in no case was a woman singled out for attack.

3. In 1980 the Chief Constable decided that contracts of women members of the RUC full-time Reserve would be renewed only in cases in which the duties being peformed could only be undertaken by a women member. The reasons for that decision were as *b*   follows. At the material time the RUC had a sufficient number of women officers for the duties normally assigned to women members. The only duties for the performance of which recruits for the RUC full-time Reserve were required were general police duties. A substantial part of such general duties consisted of security duties such as guard and escort duties which frequently involve the use of firearms. In pursuance of the Chief Constable's policy on the carrying of firearms by women members of the RUC, such *c*   duties were not to be assigned to women.

Since that decision no further contracts of full-time employment in the RUC full-time Reserve have been offered to women, save in one case. Such contracts have continued to be offered to men, as before, for service in the RUC full-time Reserve.

4. Mrs Marguerite Johnston joined the RUC as a part-time Reserve constable in March 1974. In November 1974 she became a member of the RUC full-time Reserve on a three-*d*   year contract. At the end of that contract she accepted a second contract of employment for three years. That contract expired in November 1980.

Until November 1980 Mrs Johnston was posted to Newcastle RUC station and performed normal duties of uniformed police officers, such as acting as station duty officer, taking part in mobile patrols, driving the police mobile patrol vehicle and assisting in searching persons brought to the station. She was not armed when carrying *e*   out those duties but was ordinarily accompanied in duties outside the station by an armed male member of the RUC full-time Reserve.

In November 1980 the Chief Constable refused to offer Mrs Johnston a further contract of full-time employment.

She was subsequently employed on a part-time basis in the RUC Reserve, in which she is at present employed as a communications assistant. Her salary is proportionately lower *f*   than that which she received in the RUC full-time Reserve.

It is common ground that Mrs Johnston was an efficient and valued member of the RUC full-time Reserve and had become experienced in police work and procedures, that the reason why her full-time contract of employment was not renewed was the policy decision taken by the Chief Constable in relation to women members of the RUC full-time Reserve and that if she had been a man the Chief Constable would have offered her *g*   a full-time contract.

B   *The national provisions on sex discrimination*

In Northern Ireland the Sex Discrimination (Northern Ireland) Order 1976, SI 1976/1042, lays down rules to eliminate sex discrimination and implement the principle of *h*   equal treatment for men and women as regards access to employment, vocational training and promotion and working conditions.

By art 8(1)(c) of the 1976 order it is unlawful to discriminate against a woman by refusing or deliberately omitting to offer her employment. By art 8(2)(a) it is unlawful for a person, in the case of a woman employed by him, to discriminate against her in the way he affords her access to opportunities for promotion, transfer or training, or to any *j*   other benefits, facilities or services, or by refusing or deliberating omitting to afford her access to them.

Article 10(1) of the order provides that the above provisions do not apply to any employment where being a man is a genuine occupational qualification for the job. That is the case, according to art 10(2)(a), only where—

> 'the essential nature of the job calls for a man for reasons of physiology (excluding physical strength or stamina) or, in dramatic performances or other entertainment,

for reasons of authenticity, so that the essential nature of the job would be materially different if carried out by a woman.'

The police are specifically provided for in the 1976 order. Article 19(1) provides that the holding of the office of constable is to be treated as employment and art 19(2)(a) provides that regulations made under the Police Act (Northern Ireland) 1970 are not to treat men and women differently except as regards requirements relating to height, uniform or equipment, or allowances in lieu of uniform or equipment.

Article 53 of the order provides that nothing in Pt III of the order (which part includes art 8) shall render unlawful an act done for the purpose of safeguarding national security or of protecting public safety or public order. Article 53(2) provides that a certificate signed by the Secretary of State and certifying that an act was done for those purposes shall be conclusive evidence that those conditions are fulfilled.

C   *The proceedings before the national court and the questions referred to the Court of Justice*
   1. On 27 November 1980 Mrs Johnston complained to the industrial tribunal and sought an order declaring her rights and the Chief Constable's rights in relation to: (i) her further full-time employment in the RUC full-time Reserve; (ii) access to vocational training in the handling and use of firearms; (iii) the denial of the opportunity to perform public duties in connection with the preservation of public order; and (iv) compensation.

The grounds of her application, based on the 1976 order, were that: (i) she had been unlawfully discriminated against by the Chief Constable, contrary to art 8(1)(c) of the order, in so far as he had refused or deliberately omitted to offer her further full-time employment in the RUC full-time Reserve; and (ii) she had been unlawfully discriminated against by the Chief Constable, contrary to art 8(2)(a) of the order, in so far as he had denied her access to vocational training in the handling and use of firearms and the opportunity to perform duties in connection with the preservation of public order.

   2. Before the first hearing of the case the Secretary of State issued a certificate, as provided for in art 53 of the 1976 order, stating that the refusal to offer full-time employment to Mrs Johnston in the RUC Reserve was for the purpose of safeguarding national security and protecting public safety and public order.

Before the industrial tribunal it was conceded on behalf of Mrs Johnston that, by virtue of the provisions of the 1976 order themselves, when read in isolation, the issue of that certificate deprived her of any remedy. However, she relied on the provisions of EC Council Directive 76/207 of 9 February 1976 on the implementation of the principle of equal treatment for men and women as regards access to employment, vocational training and promotion, and working conditions.

The industrial tribunal decided that questions should be referred to the Court of Justice under art 177 of the EEC Treaty but deferred the drafting of the questions until a later stage. An appeal lodged by the Chief Constable against that decision was dismissed by Lord Lowry LCJ. The Chief Constable then appealed to the Court of Appeal in Northern Ireland.

That appeal was adjourned in order for the substance of the case to be reargued before the industrial tribunal. The Chief Constable conceded that arts 10 and 19 of the 1976 order could not afford him a defence and he relied on art 224 of the EEC Treaty. The industrial tribunal decided that this defence raised further issues of interpretation of Community law which had to be submitted to the court under art 177 of the EEC Treaty.

The Chief Constable's appeal against the decision of Lord Lowry LCJ was dismissed on 13 October 1983.

   3. By a decision of 8 August 1984 the industrial tribunal submitted the following questions to the court for a preliminary ruling:

'1. On the proper construction of Council Directive No. 76/207 of 9 February 1976 on the implementation of the principle of equal treatment for men and women ("the Directive") and in the circumstances described in the agreed Statement

of Facts in this case, can a Member State exclude from the Directive's field of
application acts of sex discrimination as regards access to employment done for the
purpose of safeguarding national security or of protecting public safety or public
order?

2. On the proper construction of the Directive and in the circumstances described
in the agreed Statement of Facts in this case, is full-time employment as an armed
member of a police reserve force, or training in the handling and use of fire-arms
for such employment, capable of constituting one of those occupational activities
and, where appropriate, the training leading thereto for which, by reason of their
nature or the context in which they are carried out, the sex of the worker constitutes
a determining factor, within the meaning of Article 2(2)?

3. What are the principles and criteria by which Member States should determine
whether "the sex of a worker constitutes a determining factor" within the meaning
of Article 2(2) in relation to (a) the "occupational activities" of an armed member of
such a force and (b) "the training leading thereto", whether by reason of their nature
or by reason of the context in which they are carried out?

4. Is a policy applied by a Chief Constable of Police, charged with a statutory
responsibility for the direction and control of a police force, that women members
of that force should not carry fire-arms capable, in the circumstances set out in the
Statement of Facts in this case, of constituting a "provision concerning the protection
of women", within the meaning of Article 2(3), or an "administrative provision"
inspired by "concern for protection" within the meaning of Article 3(2)(c) of the
Directive?

5. If the answer to Question 4 is affirmative, what are the principles and criteria
by which Member States should determine whether the "concern for protection" is
"well founded", within the meaning of Article 3(2)(c)?

6. Is the applicant entitled to rely upon the principle of equal treatment contained
in the relevant provisions of the Directive before the national courts and tribunals
of Member States in the circumstances of the present case?

7. If the answer to Question 6 is affirmative: (a) Does Article 224 of the EEC
Treaty, on its proper construction, permit Member States when confronted with
serious internal disturbances affecting the maintenance of law and order to derogate
from any obligations which would otherwise be imposed on them or on employers
within their jurisdiction by the Directive? (b) If so, is it open to an individual to rely
upon the fact that a Member State did not consult with other Member States for the
purpose of preventing the first Member State from relying on Article 224 of the
EEC Treaty?'

D　*Written procedure before the court*

The industrial tribunal's decision to request a preliminary ruling was registered at the
court on 4 September 1984. In accordance with art 20 of the Protocol on the Statute on
the Court of Justice of the European Economic Community, written observations were
submitted by the following: Mrs Johnston, represented by Anthony Lester QC and David
Smyth, instructed by Murphy Kerr & Co; the United Kingdom, represented by Mrs S J
Hay, acting as agent, assisted by Anthony Campbell QC, Senior Crown Counsel in
Northern Ireland, and Richard Plender; and the Commission of the European
Communities, represented by Armando Toledano Laredo, Principal Legal Adviser, and
Julan Currall, a member of its Legal Department.

After hearing the report of the Judge Rapporteur and the views of the Advocate
General, the court decided to open the oral procedure without any preparatory inquiry.

II—*Written observations submitted to the court*

1　*Observations of Mrs Johnston*

On question 1 Mrs Johnston considers that the aims of safeguarding national security or
of protecting public safety or public order may justify a derogation from the fundamental

principle of equal treatment only in so far as the derogation is covered by the terms of art 2(2) of Directive 76/207. Only by reference to particular occupational activities is it *a* possible to ascertain whether, by reason of their nature or the context in which they are carried out, the sex of the worker constitutes a determining factor. A derogation which is general in its scope, rather than being related to particular occupational activities or their nature or the context in which they are carried out, made on the sole ground that the discriminatory measure in question was adopted for the purpose of safeguarding national security or protecting safety or public order, is not covered by that article. Were *b* this not so, a member state could determine its scope unilaterally without being subject to control by the Community institutions (see *Van Duyn v Home Office (No 2)* Case 41/74 [1975] 3 All ER 190, [1975] Ch 358).

It is not possible to answer *question 2* in the broad terms in which it is formulated. The question whether full-time employment as an armed member of a police reserve force is capable of coming within art 2(2) of the directive depends on the particular occupational *c* activity within the general category of the employment in question. Throughout her particular occupational activities Mrs Johnston performed her duties entirely satisfactorily and sex was not a determining factor. The mere fact that the Chief Constable required members of the RUC Reserve to be armed did not alter the nature of her occupational activities nor did it change the context in which they were carried out. It has never been suggested that she was incapable as a woman of being trained in the use of firearms, so it *d* was not a case in which 'the essential nature of the job calls for a man for reasons of physiology', as required by art 10(2)(a) of the 1976 order.

Employment such as that in question in this case is capable of coming within art 2(2) of the directive only in so far as particular occupational activities within the category of employment in question are activities for which the sex of the police officer constitutes a determining factor; this has not been demonstrated by the arguments advanced by the *e* Chief Constable, which are only broad generalisations, and it cannot be accepted in the case of such a broad exclusion as the exclusion of women from the RUC Reserve.

As regards *question 3* Mrs Johnston observes that in determining whether the requirements of art 2(2) of the directive are satisfied the member states must bear in mind that the provision must, as an exception to a fundamental human right, be strictly construed. The national courts must be allowed to decide whether those requirements *f* are satisfied and the member state or the employer must prove that they are satisfied. A member state may only exclude a particular occupational activity and only by reason of the nature of the activity or the context in which it is carried out. The derogation must be founded on objective reasons. In the circumstances of the present case, the sex of a police officer will only be a 'determining factor' if the nature of the particular activity would be different if carried out by a woman or if the context in which it is carried out *g* makes it essential for it to be done by a man in order to ensure respect for the fundamental right to respect for privacy, for example in carrying out body searches. The purposes asserted in the Secretary of State's certificate and the reasons given by the Chief Constable are not sufficient for this purpose.

Article 2(3) of the directive, to which *question 4* refers, on provisions concerning the protection of women, must be strictly construed and the member state or employer *h* concerned must prove that the conditions for the application of that provision are satisfied. The aim of art 2(3) is to ensure that women receive special treatment to protect their health and safety in the case of pregnancy or childbirth; it is not intended to permit women to be discriminated against by excluding them from employment in the guise of protection. It is not even contended by the Chief Constable that the requirements of the provisions of the 1976 order concerning the protection of women are satisfied in this *j* case. The fact that the Secretary of State and the Chief Constable relied on a certificate issued under art 53 of the order precludes them from asserting other purposes, such as the protection of women, which in any event was never considered before this case was brought. In any case, the blanket exclusion of women from the RUC Reserve and the denial of training in the use of firearms irrespective of the duties performed or of the *a*   individual qualities of the particular woman concerned are not proportionately related to the aim asserted. It is not necessary, in order to achieve that aim, to impose a blanket ban; other means, having a less severe impact on women, for example training women in the handling and use of firearms and deploying only police officers of either sex who are proficient in the handling and use of firearms on duties requiring such proficiency, could have been used to achieve that aim.

b   Since the answer to *question 4* must be in the negative, *question 5* does not arise. In the alternative, it is contended that art 3(2)(*c*) must be strictly construed. The member state or employer concerned must prove that the concern for the protection of women is well founded and that the means employed for the purpose of protecting women are reasonably related to and necessary for that purpose.

c   As regards *question 6*, which asks whether an individual may rely on the directive in question, art 53 of the 1976 order is contrary to the clear, complete and precise provision of art 6 of the directive and cannot therefore preclude Mrs Johnston from relying on the relevant provisions of the directive before the national courts. In the circumstances of this case the Chief Constable and the Secretary of State did not act as private persons but as persons exercising statutory powers or entrusted with public duties and the directive therefore is directly binding on them. In any event, the relevant provisions of the directive have a horizontal direct effect.

d   Article 224 of the EEC Treaty, to which *question 7* refers, does not allow the member states to derogate unilaterally and free from judicial control from any of the obligations and rights arising under the Treaties and in particular the fundamental rights guaranteed by Community law. Article 224 must be strictly construed and can only apply if all its conditions are fulfilled. A member state has a certain margin of appreciation but not an unlimited power removed from all control by the national courts and by the Court of Justice as regards the requirement relating to the maintenance of law and order and *e* serious internal disturbances. The member state must also prove that it is adopting the derogating measure for the reasons set out in art 224 and that the means used are proportionate to and necessary for the aim in view. It should have consulted the other member states and they must have together taken collective steps. In any event, it is open to an aggrieved individual to rely before a national court on any failure to comply *f* with the requirements of art 224 so as to ensure 'equality of arms' and observance of the rule of law when the member state invokes that article.

2   *The United Kingdom's observations*

With regard to *question 1* the United Kingdom considers that Directive 76/207 is in principle inapplicable to action taken by the member states for the purpose of *g* safeguarding national security or for protecting public safety or public order and the member states are free to exclude such matters from the scope of their legislation on equal treatment. That conclusion follows first of all from the principle of interpreting the directive in conformity with the rules of the Treaty and with general principles of law. The EEC Treaty itself leaves intact the power of the member states to take such measures as they may consider necessary or expedient for the above-mentioned purposes, *h* as is shown by the 'safeguard' clauses contained in arts 36, 48, 56, 66, 223 and 224. It is inconceivable that a directive may be interpreted as restricting that power of the member states which the EEC Treaty itself leaves intact. The interpretation of the directive in accordance with its objects and general scheme leads to the same result because in order to attain the directive's aims, which, as is clear from the preamble thereto, are to avoid difficulties in the operation of the Common Market owing to the competitive *j* disadvantages that the elimination of discrimination may entail and to achieve the Community's social aims, it is not necessary to restrict that power of the member states. In circumstances such as those existing in Northern Ireland, a member state is therefore entitled, for the purpose of safeguarding national security, public safety or public order, to exclude from its legislation on the implementation of the principle of equal treatment of men and women acts of the kind done by the Chief Constable.

As regards *question* 2 the United Kingdom observes that the language of art 2(2) of the directive specifically directs attention to the context in which an activity is carried out   *a* and the suitability of a person of a particular sex for employment may depend on that context as well as on the nature or inherent requirements of the post. Under art 2(2) the member states are to determine the activities which are to be excluded from the directive's field of application and they have a discretion in this regard. In interpreting the directive and determining its field of application the court and the member states must therefore take account of the need to reconcile the principle of equal treatment   *b* with other conflicting interests. The question of law submitted to the court in this case, namely whether employment of the kind in question undertaken in the circumstances described by the national court may be an occupational activity for which the sex of the worker is a determining factor, must be answered in the affirmative, taking into consideration the equally fundamental interests of national security.

The enumeration required by *question* 3 of the principles and criteria by which it   *c* should be determined whether 'the sex of the worker constitutes a determining factor' within the meaning of art 2(2) of the directive is impossible. The definition of the criteria depends on the nature of the activity and the context in which it is carried out. In order to reconcile the principle of equality of treatment with the demands of national security, public safety or public order, the member state should determine whether, by reason of the physiological differences between the sexes or by reason of the distinctions customarily   *d* drawn between the sexes, it is necessary to treat members of the two sexes differently in respect of the employment or training in question. In this regard differences in physical strength may be taken into account owing to the increased risk of the theft of firearms. It is also legitimate to take into account the probable public reaction if armed policewomen appeared on the streets, if they became targets for assassination or if they had to work with families and children. Those were the criteria applied by the Chief Constable.   *e*

With regard to *question* 4 the term 'provisions concerning the protection of women' in art 2(3) of the directive gains colour from the expression 'laws, regulations and administrative provisions' in art 3(2)(c) and covers the policy which the Chief Constable applies in the exercise of statutory powers. The aim of that policy is to protect women by preventing them from becoming targets for assassination. The breadth of the phrase 'protection of women' is not reduced by the reference to pregnancy and maternity. This   *f* is clear from art 3(2)(c) because it is unlikely that provisions governing maternity and pregnancy will cease to be inspired by a well-founded 'concern' to protect women. It is not for the court to determine whether the Chief Constable was justified in applying his policy. He might have legitimately taken into account the physical strength or social and cultural status of women, which, in time of grave emergency, are capable of warranting the adoption of a provision for the protection of women.   *g*

It is not possible to enumerate exhaustively the criteria to be taken into account for the purposes of art 3(2)(c), as requested by *question* 5. Nevertheless, in interpreting that provision some assistance might be gained by comparing it with Convention no 111 of the International Labour Organisation concerning discrimination in respect of employment and occupation (Geneva, 25 June 1958; UNTS vol 362, p 31; Cmnd 783), which permits the retention of special measures for the protection of women in specified   *h* circumstances (maternity) or at specified times (night) or in specified kinds of employment (underground), even when that employment is also arduous or dangerous for men. It authorises a state to maintain in force provisions designed to protect women when it is generally recognised by other states or by the population in question that members of that sex require special protection or assistance. Article 8(4)(b) of the European Social Charter (Turin, 18 October 1961; TS 38 (1965); Cmnd 2643) imposes an   *j* obligation to prohibit the employment of women workers on work which is unsuitable for them by reason of its dangerous, unhealthy or arduous nature. A member state may therefore take account, out of concern to protect women, of the existence and nature of a state of emergency, the arduous or dangerous nature of the employment in question and the general recognition that women require special protection or assistance.

With regard to *question 6*, which in its view calls for no answer from the court, the
a United Kingdom considers that the relevant provisions of the directive are not sufficiently
unconditional and precise to produce direct effect. Article 2(1) and art 3(1), read in the
light of the subsequent provisions of the directive and with regard to the circumstances
of the present case, are imprecise and conditional provisions since they are subject to the
exercise of a member state's power to exclude certain activities or to revise its existing
laws, regulations and administrative provisions in accordance with art 9(2) and since the
b criteria to be applied in the exercise of that power are not articulated in the directive and
defy enumeration. In any case, an individual may not rely on those provisions of the
directive as against an employer. In the present case, the Chief Constable is constitutionally
independent of the state and is involved as an employer who has to decide whether or
not to recruit a particular person. The directive does not have direct effect in such
relations. To take the opposite view would mean that there would be unwarranted and
c illogical discrimination between the public and private sectors and between member
states, depending on the distribution of functions between the public and private sectors
in the case of similar activities.

As regards art 224 of the EEC Treaty, referred to in *question 7*, it is for the member
state to determine which measures are to be taken in the event of serious disturbances.
The situation in Northern Ireland must clearly be regarded as a serious internal
d disturbance affecting the maintenance of law and order. The functioning of the Common
Market is not affected by a policy of engaging only men in armed police duties.
Furthermore, an individual may not rely on a member state's failure to consult with
other member states for the purpose of preventing it from relying on art 224. The
remedy which the Treaty makes available for an improper use of art 224 is set out in art
225. Article 224 does not confer any rights on individuals enabling them to prevent
e member states from exercising their powers under that article.

3   The Commission's observations

The Commission observes first of all that the exceptions provided for in art 2(2) and
(3) of Directive 76/207 to the prohibition of discriminatory treatment of men and
women, which relate to the nature or the context in which occupational activities or
f training are carried out and to the protection of women, are not relevant in this case.
They do not expressly refer to national security or to the maintenance of law and order.
However, in *art 224* the EEC Treaty does contemplate such cases and one cannot
therefore exclude the possibility that such reasons may justify an exception to the
principle of equal treatment either on the basis of the provisions of the directive itself or
by reason of art 224 of the EEC Treaty.

g The directive must be interpreted in the light of art 224 of the EEC Treaty. The
Commission is prepared to assume that the situation in Northern Ireland at the relevant
time, in 1980, could justify the application of art 224 on the ground of 'serious internal
disturbances affecting the maintenance of law and order'. However, for the reasons set
out later, the Commission does not think it necessary to consider whether an individual
may rely on the fact that the United Kingdom has never consulted the other member
h states on this matter. In view of art 224 of the EEC Treaty, it is not strictly necessary to
examine the exceptions provided for in the directive itself. On this point the Commission
observes however that, although no exception relating to national security or the
protection of public order or safety is expressly provided for, such considerations may
nevertheless mean that certain occupational activities can only be carried out by persons
of one sex. The Commission is therefore prepared to assume that the policy decision not
j to arm women and to reserve certain police activities to armed men in the situation
prevailing in Northern Ireland is justified and that such a policy may be adopted to
protect women police officers.

An exception created by an unchallengeable administrative decision, such as provided
for in art 53 of the 1976 order, to a fundamental principle of Community law is not
permissible, however, either under art 224 of the EEC Treaty or under the directive

itself. In any event art 224 imposes an obligation to consult. Exceptions to the directive must in particular be subject to judicial control, for which art 6 of the directive provides *a* without any possible exception. It is not therefore possible to exclude judicial control on grounds of national security or public order. It is not enough for a member state to allege that its action was taken on the basis of an exception referred to in the Treaty or in secondary legislation: it must show that the necessary conditions are met, subject to review by the court.

In the context of art 224 of the Treaty it must be shown not only that the decisions *b* taken are the result of the situation which has arisen but also that they are necessary in order to meet it and that the principle of proportionality has been observed. In this regard a parallel can be drawn with the exceptions provided for in arts 36 and 48(3) of the EEC Treaty, which do not create an area of reserved competence for the member states. The fact that an exceptional situation of the type envisaged in art 224 has arisen is not therefore sufficient for a member state to be able to derogate, without any form of *c* judicial review, from a fundamental principle of Community law. In the present case it is necessary to determine in the light of the principle of proportionality whether it was necessary and permissible in the conditions prevailing in the 1980 not only to exclude women police officers from certain duties but also to dismiss them or to refuse to renew their contracts. It has not yet been demonstrated in this case that it would not have been sufficient to assign Mrs Johnston to unarmed duties, as had been done during her six *d* years of service in the RUC full-time Reserve.

With regard to *question 2* the Commission considers that, owing to the context in which the duties described by the national court are carried out but not owing to their nature, full-time employment as an armed member of the police reserve or training in the handling of firearms may be covered by art 2(2) of the directive. It refers in this regard to the fact that elsewhere in the United Kingdom sex is not considered a *e* determining factor. The difference therefore lies in the context in which the duties and training of police officers are carried out.

As regards *question 2* it is sufficient to make the following points without giving an exhaustive list. An exception may be justified not in relation to a post as a whole but in relation to particular duties attaching to the post. Thus, Mrs Johnston could have been assigned to specific police duties which could be performed unarmed. Such a solution *f* might be imposed by the principle of proportionality. The same applies to the exclusion from certain forms of training for particular duties.

The answer to *question 4* must be in the affirmative in the circumstances of this case, at least as far as concerns art 3(2)(c) of the directive, which specifically refers to administrative provisions.

As regards *question 5* the Commission observes, without giving an exhaustive list of *g* the criteria to be taken into consideration for the purposes of art 3(2)(c) of the directive, that the necessity for a prohibition or restriction on the employment of women in a given activity may cease to be justified if the social or technical circumstances which justified it change. In the present case the concern for protection is likely to be founded for as long as the task of maintaining public order in Northern Ireland remains significantly more difficult than in the rest of the United Kingdom. *h*

With regard to *question 6* the Commission states that the Chief Constable cannot rely on the certificate issued by the Secretary of State. It is not compatible with art 6 of the directive for a member state to rely on a provision of its own legislation in order to deny individuals the right to invoke before the national courts the national provisions implementing the directive. The certificate should therefore be set aside. The national court may then deal with the matter entirely under national law. This would enable the *j* case to be resolved without its being necessary to consider whether any other provision of the directive may be directly relied on by an individual before a national court.

Question 7(a) does not arise since the only provision which it is necessary to rely on in the present case is art 6 of the directive. The obligation of the member state concerned to subject its action to control by the Community institutions and the right of individuals

to bring actions before the national courts cannot be excluded on the basis of art 224 of
a the EEC Treaty. Similarly, the answer to *question 7(b)* is negative since the Secretary of
State's certificate cannot be relied on and the merits of the case must be dealt with by the
national court.

III—*Oral procedure*
At the sitting on 9 October 1985 oral argument was presented by the following:
b *Anthony Lester QC* and *David Smyth*, Barrister, for Mrs Johnston; *Francis Jacobs QC* and
Richard Plender, Barrister, for the United Kingdom; *L Mikaelsen*, for the Danish
government; and *Armando Toledano Laredo* and *Julian Currall*, for the Commission of the
European Communities.

The Danish government's representative confined his observations to the interpretation
of art 224 of the EEC Treaty. He stated that that article makes it possible to neutralise
c any rule of Community law and leaves the member states a very wide margin of
appraisal. A member state's exercise of its discretion in that regard is not subject to
judicial review, save in the case of abuse. The powers which that article confers on
member states are to be understood in a broad sense.

28 January. **The Advocate General (M Darmon)** delivered the following opinion[1].
d Mr President, Members of the Court,
1. Let me set the scene for this case, which has come before the court by way of a
request for a preliminary ruling. We are in Northern Ireland. Public order and personal
safety are threatened by disturbances of exceptional gravity. That situation has been
recognised by the European Court of Human Rights, which, in a judgment of 18 January
1978, found that it had started in 1970 and described it as 'the longest, most violent
e terrorist campaign ever known in the two parts of Ireland'. No one claims that it is over.
In such circumstances the role of the forces of law and order, above all of the police, is
essential. As stated in the report for the hearing, to which I expressly refer for a summary
of the facts and procedure and for the preliminary questions, the Royal Ulster
Constabulary (the RUC) is placed under the authority of its Chief Constable, who may
also appoint full-time or part-time reserve constables to the Royal Ulster Constabulary
f Reserve (the RUC Reserve). As in England and Wales, the instruments governing the
organisation of the RUC and RUC Reserve make no distinction between men and women
as regards the duties to be performed.

From 1973 women have thus been recruited to the RUC Reserve, at first on a part-
time basis and then, from 1974, on a full-time basis to what may be called 'the RUC full-
time Reserve' under three-year renewable contracts. Mrs Johnston, the applicant in the
g main proceedings, who was first employed on a part-time basis and then on a full-time
basis in 1974, had her contract renewed in 1977.

Although police officers are not generally armed in the United Kingdom, the special
situation in Northern Ireland led the competent authorities to equip them with firearms
in the regular course of their duties. The change of policy applied only to male officers,
the reasons being to prevent the risk of attacks on women officers which might enable
h assailants to steal their firearms, to maintain the position of women officers in the
community and to maintain, as far as women officers were concerned, the ideal of an
unarmed police force. As a consequence of that decision it was decided not to train
women in the handling of firearms.

In 1980 the Chief Constable took an additional step. In view of the need to assign
members of the RUC full-time Reserve mainly to security duties involving the use of
j firearms, he decided not to renew the contracts of women members of the RUC full-time
Reserve when their duties could be performed by their counterparts in the RUC.
Consequently, as in the case of almost all of her female colleagues, Mrs Johnston's contract
was not renewed in 1980.

---

1 Translated from the French

It is not disputed that the measure taken by the Chief Constable, which had nothing to do with Mrs Johnston's conduct in the service, was taken solely on the ground of her sex. She therefore argued before the national court that for that reason she had suffered discrimination contrary to the provisions of EC Council Directive 76/207 of 9 February 1976 on the implementation of the principle of equal treatment for men and women as regards access to employment, vocational training and promotion, and working conditions.

2. That directive was implemented in Northern Ireland by the Sex Discrimination (Northern Ireland) Order 1976, SI 1976/1042. I shall not reproduce the résumé of that order contained in the report for the hearing but merely remind the court that: (i) art 10 concerns exceptional cases in which discrimination on grounds of sex is justified; (ii) as far as employment with the police is concerned, art 19(2) prohibits, save in matters irrelevant to this case, any discriminatory treatment on grounds of sex; (iii) art 53 provides that an act contravening that prohibition shall not be unlawful if it is done 'for the purpose of safeguarding national security or of protecting public safety or public order' (para (1)) and that a certificate signed by the Secretary of State and certifying that an act was done for such purposes shall be conclusive evidence that it was done for such purposes (para (2)).

That last provision is at the centre of the argument. On 13 May 1981 the Secretary of State issued a certificate stating that—

> 'the act consisting of the refusal of the Royal Ulster Constabulary to offer further full-time employment to Mrs Marguerite I. Johnston in the Royal Ulster Constabulary was done for the purpose of: (a) safeguarding national security; and (b) protecting public safety and public order.'

As the Industrial Tribunal of Northern Ireland points out in its decision, it is conceded (i) on behalf of the Chief Constable, that the contested measure does not have any justification under the other provisions of the 1976 order (para 40) and (ii) on behalf of Mrs Johnston, that art 53 does not allow her to challenge the certificate on the basis of national law (para 34).

The seven questions raised by the industrial tribunal in the circumstances described above make it clear that in its appraisal of the discrimination in question the court will have to examine two requirements, namely those of public order and the rule of law; judicial review is to be exercised at the point where those two concepts meet.

From that point of view it will be necessary to investigate whether a member state is entitled, for reasons of public order, to exclude all possibility of judicial review of the legality of a national measure in the light of national or Community law. If it may not do so, it will be necessary to investigate whether, and the conditions under which, the measure in question may, subject to review by the courts, be justified in Community law on the grounds of public order.

The right to obtain a judicial determination

3. Although the principle of legality is the cornerstone of the rule of law, it does not exclude consideration of the demands of public order. Indeed, they must be accommodated in order to ensure the survival of the state, whilst at the same time arbitrary action must be prevented. Review by the courts is a fundamental safeguard against such action; the right to challenge a measure before the courts is inherent in the rule of law.

Formed of states based on the rule of law, the European Community is necessarily a community of law. It was created and works on the understanding that all member states will show equal respect for the Community legal order.

Consequently, and subject to review by the courts, the Community legal order expressly incorporates the concept of public order so as to reconcile the proper functioning of the Common Market with the necessity for the member states to cope with emergencies which threaten their vital interests.

The parties have accordingly referred in particular to arts 36, 48 and 224 of the EEC
a Treaty. Each of those provisions provides an illustration of my analysis.

In the case of the provisos regarding public order contained in arts 36 and 48, the
court, having affirmed the discretion of the member states to define public order, has, in
a creative spirit, established the principle that decisions regarding public order are subject
to review by the national courts and has defined the scope of such review.

In the case of the safeguard provision in art 224, the court has not yet been required to
b rule on the conditions for its application. However, the second paragraph of art 225
expressly provides that, where a member state makes improper use of its exceptional
powers under art 224, the matter may be brought directly before the court. That
provision does not exclude all possibility of review by the national courts in such cases
or, therefore, of a reference to the Court of Justice for a preliminary ruling.

4. The Treaty, like the case law of the Court of Justice, therefore lays down the
c fundamental rule, a corollary of the principle of legality, that, whilst the demands of
public order may be allowed to modify the scope of judicial review, they cannot override
the right to obtain a judicial determination.

Therefore, a provision of national law, purportedly based on considerations of public
order, which excluded the very possibility of such review, would, in my opinion, be
incompatible with the Community legal order. By removing measures taken by the
d member states from the ambit of Community law, primary, secondary or such as
implemented by national laws, such a provision would in fact allow the national
authorities to create a 'no-go area for the law' as and when they saw fit, thus calling in
question the very foundations of that legal order.

As far as concerns more particularly the equal treatment of men and women in matters
of employment, art 6 of Directive 76/207 states:

e   'Member States shall introduce into their national legal systems such measures as
are necessary to enable all persons who consider themselves wronged by failure to
apply to them the principle of equal treatment within the meaning of Articles 3, 4
and 5 to pursue their claims by judicial process after possible recourse to other
competent authorities.'

f In its judgment in *von Colson and Kamann v Land Nordrhein-Westfalen* Case 14/83 [1984]
ECR 1891 at 1908 (para 22) the court held that

'by granting applicants for a post who have been discriminated against recourse
to the courts, [art 6] acknowledges that those candidates have rights of which they
may avail themselves before the courts.'

g The court went on to conclude that as an authority of a member state a national court
which is confronted by a provision of national legislation compromising the effectiveness
of an obligation arising under a directive (in that case Directive 76/207) and which has a
'duty under Article 5 of the Treaty to take all appropriate measures, whether general or
particular, to ensure the fulfilment of that obligation' (at 1909 (para 26)) must 'interpret
and apply the legislation . . . in conformity with the requirements of Community Law'
h (at 1909 (para 28)).

It follows that a national court cannot, without infringing art 5 of the EEC Treaty and
the directive, hold itself bound by a provision of national law which purports to exclude
on the grounds of public order all judicial review of the implementation of Community
legislation.

That duty of the national court is even more categorical where, as in this case, it is
j acting as an ordinary court responsible for applying Community law, in which regard it
must be borne in mind that the provisions of art 6, which are unconditional and
sufficiently clear, unquestionably have direct effect. Consequently, the right of recourse
to the courts for which art 6 provides may be invoked by individuals in order to challenge
any conflicting provision of national law; in this regard, the authority of the Chief
Constable cannot be separated from that of the state which confers it on him.

That having been stated, I consider that, for reasons similar to those on which the court based its decision with regard to a regulation at issue in *Amministrazione delle Finanze dello Stato v Simmenthal SpA* Case 106/77 [1978] ECR 629 at 644 (para 22): *a*

'. . . any provision of a national legal system and any legislative administrative or judicial practice which might impair the effectiveness of Community law by withholding from the national court having jurisdiction to apply such law the power to do everything necessary at the moment of its application to set aside national legislative provisions which might prevent Community rules from having *b* full force and effect are incompatible with those requirements which are the very essence of Community Law.'

I therefore consider that a member state may not be allowed for reasons of public order to exclude all review by the courts of the legality of a national measure with regard to the provisions of Community law. Consequently, in such a situation a national court *c* must—

'give full effect to those provisions, if necessary refusing of its own motion to apply any conflicting provision of national legislation . . .'

(See the operative part of the *Simmenthal* judgment [1978] ECR 629 at 645.)

d

The scope of judicial review
5. If the demands of public order may not justify the abandonment of judicial review, can they, subject to such review, justify measures of the kind taken by the Chief Constable (relating to the carrying of firearms, training in their handling and use and, ultimately, access to employment), the discriminatory character of which is not disputed? That is the outstanding issue before the industrial tribunal. *e*

Since such a justification would derogate from Community law as normally applicable, it may only be based on Community law.

Neither art 36 nor art 48(3) is relevant to this question. As far as concerns art 224, on which the United Kingdom relies and to which the second question refers, the issue is more complex. That article provides:

'Member States shall consult each other with a view to taking together the steps *f* needed to prevent the functioning of the common market being affected by measures which a Member State may be called upon to take in the event of serious internal disturbances affecting the maintenance of law and order, in the event of war or serious international tension constituting a threat of war, or in order to carry out obligations it has accepted for the purpose of maintaining peace and international security.' *g*

In contrast to the other two provisions, which constitute exceptions to specific rules, art 224 is in effect a 'safeguard clause' of general scope. Like any general rule, it applies only in the absence of special rules. As a safeguard clause, it is the ultima ratio to which recourse may be had only in the absence of any Community provision enabling the demands of public order in question to be met. *h*

In my view, the concerns of the United Kingdom can be taken into consideration, to the full extent required by the demands of public order, within the framework of Directive 76/207. Consequently, the possibility of invoking art 224 will not need to be examined.

6. The industrial tribunal is asking the court whether, having regard to the special circumstances prevailing in Northern Ireland, measures allowing only men to be (i) *j* employed as armed members of a reserve police force and (ii) trained in the handling and use of firearms may constitute permitted derogations under the directive.

In other words, the court is being asked whether reasons of public order may justify such measures either (i) because, owing to the nature of the activities involved and the context in which they are carried out, the employment in question can only be given to a man, the sex of the person employed constituting a determining factor within the meaning of art 2(2), or (ii) because the protection of women requires them and, if so, whether art 2(3) or art 3(2)(c) may be applied.

a

7. A distinction must be made here between discriminatory measures adopted before the enactment of the directive and those adopted after its enactment. Article 3(2)(c) applies to discriminatory measures adopted before its enactment, that is to say, in the case now before the court, the decision taken by the Chief Constable to arm only male members of the RUC full-time Reserve and to exclude women from training in firearms.

b

Of the grounds of justification provided by the competent authority in this regard, only the aim of preventing the risk of attacks on women could be categorised as concern for the protection of women in the wide sense of that phrase. It will be noted that the questions raised by the industrial tribunal on this point (questions 4 and 5) essentially concern the point whether the circumstances stated are of such a nature as to justify the ban on the carrying of firearms by women police officers out of concern to protect them.

c

This possibility cannot be ruled out a priori. Being measures which were in force at the time of the notification of the directive, they must, of course, be reviewed by the member states pursuant to the second subparagraph of art 9(1). The exercise of the national court's powers of review is not dependent on the performance of that obligation. If such measures are still part of positive law, it is for the national court, deriving its authority from art 6, to state whether the circumstances on which they were originally based still necessitate their maintenance and in particular to investigate whether they have become disproportionate with regard to the aim in view.

d

8. The last measure, consisting in the exclusion of women from access to the employment in question, was taken by the Chief Constable after the directive had been enacted. As such, it cannot be covered by art 3(2)(c) but only by the other two provisions referred to by the industrial tribunal.

e

Can that measure be justified by concern for 'the protection of women' referred to in art 2(3)?

This second concern (the first being the maintenance of public order) applies specifically to women police officers and not to the female population in general.

It is undeniable that the tasks of maintaining and re-establishing law and order expose the persons engaged in them to danger. Is that danger greater for women than for men for biological reasons relating to their sex?

f

If indeed art 2(3) may be invoked to reduce the rights of women, there can be no question of taking into consideration, on the basis of that provision, a need for protection, no matter how well founded, whose origin is socio-cultural or even political. In other words, it does not appear that a national authority may bar women from access to employment as armed police officers because it adopts Hamlet's rebuke: 'Frailty, thy name is woman!' That is, moreover, the interpretation to be placed on the court's judgment in *Hofmann v Barmer Ersatzkasse* Case 184/83 [1984] ECR 3047 at 3075 (para 25), in which it affirmed that the directive recognised the legitimacy of measures protecting the 'biological condition' of women during pregnancy and childbirth and their continued application in the period of the 'special relationship' formed between mother and child immediately after its birth.

g

h

9. It remains to examine whether art 2(2) may provide a justification which I have not been able to find in art 2(3).

Article 2(2) reads as follows:

j

'This Directive shall be without prejudice to the right of Member States to exclude from its field of application those occupational activities and, where appropriate, the training leading thereto, for which, by reason of their nature or the context in which they are carried out, the sex of the worker constitutes a determining factor.'

There is not the slightest reference to be found in that provision to the protection of women. Nor does it mention public order. However, such silence does not mean that those matters are excluded.

In fact, art 2(2) contains no enumeration of the reasons justifying a derogation from the principle of equal treatment. It covers a class of occupational activities whose nature *a* or the context in which they are carried out determine the sex of the persons called on to perform them. No one doubts that in some circumstances the demands of public order may constitute a legitimate ground for the authorities of a member state to permit only individuals of one sex to do certain work relating to the maintenance of law and order. The same applies to requirements concerning the protection of women other than those covered by art 2(3) (here I have in mind those of social nature (cultural, political and so *b* on)) which are themselves subject to periodic review under art 9(2) of the directive.

Public order and the protection of women may be closely linked, as the present case shows. The national court will therefore be induced to investigate whether women are more exposed to danger than men when carrying out the occupational activities of armed police officers and whether the employment of women in such activities may create a greater danger to public order, in other words whether the sex of the person employed *c* must be taken into consideration for the purposes of the activity in question. If so, it will then be for the national court to consider the contested measure in the light of the principle of proportionality in order to establish whether 'the sex of the worker constitutes a determining factor', that is to say it will be for that court to determine whether another measure could have been taken to achieve the same purpose but without excluding women from access to employment. *d*

Let me be clear: a derogation from a human right as fundamental as that of equal treatment must be appraised in a restrictive manner, having regard in particular to the exceptional circumstances characterising the situation in Northern Ireland in the relevant period.

10. In view of the generality of the sixth question I think that one last point must be made as regards the direct effect of the provisions of the directive other than those *e* contained in art 6, on which I have already given my opinion. This point only arises if the national court should decide that the circumstances relied on cannot justify the contested measures under art 2(2) or 3(2)(*c*). In such a case, the principle laid down in art 2(1) of the directive will recover all its force. The sixth question could prompt an examination of the question whether art 2(1) has direct effect. However, I do not consider such an examination necessary, since it is not disputed that the principle contained in *f* that provision has been accurately transposed into the national legislation.

Consequently, I suggest that the court should rule that:

(1) A member state may not be allowed to exclude, for reasons of public order, all judicial review of the legality of a national measure with regard to the provisions of Community law. Where a case is brought by an individual pursuant to art 6 of Directive 76/207 'on the implementation of the principle of equal treatment for men and women *g* as regards access to employment, vocational training and promotion, and working conditions' the national court trying the case must give full effect to those provisions, if necessary refusing to apply any conflicting provision of national legislation.

(2) The ban on the carrying of firearms by women police officers and on the training of women police officers in the handling and use of firearms (i) cannot be regarded as a provision concerning the protection of women within the meaning of art 2(3) of *h* Directive 76/207 and (ii) may come within the category of measures referred to in art 3(2)(*c*) if it was in force at the time when the directive was notified.

(3) The decision to exclude women from access to full-time employment as armed members of a police reserve force may, in view of exceptional circumstances relating to public order and requirements concerning the protection of those concerned, be regarded as a derogation provided for in art 2(2) of the directive. *j*

(4) As far as concerns the application of the relevant provisions of the directive to the measures concerned, it is for the national court to: (i) investigate pursuant to art 3(2)(*c*) whether the concern for protection which originally inspired the measures is well founded, if the different treatment already existed at the time when the directive was notified; (ii) investigate pursuant to art 2(2) whether the sex of the person employed constitutes a determining factor for the performance of the activity in question, if the

different treatment was not introduced until after notification of the directive; (iii) if the
a answer to those inquiries is in the affirmative, to examine in both cases whether the
measures adopted are proportionate to the aims pursued.

(5) Since the safeguard clause in art 224 of the EEC Treaty cannot be relied on by a
member state except in the absence of any other rule of Community law containing a
derogating provision based on public order, there is no need to answer the last question
referred to the court.

b
15 May. **THE COURT OF JUSTICE** delivered its judgment which, having
summarised the facts, procedure and submissions of the parties, dealt with the law as
follows.

1. By a decision dated 8 August 1984, which was received at the court on 4 September
1984, the Industrial Tribunal of Northern Ireland, Belfast, referred to the court for a
c preliminary ruling under art 177 of the EEC Treaty several questions on the interpretation
of EC Council Directive 76/207 of 9 February 1976 on the implementation of the
principle of equal treatment for men and women and of art 224 of the EEC Treaty.

2. Those questions were raised in a dispute between Mrs Marguerite Johnston and the
Chief Constable of the Royal Ulster Constabulary (the RUC). The Chief Constable is the
competent authority for appointing reserve constables to the RUC Reserve in Northern
d Ireland and to full-time posts in the RUC full-time Reserve under three-year renewable
contracts. The dispute concerns the Chief Constable's refusal to renew Mrs Johnston's
contract as a member of the RUC full-time Reserve and to allow her to be given training
in the handling and use of firearms.

3. According to the decision making the reference for a preliminary ruling, the
provisions of the Royal Ulster Constabulary Reserve (Appointment and Conditions of
e Service) Regulations (Northern Ireland) 1973, SR & O 1973/83, which govern the
appointment and conditions of service of members of the reserve police force, do not
make any distinction between men and women which is of importance in this case. It is
also clear from arts 10 and 19 of the Sex Discrimination (Northern Ireland) Order 1976,
SI 1976/1042, which lays down rules to eliminate sex discrimination and implements
the principle of equal treatment as regards access to employment, vocational training and
f promotion and working conditions, that the ban on discrimination applies to employment
with the police and that men and women are not to be treated differently in this respect,
except as regards requirements relating to height, uniform or equipment, or allowances
in lieu of uniform or equipment. Article 53(1) of the 1976 order provides that none of
its provisions prohibiting discrimination—

g   'shall render unlawful an act done for the purpose of safeguarding national
        security or of protecting public safety or public order'

whilst art 53(2) provides:

        'A certificate signed by or on behalf of the Secretary of State and certifying that an
        act specified in the certificate was done for a purpose mentioned in paragraph (1)
        shall be conclusive evidence that it was done for that purpose.'
h
4. In the United Kingdom police officers do not as a general rule carry firearms in the
performance of their duties except for special operations, and no distinction is made in
this regard between men and women. Because of the high number of police officers
assassinated in Northern Ireland over a number of years, the Chief Constable of the RUC
considered that he could not maintain that practice. He decided that, in the RUC and the
j RUC Reserve, men should carry firearms in the regular course of their duties but that
women would not be equipped with them and would not receive training in the
handling and use of firearms.

5. In those circumstances, the Chief Constable decided in 1980 that the number of
women in the RUC was sufficient for the particular tasks generally assigned to women
officers. He took the view that general police duties, frequently involving operations
requiring the carrying of firearms, should no longer be assigned to women and decided

not to offer or renew any more contracts for women in the RUC full-time Reserve except
where they had to perform duties assigned only to women officers. Since that decision, *a*
no woman in the RUC full-time Reserve has been offered a contract or had her contract
renewed, save in one case.

6. According to the decision making the reference for a preliminary ruling, Mrs
Johnston had been a member of the RUC full-time Reserve from 1974 to 1980. She had
efficiently performed the general duties of a uniformed police officer, such as acting as
station duty officer, taking part in mobile patrols, driving the patrol vehicle and assisting *b*
in searching persons brought to the police station. She was not armed when carrying out
those duties and was ordinarily accompanied in duties outside the police station by an
armed male officer of the RUC full-time Reserve. In 1980 the Chief Constable refused to
renew her contract because of his new policy, mentioned above, with regard to female
members of the RUC full-time Reserve.

7. Mrs Johnston lodged an application with the industrial tribunal challenging the *c*
decision, taken pursuant to that new policy, to refuse to renew her contract and to give
her training in the handling of firearms. She contended that she had suffered unlawful
discrimination prohibited by the 1976 order.

8. In the proceedings before the industrial tribunal the Chief Constable produced a
certificate issued by the Secretary of State in which that minister of the United Kingdom
government certified in accordance with art 53 of the 1976 order, cited above, that— *d*

'the act consisting of the refusal of the Royal Ulster Constabulary to offer further
full-time employment to Mrs Marguerite I. Johnston in the Royal Ulster Constabulary
Reserve was done for the purpose of: (a) safeguarding national security; and (b)
protecting public safety and public order.'

9. Mrs Johnston referred to Directive 76/207. The purpose of that directive, according *e*
to art 1 thereof, is to put into effect the principle of equal treatment for men and women
as regards access to employment, including promotion, and to vocational training and as
regards working conditions. According to art 2(1), the principle of equal treatment
means that there shall be no discrimination whatsoever on grounds of sex, subject,
however, to the exceptions allowed by art 2(2) and (3). For the purposes of the application
of that principle in different spheres, arts 3 to 5 require the member states in particular *f*
to abolish any laws, regulations and administrative provisions contrary to the principle
of equal treatment and to revise laws, regulations and administrative provisions where
the concern for protection which originally inspired them is no longer well founded.
Article 6 provides that all persons who consider themselves wronged by discrimination
must be able to pursue their claims by judicial process.

10. In order to be able to rule on that dispute, the industrial tribunal referred the *g*
following questions to the court for a preliminary ruling:

'1. On the proper construction of Council Directive No. 76/207 of 9 February
1976 on the implementation of the principle of equal treatment for men and
women ("the Directive") and in the circumstances described in the agreed Statement
of Facts of this case, can a Member State exclude from the Directive's field of
application acts of sex discrimination as regards access to employment done for the *h*
purpose of safeguarding national security or of protecting public safety or public
order?

2. On the proper construction of the Directive and in the circumstances described
in the agreed Statement of Facts in this case, is full-time employment as an armed
member of a police reserve force, or training in the handling and use of fire-arms
for such employment, capable of constituting one of those occupational activities *j*
and, where appropriate, the training leading thereto for which, by reason of their
nature or the context in which they are carried out, the sex of the worker constitutes
a determining factor, within the meaning of Article 2(2)?

3. What are the principles and criteria by which Member States should determine
whether "the sex of a worker constitutes a determining factor" within the meaning

of Article 2(2) in relation to (a) the "occupational activities" of an armed member of such a force and (b) "the training leading thereto", whether by reason of their nature or by reason of the context in which they are carried out?

4. Is a policy applied by a Chief Constable of Police, charged with a statutory responsibility for the direction and control of a police force, that women members of that force should not carry fire-arms capable, in the circumstances set out in the Statement of Facts in this case, of constituting a "provision concerning the protection of women", within the meaning of Article 2(3), or an "administrative provision" inspired by "concern for protection" within the meaning of Article 3(2)(c) of the Directive?

5. If the answer to Question 4 is affirmative, what are the principles and criteria by which Member States should determine whether the "concern for protection" is "well founded", within the meaning of Article 3(2)(c)?

6. Is the applicant entitled to rely upon the principle of equal treatment contained in the relevant provisions of the Directive before the national courts and tribunals of Member States in the circumstances of the present case?

7. If the answer to Question 6 is affirmative: (a) Does Article 224 of the EEC Treaty, on its proper construction, permit Member States when confronted with serious internal disturbances affecting the maintenance of law and order to derogate from any obligations which would otherwise be imposed on them or on employers within their jurisdiction by the Directive? (b) If so, is it open to an individual to rely upon the fact that a Member State did not consult with other Member States for the purpose of preventing the first Member State from relying on Article 224 of the EEC Treaty?'

11. To enable answers to be given which will be of assistance in resolving the dispute in the main proceedings, it is necessary to explain the situation in which the industrial tribunal is required to adjudicate. As is clear from the decision by which the case was referred to the court, the Chief Constable acknowledged before the industrial tribunal that, of all the provisions in the 1976 order, only art 53 could justify his position. Mrs Johnston, for her part, conceded that the certificate issued by the Secretary of State would deprive her of any remedy if national law was applied on its own; she relied on the provisions of the directive in order to have the effects of art 53 of the 1976 order set aside.

12. It therefore appears that the questions raised by the industrial tribunal are intended to ascertain first of all whether it is compatible with Community law and Directive 76/207 for a national court or tribunal to be prevented by a rule such as that laid down in art 53(2) of the 1976 order from fully exercising its powers of judicial review (part of question 6). The next object of the questions submitted by the industrial tribunal is to enable it to decide whether and under what conditions the provisions of the directive, in a situation such as that which exists in the present case, allow men and women employed with the police to be treated differently on grounds of the protection of public safety mentioned in art 53(1) of the 1976 order (questions 1 to 5). The questions submitted are also intended to enable the industrial tribunal to ascertain whether or not the provisions of the directive may, in an appropriate case, be relied on as against a conflicting rule of national law (remainder of question 6). Finally, depending on the answers to be given to those questions, the question might arise whether a member state may avail itself of art 224 of the EEC Treaty in order to derogate from obligations which the directive imposes on it in a case such as this (question 7).

The right to an effective judicial remedy

13. It is therefore necessary to examine in the first place the part of question 6 which raises the point whether Community law, and more particularly Directive 76/207, requires the member states to ensure that their national courts and tribunals exercise effective control over compliance with the provisions of the directive and with the national legislation intended to put it into effect.

14. In Mrs Johnston's view, a provision such as art 53(2) of the 1976 order is contrary to

art 6 of the directive inasmuch as it prevents the competent national court or tribunal from exercising any judicial control.

15. The *United Kingdom* observes that art 6 of the directive does not require the member states to submit to judicial review every question which may arise in the application of the directive, even where national security and public safety are involved. Rules of evidence such as the rule laid down in art 53(2) of the 1976 order are quite common in national procedural law. Their justification is that matters of national security and public safety can be satisfactorily assessed only the competent political authority, namely the minister who issues the certificate in question.

16. The *Commission* takes the view that to treat the certificate of a minister as having an effect such as that provided for in art 53(2) of the 1976 order is tantamount to refusing all judicial control or review and is therefore contrary to a fundamental principle of Community law and to art 6 of the directive.

17. As far as this issue is concerned, it must be borne in mind first of all that art 6 of the directive requires member states to introduce into their internal legal systems such measures as are needed to enable all persons who consider themselves wronged by discrimination 'to pursue their claims by judicial process'. It follows from that provision that the member states must take measures which are sufficiently effective to achieve the aim of the directive and that they must ensure that the rights thus conferred may be effectively relied on before the national courts by the persons concerned.

18. The requirement of judicial control stipulated by that article reflects a general principle of law which underlies the constitutional traditions common to the member states. That principle is also laid down in arts 6 and 13 of the European Convention for the Protection of Human Rights and Fundamental Freedoms (Rome, 4 November 1950; TS 71 (1953); Cmnd 8969). As the European Parliament, Council and Commission recognised in their Joint Declaration of 5 April 1977 (OJ 1977 C103, p 1) and as the court has recognised in its decisions, the principles on which that Convention is based must be taken into consideration in Community law.

19. By virtue of art 6 of Directive 76/207, interpreted in the light of the general principle stated above, all persons have the right to obtain an effective remedy in a competent court against measures which they consider to be contrary to the principle of equal treatment for men and women laid down in the directive. It is for the member states to ensure effective judicial control as regards compliance with the applicable provisions of Community law and of national legislation intended to give effect to the rights for which the directive provides.

20. A provision which, like art 53(2) of the 1976 order, requires a certificate such as the one in question in the present case to be treated as conclusive evidence that the conditions for derogating from the principle of equal treatment are fulfilled allows the competent authority to deprive an individual of the possibility of asserting by judicial process the rights conferred by the directive. Such a provision is therefore contrary to the princple of effective judicial control laid down in art 6 of the directive.

21. The answer to this part of question 6 put by the industrial tribunal must therefore be that the principle of effective judicial control laid down in art 6 of EC Council Directive 76/207 of 9 February 1976 does not allow a certificate issued by a national authority stating that the conditions for derogating from the principle of equal treatment for men and women for the purpose of protecting public safety are satisfied to be treated as conclusive evidence so as to exclude the exercise of any power of review by the courts.

The applicability of Directive 76/207 to measures taken to protect public safety

22. It is necessary to examine next the industrial tribunal's question 1, by which it seeks to ascertain whether, having regard to the fact that Directive 76/207 contains no express provision concerning measures taken for the purpose of safeguarding national security or of protecting public order, and more particularly public safety, the directive is applicable to such measures.

23. In *Mrs Johnston's* view, no general derogation from the fundamental principle of

equal treatment unrelated to particular occupational activities, their nature and the
a   context in which they are carried out, exists for such purposes. By being based on the
sole ground that a discriminatory act is done for purposes such as the protection of public
safety, such a derogation would enable the member states unilaterally to avoid the
obligations which the directive imposes on them.

24. The *United Kingdom* takes the view that the safeguard clauses contained in arts 36,
48, 56, 66, 223 and 224 of the EEC Treaty show that neither the Treaty nor, therefore,
b   the law derived from it apply to the fields mentioned in the industrial tribunal's question
and do not restrict the member states' power to take measures which they can consider
expedient or necessary for those purposes. The measures referred to in question 1 do not
therefore fall within the scope of the directive.

25. The *Commission* suggests that the directive should be interpreted with reference to
art 224 of the EEC Treaty so that considerations of public safety could, in the special
c   conditions envisaged by that article and subject to judicial review, justify derogations
from the principle of equal treatment even where the strict conditions laid down in
art 2(2) and (3) of the directive are not fulfilled.

26. It must be observed in this regard that the only articles in which the Treaty
provides for derogations applicable in situations which may involve public safety are arts
36, 48, 56, 223 and 224, which deal with exceptional and clearly defined cases. Because
d   of their limited character those articles do not lend themselves to a wide interpretation
and it is not possible to infer from them that there is inherent in the Treaty a general
proviso covering all measures taken for reasons of public safety. If every provision of
Community law were held to be subject to a general proviso, regardless of the specific
requirements laid down by the provisions of the Treaty, this might impair the binding
nature of Community law and its uniform application.

e   27. It follows that the application of the principle of equal treatment for men and
women is not subject to any general reservation as regards measures taken on grounds of
the protection of public safety, apart from the possible application of art 224 of the
Treaty, which concerns a wholly exceptional situation and is the subject matter of
question 7. The facts which induced the competent authority to invoke the need to
protect public safety must therefore if necessary be taken into consideration, in the first
f   place, in the context of the application of the specific provisions of the directive.

28. The answer to question 1 must therefore be that acts of sex discrimination done
for reasons related to the protection of public safety must be examined in the light of the
exceptions to the principle of equal treatment for men and women laid down in Directive
76/207.

g   *The derogations allowed on account of the context in which the occupational activity is carried out*

29. The industrial tribunal's questions 2 and 3 are concerned with the interpretation
of the derogation, provided for in art 2(2) of the directive, from the principle of equal
treatment and are designed to enable the tribunal to decide whether a difference in
treatment, such as that in question, is covered by that derogation. It asks to be informed
of the criteria and principles to be applied for determining whether an activity such as
h   that in question in the present case is one of the activities for which 'by reason of their
nature or the context in which they are carried out, the sex of the worker constitutes a
determining factor'.

30. *Mrs Johnston* takes the view that a reply to this question is not possible in terms so
general. She states that she has always worked satisfactorily in performing her duties
with the police and maintains that women are quite capable of being trained in the
j   handling of firearms. It is for the industrial tribunal to determine whether a derogation
is possible under art 2(2) of the directive, having regard to the specific duties which she
is required to carry out. That provision does not make it possible for her to be completely
excluded from any employment in the RUC full-time Reserve.

31. The *United Kingdom* submits that the member states have a discretion in deciding
whether, owing to requirements of national security and public safety or public order,

the context in which an occupational activity in the police is carried out prevents that activity from being carried out by an armed policewoman. In determining that question *a* the member states may take into consideration criteria such as the difference in physical strength between the sexes, the probable reaction of the public to the appearance of armed policewomen and the risk of their being assassinated. Since the decision taken by the Chief Constable was taken on the application of such criteria, it is covered by art 2(2) of the directive.

32. The *Commission* takes the view that, owing to the context in which it is carried out *b* but not to its nature, the occupational activity of an armed police officer could be considered an activity for which the sex of the officer is a determining factor. A derogation must, however, be justified in relation to specific duties and not in relation to an employment considered in its entirety. In particular, the principle of proportionality must be observed. The national court must look at the discrimination in question from that point of view.

c

33. In this regard it must be stated first of all that, in so far as the competent police authorities in Northern Ireland have decided, because of the requirements of public safety, to depart from the principle, generally applied in other parts of the United Kingdom, of not arming the police in the ordinary course of their duties, that decision does not in itself involve any discrimination between men and women and is therefore outside the scope of the principle of equal treatment. It is only in so far as the Chief *d* Constable decided that women would not be armed or trained in the use of firearms, that general policing duties would in future be carried out only by armed male officers and that contracts of women in the RUC full-time Reserve who, like Mrs Johnston, had previously been entrusted with general policing duties would not be renewed, that an appraisal of those measures in the light of the provisions of the directive is relevant.

34. Since, as is clear from the industrial tribunal's decision, it is expressly provided *e* that the 1976 order is to apply to employment in the police and since in this regard no distinction is made between men and women in the specific provisions that are applicable, the nature of the occupational activity in the police force is not a relevant ground of justification for the discrimination in question. What must be examined, however, is the question whether, owing to the specific context in which the activity described in the industrial tribunal's decision is carried out, the sex of the person carrying out that activity *f* constitutes a determining factor.

35. As is clear from the industrial tribunal's decision, the policy towards women in the RUC full-time Reserve was adopted by the Chief Constable because he considered that if women were armed they might become a more frequent target for assassination and their firearms could fall into the hands of their assailants, that the public would not welcome the carrying of firearms by women, which would conflict too much with the *g* ideal of an unarmed police force, and that armed policewomen would be less effective in police work in the social field with families and children in which the services of policewomen are particularly appreciated. The reasons which the Chief Constable thus gave for his policy were related to the special conditions in which the police must work in the situation existing in Northern Ireland, having regard to the requirements of the protection of public safety in a context of serious internal disturbances.

h

36. As regards the question whether such reasons may be covered by art 2(2) of the directive, it should first be observed that that provision, being a derogation from an individual right laid down in the directive, must be interpreted strictly. However, it must be recognised that the context in which the occupational activity of members of an armed police force are carried out is determined by the environment in which that activity is carried out. In this regard, the possibility cannot be excluded that in a situation *j* characterised by serious internal disturbances the carrying of firearms by policewomen might create additional risks of their being assassinated and might therefore be contrary to the requirements of public safety.

37. In such circumstances, the context of certain policing activities may be such that the sex of police officers constitutes a determining factor for carrying them out. If that is

a so, a member state may therefore restrict such tasks, and the training leading thereto, to men. In such a case, as is clear from art 9(2) of the directive, the member states have a duty to assess periodically the activities concerned in order to decide whether, in the light of social developments, the derogation from the general scheme of the directive may still be maintained.

38. It must also be borne in mind that, in determining the scope of any derogation from an individual right such as the equal treatment of men and women provided for b by the directive, the principle of proportionality, one of the general principles of law underlying the Community legal order, must be observed. That principle requires that derogations remain within the limits of what is appropriate and necessary for achieving the aim in view and requires the principle of equal treatment to be reconciled as far as possible with the requirements of public safety which constitute the decisive factor as regards the context of the activity in question.

c 39. By reason of the division of jurisdiction provided for in art 177 of the EEC Treaty, it is for the national court to say whether the reasons on which the Chief Constable based his decision are in fact well founded and justify the specific measure taken in Mrs Johnston's case. It is also for the national court to ensure that the principle of proportionality is observed and to determine whether the refusal to renew Mrs Johnston's contract could not be avoided by allocating to women duties which, without jeopardising d the aims pursued, can be performed without firearms.

40. The answer to the industrial tribunal's questions 2 and 3 should therefore be that art 2(2) of Directive 76/207 must be interpreted as meaning that, in deciding whether, by reason of the context in which the activities of a police officer are carried out, the sex of the officer constitutes a determining factor for that occupational activity, a member state may take into consideration requirements of public safety in order to restrict general e policing duties, in an internal situation characterised by frequent assassinations, to men equipped with firearms.

The derogations allowed on the ground of a concern to protect women

41. In its questions 4 and 5 the industrial tribunal then asks the court for an interpretation of the expressions 'protection of women' in art 2(3) of the directive and f 'concern for protection' in art 3(2)(c), which inspired certain provisions of national law, so that it can decide whether the difference in treatment in question may fall within the scope of the derogations from the principle of equal treatment laid down for those purposes.

42. In *Mrs Johnston's* view, those provisions must be interpreted strictly. Their sole purpose is to assure women special treatment in order to protect their health and safety g in the case of pregnancy or maternity. That is not the case where women are completely excluded from service in an armed police force.

43. The *United Kingdom* states that the aim of the policy with regard to women in the RUC full-time Reserve is to protect women by preventing them from becoming targets for assassination. The expression 'protection of women' may cover such an aim in a period of serious disturbances. The *Commission* also takes the view that an exceptional h situation such as exists in Northern Ireland and the resultant dangers for armed women police officers may be taken into consideration from the viewpoint of the protection of women.

44. It must be observed in this regard that, like art 2(2) of the directive, art 2(3), which also determines the scope of art 3(2)(c), must be interpreted strictly. It is clear from the express reference to pregnancy and maternity that the directive is intended to protect a j woman's biological condition and the special relationship which exists between a woman and her child. That provision of the directive does not therefore allow women to be excluded from a certain type of employment on the ground that public opinion demands that women be given greater protection than men against risks which affect men and women in the same way and which are distinct from women's specific needs of protection, such as those expressly mentioned.

45. It does not appear that the risks and dangers to which women are exposed when performing their duties in the police force in a situation such as exists in Northern Ireland are different from those to which any man is also exposed when performing the same duties. A total exclusion of women from such an occupational activity which, owing to a general risk not specific to women, is imposed for reasons of public safety is not one of the differences in treatment that art 2(3) of the directive allows out of a concern to protect women.

46. The answer to the Industrial Tribunal's questions 4 and 5 must therefore be that the differences in treatment between men and women that art 2(3) of Directive 76/207 allows out of a concern to protect women do not include risks and dangers, such as those to which any armed police officer is exposed when performing his duties in a given situation, that do not specifically affect women as such.

The effects of Directive 76/207

47. By its question 6 the industrial tribunal also seeks to ascertain whether an individual may rely on the provisions of the directive in proceedings brought before a national court. In view of the foregoing, this question arises more particularly with regard to arts 2 and 6 of the directive.

48. Mrs Johnston considers that art 2(1) of the directive is unconditional and sufficiently clear and precise to have direct effect. It may be relied on as against the Chief Constable acting as a public authority. In any event, the directive has horizontal direct effect even in regard to private persons.

49. In the view of the *United Kingdom*, art 2(1) of the directive is a conditional provision inasmuch as it is subject to derogations which the member state may determine in a discretionary manner. The Chief Constable is constitutionally independent of the state and in the present case is involved only as an employer; the directive has no direct effect in such relationships.

50. The *Commission* takes the view that the case may be dealt with within the scope of national law and that a ruling on the direct effect of arts 2 and 3 of the directive is not necessary.

51. On this point it must be observed first of all that in all cases in which a directive has been properly implemented its effects reach individuals through the implementing measures adopted by the member states concerned. The question whether art 2(1) may be relied on before a national court therefore has no purpose since it is established that the provision has been put into effect in national law.

52. The derogation from the principle of equal treatment which, as stated above, is allowed by art 2(2) constitutes only an option for the member states. It is for the competent national court to see whether that option has been exercised in provisions of national law and to construe the content of those provisions. The question whether an individual may rely on a provision of the directive in order to have a derogation laid down by national legislation set aside arises only if that derogation went beyond the limits of the exceptions permitted by art 2(2) of the directive.

53. In this context it should be observed first of all that, as the court has already stated in *von Colson and Kamann v Land Nordrhein-Westfalen* Case 14/83 [1984] ECR 1891 and *Harz v Deutsche Tradax GmbH* Case 79/83 [1984] ECR 1921, the member states' obligation under a directive to achieve the result envisaged by that directive and their duty under art 5 of the Treaty to take all appropriate measures, whether general or particular, to ensure the fulfilment of that obligation, is binding on all the authorities of member states, including, for matters within their jurisdiction, the courts. It follows that, in applying national law, and in particular the provisions of national legislation specifically introduced in order to implement Directive 76/207, national courts are required to interpret their national law in the light of the wording and the purpose of the directive in order to achieve the result referred to in the third paragraph of art 189 of the EEC Treaty. It is therefore for the industrial tribunal to interpret the provisions of the 1976 order, and in particular art 53(1) thereof, in the light of the provisions of the directive, as interpreted above, in order to give it its full effect.

54. In the event that, having regard to the foregoing, the question should still arise
a whether an individual may rely on the directive as against a derogation laid down by
national legislation, reference should be made to the established case law of the court (see
in particular *Becker v Finanzamt Münster-Innenstadt* Case 8/81 [1982] ECR 53). More
particularly, the court recently held in *Marshall v Southampton and South West Hampshire
Area Health Authority (Teaching)* Case 152/84 [1986] 2 All ER 584, [1986] QB 401 that
certain provisions of Directive 76/207 are, as far as their subject matter is concerned,
b unconditional and sufficiently precise and that they may be relied on by individuals as
against a member state where it fails to implement it correctly.

55. That statement was made in *Marshall's* case, with regard to the application of the
principle of equal treatment laid down in art 2(1) of the directive to the conditions
governing dismissal referred to in art 5(1). The same applies as regards the application of
the principle contained in art 2(1) to the conditions governing access to jobs and access to
c vocational training and advanced vocational training referred to in art 3(1) and 4 which
are in question in this case.

56. The court also held in *Marshall's* case that individuals may rely on the directive as
against an organ of the state whether it acts qua employer or qua public authority. As
regards an authority like the Chief Constable, it must be observed that, according to the
industrial tribunal's decision, the Chief Constable is an official responsible for the
d direction of the police service. Whatever its relations may be with other organs of the
state, such a public authority, charged by the state with the maintenance of public order
and safety, does not act as a private individual. It may not take advantage of the failure of
the state, of which it is an emanation, to comply with Community law.

57. The answer to question 6 should therefore be that individuals may claim the
application, as against a state authority charged with the maintenance of public order
e and safety acting in its capacity of an employer, of the principle of equal treatment for
men and women laid down in art 2(1) of Directive 76/207 to the matters referred to in
arts 3(1) and 4 concerning the conditions for access to posts and to vocational training
and advanced vocational training in order to have a derogation from that principle under
national legislation set aside in so far as it exceeds the limits of the exceptions permitted
by art 2(2).

f 58. As regards art 6 of the directive which, as explained above, is also applicable in
this case, the court has already held in *von Colson and Kamann v Land Nordrhein-Westfalen*
and *Harz v Deutsche Tradax GmbH*, cited above, that that article does not contain, as far as
sanctions for any discrimination are concerned, any unconditional and sufficiently precise
obligation which may be relied on by an individual. On the other hand, in so far as it
follows from that article, construed in the light of a general principle which it expresses,
g that all persons who consider themselves wronged by sex discrimination must have an
effective judicial remedy, that provision is sufficiently precise and unconditional to be
capable of being relied on as against a member state which has not ensured that it is fully
implemented in its internal legal order.

59. The answer to this part of question 6 must therefore be that the provision
contained in art 6 to the effect that all persons who consider themselves wronged by
h discrimination between men and women must have an effective judicial remedy may be
relied on by individuals as against a member state which has not ensured that it is fully
implemented in its internal legal order.

Article 224 of the EEC Treaty

60. As far as concerns question 7, on the interpretation of art 224, it follows from the
j foregoing that art 2(2) of Directive 76/207 allows a member state to take into consideration
the requirements of the protection of public safety in a case such as the one before the
court. As regards the requirement that the question whether the rules laid down by the
directive have been complied with must be amenable to judicial review, none of the facts
before the court and none of the observations submitted to it suggest that the serious
internal disturbances in Northern Ireland make judicial review impossible or that
measures needed to protect public safety would be deprived of their effectiveness because

of such review by the national courts. In those circumstances, the question whether art
224 of the EEC Treaty may be relied on by a member state in order to avoid compliance   *a*
with the obligations imposed on it by Community law and in particular by the directive
does not arise in this case.

    61. Question 7 therefore has no purpose in view of the answers to the other questions.

Costs

    62. The costs incurred by the United Kingdom, the government of Denmark and the   *b*
Commission of the European Communities, which have submitted observations to the
court, are not recoverable. Since these proceedings are, in so far as the parties to the main
proceedings are concerned, in the nature of a step in the proceedings pending before the
national tribunal, the decision on costs is a matter for that tribunal.

    On those grounds, the court, in answer to the questions submitted to it by the   *c*
Industrial Tribunal of Northern Ireland by decision of 8 August 1984, hereby rules: (1)
the principle of effective judicial control laid down in art 6 of EC Council Directive 76/
207 of 9 February 1976 does not allow a certificate issued by a national authority stating
that the conditions for derogating from the principle of equal treatment for men and
women for the purposes of protecting public safety are satisfied to be treated as conclusive
evidence so as to exclude the exercise of any power of review by the courts. The provision   *d*
contained in art 6 to the effect that all persons who consider themselves wronged by
discrimination between men and women must have an effective judicial remedy may be
relied on by individuals as against a member state which has not ensured that it is fully
implemented in its internal legal order; (2) acts of sex discrimination done for reasons
related to the protection of public safety must be examined in the light of the derogations
from the principle of equal treatment for men and women which are laid down in   *e*
Directive 76/207; (3) art 2(2) of Directive 76/207 must be interpreted as meaning that, in
deciding whether, by reason of the context in which the activities of a police officer are
carried out, the sex of the officer constitutes a determining factor for that occupational
activity, a member state may take into consideration requirements of public safety in
order to restrict general policing duties, in an internal situation characterised by frequent
assassinations, to men equipped with firearms; (4) the differences in treatment between   *f*
men and women that art 2(3) of Directive 76/207 allows out of a concern to protect
women do not include risks and dangers, such as those to which any armed police officer
is exposed in the performance of his duties in a given situation, that do not specifically
affect women as such; (5) individuals may claim the application, as against a state
authority charged with the maintenance of public order and safety acting in its capacity
as employer, of the principle of equal treatment for men and women laid down in art   *g*
2(1) of Directive 76/207 to the matters referred to in arts 3(1) and 4 concerning the
conditions for access to posts and to vocational training and advanced vocational training
in order to have a derogation from that principle contained in national legislation set
aside in so far as it exceeds the limits of the exceptions permitted by art 2(2).

Agents: *Murphy Kerr & Co*, Belfast (for Mrs Johnston); *Susan Hay*, Treasury Solicitor's   *h*
Department (for the United Kingdom); *L Mikaelsen* (for the Kingdom of Denmark);
Armando Toledano Laredo, Principal Legal Adviser (for the Commission).

                                            Mary Rose Plummer   Barrister.

a ## Bowen-Jones v Bowen-Jones and others

CHANCERY DIVISION
KNOX J
6, 7 MAY 1986

b *Costs – Order for costs – Practice – Hostile litigation – Costs on standard basis – Circumstances in which costs should be awarded on standard basis – RSC Ord 62, r 12(1).*

RSC Ord 62, r 12[a], which provides by r 12(1) for the taxation of costs on the 'standard basis' in place of the 'party and party' and 'common fund' bases and by r 12(2) for taxation on the 'indemnity basis' in place of the 'solicitor and own client' basis, is a rationalisation of the different bases of taxation of costs rather than a complete restatement of the rules c concerning awards of costs, and for the purposes of awarding costs on the standard basis under r 12(1) there is no reason in principle to depart from the established practice that, save in exceptional circumstances, the successful party in hostile litigation is not entitled to an indemnity against expenses actually incurred but only to the lower, 'standard', basis of taxation (see p 165 *e* to *j*, post).

d   Dictum of Brightman LJ in *Bartlett v Barclays Bank Trust Co Ltd (No 2)* [1980] 2 All ER at 98 applied.

Notes
For assessment of costs generally, see 37 Halsbury's Laws (4th edn) paras 744–748, and for cases on the subject, see 37(3) Digest (Reissue) 301–306, 4724–4764.

e ### Cases referred to in judgment
Bartlett v Barclays Bank Trust Co Ltd (No 2) [1980] 2 All ER 92, [1980] Ch 515, [1980] 2
    WLR 430.
Chapman, Re, Freeman v Parker (1895) 72 LT 66, [1895–9] All ER Rep 1013, CA.
EMI Records Ltd v Ian Cameron Wallace Ltd [1982] 2 All ER 980, [1983] Ch 59, [1982] 3
f   WLR 245.
Gibbs v Gibbs [1952] 1 All ER 942, [1952] P 332.

Case also cited
Baylis Baxter Ltd v Sabath [1958] 2 All ER 209, [1958] 1 WLR 529, CA.

g ### Originating summons and action
By an originating summons dated 14 December 1979, the plaintiff, Eileen Christine Bowen-Jones, the personal representative of William Alfred Bowen-Jones deceased, applied for relief pursuant to ss 30 and 203(5) of the Law of Property Act 1925 and ss 42, 44, 51 and 60 of the Trustee Act 1925, and the Judicial Trustees Act 1896 as against the defendants, John Thornton Bowen-Jones, Gordon Bowen-Jones, Alan David Bowen-Jones h and Sidney George Bowen-Jones. By a writ indorsed with a statement of claim dated 4 January 1980, the plaintiff also brought an action against the defendants for an inquiry as to what items of live and dead stock belonging to the deceased had been interfered with wrongly by the defendants and claiming damages for wrongful interference. At the trial of the action Knox J found for the plaintiff. The case is reported solely on the question of costs, which was argued following delivery of judgment in the action.

j   C A Brodie QC and Jonathan Henty for the plaintiff.
    Robert Reid QC and David Hodge for the defendants.

---

a   Rule 12, so far as material, is set out at p 164 *d e*, post

KNOX J. I now have to deal with the question of costs in these two proceedings, one by originating summons and the other by writ. I will deal with the proceedings by writ, in *a* part, first because that gives rise to no difficulty; that is on the counterclaim in the action. The parties are agreed that the counterclaim failed and therefore the defendants counterclaiming have to bear the plaintiffs' costs on the standard basis.

That expression 'standard basis' leads me to the rules (which have recently changed) on this subject. As a result of r 11 of RSC (Amendment) 1986, SI 1986/632, a new Ord 62 has, under r 7 of that statutory instrument, come into force on 28 April 1986, and is *b* made applicable to all proceedings for the taxation of costs whether begun before or after that date. It is therefore common ground between the parties that this new Ord 62 applies.

Order 62 has been amended, notably (and most relevantly for this matter) in that the bases of taxation have been given different names and have been differently defined. Rule 12 of Ord 62, as it now stands, sets out the two bases of taxation with which I am *c* concerned. I need not go into the question whether the court is in a position to order any third or other basis of taxation, since the contest has been between these two only.

First there comes the standard basis, which is defined as follows (r 12(1)):

> 'On a taxation of costs on the standard basis there shall be allowed a reasonable amount in respect of all costs reasonably incurred and any doubts which the taxing officer may have as to whether the costs were reasonably incurred or were reasonable *d* in amount shall be resolved in favour of the paying party . . .'

The other basis of taxation is dealt with in r 12(2) and is called the 'indemnity' basis. That reads as follows:

> 'On a taxation on the indemnity basis, all costs shall be allowed except insofar as they are of an unreasonable amount or have been unreasonably incurred and any *e* doubts which the taxing officer may have as to whether the costs were reasonably incurred or were reasonable in amount shall be resolved in favour of the receiving party . . .'

This new rule is an amalgam of words that were taken from the old rules and a judgment of Megarry V-C, sitting with assessors, in *EMI Records Ltd v Ian Cameron* *f* *Wallace Ltd* [1982] 2 All ER 980, [1983] Ch 59. The Vice-Chancellor set out the then existing five main bases of taxation (which now appear, at any rate at first sight, to have been reduced to two). He pointed out that the common fund basis which was set out in what was Ord 62, r 28(4) provided for there to be allowed a reasonable amount in respect of all costs reasonably incurred under that basis of taxation; and he said ([1982] 2 All ER 980 at 983, [1983] Ch 59 at 63–64): *g*

> 'The common fund basis seems to have been intended to replace the old "solicitor and client" basis (in one of the four meanings of the phrase "solicitor and client": see *Gibbs v Gibbs* [1952] 1 All ER 942 at 949, [1952] P 332 at 347), though in doing so it not very happily uses the very phrase itself.'

And further on in his judgment Megarry V-C said ([1982] 2 All ER 980 at 989, [1983] *h* Ch 59 at 71–72):

> 'On a party and party taxation, nothing will be included unless the taxing master reaches the conclusion that it satisfies the requirement of "necessary or proper". Similarly, where the taxation is on the common fund basis, the taxing master will include nothing unless he considers that it satisfies the requirement of "a reasonable amount in respect of all costs reasonably incurred". On neither basis do the rules *j* give the benefit of any doubt to the party in whose favour the order has been made. Nothing is included unless it satisfies the words of inclusion. The indemnity basis, as I would construe it, is the other way round. Everything is included unless it is driven out by the words of exclusion, namely, "except in so far as they are of an unreasonable amount or have been unreasonably incurred".'

And that, he points out, is a quotation from the old Ord 62, r 29(1), which provided on a
a solicitor and own client basis of taxation that 'all costs shall be allowed except in so far as
they are of an unreasonable amount or have been unreasonably incurred'.

It therefore seems to me that there has been something in the nature of an
amalgamation as a result of the new costs rule and that the party and party basis has
effectively disappeared and been substituted by a turn of phrase which is based on the old
common fund basis but continues with the passage in the new rule that deals with how
b doubts are to be resolved, if felt, by the taxing master, whereas the higher rate of taxation,
solicitor and own client, which is sometimes described as an 'indemnity' basis, has been
replaced by what is still called the 'indemnity basis' in Ord 62, r 12(2), as it now stands,
with the additional passage that doubts are to be resolved in the opposite direction, that
is to say in favour of the receiving party.

On the basis of this change in the rules counsel for the plaintiff submitted to me that
c this presented an opportunity for a review of the basis on which orders for taxation
should be made in favour of a successful litigant. He submitted that I should take this
opportunity to redress what he described as having been commented adversely on by a
succession of judges as something in the nature of an injustice, namely that a successful
litigant who, under the old dispensation, was awarded costs on a party and party basis
only recovered roughly two-thirds in practice of the costs to which he or she had been
d put. It was not disputed that, broadly speaking, two-thirds, as a matter of practical fact
(although it might vary from town to country), was a fair measure of the difference
between what a successful litigant would actually spend and what he might recover on a
party and party taxation. It was submitted to me that a fairer result would be to limit
that basis of taxation, which is now provided for by the standard basis under r 12(1) of
Ord 62, to those cases where there was what was described as a genuine difference of
e opinion or of recollection and there was no question of a deliberate attempt to keep the
other party out of their money or a deliberate attempt to mislead the court.

In my judgment this is not the occasion for reappraising the cases which should be
dealt with on the standard basis, which in my judgment is the successor of party and
party costs and common fund costs, and those cases where costs should be awarded on
the indemnity basis. It seems to me that there has been a rationalisation of the different
f bases of taxation rather than a complete restatement of the rules in such a way as to place
the matter entirely at large as to how costs should, in general, be dealt with between a
successful and an unsuccessful litigant.

It follows that, in general, I see no reason to depart from the practice that was stated by
Brightman LJ in *Bartlett v Barclays Bank Trust Co Ltd (No 2)* [1980] 2 All ER 92 at 98,
[1980] Ch 515 at 547, where he said:

g
> '. . . the usual rule (subject to well-recognised exceptions) in the case of fiduciary,
> contractual or tortious wrongdoing is that the defendant pays to the plaintiff only
> party and party costs. It is not, I think, the policy of the courts in hostile litigation
> to give the successful party an indemnity against the expense to which he has been
> put and, therefore, to compensate him for the loss which he has inevitably suffered,
> save in very special cases. Why this should be, I do not know, but the practice is
h > well-established and I do not think that there is any sufficient reason to depart from
> that practice in the case before me.'

Of course, there has to be a departure now, in that party and party costs are no longer
provided for by Ord 62, and so this passage needs to be read in the light of the new rule
and one has to substitute 'standard' for 'party and party' costs. But it would seem to me
j that something much more radical in the way of a recasting of the rules would be
required before that very well-established practice was, as a matter of principle, departed
from. There is nothing that I have been shown in the new Ord 62 that directly suggests
that any new principle is to be adopted by the court as a matter of general policy. I
therefore do not see that as a matter of general policy it would be right for me to depart
from that principle so stated by Brightman LJ.

That leads me to the second part of the counsel for the plaintiff's submissions on this matter which cover both the originating summons, on which the principal issue was, 'Is the plaintiff the widow of Mr Fred Bowen-Jones?' and also the claim, as opposed to the counterclaim, in the writ action in which the issues were first of all again, 'Is she his widow?' and secondly, 'To what extent was he the owner of the livestock (and to a limited extent the dead stock) at Lower House Farm when he died?' Counsel for the plaintiff submitted that there were two grounds for indemnity costs being awarded under the old practice. For one he relied on Re Chapman, Freeman v Parker (1895) 72 LT 66, [1895–9] All ER Rep 1013, which factually was similar to this case in that there was an element of suspicion of imposture which proved in the event unjustified. In that case a trustee of an express trust suspected a beneficiary, to whom he had been paying income, of not being the genuine beneficiary and persisted in that suspicion to a wholly unreasonable, and quite exceptionally unreasonable, extent, although both the Court of Appeal and the judge at first instance accepted that he held those views honestly albeit wholly unreasonable. Here too, of course, there is an element of suspected imposture in that it was claimed that the gentleman to whom Mrs Bowen-Jones was married in 1974 was not Mr Fred Bowen-Jones. But that is as far as the exact parallel goes between the present case and Re Chapman. What the court there held was that solicitor and client costs should be awarded. True it is that at that date some of the subtle distinctions in the last three of the five categories that Megarry V-C went through in his judgment in the EMI case had not been elucidated, and there is material for thinking that the Court of Appeal may well have been regarding that as giving the beneficiary in that case substantially all the costs which he had incurred.

The second basis on which counsel for the plaintiff asked for indemnity costs was that this was an appropriate case for the court to reflect, in its order for costs, its disapproval of attempts made to mislead the court by the defendants; and he referred me to an authority where a plaintiff who had been successful was disallowed his costs because his evidence was disbelieved by the judge at the trial.

As against that, counsel for the defendants submitted that there were in fact passages in the evidence of both sides which I did not accept, that the plaintiff, in some respects, was disbelieved and that her evidence must have been deliberately inaccurate. I do not propose to go through the various different aspects in which the parties strayed from the truth or to attempt to analyse the degree of deliberateness with which they left that narrow path. True it is that the defendants' departures from the truth came much closer to the heart of the matter and were (or would have been, if successful) much more determinant of the result of the case, and that many of the plaintiff's incorrect assertions in the witness box were of a relatively peripheral nature. Nevertheless I have come to the clear conclusion that this is a case where there was hostile litigation from the word go, that one party certainly has been believed, on critical matters, more than the other, but that the justice of the case requires an order for taxation on the standard basis. That is what I propose to order both in relation to the originating summons and the claim in the writ action.

Mr Alan Bowen-Jones's position was claimed to be different in relation to the action by writ in that down to day 4 it was admitted on the pleadings that he was one of those who drove off the livestock, whereas I allowed an amendment on that day in accordance with what the evidence of the plaintiff had been up to then, which was to put the responsibility for that particular episode on other defendants. Thereafter there was a difference drawn between him and the other defendants which, in substance, so far as factual matters, was accepted by the plaintiff, although not as regards legal responsibility. Here again I propose to apply a broad brush. It seems to me that day 4 is very late indeed in the day for there to be any different costs order made. It may well be that had I been minded to award costs on an indemnity basis Mr Alan Bowen-Jones might have escaped that particular fate; but, as that does not, in the circumstances, arise, I do not propose to draw any distinction between Mr Alan Bowen-Jones in this respect and the other three defendants. I shall therefore make the same order in costs in relation to all four of them.

a It seems to me that the costs thereafter were minimal, in the context of this long and expensive case.

Next I have to deal with the question of the judicial trustee's costs. It is a matter of agreement between the parties that a judicial trustee should be appointed, not only in relation to the trusts affecting property which is held on separate trusts for sale in the conveyances but also in relation to Mr Daniel Bowen-Jones's estate. A question has been raised as to the incidence of his charges. It is common ground that, to the extent to which *b* costs are not increased by the judicial trustee's appointment, for example the costs of the sale of the property which foreseeably are going to have to be incurred in any event, those costs should fall on the property the subject of the judicial trusteeship. The only question which arises is whether to the extent to which costs are increased by the appointment of a judicial trustee they should be thrown on the defendants to the exclusion of Mr Fred Bowen-Jones's estate. A complicating factor is that the judicial *c* trustee proposed to be appointed by agreement between the parties is in fact a chartered accountant and he will therefore foreseeably be doing all the accountancy work, either himself or through his staff, so that there will be a considerable overlap between costs for such work which, foreseeably again, would in any event have had to be done either by a chartered accountant or a solicitor and the costs that he is going to charge.

On balance it seems to me that it would not be right in principle for me to dissect the *d* judicial trustee's costs. They are all costs of administering the estate. He is going to act on everybody's behalf. As the trusts are now absolute trusts, and there is no prospect (so far as one can tell) of any long drawn-out process of administration over a long number of years, it seems to me that the parties may very easily be better served in the long run by not having complicated apportionments of costs but by having a simple, straightforward provision whereby all the judicial trustee's costs come out of the property the subject of *e* the judicial trusteeship; and I propose so to order.

Finally there was one question raised (which I think was eventually a matter of agreement), namely the extent to which orders for costs in the proceedings (by which, of course, I include both the originating summons and the writ, including the counterclaim) and the costs of the judicial trustee (if I threw any of them on the defendants, which I have not) should be secured on the interests of the defendants. The parties have, I think, *f* agreed (and if they have not, I order) that these should be charged on the interests of the defendants in the several properties the subject of these proceedings. That, no doubt, in practice, will lead to their being paid out of the proceeds of sale where sales take place. But I think it would be preferable for it to be expressed as a charge rather than as a direction for payment out of proceeds of sale, in case there are transactions other than sale in the strict sense of the word. That will, foreseeably, be dealt with in the minutes of *g* order, a draft (not the final draft) of which is before me, and which I direct that junior counsel should agree and lodge with the associate.

Order accordingly.

Solicitors: *Gamlens,* agents for *Beaumont Smith & Davies,* Leominster (for the plaintiff); *Maurice Putsman & Co,* Birmingham (for the defendants).

Evelyn M C Budd   Barrister.

Chatters v Burke   a

QUEEN'S BENCH DIVISION
WATKINS LJ AND TAYLOR J
17 JUNE 1986

Road traffic – Driving while unfit to drive through drink or drugs – Special reasons for not b
disqualifying – Criteria for special reasons – Respondent unfit to drive through drink – Car in
which respondent was a passenger leaving road and ending up in field – Respondent driving car
for a few yards from field to highway and parking it – Respondent intending only to park car
and not to drive it – Respondent convicted of driving while unfit to drive through drink – Whether
circumstances constituting special reasons for not disqualifying respondent – Road Traffic Act
1972, s 93(1).

c

The respondent, who had been drinking and was unfit to drive, was a passenger in a car
when the driver lost control of it. The car left the road, rolled over and stopped in a field
next to the highway. The respondent then drove the car, which had a flat tyre, for a few
yards from the field through a gateway onto the road and parked it. He was subsequently
charged with, and pleaded guilty to, driving with excess alcohol, contrary to s 6(1) of the
Road Traffic Act 1972. The magistrates fined him but did not impose a disqualification   d
under s 93(1)[a] of the 1972 Act because they considered there were 'special reasons' for not
doing so, namely that the respondent had driven the car with the intention merely of
driving it out of the field and he had not driven it any appreciable distance on the
highway. The prosecution appealed against the magistrates' refusal to disqualify the
respondent, on the ground that the brevity of the distance driven could not be a special
reason for not imposing the mandatory disqualification.   e

Held – In determining whether special reasons existed under s 93(1) of the 1972 Act for
not disqualifying a driver who was convicted of driving with excess alcohol, the matters
which were required to be taken into account by the court were (a) how far the vehicle
was in fact driven, (b) the manner in which it was driven, (c) the state of the vehicle, (d)
whether the driver intended to drive any further, (e) the prevailing road and traffic   f
conditions, (f) whether there was any possibility of danger by contact with other road
users and (g) the reason for the vehicle being driven at all. The brevity of the distance
driven was not the only, or even the major, criterion, but since the magistrates had taken
into account other factors, such as the fact that the respondent had not intended to do
more than drive the car out of the field and whether the vehicle was likely to come into
contact on the highway with other road users and be liable to give rise to any danger   g
thereby, they had been justified in their finding that there were special reasons for not
disqualifying the respondent. The appeal would therefore be dismissed (see p 171 j to
p 172 e g h, post).
    James v Hall (1968) [1972] 2 All ER 59, *R v Agnew* [1969] Crim LR 152, *Coombs v Kehoe*
[1972] 2 All ER 55, *R v McIntyre* [1976] RTR 330 and *Haime v Walklett* [1983] RTR 512
considered.   h

Notes
For special reasons for not ordering obligatory disqualification for motoring offences, see
40 Halsbury's Laws (4th edn) para 518 and for cases on the subject, see 45 Digest (Reissue)
122–126, 433–454.   j

---

a   Section 93(1), so far as material, provides: 'Where a person is convicted of an ... offence involving
     obligatory disqualification ... the court shall order him to be disqualified for such period not less
     than twelve months as the court thinks fit unless the court for special reasons thinks fit to order
     him to be disqualified for a shorter period or not to order him to be disqualified.'

a For the Road Traffic Act 1972, s 6 (as substituted by the Transport Act 1981, s 25(3), Sch 8), see 51 Halsbury's Statutes (3rd edn) 1427, and for s 93 of the 1972 Act, see 42 ibid 1744.

Cases referred to in judgments
Coombs v Kehoe [1972] 2 All ER 55, [1972] 1 WLR 797, DC.
Haime v Walklett [1983] RTR 512, DC.
b *James v Hall* (1968) [1972] 2 All ER 59, [1972] 1 WLR 797n, DC.
R v Agnew [1969] Crim LR 152, CA.
R v McIntyre [1976] RTR 330, CA.

Case also cited
Mullarky v Prescott [1970] RTR 296.

c
Case stated
John Harry Chatters appealed by way of a case stated by the justices for the county of Suffolk acting in and for the petty sessional division of Sudbury and Cosford in respect of their adjudication as a magistrates' court sitting at Sudbury whereby they fined the respondent, Timothy Paul Burke, for, inter alia, driving a motor vehicle when the proportion of alcohol in his blood exceeded the prescribed limit but declined to disqualify
d him from driving. The facts are set out in the judgment of Taylor J.

Simon Mehigan for the appellant.
Martyn Levett for the respondent.

e **TAYLOR J** (delivering the first judgment at the invitation of Watkins LJ). This is an appeal by John Harry Chatters by way of case stated by the justices for the county of Suffolk acting in and for the petty sessional division of Sudbury and Cosford in respect of their adjudication as a magistrates' court sitting at Sudbury.

The appellant preferred a charge against the respondent alleging that on Sunday 14 July 1985, in the early hours, at Glemsford in the county of Suffolk, the respondent drove
f a motor vehicle when the proportion of alcohol in his breath exceeded the prescribed limit. Other charges were also preferred against him, one of using a motor vehicle without the necessary insurance on 13 July and another on the same date of using a motor vehicle when no test certificate was in force. The justices heard the charges on 22 October, and the respondent pleaded guilty to all three of them.

The facts which were outlined on behalf of the appellant were as follows. The
g respondent was a passenger in a motor car on the evening of 13 July 1985. The reason why he was a passenger was that he had considered himself on leaving a party to be likely to have alcohol in his body above the legal limit. Accordingly, he requested someone else to drive the vehicle due to his probable impairment.

While the car was proceeding along Lower Road, Glemsford, the driver lost control of it. The car left the road, rolled over and stopped upright in a field adjacent to the
h highway. The respondent then drove the vehicle from its resting position in the field through a gateway, onto the side of the road, and immediately stopped driving the motor car and got out.

The police attended the scene, and the respondent indicated that he had driven the car to its then position on the highway. The officer formed the view that he had been drinking, and he was invited to supply a specimen of his breath. That showed that he
j was over the limit, and the Intoximeter reading was 51.

It was contended on behalf of the respondent that this was a very minor case of driving with excess alcohol and no insurance, in view of the short distance actually travelled on the highway, which was a matter of a few yards. That submission was relevant to the only issue in this case, which is whether the disqualification prescribed by s 93(1) of the Road Traffic Act 1972 might be avoided by special reasons being found. The justices were advised by their clerk that where a very short distance was travelled it was open to them to find special reasons for not disqualifying under that section.   a

The respondent gave evidence that he drove the motor car along the edge of the field, out of the gate, a matter of a few yards, and onto the roadway, facing the correct way. He left the car in that position until the police arrived. He was asked why he had so driven it, and he said because it seemed the right thing to do at the time. He later said he did not know why he had put it on the highway, but then added that it was in order to get the motor car out of the field. There was a flat tyre on the vehicle at the time that he left   b
it on the road.

On that evidence the respondent contended that the case presented on his behalf justified the justices in concluding that there were special reasons for not disqualifying. On behalf of the appellant it was contended that there were no special reasons. *James v Hall* (1968) [1972] 2 All ER 59, [1972] 1 WLR 797 was referred to. The justices came to the conclusion on the evidence that the respondent had only driven the vehicle a few   c
yards on the highway, and that the shortness of the distance was a special reason for not imposing the otherwise mandatory disqualification. They found, again as part of their opinion, that it was the respondent's intention to drive the motor car out of the field, but not to drive any appreciable distance along the highway. They rejected a submission that *James v Hall* should be distinguished on the grounds that here the vehicle was being put onto the highway rather than being moved from it, and in so finding they expressed the   d
view that the salient point was the distance travelled on the highway rather than whether the vehicle was being moved onto it or off it.

In the result the justices fined the respondent but did not disqualify him, announcing that they had found special reasons for not doing so. It is that finding of theirs regarding special reasons which is challenged on this appeal.

We have been referred to a number of authorities, first *James v Hall*, which, although   e
it was reported in 1972 as I have indicated, was in fact decided in 1968. That was a case in which the respondent had been to his daughter's wedding and had had some drink, though not very much. He accepted an invitation to stay the night with his friend and, some time after midnight, went out to move his motor car a few yards so as to take it off the street and park it in his friend's driveway. He was seen doing that by a police officer at a stage when he had stopped the vehicle in the middle of the road, and the officer then   f
cautioned him and invoked the provisions of the 1972 Act to take a breath test, which was found to be positive.

The question arose in *James v Hall* whether there ought to be a disqualification or whether the shortness of the distance and other circumstances amounted to special reasons for not disqualifying. The justices did not in fact disqualify.

Lord Parker CJ, in considering the appeal by the prosecutor, said ([1972] 2 All ER 59   g
at 60, [1972] 1 WLR 797 at 798):

'. . . it seems to me that the fact that he was only trying to drive a few yards to remove his car from the highway into his friend's driveway could amount to a special reason, being a reason special to the offence.'

The decision was therefore upheld.   h

James v Hall was considered in 1972 in the later decision in *Coombs v Kehoe* [1972] 2 All ER 55, [1972] 1 WLR 797. That was a case in which a lorry driver had parked his lorry opposite a public house. He had consumed some alcohol and subsequently decided to drive the lorry some 200 yards down a busy thoroughfare to another parking place. On his way he succeeded in colliding with two vehicles. He pleaded guilty to the offence of driving with a blood-alcohol concentration above the prescribed limit, but sought to   j
persuade the justices not to disqualify him on the grounds of special reasons. The justices found as a special reason for not disqualifying him that at the time of the commission of the offence he was only parking his lorry, and the distance involved was not more than 200 yards.

The judgment of this court was given by Lord Widgery CJ, and the headnote reads as follows ([1972] 2 All ER 55):

a
'... Although there might be a special reason for non-disqualification ... where a driver only moved his car a few yards without the likelihood of it coming into contact with other users of the road, where a vehicle was driven some 200 yards through a busy street so that it was a potential source of danger to other users of the road, the fact that the driver was only parking the vehicle and only covering a short distance for that purpose could not amount to a special reason ...'

b
Lord Widgery CJ put the matter in this way ([1972] 2 All ER 55 at 58, [1972] 1 WLR 797 at 800):

c
'It is one thing to say that a man who drives literally a few yards—by that I mean 10 or 15 yards, something of that kind—and in circumstances in which his manoeuvre is really unlikely to bring him into contact with other road users at all and thus unlikely to produce a source of danger, is a sufficient special reason in the particular circumstances, and quite a different thing to say that a man parking his lorry may be excused disqualification if he drives through busy streets for 200 yards, and inevitably in those circumstances his lorry is a potential source of danger to someone on the road.'

d
Accordingly, in *Coombs v Kehoe* the justices' decision was overruled, and it was held to be a case in which disqualification was appropriate.

We have been referred also to the more recent case of *Haime v Walklett* [1983] RTR 512. There again it was intended by a driver who had had too much to drink to move his vehicle some 200 yards towards a car park. He had only in fact gone a very few yards when he was seen by a police officer, and in that short distance he had stalled the vehicle twice and had mounted the pavement twice. The road was one in which there was a

e
public house. Ackner LJ took the view that that being so it was clearly a road which was likely to carry some traffic and, although the justices were of the opinion that there were special reasons for not disqualifying, this court reversed their decision.

In particular it is relevant to observe that Ackner LJ said (at 516):

f
'In my judgment, where the justices have clearly gone wrong is in confining their attention to the actual distance driven by the defendant. It was mere chance that he did not drive the intended 200 yards.'

Counsel for the respondent has suggested that one of the factors which it is legitimate for a court to take into account in considering this type of special reason is whether the respondent had originally had any intention of driving that evening. He drew attention to two cases. The first was *R v Agnew* [1969] Crim LR 152. That was a case in which,

g
after a collision, a passenger was invited to drive the vehicle involved some 6 feet, and it was held that as he had had no intention of driving any further than that extremely short distance that was a relevant matter to finding special reasons.

The other case was *R v McIntyre* [1976] RTR 330. Two cars were outside a public house causing an obstruction. When the appellant and his friend emerged from the public house, the appellant's car was blocking a turning, and he was under the impression that

h
a police constable who was present required him to move it. He accordingly moved the vehicle a very short distance, and again the fact that he had had no intention of driving it, as was found by the justices, was regarded as a relevant factor in considering that there were special reasons.

It is clear from these cases that there may be special reasons for not disqualifying a driver where he moves a vehicle only a short distance without any appreciable risk of

j
contact with other road users. The cases emphasise that such instances of special reasons being found will be rare and that the shortness of the distance driven is not the only or indeed the major criterion. Whether the road is a busy one and the chances of other traffic being affected by the respondent's manoeuvre are more important considerations.

In the course of this case Watkins LJ indicated seven matters which ought to be taken into account by justices if a submission is made that special reasons exist for the defendant not being disqualified. First of all they should consider how far the vehicle was in fact driven; second, in what manner it was driven; third, what was the state of the vehicle; fourth, whether it was the intention of the driver to drive any further; fifth, the *a* prevailing conditions with regard to the road and the traffic on it; sixth, whether there was any possibility of danger by contact with other road users; and, finally, what was the reason for the vehicle being driven at all.

Of those seven matters, for my part I would have thought that item six was the most important, but clearly the distance which is driven is of itself not a sufficient determinant whether special reasons should be found or not.   *b*

With those matters in mind it is necessary to look at the case stated by the justices here to see what was their true finding. It is argued by counsel for the appellant that, as in *Haime v Walklett*, the justices here based themselves simply on the shortness of the distance driven. Were that so, were we of the view that that were so, I for my part would regard the justices as having fallen into error. However, although they did say in their opinion that the shortness of the distance was a special reason for not imposing the *c* otherwise mandatory disqualification, they also indicated that they found that it was the respondent's intention to drive the car out of the field on to the highway and no more. They also took the view that the salient point was the distance travelled on the highway. It seems to me that although they did not spell it out as fully as they might have done, the justices, in saying that, were clearly having proper regard to the question of whether this vehicle was likely on the highway to be in contact with other road users and liable to *d* give rise to any danger thereby.

Those being the matters which the justices took into account, it seems to me that they were entitled on the facts of this case to come to the conclusion that they did. The distance actually driven by this respondent was very short and that which he drove on the highway was minimal. The manner of his driving is not commented on as having caused any difficulty. The state of the car, apart from its flat tyre, was without any *e* particular unusual feature. The flat tyre itself may very well have been a factor in making the justices confident that the respondent had no intention of driving any further.

So far as his intentions are concerned, he expressed the view that he was not intending to drive the vehicle further, and that was confirmed by the fact that he got out of it and was waiting out of the vehicle when the police arrived. The conditions of the road are not spelt out in the case, unhappily, and that is a matter therefore that one cannot further *f* pursue.

As to the possible risk of danger, the justices clearly had in mind the shortness of the travel on the highway; and, as to the reason for moving the vehicle, the respondent said that he had thought that it was the right thing to do in the circumstances to move the vehicle from the field onto the edge of the roadway. Whether there was any risk of it sinking in the field, or whatever other factor was operating on his mind, was not spelt *g* out in the case.

Reviewing the decision of the justices against the seven criteria to which I have made reference, it seems to me that there was more than one factor taken into account here and that the evidence was sufficient to justify the view which the justices took.

Accordingly, for my part I would dismiss this appeal.

h

WATKINS LJ. I agree. The appeal will be dismissed.

Appeal dismissed.

Solicitors: *Sharpe Pritchard & Co*, agents for M F C Harvey, Ipswich (for the appellant); *Steed & Steed*, Sudbury (for the respondent).   *j*

June Meader   Barrister.

a

Attorney General of Hong Kong v Tse Hung-lit and another

PRIVY COUNCIL

LORD BRIDGE OF HARWICH, LORD BRIGHTMAN, LORD MACKAY OF CLASHFERN, LORD ACKNER AND
LORD GOFF OF CHIEVELEY

b 22 MAY 1986

Hong Kong – Crime – Attempting to export unmanifested cargo and prohibited articles without licence – Offence to 'cause' articles to be taken out of Hong Kong – Cause – Respondents hired to convey goods to fishing boat within territorial waters of Hong Kong – Fishing boat crew intending to take goods to China – Fishing boat failing to meet respondents at rendezvous – Whether
c *respondents having control or influence over crew of fishing boat – Whether respondents 'causing' goods to be taken out of Hong Kong – Import and Export Ordinance (Hong Kong), s 18 – Import and Export (General) Regulations (Hong Kong), reg 4.*

The respondents were hired by another to load aboard a speed boat in Hong Kong video cassette recorders in respect of which there was neither an export licence nor a cargo
d manifest, and to carry them to an agreed meeting place within Hong Kong waters with the intention of transferring them to a fishing boat which was to take the recorders to China. The fishing boat never arrived and on their return journey to Hong Kong the respondents were intercepted by the police. They were tried and convicted of attempting to commit the offences of causing to be taken out of Hong Kong unmanifested cargo, contrary to s 18*ᵃ* of the Import and Export Ordinance, and causing to be taken out of
e Hong Kong articles without an export licence, contrary to reg 4*ᵇ* of the Import and Export (General) Regulations. The respondents appealed, contending that, if the fishing boat had arrived and taken the goods to China, they would not have 'caused' the goods to be taken to China. The Court of Appeal of Hong Kong allowed the appeal. The Attorney General of Hong Kong appealed to the Privy Council, contending that since the respondents knew that the goods were to be taken out of Hong Kong and had played
f their part in attempting to effect that result they would have 'caused' the goods to be taken out of Hong Kong if the plan had not miscarried.

Held – Applying the principle that an offence of 'causing' a person to carry out a prohibited act was only committed if the prohibited act was done on the actual authority, whether express or implied, of the person said to have 'caused' the act or in consequence of his exerting some influence on the acts of the other person, the respondents could not
g be said to have 'caused' the unlicensed and unmanifested cargo to be taken out of Hong Kong if the plan had been carried through, because the respondents would not have been in any position in fact or in law to control or influence the crew of the fishing boat and the crew of the fishing boat would not have been acting on the express or implied authority of the respondents. Furthermore, there was nothing in the context of the Hong Kong legislation creating the offences of causing to be taken out of Hong Kong either
h unmanifested cargo or articles without the required export licence which displaced the application of that principle. The appeal would therefore be dismissed (see p 172 *e g* to *j* and p 178 *d e*, post).

Dicta of Dixon CJ, Williams, Webb and Fullagar JJ in *O'Sullivan v Truth and Sportsman Ltd* (1957) 96 CLR at 228–229 adopted.

j **Notes**

For causing a person to commit a criminal act, see 11 Halsbury's Laws (4th edn) para 1308.

---

a   Section 18, so far as material, is set out at p 177 *e, post*

b   Regulation 4 is set out at p 177 *f g, post*

Cases referred to in judgment

McLeod (or Houston) v Buchanan [1940] 2 All ER 179, HL.
O'Sullivan v Truth and Sportsman Ltd (1957) 96 CLR 220, Aust HC.
Shave v Rosner [1954] 2 All ER 280, [1954] 2 QB 113, [1954] 2 WLR 1057, DC.
Watkins v O'Shaughnessy [1939] 1 All ER 385, CA.

Cases also cited

Alphacell Ltd v Woodward [1972] 2 All ER 475, [1972] AC 824, HL.
Bertschy v R [1967] HKLR 739.
Budenberg v Roberts (1886) LR 1 CP 575.
Goodbarne v Buck [1939] 4 All ER 107, [1940] 1 KB 107; affd [1940] 1 All ER 613, [1940]
  1 KB 771, CA.
Hardcastle v Bielby [1892] 1 QB 709.
Kelly's Directories Ltd v Gavin and Lloyds [1901] 2 Ch 763.
Klauser v R [1968] HKLR 201.
Lockhart v National Coal Board 1981 SLT 161.
Lovelace v DPP [1954] 3 All ER 481, [1954] 1 WLR 1468, DC.
Po Koon Tai v R [1980] HKLR 492.
R v Dunnington [1984] 1 All ER 676, [1984] QB 472.
R v Suen Chuen [1963] HKLR 630.
Saxton v Police [1981] 2 NZLR 186, NZ CA.
Shulton (GB) Ltd v Slough BC [1967] 2 All ER 137, [1967] 2 QB 471, DC.
Thornton v Mitchell [1940] 1 All ER 339, DC.

Appeal

The Attorney General of Hong Kong appealed by special leave of the Judicial Committee
against the decision of the Court of Appeal of Hong Kong (Huggins V-P and Cons JA,
Fuad JA dissenting) on 23 April 1985 allowing an appeal by the respondents, Tse Hung-
lit and Chan Yat-sing, from their convictions on 17 December 1984 and 2 January 1985
respectively, by the Magistrate's Court at Tsuen Wan of the offences of attempting to
export unmanifested cargo contrary to s 18(1)(b) of the Import and Export Ordinance
and attempting to export articles without a licence contrary to reg 4(1)(a) of the Import
and Export (General) Regulations. The facts are set out in the judgment of the Board.

The Director of Public Prosecutions for Hong Kong (J M Duffy QC) and P J Dykes (of the Hong
  Kong Bar) for the appellant.
Desmond Keane QC and Timothy Corner for the respondents.

22 May. The following judgment of the Board was delivered.

LORD BRIDGE OF HARWICH. This is an appeal from the majority decision of the
Court of Appeal of Hong Kong (Huggins V-P and Cons JA, Fuad JA dissenting) allowing
appeals by the respondents against their convictions by the Magistrate's Court at Tsuen
Wan of attempting to export unmanifested cargo and attempting to export articles
without the required export licence.
  The facts may be inferred from the respondents' statements and from the findings of
the magistrate. The respondents agreed for reward with a man named Ah Fai to load 34
video cassette recorders on board a speed boat, carry them to an agreed meeting place
within Hong Kong waters and there transfer them to a fishing boat. As the respondents
knew, it was intended that the crew of the fishing boat would then take the video cassette
recorders to China. The export of video cassette recorders from Hong Kong to any
country without a licence is prohibited. No licence for the export of these video cassette
recorders had been issued. Needless to say, there was no cargo manifest. In the event the
respondents took the video cassette recorders to the agreed meeting place where they
waited for some hours, but the fishing boat never arrived. On the return journey the
respondents' speedboat was intercepted by a police launch.

a   The respondents were convicted by the magistrate of the offences of attempt already
mentioned. On appeal a new point was taken, which had not been taken before the
magistrates. The respondents, it was submitted, could not be convicted of any attempt to
export the goods because, if the fishing boat had arrived and taken the goods to China,
the respondents would not have been guilty as principals of the relevant offences. This
was the argument which the majority of the Court of Appeal accepted. It is common
ground that the respondents could properly have been convicted of conspiracy to commit
b   the relevant offences. On the other hand, the prosecution do not seek to support the
convictions on the ground that, if the goods had been exported by the crew of the fishing
boat, the respondents could have been convicted of aiding and abetting or of counselling
and procuring the offences. For the purpose of both the offences which the respondents
were accused of attempting to commit the prohibited activity was to 'export' and this is
defined in s 2 of the Import and Export Ordinance as meaning 'to take, or cause to be
c   taken, out of Hong Kong any article other than an article in transit'. Nothing turns on
the degree of proximity of what the respondents did to the completion of the offences. If
the video cassette recorders had been transferred to the fishing boat within Hong Kong
waters and taken out of Hong Kong aboard that boat, it was only faintly suggested for
the appellant that the respondents could have been convicted on the basis that they
themselves had taken the goods out of Hong Kong. Their Lordships are satisfied they
d   could not. The real issue in the appeal is whether, in those circumstances, the respondents,
on the true construction of the definition of 'export' as applied to the two offences, could
properly be said to have 'caused to be taken out of Hong Kong' the unlicensed and
unmanifested cargo.
Questions of causation arise in many different legal contexts and no single theory of
causation will provide a ready made answer to the question whether A's action is to be
e   treated as the cause or a cause of some ensuing event. The approach must necessarily be
pragmatic, as is well illustrated by the many more or less imprecise distinctions which
the common law draws between what is and what is not to be treated as an effective cause
in different legal situations. When, as here, the word 'cause' is used in a statutory
definition which falls to be applied in ascertaining the ingredients of criminal offences,
care must be taken to give it no wider meaning than necessary to give effect to the
f   evident legislative purpose of the enactment.
The argument for the appellant, briefly summarised, is that the taking of goods out of
Hong Kong is an event and that any action in a chain of circumstances which foreseeably
leads to and facilitates the occurrence of that event may be said to be a cause of that event,
so as to bring the action within the relevant definition of 'export'. It is immaterial,
according to this submission, whether or not the independent action of a third party may
g   intervene between the action of the person alleged to have exported goods by causing
them to be taken out of Hong Kong and the event of the goods crossing the Hong Kong
border. So here, it is said, the respondents, if the fishing boat had kept the appointment
and taken the video cassette recorders out of Hong Kong, would have been a necessary
link in the chain of causation between Ah Fai, who planned and initiated the operation,
and the crew of the fishing boat, who brought it to fruition. The respondents knew that
h   the goods were to be taken out of Hong Kong, they played their allotted part in
attempting to effect that result and, if the plan had not miscarried, they could properly
be said to have caused the goods to be taken out of Hong Kong.
This is a formidable argument which perhaps gains in attraction from the consideration
that its application to the circumstances of the instant case would cause no injustice
whatever. The respondents have no merit and were fully alive to the criminality of the
j   enterprise in which they were prepared to participate. But it is important to bear in mind
that, if the enterprise had succeeded, the question whether the respondents caused the
video cassette recorders to be taken out of Hong Kong would have fallen to be answered
independently of their guilty knowledge of the illegality of the exportation.
The respondents rely on a line of English and Scottish authority in which a variety of
expressions have been used to limit and define the nature of the relationship which is
required to be established before one person can be convicted under a criminal statute of

'causing' another person to act in a way which the statute prohibits. The principal cases
are *Watkins v O'Shaughnessy* [1939] 1 All ER 385, *McLeod (or Houston) v Buchanan* [1940] 2   **a**
All ER 179 and *Shave v Rosner* [1954] 2 All ER 280, [1954] 2 QB 113. Their Lordships are
relieved of the duty of undertaking an independent review of these authorities since this
task has, in their Lordships' respectful opinion, been so thoroughly and admirably
performed by the High Court of Australia in *O'Sullivan v Truth and Sportsman Ltd* (1957)
96 CLR 220. The question at issue in that case was whether the respondent newspaper
publishers could properly be convicted of 'causing to be offered for sale' by a newsagent a   **b**
newspaper containing certain prohibited matter, in circumstances where the publishers
distributed the paper to the newsagent for the very purpose of making it available for
sale to the public. The High Court of Australia answered the question in the negative.
After a review of the relevant English authorities, the judgment of Dixon CJ, Williams,
Webb and Fullagar JJ contains the following statement of the principle to be derived
from them (at 228):   **c**

> 'This appears to mean that when it is made an offence by or under statute for one
> man to "cause" the doing of a prohibited act by another the provision is not to be
> understood as referring to any description of antecedent event or condition produced
> by the first man which contributed to the determination of the will of the second
> man to do the prohibited act. Nor is it enough that in producing the antecedent
> event or condition the first man was actuated by the desire that the second should   **d**
> be led to do the prohibited act. The provision should be understood as opening up a
> less indefinite inquiry into the sequence of anterior events to which the forbidden
> result may be ascribed. It should be interpreted as confined to cases where the
> prohibited act is done on the actual authority, express or implied, of the party said
> to have caused it or in consequence of his exerting some capacity which he possesses
> in fact or law to control or influence the acts of the other. He must moreover   **e**
> contemplate or desire that the prohibited act will ensue.'

Later, in considering whether the English principle should be followed, the judgment
adds (at 229):

> 'It tends to greater certainty in interpretation. It provides a sensible and workable
> test, which, at the same time, is hardly open to objection as inelastic. Without some   **f**
> such interpretation the words might be used to impose criminal sanctions in a
> manner that could not be foreseen on conduct vaguely and indefinitely described.
> But being a question of the meaning of terms the definition can provide only a
> primary meaning which context or any other sufficient indication of a different
> intention would displace. In the present case no contrary intention appears and the
> words "cause to be offered for sale or sold" in s. 35(1) should accordingly be   **g**
> understood as bearing the meaning stated.'

Their Lordships gratefully adopt both these passages, the first as an accurate and
succinct statement of the general principle prima facie to be applied, the second as a
salutary reminder that the principle may be displaced by the context in which it is made
an offence for one person to cause another to act in a particular way.   **h**

If the general principle is here applicable, it appears to their Lordships to afford to the
respondents a complete defence. Had the fishing boat kept the appointment with the
respondents and taken the video cassette recorders out of Hong Kong, there would have
been a plain inference that the crew of that boat were acting on the authority of Ah Fai,
the organiser of the forbidden exportation, and expecting no doubt, like the respondents,
to be rewarded by Ah Fai. But there was nothing in the evidence led by the prosecution   **j**
which could have justified the inference that the respondents were in any position, in
fact or in law, to control or influence the crew of the fishing boat, or that, if the plan had
been carried through, the crew of the fishing boat would have been acting on the express
or implied authority of the respondents.

The question then is whether the context of the relevant Hong Kong legislation
requires a different approach to the interpretation of the expression 'cause to be taken out

of Hong Kong'. In his dissenting judgment Fuad JA answered that question affirmatively.

a After a review of the authorities and reference to *O'Sullivan v Truth and Sportsman Ltd*, he said:

'In my respectful judgment, different considerations apply in the case before us. Here, we are not concerned with an offence of the kind discussed in the cases to which I have referred. Although it would be a rare case that an intervening human agency is not involved, the offence here essentially is not causing someone else to do

b a prohibited act, but the very act of "exporting", which can be done by the person charged either by taking the controlled goods out of Hong Kong himself, or by causing them to be taken out of Hong Kong. Put another way, there is a conceptual difference, it seems to me, between causing another to do an illegal act to which one is not a party in the usual sense, on the one hand, and being the actual perpetrator of an act which is the cause of an event taking place, on the other. It is only in the

c former case that considerations of "control, dominance or compulsion" (*Watkins v O'Shaughnessy* [1939] 1 All ER 385) are relevant. In my view, these authorities do not require us to give a restricted meaning to the words "cause to be taken out" in the context of the Import and Export Ordinance.'

It is appropriate to test this approach by reference to the statutory language creating

d the two offences which the respondents were accused of attempting to commit. The offence of exporting unmanifested cargo is created by s 18 of the Import and Export Ordinance. Read with the substitution for the word 'export' of the relevant terms of the definition s 18 provides:

'(1) Any person who . . . (b) takes, or causes to be taken, out of Hong Kong any unmanifested cargo, shall be guilty of an offence and shall be liable on conviction to

e a fine of $50,000 and to imprisonment for 6 months.

(2) It shall be a defence to a charge under this section against the owner of a vessel, aircraft or vehicle, if the owner proves that he did not know and could not with reasonable diligence have known that the cargo was unmanifested.'

The offence of exporting articles without a licence is created by reg 4 of the Import and

f Export (General) Regulations. Read with the like substitution, the regulation provides:

'(1) No person shall take, or cause to be taken, out of Hong Kong any article specified in the second column of the Second Schedule to the country or place specified opposite thereto in the third column of that Schedule except under and in accordance with a licence.

(2) Any person who contravenes paragraph (1) shall be guilty of an offence and

g shall be liable on conviction to a fine of $500,000 and to imprisonment for 2 years.'

In Sch 2 'Electrical products (powered by mains supply)' are specified in the second column and 'All countries' are specified opposite thereto in the third column.

It is unnecessary for the purposes of this judgment to express any conclusion whether a defence of lack of knowledge would be available to a defendant who was not the 'owner

h of a vessel, aircraft or vehicle' charged with causing unmanifested cargo to be taken out of Hong Kong. It is common ground that the offence created by reg 4 is one of strict liability. Their Lordships express no view whether an offence under reg 4 of causing to be taken, as opposed to taking, out of Hong Kong could theoretically be committed, as Fuad JA thought, without any intervening human agency. Let it be assumed that it could. Nevertheless the plain purpose of including among those absolutely liable for the

j export of goods without the appropriate licence persons who cause such goods to be taken out of Hong Kong, as well as those who take them out, is to apply the same criminal sanction to the consignor and his forwarding agent, who arrange and organise the illicit exportation, as to the owner of the ship, aircraft or vehicle which effects the exportation by actually taking the goods out of Hong Kong. Persons in these or similar categories would properly be held, on the narrow construction of the words 'cause to be taken out of Hong Kong', to be exporting. The goods are taken out of Hong Kong by others acting on their express or implied authority. It seems entirely appropriate that those responsible for arranging the exportation of goods, as well as those who directly perform the act of exportation, should be responsible for ensuring that any appropriate licence has been obtained and should be held criminally liable in the absence of such a licence. But what of others who merely play a physical part in the sequence of events which leads to exportation? The road haulage contractor who brings goods from the warehouse to the dockside and the stevedoring firm which loads the goods on board the ship know full well that the goods are to be exported, but are in no position to give and do not purport to give any authority to the shipowner to effect the exportation. Yet, if the appellant's construction of the language of the legislation is adopted, they too must be held to have caused the goods to be taken out of Hong Kong and will act at their peril unless they ensure in every case that the appropriate export licence has been obtained. Their Lordships fully appreciate the necessity in such a community as Hong Kong for the authorities to exercise strict control over imports and exports, but can discern no good reason why it should be necessary, in order to make such control effective, that the criminal net should be cast as widely as it would be if the construction urged by the appellant were accepted.

In the light of this analysis their Lordships cannot accept that there is anything to be found in the context of the relevant Hong Kong legislation creating the offences of 'causing to be taken out of Hong Kong' either unmanifested cargo or articles without the required export licence which is apt to displace the principle prima facie applicable to statutory offences of this kind as expressed in *O'Sullivan v Truth and Sportsman Ltd* (1957) 96 CLR 220. Nor, with respect, can their Lordships accept that there is a 'conceptual difference' between 'causing another to do an illegal act to which one is not a party in the usual sense' and 'being the actual perpetrator of an act which is the cause of an event taking place' which provides a relevant basis on which *O'Sullivan's* case and the earlier authorities there considered can properly be distinguished.

Accordingly their Lordships will humbly advise Her Majesty that the appeal should be dismissed.

Appeal dismissed.

Solicitors: *Macfarlanes* (for the appellant); *Philip Conway Thomas & Co* (for the respondents).

Mary Rose Plummer   Barrister.

Practice Direction

SUPREME COURT TAXING OFFICE

Admiralty – Costs – Taxation – Costs in Admiralty matters to be taxed in Supreme Court Taxing Office – Commencement of taxations – Summons to review taxation – Procedure.

At the request of Master Topley, Admiralty Registrar, all costs in Admiralty matters will be taxed in the Supreme Court Taxing Office.

The procedure for the commencement of taxations will be as set out in *The Supreme Court Practice 1985* vol 1, paras 62/22/1–62/22/6.

A summons to review a taxation will follow the Queen's Bench Division procedure in accordance with the Practice Direction of Lord Lane CJ dated 10 May 1984 (see *Practice Note* [1984] 2 All ER 288, [1984] 1 WLR 856, *The Supreme Court Practice 1985* vol 1, para 62/35/3).

With the agreement of the Admiralty Registrar the Practice Direction of the Admiralty Registrar dated 1 November 1973 ([1973] 3 All ER 896, [1973] 1 WLR 1424) is cancelled.

F T HORNE
Chief Taxing Master.

29 July 1986

a # James v Amsterdam-Rotterdam Bank NV
and another

CHANCERY DIVISION
WARNER AND MILLETT JJ
30 APRIL, 1, 2 MAY 1986

b

Bankruptcy – Act of bankruptcy – Non-compliance with bankruptcy notice – Execution of judgment debt not having been stayed – Execution stayed in respect of part of judgment debt – Whether balance of debt can support bankruptcy notice – Whether bankruptcy notice can be served if stay of execution lifted – Bankruptcy Act 1914, s 1(1)(g).

c *Bankruptcy – Bankruptcy notice – Service – Substituted service – Service by post – When service effected – Requirements of order for substituted service.*

On 27 June 1984 an order was made in the High Court ordering the debtor to pay a specified sum to the petitioning creditor. A stay of execution was granted in respect of part of that sum pending trial of a counterclaim brought by the debtor. The debtor failed
d to pay the balance and, on the application of the petitioning creditor, a bankruptcy notice was issued in respect of the outstanding amount and served on the debtor by means of substituted service. The order for substituted service provided for the bankruptcy notice to 'be posted to the debtor' and stated that that would be deemed 'good and sufficient service' of the notice on the debtor. The notice was posted to the debtor by first class mail on 2 May 1985. The subsequent bankruptcy petition presented by the petitioning
e creditor stated that the bankruptcy notice had been served on 3 May. On 8 January 1986 a receiving order was made against the debtor founded on the bankruptcy notice. The debtor appealed against the order on the ground that he had not committed the act of bankruptcy relied on by the creditor and contending (i) that for the purposes of s 1(1)(g)[a] of the Bankruptcy Act 1914, under which a debtor committed an act of bankruptcy if he did not comply within ten days with a bankruptcy notice served on him in respect of a
f final judgment or order 'execution thereon not having been stayed', any stay of execution, including a stay relating to part only of the amount contained in the judgment order, precluded service of a bankruptcy notice founded on the judgment or order, (ii) that the petition had incorrectly stated the date when the notice was served because in the case of substituted service by post service was effected by placing the notice in the post, which had been done on 2 May 1985 and therefore 3 May as stated in the petition was not the
g date of service. The petitioning creditor contended (i) that 'execution thereon not having been stayed' referred only to a stay of execution in respect of the whole amount of the judgment, (ii) that substituted service of a bankruptcy notice by post was not effected until the notice was delivered to the debtor and (iii) that, in any event, a mistake of one day in the date of service was so insubstantial that leave ought to be granted to amend the petition to state the correct date.

h

Held – (1) On the true construction of s 1(1)(g) of the 1914 Act service of a bankruptcy notice founded on a judgment or order was precluded on the ground of 'execution thereon not having been stayed' only if the stay of execution related to the whole of the judgment or order. Accordingly, where a stay of execution had been granted in respect of part only of a judgment debt, the balance of the debt could support the issue of a
j bankruptcy notice under s 1(1)(g). It followed that the bankruptcy notice issued against the debtor was not invalidated by the stay of execution granted in respect of the amount counterclaimed by the debtor (see p 181 *d g* to p 182 *a* and p 184 *h*, post); *Re Bates, ex p*

---

a   Section 1(1), so far as material, is set out at p 181 *e f*, post

Lindsey (1887) 57 LT 417, *Re Child, ex p Child* [1891–4] All ER Rep 899 and *Re Miller, ex p Furniture and Fine Arts Depositories Ltd* [1912] 3 KB 1 applied.   *a*

(2) The requirement in the order for substituted service that the bankruptcy notice 'be posted to the debtor' meant merely that the notice had to be placed in the course of post. Furthermore, where an order directed that service of documents be effected by a specified act then, unless the contrary was stated, service was completed when that act was carried out and, accordingly, service of the bankruptcy notice had been completed on 2 May 1985 when the notice was placed in the post, as directed by the order. The   *b* petition had therefore incorrectly stated the date of service of the bankruptcy notice. Since that error was one of substance rather than form the court would not give leave to amend the petition. Instead, the appeal would be allowed and the receiving order discharged (see p 183 *f* to *j*, p 184 *h* and p 185 *c*, post); *Re Hastings (a bankrupt)* [1985] 1 All ER 885 applied; *Austin Rover Group Ltd v Crouch Butler Savage Associates (a firm)* [1986] 3 All ER 50 considered.   *c*

Per curiam. (1) Section 1(1)(g) of the 1914 Act only prevents service of a bankruptcy notice during a subsisting stay of execution and does not preclude service of a bankruptcy notice after a stay of execution has been lifted (see p 182 *b* and p 184 *h*, post).

(2) An order for substituted service should contain express provision regarding the time at which service is to be taken to be effected, so that, when read with the bankruptcy notice, the debtor can be left in no doubt about the period which he has in which to   *d* comply with the bankruptcy notice; the time at which service should be deemed to be effected should be a stated day and should not be defined by reference to the date of posting; and the stated day should be no earlier than the date on which it can reasonably be anticipated that service would in fact be effected in the ordinary course of post (see p 184 *b f g* and p 185 *c*, post).

e

Notes

For a debtor's non-compliance with a bankruptcy notice constituting an act of bankruptcy and for stay of execution preventing the issue of a bankruptcy notice, see 3 Halsbury's Laws (4th edn) paras 255, 262, and for cases on the subject, see 4 Digest (Reissue) 91–93, 805–820.

For the Bankruptcy Act 1914, s 1, see 4 Halsbury's Statutes (4th edn) 512.   *f*

As from a day to be appointed under the Insolvency Act 1985, the Insolvency Act 1986 will make fresh provision with respect to insolvency.

Cases referred to in judgments

Austin Rover Group Ltd v Crouch Butler Savage Associates (a firm) [1986] 3 All ER 50, [1986]   *g*
    1 WLR 1102, CA.
Bates, Re, ex p Lindsey (1887) 57 LT 417, DC.
Child, Re, ex p Child [1892] 2 QB 77, [1891–4] All ER Rep 899, DC.
Debtor (No 21 of 1937), Re a [1938] 2 All ER 824, [1938] Ch 694, CA.
Debtor (No 9 of 1984), Re a (30 April 1985, unreported), DC.
H B, Re [1904] 1 KB 94, CA.   *h*
Hastings (a bankrupt), Re [1985] 1 All ER 885, [1985] 1 WLR 969, DC.
Miller, Re, ex p Furniture and Fine Arts Depositories Ltd [1912] 3 KB 1, CA.

Appeal

Robert Armand James (the debtor) appealed against a receiving order made by Mr   *j* Registrar D H C Lowis in the Exeter County Court on 8 January 1986. The respondents were the petitioning creditor, Amsterdam-Rotterdam Bank NV, and the Official Receiver of the Exeter County Court. The facts are set out in the judgment of Millett J.

Philip Hoser for the debtor.
Robin St John Knowles for the petitioning creditor.

MILLETT J (delivering the first judgment at the invitation of Warner J). This is an
a appeal from a receiving order made by the Exeter County Court on 8 January 1986. The
receiving order was founded on a bankruptcy notice dated 19 September 1984, which in
turn was founded on a judgment of the High Court dated 27 June 1984.

By that judgment it was adjudged that the defendant, the debtor, do pay to the
petitioning creditor 995,853·94 Dutch florins or the sterling equivalent at the date of
payment, and a stay of execution as to 240,000 Dutch florins was granted pending the
b trial of a counterclaim which the debtor wished to bring.

The bankruptcy notice required the debtor to pay the sum of 755,853·94 Dutch florins
or the sterling equivalent as being the amount due on a final judgment or order obtained
by the petitioner creditor against the debtor in the High Court of Justice, Queen's Bench
Division, action 1984 A No 560 dated 27 June 1984 whereon execution was not stayed.

The first submission made on behalf of the debtor is that, where execution has been
c stayed in respect of part of a judgment debt, the balance of the judgment debt cannot
support a bankruptcy notice. This submission depends on the true construction of the
words, 'execution thereon not having been stayed' which appear in s 1(1)(g) of the
Bankruptcy Act 1914. Surprisingly there is no decided case which directly covers the
point. However, in my judgment, the submission is contrary to the natural and
grammatical meaning of those words in the paragraph, would be productive of
d mischievous results, is inconsistent with the approach which has been adopted in the
decided cases and cannot be accepted.

Section 1(1) of the Act is in these terms:

> 'A debtor commits an act of bankruptcy . . . (g) If a creditor has obtained a final
> judgment or final order against him for any amount, and, execution thereon not
> having been stayed, has served on him in England, or, by leave of the court,
e elsewhere, a bankruptcy notice under this Act, and he does not, within ten days
> after service of the notice, in case the service is effected in England, and in case the
> service is effected elsewhere, then within the time limited in that behalf by the
> order giving leave to effect the service, either comply with the requirements of the
> notice or satisfy the court that he has a counter-claim set off or cross demand which
> equals or exceeds the amount of the judgment debt or sum ordered to be paid, and
f which he could not set up in the action in which the judgment was obtained, or the
> proceedings in which the order was obtained . . .'

The crucial words are: 'If a creditor has obtained a final judgment or final order against
him for any amount, and, execution thereon not having been stayed . . .'

One speaks of 'executing a judgment', not of 'executing an amount'. Grammatically,
g therefore, the word 'thereon' must refer back to the whole of the preceding phrase, 'a
final judgment or final order against him for any amount'. The judgment in question
must be the judgment for the whole amount irrespective, at this stage of the sentence,
whether execution on the whole or any part thereof has been stayed. Such a judgment
may support a bankruptcy notice, but, as the sentence goes on to provide, only if
execution thereon, that is to say on that judgment for the whole amount, has not been
h stayed. Where there has been a stay of execution on part of the judgment only, those
words are not satisfied. The debtor's submission requires further words, 'or any part
thereof', to be read into the paragraph immediately after the word 'thereon'. If those
words are read into the paragraph, the paradoxical result is then achieved that a judgment
debtor who has only a cross-claim, not amounting to a partial defence by way of set-off,
and who accordingly suffers judgment for the full amount of the creditor's claim with a
j stay of execution as to part, is in a stronger position, in that he can avoid the process of
bankruptcy until his cross-claim is determined, than he would have enjoyed if his cross-
claim gave a partial defence by way of set-off, so that he suffered judgment for part only
of the creditor's claim with leave to defend as to the balance. In this latter case the
judgment creditor would clearly have the right on any construction of the paragraph to
issue a bankruptcy notice at once without waiting for the final determination of his own
claim as to the balance. I can see no good reason why Parliament should have wished to

produce so paradoxical a result, nor can I see any good reason why Parliament should
have wished to preclude the service of a bankruptcy notice in respect of that part of a a
judgment debt on which execution has not been stayed, and therefore no good reason to
read any words into the paragraph which would be necessary to produce that result.

In fact the words 'execution . . . not having been stayed', which appear in the paragraph,
cannot be read literally, for this would preclude the service of a bankruptcy notice where
execution had formerly been stayed but the stay had since been lifted. They must be
taken to mean execution thereon not being subject to a subsisting stay. But, if the b
prohibition on issuing a bankruptcy notice is coextensive in duration with the subsistence
of a stay, there is good reason to construe the language of the paragraph so that it is
coextensive with it in amount also.

This, in my judgment, is also the approach adopted by the decided cases. In *Re Child,
ex p Child* [1892] 2 QB 77 at 81, [1891–4] All ER Rep 899 at 901 Vaughan Williams J
treated the natural view of the ratio decidendi of *Re Bates, ex p Lindsey* (1887) 57 LT 417 c
as being that a bankruptcy notice could only be served for the amount for which
execution could be issued. In *Re Miller, ex p Furniture and Fine Arts Depositories Ltd* [1912]
3 KB 1 the Court of Appeal held that a bankruptcy notice cannot issue for more than
execution can issue. Those cases do not, as counsel for the debtor cogently pointed out,
take the petitioning creditor the whole way that he must travel in this case. But, in my
judgment, it is consistent with that approach to add: but it can issue for that amount, d
and, for the reasons I have already endeavoured to give, that last step is warranted by the
terms of the paragraph itself.

It was submitted to us that the contrary conclusion is compelled by the decisions in *Re
H B* [1904] 1 KB 94 and *Re a debtor (No 21 of 1937)* [1938] 2 All ER 824, [1938] Ch 694.
In my judgment those cases were dealing with very different situations from the present.
In *Re H B* the bankruptcy notice was bad because it required payment, not in conformity e
with the judgment, but in conformity with a subsequent and purely consensual
arrangement for payment. In *Re a debtor (No 21 of 1937)* the judgment itself was in a
form which made it impossible for the bankruptcy notice to comply both with s 2 of the
Bankruptcy Act 1914 by requiring the debtor to pay in accordance with the terms of the
judgment and at the same time with the provisions of the Law Reform (Married Women
and Tortfeasors) Act 1935. f

The second point taken by the debtor is that the bankruptcy notice does not follow the
terms of the judgment in accordance with s 2 of the Bankruptcy Act 1914 because it
requires payment only of the sum in respect of which no stay had been obtained, whereas
it ought to have required payment of 755,853·94 Dutch florins, being that part of a final
judgment for 995,853·94 Dutch florins in respect of which execution has not been
stayed. g

The cases to which I have already referred of *Re Child, Re Bates* and *Re Miller* all show
that the correct form of bankruptcy notice is to require payment of the sum in respect of
which execution could issue, that is to say the lesser or reduced sum.

In the present case, the bankruptcy notice correctly identifies the judgment and states
the true amount in respect of which execution can issue and a bankruptcy notice can be
served. In my judgment, it need do no more than that. h

The third point taken by the debtor is of a different kind. The ground of appeal stated
in the notice of appeal was that it does not sufficiently appear from the bankruptcy
petition when the bankruptcy notice is alleged to have been served. In fact the bankruptcy
petition makes it abundantly clear, for it states in terms that the bankruptcy notice was
served on 3 May 1985. However, leave to amend that ground of appeal was given in the
course of the hearing and it now alleges that the bankruptcy petition incorrectly states j
the date when the bankruptcy notice was served and consequently the date of the act of
bankruptcy. We gave leave on the terms that that should not entitle further evidence to
be adduced as to what was the correct day. The point arises because the bankruptcy
notice was served by substituted service. The order for substituted service was in the
following terms:

a
'IT IS ORDERED THAT a sealed copy of this Order, together with a Bankruptcy Notice issued in this action, be posted to the debtor [giving his name and address] being the usual address of the debtor and that this shall be deemed to be good and sufficient service of the Bankruptcy Notice on the debtor.'

The evidence in support of the bankruptcy petition was that a letter containing the bankruptcy notice and a copy of the order served on the debtor by sending it on the
b previous day by ordinary post, first class mail, in a prepaid envelope. The evidence was simply that the bankruptcy notice and the order for substituted service were posted, that is to say placed in the course of the post, on 2 May.

Counsel for the debtor has submitted to us that the effect of the order for substituted service was that service should be effected by placing the letter in the post and that service was complete when the letter was posted. Accordingly, service was complete on 2 May
c and the date in the bankruptcy petition of 3 May is incorrect.

Counsel for the petitioning creditor submitted that the meaning of the phrase 'posted to the debtor' in the order for substituted service meant, not placing in the course of post, but included the whole process of transmission through the post and therefore was not complete until the letter was duly delivered to the debtor.

Some support for that submission was said to be found in a recent case in the Court of
d Appeal, *Austin Rover Ltd v Crouch Butler Savage Associates (a firm)* [1986] 3 All ER 50, [1986] 1 WLR 1102, which turned on the true construction of the phrase 'sending by post' where it appears in RSC Ord 81. In that case there was a difference of opinion between the members of the Court of Appeal. May LJ held that Ord 81 itself provided a context for construing the phrase 'sending by post' to mean the whole process of transmission by post. He said it was not complete until delivery. Lloyd LJ was able to
e find no such context and held that the natural and ordinary meaning of the phrase was to dispatch by post or place in the course of post. Sir John Megaw reached no conclusion on this matter at all, but was prepared to assume for the purposes of the judgment that the phrase meant placed in the ordinary course of post.

In *Re a debtor (No 9 of 1984)* (30 April 1985, unreported) this court was called on to deal with an order for substituted service in a similar form to that presently before us,
f but no argument was addressed to the court on the meaning of the phrase 'posted to the debtor'. However, it is pertinent to observe that both members of this court and both counsel who appeared before it appear to have assumed that the phrase meant placing in the course of post.

In my judgment that is the natural and ordinary meaning of the phrase and it requires a special context to give to it an extended meaning to embrace the whole process of
g transmission in the course of post.

Counsel for the petitioning creditor then advanced a further argument to the effect that the order for substituted service merely authorised that the service be effected in a particular manner, that is to say by placing the document in the post, and that it gave no directions as to the time when such service should be deemed to take place.

In one sense that is true. The order contains no express provision as to when service is
h to be deemed to be effected. However, in my judgment, if an order gives a direction that service is to be effected by the doing of a specified act, then it follows, unless the contrary is stated, that service must be complete when the act is done. Consequently, in my judgment, the true construction of this order for substituted service was that service should be effected by placing the document in the post and should be complete when that was done. It follows that I agree with the submissions made on behalf of the debtor
j that service in this case was in fact effected on 2 May and not 3 May and that the date stated in the bankruptcy petition was incorrect.

The next question is whether we should give leave to amend the petition in order to state the correct date on the footing that the difference of one day is so insubstantial that it can be treated as de minimis.

In my judgment, that would be inconsistent with recent decisions in this court, particularly *Re Hastings (a bankrupt)* [1985] 1 All ER 885, [1985] 1 WLR 969 and *Re a debtor (No 9 of 1984)* (30 April 1985, unreported), which show that, at any rate, once the period of three months has elapsed, an amendment of this kind cannot be allowed. I do not find it necessary to decide on this occasion whether such an amendment could be made within the three months' period.

I should, however, like to add a warning against the form of the order for substituted service which was adopted in this case, because in my view that form of order makes it very difficult and perhaps impossible to make the bankruptcy notice clear or, indeed, anything other than perplexing. The bankruptcy notice must make it clear exactly what the debtor has to do. It must not be calculated to mislead or perplex him. In this case he would have seen from the bankruptcy notice itself that he had ten days from the date of service. An ordinary debtor reading that might well conclude at first sight that he had ten days from the date on which it had reached him. However, in the same envelope he also received a copy of the order for substituted service, which stated that service could be effected by posting the document to him. From that he might well have second thoughts and, reading the order for substituted service in its ordinary and natural meaning, and, indeed, in the way in which in my judgment it has to be read, he might well conclude, correctly, that he had only ten days from the date on which it was posted and, therefore, less than the period which the Bankruptcy Act 1914 would normally make available to him. If, however, he were a sophisticated debtor or he went to a solicitor for advice, it seems to me at least possible that he or his solicitor would make precisely the mistake which the petitioning creditor's own solicitor made on this occasion, that is to say, seeing no express provision in the order for substituted service as to the date on which service should be deemed to be effected, he might well treat that order as directed only to the manner of service and not to the date on which it was to be deemed to be effected, and accordingly he might fall into the trap of concluding that after all he still had ten days from the date on which the bankruptcy notice had in fact reached him.

I would not like to part with this case without also indorsing fully what Peter Gibson J said in *Re a debtor (No 9 of 1984)*, that is to say that an order for substituted service in the form of the order made in this case is also undesirable for another reason, in that it cuts down the period which the debtor should have in order to try to make arrangements to pay or compound the debt. In my judgment, it is desirable that the order for substituted service should contain an express provision as to the time at which service is to be taken to be effected so that, when read with the bankruptcy notice, the debtor can be left in no doubt as to the period which he has in which to comply with the bankruptcy notice; the time at which service should be deemed to be effected should be a stated day and should not be defined by reference to the date of posting, which may not be ascertainable by the debtor, nor by reference to the date of delivery, which will not be ascertainable by the petitioning creditor; and the stated day should be no earlier than the date on which it could reasonably be anticipated that service would in fact be effected in the ordinary course of post.

For the reasons I have given I would allow this appeal and discharge the receiving order.

WARNER J. I agree. I will add only two things.

The first is this. There is in *Williams and Muir Hunter on Bankruptcy* (19th edn, 1979) p 34 this statement:

'But a judgment is indivisible; where one part of a judgment is unenforceable, a bankruptcy notice issued in respect of the other part is bad.'

In my view, that statement is far too wide. It rests, according to a footnote, on the authority of *Re a debtor (No 21 of 1937)* [1938] 2 All ER 824, [1938] Ch 694, to which Millett J has referred. In my view, the ratio decidendi of that case, as, indeed, Millett J indicated, was that the petitioning creditor there was in the dilemma described by Greene MR (see [1938] 2 All ER 824 at 827, [1938] Ch 694 at 703). The judgment of the county

a court did not show on its face how much of the debt was attributable to the period before the coming into force of the Law Reform (Married Women and Tortfeasors) Act 1935 and how much was attributable to the period after it. Therefore, a bankruptcy notice which complied with the Bankruptcy Act 1914 could not be drafted. If it referred to the whole judgment, as it did, it was bad because part of that judgment was not enforceable by bankruptcy proceedings, and, if it referred only to the part that was available to be enforced in bankruptcy proceedings, it did not comply with s 2 of the Bankruptcy Act

b 1914 because it did not require payment in accordance with the terms of the judgment. That difficulty does not exist in the present case. It does not exist in any case where it appears on the face of the judgment what part of it is available for enforcement in bankruptcy and what part is not.

The second thing I wish to add is my agreement with Peter Gibson and Millett JJ that registrars ought not to make orders for substituted service in the sort of form that we

c have before us here.

So I, too, would allow the appeal.

Appeal allowed. Receiving order discharged. Leave to appeal to the Court of Appeal granted.

Solicitors: Allsworth & Spears, Bishops Waltham (for the debtor); Lovell White & King (for
d the petitioning creditor).

Vivian Horvath   Barrister.

Blake v Pope

e
QUEEN'S BENCH DIVISION
STOCKER LJ AND HIRST J
13, 14 MAY 1986

Road traffic – Breath test – Requirement to take test – Prerequisite of test – 'Reasonable cause to
f *suspect' driver has consumed alcohol above prescribed limit – Police forming suspicion after person ceased driving – Whether necessary that suspicion should arise at time person was driving – Road Traffic Act 1972, ss 6(1), 7(1)(b).*

Two motorists saw the defendant driving his car erratically and forced him to stop. They considered that he had been drinking, removed the ignition keys from his car and
g telephoned the police. By the time the police arrived some ten minutes later the defendant had got out of the car. The police suspected that the defendant had been drinking and asked him to supply a specimen of breath. When he refused he was arrested. Subsequently an intoximeter reading showed that the amount of alcohol in his breath grossly exceeded the prescribed limit. He was charged with driving after consuming alcohol in excess of the prescribed limit, contrary to s 6(1)[a] of the Road Traffic
h Act 1972. At his trial the defendant submitted that the ten-minute interval between his being prevented from driving and the arrival of the police had the effect of severing the requisite connection between his driving and the intervention of the police and therefore the suspicion which the police formed about his condition when they arrived on the scene could not have arisen while he was driving. The magistrates dismissed the charge against the defendant and the prosecution appealed, contending that under s 7(1)(b)[b] of
j the Act a police officer merely had to have 'reasonable cause to suspect', regardless of how or when that suspicion was formed, that a person had been driving with excess alcohol before he could require a breath test.

---

a   Section 6(1), so far as material, is set out at p 190 *f*, post
b   Section 7(1), so far as material, is set out at p 190 *g h*, post

Held – For the purposes of s 7(1)(*b*) of the 1972 Act a police officer who intended to require a motorist to take a breath test did not have to have his suspicion aroused while *a* the motorist was driving that the motorist had been driving with excess alcohol. Furthermore, it was not necessary for there to be any nexus between the motorist's driving and the arrival of, and suspicion formed by, the police. It was therefore irrelevant that there had been an interval of ten minutes between the defendant ceasing to drive and the arrival of the police. The prosecution's appeal would accordingly be allowed (see p 191 *c* to *e* and p 192 *e* to *g*, post). *b*

Dictum of Lord Bridge in *Fox v Chief Constable of Gwent* [1985] 3 All ER at 400 applied.

Edkins v Knowles [1973] 2 All ER 503 and *R v Bates* [1973] 2 All ER 509 distinguished.

Notes

For breath tests, see 40 Halsbury's Laws (4th edn) para 489.

For the Road Traffic Act 1972, ss 6, 7 (as substituted by the Transport Act 1981, s 25(3), *c* Sch 8), see 51 Halsbury's Statutes (3rd edn) 1427, 1429.

Cases referred to in judgments

Edkins v Knowles [1973] 2 All ER 503, [1973] QB 748, [1973] 2 WLR 977, DC.

Fox v Chief Constable of Gwent [1985] 3 All ER 392, [1985] 1 WLR 1126, HL.

Patterson v Charlton [1986] RTR 18, DC. *d*

Pinner v Everett [1969] 3 All ER 257, [1969] 1 WLR 1266, HL.

R v Bates [1973] 2 All ER 509, [1973] 1 WLR 718, CA.

Sakhuja v Allen [1972] 2 All ER 311, [1973] AC 152, [1972] 2 WLR 1116, HL.

Scott v Baker [1968] 2 All ER 992, [1969] 1 QB 659, [1968] 3 WLR 796, DC.

Case stated *e*

Maurice Blake, a chief inspector of police, appealed by way of case stated by justices for the county of Norfolk, acting in and for the petty sessional division of Norwich, in respect of their adjudication as a magistrates' court on 21 May 1985 whereby they convicted the respondent, Raymond Pope, following informations laid by the appellant, on charges (1) that he drove a motor vehicle without due care and attention, contrary to s 3 of the Road Traffic Act 1972, and (2) that he failed without reasonable excuse to provide a specimen *f* of breath, contrary to s 7(4) of the Road Traffic Act 1972, and dismissed a charge that he drove a motor vehicle after consuming so much alcohol that the proportion of it in his breath exceeded the prescribed limit, contrary to s 6(1)(*a*) of the Road Traffic Act 1972. On the careless driving charge the magistrates fined the respondent £120, disqualified him from driving for three months and endorsed his licence and on the charge of failing to provide a specimen of breath they fined him £50 and endorsed his licence. The *g* question of law in the case stated was whether the magistrates were right in law in accepting the respondent's defence and dismissing the charge of driving with excess alcohol in his breath, having regard to the fact that at the same hearing: (1) they had convicted the respondent of driving without due care and attention the facts of which gave rise to the witnesses' suspicions that the respondent had been drinking alcohol; (2) the respondent was convicted on his own admission of failing to provide a specimen of *h* breath; and (3) no issue had been raised before the court on the statutory breath test procedure. The facts are set out in the judgement of Stocker LJ.

Charles Kellett for the appellant.

Jeremy Richards for the respondent.
j

STOCKER LJ. This is an appeal by way of case stated by the justices for the county of Norfolk acting in and for the petty sessional division of Norwich in respect of their adjudication as a magistrates' court sitting at the Guildhall, Norwich on 21 May 1985.

The charges before the court were these. The first one was that on 25 November 1984 at Lenwade in the county of Norfolk the respondent unlawfully drove a motor vehicle

on a certain road without due care and attention. The second charge was that on the same
a date and at the same place he drove a motor vehicle after consuming so much alcohol
that the proportion of it in his breath exceeded the prescribed limit contrary to s 6(1)(a)
of the Road Traffic Act 1972 as amended. The third charge was that on the same day and
at the same place without reasonable excuse he failed to provide a specimen of breath
when required to do so in pursuance of s 7 of that same Act. He pleaded not guilty to the
first charge and the second charge, but pleaded guilty to the third charge, that is to say,
b without reasonable excuse failing to provide a specimen. This appeal is concerned only
with the second charge of driving with excess alcohol contrary to s 6(1) of the Road
Traffic Act 1972. He was convicted on the first charge and pleaded guilty to the third
charge.

The facts found by the justices were these: that on Sunday, 25 November 1984, a Mr
Burton, who was a witness in the case, was following a Talbot Solara car on the A1067
c travelling towards Norwich at about 4 to 4.30 pm when it was dusk. He drove through
the main streets of Lenwade. The car was being driven erratically, veering from nearside
to offside of the centre line four or five times in the face of oncoming traffic. The
approaching traffic had got lights on. None of them appeared to have to brake.

Mr Burton waited until it seemed safe to overtake the Talbot and did so. He pulled in
front, bringing the other vehicle to a halt. Mr Burton then reversed close up to prevent
d the driver driving away. The respondent then got out of the Talbot and Mr Burton
formed the view that he had been drinking.

There was another witness, a Mr Blyth, who happened to be a retired traffic patrol
policeman, who had followed in his car behind the other two, and he also observed the
swerving from nearside to offside. Having formed an opinion about the cause of the
erratic driving, Mr Blyth telephoned for the police and then went to the respondent's
e vehicle and removed the ignition key. Mr Blyth then became concerned for the
respondent's safety as he appeared to be very drunk and wanted to walk away. For his
own safety he held the respondent against the adjacent river bridge until the police
arrived. Mr Blyth said he was determined to stop him driving.

The police arrived some ten to fifteen minutes later. Pc Brown observed that the
respondent was out of the car, smelled strongly of alcohol, and was unsteady on his feet.
f The respondent refused to supply a breath specimen at the roadside. He was accordingly
arrested and the Lion Intoximeter machine, which was subsequently used, showed that
he had 108 microgrammes of alcohol in 100 ml of breath. Clearly that is grossly in excess
of the maximum.

The respondent's contention before the magistrates, and his argument before us was
that since he ceased to drive some ten minutes before the arrival of the police, and since
g he had been effectively prevented from driving by the actions of Mr Burton who had
blocked the path of his car, and of Mr Blyth who had removed the ignition keys, there
was no nexus between his earlier driving and the intervention of the police because the
lapse of time between the arrival of the police and his ceasing to drive, had severed the
requisite nexus and therefore the police's suspicions as to his condition could not have
arisen while he was driving. It was contended that he could not be guilty of an offence
h under s 6(1) in accordance with authorities which were cited.

The appellant's contention before the justices need not be stated in detail. In substance
they amount to the proposition that the respondent's contentions are irrelevant, having
regard to the terms of ss 6, 7 and 10 of the Road Traffic Act 1972, as substituted by s 25(3)
of and Sch 8 to the Transport Act 1981.

The magistrates expressed their opinion in the following terms:

j   '(a) There was a clear and significant break in the sequence of events relating to
     charge (b) [the second charge], that of the Respondent's driving with excess alcohol
     in his breath.
        (b) At the time when the police officer arrived on the scene, which was a
     minimum of ten minutes from when the Respondent was stopped, he had been out
     of his vehicle for most of that time. The vehicle could not have been driven, at least,

forwards, because Mr. Burton's car had been intentionally placed close in front of it, Mr. Blyth had been for most of the time physically restraining the Respondent for *a* his own safety and the ignition keys had been removed from his vehicle.

(c) Bearing in mind the decision of *R v Bates* ([1973] 2 All ER 509, [1973] 1 WLR 718) the question of whether or not the suspicion of the police officer was aroused at the time of the respondent's driving or attempting to drive was a matter of fact to be decided at our discretion.

(d) As in that case the Respondent had been effectively prevented from driving *b* well before the policeman arrived.

(e) The evidence supporting the charge of careless driving was the manner of driving and not the cause, i.e. we were entitled to and did deal with that as a separate issue.

(f) That being so in our view *Edkins v Knowles* ([1973] 2 All ER 503, [1973] QB 748) applied, and we therefore dismissed the charge (b) of driving with excess *c* alcohol in the breath, but convicted him of charge (a) careless driving and of charge (c) failing to give a specimen of breath.'

Then they dealt with the penalty imposed.

It is clear from the terms of the opinion which I have just read that the magistrates based their decision on *Edkins v Knowles* [1973] 2 All ER 503, [1973] QB 748. In further grounds under the heading of 'opinion', they give their reasons for the proposition that *d* had it not been for a plea of guilty to the third charge, they might have dismissed that charge also on the same grounds that they gave for dismissing the second charge. I do not feel it is necessary to consider that aspect which is not relevant to this appeal.

The magistrates posed the question for the decision of this court in these terms:

'The question of law for the opinion of the High Court is:—Were we right in law *e* in accepting the Respondent's defence and dismissing the charge of driving with excess alcohol in his breath [they go on to say] having regard to [certain factors]?'

In my view the relevant part of the question is that which I have read and the remaining three sub-paragraphs do not really affect the issue.

I therefore turn to the case on which the magistrates relied in arriving at the conclusion that they did. The first such case is *Edkins v Knowles*. I shall read the headnote so that the *f* point may be made clear ([1973] 2 All ER 503):

'Two plain clothes police officers in a police car saw the respondent motorist driving a car fast and erratically. The officers followed him for three miles to a holiday camp where he lived; as they followed him they sent out a radio call requesting the attendance of a traffic patrol car. They did not attempt to overtake *g* the respondent as they thought it would be dangerous to do so. When the respondent had finally stoppped in the holiday camp they drew up beside him, identified themselves and asked him to await the arrival of the traffic patrol car. He did so remaining in the driving seat of his car. Five minutes later the traffic patrol car arrived with uniformed officers. One of the plain clothes officers then brought the respondent over to the traffic control car and in the presence of the respondent told *h* a uniformed officer how the respondent had driven. The uniformed officer noticed that the respondent's breath smelt of drink and then asked the respondent for a specimen of breath, which proved positive. A subsequent laboratory test revealed a blood-alcohol proportion above the prescribed limit. The respondent was charged with an offence under s 1(1) of the Road Safety Act 1967. The justices dismissed the charge, on a submission of no case to answer, on the ground that the uniformed *j* officer had no power under s 2(1) of the 1967 Act to require the respondent to take a breath test.'

It was held ([1973] 2 All ER 503 at 504):

'The justices had been right to dismiss the information. The uniformed officer had no power under s 2(1) to require a breath test since his suspicion that the *a*   respondent had alcohol in his body or had committed a moving traffic offence had not been formed at a time when the respondent was driving, but only some five minutes after the respondent had reached the end of his journey and when he was effectively prevented from driving by the plain clothes officers.'

In giving the judgment of the court Griffiths J said ([1973] 2 All ER 503 at 507–508, [1973] QB 748 at 755–756):

b   'The second submission was that the respondent could not lawfully have been required to take a breath test, as he had ceased driving before a constable in uniform had reasonable grounds to suspect him of having alcohol in his body or of having committed a moving traffic offence. This submission was based on the recent decision of the House of Lords in *Sakhuja v Allen* [1972] 2 All ER 311, [1973] AC 152. In that case all the members of the appellate committee held that the

c   requirement to take a breath test under s 2(1) of the Act did not have to be made whilst the motorist was driving or attempting to drive so long as it formed part of a relevant single transaction or chain of events flowing from the driving. But there was a difference of opinion as to the time at which the constable in uniform must suspect the motorist of having alcohol in his body, or of having committed a moving traffic offence. Lord Hailsham of St Marylebone LC and Viscount Dilhorne, on their

d   construction of s 2(1), held that the suspicion did not have to arise whilst the motorist was driving or attempting to drive; it sufficed if the uniformed constable had reasonable grounds for suspicion at the time he required a breath test, provided the driving, the suspicion and the requirement formed part of a continuous chain of events forming a single transaction. The majority however held that in the previous decision of *Pinner v Everett* [1969] 3 All ER 257, [1969] 1 WLR 1266 the

e   House of Lords had decided that the requirement for a breath test was not valid unless the constable in uniform formed a suspicion while the motorist was still driving that he had alcohol in his body, or had committed a moving traffic offence. Undoubtedly many of the difficult problems of fact that arise in attempting to determine whether at a given moment in time a motorist is driving would be avoided, and the Act would be much easier to administer, if this court was free to

f   follow Lord Hailsham of St Marylebone LC and Viscount Dilhorne. It would result in the conviction of the respondent, and many might see little injustice in that considering he was driving with approaching double the prescribed limit of alcohol in his blood. But we are bound by the majority, and short of reconsideration of *Pinner v Everett* by the House of Lords, it must now be taken as settled that the suspicion of a constable in uniform must arise while the motorist is driving or

g   attempting to drive, before he can be required to take a breath test.'

That case was clearly decided on the basis that the police constable had no power to require the driver to take a breath test under the terms of s 2(1) of the Road Safety Act 1967.

The other case relied on by the magistrates, and on which the respondent relies, was *R*

h   *v Bates* [1973] 2 All ER 509, [1973] 1 WLR 718. This case also turned on the provisions of the 1967 Act, s 2(1). For my part I do not feel it necessary to read more than the headnote, as the point is the same as that in *Edkins v Knowles*. The headnote to *R v Bates* reads ([1973] 2 All ER 509):

j   'S was driving his car when he was overtaken by another car driven by the appellant. Both vehicles stopped at a road junction. Thereupon S got out of his car and, telling the appellant he was drunk, physically prevented him from continuing his journey by standing in front of the appellant's car. The appellant eventually pulled into the kerb and got out of his car. Some 15 minutes later S signalled a passing police patrol car, and explained to the uniformed police officers what had happened. They administered a breath test to the appellant which proved positive. A subsequent urine test revealed a blood-alcohol proportion above the prescribed limit. The appellant was charged with an offence under s 1(1) of the Road Safety Act

1967. The jury were directed that if they found the facts proved as testified by the prosecution witnesses they should convict the appellant on the basis that, as he was *a* driving or attempting to drive at the time when the police officers formed their suspicion that he had alcohol in his body, they were entitled to require him to take a test under s 2(1) of the 1967 Act. The appellant was convicted and appealed.'

It was held:

'The issue whether or not a motorist was driving or attempting to drive at the *b* relevant time was one of fact for the jury, although in certain cases a judge, with his knowledge of the authorities, might have to indicate that the evidence was really all one way. In any event, since the appellant had been effectively prevented or dissuaded from driving before the police officers arrived, he could no longer be considered to be driving or attempting to drive for the purposes of s 2(1) of the 1967 Act. Accordingly the appeal would be allowed and the conviction quashed . . .' *c*

It is therefore appropriate to look at the terms of s 2(1) of the 1967 Act. That subsection provides:

'A constable in uniform may require any person driving or attempting to drive a motor vehicle on a road or other public place to provide a specimen of breath for a breath test there or nearby, if the constable has reasonable cause—(a) to suspect him *d* of having alcohol in his body; or (b) to suspect him of having committed a traffic offence while the vehicle was in motion. Provided that no requirement may be made by virtue of paragraph (b) of this subsection unless it is made as soon as reasonably practicable after the commission of the traffic offence.'

I therefore turn to consider the relevant sections of the Act under which this respondent was charged. They are in the Road Traffic Act 1972, as substituted by s 25(3) of and Sch 8 *e* to the Transport Act 1981. Section 6 has the heading: 'Driving or being in charge of a motor vehicle with alcohol concentration above prescribed limit', and sub-s (1) reads as follows:

'If a person—(a) drives or attempts to drive a motor vehicle on a road or other public place; or (b) is in charge of a motor vehicle on a road or other public place; *f* after consuming so much alcohol that the proportion of it in his breath, blood or urine exceeds the prescribed limit he shall be guilty of an offence.'

Section 7 is headed: 'Breath tests' and sub-s (1) reads:

'Where a constable in uniform has reasonable cause to suspect—(a) that a person driving or attempting to drive or in charge or in charge of a motor vehicle on a road *g* or other public place has alcohol in his body or has committed a traffic offence whilst the vehicle was in motion; or (b) that a person has been driving or attempting to drive or been in charge of a motor vehicle on a road or other public place with alcohol in his body and that that person still has alcohol in his body; or (c) that a person has been driving or attempting to drive or been in charge of a motor vehicle on a road or other public place and has committed a traffic offence whilst the vehicle *h* was in motion; he may, subject to section 9 below, require him to provide a specimen of breath for a breath test.'

We draw attention in particular to para (b): 'that a person has been driving or attempting to drive or been in charge of a motor vehicle on a road or other public place with alcohol in his body . . .' The legality of the respondent's arrest under sub-s (5) of s 7 *j* is not in issue on this appeal.

We also draw attention to the provisions of s 10(2). I shall read s 10(1) first. The section is headed: 'Evidence in proceedings for an offence under s. 5 or s. 6' Section 10(1) reads:

'The following provisions apply with respect to proceedings for an offence under section 5 or section 6 of this Act.'

Of course this appeal is under s 6. Section 10(2) reads:

a
'Evidence of the proportion of alcohol or any drug in a specimen of breath, blood or urine provided by the accused shall, in all cases, be taken into account, and it shall be assumed that the proportion of alcohol in the accused's breath, blood or urine at the time of the alleged offence was not less than in the specimen; but if the proceedings are for an offence under section 6 of this Act, or for an offence under section 5 of this Act in a case where the accused is alleged to have been unfit through
b
drink, the assumption shall not be made if the accused proves [certain matters which here need not be read].'

In my view it is clear from the conjoined effects of these sections that the basis on which *Edkins v Knowles* [1973] 2 All ER 503, [1973] QB 748 and *R v Bates* [1973] 2 All ER 509, [1973] 1 WLR 718 were decided no longer prevails. Section 7(2)(*b*) does not require
c that the suspicion of the officers can only justify the exercise of the power to require a breath test if the suspicion that the driver has excess alcohol arises whilst the driver is still driving or if there is a nexus between such driving and the arrival and suspicion of the police. In my view s 7(2)(*b*) is expressly to the contrary effect. Moreover, read in conjunction with s 10(2) it is clear in my view that the words 'at the time of the alleged offence' reinforce that view.
d   Counsel for the respondent argues that despite the change in the wording of the relevant sections of the 1972 Act, as opposed to s 2(1) of the 1967 Act, *Edkins v Knowles* is still applicable as indicating what the word 'drives' means in s 6(1), and that ss 6 and 7 should not be read together. For my part I am wholly unable to accept that proposition, and find support for my conclusion from part of the speech of Lord Bridge in *Fox v Chief Constable of Gwent* [1985] 3 All ER 392 at 400, [1985] 1 WLR 1126 at 1136. Lord Bridge
e said:

'It was against this background [he had pointed out the lacunae in the 1967 legislation] that Parliament by s 25 of and Sch 8 to the Transport Act 1981 replaced the old provisions by the new and radically redrafted ss 6 to 12 which are now in force and which I shall refer to as "the new provisions". It requires only a superficial comparison of the new with the old provisions to appreciate that their purpose was
f to eliminate what Parliament must have regarded as the meritless technical defences which the old provisions, as construed by the courts, had made available. My noble and learned friend Lord Fraser has already drawn attention to the omission in the definition of the offence in the new s 6 of the words in the old s 6 "as ascertained from a laboratory test for which [the accused] subsequently provides a specimen under section 9 of this Act ...." This, at a stroke, eliminated the many defences
g founded on *Scott v Baker* [1968] 2 All ER 992, [1969] 1 QB 659 and the numerous later cases in which it was affirmed and applied. The extension by the new s 7(1)(*c*) of the obligation to provide a specimen of breath for a breath test to "a person [who] has been driving" in such a way as to arouse a relevant suspicion has rendered obsolete the nice distinctions drawn by the courts to determine whether a person who was no longer at the wheel of a moving motor vehicle could or could not still
h be regarded as "driving" it under the old s 8(1). Again, the new s 10(2), which I need not here set out, has clearly removed what came to be called the "hip flask defence" by placing the onus on an accused driver who claims to have consumed alcohol after he ceased to drive to prove that, but for this subsequent consumption, the proportion of alcohol in any specimen of his breath, blood or urine proved in evidence would not have exceeded the prescribed limit.'

j
I also find directly in point a decision of this court in *Patterson v Charlton* [1986] RTR 18. Part of the headnote which relates to the decision is (at 19):

'... once the defendant had admitted to driving his car on the day of the alleged offence and also had provided specimens of breath which disclosed a proportion of alcohol exceeding the prescribed limit at the time when they were taken, it had to be assumed by virtue of section 10(2) that his breath-alcohol proportion at the time of the alleged offence was not less than in the specimen; that section 10(2) operated to transfer the burden on to the defendant to displace the assumption that his breath-alcohol proportion exceeded the statutory limit when he drove; and that, accordingly, the prosecutor had raised a prima facie case under section 6(1) and the case would be remitted to the justices with a direction to continue the hearing.'

Taylor J said (at 23):

'Looking at the circumstances of the present case, [counsel for the prosecutor] says there was a clear admission by the defendant that he had driven the vehicle on the morning of the day specified in the charge. The officer properly, under the statute, took samples which were positive and, therefore, it had to be assumed that the proportion of alcohol at the time of the alleged offence, that is to say, at the time on that day when the defendant was driving, was the same as that in the specimen. [Counsel for the prosecutor] said that there was therefore a prima facie case and the burden was transferred to the defendant, if he chose to take it up, to adduce evidence that he had consumed alcohol after he had ceased to drive, as provided by section 10. I have carefully considered the submissions made by [counsel for the defendant], but it seems to me that the argument addressed by [counsel for the prosecutor], which I have just summarised, is correct ... Once the defendant had admitted driving the vehicle on that day, which was the day charged in the offence, and once the sample showed that he had an excess of alcohol in his breath at the time of the taking of the samples, section 10 operated to transfer the burden to the defendant to displace the assumption made under that section that he was over the limit at the time when he drove.'

In my view justices misdirected themselves with regard to the proper construction of s 6(1) and s 7 of the 1972 Act, and were wrong in holding that the cases on which they relied were of assistance in construing those sections. In my view *Edkins v Knowles* [1973] 2 All ER 503, [1973] QB 748 and *R v Bates* [1973] 2 All ER 509, [1973] 1 WLR 718 are not authorities for the proper construction of the provisions of the 1972 Act, as amended by the provisions of the 1981 Act.

I would accordingly allow this appeal, and I would answer the question posed in the negative, without dealing with the sub-paragraphs of it, and would remit the matter to the magistrates with directions that they should convict.

HIRST J. I agree. I only wish to add a few words to stress the importance of the passage quoted by Stocker LJ from the speech of Lord Bridge in *Fox v Chief Constable of Gwent* [1985] 3 All ER 392, [1985] 1 WLR 1126.

The recent amendments in the statutory provisions relating to drunken driving now enshrined in ss 6 to 12 of the Road Traffic Act 1972, as substituted by s 25(3) of and Sch 8 to the Transport Act 1981, have made radical changes. Their effect is to clear away many of the minefields which previously beset the path of justice in this branch of the law. In consequence it is of great importance that magistrates trying these cases of alleged drunken driving should be on their guard against being led astray by technical defences based on cases such as *Edkins v Knowles* [1973] 2 All ER 503, [1973] QB 748 which were decided under the old law and which are now completely superseded by the new statutory code.

Appeal allowed; case remitted to magistrates with direction that they should convict.

Solicitors: *Sharpe Pritchard & Co*, agents for *David I Tomlinson*, Norwich (for the appellant); *Stanger & Co*, Aylsham (for the respondent).

Sophie Craven   Barrister.

Ratford and another v Northavon District Council

COURT OF APPEAL, CIVIL DIVISION

SLADE, RALPH GIBSON LJJ AND SIR JOHN MEGAW

28, 29, 30 APRIL, 20 MAY 1986

Rates – Rateable occupation – Occupation by receiver – Receiver appointed under debenture charging company's property – Debenture empowering receiver to take possession of property charged but not effecting transfer of possession to receiver or obliging him to take possession – Debenture and appointment of receiver containing usual agency provision deeming receiver to be company's agent – Whether receiver in rateable occupation of property – Whether rating authority having reasonable grounds for believing receiver in rateable occupation – Whether burden of proof on receiver to show that he was not in rateable occupation – General Rate Act 1967, s 97(1).

On 5 April 1983 a bank appointed receivers of a company's property under a debenture which empowered the receivers to take possession of the property and to carry on and manage the company's business. Both the debenture and the appointment contained the usual agency provision deeming the receivers to be the agents of the company in carrying on the business. The company occupied certain premises for the purposes of its business and on 6 April the receivers sent notification of their appointment to the rating authority in whose area the premises were situated. The rating authority decided that there had been a change in the rateable occupation of the premises, entered the receivers as the occupiers on the rating list and sent the receivers a demand for rates due from 5 April. The receivers refused to pay and the rating authority, acting pursuant to s 97(1)[a] of the General Rate Act 1967, made a complaint and applied for a summons 'requiring [the receivers] to appear before a magistrates' court to show why [they had] not paid the rate . . .' At the hearing of the complaint and summons the receivers acknowledged that their representatives had been on the premises from time to time, and that they themselves managed the company's business, authorised the payment of outgoings and controlled the company's assets, but they submitted that the terms of the debenture, their appointment and their letter of 6 April to the rating authority showed that they had never entered into rateable occupation of the premises. The magistrates upheld the rating authority's claim that the receivers were in rateable occupation and accordingly issued a distress warrant for the unpaid rates. On appeal by the receivers, the judge upheld the decision of the magistrates. The receivers appealed to the Court of Appeal. The issues arose (i) on whom the burden of proof lay to prove, or disprove, rateable occupation, and (ii) whether that burden had been discharged.

Held – (1) A rating authority had to have reasonable grounds for believing that the respondent was or might be in rateable occupation of the relevant premises before applying for a summons under s 97(1) of the 1967 Act for non-payment of rates. If it had such reasonable grounds and if, at the hearing of the summons, it established that it had duly made, published and demanded the rates and that they had not been paid, the burden then lay on the respondent to show sufficient cause why he should not be treated as the rateable occupier who was liable for the rates, since whether he was in actual occupation was a matter peculiarly within his knowledge. However, like the burden of proof in any litigation, the burden could shift to the rating authority if the respondent showed that prima facie he was not the rateable occupier. Since the rating authority had had reasonable grounds for believing that the receivers might be in rateable occupation of the property (because the mere appointment of a receiver under a debenture could,

---

a   Section 97(1), so far as material, is set out at p 197 *e f*, post

depending on the terms of the debenture and the receiver's appointment, effect a change
from the company to the receiver in the rateable occupation of the property charged)   *a*
and since the authority had shown that the rate had been duly made, published and
demanded from the receivers and had not been paid, it followed that the burden of proof
at the hearing of the summons lay on the receivers to show sufficient cause for the non-
payment (see p 201 *h j*, p 202 *c* to *j*, p 207 *j* to p 208 *a* and p 209 *b*, post); *Des Salles
d'Epinoix v Kensington and Chelsea Royal Borough* [1970] 1 All ER 18, *Forsythe v Rawlinson*
[1981] RVR 97 and *Verrall v Hackney London BC* [1983] 1 All ER 277 applied.   *b*

(2) Where, however, a debenture under which a receiver was appointed contained the
usual agency provision deeming him to be the company's agent, thus giving rise to a true
agency relationship between the receiver and the company, and merely empowered the
receiver to take possession of the property charged and did not effect a transfer of
possession to him or require him to dispossess the company, he could not be regarded as
being in rateable occupation of the property charged unless it was shown that he had   *c*
dispossessed the company and taken possession of the property in an independent
capacity as principal and thus otherwise than in his capacity as the company's agent.
Since the terms of the debenture and the appointment of the receivers showed merely
that they were empowered to take possession of the premises and were to be deemed to
be the company's agents, and since the only other evidence before the magistrates was
consistent with the company itself having remained in rateable occupation of the   *d*
premises during the receivership, it followed that the magistrates had not had sufficient
evidence on which to find that the receivers were in rateable occupation. The appeal
would therefore be allowed (see p 204 *b c*, p 206 *f g* and p 208 *b* to *g j* to p 209 *b*, post);
dictum of Rigby LJ in *Gaskell v Gosling* [1896] 1 QB at 697 applied; *Richards v Kidderminster
Overseers* [1896] 2 Ch 212 distinguished; *Re Marriage Neave & Co* [1895–9] All ER Rep
393, *National Provincial Bank of England Ltd v United Electric Theatres Ltd* [1916] 1 Ch 132,   *e*
Australian Mutual Provident Society v Geo Myers & Co Ltd (in liq) (1931) 47 CLR 65, *Gyton v
Palmour* [1944] 2 All ER 540 and *Taggs Island Casino Hotel Ltd v Richmond-upon-Thames
London Borough* (1966) 14 RRC 119 considered.

Quaere. Whether s 97(1) of the 1967 Act is subject to the implicit qualification that
there is no burden of proof on a respondent who receives a summons under s 97(1) when
the rating authority has no reasonable grounds for believing that he is in rateable   *f*
occupation of the property (see p 201 *j* to p 202 *a*, post).

Notes

For rateable occupation, see 39 Halsbury's Laws (4th edn) paras 15–24, and for cases on
the subject, see 38 Digest (Reissue) 325–326, 2244–2250.

For distress for rates, see 13 Halsbury's Laws (4th edn) paras 399, 409, and for cases on   *g*
the subject, see 18 Digest (Reissue) 412–413, 1369–1380.

For the liability of a receiver appointed under a debenture, see 7 Halsbury's Laws (4th
edn) paras 885–886, and for cases on the subject, see 10 Digest (Reissue) 876–879, 5071–
5085.

For the General Rate Act 1967, s 97, see 27 Halsbury's Statutes (3rd edn) 190.

  h

Cases referred to in judgments

Associated Provincial Picture Houses Ltd v Wednesbury Corp [1947] 2 All ER 680, [1948] 1
     KB 223, CA.
Australian Mutual Provident Society v Geo Myers & Co Ltd (in liq) (1931) 47 CLR 65, Aust
     HC.
Banister v Islington London BC (1972) 71 LGR 239, DC.   *j*
Briant Colour Printing Co Ltd (in liq), Re [1977] 3 All ER 968, [1977] 1 WLR 942, CA.
Bromley London Borough v Brooks (1973) 17 RRC 197, DC.
Des Salles d'Epinoix v Kensington and Chelsea Royal Borough [1970] 1 All ER 18, [1970] 1
     WLR 179, DC.
Forsythe v Rawlinson [1981] RVR 97, DC.
Gaskell v Gosling [1897] AC 575, [1895–9] All ER Rep 300, HL; *rvsg* [1896] 1 QB 669, CA.

Gyton v Palmour [1944] 2 All ER 540, [1945] KB 426, DC.

a *Holywell Union and Halkyn Parish v Halkyn District Mines Drainage Co* [1895] AC 117, [1891–4] All ER Rep 158, HL.

Lister v Reigate BC [1970] RA 1, DC.

Marriage Neave & Co, Re, North of England Trustee Debenture and Assets Corp v Marriage Neave & Co [1896] 2 Ch 663, [1895–9] All ER Rep 393, CA.

Meigh v Wickenden [1942] 2 All ER 68, [1942] 2 KB 160, DC.

b *National Provincial Bank of England Ltd v United Electric Theatres Ltd* [1916] 1 Ch 132, (1915) 85 LJ Ch 106.

Richards v Kidderminster Overseers [1896] 2 Ch 212.

Taggs Island Casino Hotel Ltd v Richmond-upon-Thames London Borough (1966) 14 RRC 119.

Verrall v Hackney London BC [1983] 1 All ER 277, [1983] QB 445, [1983] 2 WLR 202, CA.

Westminster City Council v Southern Rly Co [1936] 2 All ER 322, [1936] AC 511, HL.

c

Case also cited

Husey v Gas Light and Coke Co (1902) 18 TLR 299.

Appeal

On 21 July 1983 the Northavon District Council preferred a complaint against
d Mr W F Ratford and Mr C T E Hayward, the receivers of the property of Sabre Tooling
Ltd (the company) appointed under a debenture executed by the company in favour of a
bank, alleging that the receivers having been duly rated and assessed on a rate made on
28 February 1983 in respect of rateable property of the company at Unit 21, Cooper
Road, Thornbury Industrial Estate, Thornbury, Bristol, had failed to pay the rate
demanded. On 22 November 1983 justices for the County of Avon sitting in the petty
e sessional division of Thornbury, having considered submissions and evidence, found that
the receivers were the occupiers of the property and had undertaken the company's
liabilities and were thereby responsible for the rate demanded, and issued a distress
warrant. The receivers appealed by way of case stated by the magistrates. The case stated
raised the following questions for the decision of the High Court: (i) whether the onus of
proof lay on the receivers in the circumstances established by the evidence; (ii) whether
f the receivers were 'occupiers' of the property for the purposes of rating within the
meaning of the General Rate Act 1967; and (iii) whether having regard to ss 94 and 319
of the Companies Act 1948 the magistrates were, in the circumstances established by the
evidence, entitled to issue a distress warrant. Kennedy J, hearing the Crown Office list on
14 May 1985, answered questions (i) and (ii) in the affirmative; question (iii) did not
arise. Kennedy J therefore dismissed the appeal but granted the receivers leave to appeal.
g The receivers appealed. The grounds of the appeal were: (1) that the magistrates had
misdirected themselves in law in holding that the receivers were in rateable occupation
of the property in that (a) there was no evidence that on their appointment the receivers
had ousted the company from possession of the property, and (b) the evidence was that
the receivers had permitted the company to continue to occupy the property and to carry
on business therefrom; (2) that the magistrates had reached their conclusion by reasoning
h that was wrong in law in that (a) they failed to hold that in law the receivers' acts were
the company's acts, (b) they wrongly held that the receivers had undertaken the
company's liabilities and were thereby liable for the rates demanded, and (c) they wrongly
stated that in law there was no authority whereby the receivers could escape liability for
the rate demanded; (3) that in all the circumstances the receivers were acting as the
company's agents; and (4) that the judge had wrongly held that the burden of proof lay
j on the receivers to show they were not the rateable occupiers of the property. The facts
are set out in the judgment of Slade LJ.

Gavin Lightman QC and *Alan Boyle* for the receivers.
Christopher Cochrane for the council.

Cur adv vult

20 May. The following judgments were delivered.

SLADE LJ. This is an appeal by Mr W F Ratford and Mr C T E Hayward (the receivers)   *a*
pursuant to the leave of the judge from a judgment of Kennedy J delivered on 14 May
1985. By that judgment he dismissed an appeal by the receivers by way of case stated
from a decision of the justices for the County of Avon in respect of their adjudication as
a magistrates' court sitting at Thornbury on 22 November 1983. The complaint which
the justices had considered was one preferred on 21 July 1983 by the respondents to this   *b*
appeal, the Northavon District Council against the receivers, who at the material time
had been appointed and were acting as receivers and managers of the property of Sabre
Tooling Ltd (the company), a company whose premises were within the area of the
council. The complaint alleged that the receivers, being duly rated and assessed on a rate
made on 28 February 1983, had not paid the sum due, the property in question being
certain premises at Unit 21, Cooper Road, Thornbury Industrial Estate, Thornbury,   *c*
Bristol. The justices found the complaint was well founded. Kennedy J upheld their
decision. The receivers seek to challenge both decisions.

The sums at stake are quite small. However, the council apparently regards this appeal
as raising important questions of principle concerning the onus of proof in cases where a
person has been required, pursuant to s 97(1) of the General Rate Act 1967, to show why
he has not paid a rate specified in a complaint. On the other hand, the receivers, who are   *d*
two partners in a firm of accountants, apparently regard the appeal as raising no less
important questions of principle as to the nature and extent of the personal liability of a
receiver, appointed by a debenture holder, for rates in respect of land belonging to a
company.

The history of the matter is as follows. On 24 November 1977 the company executed
a debenture in favour of Lloyds Bank Ltd, by cl 3 of which it granted a charge over its   *e*
property present and future. By cl 7 the bank was empowered at any time after it should
have demanded payment of any money or liability thereby secured to appoint any
persons to be receivers of the premises thereby charged. Clause 7 further provided that
any receiver(s) so appointed should have power, inter alia:

> '(a) To take possession of . . . any property hereby charged . . . (b) To carry on
> manage or concur in carrying on and managing the business of the Company or any   *f*
> part thereof . . . (h) To do all such other acts and things as may be considered to be
> incidental or conducive to any of the matters or powers aforesaid and which he or
> they lawfully may or can do as Agent or Agents for the Company.'

After directions relating to the application of moneys received by such receiver(s), cl 7
finally provided:
          g
> 'Any Receiver or Receivers so appointed shall be deemed to be the Agent or
> Agents of the Company and the Company shall be solely responsible for his or their
> acts or defaults and for his or their remuneration.'

On 28 February 1983 the council made the rate in question and duly published it the
following week. The rate was due on 1 April 1983. The council initially addressed a   *h*
demand for payment to the company.

However, on 5 April 1983 the bank executed an appointment by which, in exercise of
the powers conferred on it by the debenture, it appointed the receivers 'to be Receiver(s)
and Manager(s) of the premises charged by the Debenture . . .' The appointment, after
defining the receivers' powers, provided:

> 'and so that the said Receiver(s) so appointed shall without prejudice to the extent   *j*
> of his/their said powers be deemed to be the Agent(s) of the Company . . . which
> alone shall be responsible for his/their acts or defaults.'

On 6 April 1983 Mr Ratford wrote a letter to the council telling them of the
appointment of the receivers. This letter was in the same form as letters addressed to

other persons who had had dealings with the company. In the third paragraph of this
a   letter he said:

'. . . it is my intention to permit the Company to continue to operate its business
with a view to trying to achieve a sale of the whole or part thereof . . .'

In the fourth paragraph he said:

'I must advise you that in respect of any orders placed by or on behalf of the
b   Company my personal liability thereunder will be limited to the value of the assets
within my control for the time being.'

As the justices found, the council received this letter on 11 April 1983, and in reliance
on their officers, formed the view that there had been a change in the rateable occupiers
of the premises on 5 April 1983 when the receivers were appointed. On 23 May 1983
c   the receivers were entered on the council's rating records as being occupiers of the
premises as from 5 April 1983. On 2 June 1983 the council sent out an apportioned
account for £37·22 in the name of the company made up from 1 April 1983 to 4 April
1983 and, in addition, a demand for the rates due from 5 April 1983 to 31 March 1984,
addressed to the receivers personally.
    Under s 16 of the General Rate Act 1967 the liability to be assessed for rates in respect
d   of a hereditament falls on 'every occupier of property', whoever he may be. Section 96(1)
of the Act, so far as material, provides:

'. . . if any person fails to pay any sum legally assessed on and due from him in
respect of a rate for seven days after it has been legally demanded of him, the
payment of that sum may . . . be enforced by distress . . . under warrant issued by a
magistrates' court . . .'

e   Section 97(1), so far as material, provides:

'The proceedings for the issue of a warrant of distress . . . may be instituted by
making complaint before a justice of the peace and applying for a summons
requiring the person named in the complaint to appear before a magistrates' court
to show why he has not paid the rate specified in the complaint.'

f   No payment having been made, the council on 21 July 1983 preferred a complaint
against the receivers asserting that they, being persons duly rated and assessed in the
general rate in question, had not paid it.
    On 22 September 1983, at the instance of the receivers, the company's leasehold
premises were sold.
    It is common ground that if the receivers are liable, their liability extends in respect of
g   the period from 5 April 1983 to 22 September 1983 and that the sum in question is
£1,591·26.
    Prior to the hearing of the complaint before the justices, a statement of facts was
agreed between the parties which embodied the following facts:

'(a) that the Receivers had representatives on the property from time to time
h   during their receivership; (b) that the Receivers managed the business of the
Company during their receivership; (c) that the Receivers authorised payments of
various outgoings during their receivership e.g. electricity bills, rent, wages; (d) that
the Company at the direction of the Receivers disposed of the Company's assets,
including eventually the leasehold interest in the Property; and (e) that during the
receivership, the Receivers had control of those of the Company's assets covered by
j   the debenture.'

At the first hearing before the justices on 1 November 1983 the council proved that
the rate was duly made and published, that it had been duly apportioned in accordance
with s 18 of the 1967 Act, and that the apportioned rate had been duly demanded of the
receivers and not paid. In these circumstances the council submitted that they had

established a prima facie case against the receivers that they were the rateable occupiers
and that the onus of proof lay on the receivers to show that they were not liable to pay   *a*
the rates. The justices accepted this submission and held that the onus was on the
receivers to show that they were not liable.

At the resumed hearing on 22 November 1983 the receivers submitted that, on the
basis of the evidence contained in the agreed statement of facts and the relevant
documents (namely the debenture, appointment and the letter of 6 April 1983), the
receivers never entered into rateable occupation of the premises. In para 9 of their   *b*
decision the justices held as follows:

> 'After consideration of submissions and evidence we found as a matter of fact that
> the Receivers were the occupiers of the rateable property and that they had
> undertaken the liabilities of Sabre Tooling Limited and were thereby responsible
> for the rates demanded. We were not shown and could not find any authority in
> law why the Receivers in this case could escape liability which we found was theirs   *c*
> and accordingly we ordered the issue of the Distress Warrant.'

On the application of the receivers' solicitors, the justices then stated a case which
raised the following questions for the decision of the High Court, namely:

> '(i) whether the onus of proof lay with [the receivers] in the circumstances
> established by the evidence; (ii) whether the Receivers were "occupiers" for the   *d*
> purpose of rating within the meaning of the General Rate Act of 1967; (iii) whether,
> having regard to Sections 94 and 319 of the Companies Act 1948 the Justices were
> in the circumstances established by the evidence entitled to issue a Warrant to levy
> distress.'

Kennedy J dismissed the receivers' appeal, answering questions (i) and (ii) in the   *e*
affirmative, and accordingly found it unnecessary to answer question (iii). As to the onus
of proof, he said:

> 'In the context of the present case, I am satisfied that once [the council] received
> notice of the appointment of the receivers and managers in the letter from Mr
> Ratford dated 6 April 1983 there was prima facie evidence that the receivers and
> managers had become the rateable occupiers, and it was then for them to show that   *f*
> in fact no change of rateable occupation had taken place.'

The judge then considered the evidence on which the receivers relied in order to show
that they were not in rateable occupation:

> 'First there was the debenture and the deed of appointment, but they were
> equivocal. The debenture clearly contained a power to take possession, but neither   *g*
> it nor the deed of appointment said anything as to whether or not in the instant case
> the power should be exercised.'

He then referred to the facts set out in the agreed statement of facts and continued:

> '[The receivers] chose not to give evidence and no evidence was called on their
> behalf, so in my judgment it is not surprising that the magistrates found that [the   *h*
> receivers] had failed to show that they were not in rateable occupation. Even if the
> onus of proof had been the other way round, it seems to me that the magistrates
> might well have come to the same conclusion as to who was the rateable occupier at
> the material time.'

Finally, he concluded that there was no legal barrier to the justices making the finding of   *j*
fact which he considered open to them on the evidence.

Burden of proof

It is perhaps a fair summary of the ratio of the decisions both of the justices and of
Kennedy J that (i) they regarded the onus of proof as falling throughout all the

proceedings on the receivers to show that they were not in rateable occupation of the

a premises and (ii) they considered that the receivers had not discharged this onus on the available evidence. The onus of proof is therefore of importance in the present context. Counsel on behalf of the receivers submits that this was an erroneous approach. In his submission the provisions of s 97(1) of the 1967 Act, pursuant to which the person named in the complaint is required to 'show why he has not paid the rate specified in the complaint', do not shift the burden of proof on that issue to that party; all they do is to

b call on him to show reasonable grounds (supported, if he wishes, by evidence) why he denies that he is the rateable occupier. Subject only to the person showing such reasonable grounds, the burden of proof, counsel for the receivers submits, rests on the complainant seeking the order. He reminded us of the use of a similar formula, as he submits with like effect, in various provisions of the Rules of the Supreme Court (Ord 14, r 4, Ord 62, r 8(2) and Ord 50, r 1).

c Counsel on behalf of the council began by making submissions as to the statutory purpose of s 97(1) of the 1967 Act. A rating authority, having sent out its demands for rates, may find that thousands of them remain unsatisfied. It has no right to sue for them as civil debts. It can only recover them by means of distress. It may have little or no knowledge of the actual occupation of the property in question. It has no power to call for documents or information. He accepts that a complaint can only properly be issued

d against persons who are prima facie liable to rates in respect of the property because they are known or appear to be in occupation of it. Subject only to this, however, he submits that, at the hearing of a summons before the justices of a complaint under s 97(1), all the rating authority has to show is that the rate in question has been duly made and published, that it has been demanded from the respondent and that it has not been paid; once these things have been shown, the onus falls fairly and squarely on the respondent

e to show why he should not be treated as being in rateable occupation of the premises. Any other construction, in the submission of counsel for the council, would defeat the purpose of the subsection, which was clearly intended to provide a simple and speedy method for the collection of rates.

I now turn to consider the principal authorities which have been cited to us concerning this question of onus. In *Des Salles d'Epinoix v Kensington and Chelsea Royal Borough* [1970]

f 1 All ER 18, [1970] 1 WLR 179 the Divisional Court held that the appellant was liable to rates for the year 1967–68 in respect of his former matrimonial home which he had left in November 1966. Lord Parker CJ pointed out that a man may remain in rateable occupation through deriving a beneficial use of the premises if the result is that his obligations to maintain are pro tanto discharged. He expressed his conclusion thus ([1970] 1 All ER 18 at 21, [1970] 1 WLR 179 at 182–183):

g

'Here one starts with this, that ever since 1946 the appellant has been on the valuation list as the rateable occupier. No steps have been taken by him since 9th November 1966 when he left the matrimonial home, to have his name removed from the valuation list. In addition, as I have said, when served with a summons for a distress warrant in respect of the 1967–68 rates, he never appeared to defend. In

h those circumstances it seems to me that a rating authority who can know nothing of the exact circumstances as between the appellant and his wife have really no choice open to them but to proceed against the appellant, who throughout, as far as they know, has remained the rateable occupier. It seems to me that then there must be a shifting of the burden of proof on general principles, because the only party to the proceedings who can know what the exact position is, is the appellant, and it

j seems to me that the burden then is on him to show that he has in fact ceased to be the rateable occupier. Not only do I think that that is true on general principles, but when one looks at s 97(1) of the General Rate Act 1967 it would suggest that there is this shifting of burden, because that subsection provides: [the subsection is then set out]. That as I read it contemplates that assuming that there is prima facie evidence that he is the rateable occupier, as there clearly was in this case, it is for

him then to appear and show for one reason or another why he has not paid. One
reason which he could put forward is that he had ceased to be the rateable occupier.'   *a*

Lord Parker CJ said that looked at in that way it was clear that the appellant had not
discharged the burden on him and on that ground the court dismissed the appeal.

The Divisional Court followed and applied the last-mentioned decision in *Lister v
Reigate BC* [1970] RA 1 and *Bromley London Borough v Brooks* (1973) 17 RRC 197.

In *Forsythe v Rawlinson* [1981] RVR 97 the Divisional Court had to consider an appeal
against a decision of magistrates who had authorised the issue of a distress warrant for   *b*
rates in respect of a Sunday market at Bovington Aerodrome. The only other possible
candidate for the position of rateable occupier was a company called Waterloo Galleries
Ltd. The magistrates had made a number of findings of fact. The rates in question had
been properly made and published. A demand for them had been served on the appellant.
Part of the aerodrome had been used as a regular Sunday market. The person organising
the market on the occasions when the council officers attended was the appellant. The   *c*
appellant was the only person in authority with whom the council officials had had any
contact in regard to the market in the context of a planning application. At no stage had
the appellant told council officers that he was an agen⸀ servant or officer of Waterloo
Galleries Ltd. Though, as Donaldson LJ pointed out, ⸀his was a question of mixed fact
and law, the magistrates had also found the appellant in his activities at the market was
acting for himself and not as an agent, servant or officer of Waterloo Galleries Ltd.   *d*
Evidence was given to the magistrates which tended to support the finding that the only
natural person appearing to occupy the market was the appellant. On that, the rating
authority held that it was for the appellant to show cause why he was not the rateable
occupier. The appellant declined to give evidence and submitted that no case had been
made out showing that he had been lawfully assessed and was liable. The magistrates
having overruled that submission, the appellant appealed to the Divisional Court.   *e*
Donaldson LJ, with whose judgment Mustill J agreed, referred to the provisions of s 97(1)
of the 1967 Act, and continued (at 98):

> 'Counsel for the respondent said that that section puts the burden on the person
> summoned to show cause why he should not pay the rate. So put, I regard the
> submission as frightening and the section, if properly so construed, as wholly   *f*
> oppressive, but I do not think it is to be so construed.'

Donaldson LJ then referred to *Des Salles d'Epinoix v Kensington and Chelsea Royal Borough*
[1970] 1 All ER 18 at 21, [1970] 1 WLR 179 at 182–183 from which he cited the passage
from the judgment of Lord Parker CJ dealing with the construction of s 97(1) quoted
earlier in this judgment. He continued ([1981] RVR 97 at 98):
  g

> 'The section so construed is more limited in effect. It means that the rating
> authority is only entitled to issue a complaint against people who are within the
> category of those who may prima facie be liable for the rates. In a husband and wife
> situation a prima facie case can usually be mounted against the wife because she is
> in actual occupation, and against the husband because he is the husband and because,
> as often is the case, his name appears on the rating list. I see no reason why there   *h*
> should not be prima facie cases against more than one person in the husband and
> wife field. If the local authority issues proceedings against somebody who is in that
> category, then I think s 97 itself reverses the burden of proof initially leaving the
> person complained against to show cause why a distress warrant should not be
> issued. But like all cases of the burden of proof in litigation, it is a swinging burden.
> It may be that the person concerned need at first do little more than say "I am not   *j*
> the rateable occupier" and then leave it to the rating authority to put the burden of
> proof back on to him.'

Donaldson LJ proceeded to point out that there were only two possible rateable occupiers,
namely the appellant and Waterloo Galleries Ltd. He concluded:

'For my part, it seems to me that either could be the rateable occupier, and that to that extent the appellant is within the category of person who prima facie is liable and to whom s 97(1) does apply. I say that either could be liable because the appellant might have been the *alter ego* or the servant or agent of Waterloo Galleries. In all those cases it would have been Waterloo Galleries who would be liable. On the other hand, he might himself have been running the market, in which case he would have been the occupier for rating purposes and he would have been liable. The information, as in the case of a husband and wife, is exclusively within his knowledge rather than that of the rating authority, and indeed the confidentiality between [sic] communication between a man and his company is much closer than that between husband and wife, since there is no chance of the company revealing the conversations which took place without the permission of the person concerned. In all the circumstances it seems to me that there was a case for the appellant to answer, even if his answer initially might have been extremely brief. But he did not choose to give any answer at all. In those circumstances I do not think it is possible to say that the magistrates were wrong . . .'

In *Verrall v Hackney London BC* [1983] 1 All ER 277, [1983] QB 445 this court had to consider whether a distress warrant had been properly issued to recover rates in respect of certain premises of which the rating authority asserted that an unincorporated association, the National Front, were in paramount occupation. The appellant was alleged to be a prominent member of that association. The magistrates had found that the rate had been properly made and demanded and all the necessary formalities had been complied with, that the demand for the rates had been addressed to the appellant and that the amount in question remained owing. May LJ, delivering the judgment of the court, said ([1983] 1 All ER 277 at 283, [1983] QB 445 at 459):

'These matters having been proved, in our opinion as a matter of law it was then for the appellant to show sufficient cause for not having paid the sum demanded. This, we think, is clear from the wording of s 97(1) of the 1967 Act and of the forms in Sch 12 which are referred to in s 97(2).'

However, May LJ, overruling certain earlier authorities, had held that a defence of non-occupation is capable of being raised in answer to proceedings for a distress warrant under s 97(1) (see [1983] 1 All ER 277 at 282, [1983] QB 445 at 458). He said ([1983] 1 All ER 277 at 283, [1983] QB 445 at 459):

'In the event the appellant neither gave evidence himself nor called any witness to do so on the hearing before the magistrate. A number of agreed documents were put in during the course of the opening of the case by counsel for the rating authority and a number of witnesses called on its behalf were cross-examined by counsel for the appellant. It was on this material that the appellant contended that he had been entitled not to pay the rates because he had not been the occupier of the relevant premises for the material period.'

The Court of Appeal upheld this contention and allowed the appellant's appeal.

On the basis of these authorities and on general principle, I would derive the following propositions of law as to the burden of proof in rating cases.

(1) A rating authority will not be justified in applying for a summons against a person under s 97(1) of the 1967 Act if it has no reasonable grounds for believing that he is or may be in rateable occupation of the premises in question; if it were to decide to apply for a summons in such circumstances, its decision would be open to judicial review. This I infer is what Donaldson LJ had in mind in saying in *Forsythe v Rawlinson* at 98 that 'the rating authority is only entitled to issue a complaint against people who are within the category of those who may prima facie be liable for the rates'. Thus, though for present purposes I find it unnecessary to express any concluded view on this point, it may be that s 97(1) must be read subject to the implicit qualification that it would place no onus on a

person who received a summons which so far lacked any reasonable basis that the decision
to issue it could be successfully attacked on *Wednesbury* grounds (see *Associated Provincial* *a*
Picture Houses Ltd v Wednesbury Corp [1947] 2 All ER 680, [1948] 1 KB 223). This I infer
is what Lord Parker CJ may have had in mind in saying that s 97(1) contemplates that
'assuming that there is prima facie evidence that he is the rateable occupier . . . it is for
him then to appear and show for one reason or another why he has not paid' (*Des Salles
d'Epinoix v Kensington and Chelsea Royal Borough* [1970] 1 All ER 18 at 21, [1970] 1 WLR
179 at 183).   *b*

(2) Even if this implicit qualification to s 97(1) exists, it can, in my opinion, only apply
in a case where on the facts known to the rating authority the person named in the
complaint could not have been reasonably regarded by the authority as a reasonably
possible candidate for the position of rateable occupier.

(3) Subject to (1) and (2) above, at the hearing of a summons under s 97(1), all the
rating authority has to show in the first instance is that (a) the rate in question has been *c*
duly made and published; (b) it has been duly demanded from the respondent, and (c) it
has not been paid. If these three things are shown, the burden then falls on the respondent
to show sufficient cause for not having paid the sum demanded (see *Verrall v Hackney
London BC* [1983] 1 All ER 277 at 283, [1983] QB 445 at 459 per May LJ). The question
whether a person who appears to be in occupation of a particular property is in actual
occupation of it will be peculiarly within his knowledge. It seems to me probable that *d*
the legislature, in enacting s 97(1), would have contemplated that the burden of proving
a defence based on non-occupation of the property would in the first instance fall on the
respondent.

(4) However, the standard of proof will be merely that of the balance of probabilities,
and in Donaldson LJ's words in *Forsythe v Rawlinson* at 98, 'like all cases of the burden of
proof in litigation, it is a swinging burden'. As the evidence of varying weight develops *e*
before the magistrates, the eventual burden of proof will, in accordance with ordinary
principles of evidence, remain with or shift to the person who will fail without further
evidence (see, for example, 17 Halsbury's Laws (4th edn) para 15).

Counsel for the receivers submitted that the judge erred in holding that once the
council received notice of the appointment of the receivers as receivers and managers in
the letter of 6 April 1983, the council possessed 'prima facie evidence that the receivers *f*
. . . had become the rateable occupiers, and that it was then for them to show that in fact
no change of rateable occupation had taken place'. He submitted (and I accept this
submission on the basis of the authorities referred to later in this judgment) that neither
the appointment of the receivers by the bank, pursuant to powers contained in the
debenture, nor the taking over by the receivers, when appointed, of the management of
the company's affairs, were necessarily sufficient to render the receiver's rateable occupiers *g*
in the place of the company. However, as will also appear from the authorities referred
to later in this judgment, the appointment of receivers by debenture holders, whether or
not accompanied by an assumption of the management of the company's affairs, is in
certain circumstances well capable of having this effect. As at 6 April 1983 the council
knew that the rateable occupiers must be either the company or the receivers. Their
decision to invoke the s 97 procedure against the receivers could not, in my opinion, *h*
have been successfully attacked on *Wednesbury* grounds; as I understand the facts, they
did not learn of the actual terms of the debenture or of the appointment of the receivers
until the proceedings before the justices had been instituted. In all the circumstances, at
the hearing before the justices, the onus of proof, at least in the first instance, in my
opinion fell on the receivers to show that no change of rateable occupation had taken
place. The question whether the onus shifted in the course of the hearing is another *j*
matter, and I will revert to it.

The authorities relating to the liability of a receiver for rates
With certain important statutory qualifications which have no relevance for present
purposes, a receiver appointed out of court by a debenture holder, in exercise of powers

a contained in the debenture granted by a company, in properly carrying out his functions, will ordinarily be under no personal liability. The reason is that, ordinarily, depending on the terms of his appointment, he will be acting simply as agent either for the debenture holder or for the company (see *Kerr on Receivers* (16th edn, 1983) p 259; 39 Halsbury's Laws (4th edn) para 805).

In the present case both the appointment and the debenture provided for the receiver to be deemed to be the agent of the company. Subsequently in this judgment I will from
b time to time refer to provisions of this nature as 'usual agency provisions'. I call them 'usual', because I think that provisions providing for the receiver to act as the agent of the debenture holder, though permissible, are less commonly employed in practice.

It is a general principle of rating law that where an agent is required to occupy a hereditament in order to secure the better performance of his duties as agent, his occupation is for rating purposes ordinarily treated as that of his principal. If, on the
c other hand, an agent occupies his principal's property otherwise than in his capacity as agent, the occupation will be treated as his own for rating purposes (see 39 Halsbury's Laws (4th edn) para 21).

The agency of the receivers in the present case, like that of any other receiver, was one with peculiar incidents. For instance, the company could not have dismissed them; nor could it have given them directions as to how they should carry out their activities.
d Nevertheless, the agency was, in my opinion, a real one. This is shown by the dissenting judgment of Rigby LJ in *Gaskell v Gosling* [1896] 1 QB 669 at 696, which was upheld by the House of Lords ([1897] AC 575, [1895–9] All ER Rep 300). Rigby LJ referred to the common form of words providing for the receiver when appointed to be the agent of the company. He said:

e   'These words, unless their effect is in some way controlled, are decisive of the question whether by the appointment the trustees [for the debenture holders] became principals of the receiver. They are inserted for the very purpose of preventing such a result. As appears from the statement hereinbefore contained, they express the usual intention in cases where a receiver is appointed by a mortgagee.'

f Rigby LJ concluded (at 697):

'. . . a receiver and manager appointed by a mortgagee under an agreement that he shall be the agent of the mortgagor is in the same position as if appointed by the mortgagor himself, and as if every direction given to him emanated from the mortgagor himself'.

The editor of *Kerr on Receivers* p 271 likewise states that the agency of the receiver for the
g mortgagor is a real one and draws attention to the various consequent duties owed by him to the mortgagor. He points out, however, that the receiver remains agent of the mortgagor only so long as his appointment by the mortgagee is effective, so that he ceases to be such agent when that appointment is superseded by an order of the court.

The reality and relevance of the status of a receiver as agent for a company was recognised by a decision of the Australian High Court, albeit outside the field of rating,
h in *Australian Mutual Provident Society v Geo Myers & Co Ltd (in liq)* (1931) 47 CLR 65. A section of the (Queensland) Real Property Act 1861 gave a mortgagee a right to distrain on the goods and chattels of a mortgagor who was in 'occupation' of the mortgaged land. The court held that the entry of a receiver for debenture holders appointed under a power which provided that he should be the agent of the company giving the debentures had not involved a change of possession from the company to the receiver, so that distress
j might still be levied on the company's goods and chattels. Dixon J said (at 82):

'The question whether the receiver was in control of the Company's premises in the exercise of an independent possession, or was merely in charge of the Company's undertaking on its behalf so that the Company continued in occupation, depends mainly upon the terms of the debenture deed, and perhaps to some extent upon the course actually taken by [the receiver]. The considerations which should determine the effect in such a matter of debenture deeds are dealt with in the judgment of *a* Rigby L.J. in *Gaskell* v. *Gosling* ([1896] 1 QB 669), whose view was adopted in the House of Lords ([1897] AC 575, [1895–9] All ER Rep 300), and also in *In re Marriage, Neave & Co.* ([1896] 2 Ch 663, [1895–9] All ER Rep 393). It is enough to say that, in my opinion, the true effect of the deed in this case was to render the receiver the agent of the Company and to leave its occupation or possession of its property in point of law undisturbed by his entry and by his assumption of control.' *b*

Much must clearly depend on the terms of the receiver's appointment. However, further authority apart, I would expect that the receivers in the present case, having taken up their appointment as agents for the company, would not fall to be treated as being in rateable occupation of the company's premises unless, to use Dixon J's phrase, 'they were in control of the Company's premises in the exercise of an independent possession' or, in other words, occupied them otherwise than in their capacity as agents *c* for the company, having dispossessed the company.

The authorities concerning rating law which have been cited to us, though not entirely clear or easy wholly to reconcile, in my opinion, support this view. In *Richards v Kidderminster Overseers* [1896] 2 Ch 212 a deed of floating charge on the assets of a company gave power to the trustee for the debenture holders to appoint a receiver with power to take possession of the property charged and to carry on business. The deed also *d* contained a usual agency provision and provided that the receiver should, as such agent, be deemed to be in exactly the same position as a receiver duly appointed by the mortgagee under the Conveyancing and Law of Property Act 1881. A receiver was in due course appointed and entered into possession of the property and began to carry on the business of the company. North J held that a change of occupation for rating purposes occurred when the receiver entered into possession of the property. He said (at 220): *e*

> 'The question, then, is what the construction of the deed is; and it is said that under the deed, as under the Act, the receiver was merely the agent of the mortgagor, and therefore the mortgagor continued in possession, and there was no change in possession. But in my opinion that contention is not sound. It is quite clear that the provisions of the deed do contemplate, in a particular event, and at a particular time, *f* that there either may or shall be a change of possession, in which a receiver shall enter into possession and shall carry on the business of the company; and in my opinion the provision that the receiver is to be the agent for the mortgagor is not so strong as to stultify every other provision in the deed, which says that the possession of the company shall cease and shall become the possession of the receiver . . . In my opinion, therefore, it is possible to say that the change of possession which was *g* clearly contemplated and required by the deed did not take place. It is not true to say that the company were in the occupation throughout, because the receiver on behalf of the trustee—the trustee himself, if you like to say so, on behalf of the debenture-holders—was the person from that time forward in possession.'

The ratio of the decision of North J was thus clearly based on the construction of the *h* particular trust deed, pursuant to which the receiver was appointed. He considered that, on its true construction, it required that when the receiver entered into possession of the property, the possession should cease to be that of the company and should become that of the receiver and that this requirement overrode the provision that the receiver was to be the agent of the mortgagor. If North J's construction of the trust deed was correct (as to which I need express no opinion) his ultimate decision was, in my opinion, a correct *j* one. It could not have been said that in dispossessing the company, the receiver was acting as agent for the company. This would have been a contradiction in terms.

An important decision for present purposes is the decision of this court in *Re Marriage Neave & Co* [1896] 2 Ch 663, [1895–9] All ER Rep 393 because it illustrates that the mere fact that a receiver has entered on a company's premises for the purpose of managing and carrying on its business, does not necessarily mean that he has dispossessed the company *a*   or that it has ceased to occupy the premises for rating purposes. In that case an order was made appointing a receiver and manager of a company's business, but not directing delivery up of possession to him. The receiver and manager then entered on the company's premises for the purpose of managing and carrying on its business. The Court of Appeal held that there was no change of occupation for rating purposes. Lindley LJ said ([1896] 2 Ch 663 at 671–672, [1895–9] All ER Rep 393 at 394):

b   'That order does not contain—and the omission is, to my mind, very important— any direction whatever for delivery-up of possession of the land to those gentlemen; and moreover it does not appear from the affidavits that they have taken possession of the land in any sense at all. What they have done is this: they have gone on to the property for the purpose of receiving and managing the income and business of the company, but they have not done anything to change the ostensible possession of the property in any way whatever; and, upon the facts, it appears to me that the

c   possession and occupation have not been changed at all. Counsel for the debenture holders argued that, inasmuch as corporations can only occupy by their agents, the appointment of a receiver by an order of the Court is quite enough to create a change of possession. I do not take that view of the law. A corporation can possess and can occupy. The mere fact that a receiver is appointed by an order which does not in fact order the company to give up possession does not dispossess the company.'

d   Lopes LJ said ([1896] 2 Ch 663 at 674, [1895–9] All ER Rep 393 at 396):

'It is said that, the receivers having been appointed, there was a change of occupation. It seems to me perfectly clear that that contention cannot be maintained, because, when the order is looked at, we find nothing in it which directs that possession of the land be given up to the receivers. What the receivers have to do is

e   to go there and manage the property. The occupation, in my judgment, remained in the company in precisely the same way as it did before. The company continued to occupy notwithstanding that order.'

Rigby LJ said ([1896] 2 Ch 663 at 676, [1895–9] All ER Rep 393 at 397):

'It is only where there is a change of occupation that that section has any operation. The argument that, because a receiver and manager is appointed, then ipso facto the

f   company or persons carrying on business are turned out, is neither reasonable nor plausible. It is quite conceivable that these receivers might have performed all their duties without even seeing this property. They were to carry on the business: they could have appointed a manager of that business under them, to take his instructions from them. It might never be necessary for them to go near the property at all.'

g   In *National Provincial Bank of England Ltd v United Electric Theatres Ltd* [1916] 1 Ch 132 an order was made in a foreclosure action appointing a receiver and manager and directing the tenants of those properties which were let to attorn, and the mortgagors to deliver to the receiver as such receiver and manager, all the stock-in-trade and effects of the business. The order did not contain any direction for delivery up of possession of the

h   land but the receiver subsequently stated that he had entered into possession. Astbury J, however, held that the receiver had not entered into rateable occupation of the premises. He said (see 85 LJ Ch 106 at 112):

'I think it is quite plain that in these mortgage cases, either by contract between the parties or otherwise, there may be an appointment of a receiver under such circumstances that there is a change of possession within the meaning of the Rating

j   Acts.'

Astbury J then referred to *Richards v Kidderminster Overseers* [1896] 2 Ch 212, which he distinguished by reference to the particular provisions of the debenture trust deed in that case. He then referred to *Re Marriage Neave & Co* [1896] 2 Ch 663, [1895–9] All ER Rep 393 and to the passage from Lindley LJ's judgment which I have quoted. He concluded on this point (85 LJ Ch 106 at 112):

'I think that substantially applies to the present case. It is quite true that the receiver here states that he entered into possession. But the real point is what was *a* the quality of the possession that was so taken. I think he only took the possession that he was entitled to take under the order, and that there was no change of possession as was contemplated under the statutes in question.'

In *Gyton v Palmour* [1944] 2 All ER 540, [1945] KB 426 the respondent had in February 1940 been appointed receiver and manager of the business of a company under a *b* debenture trust deed. In March 1940 he was appointed receiver and manager of all the property of the company, except uncalled capital, by a High Court order, which did not contain any direction to the company to deliver up to the respondent possession of their property. The Divisional Court found itself unable to distinguish the facts of *Re Marriage Neave & Co* from those of the case before it (see [1944] 2 All ER 540 at 542, [1945] KB 426 at 432). Viscount Caldecote CJ, however, in delivering the judgment of the court, *c* added ([1944] 2 All ER 540 at 543, [1945] KB 426 at 433–434):

> 'The nature of rateable occupation has been so frequently stated that it may seem unnecessary to repeat any of the statements which have been made. In the case, however, of *Westminster Council* v. *Southern Ry. Co.* ([1936] 2 All ER 322 at 326, [1936] AC 511 at 529), there is a passage in the opinion of LORD RUSSELL which will *d* bear repetition: "The occupier, not the land, is rateable; but, the occupier is rateable in respect of the land which he occupies. Occupation, however, is not synonymous with legal possession: the owner of an empty house has the legal possession, but he is not in rateable occupation. Rateable occupation, however, must include actual possession, and it must have some degree of permanence: a mere termporary holding of land will not constitute rateable occupation." In the present case, *e* whatever the nature of the possession into which the receiver and manager was put by the order of the court, it seems plain to me that it fell far short of the occupation which is necessary in order to constitute rateability.'

The three decisions in *Re Marriage Neave & Co*, *National Provincial Bank of England Ltd v United Electric Theatres Ltd* and *Gyton v Palmour*, though they concerned appointments *f* of receivers by the court and did not depend on the agency point, support the receivers' case on the present appeal, so far as they go. For they all clearly show that the mere fact that a receiver has entered on the company's premises for the purpose of managing and carrying on its business does not necessarily mean that the company has been dispossessed or has ceased to occupy the premises for rating purposes. If it is to be shown that a change of rateable occupation has occurred, this conclusion must be derived from the terms of *g* the receiver's appointment or from what he has actually done, or from both together.

Two decisions relied on by counsel for the council suggest that, notwithstanding the existence of an agency clause in the debenture pursuant to which the receiver is appointed, a receiver appointed out of court may conduct himself in such manner as to dispossess the company and thus render himself in rateable occupation of the property. One of these cases was *Taggs Island Casino Hotel Ltd v Richmond-upon-Thames London Borough* *h* (1966) 14 RRC 119. The case was a rather special one, not only because it was an interlocutory decision, but also because the receiver (in whose interest it was so to state on the particular facts) had deposed in an uncontroverted affidavit that he had taken possession of the company's premises (a hotel) after his appointment. The debenture pursuant to which he was appointed contained a usual agency provision. Ungoed-Thomas J reached the provisional view that on the evidence the receiver's possession had been full *j* occupation of the premises for rating purposes, notwithstanding this provision. He thought it 'highly arguable' that the provision did not have the effect of the receiver being in possession as agent for the company (at 125). By way of support to this conclusion he referred to certain observations of Viscount Caldecote CJ in *Meigh v Wickenden* [1942] 2 All ER 68, [1942] 2 KB 160, on the facts of which, notwithstanding the existence of an agency clause, the Divisional Court held a receiver to have been in

a

'occupation' of certain premises for the purpose of the Factories Act 1937 so as to impose liability on him under that Act.

In *Banister v Islington London BC* (1972) 71 LGR 239 the question arose whether a receiver was 'entitled to possession' of certain unoccupied factory premises, within the meaning of the definition of 'owner' in para 15 of Sch 1 to the General Rate Act 1967, and as such liable to be rated under para 1 of Sch 1. The debenture in question empowered the receiver to take possession of the property charged and provided that he should be

b

the agent of the company. Following his appointment he undoubtedly went into actual possession (see per Lord Widgery CJ (at 243)). An argument, however, was advanced on behalf of the appellant to the effect that although he was entitled to possession, he was entitled to possession solely qua agent of the company and was thus exempt from liability to be rated (at 244). Lord Widgery CJ referred to the decisions in *Taggs Island Casino Hotel Ltd v Richmond-upon-Thames London Borough* and *Richards v Kidderminster Overseers* as

c

illustrating what the position was in regard to receivers under the old law, before the provisions for unoccupied premises came into force. He was satisfied by the latter decision that under the old law a usual agency provision governing the receivers' appointment constituted no obstacle to a receiver who actually put himself into rateable occupation from being chargeable as such. He saw no reason 'why the plain words of Schedule 1 to the General Rate Act, 1967, should not have the same effect' (at 246).

d

The present case

On the basis of the decisions in *Richards v Kidderminster Overseers*, *Taggs Island Casino Hotel Ltd v Richmond-upon-Thames London Borough*, *Banister v Islington London BC* and *Meigh v Wickenden*, counsel for the council submitted there is no rule of law that a receiver appointed by debenture holders may not be in rateable occupation of the company's premises and that the usual agency provision does not necessarily prevent him from

e

being in occupation for rating purposes. I accept both these submissions.

He further pointed out, correctly in my opinion, that there cannot be two separate occupiers for rating purposes at one time of one hereditament (see, for example, *Re Briant Colour Printing Co Ltd (in liq)* [1977] 3 All ER 968 at 977, [1977] 1 WLR 942 at 952–953 per Buckley LJ). If there are two persons (such as the company and the receivers in the present case) each of whom is making concurrent use of the hereditament, 'it may be

f

necessary to discover which of them has the paramount position so as to be rateable as the occupier' (see [1977] 3 All ER 968 at 977, [1977] 1 WLR 942 at 953). Counsel for the council reminded us of what was said by Lord Herschell in *Holywell Union and Halkyn Parish v Halkyn District Mines Drainage Co* [1895] AC 117 at 125, [1891–4] All ER Rep 158 at 163:

g

'The question whether a person is an occupier or not within the rating law is a question of fact, and does not depend upon legal title.'

In the submission of counsel for the council the question whether or not the receivers in the present case, having power to take possession and go into occupation, did go into rateable occupation of the premises, is essentially a question of fact. He submitted that there are no grounds for holding that the justices, in finding as a fact that the receivers

h

were the occupiers of the property, erred in law or misdirected themselves or that the judge erred in upholding their decision. I find myself unable to accept this last submission, for reasons which, after the lengthy review of the authorities contained earlier in this judgment, may now be shortly stated.

(1) I respectfully agree with the justices and with the judge that the council, on

j

receiving the letter of 6 April 1983, were justified in applying for a summons against the receivers under s 97(1) of the 1967 Act. The contents of this letter gave them reasonable grounds for believing that the receivers might be in rateable occupation of the premises, since they were within the category of those who might prima facie be liable. As appears from the authorities cited above, it is possible for a receiver to be appointed on terms which involve a change of rateable occupation (see for example the *National Provincial Bank* case 85 LJ Ch 106 at 112 per Astbury J).

(2) At the first hearing before the justices, the council having shown that the rate in question had been duly made and published, that it had been duly demanded from the receivers and that it had not been paid, the burden fell in the first instance on the receivers to show sufficient cause for not having paid the sum demanded.

(3) In my judgment, however, the receivers prima facie discharged this burden by showing that they had been appointed on terms which, though empowering them to take possession of the company's premises and to carry on and manage its business, did not oblige them to take possession, and further provided that in carrying out their activities they should be deemed to be the agents of the company.

(4) This much having been shown, the onus, in my opinion, shifted to the council to show that the receivers had dispossessed the company, or, to put it another way, to show that the quality of any possession of the premises which the receivers might have enjoyed was not that of mere agents. For possession held by a person in his capacity as agent is in law the possession of his principal.

(5) The agreed statement of facts placed before the justices did no more than show that the receivers had had representatives on the property from time to time during their receivership, that they had managed the company's business and authorised the payment of various outgoings, that the company had at their direction disposed of the company's assets, including, eventually, the leasehold interest in the premises, and that during the receivership they had had control of those of the company's assets covered by the debenture. However, in my opinion, the decisions in Re Marriage Neave & Co (a decision of this court), and in the National Provincial Bank case and Gyton v Palmour show that these facts are quite consistent with the company remaining in legal possession and rateable occupation of the premises.

In my opinion, therefore, there was no sufficient evidence before the justices to justify a finding that the receivers had dispossessed the company, which had unquestionably been in possession and rateable occupation of the premises up to the date of their appointment.

The justices appear to have arrived at the conclusion expressed in para 9 of their decision from the presumption that the receivers by virtue of their appointment had assumed personal liability in general for the liabilities of the company, and in particular for the rates payable in respect of the premises. Having regard to the terms of the appointment of the receivers, no such presumptions, in my opinion, arose, save in so far as statute (e g the Companies Acts) imposed them. No reliance has been placed on statute in argument before us. With respect to all concerned, I think that, as is submitted in the notice of appeal, the judge ought to have held that the justices reached their conclusion set out in para 9 of their decision by a process of reasoning which was wrong in law, in that they failed to state that the acts of the receivers referred to in the case stated were in law the acts of the company, they wrongly held that the receivers had undertaken the liabilities of the company, and erred in stating that there was no authority in law why the receivers could escape liability for the rates. On the authorities the position is, in my opinion, rather the reverse. Save for those cases such as Richards v Kidderminster Overseers, where the terms of the receiver's appointment have effected or required dispossession of the company, I think that no case has been cited to us in which a receiver has ever been held to be in rateable occupation of occupied premises. The reason, I infer, is not far to seek. Any occupation of the relevant premises enjoyed by a receiver will normally be enjoyed by him solely in his capacity as agent for some other party. Though it is possible for him to take independent possession of the premises as principal, such cases I suspect may be comparatively rare.

Counsel for the receivers submitted that the agreed facts in this case did not indicate or establish any action on the part of the receivers in relation to the premises beyond management of the company's business and control of its assets, as in any typical receivership where the receiver decides to continue the business as a going concern. I accept this submission. The terms of the receivers' appointment having been put in evidence, and the statement of facts having been agreed, it was not, in my opinion,

incumbent on the receivers to give oral evidence. I respectfully differ from the judge's
view that inferences adverse to the receivers can be drawn from their failure to do so.

a
For the reasons given, I would allow this appeal and would answer questions (i) and (ii)
of the case stated in the negative. We have not been invited to consider question (iii).

RALPH GIBSON LJ. I agree.

b **SIR JOHN MEGAW.** I agree.

Appeal allowed. Liberty to apply to receivers to quash assessment.

Solicitors: *Wilkinson Kimbers* (for the receivers); *J Petch*, Thornbury (for the council).

c
Wendy Shockett   Barrister.

R v Secretary of State for the Home Department and another, ex parte Herbage

d
QUEEN'S BENCH DIVISION (CROWN OFFICE LIST)
HODGSON J
16, 19 MAY 1986

Crown – Relief against the Crown – Interlocutory relief – Jurisdiction – Injunction against officer
e *of Crown – Interim injunction – Judicial review proceedings – Application for interim injunction*
against officer of Crown in judicial review proceedings – Whether Crown officer's immunity from
grant of injunction in civil proceedings applying – Whether court having jurisdiction to grant
interim injunction against officer of Crown in judicial review proceedings – Crown Proceedings
Act 1947, ss 21, 38 – Supreme Court Act 1981, s 31(2) – RSC Ord 53, r 3(10).

f The Queen's Bench Division of the High Court has jurisdiction to grant, by way of
judicial review, an interim injunction against an officer of the Crown because (a) s $31(2)^a$
of the Supreme Court Act 1981 provides for the grant of relief by way of an injunction
in judicial review proceedings, (b) RSC Ord 53, r $3(10)^b$ provides for interim relief to be
granted in judicial review proceedings and (c) the immunity from the grant of an
injunction in civil proceedings enjoyed by the Crown and its officers under s 21^c of the
g Crown Proceedings Act 1947 does not apply because, by s 38^d of that Act, 'civil
proceedings' does not include 'proceedings on the Crown side of the Queen's Bench
Division' and therefore does not include judicial review proceedings (see p 212 g to j,
p 214 a b, p 215 a h j and p 216 b, post).

Notes
h For restrictions on granting injunctions against an officer of the Crown, see 11 Halsbury's
Laws (4th edn) para 1435.
For judicial review, see 37 ibid paras 567–583, and for prerogative orders, see 11 ibid
para 1451.
For the Crown Proceedings Act 1947, ss 21, 38, see 13 Halsbury's Statutes (4th edn) 30,
41.
j For the Supreme Court Act 1981, s 31, see 11 ibid 782.

---

a   Section 31 is set out at p 214 g to j, post
b   Rule 3(10) is set out at p 215 e f, post
c   Section 21, so far as material, is set out at p 212 d to f, post
d   Section 38 is set out at p 212 g, post

Cases referred to in judgment

A-G v Wilts United Dairies Ltd (1921) 37 TLR 884, CA; on appeal (1922) 91 LJKB 897, HL.

Congreve v Home Office [1976] 1 All ER 697, [1976] QB 629, [1976] 2 WLR 291, QBD and CA.

Harper v Secretary of State for the Home Dept [1955] 1 All ER 331, [1955] Ch 238, [1955] 2 WLR 316, CA.

Merricks v Heathcoat-Amory [1955] 2 All ER 453, [1955] Ch 567, [1955] 3 WLR 56.

O'Reilly v Mackman [1982] 3 All ER 1124, [1983] 2 AC 237, [1982] 3 WLR 1096, HL.

Padfield v Ministry of Agriculture Fisheries and Food [1968] 1 All ER 694, [1968] AC 997, [1968] 2 WLR 924, HL.

R v Comrs of Customs and Excise, ex p Cooke and Stevenson [1970] 1 All ER 1068, [1970] 1 WLR 450, DC.

R v Deputy Governor of Camphill Prison, ex p King [1984] 3 All ER 897, [1985] QB 735, [1985] 2 WLR 36, CA.

R v Secretary of State for the Home Dept, ex p Yaqoob [1984] 1 WLR 920, CA.

R v Secretary of State for the Home Dept, ex p Kirkwood [1984] 2 All ER 390, [1984] 1 WLR 913.

R v Secretary of State for the Home Dept, ex p McAvoy [1984] 3 All ER 417, [1984] 1 WLR 1408.

R v Secretary of State for the Home Dept, ex p Phansopkar [1975] 3 All ER 497, [1976] QB 606, [1975] 3 WLR 322, DC and CA.

R v Secretary of State for War [1891] 2 QB 326, CA.

R v Treasury Lords Comrs (1872) LR 7 QB 387.

Application for judicial review

By notice of motion dated 14 May 1986 Alex William Herbage applied pursuant to RSC Ord 53, with leave of Hodgson J given on 13 May 1986, for interlocutory relief until the hearing of the application or further order and for relief by way of judicial review in the following forms: (1) an order of mandamus directed to the governor of Pentonville Prison and to the Secretary of State of the Home Department, directing them to detain the applicant according to law; (2) a mandatory injunction directing that they should take all necessary steps forthwith to ensure that, subject only to the proper application of the Prison Rules 1964, the applicant was granted the same opportunities of association with fellow prisoners as were accorded generally to unconvicted prisoners; (3) alternatively, an injunction restraining them, whether by themselves their servants or agents or otherwise howsoever, from confining the applicant in such manner as to deprive him of the same opportunities of association with fellow prisoners as were accorded generally to unconvicted prisoners, save and except for such deprivation as was permitted by the proper application of the Prison Rules 1964; and (4) alternatively, such other interlocutory relief, whether by way of declaration or otherwise, as the court deemed appropriate. The facts are set out in the judgment.

Alan Newman and Antony White for the applicant.
John Laws for the Secretary of State and the governor.

HODGSON J. In these proceedings the applicant seeks interlocutory relief against the respondents. The form of relief sought is an interlocutory interim injunction. The respondents are the Secretary of State for the Home Department and the governor of Pentonville Prison. The relief sought is an injunction which in its mandatory form reads:

'a mandatory injunction . . . directing that they take all necessary steps forthwith to ensure that, subject only to the proper application of the Prison Rules 1964, the Applicant is granted the same opportunities of association with fellow prisoners as are accorded generally to unconvicted prisoners.'

The applicant is detained in Pentonville Prison. He is in custody awaiting an extradition warrant for surrender to the United States of America in respect of 25 charges of

dishonesty. Those proceedings the applicant is seeking to impugn in habeas corpus
a proceedings.

In his affidavit the applicant complains of the conditions under which he is detained.
There are many complaints. In the grounds on which relief is sought it is pleaded that:

'(1) The present conditions under which the Applicant is detained are detailed in
paragraphs 5 and 6 of the affidavit sworn by the Applicant which accompanies this
Notice. (2) Such conditions amount to the infliction of "cruell and unusuall
b punishment" contrary to the Bill of Rights 1668. (3) Breach of a provision in the Bill
of Rights 1688 is of itself capable of grounding an application for judicial review.
(4) Article 3 of the European Convention on Human Rights prohibits absolutely
anyone being subjected to "inhuman or degrading treatment or punishment",
although it is accepted that such Article is not directly incorporated into English
law. The conditions in which the Applicant is kept amount to breach of Article 3.
c (5) Both the Prison Act 1952 and the Prison Rules 1964 must be interpreted and
exercised so as to give effect to rights recognised by the Bill of rights 1688 and the
European Convention. (6) The Secretary of State in carrying out his duties and
powers under sections 1, 4(2) and 12 of the Prison Act 1952, and the Governor in
ensuring the proper legal custody of a prisoner pursuant to section 13(1) of the
Prison Act 1952, must act in accordance with the provisions of the Bill of Rights
d 1688 and the European Convention on Human Rights. (7) Alternatively, the
Secretary of State and the Governor, in acting under the aforementioned provisions
of the Prison Act 1952, must carry out their functions so as not to commit or permit
the commission of a tort. (8) Illegality in the performance of statutory powers or
duties under the Prison Act 1952 is judicially reviewable—and, in such exercise,
failure to have regard to the Prison Rules 1964 can be taken into account.'

e
Very briefly, the applicant's argument in the substantive application can be summarised.
The Bill of Rights 1688 is a statute. It prohibits the infliction of 'cruell and unusuall
punishment'. A breach of the provisions of the Bill of Rights can itself ground an
application for judicial review (*A-G v Wilts United Dairies Ltd* (1921) 37 TLR 884 at 886
and *Congreve v Home Office* [1976] 1 All ER 697 at 710, [1976] QB 629 at 652 are cited).
f Specific statutory duties are placed on the Secretary of State by ss 1, 4(2) and 12 of the
Prison Act 1952. Both the Prison Act 1952 and the Prison Rules 1964, SI 1964/388, made
thereunder must be interpreted and exercised so as to give effect to rights recognised by
the Bill of Rights and the European Convention on Human Rights (Convention for the
Protection of Human Rights and Fundamental Freedoms (Rome, 4 November 1950; TS
71 (1953); Cmd 8969)): see *R v Secretary of State for the Home Dept, ex p Phansopkar* [1975]
g 3 All ER 497 at 510–511, [1976] QB 606 at 626 is cited. Illegality in the performance of
statutory powers and duties by the Secretary of State and by the Governor are reviewable,
and failure to have regard to the Prison Rules can be taken into account (*R v Secretary of
State for the Home Dept, ex p McAvoy* [1984] 3 All ER 417, [1984] 1 WLR 1408 is cited).

On the basis of the applicant's affidavit and also certain medical evidence exhibited to
an affidavit sworn by the applicant's solicitor, I granted the applicant leave to move for
h judicial review by way of mandamus directed to the respondents. Since then the
respondents have filed evidence in the form of a full and detailed affidavit from the
respondent governor. It puts in issue practically everything contained in the applicant's
affidavit. The medical evidence may also be in issue.

This application for interim relief is based primarily on r 3(3) of the Prison Rules 1964,
which provides—

j 'Nothing in this Rule shall require a prisoner to be deprived unduly of the society
of other persons.'

In his affidavit the applicant deposes that throughout the whole of his seven months at
Pentonville (with minor exceptions) he has been kept in solitary confinement locked up
in his cell 24 hours a day. The governor deposes that: 'There is no inhibition at all on the
applicant's right to association with other prisoners.' If the governor is right, counsel for

the applicant submits that the granting of the interim relief sought would impose no
further obligation on the governor.

In opposing this application, counsel for the Secretary of State and the governor
submits that it fails in limini because an interim injunction does not lie against an officer
of the Crown and both the Secretary of State and the governor are such officers.

I turn first therefore to consider the question whether on a proper construction of the
relevant legislation there is jurisdiction in this court to grant an interim injunction
against an officer of the Crown.

The immunity of the Crown and its officers from injunctive relief is to be found in
s 21 of the Crown Proceedings Act 1947. Prior to the 1947 Act the remedy in private law
matters against the Crown was by way of petition of right in the High Court. It was
confined to four cases, debt due under contract or statute, unliquidated sums due by
statute, damages for breach of contract, and recovery of property. Proceedings on the
Crown side of the King's Bench Division consisted and consisted only of habeas corpus,
mandamus, prohibition, certiorari, and injunction in the nature of quo warranto. These
procedures had escaped the procedural reform of the nineteenth century although they
had been slightly modernised by the alteration of title from writ to order by the
Administration of Justice (Miscellaneous Provisions) Act 1938. There was no remedy by
way of injunction available on the Crown side of the King's Bench Division, nor was any
interim relief available.

Section 21 provides:

'(1) In any civil proceedings by or against the Crown the court shall, subject to
the provisions of this Act, have power to make all such orders as it has power to
make in proceedings between subjects, and otherwise to give such appropriate relief
as the case may require: Provided that:— (a) where in any proceedings against the
Crown any such relief is sought as might in proceedings between subjects be granted
by way of injunction or specific performance, the court shall not grant an injunction
or make an order for specific performance, but may in lieu thereof make an order
declaratory of the rights of the parties . . . [I omit para (b)].

(2) The court shall not in any civil proceedings grant any injunction or make any
order against an officer of the Crown if the effect of granting the injunction or
making the order would be to give any relief against the Crown which could not
have been obtained in proceedings against the Crown.'

By s 38 it is provided that—

'"Civil proceedings" includes proceedinga in the High Court or the county court
for the recovery of fines or penalties, but does not include proceedings on the Crown
side of the King's Bench Division.'

It follows that s 21(1) does not apply to Crown side proceedings. The proviso is a
proviso to s 21(1). Counsel for the Secretary of State and the governor submits that
because the word used is 'proceedings', not 'civil proceedings', it has a wider implication
and effectively prevents any injunction lying in Crown side proceedings against the
Home Secretary. This, with respect, seems to me to be reading far more into that
subsection than it can possibly bear. To begin with it applies to the Crown, not its
servants. Section 21(2) deals with officers of the Crown. Secondly, prerogative remedies
do not in any event lie against the Crown. The only proceedings that can be brought
against the Crown are those brought by writ or originating summons under the 1947
Act. There was no need to repeat the word 'civil' in the proviso to s 21.

Of course the prerogative orders lie against officers of the Crown including ministers,
save where the Crown's servant is merely the instrument selected by the Crown for the
discharge of the Crown's own duty (see Wade Administrative Law (5th edn, 1982) p 645
and the cases there cited). But in nearly every case mandamus will lie against a minister
or department. 'Where by statute an officer or servant of the Crown has also a duty
towards a member of the public' mandamus will lie at the suit of any member of the

public who has a sufficient interest (see *R v Comrs of Customs and Excise, ex p Cooke and*
a Stevenson [1970] 1 All ER 1068 at 1072, [1970] 1 WLR 450 at 455 per Lord Parker CJ).

Put another way, where Parliament imposes a duty on someone acting in a particular
capacity, mandamus will lie notwithstanding that he is a servant of the Crown and acting
on the Crown's behalf (see *Padfield v Ministry of Agriculture Fisheries and Food* [1968] 1 All
ER 694, [1968] AC 997, *R v Secretary of State for the Home Dept, ex p Phansopkar* [1975] 3
All ER 497, [1976] QB 606). The use of mandamus against Crown servants is specifically
b reserved by s 40(5) of the 1947 Act, which reads:

> 'This Act shall not operate to limit the discretion of the court to grant relief by
> way of mandamus in cases in which such relief might have been granted before the
> commencement of this Act, notwithstanding that by reason of the provisions of this
> Act some other and further remedy is available.'

c It is clear from that subsection that the Act contemplated the use of the new procedure
in public law matters.

Section 21(2) of the 1947 Act deals with injunctions against officers of the Crown. (In
s 38 'Officer' of the Crown is defined to include a minister of the Crown.) If I had to
construe s 21(2) in the absence of authority, I would read it as preventing the Crown
being enjoined by the expedient of enjoining a minister selected by the Crown for the
d discharge of the Crown's own duty. However, in *Merricks v Heathcoat-Amory* [1955] 2 All
ER 453, [1955] Ch 567 a mandatory injunction was sought against the Minister of
Agriculture, Fisheries and Food to make him withdraw a draft scheme for potato
marketing which had been laid before Parliament and was allegedly ultra vires. Although
the Agricultural Marketing Acts provided that it was the minister who was to make such
schemes, so that the power resided in him rather than the Crown itself, the court held
e that any remedy by way of injunction was barred by s 21(2) (see also *Harper v Secretary of*
State for Home Dept [1955] 1 All ER 331, [1955] Ch 238). It is, however, noticeable that
Upjohn J said ([1955] 2 All ER 453 at 457, [1955] Ch 567 at 575):

> 'Of course there can be an official representing the Crown and that is plainly this
> case. But if he were not, it was said he was a person designated in an official capacity
> but not representing the Crown. The third alternative was that his capacity was
> *f* purely that of an individual. I understand the conception of the first and the third
> categories, but I confess to finding it very difficult to see how the second category
> can fit into any ordinary scheme.'

It seems to me questionable whether that dictum can survive in view of later decisions
such as *Padfield v Minister of Agriculture Fisheries and Food* [1968] 1 All ER 694, [1968] AC
g 997.

The decision in *Merricks' v Heathcott-Amory* has been criticised as anomalous by
Professor Wade who points out that the minister in those circumstances would be liable
to compulsory orders in Crown side proceedings (see *Administrative Law* (5th edn, 1982)
p 519).

In *R v Secretary of State for the Home Dept, ex p Kirkwood* [1984] 2 All ER 390, [1984] 1
h WLR 913 the Secretary of State had issued a warrant under s 11 of the Extradition Act
1870 ordering the applicant to be surrendered to the United States authority. Leave to
apply for judicial review was granted and the court directed that the grant of leave should
operate as a stay of proceedings on the warrant until the application for judicial review
was determined. On the minister's application to discharge the stay Mann J held as
follows ([1984] 2 All ER 390 at 391):

j
> 'The stay would be discharged because the court was prohibited by s 21 of the
> 1947 Act from granting an injunction against an officer of the Crown and the stay
> was equivalent to an injunction restraining the Secretary of State from exercising
> his executive function. In any event, when exercising his powers under the 1870
> Act the Secretary of State was not obliged to consider the provisions of the European
> Convention on Human Rights since it was not part of the law of the United

Kingdom; and accordingly even if there had been jurisdiction to grant the stay, the
court would still have ordered it to be removed because the applicant's chances of   *a*
success by way of judicial review were negligible.'

Unfortunately no one drew Mann J's attention to s 38 of the 1947 Act and, indeed, it
was 'common ground between the parties that . . . proceedings by way of judicial review
are civil proceedings' (see [1984] 2 All ER 390 at 393, [1984] 1 WLR 913 at 917). That
seems to me to have been plainly wrong. 'Civil proceedings' in the 1947 Act are
specifically defined to exclude Crown side proceedings. Mann J felt himself bound by   *b*
the decision of Dillon LJ sitting as a single judge in the Court of Appeal in *R v Secretary
of State for the Home Dept, ex p Yaqoob* [1984] 1 WLR 920, but that was a case brought by
originating summons and so fell squarely within the Act. I note, however, that in
referring to sub-s (2) of s 21 Mann J said ([1984] 2 All ER 390 at 394, [1984] 1 WLR 913
at 917):
                                                                                       c
'In my judgment the sole purpose of sub-s (2) is to prevent the subject from
achieving indirectly a result which he could not achieve directly by reason of the
provisions of sub-s (1).'

It seems clear, however, that since 1947 the courts have construed s 21(2) as excluding
injunctive relief against an officer of the Crown even when acting under statutory powers
or duties specifically laid on him. I take leave to doubt whether the courts have been   *d*
correct in so construing s 21(2) but, as I have been referred to no case where this contrary
view has been taken, I must assume, I think, that my doubts are without foundation.

After 1947 therefore anyone wishing to pursue a public law remedy against an officer
of the Crown where Parliament has imposed a specific duty on that officer had two
avenues open to him. He could either proceed by writ or originating summons under
the 1947 Act, or he could seek a prerogative order from the Divisional Court. On the   *e*
construction placed by the courts on s 21(2) he could only obtain declaratory relief under
the 1947 Act. An interim declaration being unavailable, he could obtain no interim
relief under the Act. Interim relief was not available in Crown side proceedings for an
order of mandamus (though in certiorari and prohibition proceedings a stay could be
ordered).

In 1976 the Law Commission in their Report on Remedies in Administrative Law   *f*
(Law Com no 73) made recommendations many of which were adopted and implemented
by changes in the Rules of the Supreme Court. The new RSC Ord 53 came into force the
following year. The Law Commission had thought that legislation would be necessary
to effect the changes they recommended, and statutory backing was somewhat unusually
given to the new rules four years later by the Supreme Court Act 1981. Section 31(1) and
(2) of that Act provides:
                                                                                       g
'(1) An application to the High Court for one or more of the following forms of
relief, namely— (*a*) an order of mandamus, prohibition or certiorari; (*b*) a declaration
or injunction under subsection (2); or [and I omit (*c*), the quo warranto provision]
shall be made in accordance with rules of court by a procedure to be known as an
application for judicial review.
(2) A declaration may be made or an injunction granted under this subsection in   *h*
any case where an application for judicial review, seeking that relief, has been made
and the High Court considers that, having regard to— (*a*) the nature of the matters
in respect of which relief may be granted by orders of mandamus, prohibition or
certiorari; (*b*) the nature of the persons and bodies against whom relief may be
granted by such orders; and (*c*) all the circumstances of the case, it would be just and   *j*
convenient for the declaration to be made or the injunction to be granted, as the
case may be.'

Section 31(2) is, in all material respects, in precisely the same terms as cl 2 of the draft
bill appended to the Law Commission report. The reason why the draft clause was in
guideline terms was because the remit to the Law Commission did not include any

a examination of substantive law, but plainly the object was to ensure that, in judicial review proceedings, declarations and injunctions would only be granted in public law matters (see para 45 of the report). It is equally clear that where mandamus lies against an officer of the Crown, then a declaration or injunction does also. A final mandatory injunction is not necessary; mandamus achieves the same result.

It is perhaps pertinent here to note that there is nothing in the 1981 Act which permits judicial review proceedings to be brought against the Crown itself. In those comparatively
b rare cases therefore, such as *R v Secretary of State for War* [1891] 2 QB 326 and *R v Treasury Lords Comrs* (1872) LR 7 QB 387, where a Crown servant is merely the instrument selected by the Crown for the discharge of its own duties, proceedings can only be brought under the 1947 Act. This would seem to constitute an exception to what the House of Lords has laid down in *O'Reilly v Mackman* [1982] 3 All ER 1124, [1983] 2 AC 237.

c The Law Commission considered that it was a procedural defect that in proceedings under the 1947 Act no interlocutory relief was available. Accordingly they recommended that, in proceedings against the Crown, the court should have power to declare the terms of an interim injunction which would have been granted in proceedings between subjects alone. They recommended that this should be achieved by amendment to the 1947 Act (see para 51 of, and cl 3(2) of the draft bill appended to, the report).

d However, the specific recommendation for interim relief against the Crown and its officers in proceedings under the 1947 Act was not implemented but a general provision as to interim relief was included in the Rules of the Supreme Court. Order 53, r 3(10) reads:

e 'Where leave to apply for judicial review is granted, then— (a) if the relief sought is an order of prohibition or certiorari and the Court so directs, the grant shall operate as a stay of the proceedings to which the application relates until the determination of the application or until the Court otherwise orders; (b) if any other relief is sought, the Court may at any time grant in the proceedings such interim relief as could be granted in an action begun by writ.'

f Counsel for the applicant suggests that there are two possible meanings to r 3(10)(b): (i) mere enabling power allowing the court to grant to an applicant for judicial review all the interlocutory remedies available in an action begun by writ; or (ii) the applicant has to show that in fact he has a possible private law cause of action which he could have commenced by writ. It seems to me that the second of those meanings is quite impossible. If an applicant's cause of action is a private law one he would be in the wrong jurisdiction if seeking judicial review.

g Counsel for the Secretary of State and the governor submits a third meaning. He says, if I have understood him correctly, that the court has to do this exercise: first, decide what relief is sought and against whom; second, see whether against that person interim relief would have been available if the relief had been sought by writ. If interim relief would not have been available, then it is not available in Ord 53 proceedings.

h Applying that construction to the facts of this case the argument is that proceedings against an officer of the Crown can only be brought by writ under the 1947 Act; on the accepted construction of s 21(2) an injunction will not lie against a servant of the Crown. Therefore an interim injunction will not lie either. I find this argument unacceptable. It seems to me that, on its plain meaning, the rule merely makes available to the court the interlocutory remedies available in actions begun by writ. Judicial review proceedings can (subject to the qualification mentioned above) be brought against a minister; so long
j as the guidelines in s 31(2) of the Supreme Court Act 1981 are complied with an injunction will therefore lie against a minister, and that being so it seems to me that on its plain meaning r 3(10)(b) permits an interim injunction to be made. This partially achieves, though by a different route, the Law Commission recommendation that interim relief should be available against an officer of the Crown while retaining the immunity from interim relief of the Crown itself.

There is perhaps another argument which could be deployed by the Secretary of State, though it is not one advanced by counsel on his behalf. It could be argued that, as guideline (b) (of r 3(10)) requires the court to have regard, in deciding whether to grant an injunction, to the nature of the person against whom relief can be granted, it should not grant one against a Crown servant because such relief in actions begun by writ is not available. But that argument does not convince me and would be a construction contrary to what the Law Commission intended which, as I have pointed out, was to restrict the new power to the public law field.

I conclude therefore that the court has jurisdiction to grant an interim injunction against an officer of the Crown and that, accordingly, I would have jurisdiction to grant the interim relief sought in these proceedings against both respondents.

Even if I am right as to the jurisdiction point, I have no doubt that, in the exercise of my discretion, I ought not to grant interim relief in this case.

On this aspect of the case most of the submissions of counsel for the Secretary of State and the governor have naturally been aimed at the merits of the substantive case. In the same way as, at the outset of this judgment, I outlined the applicant's case, I now outline the case of counsel for the Secretary of State and the governor as I understand it.

So far as the governor is concerned, the decision of the Court of Appeal in *R v Deputy Governor of Camphill Prison, ex p King* [1984] 3 All ER 897, [1985] QB 735 decides that this court cannot exercise any control over a prison governor in the exercise of his managerial responsibilities, even if his actions constituted a breach of the provisions of the Bill of Rights. In any event the Bill of Rights cannot now be invoked against an officer of the Crown; nor can it be used to justify the court in making an impermissible investigation into the facts. (Incidentally, in my judgment the governor is an officer of the Crown with specific powers and duties imposed on him by Parliament.) So far as the Secretary of State is concerned, no proceedings can be brought against him. No proceedings can be brought against him unless it is shown that he has been petitioned to exercise his powers of control over the conduct of the prison and he has failed to do so, again citing *R v Deputy Governor of Camphill Prison, ex p King*. He is empowered to exercise control over the prison and its staff and must be shown to have failed in that duty. There is no evidence that he has been relevantly petitioned. In any event the court is entitled to come to the conclusion on the affidavit evidence that the applicant's case fails on the facts.

Not surprisingly there is no guidance as to the principles which ought to apply when a court is considering the granting of interim relief against officers of the Crown. Until today no one thought it could be done. I agree with counsel for the applicant that the principles governing interim injunctions in civil proceedings are not particularly helpful. Clearly the apparent strengths and weaknesses of the two opposing cases ought to be considered and, as at present advised and without deciding anything, the obstacles in the way of the applicant's substantive case seem to me to be formidable indeed. It seems to me also to be clear that it would be only in very exceptional circumstances that the court would grant interim mandatory relief in respect of the administrative functions of officers of the Crown. I agree with counsel for the applicant that there would have to be shown to be great urgency to prevent the danger of serious injury or damage occurring. The interim relief sought in these proceedings relates only to the lack of association, and I am quite unable to see how it would be a proper exercise of discretion to grant that relief. I should say that the fact that the relief can be and has been cast in a non-mandatory fashion in the alternative does not alter my view as to the circumstances which would be necessarry before the court would grant that interim relief. It follows that this application fails.

Application refused.

Solicitors: *Shone & Barker* (for the applicant); *Treasury Solicitor*.

Michael Wall Esq   Barrister.

Kerr and others v Morris

COURT OF APPEAL, CIVIL DIVISION
DILLON, LLOYD AND NICHOLLS LJJ
12, 13, 14, 15 MAY 1986

a

b *Restraint of trade by agreement – Partnership – Medical partnership – National health service practice – Mutual covenants by partners under which retiring or expelled partner would not practice within a prescribed area for two years – Whether covenant contrary to public policy – Whether covenant unlawful as infringing prohibition against sale of goodwill of national health service practice – National Health Service Act 1977, s 54(1), Sch 10, para 2(4)(5).*

c The three plaintiffs and the defendant were general medical practitioners carrying on practice in partnership within the national health service. Clause 32 of the partnership agreement provided that a partner could be compelled to retire from the partnership if, inter alia, he was given 12 months' notice in writing by all the other partners specifying the reason for which the notice was given. Clause 34 of the partnership agreement provided that for a period of two years following his expulsion from the partnership a former partner was not entitled to practise as a general medical practitioner within a radius of two miles of the place where the partnership practice was operating at the time he ceased to be a partner. Difficulties arose between the defendant and the plaintiffs and on 14 February 1985 the plaintiffs served notice on the defendant requiring him to retire from the practice on 15 February 1986 on the ground that they considered he had breached the trust necessary between partners. The defendant took the view that cl 34 was invalid and purchased a property a few doors away from the partnership surgery with the intention of setting up practice there as soon as the notice expired without waiting for the two-year period specified in cl 34 to elapse. The plaintiffs issued a writ seeking, inter alia, an injunction to restrain the defendant from acting in breach of cl 34. They also applied for an interlocutory injunction pending trial of the action. The defendant contended (i) that cl 34 was void because it would be contrary to public policy to restrain a national health service general practitioner engaged in treating national health service patients from carrying on practice where he wanted to, (ii) that cl 34 breached the contract of service between a general medical practitioner and the national health service, (iii) that since the purpose of a covenant in restraint of trade was to protect the goodwill of a business and since s 54(1)[a] of the National Health Service Act 1977 made it unlawful to sell the goodwill of a national health service medical practice, a restraint in the terms of cl 34 was either unnecessary or contrary to s 54, and (iv) that acceptance of the terms of cl 34 was valuable consideration provided by the defendant for being taken into the partnership and as such there was deemed to be an unlawful sale of goodwill under para 2(4)(a)[b] of Sch 10 to the 1977 Act, which provided that there was a deemed sale of goodwill if an outgoing partner agreed for valuable consideration to refrain from doing any act for the purpose of facilitating the succession of another medical practitioner to the practice. The judge dismissed the plaintiffs' application for an interlocutory injunction. The plaintiffs appealed.

Held – (1) A restrictive covenant in a partnership agreement between doctors practising under the national health service precluding a doctor who retired from the partnership from practising within a particular area of restraint or treating patients of the partnership was not inherently inconsistent with the national health service scheme, because a doctor's patients had no right to require him to stay in a particular area or practice to treat them and once he had resigned from a practice it was not contrary to public policy

a Section 54, so far as material, is set out at p 226 j to p 227 a, post
b Paragraph 2, so far as material, is set out at p 227 e to g, post

or the public interest for him to be subject to any reasonable restraint of trade which he had agreed to, and there was no express or implied statutory prohibition in the 1977 Act preventing contractual restraints between medical partners (see p 225 *a c d*, p 226 *c d g h*, p 230 *b* and p 232 *d e*, post); *Hensman v Traill* (1980) Times, 22 October overruled in part. *a*

(2) The goodwill of a medical practice, even though s 54(1) of the 1977 Act made it unsaleable, was nevertheless a valuable asset of the practice which the partners in the practice were entitled to protect by a reasonable restraint of trade. Furthermore, a medical practitioner was not prevented by para 2(4)(*a*) of Sch 10 to the 1977 Act from *b* entering into a valid restraint of trade covenant in a partnership agreement because entering into such a covenant would be an act done 'in pursuance of a partnership agreement' and therefore validated by para 2(5) of Sch 10 (see p 225 *j* to p 226 *a*, p 227 *h* to p 228 *a*, p 230 *d* to *f*, and p 231 *b* to p 232 *d*, post); dictum of Evershed MR in *Whitehill v Bradford* [1952] 1 All ER at 121 applied; *Hensman v Traill* (1980) Times, 22 October overruled in part. *c*

(3) The balance of convenience lay in favour of granting an interlocutory injunction against the defendant pending trial of the action. The appeal would therefore be allowed (see p 228 *h* to p 229 *d f*, p 230 *g* and p 232 *e*, post).

Notes

For restrictive covenants relating to medical practice under the national health service, *d* see 33 Halsbury's Laws (4th edn) para 22.

For the National Health Service Act 1977, s 54, Sch 10, para 2, see 47 Halsbury's Statutes (3rd edn) 839, 917.

Cases referred to in judgments

Blisset v Daniel (1853) 10 Hare 493, 68 ER 1022.

Deacons (a firm) v Bridge [1984] 2 All ER 19, [1984] AC 705, [1984] 2 WLR 837, PC. *e*

Ebrahimi v Westbourne Galleries Ltd [1972] 2 All ER 492, [1973] AC 360, [1972] 2 WLR 1289, HL.

Edwards v Society of Graphical and Allied Trades [1970] 3 All ER 689, [1971] Ch 354, [1970] 3 WLR 713, CA.

Fender v Mildmay [1937] 3 All ER 402, [1938] AC 1, HL. *f*

Hensman v Traill (1980) Times, 22 October, 124 SJ 776.

Macfarlane v Kent [1965] 2 All ER 376, [1965] 1 WLR 1019.

Whitehill v Bradford [1952] 1 All ER 115, [1952] Ch 236, CA.

Cases also cited

Breen v Amalgamated Engineering Union [1971] 1 All ER 1148, [1971] 2 QB 175, CA.

Green v Howell [1910] 1 Ch 495, CA. *g*

Liverpool City Council v Irwin [1976] 2 All ER 39, [1977] AC 239, HL.

Lyne-Pirkis v Jones [1969] 3 All ER 738, [1969] 1 WLR 1293, CA.

Peyton v Mindham [1971] 3 All ER 1215, [1972] 1 WLR 8.

Russell v Russell (1880) 14 Ch D 471.

Interlocutory appeal *h*

By a writ issued on 20 December 1985 the plaintiffs, Aubrey Robert Fawcett Kerr, William Jeffrey Mirza and Graham David Parker, who were partners in a medical practice at 7 Ladysmith Avenue, Brightlingsea, Essex, sought as against the defendant, Anthony Harcourt Morris, who was also a partner in the practice and to whom they had given notice pursuant to the partnership deed requiring him to retire from the partnership on *j* 15 February 1986, inter alia, an injunction restraining the defendant, whether by himself, his servants or agents or otherwise howsoever, for a period of two years from 15 February 1986 either on his own account or directly or indirectly for a third party, from carrying on the profession of general medical practitioner in breach of cl 34 of the partnership deed within a radius of two miles from the practice or soliciting directly or

indirectly, actively or passively, any person who was at 15 February 1986 a patient of the
a partnership to the intent or effect that such person transfer to the defendant's patient list.
By notice of motion dated 7 January 1986 the plaintiffs applied for an interlocutory
injunction as against the defendant in the terms of the writ restraining the defendant for
the period of two years from 15 February 1986 or until judgment in the action from
carrying on the profession of general medical practitioner within a radius of two miles of
7 Ladysmith Avenue, Brightlingsea, Essex. On 13 February 1986 Falconer J dismissed
b the motion. The plaintiffs appealed. On 14 February Dillon LJ refused an application by
the plaintiffs for an injunction to be granted against the defendant pending the
determination of the appeal. The facts are set out in the judgment of Dillon LJ.

F M Ferris QC and *Frank Hinks* for the plaintiffs.
Ian Croxford for the defendant.
c

DILLON LJ. This is an appeal by the plaintiffs in the action against a judgment of
Falconer J given on 13 February 1986, whereby, though directing a speedy trial, he
dismissed a motion by the plaintiffs for an interlocutory injunction.
The dispute is a dispute between doctors who are the only general medical practitioners
d with surgeries in the small Essex town of Brightlingsea, where they were formerly in
partnership together. Brightlingsea has a static population, we are told, of some 7,500
potential patients. The practice is, on the information we have been given, fairly old
established in that before 1977 a Dr Middleton, a Dr Stephens and the first plaintiff, Dr
Kerr, were in partnership as the only medical practice in Brightlingsea, practising from a
surgery at 7 Ladysmith Avenue. In 1977 Dr Middleton left and a Dr Maxwell joined Dr
e Stephens and Dr Kerr. At the end of March 1982 Dr Stephens left, leaving Dr Maxwell
and Dr Kerr, and in July Dr Mirza, the second plaintiff, who had previously acted as a
locum for some time, joined Dr Kerr and Dr Maxwell in partnership. Dr Maxwell retired
at the end of July 1982. In the course of 1982 permission had been given under statutory
provisions to which I shall have to come for a fourth partner. Consequently, on 14
September 1982 Dr Parker, the third plaintiff, joined the practice and on 2 October 1982
f Dr Morris, the defendant, joined the practice.
There then followed negotiations over terms of a partnership agreement. It had
originally been the arrangement that Dr Parker and the defendant were each coming on,
as it were, six months' approval each way to see how everyone fitted in. Ultimately,
though not until 1 March 1984, a partnership agreement was entered into between the
four of them. This provided that the four doctors, who are called 'the partners', wished
g to record the terms of their partnership as subsisting (mutatis mutandis) from 1 October
1982. There was provision that the partnership should continue unless determined under
the provisions of the agreement and that the death, retirement or expulsion of a partner
should not determine the partnership as between the continuing partners unless the
continuing partners should unanimously so agree. There were provisions as to sharing
profits which were graduated to achieve equality. Clause 26 provides:
h
> 'Each of the Partners shall be just and faithful to the other Partners and shall
> devote all his working hours diligently and to the highest medical standards in the
> Partnership business and take all reasonable and proper steps to promote the success
> thereof.'

Clause 29 provides:
j
> 'A Partner may retire from the Partnership by giving notice in writing (a
> "Retirement Notice") to all the other Partners to expire at the end of not less than
> six months or such lesser period as may be agreed between him and the other
> Partners.'

Clause 30 provides for mandatory retirement unless agreed otherwise by all the partners at the end of the financial year after any partner had attained the age of 65. Clause 32, which is very important, provides:

a

'(1) A Partner shall for the purposes of all the provisions of this Agreement relating to the retirement of a Partner from the Partnership be deemed to have retired from the Partnership forthwith unless unanimous agreement to the contrary upon:—(i) such Partner:—(a) becoming bankrupt or insolvent or compounding or making any arrangement with his creditors or (b) being struck off the professional register of the General Medical Council and be barred from practising as General *b* Medical Practitioner or (c) being incapacitated by mental or physical illness accident or otherwise from attending to the business of the Partnership for a period of twelve consecutive months or for a total of more than four hundred and fifty (450) days in any one period of twenty-four months (ii) the expiration of a Notice in writing given at any time of the other Partners' intention to cause him to retire from the Partnership such Notice being signed by all the Partners other than the one to whom *c* it is given and expiring twelve months from its being given save in the following cases when it shall expire not less than one month from its being given namely if such Notice shall be given by reason of the Partner having: (a) grossly neglected the Partnership's business or (b) been grossly or persistently negligent in the performance of his duties in the Partnership's business (c) committed or permitted any wilful and substantial breach of the provisions hereof or (d) been convicted on indictment *d* of a criminal (other than a Road Traffic) offence or (e) done or suffered any act which would be a ground for the dissolution of the Partnership by the Court

(2) Any notice under this Clause 32 shall specify the reason for which it is given.'

Clause 34, which is the other important clause, then provides for restraints. It is the first part of this clause which the plaintiffs are seeking to enforce by this appeal. The whole *e* clause reads as follows:

'No Former Partner shall for a period of two years following the date of his retirement or expulsion from the Partnership either on his own account or directly or indirectly for a third party:—(i) carry on the profession of General Medical Practitioner within a radius of two miles from any premises from which the Partnership shall be operating as General Medical Practitioners at the date upon *f* which he shall cease to be a member of the Partnership or (ii) solicit directly or indirectly actively or passively any person who was at the date of such retirement or expulsion a patient of the Partnership to the intent or effect that such person shall transfer to the patient list of that Former Partner.'

The motion was brought, in circumstances to which I shall have to come, to enforce *g* against the defendant both limbs of cl 34 but, so far as the soliciting limb in sub-cl (ii) is concerned, Falconer J found that there was no evidence at all of soliciting on the part of the defendant and that finding is not challenged on this appeal. The plaintiffs merely seek on this appeal to enforce the first limb, the area covenant over a period of two years. I shall come to the reasons why the judge declined to enforce that and why it is said for the defendant that it should not be enforced; but it is sufficient to say for the moment, *h* firstly, that the covenant is not a mere 'brass plate' covenant, which would simply ban the doctor having his surgery within the area. It would also prima facie ban his visiting from outside the area patients at their homes within the area. Next, no objection is taken to the size of the area of two miles from, in effect, 7 Ladysmith Avenue, or to the duration of the restraint, two years. It is accepted that those are reasonable if it is permissible to impose any such restraint at all on the defendant in the circumstances of this case and in *j* view of the nature of the practice as a national health service medical practice.

The partnership agreement, as I have said, was entered into in March 1984, but, during the course of that year or, at any rate, in the latter part of that year, difficulties arose between the defendant and the three other partners. The upshot was a meeting in

January 1985 when the defendant was called in by the other three partners. We have in
evidence Dr Kerr's notes of what he intended to say and to propose on that occasion, and
it seems to be common ground that he kept fairly accurately to his script. The notes
record him as intending to say this:

> 'Since [a certain event] it has shocked us into realising just what has been going
> on since you joined us and the purpose of this meeting is to inform you of our
> conclusions after many many hours of discussion and soul searching. Over the two
> years you have been with us you have consistently disappointed us and failed to
> come up to scratch as an industrious and responsible partner of considerable previous
> experience and mature years. You have not shown any motivation towards
> completing your obstetrics or note summaries and other matters spontaneously and
> without pressure despite your small list size. You have abused your position of trust
> and responsibility in the gross misuse of the telephone which you admitted to only
> under pressure . . .'

Then the proposal was that the other partners could not see how they could continue
with the defendant in the partnership, but would want to give him an opportunity for
change. They put forward one way only on which they would find it acceptable for the
defendant to stay and that is if the defendant would give them his resignation effective
in six months from the date of the meeting and would go at the end of that notice unless
the other partners were unanimously agreed that they were entirely happy with his
performance, in which case his position would be restored. The notes end:

> 'If you do not agree to these terms we will seek your immediate expulsion.'

The reference to 'the gross misuse of the telephone' was that the defendant had been
using the practice telephone at the surgery for private calls to a very considerable extent.
These were quite long distance private calls and had proved expensive. The details do not
matter. The reference to not showing 'any motivation towards completing your obstetrics
or note summaries and other matters spontaneously' was that it was thought that the
defendant had taken too long to obtain the practical qualification locally for practising
obstetrics without supervision in the area and was not sufficiently up-to-date in his
keeping of notes.

The whole conception goes back to ideas Dr Kerr had had before Dr Parker and the
defendant joined the practice. The practice had only then been a three-man practice. The
idea of turning it into a four-man practice was to increase the number of sessions in the
surgery available to patients, to introduce an appointment system for various of those
sessions, to embark on research projects, to employ a part-time nurse, to up-date the
whole system of note-taking and collating information and extend the facilities of the
practice in relation to preventive medicine and so forth. The general idea was that the
practice should be streamlined and improved to become a training practice where a
trainee general practitioner could be accepted for training under one of the doctors in the
practice and that the practice would in due course move to purpose-built premises. That
was the general nature of what was envisaged by Dr Kerr at the outset.

The defendant, having taken advice, refused to sign the notice of retirement which he
had been asked to sign and the upshot of that was that on 14 February 1985 he was served
with a notice of expulsion by his other three partners under cover of a letter from their
solicitors. The relevant paragraph of the notice of expulsion says this:

> 'In accordance with Clause 32(1)(ii) of the Partnership entered into between us on
> the First day of March 1984 for the reason that we consider that the Trust necessary
> between Partners has been breached by you we hereby give you notice that we
> require you to retire from the said Partnership on the Fifteenth day of February
> 1986.'

Certain further rights of expulsion were reserved but they do not need to be mentioned.

After that, the defendant consulted his solicitors again. In June 1985 he approached the other partners to ask them to release him from cl 34 but they refused to do so. In November 1985 he purchased a property a few doors away from the partnership surgery. This was 1 Ladysmith Avenue, Brightlingsea, for which planning permission had recently been obtained by the vendor for its use as a doctor's surgery. He has since made it absolutely plain that he wants to practise from there without waiting for two years to do so and he believes that he is in law entitled to do so because of the arguments that he puts forward, to which I shall come.

The result of that was that the writ in this action was issued by the plaintiffs on 20 December 1985 and that was followed by a notice of motion issued on 7 January 1986 and returnable for first hearing on 14 January 1986, seeking injunctions to enforce cl 34 of the partnership agreement. It was that motion which came before Falconer J for effective hearing and his order on the effective hearing of the motion of 13 February 1986 was the order which I have mentioned which directed a speedy trial but refused interlocutory relief.

I can deal quite shortly with one minor point which has been canvassed in argument for the defendant. It is said that the plaintiffs should be held to be barred from interlocutory relief because of their delay in not starting the action until December, when they had been told by the defendant in June that he wanted to be released from the covenant and was wanting to set up practice in Brightlingsea. For my part, I see nothing in that point since the defendant has said very fairly in his own affidavit that he accepts that his partners made it plain on 11 June and in the correspondence that they would seek to uphold cl 34. He went ahead with his eyes open. The matter was brought on for hearing before the year had expired and delay is not a bar to the plaintiffs' claim.

I would equally summarily reject a point which has been taken for the plaintiffs. It is said that, by continuing to work for the partnership and as one of the partners in handling the patients for the partnership during the year of the notice, the defendant affirmed the partnership agreement and disbarred himself from saying that the partners' notice was bad or that their expulsion of him from the partnership was wrongful. To put forward that argument seems to me to be devoid of all reality. It was the obviously sensible course and, indeed, the only reasonable course in the light of the patients' needs and interests that the defendant should continue working during the period of the notice as he did, and I see no basis for saying that he has thereby debarred himself from putting forward any of the arguments on which he relies in this action.

The basis of Falconer J's refusal of interlocutory relief was that he followed a decision of Bristow J in *Hensman v Traill* (1980) Times, 22 October. Bristow J held that it was contrary to public policy for there to be any restraint on a national health service general medical practitioner carrying on practice in treating national health service patients where he wanted to. Falconer J took the view, I apprehend rightly, that, as that decision had been drawn to his attention and was exactly on all fours, it was desirable that he should follow it and leave it to a higher court to decide whether *Hensman v Traill* was on this point right or wrong. He therefore took the view that, if *Hensman v Traill* was rightly decided, the plaintiffs' action was bound to fail and therefore interlocutory relief must be refused without even going into any questions of balance of convenience.

The point of law that thus arises does not depend on the particular facts of this case which would fall to be investigated at the trial of this action, and it is a point of law of some importance which would apply to all national health service general practitioner partnerships. Even though *Hensman v Traill* has not been reported in any of the recognised full law reports, it is referred to several times in *Lindley on the Law of Partnership* (15th edn, 1984). This court must decide whether this ground of decision in *Hensman v Traill* was in the judgment of this court right or wrong. If *Hensman v Traill* was right, this action is bound to fail. If *Hensman v Traill* was wrong, then it would not be right that the action should go to trial at first instance before this court had pronounced on *Hensman v Trail* because the judge at the trial would be bound, as Falconer J did, to follow *Hensman* a   v *Traill*, and the case would then have to come back to this court after trial with the possibility of a further trial if the judge had merely applied *Hensman v Traill* without making findings on other matters which are relevant to other arguments.

The basis of the decision on this point in *Hensman v Traill* was put by Bristow J as follows:

b   'As a matter of principle it is difficult to see how a contractual agreement between doctors, which, if enforceable, would have the effect of preventing a doctor from providing medical care to the patients allocated to him for that purpose by the family practitioner committee exercising its statutory obligation, could possibly be consistent with the public policy mirrored by the provisions of the National Health Service Act 1977. But since the enactment of the National Health Service Act 1946 there have been decisions on the validity or otherwise of restrictive provisions in partnership agreements between doctors with national health service practices

c   which have proceeded on the premise that such restrictions are not by their very nature unenforceable as being in restraint not of trade, but of the provision of medical services under the National Health Service Act paid for not as a matter of contract between doctor and patient, but by the state . . .'

d   He refers to certain decisions and he refers to the fact that, in the light of those decisions, counsel in *Hensman v Traill* did not think it right to argue the point at first instance but reserved it for argument thereafter. Bristow J continued, however:

'But since there is no authority binding on me, because in the cases to which I have referred the point went by default, it is in my judgment open to me to, and right that I should, come to a conclusion on it. In my judgment, when you transpose the well-known principles of common law affecting the enforcement of contracts in

e   restraint of trade to the context of doctors conducting group practices in the national health service it is not possible to regard a partnership restriction which might lead to a doctor being prevented by law from giving patients the care which he is obliged under the national health service to give them as other than contrary to the basic concept of the national health service and so contrary to public policy, and unenforceable.'

f

The scheme of the national heath service in respect of general medical practitioners is somewhat elaborate. There are restrictions on doctors seeking to set up where they wish to treat national health service patients in any locality. The relevant Act is now the National Health Service Act 1977 as amended. Section 29 of that Act provides:

g   '(1) It is the duty of every Family Practitioner Committee, in accordance with regulations, to arrange as respects their locality with medical practitioners to provide personal medical services for all persons in the locality who wish to take advantage of the arrangements.

(1A) The services so provided are referred to in this Act as "general medical services" . . .'

h   Under s 30 it is provided:

'(1) All applications made by medical practitioners in the prescribed manner to a Family Practitioner Committee for inclusion in a list kept by that Committee of the names of medical practitioners undertaking to provide general medical services for persons in the Committee's locality shall be referred by the Committee to the Medical Practices Committee and (except as mentioned in subsection (2) below) any

j   medical practitioner whose application is granted by that Committee shall be entitled to the inclusion of his name in the list [that is to say the list of those who provide general medical services within the locality or part of the locality] . . .'

The Medical Practices Committee is a nationwide committee. There is a family practitioner committee for each area. In effect, what we are concerned with here is the family practitioner committee for the county of Essex.

Section 33 of the Act as amended then provides:

'(1) The Medical Practices Committee may refuse any applications under section 30 above on the grounds that the number of medical practitioners undertaking to provide general medical services in the locality of the Family Practitioner Committee concerned or in the relevant part of that locality is already adequate . . .'

Then there is provision where, if, in the opinion of the Medical Practices Committee, additional practitioners are required for any locality or part of a locality but the number of applications exceeds the number required, the committee is to select the persons whose applications are to be granted and to refuse the other applications, but it is only to do so after consultation with the family practitioner committee concerned.

I do not need to go into further detail on that aspect. It is under those provisions or their immediate predecessors that the practice obtained permission for a fourth partner in 1982 when Dr Parker and the defendant came in, and it is common ground that, as the population of Brightlingsea is static, there would be difficulty for the practice to obtain a fourth partner in the place of the defendant if the defendant was able to practice in Brightlingsea. Conversely, there would be difficulty for the defendant coming back to practice in Brightlingsea at the end of the two-year period if in the mean time the practice had been able to replace him by another fourth partner.

The scheme of the national health service in respect of general medical services is that each doctor has his own list of patients. The sale of goodwill of a medical practice is prohibited by the 1977 Act and was prohibited by the original National Health Service Act 1946. Within the limitations of the scheme the patient has a right to the doctor of his own choice, but that is a limited right of choice because the plaintiffs and the defendant are the only doctors in Brightlingsea. Therefore, the patient cannot find another doctor with a surgery in Brightlingsea. In the present case testimonials have been put forward signed by many hundred patients on the defendant's list, expressing their desire and hope that the defendant should continue in practice in Brightlingsea and not be forced out of the area as the result of the covenant which he has entered into with the plaintiffs. I should add that under the scheme the doctor has an obligation to provide medical treatment to the patients on his list.

As against those considerations, however, the scheme recognises the existence of partnerships of doctors to treat national health service patients and it is provided that, as between partners, each may treat the other's patients. That is common form and common sense. It happens everywhere. As between the partners the patients are partnership patients and the capitation fees paid to a doctor in respect of the patients on his list are a partnership asset. That is an inevitable consequence of having a partnership in which each doctor may treat the other's patients, and in many ways they are all working together from the same surgery.

It is provided under the scheme that a doctor can refuse to accept a patient onto his list, subject to rights of appeal, and can require the removal of a patient from his list. In addition, it is provided by the National Health Service (General Medical and Pharmaceutical Services) Regulations 1974, SI 1974/160, that a doctor may withdraw his name from the medical list. Regulation 6 provides that, subject to a paragraph that is not material, a doctor may at any time give notice to the committee that he wishes to withdraw his name from the medical list and the committee shall amend the medical list accordingly three months from the date of such notice or such other period as it may agree with the doctor. Any such notice may not be withdrawn except with the consent of the committee. It follows that a doctor is free to go at any time from the area. The patients have no right to require him to stay to continue to treat them and tend their health. Therefore, as it seems to me, there can be no objection on the grounds of public policy or public interest to a doctor resigning from the partnership under cl 29 and then being under the reasonable restrictions as between the partners themselves under cl 34.

a
In my judgment it does not make any difference that the partner has, as the defendant has, bound himself to go in certain events in cl 32 and bound himself under the covenant in cl 34 if those events happened. Obviously there are differences between the position of a solicitor in private practice, even if that solicitor does legal aid work, and the position of a doctor doing national health service work in a partnership that does virtually only, or only, national health service work. In principle, however, it seems to me that the reasoning of Lord Fraser in *Deacons (a firm) v Bridge* [1984] 2 All ER 19, [1984] AC 705 is

b
applicable. The Judicial Committee there adverted to an argument that public policy required that a citizen should have the right to be advised by the lawyer of his choice and that the relationship between a solicitor and his client was a fiduciary relationship and that it would be contrary to public policy that a solicitor should be precluded from acting for a client when that client wanted the solicitor to act for him. The Judical Committee declined to accept that proposition and declined therefore to hold that a restrictive

c
covenant which precluded a solicitor from practising within a particular area of restraint was contary to public policy.

It seems to me that the same reasoning really can apply to a national health service doctor. The solicitor can go from the area at any time and can bind himself by contract that in certain events he will go. The doctor can go from the area at any time and I do not see why public policy should prevent him binding himself by contract that in certain

d
events he will go.

The alternative argument was put to the effect that a covenant in restraint of trade in a partnership agreement is only valid in so far as it protects a legitimate interest of the other partners, and historically the legitimate interest protected by a covenant in restraint of trade binding an outgoing partner is the interest of the continuing partners in the goodwill of the business. It is submitted by counsel for the defendant that, as the sale of

e
goodwill of a medical practice is now illegal, the whole foundation for holding the restraint enforceable falls away.

I should refer to *Whitehill v Bradford* [1952] 1 All ER 115, [1952] Ch 236 decided in this court. That was a case of a partnership which had existed before the national health service came into existence and there were special statutory provisions which applied to that, to which I will have to come. Evershed MR turned to consider the result of the

f
impact on that medical practice of the National Health Service Act 1946 and he said ([1952] Ch 236 at 253–254, cf [1952] 1 All ER 115 at 121):

'One plain intention of the Act provided by section 35 was that doctors who participated in the scheme of the Act by having lists of patients in accordance with the Act could no longer sell their goodwill. That formerly valuable asset of a doctor's practice became no longer saleable by the doctor in the cases mentioned—and in

g
the case with which we are concerned each of the four partners was a listed doctor. But that prohibition does not, in my judgment, have the effect of destroying the goodwill; still less does it have the effect of vesting it in the State. The goodwill remains one of the assets of the firm, but it is subject to the limitation that it cannot be sold to other people. So long as the firm carries on, the goodwill must necessarily remain one of its most valuable assets, for by goodwill in this case is meant, I take it,

h
the tendency of patients whom the doctors have treated to continue to resort to that firm for further treatment. The partners' livelihood, therefore, as doctors depends very substantially on the goodwill they have created and on the extent to which they are able to preserve it.'

j
I emphasise the last two sentences. Whether the partnership was in existence when the national health service came into existence or was created later, as in the present case, goodwill, in the sense of the tendency of patients whom the doctors have treated to continue to refer to the firm for further treatment, must remain one of the most valuable assets, albeit not a saleable asset, of the partnership on which the partners' livelihood as doctors substantially depends. Otherwise, if the patients were not satisfied, they would seek to take their names off the list and to go elsewhere, for instance, in the case of the

patients of this partnership, to the defendant, if he can set up practice in Brightlingsea, or to any other doctor who obtains permission to do that on the departure of the *a* defendant. I cannot, therefore, see that the fact that the partnership in *Whitehill v Bradford* was an old, pre-national health service, partnership substantially affects the reasoning in the case.

Evershed MR goes on to refer to special provisions of the National Health Service (Amendment) Act 1949 in respect of those old partnerships. The position was that, as the counterpart to the prohibition on the sale of goodwill, doctors in practice on the appointed *b* day were given statutory compensation for the loss of their power to sell goodwill. Parliament had to cover, and did cover by the 1949 Act, how this statutory compensation was to fit in where there were provisions in a partnership agreement providing for continuing partners to succeed to the share and interest of an outgoing partner. The effect of the provisions was that the provisions of the partnership agreement, including covenants in restraint of trade reasonably binding the outgoing partner, continued to *c* have effect, save that compensation was to come from the government and not from the continuing partners. It was necessary to have statutory provisions to show what was to happen in such cases, but the form the statutory provisions took indicates, in my judgment, that it is not inherently inconsistent with the scheme of the national health service that a doctor who quits his partnership may be subject to a reasonable restrictive covenant against practising in a particular area or against acting for former patients of *d* the partnership.

It may well be in the public interest that there should be national health service doctors in Brightlingsea to treat the patients resident there, but the public interest does not inevitably require that the defendant must be one of those doctors so long as he wishes to do so despite his contract.

Every doctor who is engaged under the national health service is engaged under terms *e* of service which are in evidence and it is said by way of further alternative submission by counsel for the defendant that the combination of cll 32 and 34 of the partnership agreement may involve a breach of the terms of service. He therefore submits that cl 34 is wholly invalid as some form of contract to procure a breach of contract, that is to say a breach of the terms of service whereby the defendant, or any of the other doctors in the partnership, is engaged as a doctor on the list to treat his patients under the national *f* health service scheme.

The instance that was particularly discussed in argument by counsel for the defendant was the instance of a partner who becomes bankrupt and is automatically expelled under cl 32. He did not dispute that the expulsion was valid. It would be difficult to conceive that the other partners should be compelled to remain in partnership with a bankrupt partner. But it was said that in such a case cl 34 would exclude the bankrupt doctor from *g* the two-mile area without any opportunity of a notice to withdraw from the national health service list and so in breach of his contract with the national health service. That is not, of course, what has happened in this case. It seems to me to be an entirely novel head of public policy for which there is no precedent to say that a contract is wholly bad if it is possible to conceive not wholly fanciful circumstances in which the operation of the contract might cause some form of breach of some other contract. I reject that *h* argument. I would hold that Bristow J was wrong in the ground he gave for that part of his decision in *Hensman v Traill* and I would overrule that part of his decision.

A further argument also based on *Hensman v Traill* which is put forward for the defendant is that it is said that the mutual agreements by the partners in the terms of cl 34 infringe the prohibition on the sale of the goodwill of a national health service medical practice. Section 54(1) of the 1967 Act provides, as did s 35(1) of the National *j* Health Service Act 1946:

'Where the name of any medical practitioner is or has been at any time entered on any list of medical practititoners undertaking to provide general medical services,

a   it shall be unlawful subsequently to sell the goodwill or any part of the goodwill of
     the medical practice of that medical practitioner . . .'

Mutual agreements by partners in terms such as those of cl 34 are not prima facie
indicative of a sale of goodwill, but s 54 has to be read with provisions in Sch 10 to the
1977 Act. Paragraph 2 is concerned with certain transactions which are deemed to be a
sale of goodwill. Paragraph 2(2) provides:

b   'Where in pursuance of any partnership agreement between medical practition-
     ers—(a) any valuable consideration, other than the performance of services in the
     partnership business, is given by a partner or proposed partner as consideration for
     his being taken into partnership . . . there shall be deemed for the purpose of section
     54(1) and paragraph 1 to have been a sale of the goodwill, or part of the goodwill, of
     the practice of any partner to whom, or to whose personal representative, the
c   consideration or any part thereof is given or, as the case may be, for whose benefit
     the services are performed, to the partner or each of the partners by or on whose
     behalf the consideration or any part thereof was given or, as the case may be, the
     partner who performed the services . . .'

It is said that every covenant which is not concerned with the performance of services in
the partners' business which is included in the partnership agreement is valuable
d consideration such that there is deemed to have been a sale of goodwill. I do not need to
consider the point mentioned in argument whether convenants in the partnership
agreement by each partner to pay his personal debts, and by each partner to maintain
membership of the British Medical Association or to be a member of the Medical Defence
Union, can be regarded as covered by the words 'the performance of services in the
partnership business'; we are only concerned here with the restraint in cl 34.
e   The answer to this point, as it seems to me, is to be found by looking at para 2(4) in
this schedule. This provides:

         'For the purposes of section 54(1) and paragraph 1—(a) if a medical practitioner
     or the personal representative of a medical practitioner agrees, for valuable
     consideration, to do or refrain from doing any act, or to allow any act to be done, for
f   the purpose of facilitating the succession of another medical practitioner to the
     practice, or any part of the practice, of the first practitioner, the transaction shall be
     deemed to be a sale of the goodwill, or part of the goodwill, of that practice by the
     first practitioner or his personal representative to the second practitioner . . .'

Then there is a further provision within the same area. Sub-paragraph (5) then provides:

g   'Sub-paragraph (4) above shall not apply to anything done in relation to the
     acquisition of premises for the purposes of a medical practice, or in pursuance of a
     partnership agreement, or to the performance of services as an assistant to a medical
     practitioner.'

Sub-paragraph (4) seems to be plainly directed, and much more plainly than sub-para (2),
to the case of a restraint of trade to facilitate continuing partners taking over the share of
h the outgoing partner under a partnership agreement. As a matter of construction, sub-
paras (4) and (2) have to be read together, and it seems to me that what is covered by sub-
para (4) and expressly validated by sub-para (5), if it is in pursuance of a partnership
agreement, cannot be illegal under sub-para (2). The two have to be read together.
     It is possible that a similar conclusion was reached by Stamp J in *Macfarlane v Kent*
     [1965] 2 All ER 376, [1965] 1 WLR 1019, but it is a bit difficult to discern from the
j slightly abbreviated reports what the judge was actually ruling in that case. Therefore, in
my judgment, the point that there has been a sale of goodwill also fails. That is a point
which also depended on *Hensman v Traill*, and Bristow J there held under the equivalent
of what is now para 2(2) of Sch 10 that those provisions rendered the restriction sought

to be imposed on the defendant in that case by the partnership agreement unenforceable. I do not agree and I would overrule that part also of Bristow J's decision in *Hensman v Traill*.

I come to the final point which has been taken by the defendant in this case, which, unlike the points to which I have been referring, depends on the particular facts of this case which will be investigated at the trial of the action. It is submitted that a 12-month notice of expulsion under cl 32 of the partnership agreement can only be given for reasonable cause and after affording the partner concerned, whom it is proposed to expel, a hearing. It is said that, if that is not complied with, then the expulsion is wrongful, it is a repudiation of the partnership agreement and, therefore, the plaintiffs, having wrongfully expelled the defendant, are not entitled to enforce cl 34 against him. It is accepted for the plaintiffs that, if they have indeed wrongfully expelled the defendant, then they would not be entitled to enforce cl 34 against him. That is trite law.

So far as general principles of law are concerned, counsel for the defendant seeks to import into partnership law propositions which have been laid down in certain trade union cases such as *Edwards v Society of Graphical and Allied Trades* [1970] 3 All ER 689 at 695–696, [1971] Ch 354 at 376–377, where it was held by Lord Denning MR that a member of a trade union cannot be expelled without reasonable cause and cannot be expelled unheard. There is, of course, also the law in relation to partnership cases laid down by Page Wood V-C in *Blisset v Daniel* (1853) 10 Hare 493, 68 ER 1022, where he held that a power of expulsion in a partnership agreement must be exercised in good faith and not against the truth and honour of the contract. That decision was approved by Lord Wilberforce in the company case of *Ebrahimi v Westbourne Galleries Ltd* [1972] 2 All ER 492 at 501, [1973] AC 360 at 380–381.

In the present case it must be emphasised that the defendant does not challenge the good faith of the plaintiffs. Clause 32(2) provides that any notice of expulsion under cl 32 has to specify the reason for which it is given. Now, the issues which arise under this heading are all issues which will fall to be resolved at the trial and I do not seek to express any concluded view on any of those issues. I merely mention them to consider what the ambit of the trial is likely to be. Prima facie it may be said, therefore, with some force that, if the other partners are giving the defendant a 12 months' notice of expulsion, they must specify a reason for giving it and, if they are to specify a reason for giving it, they must have a reason for giving it which must prima facie be a reasonable reason. In fact, they did specify a reason for giving it. They said that it was given for the reason that they considered that the trust necessary between partners had been breached by the defendant. Since their good faith is not in dispute, we can take it that they honestly believed that that was so. So it may well be that, apart from the question whether they were bound to afford him a hearing, and a hearing that went further than the January meeting which I have mentioned, before expelling him, the question at the trial will come down to whether they were justified in their honest belief that the trust necessary between partners had been breached by the defendant.

All those are matters for the trial. They depend on the facts as ultimately found, and that may be much influenced by the course of cross-examination. At the end of the day, therefore, it seems to me that in this case, as in most cases where interlocutory injunctive relief is sought, the question comes down to one of the balance of convenience pending judgment in the action for which a speedy trial has already been directed. On each side there is a risk of pecuniary loss which may be difficult to quantify. If no injunction is granted now, the defendant will be able to retain the patients on his list who want to take advantage of this skill. The trial is unlikely to take place before October or November. It is to be hoped it will not be further delayed, but that is a possibility. If there is a trial in, say, November, at which the plaintiffs succeed, the two-year period of the covenant, accepted as reasonable if the covenant is valid, will have been substantially eroded. The plaintiffs may lose patients and never recover them and suffer some financial loss in that way. Apart from that, if the trial takes place in November and the period of the restraint

has been thus eroded, there may be questions whether the plaintiffs would be allowed by
a the family practitioner committee and the Medical Practices Committee to take in a
further partner after the trial, or whether the position would be kept open until the
defendant is free to return at the end of the two years. That may affect the objects of
upgrading the practice which I have mentioned that Dr Kerr had in mind when
considering the expansion from a three-partner to a four-partner practice which might
become a training practice and might flourish sufficiently to move to a purpose-built
b surgery. Conversely, if an injunction is granted now against the defendant but he wins
at the trial and establishes that his expulsion was wrongful, he will undoubtedly have
suffered a loss of income until the trial, and one gets into imponderable questions of
whether he would be able then to get back into practice in Brightlingsea and take over
again the patients who at the present time want to go to him or whether those patients
now loyal to him will have got used in the mean time to going to the plaintiffs for their
c ailments and will prefer then to continue with the plaintiffs, and so forth.
     I take into account, for my part, the evidence we have of the wishes of the patients.
Even so, however, though I find the balancing act finely balanced, I take the view that
the balance of convenience lies in favour of granting the injunction against the defendant,
provided that the plaintiffs give the undertaking that has been offered that, until
judgment in the action or further order, they will not apply for permission to bring a
d fourth partner into the partnership in the place of the defendant.
     A further undertaking was offered by the plaintiffs to the effect that, if the injunction
is granted and the defendant sets up a surgery outside the two-mile area, they would not
object to his paying domiciliary visits, if the need arises, to patients who go to him at his
new surgery outside the area from within the area. For my part, I can see that form of
undertaking giving rise to a good deal of strife and conflict and I do not think that it is
e helpful, especially as there is no indication that the defendant has any surgery premises
available to him just outside the two-mile area. His wish on advice was to practice at
1 Ladysmith Avenue. In my judgment, until judgment in the action, he should not do
so.
     I would therefore allow this appeal and discharge the order of the judge save in so far
as it gives directions for a speedy trial. Instead, I would grant the injunction until
f judgment or further order to restrain the defendant in the terms of cl 34(i) of the
partnership agreement on the undertaking of the plaintiffs not to apply for a fourth
partner which I have mentioned.

LLOYD LJ. I agree with the order proposed by Dillon LJ. I add a few words on the two
points on which we are differing from the decision of Bristow J in *Hensman v Traill* (1980)
g Times, 22 October. I do so since that case is cited as authority in *Lindley on the Law of
Partnership* (15th edn, 1984) p 128 for the proposition that any restrictive covenant
entered into between partners, even though the sole object may be the preservation of
goodwill, must now be regarded as contrary to public policy and to the provisions of the
National Health Service Act 1977, and for that reason be void and unenforceable. There
h is a similar passage where the editors say (p 238):

     'Although in the case of medical partnerships where the partners provide a service
     under the National Health Service Act 1977 there is a prohibition on the sale of
     goodwill attaching to such service (under s. 54 of and Sched. 10 to the Act), the
     goodwill is not *per se* extinguished thereby. However, it has now been affirmatively
     established by the decision of Bristow J. in *Hensman v. Traill* that any covenant which
j purports to restrict a doctor from complying with his obligations under the Act to
     care for his patients is void and unenforceable, as being contrary to both public
     policy and the above mentioned provisions of the Act. Accordingly, in this context,
     a distinction must be drawn between National Health Service goodwill and goodwill
     attaching to private medical practice.'

Bristow J held that a restraint between partners in a national health service practice is contrary to public policy on the ground that it is contrary to what he called the basic *a* concept of the national health service. That basic concept is said to be the right of a patient to be treated by the doctor of his choice, a right which is now enshrined in s 29(2) of the 1977 Act. But that right is subject to numerous limitations, restrictions and qualifications. I am not persuaded that that right is the basic concept of the national health service, whatever precisely that may mean; but, even if it were, I would not be prepared to say that an agreement which may have the effect of thwarting that basic *b* concept is contrary to public policy. Counsel for the defendant does not suggest that he can rely on any of the well-known and well-established heads of public policy and I am certainly not prepared to contemplate creating a new head of public policy or extending an existing head of public policy to cover this case. There is no provision in the 1977 Act prohibiting contractual restraints between partners similar to the provision which prohibits the sale of goodwill under s 54 of the Act. I see no basis on which we could say *c* that a statutory prohibition is to be implied. If I were in any doubt on the matter, which I am not, then, in the words of Lord Atkin in *Fender v Mildmay* [1937] 3 All ER 402 at 407, [1938] AC 1 at 12, I would in this case give the benefit of the doubt to the contract.

The second point on which I would respectfully differ from Bristow J is in his view that the acceptance of a restraint by a doctor is the provision by him of valuable consideration as consideration for his being taken into partnership within the meaning *d* of para 2(2) of Sch 10 to the 1977 Act. If it were, then, there would be a deemed sale of goodwill which would be unlawful by virtue of s 54 of the Act. I disagree with Bristow J for this reason. As I read Sch 10, the provisions which deal specifically with an outgoing partner are to be found in para 2(4)(*a*) and (*b*). For what is is worth, those are the paragraphs (or their equivalent) which were relied on in *Macfarlane v Kent* [1965] 2 All ER 376, [1965] 1 WLR 1019. Under sub-para (4)(*a*) there is a deemed sale of goodwill if *e* an outgoing partner agrees for valuable consideration to do or refrain from doing any act for the purpose of facilitating the succession of another medical practitioner to the practice. But para 2(5) makes it clear that that sub-paragraph does not apply to anything done in pursuance of a partnership agreement. Since sub-para (4) deals specifically with the position of an outgoing partner and since sub-para (5) specifically excludes sub-para (4) in the case of a partnership agreement, I regard it as impossible to bring this case *f* within the general provisions of para 2(2) of the schedule.

In my judgment *Hensman v Traill* was wrongly decided on the two points I have mentioned, and should be overruled. It follows that the judgment of Falconer J in the present case, in which he very properly and understandably followed *Hensman v Traill*, cannot be upheld.

On all the other matters I agree with what Dillon LJ has said and have nothing to add. *g*

NICHOLLS LJ. The plaintiffs are seeking to enforce against the defendant the terms of a partnership agreement. The two relevant clauses of the agreement are in the material respects clear. Under cl 32 any partner can be compelled to retire from the partnership on being given 12 months' notice in writing at any time signed by all the other partners; under cl 34 no former partner may, for a period of two years from his expulsion, carry *h* on the profession of general medical practitioner within two miles from where the partnership practice premises are at the date when he ceases to be a partner. That agreement was signed by the four partners.

The defendant does not suggest that, when he signed, he was under any misapprehension as to the meaning or effect of those clauses. Furthermore, very frankly and fairly, the defendant does not suggest that, in this unhappy partnership dispute, *j* when his three partners gave him 12 months' written notice on 14 February 1985 requiring him to retire, they were acting in bad faith. Moreover, for the defendant it is accepted that the extent of the area and the length of the period of restraint set out in cl 34(i) are no more than those reasonably required to protect the interest of the plaintiffs

in the partnership practice. Prima facie, therefore, the defendant is bound by the terms
a of his agreement and the plaintiffs are entitled to have the assistance of the court to
require him to observe those terms.

The principal defence raised is that, because the partnership consists of medical
practitioners who are providing general medical services pursuant to the provisions of
the National Health Service Act 1977, the defendant was not able effectually or lawfully
to bind himself in the terms of cl 34(i).

b   When considering these statutory provisions, one obvious background fact is that the
practice of a medical practitioner entered on a list of medical practitioners undertaking
to provide general medical services will attract goodwill, to an extent depending on the
medical skill and other professional qualities of the individual practitioner. Equally
obviously, to my mind, such goodwill will be of value to a practitioner despite the
existence of the statutory limitation on the number of persons a doctor may have on his
c list, and despite also the control which the Medical Practices Committee has over the
number of medical practitioners practising in any particular locality and over the
selection of the practitioners for inclusion on the relevant list. The 1977 Act itself
recognises the existence of such goodwill and also, even though patients are on the lists
of individual doctors, the existence of goodwill of a partnership practice where a
practitioner practises in partnership (see, for example, para 1(8) of Sch 10).

d   The unlawfulness argument in the present case was that, when the defendant signed
the partnership agreement and thereby agreed to be bound in the terms of cl 34(i), an
unlawful sale of the goodwill or part of the goodwill of the other partners was deemed to
have been effected pursuant to para 2(2)(a) of Sch 10. I cannot accept this. Omitting
words immaterial for the present purposes, para 2(4)(a) deals with the case where—

> 'a medical practitioner . . . agrees, for valuable consideration, to . . . refrain from
e > doing any act . . . for the purpose of facilitating the succession of another medical
> practitioner to the practice . . . of the first practitioner . . .'

Of the various provisions in para 2, that provision is the one most directly aimed at a
practitioner entering into an agreement restrictive of his future activities for the benefit
of a successor. Formal partnership agreements commonly include restraint clauses such
f as cl 34 in the present case, but expressly and, in my view, significantly, para 2(4) does
not apply to anything done in pursuance of a partnership agreement.

Turning to para 2(2), 'valuable consideration' cannot be given there the width of
meaning argued for by counsel for the defendant in this case and necessary if he is to
succeed on this point because, if that phrase is given there such a wide meaning, the
argument proves too much, for it would have the result that many normal and innocuous
g obligations undertaken by a partner in a partnership agreement would be caught, with
the criminal consequence stated in para 1 of Sch 10: for example obligations on partners
to pay their own debts or not to charge their partnership shares. Reading para 2(2)(a) in
its context in Sch 10, and whatever its precise limits, I do not think that entering into a
partnership agreement containing a commonplace mutual restraint clause such as cl 34,
whether read alone or in conjunction with cl 32, constitutes giving valuable consideration
h as consideration for being taken into partnership within the meaning of para 2(2)(a).
Paragraph 2(2)(a) is not properly to be construed as applying to a transaction expressly
taken out of the ambit of para 2(4)(a) by para 2(5).

Thus, if that construction of para 2 is correct, the elaborate provisions in that paragraph
contemplate, but expressly do not make unlawful, a restraint clause in a partnership
agreement such as cl 34(i). It is against that background that the public policy submission
j of counsel for the defendant has to be considered. As to medical practitioners' goodwill,
nothing put forward in argument over the last three days has made me doubt the
correctness of the analysis of the position following the coming into effect of the National
Health Service Act 1946 set out by Evershed MR in the passage in his judgment in
Whitehill v Bradford [1952] 1 All ER 115 at 121, [1952] Ch 236 at 253–254 cited by Dillon

LJ. That judgment was given over 30 years ago. Since then many amendments have
been made to the national health service legislation, but the material provisions in s 35   *a*
of the National Health Service Act 1946 were reproduced in substantially the same terms
in the 1977 Act. In my view, in his goodwill the medical practitioner still has an asset of
value which he is entitled reasonably to protect although not to sell. Conversely, looking
at the position of the covenantor and considering the impact of a restraint clause in a
partnership agreement such as cl 34 on a doctor and his patients, and considering in
particular whether enforcement of such a clause could lead to a doctor being forced to   *b*
break his obligation (under the statutory terms of service for doctors) to render his
patients all necessary and appropriate medical services of the type usually provided by
general medical practitioners, it is to be noted that, in general, a doctor may give three
months' notice of withdrawal of his name from the medical list at any time, or require
the family practitioner committee to remove any person from his list. Moreover, I am
not persuaded that the difficulties which may be caused for patients if a restraint clause   *c*
such as cl 34 is valid and enforceable are in practice likely to be significantly different
from those arising when a doctor of his own volition, and in the absence of any restraint
clause, chooses to retire from a partnership and cease practising in the immediate
neighbourhood or altogether.

Much was sought to be made of a patient's statutory right to chose his own doctor (see,
for example, the reference to this right in s 29(2)(b) of the 1977 Act). But this right is a   *d*
qualified one: normally, the consent of the practitioner is required for a patient to be
included on his list, the allocation of patients against the will of a doctor being abnormal
rather than normal.

In these circumstances, I cannot discern a requirement of public policy that a restraint
clause such as cl 34(i) must be struck down and a doctor not be permitted to bind himself
by such a clause.
                                                                                              e
On the other defences raised, based on implied terms and delay, and on the question
of the balance of convenience, I agree with the observations of Dillon LJ. For these
reasons I, too, would allow the appeal.

Appeal allowed. Leave to appeal to the House of Lords refused. Injunction suspended for 14 days.
                                                                                              f
Solicitors: *Ellison & Co*, Colchester (for the plaintiffs); *Hempsons* (for the defendant).

                                                    Mary Rose Plummer   Barrister.

a # Secretary of State for the Home Department v Mental Health Review Tribunal for the Mersey Regional Health Authority

b # Secretary of State for the Home Department v Mental Health Review Tribunal for Wales

QUEEN'S BENCH DIVISION (CROWN OFFICE LIST)

MANN J

18, 22 APRIL 1986

c
Mental health – Mental health review tribunal – Discharge of restricted patient – Discharge – Decision directing conditional discharge of restricted patient – Direction imposing condition on discharge requiring patient to continue to reside in a hospital – Condition deferring discharge until arrangements made for admission of patient to another hospital – Whether condition valid – Mental Health Act 1983, ss 72(1), 73(1)(2)(4)(7).

d
S and G were restricted patients detained in hospital under the provisions of Pt III of the Mental Health Act 1983. The Secretary of State referred their cases to mental health review tribunals for consideration. In S's case the tribunal were satisfied under s 72(1)(b)*ᵃ* that he was not suffering from any mental illness requiring him to be detained in hospital for treatment and that it was not necessary for his health and safety or for the protection of others that he should receive such treatment but they were not satisfied under

e
s 73(1)(b)*ᵇ* that he should not remain liable to be recalled to hospital for further treatment. The tribunal therefore directed pursuant to s 73(2) that he be conditionally discharged but deferred the direction pursuant to s 73(7) until arrangements were made for his admission to another hospital prior to his subsequent discharge. In G's case the tribunal were satisfied as to the matters in s 72(1)(b)(i) on the basis that the treatment which was appropriate for him was not medical treatment within the meaning of the Act in that it

f
could be given in a hostel or in some other community facility but they were not satisfied that he should not remain liable to be recalled to hospital under s 73(1)(b). The tribunal therefore directed pursuant to s 73(2) of the Act that G should be discharged on condition that he remained in residence at a hospital. The Secretary of State sought the determination of the court on the questions whether, in S's case, the tribunal had power to defer their direction until arrangements were made for his admission to another

g
hospital and whether, in G's case, s 73(4) of the 1983 Act, which provided for the recall of patients to hospital, empowered the tribunal to direct a conditional discharge subject to a condition that the patient remain in residence in hospital.

h
Held – (1) The term 'discharge' in ss 72 to 75 of the 1983 Act meant release from hospital, although such release might be absolute or conditional. Accordingly, a condition requiring a patient who was conditionally discharged to remain in hospital was inconsistent with the duty to discharge albeit conditionally. It followed therefore that in G's case the tribunal had had no power under s 73(4) to impose on his conditional discharge the condition that he remain in residence at a hospital and that condition was accordingly unlawful (see p 237 *j* to p 238 *a*, post).

j
(2) A mental health review tribunal had no power under s 73(7) to defer their direction until arrangements were made for the patient's admission to another hospital, because such a direction ensured the patient's continued detention and was not within the powers

---

a Section 72(1), so far as material, is set out at p 235 *h j*, post.

b Section 73, so far as material, is set out at p 236 *c d*, post.

of the 1983 Act in so far as they applied to restricted patients and was therefore unlawful. Accordingly, the tribunal's decision to give S a deferred conditional discharge as a means *a* of securing his admission to another hospital was unlawful. Moreover, both the condition requiring a patient to remain in hospital in G's case, and the deferred conditional discharge in S's case, were inconsistent with the tribunal being satisfied as to the matters in s 72(1)(b)(i) or (ii), since a requirement of admission to hospital meant that the patient was to receive treatment under medical supervision (see p 238 b to f, post).

b

Notes
For the discharge from detention of restricted patients, see Supplement to 30 Halsbury's Laws (4th edn) para 1201A.

For the Mental Health Act 1983, ss 72, 73, see 53 Halsbury's Statutes (3rd edn) 1110, 1111.

c

Special cases stated

Secretary of State for the Home Dept v Mental Health Review Tribunal for the Mersey Regional Health Authority
The Secretary of State for the Home Department sought the determination by the court of certain questions of law (set out at p 237 a b, post) stated in the form of a special case *d* stated by the respondent, the Mental Health Review Tribunal for the Mersey Regional Health Authority (president his Honour Judge David QC), under s 78(8) of the Mental Health Act 1983, in respect of the tribunal's direction on 29 November 1983 that Mr S, a restricted patient within the meaning of s 79 of the 1983 Act and detained under Pt III thereof at the Moss Side Hospital, be conditionally discharged but that such discharge be deferred until arrangements had been made for Mr S's admission to another hospital *e* with a view to his subsequent discharge to a local hostel or his home. The facts are set out in the judgment.

Secretary of State for the Home Dept v Mental Health Review Tribunal for Wales
The Secretary of State for the Home Department sought the determination by the court of certain questions of law (set out at p 237 f to h, post) stated in the form of a special case *f* stated by the respondent, the Mental Health Review Tribunal for Wales (president his Honour Judge David Williams QC), under s 79 of the Mental Health Act 1983, in respect of their direction on 21 December 1983 that Mr G be conditionally discharged subject to a condition that he resided in a hospital. The facts are set out in the judgment.

John Laws for the Secretary of State.
A T Sander for the Mental Health Review Tribunal for the Mersey Regional Health *g* Authority.
The Mental Health Review Tribunal for Wales were not represented.

Cur adv vult

h

22 April. The following judgment was delivered.

MANN J. There are before the court two special cases stated under s 78(8) of the Mental Health Act 1983 by two mental health review tribunals. They were heard together. The first concerned Mr S and was stated by the Mental Health Review Tribunal for the Mersey Regional Health Authority. That tribunal was represented before the court. The second *j* case concerned Mr G and was stated by the Mental Health Review Tribunal for Wales. That tribunal was not represented before the court. In both cases, the appellant is the Secretary of State for the Home Department.

On 16 December 1976, in the Crown Court at Manchester, Mr S was convicted of an offence and was made the subject of an order under s 60 of the Mental Health Act 1959

a   for his detention in Moss Side Hospital. There was a further order making him subject
to the special restrictions set out in s 65 of the Act for an unlimited period of time. The
Crown Court had been satisfied that Mr S had been suffering from mental disorder
within the meaning of the Act, namely psychopathic disorder. On 29 November 1983
he was still detained pursuant to the order of 16 December 1976.

On 28 January 1963, at the Glamorgan Assize held at Cardiff, Mr G was found insane
on arraignment and was ordered to be detained during Her Majesty's pleasure under the
b   Criminal Lunatics Act 1800, s 2. On 12 February 1963 the Secretary of State, by warrant
under s 71(2) of the 1959 Act, directed that Mr G be detained in Ely Hospital, Cardiff.
The effect of that direction was to the same effect as an order under s 60 accompanied by
an order subjecting the patient to the special restrictions set out in s 65 of the Act for an
unlimited period of time: see s 71(4) of the 1959 Act. On 21 December 1983 Mr G was
still detained pursuant to the direction of 12 February 1963.

c   The law concerning mentally disordered persons is now to be found in the Mental
Health Act 1983, which came into force on 30 September 1983: see s 149(2). On that day
the orders in respect of Mr S came to have effect as if made under ss 37 and 41 of the
1983 Act: see Sch 5, para 3. On that day the direction in respect of Mr G came to have
effect as if made under s 46 of the 1983 Act: see Sch 5, paras 3 and 21.

Mr S and Mr G thus became restricted patients within the meaning of the 1983 Act:
d   see s 79(1). They were each to be treated as if detained under Pt III of the Act, which
relates to 'patients concerned in criminal proceedings or under sentence' as being the
subject of hospital orders, together with the restriction orders made without limitation
of time.

Section 71(2) of the 1983 Act obliges the Secretary of State to refer to a mental health
review tribunal the case of any restricted patient detained in a hospital whose case has not
e   been considered by a tribunal within the last three years. This was a new provision which
the consolidating 1983 Act took from the Mental Health Amendment Act 1982, s 28(4)
and Sch 1, para 3(2). That Act, which was repealed so far as is material by the 1983 Act,
had the commencement date of 30 September 1983. In order to meet the coming into
force of the new provision, which would have applied to both Mr S and Mr G, the
Secretary of State used his discretionary powers of reference under s 66(6) of the 1959 Act
f   in regard to both patients.

The reference in Mr S's case was determined on 29 November 1983, by which time it
had effect as if it had been made under s 71(1) of the 1983 Act: see Sch 5, para 3. The
reference in Mr G's case was determined on 21 December 1983, by which time it had
effect as had Mr S's reference. The two determinations have given rise to the two special
cases which are before the court.

g   The powers of the mental health review tribunal in regard to a reference which is
made to them are to be found in ss 72 and 73 of the 1983 Act. I must set out the material
provisions. Section 72(1) provides:

'Where application is made to a Mental Health Review Tribunal by or in respect
of a patient who is liable to be detained under this Act, the tribunal may in any case
direct that the patient be discharged, and . . . (b) the tribunal shall direct the discharge
h   of a patient . . . if they are satisfied—(i) that he is not then suffering from mental
illness, psychopathic disorder, severe mental impairment or mental impairment or
from any of those forms of disorder of a nature or degree which makes it appropriate
for him to be liable to be detained in a hospital for medical treatment; or (ii) that it
is not necessary for the health or safety of the patient or for the protection of other
persons that he should receive such treatment . . .'

j   The expression 'medical treatment' which there occurs is a term of art, which is defined
in s 145(1) in these terms: '. . . "medical treatment" includes nursing, and also includes
care, habilitation and rehabilitation under medical supervision.'

I return to s 72. Subsection (3) provides:

'A tribunal may under subsection (1) above direct the discharge of a patient on a

future date specified in the direction; and where a tribunal do not direct the
discharge of a patient under that subsection the tribunal may—(a) with a view to   a
facilitating his discharge on a future date, recommend that he be granted leave of
absence or transferred to another hospital or into guardianship; and (b) further
consider his case in the event of any such recommendation not being complied
with.'

Subsection (7) provides: 'Subsection (1) above shall not apply in the case of a restricted
patient except as provided in sections 73 and 74 below.' For present purposes, I need not   b
refer to s 74, but only to s 73. I so refer because, as will have appeared, both Mr S and Mr
G are restricted patients.
  The material provisions of s 73 are as follows:

'(1) Where an application to a Mental Health Review Tribunal is made by a
restricted patient who is subject to a restriction order, or where the case of such a   c
patient is referred to such a tribunal, the tribunal shall direct the absolute discharge
of the patient if satisfied—(a) as to the matters mentioned in paragraph (b)(i) or (ii)
of section 72(1) above; and (b) that it is not appropriate for the patient to remain
liable to be recalled to hospital for further treatment.
  (2) Where in the case of any such patient as is mentioned in subsection (1) above
the tribunal are satisfied as to the matters referred to in paragraph (a) of that   d
subsection but not as to the matter referred to in paragraph (b) of that subsection the
tribunal shall direct the conditional discharge of the patient . . .'

It is to be observed that each of those two subsections uses the mandatory word 'shall'.
The subject of conditional discharge is expanded in sub-ss (4) and (7) as follows:

'(4) Where a patient is conditionally discharged under this section—(a) he may   e
be recalled by the Secretary of State under subsection (3) of section 42 above as if he
had been conditionally discharged under subsection (2) of that section; and (b) the
patient shall comply with such conditions (if any) as may be imposed at the time of
discharge by the tribunal or at any subsequent time by the Secretary of State . . .
  (7) A tribunal may defer a direction for the conditional discharge of a patient
until such arrangements as appear to the tribunal to be necessary for that purpose   f
have been made to their satisfaction . . .'

I take first the case of Mr S. The tribunal state that they were satisfied as to the
following facts:

'(a) The patient's behaviour had improved substantially over the past six months;
(b) The patient was no longer under any medication and no longer needed any   g
medication; (c) The patient's behaviour was then such that it was no longer necessary
to detain him either for his own health or safety or for the protection of other
persons. (d) Future deterioration of the patient's mental health might occur and it
was therefore appropriate that he remain liable to be recalled to hospital for further
treatment; (e) The patient would be unable to cope upon discharge from a special
hospital straight into the community and a period in a "half way house" was essential   h
in the patient's interests and in the interests of the community.'

  The tribunal directed that Mr S be conditionally discharged, subject to two conditions,
whose terms are not material. The inference from the case stated is that the tribunal were
satisfied as to the matters in s 72(1)(b)(i) and (ii), but were not satisfied as to the matter in
s 73(1)(b). The correctness of the inference is confirmed by a letter of 10 February 1984   .
from the president of the tribunal to the clerk which, exceptionally, I was shown at the   j
request, and with the consent, of the parties. Although the tribunal directed a conditional
discharge, they made a further decision. I quote from para 7 of the case:

'Under section 73(7) of the 1983 Act we deferred the direction until arrangements
had been made for the patient's admission to Winwick Hospital with a view to the
patient's subsequent discharge to a local hostel or his home.'

On their decisions, the tribunal state the following questions of law:

'(a) Whether the Tribunal could have been properly satisfied as to the matters in section 72(1)(*b*)(i) or (ii) of the 1983 Act in the light of the facts found by them and of their decision that the patient should be admitted to another hospital while satisfactory arrangements were made for his discharge. (b) Whether in the exercise of their powers under section 73(7) of the 1983 Act or under any other part of that Act the Tribunal were able to direct that the direction to discharge be deferred until arrangements had been made for his admission to Winwick Hospital with a view to subsequent discharge to a local hostel or his home.'

I take second the case of Mr G. The tribunal said that they were satisfied as to the following facts:

'a. The patient was no longer suffering from schizophrenia, which had been diagnosed at the time of his trial. b. The patient was suffering from severe mental impairment of a degree which made it appropriate that he should continue to receive treatment in the form of supervision and guidance as to personal hygiene and rehabilitation training in elementary social skills. The patient was not at the time receiving any medication. c. The patient was incapable of looking after himself on his own and without supervision. d. None of the patient's relatives was able to provide the sort of supervision or training that he needed. e. There were at the time no suitable residential placements available which would provide the sort of supervision and rehabilitation treatment which the patient needed. f. The patient had no desire to leave Ely Hospital. g. It was appropriate that if discharged the patient should remain liable to be recalled to hospital for further treatment.'

The tribunal expressed themselves as satisfied as to the matters in s 72(1)(*b*)(i) on the basis that the treatment that they had found appropriate was not medical treatment within the meaning of the Act in that it could be given in a hostel or in some other suitable community provision. The tribunal were not satisfied as to the matter in s 73(1)(*b*) and accordingly made an order for conditional discharge, but subject to a condition that Mr G resided at Ely Hospital, which had been his home for over 21 years. On their decision, the tribunal state the following questions of law:

'a. Whether the Tribunal was correct in holding that the treatment mentioned in paragraph 5(b) above did not constitute "medical treatment" within the meaning of section 145(1) of the 1983 Act. b. Whether, on the assumption that such treatment did constitute "medical treatment", the Tribunal could have been satisfied under section 72(1)(*b*)(i) of the 1983 Act, on the facts found by it, that the patient's mental disorder was not of a nature or degree which made it appropriate for him to be liable to be detained in a hospital for medical treatment when at the same time it decided that it was appropriate for him to remain in hospital as the condition of his discharge. c. Whether, on the assumption that the Tribunal was obliged to discharge the patient conditionally under section 73(2) of the 1983 Act, it was proper for the Tribunal to discharge him on the condition that he remain in residence in Ely Hospital (or any other hospital).'

In regard to that third question, I regard the word 'proper' as being synonymous with the word 'lawful'.

In each of the two cases counsel for the Secretary of State has submitted that the tribunal had no power to do what they did. In the case of Mr S it was said that s 73(7) gave no power to defer a direction until arrangements were made for admission to another hospital. In the case of Mr G it was said that s 73(4) gave no power to condition a conditional discharge by a condition that the patient remain in residence at a hospital.

The word 'discharge', as employed in ss 72 to 75 of the 1983 Act, means, and in my judgment can only mean, release from hospital. The release may be absolute or it may be conditional. It will be conditional in the case of a restricted patient where the tribunal are not satisfied as to the matter in s 73(1)(*b*), but are satisfied as to the matters in s 72(1)(b)(i) or (ii). A condition requiring that a patient, who is conditionally discharged, should remain in hospital is, in my judgment, inconsistent with the duty to discharge albeit conditionally. Section 73(4)(a), with its reference to 'recall', strongly supports the inconsistency of such a condition with the concept of discharge. The condition imposed on the discharge of Mr G was therefore, in my judgment, not lawful.

The tribunal which considered the case of Mr S sought to use s 73(7) to secure his admission to another hospital. Counsel for the tribunal submitted that the word 'arrangements' was a word with a wide meaning and could comprehend the imposition of an interim regime prior to a direction of conditional discharge. I cannot accept that submission. Where the conditions precedent are satisfied, a tribunal is obliged to direct the conditional discharge of a restricted patient. A direction (but not the making of it) may be deferred by the tribunal 'until such arrangements as appear to the tribunal to be necessary for that purpose have been made to their satisfaction'. The purpose in question is that of discharge, albeit conditionally. In this case, the arrangement was one which when made ensured continued detention, but brought deferment of discharge to an end. In my judgment, the stipulation of such an arrangement is not within the powers of the Act in so far as they apply to restricted patients and is accordingly unlawful. I observe, in passing, that in regard to patients who are not restricted patients there is, in s 72(3), provision for the achievement of an interim regime.

The issues which I have so far discussed are issues of general importance. There are particular issues in regard to each of the two cases. In the case of Mr S there is an issue whether the decision that the patient should be admitted to Winwick Hospital as a half-way house was inconsistent with satisfaction as to the matters in s 72(1)(b)(i) or (ii). If the patient was to go to Winwick Hospital for medical treatment, as defined, then there was an inconsistency in that the absence of a case for medical treatment is implicit in satisfaction as to the matters in s 72(1)(b)(i) or (ii). Counsel for the tribunal submitted that admission to Winwick Hospital was not to be for medical treatment, but was simply in order that the patient might enjoy a half-way house. However, in my judgment, a requirement of admission to a hospital must mean that the patient is to receive treatment, in this case rehabilitation, under medical supervision. There is, thus, in my judgment, an inconsistency.

There is, on the same grounds, an inconsistency in the case of Mr G as between satisfaction as to the matters in s 72(1)(b)(i) and the requirement that the patient reside in Ely Hospital. Having given my judgment on various issues in the case, it remains to answer the questions in the cases stated. This I do as follows: in the case stated by the Mental Health Review Tribunal for the Mersey Regional Health Authority, (a) No, (b) No; in the case stated by the Mental Health Review Tribunal for Wales, (a) No, (b) No, (c) No. I was not asked to make any other order, nor was I asked to make any order as to costs. I therefore make no other order and make no order as to costs.

I wish to add this. I am confident that the two tribunals were each seeking to achieve a result which to them seemed sensible and which was in the best interests of the patients concerned. Unfortunately, and for the reasons I have given, they had no power to achieve that which they wished to achieve.

Questions answered accordingly. No order as to costs.

Solicitors: *Treasury Solicitor*; *Alsop Stevens*, Liverpool (for the Mental Health Review Tribunal for the Mersey Regional Health Authority).

Mary Rose Plummer   Barrister.

a   # R v Oxford Regional Mental Health Review Tribunal and another, ex parte Secretary of State for the Home Department and another appeal

b   COURT OF APPEAL, CIVIL DIVISION
LAWTON, STEPHEN BROWN LJJ AND SIR JOHN MEGAW
22, 23 APRIL 1986

c   *Mental health – Mental health review tribunal – Discharge of restricted patient – Discharge – Decision directing conditional discharge of restricted patient – Direction subject to arrangements being made for support of patient – Direction that tribunal reconsider case in six months' time – Whether decision directing conditional discharge a provisional or final decision – Whether tribunal having power to reconsider decision – Whether Secretary of State entitled to apply for judicial review of decision – Mental Health Act 1983, s 73(2)(7).*

d   *Mental health – Mental health review tribunal – Proceedings – Irregularity – Failure to send documents and notice of hearing to Secretary of State in case of application by restricted patient – Effect of failure – Whether failure an irregularity – Whether failure an irregularity which could be cured – Whether failure amounting to breach of rules of natural justice – Whether Secretary of State entitled to apply for judicial review – Mental Health Tribunal Rules 1983, rr 12(1), 20, 28.*

e   In two separate cases questions arose as to the powers of mental health review tribunals when directing the conditional discharge of restricted patients under s 73(2)ᵃ of the Mental Health Act 1983. In the first case C, who suffered from a mental disorder, was detained in hospital under a hospital order and was a restricted patient under the 1983 Act. He applied to a mental health review tribunal for a review of his case. The tribunal notified the Secretary of State of the application but, contrary to rr 12(1)ᵇ and 20ᶜ of the

f   Mental Health Review Tribunal Rules 1983, failed to send him a copy of the medical opinion which C intended to put before the tribunal or to inform him of the date of the hearing. At the hearing the tribunal directed pursuant to s 73(2) that C be conditionally discharged, such discharge to be deferred to enable arrangements to be made for C's support. In directing the deferment of the conditional discharge the tribunal purported to act pursuant to s 73(7)ᵈ, which allowed a tribunal to defer a direction for conditional

g   discharge until satisfactory arrangements for that purpose had been made. The Secretary of State applied for judicial review of the tribunal's decision, contending that since he had not been given an opportunity to be represented at the hearing there had been a breach of the rules of natural justice. The judge dismissed the application on the ground that even if the 1983 rules had been breached there was no need for the Secretary of State to apply for judicial review because the decision of the tribunal was merely provisional

h   and the tribunal could therefore reconvene to reconsider it. The Secretary of State appealed. In the second case L was detained in a hospital under a hospital order and was a restricted patient under the 1983 Act. She applied to a mental health review tribunal for a review of her case. The tribunal directed, pursuant to s 73(2) of the 1983 Act, that she be conditionally discharged, such discharge to be deferred pursuant to s 73(7) to

j   a   Section 73(2) is set out at p 245 d, post
    b   Rule 12(1), so far as material, provides: '. . . the tribunal shall . . . send a copy of every document it receives which is relevant to the application to . . . in the case of a restricted patient, the Secretary of State . . .'
    c   Rule 20, so far as material, provides: 'The tribunal shall give at least 14 days' notice of the date, time and place fixed for the hearing . . . to . . . in the case of a restricted patient, the Secretary of State.'
    d   Section 73(7), so far as material, is set out at p 245 g h, post

enable arrangements to be made for her support. The tribunal further directed that in the event of such arrangements not being made within six months they would reconvene to reconsider, in the light of L's progress reports during that period, whether to make the order final without the attachment of any specified arrangements. The Secretary of State applied for judicial review of the tribunal's decision, contending that the tribunal had no power under s 73(2) and (7) to reconsider their decision once it was made. The judge dismissed the application on the ground that since the tribunal's decision was provisional they could reconvene to reconsider it. The Secretary of State appealed.

Held – (1) A decision of a mental health review tribunal under s 73(2) of the 1983 Act directing that a patient be conditionally discharged was a final decision, not a provisional one, notwithstanding that they had directed pursuant to s 73(7) of the Act that the discharge be deferred to enable arrangements to be made for the support of the patient, since such arrangements were for the purpose of accomplishing the conditional discharge of the patient and not for reconsidering whether there should be a discharge at all. Accordingly, the tribunal had no power to reconsider their decision once it was made (see p 246 c to j, p 247 d f and p 248 b c, post).

(2) It followed in C's case that, the tribunal having made their decision to direct C's conditional discharge, the failure to give the Secretary of State an opportunity to make representations to the tribunal was an irregularity which could not be waived under r 28[e] of the 1983 rules since that rule applied only to the curing of irregularities which occurred before the tribunal made their decision, and because the failure amounted to a breach of the rules of natural justice the Secretary of State was entitled to apply for judicial review of the decision. In L's case the tribunal had misdirected themselves in thinking that they could reconsider her case and since their decision was wrong it could be reviewed. The appeals would therefore be allowed (see p 246 j and p 247 b to d f, post).

Per curiam. Before starting to hear any application for review when the Secretary of State is not represented a mental health review tribunal should inquire, and note, whether he has been given notice of the application and of the hearing (see p 247 c d f, post).

Notes
For the discharge from detention of restricted patients, see Supplement to 30 Halsbury's Laws (4th edn) para 1201A.

For the Mental Health Act 1983, s 73, see 53 Halsbury's Statutes (3rd edn) 1111.

For the Mental Health Review Tribunal Rules 1983, rr 12, 20, 28, see 17 Halsbury's Statutory Instruments (4th reissue) 45, 47, 49.

Case referred to in judgments
X v UK (5 November 1981, unreported), E Ct HR.

Cases also cited
Secretary of State for the Home Dept v Mental Health Review Tribunal for the Mersey Regional Health Authority [1986] 3 All ER 232.
W v L (mental health patient) [1973] 3 All ER 884, [1974] QB 711, CA.

Appeals
R v Oxford Regional Mental Health Review Tribunal and another, ex p Secretary of State for the Home Department

The Secretary of State for the Home Department appealed against the decision of Woolf J hearing the Crown Office list on 8 November 1985 whereby he dismissed an application by the Secretary of State for judicial review by way of (i) an order of certiorari to quash the decision of the first respondent, the Oxford Regional Mental Health Review Tribunal (president his Honour Judge Morrison), made on 12 February 1985 that the second

---

e   Rule 28 is set out at p 247 a b, post

respondent, Mr C, a restricted patient detained at Broadmoor Hospital pursuant to ss 37
a and 41 of and para 3 of Sch 5 to the Mental Health Act 1983, be conditionally discharged,
such discharge to be deferred until 28 June 1985 for proposals to meet the conditions to
be prepared, and (ii) an order of mandamus requiring the tribunal to redetermine Mr C's
application for review after having received such supplementary observations as the
Secretary of State might place before it. The facts are set out in the judgment of Lawton
LJ.

b
R v Yorkshire Mental Health Review Tribunal and another, ex p Secretary of State for the Home
Department

The Secretary of State for the Home Department appealed against the decision of
Kennedy J hearing the Crown Office list on 21 January 1986 whereby he dismissed an
application by the Secretary of State for judicial review by way of (i) an order of certiorari
c to quash such part of the direction made by the first respondent, the Yorkshire Mental
Health Review Tribunal (president her Honour Judge Norwood), on 1 April 1985
conditionally discharging the second respondent, Miss L, a restricted patient detained in
Stanley Royd Hospital pursuant to ss 37 and 41 of and para 3 and Sch 5 to the Mental
Health Act 1983, as directed that in the event of specified arrangements not having been
made within six months the tribunal would reconvene to reconsider in the light of Miss
d L's progress reports during the period whether the direction might be perfected without
the attachment of any specified arrangements and (ii) alternatively, a declaration that
that part of the direction was null and void and of no effect. The facts are set out in the
judgment of Lawton LJ.

John Laws for the Secretary of State.
e *Oliver Thorold* for Mr C and Miss L.
The tribunals were not represented.

LAWTON LJ. There are two appeals by the Secretary of State for the Home Department
before this court. One is against a judgment of Woolf J delivered on 8 November 1985
whereby he refused judicial review of a decision of the Oxford Regional Mental Health
f Review Tribunal made on 12 February 1985. The other appeal is against a decision of
Kennedy J refusing judicial review on 21 January 1986 of a decision of the Yorkshire
Mental Health Review Tribunal. The Oxford case arose out of an application for review
by a Mr C. The Yorkshire case arose out of an application for review by a Miss L. Both
cases substantially raise the same point, namely: what are the powers of a mental health
review tribunal under s 73(2)?

g   The facts can be stated shortly. Mr C in 1959 at the age of 17 was convicted of
manslaughter by reason of diminished responsibility and was sentenced to ten years'
imprisonment. He was released from that sentence in 1965. In 1969 he became aware
that he was suffering from some kind of mental disorder and submitted himself to
hospital treatment as an informal patient. Whilst he was in hospital it seems to have been
appreciated by the doctors treating him that he was a suitable case for compulsory
h detention in hospital pursuant to the provisions of s 26 of the Mental Health Act 1959.
Whilst undergoing treatment in hospital he confessed to two comparatively minor cases
of burglary. As a result, he was brought before the Crown Court. The Crown Court
made orders against him pursuant to s 60 of the Mental Health Act 1959 together with a
restriction unlimited in time pursuant to s 65 of that Act. He has been under care in
Broadmoor Hospital ever since. In 1971 the Secretary of State consented to his conditional
j discharge subject to arrangements being made for his supervision. It was found
impossible to make those arrangements and, as a result, the conditional discharge did not
take effect. He has applied unsuccessfully on one previous occasion for review. This was
his second application.
      The Secretary of State is entitled to notice not only that an application for review has
been made but to notice of the hearing of the application (see rr 4 and 20 of the Mental
Health Review Tribunal Rules 1983, SI 1983/942). He is also entitled to early notice of

any psychiatric reports which the applicant may be putting forward (see r 12 of the 1983
rules).

The Secretary of State, through one of the doctors at Broadmoor Hospital, submitted
in writing to the review tribunal that the Secretary of State was not satisfied that Mr C
should be released. Most unfortunately, it may be because of some administrative
mistake, the Secretary of State was not sent a copy of the medical opinion which the
applicant intended to put before the review tribunal; nor was he informed when the
hearing was to take place.

The hearing took place on 12 February 1985. The tribunal considered such information
as they had before them and came to their decision in these terms:

> 'The Tribunal has considered the Patients Application relating to the above named
> and hereby directs that:—This patient shall be conditionally discharged, such
> discharge to be deferred to Friday 28th June 1985, for proposals to meet the
> conditions to be prepared. The conditions shall be that:—1. The patient reside at
> and abide by the rules of a suitably supervised hostel which has an Active
> Rehabilitation Programme. 2. The patient shall be placed under the supervision of
> a suitable Probation Officer or suitable Social Worker, who shall report from time
> to time as requested to the Home Office and the hospital referred to in condition 3.
> 3. The patient shall attend a Psychiatric Out-Patient Clinic as directed by a Consultant
> Psychiatrist yet to be nominated. The Tribunal is satisfied about these reasons
> because:—They were satisfied that this patient continues to suffer from Psychopathic
> Disorder but not of a nature [or] degree which makes it appropriate for him to be
> liable to be detained in a hospital for medical treatment but were satisfied that this
> patient should remain liable to recall.'

It has been the submission of counsel for the Secretary of State that, on the face of it,
that order was a complete order and that all that remained to be done was for the
arrangements to be made and for the tribunal to be satisfied about them.

When the Secretary of State was sent, as he was in the ordinary course of administration,
a copy of that order, those acting for him appreciated that there had been a very serious
breakdown in the administrative arrangements which are contained in the rules made
under the Mental Health Act 1983. Because there had been that breakdown he applied
for judicial review. The answer which was put forward on behalf of Mr C to Woolf J was
as follows. There was no need for the Secretary of State to apply for judicial review, albeit
there had been an irregularity in procedure in that notices had not been given as they
should have been under the appropriate rules. The reason was that the mental health
review tribunal could reconvene, then reconsider the position and the Secretary of State
could make such representation to them as he thought appropriate. That was a submission
which, broadly, Woolf J accepted.

The facts relating to Miss L are these. In 1985, when she was a patient in the Stanley
Royd Hospital at Wakefield, she set fire to the premises in circumstances which made
her liable to be convicted of arson endangering life. She was so convicted in the Crown
Court and the Crown Court made orders under ss 60 and 65 of the Mental Health Act
1959. She is said to have made progress in hospital and, when her case came to be
considered by the Yorkshire Mental Health Review Tribunal on 1 April 1985, they came
to a decision as follows:

> 'The Tribunal has considered the application relating to the above named and
> hereby directs that the patient be conditionally discharged but the Direction therefor
> be deferred, pursuant to Section 73(7), until the following arrangements for that
> purpose have been made to our satisfaction, viz 1. that the patient be received and
> accommodated in a hostel which is supervised; 2. that she is subject to such
> periodical psychiatric out-patient treatment as may be advised and 3. that she
> remains under the supervision of an officer of the relevant Social Services
> Department.'

Counsel for the Secretary of State accepts that, if the order of the Yorkshire tribunal

had stopped there, no complaint could be made. But it did not stop there. It went on as
a follows:

> 'The tribunal directs further that in the event of the aforementioned arrangements
> not having been made within the next six months, it will reconvene to reconsider
> in the light of the patient's progress reports during this period whether the direction
> for conditional discharge may be perfected without the attachment of any specified
> arrangements.'

b
There was a reflection of that approach later in the order when it was said:

> 'There is always a possibility that at that time we may feel able to conclude that
> the statutory criteria for conditional discharge without deferment have been
> satisfied.'

c In other words, said counsel for the Secretary of State, they were taking on themselves,
having decided it was a case for conditional discharge, the right to reconsider the position
at the end of six months. It was counsel's submission that, on the proper construction of
s 73 of the Mental Health Act 1983, that tribunal had no power, just as the Oxford
tribunal had no power, to reconsider a decision once made.

One of the problems in the case has been whether either tribunal did make a decision
d which was capable of being reconsidered. It was submitted by counsel on behalf of both
Mr C and Miss L before Woolf and Kennedy JJ that a decision of the kind which was
made pursuant to s 73(2) and (7) was only a provisional one and, being only provisional,
it could be reviewed. Counsel submitted on behalf of the Secretary of State that that was
an impossible reading of the relevant sections of the 1983 Act.

I should state for completeness that both Mr C and Miss L are now restricted patients
e under the 1983 Act, although the original orders were made under the 1959 Act. That is
because of transitional provisions in the 1983 Act in para 3 of Sch 5 to that Act.

In my judgment, the problem we have to solve is one which turns on the construction
of the 1983 Act. The ordinary canons of construction apply. It may be, as counsel for Mr
C and Miss L has suggested in the course of his submissions, that the Act is not all that
well drafted. It may be that some of those provisions could have been better drafted. It is
f not for us to make any comment about either of those suggestions. What we are
concerned to do is to find out from the words what the intention of Parliament was,
nothing more; and only if there is a clear ambiguity in any particular provision are we
entitled to look behind the words used to infer in other ways what the intention of
Parliament was.

I start by reminding myself what the fundamental policy of both the 1959 and 1983
g Acts was. As a result of a series of distressing cases which came before the courts in the
1950s it became obvious, both to Parliament and to the public, that patients were being
kept in hospital long after they required treatment, largely because of the difficulty of
discharging them into the community. The second problem was that, in the 1950s and
for many years before that, those who were convicted of criminal offences but were not
insane within the meaning of the M'Naghten rules had to be sent to prison. There was
h no power in the criminal courts before 1959 to send a convicted person who was suffering
from a mental disorder to a hospital. Parliament got over both those difficulties by the
provisions of the 1959 Act.

It is relevant for the court to remind itself why it was that the courts exercising
criminal jurisdiction were given power to recommend restrictions on release from a
hospital either limited or unlimited in time. The provisions of s 65 are now substantially
j reproduced in s 41(1) of the 1983 Act. That subsection is in these terms:

> 'Where a hospital order is made in respect of an offender by the Crown Court,
> and it appears to the court, having regard to the nature of the offence, the antecedents
> of the offender and the risk of his committing further offences if set at large, that it
> is necessary for the protection of the public from serious harm so to do, the court
> may, subject to the provisions of this section, further order that the offender shall be
> subject to the special restrictions set out in this section, either without limit of time

or during such period as may be specified in the order; and an order under this
section shall be known as "a restriction order".'

Under the 1959 Act the Secretary of State was entrusted with the decision whether to
release a patient in hospital pursuant to an order under s 60. That essentially was an
executive act. The European Court of Human Rights later decided that that was contrary
to the Convention for the Protection of Human Rights and Fundamental Freedoms
(Rome, 4 November 1950; TS 71 (1953); Cmd 8969) because a patient was being detained
not as a result of a decision of a duly constituted judicial body but as a result of an
executive action on the part of a Secretary of State (see *X v UK* (5 November 1981,
unreported)). The consequence was that, when Parliament came to pass a new Mental
Health Act in 1983, provision had to be made to deal with the decision of the European
Court of Human Rights, and the scheme was that no longer could the Secretary of State
be entrusted with the duty of deciding on release from hospital, but that duty should rest
on a mental health review tribunal.

The 1983 Act came into operation on 30 September 1983. Before that date mental
health review tribunals, which had been established under the 1959 Act, only had power
to recommend release and their recommendations could be, and indeed often were,
overruled by the Secretary of State. The 1983 Act, however, envisaged that the Secretary
of State still had an interest in cases involving patients subject to restriction. Clearly he
has. He is the guardian of the public welfare in this respect. As a consequence, the Act
itself gives him certain powers and, in addition, the rules made under the Act envisage
that he shall be entitled to make representations to a mental health review tribunal. It is
said that, as a result of what may have been an administrative error, he was deprived of
that opportunity.

Counsel for the Secretary of State in this court has accepted, however, that, if Woolf J
was right in thinking that the Oxford tribunal could reconvene and listen to his
representation, no harm would be done and, on the general principle that judicial review
should not be ordered if there is another suitable remedy, counsel for the Secretary of
State has not challenged that part of Woolf J's judgment if he was right in thinking, as he
did, that the Oxford tribunal had a power to reconsider.

It is appropriate now for me to invite attention to the detailed provisions of the 1983
Act which relate to patients under restriction. Part V of the Act deals with mental health
review tribunals, their constitution and powers. They are concerned with those who are
detained by law in a mental hospital. Patients who are detained under what used to be
s 26 of the 1959 Act can still be in a mental hospital, as can, of course, those who are there
because of orders made by the Crown Court under ss 37 and 41 of the 1983 Act. Section
72 of the 1983 Act comes under the heading 'Discharge of patients' and it is in these
terms (I quote only those parts applicable to restricted patients):

'(1) Where application is made to a Mental Health Review Tribunal by or in
respect of a patient who is liable to be detained under this Act [I interpose there that
that does not refer solely to restricted patients], the tribunal may in any case direct
that the patient be discharged, and—(a) the tribunal shall direct the discharge of a
patient liable to be detained under section 2 above if they are satisfied—(i) that he is
not then suffering from mental disorder or from mental disorder of a nature or
degree which warrants his detention in a hospital for assessment (or for assessment
followed by medical treatment) for at least a limited period; or (ii) that his detention
as aforesaid is not justified in the interests of his own health or safety or with a view
to the protection of other persons; (b) the tribunal shall direct the discharge of a
patient liable to be detained otherwise than under section 2 above if they are
satisfied—(i) that he is not then suffering from mental illness, psychopathic disorder,
severe mental impairment or mental impairment or from any of those forms of
disorder of a nature or degree which makes it appropriate for him to be liable to be
detained in a hospital for medical treatment; or (ii) that it is not necessary for the
health or safety of the patient or for the protection of other persons that he should
receive such treatment . . .'

I need not read any further because the rest of the subsection is not relevant to this case.

a It is clear that the intention of Parliament under s 72(1)(b) was that people should not be detained in hospital when it was no longer appropriate that they should be there for medical treatment. It is essentially a medical question under para (b)(i) and a mixed medical and social question under para (b)(ii). But s 72(7) says:

'Subsection (1) above shall not apply in the case of a restricted patient except as provided in sections 73 and 74 below.'

b Section 73(1) is in these terms:

'Where an application to a Mental Health Review Tribunal is made by a restricted patient who is subject to a restriction order, or where the case of such a patient is referred to such a tribunal, the tribunal shall direct the absolute discharge of the patient if satisfied—(a) as to the matters mentioned in paragraph (b)(i) or (ii) of
c section 72(1) above; and (b) that it is not appropriate for the patient to remain liable to be recalled to hospital for further treatment.'

It is to be noted that that subsection is mandatory. Subsection (2), which is the important subsection for the purposes of these appeals, is as follows:

'Where in the case of any such patient as is mentioned in subsection (1) above the
d tribunal are satisfied as to the matters referred to in paragraph (a) of that subsection but not as to the matter referred to in paragraph (b) of that subsection the tribunal shall direct the conditional discharge of the patient.'

Again, as counsel for Mr C and Miss L accepts, sub-s (2) is mandatory.

Therefore, the tribunal have to ask themselves whether the criteria mentioned in para
e (b)(i) and (ii) have been established to their satisfaction. But the tribunal must confine their attention to the criteria in those two sub-paragraphs. They are not entitled, as I read the subsection, to look at any other matter. Counsel for Mr C and Miss L, in his submissions to this court, although he has accepted that the criteria in s 73(2), once established, must lead to a particular result, nevertheless contends that, when considering the criteria in s 72(1)(b)(i), the tribunal are entitled to look at the need for social support.
f It is, he submitted, a factor to be taken into consideration when deciding whether those criteria have been established.

Counsel for the Secretary of State comments and, in my judgment, rightly comments that that means writing something into s 73(2) which is not there. The riposte of counsel for Mr C and Miss L to that is to say it is there by necessary implication, which arises from the wording of s 73(7). That subsection is in two parts, the parts being divided by a
g semicolon. The first and more important part for the purposes of these appeals is as follows:

'A tribunal may defer a direction for the conditional discharge of a patient until such arrangements as appear to the tribunal to be necessary for that purpose have been made to their satisfaction . . .'

h The submission of counsel for Mr C and Miss L has been that, when the tribunal is considering the matters which they have to consider under s 73(2) and they are of the opinion that arrangements will have to be made for the support of the patient in the community and in consequence defer their direction for a conditional discharge, they are only making a provisional decision. If, afterwards and before the arrangements have been made or, indeed, after they have been made, there is any change of circumstance,
j then they can reconsider their provisional decision and decide yea or nay whether to order a discharge conditional or absolute or, indeed, not to order a discharge at all.

This was an argument which attracted Woolf J, because he was of the opinion that it was a sensible construction to put on s 73(7), particularly in the kind of circumstances to which counsel for Mr C and Miss L invited his attention, namely when between the decision to defer and the contemplated date for discharge the patient had got worse or had got better so that there was no longer any need for arrangements at all.

The answer of counsel for the Secretary of State to that before Woolf J and his argument in this court has been that, if there is a deterioration in the patients' condition after the arrangements have been approved, the Secretary of State can exercise his powers to recall, which are set out in the body of the Act, so that, from the point of view of safeguarding the patient and the public, there is no problem. Counsel for the Secretary of State also pointed out that, in practice, there is unlikely to be any difficulty about the application of sub-s (7) because in most cases, whilst negotiations are going on to establish satisfactory arrangements, those responsible for the patient and for making the arrangments will be alerted to any deterioration, and there will be no need to do anything more than to say that, in all the circumstances, the arrangements are not satisfactory. But that is a pragmatic approach to this problem.

The legal problem with which this court has to deal is: what did Parliament intend by the words it used in s 73(2)? It seems to me clear on the wording of the Act that the mental health review tribunals are only entitled to take into account those matters which are specifically referred to in s 72(1)(b)(i) and (ii), nothing else at all, and, once they have become satisfied that the criteria in those sub-paragraphs are established either, as in the case of s 73(1), under both headings or, as in the case of sub-s (2), only the first heading, then they have to make an order. They cannot do anything else. As counsel for the Secretary of State pointed out, the mental health review tribunals have three options: one is to grant an absolute discharge, one to grant a conditional discharge and one to refuse any discharge. The Oxford Mental Health Review Tribunal decided that the first of the criteria applicable in sub-s (2) had been established and they directed conditional discharge. That was their decision. They must, however, have been of the opinion that it was necessary for the purposes of conditional discharge that arrangements should be made to their satisfaction for Mr C's support in the community. That was the only matter which was outstanding. There was no power to go back on their decision that Mr C's case was other than one for conditional discharge. It might well be that, had not events taken the course they did, suitable arrangements could have been made to the satisfaction of the Oxford tribunal. Equally, it is possible that they might not have been made and, as I read the section, if they were not so made, then the conditional discharge lapsed. But that was all that could happen.

In the case of Miss L, the Yorkshire Mental Health Review tribunal persuaded themselves that they could go back over the whole case again if she made progress whilst she was awaiting the making of suitable arrangements. For the reasons I have already indicated, once they had decided that Miss L was entitled to a conditional discharge, they could not go back on that part of the order. All they could do was to see whether such arrangements as they thought necessary for her support in the community had been made to their satisfaction. It is said that this is a narrow construction of the Act, particularly having regard to the use by Parliament of the words 'such arrangements as appear to the tribunal to be necessary for that purpose'; but, as counsel for the Secretary of State pointed out, the arrangements are for the purpose of conditional discharge, not for reconsidering whether there should be conditional discharge at all.

For those reasons, it appears to me that Woolf J misdirected himself when coming to the conclusion he did that there was a power to reconsider; and Kennedy J did the same. Kennedy J's view was more narrow than Woolf J's view but in the end it came to exactly the same. That being so, it seems to me clear, on the proper construction of the 1983 Act, that there never has been a power to reconsider in either the Oxford or the Yorkshire mental health review tribunals or in any other tribunal. Once a decision has been made, they must stand by it and all that they are concerned with thereafter is the approval of such arrangements as they think necessary for accomplishing conditional discharge.

That being so, the court then has to consider, in the case of Mr C, what action should next follow. Counsel for Mr C and Miss L, rather surprisingly, submitted that the fact that the Secretary of State was not given an opportunity of making representations to the Oxford tribunal was a mere irregularity and, under the Mental Health Review Tribunal Rules 1983, it was an irregularity which could be waived. There are difficulties about that, however. Rule 28 says:

a
'Any irregularity resulting from failure to comply with these Rules before the tribunal has determined an application shall not of itself render the proceedings void, but the tribunal may, and shall, if it considers that any person may have been prejudiced, take such steps as it thinks fit before determining the application to cure the irregularity, whether by the amendment of any document, the giving of any notice, the taking of any step or otherwise.'

b
The short answer of counsel for the Secretary of State was this. Once the tribunal had made the decision which they did make on 12 February 1985, the irregularity just could not be cured. The Secretary of State had lost his right to make any representation and, as the tribunal had no power to reconvene to reconsider, it followed that there was nothing that the Secretary of State could do.

In my judgment, this was a classic case of a failure of natural justice entitling the court to intervene by ordering judicial review. In future, in order to avoid the kind of mishap
c
which occurred in this case, tribunals, before starting to hear any application when the Secretary of State is not represented, should inquire, and note, whether he has been given notice of the application and when. In Miss L's case the tribunal did misdirect themselves thinking that they had power to reconsider her case and, accordingly, to that extent their decision was wrong and can be remedied by this court.

I would allow the Secretary of State's appeals.
d

STEPHEN BROWN LJ. I agree that these appeals should both be allowed for the reasons given by Lawton LJ.

I would only add that it appears to me that the submissions of counsel for Mr C and Miss L, so attractively made to this court, would, in effect, involve a rewriting of this statute. He contends for an interpretation of s 73(7) which would involve rewriting the
e
first line by substituting the following for the first sentence: 'A tribunal may defer *consideration* of a direction for the conditional discharge of a patient until such arrangements as appear to the tribunal to be necessary for that purpose have been made to their satisfaction.' The section does not say that. The language of the section, in my judgment, assumes that the decision has already been arrived at, as indeed each of the decisions of these two tribunals indicates. In my judgment, the section has to be
f
interpreted in the way which counsel for the Secretary of State has submitted.

SIR JOHN MEGAW. I agree with the judgments which Lawton and Stephen Brown LJJ have given. I would add that I think that the terms in which the rules have been formulated provide strong support for the construction of s 73(7) which has been put forward on behalf of the Secretary of State.
g
Woolf J, in his judgment, dealing, I think, at that point with the question of the judicial review matter, said:

'What will happen on the basis of the view I have taken is that the tribunal will be required to reconsider the matter in the light of the material which the Secretary of State wants to put before the tribunal and it may be that they will as a result alter their provisional decision.'
h
With great respect, I think that that is a misconstruction of the rules.

Rule 2 of the Mental Health Review Tribunal Rules 1983, SI 1983/942, among the definitions, provides a definition of 'provisional decision'. It defines it as including a deferred direction for conditional discharge in accordance with s 73(7) of the Act. There is, therefore, no doubt that, where the rules refer to a provisional decision, they are
j
referring to a deferred direction under s 73(7).

If we turn on then in the rules to r 23, we find that, by virtue of r 23(3), the tribunal are obliged to record in writing their provisional decisions as much as their final decisions; and that record is to be signed by the president, giving the reasons for the decision. It has to be, by r 24, communicated to the parties concerned.

Then one turns on to r 25. Rules 25(1) provides quite simply, quite clearly and quite specifically:

'Where the tribunal has made a provisional decision, any further decision in the proceedings may be made without a further hearing.'

a

True, it is 'may'. True, therefore, a tribunal, having made a provisional decision, including a deferment of a direction under s 73(7), *may* thereafter require a further hearing; but, as a matter of law, under the rules they are not obliged to do so. Therefore, with great respect, I suggest that Woolf J erred in saying that the tribunal will be *required* to reconsider the matter.

When one looks at it, not from the point of view of the facts of an individual case but on the general construction of these provisions, it appears to me very unlikely that the rules would have provided that a decision under s 73(7) could be made without the necessity for a further hearing, if, indeed, as counsel for Mr C and Miss L submits, the rule permits that the 'further decision' which is to be made under s 73(7) may be a decision which can result in drastic alterations to the effect of the provisional decision. It might affect the applicant even more gravely than the Secretary of State or the public, if that were so.

b

c

For that reason also I think that the appeals must be allowed.

Appeals allowed. No order for costs save legal aid taxation. The hearing to be before a differently constituted tribunal. Leave to appeal to the House of Lords refused.

d

Solicitors: *Treasury Solicitor*; *Alexander & Partners* (for Mr C); *Irwin Mitchell*, Sheffield (for Miss L).

Mary Rose Plummer   Barrister.

e

Nanan v The State

PRIVY COUNCIL

LORD BRIDGE OF HARWICH, LORD BRIGHTMAN, LORD MACKAY OF CLASHFERN, LORD ACKNER AND LORD GOFF OF CHIEVELEY

17 MARCH, 22 MAY 1986

f

Trinidad and Tobago – Jury – Verdict – Verdict announced as unanimous – Four jurors subsequently stating they had disagreed with verdict – Verdict returned in sight and hearing of all jurors without protest – Whether evidence of jurors that they had disagreed with verdict admissible on appeal – Whether trial judge required to direct jury that verdict must be unanimous.

g

Under the law of Trinidad and Tobago the unanimous verdict of a jury of 12 persons was necessary for convictions of murder or treason whereas a majority of seven out of a jury of nine sufficed for other crimes. At the trial of the appellant for murder the judge in his summing up to the jury omitted any reference to the necessity for a unanimous verdict. When the jury returned to the courtroom after their deliberations, the clerk of the court asked the foreman in open court and in the hearing of the other members of the jury whether they had reached a unanimous verdict. The foreman clearly and unhesitatingly answered in the affirmative and then stated that they had found the appellant guilty. None of the jurors protested against either pronouncement. The next day the foreman informed the court registrar that he did not know the meaning of the word 'unanimous' and that when the clerk of the court asked him whether the jury had reached a unanimous verdict he thought he meant a majority decision. The foreman further stated that the decision to convict was in fact reached by a decision of eight to four. An application by the appellant that the trial judge state a case for the opinion of the Court of Appeal whether the verdict was valid was refused. The appellant than applied for a declaration that the verdict and his conviction and sentence were all void on the ground that the verdict was not unanimous, and supported that application by affidavits from

h

j

the foreman and three other members of the jury in which they each deposed that they
a were unaware that their decision had to be unanimous. None of the deponents stated
how he had made that error or that he did not understand the meaning of the word
'unanimous'. The application was refused on the ground that the evidence of the jurors
as to their state of mind invaded the privacy of the jury room and evidence of
misapprehension on the part of a juror was inadmissible. The appellant appealed to the
Court of Appeal, which dismissed his appeal. He appealed to the Privy Council.

b
Held – The appeal would be dismissed for the following reasons—
(1) Where a verdict had been given within the sight and hearing of the entire jury
without any expression of dissent by any member of it, there was a presumption that
they had all assented to it. That presumption could, however, be rebutted, eg if the
verdict was not pronounced in the sight and hearing of one or more members of the
c jury, who did not in fact agree with the verdict or who might not have done so, or if a
juryman was not competent to understand the proceedings. However, evidence was not
admissible from a member of the jury who simply sought to assert that he did not in fact
agree with the verdict, or that his apparent agreement with the verdict resulted from a
misapprehension on his part. Since the proffered affidavit evidence showed no more than
that for some unexplained reason four members of the jury were acting under a
d misapprehension in agreeing to a verdict of guilty, that evidence was not admissible to
rebut the presumption of assent (see p 253 *c* to *e*, p 254 *a* to *f* and p 256 *h*, post); dicta of
Atkin LJ in *Ellis v Deheer* [1922] All ER Rep at 454 and of Lord Denning MR and Harman
LJ in *Boston v W S Bagshaw & Sons* [1967] 2 All ER at 88–89 applied.
(2) Where unanimity of verdict was required by law there was no rule of law requiring
the judge to direct the jury in his summing up on the need for unanimity. Instead, the
e crucial requirement was that the verdict be taken from the jury by questions which were
so designed as to ensure beyond all reasonable doubt that the verdict was unanimous.
Accordingly, the lack of any direction by the trial judge that the verdict had to be
unanimous did not affect the validity of the verdict and, on the facts, the question put to
the jury by the clerk of the court was clear and unambiguous that the jury had to agree
on a unanimous verdict (see p 254 *j*, p 255 *c d* and p 256 *h*, post); dictum of Barwick CJ
f in *Milgate v R* (1964) 38 ALJR at 162 adopted.

Notes
For evidence by jurors, see 26 Halsbury's Laws (4th edn) para 647, and for cases on the
subject, see 30 Digest (Reissue) 348–349, 671–690.

g **Cases referred to in judgment**
Boston v W S Bagshaw & Sons [1967] 2 All ER 87, [1966] 1 WLR 1135, CA.
Ellis v Deheer [1922] KB 113, [1922] All ER Rep 451, CA.
Mansell v R (1857) 8 E & B 54, 169 ER 1048, Ex Ch.
Milgate v R (1964) 38 ALJR 162, Aust HC.
Nesbitt v Parrett (1902) 18 TLR 510, CA.
h *R v Davey, R v Davey* [1960] 3 All ER 533, [1960] 1 WLR 1287, CCA.
R v Roads [1967] 2 All ER 84, [1967] 2 QB 108, [1967] 2 WLR 1014, CA.
R v Wooler (1817) 6 M & S 366, 171 ER 589.
Raphael v Bank of England (1855) 17 CB 161, 139 ER 1030.
Ras Behari Lal v R (1933) 102 LJPC 144, [1933] All ER Rep 723.

j **Consolidated appeals**
Lalchan Nanan appealed (1) by special leave of the Judicial Committee in forma pauperis
against the judgment of the Court of Appeal of Trinidad and Tobago (Hyatali CJ, Phillips
and Kelsick JJA) on 29 June 1979 dismissing his appeal against his conviction for murder
before Warner J and a jury on 4 July 1977 and (2) with leave of the Court of Appeal
against the decision of the Court of Appeal (Hyatali CJ, Kelsick and Hassanali JJA) on 22

June 1979 dismissing his appeal from the judgment and order of Braithwaite J on 31
January 1978 dismissing an originating motion filed by the appellant and dated 23   *a*
August 1977 in which the appellant sought, inter alia, a declaration that his constitutional
rights were being infringed. The facts are set out in the judgment of the Board.

David Turner-Samuels QC, Ramesh Maharaj (of the Trinidad and Tobago Bar) and *William
Birtles* for the appellant.
George Newman QC, Mark Strachan and *The Solicitor General of Trinidad and Tobago (Lionel*   *b*
Jones) for the respondent.

22 May. The following judgment of the Board was delivered.

LORD GOFF OF CHIEVELEY. The appellant, Lalchan Nanan, was charged with
the murder of his wife, Eileen Nanan, on 26 December 1974. On 4 July 1977, following   *c*
a trial before Warner J and a jury, he was convicted of murder and sentenced to death.
    Under the law of Trinidad and Tobago, a person can only be convicted of the crimes of
murder or treason by the unanimous verdict of a jury of 12 persons, whereas, in the case
of other crimes, a person may be convicted by a majority verdict of a jury of nine persons,
the required majority being seven out of a jury of nine (see ss 16 and 24 of the Jury
Ordinance 1950 of Trinidad and Tobago). The appellant was tried by a jury of 12. The   *d*
trial judge did not, in the course of his summing up, refer to the necessity for a
unanimous verdict. On 4 July, at the conclusion of the summing up, the jury withdrew
at 2.17 pm to consider their verdict. They returned to the courtroom at 4.05 pm on the
same afternoon. After the whole jury had returned to the courtroom, the clerk of the
court asked the foreman to stand; the foreman did so. The clerk of the court then, in the
presence and hearing of the judge, of counsel, and of all the members of the jury, asked   *e*
the foreman whether he and the other members of the jury had agreed on a unanimous
verdict in respect of the accused, to which the foreman replied in the affirmative, the
reply being clear and unhesitating. The clerk of the court then asked the foreman
whether the accused was guilty or not guilty as charged, to which the foreman replied,
loudly and clearly, that the accused was guilty. There was no protest from any of the
jurors, none of whom said anything. The judge then proceeded to pass sentence.   *f*
Thereafter, on the same day, a notice of application was given for leave to appeal against
conviction, though without any grounds being given at that stage.
    On the following day, 5 July, the foreman of the jury, accompanied by another juror,
called on the registrar of the Supreme Court and informed him that, when the clerk of
the court asked him whether the jurors had arrived at a unanimous verdict, he thought
that the clerk meant a majority verdict; and that although he answered the question in   *g*
the affirmative, the jury were really divided eight to four in favour of a conviction. He
also said that he did not know the meaning of the word 'unanimous'. The other juror
informed the registrar that she was one of the four jurors who had some doubt and that
she had given the benefit of the doubt to the accused. On 11 July the registrar wrote to
counsel who had appeared for the appellant at his trial, and informed him of what had
passed. On 15 July the matter was brought to the attention of the judge, Warner J, on a   *h*
motion that he should state a case for the opinion of the Court of Appeal as to whether
the verdict was valid; but on 21 July he dismissed the motion, on the ground that the
question was based on a report made to the registrar on the day after the trial had been
concluded.
    The appellant did not appeal from that decision; but on 23 August 1977 an originating
motion was filed on his behalf, seeking declarations under s 4 of the Constitution of the   *j*
Republic of Trinidad and Tobago that (a) his constitutional right not to be deprived of
his life except by due process of law guaranteed to him by s 4(a) of the Constitution had
been, was being or was likely to be infringed, and (b) the verdict of the jury at his trial
and his consequent conviction and sentence were all void and of no effect because the
verdict was not unanimous. Affidavits were sworn in support of the application by the
foreman of the jury and by three other jurors. They were all sworn on 18 August and

were to all intent and purposes identical, each deponent stating that he or she was not
aware that all of the 12 jurors had to be agreed on the verdict, and that there was in fact a
division of eight in favour of one verdict and four in favour of another. No deponent
stated how he or she had come to make such an error, nor that he or she did not
understand the meaning of the work 'unanimous' used by the clerk of the court when
addressing the foreman of the jury. (Affidavits in similar terms had previously been
placed before Warner J on the hearing before him.)

The originating motion came on for hearing before Braithwaite J who, in a judgment
delivered on 31 January 1978, dismissed the motion. The case was presented to him on
the basis that the entire trial had been conducted according to the law of the land; as to
that, there was no disagreement expressed by counsel for the applicant (the present
appellant). Braithwaite J also stated that he could not accept that anything in the question
put by the clerk of the court to the foreman of the jury could by any stretch of
imagination have misled or confused the jury. But in any event he concluded that, on
the authorities, the evidence of the jurors as to their state of mind was inadmissible in
evidence; and that, since it followed that there was no evidence to support the motion, it
must fail.

An appeal against the decision of Braithwaite J was filed on 12 April 1978. In his
grounds of appeal, the appellant no longer contended that the verdict of the jury was
void and of no effect. On 27 April 1978 the Court of Appeal heard the appellant's appeal
against his conviction. On that appeal, which will be referred to as 'the criminal appeal',
no complaint was made about the circumstances in which the jury came to give their
verdict. The grounds of appeal consisted of allegations that the judge had erred in failing
to accede to a submission by counsel for the appellant at the close of the prosecution case;
that he misdirected the jury on identification, on alibi and on circumstantial evidence;
that he failed to put the defence case adequately to the jury. At the close of the argument
on the criminal appeal, counsel informed the court that the other appeal (which will be
referred to as 'the constitutional appeal') was being pursued, and the Court of Appeal
thereupon reserved their judgment on the criminal appeal pending the outcome of the
constitutional appeal.

Judgment was given by the Court of Appeal on the constitutional appeal on 22 June
1979. The court unanimously dismissed the appeal from Braithwaite J. Hyatali CJ
considered that two issues were raised by the appeal: first, whether the High Court had
jurisdiction to entertain the appellant's application; and, second, whether, if there was
such jurisdiction the judge was right to refuse to admit the affidavit evidence of the four
jurors. Since, however, the debate before Braithwaite J had centred on the admissibility
of the affidavit evidence, he considered that issue first. He expressed considerable
scepticism about that evidence, drawing attention to a number of factors which cast
doubt on its credibility, notably that the question put to the foreman was not whether
the jury had arrived at a verdict as suggested in the affidavits, but whether he and the
other members of the jury had agreed on a unanimous verdict; and that no member of
the jury dissented from the verdict announced by the foreman in the presence and
hearing of all the jurors when, according to the four deponents, it was a verdict on which
the foreman and the other members were not in fact agreed. Having regard to these
matters, Hyatali CJ said that 'it is difficult to resist the conclusion that the bona fides of
the four jurors herein are open to question'. However, he went on to consider the
admissibility of the affidavits. Having reviewed the authorities with great care, he
concluded, in agreement with Braithwaite J, that, in so far as the affidavits alleged that
the jury were divided eight to four on their verdict, the affidavits were inadmissible on
the ground that they sought to invade the privacy of the discussions in the jury box and
the retiring room; and in so far as they alleged misunderstanding of the kind contended
for, the authorities militated against their reception to rebut the presumption of assent.

Hyatali CJ then turned to the first of the two questions which he had identified, viz
the question of jurisdiction; and he concluded that it was tolerably clear that the High
Court had no jurisdiction to entertain the motion, first because no complaint was made
therein of an infringement of a fundamental rule of natural justice, and second because

the error alleged was one of substantive law arising out of a judgment or order of the
trial court which was liable to be, or capable of being, set aside on appeal on the ground *a*
that there was a miscarriage of justice.

Kelsick JA also concluded that the motion should be dismissed on the ground that the
matter complained of was not a contravention of one of the rules of natural justice. He
went on, however, to hold that the question of the validity of the verdict could have
been, but was not, taken on the appellant's appeal against his conviction. For that reason,
he did not feel it necessary to deal with the question whether the affidavit evidence of *b*
the jurors was admissible; but he went on to consider the point, out of deference to the
argument addressed to the court. He concluded that evidence of what had occurred in
the jury box or in the retiring room was inadmissible, but that evidence that the four
jurors were not aware, when the foreman announced his verdict, that each of the 12
jurors had to be agreed on a verdict and that they believed that the verdict could be a
majority verdict was admissible. However, he went on to point out that in none of the *c*
affidavits was it stated that the word 'unanimous' was not used by the clerk of the court,
or that the deponent was incompetent through insufficient knowledge of the English
language and in consequence of which he misunderstood the meaning of the word
'unanimous'. Indeed, in his opinion no valid reasons were stated by any of the deponents
for having been unaware of the requirement of unanimity to the verdict. In these
circumstances, notwithstanding that the evidence was in his opinion admissible in part, *d*
his conclusion was that there was no admissible evidence which rebutted the presumption
of competence or assent of any of the jurors.

Hassanali JA considered that, even assuming that there was such an error as was alleged
in the affidavits, the error did not constitute an infringement of any of the appellant's
rights guaranteed under s 4(a) of the Constitution, and the remedy for the alleged error
was by way of appeal to the Court of Appeal from the appellant's conviction. For that *e*
reason alone, in his opinion, Braithwaite J ought to have dismissed the motion. With
respect to the admissibility of the affidavit evidence, he considered that there were two
principles well established by the authorities: (a) When a verdict is delivered in the sight
and hearing of all the jury without protest, a rebuttable presumption arises that all the
jurors had assented to it, and (b) for the purposes of setting aside the verdict of a jury
evidence is not admissible from jurors to prove what discussions took place in the jury *f*
room. After reviewing the authorities, he said:

> 'Here it is not in dispute that the trial judge ascertained the jury's "unanimous
> verdict" by the time-honoured practice of addressing two questions through the
> clerk of the court to the foreman in the presence and hearing of all the jurors and
> that the answers given by the foreman unequivocally indicated that he and the
> other members of the jury had agreed on such a verdict ... It seems necessary *g*
> however only to observe that the verdict having been given in the presence and
> hearing of all the jurors, without protest, and accepted by the judge, and the jury
> discharged, the jurors are not at liberty afterwards to say that they did not mean a
> "unanimous" verdict. Counsel for the appellant remarked in the course of his
> submissions that the word "unanimous" was not used in the course of the summing
> up to the jury nor was its meaning explained to them. It is, however, immaterial *h*
> that the judge did not refer, or that the record does not show that he referred, in his
> summing up or at any time during the trial, to the word "unanimous". No rule of
> law or of practice required him to do so. On the other hand, there is nothing on the
> record to show that the trial was, up to the time that sentence was passed on the
> appellant, conducted otherwise than in accordance with the procedure prescribed to
> be followed and which ought to have been followed in his case in compliance with *j*
> all statutory and other provisions of the relevant law. The appellant does not allege
> that any one of the jurors did not understand the English language, or was otherwise
> for physical or other reasons not competent to follow the proceedings. What the
> appellant alleges in effect is that the foreman might have thought the word
> "unanimous" meant "majority"; that four jurors were under the misapprehension
> that the jury were free to return a majority verdict at the time that they gave their

a verdict in the case; and further that the jury had in fact earlier reached a majority
verdict in the jury room. As has already been noted, there is no indication as to what
was the source of the misapprehension. However, the consequence (ie the majority
verdict) which allegedly flowed from the misapprehension may be evidenced only
by reference to what transpired in the jury room. In my judgment the affidavits of
the jurors are not receivable in evidence . . .'

b For these reasons, the Court of Appeal dismissed the constitutional appeal, but gave leave
to appeal to the Privy Council.

A few days later, on 29 June 1979, the Court of Appeal also dismissed the criminal
appeal, in which no question had been raised regarding the unanimity of the jury's
verdict. Subsequently, the Privy Council granted leave to appeal in the criminal appeal,
and directed that the two appeals be consolidated.

c In presenting the appeal before their Lordships, counsel for the appellant had to face
the fact that there is indeed a well-established general principle as stated by Atkin LJ in
Ellis v Deheer [1922] 2 KB 113 at 121, [1922] All ER Rep 451 at 454 that—

'the court does not admit evidence of a juryman as to what took place in the jury
room, either by way of explanation of the grounds upon which the verdict was
given, or by way of statement as to what he believed its effect to be.'

d The same principle applies to discussions between jurymen in the jury box itself. If a
juryman disagrees with the verdict pronounced by the foreman of the jury on his behalf,
he should express his dissent forthwith; if he does not do so, there is a presumption that
he assented to it. It follows that, where a verdict has been given in the sight and hearing
of an entire jury without any expression of dissent by any member of the jury, the court
e will not thereafter receive evidence from a member of the jury that he did not in fact
agree with the verdict, or that his apparent agreement with the verdict resulted from a
misapprehension on his part.

This principle can be traced back at least as far as the decision of the Court of Queen's
Bench in *R v Wooler* (1817) 6 M & S 366, 171 ER 589; but it has been confirmed on
numerous occasions, for example, in *Raphael v Bank of England* (1855) 17 CB 161, 139 ER
f 1030, *Nesbitt v Parrett* (1902) 18 TLR 510, *Ellis v Deheer* [1922] 2 KB 113, [1922] All ER
Rep 451, *Ras Behari Lal v R* (1933) 102 LJPC 144, [1933] All ER Rep 723, *Boston v W S
Bagshaw & Sons* [1967] 2 All ER 87, [1966] 1 WLR 1135 and *R v Roads* [1967] 2 All ER
84, [1967] 2 QB 108. So the court has refused to receive evidence from a juror that he did
not understand the effect of an answer given by the foreman of the jury to a question put
by the trial judge (see *Raphael v Bank of England*), or that he did not in fact agree with the
g verdict as announced (see *Nesbitt v Parrett*), or, that he was suffering from a misapprehension when he agreed to answers given by the foreman of the jury (see *Boston v
Bagshaw*), or that he disagreed with the verdict but was too frightened to stand up and
say so (see *R v Roads*).

Two reasons of policy have been given as underlying the principle. The first is the
need to ensure that decisions of juries are final; the second is the need to protect jurymen
h from inducement or pressure either to reveal what has passed in the juryroom, or to alter
their view (see *Ellis v Deheer* [1922] 2 KB 113 at 121, [1922] All ER Rep 451 at 454 per
Atkin LJ). Lord Denning MR expressed the principle very clearly in *Boston v W S Bagshaw
& Sons* [1967] 2 All ER 87 at 88, [1966] 1 WLR 1135 at 1136 when he said:

'To my mind it is settled as well as anything can be that it is not open to the court
j to receive any such evidence as this. Once a jury have given their verdict, and it has
been accepted by the judge, and they have been discharged, they are not at liberty
to say they meant something different.'

In the same case Harman LJ said ([1967] 2 All ER 87 at 89, [1966] 1 WLR 1135 at 1137):

'It would be destructive of all trials by jury if we were to accede to this application.
There would be no end to it. One would always find one juryman who said: "that

was not what I meant" and you would have to start the whole thing anew. Interest reipublicae ut sit finis litium.'

It is, of course, entirely consistent with this principle that evidence may be given that the verdict was not pronounced in the sight and hearing of one or more members of the jury, who did not in fact agree with that verdict, or who may not have done so (see *R v Wooler* and *Ellis v Deheer*). In such a case, the confidence of the juryroom can be breached in so far as a juryman, outside whose sight and hearing the verdict was pronounced, may give evidence whether he did or did not agree with that verdict.

It is also consistent with the above principle that evidence may be given that a juryman was not competent to understand the proceedings in which event, if such evidence is accepted, the ordinary course would be to award a venire de novo: see *Ras Behari Lal v R*, in which tribute was paid to an earlier discussion on the subject by Lord Campbell CJ in *Mansell v R* (1857) 8 E & B 54 at 80, 169 ER 1048 at 1060. In such a case, as Lord Atkin pointed out in *Ras Behari Lal v R* 102 LJPC 144 at 146, [1933] All ER Rep 723 at 725:

'The objection is not that he did not assent to the verdict, but that he so assented without being qualified to assent.'

That case shows, however, that the mere fact that a verdict had been pronounced in the sight and hearing of all the jury without protest, does not lead to an irrebuttable presumption of assent. As Atkin LJ said in *Ellis v Deheer* [1922] 2 KB 113 at 120, [1922] All ER Rep 451 there will in such circumstances be—

'a prima facie presumption that all assented to it, but that presumption may be rebuted. Circumstances may arise in connection with the delivery of the verdict showing that they did not all assent.'

Ras Behari Lal v R provides an example of a case where the presumption may be rebutted. Their Lordships do not wish to be thought to exclude altogether the possibility that other cases may arise in future where the presumption may be rebutted. But they consider that, having regard to the general principle which they have stated, evidence will not be admitted simply to assert that a juror did not in fact agree with the verdict, or that his apparent agreement resulted from a misapprehension on his part.

The affidavit evidence which Braithwaite J was invited to admit in the present case was, in the opinion of their Lordships, no more than evidence which, if accepted, showed that (for some unexplained reason) four members of the jury, including the foreman, were acting under a misapprehension in agreeing to a verdict of guilty. In agreement with Braithwaite J and with Hyatali CJ and Hassanali JA in the Court of Appeal, their Lordships are of the opinion that none of the evidence was admissible, in that to admit it would have been contrary to the principle stated above. It may be said that the alleged misapprehension in the present case, if it existed, was of a fundamental kind; but the same may be said of other misapprehensions, for example as to the facts of the case or as to the applicable law, which can likewise lead to an erroneous verdict. In such cases, however, evidence of the misapprehension is equally inadmissible.

Counsel for the appellant sought to escape from this conclusion by adumbrating a possible exception to the principle. He submitted that, in all cases where a unanimous verdict is required of a jury before the accused can be convicted, it is necessary to ask the jury, after the foreman has given the verdict of the jury, whether the verdict is one on which all the members of the jury are agreed; and that, if that question is not asked at that stage, evidence can be given by a juror that he did not in fact agree to the verdict. The submission was that, only by asking such a question of the jury after the verdict has been given, can the court be certain that members of the jury have expressed their agreement to the verdict so given. Their Lordships can, however, see no basis for any such qualification to the principle.

Counsel for the appellant next submitted that it was necessary for the court to direct the jury on the need for unanimity, where unanimity is required by law. In England, before majority verdicts were introduced, it was not considered necessary for the judge a to give any such direction; all that was required was that, when the verdict of the jury was taken, it should be ensured that the verdict, if one of guilty, was one on which all the members of the jury were agreed. However, the present case can be distinguished in that, under the law of Trinidad and Tobago, unanimous verdicts are required in certain cases (murder and treason), whereas majority verdicts (of a smaller jury) are accepted in others. Even so, counsel, in advancing this submission, suffered under the handicap that no such submission was advanced below; and further that it was stated by Braithwaite J

b that counsel did not disagree with the proposition that the entire trial had been conducted in accordance with the law of the land, and by Hassanali JA that the trial judge ascertained the jury's unanimous verdict by—

> 'the time-honoured practice of addressing two questions through the clerk of the court to the foreman in the presence and hearing of all the jurors'

c and that no rule of law or practice required the judge to refer to the need for unanimity.

Their Lordships find themselves unable to accept counsel for the appellant's submission, advanced for the first time before the Board, that this time-honoured practice is defective. The crucial requirement is that the verdict should be taken from the jury by questions which are so designed as to ensure, beyond all reasonable doubt, that the verdict of the jury is a unanimous verdict. Here, the question put to the jury by the clerk of the court,

d whether the foreman and the other members of the jury had agreed on a unanimous verdict, not only reflected the words of s 16 of the Jury Ordinance but was so clear as to admit of no ambiguity. That was certainly the view of the judges involved in the case in Trinidad and Tobago. Braithwaite J said that 'it is difficult, if not impossible, for me to see that there was any ambiguity or equivocability about the clerk's question'. With that statement, Hyatali CJ agreed, and it is clear that Hassanali JA took the same view. In

e these circumstances, it would be quite wrong for their Lordships, who are not so familiar with conditions prevailing in Trinidad and Tobago, to form the opinion that the words used by the clerk of the court, which are clear on their face, were open to misunderstanding by members of the public in that country.

Their Lordships' conclusion on this point is consistent with that reached by the High Court of Australia in *Milgate v R* (1964) 38 ALJR 162. They find it helpful, moreover, to

f refer to the judgment of Barwick CJ in that case, where he said (at 162):

> 'The applicant also submitted that the failure of the trial judge expressly to tell the jury that their verdict must be unanimous was a ground for a new trial. In my opinion this is not so. There is in Queensland neither a rule of law nor a rule of practice that a jury in a criminal trial must be told by the trial judge that their verdict must be unanimous. The law and practice of England is the same. The
> g interrogation of the jury by the Clerk of Arraigns upon the return of their verdict by their foreman is the traditional method of ensuring unanimity on the part of the jury, coupled to some extent with the form of the oath individually administered to each juror. Whilst the trial judge should not leave the jury to think that a general consensus, as distinct from unanimity, will suffice (see *R. v. Davey* ([1960] 3 All ER 533, [1960] 1 WLR 1287)) there is no imperative need for him in the summing-up
> h to tell them that their verdict must be unanimous. But several factors leave me to think that great care should be exercised by the Clerk of Arraigns and by the presiding judge as to the manner in which the Clerk of Arraigns expresses to the jury the traditional formula: "Are you agreed on your verdict?" . . . "So says your foreman, so say you all?". Today probably more so than in earlier times, many decisions are taken in corporate and social life by majority or even by the expression
> j of a broad consensus of opinion without actual counting of heads. In Australia some States allow of a majority verdict in criminal cases at least in some circumstances . . . Substantial number of people move from one State to another. Also we have an increasing number of migrants who, although they become naturalised, may not be as familiar with the traditional requirements of our jury system as we expect our Australian-born citizens to be. Therefore the Clerk of Arraigns' formula on the

taking of a verdict should not be expressed in a perfunctory way nor allowed to
appear as a mere statement of an assumed or concluded state of affairs, but should   *a*
be clearly interrogative of the members of the jury. Indeed, some thought might
well be given to the modernization of its terms to remove any possibility of
misunderstanding or inadvertence. In addition, the presiding judge, depending on
the circumstances of the trial, may feel that these precautions should be fortified by
an express direction in the course of the summing-up.'

That statement of the law, their Lordships consider, is equally applicable in Trinidad and   *b*
Tobago, in those cases where a unanimous verdict is required. It may be that, like
Barwick CJ, the courts in Trinidad and Tobago may think (though it is a matter for
them) that some thought might be given to the modernisation of the formula at present
in use, to remove any possibility of misunderstanding or inadvertence, such as, for
example, by requiring the clerk of the court to conclude his questions by inquiring
whether the verdict which has been given is a verdict on which all members of the jury   *c*
are agreed, possibly fortified by an express direction by the trial judge in the course of
the summing up.

Their Lordships turn to the constitutional appeal. The relevant provision of the
Constitution of Trinidad and Tobago, which is to be found in s 4(*a*) of the Constitution,
provides as follows:

                                                                                                                             d

    'It is hereby recognised and declared that in Trinidad and Tobago there have
    existed and shall continue to exist, without discrimination by reason of race, origin,
    colour, religion or sex, the following fundamental human rights and freedoms:—
    (*a*) the right of the individual to life, liberty, security of the person and enjoyment
    of property and the right not to be deprived thereof except by due process of law
    ...'

                                                                                                                        e

The submission of counsel for the appellant was that the verdict of the jury was not in
fact unanimous, and that therefore his constitutional rights had been infringed and he
was likely to be deprived of his life other than by due process of law. This submission
therefore depended, as did his appeal against conviction in the criminal appeal, on the
admissibility of the evidence of the four jurors. Counsel submitted that, even if that
evidence was inadmissible in the criminal appeal, nevertheless it should have been held   *f*
to be admissible in the constitutional appeal, on the ground that that appeal raised a
question of fundamental rights. For, if the jurors' verdict was not in fact unanimous,
there had been a failure of due process of law; and it would be quite wrong if no
protection was given by the Constitution where there had been a failure of communication
and understanding resulting in a verdict which did not express the view of a juryman.

Their Lordships are, however, unable to accept this submission. They can see no reason   *g*
why the principle they have set out above should not be equally apt to render a juryman's
evidence inadmissiable, whether the relevant preceedings take the form of an appeal
against conviction, or the form of a declaration that a person's rights under the
Constitution have been infringed. Indeed, if counsel for the appellant's submission were
to be accepted, it would result in the principle being disregarded in any case where the
complainant had been sentenced to imprisonment, and so would to a very substantial   *h*
extent undermine the principle and the policy of the law on which it is founded.

For these reasons, their Lordships dismiss the consolidated appeals.

Appeals dismissed.

Solicitors: *Ingledew Brown Bennison & Garrett* (for the appellant); *Charles Russell & Co* (for
the respondent).

                                                              Mary Rose Plummer   Barrister.

a # Standard Chartered Bank v International Tin Council and others

QUEEN'S BENCH DIVISION (COMMERCIAL COURT)
BINGHAM J
15, 16, 17 APRIL 1986

b

Constitutional law – Foreign sovereign state – Immunity from suit – International organisation – Waiver of immunity – Bank lending money to International Tin Council – Tin Council agreeing to submit irrevocably to jurisdiction of English courts – Whether Tin Council waiving immunity – Extent of Tin Council's sovereign status – International Tin Council (Immunities and Privileges) Order 1972, para 6(1).

c

The International Tin Council (the ITC) was an international organisation operating under a series of international agreements with the object of promoting an orderly market in tin. In 1972 by a Headquarters Agreement made between the United Kingdom government and the ITC it was provided that the ITC should have legal personality and the capacity to enter into contracts and that its archives and premises should be inviolable.

d It was further provided, by art 8[a] of the agreement, that the ITC was to enjoy 'immunity from jurisdiction and execution except . . . to the extent that the [ITC] shall have expressly waived such immunity in a particular case'. Article 6(1)(a)[b] of the International Tin Council Immunities and Privileges Order 1972 provided that the ITC was to enjoy immunity 'from suit and legal process except . . . to the extent that the [ITC] shall have expressly waived such immunity in a particular case'. In July 1982 a bank lent £10m to the ITC on terms set out in a facility letter, cl 7 of which provided that the loan was to be governed by, and interpreted in all respects in accordance with, English law and the ITC was to submit irrevocably to the jurisdiction of the English courts. In 1985 the bank issued a writ against the ITC on the ground that the ITC had defaulted in repayment of the loan and interest. The ITC applied to set aside the writ and service on the ground that

f it was immune from the jurisdiction of the court, contending, inter alia, (i) that art 6(1)(a) of the 1972 order provided for a loss of immunity not by a general anticipatory waiver but only by a specific waiver made after proceedings had been begun, or at the very earliest after a particular dispute had arisen, and there had been no waiver of immunity in the circumstances and (ii) that under English law as it stood in 1972 when the order was made, a foreign sovereign could not, except in limited circumstances, be impleaded in an English court in personam and further, that a foreign sovereign could

g effectively waive his immunity only by an actual submission to the jurisdiction in the face of the court and not by agreeing in advance to submit to the jurisdiction, and accordingly it could not have been intended that the Headquarters Agreement and the 1972 order would provide for a waiver of immunity to be effective on a mere contractual undertaking to submit to the jurisdiction of the English court.

h

Held – The application would be dismissed for the following reasons—
(1) On the true construction of art 6(1)(a) of the 1972 order there was no limitation on the time at which the waiver of immunity had to be made in order to be effective. The waiver had to be express and had to be made in a particular case, but that meant no more than that it had to relate to a specific transaction and there was no reason for 'a

j particular case' to mean a particular dispute or a particular legal proceeding. It followed that cl 7 of the facility letter was an express waiver of immunity in respect of the particular transaction within the meaning of the 1972 order (see p 262 *f* to *h*, post).

---

a   Article 8 is set out at p 260 *f* to *h*, post
b   Article 6(1), so far as material, is set out at p 259 *a*, post

(2) International organisations did not enjoy sovereign status at common law and accordingly they were not entitled to sovereign or diplomatic immunity except where *a* such immunity was granted by legislative instrument, and then only to the extent of such grant. Furthermore, under the European Convention on State Immunity 1972 which came into force shortly after the 1972 Act a contracting state was expressly precluded from claiming immunity from the jurisdiction of another contracting state if it had undertaken to submit to the jurisdiction of that court by an express term contained in writing. It followed that a clear contractual waiver such as that contained in cl 7 was *b* to be given effect in accordance with its terms (see p 263 *d e g* to *j*, post).

Notes

For Headquarters Agreements and privileges and immunities of international organisations, see 18 Halsbury's Laws (4th edn) paras 1596–1597, and 5 Halsbury's Statutory Instruments (Fourth Reissue) 49–50.   *c*

Cases referred to in judgment

Arab Banking Corp v International Tin Council (15 January 1986, unreported), QBD.
Exchange (Schooner) v M'Faddon (1812) 7 Cranch 116, US SC.

Summons
                                                                              d
On 11 March 1986 the plaintiffs, Standard Chartered Bank (the bank), issued a writ against the first-named defendant, the International Tin Council (the ITC), and 24 member countries including the Commission of the European Communities (representing the European Economic Community) and the Department of Trade and Industry (representing the United Kingdom of Great Britain and Northern Ireland), claiming repayment of £10m and interest. By a summons dated 4 April 1986 the ITC applied to *e* the judge to set aside the writ and the service thereof on the ground that the ITC was immune from suit and legal process by virtue of the provisions of the International Organisations Act 1968 and the International Tin Council (Immunities and Privileges) Order 1972, SI 1972/120. The summons was heard in chambers, but judgment was delivered in open court. The facts are set out in the judgment.

                                                                              f
Nicholas Chambers QC, Rosalyn Higgins QC and *Peter Irvin* for the ITC.
Timothy Walker QC and *Mark Barnes* for the bank.

BINGHAM J. At the request of both parties and because the matter is of some general importance I am giving this judgment in open court.
    By this summons the first named defendant, the International Tin Council (the ITC), *g* applies to set aside the writ and service of the writ in proceedings started against it by Standard Chartered Bank (the bank). The issue for decision is whether the ITC is, as it contends, immune from the jurisdiction of the court in these proceedings.
    The bank's case stripped to essentials could scarcely be shorter. By a facility letter dated 19 July 1982 the bank offered to lend the ITC £10m on terms which included the following:
                                                                              h
    '7. *Governing Law and Jurisdiction.* This Facility Letter shall be governed by and interpreted in all respects in accordance with English Law and you hereby irrevocably submit to the non-exclusive jurisdiction of the High Court of Justice in England and consent to the giving of any relief and/or the issue of any process for enforcement or otherwise against you.'

                                                                              j
The offer was accepted and the loan was made and continued on the same terms in 1983, 1984 and, most recently, August 1985. The bank concluded that a default in repayment of the loan and interest had occurred and accordingly issued proceedings on 11 March 1986. Although under art 6 of the International Tin Council Immunities and Privileges Order 1972, SI 1972/120—

a
'The Council shall have immunity from suit and legal process except: (*a*) to the extent that the Council shall have expressly waived such immunity in a particular case...'

the bank submit that cl 7 of the facility letter contains an express waiver of immunity in the clearest possible terms in this particular case.

b
There is a refreshing and to my mind attractive simplicity about this argument and counsel for the ITC did not devote much of his address to elaborating the merits of the ITC's stance in this litigation. But no defendant claiming to be immune from suit can rest his case on the merits, particularly where, as here, the obligation appears on its face to be plain and the creditor may have no means of obtaining judgment save in the proceedings which he is said to be precluded from bringing. It is the legal merit of the claim for immunity which must be determined, and in determining it I must not be swayed by the apparent merits of a claim which has not yet reached the stage of adjudication.

c
To understand and evaluate the ITC's claim for immunity it is necessary to go back a little in time. Historically, the doctrine of sovereign immunity developed, in this country and elsewhere, with reference to personal sovereigns and sovereign states and governments. Diplomatic immunity grew up in parallel to protect the persons and the work of sovereigns' international agents. Cases arose in which claims to sovereign immunity were made by government departments and state-owned enterprises and provincial governments, but in each case the argument was whether the body in question shared the sovereign quality of the state which begat it. I am told that sovereign status was by international convention accorded to the League of Nations and I think there may have been earlier examples, but the wide-scale practice of according sovereign status to associations of sovereign states and international organisations seems to have been a largely post-1945 development.

d

e
The immediate precursor of this development in this country was the Diplomatic Privileges (Extension) Act 1944, which gave powers to the United Kingdom government to nominate international organisations of which it and the governments of one or more sovereign powers were members and to provide that organisations so nominated should enjoy immunities and privileges which might include among others immunity from suit and legal process.

f
In February 1946 the recently established General Assembly of the United Nations approved a General Convention on the Privileges and Immunities of the United Nations (London, 13 February 1946; TS 10 (1950); Cmd 6753), which provided in section 2 of art II:

g
'The United Nations, its property and assets wherever located and by whosoever held, shall enjoy immunity from every form of legal process except in so far as in any particular case it has expressly waived its immunity. It is, however, understood that no waiver of immunity shall extend to any measure of execution.'

h
The Diplomatic Privileges (Extension) Act 1946 amended the 1944 Act to enable effect to be given to the convention. A second convention in 1947 gave similar rights to specialised agencies of the United Nations, but those agencies did not include the ITC. Further Acts followed in 1950, in each case enabling immunity from suit and process to be conferred on nominated international organisations. The Diplomatic Privileges Act 1964, enacted to incorporate parts of the Vienna Convention on Diplomatic Relations (18 April 1961; Misc 6 (1961); Cmnd 2565) into English municipal law, was concerned with the inviolability of diplomatic missions and the immunity of diplomatic personnel, not the status of international organisations. But arts 31 and 32 are of interest:

j

'ARTICLE 31.1. A diplomatic agent shall enjoy immunity from the criminal jurisdiction of the receiving State. He shall also enjoy immunity from its civil and administrative jurisdiction except in the case of ...

ARTICLE 32.1. The immunity from jurisdiction of diplomatic agents and of
persons enjoying immunity under Article 37 may be waived by the sending State.   *a*
2. The waiver must always be express . . .
4. Waiver of immunity from jurisdiction in respect of civil or administrative
proceedings shall not be held to imply waiver of immunity in respect of the
execution of the judgment, for which a separate waiver shall be necessary.'

There was then enacted the International Organisations Act 1968. Although described
in its long title as 'An Act to make new provision . . . as to privileges, immunities and   *b*
facilities to be accorded in respect of certain international organisations and in respect of
persons connected with such organisations and other persons . . .' its effect was for present
purposes similar to the preceding Acts. The United Kingdom government was again
empowered to nominate organisations of which it or foreign sovereign powers or
governments were members and to confer on such organisations privileges and
immunities which might include immunity from suit and legal process, although the   *c*
privileges and immunities conferred were not to be greater in extent than was required
to be conferred in accordance with any agreement to which the United Kingdom was a
party.

The ITC was first established some years ago. It has operated under a series of
International Tin Agreements of which the most recent (made under the auspices of the
United Nations) is the sixth. Put very broadly, the object of the ITC has been to promote   *d*
an orderly market in tin. In order to prevent undue fluctuations in price it has, at least in
recent years, operated a buffer stock. As is very well known, it was the ITC's announcement
in October 1985 that it could or would no longer buy or pay for buffer stocks which led
to the suspension of the tin market on the London Metal Exchange and provoked a
considerable flood of litigation.

Two instruments form the immediate background to the present application. The   *e*
first of these is a Headquarters Agreement made between the United Kingdom
government and the ITC which came into force on 9 February 1972. This agreement
provided that the ITC should have legal personality and the capacity to contract and that
its archives and premises should be inviolable. It also provided in art 8 as follows:

'Immunity from jurisdiction (1) The Council shall have immunity from jurisdiction   *f*
and execution except: (a) to the extent that the Council shall have expressly waived
such immunity in a particular case; (b) in respect of a civil action by a third party for
damage arising from an accident caused by a motor vehicle belonging to or operated
on behalf of the Council or in respect of a motor traffic offence involving such
vehicle; and (c) in respect of enforcement of an arbitration award made under either
Article 23 or Article 24.
(2) The Council's property and assets wherever situated shall be immune from   *g*
any form of requisition, confiscation, expropriation, sequestration or acquisition.
They shall also be immune from any form of administrative or provisional judicial
constraint except insofar as may be temporarily necessary in connection with the
prevention of, and investigation into, accidents involving motor vehicles belonging
to, or operated on behalf of, the Council.'   *h*

I should also draw attention to arts 23 and 24 which were in these terms.

'ARTICLE 23 Contracts Where the Council enters into contracts (other than contracts
concluded in accordance with staff regulations) with a person resident in the United
Kingdom or a body incorporated or having its principal place of business in the
United Kingdom and embodies the terms of the contract in a formal instrument,   *j*
that instrument shall include an arbitration clause whereby any disputes arising out
of the interpretation or execution of the contract may at the request of either party
be submitted to private arbitration.
ARTICLE 24 Submission to an international arbitration tribunal The Council shall at the
instance of the Government, submit to an international arbitration tribunal any

a dispute (other than a dispute concerning the interpretation or application of the Fourth International Tin Agreement or any succeeding agreement): (*a*) arising out of damage caused by the Council; (*b*) involving any other non-contractual responsibility of the Council; or (*c*) involving the Executive Chairman, a staff member or expert of the Council, and in which the person concerned can claim immunity from jurisdiction under this Agreement, if this immunity is not waived.'

b The second instrument was the 1972 order made under the 1968 Act and expressed to come into force on the same date as the Headquarters Agreement. Article 4 provides that:

'[The ITC] is an organisation of which [the United Kingdom Government] and the governments of foreign sovereign Powers are members.'

c Article 6(1) reproduces exactly the language of art 8(1) of the Headquarters Agreement save that the immunity is expressed to be 'from suit and legal process' and not 'from jurisdiction and execution'. Article 6(2) differs from art 8(2) in its language but not significantly in its effect. There are a string of articles which deal with the immunity of the ITC's officers and experts and the representatives of member states which, echoing the language of art 6(1)(*a*) of the 1972 order and the 1946 General Convention on the
d Privileges and Immunities of the United Nations (Cmnd 6753), are prefaced by the words, 'Except in so far as in any particular case any privilege or immunity is waived by . . .'

Against this background the ITC makes three main submissions. Firstly, it submits on the construction of the 1972 order, read with the Headquarters Agreement, that art 6(1)(*a*) of the 1972 order should not be read as applying to contractual claims. The route
e to this conclusion is this. Article 23 of the Headquarters Agreement requires the ITC's contracts to contain an arbitration clause. If a contracting party obtains an arbitration award against the ITC, the ITC has under art 6(1)(*c*) of the 1972 order no immunity against enforcement of that award. This is a comprehensive and exclusive code for the resolution of contractual disputes. Under art 24 of the Headquarters Agreement (*b*) is concerned with the non-contractual liability of the ITC and so by necessary implication
f is (*a*). Thus an express waiver of immunity in a contractual case can never have been envisaged. This contention was supported by reference to a series of draft and final Headquarters Agreements between the United Kingdom government and the International Wheat Council, the International Coffee Organisation, the International Sugar Organisation, the International Rubber Study Group, the International Cocoa Organisation and the International Lead and Zinc Study Group made between 1968 and
g 1979 which, it was said, went to show that contractual disputes other than with the United Kingdom government were to be resolved by arbitration save where the international organisation waived its immunity in regard to the specific dispute in question.

In my judgment this argument, for all its ingenuity, is shown by the bank to be fallacious. Article 23 of the ITC Headquarters Agreement only requires the ITC to
h include an arbitration clause in a contract with a person resident in the United Kingdom or a body incorporated or having its principal place of business in the United Kingdom. A wholly foreign party falling outside this description altogether (on the ITC's argument) faces a dilemma. If he includes in his contract a clause such as the bank included, he is shut out from proceedings here unless, after a dispute has arisen and proceedings have been issued, the ITC agrees to be sued. If he includes an arbitration clause, he may obtain
j an award but will not be able to enforce it here as of right because it will not be an award falling within the exceptions from immunity contained in art 6(1)(*c*) of the 1972 order. The ITC meets that point by suggesting that such a party can protect himself by stipulating for disputes to be determined in a forum outside the United Kingdom where in all probability the ITC will not be entitled to any sovereign status at all. The bank make the two obvious comments. First, it is somewhat bizarre if a contracting party is

debarred from suing an international organisation at the place where its main and
possibly its only business is carried on. Second, even if a judgment is obtained overseas   a
that will, if unsatisfied, be valueless unless there are assets overseas, and enforcement here
where assets are (one assumes) most likely to be will depend on the consent of the ITC. It
is no answer to say that international organisations traditionally do not default on their
obligations. The question at issue is the effect of a contractual undertaking to submit,
and only contracting parties who are apprehensive or cautious will include such a term
in their contracts in the first place.   b
    The bank, as a body incorporated in England by royal charter, does not of course fall
outside art 23 of the Headquarters Agreement. The loan agreement should therefore
have contained an arbitration clause. The omission of this clause may at most have
involved an oversight by the bank, but the omission, whether deliberate or inadvertent,
was a breach by the ITC of its Headquarters Agreement with the United Kingdom
government. The ITC submits that the result of this breach by them is that the bank are   c
now precluded from suing it here, where both parties reside, without its consent. That
would indeed be a strange outcome. All these difficulties fade away if it is permissible to
give effect to cl 7 of the facility letter. I should perhaps add that I do not find the other
Headquarters Agreements to which the ITC referred of help in resolving this problem.
The same is true of the statutory instruments concerning the International Oil Pollution
Compensation Fund and the Commonwealth Telecommunications Organisation to   d
which the bank referred. There are in these various instruments strong similarities of
language and approach and some dissimilarities. There are points to be made each way.
It is safer to stick to the instruments with which the ITC is concerned.
    Secondly, the ITC submits that the language of art 6(1)(a) of the 1972 order is to be
construed as providing for a loss of immunity not by a general anticipatory waiver but
only by a specific waiver made after proceedings have been begun, or at the very earliest   e
after a particular dispute has arisen. The ITC does not argue that 'case' should be
understood in the colloquial sense familiar to any professional lawyer but as 'instance',
the context making it clear that it is an instance of suit or legal process which is referred
to. In the submission of the ITC almost every word of art 6(1)(a) supports its preferred
construction, as does a United Nations study of the language appearing in the 1946
convention.   f
    As in most questions of pure construction, much turns on the initial impression which
the words create. The language of art 6(1)(a) did not on first reading, and does not now
after detailed exegesis, strike me as containing any limitation on the time at which the
waiver, to be effective, must be made. The waiver must be express. Nothing could be
more express than cl 7 of the facility letter. The waiver must be in a particular case, but
that in my view means no more than that it must relate to a specific transaction. I find   g
no warrant in the language for reading the phrase 'a particular case' as if it meant 'a
particular dispute' or 'a particular legal proceeding'. If anything, the tense used in the
sub-clause 'shall have expressly waived' gives some slight support to the bank, but this is
a minor factor compared with the meaning which as a matter of first and continuing
impression the words convey. This point was not argued before Steyn J in *Arab Banking
Corp v International Tin Council* (15 January 1986, unreported), but it seems clear that his   h
initial reaction was the same as mine. This construction seems to me so obviously fair
and sensible and commercial that I see no reason to struggle against it. I have the greatest
doubt whether the United Nations study, not being travaux préparatoires and being very
different from the instrument I have to construe, can be relied on as a legitimate aid to
construction, but since it is in my view entirely inconclusive anyway I shall not pursue
that question.   j
    Thirdly, the ITC relies on the law of England as it stood when the 1972 order was
made. Despite the strictures of academic commentators and the divergent practice of
other states, very familiar English authorities at the highest levels at that time made plain
both that a foreign sovereign could not (save in limited and for present purposes
irrelevant circumstances) be impleaded in an English court in an action in personam, and

a also that such a sovereign could effectively waive his immunity not by agreeing in advance to submit to English jurisdiction but only by an actual submission to the jurisdiction in the face of the court. Against that background of authority, the draftsmen of the Headquarters Agreement and the 1972 order could not have intended, so the ITC contends, to provide for a waiver of immunity effective on a mere contractual undertaking to submit to the jurisdiction of the English court.

There are, I think several answers to this submission. First, the absolute doctrine of
b sovereign immunity grew up in reliance on a theory that sovereign states were characterised by what Marshall CJ in *Exchange (Schooner) v M'Faddon* (1812) 7 Cranch 116 described as 'perfect equality and absolute independence'. It followed from this that one sovereign would not insult the dignity or undermine the independence of another by seeking to assert jurisdiction over him. Whatever the merits of this doctrine as between personal sovereigns or sovereign states, it is not obviously apt to be applied to a body such
c as the ITC of which sovereign states are no more than members and whose own sovereign status is said to have a certain Cheshire cat quality. The ITC could scarcely be seen as enjoying perfect equality with the United Kingdom or the same absolute independence. It is not therefore to be assumed that the strict principles established by authority would have been applied in these different circumstances or that such application would in 1972 have been expected. Second, and perhaps more importantly, international
d organisations such as the ITC have never so far as I know been recognised at common law as entitled to sovereign status. They are accordingly entitled to no sovereign or diplomatic immunity in this country save where such immunity is granted by legislative instrument, and then only to the extent of such grant. In the present case the ITC enjoyed such immunity as was granted by s 6(1) of the 1972 order, no more and no less. That raises a question of construction on which I have already expressed an opinion. Thirdly,
e this is a field in which it is the duty of the English courts so far as possible to keep in step with the settled practice of other nations. By the early 1970s it was plain that the English courts were badly out of step. According to Dr E J Kohn in 'Waiver of Immunity' [1958] BYIL 260 at 264–265:

f 'Dr. Gmür, a Swiss lawyer, whose compendious research into the question of sovereign immunity is of the greatest value to all later workers in this field, has rightly said that—with a few insignificant exceptions—all continental legal writers have adopted the view that a waiver of immunity can be agreed in any form, that it does not have to be stated in any form, that it does not have to be stated in front of a court and that it is binding on the State which agreed to it. The European continental courts have followed this view, sometimes even without discussion. It was a point
g on which they felt no doubt.'

This consensus was reflected in the European Convention on State Immunity of 1972 (Cmnd 5081), which expressly precluded a contracting state from claiming immunity from the jurisdiction of another contracting state if it had undertaken to submit to the jurisdiction of that court by an express term contained in a contract in writing. The
h European Convention was not signed for some months after the 1972 order was made but must at that time have been in an advanced state of negotiation. When, after important decisions in the English courts departing from the absolute view of sovereign immunity, the opportunity to legislate was at last taken in the State Immunity Act 1978, provision was made for submission to the United Kingdom court by prior written agreement (see s 2(2)). Against this background and given the facts of this case, the
j draftsman of the 1972 order must in my view have intended and the court would, if called on, have held that a clear contractual waiver such as the present would be given effect in accordance with its terms.

For these reasons I conclude that the ITC's submissions fail and the summons must be dismissed. I reach that conclusion without reluctance. I cannot bring myself to suppose that the responsible officers of the ITC who accepted the terms of the facility letter on its behalf then conceived cl 7 to have the nugatory effect now contended for. My conclusion therefore enables effect to be given to the manifest intentions of the parties.

In conclusion I should express my gratitude to all counsel for the unusually interesting arguments in this particular case.

Summons dismissed.

Solicitors: *Cameron Markby* (for the ITC); *Slaughter & May* (for the bank).

K Mydeen Esq   Barrister.

Goddard and another v Nationwide Building Society

COURT OF APPEAL, CIVIL DIVISION

MAY AND NOURSE LJJ

22, 23 MAY, 27 JUNE 1986

Document – Admissibility in evidence – Privileged and confidential document – Copy coming into possession of party to litigation – Party's intention to rely on document stated in defence – Whether plaintiff seeking protection of privilege entitled to restrain defendant from relying on document – Whether rule protecting disclosure of confidential communication prevailing over rule of evidence allowing copy to be used as secondary evidence.

The solicitor acting for the plaintiffs in the purchase of a house also acted for the building society from which the plaintiffs obtained a mortgage for the purchase. While so acting for both parties, the solicitor dictated an attendance note recording information received from the building society and the substance of his conversations with one of the plaintiffs concerning that information. The attendance note was later disclosed to the building society. The plaintiffs subsequently brought an action against the building society alleging negligence on the part of its surveyor and in its defence the building society pleaded matters contained in the attendance note. The plaintiffs claimed that those matters were privileged and applied to strike out the relevant passages from the defence, and also applied for an injunction to restrain the building society from using or relying on the attendance note. The building society contended that they were entitled to use the attendance note under the rule of evidence allowing the use of secondary evidence of privileged documents. Both applications were dismissed by the judge, and the plaintiffs appealed.

Held – If a litigant had in his possession copies of documents to which legal professional privilege attached he could nevertheless use such copies as secondary evidence in his litigation. However, if he had not yet used the documents in that way, the mere fact that he intended to do so was no answer to a claim against him by the person in whom the privilege was vested for delivery up of the copies or to restrain him from disclosing or making any use of the information contained in them. Since, on the facts, the attendance note was written by the solicitor in his capacity as solicitor for the plaintiffs, who alone were entitled to claim privilege in respect of it, and since the building society had not yet used it as secondary evidence but merely intended to do so, the plaintiffs were entitled to have the passages in the defence which referred to the attendance note struck out and to an injunction restraining the building society from using or relying on the attendance note. The appeal would therefore be allowed (see p 266 *j* to p 267 *a*, p 270 *g h* and p 271 *a* to *d*, post).

Calcraft v Guest [1895–9] All ER Rep 346 and *Lord Ashburton v Pape* [1911–13] All ER Rep 708 considered.

Notes

a For legal professional privilege and confidentiality of communications between solicitor and client, see 13 Halsbury's Laws (4th edn) paras 71–78, 44 ibid para 103, and for cases on the subject, see 18 Digest (Reissue) 99–126, 741–962, 44 Digest (Reissue) 70, 656–660.

For secondary evidence of documents protected by privilege, see 17 Halsbury's Laws (4th edn) paras 141–142, 252, and for cases on the subject, see 22 Digest (Reissue) 236–237, 2028–2047.

b

Cases referred to in judgments

Ashburton (Lord) v Pape [1913] 2 Ch 469, [1911–13] All ER Rep 708, CA.
Butler v Board of Trade [1970] 3 All ER 593, [1971] Ch 680, [1970] 3 WLR 822.
Calcraft v Guest [1898] 1 QB 759, [1895–9] All ER Rep 346, CA.
c ITC Film Distributors Ltd v Video Exchange Ltd [1982] 2 All ER 241, [1982] Ch 431, [1982] 3 WLR 125.
Lamb v Evans [1893] 1 Ch 218, CA.
Lloyd v Mostyn (1842) 10 M & W 478, 152 ER 558.
Minet v Morgan (1873) LR 8 Ch App 361.
Morrison v Moat (1851) 9 Hare 241, 68 ER 492.
d Printers and Finishers Ltd v Holloway [1964] 3 All ER 731, [1965] 1 WLR 1.
R v Cox and Railton (1884) 14 QBD 153, [1881–5] All ER Rep 68, CCR.
R v Tompkins (1977) 67 Cr App R 181, CA.
R v Uljee [1982] 1 NZLR 561, NZ CA.
Rex Co and Rex Research Corp v Muirhead and Comptroller-General of Patents (1926) 136 LT 568.

e

Cases also cited

Argyll (Margaret) (Duchess) v Duke of Argyll [1965] 1 All ER 611, [1967] Ch 302.
Campbell v Tameside Metropolitan BC [1982] 2 All ER 791, [1982] QB 1065, CA.
Great Atlantic Insurance Co v Home Insurance Co [1981] 2 All ER 485, [1981] 1 WLR 529, CA.
f Jones v G D Searle & Co Ltd [1978] 3 All ER 654, [1979] 1 WLR 101, CA.
Neushul v Mellish & Harkavy (1967) 203 EG 27, CA.
Schering Chemicals Ltd v Falkman Ltd [1981] 2 All ER 321, [1982] QB 1, CA.

Interlocutory appeal

David John Goddard and June Rose appealed from a decision of Hollings J given on 16
g July 1985 whereby he dismissed (1) an application of the appellants dated 29 January 1985 to strike out those parts of the defence of the respondents, the Nationwide Building Society, based on the contents of a document for which the appellants claimed privilege, and (2) an application of the appellants dated 25 April 1985 for an injunction against the respondents restraining them for using or relying in any manner on the document and requiring the respondents to deliver up the document and any copies of it that they may
h have made. The facts are set out in the judgment of May LJ.

Gavin Lightman QC and Beverly-Ann Rogers for the appellants.
Robert Reid QC and Simon Berry for the respondents.

Cur adv vult

j

27 June. The following judgments were delivered.

MAY LJ. This is an appeal from a judgment of Hollings J of 16 July 1985 which dismissed the plaintiffs' applications of 29 January 1985 and 25 April 1985.

In 1981 the plaintiffs (the appellants) bought a house in Penarth for £19,500 with the help of a mortgage from the respondent building society. They instructed a firm of solicitors, Messrs Godfrey Evans & Co, to act for them in connection with their purchase. A Mr Graham Carson, an assistant solicitor with that firm, had the conduct of the matter on their behalf. In the usual way those same solicitors also acted as solicitors for the respondents in respect of the grant of the mortgage. Before the purchase, the respondents' surveyor carried out a survey of the house and the contents of his two reports were communicated to the appellants. These were very favourable, but recommended that £1,000 should be retained by the respondents from any advance to cover the cost of repairing a bulge in the rear wall of the property. It is contended that it was in reliance on these reports that the appellants went on with and completed their purchase. It subsequently transpired, so it is alleged, that the house was in a dangerous condition and had a value of not merely £1,000 less, but £7,500 less than the purchase price.

On 6 October 1983 the appellants issued their writ in this action and their statement of claim was served on 24 October 1983. The appellants claim damages from the respondents on the contention that the survey reports of the latter's surveyor were negligent. Alternatively, the appellants contend that in completing the purchase they relied not only on the reports but also on certain representations said to have been made by the respondents' local manager, or in the further alternative, that when making the advance the respondents warranted that the purchase price of the property was reasonable.

In the course of acting in and about the purchase and mortgage transactions Mr Carson dictated a note for the file dated 10 June 1981, recording information which he had received from the local building society manager and certain conversations that he had in consequence thereof with the male appellant. I will consider the precise capacity in which Mr Carson prepared this note later in this judgment. However, on 9 November 1983 Godfrey Evans & Co, knowing of the proceedings, wrote a letter to the respondents enclosing the note for the file on 10 June 1981 to which I have just referred. The respondents thereupon pleaded the substance of the attendance note in their defence and subsequently amended defence. The appellants challenge the accuracy of the consultations recorded in the note, but nevertheless claim that it is both confidential and privileged. Their application of 29 January 1985 was to have struck out passages from the defence based on the contents of the note on the grounds that those contents are privileged and that the pleading would embarrass the appellants in the fair trial of the action and was an abuse of the process of the court. Further, by their application of 25 April 1985 the appellants sought an injunction against the respondents to restrain them from using or relying in any manner on the note and requiring them to deliver up the document and any further copies of it that they may have made. Their applications were supported by the unchallenged expert evidence of a Mr Roger Jones that Godfrey Evans & Co owed a duty of confidentiality to the appellants, at least in respect of the note, independent of any duty which they owed to the respondents, and that the release of the note to the latter constituted professional misconduct.

The first submission of counsel on behalf of the respondents was that the judge had held, and held rightly, that on the probabilities the solicitors were acting for both parties at the time when the attendance note was dictated, although they had been separately instructed. Thus the respondents were equally entitled to know of its existence and contents with the appellants. It followed, counsel for the respondents contended, that no breach of privilege was committed when the solicitors disclosed the note to the respondents. Any legal professional privilege which attached to it was common to both parties. Consequently the appellants were in any event not entitled to the relief which they sought in respect of it.

I confess that I do not think that it is quite clear on the face of the judgment below whether the judge was indeed so finding. If he was, then with respect I think that he was in error. It is clearly undesirable to set out the terms of the note in this judgment and the judge below very properly did not do so in his judgment either. However, having considered such terms and the circumstances in which the note came into existence, I am

satisfied that the only legal professional privilege attaching to it was, and is, that of the
a present appellants.

Whether or not the judge must be taken to have made the finding to which I have
referred, he nevertheless also went on to consider the case on the basis that the disclosure
by the solicitors to the respondents of a photocopy of the note was a breach of the
appellants' privilege. Having done so, he concluded that although the appellants had no
proprietary right to the note or its contents, they did have the right to prevent the
b contents of the conversations between the appellants and the solicitors from being
revealed, either in answer to interrogatories or by the production of the note or a copy of
it. However, once the copy had come into the hands of the respondents, that was the end
of the matter and the latter were entitled to make what use of it they wished. The judge
consequently dismissed the appellants' applications and it is against that dismissal that
they now appeal.

c Before dealing with the substantive arguments which were addressed to us on the
hearing of this appeal, I should just record that, with a view to saving time and costs, the
respondents accepted that an application for an injunction made in the existing
proceedings could be regarded in the same way as separate proceedings.

In essence the opposing arguments in this case deployed both before the judge and
before us were these. For the appellants, that the content of any communication, with
d immaterial exceptions, between a solicitor and his client is confidential and only the
client can waive that confidentiality. At least where it is the solicitor who breaches his
fiduciary duty to his client in respect of such a communication, then any person who
comes into possession of that communication, or a document or a copy of a document
setting it out, can be restrained from making any use of the communications or the
original or copy documents and can be ordered to return them to the client (see Lord
e Ashburton v Pape [1913] 2 Ch 469, [1911–13] All ER Rep 708).

For the respondents it was contended that, even though communications between
solicitor and client are confidential, nevertheless if a document, original or copy,
containing or evidencing them, comes into the hands of a third party, even by dishonesty
(which of course is not alleged in the instant case), then that third party is entitled to use
that original or copy document as evidence in litigation between himself and the
f erstwhile client (see Calcraft v Guest [1898] 1 QB 759, [1895–9] All ER Rep 346).

In Lord Ashburton v Pape the latter was a bankrupt, whose discharge was opposed by
amongst others, the plaintiff. One Nocton had been Lord Ashburton's solicitor and he
employed a clerk by the name of Brooks. By a trick Pape got possession from Brooks of a
number of letters which Lord Ashburton had written to Nocton at a time when the
relationship of client and solicitor had subsisted between them. Pape's solicitors took
g copies of these letters and then handed the originals back to Pape. Lord Ashburton then
brought an action against Pape, Nocton and others for an injunction restraining them
from disclosing or parting with any letters or other documents received by or
communicated to Nocton as his solicitor, or the effects or copies of or extracts from them.

On a motion by Lord Ashburton in the action, Neville J made an order that Pape
should hand over to Nocton all the original letters which he had in his possession or
h control and restraining Pape, amongst others, until judgment or further order, from
publishing or making any use of the copies of the letters or any information contained
in them 'except for the purpose of pending proceedings in the defendant . . . Pape's
bankruptcy and subject to the directions of the Bankruptcy Court' (see [1913] 2 Ch 469
at 470). Lord Ashburton appealed asking that the order of Neville J might be varied by
striking out this exception. The Court of Appeal allowed his appeal.

j There has been a considerable amount of discussion about the decision in Lord
Ashburton v Pape since it was decided, and it is unfortunate that in one important sentence
the other reports of the case differ from that in the Law Reports (see Tapper 'Privilege
and Confidence' (1972) 35 MLR 83 and Heydon, 'Legal Professional Privilege and Third
Parties' (1974) 37 MLR 601). However, for my part I think that the ratio of the decision
in Lord Ashburton v Pape was founded on the confidential nature of the content of the

letters written by Lord Ashburton to Nocton. The Court of Appeal was concerned to protect that confidence, in the same way, for instance, as the courts protect the trade *a* secrets of an employer against the unauthorised use of them by an employee, both while he remains such, as well as after he has left the employment.

In his judgment Cozens-Hardy MR quoted with approval the following passage from the judgment of Kay LJ in *Lamb v Evans* [1893] 1 Ch 218 at 235–236 (which itself referred to an earlier judgment in *Morrison v Moat* (1851) 9 Hare 241, 68 ER 492):

> 'Then the judgment goes on to give several instances, and many of them are of *b* cases where a man, being in the employment of another, has discovered the secrets of the manufacture of that other person, or has surreptitiously copied something which came under his hands while he was in the possession of that trust and confidence, and he has been restrained from communicating that secret to anybody else, and anybody who has obtained that secret from him has also been restrained from using it.' *c*

(See [1913] 2 Ch 469 at 472, [1911–13] All ER Rep 708 at 710.)

Cozens-Hardy MR then applied that principle to the case then before him in saying ([1913] 2 Ch 469 at 472–473, [1911–13] All ER Rep 708 at 710):

> 'Apart, therefore, from these pending or threatened proceedings in bankruptcy, it seems to me to be perfectly clear that the plaintiff can obtain the unqualified *d* injunction which he asks for.'

He then went on to deal with *Calcraft v Guest* [1898] 1 QB 759, [1895–9] All ER Rep 346 in a way to which I shall refer shortly.

On the first point Kennedy LJ agreed with Cozens-Hardy MR ([1913] 2 Ch 469 at 473–474, [1911–13] All ER Rep 708 at 711):

> 'The principle which has been stated by the Master of the Rolls upon which a person would be restrained from dealing with documents or using information in documents which he has obtained wrongly, and knows he has obtained wrongly, is clear.'

In his turn Swinfen Eady LJ stated the underlying principle in this way ([1913] 2 Ch *f* 469 at 475, [1911–13] All ER Rep 708 at 711):

> 'The principle upon which the Court of Chancery has acted for many years has been to restrain the publication of confidential information improperly or surreptitiously obtained or of information imparted in confidence which ought not to be divulged. Injunctions have been granted to give effectual relief, that is not only to restrain the disclosure of confidential information, but to prevent copies *g* being made of any record of that information, and, if copies have already been made, to restrain them from being further copied, and to restrain persons into whose possession that confidential information has come from themselves in turn divulging or propagating it.'

However, in *Lord Ashburton v Pape* the defendant relied on *Calcraft v Guest* to support *h* the exception in Neville J's order. Before referring to the way in which the Court of Appeal distinguished the latter it is convenient if I first deal directly with *Calcraft v Guest*. The facts of that case were that in 1787 certain documents came into existence in respect of which the owner of a fishery on the River Frome in Dorset was entitled to legal professional privilege. In 1898 the successor in title to that fishery, Calcraft, brought an action for trespass to it, the substantial question being as to the upper boundary of the *j* fishery. He succeeded at first instance. One of the defendants appealed. Between trial at first instance and the hearing of the appeal the relevant documents came to light. They had been stored in the coach house of the grandson of the solicitor who had acted for the 1787 owner of the fishery in the 1787 litigation. That solicitor had been succeeded by his son and when he died his business was wound up and his nephew, the owner of the a coach house, acted for his executors. Soon after these documents came to light the solicitors for the appellant defendant inspected and took copies of them, but thereafter they were handed over to the plaintiff in the 1898 litigation. On the appeal, however, the appellant defendant sought to put in the copies and in the result two questions arose. First, were the original documents privileged from production? Second, even if they were, could the appellant give secondary evidence of them?

b In so far as the first question was concerned, the Court of Appeal, following the earlier decision in *Minet v Morgan* (1873) LR 8 Ch App 361, held in effect that once privileged, always privileged and that the then owner of the fishery was entitled to refuse to produce the originals. On the second question, however, the court held that secondary evidence of the documents was admissible. In his judgment, with which the other members of the court agreed, Lindley MR approved this dictum from an earlier judgment of Parke B in *Lloyd v Mostyn* (1842) 10 M & W 478, 152 ER 558:

c 'Where an attorney instructed confidentially with a document communicates the contents of it, or suffers another to take a copy, surely the secondary evidence so obtained may be produced. Supposing the instrument were even stolen, and a correct copy taken, would it not be reasonable to admit it?'

d Lindley MR then continued ([1898] 1 QB 759 at 764, cf [1895–9] All ER Rep 346 at 349):

'The matter dropped there; but the other members of the Court . . . all concurred in that, which I take it is a distinct authority that secondary evidence in a case of this kind may be received.'

e Subject to the distinction that may be drawn between letters written to a solicitor for the purpose of obtaining legal advice on the one hand, and a deed entrusted to one's solicitor to hold in confidence, the decision in *Calcraft v Guest* might have been thought to have been good authority for the admission in Pape's bankruptcy proceedings of secondary evidence of Lord Ashburton's letters to Nocton, his solicitor. However, the court distinguished the earlier authority on the basis that whereas in it the question of the admission of secondary evidence arose incidentally, in *Lord Ashburton v Pape* this issue

f of admissibility was the principal, indeed the sole, issue in the case. In his judgment Cozens-Hardy MR said ([1913] 2 Ch 469 at 473, [1911–13] All ER Rep 708 at 710):

'The rule of evidence as explained in *Calcraft* v. *Guest* ([1898] 1 QB 764, [1895–9] All ER Rep 346) merely amounts to this, that if a litigant wants to prove a particular document which by reason of privilege or some circumstances he cannot furnish by the production of the original, he may produce a copy as secondary evidence

g although that copy has been obtained by improper means, and even, it may be, by criminal means. The Court in such an action is not really trying the circumstances under which the document was produced. That is not an issue in the case and the Court simply says "Here is a copy of a document which cannot be produced; it may have been stolen, it may have been picked up in the street, it may have improperly

h got into the possession of the person who proposes to produce it, but that is not a matter which the Court in the trial of the action can go into." But that does not seem to me to have any bearing upon a case where the whole subject-matter of the action is the right to retain the originals or copies of certain documents which are privileged.'

j In my opinion Kennedy LJ followed the same path when he said ([1913] 2 Ch 469 at 747, cf [1911–13] All ER Rep 708 at 711):

'I agree that the better view seems to me to be that although it is true that the principle which is laid down in *Calcraft* v. *Guest* must be followed, yet, at the same time, if, before the occasion of the trial when a copy may be used, although a copy improperly obtained, the owner of the original can successfully promote proceedings against the person who has improperly obtained the copy to stop his using it, the owner is none the less entitled to protection, because, if the question had arisen in *a* the course of a trial before such proceedings, the holder of the copy would not have been prevented from using it on account of the illegitimacy of its origin. If that is so, it decides this case.'

Swinfen Eady LJ put the matter even more clearly in this passage from his judgment ([1913] 2 Ch 469 at 476–477, cf [1911–13] All ER Rep 708 at 712–713):

b

'There are many similar cases to the like effect, where the use of information improperly obtained has been restrained and the parties into whose possession it has come have been restrained from using or divulging it. Down to that point there can be no dispute as to the law. Then objection was raised in the present case by reason of the fact that it is said that Pape, who now has copies of the letters, might wish to give them in evidence in certain bankruptcy proceedings, and although the original *c* letters are privileged from production he has possession of the copies and could give them as secondary evidence of the contents of the letters, and, therefore, ought not to be ordered either to give them up or to be restrained from divulging their contents. There is here a confusion between the right to restrain a person from divulging confidential information and the right to give secondary evidence of documents where the originals are privileged from production, if the party has such *d* secondary evidence in his possession. The cases are entirely separate and distinct. If a person were to steal a deed, nevertheless in any dispute to which it was relevant the original deed might be given in evidence by him at the trial. It would be no objection to the admissibility of the deed in evidence to say you ought not to have possession of it. His unlawful possession would not affect the admissibility of the deed in evidence if otherwise admissible. So again with regard to any copy he had. *e* If he was unable to obtain or compel production of the original because it was privileged, if he had a copy in his possession it would be admissible as secondary evidence. The fact, however, that a document, whether original or copy, is admissible in evidence is no answer to the demand of the lawful owner for the delivery up of the document, and no answer to an application by the lawful owner of confidential information to restrain it from being published or copied.'   *f*

I confess that I do not find the decision in *Lord Ashburton v Pape* logically satisfactory, depending as it does on the order in which applications are made in litigation. Nevertheless I think that it and *Calcraft v Guest* are good authority for the following proposition. If a litigant has in his possession copies of documents to which legal professional privilege attaches, he may nevertheless use such copies as secondary evidence *g* in his litigation: however, if he has not yet used the documents in that way, the mere fact that he intends to do so is no answer to a claim against him by the person in whom the privilege is vested for delivery up of the copies or to restrain him from disclosing or making any use of any information contained in them.

We were referred to a number of other authorities and are grateful for an interesting argument on what has become known as the third party exception to legal professional *h* privilege (see the articles in the Modern Law Review to which I have already referred, and *Cross on Evidence* (6th edn, 1985) pp 400–402). Having regard to the view I take of the effect of the decision in *Lord Ashburton v Pape*, however, I do not consider it necessary to refer to the other authorities or the general argument in any detail. In *Butler v Board of Trade* [1970] 3 All ER 593, [1971] Ch 680 Goff J took the same view of *Lord Ashburton v Pape* and would have granted an injunction similar to that sought in the instant case but *j* for the fact that the defendants there were the Crown, who intended to use the copy letter in a public prosecution brought by them. However, one may just note that there is a difference between the view taken in England about the admissibility of privileged communications in criminal proceedings (see *R v Tompkins* (1977) 67 Cr App R 181) and that taken in New Zealand (see *R v Uljee* [1982] 1 NZLR 561).

Nevertheless, having regard to the decision in *Lord Ashburton v Pape*, I respectfully
a think that the judge below was wrong to reject the appellants' claim to relief. I would
allow this appeal and make the orders sought.

NOURSE LJ. I agree that this apeal must be allowed.

Two questions have been argued: first, whether the legal professional privilege
attaching to the communications recorded in Mr Carson's attendance note of 10 June
b 1981 belongs exclusively to the appellants; second, if it does, whether it has been lost in
consequence of Mr Carson's unauthorised disclosure of it to the respondents.

I wish to add little to what May LJ has said on the first question. Counsel for the
respondents bent us to a close consideration of the terms of the attendance note, but I too
am entirely satisfied that the privilege attaching to it belongs exclusively to the appellants.

The second question has confronted us, in a simple and straightforward manner, with
c the task of reconciling the decisions of this court in *Calcraft v Guest* [1898] 1 QB 759,
[1895–9] All ER Rep 346 and *Lord Ashburton v Pape* [1913] 2 Ch 469, [1911–13] All ER
Rep 708. I agree that those decisions are authority for the proposition which May LJ has
stated. However unsatisfactory its results may be thought to be, that proposition must
hold sway unless and until it is revised by higher authority.

The apparent conflict between the rule of evidence established by *Calcraft v Guest* and
d the equitable jurisdiction reaffirmed in *Lord Ashburton v Pape* was probably not fully
recognised until the later case was considered by Goff J in *Butler v Board of Trade* [1970] 3
All ER 593, [1971] Ch 680, a decision which itself made a further distinction between
most criminal and all civil proceedings. Although, for the reasons given by May LJ, I am
in no doubt that our decision must be governed by *Lord Ashburton v Pape*, the confusion
which the existing authorities have caused in this case and are liable to cause in others
e has prompted me to deal with the matter at somewhat greater length than would
otherwise have been necessary. The following observations are not made in any order of
logic or importance. They are in general confined to a case, such as the present, where
the communication is both confidential and privileged and the privilege has not been
waived.

Firstly, it is desirable to emphasise that the proceedings in which the rule of evidence
f denies protection to the confidential communication are not proceedings whose purpose
is to seek that protection. The question is an incidental one which arises when the party
who desires the protection asserts a right to it as if he was the plaintiff in an action seeking
to invoke the equitable jurisdiction. When *Lord Ashburton v Pape* was decided, the
practice and procedures of our courts were no doubt such that it was first necessary to
issue fresh proceedings. Nowadays I think that we would, at the most, require an
g undertaking to issue a pro forma writ, perhaps not even that, a consideration which no
doubt explains the agreement not to require fresh proceedings in the present case. The
crucial point is that the party who desires the protection must seek it before the other
party has adduced the confidential communication in evidence or otherwise relied on it
at trial.

Secondly, although the equitable jurisdiction is of much wider application, I have little
h doubt that it can prevail over the rule of evidence only in cases where privilege can be
claimed. The equitable jurisdiction is well able to extend, for example, to the grant of an
injunction to restrain an unauthorised disclosure of confidential communications
between priest and penitent or doctor and patient. But those communications are not
privileged in legal proceedings and I do not believe that equity would restrain a litigant
who already had a record of such a communication in his possession from using it for the
j purposes of his litigation. It cannot be the function of equity to accord a de facto privilege
to communications in respect of which no privilege can be claimed. Equity follows the
law.

Thirdly, the right of the party who desires the protection to invoke the equitable
jurisdiction does not in any way depend on the conduct of the third party into whose
possession the record of the confidential communication has come. Thus, several eminent

judges have been of the opinion that an injunction can be granted against a stranger who
has come innocently into the possession of confidential information to which he is not *a*
entitled (see *Rex Co and Rex Research Corp v Muirhead and Comptroller-General of Patents*
(1926) 136 LT 568 at 573 per Clauson J, *Printers and Finishers Ltd v Holloway* [1964] 3 All
ER 731 at 737, [1965] 1 WLR 1 at 7 per Cross J and *Butler v Board of Trade* [1970] 3 All
ER 593 at 599, [1971] Ch 680 at 690 per Goff J). This view seems to give effect to the
general rule that equity gives relief against all the world, including the innocent, save
only a bona fide purchaser for value without notice. It is directly in point in the present *b*
case and our decision necessarily affirms it.

Fourthly, once it is established that a case is governed by *Lord Ashburton v Pape*, there is
no discretion in the court to refuse to exercise the equitable jurisdiction according to its
view of the materiality of the communication, the justice of admitting or excluding it or
the like. The injunction is granted in aid of the privilege which, unless and until it is
waived, is absolute. In saying this, I do not intend to suggest that there may not be cases *c*
where an injunction can properly be refused on general principles affecting the grant of
a discretionary remedy, for example on the ground of inordinate delay.

Fifthly, in a case to which *Lord Ashburton v Pape* can no longer apply, public policy may
nevertheless preclude a party who has acted improperly in the proceedings from invoking
the rule of evidence: see *ITC Film Distributors Ltd v Video Exchange Ltd* [1982] 2 All ER
241, [1982] Ch 431 where the defendant had at an earlier hearing obtained some of the *d*
plaintiffs' privileged documents by a trick. Warner J, having expressed the view that
there were by that stage in the case difficulties in the way of his granting the plaintiffs
relief on the basis of *Lord Ashburton v Pape*, held that the greater public interest that
litigants should be able to bring their documents into court without fear that they may
be filched by their opponents, whether by stealth or by a trick, and then used in evidence,
required an exception to the rule in *Calcraft v Guest* [1898] 1 QB 759, [1895–9] All ER *e*
Rep 346, save in regard to documents at which he (the judge) had already looked (see
[1982] 2 All ER 241 at 246, [1982] Ch 431 at 440–441). I emphasise that decision
proceeded not on an exercise of the court's discretion but on grounds of public policy.

Sixthly, the distinction between civil proceedings and public prosecutions made in
Butler v Board of Trade was again one which was made on grounds of public policy. The
distinction has since been adopted and applied by the Criminal Division of this court in *f*
R v Tompkins (1977) 67 Cr App R 181. It can now be disregarded only by the House of
Lords.

Finally, it is to be noted that the Court of Appeal in New Zealand, after an extensive
consideration of the authorities, including *Calcraft v Guest, Butler v Board of Trade* and *R
v Tompkins*, recently declined to apply the rule of evidence in a criminal case and held
that the evidence of a police constable, who had happened to overhear a privileged *g*
conversation between the accused and his solicitor, ie one which was not itself part of a
criminal or unlawful proceeding (*R v Cox and Railton* (1884) 14 QBD 153 [1881–5] All
ER Rep 68) was not admissible: see *R v Uljee* [1982] 1 NZLR 561. The practical result of
the decision would seem to be to leave the spirit of *Lord Ashburton v Pape* supreme in both
civil and criminal proceedings in that jurisdiction, a supremacy for which in my
respectful opinion there is much to be said in this. *h*

Appeal allowed.

Solicitors: *Sharpe Pritchard & Co*, agents for *Grossman Hermer & Seligman*, Cardiff (for the
appellants); *Church Adams Tatham & Co* (for the respondents).

Carolyn Toulmin   Barrister.

a
Attfield and another v DJ Plant Hire and General Contractors Co Ltd

CHANCERY DIVISION
SCOTT J
11 FEBRUARY 1986

b

Sale of land – Purchaser – Purchaser in possession – Order that purchaser relinquish possession – Substantial proportion of purchase price paid – Sale including goodwill and stock-in-trade – Contract specifically regulating rights of parties – Whether vendor entitled to order that purchaser pay outstanding balance into court or relinquish possession of property – National Conditions of Sale (20th edn), condition 8.

c

The plaintiffs carried on business as builders' merchants from leasehold premises. By a contract dated 13 September 1985 they agreed to sell to the defendant their leasehold interest in the premises, the goodwill of the business, the fixtures, fittings and trade equipment, and the stock-in-trade of the business. Under the contract the purchase price of £29,000 was apportioned on the basis of £17,000 for the goodwill, £2,000 for the

d fixtures, fittings and trade equipment, £10,000 for the stock-in-trade and nil for the leasehold interest. The contract of sale incorporated the National Conditions of Sale (20th edn), condition 8[a] of which provided that where the purchaser was let into occupation of the property before the actual completion of the purchase, then on discharge or rescission of the contract or on the expiration of seven days' or such longer notice given by the vendor the purchaser was required forthwith to give up the property. The contractual

e completion date was 26 September but the plaintiffs had allowed the defendant to enter into occupation in August prior to the signing of the contract. On 16 September the defendant paid £14,500 towards the purchase price, including £2,900 as a deposit. However, the defendant was unable to complete on the completion date and in October the plaintiffs served a notice to complete requiring the contract to be completed within 16 working days after service thereof, time being of the essence. On 30 October the

f defendant paid a further £7,000 but did not complete before the expiry of the notice to complete. The plaintiffs issued a writ seeking, inter alia, specific performance of the contract, or alternatively, an order that the defendant relinquish possession, occupation or control of the assets forming the subject matter of the contract. By a notice of motion on the same day the plaintiffs sought, inter alia, payment into court by the defendant of moneys remaining payable under the contract, or alternatively, an order that the

g defendant forthwith relinquish possession, occupation or control of every asset forming part of the subject matter of the contract.

Held – The plaintiffs were not entitled to an order that the defendant purchaser either pay the outstanding balance of the purchase price into court or relinquish possession of the property because (a) where the parties had contracted that pending completion the

h purchaser could remain in possession on certain terms but had to relinquish possession on the occurrence of certain events, the contract regulated the rights of the parties and therefore the position of the plaintiffs and the defendant was covered by condition 8 of the National Conditions of Sale, (b) a substantial proportion of the purchase price had been paid and the court would not make such an order without requiring the plaintiffs to refund or pay into court the amount already paid, less the deposit, and (c) it was

j implicit in such an order that possession of the property agreed to be sold could be restored to the vendor and therefore the order was not suitable where a large part of the subject matter of the contract consisted of goodwill and stock-in-trade which, by their nature, could not be returned to the vendor in their original form (see p 277 *a* to *c* *h* *j*, p 278 *b* to *g* and p 279 *a*, post).

Greenwood v Turner [1891–4] All ER Rep 190 distinguished.

---

a   Condition 8 is set out at p 276 *g* to *j*, post

Notes

For possession before completion, see 42 Halsbury's Laws (4th edn) para 125 and for cases a on the subject, see 40 Digest (Reissue) 177, 1279–1280.

Cases referred to in judgment

Greenwood v Turner [1891] 2 Ch 144, [1891–4] All ER Rep 190.
Lewis v James (1886) 32 Ch D 326, CA.
Maskell v Ivory [1970] 1 All ER 488, [1970] Ch 502, [1970] 2 WLR 844.   b
Pearlberg v May [1951] 1 All ER 1001, [1951] Ch 699, CA; affg [1950] 2 All ER 1022, [1951] Ch 104.

Motion

By a writ dated 21 January 1986 the plaintiffs, Raymond Michael Attfield and Brian Arthur Freshwater, sought against the defendant, DJ Plant Hire and General Contractors c Ltd (i) specific performance of a contract dated 13 September 1985 for the sale of the plaintiffs' leasehold interest in premises at Waltham Abbey, Essex, together with the goodwill in the business, the fixtures and fittings, trade equipment and stock-in-trade, (ii) alternatively damages, together with all relevant accounts, directions and inquiries, (iii) alternatively an order that the defendant relinquish possession, occupation or control of every asset forming part of the subject matter of the contract, and (iv) an injunction d restraining the defendant from disposing of any such asset. By a notice of motion dated 21 January 1986 the plaintiffs sought (i) payment into court forthwith by the defendant of the moneys, including interest, remaining payable by the defendant pursuant to the contract, (ii) alternatively an order that the defendant forthwith relinquish possession, occupation or control of every asset forming part of the subject matter of the contract, and (iii) an injunction restraining the defendant from disposing in any manner of any e such asset or any item of trade equipment, plant, stock or other assets on the land forming part of the subject matter of the contract. The facts are set out in the judgment.

John Brookes for the plaintiffs.
Steven Whitaker for the defendant.

SCOTT J. This is a very interesting application. It is an application in which plaintiff f vendors seek against the defendant purchaser an order which is sometimes known as a Greenwood v Turner order. Greenwood v Turner [1891] 2 Ch 144, [1891–4] All ER Rep 190 was a case where a purchaser of land had been permitted by the vendor to go into possession of the property pending completion. The purchaser failed to complete the contract by paying the balance of the purchase price on the day agreed for completion, but none the less retained possession of the property without paying any interest thereon. g It was held by Kekewich J, applying principles of some antiquity to which I must later refer, that the court ought not to order the purchaser to pay into court the balance of the purchase money without first giving the purchaser the option to avoid that payment-in by relinquishing possession of the property to the vendors. The order made, the Greenwood v Turner order, was in the form of an option to the defendant purchaser. The h defendant purchaser was given an option either to pay the outstanding purchase money into court by a fixed date, or, if he preferred, to give up possession of the property to the plaintiff vendors. It is an interlocutory order on those lines that the plaintiffs seek in the present case.

The plaintiffs had carried on the business of a builders' merchant, under the style Abbey Building Supplies, from leasehold premises at Waltham Abbey, Essex. By a j contract dated 13 September 1985 the plaintiffs agreed to sell to the defendant for a total price of £29,000, first, their leasehold interest in the premises in question, second, the goodwill in the business, third, the fixtures, fittings and trade equipment used in connection with the business and, fourth, the stock-in-trade of the business. Under the contract, the purchase price of £29,000 was apportioned as to nil to the leasehold interest, a £17,000 to the goodwill of the business, £2,000 to the fixtures, fittings and trade equipment, and £10,000 to the stock-in-trade which was valued as at 12 August 1985.

The vendors had let the defendant purchaser, DJ Plant Hire and General Contractors Co Ltd, into possession of the leasehold premises on 12 or 13 August 1985, and since that date the defendant has been, and so far as I know still is, carrying on the business of a builder's merchant.

b The contract of sale incorporated the National Conditions of Sale (20th edn). Condition 8 thereof sets out the terms which are to apply where occupation pending completion is taken by the purchaser.

The contractual completion date specified in the contract was 26 September 1985. The contract provided for payment by the purchaser of a deposit equal to 10% of the purchase price, that is to say, £2,900. That sum was not paid on the date of the contract. In fact a cheque for £5,000 had been handed by the defendant to the plaintiffs on or about 28

c August, in advance therefore of the contract itself, but that cheque had not been honoured on presentation. On 16 September 1985, the defendant paid to the plaintiffs the sum of £14,500 on account of the price due under the contract of sale. The deposit of £2,900 was subsumed in that payment. Some of the contemporary correspondence refers to the whole of the £14,500 as a deposit. The deposit paid pursuant to the contract of sale was, however, only £2,900 part thereof.

d The defendant did not complete on the contractual completion date, 26 September 1985. Accordingly, on 7 October 1985 the plaintiffs served on the defendant a notice to complete pursuant to condition 22 of the National Conditions of Sale (20th edn). Under that notice to complete it became a term of which time was of the essence that the contract should be completed within 16 working days after service thereof. It has not been suggested that that notice to complete was not validly served and effective according

e to its tenor. It expired, I have been told, on 31 October 1985.

On 30 October 1985 the defendant paid a further sum to the plaintiffs, this time £7,000, on account of the price outstanding under the contract of sale. But the defendant did not complete on or before 31 October 1985 and was not, it seems, financially in a position to do so. So, on the expiry of the notice to complete, the defendant had paid to the plaintiffs the sum of £21,500 on account of the purchase price of £29,000. There

f was a sum of £7,500 and interest still owing.

That remains the position today, although the amount of interest outstanding has increased. Notwithstanding the failure of the defendant to complete the contract of sale in accordance with the notice to complete, the defendant has remained and remains in possession of the leasehold property, carrying on the builder's merchant's business therefrom. The plaintiffs have not yet made any election as to whether they will rescind

g the contract on account of the failure on the part of the defendant to complete or will seek specific performance thereof.

On 21 January 1986, the plaintiffs commenced the action in which the application before me is brought. The indorsement on the writ claims specific performance of the contract, together with all relevant accounts, directions and inquiries. Paragraph 4 of the indorsement on the writ seeks, alternatively to specific performance, an order that the

h defendant relinquish possession, occupation or control of every asset forming part of the subject matter of the contract. Paragraph 6 thereof seeks an injunction to restrain the defendant from disposing of any such asset as aforesaid.

By notice of motion dated 21 January 1986 the plaintiffs seek, first, payment into court forthwith by the defendant of the moneys, including interest, remaining payable by it pursuant to the contract. Alternatively, the plaintiffs seek an order that the defendant

j forthwith relinquish possession, occupation or control of every asset forming part of the subject matter of the said contract. Finally, the notice of motion seeks an injunction in the terms more or less of the injunction sought by the writ.

The notice of motion came before Knox J on 24 January. It was stood over for seven days, on the defendant undertaking not to dispose of the leasehold interest, the goodwill of the business, the fixtures, fittings and trade equipment specified in the contract or, otherwise than in the normal course of business, any stock-in-trade of the said business. The purpose of that undertaking was to preserve for the plaintiffs the assets of the business if it should transpire that the plaintiffs were entitled to resume possession thereof.

At the expiration of the seven-day adjournment, the matter came before me. I stood the motion over for a further seven days, with the undertaking by the defendant continued in the meantime. The plaintiffs' interlocutory application now comes for decision. They seek, in effect, a *Greenwood v Turner* order.

Greenwood v Turner [1891] 2 Ch 144, [1891–4] All ER Rep 190 introduced the alternative for a purchaser defendant who was in possession of the property agreed to be sold to avoid payment into court of the balance of the purchase price by electing to give up possession of the property to the vendors. The practice of requiring purchasers in possession, who were in default after the contractual completion date had passed, to pay into court the balance of the purchase price seems to have been a practice of some long standing. Kekewich J in *Greenwood v Turner* referred to some of the previous authorities and in particular *Lewis v James* (1886) 32 Ch D 326, in which Cotton LJ had dealt with the matter. Kekewich J said ([1891] 2 Ch 144 at 146, [1891–4] All ER Rep 190 at 192):

'In *Lewis v. James* Lord Justice *Cotton* states the rule, which is well known, and I only take it from that case because it is expressed in plain terms and in better language than I could frame. He says, "This is in some respects like a case where a purchaser being in possession is required to pay into Court, if he remain in possession, the purchase-money agreed upon, but it is well known that in such a case under ordinary circumstances an option is given to the purchaser to go out, and the order only is that if he continues in possession he must pay the price into Court . . .".'

There are three particular points in the present case which seem to me to require careful consideration in the context of an application for a *Greenwood v Turner* order. First, the terms of the contract between the plaintiffs and the defendant deal expressly with their respective rights and obligations in the event of the purchaser taking or retaining possession of the property pending completion. In the present case the defendant had been permitted by the plaintiffs to take possession of the property before the date of the contract. At the date of the contract, the defendant was already in possession. Condition 8 of the National Conditions deals with this situation. It provides:

'(1) If the purchaser (not being already in occupation as lessee or tenant at a rent) is let into occupation of the property before the actual completion of the purchase, then, as from the date of his going into occupation and until actual completion, or until upon discharge or rescission of the contract he ceases to occupy the property, the purchaser shall—(i) be the licensee and not the tenant of the vendor (ii) pay interest on the remainder of the purchase money at the prescribed rate (iii) keep the property in as good repair and condition as it was in when he went into occupation; (iv) pay, or otherwise indemnify the vendor against, all outgoings and expenses (including the cost of insurance) in respect of the property, the purchaser at the same time taking or being credited with the income of the property (if any) (v) not carry out any development within the meaning of the Planning Acts
(2) Upon discharge or rescission of the contract, or upon the expiration of 7 working days' or longer notice given by the vendor or his solicitor to the purchaser or his solicitor in that behalf, the purchaser shall forthwith give up the property in such repair and condition as aforesaid
(3) A purchaser going into occupation before completion shall not be deemed thereby to have accepted the vendor's title
(4) Where the purchaser is allowed access to the property for the purpose only of carrying out works or installations, the purchaser shall not be treated as being let into occupation within the meaning of this condition.'

If parties by their contract deal expressly with a particular situation, the court ought,
a in my view, to be very slow to read into the contract rights or obligations additional to
those expressed. Parties who contract on terms which incorporate the National
Conditions, and thus condition 8 thereof, contract that, if the purchaser is allowed by the
vendor into occupation pending completion, the terms that will govern his occupation
are those of condition 8. Under condition 8, the purchaser is entitled to remain in
occupation until discharge or rescission of the contract or until the expiration of such
b notice as is referred to in sub-condition (2). Where a contract contains a contractual
provision on the lines of condition 8, I find it very difficult to see how the *Greenwood v
Turner* remedy can still apply. It is, I think, accepted by counsel who appears for the
plaintiffs, that, if the contract had in terms provided that the purchaser was to be
permitted to take or to retain occupation of the property pending completion, the
plaintiffs could not have sought a *Greenwood v Turner* order. It does not seem to me that
c the case is any different where, as here, the contract expressly regulates the rights of the
parties if the purchaser is allowed into possession pending completion.

There are two authorities to which I have been referred, each of which involved a
contract incorporating the National Conditions of Sale, where the point with which I am
now dealing could have been taken but was not taken. One is *Pearlberg v May* [1950] 2
All ER 1022, [1951] Ch 104; *affd* [1951] 1 All ER 1001, [1951] Ch 699, CA. The case
d involved a contract for the purchase of land where the National Conditions had been
incorporated and where the purchaser had been allowed into possession before
completion. The purchaser was, it seems, in default and the vendor obtained against the
purchaser a *Greenwood v Turner* order. The case is not reported on that point. It is
reported, at first instance and in the Court of Appeal, on a quite separate point concerning
the effect of a *Greenwood v Turner* order on the purchaser's obligation to pay interest on
e the purchase price pending completion. There is nothing therefore in the reported
judgments that deals with the point with which I am concerned. It does, however, seem
from the recital of facts in the report that a *Greenwood v Turner* order was made against
the purchaser notwithstanding that the contract of sale had, by incorporating the National
Conditions of Sale, incorporated a condition regulating the position in the event that the
purchaser should be allowed into occupation pending completion.

f The other case is *Maskell v Ivory* [1970] 1 All ER 488, [1970] Ch 502, a decision of
Stamp J. In this case, also, the contract in question incorporated the National Conditions
of Sale. The purchaser was in occupation pending completion. The purchaser was in
default in completing. The vendor applied on motion for an order that the purchaser
pay into court the balance of the purchase money. The purchaser contended that he
ought not to be subjected to that order without being given the option of going out of
g possession, that is to say, the *Greenwood v Turner* option. The defendant was, therefore,
arguing for a *Greenwood v Turner* order and not against one. The judge acceded to the
purchaser's argument and gave him the option of going out of possession in order to
avoid paying the balance of the purchase money into court.

The question whether an order for payment of the balance of the purchase money into
court, in a case where a purchaser is in possession but in default in completing, ought to
h be made, notwithstanding that the contract itself has provided for the basis on which the
purchaser is entitled to be in possession and remain in possession, was not raised in either
of the cases I have mentioned. The point was not considered in either case.

In my view, if a vendor and a purchaser contract that the purchaser may, pending
completion, remain in possession on certain terms and must relinquish possession in
certain events, it is no longer open to the vendor to seek a *Greenwood v Turner* order.
j Where condition 8 of the National Conditions has been incorporated into the contract,
the vendor can, by giving a seven-day notice, terminate the purchaser's right to remain
in possession of the property. In *Williams on Vendor and Purchaser* (4th edn, 1936) p 565,
the rationale behind *Greenwood v Turner* orders is expressed thus:

'The Court makes such an order for the preservation of the property, which is the

subject of the action, considering it unjust to allow the purchaser to have both the
land and the purchase-money in his possession pending the trial.'   *a*

The injustice referred to is simply not present where possession is held under contractual
terms such as those incorporated by condition 8 of the National Conditions into the
contract.

The second feature of the present case which makes, in my view, the making of a
Greenwood v Turner order difficult is the fact that a substantial amount of the purchase   *b*
price has already been paid. £21,500 has been paid on account of the purchase price of
£29,000. £2,900 thereof represents the deposit, forfeitable in the event of default on the
part of the purchaser. The balance of the price paid would, however, in the event of
rescission, have to be repaid or accounted for by the vendors to the purchaser. A
Greenwood v Turner order in a case like the present would, in my view, have to be
accompanied by a requirement that the vendor either refund to the purchaser or,   *c*
perhaps, pay into court the purchase money already paid, less the deposit. Otherwise the
vendor would be in the position, described by the text in *Williams on Vendor and Purchaser*
as unjust, of being in possession both of the property and the purchase money.

Thirdly, it is implicit in *Greenwood v Turner* orders that possession of the property
agreed to be sold can be restored to the vendor. In the present case, the sale included not
simply the leasehold premises but also goodwill, the chattels used in and about the   *d*
business, and stock-in-trade. The stock-in-trade was intended to be and has been dealt
with in the ordinary course of trade by the defendant since it took possession on 12
August 1985. The evidence before me does not indicate to what extent the original stock-
in-trade has been completely turned over by the business activities of the defendant since
it took possession and commenced carrying on the business. In the nature of things,
however, a substantial quantity of the original stock-in-trade must have been sold and   *e*
the present stock-in-trade must to some extent represent replacements acquired by the
defendant in the course of carrying on the business. *Greenwood v Turner* orders were not
designed for sales of stock-in-trade nor for sales of goodwill. In the present case, although
the sale includes the leasehold premises, a nil value was attributed to them for the purpose
of apportionment of the price. The real value of the subject matter of the sale lay in the
goodwill, to which £17,000 was attributed, and the stock-in-trade, to which £10,000   *f*
was attributed. It does not seem to me that a *Greenwood v Turner* order, which
contemplates possession of the subject matter of the sale being given back by the
purchaser to the vendor, can be easily applied to a sale of the sort involved in the present
case.

All these considerations incline me to the conclusion that this is not a case in which
the plaintiffs are entitled to an order for the payment into court of the balance of the
purchase money, whether or not that relief is accompanied by the *Greenwood v Turner*   *g*
option. This conclusion does not in the least mean that the plaintiffs are without remedy.
It is plain from the undisputed facts of the case and the admissions made by counsel who
has appeared before me for the defendant, that the defendant is in breach of the contract
of sale and has still not the wherewithal to complete the contract. The plaintiffs are in a
position, and have been since the end of October, either to seek specific performance and   *h*
an order for payment of the balance of the purchase price outstanding, or to rescind,
resell and recover by way of damages any difference in price between the contract price
and the resale price. They have a substantial part of the purchase price in their hands,
which they could, I would imagine, hold as security against the damages to which they
might become entitled in the event of rescission. If they elected for specific performance,
they could, subject to landlord's consent (I do not know what the position is about that)   *j*
assign the lease to the defendant and then exercise their vendors' lien to sell it in order to
recover the balance of the purchase price outstanding. I am attempting not a definitive
exposition of the potential remedies of the plaintiffs but to illustrate that the protection
of their property interests and the need to avoid injustice being caused to them by a
purchaser in default of its obligations do not require a *Greenwood v Turner* order.

Greenwood v Turner orders were devised to avoid injustice to vendors who had not the
a protection of the contractual rights enjoyed by these plaintiffs.

Accordingly the plaintiffs have failed on this motion to establish that they are entitled
to the relief sought and I dismiss the application.

Motion dismissed.

b Solicitors: *Brian Slater & Tyers*, Waltham Abbey (for the plaintiffs); *Trefor R James*, Enfield
(for the defendant).

Jacqueline Metcalfe   Barrister.

c # Fargro Ltd v Godfroy and others

CHANCERY DIVISION
WALTON J
17, 18, 19, 20 MARCH 1986

d *Company – Minority shareholder – Action by minority shareholder – Whether minority
shareholder can bring action if company in liquidation.*

*Company – Voluntary winding up – Liquidator – Power – Power to bring minority shareholder's
action in name of company.*

e A minority shareholder's action will not lie if a company is in liquidation. The appropriate
procedure in such a situation is for the liquidator to bring the action on behalf of the
company or, if he refuses to do so, a contributory may apply to the court for an order
authorising him to bring the action in the company's name or compelling the liquidator
to do so on such terms as to indemnity as the court considers appropriate (see p 281 *b* to *e*
and p 283 *b c*, post).

f   Dictum of Cotton LJ in *Cape Breton Co v Fenn* (1881) 17 Ch D at 208 applied.
    Dictum of Lord Blanesburgh in *Ferguson v Wallbridge* [1935] 3 DLR at 83 considered.

Notes
For actions and proceedings by and against companies, see 7 Halsbury's Laws (4th edn)
paras 765–779.

g **Cases referred to in judgment**
Cape Breton Co v Fenn (1881) 17 Ch D 198, CA.
Cook v Deeks (1916) 27 DLR 1, PC.
Ferguson v Wallbridge [1935] 3 DLR 66, PC.
Foss v Harbottle (1843) 2 Hare 461, 67 ER 189.
h *Prudential Assurance Co Ltd v Newman Industries Ltd (No 2)* [1982] 1 All ER 354, [1982] Ch
    204, [1982] 2 WLR 31, CA.

Preliminary issue
The plaintiff, Fargro Ltd, suing on its own behalf and derivatively on behalf of Bridge
Produce Marketing Ltd (in liquidation), issued a writ on 17 April 1984 against the first,
j second and third defendants, Derek Godfroy, James Frank Rogers and Superior Group
Ltd, claiming (i) in its own capacity against the third defendant, Superior Group Ltd,
damages and/or compensation for breaches of (an express) contract, and (ii) derivatively
on behalf of the fourth defendant, Bridge Produce Marketing Ltd (in liquidation), against
the first, second and third defendants, damages and/or compensation. The facts are set
out in the judgment.

Gerald Godfrey QC and *Jonathan Harvie* for the plaintiff.
John McDonnell QC and *Dirik Jackson* for the first, second and third defendants.
The fourth defendant was not represented.

WALTON J. There now arises in this case a point which I must say is a novel one to me and I had assumed it to be entirely untouched by authority, but owing to the researches of counsel for the first to third defendants, it appears that that is not in fact the case.

The situation is as follows. The company with which we are concerned, that is to say Bridge Produce Marketing Ltd (Bridge), is a company in respect of which part of the relief claimed by the plaintiff is only appropriate in the case of a minority shareholders' action. The plaintiff and the third defendant (Superior Group Ltd) were equal shareholders, and still are, in the fourth defendant, Bridge, but the articles of that company were so arranged that the company itself was what is popularly known as a deadlock company. It is pleaded in para 8 of the statement of claim that, by reason of the facts and matters alleged and having regard to its articles (whereby it is specified that the chairman, whether of the board of directors or of the shareholders' meetings, shall not have a casting vote in the event of a tied vote) Bridge constitutes a deadlock company. And that is admitted in the defence.

Paragraph 28 of the statement of claim proceeds:

'[The plaintiff] sues derivatively on behalf of Bridge by reason of the facts and matters referred to . . . above . . . and that by reason of the position of Superior as a fifty % shareholder of Bridge and its wrongdoing . . . no action could be brought in the name of the company due to the ability of the wrongdoers within the company to prevent any such resolution being approved.'

Now that is not admitted in the defence. Counsel for the first to third defendants explained to me that those defendants considered that there might be concealed in that para 28 some allegation, to the effect that the liquidator of the company (for the company is now in liquidation and was at the date when the writ was issued), by reason of something done or omitted to be done by the third defendant, Superior Group Ltd, could not in fact himself bring the action.

As a result of the cross-examination of one of the plaintiff's witnesses, it became apparent to counsel for the first to third defendants that that suspicion was entirely wrong. Indeed certain correspondence with the liquidator having been disclosed by the plaintiff, it appears that the liquidator is indeed quite willing, albeit on certain terms as to indemnities and so on and so forth, to bring an action in the name of the company.

The situation therefore is that the first to third defendants have taken the position that, on the matters as pleaded in the statement of claim and as now refined by the evidence, that part of the action, which constitutes a minority shareholders' action, will not lie and that the rule in *Foss v Harbottle* (1843) 2 Hare 461, 67 ER 189 applies.

Now, as has been pointed out fairly recently in a case in the Court of Appeal, *Prudential Assurance Co Ltd v Newman Industries Ltd (No 2)* [1982] 1 All ER 354, [1982] Ch 204, the rule in *Foss v Harbottle*, although of course one applying more particularly to companies, is a rule which applies generally, in the sense that the proper plaintiff in every type and sort of action is indeed the person in whom the cause of action is vested. So that one starts from the position that, as regards a claim such as is made in the present action, which, putting it very compendiously, is that the defendants (including the third defendant, the other shareholder) have diverted assets and opportunity belonging to the plaintiff to their own use, the proper plaintiff is the fourth defendant, Bridge. It is such, because it is the company which has suffered the loss. Now if that company had not been in liquidation, it is conceded that the pleas contained in paras 8 and 28 of the statement of claim would have laid a proper foundation for a minority shareholders' action, because it would have been impossible for the plaintiff to have got the company to have taken any action against

its other shareholder or indeed the other defendants. That is quite clearly because, if the
a matter had been put to the board of the company, the board would have been equally
split. There would therefore have been no resolution to bring such an action. And if the
matter had been carried to the shareholders in general meeting, exactly the same result
would have followed.

Therefore, as a practical matter, it would have been totally impossible for the plaintiff
to set Bridge in motion to bring the action, and it is under those circumstances that a
b minority shareholders' action will lie. But once the company goes into liquidation the
situation is completely changed, because one no longer has a board, or indeed a
shareholders' meeting, which is in any sense in control of the activities of the company
of any description, let alone its litigation. Here, what has happened is that the liquidator
is now the person in whom that right is vested.

Now, that being the case, the plaintiff can take a variety of courses. The plaintiff can
c ask the liquidator to bring the action in the name of the company. Doubtless, as in
virtually all cases, the liquidator will require an indemnity from the persons who wish
to set the company in motion against all the costs, including, of course, the costs of the
defendants, which he may have to incur in bringing that action. The liquidator may ask
for unreasonable terms or, on the other hand, the liquidator may be unwilling to bring
the action, and, under those circumstances, it is always possible for the shareholders who
d wish the action to be brought to go to the court asking for an order, either that the
liquidator bring the action in the name of the company or, more usually, that they are
given the right to bring the action in the name of the company, of course, against the
usual type of indemnity which will, if there is any difficulty about the matter, be settled
by the court. And I think that this has been the practice and procedure for a very long
time indeed. It is certainly referred to by Cotton LJ in *Cape Breton Co v Fenn* (1881) 17
e Ch D 198 at 208 where he says:

> 'There is nothing in the Act of Parliament which gives the Court such power [that
> is, power to authorise somebody other than a shareholder or creditor of the company,
> to bring proceedings in the name of a company], and *primâ facie* proceedings in the
> name of the company ought to be conducted by the liquidator [in this case, of
> course, it was a compulsory liquidation]—an officer appointed by the Court and
f > subject to the supervision of the Court. There may be, no doubt, special cases where,
> although the Court does not think fit to remove the liquidator on the ground that
> his conduct in not bringing an action is improper, it may give power to other
> persons to conduct the litigation upon their giving proper indemnity against any
> consequences of that litigation. But who are the persons who can be authorized to
> take these steps? In my opinion the creditors and the contributories only, not under
g > any special clause of the Act, but because they are the persons who, under the terms
> of the Act, can intervene if they are advised that the liquidator does not properly do
> his duty. They have a right in special cases to ask the Court for leave to do that
> which the liquidator is advised not to do, or which, [and in practical terms this is
> usually the reason] because he has no funds, he does not do, viz., take proceedings
> in the name of the company, but in my opinion the power of the Court to give leave
h > to use the name of the company stops there, and is confined to those who are parties
> to the liquidation.'

So that is a course which it has always been open for the plaintiff in the present case to
take, and we know, from the correspondence that they have been having with the
liquidator, that the liquidator, subject of course to proper indemnities, has no objection
j whatsoever to the action being brought by himself in the name of the company.

Now as a matter of logic, it seems to me quite clear that, that being the situation, and
the plaintiff no longer being subject to the veto of the third defendant as the other equal
shareholder, the reason for any exception to the rule in *Foss v Harbottle* disappears. And,

if authority is wanted for that, it is to be found in a case of which I must confess I have
previously been ignorant, that of *Ferguson v Wallbridge* [1935] 3 DLR 66. And Lord
Blanesburgh, delivering the judgment of the Privy Council, first of all says, quite clearly
(at 83):

> '... in their Lordships' judgment, [the present action] could have been so
> maintained if the company were not in liquidation. *Cook* v. *Deeks* ((1916) 27 DLR 1)
> is clear authority for this. But could it be so maintained now that the company is
> assumed to be in liquidation? And the answer must again, as their Lordships think,
> be in the negative. The permissibility of the form of proceeding thus assumed,
> where the company concerned is a going concern, is an excellent illustration of the
> golden principle that procedure with its rules is the handmaid and not the mistress
> of justice. The form of action so authorised is necessitated by the fact that in the case
> of such a claim as was successfully made by the plaintiff in *Cook* v. *Deeks*—and there
> is at least a family likeness between that case and this—justice would be denied to
> him if the mere possession of the company's seal in the hands of his opponents were
> to prevent the assertion at his instance of the corporate rights of the company as
> against them. But even in the case of a going company a minority shareholder is not
> entitled to proceed in a representative action if he is unable to show when challenged
> that he has exhausted every effort to secure the joinder of the company as plaintiff
> and has failed. But *cessante ratione legis, cessat lex ipsa*. So as soon as the company goes
> into liquidation, the necessity for any such expedient in procedure disappears.
> Passing over the superficial difficulty that a company in compulsory liquidation
> cannot be proceeded against without the leave of the Court, the real complainants,
> the minority shareholders, are now no longer at the mercy of the majority, wrongly
> retaining the property of the company by the strength of their votes. If the
> liquidator, acting at the behest of the majority, refuses when requested to take action
> in the name of the company against them, it is open to any contributory to apply to
> the Court, [and then he refers to the Canadian statute and says:] and under s. 234 of
> the Provincial Companies Act, which corresponds to s. 252 of the Imperial statute
> (Companies Act, 1929 (Imp.), c. 23), it is open to the Court, on cause shown, either
> to direct the liquidator to proceed in the company's name or on proper terms as to
> indemnity, and otherwise to give to the applicant leave to use the company's name
> as plaintiff in any action necessary to be brought for the vindication of the company's
> rights. Nor is the contributory confined to that form of procedure.'

And then he suggests that there might be another method of procedure by moving for
misfeasance in the winding up, but that is a matter that one need not go into.

So there is clear authority in the Privy Council as to the vast distinction that there is
between the position where the company is a going concern and the minority
shareholders' action can be brought, and a case where when it goes into liquidation,
where there is no longer any necessity for bringing a minority shareholders' action.
Because, subject if necessary to obtaining the directions of the court, which is in itself an
excellent thing as acting as a filter against any totally wrong-headed action, the action can
be brought directly in the name of the company as it should be so brought.

Counsel for the plaintiff attempted to persuade me that there was an analogy between
the position which can occasionally arise when a beneficiary under a trust wishes for the
trustees to take some action and the trustees refuse. There under the procedure as it
applies to ordinary trustees, there is no doubt at all that in some cases, at any rate, one
may sue in one's own name as a beneficiary, making the trustees defendants in addition
to any other necessary parties. But it is quite clear, and this is referred to in the notes to
RSC Ord 15, r 14 in *The Supreme Court Practice 1985* vol 1, p 214, para 15/14/4 that where
trustees refuse to sue, beneficiaries may sue after request and refusal, but not otherwise.
And then of course the trustees must be added as defendants.

a   Here, there is no question of the liquidator refusing. So that even applying the analogy, the analogy does not hold because of the very fact that the liquidator here has not refused to sue. Now, I would go further than that, and I would say that, however accurate up to a point the analogy of the liquidator becoming a trustee for the shareholders is, it is unwise to press the parallel too far. So far as I am aware, there is no case in which the form of action with which we are here dealing has ever been allowed in a liquidation; certainly none has been pointed out to me; and it seems that, on the contrary, the
b   procedure which is adopted in the liquidation is, either that the liquidator sues in the name of the company, of course, against suitable indemnities, or that, against suitable indemnities, the would-be plaintiff is allowed himself/herself/itself to sue in the name of the company; but that in all cases, in a liquidation, the action is brought as it properly should be brought in the name of the company.

So for those reasons it appears to me that the point which has now been taken by
c   counsel for the first to third defendants is a perfectly valid one. It turns out that the action as at present constituted is improper and therefore, subject to any further discussion as to what is now to be done, that part of the action could properly be struck out. I will not expatiate on the matter further, but having got as far as we have got in the action, it will be I think a thousand pities and a great disservice to everybody if the action cannot now be reconstituted, of course, paying attention to the fact that down to date it
d   has been totally improperly constituted, in such a manner as to enable it to continue without, at any rate, too long an adjournment, and thus be brought to a satisfactory conclusion.

Leave granted for the fourth defendant to be added as co-plaintiff.

e   *Order accordingly.*

Solicitors: *Ward Bowie*, agents for *Davies Thomas & Cheale*, Worthing (for the plaintiff); *Copleys*, St Ives (for the first, second and third defendants).

Hazel Hartman   Barrister.

Westminster City Council v Government of the Islamic Republic of Iran

CHANCERY DIVISION

PETER GIBSON J

30, 31 JANUARY 1986

Land charge – Registration – Dispute regarding registration – Service of originating summons to determine dispute impossible – Diplomatic privilege – Local authority registering local land charges in respect of building formerly used as Iranian embassy – Authority issuing summons to determine whether charges could be registered in land registry – Summons unable to be served on Iranian government – Whether court could hear and determine summons in absence of service on Iranian government – State Immunity Act 1978, s 12(1) – RSC Ord 32, r 5(1).

Constitutional law – Diplomatic privilege – Immunity from legal process – Residence of diplomatic agent – Embassy of foreign state – Embassy abandoned after fire – Whether premises 'used' for purposes of diplomatic mission – Diplomatic Privileges Act 1964, Sch 1, art 22.

Originating summons – Service – Service impossible – Diplomatic privilege – Local authority issuing originating summons against Iranian government – Summons unable to be served on Iranian government – Whether court could hear and determine summons in absence of service on Iranian government – State Immunity Act 1978, s 12(1) – RSC Ord 32, r 5(1).

The Iranian government was the registered owner of premises which were used as the Iranian embassy. The premises were situated within the area of the plaintiff council. In May 1980 the property was gutted by fire and the building was left in a dangerous state. The council, in accordance with their statutory powers, shored up and secured the structure, thereby incurring expenses which were statutorily payable by the owner of the building. After unsuccessfully requesting payment from the Iranian government the council registered the expenses as local land charges and then sought registration of the charges in the land registry under the Land Registration Act 1925. The Iranian government by its solicitors objected to the registration on the ground that the property formed part of the diplomatic mission of the Iranian government and was subject to state immunity. The Chief Land Registrar referred to the court the question whether the charges could be registered and required the council to issue an originating summons or other appropriate originating process to determine the question. Accordingly, the council took out an originating summons, naming the Iranian government as defendant, but the summons could not be served in the manner prescribed by s 12(1)[a] of the State Immunity Act 1978, by being transmitted through the Foreign and Commonwealth Office to the Ministry of Foreign Affairs in Iran, because there was no British embassy in Iran. The solicitors for the Iranian government refused to accept service on its behalf. At the hearing of the summons the question arose whether the court could rule on the substantive question in view of the fact that it had not been possible to serve the summons on the Iranian government.

Held – In the absence of prior service on the Iranian government the court could not rule on the question referred to it by the Chief Land Registrar because (a) if a dispute arose regarding the registration of a charge the matter could not be described as ex parte and any party known to be interested had to be given the opportunity of appearing at the hearing before the registrar or the court if the question was referred to it, (b) although

---

a Section 12(1) is set out at p 287 *c*, post

the proceedings were not required to be commenced by originating summons and any
a appropriate originating process could have been used, whatever process was used would
have required service on the Iranian government in accordance with s 12(1) of the 1978
Act, and (c) RSC Ord 32, r 5(1)[b] did not empower the court to proceed on the basis that
the Iranian government had 'fail[ed] to attend', since r 5(1) only applied if a person failed
to attend after being served with a summons. The originating summons would therefore
be dismissed (see p 286 j, 287 b e to h and p 288 a d, post).

b   Per curiam. State immunity afforded by art 22[c] of Sch 1 to the Diplomatic Privileges
Act 1964 only applies to premises currently used for the purposes of a diplomatic mission
and does not apply to premises which have ceased to be used for diplomatic purposes (see
p 288 j to p 289 b, post).

Notes
c For diplomatic immunity accorded to the premises of a diplomatic mission, see 18
Halsbury's Laws (4th edn) para 1564.
     For the State Immunity Act 1978, s 12(1), see 10 Halsbury's Statutes (4th edn) 648, and
for the Diplomatic Privileges Act 1964, Sch 1, art 22, see ibid 563.

Originating summons
d By an originating summons issued on 4 October 1985 the Westminster City Council,
pursuant to an order dated 1 July 1985 made by the Chief Land Registrar under r 298(2)
of the Land Registration Rules 1925, SI 1925/1093, sought the determination of the
question whether five local land charges registered against premises owned by the
Government of the Islamic Republic of Iran, pursuant to s 6(1) of the London County
Council (General Powers) Act 1955 on the local land charges register could be registered
e pursuant to the proviso to s 59(2) of the Land Registration Act 1925. The facts are set out
in the judgment.

P B Mauleverer QC and *J Acton Davis* for the city council.
The Government of Iran was not represented.

f **PETER GIBSON J.** On 30 January 1979 the Provisional Revolutionary and Islamic
Government of Iran, the name then adopted by the defendant, the Iranian government,
was registered as the proprietor of 16, Princes Gate, London SW1, and the premises were
used as the Iranian embassy until May 1980. That property is within the area of the
plaintiffs, Westminster City Council. As many of us will have seen on our television
screens, those premises were stormed by the Special Air Service in May 1980 to free some
g hostages held there, but unfortunately in consequence the property was gutted by fire.
The building was left in a dangerous state. Pursuant to s 62 of the London Building Acts
(Amendment) Act 1939, the district surveyor on the 6 May 1980 certified the dangerous
state of the premises and the city council proceeded in accordance with their statutory
powers to shore up and secure the structure.
     Thereby the city council incurred expenses, and by s 66 of the 1939 Act such expenses
h are required to be paid by the owner of the building. Demands were made by the city
council on the Iranian government, but such demands were not met. The city council
then sought, in December 1981, to recover expenses which had then been incurred by
commencing proceedings in the Queen's Bench Division against the Iranian government,
but such proceedings have, by reason of the State Immunity Act 1978, to be served on
the Iranian Ministry of Foreign Affairs. There is no British embassy in Iran, and the
j Swedish embassy, which looked after British interests in Iran, was, perhaps understandably, not prepared to effect such service. Accordingly those proceedings were frustrated.
By s 6(1) of the London County Council (General Powers) Act 1955 and s 1(1)(a) of the

---

b Rule 5(1) is set out at p 287 j, post
c Article 22 is set out at p 288 g h, post

Local Charges Act 1975 the city council had the right to register the expenses as local land charges, and five local land charges were registered on dates between 5 August 1980 and 5 November 1982. Such charges by s 7 of the 1975 Act take effect as if they had been created by a deed of charge by way of legal mortgage within the meaning of the Law of Property Act 1925. By the proviso to s 59(2) of the Land Registration Act 1925, such charges cannot be realised unless registered under the Land Registration Act.

The city council sought registration of its charges under the Land Registration Act on 11 April 1983, supporting its application by the certificate of the city council's solicitor. Such an application has potentially serious consequences for the Iranian government, because of the possibility that the property might be sold by the city council if the registration is allowed. But the city council's solicitor has deposed to the fact that the purpose of the city council in seeking registration was to protect the interests of the city council in the event, in particular, of a sale by the Iranian government. Indeed, the city council has offered an undertaking that without the leave of the court it would not itself initiate action to effect a sale of the property.

The Land Registry invited the comments of the Iranian government on the application. The Iranian government, by its solicitors, Messrs Cathcart & Co, objected to the registration on the ground that the property formed part of the diplomatic mission of the Iranian government and that state immunity applied. The Land Registry confirmed to the city council that, apart from that objection, its application was in order.

On 1 July 1985 the Chief Land Registrar made an order referring to this court the question whether the charges should be registered pursuant to the proviso to s 59(2) of the Land Registration Act. The order of the Chief Land Registrar required the city council to 'take out an originating summons or such other originating process as may be appropriate for the purpose of bringing the matter before the court'. The city council took out an ordinary originating summons, using form 8 and naming the Iranian government as defendant. Under RSC Ord 10, r 5, personal service is required. No doubt the city council had the reasonable expectation that the Iranian government would want to support its objection by accepting service and appearing in these proceedings; but Cathcarts have refused to accept service on behalf of the Iranian government. They say they have no instructions to do so. Although Cathcarts have been supplied with the relevant documents and have been notified of the preliminary hearing before the master and of this hearing, the Iranian government still does not appear, and it still has not been served. Counsel appearing for the city council has therefore had the invidious task of not only presenting the city council's case but also performing his duty of drawing the attention of the court to those matters which might have been relied on by the Iranian government had it chosen to appear. I am very grateful to him for his very fair presentation of the possible difficulties in the way of the city council, and I have been much assisted by his argument.

Two questions arise, one procedural and the other the substantive question raised in the reference. The procedural question is whether the court is able to rule on the substantive question in the circumstances that it has not been possible to serve the only defendant, the Iranian government. Counsel for the city council submitted that the court can so rule. He first submitted that the hearing in this court is in effect an extension of the ex parte application before the Chief Land Registrar. It is true that the registrar, on receiving an application for registration, can, if satisfied with that application and by the evidence in support, make an order without serving the evidence on the party affected thereby. But if a dispute arises as to the registration of a charge, then the registrar comes under a mandatory obligation. Under r 298(1) of the Land Registration Rules 1925, SI 1925/1093 in that event the registrar shall hear and determine the matter, and by r 300 he must serve notice that he will hear and determine the matter at the registry on all persons appearing to be interested, stating the time of such hearing and that such persons may attend before him at that time in person or by solicitors or counsel. It is therefore to my mind clear that once a dispute has arisen the matter cannot properly be described as being ex parte, but that a party known to be interested must be given the opportunity of appearing.

The registrar, however, under r 298(2) may, if he thinks fit, instead of determining
a the question himself, refer the matter at any stage or any question thereon for the
decision of the court, and 'the Court' for that purpose means the Chancery Division, and
the matter falls to be determined by a single judge of this division: see s 138(2) of the
Land Registration Act, as amended by the Administration of Justice Act 1982 and RSC
Ord 93, r 10. Rule 298(2) therefore, allows a dispute to be resolved, if the registrar
chooses, by the court instead of by himself. One would therefore expect that the same
b obligation to serve notice of the hearing on interested parties would arise in the case of
court proceedings.

Counsel for the city council then drew my attention to s 12(1) of the State Immunity
Act 1978. By that subsection:

> 'Any writ or other document required to be served for instituting proceedings
> against a State shall be served by being transmitted through the Foreign and
> Commonwealth Office to the Ministry of Foreign Affairs of the State and service
c > shall be deemed to have been effected when the writ or document is received at the
> Ministry.'

That is subject to s 12(6), which allows the service of a writ or other document in any
manner to which the state has agreed. He submitted that despite the mandatory nature
d of s 12(1) it had no application because the originating summons was not a document
required to be served for instituting proceedings against a state, but was merely a
document chosen as a convenient method of bringing the matter before the court in
compliance with the Chief Land Registrar's order. I regret that I cannot accept this. It is
true that the Chief Land Registrar by his order was not insisting on an originating
summons and that any other appropriate originating process could have been used,
although in my judgment the originating summons was the correct form: see RSC Ord
e 5, r 3. But whatever originating process was chosen, it must have been envisaged that the
city council would be instituting proceedings as plaintiff and the only other known
interested party, the Iranian government, would be defendant, and that by analogy with
r 300 of the Land Registration Rules 1925 the Iranian government would be served with
the proceedings, so that it could participate in the hearing before the court. It seems to
f me, therefore, that the wording of the opening words of s 12(1) of the State Immunity
Act 1978 is satisfied in the present case.

There are some ex parte originating proceedings provided for under the Rules of the
Supreme Court, for example an ex parte originating summons, and counsel for the city
council submitted that I should treat the Form 8 originating summons as though it were
an ex parte originating summons. If such an ex parte application were an appropriate
originating process, the fact that another form of originating summons had been used
g would not have deterred me from exercising the power in RSC Ord 2 and from treating
the application as one made by the appropriate mode; but I find it impossible to say that
on a dispute arising under the Land Registration Act it would be appropriate for an ex
parte originating process to be used. It is known that there is a dispute between the city
council as applicant for registration and the Iranian government as objector. It seems to
h me, therefore, to be contrary to principle in those circumstances to treat the matter as
though it were an ex parte originating process. Counsel for the city council accepts that
if s 12 does apply there can be no question of ordinary substituted service, s 12 providing
the only mode of service in mandatory terms.

Counsel for the city council then argued that RSC Ord 32, r 5(1) and (2) (made
applicable to originating summonses by Ord 28, r 1) gave the court power to dispense
j with service. RSC Ord 32, r 5 provides:

> (1) 'Where any party to a summons fails to attend on the first or any resumed
> hearing thereof, the Court may proceed in his absence if, having regard to the nature
> of the application, it thinks it expedient so to do.
> (2) Before proceeding in the absence of any party the Court may require to be
> satisfied that the summons or, as the case may be, the notice of the time appointed
> for the resumed hearing was duly served on that party.'

It was submitted that r 5(1) applied because the Iranian government had failed to attend; but the failure to attend which is referred to in r 5(1) to my mind connotes that *a* someone who has been duly served with a summons has failed to attend. Rule 5(2), counsel for the city council submitted, gave the court a discretion to dispense with service because of the terms of that rule '. . . the Court may require to be satisfied that the summons . . . was duly served . . .' But I do not read this rule as a power to dispense with service. To my mind it is concerned with proof of service, and it puts a party on notice that proof of service on a person not attending may be insisted on by the court. In my *b* judgment the rule would be in a different form if it were directed at allowing dispensation with service. There are, of course, special and express provisions in the Rules of the Supreme Court allowing dispensation with service in particular cases, and the contrast with the present rule is to my mind marked.

Counsel for the city council also reminded me of the wide discretion conferred on the court by RSC Ord 2, r 1 to dispense with requirements of the rules. But I do not regard *c* it as proper in the circumstances of the present case to treat an application, which to my mind was rightly framed as an inter partes proceeding, as an ex parte application. Of course, the rules do provide for some ex parte applications (see for example RSC Ord 50, r 1(2)), but again the contrast between such a provision and the present case is marked. One would expect an express provision dealing with the matter.

In the result I find myself forced to the conclusion that I cannot rule on the question *d* referred to the court without prior service on the Iranian government. I reach this conclusion with no satisfaction whatsoever. I find it disquieting that the Iranian government, having raised an objection, can frustrate the resolution by the court of the question thereby raised by not being willing to accept service through the solicitors who raised the objection on their behalf. But, as counsel for the city council accepts, by taking a state immunity objection the Iranian government has not submitted in any way to the *e* jurisdiction (see s 2 of the State Immunity Act 1978), and further I recognise that the particular problem in the present case arises only because of the exceptional circumstance that the method of service provided for by s 12 of the 1978 Act is or may be for the time being impractical.

In case I am wrong on the procedural question, I shall express my view briefly on the substantive question. Cathcarts, in their objection on behalf of the Iranian government, *f* relied on art 22 of the 1961 Vienna Convention on Diplomatic Relations (18 April 1961; TS 19 (1965); Cmnd 2565), which is one of the articles having, by reason of the Diplomatic Privileges Act 1964, the force of law in the United Kingdom. Cathcarts claimed that the premises at 16 Princes Gate still from part of the diplomatic mission of Iran in this country. Article 22, to which Cathcarts referred, reads as follows:

　　　1. The premises of the mission shall be inviolable. The agents of the receiving *g* State may not enter them, except with the consent of the head of the mission.
　　　2. The receiving State is under a special duty to take all appropriate steps to protect the premises of the mission against any intrusion or damage and to prevent any disturbance of the peace of the mission or impairment of its dignity.
　　　3. The premises of the mission, their furnishings and other property thereon and the means of transport of the mission shall be immune from search, requisition, *h* attachment or execution.'

The references to the premises of the mission must, however, be read with the definition provided in art 1(i):

　　　'the "premises of the mission" are the buildings or parts of buildings and the land ancillary thereto, irrespective of ownership, used for the purposes of the mission *j* including the residence of the head of the mission.'

The key word, as counsel for the city council submitted, is 'used'. That must connote the present tense 'which are used'. The fact that premises have been used in the past cannot be relevant to the state immunity afforded by the Vienna Convention. The evidence is

clear that since May 1980 the premises have not been used. The premises are in such a
a state now that they could not be used without extensive rebuilding.

The Foreign and Commonwealth Office, in a letter dated the 2 November 1984,
expressed to the city council the view that the building no longer constituted the premises
of the Iran mission within the meaning of art 1(*i*). I agree. It seems to me clear beyond
argument that the premises have ceased to be used for the purposes of the mission, and
in those circumstances the provisions of art 22 have no application to the premises. But,
b for the reasons which I have endeavoured to give, I find myself unable to give a ruling
for the purposes of the reference to this court.

Order accordingly.

Solicitors: *G M Ives* (for the city council).
c

Vivian Horvath Barrister.

d
Re Charge Card Services Ltd

CHANCERY DIVISION

MILLETT J

12, 13, 15, 16, 19, 20, 21, 22, 23 MAY, 12 JUNE 1986

Sale of goods – Payment – Credit card – Nature of credit card transaction – Effect of credit card
e *company's liquidation – Company operating credit card system for purchase of petrol at garages*
– Company going into liquidation – Debts outstanding from cardholders not paid by company to
garages – Whether cardholders' debts due to company or to garages – Whether liquidator bound
to pay garages from money collected from cardholders before company had paid garages –
Whether company's right to payment from cardholders a right of reimbursement only.

f *Company – Charge – Registration – Charge on book debts – Factoring agreement – Company*
factoring debts to factoring company – Factoring company entitled to retain such amount as it
determined as security for claims, non-payment by debtors and over-payments made to company
– Whether right of retention a right of set-off or account – Whether right of retention a charge on
book debts created by the company – Whether right of retention void for non-registration or as an
attempt to contract out of rules of distribution – Bankruptcy Act 1914, s 31 – Companies Act
g *1948, s 95(1).*

A company operated a charge card scheme under which it issued charge cards to
cardholders who could obtain petrol and other products from garages by signing a sales
voucher completed by the garage. The cardholder and the garage retained a copy of the
voucher and a copy was sent to the company. The company then paid the face value of
h the voucher, less agreed commission, to the garage and the cardholder paid the full face
value to the company. The company financed its activities by factoring its debts to C Ltd
under a financing agreement whereby all present and future debts owed by cardholders
to the company were assigned to C Ltd, which paid to the company the amount of the
debts less a discounting charge. Under the terms of the factoring agreement C Ltd was
entitled in its absolute discretion to retain such amount as it determined as security for
j any claims against the company, any risk of non-payment by cardholders and any
amount prospectively chargeable to the company as a debt under the terms of the
agreement. It was a further condition of the factoring agreement that if the company
went into liquidation C Ltd could require the company to repurchase at face value any
outstanding receivables held by C Ltd under the factoring agreement. The company
subsequently went into voluntary liquidation owing almost £2m to its unsecured

creditors. At the time of the liquidation some £3m worth of receivables due from
cardholders was outstanding and the company had not then paid the garages in respect
of a substantial number of those receivables. No notice requiring the company to
repurchase outstanding receivables had been served by C Ltd. On a summons issued by
the liquidator of the company, the issues arose (i) whether the receivables due from the
cardholders were debts due to the company or to the garages, (ii) whether the right of
retention conferred on C Ltd represented an unregistered charge which was void as
against the liquidator under s 95(1)ᵃ of the Companies Act 1948 and (iii) whether, if C
Ltd required the company to repurchase the outstanding receivables, it could set off the
purchase price against any sum due from C Ltd under the agreement. In regard to the
first issue the garages contended that since a charge card transaction involved a risk of
non-payment there was a presumption that payment by a charge card was conditional
only, so that if there was a failure of the agreed method of payment the liability of the
paying party, ie the cardholder, remained undischarged and the garage was entitled to
recover payment directly from the cardholder. In regard to the second issue the company
contended that the right of retention was expressly reserved by C Ltd as security for sums
due to it by the company and that consequently it constituted a charge on book debts
created by the company which was void against the liquidator. On the third issue it
contended that in so far as the contractual right to set off extended to liabilities of the
company which were still wholly contingent at the date of the resolution to wind up it
went further than s 31ᵇ of the Bankruptcy Act 1914 and was void as an attempt to
contract out of the statutory rules of distribution on a winding up.

Held – (1) There was no general principle of law that, whenever a method of payment
was adopted which involved a risk of non-payment, there was a presumption that it was
taken as conditional payment only. Each method of payment had to be examined to see
whether such a presumption should be made (see p 301 f, post).

(2) The charge card transaction was not a tripartite agreement between the supplier,
the cardholder and the card-issuing company, but three separate bilateral contracts
between the cardholder and the company, the cardholder and the supplier, and the
company and the supplier respectively. The essence of the charge card transaction was
that the supplier and the customer had for their mutual convenience each previously
arranged to open an account with the same company and had agreed that any account
between themselves could, if the customer wished, be settled by crediting the supplier's
and debiting the customer's account with that company. That process did not depend on
the company's solvency and the customer's liability was discharged at the latest when the
supplier's account was credited, not when the supplier was paid. Furthermore, unlike
irrevocable letters of credit where the presumption was that payment was conditional,

---

a   Section 95(1), so far as material, provides: '... every charge created after the fixed date by a
    company ... and being a charge to which this section applies shall, so far as any security on the
    company's property or undertaking is conferred thereby, be void against the liquidator and any
    creditor of the company, unless the prescribed particulars of the charge together with the
    instrument, if any, by which the charge is created or evidenced, are delivered to or received by the
    registrar of companies for registration in manner required by this Act within twenty-one days
    after the date of its creation, but without any prejudice to any contract or obligation for repayment
    of the money thereby secured, and when a charge becomes void under this section the money
    secured thereby shall immediately become payable.'

b   Section 31 provides: 'Where there have been mutual credits, mutual debts or other mutual
    dealings, between a debtor against whom a receiving order shall be made under this Act and any
    other person proving or claiming to prove a debt under the receiving order, an account shall be
    taken of what is due from the one party to the other in respect of such mutual dealings, and the
    sum due from the one party shall be set off against any sum due from the other party, and the
    balance of the account, and no more, shall be claimed or paid on either side respectively; but a
    person shall not be entitled under this section to claim the benefit of any set-off against the property
    of a debtor in any case where he had, at the time of giving credit to the debtor, notice of an act of
    bankruptcy committed by the debtor and available against him.'

a payment by use of a charge card was not a conditional payment, because (a) the card was used mainly to facilitate payment of small consumer debts between parties which might not be known to each other and on terms which were not usually subject to negotiation, (b) the card had to be one which the customer was authorised to use and the supplier had to have the necessary equipment to accept, (c) the machinery for payment did not require disclosure of the customer's address to the supplier, (d) the availability of the charge card as a method of payment was advantageous to both parties and (e) the terms on which the

b supplier was entitled to payment from the card-issuing company were quite different from those on which the card-issuing company was entitled to payment from the customer and both differed from the terms on which the supplier would be entitled to payment from the customer if the latter were subject to any residual liability not discharged by his use of the card. These features of payment by means of a charge or credit card were sufficient not only to displace any presumption that payment by such

c means was a conditional payment only, but to support a presumption to the contrary. It followed that the garages had no recourse to the cardholders on the company's failure to pay their accounts (see p 300 h, p 303 e to p 304 b, post); *Richardson (Inspector of Taxes) v Worrall* [1985] STC 693, dicta of Stephenson LJ in *W J Alan & Co Ltd v El Nasr Export and Import Co* [1972] 2 All ER at 146 and of Ackner J in *Maran Road Saw Mill v Austin Taylor & Co Ltd* [1975] 1 Lloyd's Rep at 159 considered.

d (3) The company's right to payment from cardholders was not a right of reimbursement only. The agreement between the company and the cardholders authorised the company to pay the cost of any goods obtained by use of the charge card, and such authority included the further authority to incur any obligation to pay. It followed that the company's right to debit a cardholder's account was a right not only to debit it in regard to payments made but also in regard to liabilities incurred. Accordingly, the cardholders'

e liability to pay the company was not dependent on the company paying the garage (see p 304 e f and p 305 d e, post).

(4) Except in relation to the company's liability to repurchase receivables at face value, the rights of retention were not rights of set-off but of account, and accordingly were not void as an attempt to contract out of the rules of distribution on a winding up (see p 307 c d, post); dicta of Buckley LJ in *Halesowen Presswork and Assemblies Ltd v Westminster Bank*

f *Ltd* [1970] 3 All ER at 488 applied.

(5) The rights of retention contained in the financing agreement were not registrable charges which were void for want of registration under s 95(1) of the 1948 Act, because (a) it was not possible for a charge to be created in favour of a debtor over his own indebtedness to a creditor and (b) there was no relevant property capable of forming the subject matter of the charge. The only asset which the company could charge was the

g right to sue C Ltd for sums due under the agreement, but that was subject to C Ltd's right of retention which, although expressed to be by way of security, secured C Ltd against overpayment by itself rather than against default by the company in its obligations (see p 307 h to p 308 a c d, post).

(6) C Ltd could set off the purchase price of receivables against any sum due from it under the agreement, even though at the date of the winding up its claim was wholly contingent. It was enough that at the relevant date mutual dealings existed which

h involved rights and obligations, absolute or contingent, of such a nature that they could later mature or develop into pecuniary demands capable of set off. Furthermore, there was nothing in principle or on authority which drew a distinction between a liability the very existence of which was still contingent at the date of the receiving order and a liability which was then certain but the amount of which was unascertainable because its

j quantification depended on future events (see p 310 j to p 311 d, p 317 f to h and p 319 e to h, post); *Re Asphaltic Wood Pavement Co* (1885) 30 Ch D 216, *Re Daintrey, ex p Mant* [1895–9] All ER Rep 657, *Re Taylor, ex p Norvell* [1910] 1 KB 562, *Hiley v Peoples Prudential Assurance Co Ltd (in liq)* (1938) 60 CLR 468 followed; *Re Fenton, ex p Fenton Textile Association Ltd* [1930] All ER Rep 15, *Re a debtor (No 66 of 1955), ex p the debtor v Trustee of the property of Waite (a bankrupt)* [1956] 3 All ER 225 considered; *Carreras Rothmans Ltd v Freeman Mathews Treasure Ltd (in liq)* [1985] 1 All ER 155 not followed.

Notes
For set-off, see 3 Halsbury's Laws (4th edn) paras 751–761.
    For the Bankruptcy Act 1914, s 31, see 4 Halsbury's Statutes (4th edn) 552.
    As from 1 July 1985, s 95(1) of the Companies Act 1948 was replaced by s 395 of the Companies Act 1985. For s 395 of the 1985 Act, see 8 Halsbury's Statutes (4th edn) 457.
    As from a day to be appointed under the Insolvency Act 1985, s 323 of the Insolvency Act 1986 will replace s 31 of the 1914 Act.

Cases referred to in judgment
Alan (W J) & Co Ltd v El Nasr Export and Import Co [1972] 2 All ER 127, [1972] 2 QB 189, [1972] 2 WLR 800, CA.
Allen v Royal Bank of Canada (1926) 95 LJPC 17.
Asphaltic Wood Pavement Co, Re, Lee and Chapman's Case (1885) 30 Ch D 216, CA.
Barclays Bank Ltd v TOSG Trust Fund Ltd [1984] BCLC 1; *affd* [1984] 1 All ER 628, [1984] AC 626, [1984] 2 WLR 49, CA; *affd* [1984] 1 All ER 1060, [1984] AC 626, [1984] 2 WLR 650, HL.
Bolt and Nut Co (Tipton) Ltd v Rowlands Nicholls & Co Ltd [1964] 1 All ER 137, [1964] 2 QB 10, [1964] 2 WLR 98, CA.
British Eagle International Airlines Ltd v Cie Nationale Air France [1975] 2 All ER 390, [1975] 1 WLR 758, HL.
Carreras Rothmans Ltd v Freeman Mathews Treasure Ltd (in liq) [1985] 1 All ER 155, [1985] Ch 207, [1984] 3 WLR 1016.
City Life Assurance Co Ltd, Re, Grandfield's Case, Stephenson's Case [1926] Ch 191, [1925] All ER Rep 453, CA.
Daintrey, Re, ex p Mant [1900] 1 QB 546, [1895–9] All ER Rep 657, CA.
Day and Dent Constructions Pty Ltd v North Australian Properties Pty Ltd (1982) 40 ALR 399, Aust HC.
Debtor, Re a (No 66 of 1955), ex p the debtor v Trustee of the property of Waite (a bankrupt) [1956] 3 All ER 225, [1956] 1 WLR 1266, CA.
Fenton, Re, ex p Fenton Textile Association Ltd [1931] 1 Ch 85, [1930] All ER Rep 15, CA.
Halesowen Presswork and Assemblies Ltd v Westminster Bank Ltd [1970] 3 All ER 473, [1971] 1 QB 1, [1970] 3 WLR 625, CA; *revsd* [1972] 1 All ER 642, [1972] AC 785, [1972] 2 WLR 455, HL.
Hart, Re, ex p Caldicott (1884) 25 Ch D 716, CA.
Hiley v Peoples Prudential Assurance Co Ltd (in liq) (1938) 60 CLR 468, Aust HC.
Man (E D & F) Ltd v Nigerian Sweets and Confectionery Co Ltd [1977] 2 Lloyd's Rep 50.
Maran Road Saw Mill v Austin Taylor & Co Ltd [1975] 1 Lloyd's Rep 156.
National Benefit Assurance Co Ltd, Re [1924] 2 Ch 339, [1924] All ER Rep 426.
National Provincial and Union Bank of England v Charnley [1924] 1 KB 431.
Palmer v Carey [1926] AC 703, [1926] All ER Rep 650, PC.
Palmer v Day & Sons [1895] 2 QB 618.
Richardson (Inspector of Taxes) v Worrall [1985] STC 693.
Rodick v Gandell (1852) 1 De GM & G 763, 42 ER 749, LC.
Romer and Haslam, Re [1893] 2 QB 286, CA.
Sovereign Life Assurance Co v Dodd [1892] 1 QB 405; *affd* [1892] 2 QB 573, [1891–4] All ER Rep 246, CA.
Taylor, Re, ex p Norvell [1910] 1 KB 562.

Cases also cited
Blackpool Motor Car Co Ltd, Re, Hamilton v Blackpool Motor Car Co Ltd [1901] 1 Ch 77.
Bond Worth Ltd, Re [1979] 3 All ER 919, [1980] Ch 228.
Debtor, Re a (No 627 of 1936) [1937] 1 All ER 1, [1937] Ch 156, CA.
Esso Petroleum Co Ltd v Customs and Excise Comrs [1976] 1 All ER 117, [1976] 1 WLR 1, HL.
Hawkins (decd), Re (2 February 1978, unreported), Ch D.

Lloyds and Scottish Finance Ltd v Cyril Lord Carpet Sales Ltd (29 March 1979, unreported),
a   HL.
Metropolitan Police Comr v Charles [1976] 3 All ER 112, [1977] AC 177, HL.
Naoroji v Chartered Bank of India (1868) LR 3 CP 444.
Paine, Re, ex p Read [1897] QB 122.
R v Lambie [1981] 2 All ER 776, [1982] AC 449, HL.
Sale Continuation Ltd v Austin Taylor & Co Ltd [1967] 2 All ER 1092, [1968] 2 QB 849.
b   *Siebe Gorman & Co Ltd v Barclays Bank Ltd* [1979] 2 Lloyd's Rep 142.
Swiss Bank Corp v Lloyds Bank Ltd [1981] 2 All ER 449, [1982] AC 584, HL.

Originating summons

By a rereamended originating summons dated 8 March 1985, Anthony Malcolm David Bird, the liquidator of Charge Card Services Ltd (the company), sought, inter alia, the
c   following reliefs (i) as against the respondents, (1) Commercial Credit Services Ltd (Commercial Credit), (2) Henlys plc, on their own behalf and as representing all the garages which were or had been franchisees under the Motor Agents Association Fuel Card Scheme, and (3) Copes Service Stations Ltd, on their own behalf and as representing all the garages which were or had been franchisees under the Motor Agents Association Fuel Card Scheme, the determination of the question whether debts due on 21 January
d   1985 (when the company ceased to trade) or on 4 February 1985 (when the company went into creditors' voluntary liquidation) from cardholders in respect of petroleum and other products obtained by the cardholders from garage franchisees or any of them with the use of charge cards (the debts) represented (a) debts due to the company, (b) debts due to Commercial Credit or (c) debts due to the franchisee garages from which the petroleum or other products were obtained by the cardholders, (ii) as against Commercial Credit
e   only, a declaration that Commercial Credit was liable to remit to the company (acting by its liquidator) without deduction the purchase price of all receivables sold by the company to Commercial Credit pursuant to the terms of a written invoice discounting agreement dated 15 February 1983 and made between the company and Commercial Credit, and (iii) as against Commercial Credit only, a declaration that the purported right of retention conferred on Commercial Credit by standard condition 3B of the first schedule to the
f   discounting agreement represented an unregistered charge void as against the liquidator pursuant to s 95 of the Companies Act 1948. By an order dated 29 March 1985 the third respondent was appointed to represent all the garages which were members of the scheme, including the second respondents. The facts are set out in the judgment.

David Oliver QC and *Richard Hacker* for the liquidator.
g   *J M Chadwick QC* and *Richard Gillis* for the Commercial Credit.
Robin Potts QC and *Michael Todd* for the garages.

Cur adv vult

h   12 June. The following judgment was delivered.

MILLETT J. This case raises two questions. The first is one which can arise whenever goods or services are obtained by the use of a charge or credit card. The question is whether the supplier can call on the customer to pay him direct if the company which issued the card becomes insolvent before paying him. It is a question on which there is no reported decision, and on which academic writers have differed. It calls for a careful
j   analysis of the complex legal relationships arising in a familiar and everyday transaction of deceptively simple appearance.

Charge Card Services Ltd (which I shall call 'the company') was incorporated in June 1982. It ceased to trade on 21 January 1985, and entered into creditors' voluntary liquidation on 4 Febaruary 1985. On the evidence presently available there is likely to be a deficiency as regards unsecured creditors of approximately £1,932,000.

The company was promoted by the Motor Agents Association and the Scottish Motor Trades Association for the purpose of establishing and operating a charge card scheme *a* known as the Motor Agents Association Fuel Card Scheme (which I shall call 'the scheme'). Under the scheme the company issued charge cards (called Fuel Cards) to individuals and companies which had submitted written applications for the use of such cards (I shall call them 'account holders'). The cards were available for use by the account holder or by the person or persons whom the account holder had authorised to use the card (whom I shall call 'cardholders') at garages which were members of one or other of *b* the two associations and which had entered into a previous agreement with the company.

The company issued two types of charge card. The first could be used at any garage which had become a member of the scheme. The second, commonly described as an 'in-house card', could be used only at a particular garage or group of garages. For present purposes there is no relevant distinction between the two types of cards. Immediately prior to the cessation of business by the company there were some 4,666 garages which *c* were members of the scheme, of which 620 operated 'in-house cards', and there were in all some 33,500 cardholders.

The scheme was operated in a manner which would be familiar to anyone who has ever used a charge or credit card. Cardholders were entitled to use the Fuel Card to obtain petrol and other designated products from garages which were members of the scheme and which advertised their willingness to accept the card. If a cardholder decided to use *d* his card in connection with such a purchase, he would produce the card and sign a sales voucher completed by the garage. One copy of the voucher would be handed to the cardholder; one copy would be retained by the garage; and one copy would be forwarded by the garage to the company, which in due course would pay to the garage the face value of the sales voucher less an agreed commission. Weekly invoices showing the face value of the sales vouchers would be sent by the company to the account holder, who *e* would also be sent a monthly statement showing the sums invoiced and payments by the account holder (and in certain circumstances interest). The account holder was obliged to pay the amount shown as owing to the company within 14 days of receipt of the monthly statement.

The company, of course, was in no position to invoice the account holder until it had received the sales vouchers from the garage; and it was to be expected that the company *f* would pay the garage before it received payment from the account holder. Normally, no doubt, it did so. There might, however, be cases, and during the last few weeks before the company ceased trading there certainly were cases, in which the account holder was required to pay, and did pay, the company before the company paid the garage. For his part the account holder when required to pay the company would have no means of knowing, and would be unlikely to inquire, whether the company had paid the garage. *g*

Because the company would normally pay the garage before it obtained reimbursement from the account holder, it financed its activities by factoring its receivables. This was effected by an invoice discounting agreement, dated 15 February 1983 and entered into between (1) the company and (2) the first respondents, Commercial Credit Services Ltd (which I shall call 'Commercial Credit'). By that agreement all debts owing or to become owing from account holders to the company were assigned to Commercial Credit. Notice *h* of the assignment was given to account holders by a statement on each invoice sent to them.

At the date of liquidation the company's books showed some £3,000,000 of receivables due from account holders for petrol and other products supplied to cardholders against production of the Fuel Card. These receivables fell into two categories: (i) cases where the garage had been paid by the company, and (ii) cases where the garage had not been paid *j* by the company. Cases in the first of these categories cause no difficulty. It is agreed by all parties that these represented debts due to the company and that, by virtue of the invoice discounting agreement, they have been assigned to Commercial Credit. The present dispute is concerned solely with cases in the second category. In addition, for the reasons I have mentioned, there are cases where the account holder has paid the company,

but the company has not paid the garage. Such cases were not of course included in the
a company's receivables at the date of liquidation and any questions which may arise in
relation to them are not directly before me.

Shortly after the commencement of the liquidation it became apparent that difficulties
were being caused and would continue to be caused by garages, which foresaw little
prospect of a substantial dividend being received from the company or who were not
prepared to wait, seeking to recover payment direct from the account holders and not
b from the company. Among the garages which claimed to be entitled to take this course
were the second respondents, who operated an in-house scheme, and the third
respondents, who operated the general scheme. On 29 March 1985 the third respondents
were appointed to represent all garages which were members of the scheme. On the
same date the liquidator was directed to collect all sums due from account holders in
respect of petrol and other products obtained by cardholders by the use of Fuel Cards
c from garages which were members of the scheme. The liquidator was directed to pay
the moneys so collected into a separate account, and was authorised to draw on the
account for the purpose of defraying the costs of collection. That order was expressed to
be without prejudice to any necessary accounting in the light of the determination of the
questions now before the court and without prejudice to the question of the liquidator's
remuneration and the source from which it is to come. Pursuant to that order, some
d £2,234,428 has been collected by the liquidator, and after deduction of the costs of
collection a net sum of £2,034,529 remains in the account.

The first question

The first question which is raised by the summons is whether the debts due from the
account holders on 21 January 1985 (when the company ceased to trade) or on 4 February
e 1985 (when it went into creditors' voluntary liquidation) in respect of petrol and other
products obtained by cardholders from garages which were members of the scheme
represented (a) debts due to the company or (b) debts due to Commercial Credit or (c)
debts due to the garages from which the supplies were obtained, or (d) debts due to any
other persons. As I have already mentioned, it is accepted that the garages have no claim
to debts due from account holders in respect of petrol or other products for which the
f garages supplying them have been paid by the company, and that by virtue of the invoice
discounting agreement the company's receivables have been effectively assigned to
Commercial Credit. In the absence of any representative account holder before the court,
the garages have also accepted that they can make no claim in these proceedings to
moneys which were due from account holders on 21 January 1985 but were paid by
them to the company before the commencement of the liquidation. Accordingly, the
g question which I have to decide is whether debts due from account holders at the
commencement of the company's liquidation on 4 February 1985 in respect of petrol
and other products obtained by cardholders from garages which were members of the
scheme and for which the garages supplying them have not been paid by the company
represented (a) debts due to Commercial Credit or (b) debts due to the garages from
which the supplies had been obtained.

h The nature and consequence of the legal relationships created by the use of a credit or
charge card for the purchase of goods or services have not been the subject of any reported
decision.

It is clear that there are at least three parties involved: the supplier (in this case the
garage), the purchaser (the cardholder) and the company which issued the card (the
company). In the present case there are four, since cards were issued to account holders,
j who were entitled to authorise their employees or other authorised signatories
(cardholders) to make use of the cards. This is an added complication which can be
ignored for present purposes, since in such a case the account holder is liable as principal,
disclosed or undisclosed, to pay for the goods or services obtained by the use of the card,
whether or not the cardholder is also liable. The question is not who is liable to pay, but
who is entitled to receive payment.

On the use of the card, three separate contracts come into operation. First, there is the contract of supply between the supplier and the cardholder (either in his own right or as *a* agent for the account holder); second, there is the contract between the supplier and the card-issuing company, which undertakes to honour the card by paying the supplier on presentation of the sales voucher; and, third, there is the contract between the card-issuing company and the account holder by which the account holder undertakes to reimburse the card-issuing company for payments made or liabilities incurred by the card-issuing company to the supplier as a result of his or his cardholder's use of the card. *b* There are thus three separate contracts and three separate parties, each being party to two of the three contracts but neither party nor privy to the third. While the legal consequences of these arrangements must depend on the terms of the particular contracts employed, one would expect each contract to be separate and independent and to be entered into between principals. In particular, one would expect the card-issuing company to enter into both its contract with the supplier and its contract with the *c* account holder as a principal in its own right and not merely as agent for the account holder and the supplier respectively. One would also expect the supplier to be entitled to be paid whether or not the card-issuing company is able to obtain reimbursement from the account holder, and the card-issuing company to be entitled to be paid whether or not the goods or services supplied by the supplier are satisfactory. The question which arises in the present case is: on whom does the risk of default by the card-issuing company *d* fall? Does it fall on the supplier or (if the account holder has already paid the card-issuing company) on the account holder, so that he may be called on to pay twice, and (if he has not already paid the card-issuing company) on the card-issuing company's receivables' financier?

In the present case, as must be common, the two contracts to which the card-issuing company was a party were in writing, while the contract of supply was not. The terms *e* of the contract between each member garage and the company are to be found on the reverse of a franchise application form, headed 'Terms and Conditions relating to the grant and holding of a franchise'. By that agreement the company undertook to provide the equipment necessary to operate the scheme, including an imprinter and sales vouchers, and a metal double sided pole sign advertising the scheme; and to reimburse the garage for 'the cost [sic] of fuel and lubricants purchased, as shown by the relevant *f* valid sales vouchers issued by the garage, less the appropriate commission due to the Company'. Two methods of claiming and receiving reimbursement were set out, and the differing rates applicable thereto were specified. The company also undertook to establish, for the benefit of all member garages, a guarantee of its obligation to reimburse them; regrettably it never did so. Finally, it undertook to maintain records of all transactions between itself and each member garage and to forward monthly statements *g* to each such garage showing the amount of any indebtedness between them. For its part, each member garage undertook, inter alia—

> 'To honour all valid and current [Motor Agents Association] Fuel Cards presented by card holders by supplying petrol, diesel oil, liquefied petroleum gas and lubricating oil (but no other products and no services) to the card holder at the same prices and on the same terms as for cash sales displayed at the point of sale.' *h*

Each garage also undertook to display signs indicating that the Fuel Card was accepted at relevant locations and to permit the company to advertise or circulate the fact that a Fuel Card was accepted there. The company reserved the right to reject any invalid sales voucher, and the circumstances in which a sales voucher should be invalid were specified. The company also reserved the right to charge the garage with any overpayment made *j* in respect of sales vouchers and with the full amount of all payments made in respect of invalid sales vouchers.

The terms of the contract between the company and the account holder are to be found in the subscriber's agreement, by which each account holder agreed to be bound by the terms and conditions printed on the reverse of the agreement relating to the issue

of the card. So far as material these provided as follows. First, the card was to become
a valid only when it had been signed either by the person to whom it had been issued (the
account holder) or by the person whom the account holder had authorised to use the card
(the authorised signatory). The signature and/or use by the account holder or his
authorised signatory constituted agreement by the account holder to these terms and
conditions. Clause 1 of the terms and conditions of use provided:

b
'Use of the Card will authorise [the company] to pay for petrol, lpg, derv and oil
(only) supplied to the Account Holder or the Authorised Signatory by the various
garages who are members of the Motor Agents Association . . . or Scottish Motor
Trade Association . . .'

Use of the card was restricted to the account holder or the authorised signatory. The
agreement provided for monthly statements showing all accounts debited, less any
c credits or refunds, to be sent to the account holder by the company, for the account
holder to pay to the company, within 14 days from the date to which the statement was
made up, the whole of the amount shown to be owing by the statement, and for interest
to be charged on any outstanding balance after expiry of the 14-day period. The
agreement contained provisions in case the card (which remained the property of the
company) should be lost or stolen; and provided that no claim by the account holder
d against any supplier should be the subject of any set-off or counterclaim against or give
rise to any liability on the part of the company.

Each supply contract between a member garage and a cardholder will have taken place
on the garage forecourt in a manner familiar to any motorist. I have been provided with
an agreed statement of facts, from which the following can be extracted.

By promotional literature issued by the company in conjunction with the Motor
e Agents Association, retail garages were encouraged to apply to become members of the
scheme. High mileage fleet operators were similarly encouraged to apply to become
account holders. Each garage accepted as a member of the scheme was issued with a
guide to the scheme, an imprinter retail plate, sales vouchers, claim forms, promotional
literature and a metal double-sided pole advertising its membership of the scheme. The
garage would advertise its membership of the scheme, and hence its willingness to accept
f the company Fuel Card, by its signs displayed on the garage forecourt and by the
inclusion of the garage's name and address in a directory compiled by the company and
issued to all account holders. Garages operating an 'in-house' scheme would inform the
customers for whom they previously operated credit accounts of the adoption of the 'in-
house card' by sending to each such customer a letter in a standard form suggested by the
company.

g The company issued cards to an applicant only after credit references had been taken
up. An upper limit was then placed on the value of the purchases that any given account
holder could charge to his account. On issue of the cards, the account holder designated
the identity of the cardholders entitled to use them. Cards available for use at only one
garage were sent to and held by that garage. Other cards, including 'in-house cards'
available for use at more than one garage were sent to the account holders.

h A cardholder who required fuel would arrive on the garage forecourt, and at a self-
service garage would operate the fuel pump himself to put the required amount of fuel
into the vehicle's fuel tank; at a service garage the fuel pump would be operated by an
attendant acting on his instructions. The amount and price of the fuel provided would
be recorded electronically on the pump. No prior discussion as to the method of payment
would normally occur. Many petrol pumps display notices referring to the fact that it is
j an offence under the Theft Act 1968 to place fuel into a petrol tank without being able to
pay with either cash, a cheque supported by a valid banker's card or an approved credit
card.

A cardholder who required lubricating oil would normally select the oil for himself
from the garage's display or request an attendant to supply the lubricating oil for him.

At the cashier's till the cardholder (if he chose to take advantage of the scheme) would proffer his card. Alternatively the cardholder could pay by cash or cheque supported by a valid banker's card or by some other acceptable credit or charge card.

In the case of an 'in-house' scheme where the card was kept by the garage, the garage would produce the card on being informed that the cardholder wished to make use of the card in connection with the purchase.

A sales voucher, as supplied by the company, would be prepared with an imprint of the cardholder's card and sometimes the retailer's imprinter plate, giving the name (but not the address) of the account holder and the number of his account with the company, after which particulars of the date, the vehicle registration number, the amount of fuel provided and the total cost would be entered on the sale-voucher. The cardholder would sign the sales voucher (with carbons underneath). The top copy of the sales voucher would then be handed to the cardholder. Except in the case of 'in-house' schemes where the card was kept at the garage, the card would then be returned to the cardholder.

On behalf of the garages it was submitted that as soon as a cardholder puts petrol in the tank of his car, or has petrol put in the tank by a garage attendant, he thereby contracts to purchase and pay for the petrol at the price displayed on the pump. (If the cardholder is not the account holder, then the account holder also becomes liable at this stage as undisclosed principal, but this does not affect the nature or extent of the cardholder's liability.) The cardholder's liability to pay the garage for the petrol arises when the petrol is put in his tank; and his obligation, in the absence of an acceptable alternative, is to pay in cash. Credit card advertisements outside the garage constitute a standing offer to cardholders to settle their liability by means of the advertised card. The right to use his card is a right of which the cardholder can avail himself if he wishes; he may, if he prefers, pay in cash. So far these submissions adopt the analysis of Scott J in *Richardson (Inspector of Taxes) v Worrall* [1985] STC 693. If the cardholder chooses to pay by card (or, for that matter, by cheque, whether or not supported by a bank card), the argument proceeded, he is not thereby unconditionally discharged from his liability to pay. Payment by card, it was submitted, like payment by cheque, operates as a conditional payment only. A supplier who accepts payment by credit or charge card must in the first instance look to the card-issuing company for payment, and must present the sales vouchers with an appropriate claim form to the company. But if for any reason the sales voucher is not honoured by the card-issuing company, or the company defaults or becomes insolvent, then the cardholder's liability to pay the garage for the supplies he has received is not discharged. He is not discharged because, in the event, he has not paid.

The primary submission of counsel for Commercial Credit was to challenge this analysis of the forecourt transaction. It was submitted that the cardholder never becomes liable to the garage to pay for the petrol at all. His (and, if he is not the account holder, the account holder's) only obligation is to pay the company; while the garage never has any right to look to the cardholder or account holder for payment, but must from the outset look to the company. Counsel accepted the obvious fact that the cardholder enters into a contract with the garage for a supply of petrol as soon as the petrol is put into the tank of his car. But, it was submitted, his obligation is not to pay for the petrol simpliciter: it is from the outset an obligation to pay or *to provide for payment by one of the methods which the garage holds itself out as willing to accept.* One of those methods in the present case was the Fuel Card; and the terms of the agreement between the garage and the company were that the garage would honour the card by supplying the petrol, and that the company would pay the garage for the supply. The cardholder was not bound to do so, but he was entitled from the outset to accept a supply of petrol on the terms that payment to the garage would be made by the company, and that he or his account holder would not be required to pay the garage at all. There was, it was submitted, no reason to treat one method of payment, viz payment in cash, as the primary or underlying obligation, when to the cardholder's knowledge at the outset other methods, such as payment by card, were equally acceptable. The account holder and his cardholders were never at any stage under any obligation to pay the garage, it was submitted, because by arrangements made before the cardholder drove onto the forecourt they were members

of a favoured class to whom the garage would be obliged, if asked, to sell petrol and look
a for payment elsewhere.

By this means counsel for Commercial Credit sought to escape the conclusion that the
acceptance of the card by the garage discharged any pre-existing obligation on the part of
the cardholder or his account holder to pay the garage, and thus, it was hoped, avoid
altogether the question whether such discharge was absolute or conditional. For the
reasons I shall explain, I do not consider that the question can be avoided by this route.
b First, however, I must examine the analysis of the transaction made by Scott J in
Richardson (Inspector of Taxes) v Worrall.

In that case the taxpayers, a Mr Worrall and a Mr Westall, were provided with credit
cards by their employers which could be used to purchase petrol for both business and
private motoring. The credit cards had been issued to the taxpayers' employers and the
taxpayers were the authorised users. The taxpayers were assessed to income tax under
c Sch E on the footing that the provision of the petrol used for private motoring constituted
emoluments of their respective employments. Scott J upheld the Crown's claim to tax
on the ground that the credit card arrangements which the employers made available to
the taxpayers enabled them to discharge their own liabilities to pay the garage for the
petrol they had purchased.

That decision is direct authority against the approach for which counsel for Commercial
d Credit contended. It is, however, necessary to examine the arguments which were
advanced and rejected in that case, and the reasons for their rejection. The argument of
Mr Worrall's counsel is not material for present purposes. It was Mr Westall's counsel
who submitted that, when Mr and Mrs Westall purchased petrol at garages which
advertised that they accepted Barclaycard, they never incurred any liability at all to pay
for the petrol. Counsel put his argument two ways. First, he submitted that the method
e of payment was an important part of the contract of sale, and that although the petrol
had been put in the tank no contract for its purchase was concluded until, at the till,
agreement was reached on the means of payment. Not surprisingly, Scott J rejected that
argument as complete nonsense.

Counsel for Mr Westall submitted, in the alternative, that, if the contract for the
purchase of petrol was made when the petrol was placed in the tank, it was a term of that
f contract, binding on both parties, that payment would be made by Barclaycard. Scott J
described this analysis as nearly as hopeless as the first. He rejected it in these words
([1985] STC 693 at 720):

> 'Credit card advertisements outside a garage may well be regarded as a standing
> offer to motorists to settle their liability by means of the advertised credit cards. But
> a motorist whether or not he intends to use a particular credit card does not put the
> *g* petrol in his tank on the footing that he is obliged to use that card. The right to use
> the particular card, or to use any other advertised credit card, is a right of which he
> can avail himself if he wishes. He can, if he prefers, pay in cash. If an implied term
> of the contract regarding payment is to be spelled out it is, in my judgment, a term
> that payment will be made in cash but that if the motorist prefers he may settle his
> liability by a valid credit card of a sort displayed at the garage or by a cheque backed
> *h* by an acceptable bank card. The underlying obligation, however, in lieu of an
> acceptable credit card or cheque and bank card is to make payment in cash.'

I respectfully agree with Scott J that the taxpayer's contention, in the terms in which it
was put, was quite untenable. It was not a term of the contract concluded at the pump
that payment *would* be made by Barclaycard, but only that it *could* be. Right from the
j outset, however, and before incurring any liability at all, the taxpayer was entitled, if he
chose, to make payment by means of the card. In that sense, he never had any obligation
to pay the garage and, since he was not the account holder, he never had any obligation
to pay anyone. He was from the outset entitled, if he chose, to a supply of petrol on terms
that the garage would be paid by the card-issuing company, and the card-issuing company
would be paid by the account holder.

Accordingly, counsel for Commercial Credit criticised Scott J's conclusion that 'The underlying obligation . . . in lieu of an acceptable credit card or cheque and bank card, is **a** to make payment in cash'. But in my judgment this is plainly right. Scott J was merely pointing out the obvious fact that the use of a credit or bank card is an alternative to payment in cash, and that if the cardholder fails to avail himself of an acceptable alternative the obligation to pay in cash remains.

In *Richardson (Inspector of Taxes) v Worrall* [1985] STC 693 at 720 Scott J continued:

'As part of his argument counsel for Mr Westall presented to me an analysis of a **b** transaction settled by production of a credit card. His intention was to demonstrate that the card holder never becomes personally liable to pay the price of the goods or services. The liability to pay rests, he submitted, on the bank or finance company by whom the credit card was issued. The analysis depends, however, on the premise that no contract comes into existence until either the credit card is accepted by the supplier or the supplier becomes contractually bound to accept the credit card. In **c** the case of purchases of motor fuel at garages and filling stations where the normal procedure, such as that followed by Mr and Mrs Westall and, for that matter, by Mr Worrall, takes place, the premise fails. Whether the analysis of counsel for Mr Westall is sound where, as in many department stores, the goods are not finally delivered until after the credit card has been offered and accepted, I need not decide.'

d

In my judgment, the agreement which comes into existence by the cardholder's acceptance of the garage's standing offer to accept payment by means of the card has the same legal consequence whether it is made at the pump and before the contract of supply is entered into or at the till and after the contract of supply has been concluded. The agreement to accept payment by means of the card is not an independent and free-standing contract in its own right: it is merely an agreement on the method of payment **e** under the contract of supply, and this is so whether the contract of supply is already concluded or is yet to be concluded.

This follows from an analysis of the true nature of the consideration for the goods or services supplied when payment is to be obtained by the supplier by the use of a charge or credit card. Three possibilities have been canvassed. The first is that the consideration for the supply is not the price (which is to be paid by the card-issuing company, a stranger **f** to the contract of supply) but production of the card and signature of the voucher. I reject this analysis, which is quite unrealistic. Production of the card and signature of a voucher are not the consideration itself but the means of obtaining it. Moreover, a sale of goods requires a monetary consideration: see s 2(1) of the Sale of Goods Act 1979. This analysis would thus lead to the conclusion that, where payment is to be made by credit or charge card, the contract of supply is not a sale of goods, with the result that the **g** statutory conditions and warranties are not implied. The second possibility which has been suggested is that there is a sale of goods, but the contract is a tripartite contract under which the consideration for the supply to the cardholder is the undertaking of the card-issuing company to pay the price to the supplier. I reject this analysis, which confuses the result of all the arrangements made with the legal means employed to achieve it. On the use of the card, there is no tripartite agreement, but three separate **h** bilateral contracts come into operation. In my judgment, the true consideration in the contract of supply is the price, to be satisfied by the cardholder if he wishes by means of the card.

If, however, the supplier's acceptance of the use of a card is merely an agreement as to the means by which the consideration under the contract of supply may be satisfied, this must be so whether this agreement precedes or follows or is simultaneous with and **j** forms part of the contract of supply itself. If the contract of supply is entered into first, then the agreement that payment thereunder under shall be made by means of the card supersedes and discharges a pre-existing obligation to pay in cash. If not, it displaces at the outset what would, in the absence of agreement, have been an obligation to pay in cash. In either case, the question remains: what is the extent of the obligation? Is it

merely to provide a means of obtaining payment from the card-issuing company, so that
a it is satisfied simply by producing the card and signing the voucher? Or is it to provide a
means of obtaining payment from the card-issuing company which proves effective, so
that it is satisfied only if the card-issuing company honours its obligation to pay the
supplier? If the latter, then any pre-existing obligation to pay is not unconditionally
discharged by the agreed substitute and, if there was no such pre-existing obligation, the
underlying obligation to pay is not unconditionally displaced by the agreed alternative.

b   Accordingly, I turn to the real question, whether payment by charge or credit card is
an absolute payment or, like payment by cheque, is a conditional payment only. That
must depend on the terms of the contract of supply, but in the circumstances of the
present case these must be inferred. No doubt a provision in the franchise agreement
that the company's undertaking to honour the sales voucher should be taken in full
exoneration of the obligation of the cardholder or the account holder to the garage would
c be effective, as would a provision to the opposite effect in the subscriber's agreement, for
neither party to the contract of supply should be taken to contract with the other on
terms which were inconsistent with his own contract with the company. It is sufficient
to say that no such provisions are to be found in either agreement. In the course of
argument it was faintly suggested that cl B2 of the franchise agreement was such a
provision. This required the company to honour all valid and current fuel cards by
d supplying petrol and other designated products to the cardholder 'at the same prices and
on the same terms as for cash sales displayed at the point of sale'. It is, it was submitted, a
term of a cash sale that on payment the customer obtains a good discharge. But that is
not a term of a cash sale: it is simply the consequence of the performance by the customer
of all his obligations under the contract. It is the extent of those obligations where
payment is to be made by charge or credit card which is in question in the present case.
e Thus the clause is neutral on the question. In fact, the purpose of the requirement that
the cardholder is to be offered, not only the same price, but the same terms as the cash
customer is quite different: if a cash customer is given a 'free' glass or coin with each
purchase, the cardholder is to be given one too.

       It was submitted on behalf of the garages that there is a general principle of law that,
whenever a method of payment is adopted which involves a risk of non-payment, there
f is a presumption, rebuttable by proof of special circumstances, that this is taken as
conditional payment only, so that the risk of default is on the paying party. The principle,
it is said, is that in the absence of agreement, express or implied, to the contrary, failure
of the agreed method of payment leaves the liability to pay undischarged.

       In my judgment, there is no such principle. As the cases cited to me demonstrate, the
approach of the courts to this question has not been conceptual or based on any such
g supposed principle, but has been strictly pragmatic. As each new method of payment has
fallen to be considered, its nature and the surrounding circumstances have been examined
to see whether a presumption of conditional payment should be made. Indeed, only in
this way is it possible to identify those special circumstances which may take an individual
case out of the general rule applicable to payments by a particular method.

       It is long settled that the giving of a cheque operates as a conditional payment only,
h unless the parties expressly or by implication otherwise agree: see *Re Romer and Haslam*
[1893] 2 QB 286; *Bolt and Nut Co (Tipton) Ltd v Rowlands Nicholls & Co Ltd* [1964] 1 All
ER 137, [1964] 2 QB 10. Although not strictly necessary for my decision, it is right, for
reasons which will appear, that I should state my view that this presumption would not
be displaced merely by the fact that the cheque was accompanied by a bank card. A
cheque is a revocable mandate by the customer to his bank which authorises the bank, as
j his agent, to make payment out of the moneys standing to the credit of his account or
which the bank is willing to advance to him. The obligation undertaken by the bank to
the supplier, which it enters into through the agency of its customer when he uses the
bank card, is not to dishonour the cheque on presentation for want of funds in the
account, so that it is obliged if necessary to advance moneys to the customer to meet it. If
the cheque is met, the bank honours its own undertaking as principal to the supplier

and, as agent for the customer, makes payment on its behalf out of his own moneys, whether or not these have been advanced to him for the purpose. The only risk is that of *a* the default or insolvency of the bank; and this risk, though unlikely to be in the contemplation of the parties, is equally present whether or not the cheque is accompanied by a bank card. In either case, it is not unreasonable to expect the customer to take responsibility for the default of his agent.

A similar presumption has been applied to payment by bills of exchange and other negotiable instruments, whether given by the customer or a third party: see *Allen v Royal* *b* *Bank of Canada* (1926) 95 LJPC 17. This is a three-party situation, once the bill has been negotiated, for the acceptor is not the agent of a subsequent indorser, but on the contrary is liable to indemnify the indorser if he should be called on to pay. Nevertheless, the identity of the acceptor is essentially the choice of the party who proffers the bill in payment, and it is unlikely that a supplier would be content to accept the liability of an unknown acceptor, selected by the customer, in complete exoneration of his own *c* customer.

The presumption has also been applied to irrevocable letters of credit. In such cases the choice of issuing bank is essentially a matter for the buyer, and it is not unreasonable to expect him to accept responsibility if the bank fails. In *W J Alan & Co Ltd v El Nasr Export and Import Co* [1972] 2 All ER 127, [1972] 2 QB 189, where the point did not strictly arise for decision, both Lord Denning MR and Stephenson LJ expressed the view *d* obiter that in the ordinary way a letter of credit operates as a conditional payment only. Lord Denning MR said ([1972] 2 All ER 127 at 137, [1972] 2 QB 189 at 210):

'In my opinion a letter of credit is not to be regarded as absolute payment, unless the seller stipulates, expressly or impliedly, that it should be so. He may do it impliedly if he stipulates for the credit to be issued by a particular banker in such circumstances that it is to be inferred that the seller looks to that particular banker *e* to the exclusion of the buyer.'

In *Maran Road Saw Mill v Austin Taylor & Co Ltd* [1975] 1 Lloyd's Rep 156, where the issuing bank had defaulted so that the question arose directly for decision, Ackner J followed the dicta in *W J Alan & Co Ltd v El Nasr Export and Import Co* and applied the presumption. The defendants were, he said, obliged to employ a reliable and solvent *f* paymaster and if they failed to do so, despite having put him in funds, they would have to pay twice over. In *E D & F Man Ltd v Nigerian Sweets and Confectionery Co Ltd* [1977] 2 Lloyd's Rep 50 Ackner J held that the fact that the seller had agreed on the identity of the issuing bank was only one of the factors to be taken into account when considering whether there were circumstances from which it could properly be inferred that the sellers looked to that particular bank to the exclusion of the buyers, that this fact was not *g* conclusive and that there were other circumstances present which supported the presumption that the letters of credit were given as conditional payment only.

It was submitted to me that the structure of the relationship which is brought into operation when goods or services are obtained by the use of a credit or charge card is closely analogous to that established by the issue of an irrevocable letter of credit, that a similar presumption should be applied and that there were no special features of the *h* present case which would rebut that presumption.

Before dealing with this contention I must consider an argument in favour of conditional payment suggested by Stephenson LJ in *W J Alan & Co Ltd v El Nasr Export and Import Co* [1972] 2 All ER 127 at 146, [1972] 2 QB 189 at 220, and accepted by Ackner J in *Maran Road Saw Mill v Austin Taylor & Co Ltd* [1975] 1 Lloyd's Rep 156 at 159, that the buyers were not discharged because they had promised to pay by letter of *j* credit, not to provide a source of payment which did not pay. Whether or not that may be a possible ground for decision where the question turns on the true construction of the terms of payment in a written contract of supply, it cannot provide a solution in a case like the present, where the wording of the contract of supply is unknown, and indeed where the contract may have been concluded in complete silence, so that the terms of payment have to be inferred. In any case, I should respectfully have thought that the formulation begs the question, since it assumes that a promise to pay by a method which involves a risk of non-payment is satisfied only if the method results in actual payment, which is the very question to be decided. No doubt a person can be properly said to have 'paid' only when he has discharged all his obligations in regard to payment, but the extent of those obligations is the very question in issue. The fact is that the word 'pay', like the word 'payment', is ambiguous: it may refer to conditional or absolute payment, and its meaning in any given case cannot be determined merely by its use.

In my view the structure of the relationship which is brought into operation when goods or services are obtained by credit or charge card bears only a superficial resemblance to that established by the issue of an irrevocable letter of credit. In both cases the supplier looks to a third party for payment, and the third party looks to the buyer for reimbursement, each of the three parties acting as principal. But in my judgment, there all resemblance ends, for, if the surrounding circumstances are considered, the two situations are not at all alike.

Letters of credit are employed to finance international commercial transactions between traders who are normally known to each other, and the terms of which will have been the subject of negotiation. The contract will usually provide merely for payment to be made by letter of credit, the identity of the issuing bank being left to be nominated by the buyer after the contract has been concluded, and being a matter of indifference to the seller. Even where the identity of the issuing bank is agreed between the parties, there is no prior contract between the issuing bank and the seller; its obligations to the seller arise under the letter of credit itself. The sole purpose of the letter of credit is to provide security to the seller to replace that represented by the shipping documents which he gives up in exchange for the credit. Finally, the terms on which the seller is entitled to payment must be identical to those to which he is entitled under the contract with the buyer.

By contrast, credit and charge cards are used mainly to facilitate payment of small consumer debts arising out of transactions between parties who may well not be known to each other, and the terms of which are usually not the subject of negotiation. The identity of the card-issuing company is necessarily a matter for agreement, since the card must be one which the customer is authorised to use and the supplier has the necessary equipment to accept. The machinery of payment by charge or credit card does not require the disclosure of the customer's address to the supplier, and in the absence of special precautions, which are seldom taken, at least in the case of small transactions, and which were not taken in the present case, the supplier might well have difficulty in identifying the customer without the co-operation of the card-issuing company. The availability of the card as a method of payment is advantageous to both parties: the customer obtains free credit for a period longer than that which the supplier is prepared to give even to the card-issuing company, or than he himself would obtain from the use of a cheque, with or without a bank card; while the supplier obtains not only better security (as he hopes) but the convenience of having a single debtor in place of many, and the prospect of extra trade by reason of the credit facilities which he is able to extend (without providing them himself) to the customer. Finally, the terms on which the supplier is entitled to payment from the card-issuing company are quite different from those on which the card-issuing company is entitled to payment from the customer; and both differ from those on which the supplier would be entitled to payment from the customer if he were subject to any residual liability not discharged by the use of the card. The card-issuing company is liable to pay the supplier very shortly after the receipt of the sales vouchers and claim form, but is entitled to deduct its commission; while the customer is liable to pay the full face value of the voucher, but is entitled to much longer credit. If the customer is liable to pay the supplier on the failure or default of the card-issuing company, it is on terms more onerous than either, for he must be liable to make immediate payment of the full face value of the voucher. It is difficult to find any justification for imputing to the customer an intention to undertake any such liability.

The essence of the transaction, which in my view has no close analogy, is that the

supplier and customer have for their mutual convenience each previously arranged to
open an account with the same company, and agree that any account between themselves *a*
may, if the customer wishes, be settled by crediting the supplier's and debiting the
customer's account with that company. That process does not depend on the company's
solvency, and the customer must be discharged, at the latest, when the supplier's account
with the company is credited, not when the supplier is paid. But once that point is
reached, there is no logical place to stop short of the customer's signing the voucher.

The features I have described are normally present whenever payment is made by *b*
means of a credit or charge card, and they are all present in the case before me. In my
judgment, they are sufficient not only to displace any presumption that payment by such
means is a conditional payment only, but to support a presumption to the contrary.

I reach this conclusion with satisfaction, for two reasons. First, a supplier who is not
content to accept the security of the card-issuing company alone, but who wishes to
retain an additional right of recourse to the customer, has the means readily to hand: he *c*
can require payment by cheque accompanied by a bank card. Indeed, the Barclarcard
may be used to serve either function. Second, it conforms to the general understanding
of the public, that when a customer signs the voucher he has discharged his obligations
to the supplier, and that he pays for the goods or services he has obtained when he pays
the card-issuing company.

In the present case, there are no special features which support conditional payment, *d*
and one which supports the opposite view. This is the company's undertaking in the
franchise agreement to establish, for the benefit of all member garages, a guarantee of its
obligation to reimburse them. While far from conclusive, this shows that the garages
considered themselves to be giving credit to the company rather than to the account
holders.

Accordingly, I reject the submission that payment by the use of the Fuel Card operated *e*
as a conditional payment only. An alternative argument, however, was presented on
behalf of the garages to the following effect. Although the subscriber's agreement merely
authorised, and did not require, the company to pay the garage for the fuel supplied to
the cardholder, nevertheless the account holder's liability to pay the company did not
arise until the company paid the garage; the company's right was a right of
reimbursement only. Since the company had not done so, it was not entitled to retain *f*
the money collected from the account holders. Of course, it could always become entitled
to the money, simply by paying the garages. Accordingly, it was submitted, the
liquidator must either repay the money to the account holders, leaving the garages to
prove in the liquidation, or pay the garages and extinguish their claims. Since he was
under a duty to act in the interests of the general body of creditors, he was bound to take
the latter course.
                                                                                   g
This argument turns on the true construction of the subscriber's agreement, the
drafting of which is singularly inept. Its main provisions are contained in cll 1 and 3. I
have already read cl 1. That clause authorises the company to pay for the fuel supplied,
but it does not expressly authorise the company to debit the account holder with the cost.
Clause 3 is in the following terms:

'A statement showing all amounts debited, less any credits or refunds, will be sent *h*
to the Account Holder by [the company] each month. The Account Holder will pay
to [the company], within 14 days from the date to which such statement is made
up, the whole of the amount shown to be owing by that statement. Interest will be
charged at the rate of 3% (or such other rate as [the company] may notify) per month
or part of month on any balance outstanding after the expiry of such 14 day period
until settlement is received. If any amount is outstanding for more than 5 weeks *j*
after the date of first issue of the statement showing that amount or exceeds the
credit limit granted, ALL the Cards issued to the Account Holder may at the
discretion of [the company] be cancelled forthwith and under no circumstances will
the Account Holder be reinstated as a Cardholder.'

That clause, which is the clause which actually imposes on the account holder the liability

to pay the company, presupposes but does not itself confer a right to debit the account
a with the cost of the fuel. There is, of course, no difficulty in inferring such a right; the
question is whether it is a right to debit the account with liabilities incurred, or only
with payments made.

Counsel for the garages relied on cll 2 and 6. Clause 2 is concerned with the cardholder's
failure to sign the sales voucher or breach of any of the terms and conditions on which
the card is issued, and provides that this should not relieve the account holder from
b liability 'for the reimbursement of any payment made by' the company in respect of fuel
or oil supplied to the account holder or his cardholder. Clause 6 is concerned with the
theft or loss of the card, and requires this to be notified immediately and confirmed in
writing within seven days. It provides for the account holder to remain liable to the
company 'for any payment made by it to its suppliers arising from the use of the card by
any person before such confirmation is received'. Both clauses confer a right of
c reimbursement only.

Both clauses, however, deal with situations in which the company incurs no liability
to the garage, but is likely to make payments in discharge of a supposed liability. In both
situations, an obligation on the part of the account holder to reimburse the company for
payments actually made is sufficient. Neither clause provides support for the wider
proposition for which it was relied on.

d In my judgment, the answer is to be found in cl 1, which expressly authorises the
company to pay for, and by implication to debit the account holder with the cost of, fuel
and oil obtained by the use of the card. The authority to pay the garage must include
authority to incur an obligation to pay it; and, if so, then the right to debit the account
holder must be a right to debit him not only with payments made but also with liabilities
incurred. I therefore reject the argument that the account holder's liability to pay the
e company did not arise until the company had paid the garage.

Accordingly, I answer question 1 of the summons in favour of Commercial Credit.

The second question

The second question arises between the company and Commercial Credit. It is whether
f a right of retention conferred on Commercial Credit by standard condition 3B of the
invoice discounting agreement (which I shall call 'the agreement') is valid and exercisable
once the company has become insolvent and is in liquidation.

The agreement is a factoring agreement by which the company agreed to sell and
Commercial Credit agreed to purchase the company's receivables, that is to say the
benefit of the agreements with account holders. I must now describe it in some detail.

g Clause 3(a) of the agreement provides that Commercial Credit may at any time by
notice in writing require the company to repurchase any receivable in certain specified
events, for example if the debtor should dispute that the receivable is due or valid in
whole or part, or if he should become insolvent or bankrupt. Whether or not any of the
specified events has occurred, so far as I am aware no notice of repurchase under this
clause has been served.

h Clause 3(c) is of particular importance. It contains a guarantee by the company that
every debtor will duly and fully pay the receivable due from him by the end of the
permitted credit period, and an undertaking by the company to indemnify Commercial
Credit against loss by reason of the failure of any debtor for any reason to pay the full
amount of any receivable on or before the end of the permitted credit period. This is
defined as the period of 120 days beginning with the date of issue of the relevant invoice.

j Clause 4 provides that the purchase price payable by Commercial Credit to the
company for any receivable is to be the gross amount payable by the account holder less
any discount commission or other allowance due or allowable to him and less a
discounting charge calculated in the manner prescribed by standard condition 3. Clause
5 provides that the company is to be charged at the end of each calendar month with an
administration charge equal to a stated percentage of the gross amount of the receivables
purchased in that month.

Clause 6 is of crucial importance. It is in the following terms:

'Payment of the purchase price for each receivable purchased as aforesaid shall be *a*
due and made at the time and in the manner as specified in the Standard Conditions
subject to the right of debits and rights of retention, and set off as therein provided,
but shall in no event become due prior to notification of the receivable in accordance
with Standard Condition 1(a)(ii).'

Clause 10 (read with cl 11) provides, inter alia, that should the company at any time *b*
go into insolvent liquidation then Commercial Credit may by written notice determine
the agreement and thereupon the company is to repurchase at face value so much of any
receivable purchased by Commercial Credit as then remains outstanding. Commercial
Credit has not to date served any such notice, but it appears to be in a position to do so if
it chooses.

Standard Condition 3A requires Commercial Credit to maintain a current account (i) *c*
to which shall be credited (a) the purchase price of each receivable before deducting the
discounting charge, (b) the amount of any costs or expenses recovered by Commercial
Credit as a result of any proceedings against or negotiations with any account holder and
(c) any amount paid by the company to Commercial Credit under the agreement, and
(ii) to which shall be debited (a) the amount of any payment made under the agreement
by Commercial Credit to the company, (b) the amount of any credit note issued by the *d*
company to an account holder, (c) the amount of any receivables which Commercial
Credit has required the company to repurchase, inter alia, under cl 3(a) (but not under cl
10), (d) the amount of any sum payable by the company pursuant to the guarantee
contained in cl 3(c), (e) all such other amounts as are payable by the company under the
agreement including the legal costs and expenses incurred by Commercial Credit in
collecting and enforcing payment of receivables, (f) the amount of any payment, cost, *e*
damage or liability made or sustained by Commercial Credit by reason of any breach of
warranty or undertaking by the company and (g) at the end of each calendar month a
discounting charge, calculated at a specified rate on the net daily debit balance of account,
and the administration charge already referred to.

Standard Condition 3B is again of crucial importance. It is in the following terms:

'Subject to the provisions hereof and to compliance by [the company] with the *f*
requirements of Condition 1(a)(iv) [Commercial Credit] shall remit (and at any time
in [Commercial Credit's] sole discretion it may remit) to [the company] or to its
order any part of the balance for the time being standing to the credit of [the
company] in the Current Account up to the full amount thereof less any amount
which [Commercial Credit] shall in its absolute discretion decide to retain as security
for (i) any claims or defences which have arisen or may arise against [the company]; *g*
(ii) any risk of non-payment by the customer; (iii) any amount prospectively
chargeable to [the company] as a debit under paragraph (A)(ii) of this Condition.
Any balance for the time being standing to the debit of [the company] in the
Current Account shall be payable by [the company] to [Commercial Credit] on
demand.'

h
Those are the principal terms of the agreement. Commercial Credit duly maintained
the required current account, crediting and debiting the relevant items, and retained
against the risk of bad debts 15% of the balance shown thereon, together with a further
85% of receivables shown on the current aged debt analysis as being more than 120 days'
old, and accounted to the company for the balance from time to time as 'pre-payments'.
At the date of the resolution to wind up, a substantial sum was retained by Commercial *j*
Credit.

The company challenge the right of retention under standard condition 3B, and in
particular the right to retain any sum in respect of (i) the amount of the discounting
charge and administration charge for the month current at the date of the resolution to
wind up but which were not liable to be debited to the current account until the end of
that month, (ii) the amount prospectively due to Commercial Credit under the company's
guarantee in cl 3(c) where the permitted credit period had not expired at the date of the

a resolution, so that it was then only a contingent liability prospectively liable to be debited to the current account under standard condition 3A(ii)(D), and (iii) the face value of any receivables which the company may be required to repurchase if Commercial Credit serves a notice under cl 10, which is still only a contingent liability and which unlike the other items is a matter for retention under standard condition 3B(i) but is not liable to be debited to the current account.

b It was submitted on behalf of the company that the right of retention was expressly reserved by Commercial Credit as security for its prospective rights of set-off, and that in consequence it constituted a charge on book debts created by the company which was void against the liquidator for want of registration under s 95 of the Companies Act 1948 (now s 395 of the Companies Act 1985). Alternatively, it was submitted that, in so far as the contractual right of set-off extended to liabilities of the company which were still contingent at the date of the resolution to wind up, it went further than s 31 of the

c Bankruptcy Act 1914, and was void as an attempt to contract out of the statutory rules of distribution on a winding up: see *British Eagle International Airlines Ltd v Cie Nationale Air France* [1975] 2 All ER 390, [1975] 1 WLR 758.

In my judgment, and leaving aside for the moment the possible claim under cl 10, the short answer to these submissions is that Commercial Credit's right of retention under standard condition 3B(iii) in respect of any amount prospectively chargeable to the

d company as a debit to the current account is a matter not of set-off but of account. In *Halesowen Presswork and Assemblies Ltd v Westminster Bank Ltd* [1970] 3 All ER 473 at 488, [1971] 1 QB 1 at 46 Buckley LJ said:

e 'Where the relationship of the banker and customer is a single relationship such as I have already mentioned, albeit embodied in a number of accounts, the situation is not, in my judgment, a situation of lien at all. A lien postulates property of the debtor in the possession or under the control of the creditor. Nor is it a set-off situation, which postulates mutual but independent obligations between the two parties. It is an accounting situation, in which the existence and amount of one party's liability to the other can only be ascertained by discovering the ultimate balance of their mutual dealings.'

f Counsel for the company put forward a sophisticated analysis of the various provisions of the agreement to show that, despite the wording of cl 4, the discounting charge was not integral to the ascertainment of the purchase price but, like the administration charge, a true contra item. In my judgment, however, the crucial feature is not the definition of the purchase price, but the extent of Commercial Credit's obligation to pay. This is to be found in cl 6, and it is an obligation to pay, not the purchase price, which is

g merely a credit in the current account, but the balance shown on the current account subject to the right of retention. The right of retention thus constitutes a contractual limitation on the company's right to require payment of the balance on the current account. It is an essential safeguard against overpayment since, except at the end of the month when the discounting and administration charges are debited, and in the unlikely event of there being no bad debts at all, the balance on the current account can never

h represent the true amount owing by Commercial Credit. The sum made payable by cl 6, therefore, is in effect a provisional payment only and represents the best estimate that can be made at the time of the true state of account between the parties.

In my judgment, this is not a case of set-off at all, for there are no mutual but independent obligations capable of being quantified and set off against each other. There are reciprocal obligations giving rise to credits and debits in a single running account, a

j single liability to pay the ultimate balance found due on taking the account, and provisions for retention and provisional payment in the mean time.

If this analysis is correct, it also provides an answer to the company's claim that the right of retention in standard condition 3B(iii) constitutes a registrable charge, for there is no relevant property capable of forming the subject matter of the charge. The only asset which the company could charge is its chose in action, ie the right to sue Commercial Credit for the sum due under the agreement, but this already contains within it the liability to suffer a retention. Counsel for the company naturally stressed

the fact that the right of retention is expressed to be by way of security, but that is of no
avail if, as I hold, it secures Commercial Credit, not against default by the company in   *a*
the performance of its obligations, but against overpayment by itself.

This still leaves the company's liability to repurchase outstanding receivables at face
value if Commercial Credit serves a notice of termination under cl 10. The purchase
price payable by the company in this event is not available to be debited to the current
account under standard condition 3A(ii), but Commercial Credit has the right to retain
money to meet it under standard condition 3B(i). It has been conceded before me that   *b*
this is a true right of set-off. Accordingly, as well as in case I am wrong in my analysis of
the other rights of retention, I must deal with the company's contentions that the right
of retention in standard condition 3B is a registrable charge on the company's book debts,
and that in so far as it gives a right of set-off in respect of sums only contingently due
from the company at the date of liquidation it goes beyond what is permitted by s 31 of
the Bankruptcy Act 1914.

If the right of retention constitutes a charge, there is no doubt that it is a charge on   *c*
book debts and is a charge created by the company. But is it a charge at all? The sum due
from Commercial Credit to the company under the agreement is, of course, a book debt
of the company which the company can charge to a third party. In my judgment,
however, it cannot be charged in favour of Commercial Credit itself, for the simple
reason that a charge in favour of a debtor of his own indebtedness to the chargor is   *d*
conceptually impossible.

Counsel for the company conceded that a debt cannot be assigned in whole or part to
the debtor, since such an assignment operates wholly or partially as a release. Likewise, it
was conceded, it cannot be made the subject of a legal or equitable mortgage in favour of
the debtor, since this requires a conveyance or assignment by way of security, and this
operates as a conditional release. But, it was submitted, an equitable charge need involve   *e*
no conveyance or assignment of property, so that any objection on this ground falls away.

The locus classicus for the requirements of an equitable charge is the following passage
in *Palmer v Carey* [1926] AC 703 at 706–707, [1926] All ER Rep 650 at 651–652.

'The law as to equitable assignment, as stated by Lord Truro in *Rodick* v. *Gandell*
((1852) 1 De GM & G 763, 42 ER 749), is this: "The extent of the principle to be
deduced is that an agreement between a debtor and a creditor that the debt owing   *f*
shall be paid out of a specific fund coming to the debtor, or an order given by a
debtor to his creditor upon a person owing money or holding funds belonging to
the giver of the order, directing such person to pay such funds to the creditor, will
create a valid equitable charge upon such fund, in other words, will operate as an
equitable assignment of the debts or fund to which the order refers." An agreement
for valuable consideration that a fund shall be applied in a particular way may found   *g*
an injunction to restrain its application in another way. But if there be nothing
more, such a stipulation will not amount to an equitable assignment. It is necessary
to find, further, that an obligation has been imposed in favour of the creditor to pay
the debt out of the fund. This is but an instance of a familiar doctrine of equity that
a contract for valuable consideration to transfer or charge a subject matter passes a
beneficial interest by way of property in that subject matter if the contract is one of   *h*
which a Court of equity will decree specific performance.'

Similar definitions of equitable charge are to be found in *National Provincial and Union
Bank of England v Charnley* [1924] 1 KB 431 at 449–450. It is sufficient to cite the language
of Atkin LJ:

'It is not necessary to give a formal definition of a charge, but I think there can be   *j*
no doubt that where in a transaction for value both parties evince an intention that
property, existing or future, shall be made available as security for the payment of a
debt, and that the creditor shall have a present right to have it made available, there
is a charge, even though the present legal right which is contemplated can only be
enforced at some future date, and though the creditor gets no legal right of property,

a either absolute or special, or any legal right to possession, but only gets a right to have the security made available by an order of the Court.'

Thus the essence of an equitable charge is that, without any conveyance or assignment to the chargee, specific property of the chargor is expressly or constructively appropriated to or made answerable for payment of a debt, and the chargee is given the right to resort to the property for the purpose of having it realised and applied in or towards payment of the debt. The availability of equitable remedies has the effect of giving the chargee a
b proprietary interest by way of security in the property charged.

It is true, therefore, that no conveyance or assignment is involved in the creation of an equitable charge, but in my judgment the benefit of a debt can no more be appropriated or made available to the debtor than it can be conveyed or assigned to him. The objection to a charge in these circumstances is not to the process by which it is created, but to the result. A debt is a chose in action; it is the right to sue the debtor. This can be assigned or
c made available to a third party, but not to the debtor, who cannot sue himself. Once any assignment or appropriation to the debtor becomes unconditional, the debt is wholly or partially released. The debtor cannot, and does not need to, resort to the creditor's claim against him in order to obtain the benefit of the security; his own liability to the creditor is automatically discharged or reduced.

In *Halesowen Presswork and Assemblies Ltd v Westminster Bank Ltd* [1970] 3 All ER 473 at
d 487, [1971] 1 QB 1 at 46 Buckley LJ stated, in a passage subsequently approved in the House of Lords by Viscount Dilhorne, Lord Simon and Lord Cross (see [1972] 1 All ER 641 at 646, 651, 653, [1972] AC 785 at 802, 807, 810), that he could not understand how it could be said with any kind of accuracy that the bank had a lien on its own indebtedness to its customer. It is true that this comment was made in relation to a lien rather than a charge, and a lien unlike a charge can only attach to tangible property. But the reason
e why it was said that the bank did not have a lien on the credit balance in its customer's current account was clearly based on the identity of the parties rather than the particular character of the security given.

Counsel for the company relied on *Re Hart, ex p Caldicott* (1884) 25 Ch D 716, in which a partner deposited money with a bank by way of security for the indebtedness of his firm. The Court of Appeal held that the bank was not required to value its security before
f proving for its debt against the firm. It was, however, not necessary to decide whether the deposit created a charge; it was sufficient that it did not create a security on the joint estate.

It does not, of course, follow that an attempt to create an express mortgage or charge of a debt in favour of the debtor would be ineffective to create a security. Equity looks to the substance, not the form; and, while in my judgment this would not create a mortgage
g or charge, it would no doubt give a right of set-off which would be effective against the creditor's liquidator or trustee in bankruptcy, provided that it did not purport to go beyond what is permitted by s 31 of the 1914 Act.

This brings me to the last question, whether debts or liabilities which result from mutual dealings but are still only contingent at the relevant date are available to be set off under s 31.
h The relevant date in bankruptcy is the date of the receiving order. In companies liquidation, it was thought in some of the early cases to be the date on which the winding up commenced, but the correct date has now been shown to be the date of the winding-up order: see *Barclays Bank Ltd v TOSG Trust Fund Ltd* [1984] BCLC 1 at 25. Although the present is a case of company liquidation, I shall for convenience refer to the relevant date as the date of the receiving order.
j The question I am called on to decide has been the subject of some controversy. The Insolvency Law Review Committee reported (Cmnd 8558 (1982), paras 1352–1353):

'Debts payable at a future date, unliquidated claims arising out of breach of contract or breach of trust, and contingent debts can all be set off against debts presently payable Although the date for ascertaining the existence of any mutual debts, credits or dealings which may be made the subject of set-off under the section is the date of the receiving order, it is sufficient if the account prescribed by the section can be taken when the set-off arises. It is sometimes asserted that in England *a* (unlike Scotland) liabilities which at the date of the receiving order are still wholly contingent cannot be made the subject of set-off under the section; and several of those who have given evidence to us have urged that this rule be changed. If this were the law, it would indeed be defective; but it is not.'

By contrast, in *Williams and Muir Hunter on Bankruptcy* (19th edn, 1979) p 192 it is said:
b

'Since the date of the receiving order is the vital date, it follows that if there is then no "debt" due from one party to the other, but only a wholly contingent liability, as in the case of a surety who has not been called upon to pay and has not paid, there is no sum which can be set off.'

And in *Carreras Rothmans Ltd v Freeman Mathews Treasure Ltd (in liq)* [1985] 1 All ER 155 at 171, [1985] Ch 207 at 230 Peter Gibson J said:
c

'There is also no doubt that a liability existing at the relevant date but which cannot be quantified till after the relevant date is nevertheless a sum due at the relevant date for the purposes of the section: see *Re Daintrey, ex p Mant* [1900] 1 QB 546, [1895–9] All ER Rep 657. There is also no doubt that a contingent obligation to pay is not a debt due even though the contingency subsequently occurs and the *d* obligation to pay arises under the contract entered into before the due date: see *Re a debtor (No 66 of 1955), ex p the debtor v Trustee of the property of Waite (a bankrupt)* [1956] 3 All ER 225, [1956] 1 WLR 1226. Junior counsel for CR submitted that damages for a breach of contract occurring after the date of the commencement of the liquidation where there have been mutual dealings and the contractual obligations which was subsequently broken existed at that date were the proper *e* subject of a set-off. But he was unable to cite any authority which supported this proposition and in my judgment it is contrary to principle. Unless and until the breach of contract occurs, no damages could arise and hence nothing was due at the date relevant for set-off.'

In that case, the point arose on a relatively minor claim on a counterclaim, and Peter Gibson J did not have the benefit of the full and comprehensive citation of authority that *f* I have enjoyed. I am satisfied, both from the legislative history of s 31 and its predecessors and from the decided cases, that the passages I have cited from *Williams and Muir Hunter* and the *Carreras Rothmans* case cannot be supported. In my judgment, the law is correctly stated by Dixon J in *Hiley v Peoples Prudential Assurance Co Ltd (in liq)* (1938) 60 CLR 468 at 496:

g

'In the first place the general rule does not require that at the moment when the winding up commences there should be two enforceable debts, a debt provable in the liquidation and a debt enforceable by the liquidator against the creditor claiming to prove. It is enough that at the commencement of the winding up mutual dealings exist which involve rights and obligations *whether absolute or contingent* of such a nature that afterwards in the events that happen they mature or develop into *h* pecuniary demands capable of set off. If the end contemplated by the transaction is a claim sounding in money so that, in the phrase employed in the cases, it is commensurate with the cross-demand, no more is required than that at the commencement of the winding up liabilities shall have been contracted by the company and the other party respectively from which cross money claims accrue during the course of the winding up.' (My emphasis.)
j

Faced with the authorities, counsel for the company rightly did not contend that all contingent liabilities are excluded from s 31. Instead, he adopted the distinction apparently drawn by Peter Gibson J in the *Carreras Rothmans* case between a liability the very existence of which is still contingent at the date of the receiving order and a liability which is then certain but the amount of which is unascertainable because its quantification

depends on future events. (Both of course must be distinguished from a liability the
a amount of which is not yet ascertained but which is ascertainable because its quantification
does not depend on future events; such a liability is not contingent at all.)

Unless constrained by authority, I would for my own part find the suggested distinction
wholly unacceptable for present purposes. It is a difference of degree, not of kind; and of
form, not of substance. Thus a liability to pay a proportion of the future profits of a
business is wholly contingent, unless the possibility of there being no profits is remote
b and the view is taken that remote contingencies can be ignored. Again, an obligation to
pay a proportion of the future profits of a business subject to a certain minimum can be
expressed in either of two ways: as an obligation to pay £x plus 20% of the profits over
£5x, or as an obligation to pay 20% of the profits with a minimum of £x. In each case,
the only certain liability is to pay £x. In the first case, any liability to pay more is wholly
contingent. In the second, there is a single liability the quantum of which is
c unascertainable, though certain to be not less than £x. Once it is accepted, as on the
authorities it must be, that the whole amount when ascertained can be set off in the
second case, it is impossible to identify any ground of public policy, let alone any wording
in s 31, which requires the amount to be set off to be limited to £x in the first.

The legislative history of the section supports no such distinction. On the contrary, it
confirms the principle, for which there is abundant Court of Appeal authority, that
d contingent liabilities of all kinds, including liability for breaches occurring on or after
the receiving order of contracts entered into before that date, are debts provable in the
bankruptcy, and that in general all provable debts resulting from mutual dealings are
capable of set-off.

The right to set off mutual debts and liabilities arising from mutual dealings was
recognised at an early date by the courts administering bankruptcy, and was first given a
e statutory basis by the Act 4 & 5 Anne c 71 (bankrupts (1705)) s 11. Section 171 of the
Bankruptcy Act 1849, the forerunner of s 31 of the 1914 Act, expressly referred to the
set-off of provable debts. Until the 1869 Act, however, contingent debts and liabilities,
and claims to unliquidated damages, were incapable of proof and, therefore, of set-off.
Section 31 of the 1869 Act provided that, with certain exceptions not material for present
purposes:

f   'all debts and liabilities, present or future, certain or contingent, to which the
        bankrupt is subject at the date of the order of adjudication, or to which he may
        become subject during the continuance of the bankruptcy by reason of any
        obligation incurred previously to the date of adjudication, shall be deemed to be
        debts provable in bankruptcy.'

g It also defined the word 'liability' as including—

        'any obligation, or possibility of an obligation, to pay money or money's worth
        on the breach of any express or implied covenant, contract, agreement or
        undertaking, whether such breach does or does not occur, or is or is not likely to
        occur, or capable of occurring, before the close of the bankruptcy.'

h With the substitution of references to the date of the receiving order for the date of the
order of adjudication, the section was reproduced in almost identical terms by s 37(3) and
(8) of the Bankruptcy Act 1883 and s 30(3) and (8)(b) of the 1914 Act.

At the same time, s 39 of the 1869 Act introduced the present wording of s 31, adding
a reference to mutual dealings and omitting all reference to provable debts. Now that
contingent liabilities and claims for unliquidated damages for breaches after the date of
j the receiving order of contracts subsisting at that date were admissible to proof, it would
be natural to assume that they were capable of set-off, provided that they resulted from
mutual dealings and had been quantified by the time that the claim to set-off was made.

I turn finally to the authorities. The first is *Re Asphaltic Wood Pavement Co, Lee and
Chapman's Case* (1885) 30 Ch D 216. The company which was in liquidation had entered
into a contract with the Commissioners of Sewers for the reconstruction of Queen
Victoria Street. Under the contract the company was entitled to be paid a sum on

completion of the work, and was bound if so required by notice given within two years
to keep the road in repair for a further 15 years. The company had begun to make the
street when it went into liquidation, but it had apparently not sufficiently completed it
as to become entitled to payment. The winding up no doubt amounted to an anticipatory
breach of contract which could have been accepted by the commissioners, but they did
not accept it. Instead, the liquidator obtained the leave of the court to complete the
works, and the commissioners then gave notice formally requiring the company to keep
the road in repair for a further 15 years. The commissioners then treated the winding up
as a breach of this obligation and claimed damages, which were duly assessed in chambers.
The question then arose whether the commissioners could set off the amount of the
damages due from the company against the sum due from them for making the street.
Brett MR said (at 222):

> 'As between them this claim to damages can be proved in the winding-up. *The
> moment I come to that conclusion, I must hold that the Bankruptcy Act, 1869, s. 39, applies,*
> and that the claim of the Commissioners is to be treated by way of set-off . . .' (My
> emphasis.)

Cotton LJ said (at 224):

> 'At the time when the company commenced its liquidation, it was under a
> contract which implied a liability to maintain these streets if it were required. It is
> now rendered impossible . . . to do that, and in my opinion, though no notice had
> been given before the commencement of the winding-up, that is properly a liability
> the damages for which are capable of being proved, *and, if capable of being proved, are
> capable under the mutual credit clause of being set off* against any claim by the liquidator
> as against the Commissioners.' (My emphasis.)

It is to be observed that, at the date of the winding up, there was no subsisting breach
of contract on the part of the company, since notice to repair had not been given; indeed,
the contrary was not alleged. The case is, therefore, one in which at the date of the
winding up the company's liability was not merely unascertainable but wholly
contingent, and it has since been so treated: see, for example, the judgment of Warrington
LJ in *Re City Life Assurance Co Ltd, Re Grandfield's Case, Stephenson's Case* [1926] Ch 191 at
208, [1925] All ER Rep 453 at 460–461. It is direct authority for the proposition that
liability for breach occurring after the date of the receiving order of a contract subsisting
at that date, being admissible to proof, is capable of set-off. *Re Asphaltic Wood Pavement
Co Ltd, Lee and Chapman's Case* (1885) 30 Ch D 216 was not cited in the *Carreras Rothmans*
case [1985] 1 All ER 155, [1985] Ch 207; in my judgment, on this point the two cases are
completely irreconcilable.

In *Sovereign Life Assurance Co v Dodd* [1892] 1 QB 405 the defendant took out two
endowment policies on his own life with the plaintiffs, and subsequently borrowed
money from the plaintiffs on the security of the policies. The plaintiffs were compulsorily
wound up. The defendant continued to pay premiums due under the policies after the
presentation of the petition; the policies matured after that date but before the winding-
up order was made. The plaintiffs brought an action against the defendant to recover the
amount of the loans, and the defendant sought to set off against the plaintiffs' claim the
sums which but for the winding up would have been payable under the policies. In a
judgment subsequently upheld by the Court of Appeal, Charles J allowed the set-off.
Treating the date on which the petition was presented as the relevant date, he said (at
412) that there was at that date 'a debt due from the defendant, and a contract with him
which would probably result—and has in fact resulted—in a debt due to him'; and this
was enough to bring the case within the mutual dealings section. The only uncertainty,
he pointed out, was the possibility that the defendant would not pay his premiums. This
element was removed by his duly paying them (after what was taken to be the relevant
date), and thereupon the sum due to him became capable of proof in the liquidation. He
could not see why, under those circumstances, the mutual dealings section should not be
applicable.

In *Palmer v Day & Sons* [1895] 2 QB 618 the debtor instructed the defendants, a firm
a of auctioneers, to sell his house and furniture, and a sum of money became due from
him to them in respect of their charges for the sale of the furniture and an abortive sale
of the house. Subsequently he instructed the defendants to remove to their own premises
certain pictures, and to sell them on his behalf at prices approved by him. He became
bankrupt while the pictures were still unsold. The pictures were subsequently sold by
the defendants, acting on the instructions of the debtor's trustee in bankruptcy. The
b defendants claimed to set off against the proceeds of sale their own charges in respect of
the earlier sale of the furniture and the abortive sale of the house. Rejecting the argument
that, at the date of the receiving order, the debtor's claim was in detinue for the return of
the pictures and not a money claim, so that the two claims were incommensurable, the
Divisional Court allowed the set-off. Lord Russell CJ, giving the judgment of the court,
traced the history of the section and pointed out that, although 'mutual credits' was a
c wider term than 'mutual debts', the credits must be such as either must terminate in
debts or have a natural tendency to terminate in debts, and must not be such as terminate
in claims differing in their nature from debts. Similarly, the 'mutual dealings' must be
such that in the result the account contemplated by the section could be taken; in other
words, they must be such as would end on each side in a money claim. At the date of the
receiving order, the defendants were bailees of the pictures with authority to sell them,
d so that there was a mutual credit or mutual dealing then existing between the bankrupt
and themselves, a credit on the one hand by them to him in respect of the sums due to
them for the earlier sales, and a credit on the other hand by the bankrupt to them in
respect of the pictures and the money to be realised by the sale. That was enough to bring
the case within the section.

Although that case was concerned with the question whether the two claims were
e commensurable, it is to be observed that, at the date of the receiving order, both the
existence and amount of any money claim on the part of the debtor were contingent on
future events; it was not then certain that a single picture would be sold at the approved
prices. This did not preclude the right of set-off. Lord Russell CJ, indeed, expressly stated
that the section, in its current form, had been held applicable to all demands payable in
bankruptcy.

f By the turn of the century, therefore, the authorities showed that debts whose existence
and amount were alike contingent at the date of the receiving order and claims to
damages for future breaches of contracts existing at that date were capable of proof and,
being capable of proof, could be set off under the section provided that they arose from
mutual credits or mutual dealings. The only requirement was that they must in fact
have resulted in quantified money claims by the time the claim to set-off was made.

g Next came the well-known decision of the Court of Appeal in *Re Daintrey, ex p Mant*
[1900] 1 QB 546 [1895-9] All ER Rep 657. Daintrey and Mant were both solicitors.
Daintrey owed Mant £86. Daintrey sold his practice to Mant by an agreement which
fixed the price as a proportion of the profits earned from the practice during the next
three years. Shortly afterwards, a receiving order was made against Daintrey. No profits
had by then been earned from the business. At the end of the three years, a sum of £300
h was found to be due from Mant as the price of the business. Mant sought to deduct the
sum of £86 due to him from Daintrey against the £300. The Court of Appeal allowed
the set-off.

Attempts have been made from time to time to explain this decision by treating it as a
case where the debt was certain, though not yet ascertained, at the date of the receiving
order. For my own part, I fail to understand how it could be thought that, at the date of
j the receiving order, it was certain that any sum would ever become due from Mant at
all. His liability depended entirely on profits being made, and it was not certain that
profits would be made. In my judgment, Mant's liability was clearly one whose existence
and amount were both contingent at the date of the receiving order. But it does not rest
on my judgment alone; that is how Mant's liability was described by Buckley LJ in *Re
Taylor, ex p Norvell* [1910] 1 KB 562 at 580, by Lawrence LJ in *Re Fenton, ex p Fenton
Textile Association Ltd* [1931] 1 Ch 85 at 113, [1930] All ER Rep 15 at 23, and by Gibbs CJ

and Mason J in *Day and Dent Constructions Pty Ltd v North Australian Properties Pty Ltd* (1982) 40 ALR 399 at 405, 412.

Unfortunately, difficulties have been caused by certain observations of Lindley MR and Romer LJ in *Re Daintrey*. Lindley MR said ([1900] 1 QB 546 at 572, cf [1895–9] All ER Rep 657 at 672):

> 'Looking at this agreement, I fail to see that at the date of the receiving order there was nothing payable under the agreement. Under the circumstances it is clear that when this agreement was executed very considerable sums would become payable under it.'

Lindley MR can hardly have meant that very considerable sums would inevitably become payable under the agreement; and he certainly did not mean that Mant's obligation was not contingent, since later in his judgment he expressly stated that Mant was bound 'in certain conditions' to pay the money to Daintrey. Nor can he have thought that contingent liabilities were outside the section, since he had been a party to the decision in *Re Asphaltic Wood Pavement Co*. Romer LJ said ([1900] 1 QB 546 at 573–574, [1895–9] All ER Rep 657 at 672):

> 'I agree that the amount which ultimately became payable by [Mant] could not be ascertained until some time later than the date of the receiving order, and it was possible that the amount might be very small; but, whatever sum eventually became payable, became payable to Daintrey by virtue of this agreement . . . and of nothing else.'

It was submitted before me that the reason why Lindley MR and Romer LJ seemingly discounted the possibility that no profits at all would be earned from the business was that this eventuality was too remote to be considered; but in my judgment it was rightly discounted because it was irrelevant. If no profits were earned, cadit quaestio: Mant would owe nothing, and there would be nothing against which the £86 could be set off. In every case the claim to set off requires that any contingency to which the liability was still subject at the date of the receiving order has since occurred. In my view, the emphasis in the passages I have cited is not in the degree of probability that a sum would become due from Mant, but in the source of that potential liability. What was both necessary and sufficient was that any liability of Mant to Daintrey which did mature should be exclusively referable to the agreement between them already existing at the date of the receiving order, and not to any subsequent transaction.

In *Re Taylor, ex p Norvell* [1910] 1 KB 562 the debtor contracted to sell some houses to a purchaser to whom he was indebted. Afterwards, a receiving order was made against him. The purchaser brought an action for specific performance against the trustee in bankruptcy, and the question arose whether he was entitled to set off the debt owing to him against the purchase price. In a judgment whose reasoning was expressly approved by Cozens-Hardy MR in the Court of Appeal, Phillimore J sitting in the Divisional Court said (at 568):

> 'In the present case the appellant Norvell was under an obligation to the bankrupt to pay if required, upon receiving a conveyance of the land, the money due from him for the purchase of the land. It is quite true he is only liable to pay if required; but the words of s. 38 of the Bankruptcy Act, 1883, are quite wide enough to cover this, as is shewn by the judgments in *In re Daintrey* ([1900] 1 QB 546, [1895–9] All ER Rep 657). Any obligation prospective or contingent to which the bankrupt is subject, and which, if it becomes an attaching obligation, will result in a money claim, is, under s. 37, sub-ss. 3 and 4, of the Bankruptcy Act, 1883, to be estimated as at the date of the receiving order, and if the obligation arises out of mutual dealings between the debtor and a creditor it is the subject of set-off under s. 38. Any obligation of that nature, whether it binds the debtor or creditor, is capable of being set off under s. 38. It can be set off against a sum due from the other party, and similarly any sum due from the other party can be set off against it.'

In the Court of Appeal Buckley LJ said (at 580–581):

a

'Under s. 37 all liabilities, present or future, certain or contingent, to which the debtor is subject at the date of the receiving order are debts provable in bankruptcy. *All such debts and liabilities resulting from mutual dealings are within s. 38.* The latter is a section directing a statutory set-off for the purpose of ascertaining the amount which can be proved... They were debts in respect of a contract existing at the date of the receiving order, and by virtue of s. 38 there is necessarily a statutory set-off. The

b

decision of this court in *In re Daintrey* is in my opinion directly in point. It was indeed a stronger case than the present, because in that case the debt of 300*l.* which was to be the subject of set-off was a debt whose existence and amount were alike contingent at the date of the receiving order. There might have been no profits in respect of the business sold. Moreover, Lindley M.R. there stated that the liability to pay the 300*l.* was conditional although the report does not disclose what the

c

conditions were. *Sect. 38 is applicable where the mutual dealings result in a debt which is not contingent only but conditional also.*' (My emphasis.)

In *Re National Benefit Assurance Co Ltd* [1924] 2 Ch 339, [1924] All ER Rep 426 Eve J had to consider another case in which a policyholder with a life assurance company borrowed money from the company on his policy. Before the death of the assured the

d company was wound up, and the policy was valued under the Assurance Companies Act 1909. The policyholder claimed to set off the value of the policy against the debt due from him. Eve J accepted that the policyholder's claim did not come into existence until the winding-up order was made and the company thereby declared its inability to pay its debts, but he held that this did not exclude the operation of the section. After citing *Re Daintrey* and *Re Asphaltic Wood Pavement Co* he said ([1924] 2 Ch 339 at 345, [1924] All

e ER Rep 426 at 428):

'It is, I think, demonstrated by these authorities that in order to bring the mutual dealings section into operation it is not necessary that there should be mutual debts existing at the date of the winding up—that being, according to *In re Daintrey*, the material date; it is sufficient if there are contractual obligations the breach of which may give rise to a claim for damages provable in the winding up. The decision in

f *Lee and Chapman's Case* ((1885) 30 Ch D 216) goes even further, in that the winding up there did not in itself involve a breach, and there was in fact no maintainable claim for damages until the notice to repair had been given five months after the commencement of the winding up.'

Eve J's reasoning in that case was approved by the Court of Appeal in *Re City Life*

g *Assurance Co Ltd* [1926] 1 Ch 191, [1925] All ER Rep 453, which was yet another case in which a policyholder sought to set off the value of his policy against his mortgage debt. *Re Asphaltic Wood Pavement Co* and *Re Daintrey* were considered at length. Warrington LJ said that both those judgments were clear that what had to be ascertained was whether the claim in question as to which set off was raised was a claim which could be proved in the bankruptcy or the winding up as the case might be. He said ([1926] Ch 191 at 206,

h [1925] All ER Rep 453 at 459):

'Now a future debt, a debt not payable immediately, but payable in future, *even payable subject to a contingency,* is deemed to be a debt provable in bankruptcy *and is, therefore, one of the liabilities referred to in s. 31 as a debt under a receiving order ...*' (My emphasis.)

j Sargant LJ said ([1926] Ch 191 at 212, [1925] All ER Rep 453 at 462):

'When we consider s. 30, which provides what debts and liabilities are provable, and so on, I think it is impossible to avoid being struck with the extraordinary comprehensiveness of the language. Every conceivable kind of liability is made provable in bankruptcy. More than that, those liabilities when they are proved are to be deemed to be debts; they are notional debts for the purpose, of course, of applying to them the provisions of s. 31 under which the debts are to be set-off one against the other and the balance only paid. That was a feature that was very much stressed, and I think rightly stressed, by [counsel for the policyholder] in his argument. All kinds of liabilities as well as all kinds of debts are made notional statutory debts, and then are set-off against one another, so that under s. 31 the balance only is payable.'

I now come to the important decision of the Court of Appeal in *Re Fenton* [1931] 1 Ch 85. This arose from the insolvency of a surety, and was a contest between the surety and the principal debtor (unlike the present case, where the contest is between the surety and the creditor). The principal debtor was also in liquidation. The question, which was answered in the negative, was whether a surety can claim, before payment, to set off against a debt owed by him to the principal debtor his right to be protected against his liability to pay the creditor under his guarantee.

Lord Hanworth MR decided the case on two grounds. First, the two claims were incommensurable. He acknowledged that the right of a surety to be protected against his liability under the guarantee was not confined to cases in which he had paid the creditor. As soon as a definite sum had become payable to the creditor, the surety had the right to require it to be paid by the principal debtor. But the surety was not entitled to have it paid to himself, for unless he had paid the creditor he could not give a good discharge. The only order to which he was entitled was an order that the principal debtor pay the creditor. This could not be brought within the words of s 31 of the 1914 Act. Lord Hanworth MR said (at 109):

'The words of the section seem clearly to connote an account capable of ascertainment on either side if not immediately, yet based upon authority or liability definitely undertaken. I find it difficult to construe those words or adapt that system to dealings in which there was a debt on one side due to the other, and per contra there was not a debt or a certain liability, but one in respect of which there was a right of protection and no more; a liability which could not be turned into a direct contra money claim, unless and until the debt had been paid by the surety, who then, and not till then, would become entitled to give a discharge for the sum paid to him.'

It is clear that Lord Hanworth MR's conclusion was not based on the future or contingent nature of the surety's right, but on the fact that it was not a direct contra money claim for which he could give a discharge to the principal debtor.

The second ground of Lord Hanworth MR's judgment was based on the rule against double proof. As he pointed out, if the trustee of the surety's estate were allowed to set off the debt due to the creditor which the surety had guaranteed, he would exercise that right in respect of the same debt for which the creditor had proved or could prove. Worse, it would be an allowance to the surety's estate in full of a debt due to the creditor which the surety had not paid himself (and, being insolvent, would not pay in full). Lord Hanworth MR concluded that the rule against double proof also prevented the surety from setting off the liability of the principal debtor to the creditor which had not crystallised into a debt due to the surety. Again, this was not because of the future or contingent nature of the surety's right, for Lord Handworth MR expressly left open the position if, after the receiving order, the surety paid under his guarantee. The crucial fact was that, so long as the creditor remained unpaid, the surety had no direct contra provable money claim against the principal debtor at all.

Lawrence LJ decided the case entirely on the ground that to allow the set-off would contravene the rule against double proof. But for this, he would have allowed the surety's claim. He listed the requirements for set-off under s 31: that the claims must be commensurate, that they must be in the same right and that they must be between the same parties. It is to be observed that he did not suggest that they must be unconditional. He described *Re Daintrey* as a case in which set-off had been allowed in respect of a debt

whose existence and amount were alike unascertained at the date of the receiving order,
a and said that there was ample authority for the general proposition that all provable
debts resulting from mutual dealings were within s 31. The question, in his view, was
whether there was any sum due from the principal debtor to the estate of the surety at
the time when the right to set off was claimed by the surety's trustee, regard being had
to the fact that at that time nothing had been paid to the creditor by the surety and the
principal debtor was still liable for the whole sum due. He concluded that, although the
b surety's claim to be indemnified was a provable debt arising out of a mutual dealings
between the surety and the principal debtor, it could not be set off against the debt due
from the surety to the principal debtor under s 31 because, at the time when the account
under s 31 had to be taken (not, be it observed, at the date of the receiving order), the
mutual dealing had not by reason of the rule against double proof resulted in any sum
becoming due from the principal debtor to the surety which could properly be entered
c on the debit side of the account.

Romer LJ considered the case first on the supposition that the surety became bankrupt
but the principal debtor remained solvent. He rejected the claim by the surety's trustee
to set off, against the principal debtor's proof of debt, the surety's liability to the creditor.
He conceded that there were mutual dealings between the principal debtor and the
surety which resulted in a debt to the principal debtor on the one hand and a liability of
d the principal debtor to indemnify the surety against his liability to the creditor on the
other. But there was nothing to be placed to the surety's credit in the account which
would have to be taken under s 31. This was not because the surety's claim was
contingent, but because his only right was to obtain an order requiring the principal
debtor to pay the creditor.

Romer LJ then turned to consider how the position was affected by the fact that the
e principal debtor was also in liquidation. He pointed out that contingent liabilities were
in general debts provable in bankruptcy, and added (at 117): '. . . it is well settled that,
provided there be mutuality of dealings, claims provable may be set off.' The rule against
double proof, however, precluded the surety who had not yet paid the creditor from
proving in the liquidation of the principal debtor. Accordingly, he concluded, the claim
of the surety's trustee not being provable in the winding up of the principal debtor, it
f followed that it could not be set off against the debt owing to the principal debtor by the
surety.

By 1956 there was thus a long and consistent line of authority that all provable debts
which resulted from mutual dealings were capable of set-off, that these included debts
whose existence and amount were alike contingent at the date of the receiving order, as
well as liability for breaches occurring on or after the receiving order of contracts existing
g at that date, which by force of the statute were converted into provable debts, and that
the essential requirements were, first, that the liability must be one which would mature,
if it matured at all, into a quantified money claim in the natural course of events, that is
to say without any fresh agreement but solely by virtue of a contract already existing at
the date of the receiving order, and, second, that it had in fact done so by the time the
claim to set off was made. *Re Fenton* cast no doubt on these well-established principles,
h but confirmed them. The only qualifications it added were, first, that the surety's right
to require the principal debtor to pay the creditor could not be set off, because it was not
a right to require payment to himself and so was not commensurable, and, second, that
a provable debt could not be set off at a time when, by reason of the rule against double
proof, it did not rank for dividend.

In *Re Fenton* the Court of Appeal left open the question whether the surety could set
j off his claim to be indemnified by the principal debtor if, after the receiving order but
before the claim to set-off was raised, the surety had paid the creditor in full under the
guarantee. This fell to be decided in *Re a debtor (No 66 of 1955), ex p the debtor v Trustee of
the property of Waite (a bankrupt)* [1956] 3 All ER 225, [1956] 1 WLR 1266. This is the
case relied on by the editors of *Williams and Muir Hunter on Bankruptcy* (19th edn, 1979)
p 192 and by Peter Gibson J in the *Carreras Rothmans* case [1985] 1 All ER 155 at 171,

[1985] Ch 207 at 230 for the proposition that liabilities still wholly contingent at the date of the receiving order are outside s 31.

This case, like *Re Fenton*, was a contest between a surety and the principal debtor, and arose in the bankruptcy of the surety. After the receiving order, the surety's trustee paid the creditor in full in order to obtain the release of collateral security which had been given by the surety, and on his failure to obtain reimbursement by the principal debtor sought to have the principal debtor made bankrupt. The principal debtor claimed to set off a sum previously owed to him by the surety, which if allowed would bring the balance of the surety's claim against him below the amount for which a bankruptcy notice could be issued. The Divisional Court disallowed the set-off, on the ground that, until a surety is called on to pay and does pay under his guarantee, there is no debt or right at law between the surety and the principal debtor at all: the principal debtor's obligation, even as between himself and the surety, is to pay the principal debtor. *Re Daintrey* was distinguished on the ground that there was an existing obligation by Mant to Daintrey at the date of the receiving order; it was merely the amount due which came to be quantified when the accounts were subsequently taken.

For the reasons I have already given, I am unable to accept as an accurate description of *Re Daintrey* the second part of this explanation; but the first is unexceptionable. At the date of the receiving order in *Re Daintrey*, Mant's obligation, though still contingent, was an obligation to pay Daintrey, the other party to the set-off. In the two surety cases, the principal debtor's obligation, if called on by the surety, was to pay the creditor, a third party.

The Court of Appeal dismissed the principal debtor's appeal. The leading judgment was delivered by Lord Evershed MR. The central part of his reasoning is to be found in the following passage ([1956] 3 All ER 225 at 227–228, [1956] 1 WLR 1226 at 1230):

'The rights of [the bankrupt] against the appellant were the special but contingent rights of a surety who had not been called on to make any payment by the principal creditor and had not exercised what has been called the protective right of a surety to require the principal debtor to relieve him of his liability by paying the debt owed to the principal creditor. Nor was the case one in which all that remained to be done was to quantify the extent of an obligation already incurred, the amount of the indebtedness when finally ascertained being exclusively referable to an obligation to pay that sum entered into prior to the relevant date, such as was the case in *Re Daintrey, Ex p. Mant* ([1900] 1 QB 546) see per ROMER, L.J. (at 573–574). If and when a sum certain became due from the appellant to [the bankrupt] or his trustee, that debt would be referable to the contract of guarantee with the bank or to the rights flowing from such contract, entered into by [the bankrupt] with the bank subsequently to and independently (albeit in consequence) of the mutual dealings between himself and the appellant.'

I have not found that passage at all easy to follow. It may be susceptible of more than one interpretation. At first sight it appears to confirm the Divisional Court's explanation of *Re Daintrey*. But in my judgment the true ratio for the decision which emerges from the passage I have cited is that, if ever a debt became owing from the principal debtor to the surety, rather than to the creditor, the source of that obligation would be the contract of guarantee itself, a contract between the surety and the creditor, and would not be exclusively referable to any transaction between the parties to the set-off which was claimed. The true distinction between the case and *Re Daintrey* was that, in *Re Daintrey*, in the words of Romer LJ 'whatever sum eventually became payable by, became payable to Daintrey *by virtue of this agreement of December 31, 1892, and of nothing else*' (my emphasis.) (see [1900] 1 QB 546 at 573–574).

Hodson LJ's judgment is, with respect, even more difficult to follow. He certainly treated *Re Daintrey* as a case of a debt actually due, though falling to be calculated later. But he also laid stress on the words of Romer LJ which I have just quoted. In so far as I understand his judgment, it is that the reasoning in *Re Fenton* compels the conclusion

a that the change from a debt due to a third party to a debt due to the other party to the
set-off is one which must take place before the date of the receiving order; although, with
respect, this was the very point left open in *Re Fenton*.

Counsel for the company in the present case submitted that the true source of the
principal's obligation to pay the surety lay in his implied promise to indemnify him if
he was called on under his guarantee, that this was a contingent liability of the principal
debtor to pay the surety direct and that the reason it was not allowed to be set off in *Re a*
b *debtor (No 66 of 1955)* must be that it was still contingent at the date of the receiving
order.

I am unable to accept this argument. In the first place, whether or not the true source
of the principal debtor's obligation to indemnify the surety is his implied contract with
the surety to do so, rather than the contract of guarantee itself, this was not the source
identified by Lord Evershed MR. If it is the true source, this may vitiate his reasoning
c and undermine the conclusion based on it. But I am bound by the ratio decidendi of the
case, and I am neither at liberty to reject the actual ground of the decision, nor bound by
any alternative ground on which the decision could in theory be supported. In the second
place, Hodson LJ clearly based his judgment on the reasoning in *Re Fenton* which, as I
have already demonstrated, cast no doubt on the principle that provable debts, including
contingent liabilities, were capable of set-off. In my judgment, the true ratio of *Re a*
d *debtor (No 66 of 1955)* is that to come within s 31 the liability must be exclusively
referable not merely to an agreement already existing at the date of the receiving order,
but to an agreement between the same parties as the parties to the set-off, and that the
liability of the principal debtor to indemnify a surety who has paid the principal debtor
does not pass this test. Whether in fact it does so or not, there is nothing in the decision
to compel the conclusion that, contrary to all the earlier authorities, liabilities still wholly
e contingent at the date of the receiving order are, for that reason alone, outside the scope
of s 31.

The object of that section, like its predecessors, is to prevent the injustice of a man who
has had mutual dealings with a bankrupt from having to pay in full what he owes to the
bankrupt while having to rest content with a dividend on what the bankrupt owes him.
Of course, a debtor to the bankrupt must not be allowed, after the date of the receiving
f order, to gain an advantage by buying up the bankrupt's liabilities in order to obtain the
benefit of a set-off. But to disallow the set-off of a provable debt merely because it was
still contingent at the date of the receiving order, where the contingency has since
occurred and the liability which has arisen is exclusively referable to and has resulted in
the natural course of events from a transaction between the same parties entered into
before the receiving order, would in my judgment be productive of the very injustice
g the section and its predecessors were designed to prevent.

In my judgment, the passage which I have cited from the judgment of Peter Gibson J
in the *Carreras Rothmans* case [1985] 1 All ER 155 at 171, [1985] Ch 207 at 230 is not
warranted by the decision in *Re a debtor (No 66 of 1955)* [1956] 3 All ER 225, [1956] 1
WLR 1266, is contrary to both principle and authority, and is one which I must decline
to follow. On the service of a notice under cl 10 of the agreement, if a valid notice can
h still be served, therefore, Commercial Credit will be entitled to set off the purchase price
laid down by that clause against any sum due from Commercial Credit under the
agreement.

Accordingly, I answer the second question also in favour of Commercial Credit.

Declaration accordingly.

j
Solicitors: *Alsop Stevens* (for the liquidator); *Cameron Markby* (for Commercial Credit);
Sebastian Coleman & Co, agents for *Wragge & Co*, Birmingham (for the garages).

Jacqueline Metcalfe   Barrister.

Practice Direction

                   a

FAMILY DIVISION

Child − Care − Local authority − Wardship proceedings − Secure accommodation − Applications for secure accommodation − Representation of child − Guardian ad litem − Joining of ward as party to proceedings − Child Care Act 1980, s 21A(6) − Secure Accommodation (No 2) (Amendment) Regulations 1986.

                   b

The Secure Accommodation (No 2) (Amendment) Regulations 1986, SI 1986/1591, come into force on 15 October 1986 and provide, inter alia, that a ward of court may be placed and kept in secure accommodation only pursuant to the direction of a judge exercising wardship jurisdiction in the High Court or in wardship proceedings transferred to a county court under s 38 of the Matrimonial and Family Proceedings Act 1984.

                   c

    In other secure accommodation applications, dealt with in the juvenile court, s 21A(6) of the Child Care Act 1980 governs the legal representation of children for the purpose of ensuring that the views and wishes of the child can be fully argued before, and taken into consideration by, the juvenile court.

    Before making a direction to place or keep a ward in secure accommodation, the court should, unless the ward is already represented by a guardian ad litem or there are special reasons why the ward should not be so represented, join the ward as a party to the proceedings and appoint a guardian ad litem to protect his interests and ensure that his views are made known to the court.

                   d

    Issued with the approval of the President and the concurrence of the Lord Chancellor.

                   e

14 October 1986   B P TICKLE
                                         Senior Registrar.

a # Rogers and another v Essex County Council

HOUSE OF LORDS

LORD BRIDGE OF HARWICH, LORD BRANDON OF OAKBROOK, LORD MACKAY OF CLASHFERN, LORD ACKNER AND LORD OLIVER OF AYLMERTON

28 JULY, 16 OCTOBER 1986

b *Education – School attendance – Duty of parent to secure regular attendance of pupil – Failure to secure regular attendance – Proceedings against parent – Defence – Distance of home from school – Nearest available route – Shortest route dangerous to unaccompanied child – Whether route 'available' – Education Act 1944, s 39(2)(c)(5).*

c The distance of the shortest public route between the house where a 12-year-old child lived and the school where she was registered was 2·94 miles. Part of that route consisted of an isolated, unmade and unlit track which, particularly in winter, would be both difficult and dangerous for a young girl to cross on her own. The child failed to attend school regularly and her parents were convicted of failing to ensure her regular attendance, contrary to s 39[a] of the Education Act 1944. The parents appealed, relying on s 39(2)(c) of the Act which provided that it was a good defence to show that the school d was not within walking distance of the child's home and the local authority had not provided transport or alternative schooling arrangements. In the case of a child over eight years old, 'walking distance' was defined by s 39(5) as 'three miles, measured by the nearest available route'. The Crown Court dismissed the appeal but the parents' appeal to the Divisional Court was upheld on the grounds that the nearest available route was that route which the child could safely use unaccompanied. The local authority appealed to e the House of Lords, contending that the nearest available route was the shortest route usable without trespassing.

Held – For the purpose of deciding under s 39 of the 1944 Act whether a school was within walking distance of a child's home, the nearest available route between the child's home and his or her school was the nearest route along which the child could walk to f school with reasonable safety when accompanied by an adult and a route did not fail to qualify as the nearest available route because of dangers which would arise if the child was unaccompanied. The local authority's appeal would therefore be allowed (see p 322 *d* to *e*, p 325 *g h* and p 326 *a* to *e g h*, post).

Shaxted v Ward [1954] 1 All ER 336 considered.

Decision of the Divisional Court of the Queen's Bench Division [1985] 2 All ER 39 g reversed.

Notes

For the duty of parents to secure attendance of pupils and for statutory defences to proceedings against parents for non-attendance of registered pupils, see 15 Halsbury's Laws (4th edn) paras 32–33, and for cases on the subject, see 19 Digest (Reissue) 499, 503, h 3885, 3902.

For the Education Act 1944, s 39, see 15 Halsbury's Statutes (4th edn) 137.

Case referred to in opinions

Shaxted v Ward [1954] 1 All ER 336, sub nom *Farrier v Ward* [1954] 1 WLR 306, DC.

j **Appeal**

Essex County Council appealed, with leave of the Divisional Court of the Queen's Division given on 10 May 1985, against the decision of that court (Parker LJ and Tudor

---

a Section 39, so far as material is set out at p 322 *j* to p 323 *c*, post

Evans J) ([1985] 2 All ER 39, [1985] 1 WLR 700) on 19 February 1985 allowing an appeal
by the respondents, Peter Albert Rogers and Violet Rogers (the parents), by way of case   *a*
stated against a decision of the Crown Court at Chelmsford (his Honour Judge Ward and
justices) on 13 July 1984 dismissing the parents' appeal from their conviction by the
justices for the county of Essex acting in and for the petty sessional division of Colchester
on 23 May 1984 for an offence under ss 39 and 40(1) of the Education Act 1944 by reason
of the failure of the parents' daughter to attend regularly at the Stanway Comprehensive
School where she was a registered pupil. The Divisional Court certified that a point of   *b*
law of general public importance (set out at p 324 *c d*, post) was involved in its decision.
The facts are set out in the opinion of Lord Ackner.

Conrad Dehn QC and *David Mellor* for the local authority.
Gavin Lightman QC and *Edward Irving* for the parents.

c

Their Lordships took time for consideration.

16 October. The following opinions were delivered.

LORD BRIDGE OF HARWICH. My Lords, for the reasons given in the speech of
my noble and learned friend Lord Ackner, with which I agree, I would allow the appeal   *d*
and answer the certified question in the negative.

LORD BRANDON OF OAKBROOK. My Lords, I have had the advantage of
reading in draft the speech prepared by my noble and learned friend Lord Ackner. I
agree with it and for the reasons which he gives I would allow the appeal and make no
order as to costs.   *e*

LORD MACKAY OF CLASHFERN. My Lords, I have had the opportunity of
reading in draft the speech prepared by Lord Ackner. I agree with it and concur in the
order which he proposes.

LORD ACKNER. My Lords, the short question raised by this appeal is: who is to pay   *f*
for the transport to the Stanway comprehensive school of Shirley Rogers, a schoolgirl
aged 12 at the material time? Should it be the appellants, the Essex County Council,
which is the local education authority or the respondents, Shirley's parents? The local
authority have offered Shirley the use of the school bus but subject to payment of the
concessionary fare of £20 a term, the parents not qualifying for free transport on a means
test basis. The parents, on principle, have refused to make any payment for school   *g*
transport. The answer to the question is provided by the Education Act 1944 of which
only a few sections need be referred to.

Education Act 1944
    Section 36 imposes on parents the duty to secure the education of their children. It
provides: *h*

> 'It shall be the duty of the parent of every child of compulsory school age to cause
> him to receive efficient full-time education suitable to his age, ability, and aptitude
> and to any special educational needs he may have, either by regular attendance at
> school or otherwise.'

    Section 39 imposes the duty on parents to secure regular attendance of registered   *j*
pupils. Shirley was registered at the Stanway school. The section provides:

> '(1) If any child of compulsory school age who is a registered pupil at a school fails
> to attend regularly thereat, the parent of the child shall be guilty of an offence
> against this section.

a

(2) In any proceedings for an offence against this section in respect of a child who is not a boarder at the school at which he is a registered pupil, the child shall not be deemed to have failed to attend regularly at the school by reason of his absence therefrom with leave or—(a) at any time when he was prevented from attending by reason of sickness or any unavoidable cause; (b) on any day exclusively set apart for religious observance by the religious body to which his parent belongs; (c) if the parent proves that the school at which the child is a registered pupil is not within

b

walking distance of the child's home, and that no suitable arrangements have been made by the local education authority either for his transport to and from the school or for boarding accommodation for him at or near the school or for enabling him to become a registered pupil at a school nearer to his home . . .

(5) In this section the expression . . . "walking distance" means, in relation to a child who has not attained the age of eight years two miles, and in the case of any

c

other child three miles, measured by the nearest available route.'

Section 55 relates to the provision of transport and other facilities. As amended, it provides:

'(1) A local education authority shall make such arrangements for the provision of transport and otherwise as they consider necessary or as the Secretary of State may

d

direct for the purpose of facilitating the attendance of pupils at schools or county colleges or at any course or class provided in pursuance of a scheme of further education in force for their area, and any transport provided in pursuance of such arrangments shall be provided free of charge.

(2) A local education authority may pay the whole or any part, as the authority think fit, of the reasonable travelling expenses of any pupil in attendance at any

e

school or county college or at such course or class as aforesaid for whose transport no arrangements are made under this section.'

This appeal is concerned with the 'walking distance' from Shirley's home to her school and in particular whether 'the nearest available route' exceeded three miles, she being in the older age group referred to in s 39(5) quoted above. The dispute arises in the following circumstances.

f

The facts

The distance from Shirley's home to the school by the shortest route is 2·94 miles. That route involves crossing Copford Plains by an isolated and partly unmade track which is entirely unlighted. In winter this route is one of considerable danger for a young girl who would have to walk over Copford Plains in darkness. Copford Plains are

g

also extremely difficult to cross in winter and may be passable on foot in the morning but impassable by the evening. There is an alternative route by metalled roads but this is 3·2 miles in length. The parents quite reasonably regarded the Copford Plains route as unsuitable for use by Shirley, if unaccompanied. Thus, since as stated above, the local authority were only prepared to make the school bus available on payment of the concessionary fare, which the parents were not willing to pay, Shirley stayed away from

h

school during the period from 13 December 1983 until 17 April 1984. Informations were then preferred against the parents by the local authority alleging that the parents were guilty of an offence against s 39. On 23 May 1984 the justices for the county of Essex, sitting at Colchester, convicted the parents and ordered that they both be conditionally discharged for a period of 12 months. The parents appealed to the Crown Court at Chelmsford and on 13 July 1984 the appeal against conviction was dismissed.

j

The appeal against sentence was allowed, to the extent of substituting absolute discharges for the conditional discharges imposed by the magistrates. The Crown Court expressed considerable sympathy for the parents, but concluded that they were bound by the decision of the Divisional Court in *Shaxted v Ward* [1954] 1 All ER 336, [1954] 1 WLR 306.

The parents appealed by case stated to the Divisional Court (see [1985] 2 All ER 39, [1985] 1 WLR 700). I have already set out the material facts which the Crown Court *a* found. There was no finding that the route was impassable on any day that Shirley failed to attend or that the route was unsuitable, if she was accompanied. At the hearing of the appeal by the Divisional Court on 4 February 1985 the parents repeated their contention that the nearest available route of which the walking distance from a child's home to his school is to be measured for the purposes of the 1944 Act, must be, not merely the nearest route which a child can lawfully walk, but a route which a responsible parent would *b* allow a child to use *unaccompanied*. In a reserved judgment Parker LJ, with whom Tudor Evans J agreed, accepted this submission and distinguished *Shaxted v Ward*. On 10 May 1985 the Divisional Court gave leave to appeal to your Lordships' House on terms that the local authority would not seek to disturb the order for costs in the Divisional Court and would pay the parents' cost of this appeal in any event. The certified point of law of general public importance is in these terms: *c*

> 'Whether the nearest available route by which the walking distance of a school from a child's home is to be measured for the purposes of the Education Act 1944 must be not merely the nearest route which a child can walk without trespassing but a route which a responsible parent could allow a child to use unaccompanied.'

d

Shaxted v Ward
This decision is, of course, not binding on your Lordships' House and whether or not the Divisional Court was entitled to distinguish it, as it purported to do, is not an issue which need concern your Lordships. Nevertheless, it was a decision of a strong court, which has stood unchallenged for over 30 years and has been relied on over that period by local education authorities. It involved considering the crucial s 39(5) of the 1944 Act *e* and the facts of the case were similar to the facts in this appeal. It concerned two children who were under eight years of age and the route from their home to the school, at which they were registered pupils, was under two miles. The route was safe for the children to use, if escorted, but there was a particular portion of the road near the school where for small children, an escort would be desirable. The prosecutor contended that 'available route' meant a route which could be followed without committing a trespass. The *f* justices accepted this submission and the parents were convicted. They accordingly appealed by case stated.
At the outset of his judgment Lord Goddard CJ said ([1954] 1 WLR 306 at 307):

> 'The short point that arises is this: The Justices found that the route which these children had to travel was "safe for these children to use, if escorted. The bit of road near the school, where an escort would be desirable for small children, was common *g* to both the children in question." I think that the justices recognized that it would be desirable for children to be escorted or in some way conducted along or across a certain piece of road where there was probably a good deal of traffic. They found that it was usual for parents to provide escort for their children to and from school, where necessary."'

h

Having referred to s 39 of the 1944 Act Lord Goddard CJ continued ([1954] 1 WLR 306 at 308; cf [1954] 1 All ER 336 at 338):

> 'The justices have to find whether the school is within walking distance; and it is said that the route which the children took, which was under two miles, was not the "nearest available route" because part of it was said to be dangerous for children to walk along unescorted. I cannot read the word "available" as meaning necessarily *i* safe, because we can see how these words came to be included in the Act.'

Lord Goddard CJ then considered the earlier Education Acts where the words 'measured according to the nearest road' were used and concluded that the words in the 1944 Act 'measured by the nearest available route' were not intended to make any change

in the law. He then stated ([1954] 1 WLR 306 at 308–309; cf [1954] 1 All ER 336 at
a   338):

> 'To some extent I sympathize with the views of the parents in this case, and it
> may be that they would like to bring pressure upon the Kent County Council to
> have a person on the road to see that "this bit of the road", as the justices call it, is
> safe for the children to cross. Those, however, are matters for the education authority
> to consider and to put into operation if they think fit. I can only say that, if there is
b   > a road which measures not more than two miles or a route along which a child can
> walk and its measurement does not exceed two miles, that is the nearest available
> route. It may sometimes be unsafe; sometimes the route might be flooded, and, if
> that happened and the person could not walk along the road, that might be a
> reasonable excuse for not using it on that particular day, but we are not concerned
> with that but with a case where the parents think that the route is not safe.
c   > Parliament has not substituted safety as the test but the distance. Any question with
> regard to safety must be, and I have no doubt, will be taken into consideration by
> the education authority. In my opinion, therefore, the justices came to a right
> decision and the appeal fails.'

Byrne and Parker JJ both agreed.
d   It has been urged before us that in his judgment Lord Goddard CJ, when considering
whether a route was available, was discounting all safety considerations. I cannot accept
this submission. In the context in which the Lord Chief Justice made his observations,
he was concerned with a route which was said to be dangerous *only* if the children walked
along it *unescorted*.

e   *The true meaning of 'availability' in s 39(5) of the Act*
    In the submissions made to your Lordships it was common ground that 'available' in
the context of s 39(5) means 'capable of being used'. During the course of the argument
counsel for the local authority appeared reluctant to accept that for a route to be 'available'
it must be *reasonably* capable of being used. His reluctance seemed to stem from an
anxiety on behalf of his clients not to accept the responsibility, from time to time, of
f   deciding whether or not the route which is the nearest route, is reasonably capable of
being used by a child of the relevant age, notwithstanding that under s 39(2)(c) the onus
is clearly on the parent to prove that the school is not within walking distance of the
child's home. It is clear that the word 'available' qualifies the word 'route'. The availability
of the route cannot be determined by the mere study of a map. That it must be
reasonably practicable for a child to walk along it to school does not, to my mind, admit
g   of any argument. Of course, it must be free from obstructions or obstacles which would
make its use impracticable. Dangers inherent in a particular route are factors that must
be taken into account when considering its availability. A route which involved crossing
a river by means of a footbridge would, other things being equal, qualify as an available
route. However, if as a result, for example, of recent severe flooding, the bridge became
unstable and unsafe to use, that route would cease to be available.
h   The short issue in this appeal is whether 'availability' is to be measured by what is
reasonable for an *unaccompanied child* to use? Counsel for the parents was constrained to
concede that in the case of a very young school child, certainly a child of five, six or seven,
Parliament must have assumed that the child would be accompanied, however short the
distance, if there existed any real hazard, eg crossing a busy road. Accordingly, there
would be few, if any, routes in the first category provided for in s 39(5) (the two mile
j   route) which any responsible parent would allow an unaccompanied child to use. If the
availability of the route was to be measured by what is reasonable for an unaccompanied
child who had not attained the age of eight years, there would have been no point in
prescribing in the subsection the two mile route requirement. Any such child with very
few exceptions would have to be provided with free transport, although in practice, as
Parliament must have appreciated, such a child would almost always be accompanied, so

that the transport would not in fact have been necessary at all. The crucial point appears not to have been considered by the Divisional Court. It is certainly not referred to in the *a* judgment of Parker LJ.

What then was the purpose of defining 'walking distance' in relation to a child who had not attained the age of eight years? The answer, to my mind, is clear: it was simply to provide that where the nearest route from home to school was reasonably capable of being used by a child along or (in the majority of cases) with an escort and did not exceed two miles, the school was within 'walking distance' of the child's home. If, as is rightly *b* conceded, the route does not in that situation fail to qualify as 'available' because of dangers which would be consequent on the child being unaccompanied, when, if at all, would the route thus fail to qualify? Counsel for the parents submits that once the child is of sufficient age to go out on a street alone, then if the route is not reasonably safe for the child to walk along it unaccompanied the route is not 'available'. Quite apart from the fact that there are no words in the section to support such a submission, the test *c* suggested is hopelessly vague. What sort of street is one to have in mind, what sort of traffic is it to carry, what time of day, indeed what weather or season is to be assumed etc etc? Further, is the test an objective test applicable to all children of a given age or is it to be applied subjectively to the particular child whose parents have raised the issue? The complete impracticability of such a test in itself persuades me that it was never in the contemplation of Parliament. *d*

In my judgment a route to be 'available' within the meaning of s 39(5) must be a route along which a child accompanied as necessary can walk and walk with reasonable safety to school. It does not fail to qualify as 'available' because of dangers which would arise if the child is unaccompanied.

It has been argued that unless your Lordships decide that availability has to be measured by what is reasonable for an unaccompanied child, then parents who normally *e* accompany their children, but who fail to do so temporarily because of some crisis such as an illness, and as a result the child fails regularly to attend school, will have committed a criminal offence. In my judgment this submission overlooks s 39(2)(*a*) which provides that the child shall not be deemed to have failed to attend regularly if he was prevented from attending by reason of 'any unavoidable cause'.

There is a final point which I would wish to stress. Under s 55 of the Act, which is set *f* out in extenso above, the local education authority has a discretion to provide free transport where the relevant walking distance is less than three miles (or, as the case may be, two miles). The local authority in their written case fully accepted that if a local education authority failed unreasonably to exercise this discretion, it would be liable, on an application for judicial review to be ordered to carry out its statutory duty. In fact, in pursuance of their powers under s 55(2) the local authority, having been satisfied that the *g* parents did not qualify for free transport on a means test basis, in the exercise of this discretion offered the use of the school bus at the concessionary fare referred to above.

I would accordingly allow this appeal, discharge the order of the Divisional Court and would answer the certified point of law in the negative. In view of the local authority's undertaking not to disturb the order for costs made by the Divisional Court and to pay the costs of the parents of this appeal, I would make no order as to costs. *h*

LORD OLIVER OF AYLMERTON. My Lords, I have had the opportunity of reading in draft the speech delivered by my noble and learned friend Lord Ackner. I agree with it and concur in the order which he proposes.

Appeal allowed. No order as to costs. *j*

Solicitors: *R W Adcock*, Chelmsford (for the local authority); *Ellison & Co*, Colchester (for the parents).

Mary Rose Plummer Barrister.

a

R v Saunders

COURT OF APPEAL, CRIMINAL DIVISION
LAWTON LJ, DRAKE AND HIRST JJ
20, 23 MAY 1986

b Criminal law – Murder – Manslaughter – Reduction to manslaughter – Jury not agreeing on a
verdict of murder – Jury returning verdict of manslaughter – Whether jury required to acquit
defendant of murder before returning manslaughter verdict – Whether jury entitled to return
verdict of manslaughter if they cannot agree on verdict of murder – Criminal Law Act 1967,
s 6(2).

c The appellant was charged with murder. At his trial the jury were initially unable to
agree on a verdict and were directed by the judge that if at least ten of the jury were
agreed that all the ingredients of manslaughter were made out he would be prepared to
discharge the jury from returning a verdict of murder and would accept a verdict of
manslaughter. After further deliberation the foreman stated that the jury was unable to
reach a verdict on the charge of murder but unanimously found the appellant guilty of
d manslaughter. The appellant was convicted and appealed, contending that by reason of
s 6(2)ᵃ of the Criminal Law Act 1967 where a person was charged with murder it was
only open to a jury to return a verdict of manslaughter if he was 'found not guilty of
murder' and therefore an alternative verdict of manslaughter was not open to the jury
when they could not agree on a verdict of murder.

e **Held** – Having regard to the terms of s 6 of the 1967 Act, the context in which the
section appeared, and the policy of the Act, a jury could return a verdict of manslaughter
when it was unable to agree on a verdict of murder, and s 6(2) did not require the jury to
return a finding of not guilty of murder before returning the manslaughter verdict. The
jury's verdict of manslaughter was therefore valid and the appeal would be dismissed (see
p 331 *c* to *e h*, post).

f **Notes**
For alternative verdicts for murder and manslaughter, see 11 Halsbury's Laws (4th edn)
para 312, and for cases on verdicts generally, see 14(1) Digest (Reissue) 407–422, 3442–
3609.
    For the Criminal Law Act 1967, s 6, see 12 Halsbury's Statutes (4th edn) 365.

g **Cases referred to in judgment**
Mackalley's Case (1611) 9 Co Rep 61b, [1558–1774] All ER Rep 542, 77 ER 824, Exch Ch.
R v Berry (31 January 1986, unreported), CA.
R v Collison (1980) 71 Cr App R 249, CCA.
R v Rose [1982] 2 All ER 731, [1982] AC 822, [1982] 3 WLR 192, HL.
R v Stokes (1925) 19 Cr App R 71, CCA.
h *R v Walhein* (1952) 36 Cr App R 167, CCA.

Case also cited
R v Wilson [1983] 3 All ER 448, [1984] AC 242, HL.

j **Appeal**
Keith Saunders appealed against his conviction in the Crown Court at Maidstone on 12
September 1985 before Otton J and a jury of manslaughter and his subsequent sentence
of life imprisonment. The facts are set out in the judgment of the court.

James Townend QC and *James Turner* (assigned by the Registrar of Criminal Appeals) for
    the appellant.

---

a Section 6(2) is set out at p 330 *j* to p 331 *a*, post

Nicholas Purnell QC and *David Radcliffe* for the Crown.

Cur adv vult **a**

23 May. The following judgment of the court was delivered.

LAWTON LJ. The appellant appeals on a point of law against his conviction on 12 September 1985 in the Crown Court at Maidstone for manslaughter and with the leave of this court on points of mixed law and fact. He also applies for leave to appeal against **b** his sentence of life imprisonment.

The point of law is this: if on an indictment charging murder a jury cannot agree that murder has been proved and are discharged from returning a verdict on the charge of murder but they are agreed that all the elements of manslaughter have been proved, can they validly return a verdict of manslaughter having regard to the provisions of s 6(2) of the Criminal Law Act 1967?   **c**

The prosecution's case was that on 29 October 1984 the appellant killed a woman called Jeanette Lazenby by a single stab wound with a knife. This had happened in the kitchen of a house in Tunbridge Wells belonging to a man called Ayres. The appellant and the deceased had been living there for some six weeks before her death. It is unnecessary for the purposes of this appeal to recount in detail the events of 29 October. It suffices to state that on that day the appellant, who was a chronic alcoholic, had been **d** drinking heavily. Shortly after 4.50 pm Ayres, who was also a chronic alcoholic, said that he had heard screams coming from the kitchen. He went there and found Jeanette Lazenby on the floor apparently dead. A kitchen knife was in the sink. The appellant seemed dazed and kept on saying 'What have I done?' He was drunk. The degree of his drunkenness is shown by the fact that at about 10 pm that evening he had 270 mg of alcohol in 100 ml of his blood.   **e**

At the trial he put forward some fanciful defences: first, that the deceased had committed suicide; second, that she had died by accident during a scuffle over a knife; third, that some unknown person had killed her; fourth, that the appellant had killed her in self defence; fifth, that he had killed her under provocation. He also said that he was so drunk as to be unable to form an intent to kill or cause grievous or indeed any bodily harm. Counsel for the Crown before the appellant's arraignment had told counsel **f** for the appellant that, because of the appellant's drunken condition, the Crown would be willing to accept a plea of guilty to manslaughter. This was not acceptable to the appellant.

This odd mixture of defences, particularly those relating to suicide, accident and self defence, led counsel for the Crown to lead some evidence from Ayres that during a short period of between two and six weeks before 29 October the appellant had acted **g** aggressively towards the deceased. As Ayres was an unsatisfactory witness with hindsight we query whether it was worthwhile leading this evidence. Counsel for the appellant has submitted that it was inadmissible because it proved nothing more than the appellant's propensity to use violence towards the deceased. He relied on the decision of this court in *R v Berry* (31 January 1986, unreported). In our judgment it was more than evidence of propensity. It was admissible to rebut some of the defences put forward by the **h** appellant. Counsel for the appellant took other points on the evidence which had no substance.

The jury retired at 12.49 pm. At 3.50 pm they returned to court and were given a majority direction. At 4.06 pm they sent a note to the judge which was in these terms:

'The jury is split between murder and manslaughter at present and would **j** welcome further guidance on the distinction between them.'

There followed a short discussion between the judge and counsel in the absence of the jury. At 4.15 pm the jury returned to court. The judge said:

'May I ask your foreman one question. Is the matter which is troubling you a distinction between murder and manslaughter on the question of the intent in relation to the effect of drink?'

a The foreman of the jury said: 'Yes.' As a result of that answer the judge gave the jury a further direction about which no complaint is made. At 4.23 pm the jury again retired. Shortly before 5.47 pm the jury sent a note to the judge dealing with a personal problem which one of the jurors had. Before asking them to return to court the judge had a discussion with counsel as to what was to be done if the jury were still in disagreement about murder. He said that if there was no prospect of them reaching a verdict he would discharge them and order a retrial. There followed some discussion as to whether a

b verdict of manslaughter could be accepted if the jury were agreed on each of the material elements in manslaughter. In the course of this discussion the judge said:

'On the other hand would it not be possible to give them a direction that "if at least ten of you are agreed that all the ingredients of manslaughter are made out, and the only thing which is dividing you is whether the necessary intent for murder has been established, then provided at least ten of you are agreed on that, I am prepared to discharge you from returning a verdict on murder, and I am prepared to accept a verdict based on manslaughter".'

c

Counsel for the appellant said that that was a course which he would find difficult to fault. At 5.47 pm the jury returned into court and the judge gave them a *Walhein* direction (see *R v Walhein* (1952) 36 Cr App R 167) followed by a direction on the lines

d he had discussed with counsel. They then retired and came back into court at 6 pm. The following exchange then took place:

'*The clerk*. Members of the jury, will your foreman please stand. Will you answer my next question simply "Yes" or "No". In respect of the offence of murder, have at least ten of your number agreed on your verdict? *The foreman*. No.

e *The clerk*. In respect of the offence of manslaughter, have at least ten of your number agreed on your verdict? *The foreman*. Yes.

The clerk. Do you find the defendant quilty or not guilty of manslaughter? *The foreman*. We find the defendant guilty of manslaughter.

The clerk. Is that the verdict of you all or by a majority? *The foreman*. Unanimous.'

f Evidence was then called about the appellant's antecedents. Counsel for the appellant made a speech in mitigation. The judge sentenced the appellant to life imprisonment. Counsel for the Crown then asked the judge whether he would discharge the jury 'on the allegation of murder'. The transcript does not record any answer but the indictment was indorsed: 'jury failed to agree on murder but find the defendant guilty of manslaughter. Discharged from giving a verdict on murder.'

g Counsel for the appellant told us that when all this happened he was unaware of the provisions of s 6(2) of the Criminal Law Act 1967. Counsel for the Crown seems to have shared his ignorance. This is not surprising because for some reason *Archbold's Pleading, Evidence and Practice in Criminal Cases* (42nd edn, 1985) does not set out the text of this subsection. It contents itself with stating that s 6(2) lists 'the alternative verdicts available when on an indictment for murder the defendant is found not guilty of murder'.

h Now that counsel for the appellant has found out what s 6(2) provides he has submitted that the jury could not have validly returned a verdict of guilty of manslaughter because they had not acquitted the appellant of murder. This would mean, as he accepted, that the trial had ended without a valid verdict. A trial which ends without a valid verdict is no trial at all (see *R v Rose* [1982] 2 All ER 731, [1982] AC 822) with the result that this court could order a retrial on a venire de novo. Such an order might not be in the

j interests of the appellant who would be in jeopardy on a retrial of being convicted of murder and would result in a long and expensive retrial on evidence which was not improving with age. But if this is the consequence of the operation of s 6(2) properly construed this court would have no option but to quash the conviction of manslaughter. In the circumstances of this case we would be disregarding the public interest if we did not order a retrial. In order to construe s 6(2) in its context in the 1967 Act, it has been necessary for us to remind ourselves of what verdicts could be returned at common law on an indictment for murder. At least since *Mackalley's Case* (1611) 9 Co Rep 61b, [1558–

1774] All ER Rep 542 juries have been entitled to return a verdict of manslaughter on an
indictment charging murder. Both were felonies. Before 1967 it was common for the   *a*
defendants to tender pleas of manslaughter when indicted for murder, and for the
prosecution, with the consent of the judge, to accept them. That practice received
statutory recognition in relation to all offences by s 39(1) of the Criminal Administration
Act 1914. It is highly likely in the past that on indictments for murder juries sometimes
disagreed as to the adequacy of the proof of intent but were all agreed that the material
elements in manslaughter had been proved and in consequence returned a verdict to that   *b*
effect. In most cases they would have returned their verdict as 'Not guilty of murder but
guilty of manslaughter', but if they had said, as they might have done, that they could
not agree about murder but were all agreed about manslaughter, it is difficult to see why
such a verdict could not have been accepted. As far as we know there is no reported case
before 1967, nor any textbook dealing with this problem. In *R v Collison* (1980) 71 Cr
App R 249 this court had to consider a case in which at trial the jury stated that they were   *c*
not agreed about proof of the intent necessary for a charge under s 18 of the Offences
Against the Person Act 1861 but were satisfied about a charge of unlawful wounding
under s 20 of the Act. The trial judge seems to have assumed, because of the provisions
of s 6(3) of the 1967 Act, that the jury could not return a valid verdict of unlawful
wounding under s 20 of the 1861 Act because they had not acquitted the defendant of
the s 18 offence. In order to get over this difficulty, which he described as technical,   *d*
which indeed it was, he then allowed an amendment of the indictment by the addition
of a count charging a s 20 offence. In this court the argument turned solely on whether
the trial judge should have allowed the amendment. It was adjudged that he was entitled
to do so. Thompson J said (at 255):

'We can see nothing wrong or improper in what the judge did by allowing the
amendment. It may be that the difficulty that has arisen could have been otherwise   *e*
overcome. However that may be, it was right that he should take steps to permit
the jury to deliver the verdict upon which their deliberations had led them to agree.'

This case is not binding on us and shows what absurd results can follow from a literal
construction of s 6.

The power of juries to return verdicts of manslaughter on indictments charging   *f*
murder was grounded in the common law rule that on a charge of felony a defendant
might be convicted of a less aggravated felony of which the ingredients are included in
the felony charged. There was a similar rule about misdemeanours; but except under a
statute, a conviction of a misdemeanour was not allowed on a charge of felony (see *R v
Stokes* (1925) 19 Cr App R 71). By the early 1960's the old division between felonies and
misdemeanours had become an unnecessary complication in the administration of   *g*
justice. In 1964 the then Home Secretary asked the Criminal Law Revision Committee—

'whether the present division of indictable offences into felonies and misdemeanours should be retained, and if not what revision of the law should be made in
consequence of its abolition.'

That committee issued its report in 1965 and recommended abolition and consequential   *h*
changes in practice and procedure (see Cmnd 2659). The 1967 Act was based substantially
on the recommendations in that report. The division between felonies and misdemeanours was abolished. Parliament had to make provision for the procedural consequences
of the abolition. One of these was concerned with alternative verdicts. Section 6 of the
1967 Act contains these provisions. It is necessary now to construe that section. Subsection
(1), which reproduces s 39(1) of the Criminal Justice Administration Act 1914, deals with   *j*
pleas on arraignment. Section 6(3), which can conveniently be read before sub-s (2), sets
out the general rule that a defendant charged with offence A may be found guilty of any
offence B which is included in offence A or of any other offence C of which he could not
have been found guilty had there been a specific charge of offence B. Section 6(2), which
is an exception to sub-s (3), provides:

'On an indictment for murder a person found not guilty of murder may be found
guilty—(a) of manslaughter or of causing grievous bodily harm with intent to do

a so; or (b) of any offence of which he may be found guilty under an enactment specifically so providing, or under section 4(2) of this Act; or (c) of an attempt to commit murder, or of an attempt to commit any other offence of which he might be found guilty; but may not be found guilty of any offence not included above.'

Had not s 6 included sub-s (2) the operation of sub-s (3) might have enabled a jury to return on an indictment for murder a verdict of guilty of common assault and made it impossible for them to return a verdict of guilty of manslaughter when death did not *b* result from an assault. The object of sub-s (2) seems to have been partly by para (a) to limit the operation of subsection (3) and partly by paras (b) and (c) to extend it. It provides what may be done.

The problem of construction has been whether, having regard to the words used in s 6, the context in which that section appears and the policy of the Act as far as it can be ascertained from its long title, it was the intention of Parliament that a verdict of *c* manslaughter could only be returned if the defendant had been found not guilty of murder. The Act was one to amend and simplify the law in respect of matters arising from or related to the abolition of the division of crimes into felonies and misdemeanours. It was not an Act which was intended to get rid of one form of procedure and set up another; indeed s 1(2) specifically retains, subject to the provisions of the Act, the existing practice in relation to misdemeanours. We cannot discern any good reason either in legal *d* principle or common sense why a verdict of manslaughter should not be returned when the jury cannot agree about murder. Nor can we see any reason why the opening words of sub-s (2) should be read as meaning 'on an indictment for murder a person found not guilty of murder, but not otherwise, may be found guilty of manslaughter.' In our judgment the verdict of manslaughter was a valid one.

If this problem ever arises again it would be good practice for the judge to direct the *e* jury to return a verdict of not guilty of murder; but as Drake J pointed out in the course of the submission, when so directed a foreman might say: 'But some of us consider that the defendant is guilty of murder.' Something like this confronted the trial judge in this case. In our judgment he was entitled to act as he did.

In the course of his submissions counsel for the appellant made a suggestion about procedure which is worthy of comment. He suggested that in cases in which there is a *f* possibility on a count of murder of a jury returning a verdict of manslaughter, the indictment should contain two counts. This would be contrary to long established practice, would tend to confuse the jury, and would not deal with the case, not uncommon, in which the possibility of a verdict of manslaughter only becomes apparent during the course of the trial. In our opinion the present practice should continue to be followed.

g As to sentence this was clearly a case of killing by a defendant who was suffering from mental imbalance due to alcoholism. The facts of the case showed that his conduct was unpredictable because of his mental condition. A life sentence was clearly appropriate. His application for leave to appeal against sentence is dismissed. The appeal itself is dismissed.

h   *Appeal dismissed.*

The court refused leave to appeal to the House of Lords but certified, under s 33(2) of the Criminal Appeal Act 1968, that the following point of law of general public importance was involved in the decision: if on an indictment charging murder a jury cannot agree that murder has been proved and are discharged from returning a verdict on the charge of murder, but they are agreed that all
j *the elements of manslaughter have been proved, can they validly return a verdict of manslaughter having regard to the provisions of s 6(2) of the Criminal Law Act 1967?*

24 July. The Appeal Committee of the House of Lords granted leave to appeal.

Solicitors: *Director of Public Prosecutions.*

June Meader   Barrister.

Hall v Cotton and another

QUEEN'S BENCH DIVISION
STOCKER LJ AND HIRST J
15 MAY, 27 JUNE 1986

Firearms – Possession – Transfer of possession – Distinction between custodial and proprietary possession – Owner of shotguns leaving guns at home of friend who did not have shotgun certificate – Whether owner 'transferring' possession – Whether friend in 'possession' of shotguns without having certificate – Firearms Act 1968, ss 2(1), 3(2), 57(4).

The respondent C left two shotguns, which belonged to him and for which he held a certificate under the Firearms Act 1968, at the house of the respondent T for safekeeping while he and T went on holiday together and so that T could clean them after their return from holiday. T did not hold a shotgun certificate. Subsequently C was charged with having 'transferred' the shotguns to T, being a person who was not a registered firearms dealer and who did not have a shotgun certificate, contrary to s 3(2)[a] of the 1968 Act. T was charged with having in his possession a shotgun in respect of which he did not hold a shotgun certificate, contrary to s 2(1)[b] of the 1968 Act. The magistrates dismissed the informations on the ground that C had not transferred the shotguns to T because under s 57(4)[c] 'transfer' included 'lend or part with possession' and C had done neither but had merely left the guns at T's house for safekeeping and cleaning. The prosecutor appealed.

Held – On its true construction s 57(4) of the 1968 Act contained a disjunctive definition of the term 'transfer' and therefore the term 'part with possession' had to be considered on its own. Furthermore, in construing whether there had been a parting with possession custodial possession was to be distinguished from proprietary possession. Although C had retained proprietary possession of the shotguns when handing them to T he had transferred custodial possession to T, because T had physical custody of the guns coupled with knowledge of that custody. It followed that C had 'transferred' the shotguns within the meaning of s 3(2) of the Act, and that T was in 'possession' of a shotgun within the meaning of s 2(1) of the 1968 Act. The prosecutor's appeal would therefore be allowed (see p 334 *h*, p 335 *f*, p 336 *c* to p 337 *a d g* and p 338 *a*, post).

Sullivan v Earl of Caithness [1976] 1 All ER 844 distinguished.

Notes

For restrictions on the possession of firearms, see 11 Halsbury's Laws (4th edn) 875–876, 879, 36 ibid 332, and for cases on the subject, see 15 Digest (Reissue) 930–933, 8040–8057.

For the Firearms Act 1968, ss 2, 3, 57, see 12 Halsbury's Statutes (4th edn) 461, 498.

Cases referred to in judgments

Sullivan v Earl of Caithness [1976] 1 All ER 844, [1976] QB 966, [1976] 2 WLR 361, DC.
Towers & Co Ltd v Gray [1961] 2 All ER 68, [1961] 2 QB 351, [1961] 2 WLR 553, DC.
US v Dollfus Meig et Cie SA [1952] 1 All ER 572, [1952] AC 582, HL.
Woodage v Moss [1974] 1 All ER 584, [1974] 1 WLR 411, DC.

Case stated

The prosecutor, Raymond Alan Hall, appealed by way of case stated by the justices for the county of Warwick acting in and for the petty sessional division of Atherstone and Coleshill in respect of their adjudication as a magistrates' court sitting at Atherstone on

---

a   Section 3(2) is set out at p 333 *h*, post
b   Section 2(1) is set out at p 333 *h*, post
c   Section 57(4), so far as material, is set out at p 333 *j*, post

a 25 June 1985, whereby they dismissed informations against the first respondent, Samuel
   Cotton, and the second respondent, Kenneth Eric Treadwell, alleging offences contrary
   to ss 3(2) and 2(1) of the Firearms Act 1968, respectively. The facts are set out in the
   judgment of Stocker LJ.

   Richard Bray for the appellant.
   Christopher Metcalf for the first respondent.
b *Frank Chapman* for the second respondent.

                                                                          Cur adv vult

   27 June. The following judgments were delivered.

c **STOCKER LJ.** This is a prosecutor's appeal by way of case stated by justices for the
   county of Warwick acting in and for the petty sessional division of Atherstone and
   Coleshill in respect of their adjudication as a magistrates' court sitting at Atherstone.
       On 25 June 1985 the justices dismissed informations against each of the respondents.
   Against the respondent Cotton the information alleged that between 1 August 1984 and
   11 September 1984 at Ridge Lane, near Nuneaton he did transfer to the respondent
d Treadwell, who was a person in the United Kingdom other than a registered firearms
   dealer, two shotguns to which s 1 of the Firearms Act 1968 applied, the said Treadwell
   not producing a shotgun certificate authorising him to acquire it and not showing that
   he was, by virtue of the Firearms Act 1968, entitled to acquire it without holding a
   certificate, contrary to s 3(2) of the Firearms Act 1968. Against the respondent Treadwell
   the information alleged that he, on 11 September 1984 at Ridge Lane, near Nuneaton
e did have in his possession a shotgun to which s 2(1) of the Firearms Act 1968 applied, he
   then not holding a shotgun certificate in force at the time contrary to s 2(1) of the
   Firearms Act 1968.
       The justices found the following facts. (a) Some time during August 1984 the
   respondent Cotton brought the two shotguns which are the subject of the case to the
   respondent Treadwell's house. He left them there for safety's sake. Whilst he and
f Treadwell (and members of their respective families) went on holiday together, a man
   named O'Neill (who was Treadwell's lodger) remained at the house during the period of
   the holiday, but he did not inspect the shotguns or touch them. They were simply left in
   the house. (b) Cotton was the holder of a shotgun certificate, Treadwell was not. (c) On
   11 September 1984 police officers visited Treadwell's house and were shown the two
   shotguns together with 48 12-bore cartridges. This happened some weeks after Treadwell
g and Cotton had returned from holiday. (d) Treadwell agreed to clean the guns before
   returning them to Cotton.
       The relevant sections of the 1968 Act are in these terms:

       '**2.**—(1) Subject to any exemption under this Act, it is an offence for a person to
       have in his possession, or to purchase or acquire, a shot gun without holding a
       certificate under this Act authorising him to possess shot guns . . .
h   **3** . . . (2) It is an offence for a person to sell or transfer to any other person in the
       United Kingdom, other than a registered firearms dealer, any firearm or ammunition
       to which section 1 of this Act applies, or a shot gun, unless that other produces a
       firearm certificate authorising him to purchase or acquire it or, as the case may be,
       his shot gun certificate, or shows that he is by virtue of this Act entitled to purchase
       or acquire it without holding a certificate.'

j 'Transfer' is defined by the 1968 Act by s 57(4) as follows:

       '"transfer" includes let on hire, give, lend and part with possession, and "transferee"
       and "transferor" shall be construed accordingly.'

   The justices expressed their reasons in the form of a statement of their opinions in the
   following terms:

'We were of the opinion that Cotton did not transfer the shotguns to Treadwell, either before or after the holiday. He merely left them there for safety's sake and to enable them to be cleaned. In coming to our decision we had regard to the definition of "transfer" contained in Section 57 of the Firearms Act 1968, and to the decision of the Queen's Bench Division in the case of Sullivan v Earl of Caithness ([1976] 1 All ER 844, [1976] QB 966). Accordingly, we dismissed both informations.'

For the appellant it was contended, both before the justices and before us, that the respondent Cotton had transferred the shotguns to the respondent Treadwell, and that the respondent Treadwell had obtained possession of them when they were left at Treadwell's house, both during the holiday and after their return from holiday, and that each respondent was guilty of the offence under ss 3(2) and 2(1) of the 1968 Act respectively laid against him. For the respondent Cotton it was contended that by leaving the guns at Treadwell's house he did not transfer them to Treadwell, but retained possession of them himself throughout. For the respondent Treadwell it was contended that he was not at any time in possession of the guns, even though left at his house for safe keeping, even though they remained there for about a fortnight after his return from holiday until their discovery by the police.

This appeal therefore raises the question of the meaning of the words 'possession' and 'transfer' for the purposes of the 1968 Act and in the context of the facts found proved by the justices. In construing this Act it seems to me that we should keep in mind two principles of construction which may in practice be in apparent conflict. The first is that, if ambiguity arises, consideration may be given to the general intention of the Act and the mischief it seeks to prevent; and the second is that, as a penal statute, where more than one construction is possible, it should be construed in a sense favourable to an accused.

In my view the plain intention of the 1968 Act is to prevent a firearm from getting into the hands of an unauthorised and uncertified person and to enable the relevant authority, in this case the police, properly to regulate and control the certification of the persons entitled to be in possession of such firearms. It is thus important to observe in my view that what is prohibited in s 3(2) is the sale or transfer of the gun itself, the legal nature of the transfer being prescribed by the definition of the word 'transfer' in s 57(4). Counsel for the appellant has argued before us that the physical transfer of the gun must in the circumstances involve a transfer of some form of legal right and that the respondent Cotton parted with the possession of the shotguns within the ordinary and natural meaning of that phrase when he physically transferred the shotguns to Treadwell's house, not only for the duration of the holiday but also for some weeks thereafter until the police intervened on 11 September, and the fact that the arrangement involved that the respondent Treadwell should clean the guns before their return to Cotton reinforces his submissions. He argued that the converse of this proposition necessarily involved the respondent Treadwell having the shotguns in his possession. In the alternative he argued that if, in the light of the decision of this court in Sullivan v Earl of Caithness [1976] 1 All ER 844, [1976] QB 966, the respondent Cotton himself retained possession of the guns all the time on the basis that he had not in any way relinquished the right to possess, nonetheless custodial possession had been transferred to the respondent Treadwell. This argument involves the proposition that the word 'possession' can in law embrace two separate legal concepts, 'proprietary possession' and 'custodial possession'.

I therefore turn to consider Sullivan v Earl of Caithness. That case was concerned with the question whether or not the Earl of Caithness, who at the material time lived in Oxfordshire, and who was the owner of certain guns which he kept at his mother's apartment in Hampton Court Palace, was 'in possession' of the guns (unlawfully, since he had failed to renew the firearms certificate previously issued to him in respect of those guns). The contention on behalf of Lord Caithness was that since he lived in Oxfordshire and the guns were at his mother's apartment in Surrey, he was not in 'possession' of them.

In the course of giving the first judgment of the court, with which Park J and Lord Widgery CJ agreed, May J said ([1976] 1 All ER 844 at 847, [1976] QB 966 at 970):

a
'Looking at the context of the word "possession" in s 1 of the 1968 Act in the present case, I have no doubt that one can be in possession of a firearm even though one is at a place other than that at which the firearm physically is. To agree with the justices' decision in the present case would in my view effectively be to equate the word "possession" in s 1 with custody, and this I am satisfied would be wrong.'

b
After pointing out that the form of application for a certificate requires the appellant not only to state the address of his residence, but also the place where the firearm is to be kept, thus implying that the person to whom the certificate is issued may reside at a place other than the place at which the firearm is physically located, he continued ([1976] 1 All ER 844 at 847, [1976] QB 966 at 970–971):

c
'In my opinion the purpose of s 1 of the 1968 Act and its ancillary provisions is to regulate and license not merely those who have physical custody of firearms, or who keep them in the place in which they live, but also those who have firearms under their control at their behest, even though for one reason or another they may be kept at their country cottage, at the local shooting range or indeed at Bisley. As a matter of construction, therefore, which must to some extent also be a matter of first impression, and looking at the context and what I believe to have been the intent of s 1 of the 1968 Act, it may well be, I think, that the owner of a firearm

d
who does not at the relevant time have physical possession of it can nevertheless truly be said still to be in possession of it. In the present case, the respondent was at all material times the owner of the firearms. He could no doubt obtain them from his mother's flat at any time when he wanted them. She had the barest custody of them, not because she had any interest in them, but because her flat was safer than the respondent's home in Oxford. In these circumstances and on the admitted facts,

e
in my judgment the respondent was at material times in Swalcliffe in possession of those firearms for the purposes of the 1968 Act, and consequently I think the justices were wrong and should on the facts as they found them have convicted the respondent.'

Thus this case is, in my view, clear authority for the proposition that a person can be 'in possession' of a firearm at a time when he is physically not in control of it or is himself

f
not physically at the place at which it is then situated. Cases such as this must depend on their own facts, but on the facts as found by the justices in this case in my opinion the respondent Cotton retained 'possession' in the *Sullivan v Earl of Caithness* sense, which I will refer to as 'proprietary possession', at all times when the shotguns were at the house of the respondent Treadwell.

g
Does this finding therefore justify the conclusion reached by the justices that 'possession', if retained by Cotton, cannot have been transferred by him to the respondent Treadwell, contrary to s 3(2) and the consequent finding that, if not so transferred, then the respondent Treadwell cannot have been 'in possession' of the shotguns himself since such possession had not been transferred to him?

The concept of possession has not been exhaustively defined in English law and its

h
precise meaning may vary according to the context in which the concept arises and the relevant Act of Parliament in which the question arises. As Lord Parker CJ said in *Towers & Co Ltd v Gray* [1961] 2 All ER 68 at 71, [1961] 2 QB 351 at 361: 'The term "possession" is always giving rise to trouble', and in *Woodage v Moss* [1974] 1 All ER 584 at 588, [1974] 1 WLR 411 at 415, Ashworth J cited a further passage from the judgment of Lord Parker CJ ([1961] 2 All ER 68 at 71, [1961] 2 QB 351 at 361–362):

j
'For my part I approach this case on the basis that the meaning of "possession" depends on the context in which it is used . . . In some contexts, no doubt, a bailment for reward subject to a lien, where, perhaps, some period of notice has to be given before the goods can be removed, could be of such a nature that the only possession that there could be said to be, would be possession in the bailee. In other cases it may well be the nature of the bailment is such that the owner of goods who has parted with the physical possession of them can truly be said still to be in possession.'

May J, in *Sullivan v Earl of Caithness* [1976] 1 All ER 844 at 846–847, [1976] QB 966 at
969–970, cited those passages and also cited a short passage from the speech of Earl Jowitt *a*
in *US v Dollfus Meig et Cie SA* [1952] 1 All ER 572 at 581, [1952] AC 582 at 605:

> 'The person having the right to immediate possession is, however, frequently
> referred to in English law as being the "possessor" – in truth, the English law has
> never worked out a completely logical and exhaustive definition of "possession".'

I therefore turn to consider the definition of 'transfer' given in s 57(4):   *b*

> '... "transfer" includes let on hire, give, lend and part with possession, and
> "transferee" and "transferor" shall be construed accordingly.'

Clearly on the facts as found by the justices the position of neither respondent fell
within the words 'hire' or 'give'. There was no gift and no hiring. Do they fall within the
phrase 'lend and part with possession'? That this phrase is to be construed disjunctively *c*
may find some support from the definition of 'acquire' in the same section, where acquire
is defined as 'hire, accept as a gift, or borrow', which seems to me to be the mirror image
of the words 'hire, give, lend' in the definition of 'transfer' but do not reflect the words
'part with possession'. If, therefore, the words 'part with possession' are to be read
disjunctively from the word 'lend' in the definition of 'transfer', the court has to consider
whether or not the words are apt to include 'parting with possession' in some sense other *d*
than proprietary possession which was, on the authority of *Sullivan v Earl of Caithness*
[1976] 1 All ER 844, [1976] QB 966, retained by the respondent Cotton. In my opinion
the phrase is to be read disjunctively.

The definition of the word 'transfer' commences with the word 'includes' and,
therefore, subject to the ejusdem generis rule, the definition is not exclusive or exhaustive.
In my view on the facts of this case, and in particular that the shotguns were retained in *e*
the house of the respondent Treadwell for a fortnight or so after the return of the
respondents from holiday, and were still in the house when the police found them, and
were to be cleaned by him before their return to the respondent Cotton, it seems to me
the proper conclusion is that the respondent Treadwell had more than 'the barest custody'
which May J in *Sullivan v Earl of Caithness* found to be the position of Lord Caithness's
mother at Hampton Court. He was to clean them, and his physical custody of them *f*
extended beyond the period of the holiday with the respondent Cotton. What was the
nature of his interest in the guns? Whatever it was, that interest had been transferred by
the respondent Cotton. The facts in this case for the reasons indicated seem to me to be
distinguishable from those in *Sullivan v Earl of Caithness*. As a matter of law, no doubt
there is a distinction between 'custody' and 'possession', though in many cases, in my
view, the former will necessarily involve the latter. 'Custody' and 'possession' are certainly *g*
equated in drugs cases where one person knowingly has custody of drugs for another. In
my opinion, at least on the facts of this case, custody coupled with the knowledge of such
custody must be equated with 'possession'. In my opinion the submission of the appellant
is correct. The respondent Cotton retained 'proprietary possession' in the sense adjudged
in *Sullivan v Earl of Caithness*. The respondent Treadwell had 'custodial possession'. Having
regard to all the facts, for my part I am unable to accept the proposition that he had no *h*
interest at all except for the provision of his house as a place at which the shotguns were
physically located. Accordingly, such custody could only arise by at least a custodial
interest being transferred from one respondent to the other and falls within the phrase
'lend and part with possession', whether read conjunctively or disjunctively. If read
disjunctively, the respondent Cotton had parted with, and the respondent Treadwell had
acquired, 'custodial possession'. If read conjunctively, it seems to me there must have *j*
been a lending in this transaction. However, if this be wrong, and even if custody could
not, contrary to my view, be equated with 'possession', on the facts of this case the word
'includes' would be apt to include custody if the definition is construed ejusdem generis
with the express words, since 'custody' by an unauthorised person is in my view clearly
one of the mischiefs to which the 1968 Act is directed.

In my judgment the respondent Cotton transferred custodial possession to the respondent Treadwell who acquired such custodial possession.

The justices clearly directed their minds carefully to the issues, but for the reasons I have given, in my view reached a wrong conclusion in law.

The questions posed in the case stated were as follows:

'(1) Did the Respondent Cotton (who held a shotgun certificate) transfer his shotguns within the meaning of Section 3(2) of the Firearms Act 1968 to the Respondent Treadwell (who did not hold a certificate) when he left the guns at Treadwell's house whilst he and Treadwell were both on holiday and/or when the weapons remained with Treadwell for a period beyond the duration of the holiday?

'(2) Did Treadwell (who did not hold a certificate) possess a shotgun within the meaning of Section 2(1) of the Firearms Act 1968 when the shotguns were left at his house for safe keeping whilst both he and Cotton were on holiday and/or when having been left at his house during the owner's absence on holiday, they remained there beyond the duration of the holiday?'

I would answer each question in the affirmative and remit the matter to the justices with a direction that they should convict. No doubt they may reflect their findings of fact by the imposition of such penalties as they consider appropriate.

HIRST J. I agree with Stocker LJ that this appeal should be allowed for the reasons he has given. I only wish to add a few words to stress the importance of the statement which Stocker LJ has quoted from the judgment of May J in *Sullivan v Earl of Caithness* [1976] 1 All ER 844 at 847, [1976] QB 966 at 970–971 as to the purpose of s 1 of the Firearms Act 1968. That section deals with firearms. In the present case we are concerned with ss 2 and 3 of the Act, which deal with shotguns.

The purpose of s 2 is to regulate all persons who have shotguns in their possession, whether it be in their physical custody or their control, or who purchase or acquire shotguns, so as to ensure that such possession, purchase, or acquisition is unlawful without a certificate, which is of course only issued after extensive inquiries by the police as to the suitability of the applicant.

The purpose of s 3(2) is to regulate the sale or transfer by any person other than a registered firearms dealer so that, in the case of shotguns, he is prohibited from selling or transferring a shotgun to any other person unless the latter produces his shotgun certificate. This is an additional safeguard preventing shotguns passing into the hands of unlicensed persons.

The definition of 'transfer' in s 57(4) is a very wide one, and in my judgment Cotton's actions in relation to these two shotguns, as found by the justices, manifestly constituted a transfer within the scope of that definition. Having regard to the wording of s 3(2), it is immaterial whether or not Cotton himself retained possession, or at least a right to possession, of the two shotguns, though I agree with Stocker LJ that he did, in line with the decision of this court in *Sullivan v Earl of Caithness*.

So far as Treadwell is concerned, the guns were in his home and in the custody of Treadwell's lodger, presumably his agent for this purpose, during the holiday, and thereafter remained there for several weeks until the police called and found them. Meantime Treadwell had responsibility for cleaning the guns. These elements of both custody, and, to a limited extent, control, of the two guns, quite clearly to my mind demonstrate that Treadwell was in possession of them. It is not, I think, correct to equate his position with that of Lord Caithness's mother in *Sullivan v Earl of Caithness*, since their respective roles were by no means identical, and in any event the Divisional Court were not called on to consider her position under the Firearms Act 1968, apart from May J's comment that she had no more than 'the barest custody'.

In reaching these conclusions I am in no way deterred by the borderline examples cited by both counsel for the respondents. Cases of momentary delivery of a shotgun to another person in, for example, a temporary emergency or for the purpose of inspection,

could hardly be said to have involved either a transfer by the deliveror or the taking of
possession by the deliveree; equally, a spouse or servant temporarily entrusted with the *a*
custody of a shotgun by its owner would in normal circumstances be regarded as the
owner's agent; there would thus be no transfer by the latter, nor acceptance of any more
than the barest custody by the former, with no infringement of the 1968 Act in either
case.

Appeal allowed. Case remitted to the magistrates for conviction.   *b*

Solicitors: *Cocks Lloyd & Co*, Nuneaton (for the appellant); *Argyle & Sons*, Atherstone (for
the first respondent); *Pickering & Pickering*, Tamworth (for the second respondent).

Sophie Craven   Barrister.

c

Columbia Picture Industries Inc and others v Robinson and others

d

CHANCERY DIVISION
SCOTT J
4, 6, 7, 10–14, 17–21, 24, 25, 27 JUNE, 1–5, 8–12, 15–19, 22 JULY, 7–11, 14–17 OCTOBER,
19 DECEMBER 1985

Practice – Pre-trial relief – Anton Piller order – Interlocutory motion – Ex parte application – *e*
Principles relating to grant of order – Duty of plaintiff's solicitor when executing order – Cross-
undertaking as to damages by plaintiff – Award of damages for breach of undertaking –
Aggravated damages awarded for excessive and oppressive manner in which order executed.

A decision whether an Anton Piller order should be granted requires a balance to be
struck between the plaintiff's need that the remedies allowed by the civil law for the *f*
breach of his rights should be attainable by him and the requirement of justice that a
defendant should not be deprived of his property without being heard. The draconian
and essentially unfair nature of an Anton Piller order in its effect on a respondent against
whom it is made requires that it be drawn so as to extend no further than the minimum
extent necessary to achieve the purpose for which it was granted, namely the preservation
of documents or articles which might otherwise be destroyed or concealed; anything *g*
beyond that is impossible to justify. Thus an order that allows the plaintiff's solicitors to
take and retain all relevant documentary material and correspondence cannot be justified.
Once the plaintiff's solicitors have satisfied themselves what material exists and have had
an opportunity to take copies thereof, the material ought to be returned to the owner,
and should only be retained for a relatively short period for such purpose (see p 371 *d* to
f, post).

It is essential that a detailed record of the material taken should be made by a solicitor *h*
who executes an Anton Piller order before the material is removed from the respondent's
premises. So far as possible, disputes as to what material was taken, the resolution of
which depends on the oral testimony and credibility of the solicitor on the one hand and
the respondent on the other hand, ought to be avoided because, in the absence of any
corroboration of a respondent's allegation that particular material was taken, a solicitor's *j*
sworn and apparently credible denial is likely always to be preferred and such a state of
affairs is unfair to the respondent and ought to be avoided (see p 371 *g h*, post).

When an Anton Piller order is executed no material should be taken from the
respondent's premises by the executing solicitor unless it is clearly covered by the terms
of the order. In particular, it is unacceptable that the respondent be procured by the
executing solicitor to give consent to additional material being removed. In view of the
circumstances in which Anton Piller orders are customarily executed, an apparent

consent by a respondent will not be taken to have been freely and effectively given unless
a the respondent's solicitor was present to confirm and ensure that the consent is free and
informed (see p 371 *h j*, post).

It is inappropriate for seized material the ownership of which is in dispute, such as
alleged pirate tapes, to be retained by the plaintiff's solicitor pending trial. Although the
solicitor is an officer of the court, the main role of the solicitor for the plaintiff is to act
for the plaintiff. As soon as a solicitor for the defendant is on the record, the plaintiff's
b solicitor ought to deliver the material to the defendant's solicitor on his undertaking to
keep it in safe custody and produce it, if required, in court (see p 371 *j* to p 372 *b*, post).

The nature of an Anton Piller order requires that an affidavit in support of the
application for the order ought to err on the side of excessive disclosure because, in the
case of material which falls into the area of possible relevance, the judge and not the
plaintiff's solicitor should be the judge of relevance. However, provided the plaintiff, his
c solicitor and counsel make full and proper disclosure to the court when applying for an
Anton Piller order, neither the solicitor nor counsel owe a duty to the court to consider,
before applying, whether it is justifiable for the plaintiff to apply for the order or a duty
to refrain from seeking an order in unnecessarily wide or onerous terms; instead, if the
duty of full disclosure is discharged, the plaintiff's solicitor and counsel are entitled to
apply for the most favourable order they can persuade the court to grant (see p 372 *b c*
d and p 375 *c* to *g*, post).

Where in executing an Anton Piller order the plaintiff acts in breach of the cross-
undertaking as to damages given by him when applying for the order the defendant is
prima facie entitled to damages, which will be primarily compensatory and therefore
confined to compensation for damage to the defendant's legitimate interests. Damages
will therefore not be awarded for damage to or loss of illicit business. Where an Anton
e Piller order has been executed in an excessive and oppressive manner the court may order
aggravated damages against the plaintiff and, possibly, since solicitors executing such
orders do so as officers of the court, exemplary damages. However, where the order has
been executed the court need not set it aside, even if there are good grounds for doing so,
if to do so would be an empty gesture without practical effect (see p 378 *h* to p 379 *f* and
p 380 *e*, post).

f
Notes

For Anton Piller orders, see 37 Halsbury's Laws (4th edn) para 372, and for cases on the
subject, see 37(2) Digest (Reissue) 480–483, 2978–2990.

Cases referred to in judgment
g *Albert v S Hoffnung & Co Ltd* (1921) 22 SR (NSW) 75, NSW SC.
Anton Piller KG v Manufacturing Processes Ltd [1976] 1 All ER 779, [1976] Ch 55, [1976] 2
   WLR 162, CA.
Bank Mellat v Nikpour [1985] FSR 87, CA.
Booker McConnell plc v Plascow [1985] CA Transcript 137.
East India Co v Kynaston (1821) 3 Bli 153, 4 ER 561, HL.
h *Edison (Thomas A) Ltd v Bullock* (1912) 15 CLR 679, Aust HC.
EMI Ltd v Pandit [1975] 1 All ER 418, [1975] 1 WLR 302.
Entick v Carrington (1765) 2 Wils 275, [1558–1774] All ER Rep 41, 95 ER 807.
Everet v Williams (1729) 9 LQR 197.
Fields (Randolph M) v Watts (1984) 129 SJ 67, CA.
Infabrics Ltd v Jaytex Shirt Co Ltd [1978] FSR 451; *rvsd* [1980] 2 All ER 669, [1980] Ch
j   282, [1980] 2 WLR 822, CA; *rvsd* [1981] 1 All ER 1057, [1982] AC 1, [1981] 2 WLR
   646, HL.
Rank Film Distributors Ltd v Video Information Centre [1981] 2 All ER 76, [1982] AC 380,
   [1981] 2 WLR 668, HL; *affg* [1980] 2 All ER 273, [1982] AC 380, [1980] 2 WLR 273,
   CA.
RCA Corp v Custom Cleared Sales Pty Ltd [1978] FSR 576, NSW CA.
Rogers (Jeffrey) Knitwear Productions Ltd v Vinola (Knitwear) Manufacturing Co [1985] FSR
   184.

Rookes v Barnard [1964] 1 All ER 367, [1964] AC 1129, [1964] 2 WLR 269, HL.
Wardle Fabrics Ltd v G Myristis Ltd [1984] FSR 263.
WEA Records Ltd v Visions Channel 4 Ltd [1983] 2 All ER 589, [1983] 1 WLR 721, CA.   *a*

Cases also cited

Ansett Transport Industries (Operations) Pty Ltd v Halton Interstate Parcel Express Co (Aust) Pty Ltd (1979) 25 ALR 639, Aust HC.
Beloff v Pressdram Ltd [1973] 1 All ER 241.   *b*
Berger v Raymond Sun Ltd [1984] 1 WLR 625.
Customs and Excise Officers Mutual Guarantee Fund, Re, Robson v A-G [1917] 2 Ch 18.
Digital Equipment Corp v Darkcrest Ltd [1984] 3 All ER 381, [1984] Ch 512.
Evans (C) & Sons Ltd v Spritebrand Ltd [1985] 2 All ER 415, [1985] 1 WLR 317.
Falcon v Famous Players Film Co [1926] 2 KB 474, CA.
Fields (Randolph M) v Watts (1984) Times, 22 November, CA.
Fletcher Sutcliffe Wild Ltd v Burch [1982] FSR 64.   *c*
Gallery Cosmetics Ltd v Number 1 [1981] FSR 556.
Gamlen Chemical Co (UK) Ltd v Rochem Ltd [1983] RPC 1.
Ghani v Jones [1969] 3 All ER 1700, [1970] 1 QB 693, CA.
Hales v Kerr [1908] 2 KB 601.
Helliwell v Piggott-Sims [1980] FSR 356, CA.
Hoffmann-La Roche (F) & Co AG v Secretary of State for Trade and Industry [1974] 2 All ER   *d*
1128, [1975] AC 295, HL.
ITC Film Distributors Ltd v Video Exchange Ltd (No 2) (1981) 125 SJ 863; *on appeal* 126 SJ
672, CA.
Mood Music Publishing Co Ltd v De Wolfe Ltd [1976] 1 All ER 763, [1976] Ch 119, CA.
Nichols Advanced Vehicle Systems Inc v Rees [1979] RPC 127; *affd* (1985) 129 SJ 401, CA.   *e*
Smith v Day (1882) 21 Ch D 421, CA.
Stamford and Warrington (Earl), Re, Payne v Grey [1916] 1 Ch 404.
Thermax Ltd v Schott Industrial Glass Ltd [1981] FSR 289.
Yousif v Salama [1980] 3 All ER 405, [1980] 1 WLR 1540, CA.

Notice of motion

By a writ of summons issued on 18 June 1982 the plaintiffs, Columbia Picture Industries   *f*
Inc (suing on behalf of themselves and on behalf of and as representing all other members
of Motion Picture Association of America Inc (the MPAA)) and 16 other plaintiffs, all of
whom were engaged in the business of making or distributing motion picture films,
brought an action against (1) Christopher Robinson, trading as Luton Video Centre, (2)
Luton Video Services Ltd and (3) Denis Morgan, seeking, inter alia, injunctions (i)
restraining alleged breaches of copyright in respect of 104 specific films, and also of any   *g*
other films the copyright of which was, or might in the future, become vested in any of
the plaintiffs, (ii) restraining the passing off in respect of 22 of those films and
infringement of trade marks in respect of some 65 films which the defendants had
manufactured or traded in unlicensed video cassettes bearing trade marks in respect of
which one or other of the plaintiffs was the registered owner. On 18 June 1982 on the   *h*
plaintiffs' ex parte application Goulding J granted, inter alia, (i) an order restraining the
defendants from infringing any film copyright vested in or claimed by the plaintiffs, (ii)
an Anton Piller order in respect of the defendants' premises at 8 Frederick Street, Luton,
39–43 Mill Street, Luton, 30 Enderby Road, Luton and at premises at Bracknell, and (iii)
a Mareva injunction freezing the defendants' assets and bank accounts with the exception
of drawings not exceeding £200 in respect of living expenses, until 25 June 1982 or until   *j*
further order. On 21 June 1982 the order was served and executed. On 25 June 1982 the
plaintiffs' notice of motion for interlocutory relief inter partes came before Dillon J and
on 2 July the first defendant gave an undertaking in terms similar to the terms of the
order of Goulding J. By a notice of motion dated 24 February 1984 the defendants
applied, inter alia, for orders (i) that the plaintiffs' action be dismissed, (ii) that the
defendants be released from their undertakings given on 2 July 1982 and (iii) that there

a be an inquiry as to the damages the plaintiffs ought to pay pursuant to their cross-undertakings in damages contained in the orders of 18 June, 25 June and 2 July 1982. The application came before Warner J on 7 June 1984, who directed that the application should be heard at the trial of the plaintiffs' action but be listed to come on immediately before the trial. The third defendant took no further part in the proceedings after 25 June 1982. The facts are set out in the judgment.

b *John Beveridge QC, Allen Dyer* and *Sarah Munro* for the defendants.
A J Bateson QC, Hugh Laddie and *John P Baldwin* for the plaintiffs.

Cur adv vult

19 December. The following judgment was delivered.

c
SCOTT J. In this action there are 35 plaintiffs, each of whom is engaged in the business of making or distributing motion picture films. Many of the plaintiffs are or are members of groups which are household names. The first plaintiff, Columbia Picture Industries Inc, sues also on behalf of all other members of the Motion Picture Association of America Inc (the MPAA). The MPAA has some 14 members. They are all engaged in
d the business to which I have referred. The expression 'the plaintiffs' will in this judgment include not only the named plaintiffs but also the MPAA members.
The principal defendants in the action are Christopher Robinson and his alter ego, Luton Video Services Ltd, which was incorporated on 30 July 1981. Mr Robinson and, after its incorporation, the company carried on, first, a business at 8 Frederick Street, Luton, of producing and marketing prerecorded video cassettes and, second, a business
e from a shop at 39–43 Mill Street, Luton, of hiring or selling prerecorded video cassettes. The third defendant is Denis Morgan. He was immediately prior to the commencement of this action the manager of the Mill Street shop. He has taken no part in the hearing before me and, consequent on an accommodation reached between him and the plaintiffs at an early stage in this litigation, he ceased to be an active defendant. There are, in addition, 43 other named defendants. These defendants were joined for the purpose of
f compliance with s 19(3) of the Copyright Act 1956. They are defendants in form only. The real defendants are Mr Robinson and the company. References in this judgment to 'the defendants' are to be read as references to these two defendants alone.
The plaintiffs allege that Mr Robinson is a video pirate. By this they mean that he manufactures and trades in video cassettes which infringe the copyright in cinematographic films. There are 104 films in respect of which this allegation is specifically made in this action. One or other of the plaintiffs claims to be the copyright owner or the
g exclusive licensee in respect of each of these films. It is alleged in respect of each of these films that the defendants have made and then sold or hired unlicensed copies thereof and have thereby infringed the copyright therein. 154 video tapes, most of which came from the Mill Street shop, have been examined. The plaintiffs allege that these tapes are all pirate copies, that is to say copies made in breach of copyright.
h It is, in addition, alleged in respect of 22 of the 104 films that the defendants have packaged and marketed their allegedly pirate cassettes in a get-up confusingly similar to the distinctive get-up used by the respective plaintiffs entitled to market those films. Passing-off is alleged.
It is also alleged in respect of some 65 films that the defendants have manufactured or traded in unlicensed video cassettes bearing a trade mark in respect of which one or other
j of the plaintiffs was the registered owner. Infringement of registered trade marks is alleged.
It is further alleged that Mr Robinson and, through him, the company sold or hired video cassettes in the knowledge that the tapes contained therein were pirate tapes. It is alleged that Mr Robinson and, through him, the company, made copies of prerecorded tapes in the knowledge that copyright was thereby being infringed. The rereamended statement of claim alleges in para 29 that the defendants—

'exhibited a cynical disregard for the rights of the Plaintiffs and other members
of the M.P.A.A. in the hope and expectation that the profit to be made by their   *a*
unlawful acts would be greater and more immediate than any recompense they
might have to pay in respect thereof bearing in mind the risk of discovery is small
and the opportunity for concealing such unlawful acts is great.'

Consistently with this pleading the plaintiffs have maintained throughout the lengthy
hearing of this action that Mr Robinson was a video pirate operating on a large scale who   *b*
would not hesitate to make and market copies of any video cassette films that seemed to
him commercially worth while.

The plaintiffs seek wide injunctions to restrain future breaches of copyright not only
in respect of the 104 films specified in the action but also in respect of any other films the
copyright in which is now or in the future may become vested in any of the plaintiffs.
They seek injunctions to restrain also passing-off and trade mark infringement. And they   *c*
seek damages, or an inquiry as to damages, in respect of infringement of copyright,
passing-off and infringement of trade marks already committed.

The defendants' response to this attack has followed, broadly, two lines. First, the
defendants have put the plaintiffs strictly to proof of their entitlement to copyright in
the 104 specified films and to proof that the 154 video tapes are pirate copies and not
lawful copies. At the end of the evidence, however, there was little left in dispute on   *d*
either of these matters. The copyright title of one or other of the plaintiffs in nearly all
the 104 films specified in the action was, it was agreed, established. And, bar a small
handful of tapes still in dispute, Mr Robinson accepted that the 154 tapes were pirate
copies. His defence became a defence of innocence. As to the tapes that he had made at 8
Frederick Street, he believed, he said, that he had obtained the right to do so pursuant to
certain licences he had acquired. That belief could not, it was accepted, constitute a   *e*
defence to an action for infringement of copyright. It was however relied on as an answer
to the central thrust of the plaintiffs' case, namely that Mr Robinson was a major and
professional video pirate. As to the tapes hired or sold from the Mill Street shop, these,
Mr Robinson said, he had not known to be pirate tapes. He had thought them to be
genuine. This belief was put forward in part for the reason already mentioned and in
part as an affirmative defence to the plaintiffs' allegations of infringement of copyright   *f*
by the selling or hiring of pirate tapes (see s 16(3) of the 1956 Act).

There was at the end of the day little or nothing in dispute between the parties
regarding the allegations of passing-off and infringement of trade mark. As to passing-
off, the plaintiffs in the rereamended statement of claim alleged passing-off in respect of
32 films. During final speeches, the complaint was abandoned in respect of 8 films and
was accepted by the defendants in respect of 22 films. Two films only remained in   *g*
dispute, namely 'For Your Eyes Only' and 'Star Wars'. Counsel left it to me to decide
from a visual comparison of the plaintiffs' and the defendants' respective video cassettes
whether or not sufficient confusing similarity of get-up had been shown in order to
constitute the tort of passing-off. In my view, having inspected those cassettes, there is
not sufficient confusing similarity for that purpose. Passing-off is, therefore, established
in respect of 22 films.   *h*

As to infringement of trade mark, it was during final speeches agreed between counsel
that 92 of the defendants' tapes or cassette boxes bore an infringing mark.

It is, accordingly, accepted by the defendants that liability for passing-off and
infringement of trade mark has to some extent been established in the action. The tapes
and boxes, however, in respect of which passing-off or infringement of trade mark is
now admitted all derived from the Mill Street shop. None, it is said, was made by the   *j*
defendants or was known by the defendants to have been made in breach of copyright.
The established or admitted liability of the defendants for passing-off and infringement
of trade mark carried, therefore, no further the critical issue of whether or not Mr
Robinson was a flagrant and deliberate video pirate and tortfeasor.

I have outlined the issues between the parties that are raised by the causes of action on
which the plaintiffs sue. That, however, is only half the story. This litigation commenced

a with an ex parte application made on 18 June 1982 to Goulding J by counsel on behalf of the then plaintiffs, broadly the first 17 of the eventual plaintiffs. On that application Goulding J made an order to which I must refer in detail in due course. The relief thereby granted included, first, an order restraining the defendants from infringing any film copyright vested in or claimed by any of the plaintiffs. Second, the relief included an Anton Piller order in respect of 8 Frederick Street, 39–43 Mill Street, Mr Robinson's home at 30 Enderby Road, Luton, and also premises in Bracknell on which nothing now

b turns and to which I need not further refer. The Anton Piller order directed that up to five persons be permitted to enter the specified premises for the purposes of looking for and taking into the custody of the plaintiffs' solicitors, Messrs A E Hamlin & Co (to whom I will refer as 'Hamlins'), any tapes infringing any film copyright of any of the plaintiffs, any label or packaging matter intended for use with any such tapes and any documents relating thereto. Third, the relief included a Mareva injunction freezing the

c defendants' assets and bank accounts, with the exception that drawings not exceeding £200 in respect of Mr Robinson's living expenses were permitted. No exception was made in order to provide for the normal running expenses of the company. The injunctions were granted over 25 June or until further order in the mean time. Liberty was reserved for the defendants to apply to discharge or vary the order on 24 hours' notice. The order recited a number of undertakings given to the court by the plaintiffs

d or their solicitors, Hamlins, including a cross-undertaking in damages.

The order was made on a Friday. On the following Monday, 21 June, the order was served and the Anton Piller part of the order was thereupon executed. Substantial numbers of tapes and quantities of documents were removed from 8 Frederick Street, the Mill Street shop and 30 Enderby Road into the custody of Hamlins. Roughly 300 tapes in all were taken.

e On 25 June 1982, the return date specified in the ex parte order, the plaintiffs' notice of motion for interlocutory relief came, inter partes, before Dillon J. Mr Robinson appeared in person. He gave an undertaking over 2 July 1982 in terms similar to the terms of the injunction granted by Goulding J to restrain breach of copyright, passing-off and trade mark infringement. This undertaking was on 2 July continued until trial. The Mareva relief granted by Goulding J was not continued after 25 June. On 2 July,

f however, Mr Robinson gave undertakings that he would not, pending trial, dispose of his interests in 8 Frederick Street, 39–43 Mill Street and 30 Enderby Road, and the company gave undertakings that it would not, pending trial, dispose of certain motor cars. These undertakings were later discharged and other undertakings substituted for them. I need not go into any detail. The Anton Piller order granted by Goulding J had, of course, already been executed and no question as to its continuance could arise. No

g application was made on 25 June or 2 July for that Anton Piller order to be set aside.

However, by notice of motion dated 24 February 1984, the defendants applied, inter alia, for an order that the plaintiffs' action be dismissed, that the ex parte order of 18 June 1982 be set aside and that there be an inquiry as to the damages caused to the defendants by the order which the plaintiffs ought to pay pursuant to their cross-undertakings therein recited. That application came before Warner J on 7 June 1984 and was directed

h to be heard at the trial of the plaintiffs' action but to be listed to come on immediately before the trial. The consequence of this direction has been that the case was opened before me by counsel for the defendants, instead of by counsel for the plaintiffs.

The defendants contend in support of their application, first, that the evidence put before Goulding J and in reliance on which the order of 18 June 1982 was made contained serious misrepresentations and omissions. It is contended that the plaintiffs and their

j solicitors, Hamlins, failed to disclose to the judge material evidence relevant to the relief being sought and, at least arguably, favourable to the defendants, and permitted the judge to act on evidence which was in important respects misleading. These breaches of the duty owed to the court by the plaintiffs and their solicitors require, it was submitted, the order to be set aside even at this very late stage.

In addition, the defendants complain that the order was oppressively and excessively executed. They contend that more persons entered the premises than were permitted under the order to do so; they contend that tapes and material not covered by the order were removed and then retained by Hamlins; they contend that the terms of the order were misrepresented by Hamlins to the defendants' bankers; and they contend that the plaintiffs' overriding purpose in obtaining and executing the order was the improper purpose of destroying the businesses being carried on at 8 Frederick Street and at the Mill Street shop. This improper purpose, they say, was in the event achieved. They seek therefore damages pursuant to the cross-undertaking recited in the order.

The trial before me has been a combination of a trial of the plaintiffs' action and a trial of the defendants' complaints regarding the obtaining, execution and consequences of the ex parte order. Some of the defendants' complaints are, in a sense, free-standing and do not depend on the outcome of the plaintiffs' action. But the consequences, if I should find those complaints well founded, are bound to depend to some extent on the nature of the businesses being carried on by the defendants. And that matter lies at the heart of the plaintiffs' action.

I propose therefore to proceed in this way. First, I must describe the nature of the video film cassette business. Some understanding of that is essential background to a resolution of the issues between the parties. Second, I will outline the history of Mr Robinson and of his and his company's activities up to the point of service and execution of the ex parte order. Third, I will describe the manner in which the order was applied for, obtained and executed and outline the relevant events that followed. Fourth, I will deal with the issues arising in the plaintiffs' action. Fifth, I will deal with the issues arising in respect of the defendants' complaints regarding the ex parte order.

1. *The trade in video film cassettes*

Companies that make motion picture films spend very large sums of money indeed in so doing. The size of some budgets for the making of films is quite staggering. These sums are expended of course with a view of profit. The commercial exploitation of the film will usually take the form first of its release for cinema viewing. Subsequently, and particularly if the film has been a box office success at the cinema, it is likely to be reproduced in a video cassette format. Prerecorded video tapes will be made from the film and packaged in cassettes. The cassettes will be sold to the shops and to the video clubs and video libraries which offer video cassettes for sale or hire to the public. Generally, the production and marketing of video cassettes of a film will not take place until the film has run its course through the cinemas. There are two obvious reasons for this. First, the premature marketing of the film in a video cassette format may adversely affect the size of cinema audiences. If you can hire a cassette and watch the film at home, why bother to go to the cinema? Second, the success of a film in the cinemas may enable the film, when reproduced in video cassette format, to be the more easily and successfully marketed in that format.

From a commercial point of view, the ability to exploit the film by marketing it in a video cassette format is very important. The more successful a film has been in the cinema, the more valuable will be the video cassette distribution rights. In the case of a successful film the timing of the launch of a campaign to market it in video cassette format will be of great importance. If the launch is too early, it may adversely affect the film's cinema audiences. If the launch is left too late, the advantage of the publicity generated by the film's success in the cinema may be reduced. Most films do not stay popular indefinitely. They come into flower for a short time and then fade away, their place being taken by new favourites.

It is plain that the large scale unauthorised reproduction and distribution of films in video cassette format may have a devastating effect on the ability of those entitled to the distribution rights to exploit those rights. Not many people will buy or hire more than one video cassette of the same film. The market for a particular video film is a finite one and, as soon as distribution of the video cassettes has begun, a reducing one. The practice of reproducing motion picture films in a video cassette format and exploiting the film by the distribution of video cassettes of the film commenced relatively recently. The only members of the public who are in the market for buying or hiring video cassettes

are those who own or have access to video recorders. These machines are not cheap.
a Unlike television sets, video recorders are not yet so widespread that failure to own one
can be taken as a sign of social deprivation. The market is therefore a limited one. The
market for video cassettes was insignificant in the early 1970s. It seems to have begun to
grow through the 1970s until by the end of that decade it had become, for film
companies, commercially significant. The market has continued to grow through this
present decade. It has now become highly important from a commercial point of view,
b but it is still, and will always be, limited to the number of households in which a video
recorder is to be found.

With the growing commercial value in the late 1970s and early 1980s of the market
in video cassettes came the video pirates. Video pirates are those who in breach of
copyright reproduce and market motion picture films in video cassette format. In this
action the expression 'pirate' has been used to describe a video tape on which, in breach
c of copyright, a film has been reproduced or, sometimes, the cassette in which such a tape
has been packed. The expression 'counterfeit' has been used to describe a cassette whose
labelling and artwork suggest, falsely, that the tape and cassette are the produce of some
particular company, usually the company which owns, or is believed by the pirate to
own, the copyright in the film in question. Every counterfeit cassette contains a pirate
tape. Not every pirate tape is contained in a counterfeit cassette. I shall in this judgment
d use the adjective 'pirate' in the sense I have described.

In the late 1970s and the early 1980s the losses being inflicted by video pirates on those
who owned the copyright in motion picture films was very considerable indeed. Counsel
for the plaintiffs put to Mr Robinson in cross-examination that in 1980 or 1981 some
80% of the video cassettes to be found in the shops, video clubs and video libraries in this
country were pirate. Mr Robinson did not disagree with that estimate. Even if that
e estimate is taken, and I do take it, with a considerable pinch of salt, the proportion of
pirate tapes in circulation in this country must have been staggering.

This is by no means the first case in which the problems created by video piracy have
been ventilated in these courts, although it may, I understand, be the first civil case in
which there has been a full trial. There have been many cases which have had the
attention of the courts at an interlocutory stage. Some have been reported. In one, *Rank*
f *Film Distributors Ltd v Video Information Centre* [1980] 2 All ER 273 at 277, [1982] AC 380
at 403–404, Lord Denning MR described the manner in which video piracy takes place.
He said:

'A film pirate works like this. He gets hold of a technician in a cinema or in a ship
or an aircraft, any place where cinematograph films are projected on to a screen.
The pirate then bribes the technician. He pays him, say, £100. The technician then
g "borrows" a film for a night. It is simple enough. Instead of putting the film into
the cupboard, as he should, he puts it into his own case. He hands the celluloid film
to the pirate. Overnight the pirate takes the film to his "laboratory". He has there a
machine for transferring the film from celluloid onto magnetic tape. It only takes
an hour or so. Next morning the pirate returns the film to the technician. He puts
it into the cupboard. No one is any the wiser. The pirate has during the night made
h a "master tape". He uses it for making video cassettes. He then sells these cassettes
on the black market.'

I have been told that the incidence of video piracy has been much reduced since the
dark days of 1980 and 1981. But there is no doubt that at the time with which this action
is concerned video piracy was rife and flourishing and a matter of grave and legitimate
j concern to those entitled to the copyright in motion picture films.

The experience of this case has shown it to be often a very difficult matter to identify
the company, organisation or person in whom the copyright in a particular film or the
exclusive licence to reproduce and market that film for the time being vested. In the
United States of America there is, as I understand it, legislation under which entitlement
to film copyright can be registered and under which the registration constitutes either
conclusive or prima facie (I know not which) evidence of the ownership of the copyright.

That legislation does not, however, have any extra-territorial effect and it has no counterpart in this country. In this country a company which claims to be entitled to copyright or to an exclusive licence in respect of a particular film must establish, starting with the original copyright owner of the film in question and proceeding by way of assignments and grants ending up with itself, its title to those rights. It seems, from the evidence I have heard in this case, that companies which make motion picture films often enter into complex arrangements under which copyright travels down a chain of associated or nominee companies to its eventual destination. Complex arrangements are also made for the grant of exclusive licences to reproduce and distribute the film in question in different countries in the world. It has been shown by the evidence in this case to be often very difficult for the companies which claim to have film copyright or exclusive licences vested in them to prove the title which they claim. It is often correspondingly difficult for those wishing to acquire rights in particular films to be certain that those with whom they are dealing are entitled to grant the rights in question.

These difficulties are relevant in this action. First, a would-be reproducer of films may find himself purchasing rights from a company which has no right to grant them. Second, the difficulty of proving entitlement to copyright encourages video piracy. Video pirates may justifiably have some optimism that, if challenged, their challenger will fail to establish its copyright title.

There have been mentioned in evidence, and will be mentioned in this judgment, various different formats in which video films may be found. I will briefly describe them.

For the purpose of reproducing films in a video format, a master tape is required. Technically, any type of tape is capable of being used as a master. But, plainly, the better the quality of the master, the better will be the quality of the reproduction. A professional reproducer of tapes will, in practice, use a specialised form of tape as a master. One such form of tape is known as a U-matic tape. These U-matic tapes can, as I understand it, be edited with a facility not possible with tapes of more common format. This facility makes U-matic tapes particularly suitable as masters. Mr Robinson had a large number of U-matic tapes. For the purposes of the tapes which he produced in commercial quantities, he used U-matic tapes as his master tapes. There is no reason why a member of the public should not acquire a video recorder by means of which U-matic tapes could be viewed. Mr Robinson had such a machine. But these machines are a good deal more expensive than the more common video recorders and the owners of them are, more or less, confined to video enthusiasts or specialists of some sort. It follows that films which are to be reproduced in video format in commercial quantities are not reproduced in U-matic format. The master for the reproduction may, however, be a tape in U-matic format.

The evidence before me has revealed three varieties of tapes and video recorders, namely Philips 2000, VHS and Betamax. Each of these is made by a rival company. They are not interchangeable. A Philips 2000 machine can be used for viewing Philips 2000 tapes, but not for viewing VHS tapes or Betamax tapes. The same is true, mutatis mutandis, of VHS machines and Betamax machines.

It seems from the evidence that Philips was an early entrant into the video field, but that by 1981 and 1982 Philips recorders and tapes had become relatively rare. If ownership of the machines was rare, it would not be commercially worth while for video films to be reproduced in a Philips 2000 format, and it would not be worth while for shops and other outlets to keep Philips 2000 tapes in stock. And, if prerecorded tapes in that format were not kept in stock in the shops and other outlets, it would not be worth while for members of the public to buy Philips 2000 recorders. This seems to be what has happened in respect of Philips 2000 tapes and recorders. Betamax and VHS tapes, on the other hand, are stocked by most shops and outlets. But, of the two, there seems, from the evidence I have heard, to be a heavy predominance in favour of VHS. The evidence before me has indicated that Betamax does still retain a significant place in the market, but has been left a long way behind by VHS.

Mr Robinson's recorders at 8 Frederick Street were capable of reproducing tapes in a

VHS format or in a Betamax format. He did not have facilities for reproducing tapes in a
a Philips 2000 format.

There is one final feature of the use of video recorders that I should mention. Video
recorders are commonly used for the purpose of viewing on the screen of a television set
video films. The tape is inserted in the video recorder. The recorder is connected to a
television set and the film on the tape can then be viewed on the television set. But, in
addition, video recorders can be and are widely used for taking copies of programmes
b being broadcast on television. An owner of a video recorder who wants to watch a
programme or film being shown on television at some time other than the particular
time at which the film or programme is being broadcast can insert a blank tape into the
video recorder and copy the film or programme onto that blank tape. The tape on which
the film or programme has been recorded can be played and the film or programme
viewed as often as desired. This facility to copy films or programmes broadcast on
c television is one of the advantages of video recorders which has helped to give them their
popularity. Blank tapes are sold in all video shops. Their main use is for the purpose I
have described. Yet all this copying is in breach of copyright. It is a striking irony that
the growth of ownership of video recorders, on which the growth in the sales of
prerecorded video cassettes has depended and which has made so valuable the exclusive
right to reproduce films in a video format, has at the same time provided the means of
d widespread breach of that right.

2. History

[His Lordship then outlined the history of the business affairs of Mr Robinson. In 1976
Mr Robinson set up business in partnership with a Mr Wickenden under the style Direct
Maintenance Services at 8 Frederick Street, Luton, preparing and maintaining radios,
e television sets and video recorders. In February 1980 Mr Robinson became interested in
a business in a shop at 39–43 Mill Street, Luton, under the style Luton Video Centre
(LVC), which he took over in 1981, installing a Mr Gordon as manager of the shop. Also
in 1981 Mr Robinson acquired and installed at 8 Frederick Street a bank of video
recorders which enabled him to produce copies of video cassette tapes in large numbers.
It was the plaintiffs' case that 8 Frederick Street became and was at the time of the
f execution of the ex parte order a pirate factory, where reproduction of pirate tapes was
carried on systematically and on a large scale. On the execution of the ex parte order at
Mr Robinson's home at 30 Enderby Road, a large number of video cassette tapes in U-
matic format were found. It was the plaintiffs' case that those U-matic tapes were used
by Mr Robinson as master tapes for the purpose of the copying of tapes being carried on
at 8 Frederick Street. Mr Robinson's answer to the allegation that he was reproducing
g tapes in breach of copyright was that he was reproducing the tapes pursuant to licences
which he had been granted by a company or organisation called Benelux Video, operating
out of offices in Amsterdam and managed by a Mr Kooring with whom Mr Robinson
had had business dealings for some years. Benelux Video and Mr Kooring had no rights
whatsoever to grant Mr Robinson any rights at all in respect of two films with which the
action was concerned, namely 'Futureworld' and 'Russian Roulette'. The most important
h of Mr Robinson's clients was a company called Centre Video Ltd, which in 1981–82 was
the largest wholesaler of video films in England. Mr Robinson supplied Centre Video
with tapes of a film 'Carquake/Cannonball' imported by him from a Netherlands
company called Mills Video. In June 1981 Mr Percy Browne, the chief investigator for
the MPAA with the particular duty of tracking down video piracy, visited Mr Robinson
and was taken by him to 8 Frederick Street where he saw Mr Robinson's bank of 40 VHS
j and 10 Betamax video cassette recorders. Mr Robinson emphasised to Mr Browne that
he was no pirate and was reproducing tapes and marketing video cassettes in good faith
under licences he believed to be valid. The impression he gave to Mr Browne was that he
knew a good deal about the video piracy business but was not necessarily a video pirate
himself. Mr Robinson was wholly co-operative with Mr Browne on that occasion: he
voluntarily showed him his factory at 8 Frederick Street, and took him to his home at 30
Enderby Road and showed him the tapes which he had there. Mr Robinson gave evidence

that in the course of their discussions Mr Browne had asked him for assistance in discovering sources of pirate or counterfeit tapes. Mr Robinson said that he had told Mr *a* Browne that he would help if he could do so. There was evidence that Mr Robinson made several telephone calls to Mr Browne over the next month and that from time to time they met one another. On some of those occasions Mr Robinson provided Mr Browne with information about actual or suspected video piracy. Some of that information was valuable to Mr Browne. Nevertheless, the material disclosed to Mr Browne on 30 June revealed that Mr Robinson was reproducing a number of films in *b* breach of copyright. In January 1982 Mr Robinson gave one of the plaintiffs, Guild Home Video Ltd (Guild Home), an undertaking not to trade in two films, 'Slaughter' and 'Puppet on a Chain', other than through purchases from Guild Home. In March 1982 it came to the notice of the MPAA that Centre Video was advertising LVC titles which included a film entitled 'Futureworld'. In early 1982 Mr Robinson began discussions with a Mr Donnelly, a business associate, for the sale to him of the Mill Street shop, but *c* the sale ultimately fell through. The respective businesses carried on by Mr Robinson and Luton Video Services Ltd at 8 Frederick Street and at the Mill Street shop were interrupted by the execution at those premises of the ex parte order. His Lordship continued:]

I must now describe the circumstances in which that order came to be applied for and made.
d

3. *The ex parte order*

(i) *The application*

Guild Home had acquired the video cassette distribution rights in 'Futureworld' but in the spring of 1982 'Futureworld' had not yet been the subject of any legitimate release in the United Kingdom in video cassette format. However, it came to the attention of *e* Guild Home that 'Futureworld' was being advertised in the March edition of a video magazine, Popular Video, as an LVC title. The same advertisement advertised 'Slaughter' as an LVC title. After inquiries to ascertain whether licences in respect of 'Futureworld' had been granted to anyone other than Guild Home and receiving the appropriate assurances, Linda Davies, the employee of Guild Home who had visited Mr Robinson in connection with 'Slaughter' and 'Puppet on a Chain', procured a copy of a video cassette *f* of 'Futureworld' to be purchased. The packaging showed it to come from LVC, that is to say from the defendants. So, towards the end of April 1982 Miss Davies instructed Mr Hoffman, senior partner of Hamlins.

Mr Hoffman, besides being senior partner, was and is the commercial litigation partner in Hamlins. He specialises in intellectual property cases. He has had, inevitably, a very great deal of experience of Anton Piller orders since the emergence of that form of relief *g* in about 1974. Mr Hoffman estimated that since 1974 his firm had executed about 300 Anton Piller orders. Mr Hoffman was handed the copy of 'Futureworld' which Guild Home had acquired. He came to the conclusion that it was a pirate copy. He was right. On 2 June 1982 a meeting took place attended by Mr Hoffman, representatives of Guild Home and representatives of other companies. The presence at the meeting of these latter parties was because the problem Guild Home were experiencing with 'Futureworld' *h* and other titles was, it was thought, similar to problems that the other companies were experiencing with their own titles. Mr Hoffman told me that at the meeting video piracy and the Luton connection, as it was called, were discussed. Mr Percy Browne was on holiday and so was not present at this meeting. However, Mr Browne's assistant was present and told Mr Hoffman that Mr Robinson was a trusted informant of Mr Percy Browne.

Following the 2 June meeting, further test purchases were arranged. On 8 June an *j* inquiry agent instructed by Mr Hoffman purchased from the Mill Street shop a video cassette of 'Halloween' and another of 'California Suite'. In addition he hired video cassettes of 'Rocky I' and of 'Blues Brothers'. On 10 June 1982 a video cassette of 'Futureworld' was purchased from the Mill Street shop. All these video cassettes were *i* thought to be, and turned out to be, pirates. On 15 June 1982 a meeting took place

attended by representatives of Hamlins, by Mr Alistair J McGregor of counsel and by
a representatives of various film-producing companies. Mr Percy Browne was present at
this meeting. He described it in his evidence as 'the normal weekly meeting to discuss
piracy and what should be done'. Mr Robinson and Luton Video Services Ltd was one of
the matters discussed at the meeting. One of the decisions taken at the meeting was that
proceedings should be taken against the defendants for, inter alia, an Anton Piller order
and a Mareva injunction.

b   One of the matters litigated before me has been the complaint of the defendants that
the order obtained against them on 18 June and executed on 21 June 1982 was improperly
obtained and oppressively executed. It is therefore of importance to notice the basis on
which the decision to proceed was taken at the meeting of 15 June. Mr Browne was
accompanied at the meeting by his assistant, Stephen Fleming. Some five representatives
from Hamlins were present. They included Mr Hoffman, Mr Roy Brown and Mr
c Hoffman's articled clerk, Mr Burnhill. Attendance notes of what took place were
subsequently prepared by Mr Hoffman, Mr Roy Brown and Mr Burnhill. Early on in the
meeting Mr Robinson's role as an informant for Mr Percy Browne was discussed. Mr
Percy Browne told me that it was common knowledge in the industry that Mr Robinson
was his informant. He said that he told the meeting that, if there was evidence that Mr
Robinson was engaged in reproducing pirate tapes, action should be taken against him.
d Mr Percy Browne did, however, make it clear that, in view of his own personal dealings
with Mr Robinson, he would prefer not himself to take part in the execution of an Anton
Piller order at Mr Robinson's premises. Mr Hoffman's attendance note starts by recording
that Mr Percy Browne had informed the meeting that 'Chris Robinson, the owner of
LVC, had offered assistance to the M.P.A.A. and I said that had to go into the evidence'.
Notwithstanding that reference, the evidence eventually relied on for the ex parte orders
e sought contained no mention of Mr Robinson's role as an informant. It was clear to those
at the meeting that Mr Percy Browne knew more about Mr Robinson than did anyone
else at the meeting. It was therefore agreed that Mr Fleming would in the afternoon
bring over from Mr Percy Browne's office to Hamlins' offices Mr Percy Browne's file
relating to Mr Robinson. There can be no doubt but that the reason for this was to enable
those in Hamlins responsible for the collation of evidence eventually to go before the
f court on the ex parte application to be fully informed as to the background.
      It is also clear from Mr Hoffman's attendance note that at the morning meeting on 15
June a decision had been taken in principle to seek an Anton Piller order against Mr
Robinson and Luton Video Services Ltd. This decision would of course have been subject
to anything in Mr Percy Browne's file which might prompt second thoughts. Mr Roy
Brown's attendance note ends with the sentence:

g   'It was arranged that Mr. Fleming would get the file on Mr. Robinson from the
      M.P.A.A. office and I would then have the opportunity of perusing the file in the
      presence of Mr. Browne and Mr. Fleming for the purpose of my affidavit in support
      of the Anton Piller action.'

      In the afternoon of 15 June, as had been arranged, Mr Percy Browne, accompanied by
h Mr Fleming, took his file to Hamlins offices. There the file was made available to Mr Roy
Brown for his perusal. The meeting lasted half an hour to an hour and after the meeting
Mr Percy Browne took his file away with him.
      Mr Roy Brown is an experienced solicitor who has been a partner in Hamlins since
about 1966. He had not, before the meetings on 15 June, had any knowledge of Mr
Robinson. He had not previously met Mr Percy Browne. Mr Roy Brown had an
j opportunity to read the file but, I suspect, read the file only cursorily. Mr Percy Browne
and Mr Roy Brown discussed 'Futureworld', the film which had prompted the proceedings
in the first place, and Mr Percy Browne mentioned the circumstances in which he had
taken possession of a U-matic cassette of 'Futureworld' on 30 June 1981. Mr Percy Browne
mentioned also that he had been to 8 Frederick Street. Mr Percy Browne told me that he
could not remember whether or not he had told Mr Roy Brown about the bank of video
recorders that he had seen at 8 Frederick Street. He agreed, however, that that fact would

have been of particular interest to Mr Roy Brown. I think it highly likely that Mr Percy Browne, an experienced ex-police officer, would have recognised the importance of this information at the time and would have mentioned it to Mr Roy Brown.

Mr Percy Browne's file, which Mr Roy Brown read, at least cursorily, contained a list of the tapes handed over by Mr Robinson on 30 June 1981 and also a list of the tapes handed back by Mr Browne to Mr Robinson some weeks later. The file contained copies of the various licences that Mr Robinson had handed over to Mr Percy Browne, including that relating to 'Futureworld', and contained the receipt signed by Mr Kooring showing a payment of £3,000 by Mr Robinson in respect of those licences or some of them. Mr Roy Brown said in evidence that he did not ask Mr Percy Browne anything about that material.

Mr Roy Brown knew, either from the file or because he had been told by Mr Percy Browne, that Mr Robinson on 30 June 1981 had handed over his licences relating, inter alia, to 'Futureworld' and had handed over a U-matic master of 'Futureworld'. He knew that Mr Robinson had paid £3,000 to Benelux Video for the 'Futureworld' licence. He accepted in cross-examination that he may well have seen and read Mr Browne's letter to Mr Robinson of 10 July 1981. This letter listed the tapes in respect of which MPAA members claimed copyright and those in respect of which MPAA members did not claim copyright. But Mr Roy Brown told me that in looking through Mr Percy Browne's file he was not paying much attention to films other than 'Futureworld'.

Mr Roy Brown had the conduct of the ex parte application to the court for, inter alia, an Anton Piller order and a Mareva injunction. The affidavits in support were both sworn by him. He swore a substantial affidavit of some 11 pages, 27 paragraphs, on 16 June. This affidavit was settled by counsel, Mr McGregor, from instructions given to him by Mr Roy Brown. On 17 June Mr Roy Brown swore a short affidavit in order to supplement in a few respects the contents of the first affidavit.

Mr Roy Brown knew, of course, that a duty of full disclosure to the court lay on those responsible for an ex parte application. But his affidavits made no attempt to describe the occasion on 30 June 1981 when Mr Robinson had handed over a number of licences and a number of cassettes to Mr Percy Browne and when Mr Percy Browne had been shown over 8 Frederick Street. The affidavits made no mention of the fact that since 30 June 1981 Mr Robinson had been acting as an informant of Mr Percy Browne. It will be recalled that at the morning meeting on 15 June 1982 Mr Hoffman had said that the fact that Mr Robinson had offered assistance to Mr Browne had to go into the evidence. It was nowhere mentioned in Mr Roy Brown's affidavits. There was no mention of the £3,000 that Mr Robinson had paid Benelux Video for the 'Futureworld' licence.

Mr Roy Brown told me in cross-examination that he did not regard those facts as relevant. I found this an astonishing remark from an experienced solicitor.

The impression was given by Mr Roy Brown's affidavits and the exhibits thereto that the factory at 8 Frederick Street was a place of business where activities were carried on in a secretive and clandestine way. In his second affidavit in particular, Mr Roy Brown seems to be at pains to leave that impression. He said:

'In addition I would further point out that from the description of the registered office of the limited company, the second defendant, namely 8 Frederick Street, Luton, it would appear that these premises house the factory and are described as "a relatively run-down terraced house" apparently "heavily fortified" with no name plates or other identification on the outside of the premises stating that the registered office of the second defendants is in fact situate there.'

Yet, as Mr Roy Brown knew, Mr Robinson had invited Mr Percy Browne to the premises the previous June and had shown him the bank of video recorders. Moreover, it must have been known to Mr Roy Brown, for it was certainly known to his clients, that the defendants had been openly advertising their video cassettes in video magazines.

The impression that Mr Roy Brown's evidence would naturally leave on the judge must have been fortified by an exchange in court between the judge, Goulding J, and

counsel, Mr McGregor. The judge was commenting on the doorbells at the entrance to 8
a Frederick Street. The exchange proceeded thus:

> '*Goulding J.* There were three doorbells, two without any names and over the top
> one the name "Direct Maintenance Services". That is the nearest we get to it. *Mr
> McGregor.* My Lord, yes. Of course, it is not very common to find a registered office
> of a company with a front door with only a peephole in it.
> *Goulding J.* There are registered offices and registered offices. *Mr McGregor.* My
b > Lord, yes. Your Lordship may also recollect that on one occasion when Mr Hughes
> was observing 8 Frederick Street he saw a glow from it, and on another occasion
> looked through the window to see three video recording units . . .'

Mr McGregor, of course, was basing his remarks on the contents of the affidavits; but Mr
Roy Brown was sitting behind him.
c The conclusion is, in my view, inescapable that the judge received a misleading and
unfair impression of the nature of the premises at which the reproduction of tapes by the
defendants was carried out.
I regret to have to say that I do not think Mr Roy Brown paid more than lip service to
the requirement that on an ex parte application the fullest disclosure is required to be
made. But the criticism of the affidavits on the strength of which the Anton Piller order
d and Mareva injunction were obtained in this case goes further. The basis on which Anton
Piller orders are granted is that otherwise evidence essential to the plaintiffs' case may be
destroyed by the defendants. An Anton Piller order would not, I think, be granted unless
there were evidence which justified that fear. Paragraph 24 of Mr Roy Brown's first
affidavit dealt with that important matter. He said:

> 'It is my belief that the defendants named in these proceedings know full well
e > that what they are doing is unlawful and that if they are put on notice of the
> plaintiffs' complaints they will destroy any evidence which will permit the plaintiffs
> to establish their claim in damages at the trial of the action.'

That paragraph, Mr Roy Brown told me, was a common form paragraph that went into
all Hamlins' applications for Anton Piller orders and Mareva injunctions in video or
f audio piracy cases. He told me also that where video piracy on a large scale was suspected
it was the practice of Hamlins as a matter of course to seek an Anton Piller order and
Mareva injunction.
But in relation to Mr Robinson, para 24 was simply not true in the terms in which it
was couched. On 30 June 1981 Mr Robinson had been put on notice of complaints of
video piracy. He had invited the MPAA chief investigator to his business premises and
g to his home and had allowed him free rein to inspect the premises and to take away with
him what he wished. Subsequently Mr Robinson had instructed solicitors who had
conducted a short correspondence with the proprietor of the 'Futureworld' copyright.
I must return later in this judgment to consider the implications of the manner in
which the ex parte relief in this case and, I must fear, a very large number of similar
cases, was successfully applied for.

h
(ii) *The order*
The application was made to Goulding J on 18 June 1982. The judge was uneasy about
the matter.
Goulding J took the point that the company might well have a lawful trade as well as
an unlawful trade and that the Mareva injunction sought made no provision for any
j funds to be available to the company for its ordinary running expenses. In the end the
judge decided to make no provision for those expenses but to leave the company to apply
if so advised. He made the order sought by the plaintiffs. I need not read the whole of
the order but I should, I think, read the parts relevant to the matters raised by the
defendants' notice of motion.
The order contains a number of undertakings. Among them is an undertaking by the
plaintiffs—

'To abide by any Order this Court may make as to damages in case this court shall hereafter be of opinion that the Defendants shall have sustained any by reason of *a* this Order which the Plaintiffs ought to pay.'

There is also an undertaking by the plaintiffs' solicitors, Hamlins:

'(1) that they will inform the Defendants and each of them of their right to seek and obtain legal advice before complying with this Order provided that such advice is sought and obtained forthwith and (2) that all records, video cassettes, video tapes, *b* equipment documents or other articles obtained as a result of this Order will be retained in their safe custody or to their order until further Order and shall be used only in respect of this intended Action or other civil litigation.'

The order granted an injunction restraining the defendants from 'making selling offering for sale distributing or otherwise parting with possession power custody or control of or *c* destroying or defacing or hiding any . . . illicit goods' . . .' 'Illicit goods' were defined as follows:

'(i) Any complete or substantial copy (whether in the form of video cassettes or otherwise) of any film being less than 50 years old and being distributed by the Plaintiffs or any of them or any other member of the . . . MPAA . . . (a list of whom are annexed hereto), or of any film in which copyright is vested in or exclusively *d* licensed to or claimed to be so vested or licensed to the Plaintiffs or any of them or any other member of the MPAA not being a copy made by or on behalf of the Plaintiffs or any of them or any other member of the MPAA (ii) Any labels, sleeves or other printed or written matter which is for use with any illicit goods (iii) Any plates or tapes or other material used on intended to be used for making illicit goods.'   *e*

The Anton Piller part of the order was in this form:

'AND IT IS ORDERED that each Defendant (whether by himself or herself or by any person appearing to be in charge of the premises hereinafter specified) do permit the person who shall serve this Order upon him or her together with such persons being not more than 4 in number as may be duly authorised by the Plaintiffs' *f* Solicitors to enter forthwith the premises known as 30 Enderby Road, Luton, Bedfordshire, 39/43 Mill Street, Luton, Bedfordshire, 8 Frederick Street, Luton, Bedfordshire and 34 Priestwood Avenue, Bracknell, Berkshire and any other premises disclosed to the Plaintiffs pursuant to the last preceding provision of this Order or ascertained by the Plaintiffs as being premises being occupied by one or more of the Defendants together with any outhouse or any other building which *g* forms a part of the said premises and any motor vehicle owned or used by the Defendants at any hour between 8 o'clock in the forenoon and 8 o'clock in the evening for the purpose of inspecting, photographing and looking for and removing into the Plaintiffs' Solicitors' custody (i) any illicit goods (ii) any labels sleeves or other printed or written matter which is for use with any illicit goods (iii) any plates or tapes or video discs or video recording machines or other material used or *h* intended to be used for making illicit goods (iv) all or any documents relating in any way to any of the aforesaid items in (i) (ii) and (iii) above AND IT IS ORDERED that each of the Defendants whether by himself or by any person appearing to be in charge of the said premises do permit the Plaintiffs and their representatives as aforesaid to carry out such inspecting photographing looking for and removing.'

j

This order does not authorise the removal of anything that does not fall within one or other of the four sub-paragraphs. There is no authority for the removal of material for examination in order that a decision may at leisure be taken whether or not it represents 'illicit goods'.

The authority to remove documents extends to 'any documents relating in any way' to illicit goods. The breadth of this is obvious. It justifies, conceptually at least, the

removal of every document relating in any way to the defendants' business. The order
a authorised the removal of all machines and associated equipment used for making illicit
goods. I find it difficult to see how an order for the removal of the video recorders at least
could have been justified. What was the fear? That the defendants would destroy them?
It is not difficult to conclude that the purpose and likely effect of an order of this
breadth was to prevent Mr Robinson from continuing to carry on business.

A notable omission from the order is any requirement that a list, let alone a detailed
b list, of what was removed should be prepared by Hamlins and supplied to the defendants.

The Mareva injunction restrained the defendants from—

> 'removing from the jurisdiction of this Court or otherwise disposing of or dealing
> with any of their individual or joint assets within the jurisdiction and with out
> prejudice to the generality of the foregoing pledging charging or otherwise parting
> with possession of such assets save that each of the First and Third Defendants be at
c liberty to expend a sum not exceeding £200 for ordinary living expenses upon
> informing the Plaintiffs' Solicitors of the source or account from which such sum is
> to be drawn.'

Immediate full disclosure by the defendants of their assets was ordered. The order ended
with liberty to the defendants to 'move to vary or discharge this Order or any part thereof
d upon giving the Plaintiffs' Solicitors 24 hours' notice of their intention so to do.'

(iii) *The raid*

18 June 1982 was a Friday. The order was executed on the following Monday, 21 June.
It was a process that required to be and was planned with military precision. Mr Hoffman,
the senior partner of Hamlins, was in charge. There were four sets of premises at which
e the order had to be executed although only three are relevant for present purposes. A
number of people took part. Their activities all had to be co-ordinated. The personnel
from Hamlins included, in addition to Mr Hoffman, Mr Roy Brown, Mr Burnhill (Mr
Hoffman's articled clerk), Mr Cumberland (a senior legal executive with Hamlins), Mr
Baker and Mr Patel (both of whom are solicitors employed by Hamlins), Miss Anna
Kennedy (another Hamlins articled clerk). Another participant was Mr Fleming (Mr
f Percy Browne's assistant). In addition Hamlins had arranged for a number of police
officers to be in attendance. This is, I am told, normal practice where execution of an
Anton Piller order is to be effected. It is to prevent any breach of the peace.

A point was taken by counsel for the defendants that the number of persons who
executed the Anton Piller order was excessive. He construed the order as authorising
only five persons to enter the four sets of premises specified in the order. Counsel for the
g plaintiffs construed the order as limiting to five the number of persons authorised to
enter any one of the four sets of premises. In my judgment, counsel for the plaintiffs is
right. An order of this sort plainly contemplates that execution at the respective sets of
premises will take place more or less simultaneously. A requirement that the same five
persons should have to go from address to address does not make any sense and was not
what the order was contemplating. Counsel for the defendants accepted that if the order
h is to be construed as authorising a different five persons to enter each set of premises the
defendants' complaint that there was entry by an excessive number of persons cannot, on
the evidence, be sustained.

The order was executed at the Mill Street shop, 8 Frederick Street and 30 Enderby
Road. There are a number of complaints by the defendants as to what was done. Some
of these complaints rest on allegations that the plaintiffs' witnesses dispute. Some are
j based on facts that are common ground.

The witnesses who have given evidence of what took place are, on the defendants' side,
first, Mr Robinson, who was present while the order was executed at 30 Enderby Road
and for the latter part of the time during which the order was being executed at 8
Frederick Street, second, Mr Wickenden, who was present while the order was being
executed at 8 Frederick Street, and, third, Mr Gordon, who, although not present while
the order was being executed at the Mill Street shop, gave evidence about his personal

possessions and papers which were removed therefrom in the course of the raid. On the plaintiffs' side, evidence was given of what took place at 8 Frederick Street by Mr *a* Hoffman, Mr Fleming, Mr Cumberland and Mr Baker. Evidence of the raid on the Mill Street shop was given by Mr Hoffman, Mr Fleming and Mr Patel. Evidence of the raid at 30 Enderby Road was given by Mr Roy Brown, Mr Hoffman and Miss Kennedy.

Attendance notes of what occurred were made by Mr Roy Brown, Mr Baker, Mr Burnhill, Mr Cumberland and Miss Kennedy, and Mr Hoffman. These attendance notes I have found of more assistance than the oral evidence. They are significant not only for *b* their contents but also for what is not there. Some of the plaintiffs' witnesses, Mr Cumberland in particular, gave evidence of incidents occurring that find no record in any of the attendance notes. I approach the evidence on the footing that the order was being executed by some very experienced professionals. They would, I am confident, have recorded material incidents if they had occurred. Equally, I see no reason to suppose that anything fictitious would have been recorded as having happened.   *c*

The Mill Street shop. The order was executed at the Mill Street shop at about 12.55 pm. Mr Morgan, on whom the order had previously been served at his home, opened the shop and allowed Messrs Hoffman, Burnhill, Fleming and one Freeman to enter and search. The order had already been adequately explained to Mr Morgan by Mr Baker. Mr Morgan had already consulted solicitors, Messrs Tearle & Co, who had previously acted for Mr Robinson.   *d*

The shop was searched. Obviously, it contained a large number of video cassettes. These were all inspected. There was a substantial quantity of documents, including index cards on which the names of the customers and details of the tapes they had hired or purchased were recorded. Mr Hoffman himself went through the documentary material, sorting out what, in his view, should be taken. He then left the shop and went to 8 Frederick Street, leaving Mr Burnhill, Mr Fleming and Mr Freeman to sort out the video *e* cassettes that were to be taken. Mr Hoffman also entrusted Mr Burnhill with the task of drawing up a receipt of the material taken. I have no doubt that he instructed Mr Burnhill as to the form the receipt should take and that he was to require Mr Morgan to sign it.

The Mill Street receipt is in this form:

'We, A. E. Hamlin & Co., hereby acknowledge receipt of the following items *f* which have been handed to us by Mr. Denis Warden Morgan willingly and without duress.'

The tapes that were removed from the Mill Street shop are specified in the receipt either by reference to their respective titles or by reference to their respective library numbers. Empty cassette boxes are listed in the same way. In all, 218 tapes of films and 32 boxes *g* were taken. In addition, at the direction of Mr Hoffman, 29 blank tapes were taken. A considerable quantity of documents were taken. The documents were inadequately described in the receipt. The documents taken included a number of private documents belonging to Mr Gordon which he had left behind when Mr Morgan took over as manager of the shop. These private documents included his cheque book, bank paying-in book, bank statements and various letters from his bank. None of these had any *h* relevance to any 'illicit goods'. They were not returned to Mr Gordon until 3 July 1985 after trial of this action had commenced. Quite apart from the point that they ought not to have been taken at all, it would not be possible to tell from the contents of the receipt prepared by Mr Burnhill that these documents had been taken at all.

The receipt ran to five pages; each page was signed by Mr Burnhill and Mr Morgan. Neither of them gave evidence before me. Mr Burnhill's attendance note does not *j* mention the receipt or the circumstances in which Mr Morgan came to sign it. It does not indicate that Mr Morgan played any part in its preparation.

8 Frederick Street. 8 Frederick Street was entered by Mr Baker and Mr Cumberland at about noon. Mr Robinson was not present. The door was opened by and the order was served on Mr Wickenden. Mr Baker explained that the order entitled himself and Mr Cumberland to enter the premises and search for pirate tapes. Mr Wickenden allowed a them in and said that they were free to look around the premises but that he would not allow them to remove anything until Mr Robinson had arrived. At about 1.30 pm Mr Robinson telephoned, spoke to Mr Wickenden and then to Mr Cumberland. He was told of the Anton Piller order, advised to consult his solicitors and to come to the premises as soon as possible. Mr Hoffman arrived at 8 Frederick Street at about 3.00 pm and Mr Robinson arrived about half an hour later. In the mean time Mr Cumberland had inspected and been through the contents of the various rooms in the premises.

b   Mr Cumberland gave evidence, and it is not in dispute, that a number of tapes of 'Star Wars' were found on the premises. These were all pirate tapes. I shall deal later with Mr Robinson's explanation for their presence. Mr Cumberland said, however, that he found one of these 'Star Wars' tapes in the jaws of one of the video recorders. This, if true, would have been highly significant evidence. It would have carried with it an almost inescapable inference that Mr Robinson had been producing copies of 'Star Wars' on his

c bank of video recorders. Mr Robinson denied that he had done so and challenged Mr Cumberland's evidence that he had found a copy in the jaws of one of the machines.
        Following the raid, Mr Cumberland made a fairly full note of what had happened. The discovery of the 'Star Wars' tape in the jaws of a video recorder is not mentioned. Nor is it referred to in the attendance notes of any other of the persons who were at 8 Frederick Street. Nor was it mentioned by Mr Cumberland at the time to any of those

d persons. The day after the raid, 22 June 1982, Mr Cumberland swore an affidavit in order to describe what had been found at 8 Frederick Street. He does not mention a 'Star Wars' tape in the jaws of a machine. He does, however, say this about the video recorders: '. . . it was not clear that the machines were used for illicit goods.' How could he have so deposed if he had seen the 'Star Wars' pirate tape in one of the machines? How could he not have mentioned that significant circumstance? His explanation given in cross-

e examination was that the circumstance was not relevant to be included in his affidavit. The explanation is nonsense. I am unable to accept the testimony of Mr Cumberland regarding the 'Star Wars' tape in the jaws of the machine. I do not believe he found any such thing. This is, perhaps, only a small point in the scale of the evidence in this case, but it has importance in persuading me of the care with which I must examine the oral testimony of those who took part in the raid where that testimony is damaging to the

f defendants and is unsupported by any of the many contemporaneous records.
        After Mr Hoffman arrived, Mr Cumberland assisted him in sifting through the papers found in the room used by Mr Robinson as an office. Mr Cumberland told me that he went through all the papers in a filing cabinet, set aside for Mr Hoffman's perusal those which he thought of interest and put the others back in the cabinet. Mr Hoffman went through the papers that had been set aside and, he told me, he separated them into those

g that might be relevant and those which were not relevant.
        Mr Robinson has complained that all documents at 8 Frederick Street were taken, including all his personal papers, whether or not they had anything to do with his business affairs. As an example, all the papers relating to his divorce were, he said, taken. Two diaries were also, he said, taken. Mr Hoffman and Mr Cumberland denied that any divorce papers were taken. They denied that diaries were taken. They both testified that

h papers not thought to be relevant had been left behind at 8 Frederick Street.
        There is little doubt but that the criterion of relevance was very liberally applied. Mr Hoffman's evidence came, in my view, to this: he caused to be removed any documents which might, after investigation, turn out to have some relevance to the defendants' business.
        The tapes found at 8 Frederick Street were examined by Mr Cumberland and Mr

j Baker. They put aside for removal all tapes in respect of which copyright was thought by them to be vested in one or other of the plaintiffs.
        As at the Mill Street shop, a receipt was prepared for signature by Mr Robinson. It was drawn up by Mr Cumberland. Mr Cumberland was very experienced in dealing with the execution of Anton Piller orders and knew what to do. The form of the receipt was the form customarily used by Hamlins where Anton Piller orders had been executed. It was in this form:

'Received from Mr. Robinson at 8 Frederick Street, Luton, Beds, the following
items pursuant to order of Mr. Justice Goulding dated 18th June 1982 or otherwise   *a*
by consent.'

As with the Mill Street receipt, this receipt lists with particularity the tapes and video
cassette boxes that were taken. Some 23 tapes were taken. They included five of 'Star
Wars', one of 'Day of the Dolphin' and one of 'Puppet on a Chain'. In addition, a fair
volume of artwork and labels for various titles were taken. This included 25 sleeves   *b*
relating to 'Futureworld'.

It is of interest that no master tapes were taken from 8 Frederick Street. There were a
dozen or so U-matic master tapes at 8 Frederick Street, although the bulk of the U-matic
masters were kept at 30 Enderby Road.

The 8 Frederick Street receipt lists the documents taken with a good deal more detail
than the Mill Street receipt had done. There is no heading under which private   *c*
correspondence or divorce papers could be thought to fall. There is no mention of any
diaries. So, either Mr Robinson is wrong and private correspondence, divorce papers and
diaries were not taken, or the receipt was not simply inadequately particularised, as was
the case with the Mill Street receipt, but was drawn up in a positively misleading form. I
will deal later with the dispute of evidence regarding the documents that were taken
from 8 Frederick Street.   *d*

There is no doubt at all but that the form of this receipt and of the Mill Street and
Enderby Road receipts was designed by Hamlins to protect the firm against the charge
that they had taken documents or articles not covered by the order. And the practice of
the firm not simply in taking documents and things which could be seen to be covered
by the order but also to take documents or things which further and subsequent
investigation might, but might not, prove to be covered by the order made the need for   *e*
protection obvious. I have no hesitation in saying that I find this practice an objectionable
one. Conceptually at least, the consent of the respondent to an Anton Piller order might
protect the executing solicitors against a charge that things not covered by the order had
been taken. But, given the nature of Anton Piller orders and the circumstances of surprise
and shock which almost always attend their execution, there is a very real danger in
allowing the executing solicitors to go outside the terms of the order in reliance on an   *f*
alleged consent on the part of the respondent. This, too, is something to which I will
later return.

Mr Robinson signed the receipt. Mr Hoffman gave evidence that he and Mr Robinson
had expressly orally agreed that Hamlins might take from 8 Frederick Street anything
they wished. Mr Robinson denied this and I believe him. Nowhere in the attendance
notes or in the affidavit subsequently sworn by Mr Hoffman is this alleged agreement   *g*
mentioned. In his affidavit sworn on 8 August 1983 Mr Hoffman deposed that he had
set aside in a file the papers he wished to remove and had 'asked Mr. Robinson to go
through them to ensure that nothing was taken that was not relevant to the proceedings'.
This seems to me very improbable and I do not accept it. In the course of his evidence-
in-chief Mr Hoffman referred to cheque books and bank statements found at 8 Frederick
Street. He said that it was not clear whether the cheques and entries in the bank   *h*
statements related to illicit goods and that he asked Mr Robinson for his consent to their
being removed. He told me that, had Mr Robinson said no, he would have left them
there. I am unable to accept that that was his attitude. His attitude was that Mr Robinson
was a rogue, albeit, as he said, a likeable rogue, who had been operating a pirate factory
on a major scale. He intended to take away from the premises anything that might be
relevant and he intended to protect his and his firm's position by asking Mr Robinson to   *j*
sign a receipt in the form I have described. Mr Robinson did sign the receipt. He is an
intelligent man. I have no doubt that he read it and saw the reference to his 'consent'. I
will leave for later consideration the effect of that 'consent'. But the consent cannot, in
my judgment, be supplemented by any oral agreement or oral consent. I am not satisfied
that any was made or given. I think the truth of the matter is that, so far as Mr Hoffman
was concerned, Mr Robinson signified his consent by signing the receipt.

30 Enderby Road. Mr Robinson and Mr Hoffman both went to 30 Enderby Road from
8 Frederick Street. Mr Roy Brown was at the premises already. Entry was effected at
about 5.15 pm. The search of the premises took about an hour and a quarter, after which
Mr Hoffman and Mr Robinson returned to 8 Frederick Street.

In Mr Robinson's bedroom a number of U-matic tapes were found. These included U-
matic tapes of 'Futureworld', 'Slaughter' and 'Carquake', to which I have already made
reference. These particular tapes were found in a cupboard among some clothes. There
were at Enderby Road a large number of U-matic tapes besides those I have mentioned.
They related to titles the copyright in which was not vested in any of the plaintiffs. There
were a number of ordinary cassettes as well and a large quantity of artwork and labels
relating to a number of different titles. The artwork included, in particular, 'Films of the
80's' artwork and 'Fifty of the World's Best Movies' artwork. It included also a quantity
of labels, some purporting to be Mills Video labels and relating to 'Slaughter', some
purporting to be Video Universal labels and relating to 'Carquake'. The artwork and
labels relating to 'Futureworld' included the 'Films of the 80's' style, 'Fifty of the World's
Best Movies' style and Mills Video style.

An address book was found and taken. This address book was subsequently lost. It was
alleged by Mr Roy Brown that it had been surreptitiously taken back by Mr Robinson
when no one was looking. There is not a scrap of evidence for this allegation. It is
attributable to the attitude to Mr Robinson shown, I am satisfied, by all the members of
Hamlins, namely that they were dealing with a cunning rogue.

A receipt on the lines which I have already described was prepared for signature by Mr
Robinson. It read thus:

'A. E. Hamlin & Co. hereby acknowledges receipt of the following found at 30
Enderby Road, Luton, the house of Christopher Robinson pursuant to an Anton
Piller order and by consent.'

I have already referred to the U-matic master tapes that were taken. In addition, the
receipt records with particularity the other tapes that were taken. There were 58. The
receipt specifies the address book but does not descend to much detail so far as the rest of
the documents taken are concerned. There is, for example, a referent to 'Bundle of
correspondence and papers' and 'Box of assorted title cards'.

This receipt, too, was signed by Mr Robinson. Here, too, I am satisfied that he did not
enter into any agreement or give any consent to the removal of material not covered by
the Anton Piller order save to the extent that such consent was signified by the fact of his
signing the receipt.

The various articles and documents set aside for removal from the Mill Street shop, 8
Frederick Street and 30 Enderby Road respectively were put into boxes, loaded into cars
and taken to the offices of Hamlins.

It is appropriate that I should now express my findings on the factual issues between
the parties which arise out of the execution of the Anton Piller order.

1. If there is still an issue whether or not an excessive number of people attended at
any of the three sets of premises for the purpose of executing the order, I must deal with
it. There was no evidence that more than five representatives of the plaintiffs were at any
one time to be found at any one of the three sets of premises.

2. Mr Robinson has alleged that Hamlins, and Mr Hoffman in particular, failed to
explain to him the terms of the order. Mr Hoffman said that he offered the order to Mr
Robinson for him to read but that Mr Robinson was not interested in reading it or in
receiving any explanation about it. This evidence rings true. Mr Robinson does not lack
at all for self-confidence. It is clear to me that he had heard of Anton Piller orders before.
He knew they gave the executing parties the right to search premises. I can well believe
that he exuded an air of confident unconcern when faced with the Anton Piller order
and waved aside suggestions that he should sit down and read the order.

3. I do not accept the evidence of Mr Robinson that his diaries were taken from 8
Frederick Street. I have no doubt but that Hamlins would have been very pleased to have
found his diaries. If they had found them they would certainly have taken them. The

documents taken from 8 Frederick Street were reasonably well particularised in the receipt. It is improbable that, if the diaries had been taken, they would not have been listed.

4. Nor do I accept the evidence of Mr Robinson and Mr Wickenden that such personal papers as divorce papers and educational certificates were taken. Mr Hoffman's evidence on this point was clear and forthright. It was supplemented by that of other members of the firm. Mr Robinson's affidavits and letters from his solicitors sworn or written, as the case may be, after the raid do not complain about the taking of these plainly irrelevant personal papers. There were respects in which I found the evidence of Mr Hoffman, Mr Roy Brown and Mr Cumberland less than satisfactory. But I will say here and now that I did not regard Mr Robinson as a witness on whose uncorroborated evidence I could safely rely and I regard Mr Wickenden, as will later appear, as little more than Mr Robinson's stalking horse. In the circumstances, I am not prepared to disbelieve Mr Hoffman, Mr Roy Brown and Mr Cumberland's sworn denial that the personal papers in question were taken.

5. I have already said, and I repeat, that there is no evidence that Mr Robinson was responsible for the loss of the address book which Hamlins admit, by the 30 Enderby Road receipt, to have taken.

6. I have also already made clear that there was, in my judgment, no agreement reached between Mr Hoffman and Mr Robinson (save for whatever agreement may be said to be constituted by the receipts themselves) whereby Mr Robinson consented to the removal of material not covered by the Anton Piller order.

7. There is one final issue of fact with which I should deal. Mr Robinson and the company had bank accounts with Barclays Bank, Leighton Buzzard. In the course of the execution of the Anton Piller order, Mr Hoffman became aware of this. The manager of the branch, Mr Ross, gave evidence that on 21 June 1982 he received a telephone call from Mr Baker of Hamlins. Mr Baker informed him that a Mareva injunction had been made against Mr Robinson and against the company freezing their respective accounts. Mr Ross said that he was not told that Mr Robinson was allowed to draw up to £200. He did not realise that was allowed until he received a letter from Hamlins dated 22 June 1982 enclosing a copy of the order. There was thus a careless misrepresentation of the effect of the order made by Mr Baker to Barclays Bank.

Mr Robinson had, also, an account with Lloyds Bank, 60 George Street, Luton. Mr Hoffman telephoned Lloyds Bank from 8 Frederick Street, on 21 June 1982 and informed the bank that the company's and Mr Robinson's accounts had been frozen by a Mareva injunction. There is a fairly full record in Mr Burnhill's attendance note of what Mr Hoffman told the bank. On 22 June Hamlins sent Lloyds Bank a copy of the order. On 25 June Lloyds Bank wrote to Hamlins complaining that the bank had not been told on the telephone that Mr Robinson was permitted to draw up to £200 but had been told that a total freeze on the accounts had been imposed. The letter contained this sentence: 'I am most concerned as to the misrepresentation of the terms of the order.' That complaint was never, notwithstanding its serious nature, answered by Hamlins.

Mr Hoffman said that he clearly recalled telling Lloyds Bank about the £200 drawing allowance. I am sure that is what he would have wished to have said but I was not in the least convinced that he could actually remember doing so. There is no mention in Mr Burnhill's contemporaneous note that the £200 was mentioned. Lloyds Bank's letter of 25 June asserts that it was not mentioned and the absence of any reply to that assertion gives it credibility.

I am satisfied that Mr Hoffman carelessly misrepresented to Lloyds Bank the terms of the Mareva injunction.

(iv) *The events that followed the execution of the Anton Piller order*

There are a number of relevant events which I must mention. It is, I think, more convenient to deal with them under separate headings than to attempt a chronological review.

(a) *The tapes and documents taken under the order*

a   I have already mentioned the number of tapes taken from the Mill Street shop, 8 Frederick Street and 30 Enderby Road respectively. In total, about 300 tapes were taken. In addition, about 26 library boxes were taken. And the documents taken included Mr Gordon's private documents and a number of Mr Robinson's private documents taken for the purpose of further investigation.

On 4 October 1982 the defendants then solicitors, Tearle & Co, wrote to Hamlins. The
b   second paragraph said:

'The defendants' documents, papers and other items have been seized by yourselves under the Anton Piller order. This does not entitle you to keep these items belonging to the defendants indefinitely. We must require all original documents to be returned on or before 7th October 1982.'

c   Hamlins's letter in reply dated 7 October 1982 said:

'We take the view that under the terms of the order our clients are permitted to retain all documents seized from your client until trial of the action or further order.'

This answer may have been in accordance with the letter of the order. It is, however,
d   difficult to reconcile with the purpose of the order, namely to safeguard the plaintiffs against the improper destruction of evidence.

On 25 November 1982 Tearle & Co, accompanied by Mr Robinson, attended at Hamlins' office. All tapes and other seized material were produced for their inspection. They took photocopies of some of the documents. On 8 October 1982 the then plaintiffs served a statement of claim. In it, allegations of breach of copyright by the defendants in
e   respect of some 110 films were made. There were a large number of films, tapes of which had been seized on 21 June 1982 but which were not mentioned in the statement of claim.

By notice of motion dated 5 January 1983 the defendants applied, inter alia, for the return by the plaintiffs of the 29 blank tapes and the two video recorders which had been taken from the Mill Street shop and for the return of some 20 specified tapes. Mr
f   Robinson swore an affidavit in support on 22 December 1982. In para 3 he asked for the return of all tapes seized in respect of which the plaintiffs did not claim to be the copyright owners of the films recorded thereon.

Mr Roy Brown swore an affidavit on 12 January 1983. He sought to justify the seizure of the 29 blank tapes on the grounds that they 'were intended to be used for making illicit goods'. The blank tapes, it will be recalled, were found not at the 8 Frederick Street
g   factory but at the Mill Street shop. They formed a normal part of the legitimate stock that any shop selling video cassettes would be expected to carry. Mr Brown's explanation was, however, echoed by Mr Hoffman in cross-examination. Mr Brown's affidavit resisted delivery of the two video recorders on the grounds that they, too, were intended to be used in the making of illicit goods.

As to some of the tapes, return of which was sought, Mr Brown's affidavit resisted
h   return on the grounds that those entitled to the copyright, although not the plaintiffs, would be applying to be joined as plaintiffs. 'Absolution', 'The Beyond' and 'World War III' fell into this category.

By an order made on 12 January 1983 Warner J ordered the return to the defendants of the 29 blank tapes and the tapes of nine specified films. These tapes, or some of them, were returned on the same day, 12 January 1983.

j   No further returns were made until 29 April 1985. I do not understand why Hamlins did not at the first opportunity return to the defendants all the tapes in respect of which neither copyright nor an exclusive licence could be claimed by any of the plaintiffs. Mr Robinson had asked for the return of those tapes in his affidavit of 22 December 1982. The retention of these tapes by Hamlins was not capable of being justified under the terms of Goulding J's order. Their seizure in the first place was a trespass.

On 29 April 1985 Hamlins returned to the defendants 154 tapes of films in respect of which copyright was not claimed by any plaintiff. In addition, a quantity of artwork and labels relating to these films was returned. The films included two in respect of which the order of 12 January 1983 had ordered all tapes to be returned and two in respect of which Mr Roy Brown had in his affidavit of 12 January 1983 denied 'that any' tapes were held.

On 3 July 1985, nearly a month after the trial had begun, Hamlins returned Mr Gordon's private documents which had been taken from the Mill Street shop. No suggestion was made that any of these documents were relevant to any of the 'illicit goods' referred to in the order. When it was that Hamlins became aware that these documents ought not to have been taken and ought not to be retained was not made clear by the evidence.

I have dealt with the tapes and material that were returned by Hamlins. There were some 163 tapes which remained in the action. In respect of these, one or other of the plaintiffs claims copyright or an exclusive licence. In addition, a large quantity of artwork and labels relating to films in respect of which copyright or exclusive licence is claimed by one or other of the plaintiffs was in evidence in the action. And a volume of correspondence, records and sundry other documents seized on 21 June 1982 was in evidence.

But unfortunately some of the material that was seized was neither returned nor in evidence in the action. It was lost by Hamlins while in their custody. It is known from comparison of the contents of the receipts of what was taken with the details of what was returned and what was still held that 17 tapes and one cassette box have been lost. It is not known what, if any, documents have been lost. The reason for this is that the receipts were insufficiently detailed to enable a proper check to be made.

The failure on the part of Hamlins to keep safe the material taken on 21 June 1982 represents a breach of one of their undertakings given to Goulding J. Mr Hoffman was entirely candid about this regrettable failure on the part of his firm. He, as senior partner, very properly accepted responsibility. It should never have been allowed to happen and I am sure that steps have been taken by Hamlins to ensure that it does not happen again.

I will deal later with the consequences of this failure for the purposes of this litigation.

(b) The Mill Street shop

Before the raid on 21 June 1982 there were, it has been estimated, 600 to 700 tapes in stock at the Mill Street shop. About 220 were taken. Some 400-odd were, it seems, left at the shop. None the less, the shop did not reopen after 21 June 1982. Mr Donnelly was no longer interested in acquiring the business and negotiations with him fell through. The lease under which the premises were held expired and was not renewed. The stock of tapes was disposed of. There was no clear evidence as to the date of the disposal or the sum realised.

The number of tapes left at the Mill Street shop after 21 June 1982 would have been sufficient for the business to have continued; but all the records of the business were taken by Hamlins on 21 June 1982. In the circumstances it is not at all surprising that the business was not restarted.

(c) The business at 8 Frederick Street

Mr Robinson had a large number of U-matic master tapes at 8 Frederick Street and 30 Enderby Road. Of these, only those relating to 'Futureworld', 'Slaughter' and 'Carquake/Cannonball' were taken on 21 June. 'Carquake/Cannonball' was not a film in which one of the plaintiffs claimed copyright or exclusive licence. The U-matic master tapes relating to 'Carquake/Cannonball' were returned to the defendants on 29 April 1985.

So the defendants retained, after 21 June 1982, the bulk of the master tapes which had been used prior to that date for the purpose of making copies. None the less, on Mr Robinson's evidence, the business closed down. He lost its substantial capital value and the benefit of the income it had previously been producing for him.

The effect of the service of a copy of the order of 18 June 1982 on the defendants' a bankers was that, not unnaturally, they declined to extend any further credit to either of them. Prior to the order the company was £32,500-odd overdrawn on its account with Barclays Bank. This was within the overdraft limit allowed by the bank. In addition, the company owed the bank £10,475 on a loan account. After becoming aware, by reason of service of the order of 18 June 1982, of the claims being made against the defendants, the bank did not allow any further credit to them. The loan account was merged with the overdrawn current account.

b   In the absence of any credit facilities, Mr Robinson told me that he was unable to continue in business. The Mareva injunction that had been imposed on 18 June 1982 was lifted very soon thereafter. The reason for the credit restriction imposed by the bank was not any order of the court, but was the nature of the allegations being made against the defendants by the plaintiffs.

     In addition, Mr Robinson told me, his contract with Centre Video Ltd was terminated
c by Centre Video Ltd immediately on their becoming aware of proceedings being taken against him. His evidence was that by reason of the execution of the ex parte order and the aftermath thereof he had to close down his copying business. This evidence was challenged by the plaintiffs. The challenge was based on the contents of a number of documents produced by the company, Heritable Leasing Ltd, from whom Mr Robinson held his bank of video recorders on hire-purchase terms, on the contents of a number of
d documents produced by the liquidator of Centre Video Ltd and on the evidence of a Mr Boardman, an employee of Heritable Leasing at the relevant time.

     The Heritable Leasing documents appear to show that in February 1983 Mr Robinson entered into negotiations with Heritable Leasing to discharge his outstanding indebtedness of some £7,950·32 in respect of the video recorders. An agreement was reached, documented in a letter of 9 March 1983 signed by Mr Robinson, to pay off the
e indebtedness by postdated cheques over a period of six months.

     In the event seven postdated cheques of £1,000 each and one postdated cheque of £950·32 were drawn by Mr Wickenden, purporting to be trading as 'Adult Videos', and were accepted by Heritable Leasing in discharge of the defendants' indebtedness.

     Mr Boardman negotiated these arrangements with Mr Robinson. He did not deal with Mr Wickenden. In the event the cheques, or some of them, were returned to Heritable
f Leasing marked 'Refer to drawer'. Mr Boardman discussed the matter with Mr Robinson, who told him that the payments would be made if title to the machines were transferred to Mr Wickenden. There the matter rested. The payments were not made; the machines were not repossessed by Heritable Leasing. Late in 1983 several of the machines were, I was told by Mr Wickenden, damaged by water from burst pipes. He said he took them to a rubbish tip at Luton. Of those that survived the flood, five are, he said, still at 8
g Frederick Street. One is at Mr Wickenden's home.

     Mr Robinson and Mr Wickenden's evidence was that after 21 June 1982 Mr Robinson discontinued his business and Mr Wickenden commenced a separate business of his own. Mr Wickenden's business consisted of reproducing, on Mr Robinson's bank of machines, copies of video tapes with a sexual content. This business was carried on under the style 'Adult Videos'. The tapes were euphemistically described by Mr Wickenden as 'adult
h films'. An accurate and commonly used description would have been 'soft porn'. The video tapes were sold to Centre Video Ltd. This business was continued until the summer of 1983 when Centre Video Ltd went into liquidation. No doubt this liquidation was the reason why the later of Mr Wickenden's postdated cheques bounced.

     Mr Wickenden told me that Mr Robinson had no financial benefit whatsoever from the 'Adult Videos' business. This was untrue. The records of 'Adult Videos' show
j substantial payments, in excess of £5,000, made by Mr Wickenden to Mr Robinson out of the proceeds of the 'Adult Videos' business. These payments were described by Mr Robinson and Mr Wickenden as loans. I do not accept that description of the payments. The evidence shows that the arrangements for the carrying on of the 'Adult Videos' business were made by Mr Robinson. It was he who dealt with Heritable Leasing. It was he who dealt with Centre Video Ltd. It was he who arranged for U-matic master tapes to be available from which the copies might be made. It was he, not Mr Wickenden, who

was the expert technician and master producer of tapes. It was he who received substantial capital sums from the proceeds of the business.

The evidence of Mr Robinson and Mr Wickenden that the 'Adult Videos' business was Mr Wickenden's business in which Mr Robinson had no interest was, in my judgment, palpably untrue. I have no doubt but that the new business was Mr Robinson's idea. His intention was to save what he could from the wreck of his business caused by the ex parte order. He intended to continue to carry on the sleazy side of his video tape copying business using Mr Wickenden as a front. He continued to do so until the collapse of Centre Video Ltd destroyed his market. The falsity of his evidence was designed to improve his case that the plaintiffs destroyed his business by their improper use of Anton Piller procedure.

(d) *The effect of the Anton Piller order*

From the plaintiffs' point of view, the Anton Piller order achieved success. The defendants' business, which they regarded as flagrant piracy, closed down. It is the defendants' contention that the plaintiffs' object in obtaining the order and executing it was to destroy the business. I find little difficulty in accepting that that was, at least in part, the plaintiffs' motive.

On 26 July 1982 Linda Davies, whom I have already mentioned, a solicitor employed by Guild Home Video Ltd, one of the plaintiffs, wrote to Filmways Pictures Inc, a co-plaintiff, in these terms:

'I write to give you a brief outline of the results of our action against a pirate in the U.K., one Chris Robinson, who also operates under the name Luton Video Centre and Mills Video. We obtained an ex parte interlocutory court order against him and his companies and executed dawn raids, as a result of which we found he had been pirating Future World, along with many other film companies' products. As a result of the court action, his business has been destroyed and he and his businesses have been declared bankrupt. We have obviously confiscated his video master of the film Future World. We were unable to obtain any damages as neither he nor his companies had any substantial assets.'

Mr Cumberland was strongly pressed in cross-examination by counsel for the defendants to accept that the intention behind the Anton Piller order was to destroy Mr Robinson's business. This exchange took place between himself and counsel for the defendants:

'Q. The object of the plaintiffs is perhaps partly to gain damages for any wrongs that have been done them . . . but partly also, I suggest, to close down the piratical business. A. Certainly close down the piratical business, yes.

Q. So their second purpose can even be achieved without a trial, merely as a consequence perhaps of the service and enforcement of the orders themselves, can it not? A. I am sorry; I fail to see the point you are making.

Q. The mere service and execution of these orders themselves can close down many businesses, can it not? A. You mean, close down totally?

Q. Yes. A. If the business is totally illicit, yes. If it is part-illicit, part-genuine, no.

Q. You say the genuine part might still survive? A. Of course.'

(4) *The issues in the plaintiffs' action*

Copyright

[His Lordship then considered the evidence in relation to the claim in copyright and continued:]

Purchase of pirate tapes is not an infringement of copyright. Nor is possession of pirate tapes. The plaintiffs' case of breach of copyright is, first, that Mr Robinson made pirate tapes at his 8 Frederick Street factory and, second, that he sold or hired out pirate tapes from the Mill Street shop.

[His Lordship considered the evidence and continued:]

The plaintiffs' case that the sale or hire of tapes from the Mill Street shop constituted a

a breach of copyright is based on of s 16(3) of the Copyright Act 1956. Under that subsection, any person who sells or lets for hire a prerecorded video cassette infringes copyright 'if to his knowledge the making of the article constituted an infringement of that copyright'. Without that requisite knowledge the sale or letting out for hire of a video cassette is not a breach of copyright. The question, therefore, is whether Mr Robinson had knowledge that the tapes being sold or let on hire at the Mill Street shop

b were pirate tapes.

There is some useful judicial authority on the meaning of 'knowledge' for the purposes of sub-s (3).

In *Infabrics Ltd v Jaytex Shirt Co Ltd* [1978] FSR 451 at 464 Whitford J cited with approval a dictum from the judgment of Harvey J in an Australian case, *Albert v S Hoffnung & Co Ltd* (1921) 22 SR (NSW) 75 at 81. Harvey J said:

c   '"Knowledge" in the section cannot mean in my opinion any more than notice of facts such as would suggest to a reasonable man that a breach of the copyright was being committed . . . In my opinion, knowledge means notice, which would put a reasonable man on inquiry.'

In another Australian case, *RCA Corp v Custom Cleared Sales Pty Ltd* [1978] FSR 576, it

d was held by the New South Wales Court of Appeal that the requisite knowledge was actual knowledge and that constructive knowledge was not sufficient.

I accept that actual knowledge is necessary but subject to this proviso. In this area of jurisprudence, as in many others, a person who deliberately refrains from inquiry and shuts his eyes to that which is obvious cannot be heard to say that he lacked the requisite knowledge.

e   Counsel for the defendants has submitted that Mr Robinson had no actual knowledge that the tapes in question were pirate tapes. He submitted that, while Mr Gordon's knowledge might be attributed to the company, it could not be attributed to Mr Robinson and that, in any event, Mr Gordon lacked the technical expertise to test whether or not a particular tape was a pirate tape.

Counsel for the plaintiffs, on the other hand, emphasised Mr Robinson's expertise in

f the technical complexities of video tape reproduction and his undoubted deep knowledge of and acquaintance with the video piracy business. He drew my attention, in particular, to the contents of a number of memoranda made by a Mr Higginson, an employee of Twentieth Century-Fox, of telephone conversations he had with Mr Robinson in July, August and September 1981. I found Mr Higginson a reliable witness and accept his memoranda as accurate records of what was said to him by Mr Robinson. The memoranda

g certainly establish that Mr Robinson had an intimate knowledge of the video piracy business.

I have already referred in this judgment to Mr Robinson's acceptance of the suggestion that in 1981 some 80% of the video tapes in circulation were pirate tapes.

In these circumstances, I conclude that Mr Robinson knew throughout the period that he and the company were proprietors of the Mill Street shop that a large proportion of

h the stock must be pirate tapes. I do not accept that he ever made or caused to be made any check of the tapes with a view to weeding out those that were pirates. Any checks that were made had as their purpose the weeding out of those of poor quality.

If a check had been made by Mr Robinson in order to identify those tapes that were pirates he would, in my view, by reason of his professional expertise, have had a good degree of success. I do not doubt that there would have been some pirates that he would

j not have identified but he would, I think, have identified most of them.

The question for decision is whether this general knowledge on Mr Robinson's part, coupled with his ability to have made a reasonably successful check, coupled with his unconcern whether or not the shop was selling or hiring pirate tapes, is sufficient to fix him with the requisite knowledge for the purposes of s 16(3). In my judgment, it is not.

The subsection is contemplating a specific knowledge about the circumstances in which a specific article was made. A general knowledge of the sort which Mr Robinson possessed is consistent with a specific video tape being a pirate tape. It is also consistent with a specific tape being legitimate. Unless a defendant has some degree of specific knowledge about a specific tape, his general knowledge that a tape is quite likely to be a pirate does not, in my judgment, fix him with knowledge, sufficient for the purposes of s 16(3), that the tape was made in breach of copyright. A person who sells or lets on hire video tapes does not, in my judgment, have to undertake the task of checking his stock in order to protect himself from liability under s 16(3).

There were, however, some tapes in respect of which Mr Robinson *did* have some specific knowledge.

[His Lordship then considered the evidence relating to Mr Robinson's specific knowledge and continued:]

In summary, the plaintiffs' case of infringement of copyright by reproduction is, in my judgment, made good in respect of 'Futureworld', 'Slaughter', 'Day of the Dolphin', 'Russian Roulette', 'A Small Town in Texas' and 'Puppet on a Chain'. In relation to all these films I infer that the copies contained in the Mill Street stock were made at 8 Frederick Street. The plaintiffs' case is also made good in respect of the tape of 'Sleeping Beauty'.

Counsel for the plaintiffs invited me to find specifically that Mr Robinson had made copies of 'Star Wars'. There is, in my view, no satisfactory evidence of this. Counsel also invited me to infer that all tapes found at 8 Frederick Street and at 30 Enderby Road had been made on the 8 Frederick Street machines. There is, in my view, no sound basis on which I could draw that inference and, indeed, I think it unlikely that this was so. True it is that Mr Robinson had the means to copy any tape he wished. I think also that if he had wanted to copy a particular tape considerations of copyright would not have deterred him. But a person with his interest in the video trade would be likely to have a collection of tapes acquired from a variety of sources.

Remedy

(i) The main remedy sought by the plaintiffs is that of injunction. They are, in my judgment, entitled to an injunction. I am satisfied from the evidence I have seen and heard that Mr Robinson was a skilled and professional copier of video tapes. I am not satisfied that he had any real belief in the validity of the licences relating to 'Futureworld' and 'Russian Roulette' that he had obtained from Benelux Video and Mr Kooring.

I am satisfied that the Mills Video labels and the 'Films of the 80's' style were adopted by Mr Robinson to enable him, as he hoped, to continue to reproduce and sell copies of films in respect of which he was unable to do so openly under his own trading style. I think he is a highly intelligent but devious man who would not scruple to breach copyright if he thought it commercially worth while. In the circumstances, I have no doubt but that the plaintiffs have established in this case that they are entitled to the protection of an injunction.

Counsel, however, has sought on the plaintiffs' behalf an injunction of a very great breadth. He has sought an injunction restraining the defendants from knowingly infringing copyright in any film for the time belonging to any of the plaintiffs (meaning any member of the MPAA besides the named plaintiffs) or in respect of which any of them is for the time being the exclusive licensee.

It would be impossible for the defendants to know what films were covered by an injunction in that form. In my judgment it would be wrong in principle to grant an injunction the scope of which the defendants subject to it could not know and could not discover. Experience in this litigation has underlined the very great difficulty that is often experienced in ascertaining in whom copyright or exclusive rights in a particular film are for the time being vested.

I am prepared to grant an injunction protecting the copyright or exclusive rights of any of the present plaintiffs in the films in respect of which their respective titles have been established in this action. I am not prepared to extend this protection to companies who are not plaintiffs, that is to say to future MPAA members. Nor am I prepared to extend this protection to cover other films. I am, however, willing to give the present

plaintiffs or any of them liberty to apply from time to time on notice to the defendants
a to extend the injunction to other films. In order to obtain that extension, I contemplate
that the applicant would have to satisfy the court, first, that it had copyright or exclusive
rights in the film or films in question and, second, either that it had applied to the
defendants for suitable undertakings which had not been given, or that for some reason
undertakings by the defendants would not be sufficient. The costs of any such application
would of course depend on the circumstances of that application.

b The procedure I have suggested will, I hope, ensure that the plaintiffs will obtain
proper protection whilst the defendants will not be subjected to injunctions the scope of
which they cannot possibly discover.

(ii) The plaintiffs are also entitled to damages for infringement of copyright. I have
already said that I have no material before me from which I can form any estimate of the
likely number of tapes reproduced in breach of copyright by the defendants. This is
c particularly important so far as 'Futureworld' is concerned since, as I understand it, the
plaintiffs take the view that the defendants' tapes flooded the market and prevented a
profitable legitimate release of the film in video format.

In the circumstances, I direct that there be an inquiry as to damages caused by the
infringements of copyright that I have found proved.

I should, perhaps, record that a defence under s 18(2) of the Copyright Act 1956 to a
d claim for conversion damages is not, in my judgment, open to the defendants.

The plaintiffs' entitlement to damages is not a joint right. The plaintiffs have properly
combined as parties in this action but for the purposes of an inquiry as to damages the
entitlement of each plaintiff will have to be separately considered. Many of them, perhaps
most of them, will not be entitled to damages at all.

e *Passing-off and trade mark infringement*
The parties' respective counsel have agreed on the cassettes in respect of which
infringement of trade mark by the defendants has been committed. The plaintiffs whose
registered trade marks have been infringed are entitled to an injunction to restrain future
infringement. They are also entitled to an inquiry as to damages caused by the
infringements.

f The instances of passing-off, too, have, subject to the dispute as to two instances with
which I have already dealt, also been agreed. Here too, the successful plaintiffs are, in my
judgment, entitled to an injunction and an inquiry as to damages.

As with infringement of copyright, the right to damages for trade mark infringement
and the right to damages for passing-off is not a joint right. The inquiry must establish
the damage to the plaintiff whose trade mark has been infringed or whose get-up has
g been copied. Damages for copyright infringement, trade mark infringement and passing-
off must not be cumulative. The extent of the damage done to a particular plaintiff by
the tortious reproduction of a video cassette and the marketing of that cassette will not
be increased by the number of torts committed in the process.

(5) *The Anton Piller order*
h This is in many ways the most important part of this case. The damage done by the
defendants to the plaintiffs' intellectual property rights are, of course, very important to
the plaintiffs and I hope I have dealt with them accordingly. But the defendants'
complaints regarding the manner in which the Anton Piller order was obtained and
executed raise questions of general importance concerning the administration of justice.

In view of the general importance of the issues raised by the defendants' complaints, I
j allowed the defendants to adduce similar fact evidence of the manner in which Hamlins
executed an Anton Piller order against another alleged dealer in pirate tapes, a Mr Dale.
The evidence disclosed much the same pattern as was disclosed by the evidence in the
present case.

Before I come to deal with the specific complaints made by the defendants in this case,
I should, I think, review the state of the law and practice relating to Anton Piller orders.

The grant of Anton Piller orders dates from 1974. The first reported case was one in which an order was made by Templeman J in *EMI Ltd v Pandit* [1975] 1 All ER 418, [1975] 1 WLR 302. The practice received the imprimatur of the Court of Appeal in the case which has given its name to the orders, *Anton Piller KG v Manufacturing Processes Ltd* [1976] 1 All ER 779 at 782–783, [1976] Ch 55 at 60. In that case the rationale of Anton Piller orders was described by Lord Denning MR in these words:

'Let me say at once that no court in this land has any power to issue a search warrant to enter a man's house so as to see if there are papers or documents there which are of an incriminating nature, whether libels or infringements of copyright or anything else of the kind. No constable or bailiff can knock at the door and demand entry so as to inspect papers or documents. The householder can shut the door in his face and say, "Get out". That was established in the leading case of *Entick v Carrington* (1765) 2 Wils 275, [1558–1774] All ER Rep 41. None of us would wish to whittle down that principle in the slightest. But the order sought in this case is not a search warrant. It does not authorise the plaintiffs' solicitors or anyone else to enter the defendants' premises against their will. It does not authorise the breaking down of any doors, nor the slipping in by a back door, nor getting in by an open door or window. It only authorises entry and inspection by the permission of the defendants. The plaintiffs must get the defendants' permission. But it does do this: it brings pressure on the defendants to give permission. It does more. It actually orders them to give permission—with, I suppose, the result that if they do not give permission, they are guilty of contempt of court. This may seem to be a search warrant in disguise. But it was fully considered in the House of Lords 150 years ago in *East India Co v Kynaston* (1821) 3 Bli 153, 4 ER 561 and held to be legitimate.'

Lord Denning MR then went on to consider the circumstances in which an Anton Piller order could properly be made. He said ([1976] 1 All ER 779 at 783, [1976] Ch 55 at 61):

'It seems to me that such an order can be made by a judge ex parte, but it should only be made where it is essential that the plaintiff should have inspection so that justice can be done between the parties; and when, if the defendant were forewarned, there is a grave danger that vital evidence will be destroyed, that papers will be burnt or lost or hidden, or taken beyond the jurisdiction, and so the ends of justice be defeated; and when the inspection would do no real harm to the defendant or his case ... We are prepared, therefore, to sanction its continuance, but only in an extreme case where there is grave danger of property being smuggled away or of vital evidence being destroyed.'

Ormrod LJ said ([1976] 1 All ER 779 at 784, [1976] Ch 55 at 62):

'There are three essential preconditions for the making of such an order, in my judgment. First, there must be an extremely strong prima facie case. Secondly, the damage, potential or actual, must be very serious for the plaintiff. Thirdly, there must be clear evidence that the defendants have in their possession incriminating documents or things and that there is a real possibility that they may destroy such material before any application inter partes can be made.'

Finally, Shaw LJ said ([1976] 1 All ER 779 at 784, [1976] Ch 55 at 62):

'The overriding consideration in the exercise of this salutary jurisdiction is that it is to be resorted to only in circumstances where the normal processes of the law would be rendered nugatory if some immediate and effective measure was not available. And, when such an order is made, the party who has procured the court to make it must act with prudence and caution in pursuance of it.'

The practice of granting Anton Piller orders was considered obliquely by the House of Lords in *Rank Film Distributors Ltd v Video Information Centre* [1981] 2 All ER 76, [1982] AC 380. It was approved in principle. Lord Fraser said ([1981] 2 All ER 76 at 82–83, [1982] AC 380 at 444):

a

'The first four respondents are alleged to be dealers in pirated copies of many of these films, and the fifth and sixth respondents are alleged to be makers of pirate copies. The appellants are naturally concerned to protect their valuable copyright in these films. Ordinary actions against dealers in illicit films are of little avail to the copyright owners because the dealers are unlikely to be able to pay substantial damages and injunctions against them merely close down one outlet for the films and do not prevent the manufacture of more unauthorised copies which can then

b

be sold through other outlets. The main concern of the appellants is, therefore, to trace the whereabouts of the master tapes in order to take action against those who control them. For this purpose a form of order has been devised which is generally referred to as an Anton Piller order, from the case of *Anton Piller KG v Manufacturing Processes Ltd*. These orders are only made when the plaintiff produces strong prima facie evidence of infringement of his copyright. They are made on the ex parte

c

application of the plaintiff, are served on the defendants without previous notice and order the defendants to make immediate discovery of documents and to give immediate answers to interrogatories designed to find out particularly the names and addresses of their suppliers.'

There is, accordingly, no doubt at all but that Anton Piller orders have become established as part of the tools of the administration of justice in civil cases. It may be

d

thought, as, I think, Lord Denning MR thought, that they play a part not unlike that played by search warrants in the area of crime and suspected crime. But the legitimate purposes of Anton Piller orders are clearly identified by the leading cases which have established the legitimacy of their use. One, and perhaps the most usual purpose, is to preserve evidence necessary for the plaintiffs' case. Anton Piller orders are used to prevent a defendant, when warned of impending litigation, from destroying all documentary

e

evidence in his possession which might, were it available, support the plaintiffs' cause of action. Secondly, Anton Piller orders are often used in order to track to its source and obtain the possession of the master tape or master plate or blueprint by means of which reproductions in breach of copyright are being made. This purpose is, perhaps, no more than a subdivision of the first.

It is implicit in the nature of Anton Piller orders that they should be applied for ex

f

parte and dealt with by the courts in secrecy. In the Queen's Bench Division applications for Anton Piller orders are heard in chambers. Secrecy is ensured. In this division applications are heard in court but it is customary for the court to sit in camera. Otherwise there is a risk that the defendant may become aware of the litigation and the whole purpose of the Anton Piller procedure will be frustrated.

Anton Piller orders and procedure have, therefore, these characteristics: no notice to

g

the defendant of what is afoot, and secrecy. A third and, perhaps, the most significant feature of Anton Piller orders is that they are mandatory in form and are designed for immediate execution. The respondent to the order is required by the order to permit his premises to be entered and searched and, under most if not all orders, to permit the plaintiffs' solicitors to remove into the solicitors' custody articles covered by the order.

Further, Anton Piller orders are almost invariably accompanied by Mareva injunctions

h

freezing the bank accounts of the respondents and restraining them from making any disposition of their assets. Anton Piller orders and Mareva injunctions granted ex parte always reserve liberty for the respondent to apply on short notice for them to be discharged. This provides a reasonable safeguard in the case of Mareva injunctions. They can be lifted on very short notice. Harm may already have been done but can be expected to be of a limited nature. But, in relation to any Anton Piller order, the liberty to apply

j

to have it discharged is of little, if any, value to the respondent. He does not know the order has been made until it has been served on him. At the same time as the order is served, the respondent comes under an immediate obligation to consent to the entry onto and search of his premises and the removal of material from his premises specified by the order. If he does not consent, he is at risk of committal to prison for contempt of court. This is so even if the reason for his refusal to consent is his intention to apply to have the order discharged.

The peril in which respondents to Anton Piller orders are placed is exemplified by *Wardle Fabrics Ltd v G Myristis Ltd* [1984] FSR 263. There the plaintiff had obtained an *a* Anton Piller order. The defendant by its managing director refused consent to the entry onto its premises that the order required and applied for the order to be discharged on the ground that all material facts had not been disclosed to the court by the plaintiffs when applying for the order. The plaintiffs applied to punish the defendant and its managing director for contempt in failing to obey the Anton Piller order.

Goulding J, on the defendants' application, found the allegations of inadequate *b* disclosure made out and discharged the Anton Piller order. On the plaintiffs' application for contempt, Goulding J found the contempt proved and, after contemplating fining the defendants, dealt with the contempt by requiring the defendants to pay the plaintiffs' costs of the contempt application on an indemnity basis. The judge said (at 271):

> 'What is the position in those circumstances? In the absence of authority, and if I were free to look at the matter from first principles, I would have thought that if *c* the court makes an order within its jurisdiction, by which I mean in such circumstances that the purported order is not a nullity in law, then a party is bound to obey it at his risk of contempt proceedings if he does not, and that the subsequent discharge of the order as having been irregularly obtained would not in logic and principle affect the disobedient party's liability to penalties for contempt. It seems to me the system of administering justice would break down if the subjects were *d* entitled to apply their own or their advisers' ideas to the possibilities of subsequently setting aside an order and to disobey on the strength of such private judgment and then, if the judgment turned out not to have been right, be free from all penalty.'

The judge's reasoning is, if I may respectfully say so, difficult to fault. Moreover, if respondents to Anton Piller orders were to be allowed to delay their execution while *e* applications to apply to discharge were being made, the purpose of Anton Piller orders and procedure would be largely lost. Ample time would then be available to those disposed to destroy evidence or to secrete away master tapes to do so.

But notice the position that Anton Piller procedure and its logical consequences produce. A mandatory order is made in the absence of the respondent and in secret. It is served on and executed against the respondent without his having any chance to challenge *f* the correctness of its grant or to challenge the evidence on which it was granted.

Now let the possible and, perhaps, probable effects of an Anton Piller order be considered. The order is served and executed. If the order is in the terms of the order in the present case and is executed as it was in the present case, there will be a wholesale removal of all business material, whether stock-in-trade, bank statements, cheque books or correspondence. The continuance of the business by the respondent to the order is *g* thereby made impossible. How can a business be continued without records? How can it be continued without stock-in-trade? It will be recalled that, in the present case, the order authorised the removal of, inter alia, the video recorders at 8 Frederick Street. They were not, in the event, removed, but, if they had been, the whole of Mr Robinson's copying business would for that reason alone have been closed down. It is customary, on account of the Mareva injunction accompanying Anton Piller orders, for a copy of the *h* order to be served on the respondent's bankers. That was done in the present case. The almost certain effect of that being done will be that the bankers will decline to allow any further credit to the respondent. The order will throw such a question over the business of the respondent as to make any other course commercially imprudent and, therefore, unlikely. In the present case, Barclays Bank on service of the order refused to allow the defendants any further credit.

j

The service and execution of an Anton Piller order is likely to have on a respondent a personal as well as a commercial effect. Anton Piller orders are often granted not simply in respect of business premises but in respect of the respondent's home. He is required, on pain of committal, to open the doors of his house to the plaintiffs' representatives and to permit a search of the contents thereof. The plaintiffs and their representatives are at liberty to search and rummage through the personal belongings of any occupant of the house and to remove the material they consider to be covered by the terms of the order.

a   The traumatic effect and the sense of outrage likely to be produced by an invasion of home territory in the execution of an Anton Piller order is obvious.

When, in 1974 and shortly thereafter, Anton Piller orders became established weapons to combat, inter alia, copyright piracy, it was supposed that they would be relatively infrequently granted. They lay, it was said, at the very limit of the in personam jurisdiction proper to be exercised by the courts.

b   But, since 1974, Hamlins have obtained and executed, I was told, some 300 Anton Piller orders, 200 in audio piracy cases and about 100 in video piracy cases. Other firms of solicitors may perhaps be able to match those figures. Anton Piller orders are not rarities at all. They are regularly applied for and granted in all the divisions of the High Court. In no case previously, I was told, had the propriety of the obtaining and execution of an Anton Piller order been examined otherwise than in interlocutory proceedings. I

c   was told by one or other of the Hamlins witnesses (it matters not which) that this is the first case in the experience of that firm which has come to a full trial after the grant and execution of an Anton Piller order. This case provides, therefore, an opportunity, after a full hearing and after oral evidence from all the relevant participants, for a long, careful look at Anton Piller procedure and at the manner in which it is operating. It justifies, in my judgment, very grave disquiet.

d   It has to be accepted that a common, perhaps the usual, effect of the service and execution of an Anton Piller order is to close down the business which, on the applicants' evidence, is being carried on in violation of their rights. Mr Cumberland, Hamlins' experienced legal executive, accepted this. In the transcript of 12 July there is the exchange between him and counsel for the defendants to which I have already referred. But the question whether a business alleged by applicants for an Anton Piller order to be

e   illicit is in fact illicit or is genuine cannot ordinarily be answered until final judgment. Given that none of the many Anton Piller cases with which Mr Cumberland had been concerned have ever come to trial, his answers must be read as meaning that an Anton Piller order and its execution have the effect of closing down the business that the plaintiffs have, on the ex parte application, satisfied the judge is prima facie an illicit business.

f   It is a fundamental principle of civil jurisprudence in this country that citizens are not to be deprived of their property by judicial or quasi-judicial order without a fair hearing. Audi alterem partem is one of the principles of natural justice and contemplates a hearing at which the defendant can, if so advised, be represented and heard. As was said by Isaacs J in *Thomas A Edison Ltd v Bullock* (1912) 15 CLR 679 at 681, in a passage cited by Slade LJ in *Bank Mellat v Nikpour* [1985] FSR 87 at 92 and by Whitford J in *Jeffrey Rogers Knitwear*

g   *Productions Ltd v Vinola (Knitwear) Manufacturing Co* [1985] FSR 184 at 187:

> 'There is a primary precept governing the administration of justice, that no man is to be condemned unheard; and, therefore, as a general rule, no order should be made to the prejudice of a party unless he has the opportunity of being heard in defence.'

h   What is to be said of the Anton Piller procedure which, on a regular and institutionalised basis, is depriving citizens of their property and closing down their businesses by orders made ex parte, on applications of which they know nothing and at which they cannot be heard, by orders which they are forced, on pain of committal, to obey, even if wrongly made?

There are some possible answers to this criticism of Anton Piller orders and their effect.

j   One is that every Anton Piller order records an undertaking by the applicants who have obtained it to compensate the respondent for any damage caused to him by the order and for which the court thinks the plaintiff ought to pay. This is theoretically a valuable safeguard. In the present case the defendants are seeking compensation under just such an undertaking. But, in my judgment, it does not meet the main objection to Anton Piller procedure. The main objection to the procedure is that the orders made produce for the respondents damaging and irreversible consequences without any hearing at which they can be heard. The respondents may lack the means or the strength of purpose to pursue the applicants for relief under the undertaking in damages. And even villains ought not to be deprived of their property by proceedings at which they cannot be heard.

The second comment is that which Mr Cumberland gave in the course of his cross-examination. Anton Piller orders, he said, are not sought by his firm against innocent persons. Mr Hoffman, too, emphasised in his evidence the care with which Hamlins satisfy themselves that the proposed objects of Anton Piller procedure were engaged in piratical activities before applying for Anton Piller orders. This comment serves, in my opinion, not to mitigate but to underline the dangers inherent in ex parte procedure and, a fortiori, ex parte procedure where the object is to obtain a mandatory order intended for immediate execution.

It is the experience of Hamlins that, when they apply for Anton Piller orders, they almost invariably succeed in getting them. Counsel for the defendants asked Mr Cumberland how many applications for Anton Piller orders had, in his experience with the firm, resulted in failure. Mr Cumberland's answer was, 'None.' This answer did not surprise me. Hamlins are a very experienced firm in this field and they employ experienced and competent counsel. Once they have satisfied themselves that an application for an Anton Piller order ought to be made, it is to be expected that the application will be prepared and presented to the court in a form and manner that is likely to be successful. I do not imply in that remark any impropriety on the part of solicitors or counsel concerned. There is nothing inconsistent with, on the one hand, the discharge of the duty of full disclosure and, on the other hand, the presentation of the material in a manner likely to satisfy a judge that the application ought to be granted.

But the effect of this state of affairs is that it is the solicitors and counsel acting for the plaintiffs who take perhaps the critical decision. I have myself on many occasions read the material in support of a plaintiff's application for an interlocutory injuction and have formed the view that the application ought to succeed; but then, on reading the material put forward by the defendant in opposition to the grant of an injunction, have changed my mind. This is not because the plaintiff's affidavits have omitted relevant material. It is rather an indication of how the same material may be differently presented depending on the interest of the presenter. It underlines the need, if justice is to be done, for a defendant to have an opportunity to be heard.

The criticism that Anton Piller orders produce damaging and irreversible consequences for respondents without their having an opportunity to be heard is not, in my judgment, answered by pointing to the care that the plaintiff's legal advisers take to ensure that the innocent are not pursued.

The third comment is that respondents are safeguarded by the duties of full disclosure that the solicitors and counsel acting for the applicant owe to the court and that execution of Anton Piller orders is customarily required to be supervised by solicitors. This comment underlines, in my view, the unsatisfactory position in which the Anton Piller procedure places solicitors and, to a lesser extent, since they depend on solicitors for their instructions, counsel. The solicitors are retained by and owe a duty to their clients, the applicants. They satisfy themselves that their clients' interests require the protection of an Anton Piller order and are instructed by their clients to obtain one. They have a duty to see that full disclosure is made to the court of any relevant evidence. But relevance and irrelevance are not matters of white and black. There is usually a grey area of arguable relevance and arguable irrelevance. What is a solicitor's duty in respect of evidence falling into the grey area? It is to be borne in mind that the solicitor, when taking his decision as to what is relevant to be included in the affidavits in support of the Anton Piller application, will be likely already to have satisfied himself, as his clients will have been satisfied, that the respondent is a rogue against whom an Anton Piller order ought to be granted. The solicitor does not and cannot be expected to present the available evidence from the respondent's point of view.

Finally, it may be pointed out that an Anton Piller order always contains a liberty for the respondent to apply on short notice for the order to be set aside. But this cannot in practice be done until after the order has been executed. In order to obtain back his *a* business records and place his business once more in a viable position, the respondent to the order has to make a successful application to the court. There are often very real financial difficulties which stand in his way. As happened in the present case, the respondent's bankers may, on learning of the order, have cut off his funds. The obtaining of legal aid may not be possible and, even if possible, may involve lengthy delays. And the will of a respondent to take on a powerful and determined opponent in expensive litigation may waver. The respondent, often with very good reason, may lack confidence

b in the successful outcome of the litigation.

These answers to the criticism of the Anton Piller procedure do not, in my opinion, match the force of the criticism. There is and can be no adequate substitute for the right of a person against whom immediate mandatory judicial relief is sought to appear and be heard at the judicial hearing which deals with the matter. But this is not possible where Anton Piller procedure is concerned.

c I have made these general comments about Anton Piller orders not for the purpose of casting doubts on the jurisdiction of the court to make them nor for the purpose of casting doubt on the propriety, in appropriate cases, of Anton Piller orders being granted. But a decision whether or not an Anton Piller order should be granted requires a balance to be struck between the plaintiffs' need that the remedies allowed by the civil law for the breach of his rights should be attainable and the requirement of justice that a

d defendant should not be deprived of his property without being heard. What I have heard in the present case has disposed me to think that the practice of the court has allowed the balance to swing much too far in favour of plaintiffs and that Anton Piller orders have been too readily granted and with insufficient safeguards for respondents.

The draconian and essentially unfair nature of Anton Piller orders from the point of view of respondents against whom they are made requires, in my view, that they be so

e drawn as to extend no further than the minimum extent necessary to achieve the purpose for which they are granted, namely the preservation of documents or articles which might otherwise be destroyed or concealed. Anything beyond that is, in my judgment, impossible to justify. For example, I do not understand how an order can be justified that allows the plaintiffs' solicitors to take and retain all relevant documentary material and correspondence. Once the plaintiffs' solicitors have satisfied themselves what material

f exists and have had an opportunity to take copies thereof, the material ought, in my opinion, to be returned to its owner. The material need be retained no more than a relatively short period of time for that purpose.

Secondly, I would think it essential that a detailed record of the material taken should always be required to be made by the solicitors who execute the order before the material is removed from the respondent's premises. So far as possible, disputes as to what material

g was taken, the resolution of which depends on the oral testimony and credibility of the solicitors on the one hand and the respondent on the other hand, ought to be avoided. In the absence of any corroboration of a respondent's allegation that particular material (for instance, divorce papers) was taken, a solicitor's sworn and apparently credible denial is likely always to be preferred. This state of affairs is unfair to respondents. It ought to be avoided so far as it can be.

h Thirdly, no material should, in my judgment, be taken from the respondent's premises by the executing solicitors unless it is clearly covered by the terms of the order. In particular, I find it wholly unacceptable that a practice should have grown up whereby the respondent to the order is procured by the executing solicitors to give consent to additional material being removed. In view of the circumstances in which Anton Piller orders are customarily executed (the execution is often aptly called 'a raid'), I would not,

j for my part, be prepared to accept that an apparent consent by a respondent had been freely and effectively given unless the respondent's solicitor has been present to confirm and ensure that the consent was a free and informed one.

Fourthly, I find it inappropriate that seized material the ownership of which is in dispute, such as allegedly pirate tapes, should be retained by the plaintiffs' solicitors pending the trial. Although officers of the court, the main role of solicitors for plaintiffs is to act for the plaintiffs. If the proper administration of justice requires that material

taken under an Anton Piller order from defendants should, pending trial, be kept from
the defendants, then those responsible for the administration of justice might reasonably *a*
be expected to provide a neutral officer of the court charged with the custody of the
material. In lieu of any such officer, and there is none at present, the plaintiffs' solicitors
ought, in my view, as soon as solicitors for the defendants are on the record, to be
required to deliver the material to the defendants' solicitors on their undertaking for its
safe custody and production, if required, in court.

Finally, the nature of Anton Piller orders requires that the affidavits in support of *b*
applications for them ought to err on the side of excessive disclosure. In the case of
material falling into the grey area of possible relevance, the judge, not the plaintiffs'
solicitors, should be the judge of relevance. Whitford J, whose experience in these
matters probably exceeds that of any other first instance judge, has recently drawn
attention to the particular importance of full disclosure on Anton Piller applications. In
Jeffrey Rogers Knitwear Productions Ltd v Vinola (Knitwear) Manufacturing Co [1985] FSR *c*
184 at 189 he said:

'I wholly reject the suggestion . . . that when seeking an Anton Piller order, there
is no need to investigate the question whether or not in the absence of an order there
is a real possibility that infringing material or evidence will be done away with. Any
plaintiff seeking an Anton Piller order must place before the court all the information
they have relating to the circumstances of the defendant which they can suggest *d*
points to the probability that in the absence of an Anton Piller order material which
should be available will disappear.'

I now come to the specific complaints made by the defendants in this case. At an early
stage in the trial I directed the defendants and plaintiffs to prepare pleadings setting out
their respective contentions on this part of the case. I take the defendants' complaints *e*
from their pleading.

The obtaining of the order
1. The defendants complain that the plaintiffs and their solicitors and counsel 'failed
to give serious and or any adequate consideration to whether it was justifiable for the
Plaintiffs to seek' an order in the terms of that of 18 June 1982 'against the First and or *f*
Second Defendants or to whether it was sufficient for the Plaintiffs to seek negative
injunctions and or orders for the delivery up of video cassettes and or other materials'.
This complaint is based on a dictum from the judgment of Dillon LJ in *Booker McConnell
plc v Plascow* [1985] CA Transcript 137. The case is unreported but I was supplied with a
transcript of the judgments of Kerr and Dillon LJJ. Dillon LJ said:

'It follows that the making of an Anton Piller order against a trading company *g*
may well be regarded as a serious stigma on that company's commercial reputation.
Even more importantly for present purposes, it follows that there is a responsibility
in each case on the plaintiff's advisers to consider seriously whether it is justifiable
to seek an Anton Piller order against the particular defendant, or whether it would
be enough to obtain negative injunctions with, if appropriate, an order to deliver
up documents or material, for example, where, as here, the documents sought are *h*
the property of the plaintiff.'

I do not think that Hamlins did give sufficient consideration to whether Anton Piller
orders should be sought against the defendants. The practice had grown up in Hamlins
that in video piracy cases Anton Piller orders would be sought. Where Anton Piller
orders were sought, Mareva injunctions were sought as well. The affidavits in support of *j*
these applications contained pro forma paragraphs to the effect that the respondents, the
alleged video pirates, were the sort of people who would destroy evidence. I was unable
to detect anywhere in the evidence given of the meetings on 15 June 1982 that led to the
ex parte application on 18 June any indication that the solicitors at the meeting, or
counsel for that matter, had asked themselves whether Mr Robinson was in a position to
or was likely to destroy vital evidence. There was prima facie evidence that he was a

video pirate; that was enough. An Anton Piller order was to be applied for. Nevertheless,
a for reasons which I will later develop, I am not satisfied that a failure of this sort can be
represented as a breach of duty.

2. The second complaint is that the solicitors and counsel misled the court in three
specific respects.

In para 24 of his affidavit, sworn on 16 June 1982, Mr Roy Brown had deposed that 'It
is my belief that the defendants knew full well that what they are doing is unlawful' and
b that 'The defendants have a flagrant disregard for other persons' rights'. These passages
come from what I would call the pro forma parts of Mr Roy Brown's affidavit. It is
complained that no mention was made of the fact that Mr Percy Browne had asked Mr
Robinson to purchase on his behalf pirate video cassettes nor of Mr Browne's opinion
that Mr Robinson may have been an innocent dupe of others. I do not think that these
omissions had the effect of causing the passages I have cited to mislead the court. The
c licence from Benelux Video regarding 'Futureworld' was exhibited to Mr Roy Brown's
affidavit. The warning given by Mr Percy Browne to Mr Robinson on 30 June 1981 was
mentioned in the affidavit. Subsequent dealings by the defendants regarding
'Futureworld' were alleged. In the circumstances, this complaint is not, in my view,
made out. Nevertheless it is, I would accept, a thoroughly undesirable and dangerous
practice for such important allegations as those I have cited from Mr Roy Brown's
d affidavit to be made otherwise than as reasoned deductions from or opinions formed on
the actual facts of the specific case. Mr Roy Brown did not, in my view, do that. He swore
the Hamlins common form video piracy paragraphs.

Second, it is alleged that the court was misled in that the affidavit stated that Mr Percy
Browne was still investigating the defendants. This complaint is justified. Mr Percy
Browne was not still investigating the defendants. His investigation had not continued
e beyond the correspondence which followed his 30 June 1981 visit. Mr Roy Brown ought,
from his perusal of Mr Percy Browne's file, to have known this. There is no basis on
which counsel can be supposed to have known it.

Third, it is complained that Mr Roy Brown's affidavit gave the impression, contrary to
the facts, of an element of secrecy associated with the 8 Frederick Street business. This
complaint, too, is justified. Mr Roy Brown knew of Mr Percy Browne's visit to the
f premises at Mr Robinson's invitation. He had no reason to imply that there was anything
secretive or clandestine about the business carried on there. There is no basis for
supposing that counsel knew that either of the matters I have referred to was misleading.

3. The third complaint is that, in breach of their duty to the court, the plaintiffs, the
solicitors and counsel failed to disclose to the court material facts within their knowledge.
A number of particulars of alleged non-disclosure are given. There is no reason to suppose
g that counsel was aware of any of them.

(i) It was not disclosed that Mr Percy Browne had entered and inspected 8 Frederick
Street on 30 June 1981 with access to the whole of the premises. The fact of Mr Percy
Browne's visit to the premises was known to Mr Roy Brown. The details of the visit may
not have been. It was, in my judgment, a serious breach of duty for Mr Roy Brown to
fail to disclose the fact of that visit. He sought in cross-examination to say that it was not
h relevant. It was clearly relevant. Indeed, the full details of Mr Robinson's co-operation
with Mr Percy Browne on that occasion ought to have been placed before Goulding J.

Mr Percy Browne was acting for the MPAA, all of whose members are, by
representation, plaintiffs in this action. Counsel for the plaintiffs argued that failure on
the part of some plaintiffs to lay before the court relevant material known to them or
their agents ought not to prejudice the position of other plaintiffs to whom the material
j was not known. In my judgment, the reverse is the case. The Anton Piller order was
applied for by and granted to all the plaintiffs jointly. Each of them owed a duty of full
disclosure. Breach of that duty by any of them prejudices, in my judgment, the position
of all.

(ii) It was not disclosed that 'Percy Browne had in July 1981 removed approximately
30 U Matic tapes from the First Defendant at 8 Frederick Street but had shortly thereafter
returned a number thereof to the First Defendant'. This too should have been disclosed.

It was relevant to the extent to which Mr Robinson was or might be carrying on a legitimate business. This too was, or from a perusal of Mr Percy Browne's file ought to have been, known to Mr Roy Brown.   *a*

(iii) It was not disclosed that 'Percy Browne had visited one or more of the said premises on divers occasions until June 1982 being allowed the like full and free access as set out in sub-paragraph (a) above'. There is, in my judgment, nothing in this. Visits were made by Mr Percy Browne to 30 Enderby Road but these were not, in my view, of any particular significance. Here the grey shades into black.   *b*

(iv) It was not disclosed that 'Percy Browne knew that the First Defendant had a personal collection of video cassettes whether illicit or not and had approved the First Defendant's retaining the said collection in his own possession for his own personal use'. I do not think this is material, nor do I think Mr Percy Browne approved Mr Robinson's retention of the video cassettes in question.

(v) The breach of copyright actions brought against Mr Robinson by Iver Film Services   *c*
Ltd and by Helmdale Ltd were not disclosed. There were at least some of the plaintiffs by whom, or by whose agents, some facts regarding these actions were known. This was, in my judgment, relevant material to be placed before the court. It was relevant to the question whether Mr Robinson was the sort of person against whom Anton Piller relief was necessary. This was not material necessarily known to Mr Roy Brown.

(vi) It was, in my view, a serious non-disclosure that no mention was made of the fact   *d*
that Mr Robinson was an active informant for Mr Percy Browne on video piracy matters. The fact was known to Mr Roy Brown. Mr Hoffman, at the morning meeting on 15 June 1982, had said that the fact ought to be disclosed. Mr Roy Brown said in cross-examination that he did not think it relevant.

(vii) In my view, the judge ought also to have been told of the arrangement between Mr Percy Browne and Mr Robinson for the latter to purchase pirate video cassettes for   *e*
Mr Percy Browne. Mr Roy Brown may not have known of this arrangement.

(viii) It was not disclosed that 'The First Defendant was or may have been an innocent dupe of persons committing breaches of the Plaintiffs' and others copyrights'. I do not think that Mr Percy Browne's opinion to this effect, formed in June 1981, that Mr Robinson might be a dupe of Benelux Video, was material.

(ix) It is complained that it was not disclosed that Mr Robinson had made a claim of   *f*
right in respect of 'Futureworld', had paid a substantial sum of money for the Benelux licence and that his right had been corroborated by Mr Kooring. It is further complained that it was not disclosed that Mr Robinson had written to Filmways Pictures Inc threatening to recommence production of copies of 'Futureworld'. I am not satisfied that that letter was ever sent by Mr Robinson. Thereapart, the facts relating to Mr Robinson's dealings with Benelux Video and with Mr Kooring, so far as known to Mr Percy Browne,   *g*
or for that matter to Filmways Pictures Inc, ought, in my view, to have been disclosed. The Benelux Video licence had been disclosed but really very little else.

It is also complained that there was non-disclosure regarding the film 'Slaughter'. There was, in my opinion, nothing relevant to be disclosed in that connection.

(x) Non-disclosure is complained of in respect of the duration of the business carried on by Mr Robinson, in respect of the substantial nature of his assets and in respect of the   *h*
open manner in which he was carrying on business. I have already dealt with some of these matters. Mr Roy Brown's affidavit was, in my view, inadequate in that it failed to put before the judge a sufficiently full and fair picture of Mr Robinson's assets so as to enable a view to be taken whether a Mareva injunction was justified. The paragraph in Mr Roy Brown's affidavit justifying the grant of a Mareva injunction, para 25, was, like para 24, of a pro forma character. It did not, as it should have done, condescend to any   *j*
detail about his assets. But both Mr Roy Brown and Mr Percy Browne had relevant information in that connection.

In the result, the defendants' complaint of non-disclosure is, in my judgment, made out. There was, in my view, a serious failure on Mr Roy Brown's part to place before the court all the relevant material of which he knew or of which he would have known had

he read properly Mr Percy Browne's file. And it was unarguably his duty to have read
a properly that file.

4. Finally, the defendants complain that the plaintiffs, their solicitors and counsel
failed to ensure that the order sought was clear and unambiguous. This is represented as
a breach of their duty to the court. It is regrettable if an order of the court is ambiguous
or lacks clarity and it is, I would think, a breach of duty owed to the court if counsel or
solicitors, knowing of the ambiguity or lack of clarity in question, fail to draw the point
b to the attention of the judge. But nobody deliberately sets out to obtain an unclear or
ambiguous order and there is no foundation for any suggestion that the solicitors or
counsel who dealt with the ex parte application in the present case were aware of any
ambiguity or lack of clarity in the order. The complaint based on ambiguity or lack of
clarity therefore fails.

It is also alleged that a breach of duty was committed by the plaintiffs, their solicitors
c and counsel in seeking an order in unnecessarily wide and onerous terms. This, too, is
based on the dictum of Dillon LJ in the *Booker McConnell* case that I have already read. In
that dictum Dillon LJ expressed the view that it was the duty of solicitors and counsel to
give careful consideration to the necessity of seeking Anton Piller relief. It is consistent
with that view to regard the solicitors and counsel as under a duty also not to seek an
order in unnecessarily wide terms. These considerations underline the basically
d unsatisfactory nature of Anton Piller procedure. The safeguard against orders that ought
not to be made or against orders made in unnecessarily wide terms is, or ought to be, the
judge. The solicitors and counsel must obviously accept the duty of ensuring that full
disclosure of all relevant material is made to the court. But, if that duty of full disclosure
is discharged, why should not solicitors and counsel apply for the most favourable order
they can persuade the court to grant? The opinion expressed by Dillon LJ that the lawyers
e acting for the applicants on Anton Piller orders have a responsibility not to seek orders
without careful prior consideration (from which it would follow, I think, that they also
ought not to seek orders in unnecessarily wide terms) seems to me a recognition by
Dillon LJ of the very real dangers inherent in ex parte applications for mandatory orders
and a recognition that on these one-sided applications judges may very easily become too
enthusiastic.
f   Notwithstanding the dictum of Dillon LJ which I have cited, I am doubtful whether
it can really be the law that solicitors or counsel owe a duty to the court to have restraint
as to the extent of the orders they seek. In a case where there has been full and proper
disclosure I do not think an allegation of breach of duty against the lawyers, whether in
making the application in the first place or in seeking an order in onerous terms, could
ever be sustained. Still less could it be sustained if the judge had, in the event, made the
g order sought. Accordingly, I hold that this complaint, like that referred to under heading
1, has not been made out.

Execution of the order
Paragraph 7 of the pleading contains a general allegation that—

h 'the Plaintiffs by their Solicitors executed the said Order dated 18th June 1982 on
21st June 1982 onerously and with a flagrant disregard for the rights of the First and
or Second Defendants and or with the intention of preventing the First and or
Second Defendants from trading lawfully and or recklessly without due or any
regard for the probability that the consequences of their acts might be to prevent
and or inhibit the lawful trade of the First and or Second Defendants and since the
said date have further acted with a flagrant disregard for the terms of the said Order
j and or the rights of First and Second Defendants . . .'

Particulars in support of this allegation are given. I will deal with them in turn.

(a) It is alleged that an excessive number of people attended on the execution of the
order. This allegation fails.

(b) It is alleged that Hamlins failed properly to explain the terms of the order to Mr

Robinson or the evidence on which it was based. I do not find this complaint well founded. Mr Hoffman's picture given in the course of his evidence, of Mr Robinson airily waving aside explanations, rang true.

(c) The third complaint is that material was taken that was not covered by the order. This complaint is well founded and is one of substance. No attempt whatever was made by Hamlins, so far as I could tell from the evidence, to confine their seizures to material strictly covered by the order. They took everything as to which there was a question that they wished to investigate. They relied on the written consents that they intended to procure Mr Robinson or, in the case of the Mill Street shop, Mr Morgan to sign to protect themselves and the plaintiffs against the consequences of excessive seizure.

The plaintiffs rely, of course, in answer to this complaint, on the signatures contained in the written receipts. I am not prepared to allow them to do so. I am not satisfied that the signatures of Mr Robinson and Mr Morgan respectively represent a free and informed consent to the excessive seizures that Hamlins were carrying out. Hamlins' behaviour was, in my judgment, oppressive and an abuse of the position of power in which, vis-à-vis the respondents, they had been placed by the order of the court. Mr Hoffman and Mr Roy Brown attempted to justify what was done by reference to the co-operative and accommodating attitude being adopted by Mr Robinson. This was represented as signifying his consent. I do not accept that it did so. It demonstrated his resilience, good humour and remarkable apparent self-confidence.

(d) It is complained that no adequately detailed receipts recording what was taken were made. This, as a fact, was so. It represented a failure which, it is to be hoped, will not be repeated in subsequent cases. But the order did not place on Hamlins the obligation to prepare detailed, or any, receipts and their failure in this respect demonstrates neither oppressive execution of the order nor flagrant disregard of the defendants' rights.

(e) The misrepresentation of the order to Mr Robinson's bankers is complained of. It will be recalled that both Mr Baker and Mr Hoffman had respectively failed to mention on the telephone that Mr Robinson was entitled to draw £200 for living expenses. This complaint is made out. But the misrepresentation, though it should not have happened, was not deliberate and was cured within hours when the banks received copies of the order itself. I found it, however, a matter of regret that Mr Hoffman did not feel able frankly to admit his omission.

(f) The defendants complain that Hamlins failed expeditiously to return to the defendants the video cassettes and other material which had been taken. This complaint is, in my judgment, well justified in relation to the video cassettes not included in the original statement of claim. The retention of these, or most of them, for nearly three years was done by Hamlins without a shadow of right. It was, in my view, oppressive and in flagrant disregard of the defendants' rights. The plaintiffs' retention of the video cassettes specified in the statement of claim and of the documents relating thereto was in accordance with the terms of the order. Anton Piller orders ought, in my view, to make provision for the return of relevant material either to a neutral officer of the court or to the defendants' own solicitors at the earliest possible moment. But this order did not do so. The retention of this material by Hamlins cannot, in my judgment, be complained of by the defendants.

(g) The defendants complain, finally, of the breach by Hamlins of their undertaking for safe custody of the seized material in that a number of cassettes and other material were lost while in Hamlins' offices. This complaint is justified.

In the result I find that the complaint of oppressive execution of the order and flagrant disregard of the defendants' rights made out in respect of the seizure of material not covered by the order, the reliance on the so-called consents embodied in the receipts and the retention by Hamlins of material not covered by the order.

It is relevant for me here to repeat that I was satisfied by the evidence in this case that the intention of the plaintiffs and Hamlins in applying for and obtaining the Anton Piller order was by that means summarily to close down the business of reproducing tapes being carried on from 8 Frederick Street. They had, in my view, the expectation that the execution of the Anton Piller order would achieve that end. Hamlins' professional experience of the effect of executing Anton Piller orders in audio and video piracy cases

a   justified that expectation. That intention was, in my judgment, an improper one. It represented an abuse of Anton Piller procedure and it led, in my view, to an oppressive execution of the order.

Remedy

The defendants seek an order setting aside the ex parte order and damages or an

b   inquiry as to damages pursuant to the plaintiffs' cross-undertaking in damages contained in the order. I will deal first with the question whether the order should be set aside for non-disclosure.

It is a somewhat bizarre proposition. The Anton Piller order was executed on 21 June 1982, some three and a half years ago. Setting it aside now would be a gesture devoid of practical effect. The extent to which the defendants are entitled to recover damages under

c   the cross-undertaking does not, as I see it, depend on whether or not the order is formally set aside.

As to the remaining parts of the order, the negative interlocutory injunctions all expire automatically with this judgment. Final injunctions based on the result of the plaintiffs' action take their place.

Counsel for the defendants pressed me very hard with a number of authorities which

d   establish, he submitted, the principle that, where an interlocutory injunction had been obtained with inadequate disclosure of material evidence known to the applicants or their agents, the respondent was entitled to have the injunction set aside ex debito justiciae and without more ado or further inquiry. There is, in addition, clear authority that the fact that an Anton Piller order has been executed is no reason why it should not be set aside. The Court of Appeal, in *Booker McConnell plc v Plascow* [1985] CA Transcript

e   137, to which I have already referred, so held. Kerr LJ said:

'In my view, it is quite clear from these two decisions [*WEA Records Ltd v Visions Channel 4 Ltd* [1983] 2 All ER 589, [1983] 1 WLR 721 and *Randolph M Fields v Watts* (1984) 129 SJ 67] that in appropriate cases the court will discharge orders of this kind even after they have been fully executed.'

f   Dillon LJ said:

'There is next the question whether a defendant can apply to set aside an Anton Piller order on the ground that it ought never to have been made after the order has been fully executed and the search of the defendant's premises has taken place. I have no doubt that a defendant ought to be able to make such an application and to show, if he can, that the order was obtained by non-disclosure of material facts or

g   that, for other reasons, such as those indicated earlier in this judgment, the order ought never to have been made.'

Counsel for the defendants submitted that, in the present case, the order should be set aside to mark the court's disapproval of the serious breaches of duty which accompanied the obtaining of the order.

h   Counsel for the plaintiffs submitted that the order ought not to be set aside. He had, I think, in essence three reasons. First, he submitted that such non-disclosures as attended the obtaining of the order had not made any difference. If all relevant or arguably relevant material had been disclosed, Goulding J would still, he submitted, have made the order. As to this, I decline to go in for crystal ball gazing. What Goulding J would have done with the application if all relevant material about Mr Robinson, his businesses

j   and his premises had been placed before the judge it is impossible now to assess. He might or might not have granted the order. The terms of the order might or might not have been the same. I do not accept that speculation on these lines is a proper approach.

Second, counsel for the plaintiffs submitted that the evidence in this case has established that Mr Robinson was in fact a video pirate. He was in fact the sort of person who might have been expected to destroy relevant evidence of his wrongdoing. The order was, counsel submitted, looked at with the advantage of hindsight, justified, whatever might have been the deficiencies in the evidence by means of which it was obtained. Counsel reminded me of the evidence which justifies the inference that somewhere there is a master tape of 'Russian Roulette' and a master tape of 'Futureworld' the whereabouts or fate of which must be known to Mr Robinson but which he has not disclosed. I do not accept that this is the right approach either. The evidence at trial determines what orders I should now make against Mr Robinson but cannot, in my judgment, be relied on to justify ex post facto the making of the ex parte order if, at the time the order was made, it ought not to have been made or to excuse breaches of duty which attended on the obtaining of the order.

Finally, counsel for the plaintiffs took a point or points regarding the time at which the defendants' application to discharge the Anton Piller order was made, 24 January 1984. Counsel's point was in part procedural and in part one of substance. His procedural point was that an application under the liberty to apply to set aside an Anton Piller order can only be made on the return date specified in the order. The return date is the date fixed by the judge for further consideration, inter partes, of the relief granted by the order. It provides an opportunity for the respondent, if so advised, to apply to set aside the order. If the respondent does not avail himself of this opportunity then, submitted counsel for the plaintiffs, the ex parte order, or at least the wholly executed part thereof, stands unless and until set aside on appeal by the Court of Appeal. I am unable to accept these submissions. It has always been my understanding that an interlocutory application to set aside or vary an interlocutory order can be made on due notice at any time. As a matter of judicial discretion, a first instance judge will not set aside or vary an inter partes interlocutory order made by a brother first instance judge unless the application to set aside or vary is made on the basis of fresh material not before the court when the original interlocutory order was made. If no new material is relied on, or if the only new material is material that the applicant could and ought to have placed before the court on the original application (the applicant to set aside or vary being the respondent to the original application) then the original order can only be disturbed on appeal. But the respondent to an ex parte order, who, ex hypothesi, has not been heard at all on the application for the order, can, in my view, make an interlocutory application at any time for a review of the order. The significance of the return date is that it provides a fixed date on which the respondent, if so advised, can apply to vary or set aside. It does not, in my judgment, preclude a respondent who does not take advantage of the return date from applying subsequently.

The substantive point of counsel for the plaintiffs is the one to which I have already referred. How can it be right to countenance an application to set aside a mandatory interlocutory order which has been wholly executed where the application is not made until 18 months thereafter and is not dealt with until final trial of the action? The common sense of this objection seems to me overwhelming.

The many authorities to which I have already referred that establish the propriety of setting aside an executed Anton Piller order where the obtaining of the order has been attended by inadequate disclosure were all cases where the application to set aside was made reasonably soon after the execution of the order, and where it was at least possible that the setting aside of the order could have had some practical effect. I do not take the judicial expressions of opinion in those cases as a guide to the action I should take in this case, where the decision whether or not to set aside the order has to be made after final trial.

The defendants have, in my judgment, by reason of the serious defects in the evidence placed before Goulding J to which I have already referred, established grounds for the setting aside of the order. If I were satisfied that there would be any practical advantage to them in the setting aside of the order, I would do so. But I am not satisfied in this. The level of damages to which, under the cross-undertaking in damages, the defendants are entitled does not, in my judgment, depend on whether or not the order is first set aside. I do not think the setting aside of the order is necessary in order to mark my disapproval of the manner in which it was obtained, or, for that matter, of the manner in which it was executed. I hope that the terms of this judgment will have done that.

a
I am instinctively disinclined to make by judicial order what seems to me an empty gesture. I do not, therefore, propose to set aside the order.

Damages

The defendants seek damages under the cross-undertaking given by the plaintiffs. In view of my findings as to the manner in which the order was obtained and executed, the defendants are, in my judgment, prima facie entitled to damages. The problem is

b
quantum.

Damages for breach of a cross-undertaking ought, in my judgment, to be primarily compensatory. But I do not think, in the present case, that is the whole of the basis on which damages can be granted. It is well settled that an increased level of damages, sometimes described as aggravated damages, can be awarded where trespass to land or trespass to goods has been accompanied by circumstances of contumely or affront (see

c
McGregor on Damages (14th edn, 1980) paras 1082, 1127). That has been so in the present case by reason, in my judgment, of the excessive and oppressive manner in which the Anton Piller order was executed. There is not, in terms at least, any claim for exemplary damages in the present case. One of the categories of cases identified by the judgment of Lord Devlin in *Rookes v Barnard* [1964] 1 All ER 367, [1964] AC 1129 in which exemplary damages may be claimed is that of cases which involve oppressive, arbitrary or

d
unconstitutional action by servants of the government. Solicitors who execute an Anton Piller order do so, in important part, as officers of the court. It is the court which places them in a position to do that which would, without the court authority, be a flagrant and inexcusable trespass. They are placed in a position in which their actions are likely to cause shock, distress and often outrage to those against whom the orders are executed. If, in execution of these orders, they act outside the terms of the order oppressively or

e
excessively, I am disposed to think that Lord Devlin would have included the case in the category to which I have referred.

I have given thought to whether I should order an inquiry as to damages in order that the damage done by the order to the defendants' businesses at 8 Frederick Street and at the Mill Street shop may be properly assessed. I have concluded that I ought not to order an inquiry as to damages for these reasons.

f
First, the compensatory element of any damages should compensate the defendants for damage to their legitimate interests. They cannot expect to be compensated for damage to the illicit part of the businesses carried on at the Mill Street shop and at 8 Frederick Street.

The stock of video tapes at the Mill Street shop was, as I have concluded from the evidence in this case, composed largely of pirate tapes. It is true that a substantial number

g
of the tapes were not copies of films in which any of the plaintiffs is entitled to copyright or an exclusive licence. None the less, to the extent that the tapes were pirate tapes, they belonged, under s 18 of the Copyright Act 1956, to the owners of the copyright. Further, every sale of every video tape from the Mill Street shop of which evidence has been given in this case seems to have been the sale of a pirate tape. The prospect of an inquiry as to the damage caused by the Anton Piller order to such a business brings to my mind the

h
application by the highwayman against his partner for an account (see *Everet v Williams* (1725) 9 LQR 197). The court would not countenance that application and I do not think I should countenance an inquiry into the damage caused by the order to the business of the Mill Street shop. Mr Robinson will not of course suffer the fate of the highwayman, nor will Mr Beveridge suffer the fate of his counsel.

As to the business carried on from 8 Frederick Street, I find it easy to accept that the

j
business was, in part, legitimate although, as I have found, in part concerned with the reproduction of tapes in flagrant breach of copyright. But so far as the legitimate side of the business is concerned, it was, in my view, for a time carried on by Mr Wickenden. I was presented in evidence by Mr Robinson with a series of falsehoods regarding the business allegedly carried on by Mr Wickenden. He was, I think, no more than a front for Mr Robinson. The business carried on at 8 Frederick Street after the execution of the Anton Piller order terminated in July 1983 or thereabouts on account of, first, the collapse

of Centre Video Ltd and, second, the floods which damaged the majority of the video
machines. The cesser of that continued business was not attributable, directly at least, to
the Anton Piller order or its aftermath. In view of these circumstances, and particularly
in view of the false evidence given me by Mr Robinson, I am not prepared to order an
inquiry into the damage caused to the 8 Frederick Street business by the Anton Piller
order.

I propose, therefore, to make an assessment here and now of the sum that the plaintiffs
ought to pay the defendants under the cross-undertaking in damages. In spite of what I
have said, there must be some compensatory element in the damages to be awarded. The
combination of Anton Piller order and Mareva injunction made it impossible for the
defendants to obtain credit. The retention by Hamlins of all the documents of the
businesses made any continuity of business very difficult. There was a legitimate part,
both of the 8 Frederick Street business and, perhaps to a very small extent, of the Mill
Street shop business. The defendants' chance to continue on a small scale a legitimate
business was impaired by the ex parte order being obtained and executed. In addition,
this is, in my judgment, a case in which aggravated damages are justified.

I propose to order that damages of £10,000 be paid by the plaintiffs to the defendants
under the cross-undertaking in damages. If it is relevant to split the sum between the
defendants, I would allow £2,500 to the company and £7,500 to Mr Robinson. This split
recognises that contumely and affront affect individuals, not inanimate corporations.
The damages are awarded against the plaintiffs jointly.

The damages I have awarded have subsumed the matter of the breach by Hamlins of
its undertaking to keep in safe custody the material seized. Although Hamlins were
holding the material as officers of the court, they were also doing so as solicitors for the
plaintiffs. I have already commented on the unsatisfactory ambiguity of this position. In
the circumstances, the plaintiffs can, in my view, properly be held liable to the defendants
in damages for this breach by Hamlins of their undertaking. How the matter should be
dealt with as between Hamlins and the plaintiffs is not before me.

Mr Hoffman, senior partner of Hamlins, has apologised for his firm's breach of their
undertaking. I accept that apology and the matter of the breach need be taken no further.

I have uttered some strong words of displeasure about the contents of Mr Roy Brown's
affidavit and the approach by Hamlins to the obtaining and execution of the Anton Piller
order in this case. I have concluded that, in certain respects, there have been breaches of
the duties that solicitors owe the court. I hope that what I have said will help to ensure
that the defects exposed by the present case will not recur in other cases. For my part, the
matter need be taken no further.

I must deal with the costs of this litigation. I will hear submissions on that. But it may
shorten debate if I say that my provisional view is that the plaintiffs are entitled against
the defendants to the costs of the action (subject to the usual legal aid limitation) taxed
on a party and party basis, and that the defendants are entitled against the plaintiffs to
their costs of the application of 24 January 1983 and of all other applications arising out
of the Anton Piller order, taxed on a common fund basis.

It remains for me to express my appreciation to counsel for their assistance in a case
that was complicated, difficult and important.

*Judgment for plaintiffs for injunctions sought and for inquiry as to damages for infringement of
copyright. Judgment for the defendants in the sum of £10,000 (in lieu of inquiry) on plaintiffs'
cross-undertaking in damages.*

Solicitors: *Bottoms & Webb*, Luton (for the defendants); *Hamlin Slowe* (for the plaintiffs).

Jacqueline Metcalfe   Barrister.

Dutta v Westcott

QUEEN'S BENCH DIVISION
WOOLF LJ AND MACPHERSON J
3, 4 JUNE 1986

Crown Court – Appeal to Crown Court – Power of court on appeal – Sentence – Decision which is the subject of the appeal – Jurisdiction to confirm, reverse or vary sentence – Separate sentences imposed for different offences on same occasion – Appellant appealing in respect of only one offence – Whether 'decision which is the subject of the appeal' including all offences – Whether Crown Court having jurisdiction to vary or increase sentences for offences which are not subject of appeal – Supreme Court Act 1981, s 48.

The defendant was charged under various provisions of the Road Traffic Act 1972 with a number of motoring offences arising out of the same incident, namely (i) driving without insurance, (ii) failing to stop, (iii) failing to report an accident, (iv) driving a vehicle with no warrant of fitness and (v) failing to produce a driving licence. He was convicted of all five offences. In respect of the first offence he was disqualified from driving for twelve months and fined £100; no penalty points were imposed. In respect of the other offences he was fined and his licence was endorsed but because under s 19(1) of the Transport Act 1981 no penalty points could be imposed if a person was disqualified from driving, no penalty points were imposed for those offences, as would otherwise have been the case if he had not been disqualified. The defendant appealed to the Crown Court but only against his conviction for the first offence, on the ground that at the relevant time he had had an insurance certificate. The Crown Court allowed the appeal but went on to impose penalty points in respect of the second and third offences on the basis that the 'decision which is the subject of the appeal' included the whole of the magistrates' court's decision and therefore the Crown Court was entitled under s 48[a] of the Supreme Court Act 1981 to vary sentences imposed for other offences tried at the same time but which were not the subject of an appeal. On appeal by way of case stated, the defendant contended that the decision which was the subject of the appeal was the decision in respect of that particular information which was the subject of the appeal.

Held – On the true construction of s 48 of the 1981 Act the 'decision which is the subject of the appeal' referred to the whole of the decision made by the magistrates' court on the occasion when the court decided on the conviction or imposed the penalty appealed against. Accordingly, where an appellant had been convicted and sentenced by a magistrates' court for a number of offences but only appealed to the Crown Court in respect of one or some of those convictions or sentences the Crown Court had jurisdiction under s 48 to confirm, reverse or vary all the convictions and reverse, vary or increase all the sentences imposed by the magistrates' court, including those not appealed against. The Crown Court therefore had jurisdiction to impose penalty points in respect of offences which were not the subject of appeal by the defendant and his appeal would accordingly be dismissed (see p 386 *g* to *j* and p 387 *c*, post).

Notes

For the powers of the Crown Court on appeal, see 10 Halsbury's Laws (4th edn) para 879 and 29 ibid para 472.

For the Supreme Court Act 1981, s 48, see 11 Halsbury's Statutes (4th edn) 804.

Case referred to in judgments

R v Kent [1983] 3 All ER 1, [1983] 1 WLR 793, CA.

---

a   Section 48, so far as material, is set out at p 383 *j* to p 384 *d*, post

Case also cited

R v Yates [1986] RTR 64, CA.

Case stated

On 22 February 1985 the appellant, Narendra Nath Dutta, was convicted by justices sitting as a magistrates court at Highgate of driving without insurance, contrary to s 143 of and Sch 42 to the Road Traffic Act 1972, for which he was fined £100 and disqualified from driving for 12 months; failing to stop, contrary to s 25 of and Sch 4 to the 1972 Act, for which he was fined £30 and his licence was endorsed; failing to report an accident, contrary to s 25 of and Sch 4 to the 1972 Act, for which he was fined £40 and his licence was endorsed; driving a vehicle without a test certificate, contrary to s 44 of and Sch 4 to the 1972 Act, for which he was fined £25; and failing to produce his driving licence, contrary to s 161(1) of and Sch 4 to the 1972 Act, for which he was fined £5. He appealed against his conviction and sentence for the offence of driving without insurance. At the hearing of the appeal before the Crown Court at Wood Green (his Honour Judge McMullan and justices) on 3 May 1985 the court quashed the conviction and sentence and then decided that the court had jurisdiction to vary the sentence for the other offences by imposing penalty points. At the request of the appellant the court stated a case for the opinion of the High Court on the question whether the Crown Court on allowing an appeal against conviction by the magistrates on one information had jurisdiction to vary sentences imposed on conviction of other informations which were tried on the same occasion but which were not the subject of the appeal. The facts are set out in the judgment of Woolf LJ.

Beverley Lang for the appellant.
Nicholas Easterman for the respondent.

WOOLF LJ. This is an appeal by way of a case stated by his Honour Judge McMullan and two lay justices sitting at the Crown Court at Wood Green. It raises a question of the extent of the powers of a Crown Court on an appeal from a decision of the magistrates' court when a defendant has been convicted and sentenced for a number of offences, but only appeals against conviction or sentence or both in relation to some of the offences in respect of which he has been convicted. It is surprising that there has been no previous occasion on which this particular problem has been considered by the courts.

On 22 February 1985 the appellant was convicted in his absence of a series of motoring offences. The most serious offence was the offence of driving without insurance contrary to s 143 of and Sch 4 to the Road Traffic Act 1972. In respect of that offence he was sentenced to 12 months' disqualification and a fine of £100 was imposed.

He was also dealt with for failing to stop and give his name and address to the owner when required to do so by a person having reasonable grounds for so requiring, contrary to s 25 of and Sch 4 of the 1972 Act, and in respect of that matter he was fined £30, his licence was endorsed, but he was not disqualified. It was an offence in respect of which disqualification could be imposed and it is an offence which, if it stood alone, was one which would have required the imposition of between five and nine penalty points.

The third offence in respect of which he was convicted was that of failing to report an accident at a police station or to a police constable as soon as reasonably practicable within 24 hours of the occurrence, contrary to s 25 of and Sch 4 to the 1972 Act. In respect of that matter a fine of £40 was imposed and his licence was ordered to be endorsed. That again is an offence where there could have been a discretionary disqualification, and the penalty points which it would be appropriate to impose under the 1972 Act if the matter was being considered alone were between four and nine.

Fourthly, he was convicted of driving a vehicle in respect of which no test certificate had been issued within the appropriate period, contrary to s 44 of the 1972 Act. In respect of that matter a fine of £5 was imposed.

In relation to that offence there is no power to disqualify, and no question of penalty

points arises. The position is the same with regard to the final offence which was dealt
a with, which was failing to produce his licence for examination as to name and address of
the holder, date of issue etc, contrary to s 161(1) of and Sch 4 to the 1972 Act. In respect
of that matter a fine of £5 was imposed.

All the offences arose out of the same circumstances. After he had been convicted he
actually appeared before the magistrates' court having arrived late. He then had with
him an insurance certificate but the magistrates regarded themselves as having finally
b disposed of the matter which they could not reopen, and so the conviction on the first
offence to which I have referred stood, although if the magistrates had been able to
reopen the matter it would have been inevitable that they would have come to a different
conclusion, as was made apparent when the appellant appealed to the Crown Court.

The reason why no penalty points were imposed by the magistrates in respect of the
second and third offences to which I referred is because of the terms, first of all of s 19(1)
c of the Transport Act 1981, from which it is clear that if on an occasion when they are
dealing with a defendant the magistrates disqualify in respect of one offence, then they
do not order particulars of the penalty points to be endorsed on his licence under s 101 of
the 1972 Act in respect of other offences which they are also considering.

That position was dealt with by the Criminal Division of the Court of Appeal in R v
Kent [1983] 3 All ER 1, [1983] 1 WLR 793. The court, when referring to s 19(1) of the
d 1981 Act, to which I have made reference, indicated that that was the position.

The same conclusion is also to be drawn from the wording of s 101(1) of the 1972 Act,
as amended by para 6 of Sch 9 to the 1981 Act, which makes it clear that the particulars
of penalty points are only required to be endorsed on the licence if the court 'does not
order him to be disqualified'.

The magistrates, however, do not ignore the question of penalty points in dealing with
e the offender for the offences in respect of which he had not been disqualified because
they are required to take those into consideration under s 19(3) of the Transport Act 1981
in deciding whether this is a case in which to make what is colloquially called 'a totting
up' disqualification under sub-s (2) of s 19 of the Act. This is a case therefore where, if it
had not been for the disqualification that was imposed in respect of the first offence,
penalty points would undoubtly have been imposed in respect of the other offences,
f although presumably the magistrates would not have regarded this case as a case that
required them to disqualify the appellant under s 19(2).

The appellant then appealed to the Crown Court, and he limited his notice of appeal
to the first offence to which I have referred. He limited his appeal to conviction in respect
of that offence. The grounds of appeal which he set out were that he had an insurance
certificate. When the matter came before the Crown Court on 3 May 1985 on that notice
g of appeal, the Crown Court allowed the appeal and then wished to consider what was to
happen in respect of the penalty points which had not been imposed in respect of the
second and third offences to which I made reference.

The appellant was not represented on that occasion but, having heard argument, it
appears from the case stated that the Crown Court judge and the justices came to the
conclusion that they had power to look into the question of the penalty points in respect
h of the second and third offences. The powers of the Crown Court are set out in s 48 of
the Supreme Court Act 1981 as amended. It is to be noted that although those powers
are now contained in that Act, they have appeared in a similar form in earlier acts for
many, many years, and they in fact governed the powers of Quarter Sessions on appeals
from magistrates prior to the creation of the Crown Court.

Section 48 of the Supreme Court Act 1981 provides:

j   '(1) The Crown Court may, in the course of hearing any appeal, correct any error
    or mistake in the order or judgment incorporating the decision which is the subject
    of the appeal.
          (2) On the termination of the hearing of an appeal the Crown Court—(a) may
    confirm, reverse or vary the decision appealed against; or (b) may remit the matter
    with its opinion thereon to the authority whose decision is appealed against; or (c)

may make such other order in the matter as the court thinks just, and by such order exercise any power which the said authority might have exercised . . .'

The reference in s 48(2)(c) to 'the said authority' clearly refers back to the authority whose decision is appealed against, and although in the course of argument it was suggested that the word 'authority' has some special meaning, in my view it clearly is a term which applies to magistrates where the appeal is against a decision of magistrates.

The relevant subsections of s 48 provide:

'(4) If the appeal is against a conviction or a sentence, the preceding provisions of this section shall be construed as including power to award any punishment, whether more or less severe than that awarded by the magistrates' court whose decision is appealed against, if that is a punishment which that magistrates' court might have awarded.

(5) This section applies whether or not the appeal is against the whole of the decision.

(6) In this section 'sentence' includes any order made by a court when dealing with an offender, including [and then there is reference to hospital orders and recommendation for deportation].'

The argument which is advanced on this appeal, and indeed was raised by the case stated, is whether those provisions to which I have just referred are wide enough to allow the Crown Court to do what it was proposing to do, namely to look into the question of the penalty points which should be imposed in respect of the second and third offences, and presumably to impose the penalty points which it regarded as appropriate, or at least to otherwise exercise in respect of those penalty points its powers under s 48(2), notwithstanding that the only matter which was expressly made the subject of the appeal was the conviction in respect of the first of the offences which was before the magistrates.

The way the matter is put in the case stated is that the question of law to be decided by this court is whether the Crown Court, in allowing the appeal against conviction by magistrates on one information, had jurisdiction to vary sentences imposed on conviction on other informations which were tried on the same occasion but which were not the subject of appeal in a case where the magistrates had applied s 19 of the Transport Act 1981 and the case of R v Kent to which I have already made reference.

Before this court we have had the advantage of very concise and effective arguments by both counsel for the appellant and counsel for the respondent. Counsel for the respondent, in support of the conclusion of the Crown Court, makes two separate submissions. First of all he submits that the wording of s 48 of the Supreme Court Act 1981 and in particular the critical phrase 'the decision which is the subject of the appeal' (which appears in the section more than once in a slightly different form) refers to the whole of the decision of the magistrates' court on the matters which were then before the Crown Court.

Alternatively, he submits that if that is not the proper construction of s 48, in a case of dealing with offences which are subject to the provisions of s 19 of the Transport Act 1981, a decision in relation to one offence which is dealt with by the magistrates shall be treated as being so linked to the other offences which are dealt with at the same time to which s 19 of that Act also applies, that they are all subject of the same 'decision'.

In relation to his second and narrower submission he submits that that must be the result because otherwise, as this case vividly illustrates, what will happen is that if a person is successful in an appeal against conviction and sentence or both in respect of an offence in relation to which a disqualification is imposed, and that disqualification is removed, the result will be that not only does the appellant have the advantage of having the disqualification removed, but in addition he has avoided the imposition of the penalty points which the magistrates would by law have been required, in the absence of one of the exceptions, to impose in respect of the penalty points, but which they could not impose because at the time when the matter was before them they were disqualifying. Of course, if the matter had come to them on separate occasions, they could have imposed

a
penalty points, and if they had decided not to impose disqualification in respect of the offence which was the subject of the successful appeal, again they could, and indeed would, have been obliged to impose penalty points.

Counsel for the appellant forcefully submits that first of all the wording of s 48 does not permit a construction which would justify the court seeking to do what the Crown Court decided was within its power on this particular occasion. She submits that the decision which is the subject of the appeal in this case is the decision in respect of the

b
single information and cannot be regarded as being a decision in respect of the other informations and that the powers of the Crown Court are confined to dealing with that particular decision.

In addition she submits that her approach to the interpretation of s 48 is in accord with the practice adopted by the Crown Court up and down the country in dealing with appellants every day of the year.

c
Finally she submits that to adopt the interpretation which the respondents would seek to persuade this court to adopt would first of all involve this court in impermissible legislation as opposed to performing its proper role of interpreting the statutory provisions, and furthermore would involve interpreting an Act in a manner which would be prejudicial to appellants to the Crown Court; and would be prejudicial to those who have been charged with criminal offences. Counsel for the appellant also submits

d
that we should regard s 48 of the Supreme Court Act 1981 as containing in effect a penal provision. However, I am bound to say that I would personally regard it as containing a procedural provision dealing with the powers of the Crown Court on appeals.

In considering the proper interpretation of the section, it seems to me important to bear in mind that the Crown Court, when it is exercising its jurisdiction, is rehearing the matter de novo. Whether it is dealing with conviction or sentence, the Crown Court

e
looks at the matter afresh. It is also important to bear in mind that so far as conviction is concerned, the interpretation contended for by the respondents could not in any way prejudice a defendant because it is only if he chooses to seek to upset a particular conviction that the Crown Court will wish to consider that conviction. Indeed, if the Crown Court acted of its own volition in the very unlikely situation that it wanted to do so, it could not in any way prejudice a defendant who has already been convicted.

f
So far as sentence is concerned, clearly if the Crown Court can consider the question of sentence in a wider way than a particular appellant intended, this could have adverse effects on an appellant, and this court must be conscious of that. However, it has to be borne in mind that sub-s (4) of s 48 makes it clear, which is what one would expect when one bears in mind that it is a rehearing, that the Crown Court is given expressly powers of punishment whether more or less severe than those that were ordered by the

g
magistrates' court. That applies in any event in relation to the actual offence which is appealed against, and undoubtedly applies even though the appeal is against conviction only. If the Crown Court dismiss the appeal against conviction, then even on the basis of counsel for the appellant's argument, as I read s 48 it is quite clear that if the Crown Court wanted to do so, it could look into the question of sentence again. It would have jurisdiction to do so, although as a matter of practice it would not normally do so. As far

h
as jurisdiction is concerned, it would have power to do so.

So the situation is one where the result of an appeal, if the respondents are correct, could work to the disadvantage of the appellant. Against that, quite apart from the special problem which is before this court, having regard to the provisions of the Transport Act 1981, if the Crown Court is going to consider an appeal in respect of one sentence, it is going to be a great deal of difficulty in performing that task satisfactorily

j
in many cases if it cannot also consider the sentences which were imposed at the same time.

Take a situation where an appellant wishes to appeal in respect of half the offences of which he has been convicted, but has been fined in respect of all the offences. In imposing the fines on all the offences, the magistrates' court are required in accordance with good sentencing practice to consider the means of the defendant, and if the means are such that it would not be possible for him to pay the appropriate fine, the court would reduce the fines which would otherwise be appropriate, having regard to his means. The situation could therefore result that if an appeal is successful in respect of a conviction of some of the offences but there is no appeal in regard to the others, so far as the other offences are concerned an artificial result is achieved because the defendant has been fined in respect of those other offences a lesser amount than otherwise would have been the case.

There can be situations where, in order to consider whether the fines in respect of some offences are right, it is necessary for the court to look at the position in regard to the other fines. Where a court is required in the sentencing to look de novo at a situation, it is going to be very handicapped if it can be limited by a carefully drawn notice of appeal only to looking at some sentences and not looking at other sentences. It is clear because of the other provisions of s 48 that a carefully drafted notice in respect of one offence cannot prevent the court looking at the whole penalty in respect of that particular offence, but that in itself would not overcome the problem to which I have made reference.

Then there is the fact that in relation to the Transport Act 1981 the approach contended for by the appellant would have the result that a particular defendant, if his appeal against conviction is allowed on an offence in respect of which he has been disqualified, would in fact avoid penalty points which it was the court's duty as a matter of law to impose, and the whole policy of s 19 of the Transport Act 1981 would be defeated if that was the consequence.

Having regard to the respectable maturity of the provisions of s 48 of the Supreme Court Act 1981, I do not think that it is permissible to look at the latter consequence in deciding the proper interpretation of s 48 because it would be in effect looking at a later provision and construing the earlier provision in the light of the new provision. However, if the respondents are right in their contention, it does have the satisfactory result that the powers of the Crown Court are not so limited as to produce that undesirable consequence.

In addition, if the respondents are right, it would bring the position of the Crown Court in line with that of the High Court in dealing with questions of sentence. So far as the High Court is concerned, and here I refer to the Criminal Division of the Court of Appeal, there is express provision contained in s 11(2) of the Criminal Appeal Act 1968, which makes it clear that that division is not constrained in the way that counsel for the appellant submits the Crown Court is constrained. Again the provisions of the 1968 Act cannot assist in the interpretation of s 48 of the Supreme Court Act 1981.

In my view one is forced back to the meaning of the words to which I made reference, 'the decision which is the subject of the appeal'. So far as those words are concerned, it is quite clear from s 48 itself that the decision which is the subject of an appeal cannot mean merely a decision to convict or a decision to sentence. Even on counsel for the appellant's suggestion it includes both a decision to convict and then after the decision to impose a sentence. It is my view that the word 'decision' as used in s 48 is being used in a wide sense. I regard it as clear from the wording of s 48 as a whole that what was intended by the words to which I have referred, which are not in my view words of art, was that the Crown Court should have the right to confirm, reverse or vary the whole of the decision made by the magistrates' court on the occasion on which the conviction or sentence which was the subject expressly of the appeal was made. Therefore, although an appellant chooses only to appeal against part of the decision, namely, a particular conviction or a particular sentence, the Crown Court has jurisdiction in respect of all the matters which were then before the court.

I emphasise, however, that in the normal way the Crown Court will not need to investigate all the matters. Certainly with regard to sentence it does not have to approach the matter in blinkers. It can look at all the sentences. Furthermore, where as in this case an appeal against conviction affects the position in respect of the provision under the Transport Act 1981, the Crown Court can impose the penalty points which the magistrates would have been required to impose but for the sentence for the offence in respect of which the appeal was allowed.

a   In adopting that interpretation I have sought to give effect to the wording of the section as a whole, including the intent as manifested in the section, and I certainly do not regard myself as taking the course which counsel for the appellant properly counselled the court against. If, in fact, s 48 of the Supreme Court Act 1981, was not wide enough to give the Crown Court powers to remedy the situation which this appeal has thrown up, arising out of the provisions of s 19 of the Transport Act 1981, then that would be something which would be unfortunate, but it would be for Parliament to deal with, not

b   for this court. Having regard to my reading of s 48, I do not consider that intervention by legislature is necessary and that the Crown Court's powers are ample. I would explain the absence of any previous authority on the situation because, in practice, I do not believe that there have been many cases where the Crown Court would have felt itself inhibited in not passing the appropriate sentence when in circumstances such as this it allowed an appeal.

c   Accordingly, I would answer the questions posed by the Crown Court by saying that the Crown Court has the jurisdiction which it felt it had to vary the sentence in the way that is indicated in the case, and I would dismiss this appeal.

MACPHERSON J. I agree with all that Woolf LJ has said and wish to add nothing.

d   *Appeal dismissed.*

Solicitors: *Simons Muirhead Allan & Burton* (for the appellant); *R E Marsh* (for the respondent).

Michael Wall Esq   Barrister.

e

Sim v Rotherham Metropolitan Borough Council
and other actions

f

CHANCERY DIVISION
SCOTT J
17, 18, 19, 20, 21, 25, 26 MARCH, 22, 23 APRIL, 23 MAY 1986

g   *Education – Teacher – Contract of employment – Breach of contract – Refusal to cover for absent colleague – Whether teacher having contractual obligation to provide cover – Whether refusal to cover for absent colleague constituting breach of contract.*

Set-off – Cross-claim – Equitable right of set-off – Contract of employment – Teacher – Claim for salary – Teacher refusing to provide cover for absent colleague in breach of contract of employment

h   *– Employer deducting appropriate sum by way of damages from teacher's monthly salary – Teacher bringing action against employer for full salary – Whether equitable right of set-off available in action for salary under contract of employment.*

In January 1985, in the course of a long-running dispute between secondary school teachers and their employers, ie local education authorities, the teachers' union instructed

j   its members to refuse to co-operate with a practice in schools known as 'covering' whereby teachers who were not scheduled to teach during a particular teaching period were asked to stand in and take classes for absent colleagues. In compliance with these instructions, the four plaintiff teachers refused to cover for absent colleagues during a 35-minute teaching period when asked to do so by their respective head teachers. In response, the defendant education authorities deducted between £2·00 and £3·37 from the plaintiffs' monthly salaries by way of damages. The contracts under which the plaintiffs were employed contained no provisions either regarding their obligations to provide cover for absent colleagues or regarding the extent of their obligations as teachers. *a* The plaintiffs brought actions against the defendants for recovery of the sums deducted from their salaries, contending that the cover system was provided by teachers as a matter of goodwill and was not a contractual obligation and alternatively, that the defendants were not entitled to make deductions from the plaintiffs' salaries by way of equitable set-off because, inter alia, the doctrine of set-off did not apply to contracts of employment and even if it did, it did not apply in the plaintiffs' case because failure to comply with a *b* cover request for such a short period of time could not bring the doctrine into operation.

Held – (1) For the purposes of determining the ambit of teachers' contractual obligations, the correct approach was to decide whether the obligation in question was one of the professional obligations owed by a teacher to his pupils and to his school, and if it was, then failure to comply with the obligation was prima facie a breach of contract. Accordingly, since cover arrangements were administrative directions necessary for the *c* proper conduct of a school and since teachers had always accepted a professional obligation to comply with cover arrangements in the same way as they had accepted a professional obligation to comply with the school timetable, it followed that the plaintiffs had a contractual obligation to comply with the request to cover for absent colleagues and their refusal to do so was a breach of contract (see p 403 *b* to *d*, p 404 *j*, p 405 *c* to *g*, p 406 *g* to p 407 *a c* to *g j* to p 408 *b*, post); dictum of Lord Wilberforce in *Liverpool City Council v* *d* *Irwin* [1976] 2 All ER at 44 applied.

(2) Equitable set-off was available to an employer as a possible defence to an action for salary by an employee because where an employee, in breach of contract, failed or refused to perform his contractual services, his right to recover his full salary for the period during which the failure or refusal occurred could be impeached by a cross-claim by the employer for damages and to allow the employee to recover his full salary in such *e* circumstances without taking into account the loss of those services to the employer would be manifestly unjust. Furthermore, equitable set-off depended on the nature of the breach relative to the nature of the contractual claim rather than on the size of the damages (provided they were more than merely nominal damages) or the severity of the breach of contract. Accordingly, the defendants were entitled to make the deductions from the plaintiffs' salaries by way of equitable set-off and it was irrelevant that the *f* breaches of contract were of short duration and that the damages attributable to the breaches were correspondingly small (see p 415 *c* to *g* and p 416 *a g*, post); *Aries Tanker Corp v Total Transport Ltd* [1977] 1 All ER 398, dictum of Forbes J in *British Anzani (Felixstowe) Ltd v International Marine Management (UK) Ltd* [1979] 2 All ER at 1068, *Royle v Trafford BC* [1984] IRLR 184 and *Miles v Wakefield Metropolitan DC* [1985] 1 All ER 905 considered. *g*

Notes

For the discharge of contractual obligations, see 9 Halsbury's Laws (4th edn) paras 472–478.

For employment of teachers, see 15 ibid paras 211–216.

For equitable set-off, see 42 ibid paras 424–431, and for cases on set-off generally, see 41 Digest (Reissue) 4–9, 1–54. *h*

Cases referred to in judgment

Aries Tanker Corp v Total Transport Ltd [1977] 1 All ER 398, [1977] 1 WLR 185, HL; *affg* [1976] 2 Lloyd's Rep 256, CA.

Associated Provincial Picture Houses Ltd v Wednesbury Corp [1947] 2 All ER 680, [1948] 1 KB 223, CA.

British Anzani (Felixstowe) Ltd v International Marine Management (UK) Ltd [1979] 2 All ER *j* 1063, [1980] QB 137, [1979] 3 WLR 451.

Button v Thompson (1869) LR 4 CP 330.

Cia Sud Americana de Vapones v Shipnair BV, The Teno [1977] 2 Lloyd's Rep 289.

Federal Commerce and Navigation Ltd v Molena Alpha Inc, The Nanfri, The Benfri, The Lorfri [1978] 3 All ER 1066, [1978] QB 927, [1978] 3 WLR 309, CA; *affd in part* [1979] 1 All ER 307, [1979] AC 757, [1978] 3 WLR 991, HL.

Gilbert-Ash (Northern) Ltd v Modern Engineering (Bristol) Ltd [1973] 3 All ER 195, [1974]
AC 689, [1973] 3 WLR 421, HL.
Hanak v Green [1958] 2 All ER 141, [1958] 2 QB 9, [1958] 2 WLR 755, CA.
Lister v Romford Ice and Cold Storage Co Ltd [1957] 1 All ER 125, [1957] AC 555, [1957] 2
WLR 158, HL.
Liverpool City Council v Irwin [1976] 2 All ER 39, [1977] AC 239, [1976] 2 WLR 562, HL.
Mediana (owners) v Comet (owners), The Mediana [1900] AC 113, [1900–3] All ER Rep 126,
HL.
Miles v Wakefield Metropolitan DC [1985] 1 All ER 905, [1985] 1 WLR 822, CA.
Mondel v Steel (1841) 8 M & W 858, [1835–42] All ER Rep 511, 151 ER 1288.
Moorcock, The (1889) 14 PD 64, [1886–90] All ER Rep 530, CA.
National Coal Board v Galley [1958] 1 All ER 91, [1958] 1 WLR 16, CA.
Piggott v Williams (1821) 6 Madd 95, 56 ER 1027.
Redbridge London BC v Fishman [1978] ICR 569, EAT.
Royle v Trafford BC [1984] IRLR 184.
Sagar v H Ridehalgh & Son Ltd [1931] 1 Ch 310, CA.
Steam Sand Pump Dredger (No 7) (owners) v Greta Holme (owners), The Greta Holme [1897]
AC 596, [1895–9] All ER Rep 127, HL.

Cases also cited
Cherry Ltd v Wergles (1954) Times, 13 January.
Cresswell v Board of Inland Revenue [1984] 2 All ER 713.
Davis v Hedges (1871) LR 6 QB 687.
Gardner (F C) Ltd v Beresford [1978] IRLR 63.
Healey v SA Française Rubastic [1917] 1 KB 946.
Henthorn v Central Electricity Generating Board [1980] IRLR 361, CA.
Hoenig v Isaacs [1952] 2 All ER 176, CA.
Jones v Associated Tunnelling Co Ltd [1981] IRLR 477.
Le Loir v Bristow (1815) 4 Camp 134, 171 ER 43.
Mears v Safecar Security Ltd [1982] 2 All ER 865, [1983] QB 54, CA.
Pagnan (R) & Flli v Corbisa Industrial Agropacuaria Lda [1971] 1 All ER 165, [1970] 1 WLR
1306, CA.
*Secretary of State for Employment v Associated Society of Locomotive Engineers and Firemen
(No 2)* [1972] 2 All ER 949, [1972] 2 QB 455, NIRC and CA.
Sharp v Hainsworth (1862) 3 B & S 139, 122 ER 53.
Sumpter v Hedges [1898] 1 QB 673, CA.
Williams v North's Navigation Collieries (1889) *Ltd* [1906] AC 136, HL.

Actions and counterclaims

Sim v Rotherham Metropolitan Borough Council

By a writ and statement of claim dated 17 April 1985 the plaintiff, Jane Elizabeth Sim, sought as against the defendant, Rotherham Metropolitan Borough Council (Rotherham), (i) a declaration that the defendant was not entitled to make any deductions from the plaintiff's salary in respect of her refusal to teach or otherwise supervise the class of a fellow teacher employed by the defendant who continued to be absent from work for more than one day and (ii) the sum of £2·17 which the defendant had deducted from the plaintiff's salary. By a defence and counterclaim dated 13 June 1985 the defendant sought declarations (i) that by refusing to comply with the request to take a class for an absent colleague during a non-teaching period and during the first three consecutive days of absence of that colleague the plaintiff acted in breach of her terms and conditions and in breach of her contract with the defendant, (ii) that the defendants were accordingly entitled to deduct £2·17 from her salary, and (iii) that if the plaintiff again refused to comply with a request to take a class for an absent colleague during a non-teaching period and during the first three consecutive days of absence of that colleague, as in the circumstances of the present case, the defendants were entitled to employ a supply teacher to perform this duty and to deduct the cost to the defendant from the plaintiff's salary as damages (or as a sum otherwise due) for breach of contract. The facts are set out in the judgment.

Townend v Doncaster Metropolitan Borough Council

By a writ and statement of claim dated 5 June 1985, the plaintiff, Raymond Townend, sought as against the defendant, Doncaster Metropolitan Borough Council (Doncaster), (i) a declaration that the defendant was not entitled to make any deductions from the plaintiff's salary in respect of his refusal to teach, supervise or otherwise cover the class of a fellow teacher employed by the defendant at the same school as the plaintiff where (a) the teacher's absence continued for more than one day and (b) the class occurred on a day falling after the first day of such absence and (ii) the sum of £3·37 which the defendant had deducted from the plaintiff's salary. By a defence and counterclaim dated 18 July 1985 the defendant sought declarations (i) that by refusing to comply with the request or instruction to take a class for an absent colleague during a non-teaching period and during the first three days of absence of that colleague, the plaintiff acted in breach of his contract with the defendant, (ii) that the defendant was accordingly entitled to deduct £3·37 from his salary, and (iii) that if the plaintiff again refused to comply with an instruction or request to take a class for an absent colleague during a non-teaching period and during the first three consecutive days of absence of that colleague, as in the circumstances of the present case the defendant was entitled to employ a supply teacher to perform this duty and to deduct the cost to the defendant from the plaintiff's salary as damages (or as a sum otherwise due) for breach of contract. The facts are set out in the judgment.

Barnfield v Solihull Metropolitan Borough Council

By a writ and statement of claim dated 20 May 1985 the plaintiff, Denis Barnfield, sought as against the defendant, Solihull Metropolitan Borough Council (Solihull), (i) a declaration that the defendant was not entitled to make any deductions from the plaintiff's salary in respect of his refusal to teach, supervise or otherwise cover the class of a fellow teacher employed by the defendant at the same school as the plaintiff where (a) the teacher's absence continued for more than one day and (b) the class occurred on a day falling after the first day of such absence, and (ii) the sum of £2·00 which the defendant had deducted from the plaintiff's salary. By reamended defence and amended counterclaim dated 26 June 1985, the defendant sought damages for breach of contract. The facts are set out in the judgment.

Rathbone v Croydon London Borough Council

By a writ and statement of claim dated 17 June 1985 the plaintiff, Christopher Mark Seamer Rathbone, sought as against the defendant, Croydon London Borough Council (Croydon), (i) a declaration that the defendant was not entitled to make any deductions from the plaintiff's salary in respect of his refusal to teach, supervise or otherwise cover the class of a fellow teacher, employed by the defendant at the same school as the plaintiff, where the intended absence of that teacher was known in advance, and (ii) the sum of £2·11 which the defendant had deducted from the plaintiff's salary. By an amended defence and counterclaim dated 23 July 1985, the defendant sought (i) damages and interest pursuant to s 35A of the Supreme Court Act 1981 and (ii) a declaration that by refusing to cover the class of a fellow teacher as directed by the head teacher when such teacher was absent (and whether such absence was known in advance or not) the plaintiff was in breach of his contract of employment. The facts are set out in the judgment.

Eldred Tabachnik QC, Andrew Hillier and *Adrian Lynch* for the plaintiffs in all four actions.
David Donaldson QC and *David Pannick* for Rotherham and Doncaster.
James Goudie QC and *Patrick Elias* for Solihull.
Elizabeth Appleby QC and *G Caws* for Croydon.

Cur adv vult

23 May. The following judgment was delivered.

a

SCOTT J. I have before me four actions. In each action the plaintiff is a secondary school teacher and the defendant is the local education authority by which the plaintiff is or was employed. Each of the plaintiffs is, or at the relevant time was, a member of the National Union of Teachers (the NUT). The actions arise out of the long-running dispute between teachers and their employers or, depending on one's point of view, between the teachers
b and the government, as to the rates of pay applicable to secondary school teachers.

It has for a long time been the practice in secondary schools for teachers to provide cover for absent colleagues. If a member of staff is absent from school some arrangement must be made for the periods that he or she was scheduled to teach. The practice employed in secondary schools throughout the country has been that some members of the staff not scheduled to teach during the period in question would be asked to stand in
c for the absent teacher. This practice is referred to colloquially as the 'cover system'. It is contended by the NUT and by the plaintiffs that the cover system is operated by secondary school teachers as a matter of goodwill. The local education authorities, on the other hand, regard the compliance by secondary school teachers with requests to provide cover for absent colleagues as a matter of contractual obligation.

By a letter dated 30 January 1985 the general secretary of the NUT wrote a letter to the
d chief education officers in England and Wales. The letter was in these terms:

> 'I write to advise you that in the view of the decision of the management panel of the Burnham Committee to offer a salary increase for April 1985 of an insulting 4 per cent together with their indication that they saw no future in any further negotiations of this claim in the Burnham Committee, the Executive of the Union has agreed that members should, from 6 February 1985: a) refuse to cover for
e absences which are known in advance of the event or other absences after the first day of absence; b) refuse to supervise pupils during the lunch period and refuse to stay on the premises during that time; c) refuse to take part in any sporting, musical, dramatic or like events at lunchtime; d) refuse to undertake administrative or accounting tasks in connection with the school meals service; e) refuse to attend staff, departmental, year meetings etc. held outside the times of the school sessions;
f and f) refuse to attend parent consultation meetings outside the time of the school sessions. I hope, naturally, that wiser counsels will prevail and a satisfactory offer in response to the Teachers' Panel claim may be made at an early date.'

The letter refers to six different categories of services customarily provided by secondary school teachers over and above their basic teaching duties. It is contended by
g the NUT that the services referred to under these paragraphs are extra-contractual. I am not in these actions concerned with paras (b) to (f). I am only concerned with para (a) and the question whether or not secondary school teachers have a contractual obligation to provide cover for absent colleagues.

The union instructed its members to refuse to provide the services specified in the letter. Each of the plaintiffs, in compliance with those instructions, refused, when
h requested to do so, to cover for an absent colleague. The response of each of the defendants was to deduct from the refusing teacher's monthly salary a sum to represent the failure of the teacher to take the class for the period in question. The sums were all calculated on a time apportionment basis. They varied in amount: one was £2·17; another was £2·00; a third was £2·11; and the fourth was £3·37.

In each of the four actions before me, the plaintiff is suing to recover the sum deducted
j from his or her salary. But the real point of the actions is to obtain an answer to two important questions of principle. The first question is whether and to what extent secondary school teachers have a contractual obligation to provide cover for absent colleagues. The second question of principle is whether, if refusal to provide cover represents a breach of contract, it is open to the local education authorities to make deductions from the teacher's salary. The four actions have been brought as test cases to obtain answers to these questions.

The question as to the propriety of the deductions cannot arise unless the first question is answered in favour of the defendants, that is to say, unless the plaintiffs' refusal to cover *a* was a breach of contract. The propriety of the deductions must depend not simply on the question of principle that I have formulated but also on the quantum of the deductions. It is, on the pleadings in each of the four actions, an issue whether the sums deducted by the defendants were excessive in amount. The cases were opened on that footing by counsel for the plaintiffs in all four actions. He argued that, since, on the facts, the defendants had incurred no additional expenditure or been caused any actual financial *b* loss by the refusals to provide cover, no damages, bar nominal damages, could be claimed. He has, however, rightly in my judgment, accepted that authorities drawn to my attention by counsel who appears for the Rotherham Metropolitan Borough Council and for the Doncaster Metropolitan Borough Council, establish that the defendants, if deprived by breach of contract of the services of their teachers, are entitled to claim by way of damages the value of those lost services (see *Steam Sand Pump Dredger (No 7)* *c* *(owners) v Greta Holme (owners), The Greta Holme* [1897] AC 596, [1895–9] All ER Rep 127, *Mediana (owners) v Comet (owners), The Mediana* [1900] AC 113, [1900–3] All ER Rep 126 and *National Coal Board v Galley* [1958] 1 All ER 91, [1958] 1 WLR 16). Counsel for the plaintiffs also accepts that in each of the four cases the value of the services of which the defendant was deprived was at least the amount of the deduction made.

So far as the deductions are concerned, therefore, no question arises as to quantum and *d* the only question is the important one of principle, namely whether it is open to employers to make deductions on account of damages at all.

I must set out the factual background against which the two questions must be considered. I propose first to describe the administrative and other arrangements that seem, from the evidence I have heard, to be applicable to all secondary schools. Then I shall deal in turn with the position of each of the four plaintiffs. *e*

General

The employment of a secondary school teacher by a local education authority is almost invariably preceded by some form of public advertisement. The normal advertisement will specify the subject required to be taught, the standard to which it is required to be taught and the salary scale applicable to the post. Selection procedures, usually involving *f* interviews, will follow.

The selection by the local education authority of the successful applicant for the post, and the agreement by the applicant to accept the post, will be recorded either by a formal letter of appointment or by a formal written agreement.

In each of the four cases with which I am concerned, the relevant formal document had the effect of incorporating into the terms of the employment the conditions set out *g* in a booklet entitled 'Conditions of Service for Schoolteachers in England and Wales'. These conditions result from collective agreements between the teachers' organisations on the one hand and the local education authority associations on the other hand. The 60-odd pages of this booklet are bound together in a burgundy-coloured jacket. The booklet is colloquially known, and I shall refer to it as 'the Burgundy Book'. Condition 11 of the Burgundy Book is in these terms: *h*

> '*Definition of the Teacher's Day, Duties and Holiday Entitlement*   There are no existing national collective agreements on these matters beyond that affecting the school midday break which is set out in Appendix VII.'

Appendix VII a Department of Education and Science circular 16/68 issued on 15 August 1968. Paragraph 7 of the appendix says: *j*

> 'Activities which take place between sessions and after school differ in their nature from those that take place during sessions, since in general the former are voluntary and the latter compulsory.'

In the present four cases, the cover obligations of teachers for which the defendants contend relate to periods during school sessions. It is, of course, possible that a particular

teacher in a particular school may, by agreement or arrangement, be scheduled to take a
a class outside normal school hours. The question whether a teacher has any contractual
obligation to take a class outside normal school hours, whether in accordance with a
timetable or as cover for an absent colleague, has not been argued before me. The cover
obligations with which I am concerned relate only to periods within normal school
hours. Apart from the passage in the App VII circular that I have read, the Burgundy
Book is silent as to the duties of the teachers to provide cover for absent colleagues.

b   Section 17(3)(b) of the Education Act 1944 requires that—

'every county secondary school . . . shall be conducted in accordance with articles
of government made . . . by an order of the local education authority and approved
by the Secretary of State . . .'

Pursuant to this statutory requirement, each of the defendants has made articles of
c government applicable to its secondary schools. The respective articles are in much the
same form. They provide that the head teacher of a school shall control the internal
organisation, management and discipline of the school and the arrangement of classes
and shall exercise supervision over the teaching and non-teaching staff. The articles
provide also either that a copy thereof shall be given to every teacher on entry into office
or, in one case, that a copy thereof is to be available at the school for inspection by every
d teacher. Under the articles, therefore, the head teacher is the administrative head of the
school.
    It is one of the administrative duties of the head teacher to arrange for the compilation
of a school timetable for each school year. Compilation of the timetable will take place
over the first six months or so of each calendar year in order to be brought into effect at
the beginning of the new school year in September.
e   The purpose of the timetable is to inform each pupil and each teacher of the place and
time of each class that is to take place during the week. Every pupil must know to which
classroom and for which class he or she must go. Each teacher must know which class
and in which classroom he or she must teach. No school could operate without a
timetable.
    The procedure for the preparation of the timetable followed in the four schools with
f which I am concerned is, broadly, the same. The head teacher delegates the task to one
or more fairly senior members of staff. Consultations take place with members of staff,
particularly heads of departments. Before a proposed timetable becomes final,
opportunities are afforded to members of the staff to make representations about its
contents.
    The school day is divided into eight periods, each of 35 minutes. There are, therefore,
g 40 periods in the school week. The school day commences with registration of pupils at
8.45 am. Teachers are expected to arrive at school in time for this registration.
Registration is followed by school assembly. The first class of the day will usually
commence at 9.15 am, after assembly. There will be a short break in mid-morning and
a longer break at midday. The afternoon session follows the same pattern. The last period
of the day will come to an end between 3.45 pm and 4.00 pm, depending on the
h arrangements at the particular school.
    It is accepted that, in secondary schools, it is not desirable that teachers should teach
during all 40 periods of the school week. Effective teaching requires time for the
preparation of lessons and for the marking of work, whether homework or work done at
school. Accordingly, it is the practice in all secondary schools for the timetable to be so
drawn as to allow each teacher a certain number of non-teaching periods each week. The
j number of these non-teaching periods is not fixed by the local education authorities. It
will be dependent on the circumstances at each individual school and on the duties and
responsibilities of the individual teachers. Heads of department may, for instance, need
more non-teaching periods than more junior teachers.
    Inevitably from time to time teachers will be absent and unable to take the classes that,
according to the timetable, they are due to teach. Absences may result from accident or
illness and be preceded by little or no warning. It may, on the other hand, be known in

advance that absences on particular days or at particular times are going to occur. Jury service, hospital appointments, attendance at courses are examples of cases where absences are known in advance. All schools have, and must have, standing arrangements for dealing with the situation that arises when absences occur. These arrangements are the cover arrangements. The necessity for these arrangements is obvious. Classes cannot be left unsupervised, otherwise there would likely be chaos. A head teacher who allowed that to happen would be in clear breach of his obligations of management of the school.

Cover arrangements are made on two levels. There are arrangements within the school and arrangements made by the local education authority. The former arrangements are necessary in order that a class whose teacher is absent does not go unsupervised. The latter also are necessary in order that the standard of teaching in the school should not suffer by reason of the absences and so that a proper complement of teachers and a proper pupil-teacher ratio may be maintained at the school.

The arrangements made by the various local education authorities differ in detail but are in principle the same. A reserve of supply teachers is maintained. If it is known in advance that a teacher will be absent the head teacher can apply to the local education authority for a supply teacher to be sent to cover the absence. Each local education authority has its own practice as to the circumstances in which supply teachers will be sent. The most usual practice seems to be to send a supply teacher after the third day of absence of the absent teacher. But some authorities, I was told, will send supply teachers to cover on the first or second day of absence if it is thought that the absence will continue for a period exceeding three days. One authority, Sheffield, is prepared, I was told, to provide immediate cover on the first day of a teacher's absence. Whatever the practice of an authority in this regard, it is essential that the practice should be known to each head teacher; otherwise the head teacher would not know what cover arrangements must be made within the school.

Cover arrangements within individual schools vary as to detail but follow a common pattern. A member of staff is given the responsibility of supervising the arrangements although the head necessarily remains ultimately responsible. A rota is kept so that, so far as practicable, members of staff bear an equal burden one with another. The arrangements are based on and utilise the non-teaching periods provided to teachers by the school timetable. The teacher asked to take an absent teacher's class for a particular period will always be a teacher for whom that period is a non-teaching period. It follows that cover arrangements within the school have the effect of reducing the number of non-teaching periods available to teachers.

The frequency of cover requests directed to a particular teacher will vary from school to school and from time to time. Absences on account of illness tend to be more frequent during the winter months than during the rest of the year. But, as a rough guide, I was told, a teacher might be expected to be called on to cover for an absent colleague about once a week.

A teacher who provides cover for an absent colleague has, as his or her main duty, the supervision of the class for the period in question. It may or may not be practicable for the cover teacher actually to teach the class being covered. That will depend on the cover teacher's knowledge of the relevant subject. So far as is within the ability of the cover teacher, however, he or she will endeavour to teach as well as to supervise the class.

On the evidence I heard, cover arrangements broadly on the lines I have described are employed in all secondary schools and always have been. The main question in the four cases is whether the arrangements are complied with by teachers as a matter of contractual obligation or voluntarily as a matter of goodwill.

From time to time, discussions have taken place between the unions representing the teachers and the local education authority associations concerning the extent of secondary school teachers' duties under their contracts. Consensus between the two sides seems never to have been reached. The discussions are, however, valuable for the purposes of identifying areas of uncertainty.

The minutes of a meeting on 5 November 1976 record:

'The representatives of CLEA [ie the local education authorities association]

readily agreed that traditionally schools had carried out activities which went far
beyond any statutory or contractual definition of a teacher's job, eg games,
educational, recreational and cultural out of school activities. Many such activities
took place outside the hours of 9–4. But in their view some of those activities were
an integral part of a teacher's job. For example, there must be a school organisation;
therefore there must be staff meetings. With many pupils it was desirable both to
know something of their background which could only be obtained in discussion
with parents and to seek the cooperation of parents; therefore there was a need for
parents' evenings. Many teachers themselves had expressed their dissatisfaction with
the uncertainties attending their contracts and conditions of service. It was therefore
important to recognise that there was that doubt and jointly to discuss it before
positions on either side become fixed. There were two extreme positions. On the
one hand it was said that any work outside the hours of 9–4 was over and above the
teacher's contract. And on the other hand there was the view that the teacher should
be available for duty whenever so required by the head teacher or the school
authorities, indeed every day, if necessary. Neither view would commend itself to
the general public. The solution lay between the two extremes. The present position
was certainly too open-ended; but it needn't be as rigid as the first proposition.'

The NUT at its 1982 annual conference resolved, inter alia, that 'teachers on the normal
establishment of schools should no longer be required to cover for absent colleagues'.
The use of the verb 'required' reflects the long-accepted de facto position, whatever the
de jure position. A document of 14 June 1983 sets out what the teachers' unions wanted
from the local education authorities:

'*Cover* Each local authority should establish staffing formulae that contain an
element for supply provision, with teachers employed on permanent contracts who
are eligible for above scale posts. The number of teachers so employed together with
those supply teachers engaged on a daily basis should be such to ensure that there is
immediate cover available when teachers are absent making it unnecessary for
teachers on the normal establishment of the school to provide cover.'

The local education authorities were not prepared to agree to this.

Throughout the period from 1980 to 1984 the teachers' unions were asking for a
guaranteed minimum of non-teaching time to be provided to secondary school teachers.
The local education authorities were not prepared to agree to this except as part of a larger
package which would deal also with the question of teachers' contractual obligations in
respect of such matters as parents' meetings and other out of school activities.

Notwithstanding that discussions as to the ambit of teachers' contractual duties,
including their duty to comply with cover arrangements, have been continuing now for
over ten years, the parties are apparently no closer to agreement now than they were in
1974.

The main issue in the four cases with which I am concerned is, I repeat, whether or
not teachers have a contractual duty to comply with cover arrangements. The contractual
documents are silent on this point and, as I have said, the negotiations between the
unions and the associations have not reached agreement on the point. None the less,
there is an important area of common ground as to teachers' obligations.

None of the plaintiffs contends that any individual teacher is entitled to any specific
number of non-teaching periods in any week. They accept whatever the timetable
allocates. Further, while denying any contractual obligation to give up non-teaching
periods in order to comply with cover arrangements, the plaintiffs all accept a contractual
obligation to remain at the school premises during the whole of the school day unless
excused from such attendance by the head or by someone speaking with the authority of
the head. They do not contend that during their non-teaching periods they are entitled
to leave the school premises and go about their own business. It is important to notice
also that all witnesses, both on the teachers' side and on the employers' side, accepted that
a teacher, in order to do his or her job properly, would have to spend some time outside
school hours in marking school work and in preparing for classes. The allocation to

teachers of non-teaching periods recognises the teachers' need of time to carry out these essential tasks. But whether or not non-teaching periods are regarded as sacrosanct, it is accepted by teachers that, in addition to using non-teaching periods for these purposes, they will have to spend time outside school hours as well. The effect of cover arrangements, therefore, is that by eating into non-teaching periods, they increase the amount of time outside school hours that teachers must devote to the chores of marking schoolwork and preparing for classes.

All secondary school teachers are remunerated in accordance with annual salary levels laid down by the so-called Burnham scale. The salaries, although expressed as annual sums, are paid monthly in arrears. It is consistent with the status of teaching as a profession that teachers cannot claim extra payment for work they do outside school hours. The concept of overtime is inapplicable to teachers' contracts. It is an accepted feature of the teachers' profession that to some extent at least teachers have to work outside school hours without extra pay. This is common ground and, in my view, a very important part of the background against which the existence of an obligation on their part to comply with cover arrangements during the school day must be considered.

I now turn to the individual cases.

Sim v Rotherham Metropolitan Borough Council

By letter dated 4 August 1981 Miss Sim was appointed assistant teacher as from 1 September 1981 at Rawmarsh comprehensive school in Rotherham. She was an English teacher. The letter of appointment does not, however, mention her subject, English. Paragraph 1 reads:

'You are employed in the service of this Authority and you will serve on the staff of Rawmarsh Comprehensive School, or at such other place of employment as may be required.'

Paragraph 2 informed her that she would be paid in accordance with the Burnham scale and continued:

'You will be employed in full-time service exclusively in the capacity of a teacher; you will not be required to perform any duties except such as are connected with the work of the school or to abstain outside school hours from any occupations which do not interfere with the performance of your duties.'

She was given a copy of the timetable for the year 1981–82. Her timetable for the year 1984–85 was issued to her in the summer 1984. It provided her with six non-teaching periods per week: two on Monday, one on Tuesday, one on Wednesday and two on Friday.

In Rawmarsh comprehensive school special remedial teaching is arranged for pupils who need extra help. The arrangements were, when Miss Sim was at the school, made by a Mrs Hunter. Miss Sim volunteered to teach a remedial class. Period 7 on Wednesdays was, in 1984–85, one of her non-teaching periods and she agreed to take a remedial class during this period.

The cover arrangements at Rawmarsh comprehensive school were, by 1984 at least, well understood by Miss Sim. A notice was placed each morning on the notice-board in the staffroom. The notice would specify the periods and classes to be covered for colleagues absent on that day and, against each such period, the name of the member of staff who was to provide the cover. Each member of staff was expected to consult the notice on arrival at school each morning. Each teacher whose name appeared on the notice was required to place a tick against his or her name to signify that he or she had seen the notice and would take the class in question.

There were many occasions between 1981 and 1985 when, in accordance with the arrangements I have described, Miss Sim was requested to provide cover and did so. She told me that, until the industrial dispute had led to the union's request that its members refuse to cover, she had given no thought to whether or not she was contractually obliged to cover. 'Cover was just something you did' she told me.

_a_ Rotherham's policy regarding supply teachers is set out in a circular sent by the authority to all head teachers. The circular, as revised in August 1981, provides that:

'(i) In general a school must cover for an absence from its own resources for the first three days of the absence. (ii) A Special School may, at the discretion of the Head, seek a relief teacher from the first day of absence. (iii) Any school may, at the discretion of the Head, seek a relief teacher from the first day of absence arising from the attendance of a member of staff at an approved course of in-service training.

_b_ (iv) When more than one teacher is absent on the same day and the Head considers that his existing staff are unable to cover if the three day rule is applied he should immediately refer to the appropriate Branch for advice.'

The threat of industrial action having been made by the NUT's letter of 30 January 1985, the director of education sent a letter dated 14 February 1985 to all Rotherham's

_c_ teacher employees. The letter made the authority's position crystal clear in these terms:

'Teachers have a duty to employ their professional skills for the full length of the pupil day. In addition teachers have a duty to provide their professional services at times other than during the pupil day in order to enable the Authority to fulfill its statutory duty to educate pupils in accordance with age, aptitude and ability.

_d_ _Teachers will, therefore, be regarded as being in breach of contract if:_ (a) they absent themselves from school or lessons for the whole or part of the pupil timetabled day without the prior approval of the Head Teacher for good cause; (b) they refuse to take classes during non-teaching periods for absent colleagues in the period before the Authority's normal arrangements for the supply of substitute teachers come into operation, or during non-teaching periods which are created by the absence of pupils taking examinations or by being away on such activities as a school trip . . .'

_e_ I need not read paras (c) to (i), which set out additional events in which, in the view of the authority, the teachers would be in breach of contract. The letter, however, went on:

'The Authority will on and from 25th February, 1985, start deducting damages from teachers involved in the industrial action identified previously in paragraphs (a), (b), (c) and (d). Any deductions will be made by the Authority as notional

_f_ damages having regard to the pupil day; such deductions being made on the following basis . . .'

There then follows a formula.

The head of Rawmarsh comprehensive school published to his staff a memorandum dated 25 February 1985; paras 3 and 4 contain this:

_g_ '3. Agreed cover/no cover for absent colleagues is already well known and will continue, for the present. 4. Where an absence is known in advance (normally illness) the teacher next on rota for cover will be asked by the Senior Master the day before if he/she is willing to cover. A refusal will cause the class involved to be excluded (see para 8) and the teacher concerned reported in due course to the L.E.A.

_h_ as per letter to all staff dated 14th February 1985.'

The NUT prepared a letter for its members to send in answer to that of 14 February 1985. Miss Sim signed and sent a copy of that letter. It said, inter alia: 'My Union rejects entirely the Authority's view that the above actions are in breach of contract'. And in the last paragraph of the letter:

_j_ 'Therefore I must make clear that I will, as called upon by my Union, continue to take the above actions until advised to the contrary by the National Union of Teachers and I do not regard myself in any way as being in breach of contract in so doing.'

On Wednesday 26 February 1985 Miss Sim was asked to provide cover for an absent teacher during period 7. Her name was placed on the cover notice by a Mr David Hoddle, second master at the school and the person to whom arrangement of cover duties had been delegated by the head. It will be recalled that period 7 on Wednesdays was one of Miss Sim's non-teaching periods. It was also the period that she had agreed to devote to remedial teaching. Mr Hoddle was aware that some teachers had agreed to give up some of their non-teaching periods to remedial teaching. He had told Mrs Hunter that in making cover arrangements the remedial extra periods would, if possible, be left untouched. They were not, however, regarded as sacrosanct. They did not count as timetabled periods. Miss Sim saw her name on the notice. Instead of placing a tick against it, she placed a cross to show that she was not prepared to take the class. She knew that if she refused to take the class the children would be sent home. That is what happened.

There is a subsidiary issue in Miss Sim's case with which I must deal. It is said that, if otherwise Miss Sim would have been under a contractual obligation to comply with the cover arrangements for period 7 on 26 February 1985 and take the class as requested, she was not, by reason of her prior agreement to take a remedial class during that period, under that contractual obligation. Her agreement to take the remedial class is put forward as a reason why her refusal to comply with the cover request was not a breach of contract. There is no substance in this point for a number of reasons.

First, Miss Sim did not, either at the time or subsequently, put forward her remedial class commitment as a reason why she could not comply with the cover request. She was commendably frank in making clear that she declined to comply with the cover request because it was union policy that she should do so.

Second, it was clearly understood within the school that cover arrangements took precedence over remedial teaching arrangements. Miss Sim told me that if it had not been for the union's request she would, if there had been a clash between cover arrangements and her remedial teaching arrangements, have complied with the cover arrangements. This evidence is consistent with the administrative primacy of the head. It was for the head, or his authorised delegate to decide on the relative importance of Miss Sim complying with the cover request and complying with her agreement to take a remedial class. If she was otherwise under a contractual duty to comply with the cover request she could not, in my judgment, avoid that duty by relying on her remedial teaching commitment. If she had gone to Mr Hoddle and asked to be excused cover so that she might take the remedial class, he might or might not have agreed. She did not do so but simply refused to comply with the cover request.

Miss Sim having refused to comply with the request that she cover for an absent colleague during period 7 on 26 February 1985, the matter was reported to the authority, her employer. The authority deducted £2·17 from her salary for the next month. That sum was calculated by the formula I have mentioned.

In December 1985 Miss Sim left Rawmarsh comprehensive school. She left the teaching profession for other employment.

Barnfield v Solihull Metropolitan Borough Council

Mr Barnfield is, and has been since 1 September 1971, the head of the biology department at Whitesmore comprehensive school in Solihull. He was appointed by a letter of appointment dated 14 May 1971. The letter informed him that he was appointed 'in accordance with the Conditions of Service enclosed'. The conditions of service provided, inter alia, that 'hours of duty will be determined by and on behalf of the Local Education Authority. Overtime is not payable.'

The timetable for the school year 1984–85 was drawn up in the summer 1984. It followed discussions in which, in particular, heads of department participated. The time-table provided Mr Barnfield with ten non-teaching periods each week. These included period 3 on Thursdays. Two of Mr Barnfield's timetabled classes were sixth form classes scheduled to commence immediately after the last of the school's normal periods. To compensate for this he was provided with two extra non-teaching periods. Hence he had ten non-teaching periods instead of the seven or eight which would have been normal for a teacher of his seniority. Cover arrangements at Whitesmore school were dealt with by Mrs Chadbourne, the deputy head. She published each morning a list giving details

of the cover arrangements for the day. The manner in which cover arrangements
a operated was set out in a school handbook supplied to each teacher. The handbook
contains this: 'Cover for absent staff is displayed on the staff noticeboard. If the sub-list is
not on display by 8.30, notes will be sent to staff.' Mr Barnfield was naturally aware of
the cover arrangements. He had many times provided cover in accordance with them.
He told me in evidence that he had always regarded compliance with cover arrangements
as voluntary, rather than as a matter of contractual obligation. He agreed, however, that
b until the present industrial dispute he had never himself refused to comply with cover
arrangements and had never heard of any teacher doing so.

The policy of Solihull regarding supply teachers is set out in a letter dated 18 September
1980 to its head teachers. The letter reads:

> 'Supply Cover The supply cover for teachers is normally made after three days
> absence, but it has been agreed that where the absence is known in advance i.e, long
c> illness, maternity leave, or jury service, cover will be provided from the first day of
> absence.'

This policy was confirmed by a letter of 5 January 1981.

On 14 February 1985 Solihull Metropolitan Borough Council sent a letter to the
teachers at all its secondary schools, including Mr Barnfield. The letter referred to the
d notification of industrial action received from the NUT and continued thus:

> 'It is important that you should be aware that the Authority will regard you as
> being in breach of your contract if you engage in the action set out below and
> reserves its right to take whatever steps it considers appropriate. You are being
> notified of this so that you are aware of the Authority's view of the situation. It is
> not in any way seen as connected with the Authority's disciplinary procedures. The
e> action referred to is . . .'

And there follows a number of events of which (b) is: 'Refusal to cover for absent
colleagues.' On 4 March 1985, Solihull sent its teachers a further letter which referred to
the letter of 14 February 1985 and then continued:

> 'I am now writing formally to warn you of the steps being taken by the Authority
f> in respect of two of the actions listed in my earlier letter . . . (b) *Refusal to cover for*
> *absent colleagues* With effect from 5th March a deduction of £2 from your gross
> salary will be made in respect of each occasion on which you refuse a request from
> your Headteacher to cover one lesson for one absent colleague. Again, deductions
> will be made retrospectively from the next monthly payment. Deductions in respect
> of this form of action will not affect superannuation contributions or superannuable
g> service. You are being notified formally of the decision of the Authority in respect
> of these two forms of action.'

On the morning of Thursday, 14 March 1985 Mr Barnfield's name was on the cover
list. He was required to cover period 3 for an absent teacher. He went to see Mrs
Chadbourne and informed her that he would not comply with the cover request. He did
h not do so but instead used period 3 for getting on with marking schoolwork.

Mr Barnfield's refusal was reported to the authority. £2·00 was deducted from his
next salary payment. The £2·00 appears, from the letter of 4 March 1985, to be a
standard deduction figure decided on by the authority.

Townend v Doncaster Metropolitan Borough Council
j Mr Townend was appointed to teach woodwork at Stanforth boys' secondary school
with effect from 1 September 1963. The terms of his appointment were set out in a
memorandum of agreement dated 23 August 1963. Paragraph 7 of the agreement
provided that:

> 'The teacher shall be employed in full-time service and exclusively in the capacity
> of a teacher and shall not be required to perform any duties except such as are

connected with the work of the school or to abstain outside the school hours from
any occupations which do not interfere with the performance of his/her duties.'   *a*

By a letter of 28 September 1976 from the director of education, Mr Townend was
offered a post at Hatfield high school as head of woodwork and as the teacher in charge
of school transport. He accepted this appointment and still holds it. Mr Townend's duties
as head of woodwork need no explaining. His duties as the teacher in charge of school
transport required him to supervise the maintenance and use of three vehicles used for
transporting pupils to and from various extra-curricular functions.   *b*

The school timetable for 1984–85 was prepared after consultations with the school
heads of department, including Mr Townend. The timetable provided him with eight
non-teaching periods each week. These eight periods were arranged in two batches of
four consecutive periods, namely periods 5 to 8 inclusive on Monday and periods 1 to 4
inclusive on Wednesday. The purpose of this arrangement was to assist Mr Townend in
discharging his responsibilities in connection with the maintenance of the school vehicles. *c*
From time to time he had to take one or other of the vehicles to the garage for repairs,
MOT tests or servicing.

The cover arrangements employed at the school were well known to Mr Townend. A
list was placed on the staff notice-board in mid-morning. This list would contain the
details of cover arrangements for the afternoon. If a teacher was required to provide
cover during the morning session, he or she would receive a personal note to that effect *d*
from the person in charge of the cover arrangements.

Mr Townend had, during the many years he had been a teacher, provided cover
whenever requested to do so. Teachers, he told me, provided cover automatically. He
agreed that it was part of the job.

Doncaster policy regarding supply teachers was set out in a letter dated 30 August
1979 sent to all head teachers. Under the heading 'Casual Supply Staff' the letter says: *e*

> 'The general rule has been for supply staff to be allowed after three days,
> depending naturally on the particular circumstances in the schools (number of staff
> absent, total teaching staff etc.) The cost to the Authority of casual supply staff is
> considerable—in Primary/Middle Schools alone it is well in excess of £100,000 a
> year—and teachers are brought in to cover for such matters as illness, short courses, *f*
> school journeys (in termtime), educational visits, induction. The Authority have
> now decided that as a general rule cover will not be provided for the first five days
> of absence, but the particular circumstances in a school will be considered. It has
> also been agreed that NO cover will be provided for educational visits, school
> journeys (termtime), or for teachers attending short courses. These policies will also
> apply to non-teaching staffs. Heads are instructed not to bring in casual supply staff *g*
> without prior approval from the Department.'

So far as appears from the evidence before me, the authority's policy has remained
unchanged.

The authority received from the NUT a copy of the letter of 30 January 1985 to which
I have already referred. Its response to the notification of the intended industrial action
was to require the head teacher at each of its schools to give to each teacher a copy of a *h*
letter dated 8 February 1985. A copy of this letter was given to Mr Townend. It provided
as follows:

> 'This Authority has always regarded and continues to regard refusal to cover for
> absent colleagues as a breach of contract. I must make it clear to you, therefore, that
> if you take such action your Headmaster/Headmistress is required to report the facts *j*
> to us so that appropriate action can be taken. The Education Committee on 11th
> December 1984 confirmed that in respect of a refusal to cover by members of the
> N.A.S./U.W.T. action would at that stage be limited to a deduction from salary by
> way of notional damages in respect of each occasion on which the teacher refused to
> provide cover, the deduction to be calculated with regard to both the length of the
> period for which the teacher was requested to provide cover and the average length

of the pupils' timetabled day at the Authority's schools. In the case of a refusal to
accept additional pupils from the class of an absent colleague the deduction would
also have regard to the number of pupils normally registered in the class and the
number of additional pupils the teacher was asked and refused to accept. Subject to
confirmation by the Education Committee on 12th February 1985, a deduction of
salary as indicated in the preceding paragraph will be made in the case of any
member of the teaching staff who, in pursuance of industrial action, refuses to cover
the duties of an absent colleague.'

On Tuesday, 12 February the head teacher at Hatfield school personally asked Mr
Townend to cover for an absent colleague during period 4 the next morning. Mr
Townend refused. He was told that if he refused to provide cover as requested the
children in the class concerned would have to be sent home. Mr Townend gave the head
no reason for his refusal. There is no doubt, however, that the reason was the industrial
action advised by the NUT and I infer that this was known to the head.

The next morning, consistently with his refusal, Mr Townend did not take the class as
requested. Accordingly, the children were sent home. Mr Townend spent some part of
the Wednesday morning in taking one of the school vehicles to the garage. He was,
however, back at the school before the beginning of period 4. In accordance with the
intention expressed by the authority in its letter of 8 February 1985, the authority
deducted from Mr Townend's salary in March the sum of £3·37.

Rathbone v Croydon London Borough

By a letter dated 21 May 1979 the London Borough of Croydon appointed Mr
Rathbone a teacher at Purley high school for boys with effect from 1 September 1979.
He taught history, liberal studies and a civics course. On 1 September 1982 Mr Rathbone
became head of liberal studies.

Throughout the time Mr Rathbone has been at Purley high school, and indeed since
1969, the head teacher has been a Mr Ackers. Mr Ackers gave careful and valuable
evidence as to the manner in which the annual timetable was prepared and as to the
cover arrangements employed in the school.

The procedure adopted for the preparation of the annual timetable was very similar to
that adopted by the other schools. There would be discussions with heads of department;
a draft timetable would then be drawn up; the draft would be gone through with each
head of department and the final timetable would than be settled. The timetable would
provide for each teacher a certain number of non-teaching periods. However, one of
these non-teaching periods would be marked 'Reserve'. The significance of this was that
for the period marked 'Reserve' the teacher in question would be on standby to provide
cover in case an emergency should occur. The teacher would be expected to remain in
the staffroom for the first twenty minutes of the period in question so that, if an
emergency did occur, he or she could be easily found.

The timetable for 1984/85 provided Mr Rathbone with eight non-teaching periods
each week, namely periods 5 and 8 on Monday, periods 2 and 6 on Tuesday, periods 3, 7
and 8 on Thursday and period 7 on Friday. Period 7 on Thursday was marked 'Reserve'.

Cover arrangements were notified by a notice placed on the staff notice-board. All staff
members were expected to consult the notice on arrival at school in the morning. So far
as possible the persons asked to provide the cover would be taken from the same
department as that to which the absent teacher belonged.

The policy of Croydon regarding supply teachers is set out in a letter dated 1 October
1982 and repeated in a letter of 13 April 1984 sent to all head teachers. The letters say
this:

'*Supply Cover*
Head Teachers will know that the present policy regarding the appointment of
supply teachers is as follows . . .

Secondary [*schools*]
(a) Supply cover will be authorised from the fourth day;

(b) Supply cover will be authorised immediately for a second teacher absent during the same period.'

Croydon's response to the receipt of the NUT's letter of 30 January 1985 was to ask its head teachers to distribute to members of staff copies of a letter dated 5 February 1985 from the authority. The letter was to this effect:

'I have asked Head Teachers to distribute this letter to those members of staff who have indicated that they may be taking action in accordance with the National Union of Teachers' response to the continuing negotiations in regard to the pay claim which is due from 1st April, 1985. The Authority regrets that such action may occur at this time. Teachers who are contemplating such action should know, however, that the Authority regards the following as breaches of contract: (i) Refusal to cover for absent colleagues outside the Authority's normal practice ... The Authority will, therefore, make deductions from salary by way of damages as an appropriate response to any of the actions described above. Details of the way in which the damages are to be calculated will be sent to those teachers concerned. Head Teachers have been asked to inform me of the action taken by individual members of staff.'

A copy of this letter was distributed to Mr Rathbone.

By a letter dated 19 March 1985 to its teachers, Croydon explained the basis on which deductions from salary would be made.

On Friday, 15 March 1985 Mr Rathbone was asked to cover during period 7 for a Mr Wright who, like Mr Rathbone, was a member of the history department. Mr Rathbone went to see Mr Ackers, the head teacher, and told Mr Ackers he was not prepared to cover for Mr Wright. He apologised to Mr Ackers for having to refuse and made it clear that his refusal was occasioned by the industrial action. During period 7, instead of taking Mr Wright's class, Mr Rathbone marked outstanding schoolwork and prepared for his period 8 class.

I should record that Mr Rathbone, in cross-examination, expressed the opinion that the request for him to cover for Mr Wright was an unreasonable one since it was known to all concerned that he would have to refuse the request. He did not, however, express this somewhat subjective opinion to Mr Ackers.

The class which Mr Rathbone had been requested to take was not sent home. Instead, the pupils were put in a classroom adjacent to that in which Mr Ackers was teaching. With the doors of the two classrooms left open and, assisted by the authority that one would expect of a headmaster, Mr Ackers kept the two classes in order.

Mr Rathbone's refusal to comply with the cover request was reported to the authority. The sum of £2·11 was deducted from his April salary payment. The manner in which the £2·11 was calculated is unclear to me. The quantum does not, however, matter.

I now turn to the questions which arise for decision in the four actions.

Contractual duty to cover

The contracts under which secondary school teachers are employed by the respective authorities are silent as to whether there is or is not a contractual duty on teachers to cover for absent colleagues when asked to do so. The contracts are in general silent as to the extent of the teachers' obligations as teachers.

In the *Sim* case, for instance, the letter of appointment informed Miss Sim that she was to be 'employed in full-time service exclusively in the capacity of a teacher'. The letter did not expand on the obligations involved in 'full-time service' as a teacher. The documents under which the other plaintiffs were employed were no more and no less revealing. Each of the plaintiffs was employed full-time as a teacher. The provisions of the Burgundy Book were incorporated into each of the plaintiffs' contracts. But these provisions, although in many respects detailed and comprehensive, do not attempt to detail the obligations imposed on teachers by their respective contracts of service.

This feature of the teachers' contracts does not seem to me a matter of surprise. A contract for the employment of a professional in a professional capacity would not a normally be expected to detail the professional obligations expected of the employee under the employment contract. It would surprise me if a contract of employment of a solicitor by a solicitors' firm were to attempt to spell out his professional obligations owed under the contract. Nor would I expect the contract by which a doctor was employed by a hospital or by a health authority to spell out the professional obligations of the doctor. The solicitor would be employed as a solicitor; the doctor as a doctor. The plaintiffs are employed as teachers.

b   Without essaying any definition of a profession, I am firmly of opinion that schoolteachers are members of a profession, are entitled to be so regarded and ought to be so regarded. They are employed in a professional capacity. The contractual obligations of persons employed in a professional capacity are, in my view, defined largely by the nature of their respective professions and the obligations incumbent on those who follow those professions. Solicitors and doctors have professional obligations towards their

c clients and patients respectively. The duties of employed solicitors and employed doctors under their respective contracts must at least include the duty to discharge those obligations. Schoolteachers have professional obligations towards the pupils in their schools. Their contractual duties must include at the least the duty to discharge those obligations.

      These remarks in a sense beg the question that I must decide. The question in these

d four cases, namely whether the teachers have a contractual duty to cover, is not answered by posing the additional question whether teachers' professional obligations as teachers require them to comply with cover arrangements. But this latter question identifies where, in my opinion, the answer to the main question must be sought. It must be sought by examining the nature and scope of teachers' professional obligations as teachers.

      A somewhat analogous approach was adopted by the House of Lords in *Liverpool City*

e *Council v Irwin* [1976] 2 All ER 39, [1977] AC 239. The case concerned the question whether the city council, as landlords of a 15-storey tower block, owed any obligations to the tenants of the block to keep the common parts, lifts, staircases, passages and so on, in reasonable repair and condition. The contracts of tenancy under which the tenants occupied their respective flats did not in terms impose any obligations at all on the city council. The tenants contended that there was an implied obligation on the city council

f to keep the common parts in repair and the House of Lords agreed. Lord Wilberforce said ([1976] 2 All ER 39 at 42–43, [1977] AC 239 at 252–253):

      'I consider first the appellants' claim insofar as it is based on contract. The first step must be to ascertain what the contract is. This may look elementary, even naive, but it seems to me to be the essential step and to involve, from the start, an approach different, if simpler, from that taken by the members of the Court of

g   Appeal. We look first at documentary material. As is common with council lettings there is no formal demise or lease or tenancy agreement [Lord Wilberforce then described such documentation as did exist and went on:] We have then a contract which is partly, but not wholly, stated in writing. In order to complete it, in particular to give it a bilateral character, it is necessary to take account of the actions of the parties and the circumstances. As actions of the parties, we must note the

h   granting of possession by the corporation and reservation by it of the "common parts"—stairs, lifts, chutes etc. As circumstances we must include the nature of the premises, viz a maisonette for family use on the ninth floor of a high block, one which is occupied by a large number of other tenants, all using the common parts and dependent on them, none of them having any expressed obligation to maintain or repair them. To say that the construction of a complete contract out of these

j   elements involves a process of "implication" may be correct: it would be so if implication means the supplying of what is not expressed. But there are varieties of implications which the courts think fit to make and they do not necessarily involve the same process. Where there is, on the face of it, a complete, bilateral contract, the courts are sometimes willing to add terms to it, as implied terms; this is very common in mercantile contracts where there is an established usage; in that case the courts are spelling out what both parties know and would, if asked, unhesitatingly

agree to be part of the bargain. In other cases, where there is an apparently complete
bargain, the courts are willing to add a term on the ground that without it the *a*
contract will not work—this is the case, if not of *The Moorcock* (1889) 14 PD 64,
[1886–90] All ER Rep 530 itself on its facts, at least of the doctrine of *The Moorcock*
as usually applied. This is, as was pointed out by the majority in the Court of Appeal,
a strict test—though the degree of strictness seems to vary with the current legal
trend, and I think that they were right not to accept it as applicable here. There is a
third variety of implication, that which I think Lord Denning MR favours, or at *b*
least did favour in this case, and that is the implication of reasonable terms. But
though I agree with many of his instances, which in fact fall under one or other of
the preceding heads, I cannot go so far as to endorse his principle; indeed, it seems
to me, with respect, to extend a long, and undesirable, way beyond sound authority.
The present case, in my opinion, represents a fourth category or, I would rather say,
a fourth shade on a continuous spectrum. The court here is simply concerned to *c*
establish what the contract is, the parties not having themselves fully stated the
terms. In this sense the court is searching for what must be implied. What then
should this contract be held to be?'

Lord Wilberforce then referred to the relevant circumstances and expressed his conclusion
as to the approach to be adopted. He said ([1976] 2 All ER 39 at 44, [1977] AC 239 at
254):   *d*

'In my opinion such obligation should be read into the contract as the nature of
the contract itself implicitly requires, no more, no less; a test in other words of
necessity. The relationship accepted by the corporation is that of landlord and
tenant; the tenant accepts obligations accordingly, in relation, inter alia, to the stairs,
the lifts and the chutes. All these are not just facilities, or conveniences provided at *e*
discretion; they are essentials of the tenancy without which life in the dwellings, as
a tenant, is not possible. To leave the landlord free of contractual obligation as
regards these matters, and subject only to administrative or political pressure, is, in
my opinion, totally inconsistent with the nature of this relationship. The subject-
matter of the lease (high-rise blocks) and the relationship created by the tenancy
demands, of its nature, some contractual obligation on the landlord. I do not think *f*
that this approach involves any innovation as regards the law of contract. The
necessity to have regard to the inherent nature of a contract and of the relationship
thereby established was stated in this House in *Lister v Romford Ice and Cold Storage
Co Ltd* [1957] 1 All ER 125, [1957] AC 555. That was a case between master and
servant and of a search for an "implied term". Viscount Simonds made a clear
distinction between a search for an implied term such as might be necessary to give *g*
"business efficacy" to the particular contract and a search, based on wider
considerations, for such a term as the nature of the contract might call for, or as a
legal incident of this kind of contract. If the search were for the former, he said
([1957] 1 All ER 125 at 133, [1957] AC 555 at 576): "I should lose myself in the
attempt to formulate it with the necessary precision". We see an echo of this in the
present case, when the majority in the Court of Appeal, considering a "business *h*
efficacy term", ie a *"Moorcock"* term [see *The Moorcock* (1889) 14 PD 64, [1886–90]
All ER Rep 530], found themselves with five alternative terms and therefore rejected
all of them. But that is not, in my opinion, the end, or indeed the object of the
search.'

In my view, a similar approach should be adopted in considering the obligations imposed
on secondary school teachers under their contracts of service.   *j*

In considering the scope of a teacher's professional obligations as a teacher, it is
convenient to start with those matters that are common ground.

It is accepted that the teachers have an obligation to teach their classes in accordance
with the timetable from time to time in force. It is accepted that they have obligations
properly to prepare for their classes and to mark the schoolwork done by their pupils
either in class or as homework. It is accepted that these latter obligations may require

work to be done outside normal school hours. To put the point another way, a teacher
could not excuse a failure to be properly prepared for a class or a failure to mark
schoolwork within a reasonable time after it had been done by pointing out, correct
though the observation might be, that he or she had not had time within school hours to
do the work. It is, perhaps, one of the hallmarks of professional employment, as opposed
to employment in non-professional capacities, that professionals are employed to provide
a particular service and have a contractual obligation to do so properly. A worker in a car
factory or shop may clock off at 5.30 pm or, perhaps, work late on an overtime basis. An
employed professional does not usually have an overtime option. He is employed to
provide a particular service to proper professional standards. His contract may require
his attendance in an office or other place of work for particular hours but his contractual
obligations are not necessarily limited to work done within those hours. So, too, teachers'
duties are not necessarily confined to their obligation to be on school premises during
school hours and to take their classes during those hours.

The professional obligations of a teacher cannot, in my opinion, be confined to the
imparting of academic knowledge to the pupils. The relationship between a teacher and
his or her pupils goes further. There are obligations of discipline and of care. A teacher
who found two pupils fighting in a school corridor would be expected to try and deal
with it. The teacher would, in my view, be under a professional obligation to try and
deal with it, although what could or should in practice be done would obviously depend
on the circumstances. A teacher faced with a pupil who had suffered an accident, a burn
in a chemistry class or a broken arm in the school playground, would naturally be
expected to do what was possible to help the pupil. To fail to do so would not simply be
a breach of the obligations of common humanity but would also, in my view, be a breach
of the professional obligations of a teacher. I do not think any teacher would disagree.

The professional obligations of teachers relate also to the institutions in which they are
teaching. All schools need a framework of administrative rules to regulate their orderly
conduct. An example par excellence is the school timetable. No school could operate
without one. Schools, like all institutions, require some sort of administrative hierarchy.
In the case of schools, the administrative head is the head teacher. He or she is responsible
to the education authority for the proper conduct of the school. He or she has the power
and the duty within the school to give administrative directions for the proper running
of the school. The school timetable derives its authority from the position of the head
teacher. It is, in my view, a professional obligation of each teacher to co-operate in
running the school during school hours in accordance with the timetable and other
administrative regulations or directions from time to time made or given. There are, no
doubt, limitations on this obligation. It was submitted by counsel for Rotherham,
Doncaster, Solihull and Croydon that a teacher was contractually obliged to obey the
directions of the head teacher provided the directions were reasonable ones. This
approach is supported by the decision of the Employment Appeal Tribunal in *Redbridge
London BC v Fishman* [1978] ICR 569. The plaintiff had been employed 'as a full time
permanent teacher in charge of the Resources Centre'. But increasing demands were
made on her to teach English classes. Eventually her teaching load reached the point
where any further increase in it would have prevented her from doing justice to her
duties as head of the Resources Centre. So, when the head teacher asked her to take an
additional six English classes per week, she refused. It was held by the tribunal that the
head's request was an unreasonable one and that she had no contractual obligation to
comply with it. Phillips J said (at 575):

'... in our judgment, the headmaster is entitled to require teachers to do work
other than that for which they have been engaged, provided that the request is
reasonable. In fact this seems to have been the approach of the local authority, and
when she was finally dismissed it was on the ground that she had refused to accept
the *reasonable* instructions of the headmistress. In our judgment this is the correct
approach. What is reasonable will depend on the circumstances, and no doubt
amongst other things, bearing in mind the particular duties which the teacher was

engaged to undertake. And it would be relevant to take account of the custom and practice of the profession.' (Phillips J's emphasis.)

a

In the *Redbridge London BC v Fishman* the directions given by the head would have had the result of changing the character of the teacher's duties in the school. They were, therefore, unreasonable.

There was discussion by counsel before me as to what the test of the unreasonableness of particular directions ought to be. The *Wednesbury* test applicable in the area of public *b* law was mentioned in this connection (see *Associated Provincial Picture Houses Ltd v Wednesbury Corp* [1947] 2 All ER 680, [1948] 1 KB 223).

I do not think it necessary for me to attempt to formulate a definitive yardstick to be applied to any directions a head teacher might from time to time give in order to determine whether or not a teacher's professional obligations as a teacher require compliance with the directions. It is certainly not part of a teacher's professional *c* obligations as a teacher to jump whenever told to do so by the head teacher. A line must be drawn somewhere. In an extreme case, a teacher's professional obligations as a teacher might demand a refusal to accept a direction from a head teacher. I suppose a theoretical example might be a direction to discriminate against a particular pupil on racial grounds. Any direction that required the commission of an unlawful act would not have to be complied with. It is, as I understand it, accepted by the defendants that teachers' *d* professional obligations as teachers do not require them to supervise at school meals. So a direction to do so would not have to be complied with.

In these four cases, however, I am only concerned to decide on which side of the line cover arrangements fall. It is accepted, and is obvious, that all schools must have cover arrangements. Classes cannot simply be left unattended. The cover arrangements in each of the four schools had been in operation for years with, no doubt, minor adjustments *e* from time to time. The arrangements had been complied with by generations of teachers. No one had refused to comply. The requests to provide cover, the refusal of which led to these actions, were in each case made in accordance with the long-standing cover arrangements at the school in question. Neither Miss Sim, Mr Barnfield nor Mr Townend suggested that the cover request he or she refused was an unreasonable request. Mr Rathbone did make that suggestion but the ground on which he made it deprived the *f* suggestion of substance. A cover request cannot be characterised as unreasonable on the ground that it was known in advance that the recipient of the request would refuse it.

Each of the cover requests was refused, not on the ground of anything unreasonable in the request, but simply in pursuit of the NUT's industrial action.

Counsel for the plaintiffs in all four actions based his argument that the teachers had no contractual obligation to comply with the cover requests on the nature and effect of *g* the school timetable. The timetable, once settled and brought into effect at the beginning of the school year, represented, he submitted, a contractual document binding on employee and employer alike and immutable save by mutual consent. If a timetable provided a teacher with, say, six non-teaching periods per week then, he submitted, the teacher became contractually entitled during those periods to be free of classroom commitments.

These submissions are, in my judgment, unacceptable. They proceed on an erroneous *h* analysis as to the nature and effect of a school timetable. A school timetable represents administrative directions issued under the authority of the head teacher, regulating the time and the place of classes. The directions take account of the need of secondary school teachers to a certain amount of non-teaching time during the school day. But it is accepted that teachers have no contractual right to any minimum of non-teaching time. The allocation by the timetable of non-teaching time represents an administrative *j* decision taken by the head teacher.

The school timetable is not the only administrative direction or set of directions in force at the school. Cover arrangements, too, represent administrative directions issued under the authority of the head teacher. They, like the timetable, are necessary for the proper conduct of the school. The cover arrangements complement the timetable in that

they utilise some of the non-teaching periods allocated by the timetable. There is no
inconsistency between the two sets of administrative directions. It will be recalled that
the Purley high school timetable expressly marks as 'Reserved' one of each teacher's non-
teaching periods. Counsel for the plaintiffs would, consistently with his argument, have
to accept that a teacher had a contractual obligation to cover during the 'Reserved' period,
if called on to do so. It would be entirely practicable, although excessively tedious, for
each non-teaching period to be marked 'Free unless required for cover'. I suppose counsel
for the plaintiffs would have to accept that, if a timetable so marked came into effect at
the beginning of the school year, the teachers would have a contractual obligation to
cover where called on to do so. The position at each of the four schools was, in my
judgment, in practice no different. It was well known under the cover arrangements of
long-standing that non-teaching periods might have to be given up to comply with cover
requests.

The arrangements made by the timetable and the cover arrangements existed side by
side. Both represented administrative directions made by or under the authority of the
head teacher for the proper conduct of the school. The teachers at the school had, in my
judgment, a professional obligation as teachers to comply with these administrative
directions and, in my judgment, teachers have a contractual obligation under their
contracts to discharge their professional obligations as teachers towards their pupils and
their school.

The conclusions I have reached do not depend in any way on the particular policy of
the particular education authority regarding the use of supply teachers to provide cover.
Whether a supply teacher may be called for after the first day of absence, the third day of
absence or the fifth day of absence of a member of staff is a matter of policy for the
authority in question. Similarly, the number of staff to be employed at a particular school
is a matter of policy for the authority. In practice, the authorities no doubt consult with
the teachers' unions before establishing a policy or changing an established policy. No
doubt, also, the authorities should keep in mind in this regard the effect of their policy
on the teachers. But the contracts of the teachers give them, in my view, no control over
these policy matters. A change in policy by an authority may increase the burden on the
teachers. It may require the teachers at a school to cover for an absent colleague for five
days of absence rather than for three. A change in policy may, by reducing the number
of teachers, increase the size of classes or increase the number of classes to be taken. But
the teachers' professional and contractual obligations to comply with the reasonable
administrative directions given by or under the authority of the head teacher for the
purpose of organising the proper conduct of the school during school hours remain, in
my judgment, unaltered.

Counsel for the plaintiffs pointed out that the submissions made by the defendants'
counsel had failed to define the ambit of the teachers' contracts. His comment was made
as a criticism but it was, in my view, a misplaced one. These four cases are concerned
with cover arrangements. Cover arrangements relate to school periods during the school
day. It was not necessary for the defendants' counsel and it is not necessary for me to
attempt to define the teachers' contractual obligations outside school hours. As I have
said, it is accepted that teachers do have obligations that are not tied to school hours. The
obligations to prepare classes and to mark schoolwork are in point. Whether the teachers
have contractual obligations regarding such matters as meetings with parents after school
hours, staff meetings after school hours or invigilation at school examinations is not for
decision. For my part, the right approach to these and any other questions as to the ambit
of teachers' contractual obligations is to ask whether the obligation in question is a part
of the professional obligations owed by a teacher to pupils or to his or her school. If the
answer is Yes then, in my view, a person who is employed as a teacher prima facie owes
that obligation. The particular terms of the particular employment may, however, as in
the *Fishman* case, have to be taken into account.

There is obviously room for dispute as to the exact ambit of the professional obligations
owed by teachers. The standards are set both by the profession itself and by public
expectation. The evidence I have heard in this case has, however, left me in no doubt but

that teachers have always accepted a professional obligation to comply with cover arrangements just as they have always accepted a professional obligation to comply with timetable arrangements.

It follows that, in my judgment, each of the plaintiffs had a contractual obligation to comply with the request to cover, refusal of which occasioned these actions. In each case the refusal was, in my judgment, a breach of contract.

Deductions from salary

Each of the four plaintiffs was in breach of contract in refusing to comply with a cover request. Each suffered a deduction from his or her next monthly salary payment. No point is now taken on the amount of the deductions. The question is whether the defendants were entitled to make the deductions at all.

The plaintiffs contend that, even if they were in breach of contract, the defendants were not entitled to make the deductions from their salaries. The defendants' only remedy, they contend, was to bring a court action for damages.

In a sense this question is a sterile one. Even if the plaintiffs are right in saying that the deductions ought not to have been made, they cannot now recover the deductions. I have found that the plaintiffs were in breach of contract and it follows that the defendants are in law entitled to damages. It is accepted that the amount of the respective deductions did not exceed the amount of the damages to which the defendants were entitled. So no order for repayment could now be sought. But the plaintiffs and their union, the NUT, wish to establish as a matter of principle that an education authority is not entitled to deduct from a teacher's salary sums on account of damages. They seek declarations to that effect.

Counsel for the plaintiffs argued the case in this way. Firstly, he submitted that a teacher is contractually entitled to his monthly salary if he has rendered substantial performance of his contractual duties. It could not, he submitted, be argued that failure to cover for one 35-minute period prevented a teacher from claiming to have rendered substantial performance of his contractual duties.

Secondly, counsel for the plaintiffs submitted that the common law doctrine of abatement did not apply to employment contracts. The full contractual salary had to be paid.

Thirdly, he submitted that the doctrine of equitable set-off could not be used by an employer to justify deductions on account of damages from an employee's salary. Alternatively, he submitted that equitable set-off ought not to be allowed on the particular facts of the present cases.

As to counsel's first submission, the doctrine of substantial performance does not, in my view, have anything to do with these four cases. The question whether there has or has not been substantial performance of a contract only arises, in my view, where the contract is an entire contract. Where performance under an entire contract has been defective, the question may arise whether any contractual payment is due at all. Payment is conditional on performance. If there has not been complete performance there is no contractual right to payment. The severity of this approach has been mitigated by the doctrine of substantial performance. If the contract has been substantially performed, the contractual payment, subject to whatever abatement or set-off the law may allow, can be claimed.

It is an important feature of the present cases that none of the plaintiffs was dismissed on account of his or her breach of contract. The contracts of employment continued. Contractual obligations continued to be owed and duly discharged by each of the plaintiffs. Performance by each plaintiff of his or her contractual obligations continued to be accepted by the defendants. The defendants continued to be under contractual obligations to pay for the services rendered by the plaintiffs and accepted by them. This was not, in my judgment, by reason of the doctrine of substantial performance. It was because the contracts continued on foot and the services rendered thereunder continued to be accepted.

In *Button v Thompson* (1869) LR 4 CP 330 the plaintiff signed on the defendant's ship as
a mate at a monthly wage for a voyage from Shields to Alexandria. His drunkenness and
violent and insubordinate conduct resulted in his being left behind at a foreign port
before the voyage was completed. He sued for his wages up to the time he had been left
behind. Montague Smith J, with whose judgment Byles J concurred, said (at 339):

b
> 'It is contended by the defendant, that the contract was for an entire service,
> terminating on the arrival of the ship "home" at her final port of discharge; and
> that, the plaintiff having been left behind at Sulina through his own negligence, he
> cannot recover. The contract is for a succession of voyages of indefinite duration,
> although "not expected to exceed twelve months"; and the wages in the articles are
> thus provided for—"Amount of wages per calendar month, 5l. 10s.," ... The
> defendant relies on the words, "in consideration of which services to be duly
> performed," the master agrees to pay the wages, as controlling the whole contract,
c
> and creating a condition precedent to the right to recover any wages the due
> performance of the entire service contracted for. But we think that, upon articles in
> the present form, such a condition is not created; and that the monthly wages
> become vested and a debt at the end of each month of service, liable, it may be, to
> forfeiture under certain circumstances provided for by the Merchant Shipping Act,
> 1854.'
d
Later in his judgment, Montague Smith J referred to the plaintiff's misconduct and
continued (at 343): '... he was not in fact discharged; but, on the contrary, his services
were rendered and accepted up to the time of his being left behind at Sulina ...' So the
plaintiff succeeded in recovering his wages up to that time.

Similarly, in the present cases, each of the plaintiffs on the monthly payment date next
e after his or her refusal to cover was, despite the refusal, contractually entitled to be paid a
sum in respect of salary for the month. This entitlement did not depend on the relatively
short duration of the period in respect of which cover duty was refused. If an employee
were to absent himself without leave from work for a week his conduct would, I imagine,
be grounds for dismissal. But if, when he presented himself next week at his work place
ready and willing to resume his duties, his employer did not choose to dismiss him but
f accepted the resumption of his contractual services, the employer could not, when the
next monthly payment day arrived, decline to make any payment. The reason would
not be that there had been substantial performance by the employee over the month in
question. The reason would simply be that the contract had remained on foot and the
contractual obligations had continued to be owed on both sides. The question would not
have been whether the employee had a contractual entitlement to a payment on account
of salary. He clearly had that. The question would have been how much the employee
g was entitled to be paid, having regard to the fact that for a week he had done no work.

The question here is the same. In a case where the refusal to work has not brought the
contract to an end there is, in my judgment, no difference in principle whether the
refusal has continued for 35 minutes, for a day, or for a week. Substantial performance is
not relevant.

h   Prima facie the plaintiffs' contractual entitlement was to be paid the monthly salaries
due under their respective contracts. The contracts, I repeat, remained in force. The
defendants could not, in law, unilaterally vary the salary element in the contracts. For
the defendants it was contended that, since each plaintiff had failed for a 35-minute
period to do the work required under his or her contract, he or she could not claim
payment for that 35 minutes. 'No work, no pay' was put forward as a legal maxim
j applicable to cases of this sort. Whatever value the aphorism may have as a reflection of a
gut reaction, it is not, in my view, a reliable yardstick to test an employer's right to make
deductions from an employee's salary. The right to make deductions must depend on the
reason why there has been 'no work'. If the reason involves breach of contract, then
it may be that deductions can be made. But if the reason for 'no work' does not involve
any breach of contract, then why should the consequence 'no pay' follow? A teacher

locked for an hour in a school lavatory through no fault of his own would not, I imagine, be thought to be thereby losing some part of his salary.

Counsel for Solihull submitted that the real question was whether a teacher was entitled to be paid for the period of 35 minutes that he or she had not worked. Pay for that period, he said, had not been earned. In my judgment, this approach is fallacious. It involves regarding the teachers' salaries as accruing minute by minute. There is no legal or factual justification for that view of the salaries. Under the contracts, the salaries are based on a yearly scale but are paid by monthly payments. Each month a contractual right to a salary payment vests in the teacher. By reason of s 2 of the Apportionment Act 1870, the salaries are deemed to accrue day by day. If a teacher's contract were, in the middle of a month, to come to an end, by death, dismissal or some other event, s 2 would entitle the teacher, or his estate, to an apportioned part of the month's salary payment. So the salaries may be regarded as accruing day by day. But they do not accrue minute by minute. And for as long as the contract is continuing, the only payment that can be claimed by a teacher is a monthly payment and the only obligation to make a payment of salary that rests on the education authority is an obligation to make a monthly payment.

In my judgment, the correct approach in cases like the present is to start with the teachers' contractual monthly salary entitlement. If in the course of the month there has been a breach of contract by a teacher, it is necessary to consider what, if any, damages can be claimed by the employer by reason of that breach of contract. If the breach of contract has not given rise to any recoverable loss to the education authority, then, in my judgment, there is no deduction that can properly be made from the salary on account of the breach. If recoverable loss has been caused to the education authority, it is then necessary to consider whether the law allows, by way of abatement or by way of set-off, the deduction of the damages from the monthly salary. If the law does allow that deduction to be made, then the monthly salary payment can be reduced accordingly. If the law does not allow the deduction to be made, the teacher is entitled to be paid his salary in full.

As I have already said, the amount of the deduction made by each defendant in the present cases is accepted as representing not less than the amount of damages to which the defendant was entitled for the breach of contract committed by the relevant plaintiff. In each case, the deduction, although very small in amount, does not represent nominal damages. The sums were calculated so as to attribute an appropriate part of the teacher's monthly salary payment to the 35-minute period in respect of which the cover request was refused.

So there remains only the question whether the defendants were entitled to deduct the damages from the monthly salaries.

Counsel for the plaintiffs submitted that common law abatement was a remedy available only in a very restricted class of contracts that did not include contracts of employment. The remedy of abatement was authoritatively established in *Mondel v Steel* (1841) 8 M & W 858, [1835–42] All ER Rep 511. The case arose out of a contract to build a ship for an agreed price. The plaintiff contended that by reason of the defective work of the defendant an abatement of the price ought to be allowed. Parke B said (8 M & W 858 at 871, [1835–42] All ER Rep 511 at 515–516):

'It must however be considered, that in all these cases of goods sold and delivered with a warranty, and work and labour, as well as the case of goods agreed to be supplied according to a contract, the rule which has been found so convenient is established; and that it is competent for the defendant, in all of those, not to set-off, by a proceeding in the nature of a cross-action, the amount of damages which he has sustained by breach of the contract, but simply to defend himself by shewing how much less the subject-matter of the action was worth, by reason of the breach of contract; and to the extent that he obtains, or is capable of obtaining, an abatement of price on that account, he must be considered as having received satisfaction for the breach of contract, and is precluded from recovering in another action to that extent; but no more.'

In *Gilbert-Ash (Northern) Ltd v Modern Engineering (Bristol) Ltd* [1973] 3 All ER 195 at 215,
a [1974] AC 689 at 717 Lord Diplock commented that the principle of abatement had
been 'stated authoritatively in the judgment of Parke B in *Mondel v Steel* . . . who described
it as "established" by that date.' Lord Diplock then cited the passages from Parke B's
judgment that I have cited and continued:

'This is a remedy which the common law provides for breaches of warranty in
contracts for sale of goods and for work and labour . . . It is available as of right to a
b   party to such a contract. It does not lie within the discretion of the court to withhold
it. It is independent of the doctrine of "equitable set-off" developed by the Court of
Chancery to afford similar relief in appropriate cases to parties in other types of
contracts, of which a masterly account is to be found in the judgment of my noble
and learned friend Lord Morris of Borth-y-Gest in *Hanak v Green* [1958] 2 All ER
141, [1958] 2 QB 9. That it was no mere procedural rule designed to avoid circuity
c   of action but a substantive defence at common law was the very point decided in
Mondel v Steel (1841) 8 M & W 858 at 871, 872, [1835–42] All ER Rep 511 at 515,
516.'

Aries Tanker Corp v Total Transport Ltd [1977] 1 All ER 398, [1977] 1 WLR 185 was a
case concerning a voyage charter. The charterers alleged that there had been short
d delivery of the cargo and sought to make a deduction from the sum payable in respect of
freight. Common law abatement, as established by *Mondel v Steel*, was relied on to
support the deduction. The House of Lords, affirming the Court of Appeal (see [1976] 2
Lloyd's Rep 256) and the first instance judge, disallowed the deduction. Lord Wilberforce
said ([1977] 1 All ER 398 at 403, [1977] 1 WLR 185 at 189): 'That a claim in respect of
cargo cannot be asserted by way of deduction from the freight, is a long established rule
e in English law.' He then dealt with the argument that the rule was inconsistent with the
principle establishment in *Mondel v Steel* and said ([1977] 1 All ER 398 at 404, [1977] 1
WLR 185 at 190):

'. . . the two rules have been running in parallel for over a century without
difficulty, and indeed in *Mondel v Steel* (1841) 8 M & W 858, [1835–42] All ER Rep
f   511 itself Parke B specifically referred to the existence of a separate rule as regards
freight. In this House, that the rule of deduction, or abatement, is one confined to
contracts for the sale of goods or for work and labour and does not extend to
contracts generally, was recognised in *Gilbert-Ash (Northern) Ltd v Modern Engineering
(Bristol) Ltd* [1973] 3 All ER 195 at 215, [1974] AC 689 at 717, per Lord Diplock.
There is no case of its having been extended to contracts of any kind of carriage. The
rule against deduction in cases of carriage by sea is, in fact, as well settled as any
g   common law rule can be.'

On the strength of those authorities counsel for the plaintiffs submitted that common
law abatement was not available in contract of employment cases but was restricted to
contracts for sale of goods or for work and labour.
However, in *Sagar v H Ridehalgh & Son Ltd* [1931] 1 Ch 310 Lord Hanworth MR
h treated common law abatement as applicable to employment contracts. The case
concerned a piecemaker who had woven defective cloth. His employer desired to reduce
his normal wages by a sum calculated to represent the loss caused to them by reason of
his negligent weaving. The main question in the case was whether the deduction was
barred by the Truck Acts. This turned on whether the deduction was an integral part of
the machinery by means of which the employee's wages were calculated. If that were the
j case, then the Truck Acts did not bar the deductions. If, on the other hand, the deduction
for bad work was being made from ascertained wages, then the Truck Acts barred the
deduction. The Court of Appeal decided the case in favour of the mill owner. They held
that the formula for calculating the deductions was part of the machinery for calculating
the wages due to the weaver. But Lord Hanworth MR discussed also common law
abatement. He referred to *Mondel v Steel* and various other cases and then said ([1931] 1
Ch 310 at 326):

'It would seem, therefore, clear that in such a contract as that under which Sagar
was employed, the defendants would have a right to make a deduction from his   *a*
wages for bad work, unless there was some term of the contract which excluded this
right, or unless such a deduction is forbidden by statute.'

Counsel for the plaintiffs submitted, correctly in my view, that these remarks of Lord
Hanworth MR were obiter and were inconsistent with the restrictive comments about
abatement made by Lord Diplock in the *Gilbert-Ash* case and indorsed by Lord Wilberforce
in the *Aries Tanker* case. He submitted that Lord Hanworth MR was wrong. Naturally   *b*
enough all three counsel for the defendants relied on Lord Hanworth MR's dictum and
submitted that abatement of salary was a remedy available to an employer where an
employee had rendered a contractually inadequate performance of his contractual duties.

The exact scope of the common law doctrine of abatement ought, in my opinion, now
to be regarded as of academic interest only. The doctrine was evolved in the days before
the Judicature Acts. Common law set-off was available only in respect of liquidated debts.   *c*
Common law set-off provided no remedy to a party to a contract where the other party
had, by inadequate performance of his contractual duties, caused loss or damage to the
former. The former would have had a cause of action for unliquidated damages but had
no right at common law to deduct the amount of the damages from the contractual sum
owed under the contract. He would, at common law, have had no defence to an action
for the contractual sum due. Abatement may be regarded as a means whereby, in the   *d*
common law courts, the necessity for a cross-action was avoided (see Parke B in *Mondel v
Steel* 8 M & W 858 at 871, [1835–42] All ER Rep 511 at 515. Equitable set-off, on the
other hand, was developed in the courts of Chancery as a remedy for the injustice that
the narrowness of common law set-off would in many cases have caused. In *Federal
Commerce and Navigation Ltd v Molena Alpha Inc, The Nanfri, The Benfri, The Lorfri* [1978] 3
All ER 1066 at 1077–1078, [1978] QB 927 at 974 equitable set-off was described by Lord   *e*
Denning MR:

'In making the distinction between set-off and cross-claim, the courts of common
law had their own special rules. For instance in a series of cases they formulated
rules saying when there could be an abatement of rent or an abatement of the sums
due for work and labour done, or an abatement of the price of goods sold and   *f*
delivered. So that the defendant could make deductions accordingly. But the courts
of equity, as was their wont, came in to mitigate the technicalities of the common
law. They allowed deductions, by way of equitable set-off, whenever there were
good equitable grounds for directly impeaching the demand which the creditor was
seeking to enforce . . .'

Equitable set-off was not available as a defence in common law courts until after the   *g*
Judicature Acts. The position was described by Morris LJ in *Hanak v Green* [1958] 2 All
ER 141 at 149, [1958] 2 QB 9 at 23:

'The position is, therefore, that since the Judicature Acts there may be (i) a set-off
of mutual debts, (ii) in certain cases a setting up of matters of complaint which if
established reduce or even extinguish the claim and (iii) reliance on equitable set-off   *h*
and reliance as a matter of defence on matters of equity which formerly might have
called for injunction or prohibition.'

After discussing set-off of mutual debts, that is to say, common law set-off, Morris LJ
continued ([1958] 2 All ER 141 at 150, [1958] 2 QB 9 at 23–24):

'The cases within group (ii) are those within the principle of *Mondel v Steel* to   *j*
which I have referred. In these cases there is a defence to the claim which the law
recognises (compare Sale of Goods Act, 1893, s 53). The cases within group (iii) are
those in which a court of equity would have regarded the cross-claims as entitling
the defendant to be protected in one way or another against the plaintiff's claim.
Reliance may be placed in a court of law on any equitable defence or equitable
ground for relief; so also any matter of equity on which an injunction against the

a prosecution of a claim might formerly have been obtained may be relied on as a defence. This may involve that there will have to be an ascertainment or assessment of the monetary value of the cross-claim which as a matter of equity can be relied on by way of defence.'

So, before the Judicature Acts common law abatement had provided, in a restricted class of case, relief similar to that which equitable set-off provided. In both, the ingredients
b for a cross-claim were required. Both could operate not just as a cross-claim but as a defence. In my view, abatement, although developed independently, may be regarded as a common law version of equitable set-off. It was, however, developed, ad hoc in relation to certain classes of contract (see the categories mentioned by Parke B in *Mondel v Steel*). Equitable set-off, on the other hand, was based on principle. It was and is applicable to any class of case, with one or two exceptions that I must mention, provided the necessary
c ingredients are present. In my judgment, the need to consider the scope of common law abatement disappeared with the Judicature Acts. If the remedy of equitable set-off is available, abatement is not needed. If the circumstances of the case do not warrant equitable set-off, then, in my view, they would not establish an abatement.

The case law has identified certain types of transaction where, whatever the circumstances, equitable set-off is not available. Actions on dishonoured bills of exchange
d and certain actions on bank guarantees are examples. The reasons given in the *Aries Tanker* case for not permitting common law abatement to reduce the freight payable under a voyage charter would, I suppose, prevent the use of equitable set-off to achieve the same result. These exceptions may be thought to be attributable to reasons of public policy arising out of the commercial exigencies of the transactions in question.

Accordingly, in my opinion, the question whether common law abatement can be
e applied so as to reduce salaries payable under contracts of employment need not be pursued. The relevant question is whether equitable set-off can be applied to do so.

Counsel for the plaintiffs argued that it could not. He put forward two main reasons why that should be so. First, he said that equitable set-off would give an employer the power to make deductions from salary on account of supposed breaches of contract, thereby empowering him to be judge and jury in his own cause. Employees ought not,
f he submitted, to be put in a position in which, if they objected to the deductions, their only remedy would be to start an action in the courts.

I can see the force in that submission. It is true that employees whose salaries have been reduced by a purported application of equitable set-off may, in practice, find an effective remedy difficult to obtain. It may be that to allow equitable set-off to be used by employers so as to reduce the salaries paid to employees would open the door to abuse.
g Secondly, counsel for the plaintiffs pointed out that many employment contracts involve disciplinary codes and grievance procedures. Rights of set-off would, he said, place employers in a position to frustrate disciplinary codes and circumvent grievance procedures. This would be contrary to good industrial practice.

These considerations are not, however, in my judgment, sufficient to justify excluding equitable set-off across the board as a possible defence to an action by an employee for
h salary. There are several reasons why I have come to this conclusion.

First, counsel's submissions have sociological rather than legal weight. I could well understand Parliament adopting a policy of protecting employees by declining to allow set-offs against salary. That protection has for many years been provided for a certain class of employees by the Truck Acts (see s 2(2) of the Truck Act 1896). The employees protected by the Truck Acts are confined to 'workmen' (see s 2 of the Truck Amendment
j Act 1887). Teachers and other professional employees are not protected under the Truck Acts. Where Parliament has legislated to protect a certain limited class of employees, and has not extended that protection to employees generally, I doubt whether it can be right for the courts, on policy grounds, to remedy Parliament's omission.

Second, there is judicial authority which, implicitly at least, recognises the propriety of set-offs against salaries. I have already referred to Lord Hanworth MR's obiter remarks in *Sagar v H Ridehalgh & Son Ltd*. Whether or not his opinion that common law abatement could apply to reduce wages is right or wrong, he clearly saw nothing wrong in principle in allowing deductions on account of damages to be made from wages. I regard his remarks as strong authority for the applicability of equitable set-off in this field.

In *Royle v Trafford BC* [1984] IRLR 184 the plaintiff was an assistant teacher in a primary school. The defendants' education committee, in order to make economies, decided to reduce the level of teaching staff. The plaintiff's union, the National Association of Schoolmasters, instructed its members not to accept additional pupils in their classes. The plaintiff had 31 pupils in his class. He was asked to accept an additional five pupils. He refused and, for the six months' duration of the industrial action, continued to teach a class of only 31 pupils. The defendants deducted from his salary by way of damages an amount based on the period of time during which he had refused to accept the extra pupils. That meant that he had practically no salary for the period involved. The plaintiff sued for his unpaid salary. Park J held that the deductions were excessive but that deductions representing the value of the services the plaintiff had refused to render could be justified. He allowed a deduction of 5/36ths of the plaintiff's salary for the relevant period. He was, in my view, applying an equitable set-off.

In *Miles v Wakefield Metropolitan DC* [1985] 1 All ER 905, [1985] 1 WLR 822 the plaintiff was the superintendent registrar of births, deaths and marriages for Wakefield. The council was responsible for paying his salary but he was not an employee of the council. He was a servant of the Crown. In 1981 the plaintiff, as a part of industrial action taken by his union, declined to conduct any weddings on Saturday mornings. He continued, however, on Saturday mornings to carry out duties regarding the registration of births and deaths. The council made a deduction of 3/37ths from his weekly salary, the denominator being the total number of hours worked per week and the numerator being the three hours appertaining to Saturday morning. The plaintiff sued for his unpaid salary. He lost at first instance but succeeded in the Court of Appeal. Parker LJ held, as a matter of construction of the statute which obliged the council to pay the plaintiff's salary, that the council's obligation to pay was, while the plaintiff held his office, unqualified. He went on, however, to say ([1985] 1 All ER 905 at 911–912, [1985] 1 WLR 822 at 831):

'I find it unnecessary to decide whether, if the appellant had been an employee of the respondents, they would have been entitled to withhold part of his salary, but I do not accept that they would. Had that been the case, the respondents would no doubt have had a claim for any damages they could prove but, in the absence of a breach amounting to a repudiation accepted by dismissal or a specific right to suspend, there appear to me strong grounds for saying that there is no right to withhold payment and take the benefit of all work in fact done during the period in which the refusal to perform a particular function was operative.'

I do not think that in this obiter passage Parker LJ was intending to express a view on the question whether an employer would be entitled to set-off against salary the amount of damages to which the employer was entitled. Parker LJ was dealing with a case where the amount deducted from salary had exceeded any damages that could be claimed by the employer. *Royle v Trafford BC* was cited and was not disapproved. I should add that an appeal in *Miles v Wakefield Metropolitan DC* is, as I understand it, due to be heard by the House of Lords in October.

Third, the nature of equitable set-off makes it very difficult, in my view, to argue that employment contracts in general ought to be excluded from its application. In *British Anzani (Felixstowe) Ltd v International Marine Management (UK) Ltd* [1979] 2 All ER 1063 at 1068, [1980] 1 QB 137 at 145 Forbes J described the nature of equitable set-off in this way:

'It is this feature that the equity must go to the very root of the plaintiff's claim that is the essential attribute of a valid equitable set-off. An obvious example, as was emphasised in later cases, was *Piggott v Williams* (1821) 6 Madd 95, 56 ER 1027 where the fees which the solicitor claimed were in relation to a suit which would

a   never have been necessary but for the solicitor's own negligence. The principle is
clear though there may have been difficulty in applying it correctly to different sets
of circumstances. A felicitously expressed statement of the principle occurs in the
judgment of Parker J in *The Teno* [*Cia Sud Americana de Vapones v Shipnair* [1977] 2
Lloyd's Rep 289 at 297]: "...where the cross claim not only arises out of the same
contract as the claim but is so directly connected with it that it would be manifestly
unjust to allow the claimant to recover without taking into account the cross claim
b   there is a right of set-off in equity of an unliquidated claim." This statement was
expressly approved by Goff LJ in *Federal Commerce and Navigation Co Ltd v Molena
Alpha Inc* [1978] 3 All ER 1066 at 1088, [1978] QB 927 at 987 in the Court of
Appeal.'

The word used by Goff LJ in the *Federal Commerce* case to describe Parker J's statement
was 'impeccable'.

c   Why should an equitable principle of this sort not apply to employment contracts? A
fortiori, why should it not apply where the employee is suing for his contractual salary
but, in breach of contract, has failed to do all or some of the work required by his
contract? In my judgment, no sufficient reason has been shown.

In my judgment, if an employee, in breach of contract, fails or refuses to perform his
contractual services, his right or title to recover his salary for the period during which
d   the failure or refusal occurred is impeached by the employer's cross-claim for damages.
It would, in my judgment, be manifestly unjust in such a case to allow the employee to
recover his salary in full without taking into account the loss to the employer of those
services. The aphorism 'no work, no pay' expresses, in my view, the equity of the
situation.

Counsel for the plaintiffs submitted that, on the facts of the present cases, failure to
e   comply with a cover request for a 35-minute period ought not to be regarded as a breach
sufficient to impeach the plaintiffs' titles to their full contractual monthly salaries. I do
not agree. The breaches were of short duration and the damages attributable thereto
were correspondingly small in amount. But the damages were not nominal damages.
They were calculated to represent the loss caused to the defendants by the breaches of
contract and are accepted as realistic by the plaintiffs on that footing. If, in principle, the
f   nature of a breach and of the cross-claim attributable to the breach impeach a party's title
to full contractual payment, the fact that the claimable damages are small is not, in my
view, relevant. Equitable set-off does not depend on the size of the damages or on the
severity of the breach of contract. It depends, in my judgment, on the nature of the
breach relative to the nature of the contractual claim. I cannot imagine a claim which
more clearly impeaches a contractual claim to salary than a claim to damages for a refusal
g   to carry out some of the services for which the salary is being paid. If the damages had
been merely nominal damages, my opinion would have been otherwise. Nominal
damages do not represent compensation for loss. They would not, in my view, impeach
the claim to full salary. But that is not the position in these four cases.

Counsel for the plaintiffs had a further submission. He submitted that, by virtue of s 5
of the Remuneration of Teachers Act 1965 and the orders made thereunder, the plaintiffs
h   enjoyed statutory rights to be paid their salaries in full, without deductions. I reject this
submission.

Section 2 of the 1965 Act provides a procedure designed to lead to the Secretary of
State making an order 'directing that the relevant remuneration of teachers shall be
determined in accordance with the scales and other provisions set out . . .' (see s 2(4)).
j   Section 5(1) provides:

'. . . remuneration to which this Order applies shall be determined and shall be
paid to teachers by local education authorities, in accordance with the scales and
other provisions set out . . .'

These statutory provisions are concerned to identify the salary scales in accordance
with which teachers are entitled to be paid. A teacher's salary must be 'determined and

paid in accordance with' the relevant scales. These statutory provisions do not, in my judgment, bar deductions being made from a teacher's salary. Indeed, the plaintiffs' respective monthly salary slips show, as one would expect, a number of deductions in respect of a variety of matters.

The conclusions to which I have come on equitable set-off justify the deductions made by the defendants.

The defendants did, however, seek to justify the deductions on an additional ground. They rely on certain provisions to be found in the Burgundy Book.

Paragraph 5.2 in the Burgundy Book is headed 'Deduction of Salary'. Paragraph 5.2.1 provides: 'The various circumstances in which calculations shall be made for the non-payment of salary are set out in Section 9.' Section 9 is not directly relevant. It deals with such matters as maternity leave, leave for jury service and leave for various other purposes, Paragraph 5.2.2 provides:

'In addition to the provisions of Section 9, where unpaid leave of absence occurs either with the permission of the authority or without such permission (e.g. strike action) deductions of salary shall be calculated at a daily or part-daily rate based on the day's salary being 1/365th of a year for each day of the period of absence.'

It was submitted by counsel for Croydon, with whose submissions the other defendants' counsel associated themselves, that a teacher who refused to comply with a cover request was, to repeat the rather peculiar language of the paragraph, taking 'unpaid leave of absence ... without ... permission'. Absence, she submitted, denoted absence from whatever class the teacher ought to be taking. Counsel for the plaintiffs submitted in answer that, in the context of the Burgundy Book taken as a whole, 'absence' meant a total absence from school duties. Strike action is mentioned in the paragraph as an example of 'absence without permission' and would involve a total withdrawal by the teacher from his or her contractual obligations.

In the present cases the plaintiffs, although they refused to cover, remained at the school premises. They were contractually obliged to do so. They got on with marking of schoolwork or with other duties in accordance, to that extent, with their contractual obligations. The plaintiffs were not, submitted counsel for the plaintiffs, taking for themselves 'leave of absence' within the meaning of that phrase in para 5.2.2.

This is a short point of construction on which I have changed my mind more than once in the course of argument. In the end I find that I prefer the construction of counsel for the plaintiffs. I do not think that the plaintiffs' refusals to cover represented 'leave of absence'. I would not, therefore, uphold the deductions from the salaries on the para 5.2.2 ground.

In my judgment, however, the defendants can justify the deductions as equitable set-offs arising from the plaintiffs' breaches of contract. I therefore dismiss the plaintiffs' actions.

Certain of the defendants have counterclaimed for declarations. I am prepared to make declarations to reflect what I have decided and will hear counsel as to the form of any declaration.

Actions dismissed. Declarations on counterclaims granted.

Solicitors: *Hugh Pierce* (for the plaintiffs in all four actions); *Sharpe Pritchard & Co*, agents for *D Buckley*, Rotherham (for Rotherham), and agents for *W R Bugler*, Doncaster (for Doncaster); *John Scampion*, Solihull (for Solihull); *R G Hemmings*, Croydon (for Croydon).

Jacqueline Metcalfe   Barrister.

Samuelson v National Insurance and Guarantee Corp Ltd

COURT OF APPEAL, CIVIL DIVISION
O'CONNOR, ROBERT GOFF AND NOURSE LJJ
24, 25 JULY 1985

Motor insurance – Exception – Policy excluding loss or damage occurring while vehicle driven by person other than policy holder – Policy stating limitation of use of vehicle not breached by delivery of vehicle into custody or control of member of motor trade for repair – Vehicle stolen while in charge of repairer – Whether policy holder entitled to be indemnified – Whether vehicle in custody or control of member of motor trade for purpose of repair when stolen – Whether vehicle on risk while being driven by or in charge of person other than policy holder.

In March 1980 the plaintiff effected a policy of insurance with the defendant insurers in respect of his motor car, which was worth £10,500. The policy provided that the plaintiff would be indemnified against, inter alia, loss of the vehicle caused by theft. By a certificate of motor insurance issued with the policy 'use [of the vehicle] for any purpose in connection with the Motor Trade' and driving by anyone other than the plaintiff were not covered by the insurance. However, by para 1(a)(i) of the general exceptions in the policy the exclusion of use for any purpose in connection with the motor trade did not prejudice the indemnity to the plaintiff while the vehicle was 'in the custody or control of a member of the Motor Trade for the purpose of its . . . repair'. By para 1(c) of the general exceptions the insurers were not liable when the vehicle was 'being driven by or for the purpose of being driven [was] in the charge of any person other than [the plaintiff]'. The plaintiff delivered the vehicle to a car repairer for repair and in the course of those repairs the car repairer drove the vehicle to the sole agents for that make of vehicle in order to obtain spare parts for it. He parked the vehicle near the agents' premises and on his return discovered that it had been stolen. The vehicle was never recovered and the plaintiff claimed its value from the insurers, contending that the vehicle had been in the 'custody or control of a member of the Motor Trade for the purpose of its . . . repair' when it was stolen and that therefore para 1(a)(i) of the general exceptions did not apply to exclude the insurers from liability to idemnify him for its loss. The judge dismissed the plaintiff's claim on the ground that since the vehicle was, 'for the purpose of being driven', in the charge of a person other than the plaintiff when it was stolen the insurers were not liable under the policy for its loss. The plaintiff appealed to the Court of Appeal.

Held – There was nothing inherently objectionable in construing a contract of insurance in such a way as to put the insurers on and off risk at short and recurring intervals. Accordingly, the issue was whether, at the precise time it was stolen, the car was in the charge of the car repairer for the purpose of its repair or whether it was in his charge for the purpose of being driven. On the facts, when the car repairer was physically driving the vehicle to the agents, para 1(c) applied to take the car off risk. However, as soon as the car repairer parked the car outside the agents' premises to purchase spare parts, he was in charge of the car for the purpose of repairing it and para 1(a)(i) applied to put the car on risk again. It followed that at the time the car was stolen the insurers were liable for its loss. The appeal would therefore be allowed (see p 418 h to p 419 c, p 420 h j, p 421 e to g and p 422 b to h, post).

Decision of Esyr Lewis QC sitting as a deputy judge of the High Court [1984] 3 All ER 107 reversed.

Notes

For stipulations defining risks and prohibitions in policies of motor insurance, see 25 Halsbury's Laws (4th edn) paras 739–743, and for cases on the subject, see 29 Digest (Reissue) 593–599, 5198–5226.

Case referred to in judgments
Seddon v Binions (Zurich Insurance Co Ltd, third party) [1978] 1 Lloyd's Rep 381, CA.   *a*

Appeal
The plaintiff, Philip Charles Samuelson, appealed against the judgment of Mr Esyr Lewis QC sitting as a deputy judge of the High Court ([1984] 3 All ER 107) whereby he dismissed the plaintiff's claim against the defendants, National Insurance and Guarantee Corp Ltd, for £10,500 in respect of the loss of his motor car, pursuant to the terms of a *b* motor insurance policy dated 26 March 1980. The facts are set out in the judgment of O'Connor LJ.

Anthony D Colman QC and *David Joseph* for the plaintiff.
Jonathan R Playford QC and *Andrew Prynne* for the defendants.

          c

O'CONNOR LJ. In June 1980 the plaintiff, Mr Samuelson, wanted to have his De Tomaso motor car repaired, which had been damaged by vandals. He took it to Mr Ford, who was a car repairer, to have it done on 26 June 1980. Next day the car was stolen in circumstances which the judge dealt with in his judgment in this way ([1984] 3 All ER 107 at 109):

> 'On 27 June 1980 Mr Ford drove the De Tomaso to Hammersmith where the   *d*
> only agents for spare parts for this make of motor car are to be found in the United
> Kingdom. He told me, and I accept, that he needed to take the car to the agents
> because he wanted to make sure that any parts that he got, which included parts for
> some section of the electrical system, actually did suit and fit the vehicle. He parked
> the car near the agents' premises and was only away for a few minutes seeing to the
> parts. When he returned to where he had left the car, he found it had gone. The car   *e*
> had been stolen, and has never been recovered. The car was worth £10,500.'

The plaintiff held a third party fire and theft policy with the defendant insurers and he claimed for the loss of his car. Under the terms and conditions of the policy the plaintiff was the only authorised driver. The insurers refused to idemnify him on the ground that the loss was not covered by reason of general exception 1(c) in the policy. *f* That exception reads:

> 'The Corporation shall not be liable in respect of 1. any accident injury loss or
> damage occurring whilst any motor vehicle in connection with which insurance is
> granted under this Policy is ... (c) being driven by or for the purpose of being
> driven in the charge of any person other than an authorised driver described in the   *g*
> Schedule.'

Mr Ford was not an authorised driver in the schedule and the deputy judge accepted the submission by the defendants that this case was covered by the exception and that they were not bound to indemnify the plaintiff. Against that judgment he appeals to this court.

Pausing there, in my judgment the case is one of simplicity in the end. The true   *h* construction of the exception seems to me to be straightforward. When a motor car is being driven by somebody there is no ambiguity whatever, and we all know what that means. It follows that during the time that Mr Ford was driving the car from Dagenham, where this all started, to Hammersmith the exception would apply. When the journey was completed it seem to me that he ceased to be a driver. So one then has to ask, 'Was he in charge of the motor car at that stage?' The answer comes back Yes; and he was. *j* 'Was it for the purpose of driving the car?' In my judgment the answer is No. As soon as he parked outside the agents' premises in Hammersmith he was in charge of the car for the purpose of repairing it: buying the parts; seeing if they fitted; and when that exercise had been completed and as soon as he began driving back to Dagenham then he would be the driver and the policy would not be on risk.

a   Counsel for the defendants has submitted that a construction which puts the policy on and off risk in this fashion should not be adopted. For my part I see no difficulty about it because the exception envisages that the policy will indeed go on and off risk for a whole number of reasons; not only this exception, but others to which the opening words apply. For example, in para 1(*f*) there is the same opening: 'whilst any motor vehicle in connection with which insurance is granted under this Policy is', then '(*f*) being driven in an unsafe or unroadworthy condition', and quite plainly the policy would be off risk

b   while the motor car, which was in an unsafe condition, was being driven; if it caught fire during the time it was being driven, it would be not on risk. If when the journey was over it was stolen or hit by lightning, the policy is on risk. I see no difficulty about it.

That approach is really sufficient to dispose of this appeal. In my judgment the judge was simply mistaken in coming to the conclusion that he did. In fairness to him, the case was never really put in this fashion to him, and the reason may have been that the

c   plaintiff's then advisers, mesmerised by some of the breathalyser cases in which the courts have grappled with the difficulty of making everyday experience fit the language of the statute, decided that they were on risk of the court holding that para 1(*c*) prevailed, and therefore they sought to cut down the operation of para 1(*c*) by making reference to para 1(*a*)(i) of the general exceptions.

The limitation of use in this policy was:

d   'Use only for social, domestic and pleasure purposes EXCLUDING use for hiring or in connection with any trade, business or profession.'

Paragraph 1(*a*)(i) provides:

e   'The Corporation shall not be liable in respect of 1. any accident injury loss or damage occurring whilst any motor vehicle in connection with which insurance is granted under this Policy is (*a*) being used otherwise than in accordance with the "Limitations as to use" described in the Schedule except that (i) the exclusion of use for any purpose in connection with the Motor Trade shall not prejudice the indemnity to the Insured whilst any motor car described in the Schedule is in the custody or control of a member of the Motor Trade for the purpose of its overhaul

f   upkeep or repair.'

The plaintiff in the statement of claim (which, instead of being in common form, simply saying that the casualty occurred when the policy was on risk and leaving it to the insurers to set up the defence) sought to escape from a difficulty before it had arisen. Counsel for the plaintiff pleaded and argued before the judge that when those two exceptions are read together the effect of para 1(*a*)(i) was to cut down the meaning of para

g   1(*c*) so as to leave the policy on risk where a motor trader repairer to whom the car had been given for upkeep or repair was driving it and/or had it in his control. The whole argument really was devoted to that topic.

The judge, in my judgment, quite properly rejected the submission that para 1(*c*) should be cut down by para 1(*a*). On the facts of this case I think he was right so to do and I need say no more about it, but it seems to me that the simple proposition that when

h   Mr Ford parked his car at Hammersmith his journey was at an end, and that thereafter, until he began driving it back to Dagenham, he was not the person who had the charge of it for the purpose of driving it, was never put in those terms to the judge. He did, I think, consider it, but he simply came to the conclusion, having recited para 1(*c*), that there was no ambiguity in it and that this is exactly the circumstance in which the vehicle was stolen.

j   'It was, at the time it was stolen, not literally being driven. It is not necessary for me to make a finding whether the vehicle was being driven within the terms of para 1(*c*). It is arguable that it was being driven, because a vehicle can be said to be driven although it may be stopped for a while and the driver away from it. [That is the breathalyser cases.] In my judgment, however, the vehicle was, for the purpose of being driven, in the charge of a person other than the authorised driver. It was, at the time when it was stolen, in the charge of Mr Ford for the purpose of being driven by him.'

In my judgment the judge fell into error in so holding. I do not think that the car was in Mr Ford's charge at the time that it was stolen for the purpose of being driven. It was in his charge for the purpose of being repaired.

I would allow this appeal.

ROBERT GOFF LJ. Counsel for the plaintiff advanced two submissions. His first submission was concerned with the relationship between general exception 1(a)(i) and general exception 1(c). He submitted that para 1(a)(i) permits use while the motor vehicle is in the custody or control of a member of the motor trade for repair. Furthermore, since repair frequently involves the driving of the vehicle under repair, for example, shifting the vehicle from forecourt to working area and vice versa, or carrying out a test drive, para 1(a)(i) would lead an ordinary motorist to believe that he was covered while his vehicle was being so driven while in the hands of the repairer. Accordingly, in so far as para 1(c) purports to exclude cover in such circumstances, it must be read as subject to para 1(a)(i) to allow for cover to continue despite the fact that a person so driving the car at the repairer's garage is not specified as an authorised person for the purposes of the policy.

I am unable to accept this submission. I approach the matter as follows. The function of para 1(a)(i) is, as appears from its own wording, to ensure that an exclusion of use for any purpose in connection with the motor trade shall not prejudice the indemnity to the insured, while the car in question is 'in the custody or control of a member of the Motor Trade for the purpose of its overhaul upkeep or repair'. As I read it, this provision contemplates that cover under the policy will ordinarily be applicable in such circumstances. This is probably because putting one's car into a garage for overhaul, upkeep or repair is not regarded as a distinct use, as is demonstrated by the fact that it is nowhere mentioned as such among the various uses specified in the list on the back of the certificate. So the purpose of para 1(a)(i) is simply to ensure that an exclusion of use for any purpose in connection with the motor trade should not, in the specified circumstances, prejudice the cover ordinarily applicable. That being so, para 1(a)(i) does not lead to any extension of the cover. Furthermore, where it states that the exclusion in question shall not prejudice the indemnity to the insured, it is referring to the indemnity given under the policy, which must mean the cover against the specified risks subject to the other terms of the policy. Among those terms is general exception para 1(c), and I can see no reason why, as a matter of construction, para 1(a)(i) should lead to any qualification being placed on para 1(c).

Let me test the matter in this way. Suppose that the insured, using his car for one of the permitted uses, goes shopping in it and leaves his car at a car park where the car park attendant always takes the keys so that he can, if necessary, move the car. Such a state of affairs is a familiar incident of modern life; yet I can see no basis for any qualification of para 1(c) to permit the cover, if the policy is one under which the only authorised driver is the insured, to continue to apply when the car park attendant is driving the car. That being so, I can see no reason why, merely because it was thought necessary to refer in para 1(a)(i) to the car being put in for overhaul, upkeep or repair, such a circumstance should be singled out for the purpose of imposing any qualification on para 1(c).

For these reasons I cannot accept counsel for the plaintiff's first submission, and I turn then to his second. This was based on the wording of general exception 1(c), which provides as follows:

'The Corporation shall not be liable in respect of 1. any accident injury loss or damage occurring whilst any motor vehicle in connection with which insurance is granted under this Policy is ... (c) being driven by or for the purpose of being

driven is in the charge of any person other than an authorised driver described in
the Schedule.'

a

It had been accepted that the car was not being driven by Mr Ford at the relevant time.
The submission of counsel for the plaintiff was that the car was in the charge of Mr Ford
at the relevant time, not for the purpose of being driven, but for the purpose of repair.
Alternatively, he submitted that there was more than one purpose, ie the purpose of
b   repair, and the purpose of driving, and, on the approach adopted by this court in *Seddon
v Binions (Zurich Insurance Co Ltd, third party)* [1978] 1 Lloyd's Rep 381, regard should be
had to the primary purpose, which was plainly the purpose of repair. On that basis the
exception in para 1(c) had no application to the facts of the present case.

During the argument before this court there was much discussion about the meaning
of the words in the exception 'or for the purpose of being driven [is] in the charge of' an
c   unauthorised person. I was at first attracted to the idea that the purpose so referred to
was the purpose for which the car was entrusted by the insured to the person in question,
so that, if the car was entrusted to a person for, for example, the purpose of repair, it
could not be said that it was in his charge for the purpose of being driven, even though
driving was contemplated as an activity incidental to the process of repair. But I have
been persuaded by counsel for the defendant insurers that that cannot be right.

d   It seems to me that the function of the exception in para 1(c) is plain. It is essentially
directed to excluding the cover where the vehicle is driven by an unauthorised person,
but it is recognised that there are circumstances in which, although the car is not actually
being driven by an unauthorised person, nevertheless it may, for the purpose of being
driven, be in his charge. For example, an unauthorised person may be driving the car
and he may briefly pause in his journey. If so, it may be that he is no longer actually
e   driving the car, but it is nevertheless thought right that the cover should not apply
because the car is, for the purpose of being driven, still in his charge.

It is important to note that the question which is posed by these words in the exception
is not 'Why is the car in the charge of the unauthorised person?': it is whether, at the
relevant time, the car is, for the purpose of being driven, in the charge of the unauthorised
person. These questions are not, I think, the same, and the answer to the second question
f   is not dependent on ascertaining the purpose for which the insured entrusted the car to
the unauthorised person or the purpose for which that person was driving the car. We
are concerned here only with the question whether the car is, for the purpose of being
driven, in the charge of the unauthorised person. It is the immediate situation of the car
with which we are concerned. The ultimate purpose, whether of the insured or of the
unauthorised person, is, I think, irrelevant.

g   It is to be observed that the construction which I prefer is not necessarily adverse to
persons insured under a policy in these terms. It involves a fairly narrow extension of the
exclusion beyond the ordinary case where the car is actually being driven by an
unauthorised person, whereas, if the other construction which I have mentioned were
correct and the car was lent by the assured to a friend over a long period of time during
which he permitted his friend to drive the car, though he was not an authorised driver
h   under the policy, the cover might not be applicable in respect of any of the risks insured
under the policy during the whole period while the car was in the charge of that person,
even if during that period he never drove the car at all.

I therefore ask myself whether, on the facts of the present case, the car was at the time
when it was stolen 'for the purpose of being driven . . . in the charge of' Mr Ford in the
sense I have described. The relevant facts are that Mr Ford drove the car to Hammersmith.
j   He did so because it was only there that agents for spare parts for this uncommon type of
car are to be found in this country. The reason why he went in this car was that he
needed to take the car to the agents so that he could make sure that any parts that he got,
which included parts for some section of the electrical system, actually did suit and fit
the vehicle. He parked the car near the agents' premises and was only away for a few

minutes seeing to the parts. When he returned to where he had left the car he found that it was gone.

As I read the facts, which I have taken verbatim from the judgment of the judge, Mr Ford's expedition involved three elements: (1) driving to Hammersmith; (2) obtaining the spare parts for the car from the agents; and (3) driving back to his repair shop. The question then arises: During (2), was the car, for the purpose of being driven, in his charge? If Mr Ford had simply been using the car to do a little shopping, I could see that there would be a strong argument for saying that during a short time while he was in a shop the car was still, for the purposes of being driven, in his charge. But in the present case the car, while Mr Ford was in the agents' premises in Hammersmith, was there for a particular purpose independent of being driven; it was there to be used for seeing whether spare parts obtainable from the agents did 'suit and fit the vehicle'. In these circumstances it seems to me that, once the car had arrived at the agents' premises at Hammersmith, it ceased to be 'for the purpose of being driven . . . in the charge of' Mr Ford; it was there, in his charge, for another distinct purpose, which was still operative at the time when the car was stolen. My conclusion is therefore that, although I accept counsel for the defendants' submissions as to the construction of the policy, nevertheless on the facts of this particular case the insurers cannot rely on general exception 1(c).

For these reasons I too would allow the appeal.

NOURSE LJ. As I see it, this is the familiar case where the court must give the best effect it can to two potentially conflicting provisions of a contract. For the purposes of this case I see no difference between the concept of a motor car being in the custody or control of somebody within general exception 1(a)(i) and the concept of its being in his charge within general exception 1(c). At the time when it was stolen the plaintiff's car was admittedly in the charge of Mr Ford. In my view the only question which arises for decision on the two material provisions is whether the car was in his charge for the purpose of its repair or for the purpose of being driven.

At the time when the car was stolen Mr Ford had left it for a few minutes in order to see to certain spare parts which he needed to be sure did actually suit *and fit* the car. In other words, on being reunited with the car, he would have had to make some application of the parts to it in order to see whether they fitted. That was part of the process of repairing the car. When Mr Ford returned to where he had left it the car had been stolen.

On these facts I am in no doubt that at the time when the car was stolen it was in Mr Ford's charge for the purpose of its repair. That was the purpose for which it had been put into his charge and that was the purpose which was being furthered when it was stolen. The facts that he intended to drive it back from Hammersmith to Dagenham and that while he was driving to or fro the exception in para 1(c) would have applied are immaterial. There is nothing inherently objectionable in construing a contract of insurance in such a way as to put the insurers on and off risk at short and recurring intervals. That would in any event have been the result of the construction urged by the insurers in the present case.

For these reasons, which appear not to have been deployed before the deputy judge, I agree that this appeal should be allowed.

Appeal allowed. Judgment in the sum of £10,500 with interest to be agreed; failing agreement, liberty to apply.

Solicitors: *Wiseman Greenman & Lee* (for the plaintiff); *L Bingham & Co* (for the defendants).

Bebe Chua   Barrister.

a   # Attorney General of the Bahamas v Royal Trust Co and another

PRIVY COUNCIL
LORD KEITH OF KINKEL, LORD TEMPLEMAN, LORD GRIFFITHS, LORD OLIVER OF AYLMERTON AND
LORD GOFF OF CHIEVELEY

b   9, 10, 23 JUNE 1986

Charity – Education – Education and welfare – Gift for education and welfare of Bahamian children and young people – Whether gift to be construed conjunctively or disjunctively – Whether education and welfare separate objects – Whether gift charitable.

c

The will of a Bahamian testator contained a residuary bequest directing the trustees to hold the residue on trust to be used for 'any purposes for and/or connected with the education and welfare of Bahamian children and young people'. After the death of the life tenant the sole trustee issued an originating summons in the Supreme Court of the Bahamas to determine, inter alia, the validity of the residuary gift. The judge held that
d   the gift did not create a valid charitable trust because it embraced purposes connected with the 'welfare' as well as the 'education' of Bahamian children and young people, and accordingly the gift failed. An appeal by the Attorney General to the Court of Appeal of the Bahamas was dismissed and the Attorney General appealed to the Privy Council, contending that 'education and welfare' were to be construed conjunctively so that the word 'education' limited the word 'welfare' with the result that there was only one overall
e   purpose of the trust, namely educational welfare, which was charitable.

Held – On the true construction of the will, the words 'education and welfare' in the residuary bequest were to be construed disjunctively and as embracing two distinct purposes one of which, the trust for 'welfare', was non-charitable. It followed that the residuary bequest did not constitute a valid charitable trust and therefore failed. The
f   appeal would accordingly be dismissed (see p 425 g and p 426 e to p 427 a, post).
    Dictum of Sargant J in *Re Eades, Eades v Eades* [1920] 2 Ch at 356 considered.

Notes
For charities for educational purposes, see 5 Halsbury's Laws (4th edn) paras 522–527, and for cases on the subject, see 8(1) Digest (Reissue) 257–266, *112–158*.
g   For the Attorney General as a necessary party, see 5 Halsbury's Laws (4th edn) para 934, and for cases on the subject, see 8(1) Digest (Reissue) 465–466, *2213–2224*.

Case referred to in judgment
Eades, Re, Eades v Eades [1920] 2 Ch 353.

h   **Cases also cited**
A-G v Ross [1985] 3 All ER 334, [1986] 1 WLR 252.
Best, Re, Jarvis v Birmingham Corp [1904] 2 Ch 354.
Cole, Re, Westminster Bank Ltd v Moore [1958] 3 All ER 102, [1958] Ch 877, CA.
IRC v McMullen [1980] 1 All ER 884, [1981] AC 1, HL.
j   *Lloyd Greame v A-G, Re* (1893) 10 TLR 66.
London Hospital Medical College v IRC [1976] 2 All ER 113, [1976] 1 WLR 613.
Mellody, Re, Brandwood v Haden [1918] 1 Ch 228, [1916–17] All ER Rep 324.
Neville Estates Ltd v Madden [1961] 3 All ER 769, [1962] Ch 832.
Sutton, Re, Stone v A-G (1885) 28 Ch D 464.
Williams v Williams, Williams v Kershaw (1835) 5 Cl & F 111n, 7 ER 346.

Appeal

The Attorney General of the Bahamas appealed with leave of the Court of Appeal of the *a*
Commonwealth of the Bahamas against the decision of that court (Luckhoo P, da Costa
and Zacca JJA) on 26 October 1983 dismissing an appeal by the Attorney General against
part of the judgment of Blake CJ in the Supreme Court (Equity Side) given on 30 April
1982 whereby in an action by the first respondent, the Royal Trust Co, the trustee of the
will and codicils of Albert Edward Worswick (the testator), against the second respondent,
Ernest Raymond Lawson, the personal representative of the testator's widow, and the *b*
Attorney General, the judge granted a declaration that the bequest in cl 15(t) of the
testator's will was not a valid charitable bequest and was accordingly void. The facts are
set out in the judgment of the Board.

George Newman QC and *Jonathan Harvie* for the Attorney General.
J M Chadwick QC and *Lindsey Stewart* for the second respondent.   *c*
The first respondent was not represented.

23 June. The following judgment of the Board was delivered.

LORD OLIVER OF AYLMERTON. This is an appeal from an order dated 26 *d*
October 1983 of the Court of Appeal of the Commonwealth of the Bahamas (Sir Joseph
Luckhoo P, da Costa and Zacca JJA) dismissing the appellant's appeal from that part of a
decision of Blake CJ in the Supreme Court (Equity Side) dated 30 April 1982 which
declared that certain trusts contained in cl 15(t) of the will of the late Albert Edward
Worswick deceased as amended by the third codicil to his will were not charitable and
were void.   *e*
    Albert Edward Worswick (the testator) died on 20 April 1953 leaving a will dated 30
April 1951 and three codicils dated respectively 13 September 1951, 16 March 1953 and
8 April 1953. By cl 3 of his will he appointed his wife, Delphine Elizabeth Worswick, Sir
Stafford Lofthouse Sands and the first respondent, the Royal Trust Co, to be trustees of
the trusts of his will and by cl 13 bequeathed to his trustees certain shares (subsequently
replaced by shares bequeathed by the first codicil to the will) (therein and hereafter *f*
referred to as 'the trust estate') on trusts taking effect for the period of the life of his
widow. By cl 14 he directed that on the death of his widow his trustees should realise the
trust estate and pay thereout two pecuniary legacies.
    The question raised by this appeal arises from the provisions of cl 15 of the will as
varied by the third codicil. By this clause the testator directed that the remainder of the
trust estate should by held on trusts contained in paras (a) to (v) inclusive. No question *g*
arises in relation to paras (a) to (g) or (m) to (r) (inclusive) which consisted simply of
pecuniary legacies to a number of named bodies most of them, if not all, being charities.
The remaining paragraphs of the clause, however, contained trusts some of which were
arguably void for perpetuity and others of which have been revoked. Paragraph (v) was
a final gift of the residue of the trust estate to the University of Toronto, but this was
revoked by the third codicil and replaced by a further residuary trust being the trust *h*
which has given rise to this appeal.
    The provisions of the second codicil to the will are immaterial for present purposes,
but by the third codicil the testator revoked paras (s), (t), (u) and (v) of his will and
substituted therefor (in para (s)) a further pecuniary legacy to a named charity and a new
para (t) which was in the following terms:

    'All the rest residue and remainder of my Trust Estate I direct my Trustees to pay *j*
    over to the Manager of the Nassau Branch of The Royal Bank of Canada for the time
    being the Manager of the Nassau Branch of Barclays Bank (Dominion, Colonial and
    Overseas) for the time being and the said Stafford Lofthouse Sands upon trust to
    invest the same in any investments for the time being authorised by law for the
    investment of trust moneys or on mortage of any real or personal estate situate

a within the Colony and in their absolute and uncontrolled discretion to use the income therefrom and any part of the capital thereof for any purposes for and/or connected with the education and welfare of Bahamian children and young people either within or without the Colony and in all respects as they shall in their absolute discretion deem fit.'

b By cl 16 of his will the testator bequeathed the whole of the remainder of his personal estate to his widow absolutely.

The testator's will and codicils were duly proved on 8 May 1953 and the trust estate was duly vested in the trustees. The first respondent is now the sole trustee of the will. It has rightly adopted an entirely neutral attitude on this appeal. The second respondent represents the estate of the testator's widow who died on 4 April 1968.

c On 15 July 1970 an originating summons was issued in the Supreme Court of the Bahamas for the determination of a number of questions which had arisen in the administration of the trusts of the will including questions whether the bequests in paras (h), (j) and (l) of cl 15 of the will were valid charitable gifts or failed and so fell into the residuary trust declared by para (t) substituted by the third codicil. At the hearing before Blake CJ it was determined that the bequests in paras (h) and (j) were good charitable gifts but that that in para (l) failed and there has been no appeal against that part of his

d decision.

The primary question however was that of the validity of the residuary trust in the new para (t) substituted by the third codicil. It was the contention of the second respondent that the gift contained in this paragraph, inasmuch as it embraced purposes connected with the 'welfare' as well as the 'education' of Bahamian children and young people, was not a valid charitable gift and that accordingly the trusts of this paragraph

e failed and the funds subject to the trusts fell into the residuary gift contained in cl 16 of the will. That contention was accepted by Blake CJ in a carefully considered judgment and his decision was upheld by the Court of Appeal. Before Blake CJ the Attorney General had conceded that the broad principles of law relating to charities in the Bahamas were the same as the law of England but before the Court of Appeal that concession was withdrawn and it was sought to argue that the court was not bound to proceed on the

f footing that the question was governed by the English authorities. That argument was, in the event, rejected and has not been revived before their Lordships' Board.

Thus the sole question on this appeal is one of the true construction of para (t) and it is common ground between the parties that if the trusts declared in this paragraph were trusts solely for the 'welfare' of Bahamian children and young persons they would not, as the authorities stand, be valid charitable trusts. It follows that if, as both Blake CJ and the

g Court of Appeal held, the words 'education and welfare' in the pargraph are to be construed disjunctively (ie as embracing two distinct purposes) this appeal must necessarily fail, since the fund will then be capable of being applied in perpetuity to purposes some of which may be non-charitable. It is, however, the contention of counsel for the Attorney General that, reading the will and codicils as a whole, the true construction of the paragraph is one which involves reading the word 'and' in its

h conjunctive sense, that is to say, that the only purposes for which the trust moneys are authorised to be disbursed by the paragraph are purposes which are not merely for the welfare of Bahamian children and young persons but are also educational. To put it another way the word 'education' limits the word 'welfare' and there is only one overall purpose of the trust and that is the purpose of educational welfare.

In approaching the question it is helpful to bear in mind the analysis of Sargant J in Re

j Eades, Eades v Eades [1920] 2 Ch 353. He was there concerned to decide whether a gift for 'religious, charitable and philanthropic objects' constituted a good charitable bequest. In the course of his judgment, after observing that there were only two possible constructions (that is to say, either that the objects must possess all three characteristics or that there were three distinct, but possibly overlapping, characteristics the possession of any one of which would qualify an object for selection as a proper object of the trusts) he observed (at 356):

'Such a construction as the second is sometimes referred to as a disjunctive
construction, and as involving the change of the word "and" into "or". This is a short
and compendious way of expressing the result of the construction, but I doubt
whether it indicates accurately the mental conception by which the result is reached.
That conception is one, I think, which regards the word "and" as used conjunctively
and by way of addition, for the purpose of enlarging the number of objects within
the area of selection; and it does not appear to be a false mental conception, or one
really at variance with the ordinary use of language, merely because it involves in
the result that the qualifications for selection are alternative or disjunctive. Further,
the greater the number of the qualifications or characteristics enumerated, the more
probable, as it seems to me, is a construction which regards them as multiplying the
kinds or classes of objects within the area of selection, rather than as multiplying the
number of qualifications to be complied with, and so diminishing the objects within
the area of selection.'

It would be a work of supererogation to rehearse yet again the numerous reported
decisions in which testators have used somewhat similar, although not indentical,
expressions. They have been fully and helpfully reviewed in the judgment of Blake CJ
and in the judgments in the Court of Appeal and have been drawn to their Lordships'
attention by counsel for the Attorney General in the course of his able argument. In the
end, however, the question is one of the construction of the particular dispositions of this
testator and references to the construction placed on different expressions in the wills of
other testators, whilst perhaps useful as guidelines, are necessarily of limited assistance.
It is true that in the instant case there are two, and only two objects, specified, so that,
to that extent, it is the easier to adopt the conjuctive construction for which counsel for
the Attorney General contends. But there are a number of formidable difficulties about
this, and not least that it is not easy to imagine a purpose connected with the education
of a child which is not also a purpose for the child's welfare. Thus if 'welfare' is to be
given any separate meaning at all it must be something different from and wider than
mere education, for otherwise the word becomes otiose. Counsel has sought to meet this
by the submission that, in the context of the paragraph as a whole, 'welfare' is used in the
sense of 'welfare ancillary to education'. But 'welfare' is a word of the widest import and
when used in connection with a class of 'children and young people' generally is capable
of embracing almost anything which would lead to the enhancement of the quality of
life of any member of the class. Counsel's difficulty then is to find any context, either in
the paragraph itself or in other parts of the will, for subordinating this wide concept to
the object of education. Despite the helpful argument of counsel for the Attorney
General, their Lordships have been unable to discern any context from which the
inference of subordination can be drawn and that difficulty would remain even if the
trustees had been directed simply to apply the income for 'education and welfare'. The
difficulty is, however, compounded by the additional and not unimporant words 'for any
purposes for and/or connected with', for, if counsel were otherwise able to link the word
'welfare' with the preceding word 'education' in a conjunctive sense, it would then be
impossible to find a purpose which was connected with 'welfare' (used in this ancillary
sense) which was not also 'connected with' education, so that the reference to 'welfare'
would again become otiose.
The point is not one which is susceptible of a great deal of elaboration and their
Lordships need say no more than that they agree with Blake CJ and the Court of Appeal
that the phrase 'education and welfare' in this will inevitably falls to be construed
disjunctively. It follows that, for the reasons which were fully explored in the judgments
in the courts below, and as is now conceded on the footing of a disjunctive construction,
the trusts in para (t) do not constitute valid charitable trusts and that, accordingly, the
residue of the trust estate falls into the residuary gift in cl 16 of the will. In the Court of
Appeal, the costs of all parties were ordered to be taxed on the common fund basis and
paid out of the estate and it has been agreed between the parties that the cost of both
parties before their Lordships' Board should be similarly taxed and paid.

a Their Lordships will accordingly humbly advise Her Majesty that the appeal should be dismissed. The costs of the appellant and the respondents before their Lordships' Board shall be taxed and paid in the manner so agreed.

Appeal dismissed.

b Solicitors: *Charles Russell & Co* (for the Attorney General); *Shephenson Harwood* (for the second respondent).

Mary Rose Plummer   Barrister.

c

Wilkinson v Ancliff (BLT) Ltd

COURT OF APPEAL, CIVIL DIVISION
SLADE AND CROOM-JOHNSON LJJ
d 19, 23 MAY 1986

Writ – Extension of validity – Action statute-barred – Writ not served – Application for extension made after 12 months' validity had expired – Whether defendant having arguable case that he would be deprived of limitation defence if writ renewed – Whether special circumstances justifying renewal – RSC Ord 6, r 8(1)(2).

e

Limitation of action – When time begins to run – Personal injury claim – Plaintiff's knowledge – Date on which plaintiff first had knowledge that injury attributable to defendant's act or omission – Attributable – Plaintiff aware of broad failure by employer to provide safe working conditions – Plaintiff not knowing particular breaches of duty by employer – Whether time running from date when plaintiff became aware of employer's broad failure – Whether time not running until
f *defendant's acts or omissions could be particularised – Limitation Act 1980, ss 11(4)(b), 14(1)(b)(3)(b).*

The plaintiff was employed by the defendants to drive tankers containing chemicals. In April 1981 he experienced symptoms of chest congestion and in August he stopped work and claimed industrial benefit because of his condition. On 2 November he went to g hospital to have his symptoms investigated. The hospital medical report stated that he had developed bronchial asthma by inhaling chemical fumes. In late 1982 or early 1983 he consulted solicitors who issued a writ on 7 March 1984 against the defendants claiming damages for personal injury and loss arising from industrial asthma contracted by the plaintiff in the course of his employment. In May 1984 counsel advised that it would be necessary to obtain an expert's report to establish the defendants' liability. A report was h obtained from a consultant research chemist on 10 December 1984 stating that the plaintiff's asthma had been brought about by continued exposure to chemical vapours and itemising particular aspects of the defendants' failure to provide the plaintiff with safe working conditions. On the basis of that report a statement of claim was settled particularising the acts and omissions of the defendants alleged to constitute negligence. j On 29 March 1985, ie more than 12 months after the issue of the writ, the plaintiff's solicitors served the writ and statement of claim on the defendants. The defendants applied to have the service set aside and the action dismissed on the ground that the writ was no longer valid for service under RSC Ord 6, r 8(1)ᵃ. The plaintiff cross-applied for leave under Ord 6, r 8(2) to renew the validity of the writ for a further 12 months. The

---

a   Rule 8, so far as material, is set out at p 432 *h j*, post

registrar granted the defendants' application, set aside service of the writ and dismissed the action. The plaintiff appealed to the judge, who allowed the appeal and renewed the writ, thus validating the service on 29 March. The defendants appealed to the Court of Appeal, contending that when the writ was served on 29 March it was either certain or reasonably arguable that they had a limitation defence if a fresh writ were to be issued, and that in the absence of exceptional circumstances the court should not renew a writ's validity if to do so would deprive the defendant of an accrued limitation defence. The plaintiff conceded that there were no special circumstances but contended that the limitation period had not expired when the writ was served on 29 March 1985 because under ss 11(4)(b)[b] and 14(1)(b)[c] of the Limitation Act 1980 time did not begin to run until the plaintiff had 'knowledge' of his injury, which was not until he received the chemist's report on 19 December 1984 since only then did he first have 'knowledge . . . that the injury was attributable . . . to the act or omission . . . alleged to constitute negligence' because until then he could not particularise the defendants' acts and omissions.

Held – (1) Even though a defendant could only show a reasonably arguable case that he would be deprived of a limitation defence if an expired writ were to be renewed and he was unable to show that such a defence was certain to succeed, the court could nevertheless exercise its discretion by refusing to renew the validity of the writ, because the grant of leave to renew the validity of an expired writ was a substantial privilege granted to a plaintiff by the court, and in the absence of special circumstances the court would refuse to grant renewal if there was a real likelihood or substantial risk that renewal would deprive the defendant of an accrued limitation defence. However, it was always open to the court to decide that on the evidence before it the defendant would not have a good limitation defence (see p 435 h j, p 436 b c f g and p 439 h, post); Heaven v Road and Rail Wagons Ltd [1965] 2 All ER 409 applied.

(2) For the purpose of s 14(1)(b) of the 1980 Act, a plaintiff first knew that his injury was 'attributable . . . to the act or omission' of the defendant when he first knew that his injury was capable of being so attributed, bearing in mind that under s 14(3)(b) he was deemed to know facts which he could ascertain from expert medical or legal advice which it was reasonable for him to seek, though mere reasonable belief or suspicion that the injury was attributable to the defendant's act or omission was not enough to constitute 'knowledge' within s 14(1). Since the plaintiff well knew after his visit to hospital in November 1981 not only that in broad terms his injuries were capable of being attributed to the defendants' failure to provide him with safe working conditions but also that there had been particular breaches of duty by the defendants, namely exposing him to the risk of inhaling chemicals, failing to provide him with breathing apparatus and failing to monitor his health, it followed that by virtue of ss 11(3) and (4) and 14(1) of the 1980 Act the limitation period began to run in November 1981 after the hospital visit and therefore had expired before the service of the writ on 29 March 1985. Moreover, even if the evidence did not firmly establish that the limitation period had begun to run in November 1981, the defendants had a strong arguable case that that was so and it followed that the judge should have refused to renew the writ, leaving the plaintiff to issue new process if so advised. Accordingly, the appeal would be allowed, service of the writ set aside and the action dismissed (see p 437 h j and p 438 b to e h to 439 a d f h, post).

Per curiam. Where the acts and omissions complained of can be compendiously described as failure to provide the plaintiff with safe working conditions, then once the plaintiff has the broad knowledge that his injuries are attributable to the defendant's failure to provide safe working conditions the plaintiff has sufficient knowledge for the purpose of s 14(1)(b) of the 1980 Act to set time running against him, even if he does not then know the particular acts or omissions constituting the failure to provide safe working conditions and is thus not in a position to enable his lawyers to draft a fully particularised statement of claim (see p 438 e f and p 439 h, post).

---

b   Section 11, so far as material, is set out at p 434 c d, post
c   Section 14, so far as material, is set out at p 434 e to h, post

Notes

a   For renewal of a writ, see 37 Halsbury's Laws (4th edn) para 124.

For the limitation period in personal injury actions, and the plaintiff's knowledge for purposes of time running, see 28 ibid paras 691–692.

For the Limitation Act 1980, ss 11, 14, see 50(1) Halsbury's Statutes (3rd edn) 1262, 1265.

b   **Cases referred to in judgments**

Baker v Bowketts Cakes Ltd [1966] 2 All ER 290, [1966] 1 WLR 861, CA.

Chappell v Cooper [1980] 2 All ER 463, [1980] 1 WLR 958, CA.

Davis v Ministry of Defence [1985] CA Transcript 413.

Heaven v Road and Rail Wagons Ltd [1965] 2 All ER 409, [1965] 2 QB 355, [1965] 2 WLR 1249.

c   **Interlocutory appeal**

By a writ issued on 7 March 1984 the plaintiff, Robert James Wilkinson, claimed against the defendants, Ancliff (BLT) Ltd, damages for personal injury for industrial asthma disease contracted during the course of the plaintiff's employment with the defendants due to their negligence. The writ was served on the defendants after the expiry of 12

d   months from the date of the issue of the writ and thus after expiry of the writ's validity for service. Accordingly, by a summons dated 25 April 1985 the defendants applied to have service of the writ set aside and the action dismissed on the ground that to grant renewal of the validity of the writ for the purpose of service would deprive them of an accrued defence under the Limitation Acts. By a summons dated 9 May 1985 the plaintiff applied for an order that the writ should be renewed or extended to validate the service

e   on the defendants. On 24 May 1985 Mr Deputy District Registrar Stephenson, sitting in the Manchester District Registry, refused the plaintiff's application and ordered that the purported service of the writ was irregular and invalid because it occurred after the writ's validity had expired and dismissed the action. The plaintiff appealed and on 1 November 1985 Caulfield J allowed the appeal and renewed the writ so as to validate the service on the defendants. The defendants appealed seeking restoration of the registrar's order. The

f   facts are set out in the judgment of Slade LJ.

G W Wingate-Saul QC and *P A Butler* for the defendants.
M S E Grime for the plaintiff.

Cur adv vult

g   23 May. The following judgments were delivered.

SLADE LJ. This is an appeal by Ancliff (BLT) Ltd, the defendants in an action, from an order of Caulfield J made on 1 November 1985. By that order he allowed an appeal of the plaintiff in the action, Mr Robert James Wilkinson, against an order made on 24 May

h   1985 by Mr Deputy District Registrar Stephenson, who had set aside the service of the writ in the action, dismissed the action and refused to renew or extend the validity of the writ.

The chronology of the case is of some importance. I derive most of the facts in the summary of the history which follows from the affidavit evidence sworn on behalf of the respective parties. Neither side has yet had the opportunity to test its accuracy by

j   cross-examination, but I know of no reason to doubt it.

The plaintiff was formerly employed by the defendants as a road tanker driver based at their premises at Felixstowe in Suffolk. The tankers in question contained a substance known as toluene di-isocyanate (which I will call 'TDI'). As he subsequently told his medical advisers, in April 1981 he experienced symptoms of wheezing, cough and shortness of breath. In August 1981 he stopped work due to ill health. In October 1981 the Department of Health and Social Security wrote to the defendants, referring to a claim for benefit which had been received from the plaintiff, the cause of incapacity being shown as 'chest congestion', which he had told them was 'due to inhalation of chemicals due to spillage'. On 2 November 1981 he was admitted to St Bartholomews Hospital in London for investigation of symptoms of 'cough, breathlessness and wheeze'. What occurred on that occasion appears from a report by the senior registrar of that hospital, Dr Blainey, subsequently written on 20 May 1982, from which I will quote certain extracts. Dr Blainey said:

'He first developed these symptoms in April 1981 when he noticed nocturnal wheezing. Since then wheezing, cough and shortness of breath had been present during the day in addition. At that time he noticed that his symptoms were worse during the working week but improved when away from work. When he went on holiday in June 1981 his symptoms improved but recurred within three weeks of his return to work. At the time of admission he was employed as a tanker driver and in the course of his employment had encountered a number of chemicals. He told us that on several occasions during the three years of his employment he had been exposed to [TDI] at concentrations sufficiently high for him to smell the fumes during the process of loading and unloading a tanker carrying [TDI]. Since April 1981 there were occasions when he had been exposed to [TDI] at concentrations at which he was unable to detect the fumes. Nevertheless on at least two occasions he had developed wheezing, cough and shortness of breath within 20 minutes of such exposure. Since the last of these attacks, in August 1981 he had not returned to work and had as a result had no further attacks. He had no history of respiratory symptoms prior to his present employment, he had worked as an ambulance driver in Belfast before coming to England to take up his present employment. He had not smoked cigarettes since 1966. He complained of no other symptoms.'

Dr Blainey then referred to a physical examination of the plaintiff which included a chest X-ray and lung function tests and proved to be normal. He also referred to what was described in argument before us as a 'challenge test' and involved the plaintiff being exposed to TDI at a steady state concentration. Dr Blainey gave some details of the plaintiff's reaction to this challenge test and concluded:

'This reaction is conventionally regarded as a positive response to [TDI] and confirms the expression quoted from the history that this patient had developed bronchial asthma due to sensitization to [TDI].'

Following this examination, the plaintiff must in my opinion at least have been well aware that in all probability his bronchial asthma had resulted from his employment with the defendants. On or about 11 November 1981 he was advised by a social worker attached to the hospital to seek advice about compensation. On or about 13 November 1981 he contacted his trade union (the Transport and General Workers Union), who in turn put him in touch with their retained solicitors in Ipswich, Messrs Bates Wells & Braithwaite. It appears that he went to see these solicitors on 16 December 1981 and that they then sought the report from St Bartholomew's Hospital which was eventually produced on 20 May 1982.

Following the receipt of this report, Bates Wells & Braithwaite wrote to the defendants on 7 June 1982 saying that they had been consulted by the plaintiff in connection with a respiratory condition suffered by him in or about April 1981. They continued:

'According to our instructions our client who is employed by you as a Tanker Driver was exposed to [TDI] during the course of his employment. We understand that no tests were ever carried out on our client to determine his susceptibility or otherwise to the various chemicals which he was responsible for transporting. Furthermore, we are instructed that no protective clothing was supplied such as respiratory apparatus.'

They ended by saying that the plaintiff held the defendants responsible for the injury a and loss which he had suffered and asked the defendants to forward the letter to their insurers. Some further correspondence followed between Bates Wells & Braithwaite and the defendants or their insurers in June and July 1982. But it seems that eventually, in or about October 1982, that firm, for reasons which are not apparent, advised the plaintiff that he had a poor chance of succeeding in any claim against the defendants. At that point the plaintiff, whose home is in Northern Ireland, instructed a firm of solicitors in Northern Ireland, Messrs Austin Mallon. They appear to have taken a different view as

b to his prospects of success in proceedings. At the end of August 1983 they requested his present English solicitors, Messrs Livingstone & Co, to act for him in seeking to obtain legal aid and proceeding with the matter thereafter. On 29 November 1983 the plaintiff obtained legal aid.

On 7 March 1984 he issued a writ against the defendants. On the writ the plaintiff's claim was stated to be—

c

'for damages for personal injury and loss arising out of an industrial asthma disease contracted during the course of the Plaintiff's employment with the Defendants, which said disease the Plaintiff first discovered was attributable to the Defendants in November 1981 and which was contracted due to the negligence and/or breach of duty of the Defendants, their servants or agents.'

d In May 1984 counsel was asked to advise on liability. When he did so, in June 1984, he advised that it was necessary to obtain an expert's report. On 28 June 1984 Livingstone & Co instructed a firm of analytical consulting and reasearch chemists for this purpose, their principal consultant being Mr M Leitner. On 10 December 1984 Mr Leitner wrote his report. He began by referring to the plaintiff's assertion that he suffered from bronchial asthma, to the suspicion that this might be primarily, if not entirely, due to

e the fact that the plaintiff had come into contact with TDI whilst employed as a tanker driver at the defendants' premises. He referred to a written statement made by the plaintiff to his solicitors stating in precise terms the relevant circumstances during his employment with the defendants together with a number of other supporting documents. He continued:

f 'I have been asked to comment from a chemist's viewpoint on whether the circumstances, as outlined by [the plaintiff], are sufficient to lead to exposure to dangerous levels of TDI, which might in turn lead to bronchial asthma; and to further comment on the adequacy of the protective equipment used and the safety procedures generally of [the plaintiff's] employers.'

Mr Leitner then proceeded, very carefully and in great detail, to set out the information g which had been given to him by the plaintiff as to the relevant circumstances during his employment with the defendants. He summarised, from a chemist's point of view the hazards associated with exposure to TDI and expressed his 'Conclusions' thus:

'On the basis of all the facts placed before me it is my considered opinion that:
1. [The defendants] took a casual and irresponsible attitude towards their
h employee by virtue of not providing adequate warning and the hazards associated with inhalation and handling of TDI; by not providing adequate training on the safe handling of TDI; by not providing adequate warning on the importance of using breathing apparatus when handling TDI.
2. [The defendants] did not provide breathing apparatus and adequate training particularly where [the plaintiff] was expected to discharge a load of TDI at a
j customer.
3. It is my considered opinion that Felixstowe Tank Developments Limited [that was the name of the tank firm at Felixstowe Docks] should be partly responsible for [the plaintiff's] condition by virtue of the fact that [the plaintiff] was allowed to remain in the vicinity whilst road tankers were being loaded/unloaded.
4. The effects that inhalation of TDI have on the respiratory tract are well known

and adequately documented and clearly leaves little doubt that [the plaintiff's] present condition of bronchial asthma had been brought about by his continued *a* exposure to TDI vapours over a period of time.

It is not possible to estimate the exposure levels that [the plaintiff] was likely to have encountered whilst standing at the top of a tanker during discharging and not wearing breathing apparatus. However, should it be deemed necessary to ascertain typical exposure levels under such conditions, then it would be possible to set up a test operation and to monitor exposure levels with suitable equipment. In any *b* event, the exposure levels would certainly have been well in excess of the control limits by virtue of the fact that they could be detected by smell.'

On 22 January 1985 counsel's opinion and a draft statement of claim, doubtless settled partly in the light of Mr Leitner's report, were returned to Livingstone & Co. On 31 January 1985 that firm wrote to the Lloyd's underwriters concerned, asking for the address for service of the writ and statement of claim. On 1 February 1985 they wrote to *c* Austin Mallon asking them to check the draft statement of claim with the plaintiff. On 5 February 1985 the Lloyd's underwriters replied saying that they would get the relevant information. On 6 March 1986 the period of one year following the issue of the writ expired. On the next day, 7 March, the Lloyd's underwriters wrote to Livingstone & Co informing them of the defendants' registered office. On 19 March 1985 Austin Mallon wrote to them confirming the accuracy of the details in the draft statement of claim. *d*

On 28 March 1985 the writ and statement of claim were sent to the defendants at their registered office. The statement of claim, unlike the writ, did not specifically assert the date on which the plaintiff first discovered that his disease was attributable to the defendants. However, it alleged that as a result of the work which the plaintiff was employed to do for the defendants, until he ceased working due to ill-health in August *e* 1981, he had been exposed to the toxic fumes of TDI and had sustained severe personal injuries. In para 4 it alleged that his personal injuries were caused by the negligence of the defendants, their servants or agents. Particulars of negligence were then given in a number of sub-paragraphs, itemised as sub-paras (a) to (j). I will merely quote five of them:

'(a) Exposing the Plaintiff to the risk of damage or injury to his health by reason *f* of his handling of T.D.I. and inhaling the toxic fumes thereof, of which they knew or ought to have known.

(b) Failing to warn the Plaintiff adequately or at all of the dangers to which he was exposed in handling T.D.I. in particular arising from spillages and the inhalation of toxic fumes.

(c) Failing to provide the Plaintiff with any or any adequate training or instruction *g* in the safe handling of T.D.I. . . .

(g) Failing to provide breathing apparatus as part of the standard protective equipment . . .

(i) Failing to monitor the Plaintiff's health regularly or at all . . .'

It is, I think, common ground that the writ and statement of claim were received by the defendants at their registered office on 29 March 1985. *h*

RSC Ord 6, r 8, so far as material, provides:

'(1) For the purpose of service, a writ (other than a concurrent writ) is valid in the first instance for twelve months beginning with the date of its issue . . .

(2) Where a writ has not been served on a defendant, the Court may by order extend the validity of the writ from time to time for such period, not exceeding *j* twelve months at any one time, beginning with the day next following that on which it would otherwise expire, as may be specified in the order, if an application for extension is made to the Court before that day or such later day (if any) as the Court may allow . . .'

It is a well-established principle or general rule that in the absence of sufficient or good reason the court will not exercise its discretion in favour of the renewal of a writ after the period allowed for service has expired if the effect of so doing will be to deprive a

a defendant of the benefit of a limitation period which has already accrued (see the notes to RSC Ord 6, r 8, in the *The Supreme Court Practice 1985* vol 1, pp 50–51, para 6/8/3 and the cases there cited). Perhaps the locus classicus on this subject is the decision of Megaw J in *Heaven v Road and Rail Wagons Ltd* [1965] 2 All ER 409, [1965] 2 QB 355. In that case, after referring to a line of earlier authorities, he said ([1965] 2 All ER 409 at 413, [1965] 2 QB 355 at 361):

b
'In my judgment, then, subject to the question whether recent revisions of the Rules of the Supreme Court have deprived of their authority these decisions of the Court of Appeal, which would otherwise, of course, be binding on me, the principle, or the general rule, to be applied is that leave will not be given to extend the validity of a writ when application is made retrospectively after the period of twelve months prescribed by the rules has expired, if the effect of so doing would be to deprive the

c defendant of a defence which he would have had under the relevant statute of limitation, supposing that leave to extend were not given and the plaintiff were thus compelled to serve a fresh writ. To justify the exercise of the discretion there must be exceptional circumstances.'

For convenience I shall refer to the principle stated in this passage as 'the *Heaven*

d principle'.

Megaw J proceeded to explain that the recent revisions of the Rules of the Supreme Court had not deprived the earlier decisions of their authority (see [1965] 2 All ER 409 at 413–415, [1965] 2 QB 355 at 361–365), and made certain observations as to what might and might not constitute sufficient exceptional circumstances to justify a departure from the *Heaven* principle, in the course of which he said ([1965] 2 All ER 409 at 415,

e [1965] 2 QB 355 at 364–365):

'Clearly, the fact that the plaintiff will be deprived of the possibility of successfully pursuing his claim against the defendants, since the latter can plead the statute of limitation to any fresh writ, cannot be a ground. It is not an exceptional circumstance, it is the necessary consequence of applying the general rule; it is, indeed, the very fact which gives rise to the existence of the rule. Nor can the fact that the defendants

f knew of the existence of a claim, or knew that a writ had been issued, be a ground. These are in no way exceptional circumstances.'

The *Heaven* principle was approved by this court in *Baker v Bowketts Cakes Ltd* [1966] 2 All ER 290, [1966] 1 WLR 861. The later decision of this court in *Chappell v Cooper* [1980] 2 All ER 463, [1980] 1 WLR 958 shows that in an action for personal injuries the

g application of the *Heaven* principle is not inconsistent with, and remains unaffected by, the provisions of what is now s 33 of the Limitation Act 1980, which confer a power on the court to override the time limits specified by that Act.

On 25 April 1985 the defendants issued a summons seeking an order that the purported service of the writ on 29 March 1985 should be set aside and that the action should be dismissed. This application was supported by an affidavit sworn by Mr Tyson,

h the defendants' solicitor. He based his submissions on the *Heaven* principle.

On 9 May 1985 the plaintiff's solicitors issued a summons seeking an order that the writ issued on 7 March 1984 be renewed or extended to validate its service. That application was supported by an affirmation made by Mr Barr, a solicitor with Livingstone & Co, the plaintiff's solicitors. In para 10 of that affirmation Mr Barr implicitly accepted that the effect of the renewal of the writ would be to deprive the defendants of the benefit

j of a limitation period which had already accrued. Nevertheless, he submitted that in the particular circumstances of the case there were good and sufficient reasons for justifying the exercise of the court's discretion to extend the validity of the writ. It was, however, implicit in his affirmation that the failure to serve the writ in time was due to an oversight in his office.

The respective applications of the plaintiff and of the defendants fell to be heard by Mr Deputy District Registrar Stephenson on 24 May 1985. He did not accede to Mr Barr's

submissions. He made an order setting aside the service or purported service of the writ
and dismissing the action and refused the renewal or extension of the writ.

On 30 May 1985 the plaintiff gave notice of appeal to the judge against the deputy
district registrar's order.

On 19 September 1985 Mr Barr made a second affirmation in support of the plaintiff's
appeal. In this affirmation Mr Barr (who, as he said, had by then sought the advice of
counsel) submitted, that notwithstanding the implicit concession to the contrary in para
10 of his earlier affirmation, the limitation period had not expired on 29 March 1985
when the writ was served. The basis of this submission requires some explanation.
Section 11 of the Limitation Act 1980, so far as material, provides:

'(1) This section applies to any action for damages for negligence ... where the
damages claimed by the plaintiff for the negligence ... consist of or include damages
in respect of personal injuries to the plaintiff ...

(2) None of the time limits given in the preceding provisions of this Act shall
apply to an action to which this section applies.

(3) An action to which this section applies shall not be brought after the
expiration of the period applicable in accordance with subsection (4) or (5) below.

(4) Except where subsection (5) below applies, the period applicable is three years
from—(a) the date on which the cause of action accrued; or (b) the date of knowledge
(if later) of the person injured ...'

Subsection (5) has no relevance for present purposes.

Section 14(1) of the 1980 Act, so far as material, provides:

'In sections 11 and 12 of this Act references to a person's date of knowledge are
references to the date on which he first had knowledge of the following facts—(a)
that the injury in question was significant; and (b) that the injury was attributable
in whole or in part to the act or omission which is alleged to constitute negligence
... and (c) the identity of the defendant; and (d) if it is alleged that the act or
omission was that of a person other than the defendant, the identity of that person
and the additional facts supporting the bringing of an action against the defendant;
and knowledge that any acts or omissions did or did not, as a matter of law, involve
negligence ... is irrelevant.'

Subsection (2) simply contains provisions in effect defining a significant injury. Subsection
(3) reads:

'For the purposes of this section a person's knowledge includes knowledge which
he might reasonably have been expected to acquire—(a) from facts observable or
ascertainable by him; or (b) from facts ascertainable by him with the help of medical
or other appropriate expert advice which it is reasonable for him to seek; but a
person shall not be fixed under this subsection with knowledge of a fact ascertainable
only with the help of expert advice so long as he has taken all reasonable steps to
obtain (and, where appropriate, to act on) that advice.'

For present purposes the more relevant of the two dates mentioned in s 11(4) is the
date of knowledge of the plaintiff, because that would have been the later of them. A
crucial question for present purposes therefore is: did the plaintiff have the relevant
knowledge by 6 March 1982, that is to say, three years before the writ expired? Mr Barr,
in his second affirmation, withdrew the concession implicitly made in his first affirmation
to the effect that the limitation period in respect of the plaintiff's claim had expired
before the date of the service of the writ on the defendants on 29 March 1985. Having
set out further details as to the history of the matter, he stated (in para 8) that, as he was
informed by the plaintiff, it was not until after he was shown a copy of Mr Leitner's
report that the plaintiff knew that his condition was attributable to the acts or omissions
of the defendants referred to in the section of Mr Leitner's report headed 'Conclusions'.
He submitted (in para 9) that until after 10 December 1984 the plaintiff did not have

a knowledge of the facts referred to in s 14(1)(b) of the 1980 Act. He further submitted (para 10) that the plaintiff could not be fixed with earlier knowledge of these facts pursuant to s 14(3). He gave reasons for these two submissions. In the circumstances, he submitted that the *Heaven* principle did not apply. However, he went on to submit, for reasons stated (in paras 12 and 13), that an order extending the validity of the writ could cause the defendants no real prejudice.

b The plaintiff's appeal came on for hearing before Caulfield J on 1 November 1985 at Manchester, no doubt as one item in the course of a crowded list. We have been told that the hearing was a very short one, lasting in all some 12½ minutes. The judge came to a speedy and decisive view in favour of the plaintiff. We have an agreed note of his brief judgment in which he said:

c 'I think I must allow this appeal. [Counsel for the defendants] will appreciate that although the hearing might have appeared short I have allowed the appeal on the basis of the second affirmation of Mr Barr. The plaintiff is to pay the defendants' costs of this appeal in any event, such order not to be enforced without the leave of the court.'

The judge accordingly renewed the writ so as to validate the service in March 1985.

d From the summary of the second affirmation of Mr Barr, which I have already given, it will have appeared that he was there making two quite separate points, namely first, that the defendants had no good defence at all based on the Limitation Acts, so that the *Heaven* principle could have no possible application, and, second, (in paras 12 and 13) that, even if they had, the case was on its special facts an appropriate case for the court to exercise its discretion to renew the writ. Though I suspect that it was the first of these two submissions which carried weight with the judge and led him to allow the appeal,

e this is by no means clear. Since he gave no indication of the reasons for his decision beyond referring to Mr Barr's second affirmation, I think that this court is entitled to, and can only, approach the matter afresh on the basis of the evidence which was before the judge, without regarding itself as fettered by the manner in which he chose to exercise any such discretion as he may have regarded himself as possessing.

f Due to the very helpful way in which counsel on both sides made their submissions, the issues arising for decision on this appeal have become much narrower than they might otherwise have been. Counsel on behalf of the defendants has contended that the evidence shows that as at 29 March 1985, when the writ was served, the defendants either had a limitation defence which was certain to succeed, or, alternatively, that, even if they did not have a limitation defence which the court could now say was certain to succeed, they had one which was at best very strong, or, at worst, reasonably arguable. He

g submitted that, if the first of these two alternative contentions was right and the writ were to be extended, the defendants would be deprived of their defence contrary to the *Heaven* principle. On the other hand, if the defendants had a limitation defence which was merely arguable, the making of an order providing for the extension of the writ would, as counsel for the defendants pointed out, deprive them for practical purposes of the opportunity of submitting this argument at the trial. While there is no direct

h authority on the point, he contended that it is the logical extension of the *Heaven* principle that, save in exceptional circumstances, a defendant should not be deprived of a reasonably arguable limitation defence by the extension of a writ.

Counsel on behalf of the plaintiff, as I understood him, accepted that, if on the evidence before him a judge who is asked to renew a writ cannot fairly decide whether the effect of so doing would be to deprive the defendant of a possible or probable defence based on

j the Limitation Acts, then, in the absence of special circumstances, he should dismiss the plaintiff's application for renewal. Though we have been referred to no authority which directly covers this situation, this concession was in my judgment a correct one for the following reasons.

If the court grants an application for renewal of a writ in a case where the application for renewal has not been made until after the 12-month period, and with it the validity

of the writ, have expired, it is granting the applicant a substantial indulgence. If, on the
other hand, the effect of such an order is to deprive the defendant of a limitation defence,   *a*
it is depriving him of a defence which Parliament, subject to statutory exceptions,
intended he should have as of absolute right, for reasons of public policy which are
summarised by Megaw J in *Heaven's* case [1965] 2 All ER 409 at 415–416, [1965] 2 QB
355 at 365–366. With these points in mind, it seems to me that, in the absence of special
circumstances, it cannot be an appropriate exercise of the court's discretion to grant an
indulgence of this nature, if there is a real likelihood or substantial risk that in so doing   *b*
it will deprive the defendant of a good legal defence which otherwise he would possess as
of right under the Limitation Acts. Special circumstances apart, the proper course in
such a case must be to decline to renew the writ and leave the plaintiff to issue a new
writ, if so advised, and to surmount the possible time barrier in his new action as best he
can. In other words, a defendant does not necessarily have to show a cast-iron defence
based on the Limitation Acts in order to be able to invoke the *Heaven* principle. I think   *c*
the correctness of this approach is reinforced when it is borne in mind that a defendant
will usually have no proper opportunity to test a plaintiff's assertion as to his knowledge
or otherwise of material facts until after discovery in the action has taken place and the
defendant has been able to cross-examine him at the trial. In some cases, at the time
when renewal of the writ is being sought by the plaintiff, it may be difficult for the
defendant to produce conclusive proof that the limitation period has expired, even   *d*
though it may appear probable that it has done so.

Counsel for the plaintiff further accepted that if, having fully considered the evidence
in the present case, this court, despite his submissions to the contrary, were ultimately to
be of the opinion either that the relevant limitation period had expired by 7 March 1985
or that it may well have expired by that date there are no special circumstances which
would justify our failing to apply the *Heaven* principle. Again, if I may say so, I think he   *e*
was right to accept this. The first affirmation of Mr Barr shows, as I have said, that the
real reason why the writ was not served in time was an oversight on the part of the
plaintiff's legal advisers. The majority decision of this court in *Baker v Bowkett Cakes Ltd*
illustrates that an accident or mistake of this kind does not constitute a special
circumstance sufficient to justify a departure from the principle.

However, counsel for the plaintiff went on to submit, again rightly in my opinion,   *f*
that the mere fact that a defendant seeking to set aside an order for the renewal of a writ
may present argument to the effect that the renewal would deprive him of a good defence
based on the Limitation Acts does not prevent the court which hears the application
from deciding that he has no such defence, if the evidence suffices to enable it to make
this decision. Limitation Act points of this kind, he suggests (and I do not doubt) are not
uncommonly disposed of in pre-trial applications of one kind or another. In the present   *g*
case, in his submission, an analysis of the relevant evidence and the relevant provisions
of the Limitation Act 1980 shows clearly that, by virtue of ss 11(4)(*b*) and 14(1)(*b*), the
three-year limitation period did not begin to run in favour of the defendants until Mr
Leitner's report was received by the plaintiff or his legal advisers in December 1984.

The correctness or otherwise of this submission must depend on the date on which the
plaintiff first had 'knowledge . . . that the injury was attributable in whole or in part to   *h*
the act or omission which is alleged to constitute negligence . . .' within the meaning of
s 14(1)(*b*).

On the plaintiff's own case, I think it reasonably clear that, at least from the time when
he left St Bartholomew's Hospital in November 1981, he must have been well aware that
in general terms his injury was attributable to his employment with the defendants and
indeed to the conduct of the defendants. Nevertheless, counsel for the plaintiff pointed   *j*
out, s 14(1)(*b*) does not refer to the 'conduct' which is alleged to constitute negligence; it
refers, with greater particularity, to the 'act or omission' which is so alleged. The
interpretation of the latter phase in his submission is capable of raising problems in many
accident cases and is crucial on the present appeal. His contention is that the phrase in its
context can only refer to the particular acts or omissions which are alleged to constitute

negligence, that is to say, in the context of the present case, the several acts or omissions
a respectively referred to in sub-paras (a) to (j) of para 4 of the statement of claim.

In the present case, counsel for the plaintiff submits, the plaintiff acquired his
knowledge in four stages. Even before he took medical advice, he knew the bare facts of
what he had done while in the employment of the defendants and what they had done
or failed to do for him. Then, after going to St Bartholomews Hospital, he knew in broad
terms that his disease had been derived from his employment. Only after receiving Mr
b Leitner's report, however, in counsel for the plaintiff's submission, did the plaintiff
become aware of the kind of exposure to TDI to which he had been subjected while in
such employment, and of the particular things which the defendants had done to subject
him to such exposure, and of the particular steps which, as a practical matter, they could
have taken to protect him from it. The final stage in the plaintiff's knowledge arrived
when he received legal advice in the light of Mr Leitner's report. That final stage is
c irrelevant for present purposes, since the closing words of s 14(1) render irrelevant the
knowledge that any acts or omissions do or do not involve legal liability. Nevertheless,
in counsel for the plaintiff's submission, only after receipt of Mr Leitner's report did the
plaintiff first have knowledge that his injury was 'attributable in whole or in part' to the
'acts or omissions' which are alleged by the statement of claim to constitute negligence.

These submissions, which were so clearly and ably advanced by counsel for the
d plaintiff, do indeed illustrate that the wording of s 14(1)(b) of the 1980 Act may raise
difficult problems of construction and application in particular cases. The only authority
cited to us which is of direct assistance in this context is the decision of this court in *Davis
v Ministry of Defence* [1985] CA Transcript 413. We have been shown a transcript of the
judgment of May LJ in that case, with which Sir Edward Eveleigh agreed. In that case
the appellant had been employed by the respondents between 1955 and 1971. Up to
e April 1969 he had worked as a welder. At that time he contracted a localised attack of
dermatitis. In August 1971 he suffered a serious generalised attack and in the event left
the respondents' employment. More than ten years later, on 10 November 1981, the
appellant issued proceedings against the respondents, and on 8 June 1982 he served a
statement of claim which included a plea that prior to 10 November 1978 (three years
before the issue of the writ) he was unaware that the general outbreak and his subsequent
f symptoms were 'attributable' to the respondents' previously pleaded negligence and/or
breach of statutory duty. The evidence showed that the appellant had believed strongly,
throughout, that his dermatitis had been caused by his working conditions and that he
had a good claim for damages against the respondents. May LJ pointed out that the issue
between the parties turned on the proper construction of s 14(1)(b) of the 1980 Act,
supplemented where necessary by the provisions of s 14(3)(b). He continued:

g   'The "act or omission" which is alleged to constitute negligence, nuisance or breach
of duty" can be compendiously described as the respondents' failure to provide the
appellant with safe working conditions. Thus the pertinent question is: upon what
date did the appellant first know that his dermatitis was attributable in whole or in
part to his employers' failure to provide him with safe working conditions?'

h   May LJ went on to consider a submission by the appellant's counsel that the word
'attributable' in s 14(1)(b) was to be construed as meaning 'caused by'. This submission he
rejected. He considered that s 14(1)(b) required the court to ask:

       'When did the appellant first know that his dermatitis was *capable of being attributed
to* his working conditions with the respondents between 1955 and 1969, bearing in
mind that, by s 14(3)(b), the appellant is deemed to know facts which he could
j ascertain from expert medical or legal advice which it was reasonable for him to
seek?' (My emphasis.)

A little later May LJ pointed out that—

       '"Knowledge" is an ordinary English word with a clear meaning to which one
must give full effect: "reasonable belief" or "suspicion" is not enough.'

Having reviewed the evidence, he concluded:

> '. . . the combined state of mind of the appellant himself, as a layman, and that of   _a_
> his doctors and legal advisers, which must be attributed to him by s 14(3) of the
> 1980 Act, cannot, in my opinion, so surely be said to have been such that he and
> they _knew_, prior to 10 November 1978, that his dermatitis _was capable of being
> attributed_ to the appellant's working conditions.' (May LJ's emphasis.)

In there circumstances, May LJ concluded that it would be wrong to take the draconian   _b_
step of striking out the appellant's claim at that stage.

Counsel for the plaintiff relied on the _Davis_ decision to support his submission that,
until receipt of Mr Leitner's report, the plaintiff had no knowledge, as opposed to
reasonable belief or suspicion, that his injury was attributable to the acts or omissions on
the part of the defendants which are complained of. In so far as it stresses the difference
between knowledge on the one hand and reasonable belief or suspicion on the other   _c_
hand, the decision is of some assistance to the plaintiff. In two respects, however, it lends
more support to the defendants' case: firstly, in May LJ's conclusion that the word
'attributable' in s 14(1)(_b_) bears the meaning 'capable of being attributed to', rather than
the meaning 'caused by'; and, secondly, in his view, that the '"act or omission which is
alleged to constitute negligence, nuisance or breach of duty" [could] be compendiously
described as the respondents' failure to provide the appellant with safe working   _d_
conditions'.

At least so far as appears from the judgment of May LJ, it does not seem to have been
specifically argued in the _Davis_ case that each of the particular acts or omissions of the
respondents as employers which were complained of should be looked at seriatim for the
purpose of applying s 14(1)(_b_), rather than compendiously in the manner indicated by
May LJ. Nevertheless, whether or not his observations on that interlocutory appeal are   _e_
strictly binding on us, I see no reason, with respect to him, for differing from any of
them. In a case such as the present, where the acts and omissions on the part of the
defendants which are complained of are, in broad terms, the exposure of their employee
to dangerous working conditions and their failure to take reasonable and proper steps to
protect him from such conditions, I think that the employee who has this broad
knowledge may well have knowledge of the nature referred to in s 14(1)(_b_) sufficient to   _f_
set time running against him, even though he may not yet have the knowledge sufficient
to enable him or his legal advisers to draft a fully and comprehensively particularised
statement of claim. Counsel for the plaintiff suggested that the acquisition of knowledge
of additional acts or omissions on the part of the employers capable of particularising an
allegation of breach of duty under s 14(1)(_b_) would by itself take the case out of the
statute. I cannot accept this submission. If it were right, certainty would never be   _g_
achieved in cases such as the present.

I do not doubt that Mr Leitner's report was of assistance to the plaintiff's legal advisers
in drafting his statement of claim. It may well be that, until the plaintiff received that
report, he was not aware that each and every one of the particular several alleged acts or
defaults referred to in the several sub-paragraphs of para 4 of that pleading could properly
be categorised as acts or defaults which had caused, or were capable of having caused, his   _h_
illness. Nevertheless, I will refer to three of these items (sub-paras (a), (g) and (i)) by way
of example. Can it really be said that until December 1984 the plaintiff was not fully
aware that his injuries had been caused or had been capable of being caused wholly or
partially by (i) the defendants exposing him to risk of damage to his health by the
inhalation of TDI (sub-para (1)), (ii) their failure to provide him with breathing apparatus
as part of the standard equipment (sub-para (g)), (iii) their failure to monitor his health   _j_
(sub-para (i))?

Even without more, I would have been inclined to infer that the plaintiff must have
known of the significance of these three matters after his visit to St Bartholomews
Hospital in November 1981, without the need for them to be specifically drawn to his
attention in Mr Leitner's report. I do not think that report added anything substantial to

such knowledge. It is worthy of note that the writ issued on his behalf on 7 March 1984

a asserted that the plaintiff first discovered that the disease was attributable to the defendants in November 1981. Furthermore, as far back as October 1981 the plaintiff had made a claim for industrial benefit because of chest congestion said to be due to inhalation of chemicals. However, the inference that he obtained this knowledge as a result of this visit to hospital in my opinion becomes still clearer when one looks again at the second paragraph of his then solicitors' letter to the defendants of 7 June 1982, which

b I repeat:

> 'According to our instructions our client who is employed by you as a Tanker Driver was exposed to [TDI] during the course of his employment. We understand that no tests were ever carried out on our client to determine his susceptibility or otherwise to the various chemicals which he was responsible for transporting.
>
c > Furthermore, we are instructed that no protective clothing was supplied such as respiratory apparatus.'

There is no suggestion in the plaintiff's very full and detailed evidence that he obtained any relevant medical advice between his visit to St Bartholomew's Hospital and his solicitors' letter of 7 June 1982. I heed May LJ's warning that knowledge must not be equated with reasonable belief or suspicion. Nevertheless, on the basis of his own case

d and evidence, I think that the plaintiff, after his visit to hospital in November 1981, well knew that his injuries were capable of being attributed to what could be compendiously and properly described as the defendants' failure to provide him with safe working conditions. Without reference to s 14(3) of the 1980 Act, on which I do not think the defendants need to rely for present purposes, this was, in my opinion, enough to set time running against the plaintiff under the combined effect of ss 11(1), (3) and (4) and 14(1)

e of the 1980 Act. It is common ground that at all material times he had the knowledge referred to in paras (a) and (c) of s 14(1). Paragraph (b) alone in that subsection has given rise to argument, and in my opinion does not avail him.

It follows that, in my judgment, the relevant limitation period expired in November 1984 and the effect of the order of the judge was to deprive the defendants of a good defence based on the 1980 Act. However, even if I were to be wrong in concluding that

f the evidence shows surely that time began to run against the plaintiff in November 1981, the judge's order at very least in my opinion deprived the defendants of a strongly arguable defence based on the 1980 Act. The limitation point could not in my view be fairly and finally decided against them on the affidavit evidence before the judge. With the greatest respect to him, I therefore think that, in accordance with the *Heaven* principle and in the absence of exceptional circumstances justifying a contrary course, he should

g have refused to renew the writ and should have left the plaintiff to issue new proceedings if so advised.

For the reasons stated, I would allow this appeal. I would set aside the service or purported service of the writ in these proceedings, and I would dismiss the action. No doubt the plaintiff will take legal advice as to what alternative remedies may be available to him.

h **CROOM-JOHNSON LJ.** I agree with the judgment given by Slade LJ, and with its reasoning and its conclusions.

Appeal allowed. Service of writ set aside and action dismissed.

j Solicitors: *Keogh Ritson & Co*, Bolton (for the defendants); *Livingstone & Co*, Manchester (for the plaintiff).

Wendy Shockett   Barrister.

Hailbury Investments Ltd v Westminster City Council

HOUSE OF LORDS

LORD BRIDGE OF HARWICH, LORD BRANDON OF OAKBROOK, LORD GRIFFITHS, LORD MACKAY OF CLASHFERN AND LORD ACKNER

30 JUNE, I, 2, 3 JULY, 16 OCTOBER 1986

Rates – Rateable occupation – Non-occupation of premises – Liability for rates – Unoccupied hereditament – Description in valuation list – Description of premises as 'offices' – Use as offices prohibited by planning condition – Whether description of hereditament in valuation list essential element in identity of hereditament – Whether owner prohibited by law from occupying hereditament – Whether hereditament kept vacant by reason of action taken by local authority prohibiting occupation – General Rate Act 1967, Sch 1, paras 1(1), 2.

The appellants were the owners of certain units of unoccupied property described in the valuation list as 'offices'. The respondent rating authority claimed payment of rates for the property pursuant to para 1(1)[a] of Sch 1 to the General Rate Act 1967, which provided that where a relevant hereditament was unoccupied for a continuous period exceeding three months the owner was liable to be rated in respect of that hereditament. The property was kept vacant because a planning condition prohibited its use for office purposes. The appellants disputed liability for rates relying on para 2[b] of Sch 1, which provided that rates were not payable under para 1 in respect of a hereditament for any period during which '(a) the owner is prohibited by law from occupying the hereditament or allowing it to be occupied; and (b) the hereditament is kept vacant by reason of action taken by or on behalf of . . . any local or public authority with a view to prohibiting [its] occupation . . .' On an application by the local authority for the issue of distress warrants in respect of the unpaid rates, it was held that there was no impediment to the occupation of the property for residential purposes and therefore para 2 did not apply. The appellants successfully appealed to the High Court and the rating authority in turn successfully appealed to the Court of Appeal. The appellants then appealed to the House of Lords, contending that the description of a hereditament shown in the valuation list was an essential element in the identity of that hereditament, that occupation of a physical entity described as 'offices' in the valuation list for any purpose other than as offices amounted to occupation of a different hereditament from that to which the entry in the valuation list related, and that accordingly the rating authority had either to take steps to alter the entry in the valuation list or to delete the existing entry and substitute a new entry before any liability to pay rates could arise.

Held – On the true construction of para 2 of Sch 1 to the 1967 Act the word 'hereditament' merely applied to a unit of property which was sufficiently identified by an entry in the valuation list regardless of whether the description of the hereditament in that entry appropriately described the purpose for which the hereditament could lawfully be used. It followed that the fact that the appellants' hereditaments were described in the valuation list as 'offices', which was a prohibited use, did not prohibit the appellants from occupying the hereditaments nor were they kept vacant by reason of action taken by local authority with a view to prohibiting their occupation. The appeal would therefore be dismissed (see p 445 c d, p 446 b c and p 448 g to p 449 d, post).

Ravenseft Properties v Newham London Borough [1976] 1 All ER 580 and *Camden London Borough v Herwald* [1978] 2 All ER 880 considered.

---

a Paragraph 1(1) is set out at p 441 j, post
b Paragraph 2, so far as material, is set out at p 442 a b, post

Notes

a For rateable occupation, see 39 Halsbury's Laws (4th edn) paras 15–25, and for cases on the subject, see 38 Digest (Reissue) 288–293, 2048–2069.

For proceedings for the recovery of rates, see 39 Halsbury's Laws (4th edn) paras 236ff, and for cases on the subject, see 38 Digest (Reissue) 508–512, 3880–3920.

For the General Rate Act 1967, Sch 1, paras 1, 2, see 27 Halsbury's Statutes (3rd edn) 210.

b
Cases referred to in opinions
Camden London Borough v Herwald [1978] 2 All ER 880, [1978] QB 626, [1978] 3 WLR 76, CA; *rvsg* [1976] 2 All ER 808, [1977] 1 WLR 100, DC.
Langford v Cole (1910) 102 LT 808, DC.
Manchester Overseers v Headlam (1888) 21 QBD 96, DC.
c *Ravenseft Properties v Newham London Borough* [1976] 1 All ER 580, [1976] QB 464, [1976] 2 WLR 131, CA.

Appeal
Hailbury Investments Ltd appealed, with leave of the Appeal Committee of the House of Lords granted on 21 February 1985, against the order of the Court of Appeal (Eveleigh,
d Stephen Brown LJJ and Sir David Cairns) dated 13 December 1984 allowing an appeal by the respondents, the Lord Mayor and Citizens of the City of Westminster, against the order of Woolf J dated 13 July 1983 whereby he allowed an appeal by the appellants by way of case stated by Mr E G MacDermott, metropolitan stipendiary magistrate, in respect of his adjudication as a magistrate sitting at Horseferry Road whereby he held that planning restrictions which restricted the type of any future occupation of
e hereditaments belonging to the appellants to that of a domestic nature did not render the hereditament subject to the provisions of para 2(*a*) and (*b*) of Sch 1 to the General Rate Act 1967. The facts are set out in the opinion of Lord Bridge.

Charles Fay for the appellants.
Michael Burke-Gaffney QC and *Clive Newberry* for the respondents.
f

Their Lordships took time for consideration.

16 October. The following opinions were delivered.

LORD BRIDGE OF HARWICH. My Lords, the issue in this appeal is whether the
g appellants were liable to pay rates in respect of certain units of unoccupied property for the year 1978–79 and part of the year 1979–80. The respondents (the rating authority), as rating authority for the City of Westminster, applied in the Horseferry Road Magistrates Court for the issue of distress warrants in respect of the disputed rates and were successful. On appeal by case stated to the Queen's Bench Division, Woolf J reversed the decision of the stipendiary magistrate. The decision of Woolf J was in turn reversed
h by the Court of Appeal (Eveleigh, Stephen Brown LJJ and Sir David Cairns). The appellants now appeal by leave of your Lordships' House.

Liability to pay rates in respect of unoccupied property arises under the provisions of Sch 1 to the General Rate Act 1967, para 1(1) of which provides:

j 'Where, in the case of any rating area in which, by virtue of a resolution under section 17 of this Act, this Schedule is in operation, any relevant hereditament in that area is unoccupied for a continuous period exceeding three months, the owner shall, subject to the provisions of this Schedule, be rated in respect of that hereditament for any relevant period of vacancy; and the provisions of this Act shall apply accordingly as if the hereditament were occupied during that relevant period of vacancy by the owner.'

The schedule is in operation in the City of Westminster. It is accepted that this provision makes the appellants liable to pay the disputed rates unless they are exempted by para 2, which provides, so far as relevant: *a*

'No rates shall be payable under paragraph 1 of this Schedule in respect of a hereditament for . . . any period during which—(a) the owner is prohibited by law from occupying the hereditament or allowing it to be occupied; (b) the hereditament is kept vacant by reason of action taken by or on behalf of the Crown or any local or public authority with a view to prohibiting the occupation of the hereditament or *b* to acquiring it . . .'

Each of the hereditaments in respect of which the disputed rates are claimed is described in the valuation list in force for the years in question in terms which include the word 'offices' to categorise the premises and, save for a reference in one case to a 'caretaker's flat', none of the descriptions is apt to refer to residential property. At the *c* material time, as the case stated finds, each of the hereditaments in question was kept vacant by reason of a planning condition purporting to prohibit its use for office purposes. The condition had been imposed on the grant of permission for development which had not yet been implemented. One of the hereditaments was also affected by a planning condition imposed on an earlier grant of temporary permission for office use which had been implemented and which had expired in 1972. That condition required *d* discontinuance of the office use in 1972. Use of the hereditament for office purposes after 1972 would have been a breach of that condition. There are no findings of fact in the case stated relating to the physical condition of the relevant premises at the material time. The case has been argued throughout on the footing that there was no impediment to their occupation for residential purposes. The proposition which the appellants must establish to succeed is that the effect of the planning conditions referred to in relation to *e* hereditaments described in the valuation list in force at the material time as 'offices' is to entitle the owner of the hereditaments to exemption from liability to pay rates under para 2(a) or (b) of Sch 1 to the 1967 Act.

Before one reaches the main issue, the appellants confront formidable difficulties in showing, by reference to the provisions of the Town and Country Planning Act 1971, that the occupation of the hereditaments as offices was the subject of a relevant *f* 'prohibition' within the meaning of para 2(a) and (b) of Sch 1 to the 1967 Act. To succeed under sub-para (a) they would have to show that the owner of a hereditament who could only occupy it as offices in breach of a planning condition was 'prohibited by law' from so occupying it. To succeed under sub-para (b) they would have to show that the imposition of a planning condition on the grant of permission for development of which, if and when the development was carried out, it would be a breach to use a hereditament *g* for office purposes amounted to action taken by a local authority 'with a view to prohibiting the occupation of the hereditament' as offices. These aspects of the case give rise to difficult issues of construction and of planning law. For my part, like the Court of Appeal, I am content to leave them unresolved and to assume in the appellants' favour that the existence of the planning conditions which have been imposed enabled the appellants to claim either that they had been prohibited by law from occupying, or that *h* action had been taken by the local planning authority with a view to prohibiting the occupation of, any of the hereditaments in question as offices.

Starting from the basis of such an assumption, the contention advanced for the appellants may be shortly summarised. It is said that the description of a hereditament shown in the valuation list is an essential element in the identity of that hereditament; from this it follows that occupation of the physical entity described as offices in the *j* valuation list for any purpose other than as offices is the occupation of a different hereditament from that to which the entry in the valuation list relates. Before any liability to pay rates in respect of that new and different hereditament can arise, it is for the rating authority to take steps to secure an alteration of the entry in the valuation list or, more accurately, the deletion of the existing entry and the substitution of a new entry applying words of description to the new hereditament which are apt to apply to the use for which the new hereditament is or may lawfully be occupied. To this the rating a authority reply that the hereditament to which any entry in the valuation list relates is, in the case of a corporeal hereditament, simply the physical entity comprised in any unit of property identified by the description and other particulars appearing in that entry. It matters not that the description in the valuation list is no longer appropriate accurately to describe the use for which that unit of property is or may lawfully be occupied. If it is the same physical entity, it remains the same hereditament. If it may lawfully be occupied for any purpose, there is no prohibition of occupation of the hereditament to

b which para 2(a) or (b) is capable of applying so as to exempt the owner from liability for rates to which he is otherwise subject in respect of any period during which the hereditament is unoccupied.

The resolution of the issue to which these rival contentions give rise depends on the true construction of the 1967 Act. By s 115(1) 'hereditament' is defined as meaning—

c 'property which is or may become liable to a rate, being a unit of such property which is, or would fall to be, shown as a separate item in the valuation list . . .'

I shall refer to this as 'the general definition'.

Liability to pay rates in respect of unoccupied property arises only in the case of a 'relevant hereditament' which is defined by para 15 of Sch 1 as meaning—

d 'any hereditament consisting of, or of part of, a house, shop, office, factory, mill or other building whatsoever, together with any garden, yard, court or other land ordinarily used or intended for use for the purposes of the building or part . . .'

I shall refer to this as 'the Sch 1 definition'.

The general definition must be understood in the light of ss 16 and 67 of the 1967 Act, which provide, so far as presently material:

e '16. Subject to the provisions of this Act, every occupier of property of any of the following descriptions, namely—(a) lands; (b) houses . . . shall be liable to be assessed to rates in respect of the hereditament or hereditaments comprising that property according to the rateable value or respective rateable values of that hereditament or those hereditaments determined in accordance with the provisions of this Act . . .

f 67.—(1) For the purposes of rates, there shall be maintained for each rating area a valuation list prepared, and from time to time caused to be altered, in accordance with the provisions of this Part of this Act by the valuation officer.

(2) Subject to the provisions of this Act, there shall be inserted in the valuation list such particulars as may be prescribed—(a) with respect to every hereditament in the rating area and the value thereof . . .'

g Particulars required to be inserted in the valuation list are prescribed by the Valuations List Rules 1972, SI 1972/1612. As one would expect, entries in the list are required to be made in accordance with forms scheduled to the rules and in relation to each hereditament entries are required to be made under the following headings: 'Description', 'Address', 'Gross value' and 'Rateable value'. Save in certain special cases, not presently relevant, the rules make no provision as to what the entry under the heading 'Description' is to

h contain. Thus, although the use of the phrase 'unit of property' in the general definition seems to give strong support to the contention for the rating authority, the qualifying words 'which is, or would fall to be, shown as a separate item in the valuation list' prevent that phrase from having conclusive effect and in the absence of any direct indication elsewhere in the Act or rules made under it as to the significance of the description of a hereditament used in relation to an item in the valuation list, the general definition, by

j itself, fails to resolve the issue.

The Sch 1 definition, in referring to different descriptions of buildings to define the limited species of the genus hereditament in respect of which the unoccupied rate is to be payable, may seem to give some support to the appellants' contention, but is again, as it seems to me, quite inconclusive.

The resolution of the issue is to be found, in my opinion, in certain provisions relating to the preparation and alteration of valuation lists. Section 68(1) of the 1967 Act required new valuation lists to be 'prepared and made by the valuation officer so as to come into

force on 1st April in 1973 and each fifth year thereafter'. The fact that this statutory
programme was not adhered to in the event is irrelevant to the point at issue. The
valuation officer is required by s 68(2) to sign the new valuation list and transmit it to
the rating authority in advance of the date when it is to come into force normally by the
end of the preceding year. Obviously the field work of inspecting and valuing individual
properties will have been done at various dates before that. To ensure that the list is as far
as possible up to date at the moment when it comes into force, s 68(3) and (4) then
provide:

> '(3) Where, after the valuation officer has transmitted the list to the rating
> authority, but before the date on which the list is to come into force, it appears to
> him that, by reason of a material change of circumstances which has occurred since
> the time of valuation, the list needs to be altered in any respect, he shall cause the
> list to be altered accordingly before that date.
>
> (4) In subsection (3) of this section, the expression "material change of
> circumstances" means a change of circumstances which consists of—(a) the coming
> into occupation of a newly erected or newly constructed hereditament or of a
> hereditament which has been out of occupation on account of structural alterations;
> or (b) a change in the value of a hereditament caused by the making of structural
> alterations or by the total or partial destruction of any building or other erection by
> fire or any other physical cause; or (c) the happening of any event whereby a
> hereditament or part of a hereditament becomes, or ceases to be, not liable to be
> rated; or (d) a change in the extent to which any railway or canal premises within
> the meaning of section 32 of this Act are occupied for non-rateable purposes within
> the meaning of that section; or (e) property previously rated as a single hereditament
> becoming liable to be rated in parts; or (f) property previously rated in parts
> becoming liable to be rated as a single hereditament; or (g) a hereditament becoming
> or ceasing to be—(i) a dwelling-house; or (ii) a private garage or private storage
> premises within the meaning of Schedule 11 to this Act; or (h) a hereditament being,
> in accordance with Schedule 13 to this Act, used to a greater or lesser extent for the
> purposes of a private dwelling or private dwellings, and the expression "the time of
> valuation", in relation to a change of circumstances, means the time by reference to
> which the valuation officer prepared so much of the list as is affected by that change
> of circumstances.'

I find significance in what is omitted from, as well as what is contained in, this list of
what will amount to material changes of circumstances. With the exception of paras (d),
(g) and (h), no paragraph suggests that a mere change in use or mode of occupation will
amount to a material change of circumstances. If the appellants' contention were right,
one would expect a general paragraph to that effect, since a change of use effecting a
change in the appropriate description to be applied to a hereditament results, according
to the appellants' contention, in the disappearance of the old hereditament and the
creation of a new one.

Paragraphs (d), (g) and (h) are special cases. Paragraph (d) is not presently relevant, but
paras (g) and (h) are of particular significance. 'Dwelling-house' is defined in s 115(1) as
meaning—

> 'a hereditament which, in accordance with Schedule 13 to this Act, is used wholly
> for the purposes of a private dwelling or private dwellings . . .'

Whether or not a hereditament is a dwelling house as defined is of importance in
relation to the application of ss 58 to 62 which grant certain special reliefs to the occupiers
of dwelling houses. I need not examine in detail the elaborate provisions of Sch 13,
which set out various circumstances in which a hereditament is to be deemed, according
to the extent of its use for various purposes, either to be or not to be 'used wholly for the
purposes of a private dwelling or private dwellings' so as to bring it within the definition
of dwelling house. There thus appears to be a substantial overlap between para (g)(i) and
(h) of s 68(4). Be that as it may, the language of both paragraphs and of Sch 13 seems to
me quite inconsistent with the view that a hereditament changes its identity when by

reason of a change in the manner of its use it becomes or ceases to be a dwelling house as
a   defined.

Section 69, which introduces the fasciculus of sections headed 'Alterations of current
valuation list', provides as follows:

'(1) Subject to subsection (6) of this section, any person (including a rating
authority) who is aggrieved—(a) by the inclusion of any hereditament in the
valuation list; or (b) by any value ascribed in the list to a hereditament or by any
b   other statement made or omitted to be made in the list with respect to a
hereditament; or (c) in the case of a building or portion of a building occupied in
parts, by the valuation in the list of that building or portion of a building as a single
hereditament, may at any time make a proposal for the alteration of the list so far as
it relates to that hereditament . . .'

c   Here it seems to me that the words in para (b) 'any other statement made or omitted to
be made in the list with respect to a hereditament' are apt to embrace whatever is
included in or omitted from the entry in the valuation list under the heading 'Description'
and it must follow that the subsection contemplates that an alteration of the description
will not alter the identity of 'that hereditament'.

A proposal for alteration of the valuation list may be made under s 69(1) at any time
d   during the currency of the list. Where a proposal to alter the valuation of a hereditament
shown in the list or to include a new hereditament in the list is made some years after
the particular list came into force, this gives rise to a problem familiar to all rating
valuers. A general appreciation of values in a rating area can only be reflected in the
valuation list when a new list comes into force. Thus, if a hereditament were to be
valued, pursuant to a proposal made in, say, 1977, by reference to 1977 values rather
e   than to the level of values prevailing when the 1973 list was prepared, this could produce
unfairness as between one ratepayer and another. The 1967 Act sets out to provide a
solution to this problem in s 20 and, using the familiar jargon of rating valuation, aptly
gives the section the side note 'Valuation according to tone of list'. Section 20(1) provides:

'(1) For the purposes of any alteration of a valuation list to be made under Part V
of this Act in respect of a hereditament in pursuance of a proposal, the value or
f   altered value to be ascribed to the hereditament under section 19 of this Act shall
not exceed the value which would have been ascribed thereto in that list if the
hereditament had been subsisting throughout the year before that in which the
valuation list came into force, on the assumptions that at the time by reference to
which that value would have been ascertained—(a) the hereditament was in the
same state as at the time of valuation and any relevant factors (as defined by
g   subsection (2) of this section) were those subsisting at the last-mentioned time; and
(b) the locality in which the hereditament is situated was in the same state, so far as
concerns the other premises situated in that locality and the occupation and use of
those premises, the transport services and other facilities available in the locality,
and other matters affecting the amenities of the locality, as at the time of valuation.'

h   Among the 'relevant factors' enumerated by s 20(2) is '(a) the mode or category of
occupation of the hereditament' and by s 20(3) the 'time of valuation' is defined as
meaning—

'the time by reference to which the valuation of a hereditament would have fallen
to be ascertained if this section had not been enacted.'

j   To illustrate the operation of these provisions I take the example of a house formerly
shown in the valuation list as a single hereditament. It is converted into two flats which,
being in separate occupation, require separate entries in the valuation list. Proposals to
alter the list accordingly are made in the rating year 1977–78. The ceiling value for each
new hereditament is to be the value which would have been appropriate in the 1973
valuation list, i e a value assessed by reference to the level of values prevailing before 1
April 1973, on the assumption that each hereditament and its relevant surroundings
subsisted throughout the year to 1 April 1973 in the same state as on the date of the

proposal to enter the new hereditament in the list and on the further assumption that 'the mode or category of occupation of the hereditament' in 1972–73 was also as it is on the later date. If each of the two new hereditaments at the date of the proposal to alter the valuation list was occupied as a residential flat, each will be valued as such. But if one of the new hereditaments is occupied as offices, although it is the same hereditament, it will attract a different, and no doubt higher, value.

It seems to me that the inclusion of 'the mode or category of occupation of the hereditament' as a 'relevant factor' for the purposes of s 20, especially when contrasted with the absence of any analogous general reference to a change of use as a 'material change of circumstances' under s 69 (save in the special cases to which s 69(4)(d), (g) and (h) refer, is another powerful pointer to the conclusion that the purpose for which a hereditament is occupied is relevant to the valuation but not to the identity of the hereditament.

The appellants complain that it does an injustice to the owner of an unoccupied hereditament which can only be lawfully occupied for residential purposes if 'hereditament' in para 2(a) and (b) of Sch 1 is construed as referring to the physical unit of property identified in the valuation list without regard to the description of the hereditament which categorizes it as non-residential property. It was contended in the courts below that this imposed liability on the owner to pay rates at a higher rate poundage than if the hereditament were described as residential. It was, however, conceded in your Lordships' House that this was a false point. The lower rate poundage paid by occupiers of dwelling houses results from the provisions of s 48 of the 1967 Act, the purpose of which is sufficiently indicated by the side note: 'Reduction of rates on dwellings by reference to domestic element of rate support grants.' By para 1(2) of Sch 1 to the Act the amount of rates payable by the owner in respect of an unoccupied hereditament is to be one-half of the amount which would be payable if he were in occupation of it, but the sub-paragraph specifically provides that 'no reduction shall be made under s 48 of this Act in respect of any rates so payable'.

However, this aspect of the appellants' complaint may be put in an alternative way, in that the hereditaments in question clearly attracted a higher rateable value as offices than they would have done as residential property. But the answer to this point is that, in such a case, the remedy is in the hands of the owner of the unoccupied property. If a hereditament has been described and valued as offices in the current valuation list, but ceases to be occupied as offices because that use has been prohibited by law, and the only lawful use is residential, the owner has ample opportunity during the period of three months which must elapse before a relevant period of vacancy begins to propose an alteration to the valuation list. The result will be an alteration of the entry relating to the hereditament in which the new rateable value will reflect its letting value for residential use and the new rateable value will take effect retrospectively from the beginning of the rating year in which the proposal was made: see s 79(1).

Your Lordships were referred to a number of authorities. I confess that I did not derive any great help from them since, as I have already indicated, I regard the point at issue as purely one of statutory construction which has not previously been considered. There are, however, two cases to which I must refer. Woolf J founded his conclusion in favour of the appellants, to some extent at least, on some observations of my own in the Court of Appeal in *Ravenseft Properties v Newham London Borough* [1976] 1 All ER 580, [1976] QB 464. That case was concerned with the construction of para 8 of Sch 1 to the 1967 Act which operates to determine the date of completion of a newly erected building on which in turn depends the date when the owner will become liable to pay rates under Sch 1 if the new building remains unoccupied for more than three months after its completion. Paragraph 8(1) provides:

'Where a rating authority are of opinion—(a) that the erection of a building within their area has been completed; or (b) that the work remaining to be done on a building within their area is such that the erection of the building can reasonably be expected to be completed within three months, and that the building is, or when completed will be, comprised in a relevant hereditament, the authority may serve

a

on the owner of the building a notice (hereafter in this paragraph referred to as "a completion notice") stating that the erection of the building is to be treated for the purposes of this Schedule as completed on the date of service of the notice or on such later date as may be specified by the notice.'

By para 8(4) the recipient of a completion notice has the right to appeal against it to the county court if he quarrels with the date of completion of the building specified in the notice. *Ravenseft Properties v Newham London Borough* arose from such an appeal. The issue

b

was whether a newly erected office block was, on the date specified in the completion notice served by the rating authority, a completed building. The main structure was then completed, but the building had no interior partitioning and no telephone installation and the installation of electrical wiring and points was incomplete. As it stood, the building was incapable of occupation as offices. In my judgment, after referring to the Sch 1 definition of 'relevant hereditament', I said ([1976] 1 All ER 580 at

c

587–588, [1976] QB 464 at 478):

'Bearing in mind that, under the law as it stood for centuries before unoccupied property became capable of rating, occupation was always the test of liability, if, construing this provision without having regard to its wider context, I should say without hesitation that what was contemplated was that the building should be completed so as to be capable of occupation for the appropriate purposes of the

d

particular hereditament, i e as a house, shop, office etc. If the building lacks features which before it can be occupied will have to be provided and when provided will form part of the occupied hereditament and form the basis of the valuation of that hereditament, then I would take the view, unless constrained to the contrary, that that building was not within the meaning of the relevant provision of a completed

e

building.'

I do not resile from what I there said. In the case of a new, purpose-built building, the question when it is complete as a relevant hereditament, in the sense of being fit for occupation, is quite properly to be answered with regard to the purpose for which it is designed to be used. But I do not, with respect, think that this throws any significant light on the entirely different question whether a hereditament comprised in an existing

f

building changes its identity whenever there is a change in the purpose for which it is used.

In the argument before your Lordships, the authority most relied on by counsel for the appellants was *Camden London Borough v Herwald* [1978] 2 All ER 880, [1978] QB 626. The question in that case was whether the defendant was liable to pay rates in respect of a hereditament of which he occupied only a part. The Court of Appeal held that he was

g

not, reversing the decision of the Divisional Court ([1976] 2 All ER 808, [1977] 1 WLR 100). It seems to me that the difference between the Divisional Court and the Court of Appeal in that case turned not at all on any question of principle but rather on the question what was the result of applying a simple and well-established principle to the complex and somewhat obscure facts of the particular case. So far as the principle is concerned, I find it accurately stated in the following passage in the judgment of the

h

Divisional Court delivered by Robert Goff J ([1976] 2 All ER 808 at 810, [1977] 1 WLR 100 at 102–103):

'It is right that a person is only liable to be rated in respect of property of which he is the occupier: see s 16 of the General Rate Act 1967. But it does not follow that, merely because he can show that he does not in fact occupy part of premises in respect of which a rate had been made, a distress warrant should not be issued. To

j

resist the issue of a warrant, he must show that the description of the rated property in the valuation list includes on its face property which he does not occupy. The principle was stated by this court in *Overseers of the Poor of Manchester v Headlam and the London and North Western Railway Co* (1888) 21 QBD 96 at 98, in a passage which has since been frequently cited and applied: "... if one entire assessment be made in terms upon property which he does occupy, and upon other property which he does not occupy, so that upon the true state of facts being ascertained it is impossible

to satisfy the description in the rate-book without including property which he does
not occupy, the rate will be bad and ought not to be enforced." In that case, property *a*
occupied by the railway company had been assessed as "offices and land with rails",
but in assessing the amount of the rate the overseers had included certain buildings
which were not occupied by the company. It was held that, since the property in
fact occupied by the company satisfied the description in the rate-book, the rate was
good on the face of it and a distress warrant must be issued. The proper remedy of
the company in such circumstances was to appeal against the assessment; not having *b*
appealed, they could not resist the issue of a warrant. By way of contrast, in *Langford
v Cole* (1910) 102 LT 808, where a single assessment of poor rate was made on
property described in the rate-book as "mansion house and grounds" and it was
established that the mansion house itself was unoccupied at the date when the rate
was made, it was held that the rate made in respect of the whole property could not
be enforced and that a distress warrant should not therefore be issued.'
c

It would serve no purpose to examine the facts in the *Herwald* case. I need express no
concluded view whether the Divisional Court or the Court of Appeal were right in the
conclusion they reached, though I am inclined to prefer the reasoning of the Divisional
Court. The judgment of the Court of Appeal certainly provides no foundation for any
proposition of law at variance with the passage I have cited from the judgment of the *d*
Divisional Court.

What counsel for the appellants seeks to extract from the case is the proposition that,
if a person is in occupation of premises for a purpose which does not fulfil the description
of the only hereditament in the valuation list which is capable of relating to those
premises, he is not liable for rates. This is said to follow logically from the words: 'If the
person rated is in occupation of premises which fulfil the description in the valuation
list, that is sufficient for the issue of a warrant . . .' (see [1976] 2 All ER 808 at 810, [1977] *e*
1 WLR 100 at 103). Even if that half sentence is read entirely out of context, I doubt if it
serves counsel's purpose. But if one reads the passage as a whole it is perfectly clear that it
is concerned only with liability to rates arising from partial occupation of a hereditament.
No doubt the principle is well settled that if a mixed hereditament comprising property
of different kinds is described in the valuation list by reference to different elements, the *f*
occupier of part only of the hereditament who can show that a substantial element of the
hereditament as so described is not occupied by him will not be liable for rates in respect
of the hereditament as a whole and thus will escape liability altogether until the valuation
list is altered to identify and describe as a separate hereditament the property which he
does occupy. But this principle has no application to a hereditament which is fully
occupied, nor is it concerned in any way with the question whether the purpose of the
occupation does or does not correspond with the description of the hereditament in the *g*
valuation list.

For the reasons I have given I conclude that, on the true construction of the 1967 Act,
'the hereditament' referred to in para 2(*a*) and (*b*) of Sch 1 applies to a unit of property
which is sufficiently identified by an entry in the valuation list whether or not the
description of the hereditament in that entry appropriately describes the purpose for *h*
which the hereditament may lawfully be occupied. It follows that the appellants were
not at the material time prohibited from occupying the hereditaments in question, nor
were they kept vacant by reason of action taken by any local authority with a view to
prohibiting their occupation. The appellants are liable for the disputed rates.

I reach this conclusion without regret. Problems of enforcement in planning law have
shown how easily material changes of use may escape the attention of local authorities. *j*
If the appellants' contention were right, any change of use of premises might result in
the creation of a new hereditament in respect of which the occupier could only be made
liable for rates by an alteration of the valuation list. This would introduce a novel and, to
my mind, surprising doctrine into rating law. The application of the doctrine would
give rise to difficult questions as to the precise degree of correspondence between the
description of the hereditament and the purpose for which it was in fact occupied which
was necessary to an effective entry in the valuation list. I cannot see that any legitimate

a
interest of ratepayers requires the protection of such a doctrine. But it would, on the other hand, create obvious difficulty for rating authorities.

I would dismiss the appeal.

LORD BRANDON OF OAKBROOK. My Lords, I have had the advantage of reading in draft the speech prepared by my noble and learned friend Lord Bridge. I agree with it and for the reasons which he gives I would dismiss the appeal.

b
LORD GRIFFITHS. My Lords, I have had the advantage of reading in draft the speech prepared by my noble and learned friend Lord Bridge. I agree with it and for the reasons which he gives I would dismiss the appeal.

c
LORD MACKAY OF CLASHFERN. My Lords, I have had the advantage of reading in draft the speech prepared by my noble and learned friend Lord Bridge. I agree with it and for the reasons which he gives I would dismiss the appeal.

LORD ACKNER. My Lords, I have had the advantage of reading in draft the speech prepared by my noble and learned friend Lord Bridge. I agree with it and for the reasons which he gives I would dismiss the appeal.

d
Appeal dismissed.

Solicitors: *Asher Fishman & Co* (for the appellants); *G Matthew Ives* (for the respondents).

Mary Rose Plummer   Barrister.

e

GUR Corp v Trust Bank of Africa Ltd (Government of the Republic of Ciskei, third party)

f

QUEEN'S BENCH DIVISION (COMMERCIAL COURT)
STEYN J
9 APRIL, 19, 22 MAY 1986

g
COURT OF APPEAL, CIVIL DIVISION
SIR JOHN DONALDSON MR, NOURSE AND GLIDEWELL LJJ
7, 8, 9, 22 JULY 1986

Conflict of laws – Foreign government – Recognition – Locus standi to sue and be sued in English court – Republic of South Africa granting independence to dependent territory of Ciskei – British
h
government not according recognition de jure or de facto to Ciskei – British government taking no formal position regarding exercise of government authority over Ciskei – British government having dealings with South Africa in respect of Ciskei – Defendants in action in England issuing third party proceedings against Ciskei government – Whether Ciskei government having locus standi to take part in proceedings.

j
In 1981 the Republic of South Africa, by the Status of Ciskei Act 1981, purported to grant independence to its dependent territory of Ciskei. Under that Act the legislative assembly of Ciskei was empowered to make laws, including a constitution. Pursuant to that power the Ciskei assembly passed the Republic of Ciskei Constitution Act 1981, which, inter alia, authorised the President of Ciskei to establish departments of state, including a Department of Public Works, administered by ministers responsible to him. During the course or proceedings in the Commercial Court in England under a guarantee issued in London by the defendant bank in connection with a contract between the

plaintiffs, a Panamanian construction company, and the third party, the Ciskei
government, the preliminary issue arose whether the Ciskei government had locus standi   *a*
to take part in the proceedings. Certificates were obtained from the Foreign and
Commonwealth Office stating that the British government's policy was not to accord
formal recognition to governments, that it did not recognise the Republic of Ciskei de
jure or de facto, that it did not have a formal position regarding the exercise of
governmental authority over the territory of Ciskei, that it did not have any dealings
with the Ciskei government or the Ciskei Department of Public Works, but that it had   *b*
made representations to the South African government in relation to certain matters that
had occurred in Ciskei. The judge held that the effect of the certificates was that the
Republic of Ciskei did not have the capacity to sue or be sued in the English courts. The
bank and the Ciskei government appealed.

Held – On the true understanding of the certificates it was clear that although the British   *c*
government neither recognised the government of Ciskei nor took a formal position
regarding the exercise of governmental authority over the territory it nevertheless
regarded, by implication, the Republic of South Africa as being a sovereign state which
was entitled to exercise such authority, and the court was entitled to take cognisance of
the fact that by the Status of Ciskei Act 1981 the Republic of South Africa had delegated
legislative power to the Ciskei government, such power being revocable by a subsequent   *d*
legislative act of the Republic of South Africa. The delegation of legislative power
therefore constituted the requisite authority which enabled the Ciskei government to
undertake administrative and legislative acts and it followed that, as a subordinate body
set up to act on behalf of the Republic of South Africa, the Ciskei government had locus
standi and could properly be a party to the proceedings in England. The appeal would
therefore be allowed (see p 465 *b d* to p 466 *b* and p 467 *a* to *g*, post).   *e*
  Carl-Zeiss-Stiftung v Rayner & Keeler Ltd (No 2) [1966] 2 All ER 536 applied.

Notes
For recognition of states and governments generally, see 18 Halsbury's Laws (4th edn)
paras 1425–1435, and for cases on the subject, see 11 Digest (Reissue) 715–718, 409–416.
  f

Cases referred to in judgments
Adams v Adams (A-G intervening) [1970] 3 All ER 572, [1971] P 188, [1970] 3 WLR 934,
  DC.
Aksionairnoye Obschestvo A M Luther v James Sagor & Co [1921] 1 KB 456; *rvsd* [1921] 3 KB
  532, [1921] All ER Rep 138, CA.
Arantzazu Mendi, The [1939] 1 All ER 719, [1939] AC 256, HL.   *g*
Berne (City) v Bank of England (1804) 9 Ves 347, 32 ER 636, LC.
Carl-Zeiss-Stiftung v Rayner & Keeler Ltd (No 2) [1966] 2 All ER 536, [1967] 1 AC 853,
  [1966] 3 WLR 125, HL; *rvsg* [1965] 1 All ER 300, [1965] Ch 596, [1965] 2 WLR 277,
  CA.
Hesperides Hotels Ltd v Aegean Turkish Holidays Ltd [1978] 1 All ER 277, [1978] QB 205,
  [1977] 3 WLR 656, CA; *varied* sub nom *Hesperides Hotels v Muftizade* [1978] 2 All ER   *h*
  1168, [1979] AC 508, [1978] 3 WLR 378, HL.
James (an insolvent), Re (A-G intervening) [1977] 1 All ER 364, [1977] 1 Ch 41, [1977] 2
  WLR 1, CA.
Jones v Garcia del Rio (1823) 1 Turn & R 297, 37 ER 1113.
Snook v London and West Riding Investments Ltd [1967] 1 All ER 518, [1967] 2 QB 786,
  [1967] 2 WLR 1020, CA.   *j*
Transkei Republic v Europa Publications Ltd (17 January 1979 unreported), Ch D.
Upright v Mercury Business Machines Co Inc (1961) 213 NYS 2d 417, NY SC App Div.

Cases also cited
Al-Fin Corp's Patent, Re [1969] 3 All ER 396, [1970] Ch 160.
Elder Dempster Lines Ltd v Ionic Shipping Agency Inc [1968] 1 Lloyd's Rep 529.

Esal (Commodities) Ltd v Oriental Credit Ltd [1985] 2 Lloyd's Rep 546, CA.

a *Kinder v Everitt* (1823) Times, 22 December.

Luigi Monta of Genoa v Cechofracht Co Ltd [1956] 2 All ER 769, [1956] 2 QB 552.

Peru (Government), Re (1823) Times, 13 February.

Sokoloff v National City Bank of New York (1924) 239 NY 158, NY Ct of Apps.

Taylor v Barclay (1828) 2 Sim 213, 57 ER 769.

Thompson v Powles (1828) 2 Sim 194, 57 ER 761.

b *Thomson v Byree* (1824) Times, 31 May.

White Child & Beney Ltd v Simmons, White Child & Beney Ltd v Eagle Star and British Dominions Insurance Co (1922) 127 LT 571, [1922] All ER Rep 482, CA.

Yrissari v Clement (1826) 3 Bing 432, 130 ER 579.

Preliminary issue

c By a writ issued on 26 November 1985 the plaintiff, GUR Corp (a body corporate) (the contractor), claimed as against the defendants, Trust Bank of Africa Ltd, (1) a declaration that a guarantee issued on 20 April 1985 by the bank in favour of the Department of Public Works of the Republic of Ciskei for the performance and security of a contract dated 10 August 1983 between the contractor and the department in the sum of $US375,000, had expired with effect from 11.00 am London time on 15 November 1985

d and (2) the repayment of the sum of $US300,000. By a third party notice dated 20 December 1985 the defendants claimed as against the third party, the government of the Republic of Ciskei (Ciskei) a declaration that the guarantee given by the defendants had expired on 15 November 1985, that no valid demand had been made under the guarantee prior to its expiry and that the defendants were released from all liability to Ciskei under the guarantee. Ciskei served a defence and counterclaim against the plaintiff and the

e defendants to the effect that it had already made a valid demand under the guarantee before its expiry and the payment of $US375,000 or damages. On 7 March 1986 Bingham J ordered the trial of a preliminary issue, inter alia, whether Ciskei had made any valid demand under the guarantee. However, at the trial of the preliminary issue on 9 April Steyn J raised the question of Ciskei's locus standi to sue or to be sued in the English courts and the hearing was adjourned. The trial of the preliminary issue was

f heard in chambers but judgment was given by Steyn J in open court. The facts are set out in the judgment.

Mark Littman QC and *Antonio Bueno* for the contractor.
Peter Cresswell QC and *John Jarvis* for the bank.
Simon Tuckey QC and *Anthony Temple QC* for Ciskei.

g *John Laws* as amicus curiae.

Cur adv vult

22 May. The following judgment was delivered.

h
STEYN J. The principal question arising for decision in the matter is whether 'the Government of the Republic of the Ciskei' may sue, or be sued, in Her Majesty's courts of law.

The background

j The matter arises in this way. In August 1983 a contract was concluded between the plaintiff, a Panamanian company, to whom I shall refer as 'the contractor', and the third party, to whom I shall refer as 'Ciskei'. Pursuant to this contract the contractor agreed to design, construct and equip a hospital and two schools for Ciskei. Ciskei is one of the several homelands to whom the South African government has purported to grant independence. The details of the contract do not matter, save for cl 7.2.1, which obliged the contractor to furnish to Ciskei a guarantee in the sum of 10% of the building costs, such guarantee to be irrevocable for six months from the handing over of the project. The guarantee was intended to cover the cost of remedying defects. In the result the guarantee was given by the defendant, a South African bank, to whom I shall refer as 'the bank', to the Department of Public Works, Republic of Ciskei. The guarantee was dated 20 April 1985. Pursuant to it the guarantor undertook liability as guarantor for—

'. . . THE DUE PAYABLE [sic] BY GUR CORPORATION TO THE DEPARTMENT IN TERMS OF PARAGRAPH 7.2 OF THE AGREEMENT NO. 586/83 DATED 10TH AUGUST 1983 RELATIVE TO THE CONSTRUCTION OF THE 250 BED SHORT STAY HOSPITAL AND 2 SCHOOLS PROVIDED THAT THE TOTAL AMOUNT RECOVERED FROM THE GUARANTOR HEREUNDER SHALL NOT EXCEED IN THE WHOLE SUM OF US DOLL. 375,000 . . .'

The guarantor further provided as follows:

'THE GUARANTOR AGREES THAT ANY AMOUNT CLAIMABLE FROM IT HEREUNDER WILL BE PAYABLE ON RECEIPT OF A CERTIFICATE FROM THE DEPARTMENT APPROVED AND SIGNED BY REGISTERED QUANTITY SURVEYOR THAT SUCH AMOUNT IS PAYABLE BY GUR CORPORATION TO THE DEPARTMENT. THIS GUARANTEE SHALL EXPIRE AND BECOME NULL AND VOID NOT LATER THAN 11 A.M. LONDON TIME ON 30TH OCTOBER 1985 BY WHICH TIME AND DATE ANY CLAIMS HEREUNDER MUST HAVE BEEN RECEIVED. UPON ITS EXPIRATION THIS GUARANTEE SHALL CEASE TO HAVE EFFECT AND BE RETURNED TO THE GUARANTOR DULY CANCELLED.'

By agreement the operative period of the guarantee was extended until 11.00 am London time on Friday, 15 November 1985.

It would seem that the project was completed in 1985. However, there were certain disputes between Ciskei and the contractor as to alleged defects. A purported call on the guarantee was received by the bank by telex at 10.13 am on 15 November 1985. It read as follows:

'I refer to Guarantee Number PG85/3 and have to inform that the Ciskei State Attorney has instructed that the Guarantee be held as Ciskei contends that it has suffered damages in excess of amount of the Guarantee.'

The telex recorded that it was from the Director General of Finance of the Republic of Ciskei. No further call was received on the guarantee until 11.00 am on that day. The bank took the view that the telex, which it did receive, did not constitute a proper claim within the meaning of the guarantee and that the guarantee had lapsed. As security for the guarantee the bank held $US300,000 of the contractors' funds in a blocked deposit account. The contractor asked for repayment of this sum. However, in view of the fact that Ciskei contended that a proper claim in terms of the guarantee had been made, the bank refused to release the deposit.

The bank carries on business in London and is a registered banking institution under the Banking Act 1979. Accordingly, the contractor issued and served a writ within the jurisdiction against the bank claiming a declaration that the guarantee had expired and claiming repayment of the sum of $US300,000. The bank served what can best be described as a holding defence. The bank was faced with the problem that Ciskei was asserting that a proper claim had been made under the guarantee. Accordingly, the bank issued a third party notice against Ciskei. In the third party proceedings the bank claimed that the guarantee expired before any valid claim was made under it and that it is released from all liability under it. Ciskei served points of defence and counterclaim, asserting that a valid claim had been made under the guarantee. Ciskei made both the contractor and the bank parties to a counterclaim; it sought declaratory relief against both, and claimed $US375,000 against the bank together with interest.

On 7 March 1986 Bingham J ordered preliminary issues to be tried. The issues related to the question whether a valid claim had been made under the guarantee. That is how the matter came before me for hearing in April. At the hearing I raised the question whether Ciskei has any locus standi to sue, or be sued, in an English court. The bank and Ciskei submitted that Ciskei had locus standi. I was not convinced. I heard preliminary submissions on the locus standi of Ciskei and on the issues between the contractor and *a* the bank. Thereafter I adjourned the hearing in order (a) to ascertain the views of Her Majesty's government as to the status of Ciskei, (b) to request the Attorney General to appoint an amicus curiae, since that was the only way in which both sides could be argued at a resumed hearing. Earlier this week the hearing was resumed. Letters from the Foreign and Commonwealth Office were placed before the court, and Mr Laws appeared as amicus curiae. The court is grateful to him for his submissions.

b *The standing of Ciskei*

The first question is, therefore, whether Ciskei is entitled to sue, or be sued, in the English courts. It has purported to defend third party proceedings and to raise counterclaims against the contractor and the bank. Does it have any standing in an English court in any of these capacities?

The facts are simple. Ciskei is a very small territory in the eastern Cape Province of *c* South Africa. It is 'the homeland' of a small minority of the Xhosa people. In 1981 the South African Parliament enacted the Status of Ciskei Act. It recited in its preamble that 'the Government of Ciskei is desirous that Ciskei should be an independent state', and that the government of the Republic of South Africa 'deems it expedient to grant independence to Ciskei'. In s 1(1) it provided that Ciskei is 'declared to be a sovereign and independent state and shall cease to be part of the Republic of South Africa'. Section 1(2) *d* provided that the Republic of South Africa 'shall cease to exercise any authority over [Ciskei]'. Section 2 provided for the continuation of the existing laws of Ciskei. Section 3 set out the powers of the Legislative Assembly of Ciskei. Section 6 provided that the citizens of Ciskei (as defined) would cease to be South African citizens. A copy of the Republic of Ciskei Constitution Act 1981, as enacted by the Legislative Assembly of Ciskei, has also been placed before the court. It is sufficient to say that it purports to be *e* the constitution of 'a sovereign democratic, independent republic in a confederation of Southern African states'. Both these instruments were placed before me on behalf of Ciskei, and I have extracted from them what may arguably be relevant to the issues in this case.

Now I turn to the certificates of Her Majesty's government as to the status of Ciskei. In a letter dated 1 May 1986 the Foreign and Commonwealth Office, acting on behalf of *f* Her Majesty's government, addressed the following question:

'What recognition, if any, does Her Majesty's Government accord to (1) the "Government of the Republic of Ciskei" and/or (2) "the Department of Public Works, Republic of Ciskei"?'

This question was answered in the following terms:

g   '. . . consistently with the statements made in Parliament in April 1980 about the outcome of a re-examination of British policy and practice in this field, it is not the current practice of Her Majesty's Government to accord recognition to Governments. The British Government recognises states in accordance with common international practice, but so far as governments are concerned, the attitude of Her Majesty's Government is to be inferred from the nature of its dealings with the regime *h* concerned and in particular whether Her Majesty's Government deals with it on a normal government to government basis. Her Majesty's Government does not recognise the "Republic of Ciskei" as an independent sovereign state, either *de jure* or *de facto*, and does not have any dealings with the "Government of the Republic of Ciskei" or "the Department of Public Works, Republic of Ciskei".'

j The second certificate is dated 16 May 1986. The question to which it was addressed reads as follows:

'Which state, if any, does Her Majesty's Government recognise as (a) entitled to exercise or (b) exercising governing authority in respect of the territory in Southern Africa known as Ciskei. Has such recognition been de jure or de facto?'

This question was answered in the following terms:

'. . . beyond making it clear that it has not recognised as independent sovereign States Ciskei or any of the other Homelands established in South Africa Her Majesty's *a* Government has not taken and does not have a formal position as regards the exercise of governing authority over the territory of Ciskei. Her Majesty's Government does not have any dealings with the "Government of the Republic of Ciskei" or with "the Department of Public Works, Republic of Ciskei". Her Majesty's Government has made representations to the South African Government in relation to certain matters occurring in Ciskei and others of the Homelands to which South *b* Africa has purported to grant independence, notably on matters relating to individuals, but has not in general received any positive response from the South African Government.'

It is clear that, in so far as they go, these certificate are conclusive. The reason underlying this rule is that in the field of foreign relations the Crown in its executive and judicial functions ought to speak with one voice, and that the recognition of a foreign *c* state or government is a matter of foreign policy on which the executive is in a markedly superior position to form a judgment. That being the position, I proceed to consider the matters before me on the basis that what is said in the two executive certificates is determinative of the underlying facts to which they relate.

From the certificates the following four propositions can be extracted: (i) Her Majesty's government does not recognise Ciskei as an independent sovereign state; (ii) it is not the *d* current practice of Her Majesty's government to accord recognition to governments; (iii) Her Majesty's government does not have any dealings with 'the Government of the Republic of Ciskei' or with 'the Department of Public Works, Republic of Ciskei'; (iv) Her Majesty's government does not have any formal position as regards the exercise of governing authority over the territory of Ciskei.

Against this background the question is whether Ciskei has the necessary standing to *e* sue or be sued in our courts of competent jurisdiction. The critical fact, certified as it has been by the executive, is that Ciskei is not recognised by Her Majesty's government as an independent sovereign state.

The law

Two general principles of English law are clearly established. The first is that an *f* unrecognised state cannot sue or be sued in an English court: see *City of Berne v Bank of England* (1804) 9 Ves 347, 32 ER 636. The second is that the governmental acts of an unrecognised state cannot be recognised by an English court: see *Aksionairnoye Obschestvo A M Luther v James Sagor & Co* [1921] 1 KB 456, [1921] All ER Rep 138. Subject to reservations by counsel for the bank and Ciskei to argue differently elsewhere, which are too numerous to recite, neither of these general principles were called in question in *g* argument. Common sense and justice may combine to require the qualification of these general principles in certain respects. The question is whether any such gateway applies in the present case.

One qualification of the general principles may be the necessity for English courts to take cognisance of governmental acts of unrecognised states which directly affect family or property rights of individuals. There is no binding English authority supporting such *h* a qualification of the general principles. Lord Wilberforce in *Carl-Zeiss-Stiftung v Rayner & Keeler Ltd* [1966] 2 All ER 536 at 577, [1967] 1 AC 853 at 954 regarded it as a possible avenue for future development; see also *Adams v Adams* [1970] 3 All ER 572, [1971] P 188, *Re James (an insolvent)* [1977] 1 All ER 364, [1977] 1 Ch 41 and *Hesperides Hotels Ltd v Aegean Turkish Holidays Ltd* [1978] 1 All ER 277 at 282–283, [1978] QB 205 at 218. It is *j* manifest, however, that such a development, if recognised, cannot assist Ciskei in the present case. In the present case the court is not confronted with the necessity of doing justice to individuals who were caught up in a political situation which was not of their making. It is true that the principal contract was for the building of a hospital and two schools. The dispute is, however, commercial in character and involves monetary claims between Ciskei and a South African bank. Ciskei is directly impleaded, and Ciskei has brought a counterclaim.

It is necessary, therefore, to consider whether there is another gateway which avails
Ciskei. Both counsel for the bank and for Ciskei suggested that the general principles
which I have mentioned are subject to an exception created by the decision of the House
of Lords in *Carl-Zeiss-Stiftung v Rayner & Keeler Ltd*. In that case the question arose
whether the fact that the German Democratic Republic (the GDR) was not recognised de
jure or de facto constrained an English court to treat the purported state as non-existent
and to deny any effect to its acts or decrees. The Court of Appeal held in the affirmative
(see [1965] 1 All ER 300, [1965] Ch 596). The House of Lords reversed the decision of
the Court of Appeal. The existence of the above-mentioned general principles were not
questioned in any of the speeches in the House of Lords.

The House of Lords held that the acts of the GDR should be recognised by the English
courts as lawful, not as the acts of a sovereign state but as the acts of a subordinate body
set up by another state, the USSR, which was recognised as a sovereign state by Her
Majesty's government. It is right to say immediately that there are passages in the
speeches which emphasised the far-reaching and inconvenient consequences of a rigid
adherence to the principle that the acts of an unrecognised state are to be treated as of no
effect by an English court: see the observations of Lord Reid and Lord Wilberforce
([1966] 2 All ER 536 at 548, 576–577, [1967] 1 AC 853 at 907, 953–954). Much was
made of these observations. However, the *Carl-Zeiss* case was decided on the basis of the
application of principles of agency: on the materials before the House of Lords the
relevant acts were categorised as those of the USSR rather than the GDR. This route was
open to their Lordships because there was an executive certificate, which expressly stated
([1966] 2 All ER 536 at 545, [1967] 1 AC 853 at 859):

> '. . . up to the present date Her Majesty's Government have recognised the state
> and government of the Union of Soviet Socialist Republics as de jure entitled to
> exercise governing authority in respect of that zone [the GDR].'

A careful perusal of Lord Reid's speech, which was concurred in by Lord Hodson, Lord
Guest and Lord Upjohn, has persuaded me that the passage from the executive certificate
which I have quoted was the essential foundation of their Lordships' reasoning (see
[1966] 2 All ER 536 at 546, [1967] 1 AC 853 at 904). It was also critical to Lord
Wilberforce's reasoning (see [1966] 2 All ER 536 at 579, [1967] 1 AC 853 at 957).

Turning now to the present case, counsel submitted on behalf of the bank that, if the
court is bound to treat Ciskei as an unrecognised state, it follows inexorably that it must
be a subordinate body of the Republic of South Africa, which is a sovereign state.
Accordingly, he submitted that the agency argument which prevailed in the *Carl-Zeiss*
case ought also to prevail in the present case. Realistically, he recognised that it does not
follow, if this argument is right, that Ciskei can sue, or be sued, in an English court.
However, if an English court can take cognisance of the acts of Ciskei, he submitted,
then the difficulties can be cured by appropriate amendments which I will discuss below.
Counsel submitted on behalf of Ciskei that, and I quote from a helpful summary:

> 'This court therefore must regard the acts of Ciskei its government organs and
> officers as acts done with the consent of South Africa. These acts can be recognised
> by this court as lawful because they are acts done by a subordinate body which South
> Africa has set up to act on its behalf.'

This is a curious submission on behalf of an entity which purports to be an independent
and sovereign state, but I will consider it on its own merits. Counsel for Ciskei further
submitted that the court can recognise Ciskei's commercial contracts, and that Ciskei
should be permitted to litigate disputes arising out of them in this country in its own
name or at least in the name of its relevant department.

In my judgment there is an essential difference between the *Carl-Zeiss* case and the
present case. In the *Carl-Zeiss* case there was a conclusive certificate that the USSR still
exercised governing authority in the GDR. In the present case the certificate records that
Her Majesty's government 'does not have a formal position as regards the exercise of
governing authority over the territory of the Ciskei'. It was suggested that on this point

the certificate is less than clear. I disagree. It is plainly a carefully considered certificate, given by the executive to the judiciary, and its meaning is beyond question. It was also suggested that Her Majesty's government does not have a formal position on the relevant matter, because it is no longer its practice to recognise governments. This explanation may be right. The fact is, however, that there is no certification to the effect that South Africa is still the governing authority in Ciskei. Inevitably, therefore, the bank and Ciskei must rely on other evidence for the proposition that South Africa still exercises governing authority in Ciskei. In my judgment, there are no materials available before me which warrant such an inference. Indeed, such materials as have been placed before me point the other way. As I have already mentioned, Ciskei placed before me the Status of Ciskei Act 1981. It was submitted that on this point I may not look at it. Clearly, it is not permissible to have regard to any declarations of the South African state or of Ciskei in so far as they conflict with executive certificates of Her Majesty's government. However, on the point presently under consideration those executive certificates are silent. In the circumstances it is therefore permissible to refer to the Status of Ciskei Act 1981. Section 1(2) of that Act unambiguously provides that the Republic of South Africa shall cease to have any authority over Ciskei. I readily accept that there is a distinct possibility that the reality of the relationship between Ciskei and South Africa may be very different from the impression created by the South African statute. But there are no materials from which the inference can be drawn that the Republic of South Africa is still the governing authority of Ciskei. Certainly, it is impossible to infer from the mere fact that Ciskei is unrecognised by Her Majesty's government that South Africa is still the governing authority in Ciskei territory, or so viewed by Her Majesty's government. After all, recognition has in the past from time to time been withheld by Her Majesty's government on political grounds unrelated to the question whether the entity is in truth an independent state: see D W Greig 'Unrecognised Governments in English Law' [1967] LQR 96 at 97. Whether that was the motivation in the case of Ciskei, one does not know. But it does show that counsel's proposition, put forward on the basis of the inexorable march of logic, is, in fact, a non sequitur. It follows that the line of reasoning which prevailed in the Carl-Zeiss case is not apposite in the present case. The Carl-Zeiss case was decided on very special facts, which were fundamentally different from the facts in the present case.

Counsel as amicus drew my attention to an unreported decision in the Chancery Division in which Oliver J apparently held that Transkei was in principle entitled to sue, or be sued, in an English court: see Republic of Transkei v Europa Publications Ltd (17 January 1979, unreported). Transkei was the first of the so-called 'homelands' which were purportedly made independent and sovereign states by South Africa. It is apparent from the second certificate in the present case that Her Majesty's government has never recognised Transkei. In the Europa Publications case Transkei complained that the European Yearbook wrongly described it as not sovereign and independent. Its locus standi was challenged. There was no formal certificate before the court, but there was a letter from the Foreign Office saying that a certificate would be given that Transkei was not an independent sovereign state if the court asked for it. The master held that Transkei in principle had authority to sue, or be sued, in an English court but that Transkei had no cause of action, because Her Majesty's government took the view that it was not an independent and sovereign state. That was conclusive of the merits in the case, and the claim was bound to fail. On appeal Oliver J apparently upheld the master's view on both points. It is not clear whether Oliver J regarded the case as falling within the exception created by the Carl-Zeiss case. I have referred to this decision with great hesitation, because there is no judgment approved by Oliver J nor is there a note of his judgment agreed between counsel or solicitors. It is, however, my impression that the arguments, which were so carefully deployed by counsel as amicus in this case, were not fully developed in that case. While I differ from Oliver J with the greatest reluctance, I am bound to do so in this case.

Apart from the exception to established general principles which was created by the

a
Carl-Zeiss decision, no other exception was advanced which could arguably assist Ciskei in this court. Counsel for the bank did refer me to Professor Greig's article, which I have already mentioned. I have found the article illuminating and helpful. However, no proposition was extracted from it which was advanced in this court as a further substantive exception relevant to the present case. I bear in mind a point vigorously demonstrated by Professor Greig, namely that a rigid adherence to traditional principles might sometimes give rise to grave injustice as between individual litigants. That is,

b
however, a position which will have to be considered when it arises.

Counsel for the bank emphasised what he described as the unfortunate commercial consequences if Ciskei has no standing in English courts. He said that the guarantee is commercial paper issued out of the City of London. Justice demands, he suggested, that English courts should assume jurisdiction. This argument ignores the countervailing considerations of public policy, political as they are, which underlie the general principles.

c
If along the lines discussed by Lord Wilberforce in the *Carl-Zeiss* case an exception should be grafted onto the established principles in favour of individuals who have been caught up in their family and property rights in a political situation not of their own making, it hardly avails the two parties directly affected here. Neither the South African bank, versed as it is in the business of risk taking, nor Ciskei could have been ignorant of the potential effect of Ciskei's status on their remedies in foreign courts. After all, it is

d
common knowledge that the so-called independent homelands do not enjoy the courtesies and privileges of the community of nations. Moreover, it was common ground that the dispute between Ciskei and the bank can be settled in the courts of South Africa and/or Ciskei.

The parties to the contracts involved here could conceivably have structured their contractual arrangements in a different way by the intercession of other parties which

e
would have enabled them to avoid in the English courts the consequences of the lack of standing of Ciskei. That is, however, no reason to bend established rules in a way which would implicitly amount to judicial recognition of Ciskei. And recognition of a new state is the exclusive prerogative of the Crown in its executive function. On the pleadings as they stand, I conclude that it is not competent for an English court to adjudicate on the third party proceedings.

f
Counsel for the bank submitted that this result could be avoided by granting an amendment substituting for the government of the Republic of Ciskei one of the following parties: (i) the Department of Public Works, Ciskei; (ii) The Department of Public Works, Ciskei (a subordinate body); (iii) Mr C L Atwell, the director general of the above department; (iv) Mr C L Atwell, as assignee of Ciskei's rights. Counsel for Ciskei adopted these arguments, although his enthusiasm for amendments (i), (ii) and

g
(iii) was less than complete. By and large his case was that amendment (iv) solved the problem. In my judgment, counsel as amicus identified the fallacy underlying these proposed amendments. They all assume, he submitted, that one is dealing with a mere procedural rule, whereas, in fact, one is dealing with fundamental principles of English law based on important public policy considerations. Amendments (i), (ii) and (iii) are, in my judgment, without merit. Amendment (iv) requires more careful analysis. An

h
assignment of rights dated 14 May 1986 from Ciskei to Mr Atwell, a senior civil servant, was placed before the court. It had not taken effect during the hearing. It was still held in escrow. For the purposes of this judgment, however, I will assume that it had taken effect. I will further assume that according to South African law, which is expressed to be the governing law, it was a valid assignment. I also do not approach it as being a sham transaction in the sense of a transaction in which both parties assented to it only in order

j
to deceive an English court: see *Snook v London and West Riding Investments Ltd* [1967] 1 All ER 518 at 528–529, [1967] 2 QB 786 at 802. On the other hand the only purpose of this assignment to a Ciskei civil servant, after the challenge to Ciskei standing, is to avoid the consequence of Ciskei's lack of standing. If the device is upheld here, every unrecognised state would be able to circumvent the fundamental principles of our law regarding recognition of states. In a broad sense it is a colourable device which it would

be contrary to public policy to recognise. Unlike the assignment in *Upright v Mercury Business Machines Co Ltd* (1962) 213 NYS 2d 417, it was not an assignment in the ordinary *a* course of business. The act of Ciskei in assigning in these circumstances ought not to be recognised by an English court. I therefore conclude that none of these amendments ought to be allowed.

Counsel for Ciskei had one final argument. He said that Ciskei was willing to abandon its counterclaim 'if it would help'. It would not. Ciskei may also not be impleaded in this case. That has been the rule since *Jones v Garcia del Rio* (1823) 1 Turn & R 297, 37 ER *b* 1113 and there is no good reason to depart from it here.

I therefore rule that this court cannot adjudicate on the third party proceedings.

The issues between the contractor and the bank

There is, however, no reason why I should not decide the issue between the contractor and the bank. The principal issue is whether Ciskei's telex dated 15 November 1985 *c* constituted a valid claim or demand under the guarantee. This is a narrow point of construction which by express agreement must be determined in accordance with English law. The guarantee required a claim to be made by a certain date. That claim could only be made when the sum in question was payable. The sum in question only became payable on receipt by the bank of a certificate from the Department of Public Works, Republic of Ciskei approved and signed 'by a registered quantity surveyor'. Since *d* the demand was not accompanied by such a certificate it was invalid, and no valid demand was made within the operative period of the guarantee. This is, in my judgment, the clear effect of the express language of the guarantee. This construction is also consistent with the character of this demand guarantee. By its very nature it required a certain expiry date. On the contrary construction, the bank's commitment would have been open ended. That in my respectful judgment is a most implausible bargain in these *e* circumstances. If the guarantee was (contrary to my conclusion) capable of differing constructions, I would have preferred the construction which is consistent with its manifest commercial purpose. I therefore conclude that no valid claim was made on the guarantee. It is, therefore, unnecessary to consider other arguments advanced in support of the proposition that no valid demand was made under the guarantee.

f

Orders accordingly.

Solicitors: *Jeffrey Green & Russell* (for the contractor); *Durrant Piesse* (for the bank); *Barlow Lyde & Gilbert* (for Ciskei); *Treasury Solicitor*.

K Mydeen Esq   Barrister. *g*

Appeal

The bank and Ciskei appealed.

Elihu Lauterpacht QC, Peter Cresswell QC and *John Jarvis* for the bank.
Simon Tuckey QC and *Anthony Temple QC* for Ciskei. *h*
Antonio Bueno for the contractor.
John Laws as amicus curiae.

Cur adv vult

22 July. The following judgments were delivered. *j*

SIR JOHN DONALDSON MR. At first blush this might appear to have been a very ordinary commercial dispute. GUR Corp (the contractor), a Panamanian company, had contracted to build a hospital and two schools in Ciskei, Southern Africa. In connection with this construction contract, the contractor had asked the Trust Bank of Africa to issue

a bank guarantee, limited to $US375,000 and having an expiry date and time, in favour
a of the building owners, the Department of Public Works of the Republic of Ciskei. The
London branch of the bank had issued such a guarantee, but had required the contractor
to give a counter-guarantee and to deposit $US300,000 with it as security for that
obligation. In due course the building owners demanded payment under the guarantee.
The bank declined to pay on the grounds that no demand complying with the conditions
of the guarantee had been made before its expiry. The contractor not unnaturally
b supported the bank.

   In the ensuing litigation all three parties were before the court and, in a splendidly
complex set of pleadings involving claims, defences, counterclaims and third party
proceedings, every contingency was catered for. However, the basic issue was very
simple, namely whether (a) the building owners had made a valid claim under the
guarantee for $US375,000 and, if so, whether they could keep any money which they
c recovered in the proceedings or had to pay it over to the contractor as being retention
moneys no longer required for the purposes of the building contract, or (b) the bank was
under no liability under the guarantee and was therefore obliged to repay to the
contractor the $US300,000 deposited as security for its obligations under the counter-
guarantee. It was estimated that the whole matter could be heard and judgment given
within at most half a day.

d   The matter came before Steyn J, who, to the discomfiture of all three parties, raised
the question of whether it was permissible for the building owners to sue or be sued in
the English courts. Let me say at once that the judge was quite right to do so. Although
the courts in general, and the Commercial Court in particular, will always do their best
to meet the needs and wishes of the litigants, there are certain public policy constraints.
So far as is relevant, they are based on the undesirability, to put it no higher, of the
e national courts appearing to speak in terms which are not consistent with the nation's
foreign policy and diplomatic stance. And so it came about that Steyn J tried, as a
preliminary point, the issue of whether the building owner, which called itself 'The
Government of the Republic of Ciskei' had any locus standi in the courts of this country,
either as a claimant or as a respondent. He decided that it had none.

   This decision was greeted with some dismay by all three parties. Probably the most
f dismayed was the bank and for two somewhat different reasons. The first was that the
decision opened up the possibility of judgment being given against the bank in favour of
the contractor in this country, without the bank being able to obtain a judgment in its
own favour against the Republic of Ciskei, which it could use as a defence if sued by
Ciskei in the local courts or those of the Republic of South Africa. The second was of
more general import. It was that the financial institutions of the City of London which
g lend money or provide financial services to bodies in a similar position to that of the
building owners, and the 'Republic of Ciskei' is by no means unique, would have no
means of having their rights and obligations determined by the courts of this country.
Both the bank and the 'Republic of Ciskei' appealed, without opposition from the
contractor. In these circumstances we, like the judge below, sought the assistance of an
amicus in order that the arguments might be fully deployed and we, like the judge, have
h been extremely fortunate in that Mr John Laws was able to undertake this duty.

   It is now necessary to explain the problem in more detail. Ciskei is a geographical area
situated in what was once the self-governing colony of the Cape of Good Hope in
Southern Africa, that colony later becoming part of the Union of South Africa in
accordance with the South Africa Act 1909. By s 152 of that Act, the Parliament of the
Union was empowered to alter or amend it and by s 22 of the Statute of Westminster
j 1932, which applied to the Union, it was provided that no law made after 1932 by the
parliament of a dominion should be void or inoperative on the ground that it was
repugnant to the law of England. In 1961 the Union Parliament enacted the Republic of
South Africa Constitution Act, which repealed most of the 1909 Act and resulted in the
Union becoming an independent republic outside the Commonwealth, whose territory
included the territory of Ciskei. Thereafter a form of local government was established

in Ciskei, but in 1981 the Parliament of what was now the Republic of South Africa passed the Status of Ciskei Act, which purported to declare that the territory of Ciskei constituted a sovereign and independent state and was no longer a part of the Republic. The Act also purported to empower the Legislative Assembly of Ciskei to legislate in the manner provided by the Act and to make laws (including a constitution) for Ciskei. In reliance on this power, the Assembly passed the Republic of Ciskei Constitution Act 1981 which, by s 34(1), authorised the President of Ciskei to establish such departments of state as he might deem necessary for the government and to appoint persons to administer such departments, such persons being 'Ministers holding office during the pleasure of the President'. 'The Minister of Health' in fact signed the construction contract.

It appears that the Department of Public Works, which was the beneficiary named in the bank's guarantee, owes its existence to this provision and there are no materials on the basis of which it might have been argued that it and the government of Ciskei were, or might be viewed as, the same entity as the local government which existed immediately prior to the passing of the Status of Ciskei Act 1981. This is also important from another point of view. The mere fact that a party to litigation chooses to describe itself as 'The Government of the Republic of . . .' does not of itself create any problem of locus standi. This may be a trade name, a firm name, the title of an incorporated or unincorporated association, a description of what is known in the travel industry as an 'affinity group' or simply an example of what I venture to call the 'Pimlico syndrome', after the classic film 'Passport to Pimlico'. However, this is not such a case and what might otherwise be treated as mere pretentiousness cannot here be so lightly dismissed, since the Republic of Ciskei is without doubt recognised by the Republic of South Africa.

In these circumstances steps were rightly taken to inform the judge of the attitude of Her Majesty's government towards the 'Republic of Ciskei' and, to this end, Messrs Durrant Piesse, the solicitors for the bank, wrote to the Foreign and Commonwealth Office on 10 April 1986 on behalf of all parties, asking:

'1. What recognition, if any, does Her Majesty's Government accord to (1) the "Government of the Republic of Ciskei" and/or (2) "the Department of Public Works, Republic of Ciskei"?

2. Would it be contrary to the policy or attitudes of Her Majesty's Government for the English Courts to recognise either or both of such bodies as (i) contracting parties and (ii) capable of suing or being sued in an English Court under such names or either of them in respect of a commercial obligation assumed in its favour by the London branch of a bank licensed to accept deposits under the Banking Act 1979, a copy of which is annexed hereto.'

The anwer dated 1 May 1986 was as follows:

'In answer to the first of your questions, I am instructed to inform you that, consistently with the statements made in Parliament in April 1980 about the outcome of a re-examination of British policy and practice in this field, it is not the current practice of Her Majesty's Government to accord recognition to Governments. The British Government recognises states in accordance with common international practice, but so far as governments are concerned, the attitude of Her Majesty's Government is to be inferred from the nature of its dealings with the regime concerned and in particular whether Her Majesty's Government deals with it on a normal government to government basis. Her Majesty's Government does not recognise the "Republic of Ciskei" as an independent sovereign state, either *de jure* or *de facto*, and does not have any dealings with the "Government of the Republic of Ciskei" or "the Department of Public Works, Republic of Ciskei". With regard to the second question, it would appear to the Foreign and Commonwealth Office that the capacity to contract and to sue is a matter for the Court to determine having regard to the answer given to the first question and, therefore, that it would not be appropriate for the Foreign and Commonwealth Office to answer the second question.'

In a further letter dated 9 May 1986 Durrant Piesse asked a further question:

a
'Which state, if any, does Her Majesty's Government recognise as (a) entitled to exercise or (b) exercising governing authority in respect of the territory in Southern Africa known as Ciskei. Has such recognition been de jure or de facto?'

On 16 May 1986 the Foreign and Commonwealth Office answered:

b
'As stated in Mr. Prendergast's letter to you of 1 May 1986, it is not the current practice of Her Majesty's Government to accord recognition to Governments. I am therefore instructed to reply that, beyond making clear that it has not recognised as independent sovereign States Ciskei or any of the other Homelands established in South Africa Her Majesty's Government has not taken and does not have a formal position as regards the exercise of governing authority over the territory of Ciskei. Her Majesty's Government does not have any dealing with the "Government of the

c
Republic of Ciskei" or with "the Government of Public Works, Republic of Ciskei". Her Majesty's Government has made representations to the South African Government in relation to certain matters occurring in Ciskei and others of the Homelands to which South Africa has purported to grant independence, notably on matters relating to individuals, but has not in general received any positive response from the South Africa Government.'

d
In amplification and explanation of the references in that letter to the current practice of Her Majesty's government not to accord recognition to governments, it is convenient to refer to a statement made in Parliament by the Secretary of State for Foreign and Commonwealth Affairs and by the Lord Privy Seal in April 1980 and to the written answer to a parliamentary question given by the Rt Hon Sir Ian Gilmour MP on behalf

e
of the Secretary of State on 23 May 1980. The statement was in the following terms (408 HL Official Report (5th series) written answers cols *1121–1122*; 983 HC Official Report (5th series) written answers cols *277–279*):

f
'Following the undertaking of my right honourable friend the Lord Privy Seal in another place on 18th June last we have conducted a re-examination of British policy and practice concerning the recognition of Governments. This has included a comparison with the practice of our partners and allies. On the basis of this review we have decided that we shall no longer accord recognition to Governments. The British Government recognises States in accordance with common international doctrine. Where an unconsitutional change of régime takes place in a recognised State, Governments of other States must necessarily consider what dealings, if any, they should have with the new régime, and whether and to what extent it qualifies

g
to be treated as the Government of the State concerned. Many of our partners and allies take the position that they do not recognise Governments and that therefore no question of recognition arises in such cases. By contrast, the policy of successive British Governments has been that we should make and announce a decision formally "recognising" the new Government. This practice has sometimes been

h
misunderstood, and, despite explanations to the contrary, our "recognition" interpreted as implying approval. For example, in circumstances where there might be legitimate public concern about the violation of human rights by the new régime, or the manner in which it achieved power, it has not sufficed to say that an announcement of "recognition" is simply a neutral formality. We have therefore concluded that there are practical advantages in following the policy of many other countries in not according recognition to Governments. Like them, we shall

j
continue to decide the nature of our dealings with régimes which come to power unconstitutionally in the light of our assessment of whether they are able of themselves to exercise effective control of the territory of the State concerned, and seem likely to continue to do so.'

The answer to the written question added:

'In future cases where a new régime comes to power unconstitutionally our attitude on the question whether it qualifies to be treated as a Government, will be *a* left to be inferred from the nature of the dealings, if any, which we may have with it, and in particular on whether we are dealing with it on a normal Government to Government basis.'

These are the raw materials on which we have to reach a decision. Suggestions were made both in this court and below for avoiding, rather than resolving, this problem by, for example, amending the name of the third party to read 'The Department of Public *b* Works, Ciskei', substituting a named individual who happened to be an official of the department or the execution of an assignment of the building owners' rights followed by the substitution of the assignee as third party. The latter suggestion was based on an interlocutory decision of the Appellate Division of the Supreme Court for the State of New York in *Upright v Mercury Business Machines Co Inc* (1961) 213 NYS 2d 417 in which the assignee of a trade acceptance drawn in favour of a foreign corporation, said to be the *c* creature of a foreign government not recognised by the United States government, was allowed to proceed with his claims. The basis of the decision was that the lack of standing by the foreign government was not necessarily determinative, so long as the government was not a suitor. It does not assist in the present instance, because the government of Ciskei claims to be a party to the suit and the assignment has not yet been effected, although I understand that it has been executed in escrow. In these circumstances this, *d* like the other suggested methods of avoiding the problem, have to be dismissed as procedural devices which cannot be allowed to obscure the basic public policy constraint that the courts cannot take cognisance of a foreign juridical person if to do so would involve them in acting inconsistently with the foreign policy or diplomatic stance of this country.

I therefore turn to the only argument to which this objection does not apply, namely *e* that based on what has come to be referred to as the '*Carl-Zeiss* exception', although this is itself misleading, because it is not an exception to the general rule, but rather its application in unusual circumstances.

In *Carl-Zeiss-Stiftung v Rayner & Keeler Ltd (No 2)* [1966] 2 All ER 536, [1967] 1 AC 853 the issue was whether solicitors acting on behalf of the Stiftung were duly authorised so to act. This in turn involved tracing the source of their authority back to the acts of a *f* body known as the Rat (or council) of Gera, which had been established in 1952 by decree of the German Democratic Republic (the GDR). The GDR had itself been set up in 1949 by the USSR to govern that part of Germany then occupied by Russia. In doing so the USSR had purported to make the GDR an independent state. Thus there were some essential similarities between the genesis of the GDR and that of the Republic of Ciskei. In each case a sovereign state, recognised as such by Her Majesty's government, purported *g* to establish a new independent state with exclusive sovereignty over a territory which theretofore had been included in the territory of the 'mother' state. The House of Lords held that the English courts could take cognisance of the legislative authority of the GDR because, whilst they could not treat it as a sovereign state with legislative powers as such, they could and should treat it as having effective legislative powers on the footing that its legislative acts were those of a subordinate body which the USSR had set up to act on its *h* behalf. In reading the speeches in the *Carl-Zeiss* case and considering and comparing the answers of Her Majesty's government to the questions asked of them in that context and in the context of this case, it is important to bear in mind the change of practice whereby Her Majesty's government no longer formally recognises governments. In the *Carl-Zeiss* case [1965] 1 All ER 300 at 306, 307, [1965] Ch 596 at 637 the courts were told:

'Her Majesty's Government have not granted any recognition de jure or de facto *j* to (a) the German Democratic Republic or (b) its government [and] Her Majesty's Government have recognised the state and government of the Union of Soviet Socialist Republics as de jure entitled to exercise governing authority in respect of [East Germany].'

a

Lord Reid, in a speech with which Lord Hodson, Lord Guest and Lord Upjohn expressly agreed, pointed out that the House was not concerned with a situation which fitted neatly into either of the usual categories where (a) the relevant law had been made by the sovereign of a recognised state, by a legislative body established by the constitution of that state or by some person or body to whom legislative authority had been delegated by the sovereign, or (b) the law had been made against the will of the sovereign by persons engaged in rebellion or revolution (see [1966] 2 All ER 536 at 559, 564, 569,

b

[1967] 1 AC 853 at 925, 933, 941). The ratio of his, and the House's, decision is I think best explained by the following extract from his speech where, after distinguishing *Aksionairnoye Obschestvo A M Luther v James Sagor & Co* [1921] 3 KB 532, [1921] All ER Rep 138 as being a case concerned with a revolutionary situation, he continued ([1966] 2 All ER 536 at 547, [1967] 1 AC 853 at 905):

c

'The present case is, however, essentially different. The German Democratic Republic was set up by the U.S.S.R. and it derived its authority and status from the government of the U.S.S.R. So the only question could be whether or not it was set up as a sovereign state; but the certificate of our government requires us to hold that it was not set up as a sovereign state because it requires us to hold that the U.S.S.R. remained de jure sovereign and therefore did not voluntarily transfer its sovereignty

d

to the German Democratic Republic. Moreover, if the German Democratic Republic did not become a sovereign state at its inception, there is no suggestion that it has at any subsequent time attempted to deprive the U.S.S.R of rights which were not granted to it at its inception. The courts of this country must disregard any declarations of the government of the U.S.S.R. in so far as they conflict with the certificate of Her Majesty's Secretary of State, and we must therefore hold that the

e

U.S.S.R. set up the German Democratic Republic not as a sovereign state, but as an organisation subordinate to the U.S.S.R. If that is so, then mere declarations by the government of the German Democratic Republic that it is acting as the government of an independent state cannot be regarded as proof that its initial status has been altered, and we must regard the acts of the German Democratic Republic, its government organs and officers as acts done with the consent of the government of

f

the U.S.S.R. as the government entitled to exercise governing authority. It appears to me to be impossible for any de jure sovereign governing authority to disclaim responsibility for acts done by subordinate bodies which it has set up and which have not attempted to usurp its sovereignty. So in my opinion the courts of this country cannot treat as nullities acts done by or on behalf of the German Democratic Republic. De facto recognition is appropriate—and in my view is only appropriate—

g

where the new government have usurped power against the will of the de jure sovereign. I would think that where a sovereign has granted independence to a dependency any recognition of the new state would be a recognition de jure.'

Lord Wilberforce reserved for further consideration whether the non-recognition of a government or, I think, a state, would necessarily lead to the English courts treating all

h

its legislative activities as being a nullity or whether, in the interests of justice and common sense, where no consideration of public policy to the contrary has to prevail, it might not be possible to take cognisance of the actual facts or realities found to exist in the territory in question, and he instances private rights or acts of everyday occurrence or perfunctory acts of administration (see [1966] 2 All ER 536 at 577, [1967] 1 AC 853 at 954). I see great force in this reservation, since it is one thing to treat a state or government

j

as being 'without the law', but quite another to treat the inhabitants of its territory as 'outlaws' who cannot effectively marry, beget legitimate children, purchase goods on credit or undertake countless day-to-day activities having legal consequences. However, that is not this case. Lord Wilberforce's conclusion, like that of Lord Reid's, was that there was no inconsistency in accepting that there was no recognised government in the Eastern Zone apart from the governing authority of the USSR and at the same time

attributing legal validity to a law of that 'government' as a subordinate or dependent
body (see [1966] 2 All ER 536 at 582, [1967] 1 AC 853 at 961).

Steyn J, in a careful judgment of outstanding clarity, concluded that the courts should
not treat the government of the Republic of Ciskei in the same way as they had treated
the GDR and its government. He said:

> 'In my judgment there is an essential difference between the *Carl-Zeiss* case and
> the present case. In the *Carl-Zeiss* case there was a conclusive certificate that the USSR
> still exercised governing authority in the GDR. In the present case the certificate
> records that Her Majesty's government "does not have a formal position as regards
> the exercise of governing authority over the territory of the Ciskei". It was suggested
> that on this point the certificate is less than clear. I disagree. It is plainly a carefully
> considered certificate, given by the executive to the judiciary, and its meaning is
> beyond question. It was also suggested that Her Majesty's government does not have
> a formal position on the relevant matter, because it is no longer its practice to
> recognise governments. This explanation may be right. The fact is, however, that
> there is no certification to the effect that South Africa is still the governing authority
> in Ciskei. Inevitably, therefore, the bank and Ciskei must rely on other evidence for
> the proposition that South Africa still exercises governing authority in Ciskei. In
> my judgment, there are no materials available before me which warrant such an
> inference. Indeed, such materials as have been placed before me point the other
> way. As I have already mentioned, Ciskei placed before me the Status of Ciskei Act
> 1981. It was submitted that on this point I may not look at it. Clearly, it is not
> permissible to have regard to any declarations of the South African state or of Ciskei
> in so far as they conflict with executive certificates of Her Majesty's government.
> However, on the point presently under consideration those executive certificates are
> silent. In the circumstances it is therefore permissible to refer to the Status of Ciskei
> Act 1981. Section 1(2) of that Act unambiguously provides that the Republic of
> South Africa shall cease to have any authority over Ciskei. I readily accept that there
> is a distinct possibility that the reality of the relationship between Ciskei and South
> Africa may be very different from the impression created by the South African
> statute. But there are no materials from which the inference can be drawn that the
> Republic of South Africa is still the governing authority of Ciskei. Certainly, it is
> impossible to infer from the mere fact that Ciskei is unrecognised by Her Majesty's
> government that South Africa is still the governing authority in Ciskei territory, or
> so viewed by Her Majesty's government. After all, recognition has in the past from
> time to time been withheld by Her Majesty's government on political grounds
> unrelated to the question whether the entity is in truth an independent state: see D
> W Greig 'Unrecognised Governments in English Law' [1967] LQR 96 at 97.
> Whether that was the motivation in the case of Ciskei, one does not know. But it
> does show that counsel's proposition, put forward on the basis of the inexorable
> march of logic, is, in fact, a non sequitur. It follows that the line of reasoning which
> prevailed in the *Carl-Zeiss* case is not apposite in the present case. The *Carl-Zeiss* case
> was decided on very special facts, which were fundamentally different from the
> facts in the present case.'

I am not sure to what extent the judge attached importance to there being a certificate
that the USSR *still exercised* governing authority in the GDR. It may well have been a slip
of the tongue or pen, but in fact what was certified was the USSR was de jure *entitled* to
exercise governing authority in the Eastern Zone, not that it did so. In the case of Ciskei
territory, similarly there is no certificate that the Republic of South Africa in fact
exercised governing authority. What was left to be inferred from the Eastern Zone
certificate is expressed in the Ciskei certificate: 'does not have a formal position as regards
the exercise of governing authority' (my emphasis).

There is, however, an apparent contrast between the two certificates when it comes to
entitlement to exercise governing authority. In each case the certificates are conclusive that

the GDR or, as the case may be, the Republic of Ciskei are not recognised as independent

a   sovereign states. It follows from this that the courts must hold that neither the GDR or its government nor the Republic of Ciskei or its government was in law capable of an executive, administrative or legislative act at the relevant times unless enabled by some superior authority. In the case of the GDR, the certificate pointed expressly to where that superior authority was to be found, namely the sovereign state of the USSR. The question for our consideration is whether the Ciskei certificates, either alone or taken in

b   conjunction with other evidence, point to any superior authority, of which the courts can take cognisance, as supplying the requisite authority to enable the government of the Republic of Ciskei to undertake executive, administrative or legislative acts. In reviewing and evaluating that other evidence, we must disregard any declarations or acts of the Republic of South Africa or of the Republic of Ciskei which conflict with the certificates of the Secretary of State, just as the House of Lords disregarded such declarations by the

c   government of the USSR.

Where does that leave us? We must disregard s 1(1) of the Status of Ciskei Act 1981 which declares the Republic of Ciskei to be a sovereign and independent state ceasing to be part of the Republic of South Africa and s 1(2) which declares that the Republic of South Africa will cease to exercise any authority over the territory since this subsection is clearly consequential on sub-s (1). We must also disregard s 1(1) of the Republic of Ciskei

d   Constitution Act 1981. However we can, and I think must, take cognisance of the remainder of those Acts, notwithstanding that, absent those sections, they may take on a somewhat different character. Thus s 3(1) of the Status of Ciskei Act 1981, which provides:

e   'The Legislative Assembly of Ciskei, as constituted in terms of the National States Constitution Act, 1971 (Act No. 21 of 1971), may, subject to the provisions of subsection (2) [which dispenses with the need for the assent of the President of the Republic of South Africa], make laws (including a constitution) for the Ciskei in the manner prescribed by the said Act, and may in any such law provide for the making of such laws by any authority other than the said Legislative Assembly'

f   becomes a straightforward delegation of legislative power which could be revoked in the same way as it had been conferred, namely by a subsequent legislative act of the Republic of South Africa.

We also know the constitutional history of the territory of Ciskei, to which I have already referred, and we can take judicial notice of the fact that the Republic of South Africa is a sovereign state, recognised by Her Majesty's government, and that it was entitled to exercise sovereignty over the territory of Ciskei until the passing of the Status

g   of Ciskei Act 1981. If then we disregard s 1 of that Act, as we must, there are no materials from which we could infer that this situation has changed. Indeed, the certified fact that 'Her Majesty's Government has made representation to the South African Government in relation to certain matters occurring in Ciskei and others of the Homelands to which South Africa has purported to grant independence' gives rise to a clear inference that Her Majesty's government regards the Republic of South Africa as continuing to be *entitled* to

h   exercise sovereign authority over the territory. The further certified fact that the government of the Republic has not in general made any positive response gives rise only to an inference that the government of the Republic is not, in general, willing to exercise the authority which it has de jure, preferring to leave this to the government of Ciskei. This is immaterial for, as Lord Reid said, no de jure governing authority can disclaim responsibility for acts done by subordinate bodies which it has set up and which have not

j   attempted to usurp its authority (see [1966] 2 All ER 536 at 547, [1967] 1 AC 853 at 906). There is no evidence whatever that the Republic of Ciskei or its government has attempted to do that.

It follows that in my judgment the legal status of the Republic of Ciskei and its government is indistinguishable from that which obtained in the case of the GDR and its government at the time with which the *Carl-Zeiss* case was concerned.

I would therefore allow the appeal and declare that the government of the Republic of the Ciskei has locus standi in the courts of this country as being a subordinate body set *a* up by the Republic of South Africa to act on its behalf.

NOURSE LJ. I agree. The letters from the Foreign and Commonwealth Office of 1 and 16 May 1986 and the written parliamentary answers of 1980 are set out in full in the judgment of Sir John Donaldson MR and I need not repeat them.

In *The Arantzazu Mendi* [1939] 1 All ER 719 at 721–722, [1939] AC 256 at 264 Lord *b* Atkin, having stated that the correct course in a case of this kind is for a letter of inquiry to be written by the court to the Secretary of State, said this:

'I pause here to say that not only is this the correct procedure, but it is the only procedure by which the court can inform itself itself of the material fact whether the party sought to be impleaded, or whose property is sought to be affected, is a foreign sovereign state . . . The reason is, I think, obvious. Our state cannot speak *c* with two voices on such a matter, the judiciary saying one thing, the executive another. Our sovereign has to decide whom he will recognise as a fellow sovereign in the family of states, and the relations of the foreign state with ours in the matter of state immunities must flow from that decision alone.'

In the present case we have to inform ourselves of the answer to the question posed in *d* the letter to the Foreign and Commonwealth Office of 9 May 1986. That question, which was evidently drawn with the terms of the certificate in *Carl-Zeiss-Stiftung v Rayner & Keeler Ltd (No 2)* [1966] 2 All ER 536, [1967] 1 AC 853 well in mind, was in the following form:

'Which state, if any, does Her Majesty's Government recognise as (a) entitled to exercise or (b) exercising governing authority in respect of the territory in Southern *e* Africa known as Ciskei. Has such recognition been de jure or de facto?'

Although it seems that the amicus curiae may have had some reservations on the point, I think it clear that that question, being directed towards recognition of a state, was one which could have been answered without any offence to the new practice initiated by the 1980 parliamentary answers. *f*

In any event, we can only inform ourselves of the answer to the question by referring to the letters of 1 and 16 May 1986, which, so far as material, contained the following information: (1) (1 May) Her Majesty's government does not recognise the Republic of Ciskei as an independent sovereign state, either de jure or de facto; (2) (16 May) Her Majesty's government (a) has not taken and does not have a formal position as regards the exercise of governing authority over the territory of Ciskei, (b) does not have any dealings *g* with the Government of the Republic of Ciskei, but (c) has made representations to the South African government in relation to certain matters occurring in Ciskei. The clear effect of (1) above is to inform us that it is not the Republic of Ciskei which is recognised by Her Majesty's government as entitled to exercise or exercising governing authority in respect of the territory known as Ciskei. It is more difficult to be certain of what we are informed by (2) above. There may, it seems, be a conflict between (a) on the one hand *h* and (b) and (c) on the other. To say that Her Majesty's government does not have a formal position as regards the exercise of governing authority over the territory of Ciskei suggests that it has not decided with whom it will deal in relation to that territory. But to say that it does not have any dealings with the government of the Republic of Ciskei but has made representation to the South African government in relation to certain matters occurring there suggests that to date all dealings have been with the government *j* of South Africa.

The rule that the judiciary and the executive must speak with one voice presupposes that the judiciary can understand what the executive has said. In most cases there could hardly be any doubt in the matter. But in a case like the present, where there is a doubt, the judiciary must resolve it in the only way they know, which is to look at the question

and then construe the answer given. It is not for the judiciary to criticise any obscurity
a in the expressions of the executive, or to enquire into their origins or policy. They must
take them as they stand.

Reverting to the question posed in the present case and to the letter of 16 May, I have
come to a clear conclusion that we are informed by (2) above that Her Majesty's
government recognises the Republic of South Africa as de jure entitled to exercise
governing authority in respect of the territory known as Ciskei. For this purpose I find it
b unnecessary to look beyond the terms of the question and the terms of the answer. I
agree with Steyn J that what we have is plainly a carefully considered certificate. I would
also agree that once its language has been correctly understood its meaning is beyond
question. But I am of the opinion, and this is where I respectfully disagree with the
judge, that it has effectively answered the question posed.

In my view it is essential to bear in mind that the question posed distinguished
c between (a) entitlement to exercise, and (b) actual exercise of governing authority.
Accordingly, the statement that Her Majesty's government 'has not taken and does not
have a formal position as regards *the exercise* of governing authority over the territory of
Ciskei' (my emphasis) reaffirms that it has not recognised the Republic of Ciskei as de
facto exercising governing authority there and leaves the question open so far as the
Republic of South Africa is concerned. On the other hand, the statements that Her
d Majesty's government does not have any dealings with the government of the Republic
of Ciskei, but has made representations to the South African government in relation to
certain matters occurring in Ciskei, signify that it regards the latter government as being
the responsible authority in relation to matters occurring there. And it could only do
that if it recognised the Republic of South Africa as de jure *entitled to exercise* governing
authority in that territory.

e For these reasons I am of the opinion that the letters of 1 and 16 May 1986 are in
substance to the same effect as the certificates which were given in the *Carl-Zeiss* case. For
the additional reasons given by Sir John Donaldson MR I agree with him that the legal
status of the Republic of Ciskei and its government is indistinguishable from that which
obtained in the case of the German Democratic Republic and its government at the time
with which the *Carl-Zeiss* case was concerned. That is enough to dispose of this appeal in
f favour of the appellants.

It therefore becomes unnecessary to express a view on any of the other arguments
which were advanced in support of the appeal, some of which were not put to Steyn J
and some of which were of general interest and importance in the field of public
international law.

I too would allow this appeal and make the declaration proposed by Sir John Donaldson
g MR.

GLIDEWELL LJ. I agree with both the judgments which have been delivered. There
is nothing I can usefully add.

Appeal allowed. Issues to be reheard by another judge of the Commercial Court. Costs in Court of
h *Appeal and below reserved to judge.*

Solicitors: *Durrant Piesse* (for the bank); *Barlow Lyde & Gilbert* (for Ciskei); *Victor Mishcon
& Co* (for the contractor); *Treasury Solicitor.*

Diana Procter   Barrister.

Bank of Tokyo Ltd v Karoon and another

COURT OF APPEAL, CIVIL DIVISION
ACKNER AND ROBERT GOFF LJJ
3, 4, 5 APRIL, 24 MAY 1984

Conflict of laws − Foreign proceedings − Restraint of foreign proceedings − Circumstances in which court will restrain prosecution of foreign proceedings − Public policy − Bank using information obtained from New York subsidiary in evidence in proceedings in England against respondent − Respondent commencing action in New York against New York subsidiary for breach of contract − Whether New York action penalising bank for using information as evidence in English proceedings − Whether bank and New York subsidiary to be treated as single legal entity − Whether English court appropriate forum for action by respondent against New York subsidiary − Whether any principle of public policy that only nominal damages recoverable where relevant and admissible evidence is improperly obtained − Whether, if nominal damages only recoverable, grant of injunction justified − Whether New York action involving relitigation of matters already litigated in England − Whether bank entitled to injunction restraining respondent from carrying on New York action.

The respondent was an Iranian national and chief operating officer of an Iranian company, M Ltd, in which he owned nearly all the shares. He maintained a personal bank account with BTTC, a New York bank which was a wholly-owned subsidiary of the appellant, BT, a Japanese bank carrying on business in London, and he also maintained both personal and company accounts in London with BT. In 1979 the respondent left Iran following a revolution in that country. In February 1980 BT received a letter from those in control of M Ltd in Iran advising that the respondent had been sentenced in his absence to ten years' imprisonment and that his and the company's property had been taken over by the Iranian government. The letter requested BT to transfer all balances in his and the company's accounts to Iran. The respondent subsequently instructed BT to transfer all funds held by it to an account which he maintained with another bank. BT issued an interpleader summons in England to determine whether the moneys which it held were payable to the respondent or to M Ltd. The respondent issued a summons to strike out the interpleader proceedings claiming that the moneys in question were his own, that they had not emanated from M Ltd and that neither M Ltd nor those controlling it had any arguable claim to the moneys. That claim made by the respondent caused BT to make inquiries of BTTC regarding the respondent's accounts held by BTTC. BTTC supplied information about the accounts to BT, which in turn used that information in its evidence opposing the respondent's application to strike out the interpleader proceedings. The application to strike out was dismissed by a judge, who ordered that the interpleader issue be tried. The respondent then commenced proceedings in New York against both BT and BTTC claiming damages for, inter alia, breach of confidence, breach of contract, violation of privacy, conspiracy and wrongful inducement of breach of contract. BT applied to the High Court in England for an injunction restraining the respondent from carrying on the New York action. The judge hearing the application decided that the New York proceedings against BT ought to be restrained but that the proceedings against BTTC need not to be restrained, and he made orders having that effect. BT appealed, contending that the injunction should extend to the action against BTTC on grounds of public policy because (i) arising out of the principle that a litigant should be able to take all proper steps to put relevant evidence before the court, there was an overriding public policy that the court should protect its own jurisdiction by ensuring that BT was not penalised by means of the New York action for having obtained relevant evidence for the interpleader proceedings, (ii) even if BT had improperly obtained information from BTTC that information was relevant and admissible evidence in the interpleader proceedings and accordingly the respondent would only be entitled to nominal damages in England, and (iii) public policy required

that there should be finality of litigation and the New York action would involve
a relitigating matters already litigated in the interpleader proceedings. BT further
contended that the English court was the appropriate forum for the trial of any breach of
duty owed by BTTC to the respondent.

Held – The appeal would be dismissed for the following reasons—
(1) The court would not treat BT and BTTC as one and the same, and on the basis that
b they were separate legal entities the respondent's New York action against BTTC did not
infringe English public policy, because whereas BT had put the confidential information
before the court and was seeking the protection of the court for doing so the respondent's
cause of action was against BTTC for breaches of duty in divulging the information to
BT in the first place and that action against BTTC could not be said to penalise BT for
using the information in the interpleader proceedings (see p 476 *a* to *d* and p 486 *d e*,
c post); *Laker Airways Ltd v Sabena Airlines and KLM Airlines* (1984) 731 F 2d 909 considered.
(2) The English court was not the appropriate forum for the action brought by the
respondent against BTTC because the action was in every sense a United States action,
since the contract on which the claim was based was made in New York with a New York
bank, the proper law of the contract was New York law, any breach of contract arising
out of the divulgence of the information took place in New York, and the balance of
d juridical advantage was in favour of the respondent's action remaining in New York (see
p 477 *a* to *e* and p 486 *h* to p 487 *b*, post).
(3) (Per Ackner LJ) It was doubtful whether there was a principle of public policy
preventing damages other than nominal damages from being recovered where evidence
which was relevant and admissible had been improperly obtained, but even if there was
the fact that damages would be limited to nominal damages did not justify the grant of
e an injunction since the respondent would still have a good cause of action (see p 476 *d e j*,
post).
(4) (Per Robert Goff LJ) The principle of finality of litigation did not apply because the
respondent was not seeking to relitigate in the New York proceedings a matter which
had been the subject of a judgment in England but was instead seeking to obtain redress
from a bank in New York, in respect of the disclosure of confidential information by that
f bank in New York, and that cause of action had not been the subject of a judgment in
England (see p 485 *f h j*, post).
Per Robert Goff LJ. Observations on whether the same principles ought to govern the
grant of a stay of English proceedings and grant of an injunction restraining a party from
instituting or prosecuting foreign proceedings (see p 483 *e f*, 484 *a* to *c j* to p 485 *e*, post);
dictum of Lord Scarman in *Castanho v Brown & Root (UK) Ltd* [1981] 1 All ER at 151
g considered.

Notes
For general principles governing stay of proceedings, see 8 Halsbury's Laws (4th edn)
paras 787, 788, and for cases on the subject, see 11 Digest (Reissue) 631–633, 1686–1689.

h **Cases referred to in judgment**
Abidin Daver, The [1984] 1 All ER 470, [1984] AC 398, [1984] 2 WLR 196, HL.
Armstrong v Armstrong [1892] P 98.
Atlantic Star, The Atlantic Star (owners) v Bona Spes (owners) [1973] 2 All ER 175, [1974]
   AC 436, [1973] 2 WLR 795, HL.
Bethell v Peace (1971) 441 F 2d 495, US Ct of Apps.
j *Booth v Leycester* (1837) 1 Keen 579, 48 ER 430.
British Airways Board v Laker Airways Ltd [1983] 3 All ER 375, [1984] QB 142, [1983] 3
   WLR 544, CA.
Bushby v Munday (1821) 5 Madd 297, [1814–23] All ER Rep 304, 56 ER 908.
Carron Iron Co v Maclaren Dawson & Stainton (1855) 5 HL Cas 416, 10 ER 961, HL.
Castanho v Brown & Root (UK) Ltd [1981] 1 All ER 143, [1981] AC 557, [1980] 3 WLR
   991, HL.

Chapman v Honig [1963] 2 All ER 513, [1963] 2 QB 502, [1963] 3 WLR 19, CA.
Christian v Christian (1897) 67 LJP 18.
Cohen v Rothfield [1919] 1 KB 410, [1918–19] All ER Rep 260, CA.   *a*
Cole v Cunningham (1890) 133 US 107, US SC.
Distillers Co (Biochemicals) Ltd v Thompson [1971] 1 All ER 694, [1971] AC 458, [1971] 2
    WLR 441, PC.
Distin, Re, ex p Ormiston (1871) 24 LT 197.
Ellerman Lines Ltd v Read [1928] 2 KB 144, [1928] All ER Rep 415, CA.   *b*
Enoch v Zaretzky Bock & Co [1910] 1 KB 327, CA.
European Asian Bank AG v Punjab Sind Bank [1982] 2 Lloyd's Rep 356, CA.
Fallon v Calvert [1960] 1 All ER 281, [1960] 2 QB 201, [1960] 2 WLR 346, CA.
Graham v Maxwell (1849) 1 Mac & G 71, 47 ER 1043, LC.
Gulf Oil Corp v Gilbert (1947) 330 US 501, US SC.
Hyman v Helm (1883) 24 Ch D 53, CA.   *c*
Laker Airways Ltd v Sabena Airlines and KLM Airlines (1984) 731 F 2d 909, US Ct of Apps.
Lett v Lett [1906] 1 IR 618.
McHenry v Lewis (1882) 22 Ch D 397, CA.
MacShannon v Rockware Glass Ltd, Fyfe v Redpath Dorman Long Ltd [1978] 1 All ER 625,
    [1978] AC 795, [1978] 2 WLR 362, HL.
Moore v Moore (1896) 12 TLR 221, CA.   *d*
North Carolina Estate Co, Re (1889) 5 TLR 328.
Peruvian Guano Co v Bockwoldt (1883) 23 Ch D 225, [1881–5] All ER Rep 715, CA.
Piper Aircraft Co v Reyno (1981) 454 US 235, US SC.
St Pierre v South American Stores (Gath & Chaves) Ltd [1936] 1 KB 382, [1935] All ER Rep
    408, CA; *subsequent proceedings* [1937] 3 All ER 349, CA.
Sim v Robinow (1892) 19 R 665, Ct of Sess.   *e*
Smith Kline & French Laboratories Ltd v Bloch [1983] 2 All ER 72, [1983] 1 WLR 730, CA.
Société du Gaz de Paris v SA de Navigation Les Armateurs Français 1926 SC(HL) 13.
Tournier v National Provincial and Union Bank of England [1924] 1 KB 461, [1923] All ER
    Rep 550, CA.
Trapp v Mackie [1979] 1 All ER 489, [1979] 1 WLR 377, HL.
Trendtex Trading Corp v Crédit Suisse [1980] 3 All ER 721, [1980] QB 629, [1980] 3 WLR   *f*
    367, CA; *affd* [1981] 3 All ER 520, [1982] AC 679, [1981] 3 WLR 766, HL.
Tropaioforos, The (No 2) [1962] 1 Lloyd's Rep 410.

Interlocutory appeal
Bank of Tokyo Ltd (BT) appealed against the decision of Bingham J on 7 November 1983
whereby he refused BT's application for an injunction restraining the first respondent,
Majid Karoon, from taking any further steps in an action begun by Mr Karoon in New   *g*
York against BT and Bank of Tokyo Trust Co (BTTC), a wholly-owned subsidiary of BT.
The second respondent was Maritime Co Ltd. The facts are set out in the judgment of
Ackner LJ.

Leonard Hoffmann QC and *D T Donaldson* for BT.   *h*
Nicholas Strauss for Mr Karoon.
The second respondent was not represented.

                                                              Cur adv vult

24 May. The following judgments were delivered.   *j*

ACKNER LJ. The respondent, Mr Karoon, is neither a national of nor resident in this
country. He is an Iranian citizen who left Iran at the time of the revolution in November
1979 and is now living in France. The Bank of Tokyo Trust Co (BTTC) is a New York
corporation which is a wholly-owned subsidiary of the Bank of Tokyo Ltd (BT), the
appellants, a Japanese bank carrying on business in London.

On 7 November 1983 Bingham J refused to grant an injunction restraining Mr Karoon
a from taking any further steps in an action that he had begun in New York against BTTC,
or commencing or prosecuting any other proceedings relating to the same subject matter
before any other court than the English High Court. It is against this refusal that BT now
appeals. He did however order that Mr Karoon be restrained from continuing the
proceedings against BT, who had been joined as co-defendants with BTTC. Against this
decision there is no cross-appeal.

b   The circumstances out of which his claim in the New York action arose can be shortly
stated. Although Mr Karoon and his wife and children were able to leave Iran, the rest of
Mr Karoon's family and his wife's family are still in Iran and he has fears for their safety.
From 1961 onwards he was the chief operating officer of an Iranian company called
Maritime Co Ltd (Maritime) in which he owned nearly all the shares. Maritime carried
on a shipping business. For some years prior to his departure from Iran he maintained a
c personal bank account with BTTC. He also maintained both a personal and a company
account with BT. Following his departure from Iran, Mr Karoon transferred
approximately $685,000 from his personal account with BTTC to his personal account
with BT. He also instructed BT to transfer all moneys from the company account to his
personal account.

In February 1980 BT received a letter from Maritime in Iran to advise them that on 3
d February 1980 Mr Karoon had been sentenced in absentia to ten years' imprisonment
and that his and the company's property had been taken over by the government of Iran.
BT was asked to transfer all balances to Iran. BT responded to the effect that all the
company's accounts had been closed prior to their receipt of this letter, on the instructions
of the account's sole signatory (Mr Karoon), and that under English law it would be a
breach of confidence to make any disclosure regarding a customer's personal affairs
e without his prior authorisation. They also advised Mr Karoon of their receipt of this
letter and their response. He thereupon instructed them to transfer funds they were
holding to an account which he maintained with another bank. BT was concerned with
its position. If it did not carry out his instructions it might be liable to him. On the other
hand, if it did carry out his instructions it might be liable to those now in charge of
Maritime. Accordingly, on 21 March 1980 BT issued an interpleader summons to
f determine whether the money which it held was payable to Mr Karoon or to Maritime.

On 15 April 1980 Mr Karoon issued a summons to strike out the interpleader
proceedings under RSC Ord 18, r 19. In his affidavit he swore, inter alia, that 'On 3rd
December 1979 I remitted $US685,800 of my own money from my account at the
bank's branch in New York to the bank . . . These moneys had not originated from the
company'.

g   He explained how they were placed on deposit and that on 27 December 1979 there
was due to him $US689,421·88. He contended that Maritime could have no arguable
claim to these moneys, even if proceedings were appropriate in respect of the English
funds. He also expressed concern that, if the Iranian government knew about the funds
in London, his relations would be used as a lever to force him to remit the money to Iran.

In reply to this affidavit Mr Saunders, an officer of BT, swore another affidavit in
h which he said:

'1. Inquiries have been made of The Bank of Tokyo Trust Company, New York
in respect of a remittance in the sum of U.S. Dollars 685,800 credited to the First
Defendant's External Savings Account Number 61817-3 on 5th December 1979 in
order to establish the source of the said money.

j   2. I am informed and verily believe that the said sum was made up from two
fixed deposits ((a) and (b) respectively) which were automatically renewable every
three months and which had been pre-matured and credited to the First Defendant's
New York checking account (Number 121-004-775) in order to cover the said
payment. Fixed deposit (a) was valued at U.S. Dollars 183,797·83 and (b) at U.S.
Dollars 497,803·98.

3. Fixed Deposit (a) was opened on 14th December 1978 with a transfer of U.S.

Dollars 170,000 from a savings account maintained by the First Defendant, which
account was opened on 5th April 1976 with initial funds of U.S. Dollars 425,000 by a
means of a transfer from the First Defendant's Checking Account Number 121–
004–775. I am informed that the sum of U.S. Dollars 511,000 had been credited to
the said checking account on 30th December 1975 by order of Fairfield International
Limited of 227 Park Avenue New York. Prior to 14th December 1978, the said
savings account had been credited with U.S. Dollars 115,200, being the proceeds of
a cheque drawn on Midland Marine Bank, New York by order of Mowbrays Tug b
and Barge Sales Corporation.

4. Fixed Deposit (b) was opened on 23rd April 1979 with a transfer of U.S. Dollars
473,000 from the said savings account maintained by the First Defendant. The
account had been credited on 11th April with the proceeds of a cheque for U.S.
Dollars 32,569·75 drawn on Wells Fargo Bank New York by order of Utah House
Fire Insurance Company and on 23rd April with the proceeds of a cheque for U.S. c
Dollars 441,992·01 drawn on Chase Manhattan Bank by order of Adams and Porter
Incorporated.'

The affidavit was never served on Maritime, who were at that time not party to the
proceedings to strike out. The application, which was heard by Robert Goff J, failed. A
note of his judgment was before Bingham J, and the relevant part to the proceedings
before him was quoted by the judge as follows: d

'There were certain accounts in the name of Majid Karoon and certain accounts
in the name of Maritime Co. Certain moneys were transferred from New York
which Majid Karoon says are his. There has been an amalgamation of accounts
carried out in accordance with instructions given on 24 December 1979 and 20
February 1980 . . . Finally I am asked to look at the evidence to find that a substantial e
part of the moneys must belong to Majid Karoon. I am invited to look at the letter
and to find that it makes no claim on Majid Karoon's assets. The difficulty is that I
am faced with one party's evidence. The bank is in the middle and can only act
fairly, which it cannot do not knowing the full facts. It would be quite wrong for
me to pre-empt the situation on one party's evidence, especially having regard to
the history which shows that Majid Karoon has not sought to keep his own and f
Maritime's moneys separate. No accurate assumptions on a split can be made. It
seems to me that the workers council letter is written in such English as the bank
has reasonable grounds to assume that a claim may be pressed not only against
Maritime's accounts but also against Majid Karoon's accounts in so far as the money
is in origin Maritime's money which he has transferred into his own account. He
may have acted in breach of his obligations to the company. In my judgment there g
are reasonable grounds that the bank may be sued for not only Maritime's money
but also that money held by Majid Karoon. The bank was fully entitled to interplead.
I cannot accede to the application. To interplead was a natural reflex of the bank.'

On 4 March 1983 an interpleader issue was eventually ordered. The order was by
consent, no attempt being made to limit the order to the English as opposed to the
American moneys. It reads as follows: h

'1. The Plaintiffs [BT] be forthwith discharged from any liability to either of the
Defendants in respect of any monies the subject matter of these proceedings and
that no action be brought in respect thereof against the Plaintiffs by either of the
Defendants, including an action by the First Defendants acting in the name of the
Second Defendants.
2. The Plaintiffs do pay the monies the subject matter of these proceedings after j
deduction of their usual banking charges into Court as and when each of the current
Special Deposits matures and that the monies presently held on call be paid together
with the first Special Deposit money on maturity thereof and that meanwhile the
Plaintiffs hold the said monies to the direction of the Court.'

The complaint in the New York proceedings is based on BTTC's voluntary disclosure
a   to BT of information relating to his account in New York. This disclosure is alleged to
have been a breach of its contractual duty of confidence to Mr Karoon, to have violated
Mr Karoon's 'right of privacy', and made in conspiracy with BT to injure Mr Karoon. A
total of $4m damages is claimed, $1m as punitive damages for the breach of the 'right of
privacy' and the conspiracy, additional to the $1m claimed for 'special damage' for each
of the three causes of action.

b   Before Bingham J counsel for BT submitted that the New York proceedings would
cause injustice to his clients for a number of reasons, which the judge summarised under
five headings. The first two can be taken together, it being submitted: whatever the
prospects of success, the New York action is an attempt to penalise BT for availing itself
of the interpleader procedure in England and complying with the Rules of the Supreme
Court; the New York action would involve relitigating a matter already litigated in
c   England, ie whether an interpleader should have been ordered in respect of moneys
remitted from the United States; as such, the action is vexatious and oppressive. It is in
truth doubly vexatious and oppressive because it has no reasonable prospect of success,
since Mr Karoon will be quite unable to show that he has suffered any damage, because
Robert Goff J would have made the selfsame order if BT had not relied on the information
provided to it by BTTC.

d   The three further points of counsel for BT submitted to the judge can again be stated
as one proposition, namely that an English court is the forum conveniens because it can
without difficulty resolve what duty of confidence, if any, was owed by the New York
bank in these circumstances to its client Mr Karoon. *Tournier v National Provincial and
Union Bank of England* [1924] 1 KB 461, [1923] All ER Rep 550 is the source of the law in
both jurisdictions. By contrast, a New York judge would be faced with difficult questions
e   concerning the duty of an English litigant in an English interpleader. Moreover, if Mr
Karoon were able to establish that he would have succeeded in striking out the
interpleader proceedings had not BTTC provided the information to BT, he would still
have to establish, in order to claim damages, that the money in London belonged to him
and that issue has to be decided in London. Mr Karoon, moreover, has no legitimate
juridicial advantages in proceedings in New York.

f   Before Bingham J no submission appears to have been made to the judge that a
different approach might be justified to the New York action, according to whether one
was considering the position of BTTC or the position of BT. Neither party asked the
judge to differentiate between BT and BTTC in any order he made. However, in his
judgment, viewing the two companies as two separate legal entities, Bingham J concluded
that they should be treated separately. In regard to the New York action, in so far as it
g   related to BTTC, he said:

'It is an action brought in New York against a bank incorporated and carrying on
business there. Mr Karoon, an Iranian citizen resident in France, had an account
with that bank. Although Mr Karoon has advanced three causes of action against
BTTC (breach of confidence, invasion of privacy and conspiracy) it seems plain that
h   his central complaint against BTTC arises from its voluntary disclosure to BT of
information relating to his account. Whether this disclosure involved a breach of
contractual duty, or of Mr Karoon's right to privacy, on the part of BTTC must be
determined according to the law of New York. Whether BTTC was guilty of an
actionable conspiracy may also fall to be decided under that law, although this cause
of action appears to be something of a makeweight. The disclosure by BT to the
j   English court forms no part of Mr Karoon's cause of action against BTTC. That
disclosure does have a significant bearing on Mr Karoon's ability to prove actual
damage flowing from the disclosure, since he could show none if Robert Goff J
would have made the same order even without the information concerning Mr
Karoon's American transactions in Mr Saunders's affidavit. To that extent the action
does involve inquiry into what Robert Goff J would have done on different evidence,

an inquiry which would be best carried out by this court. It is, however, an inquiry which a New York court could doubtless undertake and resolve. Mr Karoon may have a cause of action for invasion of privacy available to him in New York which is not available here. It would certainly appear that his chances of obtaining substantial damages on a punitive or exemplary basis are better there. His ability to sue in New York on a contingency fee basis may not be a juridical advantage (see *Smith Kline & French Laboratories Ltd v Bloch* [1983] 2 All ER 72 at 86, [1983] 1 WLR 730 at 747) and is, in my view, counterbalanced by BTTC's inability to recover costs if successful, but is certainly not an argument against allowing the New York action to proceed against BTTC. Overall, I do not regard an injunction as appropriate to restrain the action in so far as it lies against BTTC. If the action were to proceed, BTTC might, of course, win or lose; and if it lost the damages might be large, or nominal, or even non-existent. But all these seem to me to be matters best entertained and resolved in the New York court which would be applying its own law to events very largely occurring within its own jurisdiction.'

In reaching his decision relative to BTTC, Bingham J was applying the principles to which he made specific reference, as laid down or reflected in the decisions of *The Atlantic Star, Atlantic Star (owners) v Bona Spes (owners)* [1973] 2 All ER 175, [1974] AC 436, *MacShannon v Rockware Glass Ltd* [1978] 1 All ER 625, [1978] AC 795, *Castanho v Brown & Root (UK) Ltd* [1981] 1 All ER 143, [1981] AC 557 and *Trendtex Trading Corp v Crédit Suisse* [1980] 3 All ER 721, [1980] QB 629. These principles were not in dispute between the parties.

He then turned his attention to the New York action against BT, commenting that the claim assumed a somewhat different aspect. He said:

'The crux of Mr Karoon's complaint against BT is that it acted unlawfully in seeking information from BTTC. The allegation is made that BT gratuitously revealed this information, but counsel for Mr Karoon accepted that the revelation was not gratuitous and acknowledged the difficulty of maintaining that BT had no interest in revealing that information. BT is also accused of conspiracy and inducement of breach of contract by BTTC, but these complaints arise out of the same factual premise, namely the request for information made by BT to BTTC. This was a request made by BT in the context of its role as a party seeking to interplead under RSC Ord 17. In his original affidavit, Mr Saunders had made no overt reference to these moneys transferred by BTTC to BT. Mr Karoon raised a clear issue concerning them in his affidavit of 25 April. BT had either to let the matter (and the moneys) go, with the risk that it might later be held accountable for the moneys, or make such enquiries as it could (or, if it had already made inquiry, inform the court of the result). Leaving entirely on one side the question whether, on information being requested, BTTC should, as a matter of New York law, have complied with the request, I think that two significant questions of English law arise in respect of BT's conduct: whether it was reasonable and proper for BT, in seeking to protect its own interests, to request information from BTTC; and whether, in pursuance of its duty as a party applying to interplead it was proper for BT to seek to lay before the court all evidence within its power relevant to the application. This is a lis between a bank carrying on business in London and a London customer of that bank arising out of English interpleader proceedings to which both were party. Moreover, it directly touches on a matter with which this court must be very closely concerned, the proper conduct of a party to English interpleader proceedings. I should not and do not form or express any opinion whether BT's conduct was proper or improper. That is not an issue before me. I am, however, of the opinion that BT would be exposed to the risk of real injustice if the propriety of its conduct were to be judged in any court other than that in which the interpleader proceedings took place. It furthermore appears to me that England is in every way a more appropriate forum than New York for trial of the issues between Mr Karoon and BT and that Mr Karoon would lose no legitimate juridical or personal advantage by suing here. The New York forum would afford him no additional cause of action and the chance of an improved measure of damage would be problematical. These considerations are, however, in my judgment, of less weight in this than in the usual case because the overriding consideration of what justice demands points strongly towards restraint of Mr Karoon's action against BT in New York. If BT were the only New York defendant, I would, even bearing in mind the need for great caution in restraining prosecution of a foreign action, think it right to grant an injunction.'

The difficulty which then faced Bingham J was the combination in one set of New York proceedings of claims against BTTC, which he was not willing to restrain, and claims against BT, which he was. He concluded that it would not be right to grant an excessive injunction, which would be the case if he restrained the prosecution of an action which he regarded as properly brought against BTTC in New York, nor would it be right to expose BT to an unacceptable risk of injustice. He therefore made no mandatory order that Mr Karoon discontinue his New York proceedings, but he continued the negative injunction made ex parte on 13 September 1983, restraining Mr Karoon from taking any further steps in the New York action so far as it related to BT. Mr Karoon thus remained free to prosecute the New York action against BTTC. Counsel on behalf of Mr Karoon is content with that position because BT is not a necessary party to the New York action. Mr Karoon can obtain all the remedies to which he is entitled with the New York action limited to BTTC.

Before us counsel for BT has stressed the distinction between his two lines of argument, and reinforced the distinction by reference to the recent decision of the United States Court of Appeal for the District of Columbia Circuit in *Laker Airways Ltd v Sabena Airlines and KLM Airlines* (1984) 731 F 2d 909. His first line of argument is that, as a matter of English public policy, the claims in New York should not be allowed to be brought at all. Citing the American *Laker* case (at 929) per Judge Wilkey:

'Courts have a duty to protect their legitimately conferred jurisdiction to the extent necessary to provide full justice to litigants . . . the court may freely protect the integrity of its judgments by preventing their evasion through vexatious or oppressive relitigation'

he maintained: (1) that there is 'an overriding public policy' that a litigant should be able to take all proper steps to put relevant evidence before the court; (2) that it is in the public interest that there should be finality in litigation, and, since Mr Karoon had not objected to Mr Saunders's affidavit being put before Robert Goff J, he should not now be allowed to bring an action for damages allegedly arising from the use of that affidavit.

As regards the latter point, counsel for BT expressly accepted that any objection by Mr Karoon would have been doomed to failure and in such circumstances it seems to me plain that Mr Karoon cannot be blamed for having failed to take what is accepted would have been futile action.

Thus, counsel for BT's first and main criticism of Bingham J's decision is that he treated the case as being an ordinary case of competition between two jurisdictions where the question was which was the most appropriate forum.

It is however quite fundamental to counsel's submission (and he readily accepts this) that the public policy on which he relied requires the court to overlook the corporate distinctions in law between BT and BTTC. While accepting that BT and BTTC are separate legal entities, counsel contends that from a practical point of view it makes no difference whether BTTC was a branch of BT or a subsidiary. He argues that if one looks at the substance of the matter, BT are being sued in New York on account of the evidence which they gave in their own defence in proceedings brought against them by Mr Karoon in London. The protection of BT's own interests required the giving of this information and accordingly BT, which must in practice be treated as having this information in their possession, was not in breach of its implied obligation of secrecy (see *Tournier v National Provincial and Union Bank* [1924] 1 KB 461, [1923] All ER Rep 550).   *a*

The reality of the matter is that BTTC is not a branch of BT. That is not the way in which BT has chosen to organise its business as a bank. Of course, BT is entitled to take all proper steps to obtain evidence to resist Mr Karoon's application to strike out the interpleader summons, but the issue remains, were these steps proper ones? If, as Mr Karoon maintains, BTTC owed him a duty of confidence and was therefore not entitled to communicate to another separate legal entity any information concerning his account   *b* with them without his approval, then BTTC was in breach of its duty and it would follow that BT induced a breach of contract. Counsel for BT accepted that if BTTC was not a subsidiary of BT but was another bank, then Mr Karoon would certainly have a cause of action, although he maintained his contention that his damages would be purely nominal.

I can see no valid basis, and certainly no authority was provided to us by counsel for   *c* BT, for the contention that we must ignore the separate legal existence of BTTC. Once the corporate distinction in law between BT and BTTC has to be recognised, the foundation of counsel's submission that there is an English rule of public policy which requires that this action should not be allowed to be brought disappears. There is an arguable case that BTTC, a separate juridical entity, owing Mr Karoon an obligation of secrecy, broke that obligation when, without his consent, they revealed to BT the material   *d* referred to above concerning his account in New York.

In his reply, counsel for BT formulated a further issue of public policy, namely that damages cannot be recovered, other than nominal damages for breach of contract, as a result of there being introduced into litigation in England relevant and admissible evidence, *even though such evidence has been improperly obtained*. He submitted that as a matter of public policy it is so essential to the administration of justice that all relevant   *e* and admissible evidence is placed before the courts that, even though such evidence may have been provided in breach of a contract not to divulge such material and damage can be established to have resulted from this wrongful disclosure, the plaintiffs' remedy is limited to nominal damages for breach of contract, and he has no remedy against the person who wrongfully induced the breach of contract.

Counsel for BT was at pains to make quite clear that he was not limiting this rule of   *f* public policy to the case of a plaintiff who had wrongfully concealed evidence or sought to mislead the court, and had ultimately failed in his claim because evidence improperly obtained had ultimately been put before the court. That would merely be an example of the well-established principle, ex turpi causa non oritur actio. Counsel for BT was unable to produce any authority in support of the existence of this rule of public policy and it became apparent in the course of his submissions that it would not be difficult to imagine   *g* examples where such a rule would operate contrary to accepted notions of justice and fairness. Moreover, it is of the very essence of our adversarial system that the court decides the dispute on the material placed before the court, it being for the parties and not for the court to decide of what that material should consist. Hence the well-established principle that in civil litigation the judge is not entitled, without the consent of the parties, to call a witness, although he may have every reason to believe that such a   *h* witness might well enable him the better to reach a just decision (see *Enoch v Zaretzky Bock & Co* [1910] 1 KB 327 and *Fallon v Calvert* [1960] 1 All ER 281, [1960] 2 QB 201).

I am therefore far from satisfied that such a wide principle of public policy exists. But, even were it to exist, it would not justify the *striking out* of the action. Ex hypothesi, the plaintiff would have a good cause of action for breach of contract, and the fact that his damages might well be nominal still entitles him to bring his action. He might well be   *j* content with a declaration which established that the defendant broke some important duty of secrecy and was therefore not to be trusted. Accordingly, this rule of English public policy, were it to exist, cannot support the contention of counsel for BT that the action against BTTC should never have been brought and therefore that the proceedings should be stopped in limine. It would merely preclude the right to recover more than nominal damages.

The action brought by Mr Karoon against BTTC is in every sense an American action.
a The contract on which the contractual claim is based was made in New York with a New York corporation. The proper law of that contract is American law and if according to American law a breach of that contract took place when BTTC divulged information to BTTC, then the breach of that contract took place in New York. So far as the tort of conspiracy is concerned, the alleged conspirator who is being sued is a New York corporation, and for an alleged conspiracy that took place in New York because it was *b* there that both the agreement and the overt acts in pursuance of that conspiracy were made and carried out. It will be for American law to determine whether the tort of conspiracy was committed and for this decision the New York court is the natural forum (see *Distillers Co (Biochemicals) Ltd v Thompson* [1971] 1 All ER 694, [1971] AC 459). Further, the alleged invasion of privacy occurred in New York. It is a cause of action as yet unknown to English law and will have to be determined in accordance with New *c* York law. In the result New York law will be the proper law for the determination of whether or not there has been a breach of contract and whether or not BTTC has committed the two torts alleged. New York law will also be the lex fori. In such circumstances it seems to me to be irrelevant that in England, assuming the submission of counsel for BT to be correct, Mr Karoon would have recovered only nominal damages for breach of contract.

d As regards the second line of attack of counsel for BT, he ultimately conceded that, if the corporate distinctions in law must not be overlooked and BTTC must be treated as a separate legal entity (as is indeed my view), then New York is the natural forum for the reasons to which I have recently referred. In such circumstances there is no need to consider the balance of legitimate juridical advantages. However, were we obliged to consider that matter, I do not think that counsel would have seriously contended that the *e* balance was other than in favour of the action remaining in New York. Mr Karoon alleges on affidavit that as a result of BT successfully interpleading he has no funds to support his litigation. However, in America he can bring his claim because of the contingency fee system. *Smith Kline & French Laboratories Ltd v Bloch* [1983] 2 All ER 72, [1983] 1 WLR 730 was a decision on its own very special facts, where the Court of Appeal was clearly of the view that the plaintiff, who had legal aid in England, was abusing the *f* contingency fee system in order to bring proceedings in America against the American parent corporation, against which he had no real cause of action. His cause of action, if any, lay against the English subsidiary and his conduct in bringing the American proceedings was clearly vexatious. Thus, in that case it was not a *legitimate* judicial advantage. Moreover, were Mr Karoon to bring proceedings in England, he would inevitably be met with a claim for security of costs, being resident out of the jurisdiction, *g* and this he could not, or would have great difficulty in meeting. He is of course faced with no such problems in the United States. It is common ground that under New York law he may well have a claim for exemplary damages. Although this is certainly not accepted by BT, Mr Karoon might, under New York law, be able to recover exemplary damages, even though he only obtained nominal damages for the alleged breach of contract and/or no actual damage for the torts of invasion of privacy or conspiracy.

h In the end there is left only one unusual feature which will face the New York court. It will have to decide whether the provision by BTTC to BT of the information which BT subsequently put before the court in fact resulted in Mr Karoon losing any real chance of either striking out the interpleader summons or obtaining summary relief under Ord 17, r 5, in short, what probably would have happened in England if BTTC had not made the information available to BT. Although this is an unusual inquiry for a New York court *j* to make, it will, if and when required, be provided with expert evidence as to English law and procedure and should ultimately have no difficulty in resolving this issue.

I would accordingly dismiss this appeal.

ROBERT GOFF LJ. Bingham J was faced with the following situation. The Bank of Tokyo Ltd, the appellant before this court (which I shall refer to as 'BT'), had commenced interpleader proceedings in this country. It had done so because there were moneys credited to accounts at its London branch to which competing claims were being made, on the one hand, by an Iranian company, Maritime Co Ltd (Maritime), through a workers' council in Iran which, following the revolution in that country, appeared to have gained control of Maritime; and, on the other hand, by an Iranian gentleman, Mr Karoon, the respondent before this court, who formerly controlled Maritime but who has, since the revolution in Iran, left that country and taken up residence in France. The interpleader proceedings have been complicated by the fact that Mr Karoon, fearing that disclosure to Maritime of the existence of certain of these moneys might have an adverse effect on his family in Iran, sought to persuade the English court that no such disclosure should be allowed. That attempt has in fact failed, because disclosure was necessary to enable the interpleader issue to be tried. However, one of the steps which Mr Karoon at one time took was to ask the English court to strike out the interpleader proceedings under RSC Ord 18, r 19, his submission being that certain moneys which had been transferred to BT's London branch from Mr Karoon's personal account with the Bank of Tokyo Trust Co, the New York subsidiary of BT (which I shall refer to as 'BTTC'), were his own and were moreover moneys to which Maritime could have no arguable claim, so that they should not be the subject of the interpleader proceedings.

The commercial judge (who, it so happens, was myself) dismissed that application. A note of the judgment is before this court and shows that the basis of the decision was that the court considered that, having regard in particular to a letter emanating from the workers' council, BT had reasonable grounds for thinking that it might be sued by Maritime not only in respect of moneys of Maritime but also in respect of moneys of Mr Karoon on the ground that they had emanated from Maritime, and that it would be wrong for the court to pre-empt the situation on the evidence of one party only. At all events, for the purposes of his application to strike out, Mr Karoon swore an affidavit concerning the moneys which had been transferred from BTTC, stating that those moneys had not originated from Maritime. As a result, BT made inquiries of BTTC about those moneys. BTTC then supplied information about the moneys to BT, some of which was embodied in an affidavit sworn by Mr Saunders of BT for the purpose of laying the information before the commercial judge when he dealt with Mr Karoon's application to strike out.

Mr Karoon has taken objection to his bankers in New York, BTTC, supplying this information to BT, and indeed he has objected to BT seeking to obtain the information from BTTC. So, on 7 July 1983, he commenced proceedings in New York against both BT and BTTC. In those proceedings he alleged (1) breach by BTTC of its contractual duty of confidence to him, in revealing the information to BT, (2) breach of contract by BT in obtaining the information, (3) violation by BTTC of Mr Karoon's right of privacy, (4) conspiracy by BT and BTTC and (5) that BT wrongfully induced BTTC to break its contract with Mr Karoon.

On its application before Bingham J, BT asked for an order directing Mr Karoon to discontinue the action in New York against BT and BTTC and/or an injunction restraining Mr Karoon from taking any further steps in the New York action or 'commencing or pursuing any other proceedings relating to the same subject matter before any other court than this Honourable Court'. The judge declined to make a mandatory order, but he maintained an injunction (which had earlier been granted ex parte) in terms expressly limited to the New York proceedings against BT. The effect was that Mr Karoon was free to prosecute his New York action against BTTC, but not against BT.

The reasoning of Bingham J was as follows. Having set out the applicable principles, he first considered the New York action against BTTC. He then concluded:

'Overall, I do not regard an injunction as appropriate to restrain the action insofar as it lies against BTTC. If the action were to proceed, BTTC might, of course, win or lose; and if it lost the damages might be large or nominal, or even non-existent. But all these seem to me to be matters best entertained and resolved in the New York court which would be applying its own law to events very largely occurring within its own jurisdiction.'

a However, when the judge turned to the New York action as against BT, the case appeared to him to assume a somewhat different aspect. He drew attention to the fact that BT's request to BTTC was made by it in the context of its role as a party seeking to interplead in the English court, following Mr Karoon's reference to the moneys in his own affidavit. He continued:

'Leaving entirely on one side the question whether, on information being requested, BTTC should, as a matter of New York law, have complied with the
b request, I think that two significant questions of English law arise in respect of BT's conduct: whether it was reasonable and proper for BT, in seeking to protect its own interests, to request information from BTTC; and whether, in pursuance of its duty as a party applying to interplead, it was proper for BT to seek to lay before the court all evidence within its power relevant to the application. This is a lis between a bank carrying on business in London and a London customer of that bank arising out of
c English interpleader proceedings to which both were party. Moreover, it directly touches on a matter with which this court must be very closely concerned, the proper conduct of a party to English interpleader proceedings. I should not and do not form or express any opinion whether BT's conduct was proper or improper. That is not an issue before me. I am, however, of the opinion that BT would be exposed to the risk of real injustice if the propriety of its conduct were to be judged
d in any court other than that in which the interpleader proceedings took place. It furthermore appears to me that England is in every way a more appropriate forum than New York for trial of the issues between Mr Karoon and BT and that Mr Karoon would lose no legitimate juridical or personal advantage by suing here. The New York forum would afford him no additional cause of action and the chance of an improved measure of damage would be problematical. These considerations are,
e however, in my judgment, of less weight in this than in the usual case because the overriding consideration of what justice demands points strongly towards restraint of Mr Karoon's action against BT in New York. If BT were the only New York defendant, I would, even bearing in mind the need for great caution in restraining prosecution of a foreign action, think it right to grant an injunction.'

f BT has appealed to this court against the judge's decision, in so far as he failed to restrain Mr Karoon from pursuing the New York action as against BTTC. There is no cross-appeal by Mr Karoon. This is for the simple practical reason that Mr Karoon's New York action can continue just as well against BTTC alone. However, in so far as it may be necessary for the purposes of resisting BT's appeal, Mr Karoon has by his respondent's notice taken the point that the judge was wrong to continue the injunction restraining
g Mr Karoon from further prosecuting the New York action against BT.
Before the judge, counsel for BT had argued that the New York proceeedings would cause injustice to his clients for a number of reasons, viz: (1) the New York action was vexatious because (a) it was an attempt to penalise BT for availing itself of the interpleader proceedings in England, (b) it would involve relitigating the question (already litigated here) whether an interpleader issue should have been ordered and (c) it had no reasonable
h prospect of success; and (2) any action should be tried in England because (a) the interpleader proceedings were already here, (b) an English court could, without difficulty, resolve what duty of confidence is owed by a New York bank to its client, whereas a New York judge would be faced with difficult questions regarding English interpleader proceedings, (c) the question of ownership of the moneys had to be decided first anyway and (d) the availability of a contingency fee to Mr Karoon could not, on the authorities,
j be regarded as a juridical advantage to him. Before this court, however, Mr Hoffmann's argument was somewhat different. The reason for the development of his argument was the intervening decision of the US Court of Appeals in *Laker Airways Ltd v Sabena Airlines and KLM Airlines* 731 F 2d 909, which was only decided on 6 March 1984 and so was not available to Bingham J in the present case. Counsel for BT drew on the analysis of Judge Wilkey, who delivered the majority judgment in that case, and urged this court to do likewise in considering the problem in the present case. In order to place counsel's

submissions in their context, it will be necessary briefly to summarise the relevant
principles stated by Judge Wilkey. This is no easy task. The judgment is substantial both *a*
in content and in length. I have studied it with interest and, indeed, respect.

Laker Airways Ltd v Sabena Airlines and KLM Airlines is concerned with the unhappy
clash of jurisdiction which has occurred between courts in this country and courts in the
United States, following on the commencement by the liquidators of Laker of antitrust
proceedings in the United States against a number of international airlines, alleging that
their combined activities were the cause of Laker's downfall. Among the airlines so sued *b*
were two British airlines, British Airways and British Caledonian. Following the making
of an order by the Secretary of State for Trade and Industry in this country (acting under
powers conferred on him by Act of Parliament) which had the effect of prohibiting the
two British airlines from complying with 'United States antitrust measures', the Court of
Appeal in this country granted an injunction restraining Laker from taking any steps
against British Airways and British Caledonian in the United States action (see *British* *c*
Airways Board v Laker Airways Ltd [1983] 3 All ER 375, [1984] QB 142). Meanwhile, in
the United States Laker obtained temporary restraining orders from the District Court
restraining other airlines from instituting in the courts of this country similar proceedings
for an injunction. Two of those airlines, KLM and Sabena, challenged the District Court's
preliminary injunction on appeal to the Court of Appeals. The Court of Appeals, by a
majority, declined to overturn the injunction so granted. *d*

In the course of his judgment Judge Wilkey analysed in depth the applicable principles
of law. I am only concerned, for present purposes, with his consideration of the propriety
of what he called 'the antisuit injunction'. I shall summarise the principles stated by him
as briefly as I can, though I realise that so brief a summary cannot do justice to his
reasoning.

(1) He observed that the sufficiency of jurisdictional contacts with both the United *e*
States and England resulted in concurrent jurisdiction to prescribe, but he continued (at
926–927):

> 'However, the fundamental corollary to concurrent jurisdiction must ordinarily
> be respected: parallel proceedings on the same in personam claim should ordinarily
> be allowed to proceed simultaneously, at least until a judgment is reached in one *f*
> which can be pled as res judicata in the other ... For this reason, injunctions
> restraining litigants from proceeding in courts of independent countries are rarely
> issued [though] a second reason cautioning against exercise of the power is avoiding
> the impedance of the foreign jurisdiction.'

And (2):
  g
> 'There are no precise rules governing the appropriateness of antisuit injunctions.
> The equitable circumstances surrounding each request for an injunction must be
> carefully examined to determine whether, in the light of the principles outlined
> above, the injunction is required to prevent an irreparable miscarriage of justice.'

However, (3) injunctions are most often necessary (a) to protect the jurisdiction of the *h*
enjoining court or (b) to prevent the litigant's evasion of the important public policies of
the forum.

(4) With regard to (3)(a) above, viz protection of the jurisdiction of the enjoining
court, a distinction was drawn between cases where the enjoining court has proceeded to
judgment on the merits, and cases where an injunction is requested to protect the court's
jurisdiction before a judgment has been reached. In the former case there is little *j*
interference with the rule favouring parallel proceedings in matters subject to concurrent
jurisdiction so a court may protect the integrity of its judgments by preventing their
evasion through vexatious or oppressive relitigation (see, eg, *Bethell v Peace* (1971) 441 F
2d 459). In the latter case the factors which might support the issue of an injunction do
not usually outweigh the importance of permitting foreign concurrent actions; and the
policies underlying the rule permitting parallel proceedings in concurrent in personam

_a_ actions are more properly considered in a motion for dismissal for forum non conveniens. Even so, there must be circumstances in which an antisuit injunction is necessary to conserve the court's ability to reach a judgment, and the District Court's injunction was proper on that basis.

(5) With regard to (3)(b) above, viz preventing the litigant's evasion of the important public policies of the forum, an antisuit injunction will issue to preclude participation in the litigation only when the strongest equitable factors favour its use. Among the

_b_ authorities cited by Judge Wilkey where such an injunction has issued was _Cole v Cunningham_ (1890) 133 US 107, a case concerned with protecting the exercise of bankruptcy jurisdiction. Judge Wilkey further considered that the District Court's injunction properly prevented KLM and Sabena from attempting to escape the application of the United States antitrust laws to the conduct of business in the United States.

Counsel for BT urged us to adopt a similar approach in the present case to that adopted

_c_ by Judge Wilkey in his analysis, and in particular to distinguish, on the basis of both English and United States authorities, the two groups of cases where injunctions may be granted, viz to protect the jurisdiction of the court and to prevent the litigant's evasion of the important public policies of the forum. The present case before us fell, submitted counsel for BT, within these principles. He asked us to approach the case by considering first whether, if BT in London and BTTC in New York had been a single entity and all

_d_ relevant events had happened in England, proceedings in this country similar to those commenced by Mr Karoon in New York would have been struck out as an abuse of process. He submitted that they would, because such proceedings would have infringed both the public interest in making available all relevant evidence for the court and the public interest that there should be finality in litigation. That being so, he submitted that it made no difference that Mr Karoon had commenced his proceedings not in this

_e_ country but in New York, because the English court, in protecting the integrity of its own jurisdiction, should now allow a litigant, subject to its jurisdiction, to bring such an action in a foreign jurisdiction. Furthermore, he submitted, having regard to the basis of the jurisdiction, the court should not be deflected from giving effect to its public policy by the fact that BT and BTTC are different legal entities; otherwise it would be sacrificing substance to form.

_f_ As an alternative to this main line of argument, counsel for BT invoked the principles enunciated by the House of Lords in recent cases concerned with alternative forums, viz _MacShannon v Rockware Glass Ltd_ [1978] 1 All ER 625, [1978] AC 795 and _Castanho v Brown & Root (UK) Ltd_ [1981] 1 All ER 143, [1981] AC 557, and submitted that, on the 'critical equation' referred to in those cases, the balance pointed towards requiring Mr Karoon to litigate in England.

_g_ In considering the submissions of counsel for BT, I recognise that it is not merely legitimate but desirable that courts in this country should pay due regard to developments in sister common law jurisdictions, notably the United States; this is especially desirable when the court is concerned with principles of law affecting the relationship between our two jurisdictions and when we are presented with an analysis as profound as that of Judge Wilkey in _Laker Airways Ltd v Sabena Airlines and KLM Airlines_. Even so, we have

_h_ to proceed with due caution. Not only do we have to operate within the confines of the doctrine of precedent in this country, but we have to bear in mind that the development of the relevant principles of law in our two countries may not be identical. Frequently, however, under the influence of history and of practical pressures to which both jurisdictions are subject, it transpires that there have taken place in our two jurisdictions parallel developments which, though neither simultaneous nor identical, reveal a very

_j_ similar trend.

This is just what we find in the case of what American lawyers call 'antisuit injunctions'. At bottom, the fundamental principles appear to have developed along similar lines. Thus, the jurisdiction is very wide, being available for exercise whenever justice demands the grant of an injunction. Again, the English court does not attempt to restrain the foreign court, but operates in personam, restraining a party from instituting or prosecuting the suit in the foreign jurisdiction; though an injunction will only be granted to restrain a person who is regarded as being properly amenable to the jurisdiction of the English courts. Furthermore, it has been repeatedly stated that the jurisdiction *a* must be exercised with extreme caution, indeed sparingly: this is partly because concurrent proceedings in different jurisdictions are tolerated, but also because of a desire to avoid conflict with other jurisdictions. For it is accepted, as is indeed obvious, that courts of two different jurisdictions, one in this country and one in a foreign country, can have jurisdiction over the same dispute. It is not prima facie vexatious for the same plaintiff to commence two actions relating to the same subject matter, one in England *b* and one abroad; but the court may be less ready to tolerate suits in two jurisdictions in the case of actions in rem than it is in the case of actions in personam. All these principles are well established, and indeed non-controversial, and appear to be common to both the English and the United States jurisdictions.

But the jurisdiction to grant such an injunction has only rarely been exercised in this country. The earliest cases in which the jurisdiction was established do not necessarily *c* provide authoritative examples of its exercise today; indeed one of them (*Bushby v Munday* (1821) 5 Madd 297, [1814–23] All ER Rep 304) was later to be described by Lord Brougham as going to the 'very verge of the law' (see *Carron Iron Co v Maclaren Dawson & Stainton* (1855) 5 HL Cas 416 at 446, 10 ER 961 at 973). In the course of the nineteenth century, there developed a line of cases in which assets were being administered by the English court, and one interested person sought to gain an advantage over other interested *d* persons by prosecuting proceedings in a foreign country where part of the assets were situated. In such cases, for example, where a person sought in this way to gain the benefit of foreign assets of an estate after a decree of administration (see, eg, *Graham v Maxwell* (1849) 1 Mac & G 71, 47 ER 1043), or of a bankrupt after his petition in bankruptcy (see, eg, *Re Distin, ex p Ormiston* (1871) 24 LT 197), or of a company after winding-up proceedings had been commenced (see, eg, *Re North Carolina Estate Co* (1889) 5 TLR 328), *e* such a person has been restrained by injunction from pursuing foreign proceedings, but only if he were a domiciled Englishman or otherwise amenable to the jurisdiction of the English court. In the later nineteenth century, however, following the decisions of the Court of Appeal in *McHenry v Lewis* (1882) 22 Ch D 397 and *Peruvian Guano Co v Bockwoldt* (1883) 23 Ch D 225, [1881–5] All ER Rep 715, it became accepted that, at least in the case of actions in personam, concurrent proceedings by the same party in this *f* country and abroad were not prima facie vexatious, and the proceedings abroad should not therefore be restrained. It was for the party seeking an injunction to prove that the proceedings abroad were vexatious; for that purpose, he had generally to show that the plaintiff in the foreign court could not obtain an advantage from the foreign procedure which he could not obtain in the English court (see in particular *Hyman v Helm* (1883) 24 Ch D 53 and *Cohen v Rothfield* [1919] 1 KB 410, [1918–19] All ER Rep 260). That criterion *g* was very rarely fulfilled; for examples where it was fulfilled see *Armstrong v Armstrong* [1892] P 98, *Moore v Moore* (1896) 12 TLR 221 and *Christian v Christian* (1897) 67 LJP 18.

Injunctions have however also been granted to restrain proceedings brought in breach of contract (see *Lett v Lett* [1906] 1 IR 618 and *The Tropaioforos (No 2)* [1962] 1 Lloyd's Rep 410), and to restrain enforcement of a judgment obtained fraudulently (see *Ellerman Lines Ltd v Read* [1928] 2 KB 144, [1928] All ER Rep 415). Putting aside these latter cases, *h* however, and without attempting to cut down the breadth of the jurisdiction, the golden thread running through the rare cases where an injunction has been granted appears to have been the protection of the jurisdiction; an injunction has been granted where it was considered necessary and proper for the protection of the exercise of the jurisdiction of the English court. This can be said not only of cases where assets were being administered by the English court but also of cases where proceedings abroad were restrained as *j* vexatious, for a party who attempts to reap the benefit of proceeding vexatiously is interfering with the proper course of administration of justice here (for an example, see *Armstrong v Armstrong* [1892] P 98 at 101 per Jeune J). But there was this difference between these two groups of cases: that, whereas in the latter group the foreign proceedings were regarded as vexatious because the plaintiff could derive no advantage *a* from them, in the former group he was restrained precisely because he might gain an advantage from the foreign proceedings.

Now at one time it was thought that the requirement that proceedings must be vexatious was applicable, not only to the exercise of the court's jurisdiction to restrain a party from instituting or prosecuting foreign proceedings, but also to the exercise of the court's jurisdiction to stay proceedings commenced in this country: see again *McHenry v Lewis* and *Peruvian Guano Co v Bockwoldt*. A stay would only be granted if the continuance

b of the action in this country would be oppressive or vexatious to the defendant or otherwise an abuse of the process of the court, and if a stay would not cause an injustice to the plaintiff: see *St Pierre v South American Stores (Gath & Chaves) Ltd* [1936] 1 KB 382 at 398, [1935] All ER Rep 408 at 414 per Scott LJ. Again, these criteria were rarely fulfilled. However, in *The Atlantic Star, Atlantic Star (owners) v Bona Spes (owners)* [1973] 2 All ER 175, [1974] AC 436, the House of Lords recognised that this very restrictive

c criterion for staying proceedings in this country was too nationalistic: Lord Reid referred to it as a 'rather insular doctrine' (see [1973] 2 All ER 175 at 181, [1974] AC 436 at 453). In that case the court relaxed the criteria of 'oppression' and 'vexation'. Four years later, in *MacShannon v Rockware Glass Ltd* [1978] 1 All ER 625, [1978] AC 795, the House of Lords relaxed the criteria still further, abandoning altogether the criteria of 'oppression' and 'vexation', and adopting a principle which is now accepted to be indistinguishable

d from the principle of forum non conveniens as accepted in Scottish law (see *The Abidin Daver* [1984] 1 All ER 470, [1984] AC 398. A parallel development has taken place in the United States: see *Gulf Oil Corp v Gilbert* (1947) 330 US 501, and *Piper Aircraft Co v Reyno* (1981) 454 US 235.

On these authorities it may be observed that there are strong similarities in the way in which the law on this topic has developed in both countries. However, in 1981 there

e occurred a development in this country which has sharply differentiated the two jurisdictions. In *Castanho v Brown & Root (UK) Ltd* [1981] 1 All ER 143, [1981] AC 557, Lord Scarman (who delivered a speech with which the remainder of the Appellate Committee agreed) treated the criteria applicable to the exercise of the court's discretion to impose a stay or grant an injunction as identical. He said ([1981] 1 All ER 143 at 150, [1981] AC 557 at 574):

f
> 'It is unnecessary now to examine the earlier law. The principle is the same whether the remedy sought is a stay of English proceedings or a restraint upon foreign proceedings.'

After referring to *The Atlantic Star*, he quoted a passage from Lord Diplock's speech in *MacShannon v Rockware Glass Ltd* [1978] 1 All ER 625 at 630, [1978] AC 795 at 812 as

g embodying his distillation of principle in the case of a stay, which reads as follows:

> 'In order to justify a stay two conditions must be satisfied, one positive and the other negative: (a) the defendant must satisfy the court that there is another forum to whose jurisdiction he is amenable in which justice can be done between the parties at substantially less inconvenience or expense, and (b) the stay must not

h deprive the plaintiff of a legitimate personal or juridical advantage which would be available to him if he invoked the jurisdiction of the English court.'

Lord Scarman then said ([1981] 1 All ER 143 at 151, [1981] AC 557 at 575):

> 'Transposed into the context of the present case, this formulation means that to justify the grant of an injunction the defendants must show (a) that the English
j court is a forum to whose jurisdiction they are amenable in which justice can be done at substantially less inconvenience and expense, *and* (b) that the injunction must not deprive the plaintiff of a legitimate personal or juridical advantage which would be available to him if he invoked the American jurisdiction. The formula is not, however, to be construed as a statute. No time should be spent in speculating what is meant by "legitimate". It, like the whole of the context, is but a guide to

solving in the particular circumstances of the case the "critical equation" between advantage to the plaintiff and disadvantage to the defendants.' (Lord Scarman's emphasis.)

Lord Scarman did not apparently consider it necessary to give reasons for his opinion that the principle is the same whether the remedy sought is a stay of English proceedings or a restraint on foreign proceedings, and that it was therefore unnecessary, having regard to the decisions of the House of Lords in *The Atlantic Star* and *MacShannon's* case, both of which related only to a *stay* of *English* proceedings, to examine earlier case law on *restraint* of *foreign* proceedings. As I have recorded, it is now recognised that the principle applicable in the case of a stay of foreign proceedings is indistinguishable from the Scottish principle of forum non conveniens. This latin tag is, like many others, misleading: proceedings in the English forum are stayed not because *England* is an *inconvenient* forum, but because there is another clearly more *appropriate* forum *abroad*. The classic statement of principle is to be found in the judgment of Lord Kinnear in *Sim v Robinow* (1892) 19 R 665 at 668, when, after stating that the court would not refuse to exercise its jurisdiction 'upon the ground of a mere balance of convenience and inconvenience', he said that:

> 'The plea can never be sustained unless the court is satisfied that there is some other tribunal, having competent jurisdiction, in which the case may be tried more suitably for the interests of all the parties and for the ends of justice.'

A similar principle was adopted by Lord Sumner in *Société du Gaz de Paris v SA de Navigation Les Armateurs Français* 1926 SC(HL) 13 at 22, when he said that the object was to find 'that forum which was the more suitable for the ends of justice'.

It follows that the policy underlying the principle of forum non conveniens is a policy of declining to exercise jurisdiction where there is another clearly more appropriate forum; though, if in such circumstances trial in England would offer the plaintiff a real advantage, a balance must be struck and the court must decide in its discretion whether justice requires a stay. This policy, avowedly less nationalistic than the old principle of vexation or oppression as applied in the past in cases of stay of proceedings, is one which is given effect to, on an application by the defendant, by a court of the forum in which there have been commenced proceedings over which the court has jurisdiction. It is a self-denying ordinance. The principle (derived from the speeches of their Lordships in *MacShannon's* case) was so interpreted and applied in *Trendtex Trading Corp v Crédit Suisse* [1980] 3 All ER 721, [1980] QB 629, with the approval of the House of Lords in that case, Lord Roskill describing the judge's approach as 'entirely correct in principle' (see [1981] 3 All ER 520 at 532, [1982] AC 679 at 705). Furthermore, the exercise of the judge's discretion, so approved, in that case involved the granting of a stay, although the plaintiff was thereby deprived of a most valuable juridical advantage in this country, viz discovery of documents in accordance with English rules of procedure. It appears therefore that a juridical advantage of the plaintiff in this country will not necessarily be decisive. (That this is indeed so can be illustrated by the often-quoted example of a road accident involving two motorists in a foreign country, both being resident nationals of that country: one seizes the opportunity given by the casual presence of the other in this country to serve proceedings on him here, with the aim of recovering the higher damages available in the English courts. The English court would surely order a stay of proceedings on the application of the defendant, though the plaintiff's whole purpose in proceeding here was to obtain the juridical advantage of higher damages.) The decision of the House of Lords in the *Trendtex* case was followed by the Court of Appeal in *European Asian Bank AG v Punjab and Sind Bank* [1982] 2 Lloyd's Rep 356. The principles in these two cases, derived from all the speeches of the House of Lords in *MacShannon's* case and approved by the House of Lords in the *Trendtex* case, are, I understand, regularly followed in the Commercial Court, where cases of this kind tend to arise for decision.

In *Castanho v Brown & Root (UK) Ltd* Lord Scarman has taken the principle of forum a non conveniens as developed in relation to a stay of English proceedings where it was expressly developed in order to adopt a *less* nationalistic approach, i e to render the English courts *less* tenacious of proceedings started within its jurisdiction, and has applied it *inversely* in cases of restraint by the English courts of foreign proceedings. The effect would appear to be, not only that in cases of restraint of foreign proceedings the very restrictive principle of protection of the English jurisdiction has been abandoned, but also that the English court will now be more free to grant injunctions restraining foreign

b proceedings than it was in the past under the old case law. We should perhaps not be surprised to discover that the approach of Lord Scarman in *Castanho*'s case is different from the approach of courts in the United States. There, as here, the grant of a stay of proceedings depends on the application of the principle of forum non conveniens (see, e g, *Piper Aircraft Co v Reyno* (1981) 454 US 235). But the grant of an injunction restraining foreign proceedings depends on the twin principles of protection of the

c jurisdiction of the court of the forum, and of preventing evasion of important public policies of the forum; and in each case the principles have been stated and applied in restrictive terms. So cases of stay of proceedings and of restraint of foreign proceedings are regarded as being founded on different principles. Furthermore, as appears from Judge Wilkey's opinion in *Laker Airways Ltd v Sabena Airlines and KLM Airlines* (1984) 731 F 2d 909, in the United States it is considered more appropriate, where there is a clash of

d jurisdiction, for a stay of proceedings to be considered by the court seised of the matter rather than for a court to establish its own forum as the more appropriate forum by granting an injunction restraining proceedings in a foreign court.

Given the present divergence between the principles applicable in our two countries, it is, I fear, very difficult for this court to respond to the submission of counsel for BT that we should proceed on the basis of Judge Wilkey's analysis in *Laker Airways Ltd v*

e *Sabena Airlines and KLM Airlines*. I can only console myself with the reflection that in any event counsel's submission appears to me to involve an illegitimate extension, in at least two respects, of the principles as stated by Judge Wilkey, and indeed of the principle as developed in the long line of English cases before *Castanho*.

I first address myself to the public interest that there should be finality in litigation. Such a public interest no doubt exists. Moreover, authorities can be found, both in this

f country and in the United States, in which courts have gone so far as to grant injunctions restraining persons properly amenable to their jurisdiction from relitigating abroad matters which have already been the subject of a judgment of the court of the forum. For an English example, see the old case of *Booth v Leycester* (1837) 1 Keen 579, 48 ER 430; and for an American example, see *Bethell v Peace* (1971) 441 F 2d 495. *The Tropaioforos (No 2)* [1962] 1 Lloyd's Rep 410 could perhaps also be treated as falling under this head,

g though it contained the exceptional feature that the litigant sought to be restrained had entered into an agreement with all underwriters to be bound by the outcome of the proceedings, thereby providing a contractual basis for the grant of the injunction. However, I do not regard the present case as falling under this head of public policy. In the New York proceedings, Mr Karoon is not, as I understand it, seeking to relitigate a matter which has been the subject of a judgment in this country. He is seeking rather to

h obtain redress from a bank in New York in respect of disclosure of confidential information by that bank in New York. I cannot see that the mere fact that Mr Karoon had an opportunity, which he did not take, to object to Mr Saunders's affidavit being put in evidence on the striking out application in London has any effect on the situation. The simple fact is that the cause of action alleged by Mr Karoon against BTTC has not been the subject of a judgment in this country. I can therefore see no basis for this submission

j of counsel for BT.

The second submission of counsel for BT however raises more difficult problems. He asserted a public interest in making available all relevant evidence for the court. This public interest was, he submitted, exemplified by the rule that statements in affidavits are absolutely privileged in defamation proceedings (see *Trapp v Mackie* [1979] 1 All ER 489 at 491, [1979] 1 WLR 377 at 378–379 per Lord Diplock), and by the rule that victimisation of a witness on account of evidence he has given is a contempt of court (see *Chapman v Honig* [1963] 2 All ER 513 at 517, [1963] 2 QB 502 at 512 per Lord Denning *a* MR). His original submission before us was that, on this principle, BT could not be sued for adducing evidence in the interpleader summons. However, in the course of argument he recognised that the gravamen of his submission lay in a litigant seeking to recover damages in respect of the disclosure of material evidence in proceedings, when the only damage suffered was (it was submitted) a failure to achieve a result which would have been achieved had the material evidence not been disclosed. As a matter of public policy *b* such damages should not, submitted counsel for BT, be recoverable in law.

Now this submission does indeed raise novel and difficult problems. It cannot be said to be entirely without substance, but it was not founded on any authority cited to us, either from this country or from the United States. Furthermore, if any such policy exists, as proposed by counsel, it may be given effect to as part of the lex fori; and it does not necessarily follow that a court of this country would give effect to it by an injunction *c* restraining proceedings in another jurisdiction. We have also always to bear in mind the restraint we must impose on ourselves before taking any steps which might bear on the exercise by the courts of another country of its own jurisdiction. However, in the present case, I must desist from exploring this interesting and novel proposition, because there is in my judgment a fatal obstacle to the argument of counsel for BT. This is that the evidence in question was adduced in a court of this country not by BTTC, but by BT. *d* The proceedings which counsel is asking this court to restrain are proceedings by Mr Karoon against BTTC, in respect of their having divulged confidential information not to the English court but to BT. I cannot for my part see that the public policy now asserted by counsel should (assuming that it exists) provide any ground for restraining those proceedings. Counsel suggested beguilingly that it would be technical for us to distinguish between parent and subsidiary company in this context; economically, he *e* said, they were one. But we are concerned not with economics but with law. The distinction between the two is, in law, fundamental and cannot here be bridged. For this reason, I should in any event have dismissed this argument.

I turn then to consider the alternative submission of counsel for BT, which was founded on Lord Scarman's speech in *Castanho's* case [1981] 1 All ER 143, [1981] AC 557. This was to the effect that, applying the principles in *MacShannon's* case [1978] 1 All ER *f* 625, [1978] AC 795, the balance points towards requiring Mr Karoon to litigate in England. He relied in this connection in particular on the following factors: proceedings were already on foot in London between BT and Mr Karoon; the issue whether Mr Karoon was entitled to the moneys in question will in any event have to be decided in the interpleader issue in London; there is no dispute of fact over what happened in New York, and the principles of law on bankers' confidentiality in New York and London are *g* substantially the same; the critical question whether the provision of information caused any loss to Mr Karoon would be better decided here; and Mr Karoon has no legitimate juridical advantage in New York.

I have to confess that I find the consequences of this argument to be startling. There is no pending litigation in this country between Mr Karoon and BTTC; that of itself would render any order by the English court restraining the action in New York a remarkable *h* restraint on the prosecution of proceedings in that state. Even if England were to be regarded by the English court as a clearly more appropriate forum, or the natural forum, for the trial of the action, I feel the gravest reservations about an English court granting an injunction restraining Mr Karoon from proceeding in New York rather than allowing a court of that state, being the forum having jurisdiction where an action has already been commenced, making its own decision whether England is the more appropriate *j* forum and whether it should in the circumstances grant a stay of proceedings. But in any event I am not prepared to hold that England is a clearly more appropriate forum for the trial of the action between Mr Karoon and BTTC. The cause of action arose in New York. One of the parties is a New York corporation: the other is an Iranian citizen resident in France. The applicable law is the law of the State of New York; and, even if

New York law on breach of confidence by a banker shares a common origin with our
a own law on the subject, I am not prepared to assume in the present case that they are
identical, and in any event there are other legal issues in the case (for example, a claim to
penal damages). Taking into account the factors relied on by counsel for BT, I cannot see
that they displace the strong connection with the New York jurisdiction. That being so,
on the principles expounded by the House of Lords in MacShannon's case, as interpreted
with the approval of the House of Lords in the Trendtex case [1981] 3 All ER 520, [1982]
b AC 679, there can be no basis, on the inverse application of the principle of forum non
conveniens, to grant an injunction restraining Mr Karoon from continuing with his
proceedings against BTTC in New York.
    For these reasons, I would dismiss the appeal.

Appeal dismissed. Leave to appeal to the House of Lords refused. Injunctions to continue over
c *hearing of any petition for leave to appeal.*

Solicitors: *Herbert Smith & Co* (for BT); *Baker & McKenzie* (for the respondents).

Carolyn Toulmin   Barrister.

d

South Carolina Insurance Co v Assurantie Maatschappij 'de Zeven Provincien' NV

e
South Carolina Insurance Co v Al Ahlia Insurance Co and others

HOUSE OF LORDS
LORD BRIDGE OF HARWICH, LORD BRANDON OF OAKBROOK, LORD BRIGHTMAN, LORD MACKAY OF
CLASHFERN AND LORD GOFF OF CHIEVELEY
f 6, 7 MAY, 29 JULY 1986

Conflict of laws – Foreign proceedings – Restraint of foreign proceedings – Circumstances in
which court will restrain prosecution of foreign proceedings – Defendants to actions in England
seeking discovery against plaintiffs by bringing proceedings for discovery in foreign court –
Whether injunction would be granted restraining defendants from continuing foreign proceedings.

g
The plaintiffs, a United States company, entered into contracts of reinsurance with a
number of insurance companies in London, including the defendants. Subsequently the
plaintiffs began two actions in England claiming substantial sums due from the
defendants. The defendants intimated that their defence would allege misrepresentation
and non-disclosure on the part of the plaintiffs, and in order to investigate and make
h good those defences the defendants requested discovery of documents held by the
plaintiffs' business associates and underwriting agents in the United States. When that
request was refused the defendants lodged a petition for discovery in the United States
district court with a view to using the United States procedure for pre-trial discovery to
obtain the documents. The plaintiffs applied to the English court for, inter alia, an
injunction restraining the defendants from taking any further step in the United States
j proceedings. The judge granted the injunction. The defendants appealed to the Court of
Appeal, which affirmed the decision on the ground that, unless the circumstances were
wholly exceptional, the court would exercise its inherent jurisdiction to control its own
proceedings by restraining a party to an action begun in England from invoking foreign
procedural remedies to assist in preparing his case in the English action. The defendants
appealed to the House of Lords.

Held – The appeal would be allowed for the following reasons—

(1) (Per Lord Bridge, Lord Brandon and Lord Brightman; Lord Mackay and Lord Goff dubitante). Although s 37(1)^a of the Supreme Court Act 1981 on its face gave the court very wide powers to 'grant an injunction . . . in all cases in which it appears to the court to be just and convenient to do so', that discretion to grant an injunction was (subject to two immaterial exceptions) limited to two situations, namely (a) where a party to an action had invaded or threatened to invade a legal or equitable right of another party which was amenable to the jurisdiction of the court, and (b) where one party had behaved or threatened to behave in a manner which was unconscionable. In the exercise of that discretion the court had power to grant an injunction restraining a party from beginning or continuing proceedings against another party in a foreign court but only if it could be shown that the foreign proceedings invaded or threatened the other party's rights or amounted to unconscionable conduct and, in any event, the jurisdiction would be exercised with caution because it involved indirect interference with the process of a foreign court (see see p 489 *e* and p 499 *a*, post).

(2) On the facts (Lord Mackay and Lord Goff concurring), it was not necessary to protect the jurisdiction of the English court by granting the plaintiffs an injunction restraining the defendants from continuing the United States proceedings, because (a) the plaintiffs had not shown that the United States procedure for pre-trial discovery would invade a legal or equitable right of the plaintiffs, (b) the defendants' conduct in starting the United States proceedings with a view to using that jurisdiction's pre-trial discovery procedure did not amount to unconscionable conduct which interfered with the English court's control of its own process because in civil proceedings the court did not, in general, exercise any control over the manner in which a party obtained the evidence needed to support his case and the defendants were doing no more than adhere to the principle that it was up to a party to obtain by his own means the evidence he needed to present his case, provided such means were lawful in the country in which they were used, (c) the defendants' conduct in seeking to exercise a right potentially available to them under United States law did not in any way depart from or interfere with the procedure of the English court, (d) any liability on the part of the plaintiffs for increased costs was self-imposed and would not have been incurred if they had not refused the defendants access to the relevant documents, (e) any inconvenience caused by the United States proceedings was likewise self-inflicted on the plaintiffs and was subordinate to justice being fully done in the two English actions, and (f) furthermore, the extra costs and inconvenience could not amount to an interference with the court's control of its own process (see p 489 *e*, p 496 *f* to *j*, p 497 *b* to p 498 *h* and p 499 *a* to *c f g*, post).

Decision of the Court of Appeal [1985] 2 All ER 1046 reversed.

Notes

For the general principle governing the stay of foreign proceedings, see 8 Halsbury's Laws (4th edn) paras 787–788, and for cases on the subject, see 11 Digest (Reissue) 637–641, 1720–1746.

Cases referred to in opinions

Bank of Tokyo Ltd v Karoon [1986] 3 All ER 468, CA.

British Airways Board v Laker Airways Ltd [1984] 3 All ER 39, [1985] AC 58, [1984] 3 WLR 413, HL.

Castanho v Brown & Root (UK) Ltd [1981] 1 All ER 143, [1981] AC 557, [1980] 3 WLR 991, HL.

Court of the Comr of Patents for the Republic of South Africa, Re, Re Selas Corp of America and Electric Furnace Co (1980) 88 FRD 75, US DC.

Deere (John) Ltd and Deere & Co v Sperry Corp (1985) 754 F 2d 132, US Ct of Apps, 3rd Cir.

---

a Section 37(1), so far as material, is set out at p 495 *g* to p 496 *b*, post.

MacShannon v Rockware Glass Ltd [1978] 1 All ER 625, [1978] AC 795, [1978] 2 WLR
a   362, HL.
Siskina (cargo owners) v Distos Cia Naviera SA, The Siskina [1977] 3 All ER 803, [1979] AC
210, [1977] 3 WLR 818, HL.

Interlocutory appeal
The defendants, Assurantie Maatschappij 'de Zeven Provincien' NV, Al Ahlia Insurance
b   Co and Arabian Seas Insurance Co, appealed with leave of the Appeal Committee of the
House of Lords granted on 19 November 1985 against the decision of the Court of Appeal
(Griffiths, Slade and Lloyd LJJ) ([1985] 2 All ER 1046, [1986] QB 348) on 23 May 1985
dismissing the defendants' appeal from the judgment of Hobhouse J dated 25 April 1985
whereby on two applications of the plaintiffs, South Carolina Insurance Co, he ordered
that the defendants be restrained (i) from taking any further step in their motion before
c   the United States District Court, Western District of Washington at Seattle and (ii) from
enforcing any order of the United States court. The facts are set out in the opinion of
Lord Brandon.

Robert Alexander QC and *Jonathan Sumption QC* for the defendants.
Kenneth Rokison QC, Christopher Symons and *Thomas Weitzman* for the plaintiffs.
d
Their Lordships took time for consideration.

29 July. The following opinions were delivered.

LORD BRIDGE OF HARWICH. My Lords, for the reasons given in the speech of
e   my noble and learned friend Lord Brandon, with which I agree, I would allow this
appeal.

LORD BRANDON OF OAKBROOK. My Lords, the question for decision in this
appeal is a novel one and can be stated in this way. An action between A and B is pending
before an English court. While it is pending B, exercising a statutory right potentially
available to him under the Federal law of the United States, applies to a district court of
f   the United States for an order that persons resident in the United States, who are not
parties to the action before the English court, should give him pre-trial discovery of
documents relevant to the issues in that action. In those circumstances, is it right for the
English court, on the application of A, to grant an injunction against B prohibiting him
from prosecuting further his proceedings in the United States district court? Hobhouse J,
at first instance, and the Court of Appeal (Griffiths, Slade and Lloyd LJJ) ([1985] 2 All ER
g   1046, [1986] QB 348) on appeal from him, have held that it is right for such an injunction
to be granted. The parties enjoined (for in the instant case there are three of them) now
bring a further appeal with the leave of your Lordships' House.
   The background of the case is to be found in what can conveniently be described as a
three-tier insurance arrangement. The company which first insured the relevant risks
h   was a United States company, United National Insurance Co (United National). United
National reinsured the risks which it had insured with another United States company,
South Carolina Insurance Co (the plaintiffs). The plaintiffs in turn rereinsured the risks
which they had reinsured with a number of other insurance companies in the London
market. These other insurance companies included a Dutch company, Assurantie
Maatschappij 'de Zeven Provincien' (Seven Provinces) and two Middle or Far Eastern
companies, Al Ahlia Insurance Co (Al Ahlia) and Arabian Seas Insurance Co (Arabian
j   Seas) (the defendants). In or about 1984 the plaintiffs called on the defendants to pay
substantial sums which the plaintiffs claimed to be due from them under the contracts
of rereinsurance concerned. The defendants refused to make the payments asked for,
denying that they were liable to do so.
   As a result the plaintiffs brought two actions in the Commercial Court here in order to
recover the sums which they claimed to be payable, together with interest on such sums.

In the first action, which was begun on 12 December 1984, Seven Provinces is the sole defendant. In the second action, which was begun on 28 February 1985, Al Ahlia is the first defendant and Arabian Seas is the second defendant. It was the original intention of the solicitors acting for the plaintiffs to seek summary judgment in both actions under RSC Ord 14. However, at an application to fix a date for the hearing of the Ord 14 proceedings against Seven Provinces, counsel for the latter indicated that a number of substantial defences would be raised to the plaintiffs' claim. These defences included: (1) misrepresentation or non-disclosure regarding the retention position on the part of the plaintiffs; (2) non-disclosure of a previous bad loss record on the business concerned; (3) excessive deductions from premiums; and (4) payment of claims outside the limits of the relevant treaty.

The underwriting agent for United National through whom business was placed with it was Pacific General Agency Inc (PGA). The loss adjusters who investigated the claims made against United National were Arthur Campbell-Husted & Co (Campbell-Husted). The principal place of business of both PGA and Campbell-Husted is in the State of Washington.

My Lords, the defendants are, by reasons of their position, remote from the facts in dispute, and obliged to rely for detailed information about them on such documents as they can obtain from the plaintiffs or PGA and Campbell-Husted. The latter two, however, were not the agents of the plaintiffs in connection with the relevant transactions; it follows that discovery of documents by the plaintiffs in the two actions in England would not extend to relevant documents held by them. In this situation, if the defendants are to achieve their legitimate object of inspecting and copying where necessary, relevant documents held by PGA and Campbell-Husted, some other means have to be found to enable them to do so.

In November 1984, after the plaintiffs had put forward their claims against the defendants, but before the two actions in England were begun, the latter had asked PGA if they could inspect the documents in which they were interested at Seattle on 7 December 1984. PGA referred the request to their principal, United National, which in turn consulted the plaintiffs. It appears that, on the advice of the plaintiffs' English solicitors, the request for inspection was, in effect, refused. The two actions in England were subsequently begun.

My Lords, 28 United States Code § 1782 provides:

'Assistance to foreign and international tribunals and to litigants before such tribunals.

(a) The district court of the district in which a person resides or is found may order him to give his testimony or statement or to produce a document or other thing for use in a foreign or international tribunal. The order may be made pursuant to a letter rogatory issued, or request made, by a foreign or international tribunal or upon the application of any interested person and may direct that the testimony or statement be given, or the document or other thing be produced, before a person appointed by the court. By virtue of his appointment, the person appointed has power to administer any necessary oath and take the testimony or statement. The order may prescribe the practice and procedure, which may be in whole or in part the practice and procedure of the foreign country or the international tribunal, for taking the testimony or statement or producing the document or other thing. To the extent that the order does not prescribe otherwise, the testimony or statement shall be taken, and the document or other thing produced, in accordance with the Federal Rules of Civil Procedure . . .'

On 28 March 1985, before the defendants had served their points of defence and counterclaims in the two actions against them in England, they applied by motion to the United States District Court, Western District of Washington at Seattle for an order under § 1782 above. The motion, the title of which referred to the two actions in England, asked for an order against PGA and Campbell-Husted involving two matters. The first

a
matter was the production and inspection of numerous specified classes of documents of
the kind which could reasonably be expected to have come into being in the course of
the transaction of the insurance business which had led to United National, having settled
claims itself, to recover from the plaintiffs as its reinsurers, and to the plaintiffs then
claiming to recover over from the defendants, the rereinsurers. The second matter was
the appearance of three named persons from PGA and Campbell-Husted to give testimony
by deposition. The motion was supported by a memorandum and an affidavit.

b
Notice of the defendants' motion was served on PGA and Campbell-Husted. The
plaintiffs were also served with notice of the motion, or otherwise made aware of its
having been lodged. Neither PGA nor Campbell-Husted appeared before the district
court to resist the application. The plaintiffs, however, did so appear, and having indicated
their objection to it, were given until 29 April 1985 to file their affidavit in opposition.
It is to be inferred from the foregoing that neither PGA nor Campbell-Husted objects to
c
producing the documents listed in the motion for inspection, and where necessary for
copying, by the defendants, and that it is only the plaintiffs' objection that has stood in
the way of their doing so.

On 24 April 1985, before the date fixed for filing their affidavit in opposition in the
United States district court, the plaintiffs issued summonses in the two actions in England.
By their summonses they sought (1) an order that the defendants should withdraw their
d
application to the United States district court, (2) an injunction restraining the defendants
from proceeding further with such application, and (3) a declaration that the application
was an abuse of the process of the English court.

My Lords, the summonses were heard by Hobhouse J on 25 April 1985. He declined
to make the declaration asked for, but granted the plaintiffs injunctions restraining the
defendants until further order from taking any further steps in their motion before the
e
United States district court and from enforcing any order made by that court on such
motion. The main ground on which Hobhouse J decided to grant such injunctions
appears from his judgment where, having set out what he called the framework of the
matter, he said:

f
'It involves a question of principle as to whether or not the English court should
retain the control of its own procedure and the proceedings that are before it. I have
no doubt that the answer to be given to that question is that the English court
should retain that control.'

The decision of Hobhouse J was, as I indicated earlier, affirmed by the Court of Appeal.
Griffiths LJ gave the principal judgment, with which Slade and Lloyd LJJ both agreed.
The main reason which Griffiths LJ gave for his decision was similar to that relied on by
g
Hobhouse J. He said ([1985] 2 All ER 1046 at 1052, [1986] QB 348 at 358):

'Once the parties have chosen or accepted the court in which their dispute is to be
tried they must abide by the procedure of that country and that court must be
master of its own procedure. Litigation is expensive enough as it is, and if a party
fighting a case in this country has to face the prospect of fighting procedural battles
h
in whatever other jurisdiction his opponent may find a procedural advantage it may
impose intolerable burdens, and encourage the worst and most oppressive form of
procedural forum shopping. We should set our face against any such situation
developing. Severe dislocation to the timetable of the English litigation is a readily
foreseeable consequence of unrestrained access to foreign procedural remedies. This
is likely to cause hardship or inconvenience not only to the other party to that
j
litigation but will also affect other litigants whose cases are listed on forecasts
dependent on litigation being conducted in accordance with our own rules of
procedure. As the judge said, the court will lose control of its own proceedings.
Furthermore, one party might be able to gain a very unfair advantage in the English
procedure if he were able to take the deposition of and cross-examine a witness
whom he would never call on his own behalf at the trial, for example the employees

or business associates of his opponent. I think counsel for the defendants recognised
this when he said he would be content to accept the stay in respect of his application
to take the depositions of the witnesses from PGA and Arthur Campbell-Husted &
Co. I am therefore satisfied that as a matter of principle the court must have an
inherent jurisdiction to make any necessary order to ensure that the litigation is
conducted in accordance with its own procedures.'

My Lords, before examining the question whether Hobhouse J and the Court of
Appeal were right or wrong to grant the injunctions now appealed against, it is necessary
to draw attention to a number of preliminary matters.

The first matter to which attention needs to be drawn is the existence of an essential
difference between the civil procedures of the High Court in England on the one hand,
and of courts of the United States on the other, with regard to what may be compendiously
described as pre-trial discovery. Under the civil procedure of the High Court in England,
pre-trial discovery may take two forms. The first form, which is far and away the more
common, is by way of disclosure and inspection of relevant documents under RSC Ord
24. The second form, which is comparatively rare, is by way of the asking and answering
on oath of interrogatories under RSC Ord 26. Such discovery is, however, subject to two
important limitations, one relating to its scope and the other to the stage of an action at
which it normally takes place. So far as the scope of discovery is concerned, it is limited
to the disclosure and inspection of documents in the possession or power of the parties to
the action, or to the asking and answering on oath of interrogatories as between such
parties. So far as the stage of an action at which discovery normally takes place is
concerned, it is the general rule that the two forms of discovery to which I have referred
do not take place until the formal pleadings by both sides have been completed and the
issues in disputes thereby fully and clearly defined. In this connection, however, it is
right to say that the court has power to order either form of discovery at any stage of an
action, including a stage earlier than the completion of pleadings; but such power is
rarely exercised and then only on special grounds, for instance when discovery is needed
in order that jsutice may be done in interlocutory proceedings.

Because of the first limitation to which I have referred, there is no way in which a
party to an action in the High Court in England can compel pre-trial discovery as against
a person who is not a party to such action, either by way of the disclosure and inspection
of documents in his possession or power, or by way of giving oral or written testimony.
I would, however, stress the word 'compel' which I have used in the preceding sentence,
for there is nothing to prevent a person who is not a party to any action from voluntarily
giving to one or other or both parties to it either disclosure and inspection of documents
in his possession or oral or written testimony.

The procedure of the High Court in England, while not enabling parties to an action
to compel pre-trial discovery as against a person who is not a party to such action,
nevertheless affords ample means by which such a person, provided that he is within the
jurisdiction of the court, can be compelled either to give oral testimony, or to produce
documents in his possession or power, at the trial of the action itself. Under RSC Ord 38,
Pt II (rr 14–19), such a person may be compelled to give oral testimony at the trial by the
issue and service on him of a subpoena ad testificandum, or to produce documents in his
power or possession (so long as they are adequately described and defined) by the issue
and service on him of a subpoena duces tecum. The issue of such subpoenas is in the first
instance a ministerial rather than a judicial act, and a party may therefore issue subpoenas
of either kind as he thinks fit; the court, however, has power to set aside any subpoena
on proper grounds, for instance, irregularity of form, irrelevance, oppressiveness or abuse
of the process.

The procedure of the High Court in England includes a further power of the court,
conferred on it by RSC Ord 38, r 13, to order any person to attend any proceedings in a
cause or matter and produce any document to be specified or described in the order, the
production of which appears to the court to be necessary for the purpose of that
proceeding. It has, however, long been established that this rule is not intended to be

a used, and cannot properly be used, to enable a party to an action to obtain pre-trial disclosure and inspection of documents in the possession or power of a person who is not a party to such action. It is a rule of limited application, involving the production of a document or documents to the court itself rather than to either of the parties to an action.

My Lords, the civil procedure of courts in the United States differs essentially from that in the High Court in England in that under it parties to an action can compel, as against persons who are not parties to it, a full measure of pre-trial discovery, including b both the discloure and production for inspection and copying of documents, and also the giving of oral or written testimony. This power of compulsion can be, and regularly is, used at an early stage of an action.

The second matter to which attention needs to be drawn is that 28 United States Code §1782, as appears from its terms which I set out earlier, expressly provides that an order made under it may prescribe the practice and procedure, which may be in whole or in c part the practice and procedure of the foreign country or the international tribunal, for taking the testimony or statement or producing the document or other thing; and that, to the extent that the order does not prescribe otherwise, the testimony or statement shall be taken, and the document or other thing produced, in accordance with the Federal Rules of Procedure.

Reference was made in the two courts below and again in your Lordship's House to d certain United States authorities which bear on the exercise of a district court's powers under §1782. In a decision of the United States District Court of Pennsylvania, *Re Court of the Comr of Patents for the Republic of South Africa, In the matter between Selas Corp of America and the Electric Furnace Co* (1980) 88 FRD 75 at 77, Judge Newcomer said:

'[1, 2] It is of great concern to this Court that counsel for Opponents have not been able to represent to this Court that the documents and testimony for which e Opponents request a discovery order are discoverable under South African law. Indeed, discussions with counsel lead this Court to suspect that these materials would *not* be available through South African procedures. Clearly, this Court should not by its exercise of the discretion allowed it under section 1782 allow litigants to circumvent the restrictions imposed on discovery by foreign tribunals. Few actions could more significantly impede the development of international cooperation f among courts than if the courts of the United States operated to give litigants in foreign cases processes of law to which they are not entitled in the appropriate foreign tribunals.'

Further, in *John Deere Ltd and Deere & Co v Sperry Corp* (1985) 754 F 2d 132 at 135 Judge Garth, giving the judgment of the United States Court of Appeals for the Third Circuit, g said:

'As a cooperative measure, §1782 cannot be said to ignore those considerations of comity and sovereignty that pervade international law. A grant of discovery that trenched upon the clearly established procedures of a foreign tribunal would not be within §1782.'

h My Lords, it was contended for the plaintiffs, on the basis of these authorities, that the defendants' application to the district court of the United States was bound to fail. The ground relied on was that, since the procedure of the High Court in England did not enable parties to an action to compel pre-trial discovery against persons not parties to it, the district court would not permit the defendants to circumvent that limitation by granting them an order for such discovery under §1782.

j It appears to me that there may well be considerable force in this contention. It is not possible, however, for your Lordships, on the limited material before you, to decide for yourselves in advance how the United States district court would see fit to exercise the discretion conferred on it by §1782, in the particular circumstances of this case, and having regard to the characteristics of civil procedure in the High Court in England which I endeavoured to summarise earlier.

The third matter to which attention needs to be drawn concerns certain changes in the positions of the parties which have occurred since the original hearing of the plaintiffs two summonses before Hobhouse J. The first change of position relates to the *a* memorandum lodged in support of the defendants' application to the United States district court, in which they asserted:

> 'As evidenced by the attached affidavit of Francis Otley Mackie, the petitioners herein are seeking this court's assistance in obtaining information and documentation which is necessary, material and relevant to litigation pending in the courts of England for use in those proceedings. The affidavit further establishes that were all *b* the parties residents of England, the requested discovery would be permitted pursuant to the rules of procedure and discovery in England. Accordingly, the petitioners' motion for taking of testimony and the production of documents should be granted.'

Mr Mackie, whose affidavit is referred to at the beginning of the above passage, is a *c* partner in the firm of solicitors acting for the defendants in the two actions in England. The relevant part of that affidavit is para 12, in which Mr Mackie deposed, inter alia, as follows:

> 'Discovery of such documentation and testimony is permitted according to the English rules of procedure . . . Petitioners would be able to obtain writs of subpoena duces tecum issued by the High Court of England . . . directing these entities to *d* produce the documents requested and directing them individually to appear and give testimony at depositions.'

These statements in the defendants' memorandum and Mr Mackie's affidavit were criticised by Hobhouse J and by Griffiths LJ in the Court of Appeal as giving such an incomplete and inaccurate account of the procedure of the High Court in England with *e* regard to discovery as seriously to mislead the United States district court. Griffiths LJ, however, expressly acquitted Mr Mackie of any deliberate intention to mislead. Before your Lordships leading counsel for the defendants accepted unreservedly that the passages in question were incomplete and inaccurate, and as a consequence liable to mislead. The main error, as will be apparent, is the failure to distinguish clearly between compelling a person not a party to an action to give pre-trial discovery on the one hand, and compelling *f* him to give oral evidence and produce documents at the trial itself on the other hand. I think that it is right for your Lordships to say that the criticisms of that error made by the two courts below were fully justified and that it is most unfortunate that it should ever have occurred. That said, however, having regard to the admission of such error freely made by leading counsel for the defendants, and having regard further to the summary which I endeavoured to give earlier of the relevant procedure of the High *g* Court in England, it seems to me that the error is no longer of significance in the consideration of this appeal.

The second change of position concerns the scope of the defendants' application to the United States district court. As I indicated earlier, that application as originally framed covered two distinct matters: first, the production and inspection of specified classes of documents; and, second, the appearance of three named persons from PGA and Campbell- *h* Husted to give testimony by depositions. On the face of the motion it appeared that what the defendants were seeking in relation to the second of these matters was the taking of oral evidence from the persons named relevant to the issues in the English actions, such evidence to be recorded in depositions. Before the Court of Appeal, however, counsel for the defendants expressly abandoned any intention to achieve this end, and before your Lordships leading counsel for the defendants made it clear that the appearance of the *j* named persons was only sought for the purpose of their producing and identifying the relevant documents held by PGA and Campbell-Husted, and in no way for the purpose of their giving oral evidence to be recorded in depositions with regard to issues of fact arising in the English actions.

The third change of position arises from the stage which the two actions in England

have now reached. At the time when the plaintiffs' applications first came before
a Hobhouse J the defendants had not yet served their points of defence and counterclaim,
so that the issues between the parties had not yet been defined by pleadings and no
discovery of documents as between the parties had yet taken place. Hobhouse J regarded
this as a significant matter in exercising the discretion to grant injunctions which he held
that he had. During the hearing before the Court of Appeal, however, the defendants
served points of defence and counterclaim, and since then discovery of documents as
b between the parties has taken place. The actions in England are, therefore, much further
advanced than they were when the plaintiffs' applications first came before the judge.

The fourth change of position is this. Following the decision of the Court of Appeal
the plaintiffs arranged for the defendants to have controlled access to certain documents
held by PGA and Campbell-Husted. According to the defendants, however, substantial
restrictions were imposed by the plaintiffs on the documents which they were allowed
c to inspect under this arrangement. It is the defendants' case, therefore, that their
application to the United States district court remains necessary in order to enable them
to have inspection of other documents to which, by reason of the control exercised by
the plaintiffs, they have not so far had access. Your Lordships were not asked to go into
the details of these matters, which are in dispute between the parties, and it is right, I
think, for the purposes of this appeal for your Lordships to proceed on the basis that the
d defendants have at least an arguable case with regard to them.

The fifth and final matter to which attention should be drawn is that the judge of the
United States district court before whom the defendants' application under §1782 is
pending has helpfully directed that further proceedings in that application should be
stayed until the determination first of the defendants' appeal to the Court of Appeal, and
then of their further appeal to your Lordships' House.

e   My Lords, having drawn attention to these various preliminary matters, I turn to
consider whether the injunctions granted by Hobhouse J and affirmed by the Court of
Appeal should be allowed to stand. I put the question in that form because of the various
ways described by me above in which the positions of the parties have changed since the
original hearing before Hobhouse J.

As appears from the passages from the judgments of Hobhouse J and Griffiths LJ
f which I set out earlier, both courts below treated the plaintiffs' applications for injunctions
as raising matters of principle for decision. I have no doubt that they were right so to
treat them. Putting the point differently, the question which your Lordships have to
decide is whether the circumstances of the case are such as to give the court power to
grant the injunctions at all, and not whether, there being such power, it was a proper
exercise of discretion to grant them rather than to refuse them.

g   In considering the question which I have formulated, it will be helpful in the first
place to state certain basic principles governing the grant of injunctions by the High
Court. The first basic principle is that the power of the High Court to grant in injunctions
is a statutory power conferred on it by s 37(1) of the Supreme Court Act 1981, which
provides:

h   'The High Court may by order (whether interlocutory or final) grant an injunction
        . . . in all cases in which it appears to the court to be just and convenient to do so.'

That provision is similar to earlier provisions of which it is the successor, namely s 45(1)
of the Supreme Court of Judicature (Consolidation) Act 1925 and s 25(8) of the Supreme
Court of Judicature Act 1873. The second basic principle is that, although the terms of
s 37(1) of the 1981 Act and its predecessors are very wide, the power conferred by them
j has been circumscribed by judicial authority dating back many years. The nature of the
limitations to which the power is subject has been considered in a number of recent cases
in your Lordships' House: see *Siskina (cargo owners) v Distos Cia Naviera SA, The Siskina*
[1977] 3 All ER 803, [1979] AC 210, *Castanho v Brown & Root (UK) Ltd* [1981] 1 All ER
143, [1981] AC 557 and *British Airways Board v Laker Airways Ltd* [1984] 3 All ER 39,
[1985] AC 58. The effect of these authorities, so far as material to the present case, can be

summarised by saying that the power of the High Court to grant injunctions is, subject to two exceptions to which I shall refer shortly, limited to two situations. Situation (1) is when one party to an action can show that the other party has either invaded, or threatens to invade, a legal or equitable right of the former for the enforcement of which the latter is amenable to the jurisdiction of the court. Situation (2) is where one party to an action has behaved, or threatens to behave, in a manner which is unconscionable. The third basic principle is that among the forms of injunction which the High Court has power to grant is an injunction granted to one party to an action to restrain the other party to it from beginning, or if he has begun from continuing, proceedings against the former in a foreign court. Such jurisdiction is, however, to be exercised with caution because it involves indirect interference with the process of the foreign court concerned.

The latter form of injunction may be granted in such circumstances as to constitute an exception to the second basic principle stated above. This may occur where one party has brought proceedings against another party in a foreign court which is not the forum conveniens for the trial of the dispute between them, as that expression was defined and applied in *MacShannon v Rockware Glass Ltd* [1978] 1 All ER 625, [1978] AC 795. In such a case the party who has brought the proceedings in the foreign court may not, by doing so, have invaded any legal or equitable right of the other party, nor acted in an unconscionable manner. The court nevertheless has power to restrain him from continuing his foreign proceedings on the ground that there is another forum in which it is more appropriate, in the interests of justice, that the dispute between the parties should be tried. The present case, however, is not concerned with a choice between two competing forums for the trial of a dispute, and the exception to which I have just referred is therefore not relevant to it.

The power of the court to grant Mareva injunctions may also, before it was statutorily recognised, have been a further exception to the second basic principle stated above. That power, however, has now been expressly recognised by s 37(3) of the Supreme Court Act 1981, and again the present case is in no way concerned with it.

Ignoring these exceptions, therefore, and applying the basic principles which I have stated to the present case, the first question for consideration is whether the plaintiffs have shown that what I have described above as situation (1) exists. Have the plaintiffs shown that the defendants, by beginning and intending to prosecute their application to the United States district court, have invaded, or threatened to invade, a legal or equitable right of the plaintiffs for the enforcement of which the defendants are amenable to the jurisdiction of the court? It was contended by counsel for the plaintiffs that the plaintiffs did indeed have such a legal or equitable right, but it appeared to me that he had great difficulty in formulating the legal or equitable right on which he relied. Neither of the courts below decided as they did on the basis that the defendants had by their conduct invaded a legal or equitable right of the plaintiffs, and I cannot see how such a case can be made out. I would therefore hold that the plaintiffs have not shown that situation (1) exists.

The second question for consideration is whether the plaintiffs have shown that what I have described above as situation (2) exists. Have the plaintiffs shown that the defendants, by beginning and intending to prosecute their application to the United States district court, have acted in a manner which is unconscionable? It is difficult, and would probably be unwise, to seek to define the expression 'unconscionable conduct' in anything like an exhaustive manner. In my opinion, however, it includes, at any rate, conduct which is oppressive or vexatious or which interferes with the due process of the court.

Although neither Hobhouse J at first instance nor Griffiths LJ in the Court of Appeal stated in terms that they thought it right to grant injunctions on the ground that the defendants' conduct in making their application to the United States district court was unconscionable, it seems to me to be implicit in their reasons that they regarded it as being so. Hobhouse J based his decision expressly on the need for the court to retain control of its own process, with the necessary implication that the defendants' conduct *a* was an interference with such control and therefore an interference with the due process of the court. Griffiths LJ based his decision on three grounds: first (like Hobhouse J), that the court must retain control of its own process; second, that the civil procedure of United States courts is significantly different from that of English courts, and the parties, by submitting to the jurisdiction of an English court, must be taken to have accepted its procedure; and, third, that unrestricted access to foreign procedural remedies was liable to produce hardship in the form of increased costs and inconvenience. I shall consider

b each of these grounds in turn.

I consider, first, the ground that the defendants' conduct was an interference with the court's control of its own process. It is not clear to me why this should be so. Under the civil procedure of the High Court the court does not, in general, exercise any control over the manner in which a party obtains the evidence which he needs to support his case. The court may give him help, certainly; for instance by discovery of documents inter

c partes under RSC Ord 24; by allowing evidence to be obtained or presented at the trial in various ways under Ords 38 and 39; and by the issue of subpoenas under Pt II (rr 14–19) of Ord 38, to which I referred earlier. Subject, however, to the help of the court in these various ways, the basic principle underlying the preparation and presentation of a party's case in the High Court in England is that it is for that party to obtain and present the evidence which he needs by his own means, provided always that such means are lawful

d in the country in which they are used. It was not in dispute that, if PGA and Campbell-Husted, uninfluenced by the control exercised over them by the plaintiffs on the advice of the latter's English solicitors, had freely and voluntarily allowed the defendants to inspect, and where necessary to copy, all the documents referred to in the latter's application, it could not possibly have been said that there had been any interference with the English court's control of its own process. That being so, I cannot see why, since

e the Federal law of the United States authorises an application of the kind made by the defendants in this case, the making of such application, which may or may not succeed in whole or in part, should be regarded as being such an interference either. I cannot, therefore, agree with the first ground of decision relied on by the Court of Appeal.

I consider, second, the ground that the procedure of United States courts is significantly different from that of English courts, and the parties, by submitting to the jurisdiction

f of an English court, must be taken to have accepted its procedure. It is, no doubt, true that the defendants, by entering unconditional appearances in the two English actions, can be said in a certain sense to have accepted the procedure of that court. Your Lordships were not, however, informed of any ground on which the defendants could, with any prospect of success, have contested the jurisdiction of the High Court in England in respect of the disputes which are the subject matter of the two actions concerned. Be that

g as it may, I cannot see that the defendants, by seeking to exercise a right potentially available to them under the Federal law of the United States, have in any way departed from, or interfered with, the procedure of the English court. All they have done is what any party preparing his case in the High Court here is entitled to do, namely to try to obtain in a foreign country, by means lawful in that country, documentary evidence which they believe that they need in order to prepare and present their case. It was said

h that the defendants could have applied to the High Court under RSC Ord 39, r 2, for letters of request to issue to the proper judicial authorities in the United States. But 28 United States Code §1782 allows an application to be made either indirectly by the foreign court concerned or directly by an interested party, and I can see no good reason why the defendants should not have chosen whichever of these two alternatives they preferred. It is, I think, of the utmost importance to appreciate that the reason why

j English procedure does not permit pre-trial discovery of documents against persons who are not parties to an action is for the protection of those third parties, and not for the protection of either of the persons who are parties to the action. I cannot, therefore, agree with the second ground of decision relied on by the Court of Appeal.

I consider, third, the ground that unrestrained access to foreign procedural remedies was liable to cause hardship in the form of increased costs and inconvenience. So far as increased costs are concerned, Griffiths LJ was referring to increased costs incurred or to be incurred by the plaintiffs in contesting the proceedings in the United States district court. If, however, the defendants are right in their contention that they have not yet, by reason of the control exercised by the plaintiffs, had access to all the documents to which they believe that they need access in order to prepare their case in the two English actions, it can reasonably be said that any liability for increased costs incurred by the plaintiffs is in a sense self-imposed. If they had been willing to permit PGA and Campbell-Husted to allow the defendants to inspect, and where necessary copy, all the documents to which the latter had sought access, the making or prosecution of the defendants' application to the United States district court would not have been necessary. In this connection it is right to stress what I have already stated earlier, that PGA and Campbell-Husted, left to themselves, would voluntarily have given the defendants permission to inspect, and where necessary copy, all the documents to which the latter sought access. It was said for the plaintiffs that the documents not so far disclosed were not relevant to the issues in the two English actions. If that is so, I cannot help asking myself why the plaintiffs have gone to such lengths to prevent the disclosure of such documents. So far as inconvenience is concerned, it is apparent that Griffiths LJ had two kinds of inconvenience in mind: first inconvenience in relation to the two actions immediately concerned in the form of delay in getting them tried and possible prolongation of the trial when it took place; and, second, inconvenience to other litigants by reason of the consequent dislocation of the timetable for the trial of other cases in the congested list of the Commercial Court. So far as delay is concerned, it is perhaps ironical that the only result of the plaintiffs seeking to obtain injunctions against the defendants has been to increase greatly whatever delay the defendants' application, if allowed to proceed unopposed, might otherwise have caused. I recognise that the defendants' application may result in some increased costs to the plaintiffs, but these could, as I indicated earlier, have easily been avoided by a different attitude on the plaintiffs' part. I recognise also that some inconvenience of the two kinds to which I have referred may arise from the defendants' application; but, if there is a reasonable possibility that such inconvenience is the price of justice being fully done at the trial of the two English actions, then it seems to me to be a price which must necessarily be paid. In any event, I cannot see how the defendants' application, made in what may prove to be a just cause, can, solely on the ground that it occasions the extra costs and inconvenience under discussion, be categorised as an interference with the court's control of its own process. The court can control any excessive delay by fixing such date for the trial of the two actions as may be just, and nothing which the defendants can do can take away or interfere with the court's control in this respect. As to increased costs these will, no doubt, be a matter for the consideration of the Commercial judge at the conclusion of the trial, and I do not think it would be right for your Lordships to express any views, one way or the other, about such matter. For these reasons I cannot agree with the third ground of decision relied on by the Court of Appeal.

My Lords, the result of the views which I have expressed is that there was, in my opinion, no such interference with the procedure of the English High Court by the defendants as would amount to unconscionable conduct on their part, and so justify, in accordance with the basic principles which I stated earlier, the exercise of the court's power to grant injunctions against them. It follows that I would allow the appeal and set aside the orders of Hobhouse J dated 25 April 1985 and of the Court of Appeal dated 23 May 1985. As regards costs in your Lordships' House, I have no doubt that the plaintiffs should pay the costs of the defendants. As regards costs in the two courts below, different considerations may apply, first, because of the breadth of the defendants' application to the United States district court as originally framed, and, second, because of the misleading nature, in the respect to which I referred earlier, of the memorandum and affidavit lodged in support of such application. I therefore think it desirable that, in relation to those costs, your Lordships should have the assistance of further argument from counsel on either side.

LORD BRIGHTMAN. My Lords, in this appeal I respectfully differ from the
conclusion reached by the Court of Appeal. I have had the privilege of studying in
advance the speech of my noble and learned friend Lord Brandon, and I find myself
wholly convinced by his reasons for moving that this appeal should be allowed. I agree
with the orders that he proposes should be made.

LORD MACKAY OF CLASHFERN. My Lords, I have had the advantage of reading
in draft the speeches prepared by my noble and learned friends Lord Brandon and Lord
Goff. I agree that it would be wise to to make the reservation on the matter to which
Lord Goff has drawn attention but, like him, I agree with the conclusion reached by Lord
Brandon and with the reasons he has given for reaching that conclusion.

LORD GOFF OF CHIEVELEY. My Lords, I find myself to be in respectful
agreement with the conclusion reached by my noble and learned friend Lord Brandon,
on this appeal, and with the reasons given by him for reaching that conclusion. I wish,
however, to draw attention to one matter on which I have certain reservations, and to
which I attach importance.

I am reluctant to accept the proposition that the power of the court to grant injunctions
is restricted to certain exclusive categories. That power is unfettered by statute; and it is
impossible for us now to foresee every circumstance in which it may be thought right to
make the remedy available. In particular, I do not regard the exercise of the power to
restrain a person from commencing or continuing proceedings in a foreign forum as
constituting an exception to certain limited categories of case in which it has been said
that the power may alone be exercised. In my opinion, restraint of proceedings in a
foreign forum simply provides one example of circumstances in which, in the interests
of justice, the power to grant an injunction may be exercised. I have elsewhere explained
in detail, for reasons which it is unnecessary for me to repeat in the present case, why, on
the basis of a line of established authority, I am at present inclined to the opinion that an
injunction has generally been granted in such circumstances for the purpose of protecting
the English jurisdiction, and why I doubt, with all respect, whether the speech of my
noble and learned friend Lord Scarman in *Castanho v Brown & Root (UK) Ltd* [1981] 1 All
ER 143, [1981] AC 557, contains the last word on the subject. I refer, in this connection,
to my judgment in *Bank of Tokyo Ltd v Karoon* [1986] 3 All ER 468.

Even so, I can see no basis for the grant of an injunction in the present case. In
particular, in agreement with my noble and learned friend Lord Brandon, and respectfully
differing from Hobhouse J and the Court of Appeal, I do not consider that the grant of
the injunction can be justified as necessary to protect the English jurisdiction on the facts
of the present case. In this, I find myself entirely in agreement with the reasons expressed
in the speech of my noble and learned friend Lord Brandon. I therefore agree that the
appeal should be allowed.

Appeal allowed.

Solicitors: *Clyde & Co* (for the defendants); *Herbert Smith & Co* (for the plaintiffs).

Mary Rose Plummer   Barrister.

Food Corp of India v Marastro Cia Naviera SA
The Trade Fortitude

COURT OF APPEAL, CIVIL DIVISION
DILLON, LLOYD AND NICHOLLS LJJ
21, 22, 23 APRIL, 19 MAY 1986

Arbitration – Award – Interest – Payment before award – Power of arbitrator to award interest on sum paid prior to date of award – Statutory power to award interest coming into force after payment made – Whether arbitrator having power to award interest on sums paid prior to award – Arbitration Act 1950, s 19A.

By a voyage charterparty dated 12 September 1974 the owners chartered a vessel to the charterers for the carriage of a cargo of wheat from the United States Gulf to India. Subsequently a dispute arose between the parties over demurrage which was referred to arbitration in England under the terms of the charterparty. In April 1985 the arbitrator published his award in the form of a special case in favour of the owners. He included interest under s 19A[a] of the Arbitration Act 1950 on a payment on account of demurrage which the charterers had made to the owners in April 1982. The charterers applied for remission on the ground that the arbitrator had made an accidental slip in the calculation of demurrage. On the special case, the question arose whether an arbitrator had power under s 19A to award interest on sums paid prior to the date of the award since s 19A, which was introduced by s 15 of and Sch 1 to the Administration of Justice Act 1982, had not come into force until 1 April 1983. The judge refused to remit the award. On the special case he held that s 19A only applied to arbitration agreements entered into after s 19A came into force and that accordingly the arbitrator had no power to award interest on the sum paid by the charterers in April 1982. The owners appealed.

Held – (1) The charterers had failed to establish a strong prima facie case that the arbitrator had made an accidental slip, and remission would therefore be refused (see p 502 g to j, p 508 e to p 509 a and p 512 d, post); *Mutual Shipping Corp of New York v Bayshore Shipping Co of Monrovia, The Montan* [1985] 1 All ER 520 distinguished.

(2) It was an implied term of the arbitration agreement that the arbitrator should conduct the reference in accordance with the law in force at the time of the hearing. Accordingly, the arbitrator had power under s 19A of the 1950 Act to award interest on sums paid prior to the date of the award in respect of arbitration agreements made before 1 April 1983. It followed that the owners' claim for interest on a payment on account of demurrage paid by the charterers had been correctly allowed. The appeal would therefore be allowed in part (see p 503 j, p 504 j to p 505 a c, p 510 j to p 511 c e to g and p 512 d, post); *Chandris v Isbrandtsen Moller Co Inc* [1950] 2 All ER 618 considered.

Notes

For claims for interest, see 32 Halsbury's Laws (4th edn) paras 106–109, and for cases on the subject, see 34 Digest (Reissue) 541–550, 4308–4410.

For the power of an arbitrator to award interest, see 2 Halsbury's Laws (4th edn) para 580, and for cases on the subject, see 3 Digest (Reissue) 201–203, 1235–1243.

For the Arbitration Act 1950, s 19A, see 2 Halsbury's Statutes (4th edn) 554.

Cases referred to in judgments

Atlantic Lines and Navigation Co Inc v Italmare Spa, The Apollon [1985] 1 Lloyd's Rep 597.

Baxters and Midland Rly Co, Re (1906) 95 LT 20, CA.

Chandris v Isbrandtsen Moller Co Inc [1950] 2 All ER 618, [1951] 1 KB 240, CA.

---

a   Section 19A is set out at p 510 a b, post

Fuga AG v Bunge AG [1975] 2 Lloyd's Rep 192.

a *GKN Centrax Gears Ltd v Matbro Ltd* [1976] 2 Lloyd's Rep 555, CA.

London Chatham and Dover Rly Co v South Eastern Rly Co [1893] AC 429, HL.

Montgomery Jones & Co and Liebenthal & Co, Re (1898) 78 LT 406, CA.

Mutual Shipping Corp of New York v Bayshore Shipping Co of Monrovia, The Montan [1985] 1 All ER 520, [1985] 1 WLR 625, CA.

President of India v La Pintada Cia Navegacion SA [1984] 2 All ER 773, [1985] AC 104,

b [1984] 3 WLR 10, HL.

Ramdutt Ramkissen Das v E D Sasson & Co (1929) 98 LJPC 58, [1929] All ER Rep 225.

Sutherland & Co v Hannevig Bros Ltd [1921] 1 KB 337, [1920] All ER Rep 670, DC.

Tersons Ltd v Stevenage Development Corp [1963] 3 All ER 863, [1965] 1 QB 37, [1964] 2 WLR 225, CA.

Tracomin SA v Sudan Oilseeds Co Ltd (No 1) [1983] 3 All ER 137, [1983] 1 WLR 1026, CA.

c

Cases also cited

Bremer Vulkan Schiffbau Und Maschinenfabrik v South India Shipping Corp [1981] 1 All ER 289, [1981] AC 909, HL.

Cia Martima Zorroza SA v Maritime Bulk Carriers Corp, The Marques de Bolarque [1980] 2 Lloyd's Rep 186.

d *Cie Financière pour le Commerce Extérieur SA v OY Vehna AB* [1963] 2 Lloyd's Rep 178.

Contishipping v Victor Shipping and Trading Ltd, The Gina Juliano [1984] 2 Lloyd's Rep 477.

Faure Fairclough Ltd v Premier Oil and Cake Mills Ltd [1968] 1 Lloyd's Rep 237.

Flynn v Robertson (1869) LR 4 CP 324.

Frobisher (Second Investments) Ltd v Kiloren Trust Co Ltd [1980] 1 All ER 488, [1980] 1 WLR 425.

e *Government Insurance Office of New South Wales v Atkinson-Leighton Joint Venture* (1980) 31 ALR 193, Aust HC.

Intermare Transport GmbH v International Copra Export Corp, The Ross Isle and Ariel [1982] 2 Lloyd's Rep 589.

Ismail v Polish Ocean Line (No 2), The Ciechocinek [1980] 1 Lloyd's Rep 97.

Moran v Lloyd's [1981] 1 Lloyd's Rep 423, CA.

f *President of India v Lips Maritime Corp, The Lips* [1985] 2 Lloyd's Rep 180.

Salzer (Robert) Constructions Pty Ltd v Barlin-Scott Air Conditioning Pty Ltd [1980] VR 545, Vic Full Ct.

Stock v Frank Jones (Tipton) Ltd [1976] 3 All ER 218, [1976] 1 WLR 694; *affd* [1978] 1 All ER 58, [1977] 1 WLR 1288, CA; *affd* [1978] 1 All ER 948, [1978] 1 WLR 231, HL.

Techno-Impex v Gebr van Weelde Scheepvartkantoor BV [1981] 2 All ER 669, [1981] QB 648,

g CA.

Temple Steamship Co Ltd v V/O Sorfracht (1943) 76 Ll L Rep 35, CA.

Ward v Chief Constable of Avon and Somerset (1985) 129 SJ 606, CA.

Yew Bon Tew v Kenderaan Bas Mara [1982] 3 All ER 833, [1983] 1 AC 553, PC.

Appeal and application for leave to appeal

h Marastro Cia Naviera SA, the owners of the vessel Trade Fortitude, appealed against the judgment of Leggatt J dated 29 July 1985 allowing an appeal by Food Corp of India (the charterers) against an award in the form of a special case by Mr Clifford Albert Lawrence Clark as arbitrator dated 3 April 1985 whereby he awarded the owners interest on a payment on account of demurrage which the charterers had paid to the owners on 13 April 1982. The charterers applied for leave to appeal against the decision of Leggatt J on

j 30 July 1985 refusing (1) to remit the arbitrator's final interim award to the arbitrator for reconsideration with a view to correcting an alleged mistake or error in the award and (2) to declare that the arbitrator had power to correct that mistake or error. The facts are set out in the judgment of Dillon LJ.

Michael G Collins for the owners.
Giles Caldin for the charterers.

Cur adv vult

19 May. The following judgments were delivered.

DILLON LJ. On the application by the charterers for leave to appeal against the *a*
judgment of Leggatt J of 30 July 1985, whereby he refused to remit the arbitrator's final
interim award to the arbitrator for reconsideration with a view to correcting an alleged
mistake or error in the award, and refused also to declare that the arbitrator had power to
correct that mistake or error, I would grant leave to appeal, since the application for leave
has been fully argued on the merits of the appeal and the argument has ranged over *b*
questions of law of considerable importance in relation to the remission and correction
of arbitrators' awards.

At the end of the day, however, I do not find it necessary to decide any of those
questions. The appeal falls to be decided on the facts. On the facts, it is not possible to say
what error, if any, the arbitrator has made, and therefore it is not possible for this court
either to declare that the arbitrator has power to correct the error or to remit the award *c*
with a view to the arbitrator correcting the error.

The owners' adjusted claim for demurrage was for 159 days 21 hours 31 minutes. The
arbitrator awarded demurrage for 153 days 4 hours 18 minutes. Assuming, without
deciding, that the arbitrator's confidential reasons can be looked at to see if he has made a
mistake which ought to be corrected, I find that he has held that the steaming time
(amounting to 4 days 13 hours 20 minutes) of five of the lighters to Calcutta is not to *d*
count against laytime, and a time for a winch breakdown of 1 hour 53 minutes is likewise
not to count. These give a total of 4 days 15 hours 13 minutes.

The charterers say that, if 4 days 15 hours 13 minutes are not counted against laytime,
the laytime extended into the weekend of 21–22 December 1974, which was also not to
be counted against the charterers as the vessel was not on demurrage when the weekend
began. They pray in aid an extra 10½ days, being Saturday afternoon and Sunday for each *e*
of seven lighters. They submit that the arbitrator has made the mistake of adjusting for
the 4 days 15 hours 13 minutes, which are not to count against laytime, by simply
deducting that amount from the 159 days 21 hours 31 minutes demurrage claimed
without addressing his mind to the weekend. But, if the arbitrator had only done that,
he would have arrived at a figure of 155 days 6 hours 18 minutes demurrage. In fact, he
has arrived at a figure of 153 days 4 hours 18 minutes, which is 2 days 2 hours lower. *f*
Whatever process led him to this figure, it is a figure between what the charterers say he
should have awarded and what he would have awarded if he had made the mistake
which the charterers say he made.

I may suspect that the arbitrator has made a mistake or mistakes, but I cannot say what
the mistake was and therefore I clearly cannot say that it was an accidental slip or
omission within the meaning of the slip rule, s 17 of the Arbitration Act 1950, which *g*
the arbitrator has power to correct.

As to remission, I find directly applicable the comments of Stephenson LJ in *GKN
Centrax Gears Ltd v Matbro Ltd* [1976] 2 Lloyd's Rep 555 at 576, where he said:

'To send an award back to enable justice which has certainly not been done to be
done . . . is one thing; to send it back to make sure that justice which may possibly
not have been done is done is quite another, and, as it seems to me, would, in the *h*
words of Lord Justice Willmer in *Tersons Ltd. v. Stevenage Development Corporation*
([1963] 3 All ER 863 at 867, [1965] 1 QB 37 at 47): ". . . cut at the root of the whole
purpose of arbitration, the basic idea of which is that the arbitrator's decision shall
be final."'

Accordingly, I would dismiss the charterers' appeal.

I turn to the appeal of the owners against the decision of Leggatt J of 29 July 1985 *j*
whereby, on that part of the arbitrator's award which, pursuant to earlier directions, was
in the form of a special case, he held that the arbitrator did not have power to award the
owners' interest on a payment of $US39,809·10 on account of demurrage which the
charterers had paid to the owners on 13 April 1982.

This was a voluntary payment by the charterers not under any order or award, made
a while the arbitration was pending. The judge held that the only power of an arbitrator
to award interest on such a voluntary payment was the power conferred by the new s 19A
of the Arbitration Act 1950, which was introduced into that Act by the Administration
of Justice Act 1982. He further held that that power only applied to arbitrations under
arbitration agreements entered into after the relevant provisions of the Administration
of Justice Act 1982 had come into force, viz after 1 April 1983.

b   If the judge was right in that conclusion of law, his decision that the arbitrator had no
power to award interest on this voluntary payment would follow on the dates in this
case. The charterparty, which includes the arbitration clause and constitutes the
arbitration agreement, was entered into on 12 September 1974. Final discharge of the
cargo on completion of the voyage took place in January 1975. The arbitration was
commenced on 9 January 1976. It proceeded at a pace which seems to have satisfied both
c parties (though it can hardly be said to demonstrate that expedition which is supposed to
be a main advantage of the process of arbitration) and came on for hearing in March
1984. The arbitrator's award was ultimately made on 3 April 1985. In the mean time,
the voluntary payment in question had been made on 13 April 1982, and s 19A had come
into force on 1 April 1983.

    Section 19A was introduced by s 15 of and Sch 1 to the Administration of Justice Act
d 1982. These provisions of the 1982 Act, as Lloyd LJ has explained in his judgment, also
introduced a new s 35A into the Supreme Court Act 1981 and a new s 97A into the
County Courts Act 1959. The new s 35A and the new s 97A gave power to the High Court
and to the county court to award interest, in proceedings for the recovery of a debt or
damages, on all or any part of the debt or damages in respect of which judgment is given
or payment is made before judgment. This covers a voluntary payment while proceedings
e are pending, and the wording of the sections makes it clear that they apply to proceedings
whenever instituted. Before these sections came into force, the only relevant power of
the courts to award interest was the power conferred on courts of record by s 2 of the
Law Reform (Miscellaneous Provisions) Act 1934 to award interest on any sum by way
of debt or damages for which judgment was given at the trial of the proceedings. Section
15(4) of the 1982 Act provided that s 3 of the 1934 Act should cease to have effect in
f relation to the High Court and the county courts because it was superseded, so far as
applicable to those courts, by the provisions of the 1982 Act.

    Section 19A of the Arbitration Act 1950 states that, unless a contrary intention is
expressed therein, every arbitration agreement shall, where such a provision is applicable
to the reference, be deemed to contain a provision that the arbitrator may award interest
on any sum which he awards and on any sum which is the subject of the reference but
g which is paid before the award. The formula 'Unless a contrary intention is expressed
therein, every arbitration agreement shall, where such a provision is applicable to the
reference, be deemed to contain a provision that . . .' is common in the Arbitration Act
1950: see ss 8(2), 12(1) and (2), 14, 15 and 16. That is, as it seems to me, why the formula
was used in s 19A. Section 19A does not refer in terms to 'every arbitration agreement
(whenever made)', but nor do the other sections in the 1950 Act which I have mentioned;
h it was not necessary to include the words '(whenever made)' in those sections because s 33
of the 1950 Act has provided that Pt I of the Act (which comprises ss 1 to 34) shall not
affect arbitrations commenced before the commencement of the Act but shall apply to
arbitrations commenced after the commencement of the Act under agreements made
before the commencement of the Act. On coming into force, s 19A has to be read in its
context in Pt I of the 1950 Act and in conjunction with s 33. Prima facie, therefore, it
j applies to any arbitration commenced after the commencement of the 1950 Act, which
was in 1950. I cannot read the words 'commencement of this Act' in s 33 as meaning in
relation to s 19A the coming into force of s 15 of the 1982 Act by which s 19A was inserted
into the 1950 Act. Counsel for the charterers sought to found an argument in relation to
s 33 on s 20(2) of the Interpretation Act 1978 but that subsection is directed to a different
purpose, and s 33 has not been amended by the 1982 Act.

Parliament could have made the position clearer, if it was intended that s 19A should have fully retrospective effect, by providing in the 1982 Act in terms that it was to apply *a* to arbitration agreements whether entered into before or after the coming into force of s 15 of the 1982 Act, as Parliament did in relation to s 58 of the Administration of Justice Act 1985 (which also amended the 1950 Act) by para 15 of Sch 9 to the 1985 Act. Conversely, however, if Parliament had intended to limit the effect of s 15A so that it would not be fully retrospective, Parliament could have made the position clearer by the wording, eg of the commencement order, as was done in relation to the Arbitration Act *b* 1979, where the commencement order provided that the Act should come into operation on an appointed day but should not apply to arbitrations commenced before that date. I do not derive assistance, however, in construing what Parliament has provided, from considering how it might have been done better either way.

I do, however, find it helpful to consider what powers the arbitrator would have had in this arbitration to award interest on the sum for demurrage which he actually awarded *c* to the owners (as opposed to the interim voluntary payment) if the judge is right that s 19A only applies to arbitration agreements entered into after s 19A had come into force, and so was not available to the arbitrator.

Before s 19A there was no general statutory provision empowering arbitrators to award interest on the sums they awarded. But it was held by this court in *Chandris v Isbrandtsen Moller Co Inc* [1950] 2 All ER 618, [1951] 1 KB 240 that, just as before the 1934 Act came *d* into force an arbitrator had been held entitled to award interest in the circumstances in which, under the Civil Procedure Act 1833, a jury could have awarded interest, so equally, after the 1934 Act came into force, an arbitrator had impliedly the power to award interest which s 3 had conferred on courts of record.

The decision in the *Chandris* case was approved by the House of Lords in *President of India v La Pintada Cia Navegacion SA* [1984] 2 All ER 773, [1985] AC 104. There, Lord *e* Brandon said that, where parties refer a dispute between them to arbitration in England, they impliedly agree that the arbitration is to be conducted in accordance in all respects with the law of England, unless the agreement of reference provides otherwise. Thus, although s 3 of the 1934 Act by its terms empowered only courts of record to include interest in sums for which judgment was given for damages or debt, arbitrators were nevertheless empowered, by the agreement of reference, to apply English law, including *f* so much of that law as was to be found in s 3 of the 1934 Act.

In my judgment, this implied agreement in the arbitration agreement is naturally to be understood as empowering arbitrators to apply English law as it is from time to time during the course of the reference (and in particular in the context of the present case as it was at the time of the hearing and the award) and not as an agreement empowering the arbitrator to apply English law crystallised as at the date of the arbitration agreement. *g* As it was put by Cohen LJ in the *Chandris* case [1950] 2 All ER 618 at 624, [1951] 1 KB 240 at 264 (though admittedly without having his mind addressed to transitional problems):

'In my opinion, the right of arbitrators to award interest was not derived from the Civil Procedure Act, 1833, s. 28 and s. 29, but from the rule that arbitrators had the powers of the appropriate court in the matter of awarding interest. In my *h* opinion, therefore, the effect of the Act of 1934 is that, after it came into force, an arbitrator had no longer the powers of awarding interest [on] damages conferred on juries by the Civil Procedure Act, 1833, s. 28 and s. 29, but he had the power conferred on the appropriate court, in the Act of 1934 described as a court of record.'

In the present case, the power of the court under s 3 of the 1934 Act to award interest *j* on a judgment at the trial of proceedings which the arbitrator would by implication prospectively have had at the time of the arbitration agreement had been superseded by the time of the hearing, and a fortiori by the date of the award, by the wider powers of the court as a result of s 15 of the 1982 Act. It is those wider powers which, by the *Chandris* process of implication, the arbitrator would have had when he made the award if s 19A had not been inserted into the 1950 Act. The purpose of s 19A is to make explicit

powers to award interest which had previously rested on implication. There is thus a
a further strong pointer to holding that s 19A has retrospective effect and applies to pending
and future arbitrations under arbitration agreements whenever made, just as the powers
of the High Court and of the county courts under s 35A of the 1981 Act and s 97A of the
1959 Act apply to proceedings whenever instituted.

In reaching the opposite view, the judge attached particular importance to the words
in s 19A 'Unless a contrary intention is expressed therein', which he felt showed that the
b section could only apply to arbitration agreements entered into after the section had
come into force. I do not attach so much importance to those words. I regard them as
part of a standard formula in sections in the 1950 Act and sufficiently satisfied by their
effect in relation to future agreements, coupled with the effect of any relevant provisions
there may be in existing agreements, eg provisions which there might theoretically be
excluding or limiting an arbitrator's power to award any interest at all.

c   For the foregoing reasons, I would, for my part, allow the owners' appeal, and would
hold that the arbitrator had power to award interest, as he did, on the voluntary interim
payment with which the court is concerned.

LLOYD LJ. On 12 September 1974 the Food Corp of India chartered the Trade
Fortitude for the carriage of a cargo of wheat in bulk from US Gulf to India. She arrived
d off Calcutta in early December 1974, where she discharged into lighters. There was a
provision in the charterparty whereby the time taken in discharging the cargo was to be
calculated, not by reference to the Trade Fortitude, but by reference to the lighters. There
were ten such vessels in all. There was severe congestion in the port of Calcutta at the
time, as a result of which the last of the lighters did not complete discharge until 23
January 1975. The owners claimed 159 days 21 hours 31 minutes demurrage at $US1,000
e a day. The charterers at first admitted 88 days demurrage. Subsequently, they admitted
114 days. They paid about $40,000 on 18 July 1975. They paid a further $39,000 or
thereabouts seven years later on 13 April 1982.

Meanwhile, in March 1975, the owners had appointed Mr Cedric Barclay as their
arbitrator. They did not communicate that appointment to the charterers until January
1976. On 18 March 1976 the charterers appointed Mr Clifford Clark. On 4 July 1983 Mr
f Barclay resigned. Mr Clark was thereupon appointed sole arbitrator. The hearing took
place on 21 March 1984. Two questions fell from Mr Clark's determination. There was
first the balance of the owners' claim for demurrage amounting to about $75,000.
Second, there was a claim for interest on the second instalment of $39,000 paid by the
charterers on 13 April 1982.

On the first question Mr Clark made a final award in favour of owners in the sum of
g $66,630·05. On the second question he held, subject to the decision of the court on the
hearing of a special case, that the owners were entitled to interest on the sum in question
from 1 June 1975 to 13 April 1982. The question of law for the opinion of the court, as
stated by the arbitrator, was whether he had power to award interest on sums paid prior
to the date of the award, under s 19A of the Arbitration Act 1950, as inserted by s 15(6) of
and Pt IV of Sch 1 to the Administration of Justice Act 1982.

h   Returning to the first question, the arbitrator furnished the parties with reasons for
his award, in accordance with the usual practice of London maritime arbitrators. The
reasons were provided on the usual basis, namely that they were not to be used in
connection with any proceedings on the award. There was an issue between the parties
whether we should look at the reasons or not. I will assume that we are entitled to look
at the reasons, at least for the purpose of this narrative.

j   One of the issues for the arbitrator's decision was whether steaming time was to count.
By steaming time I mean the time taken by the lighters from the point of discharge from
the Trade Fortitude to the discharging berth at Calcutta. The arbitrator decided that
point in favour of the charterers. The figure for steaming time was agreed by the parties
as 4 days 13 hours 20 minutes. The arbitrator also decided another minor item in favour
of the charterers, for which the agreed figure was 1 hour 53 minutes.

We do not know what calculations the arbitrator carried out. But from his reasons we know that he arrived at a final figure of 153 days 4 hours 18 minutes on demurrage, compared with the owners' claim of 159 days 21 hours 31 minutes.

The arbitrator published his award on 3 April 1985. On 25 April the charterers sent a telex to the arbitrator. In it they claimed that Mr Clark must have made a mistake. He must have held that laytime expired before the weekend of 21–22 December 1974. According to the charterers, the effect of steaming time not counting as laytime was that laytime did not expire until after the weekend. They sent a fresh timesheet to the arbitrator to prove their point. If laytime expired before the weekend, so that the lighters were already on demurrage, then the weekend would count in the owners' favour; but not otherwise. This consideration, when applied to the seven lighters then in use, would, according to the charterers, make a difference of about ten days. Instead of 153 days on demurrage, the arbitrator should have arrived at a figure of 143 days on demurrage, thereby reducing his award in owners' favour by about $22,000.

The charterers invited the arbitrator to amend his award, presumably under s 17 of the 1950 Act, since an arbitrator has no other power to amend once he has published his final award. But the owners, to whom the charterers had sent a copy of their telex of 25 April 1985, did not agree that the award should be amended; nor, despite increasingly urgent telex messages from the charterers to the arbitrator, did the arbitrator. Indeed, on 9 May 1985, the arbitrator replied that he had not looked at the case again since the publication of his award.

Having failed to persuade the arbitrator that there was any error in his award, the charterers applied to the Commercial Court. They asked for remission on the ground that the arbitrator had made a mistake or on the ground that he had misconducted himself in failing to correct his mistake when it was pointed out. Leggatt J refused relief, and refused leave to appeal.

On the argument of the special case Leggatt J held, contrary to the arbitrator's view, that the arbitrator had no power to award interest on the sum paid by the charterers in April 1982. Accordingly, he upheld the arbitrator's alternative award and dismissed the owners' claim for interest.

There are now two appeals to this court: the charterers' appeal against the judge's refusal to remit; the owners' against his judgment in favour of the charterers on the special case. It is convenient to take the charterers' appeal first.

Strictly, the charterers need leave to appeal. But, since we have now heard full argument from both sides, we propose to grant leave and, with counsel's consent, treat the hearing of the application as the hearing of the appeal.

The outcome of the appeal turns on the construction of s 17 of the 1950 Act. Section 17 provides:

'Unless a contrary intention is expressed in the arbitration agreement, the arbitrator or umpire shall have power to correct in an award any clerical mistake or error arising from any accidental slip or omission.'

Section 17 has been considered very recently by this court in *Mutual Shipping Corp of New York v Bayshore Shipping Co Ltd of Monrovia, The Montan* [1985] 1 All ER 520, [1985] 1 WLR 625. That case happened also to arise out of an award of Mr Clifford Clark, as sole arbitrator. One of the questions depended on the vessel's fuel consumption. The owners' evidence was that there was a saving of seven tons of fuel as compared with the vessel's warranted fuel consumption. The charterers' evidence was that the saving was only 4·5 tons. The arbitrator preferred the charterers' evidence. But, unfortunately, he took the owners' figure instead of the charterers' figure, thus rendering the charterers liable to pay much more than he intended. In that case the arbitrator admitted his mistake. This court held that the mistake was 'an error arising from an accidental slip' within the meaning of s 17. The arbitrator could have corrected the mistake himself, if he had wished, but, as he had not, the court would remit the award to enable him to do so.

Counsel for the charterers relied on *The Montan* for three submissions. His first submission was that we are free to look at the arbitrator's reasons in the present case even though he has furnished them on a restricted or confidential basis, that is to say on the

basis that they are not to be used in connection with any proceedings on the award. Sir
a John Donaldson MR said that an agreement or understanding between parties whereby
they agree not to place the arbitrator's reasons before the court would be an attempt to
oust the jurisdiction of the court. Accordingly, he held that the reasons could be looked
at, but only for an extremely limited purpose. In taking that view he went beyond the
ground on which Hobhouse J had decided the case in favour of the charterers. Robert
Goff LJ found it unnecessary to express any view on the question whether the reasons
b could be looked at, since he held that the existence and nature of the arbitrator's admitted
mistake emerged sufficiently clearly from the correspondence, without reference to the
reasons. Sir Roger Ormrod held that the status of confidential reasons was a matter for
discussion. But the parties could not blindfold the court. Only the court could do that.

Counsel for the owners argued strenuously that the court should only look at the
confidential reasons in the case of alleged fraud or impropriety, neither of which, I hasten
c to add, is suggested here. An assertion of error, unadmitted by the arbitrator, is not
enough.

The second submission of counsel for the charterers was that the decision in *The
Montan* applies whether or not the arbitrator admits his mistake. In that connection
counsel relied on the following paragraph from Sir John Donaldson MR's judgment
([1985] 1 All ER 520 at 525–526, [1985] 1 WLR 625 at 632):

d 'In the instant case, as in *Fuga AG v Bunge AG* [1975] 2 Lloyd's Rep 192, the
arbitrator admits that he made an accidental error, but I should not like it to be
thought that such an admission is a prerequisite to the exercise of the court's
jurisdiction to remit. If the arbitrator says nothing and there is a strong prima facie
case that there has been an accidental error, the award could be remitted to him
with a direction to reconsider it and to revise it if, but only if, there was such an
e error. If the arbitrator denies that he made any error or that the error was accidental,
there would still be jurisdiction to remit, but I cannot think that any court would
consider it appropriate to do so, unless there were other factors present.'

He also relied on the following passage from the judgment of Robert Goff LJ, and in
particular the words which I have emphasised ([1985] 1 All ER 520 at 530, [1985] 1 WLR
f 625 at 638):

'Without laying down any hard and fast rule, I think that as a general rule the
court should not intervene in cases of simple mistake unless there is a clear admission
by the arbitrator that he has made a mistake. Nowadays, arbitrators should be able
to correct any clerical mistakes in their awards, or any mistakes in their awards
arising from accidental errors or omissions, under s 17. The most likely case which
g may arise in which the court may be asked to exercise its power to remit an award
on grounds of error will be where an arbitrator, having made a mistake, is not
certain whether he has power to correct his award under s 17, as he may not be
when one party disputes his power to do so. In such a case, *or if the arbitrator otherwise
declines to exercise his power*, the aggrieved party may apply to the court for a
remission. Such cases apart, I cannot but think that the court's power of remission
h will be very rarely exercised in cases of mistake; but, as I have said, I do not wish to
restrict the width of the power to order remission in the interests of justice.'

Counsel for the owners submits that, though the court's power to remit under s 22 of
the 1950 Act, as under its predecessors, is unlimited, nevertheless the court will not in
practice go outside the four grounds accepted as correct in *Re Montgomery Jones & Co and
j Liebenthal & Co* (1898) 78 LT 406. The third of the four grounds is admitted mistake.
The distinction between an admitted mistake and a mistake which is not admitted or
denied is the obvious one that it would be a reproach to the law if the court were
unwilling to remit where the arbitrator has admitted his mistake, particularly if he has
asked for the reward to be remitted. Counsel for the owners relies in that connection on
the recent decision of Webster J in *Atlantic Lines and Navigation Co Inc v Italmare Spa, The
Apollon* [1985] 1 Lloyd's Rep 597, in which, after a most helpful review of all the cases,

Webster J felt compelled not to follow the dicta in *The Montan* to which I have already
referred, on the ground that they are inconsistent with a previous unreported decision of
the Divisional Court in *Re Baxters and Midland Rly Co*, and also by inference (I think he
would say) with the dicta of the Court of Appeal in that case ((1906) 95 LT 20). Since the
arbitrators had not admitted any error in *The Apollon*, Webster J declined to remit the
award.

I understand that *The Apollon* is under appeal to this court.

For reasons which will appear in a moment, I do not find it necessary to arrive at any
decision on the first or second submission of counsel for the charterers. I am prepared to
assume in his favour that we are permitted to look at the arbitrator's reasons in this case.
I am further prepared to assume that the court will in a proper case remit an award to an
arbitrator, where he has made an accidental slip, even though the accidental slip is not
admitted. But at the very least in such a case there must, as Sir John Donaldson MR
pointed out, be strong prima facie evidence of the accidental slip in question.

That brings me to the third submission of counsel for the charterers. Just as there was
held to be an accidental slip in *The Montan*, by the transposition in the arbitrator's mind
of the evidence given on each side, so also, it is said, there was an accidental slip here. The
slip was not so obvious, but its nature was the same. The arbitrator found in favour of
the charterers on the issue of steaming time. But he then failed to carry through the
effect of that finding into his award. If he had been thinking at all, the arbitrator must
have realised that his finding would have the effect that the expiry of laytime would be
postponed until after the weekend of 22 December 1974, with the result that that
weekend would not count. According to counsel for the charterers, the only explanation
is that the arbitrator made an accidental slip.

I cannot accept counsel's third submission. It rests on the assertion that the arbitrator
has failed to 'carry through' his two findings in favour of the charterers, to which I have
referred. On the agreed figures the total time saved amounts to 4 days 15 hours 13
minutes. If the arbitrator had made the simple error which he is said to have made, he
would have deducted 4 days 15 hours 13 minutes from 159 days 21 hours 31 minutes,
in which case he would have arrived at 155 days 6 hours 18 minutes. But he did not
arrive at that figure: he arrived at 153 days 4 hours 18 minutes, a difference of 2 days 2
hours. Nobody has been able to explain that difference. Either the arbitrator did not
make the simple error which he is said to have made or he has made some other error as
well. On either view, the charterers have failed to establish a strong prima facie case that
the arbitrator has made the error he is said to have made. The most they have established
is that he has made an error. The nature of that error remains a mystery.

Even if the arithmetic had added up, so that we could be sure that what the arbitrator
did was to subtract the steaming time from time on demurrage instead of adding it (as it
were) to laytime, I would hesitate to describe that error as arising from an accidental slip.
In one sense, of course, all errors are accidental. You do not make a mistake on purpose.
But here the words take their colour from their context. I do not suggest that s 17 is
limited to clerical mistakes. But, in general, the error must, in the words of Rowlatt J in
Sutherland & Co v Hannevig Bros Ltd [1921] 1 KB 336 at 341, be an error affecting the
expression of the arbitrator's thought, not an error in the thought process itself. Assuming
the arbitrator made the mistake he is said to have made, I would regard it as having been
an error in his thought process, not an error in the expression of his thought. The fact
that the error, if he made it, was an elementary error is not sufficient to make it
accidental.

In *The Montan* Robert Goff LJ referred to a number of cases which showed that the
High Court slip rule, RSC Ord 20, r 11, is not confined to an accidental slip on the part of
the court. It also covers accidental slips by one of the parties, or by his counsel or by his
solicitor. But none of the cases referred to comes near the present case. I will not attempt
to define an accidental slip or omission where others before me have found the task so
difficult. The animal is, as Robert Goff LJ said in *The Montan* [1985] 1 All ER 520 at 529,
[1985] 1 WLR 625 at 627, usually recognisable when it appears on the scene. Even if
there were strong prima facie evidence that the arbitrator had made the error which he

a is said to have made, which I do not think there is, I would not regard that error as having arisen from an 'accidental slip or omission' within the meaning of s 17.

The second ground on which counsel for the charterers seeks remission is misconduct. He submits that it is misconduct on the part of an arbitrator, who has the power to correct an error under s 17, not to consider exercising that power when asked. The factual basis for that submission in the present case is the arbitrator's telex of 9 May 1985, in which he said that he had not looked at the case since the publication of his award.

b I am reluctant to add to the burdens of arbitrators, who are already overburdened. But I am bound to say that an arbitrator should always reconsider his award when it is alleged by one side or the other that he has made an accidental slip. When the other side accepts that he has made an accidental slip, or a slip that may be accidental, failure by the arbitrator to reconsider his award would normally amount to misconduct. Even where the other side do not accept that he has made an accidental slip, an arbitrator should

c reconsider his award, at least as a matter of sound practice.

In the present case, even if the arbitrator had been guilty of misconduct, I would be unwilling to remit the award. For remission is a discretionary remedy. If I am right that the error which the arbitrator is alleged to have made was not an accidental error within the meaning of s 17, then the arbitrator would have no power to amend his award, and remission would be pointless. The possibility of the arbitrator having made some *other*

d error, which arose from an accidental slip, does not justify remission. As Stephenson LJ said in *GKN Centrax Gears Ltd v Matbro Ltd* [1976] 2 Lloyd's Rep 555 at 576, remission where justice has certainly not been done is one thing; remission where it may not have been done is another. I would dismiss the charterers' appeal.

I now turn to the owners' appeal. It raises more difficult questions, on which a number of current arbitrations are said to depend.

e The arbitrators held, as I have already mentioned, that the owners are entitled to recover interest on the sum of about $39,000 from 1 June 1975 until the date of payment on 13 April 1982. Leggatt J took a different view. Before summarising his reasons I should first set out the relevant provisions of s 15 of and Sch 1 to the Administration of Justice Act 1982, confining my quotation to what is necessary to appreciate the judge's reasons. Section 15 provides:

f

'(1) The section set out in Part I of Schedule 1 to this Act shall be inserted after section 35 of the Supreme Court Act 1981.

(2) The section set out in Part II of that Schedule shall be inserted after section 97 of the County Courts Act 1959 . . .

(6) The section set out in Part IV of Schedule 1 to this Act shall be inserted after section 19 of the Arbitration Act 1950.'

g

Schedule 1 to the 1982 Act, referred to in s 15(1) and (2) of that Act, is in these terms:

'INTEREST ON DEBTS AND DAMAGES

PART I

SECTION INSERTED IN SUPREME COURT ACT 1981

h 35A.—(1) Subject to rules of court, in proceedings (whenever instituted) before the High Court for the recovery of a debt or damages there may be included in any sum for which judgment is given simple interest, at such rate as the court thinks fit or as rules of court may provide, on all or any part of the debt or damages in respect of which judgment is given, or payment is made before judgment, for all or any part of the period between the date when the cause of action arose and—(a) in the case of any sum paid before judgment, the date of the payment; and (b) in the case

j of the sum for which judgment is given, the date of the judgment . . .

PART II

SECTION INSERTED IN COUNTY COURTS ACT 1959

[Here there follow provisions applicable to county courts of the same kind as those applicable to the High Court by virtue of Pt I] . . .

PART IV

SECTION INSERTED IN ARBITRATION ACT 1950

19A. (1) Unless a contrary intention is expressed therein, every arbitration agreement shall, where such a provision is applicable to the reference, be deemed to contain a provision that the arbitrator or umpire may, if he thinks fit, award simple interest at such rate as he thinks fit—(a) on any sum which is the subject of the reference but which is paid before the award, for such period ending not later than the date of the payment as he thinks fit; and (b) on any sum which he awards, for such period ending not later than the date of the award as he thinks fit . . .'

By art 2 of the Administration of Justice Act 1982 (Commencement No 1) Order 1983, SI 1983/236, s 15 came into force on 1 April 1983.

The argument before the judge turned on the question whether s 19A had retrospective effect on arbitration agreements made before 1 April 1983. He held not. Counsel for the charterers identified four separate strands in the judge's reasoning. First, neither s 15 of the 1982 Act nor s 19A of the 1950 Act contain any express provision that s 19A was to have retrospective effect. Second, the express language of s 19A, and in particular the opening words 'Unless a contrary intention is expressed therein', suggests strongly that the section was to have prospective effect only. Third, there is a marked contrast between the language of s 35A of the Supreme Court Act 1981, incorporated by Pt I of the schedule, and the language of s 19A of the 1950 Act, incorporated by Pt IV. Section 35A covers proceedings whenever instituted, that is to say before or after 1 April 1983. There are no equivalent words in s 19A. Fourth, it would be bad law as well as bad logic to imply a new term into an existing contract.

Counsel for the owners criticised the judge's reasoning in a number of respects. Section 19A by its express terms applies to every arbitration agreement. Even if the language were not clear enough in itself to give s 19A retrospective effect, nevertheless it is plain that it was intended to have retrospective effect by necessary implication. He relied in that connection on Tracomin SA v Sudan Oil Seeds Co Ltd (No 1) [1983] 3 All ER 137, [1983] 1 WLR 1026. Nor do the words 'Unless a contrary intention is expressed therein' necessarily indicate a prospective effect only. The presence of those words can be sufficiently explained by the fact that the new section was to take its place in an existing Act, in which these very words can be found in at least nine other sections or subsections. As for the contrast between s 35A of the 1981 Act and s 19A of the 1950 Act, counsel for the owners relies on the same explanation. Unlike the jurisdiction of the High Court, the arbitrators' jurisdiction is consensual. One would not have expected to find precisely the same language in each case. The absence of the words 'whenever instituted' in s 19A carries little weight. On the contrary, the inclusion of those words would have created an awkward inconsistency with s 33 of the 1950 Act, once s 19A had taken its place in Pt I of the Act. For s 33 provides:

'This Part of this Act shall not affect any arbitration commenced . . . before the commencement of this Act, but shall apply to an arbitration so commenced after the commencement of this Act under an agreement made before the commencement of this Act.'

If it had been intended that s 19A was not to have effect in relation to agreements made 'before the commencement of this Act', that is to say before the commencement of the 1950 Act, but only after 1 April 1983, the most elegant way of achieving that result, and perhaps the only correct way, would have been to make express provision in the Administration of Justice Act 1982 (Commencement No 1) Order 1983, as was done when the new s 10(3) and (4) of the 1950 Act were inserted by s 58 of and Sch 9 to the Administration of Justice Act 1985.

I find these arguments evenly balanced. On the whole, I would have come down in favour of the judge's view, but for one argument which I have not so far mentioned. It is an argument which was not advanced strongly before us and may not have been advanced at all before the judge. It approaches the problem from a different angle. The question is

not: is s 19A, by its terms or necessary implication, retrospective? but rather: what was
a the term implied when the original arbitration agreement was made? If the implied
term was that the arbitrator was to conduct the arbitration and have all such powers as
he would have had in accordance with the law as it stood when the arbitration agreement
was entered into in September 1974, then the answer to the question raised by the special
case would indeed depend on whether s 19A is retrospective in the strict sense. But, if the
implied term was that the arbitration was to be conducted and the arbitrator to have all
b such powers as he might have at the time of his award, then it is immaterial whether
s 19A is retrospective or not. The owners succeed, not by virtue of a term to be implied
retrospectively, but by virtue of a term which has been there all along. In other words, it
is not a question, as the judge thought, of implying a *new* term into an *existing* contract,
but of ascertaining what the true intention and effect of the existing contract is.

The only authority which comes near the question is *Chandris v Isbrandtsen Moller Co
c Inc* [1950] 2 All ER 618, [1951] 1 KB 240. In that case it was argued that an arbitrator
had no power at all to award interest, since his original power derived from s 28 of the
Civil Procedure Act 1833, and that section had been repealed by s 3 of the Law Reform
(Miscellaneous Provisions) Act 1934. The Court of Appeal rejected that argument. The
court held that an arbitrator's power to award interest derived, not directly from the
language of the 1934 Act, but indirectly from the submission to arbitration. Adapting
d the words of Lord Salvesen in *Ramdutt Ramkissen Das v E D Sassoon & Co* (1929) 98 LJPC
58 at 62, [1929] All ER Rep 225 at 229, Tucker LJ said ([1950] 2 All ER 618 at 623,
[1951] 1 KB 240 at 262):

'Although the Law Reform (Miscellaneous Provisions) Act, 1934, does not in
terms apply to arbitrations, I think that in mercantile references of the kind in
question it is an implied term of the contract that the arbitrator must decide the
e dispute according to the existing law of contract, and that every right and
discretionary remedy given to a court of law can be exercised by him.'

What is meant by 'existing law'? Does it mean the law existing at the date of the
arbitration agreement? Or does it mean the law existing at the date of the hearing or, if
it be different, at the date of the award? I have no doubt that the latter view is correct.
f As far as the substantive law is concerned, any other view would be unworkable.
When leave to appeal is given on a question of law under s 1 of the Arbitration Act 1979,
the Commercial Court applies the law as it stands. No one would suggest that the court
should apply the law as it stood at the date of the arbitration agreement, ignoring any
decisions of the courts in the mean time. It must follow that the arbitrator, too, is obliged
to apply case law at the time of his award. That is what the parties must have intended
g by their submission. I see no reason why the parties should have intended to draw any
distinction between case law and statute law. It is sometimes said that the difference
between case law and statute law is that, whereas a statute can change the law, cases can
only change what was thought to be the law. But I doubt if two commercial men
entering into a charterparty would appreciate that distinction.

Nor would they draw any distinction between substantive law and procedural law,
h assuming (for the sake of argument) that the power of an arbitrator to award interest is a
matter of procedure and not substance. Arbitration clauses frequently provide that the
arbitration is to be conducted in accordance with the 1950 Act 'and any statutory
modification or re-enactment thereof'. The absence of those words in the present case
does not lead me to conclude that the parties did not intended to be bound by procedural
law at the date of the award.

j Counsel for the charterers argued that, if the above view be correct, then s 19A is otiose.
If arbitrators have an implied power to follow the law, then they do not need s 19A. They
can apply s 35A by analogy. Secondly, he argued that an arbitrator appointed under
arbitration agreements entered into after 1 April 1983 will have two sources of power:
an express power under s 19A of the 1950 Act and an implied power to follow the High
Court under s 35A. This was said to be contrary to the reasoning of Lord Brandon in
President of India v La Pintada Cia Navigacion SA [1984] 2 All ER 773 at 790, [1985] AC

104 at 131, where he rejected a solution which would have resulted in parallel but inconsistent remedies.

I cannot accept either of these arguments. Section 12 of the 1950 Act contains a number of express provisions relating to the conduct of proceedings which, in the absence of express provision, might well have been implied. It does not mean that s 12 is otiose. No more is s 19A. As for the second argument, there would, in *La Pintada*, have been an inconsistency between two remedies. One remedy would have been discretionary; the other as of right. There is no such inconsistency here.

For the reasons I have given, I would hold that s 19A of the 1950 Act applies to all arbitration agreements under that Act, whenever made. I would therefore allow the owners' appeal in the special case and restore the award of the arbitrator. I am glad to have been able to reach that result. In the first place, it means that so far as the power to award interest is concerned, there is no difference between arbitrations and actions. In the second place, it serves to exclude the rule in *London Chatham and Dover Rly Co v South Eastern Rly Co* [1893] AC 429, the justice of which was never very apparent, in the few remaining arbitrations to which this decision will apply.

NICHOLLS LJ. I agree with the judgments of both Dillon and Lloyd LJJ and I wish to add only one observation with regard to the interest claim. Before the coming into force of s 15 of the Administration of Justice Act 1982, at common law the court had no power to award interest when a debt was paid late after proceedings for its recovery had begun but before they were concluded, but courts of record did have a statutory power to award interest where a debt remained unpaid and a money judgment was obtained thereon: see *President of India v La Pintada Cia Navegacion SA* [1984] 2 All ER 773, [1985] AC 104. The statutory power of the court stemmed, in recent years, from s 3 of the Law Reform (Miscellaneous Provisions) Act 1934. By implication arbitrators had the like power, even though s 3 in terms empowered only courts of record to award interest (see *Chandris v Isbrandtsen Moller Co Inc* [1950] 2 All ER 618, [1951] 1 KB 240).

It is not in dispute that the purpose of s 15 of the 1982 Act was to enlarge the powers of courts and arbitrators to award interest. But s 3 of the 1934 Act was superseded in relation to the High Court and the county court by the new s 35A of the Supreme Court Act 1981 and a corresponding new section of the County Courts Act 1959: see s 15(4) of the 1982 Act. If, as contended by the charterers, the new s 19A of the Arbitration Act 1950 only applies to arbitration agreements made after that section came into operation, I can see no escape from the conclusion that, when s 15 of the 1982 Act took effect and s 3 of the 1934 Act was superseded as mentioned, the effect was to cut down arbitrators' existing powers regarding the award of interest in that, and to the extent that, with the disappearance of s 3 (the source by implication of the arbitrators' existing powers), for the future arbitrators would have no power to award interest where the arbitration agreement had been entered into before s 19A of the 1950 Act came into operation. This conclusion manifestly cannot have been intended by Parliament.

This difficulty cannot be avoided by looking to the new section which replaced s 3 of the 1934 Act without fatally undermining the charterers' case, because the new section, s 35A, is all embracing in its terms, applying as much to existing proceedings as to new proceedings. To my mind, this consideration provides further support for the construction of s 15 of the 1982 Act, and s 19A of the 1950 Act introduced thereby, set out in the judgments of Dillon and Lloyd LJJ.

Leave to appeal by charterers against order of Leggatt J of 30 July 1985 granted but appeal dismissed. Owners' appeal against order of Leggatt J of 29 July 1985 allowed; question in special case answered in affirmative and owners' claim for interest on interim payment upheld. Leave to appeal to the House of Lords refused.

Solicitors: *Sinclair Roche & Temperley* (for the owners); *Zaiwalla & Co* (for the charterers).

Celia Fox   Barrister.

a ## Posner and others v Scott-Lewis and others

CHANCERY DIVISION
MERVYN DAVIES J
26, 27 NOVEMBER, 4 DECEMBER 1985

b *Specific performance – Personal services – Service agreement in lease – Covenant in lease to execute service agreement – Landlord covenanting to employ resident porter to carry out specified duties – Landlord employing part-time non-resident porter – Whether landlord in breach of covenant – Whether covenant capable of being enforced by specific performance.*

The plaintiffs were tenants in a block of flats owned by the defendant landlords. Each plaintiff held his tenancy on the terms of a written lease which contained in cl 3(11) a
c covenant by the defendants to employ a resident porter to keep the communal areas clean, to be responsible for the central heating and boilers, and to collect rubbish from the flats. In 1985 the then resident porter left the defendants' employment but by arrangement with the defendants continued to carry out on a part-time basis the duties specified in cl 3(11). The plaintiffs sought specific performance of the covenant in cl 3(11) compelling the defendants to employ a porter who was resident, contending that the
d porter's duties were being carried out inadequately. The defendants contended that they were not in breach of cl 3(11) since although they were not employing a resident porter all the duties required to be performed under cl 3(11) were in fact being discharged. The question arose, inter alia, whether an order for specific performance could be made if the defendants were in breach of cl 3(11).

e **Held** – (1) On its true construction cl 3(11) of the leases indicated that there would be a porter in residence and that he would perform certain functions, and the defendants could not discharge their duty to keep a porter in residence by arranging for his functions to be carried out by a non-resident porter, since a resident porter was valuable not only for the duties he was expected to perform but also by his very presence. It followed that the defendants were in breach of cl 3(11) (see p 519 c to e, post).

f   (2) In the circumstances it was open to the court to consider the making of an order for specific performance. The making of such an order depended on whether there was sufficient definition of what had to be done by way of compliance with the court's order, whether enforcing compliance would involve superintendence by the court to an unacceptable degree, and the amount of prejudice and hardship that would be suffered by the respective parties if the order was made. On the facts, an order that the defendants
g employ within a specified period a resident porter for the purposes of carrying out the cl 3(11) duties would not occasion any protracted superintendence by the court and if the defendants without good cause failed to comply with the order in due time the plaintiffs could then take appropriate enforcement proceedings against the defendants. Furthermore, there would be no hardship or prejudice caused to the defendants by the order since they would simply be performing what they had promised to do and what they
h had in fact done in the past. On the other hand, there would be considerable inconvenience, if not hardship, to the plaintiffs if having bargained for a resident porter and having enjoyed his presence in the past they had in the future to be content with a non-resident porter. An order for specific performance would accordingly be made (see p 521 b to g, post); *Ryan v Mutual Tontine Westminster Chambers Association* [1893] 1 Ch 116 distinguished; dicta of Megarry J in *C H Giles & Co Ltd v Morris* [1972] 1 All ER at
j 969–970 and of Megarry V-C in *Tito v Waddell (No 2)* [1977] 3 All ER at 307–308 considered.

Notes

For specific performance of contracts for personal work or services, see 44 Halsbury's Laws (4th edn) para 407, and for cases on the subject, see 45 Digest (Reissue) 16–20, 99–124.

For a landlord's undertaking as to employees, see 27 Halsbury's Laws (4th edn) para 141, and for cases on the subject, see 31(1) Digest (Reissue) 315, *2535–2536*.

Cases referred to in judgment

Federated Homes Ltd v Mill Lodge Properties Ltd [1980] 1 All ER 371, [1980] 1 WLR 594, CA.

Giles (C H) & Co Ltd v Morris [1972] 1 All ER 960, [1972] 1 WLR 307.

Ryan v Mutual Tontine Westminster Chambers Association [1893] 1 Ch 116, CA.

Shelfer v City of London Electric Lighting Co [1895] 1 Ch 287, [1891–4] All ER Rep 838, CA.

Shiloh Spinners Ltd v Harding [1973] 1 All ER 90, [1973] AC 691, [1973] 2 WLR 28, HL.

Tito v Waddell (No 2), Tito v A-G [1977] 3 All ER 129, [1977] Ch 106, [1977] 2 WLR 496.

Wolverhampton Corp v Emmons [1901] 1 QB 515, CA.

Motion

By a notice of motion dated 24 October 1985 the plaintiffs, (1) Morris Posner, (2) Leslie Dayan, (3) Sigrid Nagel, (4) Eric Nagel, (5) Julia Bennett, (6) E Cantor, (7) Audrey Newsome, (8) Emot Ltd and (9) Anne Benn, sought as against the defendants, (1) Richard James Scott-Lewis, (2) Jeanette Angela Scott-Lewis, (3) Kestie Fiona Scott-Lewis, and (4) Russell Scott-Lewis, the following relief: (i) specific performance of the defendants' covenant in cl 3(11) of the plaintiffs' respective leases of their respective flats (and garages in the case of the third and fifth plaintiffs) in Danes Court, 1–5 St Edmunds Terrace, London NW8 to employ (so far as in the defendants' power) a resident porter for the purposes set out in cl 3(11), (ii) an injunction restraining the defendants and each of them by themselves their servants agents or otherwise howsoever from selling, agreeing to sell leasing or agreeing to lease or otherwise disposing of or parting with possession of the porter's flat situated on the ground floor of Danes Court, save in respect of giving possession of the flat to a resident porter employed by the defendants for the purpose and in accordance with the provisions of cl 3(11), and (iii) for interlocutory judgment for damages in breach of the defendants' covenant in cl 3(11), to be assessed by the master, alternatively that there be an inquiry as to damages for breach of the covenant. The facts are set out in the judgment.

Romie Tager for the plaintiffs.
Andrew Hochhauser for the defendants.

Cur adv vult

4 December. The following judgment was delivered.

MERVYN DAVIES J. I have before me two motions by the plaintiffs in this action: the first motion dated 24 October 1985 seeks final judgment under RSC Ord 14 with an alternative claim for interlocutory relief; the second motion dated 7 November 1985 seeks as a further alternative the appointment of a receiver. The writ is dated 29 August 1985. There are nine plaintiffs. The plaintiffs are members of the Danes Court resident's association. Danes Court is a block of residential flats in St Edmunds Terrace, London NW8. Each of the plaintiffs is a tenant of a flat in the block. Thus the first plaintiff, the chairman of the resident's association, is the lessee of 4 Danes Court, the second plaintiff Mr Dayan, the secretary, is the lessee of 2 Danes Court, and so on. There are 25 flats in the block together with a flat that has until recently been occupied by a resident porter.

At the issue of the writ the first defendant, Richard James Scott-Lewis, was made sole defendant on the footing that he was the lessor or landlord to the plaintiff tenants. On 1 October 1985 the writ was amended to add the second, third and fourth defendants since it is common ground that the four defendants together are the landlords of the flats in Danes Court. The defendants have been the landlords since about 1982.

Each of the plaintiffs holds his or her tenancy on the terms of a lease in writing. It is
a common ground that all the Danes Court leases are in terms similar to the lease which is
exhibited to an affidavit of Mrs S Nagel, the third plaintiff, sworn on 2 September 1985.
This particular lease is that of Mr Dayan, the second plaintiff. The lease is dated 6 April
1964 and is made between Boyton Developments Ltd—

b
'(hereinafter called "the Lessor" which expression where the context so admits
includes the estate owner or estate owners for the time being entitled to the
immediate reversion to the property hereby demised expectant on the term hereby
granted) of the one part and Mr Dayan (hereinafter called the "lessee" which
expression where the context so admits includes his assigns and successors in title
and the persons deriving title under him)'

of the other part. As I have mentioned the defendants are now the lessors.
c   The lease witnesses that in consideration of the sum of £8,500 the lessor demises flat 2
on the ground floor of Danes Court to Mr Dayan (together with and subject to various
rights which I need not mention) for 99 years from 25 December 1963 at a yearly rent of
£100.
There follow various covenants by the lessee including these:

d
'(4) To use the property exclusively as a private dwelling or residence in single
occupation only and the garage as a garage incidental to the enjoyment of the
property . . .
(6) Not to use or permit or suffer the property to be used for any trade business
or profession or for any meeting thereon or for any illegal or immoral purpose or in
any manner whereby the character of the properties in the building as high class
residential properties may be prejudiced or injured . . .
e   (18) To observe and perform and conform to the Management Regulations set
forth in the Schedule hereto and to such other reasonable rules and regulations as
the lessor may from time to time properly make for the orderly and better
management of the building and the grounds thereof upon being given notice in
writing of such other reasonable rules.'

f   There are also covenants by the lessor. These covenants include: cl 3(2), where the
lessor promises to maintain etc the main hall, staircases, lift, the central heating system
and the internal telephone system (which connects with the porter's flat); cl 3(7), a
promise by the lessor to see that the common parts are kept clean and lighted and (see
cl 3(1)) to supply and maintain hot water and central heating. There is a lessor's covenant
that I must quote in full. Clause 3(11) reads:

g
'To employ (so far as in the Lessor's power lies) a resident porter for the following
purposes and for no other purposes:—(a) To keep clean the common staircases and
entrance hall landings and passages and lift (b) To be responsible for looking after
and stoking the central heating and domestic hot water boilers (c) To carry down
rubbish from the properties to the dustbins outside the building every day.'

h   Clause 3(12) reads: 'To maintain repair and meet all overheads outgoings and expenses
in respect of the porter's flat.'
Clause 4 of the lease provides for the lessee paying a proportion of the expenditure
incurred by the lessor in connection with the fulfillment by the lessor of the obligations
undertaken by cl 3 of the lease. I need not set out these detailed provisions, but the effect
is, inter alia, that the cost to the lessor of providing a resident porter under cl 3(11) is
j recoverable in part from the lessee. Thus with a similar provision in all the leases the
lessor will recover all his cl 3 expenditure. The cl 3 covenants are binding on the lessor
only while holding title to the reversion (see cl 5). I need not mention the stipulations in
the schedule, ie the management regulations, save to quote reg 1:

'The entrance doors of properties shall be kept shut and no owner shall on any

account whatsoever leave or permit to be left any invalid carriage or chair or any
bicycle perambulator box parcel refuse rubbish or any article whatsoever upon or   *a*
obstructing any part of the building used in common with other occupiers but
lessees shall each morning before Nine a.m. have ready within their properties for
removal in a proper receptacle the refuse of the previous day.'

The writ claims specific performance of the lessor's covenant in cl 3(11) of the plaintiffs'
respective leases of their respective flats, that is to say the plaintiffs seek to compel the
defendants to employ a resident porter for the purposes itemised in cl 3(11). There is also   *b*
a claim for damages by reason of the defendants' failure to employ a resident porter since
1 June 1985. The issue of the writ on 29 August 1985 was followed by an ex parte order
made by Walton J on 5 September 1985. The defendants were restrained until judgment
or further order from selling or leasing the porter's flat. That order was made, as I
understand, because it was then supposed that the defendants were about to dispose of
the porter's flat, and if that were done then the relief sought in the writ might not be   *c*
available.

The next step to mention is that the plaintiffs served a statement of claim on 2 October
1985. Particulars of the plaintiffs' and defendants' titles are given, and complaint is made
of the defendants' failure to employ or seek to employ a resident porter since 1 June
1985.

There followed on 24 October 1985 the first notice of motion seeking, pursuant to   *d*
Ord 14, specific performance as mentioned in the writ, with damages. In the alternative
there is a claim for an interlocutory mandatory order requiring the defendants to take
steps to employ a resident porter. Then, as I have said, there is the second notice of
motion, dated 7 November 1985, whereby there is sought, pending trial, a receiver of all
the rents profits service charges and other moneys payable by the lessees of all the Danes
Court flats.   *e*

I will now mention some of the affidavit evidence read to me. The principal affidavit
in support of the motion was sworn by the honorary treasurer of the resident's association,
Mrs Nagel, the third plaintiff. In para 3 Mrs Nagel describes Danes Court as a modern
luxury block of flats ('in the true sense of the term') which was completed in 1964,
comprising 26 flats including the porter's flat, on eight floors. Some of the flats in the
block have been sublet but all the plaintiffs are residents save that Mrs Nagel, living in   *f*
no 19 with her husband, has sublet no 18. Mrs Nagel says she receives a rent of £1,300 a
month for the subletting of no 18. Mrs Nagel states that Danes Court—

'has until recently been maintained to the highest standards with the recognised
amenity of a resident porter which distinguishes the true luxury flat from other
flats in the neighbourhood which do not offer this particular service.'
                                                                                      g

In para 8 Mrs Nagel says that there is a flat on the ground floor which has been occupied
by the resident porters, who have been employed successively since 1964. The flat ceased
to be so occupied on 31 May 1985. The porter then in residence, Mr Bewsher, ceased to
be employed by the defendants on that date. Mr Bewsher took up employment at a
nearby block of flats called Kings Court. That is not in the defendant's ownership.
However, it seems that there was some arrangement between Mr Bewsher and the first   *h*
defendant, because since 1 June 1985 Mr Bewsher has, to some extent at any rate,
continued to carry out the words specified in (a), (b) and (c) of cl 3(11). According to Mrs
Nagel the work is done inadequately and clearly it must be done on a part-time basis
since Mr Bewsher now has duties at Kings Court, where he resides.

There was a meeting of some of the residents on 11 July 1985. The first defendant
attended. In para 18 of the affidavit Mrs Nagel says: *j*

'... the defendant said that he had made efforts to find a replacement for Mr.
Bewsher and he said he had interviewed 11 applicants.'

There was a discussion at the meeting of certain repair works which the defendants said
would have to be carried out.

In this connection Mrs Nagel says in para 19:

'At this point, the defendant returned to the earlier discussion about the required remedial works and their cost. He said that in order to finance the building works it would be necessary for him to consider selling the resident porter's flat. Mr. Bennett intervened once again and asked the defendant why he had bothered to interview 11 applicants for the job if he was proposing to sell off the porter's flat. To everyone's astonishment, the defendant then conceded that he had not in fact interviewed any applicants for the job, had not made any efforts to do so, and had no intention of doing so. The defendant then put forward a proposal that the lessees should pay him in advance the monies which would be required for the remedial works. He suggested that if an appropriate scheme could be worked out it would not be necessary to sell the porter's flat.'

There is some correspondence exhibited to Mrs Nagel's affidavit extending over the period 6 June to 20 August 1985. It illustrates the tenants' concern at being left without a resident porter, and in a letter dated 16 August 1985 assurances are sought that the porter's flat will not be sold and that a new porter will be put in residence. No assurances being forthcoming, the writ was issued.

There is then a second affidavit of Mrs Nagel sworn on 4 September 1985 exhibiting other correspondence. I do not propose to refer to that exhibit since the correspondence relates to old complaints. There is, however, one recent letter there, dated 2 July 1985, written by the first defendant, in which he was then saying that he would be interviewing another caretaker on 15 July and that Mrs Nagel had assurance that it was not the intention to sell the caretaker's flat 'at this juncture'. That letter was of course written before the meeting dated 11 July 1985 that I have mentioned.

A third affidavit of Mrs Nagel sworn on 24 October 1985 sufficiently verifies the facts alleged in the statement of claim.

The first plaintiff, Mr Posner, swore an affidavit on 7 November 1985. Therein he seeks to show the inconveniences suffered by reason of there being no resident porter at Danes Court. The inconveniences include: (a) automatic timing of the central heating system deprives the tenants of the benefits resulting from a resident porter exercising his discretion when heating should be put on and off having regard to the prevailing weather conditions, (b) breakdowns in the lift with the consequence that residents outside the lift have to seek help for residents trapped in the lift, (c) there is difficulty in obtaining access to the block since access has to be obtained by disturbing a resident rather than a porter, (d) recorded mail is sometimes difficult to deliver and (e) milk and newspapers often have to be left in the open outside the main door.

On the defendants' side there are three affidavits, one by Mr Kenneth John Bewsher, who was the resident porter until 31 May 1985, and the other two by the first defendant. Mr Bewsher bears out that he is now a resident caretaker at Kings Court, 31 Prince Albert Road, London NW8, and that prior to May 1985 he was the caretaker at Danes Court, living in a flat there. He left Danes Court for Kings Court because he was offered better pay. He says he resigned from his position at Danes Court. Mr Bewsher goes on to say this in para 3: 'Mr Scott-Lewis asked me to stay on as I was only going to be approximately one minute away in the adjacent block, and I agreed to do so.' This means, as I understand, that while Mr Bewsher is employed as a resident caretaker at Kings Court, he also works for Mr Scott-Lewis, so apparently he is paid by two employers in respect of the same time. He says in paras 5 and 6:

'I am therefore in a position to act as caretaker for both Kings Court and Danes Court. I spend approximately 2 hours in the morning at Danes Court collecting the rubbish and cleaning the common parts, and I also patrol in the afternoon and in the evening. The central heating is on automatic and I order oil when appropriate. I also continue to help out the various tenants from time to time and so far as I am concerned I do exactly the same job now as I was doing when I was actually resident in the premises, with no decline in standards whatsoever.

(6) All the tenants know where I am, which is approximately one minute away, and they either telephone me or pop in to see me to ask me to assist, which of course I am always willing to do.'

The first defendant in his first affidavit sworn on 15 November 1985, gives evidence to the same effect as Mr Bewsher, and indeed states that Mr Bewsher was asked to carry out after May 1985 the same duties as he had carried out before that date 'albeit on a non resident basis'. In his second affidavit sworn on 20 November 1985, the first defendant refers to the fact that in his first affidavit he said he had made efforts to obtain an 'alternative porter which came to nought'. He goes on to say:

'It is totally incorrect to say that I am not performing the covenant set forth in cl 3(11) of the leases, as Mr. Bewsher is doing exactly the same job to perform the convenants as he was doing prior to 31 May, 1985 albeit that he lives approximately 1 minute away from the block.'

I say now that I do not understand this statement because cl 3(11) obliges the defendants to employ a resident porter and this they are not doing. I need not deal with other matters in the first defendant's affidavit since it is largely concerned with a denial of any falling-off in standards since Mr Bewsher ceased to reside.

There is reply evidence by the plaintiffs. It is an affidavit by Mr Dayan sworn 22 November 1985. Mr Dayan says that it is not the case that Mr Bewsher is now carrying out the same duties as he did when resident. Dealing with the specific duties mentioned in cl 3(11), Mr Dayan complains: (1) of a deterioration in the maintenance of the common parts, which 'are beginning to look decidedly shabby'. He comments on para 3 of the first affidavit of the first defendant where it is suggested that the cleaning of the common parts and the emptying of rubbish can be done in about two hours. Mr Dayan says that this is an unrealistic estimate since there are 26 flats on eight floors. He is satisfied that it used to take Mr Bewsher, when he was in residence, considerably longer than two hours to carry out those duties; and (2) that the change to automatic time switching for the central heating means that the central heating system is operated much less satisfactorily.

As well as making those references to the cl 3(11) tasks, Mr Dayan also refers to the fact that in the past the resident porters at Danes Court have always performed functions and services which have added to 'the general amenity of the residents of the block and the efficiency of the day to day running thereof'.

He itemises some obvious advantages arising from the presence of a resident porter in the way of giving access to tradesmen, deliveries and a better feeling of security. Mr Dayan takes up the first defendant's statement in para 4 of his first affidavit where he says:

'I am surprised by the allegation that I stated that I had not interviewed people for the post. I instructed my secretary to ask Park Estates to advertise for a new caretaker and as a result 11 people were interviewed. There was not one suitable applicant.'

Mr Dayan says there will be no difficulty in finding a resident porter for Danes Court. Mr Dayan advertised in the Standard newspaper on 2 September 1985. There were 20 applications received in response to that advertisement.

The plaintiffs' principal claim, pursuant to Ord 14, is in these terms:

'(1) Specific performance of the lessors' covenant in cl 3(11) of the plaintiffs' respective leases of their respective flats (and garages in the case of the third and fifth plaintiffs) in Danes Court, Nos. 1–5 St. Edmunds Terrace, London NW8 to employ (so far as in the defendant's power lie) a resident porter for the purposes more particularly set forth in the said cl 3(11).'

That is to say the plaintiffs claim in effect that the defendants are now failing to employ, pursuant to cl 3(11), a resident porter for the purposes specified in cl 3(11), and that the defendants ought to be ordered so to employ. It is admitted that the defendants do not

now employ a *resident* porter for the purposes specified or for any purpose. Counsel for
a the defendants accepted that no resident porter is employed, and so much is to be inferred
from para 2 of the first defendant's second affidavit. However, counsel submitted that
the defendants were not in breach of cl 3(11) since, he said, all the duties that are to be
performed in (a), (b) and (c) of cl 3(11) are in fact being discharged, and the fact that those
duties are being discharged by a non-resident as opposed to a resident porter does not
justify the view that there is a breach of cl 3(11). Counsel for the defendants went on to
b say that at least the defendants should have the opportunity of a trial, so that, in so far as
there is in the affidavit evidence a conflict about the present adequacy of the porterage
(within (a), (b) and (c) of cl 3(11)), the position can be clarifed by oral evidence.

I do not accept counsel's submission. If one assumes, as the defendants allege, that Mr
Bewsher is discharging his (a), (b) and (c) duties now as he did before 31 May 1985, there
is in my view still a clear breach of cl 3(11). Clause 3(11) indicates that (a) there will be a
c porter in residence and (b) that he will perform certain functions. To arrange for his
functions to be carried out by a non-resident cannot in my view discharge the defendants
from their duty to keep a porter in residence. There is, to my mind, a world of difference
between living in a block with a porter in residence and living in a block where there is
no porter in residence. A tenant in a block of flats understandably attaches great
importance to the presence of a resident porter. While the tenant no doubt appreciates
d the manual work that the porter may perform, he equally appreciates the feeling of
security (and the opportunities to ask for help) that arise from the presence of a resident
porter. In other words, a resident porter is valued not only for the duties he is expected
to perform, but also for his very presence.

I am therefore of the view that the defendants are in breach of cl 3(11). I see no reason
for sending the matter for trial to discuss that matter.

e Since I am of the view that the defendants are in breach of cl 3(11), the question arises
whether or not cl 3(11) is a provision susceptible of specific performance.

I was referred to *Ryan v Mutual Tontine Westminster Chambers Association* [1893] 1 Ch
116. That is a case where the Court of Appeal considered a contract between a landlord
and his tenant by which the landlord undertook to employ a porter to perform certain
services for the benefit of the tenant. The contract was held to be not specifically
f enforceable. One ground of the decision was that the execution of the contract would
require 'constant superintendence by the court' (at 123, 125).

A close examination of the facts in *Ryan's* case (at 117–120) shows the situation in that
case differs in some respects from the situation before me. For example, in *Ryan's* case
the porter was to 'be and act as the servant of the tenants'. That is not so at Danes Court.
Again the Danes Court lease has, but the *Ryan* lease had not, covenants by the lessor
g whereby the porter's duties are, at any rate as to (a) and (b) of cl 3(11), elsewhere in the
lease seen as direct obligations of the lessor to the lessee (see cl 3(2), (7), (10) and (13)).
There is also the fact that the scheme of apportioning service charges between the Danes
Court tenants involves taking account of the costs of maintaining and repairing the
porter's flat: see cl 3(12).

Drawing attention to these differences between *Ryan's* case and the present case,
h counsel for the plaintiffs submitted that *Ryan's* case should be distinguished. In short, he
said that since the resident porter's functions at Danes Court were already obligations of
the lessor to the lessees, there were no duties on the part of the porter towards the tenants
that the tenants were seeking to enforce. All that was required was the appointment of a
resident porter, whereas in *Ryan's* case the plaintiff was in effect seeking to enforce
performance of duties said to be owed by the porter to the plaintiff. I do not accept or
j reject counsel for the plaintiffs able argument. I suspect that it is difficult to distinguish
Ryan's case. However that may be, *Ryan's* case has been remarked on in many later
authorities.

In *C H Giles & Co Ltd v Morris* [1972] 1 All ER 960 at 969–970, [1972] 1 WLR 307 at
318–319 Megarry J, after referring to *Ryan's* case, said:

'One day, perhaps, the courts will look again at the so-called rule that contracts for personal services or involving the continuous performance of services will not be specifically enforced. Such a rule is plainly not absolute and without exception, nor do I think that it can be based on any narrow consideration such as difficulties of constant superintendence by the court. Mandatory injunctions are by no means unknown, and there is normally no question of the court having to send its officers to supervise the performance of the order of the court. Prohibitory injunctions are common, and again there is no direct supervision by the court. Performance of each type of injunction is normally secured by the realisation of the person enjoined that he is liable to be punished for contempt if evidence of his disobedience to the order is put before the court; and if the injunction is prohibitory, actual committal will usually, so long as it continues, make disobedience impossible. If instead the order is for specific performance of a contract for personal services, a similar machinery of enforcement could be employed, again without there being any question of supervision by any officer of the court. The reasons why the court is reluctant to decree specific performance of a contract for personal services (and I would regard it as a strong reluctance rather than a rule) are, I think, more complex and more firmly bottomed on human nature. If a singer contracts to sing, there could no doubt be proceedings for committal if, ordered to sing, the singer remained obstinately dumb. But if instead the singer sang flat, or sharp, or too fast, or too slowly, or too loudly, or too quietly, or resorted to a dozen of the manifestations of temperament traditionally associated with some singers, the threat of committal would reveal itself as a most unsatisfactory weapon; for who could say whether the imperfections of performance were natural or self-induced? To make an order with such possibilities of evasion would be vain; and so the order will not be made. However, not all contracts of personal service or for the continuous performance of services are as dependent as this on matters of opinion and judgment, nor do all such contracts involve the same degree of the daily impact of person on person. In general, no doubt, the inconvenience and mischief of decreeing specific performance of most of such contracts will greatly outweigh the advantages, and specific performance will be refused. But I do not think that it should be assumed that as soon as any element of personal service or continuous services can be discerned in a contract the court will, without more, refuse specific performance. Of course, a requirement for the continuous performance of services has the disadvantage that repeated breaches may engender repeated applications to the court for enforcement. But so may many injunctions; and the prospects of repetition, although an important consideration, ought not to be allowed to negative a right. As is so often the case in equity, the matter is one of the balance of advantage and disadvantage in relation to the particular obligations in question; and the fact that the balance will usually lie on one side does not turn this probability into a rule. The present case, of course, is a fortiori, since the contract of which specific performance has been decreed requires not the performance of personal services or any continuous series of acts, but merely procuring the execution of an agreement which contains a provision for such services or acts.'

Those observations do not of themselves enable me to disregard *Ryan's* case. But then one comes to *Shiloh Spinners Ltd v Harding* [1973] 1 All ER 90, [1973] AC 691. Lord Wilberforce seems to say that 'the impossibility for the courts to supervise the doing of work' may be rejected as a reason against granting relief (see [1973] 1 All ER 90 at 102, [1973] AC 691 at 724). Finally there is *Tito v Waddell (No 2)*, *Tito v A-G* [1977] 3 All ER 129 at 307–308, [1977] Ch 106 at 321. Megarry V-C said:

'In cases of this kind it was at one time said that an order for the specific performance of the contract would not be made if there would be difficulty in the court supervising its execution: see, e g, *Ryan v Mutual Tontine Westminster Chambers Association* [1893] 1 Ch 116 at 123, 125, 128. Smith MR subsequently found himself unable to see the force of this objection (see *Wolverhampton Corpn v Emmons* [1901]

1 QB 515 at 523); and after it had been discussed and questioned in *C H Giles & Co Ltd v Morris* [1972] 1 All ER 960 at 969–970, [1972] 1 WLR 307 at 318, the House of Lords disposed of it (I hope finally) in *Shiloh Spinners Ltd v Harding* [1973] 1 All ER 90 at 101–102, [1973] AC 691 at 724. The real question is whether there is a sufficient definition to what has to be done in order to comply with the order of the court. That definition may be provided by the contract itself, or it may be supplied by the terms of the order, in which case there is the further question whether the court considers that the terms of the contract sufficiently support, by implication or otherwise, the terms of the proposed order.'

In the light of those authorities it is, I think, open to me to consider the making of an order for specific performance in this case, particularly since the order contemplated is in the a fortiori class referred to by Megarry J in the last sentence of the extract from the *Giles* case [1972] 1 All ER 960 at 970, [1972] 1 WLR 307 at 318 quoted above. Damages here could hardly be regarded as an adequate remedy.

Whether or not an order for specific performance should be made seems to me to depend on the following considerations: (a) is there a sufficient definition of what has to be done in order to comply with the order of the court; (b) will enforcing compliance involve superintendence by the court to an unacceptable degree; and (c) what are the respective prejudices or hardships that will be suffered by the parties if the order is made or not made?

As to (a), one may in this case sufficiently define what has to be done by the defendants by ordering the defendants, within say two months, to employ a porter to be resident at Danes Court for the purpose of carrying out the cl 3(11) duties. It is to be borne in mind that there is still a vacant flat available for a resident porter. As to (b), I do not see that such an order will occasion any protracted superintendence by the court. If the defendants without good cause fail to comply with the order in due time, then the plaintiffs can take appropriate enforcement proceedings against the defendants. As to (c), I see no hardship or prejudice resulting to the defendants from the order. They will simply be performing what they have promised to do and what has been carried out by the lessors over the past 20 years. On the other hand I see considerable inconvenience, if not exactly hardship, for the plaintiffs if, having bargained for a resident porter and paid a premium and having enjoyed his presence for 20 years, they are to be expected for the future to be content with a porter who simply walks up and down the stairs for two hours only during the day doing his cleaning and refuse collection. It follows that there should be an order for specific performance. I should add that counsel for the defendants referred to the four conditions in *Shelfer v City of London Electric Lighting Co* [1895] 1 Ch 287, [1891–4] All ER 838 as set out in *Federated Homes Ltd v Mill Lodge Properties Ltd* [1980] 1 All ER 371 at 381, [1980] 1 WLR 594 at 607, where Brightman J said:

'There remains only the question whether we ought to interfere with the remedy granted by the judge of an injunction against the building of the 32 extra dwellings. *Shelfer v City of London Electric Lighting Co* is authority for the proposition that a person who has the benefit of a restrictive covenant is, as a general rule, entitled to an injunction on the trial of the action as distinct from an award of damages unless (1) the injury to the plaintiff's legal rights is small, (2) it is capable of being estimated in terms of money, (3) it can adequately be compensated for by a small payment, and (4) it would be oppressive to the defendant to grant an injunction. In my view, the first, third and fourth of these conditions have not been shown to be satisfied.'

Counsel for the defendants said that all four conditions were satisfied so that the appropriate remedy for breach of cl 3(11) was damages and not the specific relief. If and in so far as it is appropriate to consider the four conditions in the circumstances of this case, I am satisfied that not one of the four conditions can be answered in the defendants' favour.

Counsel for the plaintiffs at my invitation in the course of the hearing drafted a proposed order. The draft is elaborate. I am content to make an order based on that form, but since it is so extremely detailed I think I will give counsel the opportunity of putting it in a minute with a simpler form of order. He may be able to do that with the collaboration of counsel for the defendants. Counsel for the defendants may wish to collaborate since a simpler order will save the cost of working out the details involved in the original draft of counsel for the plaintiffs. The order will provide for an inquiry as to damages in respect of the time since 31 May 1985.

In the light of the order for specific performance, it is not necessary for me to say anything about the other relief claimed in the first notice of motion or about the relief claimed in the second notice of motion.

Order accordingly.

Solicitors: *Beckman & Beckman* (for the plaintiffs); *Malkin Cullis & Sumption* (for the defendants).

Jacqueline Metcalfe   Barrister.

Paterson Zochonis & Co Ltd and others v Merfarken Packaging Ltd and others

COURT OF APPEAL, CIVIL DIVISION
OLIVER, FOX AND ROBERT GOFF LJJ
4, 5, 29 OCTOBER 1982

Copyright – Infringement – Damages – Passing off by third party facilitated by defendant's infringement – Use made by third party of infringing material – Whether damages including damage resulting from use made by third party of infringing material – Copyright Act 1956, s 17.

Copyright – Infringement – Negligence – Duty not to infringe – Duty to take reasonable care to prevent infringement – Whether parallel common law duty existing alongside statutory duty not to infringe.

Pleading – Striking out – Embarrassing material – Pleaded facts not within defendant's knowledge – Whether pleadings should be struck out as embarrassing – RSC Ord 18, r 19(1)(c).

The plaintiffs were a group of companies who manufactured and sold a complexion cream. The cream was sold in tubes packed in oblong cartons which had a distinctive design and which also contained an advertising leaflet. Two competitors decided to manufacture and sell their complexion cream by fraudulently copying the plaintiffs' design and get-up, and placed orders with the defendants, who were printers and manufacturers of packaging, for the production of cartons and leaflets which were exact copies of those used by the plaintiffs and which were copied from samples supplied by the two competitors. The defendants fulfilled the orders, and subsequently counterfeit tubes of cream were packed into the cartons supplied by the defendants and then sold. The plaintiffs brought an action against the defendants for damages for passing off, on the grounds (i) that the defendants had infringed the plaintiffs' copyrights and (ii) that the defendants had negligently failed to make inquiry whether the competitors had authority to order the cartons to be printed and ought to have foreseen that damage would flow from the use made of the cartons and leaflets by the competitors. The defendants sought to strike out that part of the statement of claim alleging negligence. The judge granted the application, holding (i) that parts of the statement of claim should

a be struck out under RSC Ord 18, r 19(1)(c)[a] as being 'embarrassing' to the defendants
because they related to a series of transactions to which the defendants were not party
and of which they could not possibly have known, (ii) that there could be no liability in
negligence because the defendants could not reasonably have foreseen that the supply of
the infringing material would lead to damage of the sort which had occurred, and there
was no reason why the supply of a specimen carton by the competitors should have put
the defendants on inquiry, and (iii) that the fact that the defendants had put into the
b hands of the competitors the essential material which enabled them to carry out the
alleged fraud was not a circumstance giving rise to any possible liability in the absence of
knowledge that the goods would be improperly used. The plaintiffs appealed, contending
(i) that the Copyright Act 1956 created a tort of strict liability for which damages were at
large, that under s 17[b] of the Act damages for infringement of copyright included
damages 'available . . . in respect of infringements of other proprietary rights' and that
c such damages therefore included any damage which could reasonably have been foreseen
as the likely consequence of the infringement even though the defendants may not have
realised that they were infringing or may not even have been reasonably able to foresee
that their action would be an infringement, and (ii) that in any event the defendants
were liable in negligence since a reasonable printer would have foreseen that the material
which he printed was likely to be used for the purpose for which it was in fact used and
d that therefore the defendants were under a duty of care to the plaintiffs.

Held – (1) The mere fact that a pleaded fact could not have been within the knowledge
of the defendant did not make the pleading 'embarrassing' for the purposes of RSC
Ord 18, r 19(1)(c). The judge had therefore been wrong to strike out parts of the
statement of claim on the grounds that they were embarrassing to the defendants (see
e p 527 d, p 532 a b and p 536 b, post).
(2) Since the measure of damages under s 17 of the 1956 Act for infringement of
copyright was the depreciation caused by the infringement to the value of the copyright
as a chose in action, such damages did not extend to damage resulting from the use made
by a third party, without the defendant's authority, of the infringing material.
Accordingly, since the plaintiffs in their copyright claim were not claiming damages for
f the depreciation of their copyright but were instead seeking damages for the passing off
of other goods as their own on the basis that such passing off had been facilitated by the
defendants' infringement of their copyright, the judge had been right to strike out the
copyright claim (see p 528 f g, p 529 b to d, p 532 f to p 533 b and p 537 j to p 538 b d e h,
post); dictum of Lord Wright MR in *Sutherland Publishing Co Ltd v Caxton Publishing Co
Ltd* [1936] 1 All ER at 180 applied.
g (3) There did not exist, alongside the statutory duty not to infringe, a parallel common
law duty owed by a printer to take reasonable care to prevent infringement, because,
although, exceptionally, a duty of care could arise where a defendant provided a third
party with the means of committing a tort against the plaintiff, as a matter of policy the
law did not oblige a printer or manufacturer to inquire into the purpose to which
material printed or manufactured by him was going to be put by the person for whom
h he printed or manufactured it or (per Robert Goff LJ) if there was a sufficient relationship
of proximity for a duty of care to exist there were special circumstances negativing that
duty. The plaintiffs' statement of claim accordingly disclosed no cause of action in
negligence and that part of the claim had been correctly struck out. The appeal would
therefore be dismissed (see p 529 e to g, p 530 c d, p 531 e f h j, p 533 g to j, p 534 c e f,
p 535 b c, p 539 f to h and p 541 g to p 542 a e f j to p 543 a f, post); *Home Office v Dorset
j Yacht Co Ltd* [1970] 2 All ER 294 and *Anns v Merton London Borough* [1977] 2 All ER 492
applied.

---

a   Rule 19(1), so far as material, provides: 'The Court may at any stage of the proceedings order to be
struck out . . . any pleading or the indorsement of any writ . . . on the ground that . . . (c) it may
prejudice, embarrass or delay the fair trial of the action . . . and may order the action to be stayed
or dismissed or judgment to be entered accordingly, as the case may be.'
b   Section 17, so far as material, is set out at p 527 j, post

Notes
For passing off, see 9 Halsbury's Laws (4th edn) para 806, and for cases on the subject, see *a*
13 Digest (Reissue) 137–138, 1127–1135.
For striking out pleading on ground of embarrassment, see 36 Halsbury's Laws (4th edn) para 74.
For the Copyright Act 1956, s 17, see 11 Halsbury's Statutes (4th edn) 272.

Cases referred to in judgments

b

Anns v Merton London Borough [1977] 2 All ER 492, [1978] AC 728, [1977] 2 WLR 1024, HL.
Banco de Portugal v Waterlow & Sons Ltd [1932] AC 452, [1932] All ER Rep 181, HL.
Belegging- en Exploitatiemaatschapij Lavender BV v Witten Industrial Diamonds Ltd [1979] FSR 59, CA.
Birn Bros Ltd v Keen & Co Ltd [1918] 2 Ch 281.

c

CBS Inc v Ames Records and Tapes Ltd [1981] 2 All ER 812, [1982] Ch 91, [1981] 2 WLR 973.
Dunlop Pneumatic Tyre Co Ltd v David Moseley & Sons Ltd [1904] 1 Ch 612, CA.
General Tire and Rubber Co v Firestone Tyre and Rubber Co Ltd [1975] 2 All ER 173, [1975] 1 WLR 819, HL.

d

Hadley v Baxendale (1854) 9 Exch 341, [1843–60] All ER Rep 461, 156 ER 145.
Hedley Byrne & Co Ltd v Heller & Partners Ltd [1963] 2 All ER 575, [1964] AC 465, [1963] 3 WLR 101, HL.
Home Office v Dorset Yacht Co Ltd [1970] 2 All ER 294, [1970] AC 1004, [1970] 2 WLR 1140, HL.
Infabrics Ltd v Jaytex Ltd [1981] 1 All ER 1057, [1982] AC 1, [1981] 2 WLR 646, HL.

e

Junior Books Ltd v Veitchi Co Ltd [1982] 3 All ER 201, [1983] 1 AC 520, [1982] 3 WLR 477, HL.
M'Alister (or Donoghue) v Stevenson [1932] AC 562, [1932] All ER Rep 1, HL.
Morton Norwich Products Inc v Intercen [1976] 2 FSR 513.
Ontario Hospital Services Commission v Borsoski (1974) 54 DLR (3d) 339, Ont HC.
Smith v Leurs (1945) 70 CLR 256, Aust HC.

f

Stansbie v Troman [1948] 1 All ER 599, [1948] 2 KB 48, CA.
Sutherland Publishing Co Ltd v Caxton Publishing Co Ltd [1936] 1 All ER 177, [1936] Ch 323, CA; *affd* [1938] 4 All ER 389, [1939] AC 178, HL.
Townsend v Haworth (1875) 48 LJ Ch 770, CA.
Walker (John) & Sons Ltd v Henry Ost & Co Ltd [1970] 2 All ER 106, [1970] 1 WLR 917.
Weld-Blundell v Stephens [1920] AC 956, [1920] All ER Rep 32, HL.

g

Yachuk v Oliver Blais Co Ltd [1949] 2 All ER 150, [1949] AC 386, PC.

Interlocutory appeal
The plaintiffs, Paterson Zochonis & Co Ltd, Paterson Zochonis (UK) Ltd, Parnon Ltd and Paterson Zochonis Industries Ltd, appealed against the decision of Whitford J on 29
h
January 1982 granting an application by the defendants, Merfarken Packaging Ltd, Ratcliffe & Son (Printers) Ltd and Roding Valley Paper Ltd (trading together as the Merfarken Group), to strike out paras 18 to 36 of the statement of claim served on 31 July 1981 in an action commenced by the plaintiffs against the defendants on 5 November 1980 for damages for infringement of copyright. The facts are set out in the judgment of Oliver LJ.
j

Robin Jacob QC and *Martin Howe* for the plaintiffs.
John P Baldwin for the defendants.

Cur adv vult

29 October. The following judgments were delivered.

a

OLIVER LJ. This is an interlocutory appeal with the leave of this court from an order of Whitford J made on 29 January 1982 striking out a substantial part of the plaintiffs' statement of claim in an action for damages for infringement of copyright.

The relevant facts are these. The plaintiffs are a group of companies whose business consists of the manufacture and sale of a complexion cream specially adapted for those

b with dark skin and sold under the name Venus de Milo. It has had, so it is said, a wide commercial success, particularly among the immigrant community and the plaintiffs claim to have acquired a substantial goodwill and reputation in the United Kingdom. The cream is sold in tubes which are pink in colour and carry brown and white lettering and a small representation of an armless statue on a brown background.

Each tube is contained in an oblong carton similarly coloured and designed which also

c contains an advertising leaflet. The plaintiffs claim (and their claim must be considered valid for the purposes of the present application) to be the owners of the copyright in the design of the carton and the contents of the leaflet.

The defendants are three companies forming part of a group and their business is that of printing and producing packaging. Their precise individual roles are not entirely clear but for present purposes they can be treated as one entity. The present action arises from

d the activities of certain competitors of the plaintiffs who, it is alleged, have deliberately and fraudulently set about seeking to filch the plaintiffs' goodwill by passing off as the plaintiffs' Venus de Milo complexion cream some other and counterfeit cream manufactured by or for the competitors. It is not suggested that the defendants are involved in this except to the extent that, as will be seen, they innocently accepted and executed orders for the printing and manufacture of cartons.

e The action was commenced on 5 November 1980 and the statement of claim was served on 31 July 1981. It may be conveniently divided into sections according to its matter. After describing the plaintiffs and their business (in paras 1 and 2) it proceeds to lay the foundation for a passing-off action by pleading (in paras 3 to 6 inclusive) the development of the business and its reputation and goodwill. Paragraphs 7 to 11 inclusive plead the production of the design and get-up and the subsistence of literary and artistic

f copyright in, inter alia, the cartons and advertising leaflet, which copyright is claimed to be owned by the plaintiffs.

Paragraphs 12 and 13 allege the formation by two individuals known as 'the Hollands' of a scheme for the manufacture and sale of complexion cream copying the plaintiffs' get-up. The next section is concerned with the defendants and covers paras 14 to 17 inclusive. It sets out that orders were placed by the Hollands with the defendants for the

g production of numbers of inner and display cartons and leaflets which were exact copies of the plaintiffs' designs and which were to be copied from samples supplied by the Hollands. There were, it is alleged, two orders the first of which (placed in March 1980) was fulfilled, the cartons and leaflets having been delivered by the defendants to the premises of a company called C B Baggs Ltd in August 1980. The second order was partly fulfilled but the goods were in fact delivered into the custody of the plaintiffs' solicitors,

h I infer as a result of an Anton Piller order. There follows a long section (paras 18 to 29 inclusive) which sets out a series of transactions between the Hollands, C B Baggs Ltd, a firm called Gemini Products and Flexile Ltd, the substance of which is that cream was supplied through Gemini Products to Baggs and was inserted by Baggs into counterfeit tubes produced by Flexile on Baggs' order and then packed into the cartons which had been supplied by the defendants. When thus packed they were delivered to the Hollands

j who disposed of them on the market, thus passing the resultant product off as the plaintiffs' product. Paragraph 30 alleges that all this was done without the plaintiffs' licence or consent. Paragraph 31 alleges (with appropriate particulars) guilty knowledge and complicity on the part of Baggs, the Hollands, Gemini and Flexile (but not on the part of the defendants).

So far, there is nothing in all this which appears to concern the defendants but there

then comes in para 32 an allegation that the defendants ought to have realised that the Hollands were not entitled to authorise the reproduction of the plaintiffs' packaging and   *a*
leaflets and ought to have foreseen that printing and supplying them would result in loss and damage to the plaintiffs of the type which has occurred (which is extensively pleaded in para 38 and which may be summarised as covering loss of sales and damage to reputation as a result and costs of investigatory and preventive measures in addition specifically to damages for conversion).

Particulars under para 32 are given and they amount to the following. (i) The leaflets   *b*
bore the words 'Made in Nigeria' and a device containing the letters AIL (standing for Associated Industries Ltd, the plaintiffs' previous title). The defendants made no inquiries about whether the Hollands were connected with AIL or had any authority to order the cartons to be printed. (ii) The cartons contained the letters PZ and this ought to have put the defendants on inquiry. (iii) The defendants ought to have been put on inquiry by the fact that they were supplied with specimens of actual cartons rather than artwork.   *c*

Paragraphs 33 and 34 plead infringement of the plaintiffs' copyright. Paragraph 35 pleads that the Hollands, Gemini, Baggs and Flexile were all knowingly engaged in a joint venture and para 36 alleges that the defendants are also jointly liable 'because the said joint venture flowed from their acts of infringement of copyright and conversion and because they were negligent as aforesaid'.

Thus the action is, in effect, an action for damages for passing off without any allegation   *d*
that the defendants themselves have passed off or been knowingly privy to passing off the plaintiffs' goods, indeed that was expressly disclaimed in the argument before the judge, the basis for the claim being (a) that the defendants have infringed the plaintiffs' copyright and (b) that they negligently failed to make inquiry and ought to have foreseen that the damages claimed would flow from the use made by the Hollands of the cartons and leaflets.   *e*

On 26 October 1981 the defendants issued a summons to strike out the bulk of the statement of claim, effectively everything except the essential allegations of copyright and infringement. Whitford J acceded to the defendants' application. He was prepared to assume that it could be established that the passing off had taken place and would not have taken place if the infringing material had not been supplied by the defendants, but he held that the form of the pleading was embarrassing. The allegations of passing off,   *f*
he said, related to matters which must be outside the defendants' knowledge and would increase costs. He rejected the suggestion that there could be any liability in negligence because, as I read his judgment, he did not consider that the particulars under para 32 supported any case for arguing that the defendants could reasonably have foreseen that the supply of the infringing material would lead to damage of the sort which has occurred. He could not see why printers should make any inquiries and from his   *g*
experience of copyright cases he indicated that he could see no reason why the supply of a specimen carton, rather than artwork, should put anyone on inquiry. So far as concerned the suggestion that the defendants had put into the hands of the Hollands the essential materials which enabled them to carry out the alleged fraud, he did not regard that as a circumstance giving rise to any possible liability in the absence of knowledge that the goods were going to be improperly used.   *h*

Accordingly, he made an order striking out, in effect, the whole statement of claim apart from the bare allegations of infringement of copyright and conversion and the claim for damages on that basis.

The plaintiffs now appeal to this court and their counsel puts their case in two ways. First, he says that the Copyright Act 1956 creates a tort of strict liability for which damages are recoverable at large. True it is that the defendants may not have realised   *j*
that they were infringing and may not even have been able reasonably to foresee that what they were doing was an infringement; but, granted that a tort was committed by the printing of the cartons and leaflets, the consequence that those cartons and leaflets would be used to the damage of the plaintiffs in passing off spurious goods as their goods was one which a reasonable man would have foreseen and the defendants are accordingly

a liable for the damage so suffered by the plaintiffs. Paragraphs 18 to 29 and 31, which the judge directed to be struck out, were merely pleading the factual material supporting the allegation of damage for which the defendants are liable and therefore should not have been struck out.

His second and alternative argument is that in any event there is a liability in negligence. A reasonable printer would have foreseen that the material which he printed was likely to be used for the purpose for which it was in fact used and thus came under a
b duty of care to the plaintiffs. Paragraphs 32, 35 and 36 of the statement of claim, in conjunction with the paragraphs mentioned above, thus plead, counsel for the plaintiffs argues, an arguable case of negligence against the defendants which ought not to have been struck out.

I confess that, speaking only for myself, I find difficulty in following the reasoning of the judge in striking out the portions of the statement of claim mentioned as
c 'embarrassing'. There is, so far as I can see, no particular difficulty in pleading to them nor is there any equivocation about what the pleaded case is. The judge, if I read his judgment correctly, considered that they were embarrassing because they related to a series of transactions to which it was not alleged that the defendants were party and of which they could not possibly have had any actual knowledge. But the mere fact that a defendant is called on to meet allegations of fact of which he had no previous knowledge
d does not appear to me to constitute an embarrassment justifying the striking out of a plaintiff's statement of claim so long as the facts pleaded are relevant to what is claimed against the defendant. It is true that, assuming that the transactions between the Hollands and their associates have any materiality to a claim against the defendants, they are perhaps set out in rather greater detail than is strictly necessary, for if the defendants are liable on the footing that their infringement of copyright facilitated a passing off by the
e Hollands of the plaintiffs' goods, it hardly matters whether that passing off was done by the Hollands alone or as part of a joint venture with others. To that extent I think that, on any view, a good deal of the material contained in paras 18 to 29 is not strictly necessary for establishing the case against the defendants and could be more concisely dealt with. But the real nub of the defendants' case is not that the story of the plaintiffs' misfortune is related with too much unnecessary detail, but that it is, as a whole, totally
f irrelevant to any possible claim against them for damages and discloses no reasonable cause of action against them. They therefore say that, whether or not the judge correctly described the statement of claim as embarrassing for the reason given by him, the decision to strike out was right and they ought not to be called on to plead to any case beyond that of simple infringement of the plaintiffs' claimed copyright.

I turn therefore to the first proposition of counsel for the plaintiffs which rests wholly
g on the allegation that what the defendants did, that is to say printing and delivering the cartons and leaflets in accordance with the order given to them, constituted an infringement of the plaintiffs' copyright. That right, which must be assumed for present purposes to exist and to be vested in the plaintiffs, is simply the exclusive right to do certain acts in relation to the copyright material; that is to say, so far as relevant to the present case, reproducing it in any material form.

h Now the right to recover damages for an infringement of copyright is statutory and it rests on ss 17 and 18 of the 1956 Act (reproducing ss 6 and 7 of the Copyright Act 1911). Section 17(1) provides that infringements shall be actionable at the suit of the owner of the copyright and continues:

> 'and in any action for such an infringement all such relief, by way of damages, injunction, accounts or otherwise, shall be available to the plaintiff as is available in
j any corresponding proceedings in respect of infringements of other proprietary rights.'

Section 18 gives an additional and, on the authorities, cumulative right to the copyright owner to claim damages for the conversion or detention of any infringing copy as if he were the owner of the copy when it was made. What counsel for the plaintiffs contends

is that the right to recover damages 'available in any corresponding proceedings in respect
of infringements of other proprietary rights' referred to in s 17(1) is a right to recover
any damages which flow from the infringement subject to the ordinary rules of
remoteness of damage, that is to say that the plaintiff can recover any damage which
could reasonably have been foreseen as the likely consequence of the infringement. If
the defendants had realised (which it is not alleged for a moment that they did) that the
material which they produced constituted an infringement of the plaintiffs' copyright,
then they, as reasonable persons, could have foreseen that a likely use to be made of the
infringing material was in connection with the sale by their customer of goods bearing a
spurious resemblance to the plaintiffs' goods. Passing off by a user of the infringing copy
was therefore a reasonably foreseeable consequence of the statutory tort, even though
foreseeability played no part in the tort itself, and accordingly the defendants have made
themselves liable for damages occasioned by the passing off.

Counsel for the defendants meets this in this way. What the defendant is liable for, he
argues, is the loss caused by the infringement. The only infringement here is that which
is referred to in ss 2 and 3 of the Act, that is the unauthorised reproduction of copyright
material. The damages for that can only be nominal and cannot include any damage
flowing from the delivery of the infringing material to Baggs. That might be an
infringement under s 5 but if that were relied on the defendants would have a complete
defence because it would be necessary for the plaintiffs to prove actual knowledge, at the
time of delivery, that the material was infringing material. The only claim, therefore,
that the plaintiffs could sustain in respect of this delivery would be a claim for conversion
under s 18, where again the damages would be merely the value of the goods: in this case
a nominal figure. Thus, on this argument, what happens to the copy once it has been
produced is, so far as a claim for damages against the copier is concerned, entirely
immaterial except in so far as any dealing by him constitutes a conversion or a further
case of infringement can be proved under s 5. For my part, I find myself unable to accept
this as a correct view of the relationship between ss 2 and 3 and s 5. The latter section is,
as it seems to me, directed to the position of the innocent third party unwittingly dealing
with infringing material supplied to him and it is not, as the argument of counsel for the
defendants would suggest, concerned with protecting the person who, however
innocently, himself makes and sells the infringing material.

I do not, therefore, find, as counsel for the defendant suggests, that ss 2, 3 and 5 provide
a complete answer to the plaintiffs' claim. On the other hand, it does not at all follow, in
my judgment, that the statutory right to recover damages from one who unwittingly
infringes a copyright extends to the recovery of loss which may be caused by the use
made by a third party of the infringing material, a claim which, as counsel for the
plaintiffs conceded, goes a great deal further than any reported case that the industry of
counsel has succeeded in uncovering. Counsel for the plaintiffs argues that the present
claim is analogous to that made in *Banco de Portugal v Waterlow & Sons Ltd* [1932] AC
452, [1932] All ER Rep 181, where the plaintiff bank recovered, as damages for the
unauthorised reproduction by Waterlows of banknotes, the face value of the notes which
had been put into circulation by those who had procured their production. Speaking for
myself, however, I do not find that analogy helpful. The *Banco de Portugal* case, whilst no
doubt it involved an infringement of the bank's copyright, was argued and decided as a
claim for breach of contract and the damages were just such as would have been
contemplated by the parties at the time when the contract was made as the likely
consequence of the breach of the implied negative obligation not to print and deliver
notes without the bank's authority. What the instant case is concerned with is the extent
of the statutory right to recover damages for the invasion of the plaintiffs' *proprietary*
right, that is the exclusive right to do or authorise the acts referred to in the statute. The
normal measure of damages under s 17 for such an infringement is the depreciation
caused by the infringement to the value of the copyright as a chose in action (see the
judgment of Lord Wright MR in *Sutherland Publishing Co Ltd v Caxton Publishing Co Ltd*
[1936] 1 All ER 177 at 181, [1936] Ch 323 at 337 and the speech of Lord Scarman in

Infabrics Ltd v Jaytex Ltd [1981] 1 All ER 1057 at 1068–1069, [1982] AC 1 at 26–27).

a There may, of course, as Lord Scarman recognised, be special circumstances where damages are not so limited, for instance in *Birn Bros Ltd v Keen & Co Ltd* [1918] 2 Ch 281, a case in which the defendants had deliberately and knowingly both copied the plaintiffs' cards and sold infringing copies as part of a policy of trade piracy, the plaintiffs, whose trade consisted in the exploitation of the copyright material, recovered damages for general loss of trade as a result of the defendants' activities. What the plaintiffs seek to do

b here, however, is something very much more extensive. Their claim is to include in damages for the defendants' invasion of their statutory proprietary right damages for the invasion by a quite different person of a quite different right, namely their right to the goodwill and reputation of a business. The only connecting link which can be suggested between paras 14 to 17 of the statement of claim which plead the infringement and the history of the third parties' activities set out in paras 18 to 31 is the allegation in para 32

c that the defendants ought to have made inquiries which would or might have disclosed that they were infringing the plaintiffs' copyright. In effect this is saying no more than the defendants owed a duty of care to the plaintiffs not to infringe and it provides, in my judgment, no foundation for what is acknowledged to be a wholly novel claim for damages under s 17 of the 1956 Act.

That, however, does not conclude the matter, because counsel for the plaintiffs

d advances as his alternative justification of the pleading a simple common law claim in negligence. Essentially the proposition is this. The material which the defendants were requested to and did produce was capable of being used to assist in passing off someone else's product as the plaintiffs' product. If the defendants had inquired they would have realised that it might be used for that purpose. In failing so to inquire they were in breach of a duty of care owed to the plaintiffs and the plaintiffs have suffered damage as

e a result of such breach. As I understand the argument of counsel for the plaintiffs, the fact that what the defendants were asked to do involved an infringement of copyright is really an irrelevance, on this way of putting the case, except in so far as, possibly, it points to a greater probability of the material being misused. There is a duty not to infringe and you do not add to it by calling it a duty to take reasonable care not to infringe. Thus the claim would equally subsist if what the defendants had been asked to produce did not

f infringe any copyright of the plaintiffs and this way of putting the case appears to me, therefore, to involve the general proposition that a printer or manufacturer is under a general common law duty of care which obliges him to inquire into the purpose to which that which he prints or manufactures is going to be put by the person for whom he prints or manufactures it.

Counsel for the defendants submits that the existence of the duty of care claimed by

g counsel for the plaintiffs, a duty to take reasonable care not to supply to another goods which that other may or will use for a wrongful purpose to the injury of the plaintiff, is simply not a tenable proposition. This pleading cannot, he submits, support a claim that the defendants are jointly liable with the Hollands and their associates as para 32 suggests. That is to make them joint tortfeasors and that cannot stand in the absence of an allegation of knowledge and a common design (see, for instance, *Morton Norwich Products*

h *Inc v Intercen* [1976] 2 FSR 513 at 521). That must, I think, be correct but it does not entirely dispose of counsel for the plaintiffs' case for there may still be a claim, quite independently of common design, for damages for common law negligence if a proper foundation is laid for it. Counsel for the defendants argues that in the absence of actual procurement there is no liability even for knowingly supplying to a tortfeasor the material for the commission of a tort. Thus, if there is no duty not deliberately to supply

j the means of commission of a tort, a fortiori there can be no duty not to do it unwittingly but carelessly. In this context he has drawn our attention to two recent cases. In *Belegging-en Exploitatiemaatschapij Lavender BV v Witten Industrial Diamonds Ltd* [1979] FSR 59 it was held by this court that a defendant in a patent action was not an infringer simply by reason of the sale by him of material which he knew was going to be incorporated in an infringing article, a matter now expressly dealt with by the Patents Act 1977. The point is not a new one. It has long been settled that the supply of materials for incorporation in an infringing article did not of itself cause the seller to be an infringer. In *Dunlop Pneumatic Tyre Co v David Moseley & Sons Ltd* [1904] 1 Ch 612 Vaughan Williams LJ quoted with approval the following passage from the judgment of Mellish LJ in *Townsend v Haworth* (1875) 48 LJ Ch 770 at 773:

> 'Selling materials for the purpose of infringing a patent to the man who is going to infringe it, even although the party who sells it knows that he is going to infringe it and indemnifies him, does not by itself make the person who so sells an infringer.'

He went on to express the view obiter that the action would fail even if the plaintiffs could show that the goods supplied could not be used for any purpose other than an infringing purpose. Similarly, in *CBS Inc v Ames Records and Tapes Ltd* [1981] 2 All ER 812, [1982] Ch 91 a supplier who hires out records with the knowledge that they may be used for the purpose of making infringing copies does not authorise the infringement and is not himself liable as an infringer.

These cases do, it is true, establish the proposition that to supply goods which to the knowledge of the supplier will be used by a third party for the production of an article which constitutes an infringement of patent or copyright does not make the supplier himself an infringer. Speaking for myself, I am not convinced that they are necessarily also authority for the further proposition that knowingly to supply goods for the purpose of enabling a tort to be committed can never involve any liability on the part of the supplier short of inducement or common design.

Clearly the circumstances may be so strong as to make an inference of common design or of the commission of a tort by the supplier irresistible. A case in point is *John Walker & Sons Ltd v Henry Ost & Co Ltd* [1970] 2 All ER 106, [1970] 1 WLR 917. But whether, short of this, knowledge simpliciter can never involve liability is not a question which needs to be decided on this application, where knowledge (much less complicity) is not alleged, and I desire to guard myself against expressing any concluded view. The question here is whether the innocent but, let it be assumed, careless supply of such material can be a ground of liability. In support of the proposition that it can reliance is placed by the plaintiffs on the speech of Lord Reid in *Home Office v Dorset Yacht Co Ltd* [1970] 2 All ER 294 at 297, [1970] AC 1004 at 1026, where he said:

> '... when a new point emerges, one should ask not whether it is covered by authority but whether recognised principles apply to it. *Donoghue v Stevenson* [1932] AC 562, [1932] All ER Rep 1 may be regarded as a milestone, and the well-known passage in Lord Atkin's speech (see [1932] AC 562 at 580, [1932] All ER Rep 1 at 11) should I think be regarded as a statement of principle ... I think that the time has come when we can and should say that it ought to apply unless there is some justification or valid explanation for its exclusion ... where negligence is involved the tendency has been to apply principles analogous to those stated by Lord Atkin (cf *Hedley Byrne & Co Ltd v Heller & Partners Ltd* [1963] 2 All ER 575, [1964] AC 465).'

The boundaries of an action for tortious negligence are thus not fixed, and counsel for the plaintiffs argues that whilst it may be that counsel for the defendants will ultimately prove to be right, the point is a difficult and arguable one and the statement of claim ought not, therefore, to be struck out at this stage. After all, says counsel for the plaintiffs, a printer who prints a libel finds himself under a liability and, by analogy, there is no greater hardship in placing him under a duty to take reasonable care to consider other possible consequences. As to that argument, I think it misses the point. The printer who prints a defamatory statement is liable not because he fails to take reasonable care to see that what he prints is not defamatory (indeed, it does not matter how careful he is) but because he is a publisher either to his compositors or staff or to the person to whom he supplies the printed material. I get no help from that analogy and one comes back,

therefore, to the question: on what basis is it to be said that a supplier of goods or services
a is under a duty to inquire into the possible use which may be made of the goods he
supplies or of the results of the services which he renders? Even allowing that recent
developments in the law have expanded the field of claims in negligence, I cannot, for
my part accede to the extreme proposition for which counsel for the plaintiffs contends.
The judge found it unnecessary to consider this point in detail because he held that the
particulars delivered under para 32 of the statement of claim provided no foundation at
b all for the suggestion that, assuming a duty, it had been broken, for there was nothing to
put the defendants on inquiry. I confess to considerable sympathy with the judge's view,
for I am, at the moment, quite unable to see how the appearance on the plaintiffs'
literature and carton of the letters AIL and PZ and the absence of separate artwork could
or should have led the defendants to think, not that there was, but even that there might
be something suspicious about the order which they were asked to fulfil. Nevertheless, if
c the matter turned on that alone, I am not sure that I would have precluded the plaintiffs
from seeking to prove the contrary at a trial, for the issue must be one of fact. But there
is, of course, no point in allowing such an issue to proceed to trial if even a successful
outcome carries the plaintiffs no further. For myself, I am prepared to assume that the
inquiring mind of the reasonable man would have been aroused by the indicia on which
the plaintiffs claim to rely in their particulars. But even making that assumption, where
d does it lead them? Counsel for the plaintiffs argues thus. If, as they should have done,
those indicia had aroused the defendants, they ought to have inquired as to the plaintiffs'
authority. If they had inquired, they might, not certainly would (for that depends on the
ingenuity of their customers or their capacity for convincing mendacity) but might,
have discovered that the material which they were asked to print was the subject matter
of a copyright in somebody else. If they had discovered that, it would probably have led
e them to consider that the material would be likely to be used for some such venture as
that in which the Hollands are alleged to have engaged. So that one comes back to this,
that the plaintiffs' case ultimately depends on the existence, alongside the statutory duty
not to infringe copyright, of a parallel common law duty owed to the copyright owner
to take reasonable care not to infringe copyright. For my part, I find myself wholly
unable to accept the existence of such an additional or parallel duty.
f   The particulars pleaded under para 32 for what they are worth (and I have already
indicated my agreement with the judge's view that they are worth very little) are, on the
face of them, merely particulars supporting, so far as they go, the suggestion that the
defendants ought to have realised that the Hollands had no authority from the plaintiffs
to order the printing. They go, so far as I can see, no way at all to amplifying the bald
allegation that the defendants ought to have foreseen that the plaintiffs would suffer loss
g as a result of the subsequent activities of persons for whose actions the defendants were
in no way responsible. That bald allegation stands alone and unsupported as the
foundation for the case based on tortious negligence, and even assuming (which I doubt)
that this generalised allegation is a sufficient pleading that the acts of these persons
constituted a foreseeable risk capable of creating a relationship between the defendants
and the plaintiffs of sufficient proximity to give rise to any duty of care, I find myself, for
h the reasons given by Robert Goff LJ, in his judgment which I have had the advantage of
reading in draft, wholly unpersuaded that the facts pleaded disclose in the circumstances
of this case a breach of duty giving rise to liability for negligence.
I quite take the point of counsel for the plaintiffs that to strike out a pleading is a
serious step and ought not to be taken if there is a reasonably arguable case, but the
matter has been fully argued before us and it does not, as I see it, depend on the resolution
j of any issues of fact. In those circumstances it would do no service to the parties to permit
the action to go on so that the same point would fall to be determined by the judge and
then, perhaps, come back again before this court. I have, speaking for myself, formed a
clear view that the plaintiffs' claim against the defendants for damages for passing off
cannot succeed even if they prove all the allegations in their pleading and accordingly I
would dismiss the appeal.

FOX LJ. The judge decided that those parts of the statement of claim which describe the acts of those concerned in the alleged passing off (Baggs, the Hollands, Flexile and *a* Gemini) were embarrassing. His reason for that, as I understand the judgment, was that those matters were not within the knowledge of the defendants. In my opinion, the mere fact that a matter pleaded against a defendant cannot be within his knowledge does not make the pleading embarrassing. A pleading may be embarrassing if it is obscure or irrelevant. But if what it alleges is material to the cause of action I do not think the other party's absence of knowledge of the fact pleaded has a bearing on the matter. The *b* pleading, I may add, is lengthy. But even if length passes into prolixity it may not necessarily justify striking out: the matter may be dealt with as one of costs.

The pleading, if long, is not obscure and accordingly I think that the matter resolves itself into a question of identifying the causes of action which are alleged and, if a valid cause of action is demonstrated, of determining whether the matters pleaded are relevant or not. If no valid cause of action is shown then the pleading is bad anyway. *c*

The plaintiffs assert causes of action under two heads. The first is infringement of copyright. The argument runs thus. The defendants infringed the plaintiffs' copyright by reproduction of the boxes and the leaflets. The resulting tort is a tort of strict liability. A reasonable man could have foreseen that the boxes and leaflets would be used to damage the plaintiffs by passing off. Damages are at large and this damage was reasonably foreseeable. The paragraphs in the statement of claim which the defendants object to *d* merely relate the facts showing how damage was caused to the plaintiffs.

Counsel for the plaintiffs in support of this argument referred us to *Banco de Portugal v Waterlow & Sons Ltd* [1932] AC 452, [1932] All ER Rep 181. It is correct that, in that case, the bank recovered from Waterlows the face value of the spurious bank notes innocently printed by Waterlows. But if it be the case that Waterlows infringed the bank's copyright in the notes, that was not the basis on which the case was decided. *e* Waterlows were in direct contractual relations with the bank. The basis of the decision was breach of contract. The damages recovered were the exchange value of the genuine currency of the same denomination which the bank gave in return for the spurious notes. Such damage must have been within the contemplation of the parties when the contract was made. That is to say it would have been within the contemplation of the parties when the contract was made that if Waterlows printed without authority and *f* handed over Portuguese bank notes to a third party the bank would suffer damage of that extent.

The present case is quite different. The cause of action is not in contract at all. It is a cause of action under the Copyright Act 1956 for infringement. The 1956 Act confers remedies of two kinds. The first is under s 17 which provides that infringement shall be actionable at the suit of the owner of the copyright and in any action for such *g* infringement 'all such relief by way of damages injunction accounts or otherwise shall be available to the plaintiff as is available in any corresponding proceedings in respect of infringements of other proprietary rights'. In *Sutherland Publishing Co Ltd v Caxton Publishing Co Ltd* [1936] 1 All ER 177 at 180, [1936] Ch 323 at 336 Lord Wright MR said that the measure of damages for infringement 'is the depreciation caused by the infringement to the value of the copyright as a chose in action'. But what the plaintiffs *h* are seeking to recover in this case is the loss which they suffered by reason of the passing off. That is something quite different from the loss which they suffered by the diminution in value of the copyright consequent on the infringement. The plaintiffs seek to bridge that gap by saying (see para 32 of the statement of claim) that the defendants were put on notice by the circumstances set out in the particulars under para 32. That, however, is introducing a quite new factor into the matter which is not contemplated by s 17 at all. *j* I do not think that, applying Lord Wright MR's test, damages for infringement of the proprietary right which is copyright can be inflated by reference to the infringement by a third party, without the authority of the defendants, of the right of the plaintiffs not to have the goods passed off as theirs. It may be the purpose of the law is to compensate the owner of a copyright for the loss he has suffered by the infringement but, as I see it, the loss suffered by the infringement here does not include the loss suffered by the passing

off. If the matters pleaded in para 32 are relevant at all they are relevant to a quite separate
a cause of action.

In my view, therefore, the paragraphs which the judge ordered to be struck out,
relating as they do to the history of the alleged passing off, have no relevance to any cause
of action for infringement under s 17.

Nor, in my view, are they relevant to any claims by the plaintiffs in respect of the
goods converted, which would be the boxes and the leaflets only.

b Counsel for the defendants raised a further point on the 1956 Act. He said that what
the plaintiffs are complaining of is, in substance, distribution and that, under s 5(3), there
is only liability if to the knowledge of the defendant the making of the article constituted
an infringement of the copyright (of which there is no allegation in the statement of
claim). I do not accept that. Section 5 is dealing with secondary infringement. In the
present case the plaintiffs' claim, as pleaded, shows a case of primary infringement under
c s 2. The defence provided by s 5(3) to the innocent dealer is not available in a case of
primary infringement. I would, therefore, reject the argument of counsel for the
defendants on this though, in the event, it is of no consequence since, for the reasons
which I have given, I do not think that the matters asserted in the parts of the statement
of claim struck out by the judge are material to any claim of the plaintiffs under the Act.

Counsel for the plaintiffs, however, advances a further contention. He says that the
d defendants are liable in negligence for failing to inquire as to the purpose to which the
Hollands intended to put the goods supplied by the defendants.

Where there is a breach of a duty of care arising from a proximity relationship within
the principles of *M'Alister (or Donoghue) v Stevenson* [1932] AC 562, [1932] All ER Rep 1,
Hedley Byrne & Co Ltd v Heller & Partners Ltd [1963] 2 All ER 575, [1964] AC 465 and
Home Office v Dorset Yacht Co Ltd [1970] 2 All ER 294, [1970] AC 1004 damages are
e recoverable for economic loss sustained for the breach of that duty (see *Junior Books Ltd v
Veitchi Co Ltd* [1982] 3 All ER 201, [1983] 1 AC 520).

The latter case was not discussed before us but, as I understand it, the House of Lords
accepted that the matter must be considered in the two stages indicated by Lord
Wilberforce in *Anns v Merton London Borough* [1977] 2 All ER 492 at 498, [1978] AC 728
at 751. The first question is whether there is a sufficient relationship of proximity
f between the parties that in the reasonable contemplation of the alleged wrongdoer
carelessness on his part may be likely to cause damage to the plaintiff. Second, if the
answer to that question is affirmative, the court must consider whether there are any
circumstances which ought to negative or limit the ambit of the duty.

The contention of counsel for the plaintiffs is that the circumstances were such that
the defendants did owe a duty of care to the plaintiffs. He says that the facts particularised
g in para 32 of the statement of claim were such as to raise a doubt as to the authority of
Hollands to give an order for the work. If the defendants had made inquiries they would
probably have discovered the existence of the copyright and the consequent likelihood
of some improper dealing which would damage the copyright owners. The argument as
thus formulated depends on possible lack of authority in relation to copyright material.
I do not, however, see why a printer should owe a duty of care to inquire about copyright.
h The 1956 Act confers remedies for breach of copyright including some innocent breaches.
A printer who infringes by reproduction exposes himself accordingly. But I see no reason
why, in addition, he should owe any duty of care in respect of possible infringement. I
think that, if it be that at the first of the two stages which I have mentioned it could be
concluded that a duty of care existed, such duty should, at the second stage, be negatived
having regard to the existence of the statutory duty not to infringe copyright.

j In my view, therefore, the argument, as formulated, fails. There is, however, a wider
aspect of the matter. The damage which the plaintiffs have suffered is really in
consequence of the passing off. And one can imagine cases of damage suffered by passing
off where there is no breach of copyright at all. Is there some duty on a trader to take
reasonable care, in the disposal of his goods, not to facilitate a passing off? There are two
preliminary matters to which I should refer.

First, it is the law that to sell materials to a person who is to your knowledge intending to use them to infringe a patent does not constitute an infringement of the patent by you (see *Belegging- en Exploitatiemaatschapij Lavender BV v Witten Industrial Diamonds Ltd* [1979] FSR 59). That, however, does not assist in the present problem, it merely determines what is an infringement and not what is the tort of negligence.

Second, this is not an area in which it can be said, realistically, that the complainant relied on the skill or judgment of the alleged wrongdoer. Lord Roskill in *Junior Books Ltd v Veitchi Co Ltd* [1982] 3 All ER 201 at 214, [1983] 1 AC 520 at 546–547, while observing that the concept of proximity must involve, in most cases, some degree of reliance, evidently did not regard it as being in all cases, a prerequisite to the establishment of a duty of care under the principles stated in the *Junior Books* case.

I come then to the question whether in the circumstances of this case a duty of care by the defendants existed. I take the general rule to be that a person is under no duty of controlling another to prevent him from doing harm to a third. And one cannot apply rigidly the language of Lord Atkin in *M'Alister (or Donoghue) v Stevenson* [1932] AC 562 at 580, [1932] All ER Rep 1 at 11: 'You must take reasonable care to avoid acts or omissions which you can reasonably foresee would be likely to injure your neighbour'. As Lord Diplock observes in *Home Office v Dorset Yacht Co Ltd* [1970] 2 All ER 294 at 326, [1970] AC 1004 at 1060, English law—

> 'abounds with instances of acts and, more particularly, of omissions which give rise to no legal liability in the doer or omitter for loss or damage sustained by others as a consequence of the act or omission, however reasonably or probably that loss or damage might have been anticipated.'

In the end, the question whether a duty of care is to be held to exist is to some extent one of policy depending on practical considerations. There cannot be a general duty of care imposed on traders to satisfy themselves that the goods which they sell will not be used to facilitate some dishonest purpose which will damage others. That would impose an impossible burden on traders.

If, on the other hand, a trader has actual knowledge of a dishonest purpose and it is reasonably foreseeable by him that, if goods are supplied, they will be used for that purpose so as to cause damage to a third party, it may be that a duty of care would exist. Thus there may be circumstances falling short of those which would constitute a person a joint tortfeasor but where his degree of knowledge and involvement make it desirable as a matter of policy that he should incur liability for his acts or omissions. That, however, is not this case and it is not necessary to decide it. It is not alleged that the defendants had any knowledge of the alleged purposes of the Hollands or of their associates.

What is said is that the defendants should have suspected that something was, or might be, wrong and that some unlawful purpose was in prospect. But here again I think that, in a case where no knowledge of an improper purpose is alleged, one must beware of imposing unreasonable burdens on traders. The first question is whether there was a sufficient relationship of proximity between the defendants and the plaintiffs that it was in the reasonable contemplation of the defendants that carelessness on their part would be likely to cause damage to the plaintiffs. I do not think there was. In *Home Office v Dorset Yacht Co Ltd* [1970] 2 All ER 294 at 300, [1970] AC 1004 at 1030 Lord Reid said:

> 'I do not think that a mere foreseeable possibility is or should be sufficient, for then the intervening human action can more properly be regarded as a new cause than as a consequence of the original wrongdoing. But if the intervening action was likely to happen I do not think it can matter whether that action was innocent or tortious or criminal.'

In the present case if the goods were printed and delivered to Hollands without further inquiry it was possible that they would be improperly used to damage a third party. But I do not think that can be said to be 'likely'. The indicia referred to in para 32 are by themselves inconclusive. They are quite consistent with the Hollands having authority to place the order. What is the honest trader to do in such circumstances? Let me suppose

that he is to inquire of his customer by asking about his authority. If he asks the customer
a and the latter confirms that he has authority, is the trader entitled to believe him? If he
is, the supposed duty of care is not likely to be of great value to the injured party since
the dishonest customer will generally assert authority. If, on the other hand, the trader is
not entitled to believe the customer, must the trader require him to prove, by documents,
his title to give the order? In cases involving copyright, most traders would, without
legal advice, be altogether ill-equipped to judge what the rights and wrongs of the
b problem were. I do not think that ordinary trading can really be conducted on this basis.
It seems to me that in a case where the trader has no knowledge of an improper purpose
and, at any rate, where the possible indications of an improper purpose are consistent
with the order being, in fact, a perfectly lawful one, it would in practical terms be
unsatisfactory and burdensome on traders for the law to impose a duty to inquire into
the intentions and purposes of the customer. I would conclude that, if any prima facie
c duty of care exists it is negatived in the circumstances. I add that in a passing-off case, the
complainant is not without remedy. He has a full cause of action against those conducting
the passing off.

I think the judge's order was right. I would dismiss the appeal.

ROBERT GOFF LJ. The plaintiffs in this action, to whom we have already given leave
d to appeal, are appealing against an order made by Whitford J on 29 January 1982, under
which he ordered that a substantial part of the statement of claim should be struck out.

The matter arises in the following way. The plaintiffs are companies who, inter alia,
make and sell, in West Africa and elsewhere, a complexion cream under the name Venus
de Milo. The defendant companies are printers. It is not necessary for the purposes of
this appeal to distinguish between the various plaintiffs and defendants. The case of the
e plaintiffs, as set out in their statement of claim, is that certain persons, and in particular a
certain Patricia Holland and Richard Peter Holland, formed the intention of having
made and of selling a complexion cream in tubes and packaging designed to be as similar
as possible to the plaintiffs' Venus de Milo cream. For that purpose, the plaintiffs allege,
these persons ordered from the defendants a large quantity of cartons, to be copied from
a sample of the plaintiffs' cartons which they supplied to the defendants, together with
f leaflets for inclusion in the cartons which were substantially exact copies of the plaintiffs'
leaflets. Pursuant to this order, the defendants manufactured and delivered over 100,000
cartons and 100,000 leaflets to the order of the Hollands; many more cartons and leaflets,
manufactured or part manufactured, were subsequently taken into the custody of the
plaintiffs' solicitors under Anton Piller orders.

In these circumstances, the plaintiffs claim that the defendants have committed an
g infringement of their copyright, in relation to both the cartons and the leaflets. They are
claiming the ordinary relief in respect of such infringement. But, in their statement of
claim, they have advanced two claims which go beyond the ordinary relief claimed in
actions for infringement of copyright; it is the part of the statement of claim relating to
these two matters which, on the application of the defendants, the judge has ordered to
be struck out. First, the plaintiffs have claimed, as loss and damage suffered by them by
h reason of the defendants' infringement of copyright, the damage which would ordinarily
be attributable to the alleged passing off by the Hollands and others of their goods as the
plaintiffs' goods, including, for example, damages for loss of sales assessed on the basis of
the additional profit per tube which the plaintiffs would have earned if they had
themselves sold the number of tubes of Venus de Milo cream which the Hollands and
others sold, and damage to the reputation and goodwill of Venus de Milo cream in the
j United Kingdom and elsewhere caused by the inferior quality of the cream sold in the
counterfeit tubes. Second, in the alternative, the plaintiffs claim that the defendants are
liable to them in negligence. They claim that the defendants owed to the plaintiffs a duty
of care; and that the defendants were negligent in that they ought to have realised (from
words and devices which appeared on the cartons, and from the fact that they were asked
to make up artwork from specimens instead of being supplied with artwork) that the

Hollands were not entitled to authorise the reproduction of the plaintiffs' packaging and leaflets, and ought to have foreseen that printing and supplying them would result in loss and damage to the plaintiffs of the kind which they allege occurred.

The judge approached the matter as follows. He first concluded that the paragraphs in the statement of claim concerned with the actions of those who caused the alleged passing off must be embarrassing, in that they related to matters which could not be within the knowledge of the defendants who, the plaintiffs accepted, were wholly innocent so far as any question of passing off was concerned. With great respect to the judge, however, the mere fact that these pleaded facts would not have been within the knowledge of the defendants cannot render that part of the pleading embarrassing within the meaning of that word as used in RSC Ord 18, r 19. Indeed, it was accepted in argument before this court that the principal issue which arose on the defendants' application, and on the appeal, was not whether the relevant parts of the statement of claim were embarrassing, but whether they should be struck out as not disclosing any reasonable cause of action. The judge formed the view that they did not. He regarded the crucial question as being, in relation to both the relevant heads of claim, whether there was anything in the pleading which supported the proposition that 'a reasonable man would foresee that one of the consequences of the printing of the words in dispute, if in fact they were wrongly printed, would be that passing off might result'. That question he answered in the negative, and therefore ordered the parts of the pleading relevant to both points to be struck out.

Before this court, counsel for the plaintiffs put his case as follows. I take first the point on infringement of copyright. First, he said, the act complained of was the act of reproducing the 'artistic work', in which the plaintiffs owned the copyright, in a material form. It followed that the infringement on which the plaintiffs relied was the commission of an act restricted by virtue of s 3(5)(a) of the Copyright Act 1956; the plaintiffs did not rely on any infringement by the defendants under s 5 of the Act, which prohibits importation of articles and their distribution (in particular by sale) in certain circumstances, but which also provides that there shall only be an infringement if to the defendant's knowledge the making of the articles constituted an infringement of the relevant copyright. Next, counsel for the plaintiffs submitted that, on the facts pleaded in the statement of claim, the infringement caused the damage claimed, including the loss of sales and damage to goodwill. In this connection, he adopted as part of his argument a passage in 12 Halsbury's Laws (4th edn) para 1140, note 2, to the effect that, in the case of a tort of strict liability (such as infringement of copyright under s 3(5) of the 1956 Act), the tortfeasor will be liable for damage which, if he was aware of the facts constituting the commission of the tort, he could reasonably have foreseen as flowing from it. Here, submitted counsel for the plaintiffs, if the defendants had been aware that they were committing an infringement of the plaintiffs' copyright, they could reasonably have foreseen that the damage claimed by the plaintiffs would have resulted from the infringement. He cited, in support of his argument, the decision of the House of Lords in *Banco de Portugal v Waterlow & Sons Ltd* [1932] AC 452, [1932] All ER Rep 181. In that case it was held that the defendant printers, who were parties to a contract with the plaintiff Portuguese bank to print certain Portuguese bank notes, were liable to the Portuguese bank in damages when they innocently printed and delivered to a third party a quantity of the bank notes, because they had committed a breach of an absolute duty under their contract with the Portuguese bank only to print and deliver such notes with the authority of the bank; and it was further held that the damages recoverable from the printers were not nominal but were the exchange value expressed in sterling of the genuine currency given in exchange for the counterfeit notes, together with the cost of printing the genuine notes which had to be withdrawn. Such damage was held to be within the reasonable contemplation of both parties at the time of making the contract as the probable result of the breach, within the rule in *Hadley v Baxendale* (1854) 9 Exch 341, [1843–60] All ER Rep 461. So here, submitted counsel for the plaintiffs, the damages claimed by the plaintiffs were reasonably foreseeable by the defendants, if aware of the facts constituting the infringement. There was no question of novus actus interveniens,

a any more than there was in *Banco de Portugal v Waterlow & Sons Ltd*, since the act of the
Hollands in causing the printed cartons and leaflets to be used for marketing counterfeit
goods was precisely the thing which could have been foreseen by the defendants, if aware
of the infringement, as likely to occur as a result of it, as the circulation of the bank notes
could have been foreseen by the defendant printers in the *Banco de Portugal* case, if aware
of the facts constituting their breach of contract.

b In answer to this submission, counsel for the defendants submitted that the effect of
the argument of counsel for the plaintiffs was that the plaintiffs were seeking to recover
damages which were not recoverable under the 1956 Act. The alleged infringement was
simply reproducing the relevant work in a material form. The only damages recoverable
for such infringement were (1) damages under s 17 of the 1956 Act, viz such relief by
way of damages as was available in any corresponding proceedings in respect of
infringements of other proprietary rights, and (2) damages under s 18 of the 1956 Act,
c viz damages in respect of the conversion or detention of an infringing copy, or of any
plate used or intended to be used for making infringing copies, as the plaintiffs would be
entitled to if they were the owners of every such copy or plate and had been the owners
thereof since the time when it was made. As to the former, submitted counsel for the
defendants, damages were not recoverable in respect of the delivery of infringing copies,
when the only infringement alleged was the reproduction of the relevant work. If a
d plaintiff wished to recover such damages, he had either to proceed under s 5, when the
defendant would be able to rely on the statutory restriction on liability which I have
already set out; or to claim damages for conversion under s 18. Neither of these claims
has been advanced in the present case.

I find myself unable to accept the submission of counsel for the defendants. I read the
Act somewhat differently, and in particular I differ from him as to the construction of s 3
e of the 1956 Act. As I read s 3, which is concerned with artistic works, the function of the
section, in defining in s 3(5) the acts restricted by the copyright in an artistic work, is to
impose an absolute liability on any person who commits an infringement of copyright
by the commission of any such act, subject only, where damages for infringement are
claimed, to the very limited defence available generally under s 17(2), viz that at the time
of the infringement the defendant was not aware, and had no reasonable grounds for
f suspecting, that copyright subsisted in the work. Furthermore, the acts restricted by
s 3(5) may be loosely described as acts which constitute a primary infringement of
copyright, in contradistinction to the infringements legislated for under s 5, which may
loosely be described as dealing in infringing articles, whether by importation or
distribution. In these circumstances, it is understandable that there should be available,
under s 5, to those who deal in infringing articles, the restriction on liability which is not
g available to those who commit a primary infringement under s 3, viz that they did not
know that the making of the article constituted an infringement of the relevant
copyright. It follows, as a matter of construction, that a person who commits an
infringement of copyright by reproducing an artistic work in a material form, contrary
to s 3(5)(a), for another person, and delivers the reproduction up to that other person, is
absolutely liable for so doing (subject only to the limited defence under s 17(2)), just as
h he would be if he published the work, or included the work in a television broadcast, or
caused a television programme which included the work to be transmitted to subscribers
to a diffusion service, contrary to s 3(5)(b), (c) and (d) respectively. This construction of
s 3(5)(a) appears to be consistent with the decision of Peterson J in *Birn Bros Ltd v Keen &
Co Ltd* [1918] 2 Ch 281. Furthermore, it cannot be right that the only remedy available
to a plaintiff against a person who disseminates copies of artistic works which, in breach
j of copyright, he has reproduced, is the remedy of conversion; because, under s 18, there
are defences available to an action for damages for conversion which are not generally
available in the case of an action for damages for an infringement of copyright under
s 3(5). The construction of counsel for the defendants imposes, in my judgment, a
construction of s 3(5)(a) which is too restrictive and which takes insufficient account of
the context within which that subsection is set.

However, although I feel unable to accept the submission of counsel for the defendants

as providing a sufficient answer to the argument of counsel for the plaintiffs, I consider
that the latter goes too far. The general remedy for damages for infringement of a
copyright is legislated for by s 17 of the 1956 Act, and is there described as being 'such
relief, by way of damages . . . as is available in any corresponding proceedings in respect
of infringements of other proprietary rights'. These words have been considered in
certain authorities, and in particular by the Court of Appeal in *Sutherland Publishing Co
Ltd v Caxton Publishing Co Ltd* [1936] 1 All ER 177 at 181, [1936] Ch 323 at 336, in which
Lord Wright MR described the measure of damages arising under s 6 of the Copyright b
Act 1911 (the precursor of s 17 of the 1956 Act) as 'the depreciation caused by the
infringement to the value of the copyright as a chose in action', a description which is, if
I may say so with respect, consistent with the wrong being the infringement of a
proprietary right. No doubt, if the effect of the infringement is to divert profits from the
owner of the copyright to the infringer, the measure of damages will normally be the
profit which would have been received by the owner of the copyright if the sale had been c
made by him: cf *General Tire and Rubber Co v Firestone Tyre and Rubber Co Ltd* [1975] 2
All ER 173 at 177, [1975] 1 WLR 819 at 824 per Lord Wilberforce (a case concerned with
the damages recoverable in the case of an infringement of a patent). Furthermore,
additional damages may be awarded under s 17(3) of the 1956 Act in the special
circumstances specified in that subsection. But it does not follow, in my judgment, that
the measure of damages extends to include damages of the type claimed in the present d
case. Here the plaintiffs are in truth claiming not damages for the depreciation of their
copyright, but damages for the passing off of other goods as their own on the basis that
such passing off has been facilitated by the defendants' infringement of their copyright
in the cartons and accompanying leaflets. When pressed on this point, counsel for the
plaintiffs submitted that the damages so claimed were recoverable as parasitic damages. I
know, however, of no principle that, whenever one interest of a plaintiff has been e
wrongfully damaged, consequential damage to another interest of the plaintiff is
necessarily recoverable. In each case it has to be considered whether, as a matter of policy,
the latter damages should be recoverable in an action founded on the wrongful invasion
of the plaintiff's first interest. I know of no authority which enables a plaintiff, suing for
damages for infringement of his copyright, to recover as part of such damages loss he has
suffered because the commission by a third party of the tort of passing off has been f
facilitated by the defendant's infringement of his copyright; and as a matter of policy it
is, in my judgment, undesirable to extend the scope of recoverable damages in an action
for infringement of copyright in this way. The law of copyright is a self-contained branch
of the law, concerned with the protection of a particular proprietary right. The provisions
regulating the protection of that right, including, for example, those which provide for
strict liability or liability based on fault, are framed with regard to a particular interest, g
viz the proprietary right in question. It would be undesirable as a matter of policy to
extend the statutory remedies available for the protection of that interest to the recovery
of damages in respect of the invasion of a different interest.

It follows that I am unable to accede to the argument of counsel for the plaintiffs on
the first point. I turn therefore to his argument on negligence. His submission on this
point was simple. It was to the effect that printers should be under a duty of care to avoid h
damage caused by the printing of packaging and other similar material in breach of
copyright which might foreseeably be used by others to pass off their goods as those of
the owners of the copyright in the packaging or other material. He recognised that he
could cite no authority in support of his proposition; but he submitted that, as a matter
of policy, the duty of care should be extended to apply in such cases. It was however
apparent from his argument that a breach of copyright by the defendant was not to be a j
prerequisite of liability; it was enough that, by printing material for another, he
negligently facilitated the commission by him of the tort of passing-off his goods as those
of the plaintiff.

Counsel for the defendants, on the other hand, submitted that any such extension of
the duty of care was contrary to authority and to good practice. Certainly, as he was able

a to show, it is at least implicit in certain authorities which he cited that no action lay against a person who merely facilitated passing off by another, as opposed to being sufficiently involved in the commission of the tort to become a joint tortfeasor. Thus in *Belegging- en Exploitatiemaatschapij Lavender BV v Witten Industrial Diamonds Ltd* [1979] FSR 59 the Court of Appeal had to consider whether a statement of claim which alleged, in very vague terms, that the defendants had infringed the plaintiffs' patent, or counselled, aided or procured the infringement of that patent, should be struck out as disclosing no
b reasonable cause of action. The court appears to have regarded the only relevant allegation as being that of infringement of the patent, and in the course of his judgment Buckley LJ (at 64) referred to, and relied on, the following statement of principle by Mellish LJ in *Townsend v Haworth* (1875) 48 LJ Ch 770 at 773:

c 'Selling materials for the purpose of infringing a patent to the man who is going to infringe it, even although the party who sells it knows that he is going to infringe it and indemnifies him, does not by itself make the person who so sells an infringer. He must be a party with the man who so infringes, and actually infringe'.

Again, in *CBS Inc v Ames Records and Tapes Ltd* [1981] 2 All ER 812, [1982] Ch 91 the argument and the decision of the court appear to have proceeded on the assumption that no action lay for negligently facilitating a breach of copyright by a third party.
d Even so, the scope of the duty of care has developed to such an extent over the past fifty years that authorities such as these, while providing a valuable indication of the attitude of the courts in the past, cannot be taken as excluding, as a matter of authority, the existence of a duty of care in a case such as the present. Whether such a duty of care exists is a point on which there is no conclusive authority; and this court has to consider whether, in the light of the development of the duty of care, it should be held to apply
e in a case such as the present.

I hope that I do not do injustice to the argument of counsel for the plaintiffs if I summarise it as follows. A printer who prints a libel can find himself liable in damages to the person so defamed; this imposes a thoroughly healthy restraint on the activities of printers; and it would be an admirable development if printers who negligently facilitate the commission by others of the tort of passing off were similarly restrained. For myself,
f however, I do not find the analogy of libel helpful. The printer who prints defamatory material may, in certain circumstances, commit the tort of libel. But he is liable because he has himself committed that tort: he is not liable because he has by his negligence facilitated the commission of some other tort by a third party.

The true starting point for the inquiry in the present case must now be the authoritative statement of Lord Wilberforce in *Anns v Merton London Borough* [1977] 2 All ER 492 at
g 498, [1978] AC 728 at 751–752, where he said:

'. . . the position has now been reached that in order to establish that a duty of care arises in a particular situation, it is not necessary to bring the facts of that situation within those of previous situations in which a duty of care has been held to exist. Rather the question has to be approached in two stages. First one has to ask whether, as between the alleged wrongdoer and the person who has suffered damage
h there is a sufficient relationship of proximity or neighbourhood such that, in the reasonable contemplation of the former, carelessness on his part may be likely to cause damage to the latter, in which case a prima facie duty of care arises. Secondly, if the first question is answered affirmatively, it is necessary to consider whether there are any considerations which ought to negative, or to reduce or limit the scope of the duty or the class of person to whom it is owed or the damages to which a
j breach of it may give rise . . .'

This statement (which was foreshadowed by more tentative remarks of Lord Reid in *Home Office v Dorset Yacht Co Ltd* [1970] 2 All ER 294 at 297, [1970] AC 1004 at 1026) marked the coming of age of the law of negligence. There is now a prima facie duty of care in those cases where the prerequisite, that the defendant ought reasonably to have foreseen that his act or omission was likely to cause damage of the relevant type to a person in the position of the plaintiff, has been fulfilled. When new cases come before *a* the court the inquiry is no longer whether the duty of care should be extended to the new situation; it is rather whether, given the fulfilment of the prerequisite, there are circumstances which require that the prima facie duty of care should be negatived, or reduced or limited in scope. Moreover, as is apparent from the recent decision of the House of Lords in *Junior Books Ltd v Veitchi Co Ltd* [1982] 3 All ER 201, [1983] 1 AC 520, the same approach applies whether the damage claimed by the plaintiff arises from *b* physical loss or damage suffered by him (sometimes together with parasitic economic loss), or from purely economic loss.

Even so, it is necessary to sound a note of caution. There is a not insignificant number of cases in which the courts have held that no duty of care exists; there are others where they have held that the duty must be limited. Moreover, in considering new cases as they arise the courts have, as must surely be right, recognised that a heavy duty of care rests *c* on them to ensure that they themselves do not overstep the bounds of reasonableness by imposing too onerous legal duties on members of the public. Vivid examples of this circumspection are to be found in two of the leading cases, *Hedley Byrne & Co Ltd v Heller & Partners Ltd* [1963] 2 All ER 575, [1964] AC 465 and the *Dorset Yacht* case itself. It is plain that, in considering whether the duty of care should be negatived or limited in any new situation, the courts are making what it usually called a decision of policy (see the *d* *Dorset Yacht* case [1970] 2 All ER 294 at 325, [1970] AC 1004 at 1059 per Lord Diplock). Presented with such a case, the courts have to do their limited best. They have no secretariat, or apparatus for inquiry. They have to derive all the guidance they can from the authorities, and from the writings of scholars; and they have the inestimable benefit of the assistance of counsel. But they are also fully entitled to, and do, draw on their own professional and practical experience. In the end, the choice must be one of judgment, in *e* the balancing of conflicting interests; and in the exercise of that judgment the courts must strive neither unjustifiably to deprive potential plaintiffs of remedies for their injuries, nor unjustifiably to impose too heavy a legal responsibility on potential defendants.

In a case such as the present, there may well be circumstances in which a printer of packaging or other similar material may reasonably foresee that, in carrying out such *f* work for another, it is likely that that other may use the material so provided to him for the commission of the tort of passing off. Given the appropriate facts, therefore, a sufficient relationship of proximity may exist. The question for consideration is whether the prima facie duty of care to avoid such a consequence should, for some special reason, be negatived or limited. As I have already indicated, the existing authorities (such as they are) proceed on the assumption that there is no such duty of care. This factor has served *g* to reinforce my own instinctive caution in this matter. But it cannot be decisive; and if, as I do, I feel hesitation in holding that the facts pleaded in the present case disclose a cause of action, I have to analyse the causes of that reaction with some care. For that purpose, it is necessary to isolate each special feature of a case of this type, and to consider whether, and if so to what extent, that feature should inhibit the imposition of liability.

The first special feature is that there is here said to be a duty of care on the defendant *h* to avoid providing a third party with the means of committing a tort against the plaintiff. Is there any general principle which excludes or limits liability in such a case? In my judgment, there is no principle which excludes liability. It is only necessary to give examples such as handing a loaded gun to a small boy or a simpleton, who then 'has a go' and shoots the plaintiff, or entrusting a car to a man who is obviously drunk or even incompetent, to realise that there are cases in this category where there is a duty of care. *j* It is implicit in the decision of the Privy Council in *Yachuk v Oliver Blais Co Ltd* [1949] 2 All ER 150, [1949] AC 386 that there may be liability in the first of these examples; and the Canadian case of *Ontario Hospital Services Commission v Borsoski* (1974) 54 DLR (3d) 339 provides strong persuasive authority that there may be liability in the second. But even so a note of caution has to be sounded. Take the case of a dealer in cars who sells a

a   car to a man whom he knows to be an alcoholic, or to be the husband of an alcoholic who
to his knowledge drives her husband's car; it is difficult to believe that he would be held
liable when, a few weeks later, the husband or wife (as the case might be) was involved,
while in a state of intoxication, in a collision with the plaintiff's car. Clearly there is a
line to be drawn.

b   Furthermore, the examples I have so far given are of cases where the third party
commits the tort of negligence, not where he is involved in deliberate wrongdoing. Once
again, however, a duty of care cannot be negatived. A case such as *Stansbie v Troman*
[1948] 1 All ER 599, [1948] 2 KB 48 suggests examples, and the *Dorset Yacht* case itself
provides an example, where the defendant may be held liable in such circumstances.
However, both these authorities exhibit special features. In particular, there was in the
Dorset Yacht case a special relationship, involving a degree of control, which provided the
foundation for liability. Moreover, once again a note of caution has to be sounded. This
c   is because, for example, I do not consider that a dealer in sporting tackle, including
shotguns, who lawfully sold a shotgun to a notorious poacher, would be held liable when,
a few weeks later, the poacher used the gun to deprive the plaintiff of game from his
estate. Once again, a line has to be drawn.

It is tempting to conclude that, in the absence of some special relationship, there can
be no liability for damage caused to the plaintiff by the deliberate wrongdoing of a third
d   party. That this is so in cases where the defendant fails to prevent a third party causing
loss or damage to the plaintiff is demonstrated by the *Dorset Yacht* case, and by the dictum
of Dixon J in *Smith v Leurs* (1945) 70 CLR 256 at 262 cited with approval in that case,
both primarily concerned with circumstances where the third party was under the
defendant's control. Moreover, as long ago as 1920, Lord Sumner said in *Weld-Blundell v
Stephens* [1920] AC 956 at 986, [1920] All ER Rep 32 at 47:

e   'In general (apart from special contracts and relations and the maxim Respondeat
superior), even though A. is in fault, he is not responsible for injury to C. which B.,
a stranger to him, deliberately chooses to do.'

However, the analogy of cases where the defendant fails to prevent a third party from
causing injury to the plaintiff is not exact; and in the changed climate of today, Lord
f   Sumner's dictum must be regarded as too sweeping. If the defendant hands a gun to a
man, with the knowledge that he intends deliberately to shoot the plaintiff, I can see no
reason why liability of the defendant to the plaintiff for the injuries he suffers when the
third party shoots him should inevitably be excluded; after all, 'the action of negligence
lies not only for carelessness but also for intentional conduct' (see *Salmond and Heuston on
Torts* (18th edn, 1981) p 181. The solution to the problem appears to lie in a passage from
g   the speech of Lord Reid in the *Dorset Yacht* case [1970] 2 All ER 294 at 300, [1970] AC
1004 at 1030 where, after citing certain authorities, he said:

        'These cases show that, where human action forms one of the links between the
original wrongdoing of the defendant and the loss suffered by the plaintiff, that
action must at least have been something very likely to happen if it is not to be
regarded as novus actus interveniens breaking the chain of causation. I do not think
h   that a mere foreseeable possibility is or should be sufficient, for then the intervening
human action can more properly be regarded as a new cause than as a consequence
of the original wrongdoing. But if the intervening action was likely to happen I do
not think it can matter whether that action was innocent or tortious or criminal.
Unfortunately tortious or criminal action by a third party is often the 'very kind of
thing' which is likely to happen as a result of the wrongful or careless act of the
j   defendant.'

Of course, in the law of negligence the common criterion of foreseeability creates
some overlap between the various constituent parts of the tort; and the point made by
Lord Reid can perhaps be as legitimately made at the stage of breach of the duty of care
as it can at the stage of causation. Even so, the effect of Lord Reid's observation is that

there is no principle of law excluding liability in negligence for damage caused by the deliberate wrongdoing of a third party; but only in the limited circumstances indicated *a* by Lord Reid will liability attach for such damage.

However, that is not the only special feature of the present case. The second feature I have to consider is that the loss alleged to have been suffered by the plaintiff is purely economic loss. Now it is true that, nowadays, the prima facie duty of care which exists to avoid reasonably foreseeable damage to persons in the category of the plaintiff applies to economic loss as well as to physical loss or damage; even so, it is plain from the cases that *b* there are numerous circumstances in which liability in negligence for economic loss is excluded altogether (see the examples given in *Salmond and Heuston on Torts* p 192), and in others, of which the *Hedley Byrne* case provides the most noteworthy example, it is restricted to special circumstances. However, although the fact that the loss is economic is a common feature of these examples, it does not appear to provide of itself the reason why liability is excluded or restricted. The primary reason appears rather to be an *c* understandable reluctance on the part of the courts to impose legal responsibility for injury suffered by persons of too wide, or too indeterminate, a category. The cases fall into the group where, in the delicate balancing operation which the courts have to perform, the scales of policy tip in favour of potential defendants rather than potential plaintiffs. No such feature, however, is present in the case now under consideration. The danger to be averted is not one which may affect numerous persons, but simply one *d* person who may suffer from a third party passing off goods as his. I can see no reason why the fact that the loss suffered in such a case is purely economic should of itself have the effect of excluding, or even restricting, liability in such a case.

There is a third special feature of the present case to which I must refer. This is that the alleged negligence is of a kind which occurs in the course of the defendant's ordinary business, in this case in the course of his trade as a printer. It is difficult to resist the *e* feeling that, if a person approaches a printer and asks him to carry out certain work, there must be some limit to the extent to which the printer should be expected to, so to speak, look over his shoulder and consider whether or not the material when printed might be used by the customer for passing-off his goods as another's. However, considerations of this kind should not, in my judgment, affect the existence or scope of the duty of care. They are rather circumstances to be taken into account when considering whether the *f* defendant has complied with the standard of care appropriate in the particular case.

With these principles in mind I turn to the facts pleaded in the present case. The allegation of negligence is founded on the following facts pleaded in para 32 of the statement of claim:

> '[The defendants] ought to have realised that the Hollands were not entitled to authorise the reproduction of the plaintiffs' packaging and leaflets, and ought to *g* have foreseen that printing and supplying them would result in loss and damage to the plaintiffs of the kind which has occurred. Particulars: (a) The leaflets printed by [the defendants] bore the words "Made in Nigeria" and a device containing the letters AIL. The Hollands had no connection with any company or form with initials AIL, and [the defendants] ought to have been put on enquiry by this. In fact, they made no inquiries into the Hollands' right to authorise printing of the cartons. *h* (b) The cartons printed by [the defendants] bore a device mark containing the letters PZ, and [the defendants] ought to have been put on enquiry by this fact. (c) [The defendants] ought to have been put on enquiry by the fact that they were asked to make up artwork from specimens instead of being supplied with artwork.'

I have no hesitation in holding that these allegations fall far short of facts capable of *j* giving rise to liability in negligence in a case of this kind. I accept that in these circumstances, as no doubt in many other comparable circumstances, there might be a risk that the printed material could be used by the customer for the purpose of passing off his goods as another's. But the printer may know nothing about the customer's rights, by virtue of his own title or possibly some licensing or agency arrangement, to market a the relevant goods; and, in my judgment, it would impose far too heavy a burden on printers to require them, on the basis of such information as is here pleaded, to make inquiries of the kind suggested. I feel fortified in this conclusion by the approach of the judge, who has far greater experience than I in matters of this kind. Referring to the devices 'AIL' and 'PZ', he said in his judgment:

b 'I cannot for the life of me see why [the defendants] should ever have taken into consideration the question whether or not the Hollands had any connection with any company or firm with the initials AIL at all. Let me assume that they made no inquiries. I cannot see why they should. Secondly, it is said: "The cartons printed by [the defendants] bore a device mark containing the letters PZ, and [the defendants] ought to have been put on inquiry by this fact". Again I cannot for the life of me see why.'

c I cannot help suspecting that cases of this type in which a printer may be held liable in negligence are likely to be rare, involving as they must a degree of knowledge which far transcends the facts pleaded in the present case. An example of a case in which such liability may be imposed can be inferred from the decision of Foster J in *John Walker & Sons Ltd v Henry Ost & Co Ltd* [1970] 2 All ER 106, [1970] 1 WLR 917, in which the first defendants shipped to Ecuador large numbers of empty bottles, cartons and labels, and a
d large quantity of malt whisky. The first defendants knew and intended that, by using these particular labels, whisky was to be marketed in Ecuador as Scotch whisky, and they also knew that the whisky to be so marketed would be a debased blend including an admixture of local spirits. Foster J held, inter alia, that, having regard to the knowledge and intention of the first defendants in these circumstances, the sale by them in England of the goods and labels was tortious. In granting an injunction restraining the first
e defendants from continuing with this form of activity, however, the order was expressed to be subject to the proviso that it should not apply if the first defendants had reasonable grounds for believing, and did in fact believe, that any such admixture would not be passed off as and for Scotch whisky. The terms of the order appear, therefore, to have been consistent with a conclusion that liability for activities of this kind might sound in negligence.
f However, in the present case, for the reasons I have given, I am satisfied that the statement of claim as pleaded discloses no cause of action in negligence. I would therefore dismiss the appeal.

Appeal dismissed. Leave to appeal to the House of Lords refused.

Solicitors: *Pothecary & Barratt*, agents for *Leak Almond & Parkinson*, Manchester (for the plaintiffs); *Franks Charlesly & Co* (for the defendants).

Mary Rose Plummer   Barrister.

King v Liverpool City Council *a*

COURT OF APPEAL, CIVIL DIVISION
PURCHAS, NICHOLLS LJJ AND CAULFIELD J
17, 18 FEBRUARY 1986

Negligence – Duty to take care – Act of third party – Duty of owner of building to occupier of *b*
adjoining building in respect of act of third party – Vandals gaining access to defendant's
unoccupied and unsecured premises and damaging water system – Plaintiff's adjacent property
flooded – Whether defendant owing duty to plaintiff for acts of third party – Whether defendant
liable for plaintiff's loss.

The plaintiff was the tenant of a council flat. In August 1982 the flat directly above the
plaintiff's flat became vacant when the tenants left and on 2 September the plaintiff *c*
notified the council that the vacant flat was unoccupied and unprotected against vandals.
The council failed to take any action and between 10 and 12 September vandals entered
the vacant flat and removed copper piping and other parts of the water system, causing
water to flood the plaintiff's flat. The council failed to board up the vacant flat or if it did
so it did not do so effectively and on two further occasions vandals broke into the vacant *d*
flat and damaged the water supply causing the plaintiff's flat to be flooded again. The
plaintiff brought an action against the council alleging that the council had been
negligent in failing to secure the vacant flat thereby entitling the plaintiff to damages in
negligence or nuisance. The judge dismissed the plaintiff's claim and she appealed.

Held – In the circumstances, and having regard to the fact that it was not possible for the
council to take effective steps to defeat the actions of trespassing vandals, the council did *e*
not owe a duty of care to the plaintiff in respect of the damage caused by the actions of
the vandals (see p 552 *g* to p 553 *b* and p 554 *a*, post.

P *Perl (Exporters) Ltd v Camden London BC* [1983] 3 All ER 161 followed.
Lamb v Camden London Borough [1981] 2 All ER 408 and dictum of Robert Goff LJ in
Paterson Zochonis & Co Ltd v Merfarken Packaging Ltd (1982) [1986] 3 All ER at 540–542
considered. *f*

Notes
For the duty of care of occupiers, see 34 Halsbury's Laws (4th edn) paras 18–52, and for
cases on the subject, see 36(1) Digest (Reissue) 75–151, 299–577.

Cases referred to in judgments *g*
A-G v Corke [1933] Ch 89, [1932] All ER Rep 711.
Anns v Merton London Borough [1977] 2 All ER 492, [1978] AC 728, [1977] 2 WLR 1024,
   HL.
Davies v Liverpool Corp [1949] 2 All ER 175, CA.
Harris v Birkenhead Corp (Pascoe, third party, Alliance Assured Co Ltd, fourth party) [1976] 1
   All ER 341, [1976] 1 WLR 279. *h*
Haynes v Harwood [1935] 1 KB 146, [1934] All ER Rep 103, CA.
Hedley Byrne & Co Ltd v Heller & Partners Ltd [1963] 2 All ER 575, [1964] AC 465, [1963]
   3 WLR 101, HL.
Home Office v Dorset Yacht Co Ltd [1970] 2 All ER 294, [1970] AC 1004, [1970] 2 WLR
   1140, HL.
Hosie v Arbroath Football Club Ltd 1978 SLT 122. *j*
Lamb v Camden London Borough [1981] 2 All ER 408, [1981] QB 625, [1981] 2 WLR 1038,
   CA.
Newby v General Lighterage Co Ltd [1955] 1 Lloyd's Rep 273, CA.
Noble v Harrison [1926] 2 KB 332, [1926] All ER Rep 284, DC.
Ontario Hospital Services Commission v Borsoski (1974) 54 DLR (3d) 339, Ont HC.

Paterson Zonchonis & Co Ltd v Merfarken Packaging Ltd (1982) [1986] 3 All ER 522, CA.

a *Perl (P) (Exporters) Ltd v Camden London BC* [1983] 3 All ER 161, [1984] QB 342, [1983] 3
    WLR 769, CA.

Rylands v Fletcher (1868) LR 3 HL 330, [1861–73] All ER Rep 1, HL.

Sedleigh-Denfield v O'Callaghan (Trustees for St Joseph's Society for Foreign Missions) [1940] 3
    All ER 349, [1940] AC 880, HL.

Smith v Leurs (1945) 70 CLR 256, Aust HC.

b *Stansbie v Troman* [1948] 1 All ER 599, [1948] 2 KB 48, CA.

Ward v Cannock Chase DC [1985] 3 All ER 537.

Weld-Blundell v Stephens [1920] AC 956, [1920] All ER Rep 32.

Yachuk v Oliver Blais Co Ltd [1949] 2 All ER 150, [1949] AC 386, PC.

Cases also cited

c *Stevens v Woodward* (1881) 6 QBD 318, DC.

Wells v Metropolitan Water Board [1937] 4 All ER 639.

Appeal

The plaintiff, Mary King, appealed from the decision of his Honour Judge Sachs given on
12 December 1984 in the Liverpool County Court dismissing the plaintiff's claim for
d damages against the defendant, Liverpool City Council. The facts are set out in the
judgment of Purchas LJ.

David Marshall Evans QC and *Graham Wood* for the plaintiff.
John Kay QC and *William Braithwaite* for the council.

e **PURCHAS LJ.** This is an appeal by the plaintiff from a judgment of his Honour Judge
Sachs given at the Liverpool County Court on 8 January 1985. The judge dismissed the
plaintiff's claim against the respondents, Liverpool City Council, for damage caused to
her property by water escaping from a flat owned by the council. The plaintiff was a
tenant of a neighbouring flat owned by them. The premises were at 16 Great Mersey
Street, Liverpool. The plaintiff's flat was no 16 and immediately above it was flat 16A,
f which at the material time was vacant but for which the council were responsible.

The short facts leading up to this matter are as follows. The plaintiff, first under a joint
tenancy and later, after her divorce, as sole tenant, had been in flat 16 since 1978. At the
end of August 1982 the tenants of flat 16A left the premises and on 2 September the
plaintiff, noticing that the flat above was unoccupied and not protected in any way
against trespassers or vandals, telephoned the appropriate department of the council to
g this effect. That message was received and passed to the appropriate department, the
depot at Shaw Street, Liverpool, where it was recorded and various steps were taken
which, in the event, were not successful.

Between 10 and 12 September 1982 vandals entered flat 16A and removed copper
piping and other parts of the water supply equipment in that flat. In the result water
escaped from the damaged system and flooded the plaintiff's premises. The council sent
h a plumber who did some repair work, but again the flat was not boarded up either by
plywood or, as is sometimes done, with metal sheeting.

Two days later on 14 September 1982 there was another flood and this was sufficiently
serious to cause the plaintiff, understandably, to leave the flat. It appears very probable
that that again was as a result of vandals invading flat 16A. Thereafter the plaintiff lived
with her sister until December 1982, when she was rehoused by the council.

j In the meanwhile there had been a third flood, which appears to have occurred again
probably as a result of invasion by vandals between 16 and 17 September 1982.

Those are the facts, about which there is no dispute. Work records etc were produced
by the council, indicating that boarding or sheeting work had been carried out to flat
16A, although that was not seen by the plaintiff on her visits, and it was accepted by
witnesses for the council that it was not certain that the sheeting work had been

completed or effectively done. But their records certainly indicated that steps had been
taken to that end.

    a

   The plaintiff brought an action in the Liverpool County Court in June 1983. She
alleged negligence against the council in the first instance and the council counterclaimed
for arrears of rent. Later, in February 1984, her particulars of claim were amended. Then
the plaintiff alleged a breach of covenant for the quiet enjoyment of her flat (she was, of
course, a tenant of the council), alternatively negligence, which was her original cause of
action, or alternatively nuisance. The claim for breach of covenant was abandoned at the
trial below, but the plaintiff continued her claim in nuisance and negligence.

    b

   The facts material to this appeal, as found by the judge, can be shortly summarised. It
was accepted that the reason for the plaintiff's request, although not necessarily the same
as the motive for the defendants' action 'was that unhappily, as in many areas of
Liverpool, vandals readily discover that premises have been vacated, quickly descend on
them and cause substantial damage. From documents supplied by the defendants
housing department there is a card relating to 16A Great Mersey Street which shows that
on 2 September a request for two sorts of work to be undertaken: '(1) to sheet up and (2)
to remove services.' The judge listened to a considerable body of evidence from, amongst
others, the superintendent of the Shaw Street depot and the assistant district housing
manager.

    c

   The superintendent of the Shaw Street depot, Mr Peter Gibney, said this in evidence:

    d

> 'I know hundreds of tenants suffer from vandal damage. We sheet up and remove
> services. I know they have a rising main in a vulnerable position. We do not go
> looking for work. We used plywood albeit ineffective because we are told to. It
> looks like a burst on rising main [that is referring to the events in flat 16a]. Rising
> main would be made out of copper, basically the vandals go for the cylinder—
> sometimes for the rising main. There is a stop tap for each flat—can't remove
> pipe—would effect [occupants of the other flats].'

    e

The evidence of Stephen Alan Guy, the assistant district housing manager, was much to
the same effect:

> 'Sheeting up regarded as urgent—accepted by both departments as such. Wouldn't
> expect 10/12 days to elapse. Many properties are not sheeted up—works department
> slow or not reported. If properties not boarded up—vandals would get to know in
> short time. Services would be interfered with in unprotected premises. No steps
> taken apart from boarding up and remove rubbish.'

    f

Then, in relation to flooding:

> 'Three floods uncommon—normally one. Local Authority can remove services
> and secure premises. Particularly vulnerable if attacked once because not sheeted
> up.'

    g

Then in re-examination a finding on which the judge relied, he said:

> 'No guarantee sheeting up will stop vandals. Sheet steel is the answer. Quite often
> vandals get to know premises vacant within day or so.'

    h

The judge's findings on this evidence are recorded in the notes of his judgment in
these terms:

> 'Further evidence was called by the [council] being the evidence of Mr Guy the
> assistant district housing manager. His is an administrative post and he explained
> the procedures to which I have referred. He accepted that at the time there would
> be no record sent to his department that completion of the work had taken place.
> He agreed that unprotected premises would be likely to be the victims of vandals.
> He also told me that there was no guarantee that sheeting up would stop the vandals,
> although he would be more optimistic if steel sheeting was used and he accepted

    j

that vandals get to know of vacant premises within a day or so of them becoming
vacant. I have to find as a matter of fact what occurred in respect of these vacated
premises. I accept the evidence of the plaintiff bearing in mind that I find facts on a
balance of probabilities. I accept she informed the department of the various events,
that there were the three floods in the sequence to which she refers and that certainly
whenever she went to look at the flat 16A there was no sign of boarding up. If
therefore boarding up was done (of which I am not persuaded) clearly it was
ineffective as it was never observed by the plaintiff. I have no reason to doubt either
her description of the floods that occurred or the damage done. Equally I accept the
evidence called by the council that it is impossible to turn off the rising main supply
of drinking water without affecting other tenant. I also accept that damage done to
the flat 16A was damage done by vandals.'

The judge's finding on nuisance was in the following terms. Having referred to the
judgment of Lord Wright in *Sedleigh-Denfield v O'Callagan (Trustees for St Joseph's Society
for Foreign Missions)* [1940] 3 All ER 349, [1940] AC 880, he said:

'The facts that I find are that regrettably boarding up is ineffective and further it
is not possible to block off the rising main for the reasons I have given. I do not find
therefore the defendants in this case have adopted or continued a nuisance.
Regrettably in the circumstances I find that it is not possible for effective steps to be
taken in a situation like this which could defeat the activities of vandals. I find on
the evidence of the plaintiff that following the first flood a plumber did come to
visit the premises. As the case is pleaded the plaintiff maintains that the nuisance
was created by the failure to board up as opposed to the failure to rectify the
plumbing. For these reasons I am satisfied that the [council] abated the situation by
sending the plumber and did all that they could in that respect for the reasons I have
given. Counsel for the plaintiff sought to say that the nuisance was not an escape of
water but the condition of the premises. I was unpersuaded by the argument and
found it of no significance.'

As regards the claim in negligence, the judge based his finding on passages from the
judgments in *P Perl (Exporters) Ltd v Camden London BC* [1983] 3 All ER 161 esp at 164,
[1984] 1 QB 342 esp at 349 per Waller LJ, dealing with liability for the acts of third
parties, where he said:

'But no case has been cited to us where a party has been held liable for the acts of
third party when there was no element of control over the third party. While I do
not take the view that there can never be such a case I do take the view that the
absence of control must make the court approach the suggestion that there is
liability for a third party who was not under the control of the defendant with
caution.'

The judge then referred to a passage from the judgment of Oliver LJ in *Lamb v Camden
London Borough* [1981] 2 All ER 408 at 419, [1981] QB 625 at 644 to this effect:

'There may, for instance, be circumstances in which the court would require a
degree of likelihood amounting almost to inevitability before it fixes a defendant
with responsibility for the act of a third party over whom he has and can have no
control.'

The judge based himself on those judgments and found against the plaintiff on her claim
in negligence.

Counsel who has appeared for the plaintiff on this appeal has based his submissions in
negligence. He concedes, in my judgment rightly, that where nuisance was concerned
he could only establish the second of the three grounds of liability in nuisance, namely
'if by the neglect of some duty he [the tortfeasor] allowed it to arise' (see *Noble v Harrison*
[1926] 2 KB 332 at 338, [1926] All ER Rep 284 at 287 per Rowlatt J). Counsel for the

plaintiff submitted that the judge was wrong in considering that he was bound to find
for the defendants by the decision of this court in *P Perl (Exporters) Ltd v Camden London* a
BC. He distinguished that case on the basis that in the *Perl* case the failure to secure the
premises had the result that mischievous third parties gained access to neighbouring
premises and there caused the damage in a way that was not readily foreseeable. Here,
counsel for the plaintiff submits, the failure to secure the premises did not allow access to
neighbouring premises, but allowed vandals to come on the very same premises as those
occupied by the defendants, to behave in a foreseeable and wrongful manner, which led b
to water escaping from the water system in that council flat, thus doing damage to the
plaintiff's flat and property.

Counsel for the plaintiff relied on the findings and evidence to which I have already
referred, namely that, if premises were left unsecured, it was likely if not highly likely
that vandals would invade those premises and would cause damage thereto. Further,
counsel for the plaintiff submitted that it was foreseeable that they would be attracted to c
the valuable parts of the fittings of the flat, namely the copper piping and the cistern and
metal attachments, and that in breaking these out from the premises they would release
waters from the rising main; therefore, says counsel for the plaintiff, the damage to the
plaintiff's property and the flat was entirely foreseeable.

Encapsulated (I hope without doing injustice to counsel's able submissions) he puts his
case in this way: these circumstances placed a duty on the council owed to the occupier d
of neighbouring premises, because there was a potential hazard in flat 16A constituted by
the pipes and water system, in respect of which the occupier was under a duty of care to
prevent that potential hazard materialising in a way reasonably foreseeable, ie as a result
of the invasion of vandals if the premises were not secure, or the water cut off.

With reference to *Perl's* case counsel for the plaintiff submitted that the effect of that
case in no way bound the judge. He referred the court to a number of cases where it was e
submitted that liability was established for the act of a third party.

This is an area of the development of the law of tort and negligence which has received
considerable attention in recent years. It is not necessary in this judgment to rehearse in
detail the cases to which counsel for the plaintiff drew our attention and I hope that by
dealing with them summarily, that will not be considered a discourtesy to his submissions.

First of all reference was made to the well-known *Home Office v Dorset Yacht Co Ltd* f
[1970] 2 All ER 294, [1970] AC 1004. That case involved damage done by inmates of a
Borstal institution, who escaped to a nearby yacht harbour, took a yacht and caused
damage. The basis of liability in that case, however, was an established duty on the
warders employed in the establishment to control the acts of the wrongdoers (the third
parties) and that, as a result of that breach of duty properly to contain the Borstal inmates,
the damage caused by interference with the yachts was foreseeable and therefore g
recoverable. But, in considering that case, Watkins LJ in *Lamb v Camden London Borough*
[1981] 2 All ER 408 at 421, [1981] QB 625 at 646 drew the distinction between the
proximity between the Borstal institute and the yacht basin and the more remote
possibility of one of the inmates escaping to John o Groat's and there doing damage. It is
in each case necessary for the court to look at the scope of the duty in relation to the
context in which it arises, and in the *Dorset Yacht* case the circumstances were clearly h
established, showing a breach of duty on the part of the warders for whom the defendants
were responsible.

In *Harris v Birkenhead Corp (Pascoe, third party, Allowance Assurance Co Ltd, fourth party)*
[1976] 1 All ER 341 at 349, [1976] 1 WLR 279 at 288, as appears from the judgment of
Megaw LJ it was conceded by counsel for the corporation that there was a duty owed to
the child trespasser who was injured as a result of his trespassing on property for which j
the defendant corporation were responsible.

Again, in *Ward v Cannock Chase DC* [1985] 3 All ER 537, to which we were referred,
the council admitted liability for negligence, as appears from the headnote in that case.

These cases were dealing with the remoteness of the damage sustained in the context
of the facts and an established duty.

Davies v Liverpool Corp [1949] 2 All ER 175, to which we were referred, does not, with
respect to the submissions of counsel for the plaintiff, assist. It is based on the vicarious
responsibility of the corporation for the negligent discharge of his duty by the tram
conductor and, in my judgment, does not take the matter any further.

Newby v General Lighterage Co Ltd [1955] 1 Lloyd's Rep 273 was also referred to us.
There a barge had been moored, but not securely moored, on a fast-running waterway.
There was interference, and predictable interference, by passers-by on the towpath, and
liability was established.

As with *Haynes v Harwood* [1935] 1 KB 146, [1934] All ER Rep 103, the leading case in
this area, duties existed as between the users of either a highway or a waterway and the
existence of that duty was accepted. In this case the court is concerned with the existence
of the duty on an occupier of land so to control access to that land by strangers as to
prevent injury to neighbouring property.

The authorities already mentioned in this judgment, in particular that judgment of
Waller LJ, in *P Perl (Exporters) Ltd v Camden London BC*, indicate that there is no direct
authority on this point. Waller LJ referred to the decision of this court in *Lamb v Camden
London Borough* [1981] 2 All ER 408, [1981] QB 625 and in particular to the judgment of
Oliver LJ and then said ([1983] 3 All ER 161 at 166, [1984] QB 342 at 352):

> 'I agree with Oliver LJ that the foreseeability required to impose a liability for the
> acts of some independent third parties requires a very high degree of foreseeability.
> Adapting the words of Lord Atkin, ought the appellants to have had the respondents,
> as occupiers of no 142, in contemplation as being affected when directing their
> minds to the question of repairing the doors and locks of no 144? It is not sought
> here to make the appellants liable for any act, it is sought to make the appellants
> liable for an omission to act. Can it be said that the appellants ought reasonably to
> have had in contemplation the fact that third parties would go into the empty
> basement of no 144, make a hole in an 18-inch wall large enough for somebody to
> climb through and steal a large number of articles of clothing from within? I would
> unhesitatingly answer No. Whether or not an occupier of a house can ever be liable
> to a neighbour for an omission to act is doubtful. I do not however have to consider
> whether such a case may possibly arise. It is sufficient to say that in this case I am
> satisfied that there was no breach of duty by the appellants to the respondents and
> accordingly I would allow this appeal.'

Oliver LJ in the *Perl* case [1983] 3 All ER 161 at 168–169, [1984] QB 342 at 355, referring
to the *Dorset Yacht* case, said:

> 'The *Dorset Yacht* case does not, therefore, in my judgment support the conclusion
> as which the deputy judge arrived, unless it can be said that there was here some
> special relation taking the case out of the general rule which excludes liability for
> the acts of independent third parties. Counsel for the respondents has submitted
> that that special relation is to be found from a number of factors combined that is to
> say (a) geographical propinquity, (b) the appellants' knowledge that the respondents
> used their premises to store goods which might be attractive to thieves, (c) the
> appellants' knowledge or means of knowledge that there had been frequent
> incursions by trespassers (including burglaries in some of the flats in no 144) and (d)
> the relatively simple steps required to impede the entry of trespassers by fitting an
> effective lock on the front door. These factors, however, whilst they are, no doubt,
> relative as regards remoteness of damage and may possibly be said to give rise to a
> relation between the appellants and the respondents, go nowhere towards establishing
> the sort of relation referred to by the majority in the *Dorset Yacht* case and clearly
> envisaged by Dixon J in the passage from his judgment in *Smith v Leurs* (1945) 70
> CLR 256, namely a relation between the defendant and the third party for whose
> act he is said to be responsible.'

Oliver LJ then went on to consider other cases, to which we were also referred by counsel for the plaintiff. Returning to the point, he said ([1983] 3 All ER 161 at 170–171, [1984] QB 342 at 357):

> 'Speaking for myself, I am unable to see here any circumstances from which there could properly be inferred any duty on the appellants so to protect their own premises as to prevent trespassers from entering the respondents' premises beyond the fact that such entry was, as it plainly was, a foreseeable possibility. In my judgment that is not, by itself, sufficient to raise the duty for which the respondent contends. Indeed the contrary position would, I think, lead to the most startling and far-reaching consequences.'

Robert Goff LJ in his judgment refered to the question where the intervention of a third party wrongdoer is involved. He said ([1983] 3 All ER 161 at 171–172, [1984] QB 342 at 359):

> 'The vital feature in the type of case under consideration is, as I see it, that the respondents are seeking to render the appellants liable in negligence for the wrongdoing of a third party. Now there may indeed be circumstances where a person may be liable for a third party's wrongdoing. He may of course be liable in contract (see *Stansbie v Troman* [1948] 1 All ER 599, [1948] 2 KB 48); he may be liable under the Occupiers' Liability Act 1959, for example, where he invites a crowd of persons onto his land and part of his premises, designed to control the crowd, are unfit for that purpose and collapse, with the result that the plaintiff is injured (see *Hosie v Arbroath Football Club Ltd* 1978 SLT 122); he may be liable in nuisance if he causes or permits persons to gather on his land, and they impair his neighbour's enjoyment of his land (cf *A-G v Corke* [1933] Ch 89, [1932] All ER Rep 711, though that case was expressed to be decided on the principle in *Rylands v Fletcher* (1868) LR 3 HL 330, [1861–73] All ER Rep 1); and he may be vacariously liable for the third party's wrongdoing. He may even be liable in negligence, when the wrongdoer is a person who, by virtue of a special relationship, is under his control: see *Home Office v Dorset Yacht Co Ltd* [1970] 2 All ER 294, [1970] AC 1004. Speaking for myself, I do not rule out the possibility that there are other circumstances in which a person may be liable in negligence for the wrongdoing of a third party. This is a matter which this court considered recently in *Paterson Zochonis & Co Ltd v Merfarken Packaging Ltd* (1982) ([1983] 3 All ER 522), and which I need not therefore dwell on in this judgment. In particular, I have in mind certain cases where the defendant presents the wrongdoer with the means to commit the wrong, in circumstances where it is obvious or very likely that he will do so, eg where he hands over a car to be driven by a person who is drunk, or plainly incompetent, who then runs over the plaintiff . . . But such cases are very different from the present case, where the allegation is that the appellants failed to exercise reasonable care to prevent a third party from causing damage to the respondents. In *Smith v Leurs* (1945) 70 CLR 256 at 261–262, in a passage which was cited with approval in *Home Office v Dorset Yacht Co Ltd*, Dixon J said: "The general rule is that one man is under no duty of controlling another to prevent his doing damage to a third. There are, however, special relations which are the source of a duty of this nature." It is of course true that in the present case the respondents do not allege that the appellants should have controlled the thieves who broke into their showroom. But they do allege that the appellants should have exercised reasonable care to prevent them from gaining access through their own premises; and in my judgment the statement of principle by Dixon J is equally apposite in such a case. I know of no case where it has been held, in the absence of a special relationship, that the defendant was liable in negligence for having failed to prevent a third party from wrongfully causing damage to the plaintiff.'

Although we were not referred to *Paterson Zonchonis & Co Ltd v Merfarken Packaging Ltd* [1986] 3 All ER 522 it is helpful to look at that case in amplification of the passage

from the judgment of Robert Goff LJ to which both counsel for the plaintiff and counsel
a for the council referred. The facts of that case are entirely different from those in the
present case. The main action was an action to strike out parts of the pleadings in a claim
involving infringement of copyright. For the purposes of this appeal it is necessary only
to consider the second claim, which based itself on negligence. The summons was to
strike out, inter alia, a claim for damages for negligence brought by the holders of a
copyright against the printers whose products (ie the packaging and label) enabled a third
b party (the tortfeasor) to infringe the copyright. Whitford J struck out that part of the
claim and on appeal the appeal was dismissed. The court consisted of Oliver, Fox and
Robert Goff LJJ. All the judgments were to the same effect, but in the context of this
appeal it is perhaps only necessary, with respect to the other members of the court, to
refer to the judgment of Robert Goff LJ. I quote a few passages from that judgment.
Having dealt with the general claim in negligence and referring to the classical statement
c of Lord Wilberforce in *Anns v Merton London Borough* [1977] 2 All ER 492 at 498, [1978]
AC 728 at 751–752 Robert Goff LJ said ([1986] 3 All ER 522 at 540–542):

> 'Even so, it is necessary to sound a note of caution. There is a not insignificant
> number of cases in which the courts have held that no duty of care exists; there are
> others where they have held that the duty must be limited. Moreover, in considering
d > new cases as they arise the courts have, as must surely be right, recognised that a
> heavy duty of care rests on them to ensure that they themselves do not overstep the
> bounds of reasonableness by imposing too onerous legal duties on members of the
> public. Vivid examples of this circumspection are to be found in two of the leading
> cases, *Hedley Byrne & Co Ltd v Heller & Partners Ltd* [1963] 2 All ER 575, [1964] AC
> 465 and the *Dorset Yacht* case itself. It is plain that, in considering whether the duty
e > of care should be negatived or limited in any new situation, the courts are making
> what is usually called a decision of policy (see the *Dorset Yacht* case [1970] 2 All ER
> 294 at 325, [1970] AC 1004 at 1059 per Lord Diplock). Presented with such a case,
> the courts have to do their limited best. They have no secretariat, or apparatus for
> inquiry. They have to derive all the guidance they can from the authorities, and
> from the writings of scholars; and they have the inestimable benefit of the assistance
f > of counsel. But they are also fully entitled to, and do, draw on their own professional
> and practical experience. In the end, the choice must be one of judgment, in the
> balancing of conflicting interests; and in the exercise of that judgment the courts
> must strive neither unjustifiably to deprive potential plaintiffs of remedies for their
> injuries, nor unjustifiably to impose too heavy a legal responsibility on potential
> defendants . . . The first special feature is that there is here said to be a duty of care
g > on the defendant to avoid providing a third party with the means of committing a
> tort against the plaintiff. Is there any general principle which excludes or limits
> liability in such a case? In my judgment, there is no principle which excludes
> liability. It is only necessary to give examples such as handing a loaded gun to a
> small boy or a simpleton, who then "has a go" and shoots the plaintiff, or entrusting
> a car to a man who is obviously drunk or even incompetent, to realise that there are
h > cases in this category where there is a duty of care. It is implicit in the decision of
> the Privy Council in *Yachuk v Oliver Blais Co Ltd* [1949] 2 All ER 150, [1949] AC 386
> that there may be a liability in the first of these examples; and the Canadian case of
> *Ontario Hospital Services Commission v Borsoski* (1974) 54 DLR (3d) 339 provides strong
> persuasive authority that there may be liability in the second. But even so a note of
> caution has to be sounded. Take the case of a dealer in cars who sells a car to a man
j > whom he knows to be an alcoholic, or to be the husband of an alcoholic who to his
> knowledge drives her husband's car; it is difficult to believe that he would be held
> liable when, a few weeks later, the husband or wife (as the case might be) was
> involved, while in a state of intoxication, in a collision with the plaintiff's car.
> Clearly there is a line to be drawn. Furthermore, the examples I have so far given
> are of cases where the third party commits the tort of negligence, not where he is

involved in deliberate wrongdoing. Once again, however, a duty of care cannot be negatived. A case such as *Stansbie v Troman* [1948] 1 All ER 599, [1948] 2 KB 48 *a* suggests examples . . . [Robert Goff LJ then considered further such examples, and continued on the principle in these words:] It is tempting to conclude that, in the absence of some special relationship, there can be no liability for damage caused to the plaintiff by the deliberate wrongdoing of a third party. That this is so in cases where the defendant fails to prevent a third party causing loss or damage to the plaintiff is demonstrated by the *Dorset Yacht* case, and by the dictum of Dixon J in *b* *Smith v Leurs* (1945) 70 CLR 256 at 262 cited with approval in that case, both primarily concerned with circumstances where the third party was under the defendant's control. [Robert Goff LJ then referred to Lord Sumner's judgment in *Weld-Blundell v Stephens* [1920] AC 956 at 986, [1920] All ER Rep 32 at 47 and continued:] However, the analogy of cases where the defendant fails to prevent a third party from causing injury to the plaintiff is not exact; and in the changed *c* climate of today, Lord Sumner's dictum must be regarded as too sweeping. [His Lordship then referred again to the *Dorset Yacht* case, to which I need not refer, and continued:] Of course, in the law of negligence the common criterion of foreseeability creates some overlap between the various constituent parts of the tort; and the point made by Lord Reid can perhaps be as legitimately made at the stage of breach of the duty of care as it can at the stage of causation. Even so, the effect of *d* Lord Reid's observation is that there is no principle of law excluding liability in negligence for damage caused by the deliberate wrongdoing of a third party; but only in the limited circumstances indicated by Lord Reid will liability attach for such damage.'

And I revert to the observations of Lord Reid's in the *Dorset Yacht* case [1970] 2 All ER 294 at 300, [1970] AC 1004 at 1030 to which Robert Goff LJ is referring: *e*

'These cases show that, where human action forms one of the links between the original wrongdoing of the defendant and the loss suffered by the plaintiff, that action must at least have been something very likely to happen if it is not to be regarded as novus actus interveniens breaking the chain of causation. I do not think that a mere foreseeable possibility is or should be sufficient, for then the intervening *f* human action can more properly be regarded as a new cause than as a consequence of the original wrongdoing. But if the intervening action was likely to happen I do not think that it can matter whether that action was innocent or tortious or criminal. Unfortunately, tortious or criminal action by a third party is often the "very kind of thing" which is likely to happen at a result of the wrongful or careless act of the defendant.' *g*

Bearing those authorities in mind, I return to the findings of the judge, which I have already cited in this judgment. The judge considered the general system adopted by the council in the context of the extensive area of their responsibility and the regrettable, but established, social climate at present being experienced in that city, and indeed in other cities. The judge considered with great care the effectiveness, or lack of effectiveness, of *h* 'boarding up' as being one of the courses which admittedly the council from time to time took as they could, although not in this specific context of flooding; nevertheless flooding was a recognised result.

The judge's finding is, in my judgment, determinative of this appeal. Summarising his judgment, he said:

'Regrettably . . . I find that it is not possible for effective steps to be taken in a *j* situation like this which could defeat the activities of vandals.'

Whether this finding, together with the established circumstances of the defendants, should operate to restrict the ambit of the duty to take any positive steps to secure the

property, or duty arising in relation to an omission to take such steps; or whether it
a operates to break the chain of causation, may, as Robert Goff LJ suggested in the passage
which I have just cited from the *Paterson Zochonis* case, not be essentially material.
Personally I prefer the former approach and would limit the area of the duty itself in the
circumstances prevailing in this case. In either event, in my judgment the judge was
right to hold that the council owed no duty to the plaintiff in respect of the acts of the
vandals in this case and accordingly I would dismiss this appeal.

b
NICHOLLS LJ. I agree, and I add observations only on two points.
The first is this. Counsel for the plaintiff sought to distinguish this case from the
decision of this court in *P Perl (Exporters) Ltd v Camden London BC* [1983] 3 All ER 161,
[1984] QB 342 on the ground that the ratio decidendi of that case was that an occupier of
property owed no duty so to use his property as to prevent third parties from getting on
c to his property, and thence onto the plaintiff's property, because an occupier is not liable
for the escape of burglars from his land. Contrast the present case, it was submitted,
where the plaintiff does not have to set up the existence of a novel duty of care. An
occupier is under a duty to take reasonable care to ensure that water on his property,
which is a potential hazard to neighbouring properties, does not escape and damage those
properties. Here it was reasonably foreseeable that a failure by the defendant to follow its
d normal practice of boarding up empty property, would be very likely to result in vandals
entering, and stripping away and removing the copper water pipes and cistern, with the
escaping water then causing damage to the plaintiff's property.
I am unable to accept that any material ground of distinction exists between the two
cases. In the *Perl* case, as in the instant case, the plaintiff sought to make the defendant
occupier liable in negligence for the wrongdoing of a third party. In his judgment Robert
e Goff LJ ([1983] 3 All ER 161 at 171–172, [1984] QB 342 at 359) set out, in a passage
already cited by Purchas LJ, some examples of circumstances where there may be liability
for a third party's wrongdoing, and concluded that those instances were very different
from that case where, as in the present case, the allegation was that the defendant failed
to exercise reasonable care to prevent a third party from causing damage to the plaintiff.
In his preface to that passage Robert Goff LJ assumed that there might well be cases
f where the occupier could reasonably foresee that thieves might use the unprotected
property as a means of access to neighbouring property. But he, in common with the
other members of the court, rejected the existence of the broad duty of care contended
for by the plaintiff's counsel, and his conclusion was to the effect that in the absence of a
special relationship, there was no duty to prevent thieves from so using one's property.
I cannot see any distinction in principle between a case where the damage arises from
g the third party using the defendant's property as a means of obtaining unauthorised
access to the plaintiff's property and there committing theft, and one where the damage
arises from the third party so conducting himself on the defendant's property as to
damage the plaintiff's property by causing water to escape from the former property to
the latter. Nor can I see that it is material that the defendant had a responsibility to take
reasonable steps to prevent the escape from its property of water in an ordinary domestic
h water system. I do not consider that there is a greater responsibility on the defendant
because the third party caused damage by creating an escape of water than if the damage
had been caused by the third party lighting a fire on the defendant's property or, if the
defendant's property had been on the top floor of the building, by the third party
stripping lead from the roof and thereby permitting rain to enter and eventually to reach
and damage the plaintiff's property.
j Secondly, although in the *Perl* case the plaintiff seems to have been relying on a claim
in negligence alone, and nuisance is relied on in the present case, before us it was accepted
that, for the plaintiff to succeed in nuisance, she had to establish a breach of a duty of
care. In this regard I add that this is not a case where the acts of a trespasser have been
continued or adopted by the defendant as occupier of its land.

CAULFIELD J. I agree with both judgments from Purchas and Nicholls LJJ and do not wish to add anything.

Appeal dismissed. No order for costs. Leave to appeal to the House of Lords refused.

24 July. The Appeal Committee of the House of Lords (Lord Bridge of Harwich, Lord Brandon of Oakbrook and Lord Ackner) dismissed a petition by the plaintiff for leave to appeal.

Solicitors: *Charles Frais,* Liverpool (for the plaintiff); *W I Murray,* Liverpool (for the council).

Carolyn Toulmin   Barrister.

The Speedlink Vanguard and the European Gateway

QUEEN'S BENCH DIVISION (ADMIRALTY COURT)

STEYN J

17, 21, 23, 24 APRIL, 21 MAY 1986

Estoppel – Issue estoppel – Shipping – Collision – Court of formal investigation – Findings of court of formal investigation – Court of formal investigation establishing negligence of one party causing ships to collide – Whether findings of court of formal investigation binding in subsequent collision or limitation action – Whether abuse of process to relitigate findings – Merchant Shipping Act 1894, s 466 – Shipping Casualties and Appeals and Re-hearing Rules 1923.

On 19 December 1982 two cross-channel ferries, the Speedlink Vanguard and the European Gateway, collided causing the European Gateway to capsize. In order to determine the cause of the collision a court of formal investigation was set up by the Secretary of State for Transport under s 466 of the Merchant Shipping Act 1894. Procedure at the court of formal investigation, which had all the powers of a magistrates' court, was governed by the Shipping Casualties and Appeals and Re-hearing Rules 1923 which provided for the Secretary of State to decide on and put questions for the opinion of the court and direct the examination of witnesses as necessary. The formal investigation concluded that the actions of the European Gateway's master were the major cause of the collision. Subsequently, the owners of the Speedlink Vanguard (the plaintiffs) began proceedings against the owners of the European Gateway (the defendants) for damages, basing their claim on the findings of the formal investigation. The defendants denied all liability in a defence and counterclaim which took issue with the findings of the formal investigation. The plaintiffs contended that the defendants were precluded by the doctrine of issue estoppel from in effect relitigating the findings of the formal investigation and that it would be an abuse of process to do so. On the trial of a preliminary issue whether the findings of a court of formal investigation could give rise to issue estoppel in a subsequent Admiralty action, the question arose whether such a court was a court of competent jurisdiction between contending shipowners.

Held – A court of formal investigation into a shipping casualty was not a court of competent jurisdiction for the purposes of determining issues between contending shipowners because, having regard to the provisions of the 1894 Act and the 1923 rules, which did not provide for a properly constituted lis between the parties, and to the primary function of a court of formal investigation, which was the preservation of a reasonable standard of safety of life and property at sea rather than the determination of *a* civil liability between shipowners, it was clear that despite its formal procedure and apart from its disciplinary function with regard to masters of vessels, the functions of a court of formal investigation were entirely investigatory. It followed that the findings of such a court could not give rise to issue estoppel (see p 562 *g* to p 563 *b e f*, p 564 *e* to *h* and p 565 *a b h j*, post).

Dictum of Lord Brandon in *DSV Silo- und Verwaltungsgesellschaft mbH v Sennar (owners), The Sennar* [1985] 2 All ER at 110 applied.

b
Notes

For formal investigations into shipping casualties, see 43 Halsbury's Laws (4th edn) paras 64–68.

For issue estoppel, see 16 ibid para 1530, and for cases on the subject, see 21 Digest (Reissue) 37–64, 232–403.

c For s 466 of the Merchant Shipping Act 1894, see 31 Halsbury's Statutes (3rd edn) 305.

For the Shipping Casualties and Appeals and Re-hearings Rules 1923, see 20 Halsbury's Statutory Instruments (4th reissue) 180.

As from 1 July 1983 s 55 and 56 of the Merchant Shipping Act 1970 make fresh provision for inquiries and investigations into shipping casualties.

As from 1 August 1985 the Merchant Shipping (Formal Investigations) Rules 1985, SI
d 1985/1001, make new provision for formal investigations into shipping casualties and incidents.

Cases referred to in judgment

Carl-Zeiss-Stiftung v Rayner & Keeler Ltd (No 2) [1966] 2 All ER 536, [1967] 1 AC 853, [1966] 3 WLR 125, HL.
e *City of London, The* (1855) Swab 245, 300, 166 ER 1119, 1148.
DSV Silo- und Verwaltungsgesellschaft mbH v Sennar (owners), The Sennar [1985] 2 All ER 104, [1985] 1 WLR 490, HL.
Freisland, The (1922) 11 Ll L Rep 157.
Golden Sea, The (1882) 7 PD 194.
Hull v Clifford, Clifford v Timms, Clifford v Phillips [1907] 2 Ch 236, CA.
f *Labour Relations Board of Saskatchewan v Joint East Iron Works Ltd* [1949] AC 134, PC.
Mangerton, The (1856) Swab 120, 166 ER 1051.
Princess Victoria, The [1953] 2 Lloyd's Rep 619, NI, HC.
Swallow, HMS (1855) Swab 30, 166 ER 1002.
Waddle v Wallsend Shipping Co Ltd [1952] 2 Lloyd's Rep 105.

g ### Cases also cited

Barnett v Cohen [1921] 2 KB 461, [1921] All ER Rep 528.
Bird v Keep [1918] 2 KB 692.
Caine v Palace Steam Shipping Co [1907] 1 KB 670, CA; *affd* [1907] AC 386, HL.
Calmenson v Merchant's Warehousing Co Ltd (1921) 125 LT 129, HL.
Corchester, The [1956] 3 All ER 878, [1957] P 84, DC.
h *DPP v Humphrys* [1976] 2 All ER 497, [1977] AC 1, HL.
Fidelitas Shipping Co Ltd v V/O Exportchleb [1965] 2 All ER 4, [1966] 1 QB 630, CA.
Henry Coxon, The (1878) 3 PD 156.
Hoystead v Taxation Comr [1926] AC 155, [1925] All ER Rep 56, PC.
Hunter v Chief Constable of the West Midlands [1981] 3 All ER 727, [1982] AC 529, HL.
Hutton v Ras Steam Shipping Co Ltd [1907] 1 KB 834, CA.
j *Little Lizzie, The* (1870) LR 3 A & E 56.
Lord Seaton, The (1845) 2 Wm Rob 391, 166 ER 802.
Marginson v Blackburn BC [1939] 2 KB 426, CA.
Mills v Cooper [1967] 2 All ER 100, [1967] 2 QB 459, DC.
Nothard v Pepper (1864) 17 CBNS 39, 144 ER 16.
R v Secretary of State for the Environment, ex p Hackney London BC [1983] 3 All ER 358, [1983] 1 WLR 524, DC; *affd* [1984] 1 All ER 956, [1984] 1 WLR 592, CA.

Ribble (River) Joint Committee v Croston UDC [1897] 1 QB 251, DC.
Robinson v Robinson [1943] 1 All ER 251, [1984] P 43.
Spain v Union Steamship Co of New Zealand Ltd (1923) 33 CLR 555, Aust HC.
Steelmet Inc v Caribe Towing Corp (1984) 747 F 2d 689, US Ct of Apps.
Thoday v Thoday [1964] 1 All ER 341, [1964] P 181, CA.
Warren v Warren [1962] 3 All ER 1031, [1962] 1 WLR 1310.

Preliminary issue
By a writ dated 9 February 1983 and statement of claim served on 7 June 1985 the plaintiffs, the owners of the ship Speedlink Vanguard, claimed against the defendants, the owners of the ship European Gateway, inter alia, 80% of the damage caused to the plaintiffs' ship arising out of a collision between the two ships on 19 December 1982. By a defence and counterclaim the defendants denied liability and sought judgment against the plaintiffs. In their amended reply and defence to the counterclaim the plaintiffs contended, inter alia, (i) that the defendants were estopped from denying that the collision was caused by the negligence of the defendants, their servants or agents, and (ii) that it was an abuse of the process of the court and/or contrary to public policy for the defendants to relitigate the findings of a court of formal investigation held to determine the cause of the collision pursuant to s 466 of the Merchant Shipping Act 1894. By a writ and statement of claim served on 7 June 1985 the plaintiffs, Sealink Ltd (demise charterers of the ferry Speedlink Vanguard), began a limitation action pursuant to s 503 of the Merchant Shippping Act 1894 against the defendants, (1) the owners of the ship European Gateway, (2) Small & Co (Engineering) Ltd, (3) Eva Mary Bewley (administratrix of the estate of the late Joseph Topp deceased), (4) Anthony Stinsas and (5) all other persons claiming or being entitled to claim damages by reason of, or arising out of, the collision between the two ships on 19 December 1982. On 5 December 1985 Sheen J ordered the hearing of a preliminary issue whether, as between contending parties, the findings of a court of formal investigation could give rise to an issue estoppel in a subsequent Admiralty action; alternatively, whether it was an abuse of the process of the court or contrary to public policy to attempt to relitigate such findings. The facts are set out in the judgment.

J Franklin Willmer QC and *Simon Gault* for the owners of the Speedlink Vanguard.
Anthony Clarke QC and *Nigel Teare* for the owners of the European Gateway.

Cur adv vult

21 May. The following judgment was delivered.

STEYN J.

Introduction
    Formal investigations into shipping casualties or wreck inquiries have taken place in this country since the middle of the last century. In the case of collisions between ships the formal investigation almost invariably preceded a collision action in the Admiralty Court. Indeed, it would seem that a pending action in the Admiralty Court was regarded as a good reason not to hold an inquiry (see Murton *Wreck Inquiries* (1884) pp 43–44). On the other hand, while the report of a formal investigation frequently led to a settlement between contending owners in collision cases, the settled practice was not to receive the report in evidence for any purpose whatsoever. Now, some 130 years since the creation of the system of formalised wreck inquiries, the question is raised for the first time whether as between contending shipowners the findings of a court of formal investigation can give rise to an issue estoppel in a subsequent Admiralty action, or alternatively, whether it is an abuse of the process of the court or contrary to public policy for a party to seek 'to attempt to relitigate' those findings. It was said that these are novel propositions. The novelty of the propositions does not trouble me. After all, the law reports show that the heresy of yesterday frequently becomes the orthodoxy of today.

The collision

a   On the night of 19 December 1982 the Speedlink Vanguard was inward bound to the Harwich train terminal and the European Gateway was outward bound from Felixstowe. Both vessels were engaged in the cross-channel ferry service. The European Gateway collided with the Speedlink Vanguard in the approaches to the port of Harwich. The collision caused a breach in the starboard side of the European Gateway. Fortunately the collision took place in shallow water. Within ten minutes of the collision the European

b   Gateway was lying on her starboard side with her portside clear of the water. The rescue attempts were remarkably successful but two passengers and four crew members lost their lives.

The formal investigation

c   Immediately after the collision preliminary inquiries took place. On 29 June 1983 the Secretary of State for Transport, acting under the powers conferred on him by s 466 of the Merchant Shipping Act 1894, directed that a formal investigation be held into the collision by a wreck commissioner. Mr Nicholas Phillips QC was appointed as the wreck commissioner. He was assisted by four assessors with nautical, engineering and other relevant experience. The court had all the powers of a magistrates' court when acting as

d   a court in the exercise of its ordinary jurisdiction (see s 466(10)).

Pursuant to s 466(1) counsel and solicitors acting on behalf of the Secretary of State for Transport were effectively in charge of 'superintending the management of the case', and were charged with the duty of 'assisting . . . the court', both expressions being taken from s 466(5). When the formal investigation was constituted, the Shipping Casualties and Appeals and Re-hearings Rules 1923, SR & O 1923/752, were applicable to it. These rules

e   were repealed in July 1983. New rules did not come into force until 1985, when the Merchant Shipping (Formal Investigations) Rules 1985, SI 1985/1001, were promulgated pursuant to s 58 of the Merchant Shipping Act 1970. However, during the course of the formal investigation everybody proceeded on the basis that the 1923 rules were applicable. It is now common ground that the 1923 rules did apply to the formal investigation, which was constituted before the repeal of those rules in July 1983. In

f   accordance with the procedure established by the 1923 rules, the Secretary of State caused notices of investigation to be served on the owners of the European Gateway, on the disponent owners of the Speedlink Vanguard, and on the masters of both vessels. The 1923 rules contain the following provisions regarding participation in the conduct of the proceedings:

g   '4. The [Secretary of State], the owner, the master, and any certificated officer or other person upon whom a notice of investigation has been served, shall be deemed to be parties to the proceedings.

5. Any other person may, by leave of the judge, appear, and any person who appears under this Rule shall thereupon become a party to the proceedings.'

In the result, apart from the Secretary of State for Transport, the owners of the vessels,

h   their masters, and cargo interests became parties to the proceedings. It is right, however, to add that although counsel appearing for the Secretary of State had the general duty of superintending the case, acting pro bono publico, separate counsel was instructed to appear on behalf of the Secretary of State because the owners of the Speedlink Vanguard wished to raise certain criticisms of the Department of Transport. So much for the parties who were represented at the formal investigation.

j   The hearing took place between November 1983 and March 1984, occupying in all 35 days. All parties were throughout represented by counsel and solicitors. The procedure adopted was that set out in the following provisions of the 1923 rules:

'11. When the examination of the witnesses produced by [the Secretary of State] has been concluded, [the Secretary of State] shall state in open Court the questions in reference to the casualty, and the conduct of the certified officers, or other persons connected therewith, upon which the opinion of the Court is desired . . .

12. After the questions for the opinion of the Court have been stated, the Court shall proceed to hear the parties to the investigation upon, and determine the questions so stated. Each party to the investigation shall be entitled to address the Court and produce witnesses, or recall any of the witnesses who have already been examined for further examination, and generally adduce evidence. The parties shall be heard and their witnesses examined, cross-examined, and re-examined in such order as the Judge shall direct. [The Secretary of State] may also produce and examine further witnesses, who may be cross-examined by the parties, and re-examined by [the Secretary of State].

13. When the whole of the evidence in relation to the questions for the opinion of the Court has been concluded, any of the parties who desire so to do may address the Court upon the evidence, and [the Secretary of State] may address the Court in reply upon the whole case.'

In this case the questions were stated in open court only on the 23rd day of the hearing. Realistically, it must be accepted that none of the questions then formulated came as any great surprise to those present at the hearing. Turning now to the course which the formal investigation took, it appears from the report of the formal investigation that the first purpose of the investigation was to seek answers to two basic questions (para 2.2):

'(i) Why did the collision occur? (ii) Why did the "EUROPEAN GATEWAY" capsize so rapidly?'

The report continued:

'2.3 The second purpose of this investigation is to consider what lessons for the future can be learnt from the casualty. Such an exercise is the primary justification for any Formal Investigation and that is particularly so in this case. The investigation raised one question with implications for the safety of all passenger vessels: is it better that watertight doors between compartments should be kept open or closed at sea? Much of the investigation has been devoted to considering this important question.

2.4 The final, and subsidiary, purpose of this investigation is to consider whether the loss of the "EUROPEAN GATEWAY" and the consequent loss of life were caused by the wrongful act or default of any persons and, if so, whether the Court should impose penalties on those at fault.'

There were a large number of issues of fact. The most important question however related to the exact place of the collision. The conclusions of the court of formal investigation are set out in the answers to the questions posed by the Secretary of State for Transport. The following conclusions are relevant:

'Question 1(a) What caused the collision between the "EUROPEAN GATEWAY" and the "SPEEDLINK VANGUARD" on the 19th December 1982? (b) What caused the "EUROPEAN GATEWAY" to capsize following the collision?

Answer 1(a) Negligence in navigation of both vessels. (b) Ingress of water into the generator room, the stabilizer room, the main engine room and the gearbox room would have caused the vessel to sink had the depth of water permitted this. The list which resulted in capsize was caused by transient asymmetric flooding.'

Turning to the question whether conduct of those in charge of the navigation of the European Gateway (Captain McGibney) and the Speedlink Vanguard (Captain Bolton) was culpable, the conclusions were as follows:

'Question 6 Was the collision caused or contributed to by the wrongful act or default of any person or persons, and if so whom and in what respects?

Answer 6 Yes, the collision was caused by wrongful acts and default on the part of both Captain McGibney and Captain Bolton in the following respects: *Captain McGibney* (i) Failed to keep a good look-out; (ii) Attempted to cross ahead of the

a
"SPEEDLINK VANGUARD" when it was unsafe to do so. *Captain Bolton* Altered course to starboard, initially without reduction of speed, at a time when he should instead have taken off his way.'

Dealing with the relative culpability of the two masters, the court concluded (para 12.29 of the report):

b
'... It is no part of our task to apportion fault but ... it was the action of Captain McGibney in standing on across the channel in front of the "SPEEDLINK VANGUARD" that provoked, and was the major cause of, this collision.'

The owners of the Speedlink Vanguard had therefore succeeded in satisfying the court of formal investigation that the preponderant blame was that of the master of the European Gateway.

c
The collision action
In February 1983 a writ was issued by the owners of the Speedlink Vanguard against the owners of the European Gateway, ie before the formal investigation was constituted. The plaintiffs' statement of claim was only served in June last year. In that pleading the owners of the Speedlink Vanguard squarely based their case on the findings of the formal d court of investigation. Bearing in mind that their master had been found to be culpable, although less so than the master of the European Gateway, they asked for judgment for 80% of the damage sustained. The owners of the European Gateway served a defence and counterclaim in which they denied all liability and asked for judgment in their favour. Without condescending to detail, it should be said that the denials and averments in the defence and counterclaim are in many material respects at variance with the findings of e the court of formal investigation. The plaintiffs in their reply and defence to the counterclaim pleaded that the owners of the European Gateway are precluded by the doctrine of issue estoppel or the principles of abuse of the process of the court from 'reopening' the findings of the formal investigation. In their rejoinder the owners of the European Gateway raised a counter-estoppel, based on the 'fact that the owners of the Speedlink Vanguard raised the question of issue estoppel almost one year after the report f of the formal investigation had been made available in draft to the parties. For reasons which will subsequently emerge, I did not hear argument on the counter-estoppel.

The limitation of liability action
In March 1986 a limitation of liability action was commenced by the owners of the Speedlink Vanguard in the Admiralty Court. The owners of the European Gateway are g the defendants in that action. At issue in that action is the question whether the collision took place without the actual fault or privity of the owners of the Speedlink Vanguard. The owners of the Speedlink Vanguard again rely on issue estoppel and abuse of the process of the court, and assert that the owners of the European Gateway are precluded by the findings of the court of formal enquiry from contending that there was actual fault or privity on the part of the owners of the Speedlink Vanguard and/or that any h actual fault or privity on their part caused or contributed to the collision. By way of rejoinder a counter-estoppel similar to that pleaded in the collision action has been raised. The issues in the collision action and in the limitation action are different. For reasons which I will subsequently mention I did not hear argument on the materiality of the differences. Similarly, I did not hear argument on the counter-estoppel pleaded in this j action.

The procedural position
The present position is that both the collision action and the limitation of liability action are due to be heard in October 1987. Plainly, it is essential that an early decision be obtained on the plea of issue estoppel. If it is upheld, the trial will be substantially shortened. If it fails, wide-ranging preparations will have to take place. Accordingly, the

Admiralty judge ordered the hearing of preliminary issues on the questions of issue estoppel in both actions. That is how the matter came before me. At the hearing before *a* me the owners of the Speedlink Vanguard were by consent granted leave to rely, in the alternative, on abuse of the process of the court. Counsel for the owners of the Speedlink Vanguard candidly explained that it was not easy to see how, if his clients failed on issue estoppel, they could succeed on abuse of the process of the court. My judgment will therefore concentrate on the substantial arguments addressed to me on issue estoppel, but I will briefly refer to the question of abuse of the process of the court at the end of *b* this judgment.

With regard to the present procedural position I should add, however, that the owners of the European Gateway did not appeal (as they were entitled to do under s 57(4) of the Merchant Shipping Act 1970) against the findings of the court of formal investigation: they relied on what they described as the 'generally accepted view' that the parties were not bound by the findings of a formal investigation. Faced with the plea of issue estoppel, *c* they sought to appeal out of time. This application was dismissed in December 1985, and leave to appeal was refused. However, in February this year leave to appeal was granted by Neill LJ. That appeal has not been heard.

The requirements of issue estoppel

In the present case one is concerned with a kind of estoppel which is known as issue *d* estoppel per rem judicatam. In *DSV Silo- und Verwaltungsgesellschaft mbH v Sennar (owners)*, *The Sennar* [1985] 2 All ER 104 at 110, [1985] 1 WLR 490 at 499 Lord Brandon, speaking for all their Lordships, stated the requirements of this kind of estoppel as follows:

'The first requirement is that the judgment in the earlier action relied on as creating an estoppel must be (a) of a court of competent jurisdiction, (b) final and conclusive and (c) on the merits. The second requirement is that the parties (or *e* privies) in the earlier action relied on as creating an estoppel and those in the later action in which that estoppel is raised as a bar must be the same. The third requirement is that the issue in the later action in which the estoppel is raised as a bar must be the same issue as that decided by the judgment in the earlier action.'

Pertinent as Lord Brandon's language was to the question before the House of Lords, *f* namely, whether the judgment of a foreign court could create an issue estoppel, it is right to add that in Lord Brandon's formulation a broad interpretation should be given to the concept of an 'action'. It includes, for example, an award resulting from arbitration proceedings. Subject to this qualification, which was not in issue, it is my task to assess the validity of the plea of issue estoppel in the light of the requirements stated by Lord Brandon. In doing so I bear in mind the objects of the rule of res judicata, namely that in *g* the interests of the state there should be an end to litigation, and that a party ought not to be subjected to the hardship of twice contending the same issue (see *Carl-Zeiss-Stiftung v Rayner & Keeler Ltd (No 2)* [1966] 2 All ER 536 at 549–550, [1967] AC 853 at 909).

The issue

Turning now to the application of the principles enunciated in *The Sennar*, it was *h* common ground that the real issue was whether Lord Brandon's first requirement was established. If it was, the second requirement (the same parties) and the third requirement (the same issue) would present no real difficulty. Ultimately, I believe, it was agreed that the critical question was as follows: was the court of formal investigation a court of competent jurisdiction as between contending owners in relation to the findings of fact, contained in the report, on which the owners of the Speedlink Vanguard seek to rely? *j* With regard to the question whether the certificate of a master or certificated officer ought to be suspended or cancelled, it was agreed that a court of formal investigation fulfils a true adjudicative function, and that it acts as a court of competent jurisdiction. I respectfully agree. The true question is therefore whether the court of formal investigation acted as a court of competent jurisdiction as between contending

a
shipowners. Conceivably, another way of looking at the matter is to say that the court is
a court of competent jurisdiction for some purposes, and that the only question is
whether quoad its findings of fact, to the extent to which those findings are relied on in
the present case, they are final and conclusive. In my judgment the former way is the
correct way of approaching the matter, but it will be apparent from this judgment that
the latter approach should in my judgment lead to the same result.

b   *The received wisdom*
On behalf of the owners of the European Gateway it was argued that Admiralty judges,
and authors well versed in this field, have always accepted that the findings of a formal
investigation are not binding in a subsequent Admiralty action. The evidence marshalled
in support of this proposition is substantial. In a number of cases Dr Lushington (the
judge of the High Court of Admiralty from 1838 to 1867) expressed his firm view that
c   the report of a formal investigation is not admissible in a subsequent collision action (see
HMS Swallow (1855) Swab 30, 166 ER 1002, *The Mangerton* (1856) Swab 120, 166 ER
1051 and *The City of London* (1855) Swab 245, 166 ER 1119). In *Hull v Clifford, Clifford v
Timms, Clifford v Phillips* [1907] 2 Ch 236 the Court of Appeal had to consider the
admissibility of a finding of the General Medical Council against a dentist in disciplinary
proceedings in subsequent partnership disputes which were litigated in the High Court.
d   The decision is not in pari materia. However, one of the members of the court was
Barnes P who was the President of the Admiralty Court from 1892 to 1909. He gave the
following illustration (at 251–252):

'I may give an instance, arising in cases with which I was at one time familiar, of
an order which, in its effect the order in question somewhat resembles, viz., the
order of a Court holding a formal investigation into a shipping casualty under the
e   Merchant Shipping Acts. If in such a case the Court should find that the loss or
abandonment of or serious damage to a ship or loss of life has been caused by the
wrongful act or default of a master mate or engineer, it may cancel or suspend his
certificate: Merchant Shipping Act, 1894 (57 & 58 Vict. c. 60), s. 470. Numerous
cases have been dealt with under this Act and the Acts which it replaces, and in
many cases actions have been brought by cargo owners and others against the
f   shipowners in respect of the loss, but it has never so far as I am aware been suggested
that the decision of the Court cancelling or suspending an officer's certificate could
be used either as conclusive or any evidence against the owners to prove the loss and
that it was caused by the officer's act or default, although his status as an officer is
altered by the order, and although the order would no doubt be admissible upon a
question as to what was the status of the officer and would probably be conclusive
g   upon the point. Nor have I ever heard it suggested that such a decision could be
used against a captain whose certificate had been cancelled or suspended if he had
been in a position to be sued for the loss.'

It is clear that Duke P, who was the Admiralty judge from 1919 to 1933, took a similar
view (see *The Friesland* (1922) 11 Ll L Rep 156 at 159). In *Waddle v Wallsend Shipping Co
h   Ltd* [1952] 2 Lloyd's Rep 105 at 131 Devlin J expressed the same view. See also *The
Princess Victoria* [1953] 2 Lloyd's Rep 619 at 628. Similar views were expressed in Murton
Wreck Inquiries (1884) p 111, in McMillan *Shipping Inquiries and Courts as regulated by the
Merchant Shipping Acts* (1929) p 105 and in *The Law of Collisions at Sea* (11th edn, 1961)
para 362.
Counsel for the owners of the Speedlink Vanguard emphasised four points. Firstly, in
j   relation to the dicta of Dr Lushington he pointed out that the procedure at formal
investigations became much more formal and judicial in character after Dr Lushington's
period as Admiralty judge. He particularly emphasised that a limited right of appeal was
only introduced in 1879. That leaves, of course, a substantial body of opinion to the same
effect after Dr Lushington's tenure of office. Secondly, it was said that the observations
in question were all directed to the inadmissibility of the report of the formal

investigation. That is so. It is right, however, to bear in mind that the doctrine of issue estoppel is part of the law of evidence. If the law is that such a report is inadmissible in evidence, it can be said a fortiori not to found an issue of estoppel. It is inconsistent with the notional existence of issue estoppel in this field. Thirdly, it was submitted that the doctrine of issue estoppel (as opposed to cause of action estoppel) is of recent origin. This factor must, it is said, detract from the judicial observations which I have mentioned. In *Carl-Zeiss-Stiftung v Rayner & Keeler Ltd (No 2)* [1966] 2 All ER 536 at 552, [1967] 1 AC 853 at 913 Lord Reid said that issue estoppel is a comparatively new phrase but he pointed out that the principle underlying it was already recognised in the eighteenth and nineteenth centuries. Lastly it was submitted that the judicial observations which I have mentioned were all made in cases in which the question of issue estoppel was not argued. It is therefore submitted that undue weight ought not to be attached to this corpus of judicial views. I respectfully agree. It will therefore be necessary to examine the question with some care.

The legislative history of wreck inquiries

The question whether the findings of the court of formal investigation as between contending shipowners gives rise to an issue estoppel must ultimately depend on the true function of that tribunal under s 466 of the Merchant Shipping Act 1894 and the 1923 rules, and the way in which the present inquiry was conducted. However, counsel for the owners of the European Gateway carefully traced the history of the legislation, primary and subordinate, governing wreck inquiries. Undoubtedly, as I have said, during the period 1854 to 1894, the mode of conducting wreck inquiries gradually became more formal. There is, however, not a great deal of dispute about the purpose of such an inquiry. It is common ground that the primary purpose of any such inquiry is (as was explicitly recognised in para 2.3 of the report in the present case) to assist in the preservation of a reasonable standard of safety of life and property at sea. The second purpose is to determine why a casualty occurred. The third purpose is to consider whether the casualty was caused by the wrongful act or default of any person and, if so, whether the court should impose penalties on those at fault (see *McMillan* pp 1–8). It is clear that the first function of the inquiry is purely investigatory. It is to be contrasted with the third function of the inquiry which is adjudicative. While the procedure adopted at the inquiry differs from criminal and civil proceedings in an ordinary court, it is nevertheless clear that in so far as the inquiry is called on to decide the issue whether the certificate of a master, or other certificated officer, ought to be cancelled or suspended it is, subject to appeal, making a final and conclusive decision, which is judicial in character. What, however, is the character of the inquiry into the cause of the casualty? It overlaps with both the investigatory and disciplinary functions of the inquiry. But there is nothing in the legislative history to show that *a* purpose of inquiring into the cause of a collision was to determine civil liability as between contending shipowners.

The law governing the present inquiry

Ultimately, the question whether there is, or can be, an issue estoppel in this case must depend on the *function* of the court of formal investigation, as between contending shipowners, seen in the light of the applicable legislation, primary and subordinate. Both sides relied on a number of features relating to the trappings and procedure of the inquiry which was said to support their submissions. It will be necessary to consider the relevance of these points. In my judgment, however, there is a more fundamental question involved: what do the 1894 Act and the 1923 rules provide in relation to the determination of civil liability as between contending shipowners? It is difficult to visualise that, as between contending shipowners, the court of formal investigation can be acting as a court of competent jurisdiction trying an issue of civil liability unless there is in such an inquiry a properly constituted lis between the contending shipowners. Section 466 of the 1894 Act prescribes the procedure to be adopted at a wreck inquiry only in the broadest outline. Significantly, however, it provides in sub-s (5) that the person who has applied to a court to hold a formal investigation shall be duty bound 'to

superintend the management of the case'. In relation to a master or other certificated
a officer, there is a power to cancel or suspend a certificate (see s 470 of that Act). By long-
standing custom the court of formal investigation can also censure or admonish a master
or certificated officer. No sanctions can be imposed on a shipowner, who is personally or
vicariously liable, other than by an appropriate order for costs under sub-s (8) of s 466.
Section 466 does not provide for the trying of questions as to civil liability between
contending shipowners. Prima facie, therefore, apart from its disciplinary function, the
b functions of a court of formal investigation are entirely investigatory.

In order to appreciate the shape of a wreck inquiry it is, however, necessary to turn to
the detailed provisions of the 1923 rules. The parties to a formal investigation are the
Secretary of State for Trade, the owners, the master, and any certificated officer or other
person on whom a notice of investigation has been served (r 3). In other words, the
Secretary of State for Trade has a discretion to decide who shall be parties to the formal
c investigation. It is right to add, however, that the judge may grant leave to other persons
to appear (r 5). More important is the fact that the notice of investigation states the
questions which the Secretary of State for Trade intends to raise (r 3). He may amend,
add to, or omit any of those questions (r 3). The proceedings commence with the
production and examination of witnesses by the Secretary of State for Trade (r 10). It is
important to note, however, that the investigation is not confined to the questions in the
d notice of investigation. That brings me to rr 11, 12 and 13, which are quoted in extenso
earlier in this judgment. There is no provision for the framing of questions by, for
example, two contending shipowners. Indeed, even the judge has no power, on
application by both parties, to define such questions. It is the exclusive prerogative of the
Secretary of State for Trade to frame such questions as he deems fit.

The court of formal investigation must then answer those questions, and may not
e consider any other questions. It would, for example, be perfectly proper for the Secretary
of State for Trade to confine the questions to matters relevant to the promotion of safety
at sea. What could be inferred from the general tenor of s 466 of the 1894 Act, is made
explicit by the 1923 rules: there is no lis between contending shipowners. Prima facie
this factor militates cogently against the submission that the court of formal investigation
was acting as a court of competent jurisdiction between the two contending shipowners.
f After all, the conception of a judicial function is inseparably bound up with the idea of a
suit between parties, which it is the duty of the court to decide between those parties (see
Labour Relations Board of Saskatchewan v Joint East Iron Works Ltd [1949] AC 134 at 149).

The procedure adopted

It was, however, submitted that in considering whether an issue estoppel arises it is
g permissible to look not only at the report but also at the way in which the inquiry was
conducted (see *Carl-Zeiss-Stiftung v Rayner & Keeler Ltd (No 2)* [1966] 2 All ER 536 at 584,
[1967] 1 AC 853 at 965). It was further submitted that the fact that proceedings at the
formal investigation were conducted partly in an inquisitorial fashion, as opposed to the
traditional adversarial system adopted in ordinary courts of law in this country, does not
preclude an issue estoppel arising. The terms 'inquisitorial' and 'adversarial' are imprecise,
h and often cause confusion. I use the term inquisitorial to denote a *mode* of trial, where
the judge plays a large part in the exploration of issues and deployment of evidence, as
opposed to an adversarial *mode* of trial when the parties control the exploration of issues
and deployment of evidence. In both cases, when used in connection with ordinary
courts of law, the *function* of the court is adjudicative and not investigatory. The
proposition that a partly inquisitorial procedure does not by itself preclude an issue
j estoppel arising can readily be accepted (see *The Sennar* [1985] 2 All ER 104, [1985] 1
WLR 490). It is submitted, however, that at the formal investigation the contending
shipowners in fact adopted an adversarial approach: each sought to put the blame on the
master of the other's vessel. This submission was made good by detailed references to the
transcripts. It was not challenged. It cannot, however, by itself sustain an issue estoppel
if, on a proper interpretation of the relevant primary and subordinate legislation, the
court of formal investigation is not a court of competent jurisdiction. In other words, it

is an indispensible part of the case in favour of an issue estoppel arising. But it is not sufficient in law.

The owners' right of appeal

That brings me to a point which counsel for the owners of the Speedlink Vanguard put in the forefront of his submissions. He pointed out that an owner, having an interest in the inquiry, and who appeared at the hearing and is affected by the decision of the court, may appeal from that decision to the High Court (see s 66 of the Merchant Shipping Act 1906). It shows, he submits, that a judicial decision is involved as between shipowners. Moreover, he emphasised that if the High Court's decision on an appeal can give rise to an issue estoppel, it would be strange if the court of formal investigation's decision as between contending shipowners cannot do so. An appeal presupposes, he argued, a judicial decision appealed. This is a formidable argument. It needs to be remembered, however, that until 1906 an owner had no right of appeal (see *The Golden Sea* (1882) 7 PD 194). If from 1894, when s 466 was enacted, until 1906, when the right of appeal in favour of an owner was created, the relevant function of the court of formal investigation was investigatory, it would be strange if it became adjudicative merely by the creation of a right of appeal. In my judgment the explanation is that given by *McMillan* p 21, namely that an owner's ability to obtain insurance cover can be gravely affected by findings of a court of formal investigation. It was therefore considered fair that an owner should have a right of appeal when he is affected. It is a limited right of appeal: an owner would, for example, not be able to say that he is 'affected' by a finding that the other vessel was seaworthy or that her master was not at fault. The existence of a right of appeal does not therefore alter my view that there is no lis between the contending shipowners, and that the function of the court of formal investigation does not extend to pronouncing on the civil liability of those parties.

Other indicia in the Merchant Shipping Act 1894

There are two provisions in the 1894 Act, which in my judgment lend support to the view that the findings of the court of formal investigation are not intended to be conclusive as between contending owners. The first is s 483(2), which provides that all orders made by a naval court shall in any subsequent legal proceedings be conclusive as to the right of the parties. It differs from the submission advanced in favour of an issue estoppel in this case inasmuch as such an order by a naval court also binds someone who was not a party to the naval court proceedings. While I do not attach great weight to the absence of a similar provision in s 466, it is arguably of some relevance, in so far as it possibly shows that the legislature chose not to provide that a report under s 466 shall be conclusive in subsequent proceedings (see also s 484(2) of the 1894 Act). The other provision is more important. Section 475 provides, inter alia, that the Secretary of State for Trade *may*, in any case in which a formal investigation has been held into a shipping casualty, order the case to be reheard. If the functions of the court of formal investigation, apart from its limited disciplinary function, are regarded as investigatory only, this provision is explicable. On the other hand, if the findings of the court of formal investigation as between contending owners are regarded as judicial in character, it is difficult to see why a third party should have the absolute right to order a rehearing, inter alia, of those very findings.

Other indicia in the 1923 rules

There are other features of the procedure under the 1923 rules which are very different from the procedure adopted in civil proceedings. Firstly, there appears to be no direct power to order and enforce general discovery of documents (see r 6). Secondly, rr 12 and 13 do not in terms place contending parties in the position of plaintiffs and defendants, with consequential rights in one to open, in the other to answer and in the former to reply (r 12). Instead, the first and final word rests with the Secretary of State for Trade. Thirdly, it is relevant to bear in mind that the owners' witnesses, such as the master and certificated officers, can be compelled to testify and there is no privilege against self-

incrimination before the court of formal investigation (see *McMillan* p 104). Fourthly, it
a is noteworthy that where a certificate of an officer is cancelled or suspended the decision
must be given in open court. To that extent, of course, a judicial decision directly
affecting private rights is involved. In all other cases decisions may be communicated in
writing to the parties. That is indeed what happened in the present case. I regard none of
these matters as of decisive importance. Cumulatively, however, they tend to support
the conclusion that, apart from its limited disciplinary functions, the court of formal
b investigation fulfils a purely investigatory function.

Policy considerations

Both sides prayed in aid policy considerations. It will be necessary to measure the
consequence of one decision against the other. The owners of the Speedlink Vanguard
stressed the wastefulness which would result if the findings of a wreck commissioner,
c specially selected for his experience, and assisted by expert assessors, could be 'relitigated'
in the Admiralty Court. There is force in this submission, and I will revert to it at the
end of this judgment. In my opinion, however, this consideration is outweighed by the
factors relied on by the owners of the European Gateway. In my judgment they are right
in asserting that, if it be held that the findings of fact of a court of formal investigation
are conclusive as between contending owners, this will have a detrimental effect on the
d effective functioning of such investigations. It will lead to a shift from safety at sea to the
determination of civil liability as between shipowners and others as the major purpose of
the inquiry. Here I pause to point out that if issue estoppel can apply between owners, it
may also apply in the case of cargo owners or personal injury claimants. It will probably
also tend to have an inhibitory effect on parties who would otherwise seek to be joined
with the leave of the judge under r 5. Such parties would have to consider carefully
e whether they wish to have their potential civil rights and liabilities determined at a
wreck inquiry or in the Admiralty Court.

One can also visualise other ways in which the effectiveness of wreck inquiries would
be hampered. It would necessarily involve each party putting forward his case on all
issues, and sub-issues, whereas at present a party is fully entitled to concentrate on
essentials. Moreover, it must be remembered that foreign owners are within the scope of
f the jurisdiction of a court of formal investigation (see s 464 of the 1894 Act). If it were to
be held that the doctrine of issue estoppel applies, it is probable that foreign owners who
are potentially exposed to civil liability will be less likely to afford assistance to a court of
formal investigation. In so far as there may arguably be a choice between differing
constructions I unhesitatingly choose the construction which best meets the purpose of
the legislation as to wreck inquiries. In my judgment, however, the provisions of the
g 1894 Act and of the 1923 rules convincingly show that a court of formal investigation
was not intended to act as a court of competent jurisdiction. That is also the position on
an appeal to the High Court.

Conclusions

It follows that I have come to the conclusion that no issue estoppel arises. The
h alternative submission that it would be an abuse of court to relitigate the court of formal
investigation's findings must also fail. After all, it cannot possibly be an abuse in this case
to re-open matters, in circumstances where the law permits it. For the avoidance of doubt
I record that in my judgment it is quite clear that the owners of the European Gateway
and their representatives at all material times proceeded on the basis that the findings of
the court of formal investigation would not be conclusive.

j

Alternative arguments

Having come to a firm and clear conclusion on the above matters, I did not hear
argument on certain alternative issues, such as: (a) the counter-estoppel; (b) the measuring
of particular findings of fact against allegations in the pleadings; (c) the different
considerations which arise in the limitation action.

It was agreed that if I was against the owners of the Speedlink Vanguard on the principal points, it would be an unnecessarily time-consuming exercise to hear argument on those matters.

a

Recommendation regarding wreck inquiries
  Finally, I wish to draw attention to a recommendation made by Devlin J in *Waddle v Wallsend Shipping Co Ltd* [1952] 2 Lloyd's Rep 105 at 131. He said:

> 'I think that the competent authorities might consider whether the useful purposes that Wreck Inquiries serve would not be increased if the report was made *b* available to any Court which had to determine the cause of the loss. It is not necessary that the findings of fact in the report should be treated as binding. The opinion of the Commissioner based on the facts he finds has at least as high a value as that of an expert based on the facts which he assumes to be proved; and it has the advantage of being quite independent of either side'

c
Thirty-four years later I now respectfully repeat and indorse this recommendation. What is needed is a statutory provision enabling the judge hearing the collision or limitation action to make such evidential use of the report as a whole as he thinks fit.

Declaration in favour of the plaintiffs.

d
Solicitors: *Ingledew Botterell Roche & Pybus*, Newcastle-upon-Tyne, (for the owners of the Speedlink Vanguard); *Norton Rose Botterill & Roche* (for the owners of the European Gateway).

N P Metcalfe Esq   Barrister.

e

S v S

FAMILY DIVISION
WAITE J
4, 5, 6 JUNE, 1 JULY 1986

f

Divorce – Financial provision – Variation of order – Discharge – Husband applying to have maintenance order discharged on payment of capital sum – Wife objecting to discharge – Whether court having jurisdiction to discharge periodical payments order on payment of capital sum – Matrimonial Causes Act 1973, s 31(5)(7).

g

The parties were divorced in 1975. A consent order was made whereby the husband, who was very wealthy, was ordered to pay a lump sum of £125,000 and to make periodical payments of £23,000 per year to the wife, who consented to the dismissal of all her claims for financial provision and thereby gave up any right to claim capital relief *h* in the future. Provision was also made for the three children of the family. In 1986 the wife applied under s 31 of the Matrimonial Causes Act 1973 for an increase in the periodical payments. By that time only one of the children was still a minor. The husband cross-applied to have the consent order discharged completely on payment by him of a capital sum of £120,000 thereby achieving a clean and final break between the parties. He contended that the court could make such an order against the wishes of the maintained spouse under the jurisdiction contained in s 31(7)[a] which enabled the court *j* to vary a periodical payments order by limiting the payments to 'such further period as will . . . be sufficient to enable the [maintained spouse] to adjust without undue hardship to the termination of those payments'. The wife contended that, having regard to the

---

a Section 31(7) is set out at p 569 *e*, post

prohibition in s 31(5)[b] against the making of a lump sum order on an application for
a variation of a periodical payments order, the court had no power, in the absence of
agreement between the parties, to compel a spouse to accept a capital sum, however large,
in return for what would amount to compulsory commutation of her right to periodic
payments, and that in any event the amount offered by the husband to terminate his
liability for periodic payments was too low.

b **Held** – The court was faced with a choice between a broad and a narrow construction of
s 31(5) of the 1973 Act and since the broad construction assisted, whereas the narrow
construction could inhibit, the modern approach of alleviating the consequences of
matrimonial breakdown, the court would adopt the broad construction, because,
applying the clean break principle, Parliament was to be presumed to have intended that
the courts should be allowed the maximum freedom to help former spouses to pursue
c independent lives without the burden of financial interdependence. Accordingly, the
court had jurisdiction under s 31(7) to terminate the wife's periodical payments on the
basis of a capital offer by the husband, provided the court was satisfied that such a course
would accord with the paramount requirements of the welfare of any under-age child of
the family and that the effect of the offer would be such as to enable the wife to adjust,
within an appropriate period, to the termination of her periodical payments without
d undue hardship. In the circumstances, a capital offer by the husband as the quid pro quo
for the termination of periodic maintenance would in principle be accepted by the court,
since it would accord with public policy, with common sense and fairness, and most
importantly, with the welfare of the child of the family in removing the sole remaining
source of serious dispute between her parents. However, on the facts, the husband's
proposals were not sufficient in amount to justify a termination of the wife's periodic
e maintenance but, on principle and having regard to the paramount interest of the child
of the family in having her parents' financial differences disposed of once and for all, it
would be appropriate to allow the husband the opportunity of increasing his capital offer
to that amount which the court considered appropriate, which was £400,000. In any
event, the periodical payments order would be varied by increasing the payments made
to the wife to £70,000, back-dated to 1979 (see p 574 *h* to p 576 *g*, post).
f

Notes
For the court's power to vary maintenance agreements, see 22 Halsbury's Laws (4th edn)
paras 1152–1157, and for cases on the subject, see 27(1) Digest (Reissue) 85–86, 652–653.
For the Matrimonial Causes Act 1973, s 31(5), see 43 Halsbury's Statutes (3rd edn) 576,
and for s 31(7) of that Act (as substituted by the Matrimonial and Family Proceedings Act
g 1984, s 6(3)), see 54(1) ibid 770.

Cases referred to in judgment
Minton v Minton [1979] 1 All ER 79, [1979] AC 593, [1979] 2 WLR 31, HL.
Morris v Morris (1985) 6 FLR 1176, CA.

h **Cases also cited**
M H v M H (1982) 3 FLR 429.
Morley-Clarke v Jones [1985] 3 All ER 193, [1986] Ch 311, CA.
Preston v Preston [1982] 1 All ER 41, [1982] Fam 17, CA.
Warden v Warden [1981] 3 All ER 193, [1982] Fam 10, CA.

j **Summons**
The husband and the wife cross-applied under s 31 of the Matrimonial Causes Act 1973
for the variation of a consent order dated 26 September 1975 providing for periodic
payments to be made to the wife. By a summons issued on 4 June 1986 the husband
sought an order terminating the wife's periodic maintenance on the payment of £120,000

---

b   Section 31(5) is set out at p 569 *b c*, post

by him in commutation of the wife's periodic payments and releasing his outstanding charge of £56,000 on the wife's home. The summons was heard and judgment was given in chambers. The case is reported by permission of Waite J. The facts are set out in the judgment.

T Scott Baker QC and *Susan Solomon* for the wife.
Robert L Johnson QC and *Nicholas Wilson* for the husband.

Cur adv vult

1 July. The following judgment was delivered.

WAITE J. These cross-applications both invoke the jurisdiction of the court under s 31 of the Matrimonial Causes Act 1973 (as amended) to vary or discharge an order for periodical payments. The wife asks for an upward variation to increase the amount of the existing order in her favour. The husband asks that the order may be discharged altogether on his tendering a sum of capital, with the intention of wholly supplanting his future liability for periodic maintenance and thus achieving a clean break.

The background is one of exceptional wealth. [His Lordship described the circumstances relating to the marriage and continued:] At the time of the divorce there had been a settlement of financial issues, under which the parties consented to an order for periodic payments to the wife, together with a lump sum order, on the strength of which the wife consented to the dismissal of all her future claims to capital provision. Their differences have thus centred since then upon the extent to which the periodical payments thereby ordered may require to be varied to meet the wife's current needs. It has proved to be an intractable problem involving prolonged, though in the end unsuccessful, efforts towards a negotiated settlement and very protracted proceedings, of which this hearing is the culmination.

It was a hearing in which the stage was set, until very recently, for a conventional contest devoted solely to the issue of the amount by which the periodical payments ordered by consent in the wife's favour at divorce fell to be increased in the light of her current needs. Very much at the last moment, however, the husband has come forward with the capital proposal already mentioned, offering it as the quid pro quo for an order terminating the wife's right to be maintained on any periodic basis at all. He claims that the recent amendments to the 1973 Act, introduced by the Matrimonial and Family Proceedings Act 1984, give the courts jurisdiction to make such an order even against the wishes of the maintained spouse. The wife contends that there is no power in the court, in its variation jurisdiction, to compel a spouse in the absence of agreement to accept a capital sum, however large, in what she claims would amount to compulsory commutation of her right to periodic maintenance. That is, of course, being a matter of jurisdiction, an issue of pure law. Counsel are satisfied that it is one on which there is no current authority.

The wife contends, in the alternative, that if there is jurisdiction in the court to accept the husband's proposal, the sum which he has proffered is in any event far too small. The alternative argument on the husband's side is that if for any reason he has to go on paying periodic maintenance, the figure claimed by the wife is far too high. These alternative arguments give rise of course to issues of pure discretion, in the exercise of which the governing legislation decrees that all the circumstances of the case are to be taken into account. It will, therefore, be as well to pause for a moment in the narrative and consider the legislative framework against which this survey has to be undertaken.

The 1973 Act followed a long established legislative tradition in maintaining a distinction between originating maintenance orders on the one hand, and the procedure for their variation on the other. It was a distinction principally drawn in three ways.

Firstly, variation was made the subject of a self-contained statutory procedure laid down in s 31 of the Act. That section begins by defining the limited categories of

financial provision order which are capable of being varied at all, a definition from which
_a_ orders of a capital nature are, for the most part, excluded, and then prescribes the limits
of the variation jurisdiction and the criteria which are to be applied in its exercise.

Secondly, the distinction between the two jurisdictions was emphasised by an express
prohibition against the making of a lump sum order on an application to vary periodical
payments. That is contained in s 31(5) of the 1973 Act in these terms:

_b_   'No property adjustment order shall be made on an application for the variation
of a periodical payments or secured periodical payments order made (whether in
favour of a party to a marriage or in favour of a child of the family) under section
23 above, and no order for the payment of a lump sum shall be made on an
application for the variation of a periodical payments or secured periodical payments
order in favour of a party to a marriage (whether made under section 23 or under
section 27 above).'

_c_
Thirdly, the criteria for the exercise of the respective discretions of the court in the
originating and in the variation jurisdictions were differently expressed. In both
jurisdictions the court was required to have regard to all the circumstances of the case.
The originating jurisdiction, however, was circumscribed by the need to apply the
statutory objective set out at the end of s 25(1) of the 1973 Act, the objective, that is to
_d_ say, of putting the parties in the same position financially as they would have enjoyed
under a deemed rehabilitation of the marriage. This artificial concept had never had any
counterpart in s 31, where the criteria for the exercise of the variation jurisdiction were
expressed in sub-s (7) as follows:

_e_   'In exercising the powers conferred by this section the court shall have regard to
all the circumstances of the case, including any change in any of the matters to
which the court was required to have regard when making the order to which the
application relates and, where the party against whom that order was made has died,
the changed circumstances resulting from his or her death.'

The amendments to the 1973 Act made by the Matrimonial and Family Proceedings
_f_ Act 1984 have preserved the first two of these distinctions intact. Variation is still
exhaustively governed by a self-contained code in s 31, and the embargo in s 31(5) on the
making of a lump sum order on a periodical payments variation application has been
preserved.

The third distinction, the criteria for exercise of the respective jurisdictions, has,
however, become more blurred as a result of the following amendments.

In the originating jurisdiction, s 25 has been altered in two substantial respects. Firstly,
_g_ the generality of circumstance to which the court is still required to have regard is now
made subject to a duty to give primacy to the welfare of any minor child of the family.
Secondly, the former statutory objective governing original orders under s 25, with its
difficult concept of the deemed rehabilitation of the marriage, has been brought to an
unlamented end. In its place the new s 25A has enacted the entirely different objective of
the clean break, thus giving the stamp of Parliamentary approval to a purpose which had
_h_ already been authoritatively upheld in case law (_Minton v Minton_ [1979] 1 All ER 79,
[1979] AC 593 and see _Morris v Morris_ (1985) 6 FLR 1176).

Section 25A reads as follows:

'(1) Where on or after the grant of a decree of divorce or nullity of marriage the
court decides to exercise its powers under section 23(1)(_a_), (_b_) or (_c_), 24 or 24A above
_j_ in favour of a party to the marriage, it shall be the duty of the court to consider
whether it would be appropriate so to exercise those powers that the financial
obligations of each party towards the other will be terminated as soon after the grant
of the decree as the court considers just and reasonable.

(2) Where the court decides in such a case to make a periodical payments or
secured periodical payments order in favour of a party to the marriage, the court

shall in particular consider whether it would be appropriate to require those
payments to be made or secured only for such term as would in the opinion of the
court be sufficient to enable the party in whose favour the order is made to adjust
without undue hardship to the termination of his or her financial dependence on
the other party.

(3) Where on or after the grant of a decree of divorce or nullity of marriage an
application is made by a party to the marriage for a periodical payments or secured
periodical payments order in his or her favour, then, if the court considers that no
continuing obligation should be imposed on either party to make or secure periodical
payments in favour of the other, the court may dismiss the application with a
direction that the applicant shall not be entitled to make any further application in
relation to that marriage for an order under section 23 (1)(a) or (b) above.'

Turning from the originating to the variation jurisdiction, the changes made by the
1984 Act have been to s 31(7). That has been repealed and substantially re-enacted in a
form which still retains the generality of language of the original, but now mentions for
mandatory consideration two specific topics which had not previously been picked out
from the totality of circumstances to which the court was required to have regard.
The new s 31(7) reads as follows:

'In exercising the powers conferred by this section the court shall have regard to
all the circumstances of the case, first consideration being given to the welfare while
a minor of any child of the family who has not attained the age of eighteen, and the
circumstances of the case shall include any change in any of the matters to which
the court was required to have regard when making the order to which the
application relates, and—(a) in the case of a periodical payments or secured periodical
payments order made on or after the grant of a decree of divorce or nullity of
marriage, the court shall consider whether in all the circumstances and after having
regard to any such change it would be appropriate to vary the order so that payments
under the order are required to be made or secured only for such further period as
will in the opinion of the court be sufficient to enable the party in whose favour the
order was made to adjust without undue hardship to the termination of those
payments; (b) in a case where the party against whom the order was made has died,
the circumstances of the case shall also include the changed circumstances resulting
from his or her death.'

The two topics thus picked out for mandatory consideration are, firstly the welfare of
a minor child of the family, which must now be given primacy, and secondly the
possibility of a termination of periodic payments after a period sufficient to enable the
maintained spouse to adjust to it. The factor which has blurred the former sharp
distinction drawn between the originating and the variation jurisdictions is that these
two requirements are introduced into both jurisdictions in identical terms. The issue of
law in this case turns principally on the statutory implications of these changes for the
light that they may throw upon the Parliamentary intention.

Before coming to that, however, it will be convenient now to return to a more detailed
description of the background circumstances, because of course it is to them that the
legislation (in both its original and its amended form) requires the court in any event,
whether its jurisdiction be broad or narrow, to have regard.

[His Lordship then referred to the marriage of the parties and the circumstances of
their three children and continued:] In 1975 the marriage broke down. The wife
consulted a solicitor well known as a specialist in matrimonial cases. The marriage was
dissolved on her undefended petition by decree absolute dated 4 September 1975. On
the 26th of that month a consent order was made in the matrimonial proceedings in
terms which had been negotiated between the parties' respective solicitors, the broad
effect of which was as follows.

(1) There was to be a lump sum payment to the wife of £125,000, of which £75,000

was payable forthwith and the balance by five annual instalments of £10,000, beginning
in September 1976, with in abatement provision in the event (which has not happened)
of the wife remarrying before the instalments had been paid in full. The fact that the
lump sum payment was, in part, the subject of an instalment order has not been relied
on by either side except as part of the relevant background circumstances, and neither
party has sought to take any jurisdictional point on the footing that this is a case to which
s 31(2)(d) of the 1973 Act does or does not apply.

(2) A periodical payments order in favour of the wife at the rate of £23,000 pa less tax
until remarriage or further order.

(3) A periodical payments order in favour of each of the three children until the age
of 18 in the sum of £2,500.

(4) Those orders were made on the basis of an undertaking by the wife to settle the
£50,000 balance of the lump sum payable by instalments on the trusts of a settlement
which gave her a life interest in them with remainder to the children, subject to a power
in the wife, which has been fully exercised, to call on the trustees to advance up to half
the trust fund to herself absolutely. The remaining moiety of the fund is held subject to
a power, which has not been exercised, to advance capital to her at the trustees' discretion.

(5) The wife's claims for secured provision, transfer of property order and variation of
settlement were all dismissed. It is common ground that the effect of that has been to
put the wife out of court to claim as of right any further relief of a capital nature, whether
by lump sum or otherwise.

The wife is currently suing the solicitor who advised her to agree to the 1975 consent
order, alleging that his advice was negligent; and she is maintaining an associated claim
against the firm she subsequently consulted, for failing to advise her that she was entitled
to make such a claim against her first solicitor or that such claim was liable to become
time-barred.

Although a good deal of argument was addressed to me on the issue of whether the
settlement incorporated in the 1975 consent order was a good one or a bad one from the
wife's point of view, I do not regard this as an aspect of the case which calls for any great
prominence. It is sufficient, in my judgment, to say that the outcome of the pending
negligence litigation appears to me to be too uncertain to justify making any assumptions
about possible benefits which the wife may derive from it if she is successful.

As to the general merits of the settlement itself, questions of alleged negligence apart,
I think it is relevant and proper for me to take account of the fact that, so far at least as
the lump sum element is concerned, that settlement does not appear, even allowing for
the effect of inflation in the meantime, to have been a particularly generous one when
hindsight is applied to it with the benefit of the subsequently reported Court of Appeal
decisions in financial cases involving husbands with substantial capital assets. However,
that will be only one of the numerous factors in the case which I am called on to consider,
and in the end it will have to be given whatever place it deserves in the whole picture.

There was an informal understanding, implemented for three years, that the wife
would have an additional £2,000 paid to her as a consultancy fee from one of the
husband's corporate interests; and the £75,000 proportion of the wife's lump sum
payable to her outright was applied, by agreement, in the purchase of a home for herself
and the children (of whom she had care and control by consent). A property was bought
for £100,000, the balance being provided by a £25,000 mortgage from the husband.

In 1979 a new property was purchased, which I shall refer to as the 'Paddington home'.
It is a spacious house standing in an area of London to which the property market has
astutely given the title of 'Little Venice'. The parallel has, in one respect certainly proved
an apt one in the case of this particular property; for its fabric seems to have been in
constant peril. It has been subject to many structural problems, has needed to have large
sums spent on it, and still (as will appear) requires a lot more work to put it in proper
order. The Paddington home was paid for as to one half of the purchase price out of the
net proceeds of sale of the first home and, as to the other half, by the trustees of a
discretionary settlement established for the purpose by the husband for the benefit of the

children. It was duly registered in the joint names of the wife and of a corporation wholly owned by the discretionary settlement trustees. The purchase was assisted by a mortgage from the husband, on which approximately £56,000 remains outstanding.

During the first five years following the divorce, the wife managed her single parent household on very similar lines to those that had applied during marriage. She simply spent what she needed, regardless of the amount payable to her under the maintenance order. Whenever that policy ran her into difficulty she applied to the husband for help which he, in his easy-going fashion, was for the most part willing to provide, mainly because his children were then still young and in her care and he was himself living abroad, for reasons of fiscal prudence.

That picture began to change in 1981, when the husband had remarried and returned to live in this country. He wanted the maintenance of the wife and children put on a proper footing, so in December 1981 he himself made an application for an upward variation of the periodical payments order with the object of providing the wife with a fair measure of cloth according to which she would in future have to cut her coat.

Those proceedings moved at a leisurely pace, partly because by then the wife had changed her solicitors, and there were detailed and protracted negotiations between the solicitors on each side in the hope of achieving an agreed variation of the consent order. The proceedings took a more hostile turn in February 1983, when the wife issued her own cross-application for variation of the periodic payments order and followed it up in April with an application for detailed discovery of the husband's sources of wealth. That discovery was successfully resisted by the husband, both before the registrar and on the wife's appeal to Hollis J heard on 16 June 1983, on the basis of what has come to be known colloquially in the profession as the 'millionaire's defence'. The husband, that is to say, conceded that his wealth was more than sufficient to support any order that the court might make for the wife's reasonable maintenance requirements, and on that basis submitted that it would be oppressive for him to have to incur the expenditure of time and money involved in giving discovery of the diffuse and complex details of his wealth holdings.

That concession still stands today and it is common ground that I should approach this case on the basis, recently confirmed by his solicitors in correspondence, that his wealth is large enough and liquid enough to fund any order I might make to satisfy the wife's reasonable maintenance needs.

The opportunity was taken at the appeal hearing before Hollis J of obtaining by consent an agreed order for an interim variation of maintenance pending the final hearing of the issue of variation. The wife's periodical payments were increased on that interim basis consensually to £44,000 and those for the children to £10,000 pa, subject to tax in both cases. The wife restored the proceedings early in 1985 but did not take any step to bring them on until the beginning of this year. Very shortly before this hearing began before myself on 4 June 1986, the husband took out a summons for a permanent discharge of any liability to periodic maintenance, on the basis of the proposals of a capital nature whose detail I shall later describe.

The wife's pattern of expenditure since 1980 has gone on very much as it did before. She still professes an ignorance of, and certainly takes as little interest as possible in, the details of household budgeting. For the three years down to the order of 16 June 1983 the husband tried to help her by arranging for a firm of accountants to control and monitor her expenditure, but she found that control irksome and it was discontinued at her request.

Since 1983 her own accountants have relieved her of all the details of day-to-day household accounting by paying all the expenses of her home. She maintains complete control, however, of all her personal spending, including travel and holidays, and her accountants' brief does not extend to provision for matters of substantial expenditure, such as the heavy charges she has faced for repairs to the Paddington home. She has continued to call on the husband for help from time to time with the children's expenses, including the cost of their travel and holidays. He has been increasingly reluctant to

respond to such demands, at all events without enquiries, which she has found irksome,
a into the details of how they were incurred.

So it has come about that money has developed into a major issue between these two
otherwise congenially disposed people. The wife feels that as the divorced spouse of so
rich a man, and as the mother of his children, she ought to be wholly relieved of financial
anxiety. As her anxieties have increased, so her resentment has mounted at what she
condemns as meanness on his part. Those anxieties have now become considerable. She
b has substantial personal debts, including a disputed bill of costs rendered by her second
firm of solicitors, who have now been joined in the negligence proceedings already
mentioned. She owes the Inland Revenue £61,000 for accumulated arrears of tax at the
higher rates, the enforcement of which is imminent. A total of £80,000 would now be
needed to put the Paddington home into a proper state of decoration and repair,
complying with the covenants in the ground lease under which it is held.

c   Turning next to the other members of the family, the eldest son is now married and a
father, and lives in accommodation provided for him by the husband in the latter's
property in the home counties. He has had only modest success so far in attempting to
make a career as a musician. The younger son came of age in August 1985, when the
husband ceased to be under any legal liability to maintain him. He lives with the wife at
the Paddington home. He has no job or training, a state of affairs which he is not at
d present actively seeking to change. He is dependent on his mother for his keep and his
modest pocket money allowance.

The daughter attends an independent girls' day school, where her academic progress
has been reasonably satisfactory but she has no wish to continue her education for a
moment longer than she has to. She plans to leave after her sixteenth birthday at the end
of this year and wants to train to become a model.

e   While the younger son remains with his mother, the husband is willing, voluntarily,
to pay for his maintenance whatever sum is suggested by the court. He is willing to
consent to any suitable order for the daughter's maintenance until she attains 18.
Therefore, the wife has no direct maintenance responsibilities in respect of the two
younger children, save to the indirect extent that the Paddington home is a roof that has
to be maintained over their heads as well as hers, at considerable expense.

f   The nanny still lives with the wife, who pays her wages and provides her with a car.
She takes charge of the household and provides care, so far as they still need it, for the
younger son and the daughter during the wife's fairly frequent absences from home.
The husband has always generously maintained the wife's parents, and her mother (now
a widow) lives near the Paddington home where she continues to receive a generous
contribution to her maintenance from her ex-son-in-law.

g   The wife has, for a number of years past, been a good deal in the company of a man
for whom she was prepared to accept as accurate the description of 'boyfriend'. That does
not, by itself, provide any very clear picture of the relationship, because the expressions
'boyfriend' and 'girlfriend' have lost their original association with the first tender
overtures of courting youth and have developed, in modern speech, a curious elasticity
which may not have anything at all to do with age or very much to do with friendship.

h [His Lordship referred to their association and continued:] He has been extremely
generous to her over the years, not only giving her personal gifts of great value,
exemplified by a fur coat worth £10,000, but also making substantial payments on her
behalf including, for example, a £23,000 builder's account for urgent repairs to the
Paddington home and a contribution, amounting to much the same figure, towards the
costs of this litigation and of the negligence actions which she is pursuing against her
j former solicitors. I accept the wife's evidence that the association, though enduring, has
had its ups and downs and its interruptions and that she has no intention of allowing it
to develop into marriage.

The husband's counsel cited a number of cases in which judges have been called on to
deal with the impact on a husband's maintenance liability of relationships maintained by
particular claimants, in varying degrees of intimacy or dependence, with a third party.

No principle is in my judgment to be deduced from them; nor, with respect, do I see how such issues can ever be concluded by authority. In a jurisdiction as discretionary as this one, such relationships are certainly to be taken into account as one of the many factors to which the court is bound to have regard, but in the delicate weighing process which the discretion involves of one factor against the other, they are not entitled to any advance marking on the scales.

The appropriate finding to be made on this aspect of the case is, in my judgment, simply that the wife has a rich and generous boyfriend of long standing whose loyalty and generosity she may reasonably expect to continue for a number of years still to come. That is something which is relevant, certainly, to any sensible assessment of her maintenance requirements. Its influence on the final arithmetic will not, however, depend on any rule of thumb approach; it is simply something to be taken into account with all the other numerous factors in the case.

It does not seem to me to be desirable, particularly in a case like the present where very large sums are under consideration, that I should attempt to specify all the factors relevant to the exercise of the discretion, for they are legion. They range from matters of comparatively minor detail, such as the income which the wife still receives from the settled proportion of the lump sum payment of which she is life tenant, to such broader issues as the changes in the purchasing power of the pound (and the competing methods of assessing them) which have occurred since the date of the consent order. All have been touched on in the speeches of counsel, and I hope it is sufficient, in the interests of keeping this description of the background circumstances as succinct as possible, to say that they have all been taken into account.

Turning then from the factual background to the contentions of the parties, the issues which appear to me to be raised by the arguments on each side are the following. (1) Does the court, as a matter of law, have jurisdiction to accept the husband's capital proposals as the basis for an order terminating the wife's periodic payments under the amended s 31(7)? (2) If the answer to (1) is Yes, should the court, as a matter of discretion, accept the husband's proposals in principle? (3) If the answer to both (1) and (2) is Yes, are the husband's proposals sufficient in amount to justify their acceptance in the particular circumstances? (4) If the answer to (1) and (2) is Yes but to (3) is No, should the husband be given any, and if so what, opportunity of making an improved proposal? (5) In any event, what sum should now be provided by a periodical payments order to the wife to cover the interval down to the date of their termination or (as the case may be, depending on the answers to the previous issues) to cover her future maintenance until further order?

I will deal with those issues consecutively. On the question of jurisdiction, each side relies on the indications of legislative policy to be inferred from the changes to s 31 to which I have already drawn attention. Counsel for the wife relies on the retention of the embargo in s 31(5) against capital orders being made on a variation application. That is the plainest possible indication, he says, of parliamentary purpose; and the Act should not therefore be construed, in the absence of express words of authorisation, as permitting the same result to be achieved by the side route of a voluntary capital offer as would be achieved through the direct but prohibited route of an outright lump sum payment.

On the other hand, counsel for the husband contends that the new s 31(7), linked as it was obviously intended to be with the new 'clean break' objective introduced by s 25A, shows the clearest possible parliamentary intention that the clean break should be in the forefront of the court's mind as much when it is exercising its jurisdiction to vary as when it is exercising its originating jurisdiction. What break could be cleaner, he asks, than that which is achieved by providing the wife with sufficient capital to enable her to adjust, without undue hardship, to the termination of her right to periodic maintenance?

I have found these arguments very finely balanced. The legislation is not easily construed, and counsel for the wife has every justification for saying that if Parliament did indeed intend the court to have jurisdiction to act as the husband proposes, then it has adopted an extraordinarily roundabout method of conferring it.

In my judgment, it comes down in the end to making a choice between a broad or a

narrow construction of the embargo in s 31(5). If a broader construction assists, and the
a   narrower inhibits, the application of the clean break principle, then the modern approach
to the law, centred as it is on alleviating the consequences of matrimonial breakdown,
demands that the broader construction should prevail. Parliament must be presumed to
have intended, in other words, that the courts should be allowed the maximum freedom
to help former spouses to pursue independent lives, liberated from the running irritant
of financial interdependence.

b   On those grounds I prefer the construction urged by counsel for the husband and I
hold that I have jurisdiction to terminate the wife's periodical payments on the basis of a
capital offer by the husband. That is of course subject to the qualification that I have no
jurisdiction to order termination, unless I am first satisfied that such a course would
accord with the paramount requirements of the welfare of any child of the family under
age and that the effect of the offer is such as to enable the wife to adjust within an
c   appropriate period to the termination of her payments without undue hardship.

        That brings me to the second issue. In exercising the discretion under s 31(7) I must
have regard to all the circumstances of the case, including any material change in those
particular features to which the court was required to have regard on the making of the
original consent order in 1975. I must give first consideration to the welfare of the
daughter as the only remaining minor child of the family. I must ask myself whether
d   the husband's proposals are such as to enable the wife to adjust, without undue hardship,
to the termination of her periodical payments and, if so, what period would be required
to enable her to do so.

        That all adds up to a wide-ranging survey of the background circumstances. There are
many pieces to be fitted into the mosaic but, when they are all finally in place, the pattern
which emerges is, in my judgment, a clear one. I have no hesitation in saying on the
e   second issue that a capital offer from the husband as the quid pro quo for a termination
of periodic maintenance ought, in principle, to be accepted. It would accord with public
policy, with common sense and fairness and, most important of all, with the welfare of
the daughter in removing a source of dispute, the sole remaining source of serious
dispute, between her parents.

        Coming now to the third issue, are the husband's proposals sufficient to justify an
f   exercise of the discretion in that way? The proposals he makes are these. The Paddington
home, even in its present state of disrepair, could be sold for £600,000. The husband
offers to pay the wife a capital sum of £120,000 and to release his outstanding charge of
£56,000 on the Paddington home. That would leave her, in effect, with assets of
£420,000 when the proffered sum is added to her £300,000 share of the equity in the
Paddington home. I should say at once, and I do not think it is necessary to give detailed
g   reasons for my view, that I do not regard that as anything like enough to justify a
termination of her periodic maintenance rights.

        The fourth issue therefore arises. Should the husband be permitted an opportunity of
improving on that offer? Counsel for the wife argues that it would be wrong in principle
to allow him to do so. If a husband has been granted an opportunity, at or before the
hearing, of making an offer high enough to hit the discretionary target and if he turns
h   out to have aimed too low and missed it, then that, says counsel, should be that.

        I would be sorry to think that the exercise of the discretion should be so inflexible as
to produce a result of that kind. Both on general grounds of principle and having regard
again to the paramount interest of the daughter in having her parents' financial
differences disposed of once and for all, I think it would be appropriate to allow the
husband the option of obtaining an order terminating the wife's rights to periodic
j   maintenance on payment within a suitable time limit of that sum of money or money's-
worth which I consider to be proper.

        I should say straightaway what I think that figure should be. It is £400,000. If he were
to pay that amount within an appropriate period, then I would regard that as a proper
basis for terminating his liability for periodic payments to the wife within a reasonable
period thereafter.

        She would doubtless experience some hardship in adjusting to such termination, but I am satisfied that it would not be an undue hardship. On the contrary, it might in the end prove to have been beneficial. It may be hard for her at first, should that become *a* necessary as I anticipate it would, to have to leave the Paddington home and settle somewhere a little less grand and spacious but a little more easy to maintain. It may also be hard for her at first to leave the privilege of maintaining a mind above money to be enjoyed by the monks and the monarchs to whom it traditionally belongs, and settle down to the sort of sensible budgeting that everyone else has to undertake, and which she, I am entirely satisfied, could perfectly well undertake herself if she was prepared to *b* put her mind to it. That is the kind of hardship, however, which in the end can do her nothing but good and which certainly could not be called undue. For the avoidance of doubt, I should mention in passing that in arriving at the figure of £400,000 I have treated the husband's existing offer as superseded for all purposes, including his offer to release the mortgage on the Paddington home.

I come to the fifth and final issue. Whether the husband takes up the option given to *c* him by this court or not, some order for periodical payments to the wife will be required. I consider that the proper figure, in all the circumstances, would be £70,000 per annum and I think it would be appropriate to back-date it to the commencement of the financial year beginning 5 April 1979, credit being given in that and every subsequent fiscal year for all sums actually paid by way of maintenance by the husband, whether under an order of the court or otherwise.

d

I order the £10,000 annual payments for maintenance for the daughter to continue while she remains a minor, and I respond to the husband's request for a judicial opinion as to the appropriate figure for the younger son's maintenance while he remains with the mother by naming the sum of £5,000 pa. If that encourages him to set off and do some of the good work that is still waiting to be done in the world, with or without financial reward, so much the better.

e

The order which I propose to give effect to this judgment, subject of course to any submissions as to its form, on which I shall be pleased to hear counsel in a moment, is the following. (1) I order periodical payments to the wife at the rate of £70,000 pa, subject to tax, back-dated to the commencement of the financial year beginning 5 April 1979, credit being given in that and every subsequent fiscal year for all sums actually paid by way of maintenance, whether under order of the court or otherwise. (2) The *f* periodical payments at the rate of £10,000, subject to tax, for the daughter are to continue during her minority. (3) I give liberty to the husband to apply to the registrar in chambers at any time within three months from the date of this judgment for an order directing that if he shall within 28 days pay to the wife the sum of £400,000, the said periodical payments ordered for the wife shall terminate three months after the date of payment of the said sum.

g

Order accordingly.

Solicitors: *Eric Cheek & Co*, Harrow (for the wife); *Frere Cholmeley* (for the husband).

Bebe Chua   Barrister.

Khashoggi v IPC Magazines Ltd and another

COURT OF APPEAL, CIVIL DIVISION
SIR JOHN DONALDSON MR AND SLADE LJ
10 OCTOBER 1986

b *Libel and slander – Injunction – Interlocutory – Justification – Inseparable allegations – Common sting – Article containing a number of inseparable allegations – Defendants unable to prove particular allegation complained of – Defendants intending to justify common sting of allegations – Whether plaintiff entitled to interlocutory injunction restraining publication of article.*

The defendants were the proprietors of a magazine in which an article was published associating the plaintiff with a number of men, including a foreign head of state. The plaintiff brought an action for defamation against the defendants in respect of her alleged affair with the head of state, and obtained an interlocutory injunction restraining the defendants from further publication until trial of the action. The defendants subsequently applied for the injunction to be discharged on the ground that although they were unable to prove the particular allegation complained of, it was inseparable from the other allegations in the article, the common sting of which, namely general promiscuity, they intended to justify. The plaintiff contended that since the particular allegation complained of could not be proved the injunction should not be discharged. The judge dismissed the defendants' application and they appealed to the Court of Appeal.

Held – The principle that an interlocutory injunction would not be granted in a defamation action if the defendant intended to plead justification extended to allegations which could not be proved but which were inseparable from other allegations the common sting of which the defendant intended to justify, since the court's injunctive powers could only be invoked to defend a right or protect an interest and if the defendant were to succeed in his plea of justification the plaintiff would have no right and therefore he could not expect to have it defended. Since the defendants might succeed in their plea of justification of the common sting it was inappropriate for the interlocutory injunction to be continued. The appeal would therefore be allowed (see p 581 *b* to *f j*, post).

Bonnard v Perryman [1891–4] All ER Rep 965 and *Polly Peck (Holdings) plc v Trelford* [1986] 2 All ER 84 applied.

Notes

For the exercise of the court's jurisdiction regarding interlocutory injunctive relief in libel actions, see 24 Halsbury's Laws (4th edn) para 984 and 28 ibid paras 166–168, and for cases on the subject, see 32 Digest (Reissue) 323–324, 2686–2700.

Cases referred to in judgments

American Cyanamid Co v Ethicon Ltd [1975] 1 All ER 504, [1975] AC 396, [1975] 2 WLR 316, HL.
Bonnard v Perryman [1891] 2 Ch 269, [1891–4] All ER Rep 965, CA.
Coulson (William) & Sons v James Coulson & Co (1887) 3 TLR 846, CA.
Polly Peck (Holdings) plc v Trelford [1986] 2 All ER 84, [1986] 2 WLR 845, CA.

Interlocutory appeal

The defendants, IPC Magazines Ltd and Bridget Rowe, appealed against the decision of Sir Neil Lawson, sitting in chambers as a judge of the High Court, on 10 October 1986, whereby he refused to discharge an interlocutory injunction granted to the plaintiff, Soraya Khashoggi, on 7 October 1986 by the Court of Appeal (Sir John Donaldson MR and Croom-Johnson LJ) when allowing her appeal from the decision of Saville J on 7 October 1986 refusing her application for an injunction until trial of an action for defamation brought by the plaintiff against the defendants restraining them from further publishing an article entitled 'What makes you divorce the richest man in the world' in their magazine Woman's Own dated 11 October 1986. The facts are set out in the judgment of Sir John Donaldson MR.

G P Shaw for the defendants.
Roger Buckley QC and *Richard Rampton* for the plaintiff.

SIR JOHN DONALDSON MR. This dispute between Mrs Khashoggi as plaintiff and IPC Magazines Ltd and Bridget Rowe as defendants has occupied a disproportionate amount of the time of the courts during the last week. It began on Monday or Tuesday with an application to Saville J for an ex parte injunction restraining the publication of an article in Woman's Own misleadingly dated 11 October, although I hasten to add that it is a habit for weekly magazines to put a date for publication which seems to be quite a long time after the magazine is first on sale to the public. The plaintiff was seeking an ex parte injunction to restrain the publication of an article about her headed 'What makes you divorce the richest man in the world' which related a somewhat highly-coloured account of her life with her husband before and after the dissolution of their marriage which certainly, read as a whole, is capable of carrying the meaning that she was a lady of considerable sexual enthusiasm. This is not the first time that this sort of allegation has been made against Mrs Khashoggi, and I shall have to mention that briefly in a moment.

In the previous week's issue of Woman's Own there had been a trailer foreshadowing the publication of this article, and that had caused Mrs Khashoggi to get in touch with IPC Magazines and to explain in no uncertain terms that she objected to the publication of any such article and would take the necessary steps to prevent its publication. That led to a letter being written by Mr John Kensit, IPC's legal adviser, to Mrs Khashoggi, saying:

> 'Further to our telephone conversation this afternoon, I write to confirm that I am informed that we will not be publishing anything about you in Woman's Own next week that we are not able to justify.'

That letter was of crucial importance for this reason. Under the rule of law contained in *Bonnard v Perryman* [1891] 2 Ch 269, [1891–4] All ER Rep 965 it is well established that, if a publisher is going to justify, no interlocutory injunction will be granted, and it is a reasonable inference that, faced with that letter, Mrs Khashoggi was advised (if she was not advised, she should have been) that she would have no chance of obtaining an ex parte interim injunction.

Thus nothing happened until earlier this week when she obtained a copy of the issue of 11 October, whereupon she read the following passage, which is quite a short passage, in the article, saying: 'For Khashoggi [meaning Mrs Khashoggi's husband], the last straw was a report relayed to his London office by MI5, the British secret service, that Soraya was having an affair with his friend' who is the president of another nation. That is the passage which Mrs Khashoggi has pointed to as being defamatory of her. She makes no allegation that any of the rest of the article is defamatory about her, or if she does feel that way about it she is not making any legal complaint. However, she says that this allegation is wholly untrue and completely defamatory, and on that basis she went to Saville J.

What was said to Saville J earlier this week by or on behalf of the defendants was: 'We cannot plead justification, but, so far as any injunction is concerned, it is much too late now. All these copies of Woman's Own have already been distributed.' That view prevailed with Saville J. The matter then came before the Court of Appeal consisting of myself and Croom-Johnson LJ, and we took the view that that was too simplistic an approach, because the only reason why it was too late, in the sense that the magazine had already been distributed, was that Mrs Khashoggi had been deterred from applying to the court for relief by the letter from Mr Kensit. Let me make it clear that I did not understand at the last hearing that an allegation of mala fides was being levelled at Mr

Kensit. I now understand the word 'lying' was used, which would certainly carry with it
an imputation of mala fides, but in so far as I appreciated that it had been said, and I am
not sure that I did, I must merely have thought that it was forensic licence.

However, the nub of the matter, as I understood it, was that it was being said, and
certainly it was my view, that this letter was written recklessly in view of the fact that by
the time the matter came before this court and Woman's Own were for the first time
represented, it was said that on the information then available to them they could not
justify the allegation complained of. Both members of the court felt that in those
circumstances, had Mrs Khashoggi been given her opportunity of applying to the court
before publication, she would have succeeded in obtaining an injunction, and it was not
right that Woman's Own should be able to take advantage of their own wrong and say,
'It is now too late.' That is not entirely a theoretical or impractical view, because although
the magazine had been distributed it was probable that a number of copies had not yet
gone the full length of the chain of distribution and would in practice be prevented from
further circulation by our injunction. So it has proved, because today there is a complaint
by the magazine that they are liable to suffer damage to the tune of £150,000, which is
not of course consistent with their having distributed all their magazines. I do not mean
to say that they suggest that all the copies are still in their hands, but they rightly say that
the distributors are withdrawing them and they will be returned.

We made that order, and leaving apart details such as security for the counter-
undertaking and various visits to the court which there have been in that connection, the
position changed when this morning the defendants applied to Sir Neil Lawson sitting as
a judge in chambers to have the injunction discharged. He refused that application and
they now appear before this court pursuing the same application on appeal from him.

The reasons which are advanced by counsel for the defendants are twofold. He does
mention the question of the letter from Mr Kensit, but I have already dealt with that and
I need not deal with it again. First of all, he says that there was a remarkable lack of
candour on the part of Mrs Khashoggi when she applied for the injunction originally, and
second he says that it has now been discovered that Woman's Own has a full defence
to this action and in those circumstances the injunction should be withdrawn and they
should be allowed to resume publication.

I think I can deal with lack of candour fairly briefly. It is said that Mrs Khashoggi
should have revealed that very serious allegations had been made against her in
newspapers in 1980 and that on that occasion she had sued for libel but had not thought
it right to go beyond the stage of delivering a statement of claim. That was in fact
mentioned to us at the previous hearing. We were told that there were financial problems
in her way, and indeed that was used by the defendants as a basis for persuading us to
require security for her counter-undertaking in damages. Then it was said that she had
twice sold her story to newspapers, once for some £75,000, and that recently she had
given an interview relating to what were described by counsel as her 'sexual adventures'.
It was said that all those things should have been revealed to the court. Third, it was said
that the court should have been told or she should have remembered that, when she
applied in December 1985 for an injunction in a different context, the judge in chambers
found her guilty of a lack of candour, although he thought that in all the circumstances
it was nevertheless right to grant an injunction.

I would not want anything that I say to be thought to derogate from the undoubted
duty of an ex parte applicant for relief to be utterly candid. In a different context, that of
Anton Piller orders and Mareva injunctions, I have already made clear my total dedication
to that principle. Nevertheless, I think one has got to take account of the circumstances
in which Mrs Khashoggi was applying to the court. We have already heard from her
solicitor, Mr Peter Carter-Ruck, that he knew from her a great deal of the previous
history and matters which should have been revealed in this context. However, he
rightly points out that the letter from Mr Kensit prevented any proceedings until after
publication, and thereafter time was absolutely of the essence. The copies of Woman's
Own were trickling down the distribution chain at a rate of knots, and every minute
gone probably meant several hundred further copies on the streets. In those circumstances

I think it would be unrealistic to complain that there was not full disclosure at that stage. However, I do not think that this appeal ought to turn on that aspect of the matter at all. I believe that this appeal really turns on the position which has now been reached in relation to the plea of justification. *a*

Bonnard v Perryman is of course a classic authority. Lord Coleridge CJ, reading a judgment of the court with which Lord Esher MR and Lindley, Bowen and Lopes LJJ concurred, said ([1891] 2 Ch 269 at 284, [1891–4] All ER Rep 965 at 968):

> 'The right of free speech is one which it is for the public interest that individuals *b*
> should possess, and, indeed, that they should exercise without impediment, so long
> as no wrongful act is done; and, unless an alleged libel is untrue, there is no wrong
> committed; but, on the contrary, often a very wholesome act is performed in the
> publication and repetition of an alleged libel. Until it is clear that an alleged libel is
> untrue, it is not clear that any right at all has been infringed; and the importance of
> leaving free speech unfettered is a strong reason in cases of libel for dealing most *c*
> cautiously and warily with the granting of interim injunctions. We entirely approve
> of, and desire to adopt as our own, the language of Lord *Esher*, M.R., in *Coulson* v.
> *Coulson* ((1887) 3 TLR 846)—"To justify the Court in granting an interim injunction
> it must come to a decision upon the question of libel or no libel, before the jury
> have decided whether it was a libel or not. Therefore the jurisdiction was of a
> delicate nature. It ought only to be exercised in the clearest cases, where any jury *d*
> would say that the matter complained of was libellous, and where, if the jury did
> not so find, the Court would set aside the verdict as unreasonable".'

In the present instance the defendants do not say that they can prove the facts alleged in the paragraph to which exception is taken and which I have read. What they do say is that they are not limited to those facts in seeking to justify the libel. They can rely on other facts by way of justification, and if they succeed there would have been no cause of *e* action available to Mrs Khashoggi and in that sense there was no libel.

Counsel for the plaintiff says that the rule in *Bonnard v Perryman* applies in what might be described as the simple or classic case of justification where somebody sets out an allegation and, on being challenged, says, 'I will prove the truth of that particular allegation.' He says it has never been extended beyond that. Counsel for the defendants *f* on the other hand says, 'Why not?'

Let us start with the decision of this court in *Polly Peck (Holdings) plc v Trelford* [1986] 2 All ER 84 at 102, [1986] 2 WLR 845 at 869, where O'Connor LJ sets out the relevant parts of the law of the defence of justification. He said:

> 'Where a publication contains two or more separate and distinct defamatory
> statements, the plaintiff is entitled to select one for complaint, and the defendant is *g*
> not entitled to assert the truth of the others by way of justification.'

Applying that to this article, Mrs Khashoggi was entitled to select this allegation that she had an affair with the president of a friendly foreign state and to complain of that notwithstanding that she makes no complaint of the various other allegations of a not dissimilar nature made in the same article.

The judgment of O'Connor LJ goes on to say: *h*

> 'Whether a defamatory statement is separate and distinct from other defamatory
> statements contained in the publication is a question of fact and degree in each case.
> The several defamatory allegations in their context may have a common sting, in
> which event they are not to be regarded as separate and distinct allegations. The
> defendant is entitled to justify the sting, and once again it is fortuitous that what is *j*
> in fact similar fact evidence is found in the publication [I think he means in the
> publication itself].'

What is said here is that that principle can be applied and the sting of the article is promiscuity generally. It is submitted that it would be very difficult for the plaintiff, when her statement of claim comes to be prepared, to make any complaint about this

particular allegation which could not equally be made about the other allegations
contained in the same article. In those circumstances the *Polly Peck* principle applies and,
notwithstanding that the defendants may not be able to prove the particular affair
complained of, they will be able to adduce evidence which will justify the sting of the
article and the sting of that statement on the footing, I suppose, that it is not more
defamatory to have an extra-marital affair with one person rather than another in the
circumstances of this case.

However, it is not for us, as I think, to decide whether that is true and what the jury
would make of it, because it is clearly a jury case. We have to apply the *Bonnard v
Perryman* principle even if, as far as counsel's researches go, it has never before been
applied to this extended view of justification: what one might describe as, though I am
sure it did not start as, the *Polly Peck* form of justification.

I cannot see why it should not be applied. Quite apart from any question of public
interest in the freedom of the press, there is a much wider principle which covers it, and
that is this. The injunctive powers of the court can only be invoked in support of a right
or in defence of an interest. If the *Polly Peck* defence were to succeed Mrs Khashoggi
would have no right. She therefore cannot expect to have it defended. That does not of
course answer the question which arises as to how likely she is to succeed. That is a
problem which always arises in libel and elsewhere. The point is that *Bonnard v Perryman*,
apart from its reference to freedom of speech, is based on the fact that courts should not
step in to defend a cause of action in defamation if they think that this is a case in which
the plea of justification might, not would, succeed. I see no reason why that principle
should be confined to justification in its primary meaning as compared with justification
in an extended sense, the *Polly Peck* sense.

Counsel for the plaintiff says that that is all wrong and that the true test to be applied
is that in *American Cyanamid Co v Ethicon Ltd* [1975] 1 All ER 504 at 510, [1975] AC 396
at 407–408. For the reasons I have given I do not think he is right, but if he was right I
still do not think that Mrs Khashoggi would succeed. The first question to be asked
would be: is there a serious question to be tried? The answer is Yes. The next questions
would be: if the plaintiff succeeded at the trial in establishing a right to a permanent
injunction, would she be adequately compensated by an award of damages for the
continued publication of the libel meanwhile and would the defendants be in a position
to pay those damages?' The answer in each case would be Yes and no interim injunction
would be granted.

For my part I would now discharge the injunction, but in doing so I would like to
make it absolutely clear that I am not expressly or impliedly saying that Mrs Khashoggi
was not entitled to the interim injunction which she obtained up to this morning when
a wholly different situation resulted from the defendants coming forward and saying,
with particularity and with the support of their own experienced counsel, that they now
intended to plead justification and giving reasons why it was possible that they might
succeed in that plea. Thus any question of a claim on the counter-undertaking as to
damages must stand over until the dust has settled and the matter has been investigated
much more fully. We could have a situation undoubtedly in which Mrs Khashoggi was
under no liability whatever under the counter-undertaking up to this moment. We
could have a situation in which she was liable up to this moment. That is a matter for
someone else to investigate at a future time, and certainly not for us to investigate this
afternoon. For those reasons I would now set the injunction aside.

SLADE LJ. I agree and do not wish to add anything of my own.

Appeal allowed.

Solicitors: *William Charles Crocker* (for the defendants); *Peter Carter-Ruck & Ptnrs* (for the
plaintiff).

Diana Procter   Barrister.

Notcutt v Universal Equipment Co (London) Ltd

a

COURT OF APPEAL, CIVIL DIVISION
DILLON LJ AND SHELDON J
11, 12 FEBRUARY, 14 MARCH 1986

b

Employment – Contract of service – Frustration – Sickness of employee – Short-term periodic contract – Absence from work – Employee absent from work because of heart attack and unable to resume employment – Whether contract terminated by frustration because of employee's illness – Employment Protection (Consolidation) Act 1978, s 49(1), Sch 3, para 3.

The appellant entered into employment with the respondent in 1957. He was paid at an *c* hourly rate and his employment was, by virtue of s 49(1)[a] of the Employment Protection (Consolidation) Act 1978, terminable by 12 weeks' notice. It was a term of his contract of employment that no remuneration would be paid for periods of absence from work because of sickness, injury or incapacity or for any reason other than agreed holidays. In 1983 the appellant suffered a heart attack and was thereafter off work. A medical report in July 1984 made it clear that he would be unable to work again. On 26 July 1984 the *d* respondent gave notice to the appellant terminating his employment on 19 October 1984. The appellant brought an action claiming that he was entitled to sick pay during the period of the notice by virtue of para 3[b] of Sch 3 to the 1978 Act. The respondent contended that the contract of employment had been frustrated by the appellant's illness before the purported notice of termination. The judge dismissed the action and the appellant appealed. *e*

Held – Since a periodic contract of employment determinable by short or relatively short notice could none the less be intended in many cases by both parties to last for years, and since the power of the employer to terminate the contract by notice was subject to the provisions of the 1978 Act which provided protection for employees against unfair dismissal, such a periodic contract could, in appropriate circumstances, be *f* terminated without notice by frustration because of, for example, an employee's illness or incapacity. The mere fact that the contract could be terminated by the employer by relatively short notice did not of itself render the doctrine of frustration inapplicable. On the facts, the heart attack suffered by the appellant had rendered the performance of his contractual obligations impossible and had brought about such a change in the

g

---

a Section 49(1), so far as material, provides: 'The notice required to be given by an employer to terminate the contract of employment of a person who has been continuously employed for one month or more . . . (*c*) shall not be less than twelve weeks' notice if his period of continuous employment is twelve years or more.'

b Paragraph 3, so far as material, provides:

'(1) If an employee does not have normal working hours under the contract of employment in *h* force in the period of notice the employer shall be liable to pay the employee for each week of the period of notice a sum not less than a week's pay.

(2) Subject to sub-paragraph (3), the employer's obligation under this paragraph shall be conditional on the employee being ready and willing to do work of a reasonable nature and amount to earn a week's pay.

(3) Sub-paragraph (2) shall not apply—(*a*) in respect of any period during which the employee is incapable of work because of sickness or injury, or (*b*) in respect of any period during which the *j* employee is absent from work in accordance with the terms of his employment relating to holidays, and any payment made to an employee by his employer in respect of such a period, whether by way of sick pay, statutory sick pay, holiday pay or otherwise, shall be taken into account for the purposes of this paragraph as if it were remuneration paid by the employer in respect of that period . . .'

a significance of the mutual obligations between employer and employee that the contract if performed would be a different thing from that contracted for. It followed that the contract of employment had been frustrated by the appellant's illness. The appeal would accordingly be dismissed (see p 586 d to e and p 587 f g j to p 588 b, post).

Dicta of Lord Reid and Lord Radcliffe in *Davis Contractors Ltd v Fareham UDC* [1956] 2 All ER at 154, 160 applied.

Dictum of Bristow J in *Harman v Flexible Lamps Ltd* [1980] IRLR at 419 disapproved.

b **Notes**

For the termination of a contract of employment due to illness of an employee, see 16 Halsbury's Laws (4th edn) para 645.

For the doctrine of frustration generally, see 9 ibid paras 450–459, and for cases on the subject, see 12 Digest (Reissue) 482–484, 3426–3434.

c For the Employment Protection (Consolidation) Act 1978, s 49, Sch 3, para 3, see 16 Halsbury's Statutes (4th edn) 430, 556.

Cases referred to in judgments

Davis Contractors Ltd v Fareham UDC [1956] 2 All ER 145, [1956] AC 696, [1956] 3 WLR 37, HL.

d *Denny Mott & Dickson Ltd v James B Fraser & Co Ltd* [1944] 1 All ER 678, [1944] AC 265, HL.

Egg Stores (Stamford Hill) Ltd v Leibovici [1977] ICR 260, EAT.

Hare v Murphy Bros Ltd [1974] 3 All ER 940, CA.

Harman v Flexible Lamps Ltd [1980] IRLR 418, EAT.

Hart v A R Marshall & Sons (Bulwell) Ltd [1978] 2 All ER 413, [1977] 1 WLR 1067, EAT.

e *Marshall v Harland & Wolff Ltd* [1972] 2 All ER 715, [1972] 1 WLR 899, NIRC.

National Carriers Ltd v Panalpina (Northern) Ltd [1981] 1 All ER 161, [1981] AC 675, [1981] 2 WLR 45, HL.

Westwood v Secretary of State for Employment [1984] 1 All ER 874, [1985] AC 20, [1984] 2 WLR 418, HL.

f **Case also cited**

Hebden v Forsey & Son [1973] ICR 607, NIRC.

Appeal

Derek Notcutt appealed against the order of his Honour Judge Birks sitting in the Brentford County Court on 22 March 1985 whereby he dismissed the appellant's claim for sick pay under para 3 of Sch 3 to the Employment Protection (Consolidation) Act g 1978 on the ground that his contract of employment with the respondents, Universal Equipment Co (London) Ltd, had been frustrated. The facts are set out in the judgment of Dillon LJ.

Robin Allen for the appellant.
h *Andrew Hillier* for the respondents.

Cur adv vult

14 March. The following judgments were delivered.

j **DILLON LJ.** This is an appeal by the plaintiff in the action, Mr Notcutt, from a decision of his Honour Judge Birks given in the Brentford County Court on 22 March 1985 whereby he dismissed the appellant's action with costs. The appeal was brought on at very short notice to fill an unexpected gap in the court's list. Each side had therefore to instruct counsel who had not appeared in the court below. In the result we have had the benefit of an extremely high standard of advocacy from both counsel who have appeared

before us and I am most grateful to them for the clarity and conciseness of their
arguments. Their arguments brought out that the appeal raises issues of considerable
general importance in that it seems that this is the first case in which the Court of Appeal
has been required to consider the application of the doctrine of frustration to a periodic
contract of employment which is determinable by short or relatively short notice where
the contract is said to have been frustrated by the illness or incapacity of the employee.
Had this been appreciated before the hearing began, arrangements would have been
made for the appeal to be heard by a three-judge court. As, however, the importance of
the case only emerged as the argument developed, I did not think it right to put the
parties to the extra expense which would have been involved if we had directed that the
appeal be adjourned to come on before a three-judge court.

The appellant, who was born in December 1920, entered the employment of the
respondents, who are a relatively small company with two directors and about a hundred
employees, in December 1957. He remained in their employment until 1984. He was a
skilled workman whose job was to operate a universal milling machine, whereby metal
was milled to make parts for aircraft or for other plant and equipment. His wages were
at an hourly rate. Subject to statute, his employment was originally terminable by a
week's notice, and it was a term of his contract that no remuneration would be paid for
periods of absence from work because of sickness, injury or incapacity or for any other
reason other than agreed holidays.

However, certain further terms are incorporated (see *Westwood v Secretary of State for
Employment* [1984] 1 All ER 874 at 877, [1985] AC 20 at 41) into the contract of
employment by the Employment Protection (Consolidation) Act 1978 as amended.
Apart from the provisions of that Act which record the right of every employee, not here
in question, not to be unfairly dismissed, s 49 of the Act gives employees a right to a
minimum period of notice if their contract of employment is to be terminated by notice
by their employer. In the appellant's case by 1984 the notice required to terminate his
contract had to be not less than 12 weeks' notice. Moreover under s 50(1) of the 1978
Act, if an employer gives notice to terminate the contract of employment of a person
who has been continuously employed for one month or more, the provisions of Sch 3 to
the Act are to have effect as respects the liability of the employer for the period of notice
required by s 49. These provisions include under para 3 of Sch 3 an obligation on the
employer to pay the employee at his average hourly rate in so far as during the period of
his notice he is incapable of work because of sickness or injury.

What actually happened is that the appellant had a coronary infarction in October or
November 1983, when he was nearly 63 years old, and was thereafter off work. The
respondents for a time sub-contracted the appellant's work on a temporary basis, but this
was not wholly satisfactory, and, not unnaturally, by July 1984 they were minded to
employ another miller in the appellant's place if the appellant was not going to return to
work. They therefore arranged with the appellant for him to authorise his doctor, Dr
Menzies, to write a report to the respondents on the appellant's state of health. That was
done. The report is dated 24 July 1984 and the relevant parts read as follows:

'This man had a Coronary Infarct in November 1983. He also suffers from
arthritis of shoulders, hips and spine. He is unlikely to be able to resume work in
the near future. In fact, I doubt whether he will ever be able to work again.'

On receipt of this report, the respondent's shop foreman, Mr Johnson, who was
handling the matter for the respondents, had a telephone conversation with the appellant
in which they discussed the report. The judge found as a fact that both sides accepted
that the report made it clear that the appellant was not going to work again. There is
evidence to support that finding, not least, so far as the appellant himself is concerned, in
that he himself said in evidence that after the report he knew he could not go on working.
I regard that finding as crucial to this appeal.

Accordingly, after consulting ACAS as to the length of notice, Mr Johnson on the

respondents' behalf by a letter of 26 July 1984 gave the appellant notice to terminate his
a   employment on 19 October 1984.

The appellant took advice, and a law centre on his behalf claimed that he was entitled
to sick pay under para 3 of Sch 3 to the Act while absent from work during the period of
his notice. This took the respondents by surprise. Their first reaction was to suggest that
the appellant might wish to be re-engaged, presumably without pay unless he
unexpectedly became fit to work. This was not accepted. The respondents then suggested
b   that the notice of termination was really a sham, designed to enable the appellant to
obtain extra social security benefits when his contract of employment had in truth been
determined without notice by mutual consent on 25 or 26 July 1984; this, however, the
judge rejected on the facts. The respondents also contended, however, that the contract
of employment had been frustrated by the appellant's illness before the purported notice
of termination of 26 July. That argument, of frustration, the judge accepted; he
c   accordingly dismissed the action, in which the appellant has claimed payment of his sick
pay under Sch 3 to the Act during the period of that notice, and it is against that decision
that the appellant now appeals.

I have found it impossible to discern from the wording of the Act why Parliament
should have required an employer to pay sick pay to an employee who is off work because
of sickness or injury while under notice of termination of his contract, although the
d   employer is under no such obligation while the employee is not under notice. Possibly it
may have been thought that a good employer who, even if not obliged to, would pay
sick pay to a man off sick would not be willing to do so if the man was under notice;
even this speculation, however, is difficult to fit in with sub-s (3) of s 50 of the Act (which
does not apply in this particular case). Whatever the reason, however, it is clear that the
Act has imposed such an obligation on employers. The obligation is incorporated into
e   the contract of employment. Both counsel are therefore agreed that, if the appellant's
contract was terminated by the notice of 26 July, he is entitled to the moneys which he
has claimed. Conversely both counsel are equally agreed that, if the appellant's contract
of employment had been frustrated before the notice of 26 July was given, that notice
was of no effect and the appellant cannot make any claim under s 50 of or Sch 3 to the
Act.

f   The arguments of counsel for the appellant are firstly, and generally, that the doctrine
of frustration can have no application to a periodic contract of employment because there
is no need for it, the contract can always be terminated by short or relatively short notice,
and secondly that in the circumstances of the present case there was no frustration as
absence for sickness, injury or incapacity was envisaged by the contract and also by para
3 of Sch 3 to the Act.

g   In *Harman v Flexible Lamps Ltd* [1980] IRLR 418 at 419 Bristow J commented as
follows:

> 'In the employment field the concept of discharge by operation of law, that is
> frustration, is normally only in play where the contract of employment is for a long
> term which cannot be determined by notice. Where the contract is terminable by
> notice, there is really no need to consider the question of frustration and if it were
h   > the law that, in circumstances such as are before us in this case, an employer was in
> a position to say "this contract has been frustrated" then that would be a very
> convenient way in which to avoid the provisions of the Employment Protection
> (Consolidation) Act. In our judgment that is not the law in these sort of
> circumstances.'

j   In the present case, the argument of frustration is of course unashamedly put forward
to avoid the provisions of the Act; in that it has succeeded in the court below.

Notwithstanding the views expressed by Bristow J, however, there have been several
cases in the National Industrial Relations Court and the Employment Appeal Tribunal in
which those courts have considered that a contract of employment which is terminable

by relatively short notice is in law capable of being terminated, without notice, by
frustration as a result of the illness of the employee, and those courts have endeavoured
to list by way of guideline the factors of which account should be taken in considering
whether a particular such contract has been so frustrated: see *Marshall v Harland & Wolff
Ltd* [1972] 2 All ER 715, [1972] 1 WLR 899, *Egg Stores (Stamford Hill) Ltd v Leibovici* [1977]
ICR 260 and *Hart v A R Marshall & Sons (Bulwell) Ltd* [1978] 2 All ER 413, [1977] 1 WLR
1067. The judge in the present case was in his judgment endeavouring to apply the
guidelines laid down in these cases to the facts of the present case.

In this court, in *Hare v Murphy Bros Ltd* [1974] 3 All ER 940 Lord Denning MR held
that a contract of employment of a workman was frustrated when the man was sentenced
to imprisonment for 12 months. In reaching that conclusion Lord Denning MR
considered by way of analogy that if the man had been grievously injured in a road
accident and incapacitated for eight months his contract of employment would be
frustrated. However, though the man's contract was presumably determinable on short
notice, no argument was founded on this: the discussion seems to have been over
whether the contract was terminated by frustration or by repudiatory breach on the part
of the man in committing the offence for which he was imprisoned.

For my part, as a periodic contract of employment determinable by short or relatively
short notice may none the less be intended in many cases by both parties to last for many
years and as the power of the employer to terminate the contract by notice is subject to
the provisions for the protection of employees against unfair dismissal now in the 1978
Act, I can see no reason in principle why such a periodic contract of employment should
not in appropriate circumstances be held to have been terminated without notice by
frustration according to the accepted and long-established doctrine of frustration in our
law of contract. The mere fact that the contract can be terminated by the employer by
relatively short notice cannot of itself render the doctrine of frustration inevitably
inapplicable. Accordingly, the words of Bristow J cited earlier in this judgment must be
taken as no more than a warning that the court must look carefully at any submission
that a periodic contract of employment has been discharged by frustration if that
submission is put forward to avoid the provisions of the 1978 Act; if Bristow J intended
to go further than that I cannot agree with him.

The principles that govern the doctrine of frustration are conveniently to be found in
the speeches of Lord Reid and Lord Radcliffe in *Davis Contractors Ltd v Fareham UDC*
[1956] 2 All ER 145 at 154, 160, [1956] AC 696 at 721, 728–729. Lord Reid said:

'In my view, the proper approach of this case is to take . . . all facts which throw
light on the nature of the contract or which can properly be held to be extrinsic
evidence relevant to assist in its construction and then, as a matter of law, to construe
the contract and to determine whether the ultimate situation . . . is, or is not, within
the scope of the contract so construed.'

Lord Radcliffe, in a much quoted passage, said:

'So, perhaps, it would be simpler to say at the outset that frustration occurs
whenever the law recognises that, without default of either party, a contractual
obligation has become incapable of being performed because the circumstances in
which performance is called for would render it a thing radically different from that
which was undertaken by the contract. Non haec in foedera veni. It was not this
that I promised to do. There is, however, no uncertainty as to the materials on
which the court must proceed. "The data for decision are, on the one hand, the
terms and construction of the contract, read in the light of the surrounding
circumstances, and, on the other hand, the events which have occurred" (*Denny,
Mott & Dickson, Ltd. v. James B. Fraser & Co., Ltd.* ([1944] 1 All ER 678 at 683), per
LORD WRIGHT). In the nature of things there is often no room for any elaborate
inquiry. The court must act on a general impression of what its rule requires. It is
for that reason that special importance is necessarily attached to the occurrence of

a any unexpected event that, as it were, changes the face of things. But, even so, it is not hardship or inconvenience or material loss itself which calls the principle of frustration into play. There must be as well such a change in the significance of the obligation that the thing undertaken would, if performed, be a different thing from that contracted for.'

Counsel for the appellant urges that there is a further factor which must be satisfied before it can be said that a contract has been terminated by frustration: it must be shown
b that it would be unjust to hold the parties to the literal terms of their contract. He therefore submits that there is no injustice in holding the parties in this case to their contract, despite the doctor's report and the subsequent conversation between the appellant and Mr Johnson, because the respondents were under no obligation under the contract to pay the appellant while he was away sick, and if they chose to terminate his contract by notice there could be no injustice in requiring them to pay him sick pay
c which the statute in that event required them to pay.

To establish this further factor, counsel for the appellant relies on various statements in the authorities, such as the passages in the speech of Lord Simon in *National Carriers Ltd v Panalpina (Northern) Ltd* [1981] 1 All ER 161 at 175, [1981] AC 675 at 700:

> 'Frustration of a contract takes place when there supervenes an event ... which so
d > significantly changes the nature (not merely the expense or onerousness) of the outstanding contractual rights and/or obligations from what the parties could reasonably have contemplated at the time of its execution that it would be unjust to hold them to the literal sense of its stipulations in the new circumstances ...'

And again that the doctrine of frustration is—

e > 'on the face of it apt to vindicate justice wherever owing to relevant supervening circumstances the enforcement of any contractual arrangement in its literal terms would produce injustice.'

(See [1981] 1 All ER 161 at 176, [1981] AC 675 at 701.)

I do not for my part see that these references to justice or injustice introduce any further factor. If the unexpected event produces an ultimate situation which, as a matter
f of construction, is not within the scope of the contract or would render performance impossible or something radically different from that which was undertaken by the contract, then it is unjust that the contracting party should be held to be still bound by the contract in those altered circumstances. I approach the facts of this case on the footing that the test to be satisfied is that explained by Lord Reid and Lord Radcliffe in the passages above set out.

g   The appellant's contract provided that the respondents were not bound to pay the appellant while he was absent from work because of sickness, injury or incapacity. The contract thus envisaged the possibility that he might be away from work because of sickness, injury or incapacity. But as a matter of construction of the contract I cannot hold that the reference to injury would cover an injury which totally disabled him from performing his work under the contract, eg if the operation of the milling machine
h requires the use of his right hand and he lost his right arm, or was rendered quadriplegic in an accident away from work which was not his fault and had nothing to do with his employers. In such a case his accident would have caused his contract of employment to be frustrated as a matter of law. Again, if sickness or incapacity are considered rather than injury, the result would be the same if, for example he had a stroke which left his right side permanently paralysed.

j   On the actual facts of the present case, the effect of his coronary could not initially be assessed. But, when more than six months later the doctor made his report, both parties appreciated, on the judge's findings, that he was not going to work again. He was totally incapacitated from performing the contract. That was a situation which, in my judgment, was outside the scope of the contract properly construed. To put it another way, the

coronary which left him unable to work again was an unexpected occurrence which
made his performance of his contractual obligation, to work, impossible and brought   *a*
about such a change in the significance of the mutual obligations that the contract if
performed would be a different thing from that contracted for.

In these circumstances I am unable to accept the arguments for the appellant. The
judge approached the case on a correct basis and I agree with his conclusion. Accordingly,
though I feel much sympathy with the appellant in that his working life has been cut
short by illness or incapacity, I would dismiss this appeal.   *b*

SHELDON J. I agree. Indeed I agree so entirely both with Dillon LJ's conclusion and
with his reasons that there is little that I can usefully add. I would, however, refer to and,
with respect, adopt the following passage from the judgment of Phillips J in *Egg Stores
(Stamford Hill) Ltd v Leibovici* [1977] ICR 260 at 265:

> 'It is possible to divide into two kinds the events relied upon as bringing about   *c*
> the frustration of a short-term periodic contract of employment. There may be an
> event (e.g. a crippling accident) so dramatic and shattering that everyone concerned
> will realise immediately that to all intents and purposes the contract must be
> regarded as at an end. Or there may be an event, such as illness or accident, the
> course and outcome of which is uncertain. It may be a long process before one is
> able to say whether the event is such as to bring about the frustration of the contract.   *d*
> But there *will* have been frustration of the contract, even though at the time of the
> event the outcome was uncertain, if the time arrives when, looking back, one can
> say that at some point (even if it is not possible to say precisely when) matters had
> gone on so long, and the prospects for the future were so poor, that it was no longer
> practical to regard the contract as still subsisting.' (Phillips J's emphasis.)
>   *e*

In the present case, that time arrived when, following the medical report, as the judge
found, both sides accepted that the appellant was not going to work again. From that
moment, at the latest, the frustration of their contract was established, so that the service
thereafter of a notice purporting to terminate his employment was otiose and of no legal
effect.

                                                                                          f
Appeal dismissed. Leave to appeal to House of Lords refused.

Solicitors: *Hilary Plews*, Hounslow (for the appellant); *Roebuck & Co*, Hounslow (for the
respondents).

                                                          Celia Fox   Barrister.

F C Shepherd & Co Ltd v Jerrom

COURT OF APPEAL, CIVIL DIVISION
LAWTON, MUSTILL AND BALCOMBE LJJ
10, 11, 12 DECEMBER 1985, 23, 24 JUNE, 21 JULY 1986

Employment – Contract of service – Frustration – Imprisonment of employee – Apprentice sentenced to borstal training for not less than six months – Apprentice half way through four-year apprenticeship when sentenced – Whether apprentice guilty of 'serious misconduct' in his apprenticeship – Whether sentence frustrating contract of apprenticeship – Whether frustration self-induced – Whether apprentice repudiating contract – Whether apprentice unfairly dismissed – Whether apprentice contributing to his dismissal – Whether unreasonable to award maximum compensation where employee contributing to his unfair dismissal – Employment Protection (Consolidation) Act 1978, s 74(6).

The employers were builders who engaged an apprentice plumber under a four-year training service agreement incorporating the rules of a joint industry board governing the recruitment of apprentices. The rules contained provision for the termination of the apprenticeship by the board in cases of 'serious misconduct warranting dismissal'. The apprentice had more than half the period of his apprenticeship to serve when he was convicted of affray and conspiracy to assault and was sentenced to borstal training for an indeterminate period of between six months and two years. On his release from borstal six months later the employers refused to take him back and he complained to an industrial tribunal that he had been unfairly dismissed. The employers contended that he had not been dismissed because the apprenticeship agreement had been frustrated by the apprentice's conviction and custodial sentence. The tribunal held that the agreement had not been frustrated by the apprentice's sentence, that the employers had repudiated the contract by refusing to take the apprentice back into their employment, that their repudiation amounted to constructive dismissal which was unfair because termination of the apprentice's employment was governed by the board's termination procedure and that the apprentice was entitled to £7,000 compensation, being the maximum that could be awarded. The Employment Appeal Tribunal affirmed that decision and the employers appealed. At the hearing of the appeal the apprentice contended (i) that it was not open to the employers to rely on the doctrine of frustration, because if performance of the contract had been radically affected that had been caused not by some outside event but by the fault of one of the parties, namely the apprentice himself in being sent to borstal, and (ii) that, although he himself had repudiated the contract by his conduct, in the absence of acceptance of that repudiation by the employers he was ready to resume the performance of his obligations.

Held – The appeal would be allowed for the following reasons—

(1) (Per Lawton and Balcombe LJJ) The 'serious misconduct' which the joint industry board's termination procedure was aimed at was conduct which directly related to an apprentice's work and training and would normally be restricted to conduct occurring in the course of his work and training as such, although (per Balcombe LJ) in some types of employment conduct outside work might be relevant to the employee's fitness to perform the work for which he was employed. Since the actions of the apprentice in getting involved in an affray and being sent to borstal had nothing to do with his work and training the board's termination procedure was irrelevant (see p 594 *f* to *h* and p 605 *g* to *j*, post).

(2) A custodial sentence imposed on an employee was capable of frustrating the employee's contract of employment if the sentence was such that it rendered the performance of the contract radically different from that which the parties contemplated when they entered into the contract. Having regard to the length of the sentence imposed on the apprentice in relation to the length of his apprenticeship, the sentence of borstal

training had frustrated the contract and there had therefore been no dismissal, actual or
constructive, of the apprentice by the employers. Accordingly, the industrial tribunal
had had no jurisdiction to entertain the apprentice's claim for unfair dismissal (see p 595
c, p 597 *g h*, p 603 *j* to p 604 *a g*, p 606 *d e*, p 608 *h j* and p 609 *g h*, post); *Notcutt v
Universal Equipment Co (London) Ltd* [1986] 3 All ER 582 followed.

(3) The apprentice was not entitled to rely on the defence that the frustration was self-
induced, because (a) (per Lawton and Mustill LJJ) he could not plead his own default in
order to establish his right to compensation for unfair dismissal, since a promisor would
not be permitted to improve his position by asserting that an event which would
otherwise bring about a mutual discharge by frustration was caused by his own fault, (b)
(per Mustill LJ) similarly, he was not entitled to improve his position by asserting that he
himself had repudiated the contract, (c) (per Lawton LJ) although his criminal conduct
had been deliberate what had affected his ability to perform the contract was not his
conduct but the outside event of the court sentencing him to borstal training and (d) (per
Balcombe LJ) in the context of employment law it was irrelevant whether imprisonment
amounted to 'self-induced' frustration (see p 596 *e f j* to p 597 *b*, p 601 *b* to p 602 *a c d* and
p 608 *f g*, post); *Joseph Constantine Steamship Line Ltd v Imperial Smelting Corp Ltd, The
Kingswood* [1941] 2 All ER 165 and *Universal Cargo Carriers Corp v Citati* [1957] 3 All ER
234 considered.

Per curiam. Where unfair dismissal arises out of imprisonment it would be
unreasonable for a tribunal to find that the complainant had not contributed to his
dismissal, within s 74(6)ᵃ of the Employment Protection (Consolidation) Act 1978, and
would therefore be unreasonable to award him the maximum amount of compensation
(see p 598 *a* to *c* and p 611 *b*, post).

Notes

For dismissal of an employee on grounds of misconduct, see 16 Halsbury's Laws (4th
edn) paras 616, 628–630, and for cases on the subject, see 20 Digest (Reissue) 434–442,
3530–3623.

For the doctrine of frustration generally, see 9 Halsbury's Laws (4th edn) paras 450–
459, and for cases on frustration of contracts of employment, see 12 Digest (Reissue) 508–
509, 3519–3528.

For the Employment Protection (Consolidation) Act 1978, s 74, see 16 Halsbury's
Statutes (4th edn) 464.

Cases referred to in judgments

Appleby v Myers (1867) LR 2 CP 651, [1861–73] All ER Rep 452, Ex Ch.
Bank Line Ltd v Arthur Capel & Co [1919] AC 435, [1918–19] All ER Rep 504, HL.
Chakki v United Yeast Co Ltd [1982] 2 All ER 446, EAT.
Constantine (Joseph) Steamship Line Ltd v Imperial Smelting Corp Ltd, The Kingswood [1941] 2
    All ER 165, [1942] AC 154, HL.
Cutter v Powell (1795) 6 Term Rep 320, [1775–1802] All ER Rep 159, 101 ER 573.
Dahl v Nelson Donkin & Co (1881) 6 App Cas 38, [1881–5] All ER Rep 572, HL.
Davis Contractors Ltd v Fareham UDC [1956] 2 All ER 145, [1956] AC 696, [1956] 3 WLR
    37, HL.
Hare v Murphy Bros Ltd [1974] 3 All ER 940, CA; *affg* [1973] ICR 331, NIRC.
Harman v Flexible Lamps Ltd [1980] IRLR 418, EAT.
Harrington v Kent CC [1980] IRLR 353, EAT.
Heyman v Darwins Ltd [1942] 1 All ER 337, [1942] AC 356, HL.
Hochster v De la Tour (1853) 2 E & B 678, [1843–60] All ER Rep 12, 118 ER 922.
Hong Kong Fir Shipping Co Ltd v Kawasaki Kisen Kaisha Ltd [1962] 1 All ER 474, [1962] 2
    QB 26, [1962] 2 WLR 474, CA.
Howell v Coupland (1874) LR 9 QB 462; *affd* (1876) 1 QBD 258, [1874–80] All ER Rep
    878, CA.
Jackson v Union Marine Insurance Co Ltd (1874) LR 10 CP 125, [1874–80] All ER Rep 317.

---

a   Section 74(6) is set out at p 598*b*, post

a *London Transport Executive v Clarke* [1981] ICR 355, CA.
Maritime National Fish Ltd v Ocean Trawlers Ltd [1935] AC 524, [1935] All ER Rep 86, PC.
Mertens v Home Freeholds Co [1921] 2 KB 526, [1921] All ER Rep 372.
Nelson v BBC (No 2) [1980] ICR 110, CA.
Norris v Southampton City Council [1982] ICR 177, EAT.
Notcutt v Universal Equipment Co (London) Ltd [1986] 3 All ER 582, [1986] 1 WLR 641, CA.
Paal Wilson & Co A/S v Partenreederei Hannah Blumenthal, The Hannah Blumenthal [1983] 1
b   All ER 34, [1983] 1 AC 854, [1982] 3 WLR 1149, HL.
Paradine v Jane (1647) Aleyn 26, [1558–1774] All ER Rep 172, 82 ER 897.
Pioneer Shipping Ltd v BTP Tioxide Ltd, The Nema [1981] 2 All ER 1030, [1982] AC 724,
     [1981] 3 WLR 292, HL.
O'Kelly v Trusthouse Forte plc [1983] 3 All ER 456, [1984] QB 90, [1983] 3 WLR 605, CA.
Robinson v Davison (1871) LR 6 Exch 269, [1861–73] All ER Rep 699.
c *Taylor v Caldwell* (1863) 3 B & S 826, [1861–73] All ER Rep 24, 122 ER 309.
Universal Cargo Carriers Corp v Citati [1957] 2 All ER 70, [1957] 2 QB 401, [1957] 2 WLR
     713; affd [1957] 3 All ER 234, [1957] 1 WLR 979, CA.
Wiseman v Salford City Council [1981] IRLR 202, EAT.

Cases also cited
d *Edwards (Inspector of Taxes) v Bairstow* [1955] 3 All ER 48, [1956] AC 14, HL.
Egg Stores (Stamford Hill) Ltd v Leibovici [1977] ICR 260, EAT.
Gunton v Richmond upon Thames London Borough [1980] 3 All ER 577, [1981] Ch 448, CA.
Hanks v Ace High Productions Ltd [1978] ICR 1155, EAT.
Hollier v Plysu Ltd [1983] IRLR 260, CA.
Jowett v Earl of Bradford [1977] 2 All ER 33, EAT.
e *Kodros Shipping Corp v Emp Cubana de Fletes, The Evra* [1982] 3 All ER 350, [1983] 1 AC
     736, HL.
Kumchyk v Derby City Council [1978] ICR 1116, EAT.
Lamont v Fry's Metals Ltd [1985] ICR 566, CA.
Marshall v Harland & Wolff Ltd [1972] 2 All ER 715, NIRC.
National Carriers Ltd v Panalpina (Northern) Ltd [1981] 1 All ER 161, [1981] AC 675, HL.
f *Nikitas v Solihull Metropolitan BC* (17 February 1982, unreported), EAT.
Southern Foundries (1926) Ltd and Federated Foundries Ltd v Shirlaw [1940] 2 All ER 445,
     [1940] AC 701, HL.
Tarnesby v Kensington and Chelsea and Westminster Area Health Authority (Teaching) [1981]
     ICR 615, HL.
Trimble v Supertravel Ltd [1982] ICR 440, EAT.
g *Union of Construction Allied Trades and Technicians v Brain* [1981] ICR 542, CA.
Varndell v Kearney & Trecker Marwin Ltd [1983] ICR 683, CA.

Appeal
F C Shepherd & Co Ltd (the employers) appealed against the decision of the Employment
Appeal Tribunal (Waite J, Mr A C Blyghton and Mr G A Peers) ([1985] ICR 552) on 26
h April 1985 dismissing an appeal against the decision of an industrial tribunal (chairman
Mr N F Stogdon) sitting at London (Central) on 2 August 1983 awarding the applicant,
Mark Terrence Jerrom (the apprentice), the sum of £7,000 for unfair dismissal. The facts
are set out in the judgment of Lawton LJ.

Elizabeth Slade for the employers.
j *Peter Clark* for the apprentice.

                                                                    Cur adv vult

21 July. The following judgments were delivered.

LAWTON LJ. This is an appeal by employers, F C Shepherd & Co Ltd, against the
affirmation by the Employment Appeal Tribunal (Waite J, Mr A C Blyghton and Mr G A

Peers) ([1985] ICR 552) of a decision of an industrial tribunal whereby they had adjudged
that an apprentice, Mark Terence Jerrom, had been unfairly dismissed because the *a*
employers would not take him back as an apprentice after his release from sentences of
borstal training passed on him for conspiracy to assault and affray. To compensate him
for this refusal, the industrial tribunal has awarded him the maximum amount for a
compensatory award, namely £7,000. The Employment Appeal Tribunal also affirmed
this award. Many members of the public may think, learning what has happened, that
the works of justice are wonderful to behold. Seldom can an appeal from an industrial *b*
tribunal have raised more difficult points of law.

The employers are builders trading from premises in Lambeth. They employ between
50 and 60 men. On 10 September 1979 the employers, who are members of the National
Federation of Building Trades Employers, took on Mark Jerrom as an apprentice. On 20
June 1980 both the employers and apprentice entered into a training service agreement,
whereby the apprentice undertook to serve a full term as the employers' apprentice. This *c*
would have been for four years. The apprentice's father was a party to the agreement, as
was the Joint Industry Board for Plumbing Mechanical Engineering Services in England
and Wales (the joint industry board). Incorporated in the agreement were the joint
industry board's regulations relating to apprentices.

Some time between June 1980 and 25 June 1981 the apprentice conspired with other
members of the social group to which he belonged to have a 'punch-up' with a rival *d*
group. Later, pursuant to that conspiracy, he took part in an affray. In the course of it a
youth was killed. The apprentice was indicted for manslaughter, conspiracy to assault
and affray. On 25 June 1981 he was acquitted of manslaughter but convicted of the other
two offences. He was sentenced to borstal training, that is to say to an indeterminate
period involving the loss of liberty for not less than six months nor more than two years.
At the date when sentenced, the probability was that he would serve 39 weeks, less if his *e*
behaviour in custody was excellent (as it was) or more if it was not.

In September 1981 the apprentice's father asked a probation officer to find out whether
the employers would allow the apprentice to continue his training when he was released
from borstal. The employers said they would not. This answer was communicated to the
father by the probation officer by letter dated 16 September 1981. By letter dated 17
September 1981 the employers told the joint industry board that the apprentice had been *f*
sentenced to borstal training and that they would like to terminate the apprentice's
training agreement and asked them to make 'the necessary arrangements'. The industrial
tribunal made no specific finding with regard to the effect of the employer's conversation
with the probation officer on 16 September or of their letter dated 17 September; but on
the facts the Employment Appeal Tribunal adjudged that in September 1981 the
employers 'had not yet made their attitude towards [the apprentice's] return sufficiently *g*
clear and unequivocal to constitute an implied acceptance of the contract's repudiation
. . .' (see [1985] ICR 552 at 563–564). In my opinion this was a surprising finding but the
terms of the letter provided some evidence for it.

On 6 January 1982 the apprentice was released from borstal. Soon afterwards he asked
the employers by letter and telephone to allow him to continue his training as an
apprentice. They refused to do so. On 26 March 1982 he applied to the secretary of *h*
tribunals for a decision whether he had been unfairly dismissed. On the standard form
of application he stated that his employment had ended on 25 June 1981 and that 'at a
later date' (which had been 16 September 1981) his employers had informed his probation
officer that his services had been terminated. The employers gave a notice of appearance
dated 6 April 1982. In it they stated that the apprentice had been dismissed for
'repudiatory conduct'. They gave particulars of the 'repudiatory conduct' in these terms: *j*
'We considered the impossibility of performance arising from the [apprentice's] absence
from work . . . to be repudiatory conduct.' When sending this notice of appearance to
the secretary of tribunals, the employers' national federation asked that there should be a
preliminary hearing to decide whether the industrial tribunal had jurisdiction to hear
the apprentice's application, which they alleged was out of time, as it clearly was if 'the

dismissal' which the notice of appearance referred to had occurred at any time before 26
a December 1981. By notice dated 21 April 1982 the regional office told both the
employers and the apprentice that on 7 May 1982 there would be a hearing limited to
consideration of a preliminary issue, viz:

> 'Whether, having regard to the time limit contained in section 67(2) of the
> Employment Protection (Consolidation) Act 1978, a tribunal has jurisdiction to
> consider the [apprentice's] complaint of unfair dismissal'.

b
The hearing of the preliminary issue was in fact held on 18 June 1982. The apprentice
attended, represented by his father. The employers were represented by an officer of the
National Federation of Building Trades Employers who was qualified as a solicitor. No
oral evidence was given. The employers' representative put in evidence a bundle of
correspondence and the joint industry board's rules. The industrial tribunal, of their own
c motion, suggested 'that it is not usually possible to dismiss an apprentice unless there is
first an investigation and consent by the board for the trade under the terms of the
apprenticeship deed'. The chairman asked to see the training service agreement. The
employers produced it. Their representative, sensing that the industrial tribunal might
be thinking that the sentence of borstal training had not brought the apprenticeship to
an end, submitted that there had not been a dismissal. If the apprentice had not been
d dismissed he had no claim against his employers. It seems, from the chairman's note
made long afterwards, that the industrial tribunal were of the opinion that they 'should
adjourn sine die while the parties returned to the board to prevent injustice on a
technicality'.
The first question to be decided in this appeal is whether the industrial tribunal did
adjourn the hearing of the preliminary issue. Counsel for the apprentice submitted that
e they did; counsel for the employers submitted that they purported to adjourn after
having made a finding that the apprentice had never been dismissed. That two
experienced members of the Bar should each be able to put forward these divergent
submissions arises from the inept way in which the chairman recorded the industrial
tribunal's decision. Under the heading 'Decision' came these words:

> 'The unanimous decision of the tribunal is that the [apprentice] has never been
> *f* dismissed and is still employed as an apprentice under the terms of his apprenticeship
> agreement with the [employers] dated 20 June 1980. These proceedings are
> adjourned sine die for the reasons appearing below.'

Under the heading 'Reasons', the chairman wrote that the agreement had not been
ended and that there had been no dismissal. Nevertheless I am satisfied, when this
g document is read as a whole, and in the light of what had happened on 18 June 1982,
that the industrial tribunal did not intend to give a final decision on the preliminary
issue.
On 7 July 1982 the local conciliation panel of the joint industry board met to consider
whether to accede to the employer's request that the apprentice's training service should
be terminated. The apprentice was present, as were representatives of the employers.
h The panel decided that the termination of the agreement should be refused on the
ground that the offences of which the apprentice had been convicted had no relevance to
the performance of his work as a plumber's apprentice.
This decision was unacceptable to the employers. They consulted their solicitors, who,
by letter dated 4 February 1983, wrote to the Central Office of Tribunals recounting
what had happened and recording that at the hearing on 18 June 1982 it had not been
j argued either that the training service agreement had been frustrated or alternatively
that the apprentice had repudiated it by committing the offences of which he was
convicted. They ended their letter by asking for the industrial tribunal to reconvene,
since the original hearing had been adjourned sine die, or to agree to review such decision
as they had made. The assistant secretary decided that the parties should return to the
industrial tribunal for a full hearing. When the industrial tribunal did reconvene on 17

June 1983 they purported to hear the apprentice's claim in full. If, as I adjudge, the first hearing had been adjourned there was no decision to be reviewed: see the definition of 'decision' in reg 2 of the Industrial Tribunals (Rules of Procedure) Regulations 1980, SI 1980/884, and para 10 of Sch 1 thereto. The apprentice was once again represented by his father; the employers were represented by their solicitor.

The employers submitted that they had not dismissed the apprentice because the training service agreement had been frustrated by his convictions and custodial sentence, alternatively that by his conduct resulting in his convictions and sentence he had repudiated the training service agreement and that they had accepted the repudiation.

The apprentice's case, probably put for him by the chairman, was that the employers never had any right to dismiss him because only the joint industry board could terminate his contract and that by refusing to take him back into their employment in January 1982 they had repudiated the agreement themselves and that he had impliedly accepted that repudiation by starting proceedings for unfair dismissal on 26 March 1982.

The industrial tribunal decided that the training service agreement had not been frustrated, that the employers had repudiated it by refusing to take the apprentice back into their employment and that the apprentice had accepted that repudiation. The consequence was that there had been unfair dismissal.

Their written reasons for their decision were not as lucid as they could have been. What seems clear, however, is that the rules of the joint industry board relating to apprentices dominated their thinking. Counsel for the apprentice submitted that these rules did govern the case.

The rules relating to apprentices come under a heading 'Training' and are part of a large body of rules setting out national working rules for those engaged in the plumbing and allied trades. The heading shows that the rules were concerned, inter alia, with what a youth did as an apprentice. Rule 26 deals with the suspension and dismissal for misconduct. A distinction is drawn between 'misconduct', which may attract suspension, and 'serious misconduct' which may lead to the termination of a training service agreement by the joint industry board. The employer has to apply for termination and the application has to be supported 'by a full report on the apprentice's conduct' and submitted within 48 hours to the regional secretary. Immediately on receipt of the application form from the employers he must seek an explanation in writing from the apprentice and his guardian in response to the accusations. In my judgment the 'serious misconduct' which is within the contemplation of the rules is that which occurs in the course of the apprentice's work and training as such. It cannot have been intended that a training service agreement continued until termination by the joint industry board if the apprentice had been sentenced to life imprisonment or to a term which was longer than the unexpired period of his apprenticeship. Further, the requirement for the employer to submit a report on the apprentice's conduct is inappropriate when such conduct has nothing to do with his employment and which may have occured, and probably did, in circumstances about which the employer knew nothing. I am satisfied that the industrial tribunal misdirected themselves in deciding that the rules had any application to the facts of this case. The Employment Appeal Tribunal were of the same opinion as the industrial tribunal, stating ([1985] ICR 552 at 563) that termination was—

'a matter to be determined by the board under the termination procedure . . . When parties have stipulated their own procedure to govern complaints of absence (however caused) on the part of the employee, they must be taken as having intended to exclude (to that extent) any principle of common law under which absence falls to be treated as a repudiation of the work contract'.

Both tribunals for this reason adjudged that the apprenticeship contract had not been frustrated.

Since both tribunals decided as they did for reasons which I consider to be wrong, it is for this court to decide what were the consequences in law of the events which happened. The first question is whether what happened was capable in law of frustrating the

a

b

c

d

e

f

g

h

j

contract. The second is whether it did frustrate it; this is a question of fact (see *Pioneer Shipping Ltd v BTP Tioxide Ltd, The Nema* [1981] 2 All ER 1030 at 1047, [1982] AC 724 at 752 per Lord Roskill). Had the two tribunals considered the undisputed facts in the right way this court would only have been able to differ from them if they had reached conclusions which were clearly unreasonable. As they approached the undisputed facts in the wrong way, in my judgment, this court is entitled to decide what inference should be drawn from the facts without remitting the case to an industrial tribunal to find them: see the Employment Protection (Consolidation) Act 1978, Sch 11, para 21 and RSC Ord 59, r 10(3).

As to the first of these questions, there was an event, namely the sentence of borstal training, which was not foreseen or provided for by the parties at the time of contracting. It was a question of fact, to which I shall return later, whether it rendered the performance of the contract radically different from what the parties had contemplated when they entered into it. What has to be decided is whether the outside event and its consequences in relation to the performance of the contract occurred without either the fault or default of either party to it. I have based this dissection of the problem on the speech of Lord Brandon in *Paal Wilson & Co A/S v Partenreederei Hannah Blumenthal, The Hannah Blumenthal* [1983] 1 All ER 34 at 44, [1983] 1 AC 854 at 909.

There was no fault or default on the part of the employers. They were alleging that because of the unforeseen outside event the contract had been frustrated. If it had been, there had been no dismissal as defined in s 55 of the 1978 Act. The oddity of this case is that the apprentice, for his own purposes, is seeking to allege that he was in default so as to keep in being a contract which the employers would otherwise have been able to say had been terminated by operation of law. Through his counsel he has submitted, relying on *Universal Cargo Carriers Corp v Citati* [1957] 2 All ER 70, [1957] 2 QB 401, that his conduct, resulting as it did in a sentence of borstal training, amounted to a repudiation of the contract which the employers did not accept until January 1982. It seems to me that the apprentice is seeking to rely on his own default, if in law it should be regarded as such, to establish his right to claim for unfair dismissal.

This is the opposite of what happened in two of the leading cases dealing with the consequences of default in relation to the frustration of contracts, namely *Maritime National Fish Ltd v Ocean Trawlers Ltd* [1935] AC 524, [1935] All ER Rep 86 and *Mertens v Home Freeholds Co* [1921] 2 KB 526, [1921] All ER Rep 372. In each of these cases the plaintiff had sought to enforce the contract and the defendants had pleaded frustration because of change of circumstances. It was adjudged in both cases that these pleas failed because the defendants' own acts had caused or contributed to what had made performance impossible. The frustration which the two defendants had sought to rely on were self-induced and in consequence in law there had been no frustrations. In the *Maritime National Fish Ltd* case the act had been an election; in the *Mertens* case, reprehensible conduct which could fairly be described as a default. As Lord Brandon commented in the *Paal Wilson & Co* case [1983] 1 All ER 34 at 44, [1983] 1 AC 854 at 909: '... the courts have never defined with precision the meaning of the expression "default" in this context.' This case does call for this court to decide whether the apprentice's conduct resulting in a sentence of borstal training was a default which prevented the contract from being frustrated.

The classic formulation of the concept of 'self-induced frustration' is to be found in the speech of Lord Summer in *Bank Line Ltd v Arthur Capel & Co* [1919] AC 435 at 452 when he said:

> 'I think it is now well settled that the principle of frustration of an adventure assumes that the frustration arises without blame or fault on either side. Reliance cannot be placed on a self-induced frustration; indeed, such conduct might give the other party the option to treat the contract as repudiated.'

In *Joseph Constantine Steamship Line Ltd v Imperial Smelting Corp Ltd, The Kingswood* [1941] 2 All ER 165, [1942] AC 154 the House of Lords had to adjudge whether in a claim by

charterers against shipowners for damages for failure to load a cargo when the shipowners
pleaded that the contract had been frustrated by an explosion, for which no cause was
ascertained, they had to prove that it had not been caused by their act or default. Their
Lordships adjudged that they did not have to do so. At the end of his speech 'For purposes
of clearness, and to avoid possible misunderstanding hereafter' Viscount Simon LC said
([1941] 2 All ER 165 at 173, [1942] AC 154 at 166):

> '. . . I do not think that the ambit of "default" as an element disabling the plea of
> frustration to prevail has as yet been precisely and finally determined. "Self-induced"
> frustration, as illustrated by the two decided cases already quoted [that is the
> *Maritime National Fish Ltd* and *Mertens* cases], involves deliberate choice, and those
> cases amount to saying that a man cannot ask to be excused by reason of frustration
> if he has purposely so acted as to bring it about. "Default" is a much wider term,
> and in many commercial cases dealing with frustration is treated as equivalent to
> negligence. Yet in cases of frustration of another class, arising in connection with a
> contract for personal performance, it has not, I think, been laid down that, if the
> personal incapacity is due to want or care, the plea fails. Some day it may have to be
> finally determined whether a *prima donna* is excused by complete loss of voice from
> an executory contract to sing if it is proved that her condition was caused by her
> carelessness in not changing her wet clothes after being out in the rain. The implied
> term in such a case may turn out to be that the fact of supervening physical
> incapacity dissolves the contract without inquiring further into its cause, provided,
> of course, that it has not been deliberately induced in order to get out of the
> engagement.'

The apprentice's criminal conduct was deliberate but it did not by itself have any
consequences on the performance of his contract. What affected performance was his
sentence of borstal training, which was the act of the judge and which he would have
avoided if he could have done so. It cannot be said, I think, that the concept of 'self-
induced frustration' can be applied to this case. What can be said, however, is that when
the apprentice acted in the criminal way he did he was recklessly putting at risk his
ability to perform his contract. He should have appreciated that if he joined in an affray
he might lose his liberty. I doubt, however, whether as a matter of contract he had
impliedly agreed with his employers that outside working hours he would never behave
in a way which might interrupt for a substantial period his ability to go to work.

Lord Wright, in the same case, after having referred to some of the undecided aspects
of the law relating to frustration, said ([1941] 2 All ER 165 at 190, [1942] AC 154 at 192):

> 'The appeal can, I think, be decided according to the generally accepted view that
> frustration involves as one of its elements absence of fault, by applying the ordinary
> rules as to onus of proof. If frustration is viewed, as I think it can be, as analogous to
> an exception, since it is generally relied upon as a defence to a claim for failure to
> perform a contract, the same rule will properly be applied to it as to the ordinary
> type of exceptions. The defence may be rebutted by proof of fault, but the onus of
> proving fault will rest on the plaintiff. This is merely to apply the familiar rule
> which is applied, for instance, where a carrier by sea relies on the exception of perils
> of the seas. If the goods owner then desires to rebut that prima facie defence on the
> ground of negligence or other fault on the part of the shipowner, it rests on the
> goods owner to establish the negligence or fault.'

This line of reasoning was discussed by Lord Porter (see [1941] 2 All ER 165 at 196–197,
[1942] AC 154 at 200–202). He queried whether an accidental injury to a contractor
preventing performance would be regarded as caused by his default.

In the absence of any binding, or even persuasive, authority dealing with this problem
I approach it in this way. The employers wanted to establish that the contract had been
frustrated. They had to prove that there had been some outside event which rendered
performance of the contract radically different from what the parties had contemplated

when they made it. They proved an outside event which had occurred because of the

a sentence which the judge had imposed. They claimed that performance would have
been radically different. The apprentice did not suggest that they had been at fault. In
my judgment the apprentice should not be allowed to plead his own 'default' in order to
establish his right to claim compensation for unfair dismissal.

In my judgment the principle of law is that he who asserts that the performance of a
contract had been frustrated must prove not only the two essential elements to which

b Lord Brandon referred but that the outside event or extraneous change of situation was
not caused by any default on his part. If the party against whom frustration is asserted
can by way of answer rely on his own misconduct, injustice results, as is shown by the
following example which was discussed in argument. A butler is convicted of stealing
his employer's silver and is sentenced to two years' imprisonment. If this is no more than
repudiatory conduct on his part and his employer does not tell him either expressly or

c by implication (see *London Transport Executive v Clarke* [1981] ICR 355) that he has been
dismissed, he could claim on release from prison that he was still employed as a butler.
Such a contention would surprise the employer, but perhaps not his solicitors.

The only decision of this court which deals with the effect of a custodial sentence on a
contract of employment, *Hare v Murphy Bros Ltd* [1974] 3 All ER 940, was decided before
the decision of this court in *London Transport Executive v Clarke*. In *Hare's* case [1973] ICR

d 331 the National Industrial Relations Court had adjudged that the employee's criminal
conduct which had resulted in his being sentenced to 12 months' imprisonment
amounted to a breach of his contract of employment of so serious a nature that it
constituted a unilateral repudiation of that contract at the date when he was convicted
and sentenced. That made it impossible for him to claim unfair dismissal because at that
date the Industrial Relations Act 1971 was not in force. The National Industrial Relations

e Court has said that the sentence was not an event frustrating the contract of employment
because it had been brought about by the employee's own conduct. In this court the
employee submitted that the contract had not been determined until his repudiatory
conduct by being sent to prison had been accepted by his employers, which, he submitted,
was within time for the purpose of claiming that he had been unfairly dismissed. Lord
Denning MR, who delivered the leading judgment, said that he could not accept that by

f becoming involved in a brawl the employee had been in breach of contract. He thought
that the sentence of imprisonment was a frustrating event which brought his contract of
employment to an end. Stephenson LJ thought that the contract had been brought to an
end in one of four ways, but he did not find it necessary to say which was the appropriate
label to apply. I was a member of the court. I agreed that the appeal should be dismissed
on what I called the 'common sense of the situation', which was not an example of sound

g legal reasoning. Since it is not clear on what grounds the court as such decided *Hare's* case
I do not regard it as a binding authority. In my opinion this court can reconsider the
problem of the effect of a custodial sentence on a contract of employment. In my
judgment such a sentence is capable in law of frustrating the contract.

The next question is whether on the facts of this case the sentence of borstal training
did frustrate the contract. In my judgment it did. The parties must have contemplated

h that four years' training was necessary for producing a qualified plumber. The passing of
the sentence meant that there was going to be a substantial break in the period of
training, probably 39 weeks, possibly six months but also possibly more than 39 weeks.
At the end of the contract period the apprentice was not going to be as well trained as the
parties had contemplated he would be.

Much time was spent in this court discussing whether the apprentice's conduct,

j resulting as it did in his being sentenced to borstal training, was repudiatory of the
contract. He broke no term of it. His conduct can only be said to be repudiatory on the
grounds set out by Devlin J in *Universal Cargo Carriers Corp v Citati* [1957] 2 All ER 70 at
84, [1957] 2 QB 401 at 436. Even if that case states the law relating to commercial
contracts correctly (and I make no comment on that) I doubt whether the principle it
establishes applies to contracts of personal service. The apprentice's criminal conduct

itself would have had no effect on his performance of it had he not been arrested, convicted and sentenced. The sentence was a consequence of the disorderly conduct; *a* probably a foreseeable one; but not an inevitable one. As I would decide this appeal on the frustration point I do not find it necessarry to say more about repudiation.

If, however, I am wrong about frustration and it should be adjudged that the employers had not accepted the apprentice's repudiatory conduct before 26 December 1981, I am of the opinion that the award of £7,000 compensation cannot be supported. Section 74(6) of the 1978 Act provides as follows: *b*

'Where the tribunal finds that the dismissal was to any extent caused or contributed to by any action of the complainant it shall reduce the amount of the compensatory award by such proportion as it considers just and equitable having regard to that finding.'

In my judgment no reasonable industrial tribunal would have found as this tribunal *c* did that there was 'no contributory fault affecting the constructive dismissal'. Accepting, as I must because there has been no appeal on the issue, that the dismissal was unreasonable, it would never have happened had not the apprentice behaved in the criminal way he did. I would reduce the award by 75%.

I would allow the appeal.

d

MUSTILL LJ. The problem in this case arises from the coexistence in employment law of two barely consistent regimes: the general principles of contract developed by the common law and the superimposed system created by the statutory law of unfair dismissal. The result has been that the parties have advanced in argument propositions founded on the common law from standpoints diametrically opposed to those which would have been taken up if this had been an action for wrongful dismissal in the county *e* court. The apprentice asserts that he himself repudiated the contract, a proposition which of course he would never ordinarily advance. Instead of gratefully acknowledging this candour as a concession that they could not possibly be liable for refusing to take him back, the employers allege that the contract was frustrated, and when he claims that it was not, because by his criminal conduct and the resulting sentence he had brought his inability on himself, they respond that his conduct did not have a sufficiently close *f* connection with the contract to bring into play the concept of self-induced frustration.

The fact that this case reflects a mirror image of the ordinary position makes it essential to recognise that 'frustration' and 'repudiation' are not events which happen to a contract in the abstract. Rather, these terms denote, respectively, circumstances which discharge a promisor from future performance of his contract and hence give him a defence to any proceedings brought to enforce his obligations and circumstances which entitle a *g* promisee both to treat himself as discharged from the performance of his own counter-promise and to recover damages from the promisor for loss of the bargain. I believe that many of the difficulties in the present case stem from the fact that the parties have called up these doctrines without addressing the question who was the promisor and who the promisee in regard to the particular obligation relied on, and without reference to the purpose which the pleas of frustration and repudiation are intended to serve. *h*

It is convenient to look briefly at the history of these pleas. Valuable accounts can be found in the judgment of Diplock LJ in *Hong Kong Fir Shipping Co Ltd v Kawasaki Kisen Kaisha Ltd* [1962] 1 All ER 474 at 485–488, [1962] 2 QB 26 at 65–71, and in *Smith's Leading Cases* (2 Smith LC (13th edn, 1929) 9, 611), the notes to *Cutter v Powell* (1795) 6 Term Rep 320, [1775–1802] All ER Rep 159 and *Taylor v Caldwell* (1863) 3 B & S 826, [1861–73] All ER Rep 24. The relevant passages are too long to cite here, but I believe *j* them to be consistent with the following summary.

First, as to frustration. The starting point was the principle laid down by *Paradine v Jane* [1647] Aleyn 26, [1558–1774] All ER Rep 172 that a party who had created a duty on himself was bound to perform it or pay damages even if his non-performance was brought about by a supervening event beyond his control. By the middle of the

nineteenth century it had become firmly established that this principle was subject to
a three exceptions (amongst others): (1) where the contract was subject to an express
condition precedent which had failed; (2) where the promisee had been guilty of a failure
of performance going to the root of the consideration; and (3) where the promisee had
prevented the promisor from performing the obligation sued on. In these three instances
the promisor was not liable to the promisee for his non-performance. But the first
instance was itself subject to exception in the case where the failure of the condition
b precedent was brought about by the promisor's own act.

In *Taylor v Caldwell* the law moved a great step forward when the Court of Queen's
Bench recognised that the contract could be discharged by the failure of an implied
condition precedent, and that in appropriate circumstances a condition could be implied
to the effect that a particular person or thing should continue to exist. In due course, the
scope of the implied condition was extended to comprise the continued possibility of
c performance, so that if the promisor was prevented from performing by supervening
impossibility, he was discharged from liability.

There were thus, as pointed out in *Smith's Leading Cases* (2 Smith LC (13th edn, 1929)
612), two distinct situations in which impossibility of performance might discharge the
promisor. First, where the impossibility was created by the promisee himself; in this case
there was no need to have recourse to what is now called frustration. Second, where the
d impossibility arose from a supervening external event.

In due course, the implied condition was extended beyond cases of outright
impossibility to embrace those where the supervening event put an end, in a business
sense, to the engagement of the parties and frustrated the object of that engagement.
This expression seems first to have appeared in *Jackson v Union Marine Insurance Co Ltd*
(1874) LR 10 CP 125 at 145, [1874–80] All ER Rep 317 at 323. The case was concerned,
e not with the failure of an implied condition which prevented the promisor from
performing and hence excused him, but with a situation where there was a delay in
performance by the promisee long enough to put an end, in a commercial sense, to the
speculation entered on by the parties. The delay was due to an excepted peril, so that the
promisee could not have been liable in damages under a cross-claim by the promisor, but
the promisee's non-performance was enough to discharge the promisor from his
f obligations. Strictly speaking therefore the case was not analysed in terms of the modern
doctrine of frustration, but the practical result was the same, and the concept of
frustration of the adventure became the touchstone of the type of event which would
discharge the promisor.

More recently, the doctrine has been modified as regards both rationalisation and
terminology. The idea of the implied term that the promisor's obligation will be capable
g of performance without alterations which frustrate the adventure is no longer in favour.
Since *Davis Contractors Ltd v Fareham UDC* [1956] 2 All ER 145, [1956] AC 696 the
procedure has been to construe the contract and then see whether if the contract is
enforced in its literal sense the performance in the changed circumstances will involve a
radically different thing from that which was contemplated by the contract, so construed.
Nevertheless, the doctrine of frustration retains its original shape. It operates to discharge
h the promisor from further performance, and furnishes him with a defence if he is sued.
True it is that a contract involves obligations on both sides. Each party is promisor in
respect of his own set of obligations. If the frustrating event occurs without fault, each
party is discharged from his own obligations, neither can be sued for non-performance,
and the contract becomes empty of content. Thus, it is convenient to say that the 'contract
is frustrated' on the occurrence of the relevant event. Strictly, however, it is the adventure
j which is frustrated, not the contract: see per Lord Wright in *Joseph Constantine Steamship
Line Ltd v Imperial Smelting Corp Ltd, The Kingswood* [1941] 2 All ER 165 at 184, [1942] AC
154 at 182. The effect of the frustration is to discharge one promisor, or the other, or
both, depending on the existence and location of any fault giving rise to the event.

I now turn to repudiation. Whereas frustration is a plea which is called in aid by the
promisor, repudiation may be relied on by the promisor or by the promisee. Originally,

the plea operated by way of defence and was available in two different situations: (1) where the promisee had by his words or conduct evinced an intention no longer to perform his contract (ie where he had renounced it), and (2) where the promisee had disabled himself from performing his own obligations. (I am not here dealing with the case of a breach of condition or other actual breach going to the root of the contract.) In these situations, the promisor is entitled to choose between continuing performance of the contract or electing to treat the repudiation as a discharge of any further obligation on his one part, and a defence to any claim for non-performance.

A repudiation may however also be the basis of a claim by a promisee. If the promisor renounces the contract, or disables himself from performing it, the promisee may elect to treat the contract as broken by anticipation, and may sue for damages without waiting for the time for performance to arrive: see *Hochster v De la Tour* (1853) 2 E & B 678, [1843–60] All ER Rep 12 and many subsequent cases.

Finally, in *Universal Cargo Carriers Corp v Citati* [1957] 2 All ER 70, [1957] 2 QB 401 two further steps were taken. The first was to recognise that the test for the kind of breach, either actual or anticipatory, which constitutes a repudiation is the same as in relation to frustration (now see the *Hong Kong Fir* case). Second, that a party is taken to have repudiated his obligations if he is unable to perform them. The first proposition is now established law. The second is more debatable. I return to it briefly later.

In the light of these commonplace statements of principle we may consider what the case would look like if, for instance, an action for wrongful dismissal were to be brought at common law. The action would take place against the background of mutual dependent obligations: the employee was obliged to provide good and faithful service, the employer to give him the opportunity to provide such service and to improve his skills by serving his time. The employee (qua promisee) would plead that he had tendered himself, on release from custody, ready, willing and able to perform his part of the bargain, and would allege that the employer (qua promisor) had repudiated the contract by refusing him the chance to perform, thus rendering himself liable in damages. The employer might say that the employee (qua promisor) had by his conduct disabled himself from performing to an extent which frustrated the venture, or (on the *Citati* basis) that he was to that extent simply unable to perform, and that the employer had elected to treat this as a wrongful repudiation. But equally the employer might decide that since he was not claiming damages from the employee there was no point in alleging repudiation, with the need to prove that the repudiation was accepted, and would simply fall back on frustration. Or he might plead both. In response the employee would deny that the duration and circumstances of his absence from work were sufficient to make the absence a frustrating event. He would obviously not go on to allege that his absence was his own fault.

The introduction of the statutory remedies for unfair dismissal quite transforms the position, because it now makes all the difference whether the case is one of repudiation or frustration. If the Employment Protection (Consolidation) Act 1978 had been expressed in rather different terms, the present difficulties might have been avoided by giving 'dismissal' a loose meaning, wide enough to comprise every case in which the employer refuses, on the ground of an interruption in the employee's service, to take him back when the interruption is over. The distinction between frustration and repudiation might still be relevant to liability, but would not affect the jurisdiction of the industrial tribunal. It is, however, quite clear from the words 'but only if' in s 55(2) of the 1978 Act that the list contained in that subsection is an exhaustive statement of the circumstances amounting to dismissal; and it is accepted by both sides on this appeal that a discharge of the employer's obligations by frustration, followed by a refusal on his part to take the employee back, cannot be by any stretch regarded as a dismissal.

Furthermore, the statutory concepts of 'dismissal' and 'unfairness' interact in a way which have no counterpart in the common law. An acknowledgment, or even assertion, of serious fault on the part of the employee is not so fatal, and hence not so tactically inconceivable, as it would be if the claim were pursued in court.

The statute, and its associated time-barring provisions, thus forces the parties to take
a an unnatural stance. If the employer wished to deny the jurisdiction of the tribunal, he
would have to be careful to justify his refusal to take back the employee on the ground
of frustration, and not to add repudiation as a natural second string. On the other side,
the employee is driven to say that the effect of his own conduct is to exclude the
possibility of frustration, and to assert that although he had himself repudiated the
contract it remained in being until (absent a timely acceptance of repudiation by the
b employer) he was again ready to resume the performance of his obligations.

Finding itself in what, from the common law standpoint, is a looking-glass world, the
court must answer two questions. First, can a promisor be permitted to improve his
position by asserting that an event which would otherwise bring about a mutual
discharge by frustration was caused by his own fault, keeping open the obligations to
perform not only of himself but also of the promisee? Second, can a promisor be
c permitted to improve his position by asserting that he has himself repudiated the
contract? It is convenient to take the second question first. No authority has been cited
to us which provides an answer, and further researches have disclosed none. This is not
surprising. In a conventional legal context the question is simply nonsense, and arises
here only because of the jurisdictional paradox created by s 55(2) of the 1978 Act. The
question must therefore be approached at large. For my part, I cannot see how the answer
d could be anything other than No. On the facts of the present case, if the man in the street
were to be asked whether, for the purposes of claiming compensation from his employers,
the apprentice should be better off because his actual and prospective absence from work
was caused by his having committed a criminal act and being punished for it, than if it
was due to an event not of his own making, he would not pause long to reply. In my
judgment he would be right, for such a result would be an affront to common sense, an
e infringement of what Diplock LJ described in the *Hong Kong Fir* case [1962] 1 All ER 474
at 485, [1962] 2 QB 26 at 66 as 'the fundamental legal and moral rule that a man should
not be allowed to take advantage of his own wrong'.

In my opinion the first question calls for the same answer, because in reality the two
questions are the same. It is long-established law that—

f   'Where a party has incapacitated himself from performing his side of the contract,
       the same consequence follows as if he had absolutely refused to perform it . . . A
       party is deemed to have incapacitated himself from performing his side of the
       contract, not only when he deliberately puts it out of his power to perform the
       contract, but also when by his own act or default circumstances arise which render
       him unable to perform his side of the contract or some essential part therof.'

g (See 2 Smith LC (13th edn, 1929) 38–40, and the numerous authorities there cited.)

Thus, by asserting that the frustration was self-induced, the employee asserts that he
himself had repudiated it; and this is something which, in my judgment, he should not
be allowed to do.

I would therefore conclude that the apprentice should not be allowed to introduce into
the dispute the issues of repudiation and self-induced frustration. I must, however, deal
h with two questions which were much pressed in argument.

The first involves the proposition that there can be no frustration unless the event in
question happened without fault on either side, so that an assessment of the employers'
case on frustration must involve an inquiry into the blameworthy character of his
unavailability for work. Support for the proposition, although not for the use sought to
be made of it in the present case, may be found in authorities beginning with the
j judgment of Blackburn J in the foundation case of *Taylor v Caldwell* (1863) 3 B & S 826,
[1861–73] All ER Rep 24 and continuing through *Dahl v Nelson Donkin & Co* (1881) 6
App Case 38 at 53, [1881–5] All ER Rep 572 at 580, *Jackson v Union Marine Insurance Co
Ltd* (1874) LR 10 CP 125 at 144, [1874–80] All ER Rep 317 at 322, *Appleby v Myers* (1867)
LR 2 CP 651, [1861–73] All ER Rep 452 and *Bank Line Ltd v Arthur Capel & Co* [1919] AC
435 at 452 per Lord Sumner. The reference to absence of fault 'on either side' must

however be properly understood, and I do not believe it can mean that the promisor is
disentitled from alleging frustration if his promisee is at fault. There are two explanations *a*
of these words, consistent with principle.

The first is that the promisor is, indeed, entitled to treat himself as discharged if a
frustrating event is brought about by his promisee; but not by frustration, so much as
the simpler expedient of the old rule that prevention by the promisee discharges the
promisor. This was, I believe, the explanation favoured by Viscount Maugham in *Joseph
Constantine Steamship Line Ltd v Imperial Smelting Corp Ltd, The Kingswood* [1941] 2 All ER *b*
165 at 176–177, [1942] AC 154 at 171. So long as it is not taken to involve the proposition
that a promisor may not be discharged both by frustration and by an accepted repudiation,
arising out of the same circumstances, this explanation is in harmony with general
principle.

For my part, however, I would prefer the alternative explanation, which looks to each
party as promisor in respect of the counter-promises created by the contract. I believe *c*
that if the words relied on are read in the light of the judgments from which they are
culled, it can be seen that they are concerned with the position of each promisor in
relation to his own promise. He is disentitled to treat himself as discharged if the
frustrating event is self-induced; but this will not affect the position of the other party,
for whom the event is not 'self'-induced. Thus, the words of Lord Porter, in the *Joseph
Constantine* case [1941] 2 All ER 165 at 195–196, [1942] AC 154 at 199–200: *d*

> 'If the words "without fault on either side" be strictly interpreted, it would appear
> that the contract is not at an end unless neither party is in fault. If the contract is
> *prima facie* put an end to by impossibility of performance without further proof,
> and if that result is only avoided provided fault be proved in one party or the other,
> no difficulty arises. If the view were to prevail, however, that the party alleging
> frustration has to prove that neither party is in fault, he would be in considerable *e*
> difficulty. Not only would he have to prove that he was not in fault himself, but he
> would have to establish also that his opponent was not in fault, and, if he were
> unable to do so, he would have failed to proved frustration. However, I do not think
> the expression should be so strictly interpreted. Even in *Taylor* v. *Caldwell* ((1863) 3
> B & S 826 at 833, 835, [1861–73] All ER Rep 24 at 27), BLACKBURN, J., speaks of the
> "perishing of the thing without the fault of the contractor," and, quoting Pothier *f*
> [*Traité des Obligations* (1806) partie 3, ch 6, art 668]: ". . . the debtor *corporis certi* is
> freed from his obligation when the thing has perished neither by his act, nor his
> neglect and before he is in default . . ." In *Robinson* v. *Davison* ((1871) LR 6 Exch 269
> at 277; cf [1861–73] All ER Rep 699 at 701) BRAMWELL, B., says: ". . . incapacity
> either of body or mind in the performer without default on his or her part is an
> excuse for non-performance." In *Howell* v. *Coupland* ((1874) LR 9 QB 462 at 465), *g*
> BLACKBURN, J., says: "Of course if the perishing were owing to any default of the
> seller, that would be quite another thing." In the same case (at 467), QUAIN and
> ARCHIBALD, JJ., speak of a cause over which the defendant has no control. Similar
> expressions can be found in the later cases, and I think that in all of them stress is
> laid, not upon the freedom from blame of both parties, but upon the fact that a
> party who has been in fault cannot rely upon frustration due to his own wrongful *h*
> act. If the meaning be that impossibility excuses performance, the change of
> expression is comprehensible enough. It signifies only that the party in default
> cannot take advantage of his own wrong. It is a personal disqualification preventing
> him from taking advantage of a frustration which has automatically occurred, not a
> condition of its occurrence.'

The second matter raised in argument was founded on the statement, so often made *j*
in the cases as to be axiomatic, that frustration operates automatically. The conclusion
invited was that a contract is either frustrated or it is not, and that its fate cannot depend
on the accident of who happens to be the plaintiff in subsequent proceedings, or, indeed,
on whether such proceedings are ever brought. I do not accept this argument, for it

overlooks two points. First, that the significance of the automatic discharge is not that
the contract has necessarily disappeared in its entirety, but that a promisor is entitled to
treat himself as discharged, without (as in the case of repudiation) giving notice of his
election to the promisee. Second, that in strict law it is the adventure, not the contract,
which is frustrated, the mutual discharge usually following from the fact that the
frustration of the adventure discharges each promisor alike. What matters, however, in
the case of self-induced frustration is that the party who is the 'self' cannot treat himself
as being discharged. Thus, the frustration of the adventure is, indeed, an objective fact,
the same for both parties, irrespective of the positions which they occupy in any
subsequent dispute. But the effect of this objective fact on the mutual obligations of the
parties is not the same for both parties. The party not in default will have an excuse for
non-performance, if sued, but the other party will not. So also in the present case. The
frustrating event, if such it was, discharged the employers, which is all that matters here.
But it would not have discharged the employee, if it has arisen through his fault.

For these reasons, therefore, I consider that the issues in the present case are whether
the apprentice's absence through imprisonment was capable of discharging the employers
from their obligation to keep him in their service; and, if so, whether on the facts of the
present case it actually did so. It is not to my mind necessary to explore the difficult
question whether the concept of self-induced frustration involves that the act or omission
leading to the frustrating event should be in the nature of an election or deliberate choice,
or whether it must have some element of blameworthiness, or whether it is sufficient if
the act or omission results from some conscious act. Nor need it be considered whether
the inducing act or omission must in some way be directed to the performance of the
contract.

Furthermore, there is no need to discuss the problem, by no means easy, whether if
this had been a case where the absence of the employee had caused the employers to
suffer damage, so that it would have been to their advantage to allege repudiation rather
than frustration, they would have been able to establish a claim. A decision on this point
would require the court to consider whether *Universal Cargo Carriers Corp v Citati* was
rightly decided, and if so how far the principle which it embodies can be taken, a
complex question on which the arguments in the present case did not embark. I would,
however, just add this. In the *Citati* case, the defendants were throughout the relevant
period doing their best to perform but were let down by the ultimate suppliers of the
goods. This might lead *Citati* to be read as deciding inferentially that every case of
anticipated inability to perform is a case of repudiation. This cannot be right, for, if it
were, the promisor would never be able to allege frustration. This branch of the law
cannot, I believe, be made to work unless repudiation of the *Citati* kind and self-induced
frustration are opposite sides of the same coin. This could be achieved by qualifying the
doctrine that anticipated inability to perform in a degree going to the root of the contract
is a repudiation with the words 'unless it is due to an excepted peril', an idea foreshadowed,
in the case of actual rather than anticipated breach, in *Jackson v Union Marine Insurance Co
Ltd* (1874) LR 10 CP 125, [1874–80] All ER Rep 317. In the *Citati* case it appears to have
been taken for granted that the procuring of goods in time to ship was an absolute
obligation. The present case is different. The obligation of the employee is not absolute,
for he could not be held in breach if his failure to present himself for work had been due
to illness, unless, perhaps, he had brought the illness on himself (a point left open in the
Joseph Constantine case). Whether the implied exception would extend to a situation
where, as here, the ultimate cause of the absence was a conscious and wrongful act, but
one which was in no sense directed towards the contract, is a difficult question which it
is unnecessary to decide, but my present inclination is to consider that it would.

Before leaving this part of the case, I should mention that, in company with Lawton
LJ, I have felt free to approach the issue of law afresh, without being constrained by
anything said in *Hare v Murphy Bros Ltd* [1974] 3 All ER 940.

I now turn to the next question, namely whether the employers' obligations under the
contract of apprenticeship were capable of being discharged by frustration, on the

happening of an event disabling the apprentice for a long period from attending at work. Notwithstanding the observations of the Employment Appeal Tribunal in *Harman v Flexible Lamps Ltd* [1980] IRLR 418 at 419, I can see no reason in principle why it should not, and I would in this respect adopt the reasoning of Dillon LJ in *Notcutt v Universal Equipment Co (London) Ltd* [1986] 3 All ER 582, [1986] 1 WLR 641. I accept that the considerations applying to the relationship between apprentice and master are not precisely the same as those of an ordinary employment, and that the importance to the apprentice of having the opportunity to qualify by serving his time and conversely the *b* importance to both parties of the apprentice preserving continuity of attendance so as not to break the thread of his instruction require the issue of frustration to be approached in a rather special light. But this is no reason to hold that a contract of apprenticeship is incapable of being frustrated. Nor does the reason advanced by the industrial tribunal provide any answer, for the interposition of the procedure for termination under r 26.2 of the joint industry board's rules cannot mean that the obligations of the employer are incapable of being discharged by frustration. It would patently be absurd if, for example, in a case where it was plain that through some mishap the apprentice was going to be prevented from ever again attending for work, the employer had to go through the empty formality of obtaining a ruling from the officers of the regional board before he could treat his obligations as at an end. On the other hand, I accept that the presence of a termination provision should inhibit the court from being too ready to find in favour of *d* frustration.

This leads to the final question: whether on the facts the agreement was frustrated. In the ordinary way, this is a question for the fact-finding tribunal: see *Pioneer Shipping Ltd v BTP Tioxide Ltd, The Nema* [1981] 2 All ER 1030, [1982] AC 724. In the present instance, however, I consider that we are entitled to approach it afresh, notwithstanding the decision of the industrial tribunal, since it appears to have been assumed that the presence *e* of r 26.2 prevented the employer from alleging frustration. Here there was a contract for a period of four years, plus time added for illness under r 27.2. By the time the apprentice's sentence was imposed there remained rather more than half this period still to run. The sentence was indeterminate, having the various foreseeable durations which Lawton LJ has described. His training would inevitably suffer really substantial disruption, as would the timetable of the employers, who had planned to train him up *f* to replace one of their full-time plumbers who was due to retire. If this were a commercial contract, of the type from which many of the reported decisions on frustration have sprung, it would be debatable whether an interruption of this duration would be enough to frustrate the object of the adventure. But an apprenticeship is a long way from a charterparty, and I conclude that in the special circumstances of this case the likely interruption was sufficient to discharge the employers from any further obligation, from *g* the moment when the sentence of borstal training was imposed.

In conclusion I would add one comment on the question of contribution. The tribunal has found no contributory fault on the part of the apprentice. Yet the whole thrust of his argument has been that he was at fault, to a degree which placed him in repudiation of the contract and caused any frustration of the adventure to be self-induced. I do not see how he can allege fault for one purpose and deny it for another. The tribunal ought to *h* have taken this into account. I would have thought it justifiable, in the circumstances, to reopen the tribunal's decision on this point, if I had come to a contrary conclusion on the issues discussed above, and like Lawton and Balcombe LJJ would have considered that a substantial reduction in the sum awarded would have been called for.

In the result, I too would allow the appeal.

j

BALCOMBE LJ. The facts of this case are fully set out in the judgment of Lawton LJ and I need not repeat them. Nor do I wish to add anything on the procedural tangle brought about by the ineptitude of the chairman of the industrial tribunal; I am satisfied that the tribunal did not reach a final conclusion at their intital hearing on 18 June 1982 and accordingly that they were able to proceed to a full hearing on 17 June 1983.

The following questions arise on this appeal: (1) the construction of r 26 of the rules governing recruitment etc of apprentices laid down by the Joint Industry Board for Plumbing Mechanical Engineering Services in England and Wales: (2) whether a custodial sentence imposed on an employee is capable of frustrating a contract of employment; (3) if the answer to question 2 is in the affirmative, whether the apprentice's training service agreement in this case was frustrated when he was sentenced to borstal training; (4) if the answer to either question 2 or question 3 is in the negative, whether the apprentice by his conduct 'repudiated' his training service agreement; (5) if the answer to question 4 is in the affirmative, whether the employers accepted that repudication and, if so, when; (6) if the apprentice was dismissed by the employers, was his dismissal to any extent caused or contributed to by any action of the apprentice?

Of these questions, question 2 raises an issue of considerable general importance. Further, it is relevant to note that the questions all arise in the context of an application by the apprentice for compensation for unfair dismissal under Pt V of the Employment Protection (Consolidation) Act 1978, so that to found the jurisdiction of the industrial tribunal to consider his claim the apprentice must establish that he was dismissed by the employers within the meaning of s 55 of that Act. An employee whose contract of employment is brought to an end by operation of law, eg by frustration, is not dismissed. That is why we have been faced with the spectacle, apparently unusual to those used to the application of the doctrine of frustration to commercial contracts, of the apprentice seeking to establish that he was at fault, that he had therefore repudiated his contract and that when that repudiation was accepted by the employers they dismissed him; whereas the employers, the innocent parties on this way of looking at the matter, were seeking to maintain that the contract had been frustrated.

1 *The construction of r 26*

Rule 26.1 provides:

'An employer may suspend an apprentice for a maximum of two weeks without pay on each occasion for misconduct, including wilful absence without permission, at any time during the apprenticeship . . .'

Rule 26.2 provides:

'In the event of continued misconduct after suspension under Rule 26.1 and after disciplinary warnings have been given *or in the case of serious misconduct warranting dismissal* the employer may suspend the apprentice under Rule 26.1 and apply for termination of the Training Service Agreement . . .' (My emphasis.)

The rule continues with the procedure governing any such application.

In my judgment the 'serious misconduct warranting dismissal' within the meaning of r 26.2 is conduct which directly relates to the apprentice's work and training. Normally that will mean conduct which occurs during the course of the apprentice's work and training as such, although it is possible that in some types of employment conduct outside work may be relevant to the employee's fitness to perform the work for which he is employed: cf *Wiseman v Salford City Council* [1981] IRLR 202. However, the actions of the apprentice in becoming involved in an affray with members of a rival motorcycle gang cannot in my judgment be conduct which related directed to this work and training, notwithstanding the natural distaste of the employers for crimes of violence. More especially the imposition of a sentence of borstal training could not have been 'misconduct' within r 26.2: 'conduct' connotes some action on the part of the apprentice, whereas he was the passive recipient of the sentence.

So on this issue I am satisfied that both the industrial tribunal and the Employment Appeal Tribunal erred as a matter of law.

2 *Can frustration apply?*

The classic statement of the doctrine of frustration is in the speech of Lord Radcliffe in *Davis Contractors Ltd v Fareham UDC* [1956] 2 All ER 145 at 160, [1956] AC 696 at 729:

'. . . frustration occurs whenever the law recognises that, without default of either party, a contractual obligation has become incapable of being performed because the circumstances in which performance is called for would render it a thing radically different from that which was undertaken by the contract . . . it is not hardship or inconvenience or material loss itself which calls the principle of frustration into play. There must be as well such a change in the significance of the obligation that the thing undertaken would, if performed, be a different thing from that contracted for.'

A modern statement of the principle is to be found in the speech of Lord Brandon in *Paal Wilson & Co A/S v Partenreederei Hannah Blumenthal, The Hannah Blumenthal* [1983] 1 All ER 34 at 44, [1983] 1 AC 854 at 909:

'. . . there are two essential factors which must be present in order to frustrate a contract. The first essential factor is that there must be some outside or extraneous change of situation, not foreseen or provided for by the parties at the time of contracting, which either makes it impossible for the contract to be performed at all, or at least renders its performance something radically different from what the parties contemplated when they entered into it. The second essential factor is that the outside event or extraneous change of situation concerned, and the consequences of either in relation to the performance of the contract, must have occurred without either the fault or the default of either party to the contract.'

It is relevant that both these cases concerned commercial contracts.

So far as the first of Lord Brandon's factors is concerned, it is easy to see that a sentence of imprisonment, particularly if for a lengthy or indeterminate term, could render the performance of a contract of employment of the man imprisoned something radically different from what the parties contemplated when they entered into it. It is the application of the second factor which poses a problem: clearly in one sense the frustrating event, the sentence of imprisonment, is attributable to the fault or default of the man imprisoned.

In all the cases to which we were referred in which Lord Brandon's second factor was applied it was clear that the party seeking to rely on frustration had brought about the alleged 'frustrating' event, either with the intention of bringing the contract to an end or at the very least in the knowledge that it was likely to have that effect. Thus in *Mertens v Home Freehold Co* [1921] 2 KB 526, [1921] All ER Rep 372 the defendant deliberately acted in such a way as to ensure that the governmental licence, necessary for the carrying on of certain building work, should be revoked. The Court of Appeal held that he could not rely on the absence of the licence as an excuse for his failure to perform his obligations under the building contract. In *Maritime National Fish Ltd v Ocean Trawlers Ltd* [1935] AC 524, [1935] All ER Rep 86 the owners of a trawler fitted with an otter trawl, which needed a ministerial licence to leave port with such a trawl, were not entitled to rely on the absence of a licence as frustrating a charterparty of the trawler, when they had deliberately omitted the trawler from the list of three trawlers named in their application for licences, and they had been told that only three licences would be granted.

The problem of what amounts to fault or default in excluding the application of the doctrine of frustration was considered, but not decided, in the speeches in the House of Lords in *Joseph Constantine Steamship Line Ltd v Imperial Smelting Corp, The Kingswood* [1941] 2 All ER 165, [1942] AC 154. Viscount Simon LC said ([1941] 2 All ER 165 at 173, [1942] AC 154 at 166):

'I do not think that the ambit of "default" as an element disabling the plea of frustration to prevail has as yet been precisely and finally determined. "Self-induced" frustration, as illustrated by the two decided cases already quoted [that is the *Mertens* and *Maritime National Fish Ltd* cases], involves deliberate choice, and those cases amount to saying that a man cannot ask to be excused by reason of frustration if he has purposely so acted as to bring it about. "Default" is a much wider term and in

a
many commercial cases dealing with frustration is treated as equivalent to negligence. Yet in cases of frustration of another class, arising in connection with a contract for personal peformance, it has not, I think, been laid down that, if the personal incapacity is due to want of care, the plea fails. Some day it may have to be finally determined whether a *prima donna* is excused by complete loss of voice from an executory contract to sing if it is proved that her condition was caused by her carelessness in not changing wet clothes after being out in the rain.'

b
See also per Lord Russell, Lord Wright and Lord Porter ([1941] 2 All ER 165 at 182, 192–193, 196–197, [1942] AC 154 at 179, 195–196, 201–202).

The only case in the Court of Appeal in which the question has been considered is *Hare v Murphy Bros Ltd* [1974] 3 All ER 940. That is not a very satisfactory decision: one side was not represented and did not appear, so the court heard argument from one side only. Lord Denning MR held that a sentence of imprisonment did frustrate the contract of

c
employment; Stephenson LJ held that the sentence of imprisonment did terminate the employment, and it mattered not whether the termination was labelled a frustrating event, repudiatory conduct, a breach going to the root of the contract of employment or impossibility of performance. Lawton LJ did not deal with this question. In my judgment *Hare v Murphy Bros Ltd* is not a decision which binds this court to hold that a sentence of imprisonment is capable of frustrating a contract of employment. Nevertheless

d
I find the reasoning of Lord Denning MR (at 942–943) highly persuasive. There are decisions of lower courts that a sentence of imprisonment is capable of frustrating a contract of employment: see *Harrington v Kent CC* [1980] IRLR 353, *Chakki v United Yeast Co Ltd* [1982] 2 All ER 466; to the contrary effect is *Norris v Southampton City Council* [1982] ICR 177; but none of these decisions is binding on us.

In *Universal Cargo Carriers Corp v Citati* [1957] 2 All ER 70 at 84–85, [1957] 2 QB 401

e
at 436–438 Devlin J considered the law relating to anticipatory breach of contract:

'The law on the right to rescind is succinctly stated by LORD PORTER in *Heyman v. Darwins, Ltd.* ([1942] 1 All ER 337 at 359, [1942] AC 356 at 397), as follows: "The three sets of circumstances giving rise to a discharge of contract are tabulated by ANSON (*Law of Contract* (20th edn, 1952) p 319) as: (i) renunciation by a party of his

f
liabilities under it; (ii) impossibility created by his own act . . . In the case of the first two the renunciation may occur or impossibility be created either before or at the time for performance . . ." . . . the first two state the two modes of anticipatory breach . . . A renunciation can be made either by words or by conduct, provided it is clearly made. It is often put that the party renouncing must "evince an intention" not to go on with the contract. The intention can be evinced either by words or by

g
conduct. The test of whether an intention is sufficiently evinced by conduct is whether the party renouncing has acted in such a way as to lead a reasonable person to the conclusion that he does not intend to fulfil his part of the contract . . . Since a man must be both ready and willing to perform, a profession by words or conduct of inability is by itself enough to constitute renunciation. But unwillingness and inability are often difficult to disentangle, and it is rarely necessary to make the

h
attempt. Inability often lies at the root of unwillingness to perform. Willingness in this context does not mean cheerfulness; it means simply an intent to perform. To say "I would like to but I cannot" negatives intent just as much as "I will not" . . . If a man says "I cannot perform", he renounces his contract by that statement, and the cause of the inability is immaterial.'

j
Counsel for the apprentice submits that this principle enunciated by Devlin J, that impossibility of performance of a contractual obligation created by the act of a party, to the contract amounts to the renunciation (or repudiation) of the contract by that party is but the obverse of the coin, where the reverse is Lord Brandon's second factor in *Paal Wilson & Co A/S v Partenreederei Hannah Blumenthal*. Accordingly, he submits that, if we are against him on the construction of r 26, this cannot be a case of frustration: it must a case of repudiation by the apprentice.

While I can see the logical attraction of that submission, and whatever may be the rule in the case of a commercial contract, I find difficulty in applying it to the case of a *a* contract of employment and the imprisonment of the employee. What is the conduct of the employee by which he 'evinces an intention' not to go on with the contract? It cannot be the commission of the criminal offence, since in most cases it will not follow that he will necessarily suffer a sentence of imprisonment. What is the position between the commission of the offence and trial, while it remains uncertain whether the employee will be imprisoned, or will suffer some other punishment which will not necessarily *b* prevent him from fulfilling his obligations under his contract of employment? What is the position of an employee who is remanded in custody pending trial: does this 'evince an intention' not to go on with the contract? For myself, I find it impossible to give a sensible answer to these question. Further, I agree with Lord Denning MR's analysis of the position in *Hare v Murphy Bros Ltd*. In that case the National Industrial Relations Court had held that Mr Hare's sentence of imprisonment was not a frustrating event *c* because it was brought about by his own act in committing the offence for which he was sentenced to imprisonment (see [1973] ICR 331). It was, however, a breach by him of his contract of so serious a nature, bearing in mind the length of time during which he would be away from work and the importance of his position as foreman, that it went to the root and constituted a repudiation of his contract of employment. In criticising that decision Lord Denning MR said ([1974] 3 All ER 940 at 942): *d*

> 'I cannot agree with that reasoning. In the first place, I do not think that Mr Hare was guilty of any breach of contract. Take the brawl in March 1971 when Mr Hare struck a blow by which he unlawfully wounded someone or other. That was quite unconnected with his employment. It was no breach by him of his contract of employment. Take next the sentence of imprisonment for 12 months in June 1971. That, too, was not a breach by him. If he had been given a suspended sentence or *e* put on probation he would not be guilty of any breach of his contract of employment. Nor is it when he is sentenced to 12 months. That was the act of the court which sentenced him. It was no breach by him. But nevertheless—contrary to the Industrial Court—I think there was a frustrating event. The sentence of 12 month's imprisonment frustrated the contract of employment. I know that it was brought about by his own act, namely, the unlawful wounding. In that way it may *f* be said to be "self-induced"; but still it was a frustrating event.'

In my judgment that analysis is entirely consistent with the realities of the situation.

I appreciate that mine may be a simplistic approach to a difficult jurisprudential problem, but I am conscious that employment law is today largely administered by industrial tribunals, often without the benefit of legal representation of some or all of the *g* parties before them. In my view it is important that, if possible, the legal concepts relating to the existence and termination of a contract of employment should be readily comprehensible. If that approach involves a degree of inconsistency between contracts of employment and commercial contracts, then that is a price I am prepared to pay.

Accordingly, I answer question 2 above in the affirmative: a custodial sentence imposed on an employee is capable of frustrating a contract of employment. *h*

3 Does frustration apply?

Whether a particular event is capable of frustrating a contract is a matter of law. It follows from my answer to question 2 that in my judgment the sentence of borstal training imposed on the apprentice was capable of frustrating his training service *j* agreement. Whether a particular event does frustrate the contract in question is a question of fact to be decided by the tribunal to which is entrusted the task of deciding issues of fact, in this case the industrial tribunal: see *Pioneer Shipping Ltd v BTP Tioxide Ltd, The Nema* [1981] 2 All ER 1030 at 1047, [1982] AC 724 at 753. Provided the industrial tribunal applied the right legal test, an appellate court should not interfere. In this case the industrial tribunal did not apply the right legal test. The industrial tribunal's finding *a* on this question is to be found in the following passage from the reasons for the decision given on 20 June 1983:

> *b* 'We find there was no frustration. Apprentices are not to be treated in exactly the same way as ordinary employees. Some 18 months of the four years contract had been served. It was extendable expressly for such matters as illness. Further, it has machinery for ending it in the contract which has been used. We have no need to quote authorities. There are none exactly in point for apprentices. The facts relied on for frustration must be as they actually were, not what either party wrongly believed them to be. For example the [employers] say they thought borstal could be for 18 months. In effect it is very rare for more than eight months to be served and in this case it was less than that.'

c Apart from the error as to the period of his contract which the apprentice had served before being sentenced to borstal training (10 September 1979 to 28 June 1981 is 21 months, not 18 months) and apart from the somewhat didactic statement as to the usual length of a period of borstal training (the relevant point being that it was an indeterminate period) it is apparent that the industrial tribunal founded their decision on this point on their finding that the contract contained machinery for ending it which was operative in the circumstances. I have already said that was wrong as a matter of law.

d The industrial tribunal applied the wrong test and in this they were followed by the Employment Appeal Tribunal (see [1985] ICR 552 at 562–563). Accordingly, it is open to us to review its decision on this issue. We do not have to send the case back to the industrial tribunal for a fresh finding; we have power to make the necessary findings if we have sufficient material to enable is to do so: see para 21(1) of Sch 11 to the 1978 Act and RSC Ord 59, r 10(3). The relevant facts are to be found in the judgment of the *e* Employment Appeal Tribunal (at 556–557):

> *f* 'The company is a medium-sized building firm with 40 to 50 employees. They normally employ two full-time plumbers. One of them, Mr. Jury, was due to retire on reaching the age of 65 in May 1985. Good plumbers are not easy to find these days. The employers' intention when they took on the [apprentice] in September 1979 was to train him up as a successor to Mr. Jury. If everything went according to plan, his four-year apprenticeship would be due to end in 1983, and then he would have some 20 months working with Mr. Jury preparatory to taking over his job . . . The [apprentice] came up for trial on 25 June 1981—by which date his apprentice training had proceeded for one year and nine months. He was convicted and sentenced to borstal training for a period of six months to two years.'

g In my judgment, on these facts, the sentence of borstal training did frustrate the training service agreement.

Accordingly, I answer question 3 in the affirmative. That is enough to dispose of this appeal: frustration = no dismissal = no jurisdiction to hear an application for unfair dismissal; but in case this should go further, and in deference to the very full and careful arguments before us, I will attempt to answer the remaining questions.

h
4 Repudiation

Counsel for the apprentice contended that, if we were against him on the construction of r 26, then the apprentice, by his conduct in committing the offence which led to a sentence of borstal training, repudiated his training service agreement. If I were wrong in my view that the training service agreement was frustrated, then this contention must *j* be correct; it then represents the only possible alternative to frustration.

5 Acceptance of repudiation

This is a question of mixed law and fact. An appellate court should not interfere with the finding of the industrial tribunal if they reached a decision after having applied the right test. However the industrial tribunal reached no decision on this particular matter. In their reasons they say:

'The [employers] have never had the right to dismiss because it was for the Joint
Industry Board to decide if the agreement is at an end. Therefore, if they treat the *a*
[apprentice] as dismissed they repudiate the contract. It is then for the [apprentice]
to decide whether there has been such repudiation and whether he will accept it as
ending the contract.'

They then found that the apprentice accepted what they termed the employers'
repudiation by his application to the industrial tribunal. As will be apparent from what
I have already said, the error in this approach lies in the words 'because it was for the *b*
Joint Industry Board to decide if the agreement is at an end'. For the reasons given in my
answer to question 1, it was not. But because of the way in which they approached the
whole question of repudiation, the industrial tribunal never made a finding on the
question whether the employers accepted the apprentice's repudiation and, if so, when.
    The Employment Appeal Tribunal attempted to grasp this nettle. It said ([1985] ICR
552 at 563–564):   *c*

    'They [the industrial tribunal] were fully within their rights in holding (as by
    implication they must be deemed for this purpose to have held) that by their
    conduct in September 1981 the employers had not yet made their attitude towards
    the [apprentice's] return sufficiently clear and unequivocal to constitute an implied
    acceptance of the contract's repudiation, and that such acceptance was not made *d*
    plain until they barred their doors to him after his return in January 1982. The
    question whether particular words or conduct on the part of an employer did or did
    not amount to an acceptance of an antecedent repudiation of the contract by the
    employee is one of those questions which, though technically a question of law,
    contains a very sustantial element of fact.'

Then, after a reference to *O'Kelly v Trusthouse Forte plc* [1983] 3 All ER 456, [1984] QB *e*
90, it continued:

    'It was equally a question of fact and degree in the present case for the industrial
    tribunal to determine whether the employers had by conduct accepted the
    [apprentice's] repudiation of the contract. We regard it as entirely open to them to
    have found upon the evidence that acceptance of the [apprentice's] repudiation of *f*
    the contract . . . did not take place until January 1982.'

    But the industrial tribunal never did make such a finding on the evidence. In the
earlier part of the passage cited the Employment Appeal Tribunal held that by implication
they must be deemed to have made such a finding. A deemed finding by implication on
a question to which the fact-finding tribunal never addressed its mind is not a finding by
which an appellate tribunal, whether the Employment Appeal Tribunal or this court, is *g*
bound. However on this question we do not have the material necessary to make a
finding. For my part, I would have considered the employers' actions, in September
1981, in telling the apprentice's probation officer that they had decided to terminate the
apprenticeship, could be a sufficient indication that they accepted a repudiation of the
agreement by the apprentice, notwithstanding their then belief that r 26.2 applied. But
that still leaves open potentially difficult questions whether this decision was *h*
communicated to the apprentice and, if so, when, or whether the probation officer or the
apprentice's father (to whom the decision was communicated by the probation officer)
were his agents for the purpose of receiving the acceptance. Had this been a live issue I
would have thought it right to remit the case to the industrial tribunal for a finding,
since, if the employers accepted the apprentice's repudiation in September 1981, his *j*
application to the industrial tribunal in March 1982 was out of time. However, in view
of any answer to question 3, this is unnecessary.

6 *Contribution*
    Again, the finding on this question of the industrial tribunal, acting as an industrial
jury, would be unappealable as raising no question of law, had the industrial tribunal
applied the right test. Again they did not. They said:

a

'. . . we also find no contributory fault affecting the constructive dismissal which arose from the [employers'] fundamental breach in treating the [apprentice] as dismissed when they should have gone to the Joint Industry Board.'

So it would be open to an appellate court to review this question. Had the issue been material, i e on the basis that the apprentice repudiated his agreement, that his repudiation was accepted by the employers not earlier than January 1982, and that this constituted an unfair dismissal (there having been no appeal on this point), then I agree with the

b view of Lawton LJ that the award should be substantially reduced: see *Nelson v BBC (No 2)* [1980] ICR 110 at 121.

I too would allow this appeal.

Appeal allowed. Leave to appeal to the House of Lords refused.

c Solicitors: *Capstick Hamer & Co* (for the employers); *Brian Thompson & Partners* (for the apprentice).

Mary Rose Plummer   Barrister.

d

R v Steer

COURT OF APPEAL, CRIMINAL DIVISION
e NEILL LJ, PETER PAIN AND GATEHOUSE JJ
13, 15 MAY 1986

Criminal law – Damage to property – Damage to property with intent to endanger life or being reckless whether life would be endangered – Causal connection between damage and danger – Appellant firing shots at house – Persons inside house endangered by bullets but not by damaged
f *property – Whether necessary to prove danger to life resulting from damage to property – Criminal Damage Act 1971, s 1(2).*

The appellant went to the house of his business partner, with whom he had quarrelled, and fired several shots at the house. No injuries were caused to the partner or his family inside the house. The appellant was charged, inter alia, with damaging property being reckless whether the life of another would be endangered thereby, contrary to s 1(2)[a] of
g the Criminal Damage Act 1971. He was convicted and appealed, contending that s 1(2) only applied if property was damaged and the damage in turn caused danger to life whereas any danger to the appellant's partner and his family had been directly caused by the bullets fired by the appellant and not by damaged property. The Crown contended that the 'damage' which caused the danger referred to the act of damage and not the
h damaged property and that it was not necessary to prove that the damaged property itself was likely to cause danger to life.

Held – On the true construction of s 1(2) of the 1971 Act a person could only be convicted of recklessly endangering the life of another by damaging or destroying property if it was proved that the danger to life resulted from the destruction of or damage to property, since s 1(2) was directed to the possible dangers caused by the
j damaged or destroyed property and a causal link had to be shown connecting the damage to the property to the danger to life. Dangers inherent in the method of causing the destruction of or damage to property were therefore irrelevant in proving an offence under s 1(2). The appeal would therefore be allowed (see p 614 g to j and p 615 e, post).

a   Section 1(2) is set out at p 613 f, post

Notes

For the offence of destroying or damaging property, see 11 Halsbury's Laws (4th edn) *a*
para 1306, and for cases on the subject, see 15 Digest (Reissue) 1439–1440, 12690–12693.
    For the Criminal Damage Act 1971, s 1, see 12 Halsbury's Statutes (4th edn) 557.

Cases referred to in judgment

R v Caldwell [1981] 1 All ER 961, [1982] AC 341, [1981] 2 WLR 509, HL.
R v Hardie [1984] 3 All ER 848, [1985] 1 WLR 64, CA.   *b*
R v Miller [1983] 1 All ER 978, [1983] 2 AC 161, [1983] 2 WLR 539, HL.

Appeal

Dennis Steer appealed against his conviction on 15 May in the Crown Court at Lincoln
before his Honour Judge Wilcox and a jury on an indictment charging him with, inter
alia, damaging property with intent, contrary to s 1(2) of the Criminal Damage Act 1971. *c*
He was sentenced on that count to two years' imprisonment, with 16 months of the
sentence suspended. The facts are set out in the judgment of the court.

Michael Mettyear (assigned by the Registrar of Criminal Appeals) for the appellant.
Keith Jackson for the Crown.

                                                                                            d
NEILL LJ (delivering the judgment of the court). This appeal raises a question as to the
proper construction of s 1(2) of the Criminal Damage Act 1971.
    On 16 December 1985 the appellant appeared in the Crown Court at Lincoln on an
indictment containing three counts. The third count charged the appellant with
damaging a bungalow without lawful excuse contrary to s 1(1) of the 1971 Act. To this
count the appellant pleaded guilty. To the other two counts, however, the appellant *e*
pleaded not guilty. In the first count, which charged the appellant with an offence
contrary to s 16 of the Firearms Act 1968, it was alleged that on 8 June 1985 he had in
his possession an automatic rifle with intent by means thereof to endanger life. In the
second count, which was amended at the trial and which was treated by the prosecution
as an alternative count to count 1, the appellant was charged with damaging property
with intent contrary to s 1(2) of the 1971 Act, it being alleged that on 8 June without *f*
lawful excuse he damaged a bungalow belonging to David Gregory, intending to damage
such property or being reckless as to whether such property would be damaged and
being reckless whether the lives of David Gregory and Tina Gregory would thereby be
endangered.
    The trial of the appellant on these two counts took place before his Honour Judge
Wilcox and a jury. At the conclusion of the case for the prosecution, however, it was *g*
submitted on behalf of the appellant that he had no case to answer on the second count.
Following legal argument this submission was rejected by the judge, and the appellant
then changed his plea on this count to one of guilty. A formal verdict of guilty on the
second count was then returned, and on the direction of the judge a formal verdict of not
guilty was returned on the first count. Following these verdicts the appellant was then
sentenced on 18 December as follows: on count 2, the offence contrary to s 1(2) of the *h*
1971 Act, to two years' imprisonment, with 16 months of the sentence being suspended,
and on count 3, the offence contrary to s 1(1) of the 1971 Act (to which he had earlier
pleaded guilty) to eight months' imprisonment, such term to be concurrent with the
sentence on count 2. The appellant now appeals to this court on a question of law in
accordance with s 1(2)(a) of the Criminal Appeal Act 1968. An extension of time for the
appeal was granted by the single judge.   *j*
    The events which led to the trial of the appellant on these charges can be stated quite
shortly. The appellant had had a number of disagreements with his business partner, Mr
David Gregory, and by the beginning of June 1985 there was very considerable ill-feeling
between them. At some time after midnight in the early hours of 8 June the appellant
went to Mr Gregory's bungalow where Mr Gregory lived with his wife and two children.

He had with him an automatic .22 rifle. He rang the door bell. Mr and Mrs Gregory
a woke up and looked out of their bedroom window. They saw the appellant at the door.
He pointed the rifle at the bedroom window and fired at it. Mr Gregory heard the
window being smashed and went to telephone the police. He then heard two further
shots. Later, bullet holes were found in the bedroom window, in the window of the
lounge and in the front door. No injuries, however, were caused to those inside the
bungalow.

b The case for the Crown at the trial was that one or more of the bullets might have
endangered the lives of Mr and Mrs Gregory. The bullets were discharged at short range,
and, even if not directly aimed at anyone, they might have ricocheted or split in some
way so as to strike Mr Gregory or his wife. It was said that it was sufficient to show that
the appellant's acts which damaged the property also endangered life. In this context
reliance was placed on *R v Hardie* [1984] 3 All ER 848, [1985] 1 WLR 64. It was not
c suggested, however, at the trial or in this court, that the lives of Mr and Mrs Gregory
were likely to be endangered by any fragment of glass, plaster or any other part of the
bungalow or its contents which might have been damaged by the bullets.

The case for the appellant, on the other hand, was that s 1(2) of the 1971 Act is
concerned with the situation where property is damaged and that damage in turn causes
danger to life. In the present case, it was said, the danger to life was caused by the bullets
d and not by the damaged property.

In order to consider these submissions, which have been succinctly repeated before us,
it is necessary to start by setting out the provisions of s 1 of the 1971 Act, which are in
these terms:

'(1) A person who without lawful excuse destroys or damages any property
belonging to another intending to destroy or damage any such property or being
e reckless as to whether any such property would be destroyed or damaged shall be
guilty of an offence.

(2) A person who without lawful excuse destroys or damages any property,
whether belonging to himself or another—(*a*) intending to destroy or damage any
property or being reckless as to whether any property would be destroyed or
damaged; and (*b*) intending by the destruction or damage to endanger the life of
f another or being reckless as to whether the life of another would be thereby
endangered; shall be guilty of an offence.

(3) An offence committed under this section by destroying or damaging property
by fire shall be charged as arson.'

Before we attempt to deal with s 1(2) in detail it is convenient to draw attention to
g three matters. First, the title to the 1971 Act begins with these words: 'An Act to revise
the law of England and Wales as to offences of damage to property . . .' Second, in the
Act 'property' means property of a tangible nature, whether real or personal, including
money and other items, specified in s 10(1), to which it is not necessary further to refer.
Third, a person who at the time of committing an offence under s 1 of the 1971 Act has
in his possession a firearm or an imitation firearm is guilty of an offence under s 17(2) of
h the Firearms Act 1968: see para (1) of Sch 1 to the Firearms Act 1968, as substituted by
s 11(7) of the 1971 Act.

We return to s 1(2) of the 1971 Act. The submissions advanced on behalf of the Crown
were on these lines: (a) the words 'destruction' or 'damage' in the phrase 'intending by
the destruction or damage' in s 1(2)(*b*) meant the act of destruction (or the 'destroying')
or the act of damage (or the 'damaging'), and not the destroyed or damaged property;
j (b) although it was conceded that the destruction of or damage to the property had to
precede in point of time or coincide with the endangering of life, so that no offence
under s 1(2) would have been committed if Mr and Mrs Gregory had been standing
outside the damaged bungalow, it was not necessary to prove that the destroyed or
damaged property itself was likely to cause any danger to life; (c) accordingly, if a
burning firebrand were tossed into a building, it was sufficient on the issue of intent to

prove that the firebrand was likely to damage the building and to endanger life, and it was unnecessary to show that the danger to life would be due to the burning building rather than to the burning firebrand.

 It will be apparent that submissions on those lines were accepted by the trial judge. We shall refer to part of his ruling. He said:

> 'The contention of the defence is this, that there must be proved to be a destruction or damage of property which, as a consequence of that destruction or damage, either deliberately endangers life or recklessly endangers life. They rely, for instance, on the examples cited where a car or rather where a man may criminally damage the brake lights of a motor car, knowing or not addressing his mind to the possibility that he may subsequently drive that motor car and be injured or his life may be endangered thereby. The defence submit that where the causation of the damage is as in this case, for instance, by the firing of bullets through a window which causes damage and which may also endanger life by reason of the impact or the effect of the bullets, it does not fall within the subsection, that is sub-s (2)(b). In my judgment that argument is fallacious. If a firebrand is tossed on to the thatched roof of a dwelling-house known to be occupied and the roof catches fire and threatens or injures the occupants the section is fulfilled. The same act may have a number of consequences. In my judgment there is no logical necessity to separate the conduct which causes deliberate damage from the consequences of its reckless effect. I am fortified in my view on this occasion by the approach adopted by the Court of Appeal, albeit considering a matter that is not directly on the point of the case. *R v Hardie* [1984] 3 All ER 848, [1985] 1 WLR 64 set out the approach that a jury should take here when they are concerned with the state of mind. Parker LJ said ([1984] 3 All ER 848 at 851, [1985] 1 WLR 64 at 67): "They are, however, concerned with that state of mind at one stage only, namely when he does the relevant act. If, when doing that act, he creates an obvious risk both that property will be destroyed and that the life of another will be endangered and gives no thought to the possibility of there being either risk, the requirements of the sub-s (2) are in our judgment clearly satisfied. [Then Parker LJ gave an example:] If, for example, a person drops a lighted match at a petrol station into a bin containing an oily rag by a pump in use by the attendant to fill a car and he thereby creates an obvious risk both that property will be damaged and that the life of the attendant will be endangered, but has given no thought to either matter, it would be farcical to say that the elements of the offence in sub-s (1) had been fulfilled but those of sub-s (2) had not." That is an example of one act which has a number of consequences.'

 With all due respect to the judge and the valuable argument of counsel for the Crown, we are unable to accept this construction of s 1(2). The statute is concerned with criminal damage to property. Section 1(2) creates an aggravated offence where property is destroyed or damaged and the defendant intends by the destruction or damage to endanger the life of another or is reckless whether the life of another would be thereby endangered. The words 'by' and 'thereby' are important. In the present case we are concerned only with *damage* to property and a charge of recklessness rather than with one involving a specific intent to endanger life.

 The relevant words of s 1(2) therefore become: 'A person who without lawful excuse damages any property . . . being reckless as to whether the life of another would be thereby endangered . . .' It seems to us to be clear from the wording of s 1(2) that a causal link has to be shown between the damage to the property and the danger to life. The word 'thereby' relates to the damage to the property and not to the act which causes the damage.

 This approach appears to us to be wholly consistent with the guidance given by Lord Diplock in *R v Caldwell* [1981] 1 All ER 961 at 967, [1982] AC 341 at 354–355, where, in a passage cited by this court in *R v Hardie* [1984] 3 All ER 848 at 851, [1985] 1 WLR 64 at 67 he said:

a   'Where the charge is under s 1(2) the question of the state of mind of the accused must be approached in stages, corresponding to paras (*a*) and (*b*). The jury must be satisfied that what the accused did amounted to an offence under s 1(1), either because he actually intended to destroy or damage the property or because he was reckless (in the sense that I have described) whether it might be destroyed or damaged. Only if they are so satisfied must the jury go on to consider whether the accused also either actually intended that the destruction or damage of the property should endanger someone's life or was reckless (in a similar sense) whether a human
b   life might be endangered.'

Moreover, it is apparent that offences under s 1 of the 1971 Act are result-crimes in the classification adopted by Professor Gordon in his work *The Criminal Law of Scotland* (2nd edn, 1978), so that an offence under s 1(2) is not complete unless and until the conduct of the accused has caused the property to be destroyed or damaged (see *R v Miller* [1983]
c   1 All ER 978 at 980, [1983] 2 AC 161 at 174–175). Accordingly, it is logical that the state of mind with which the statute is concerned in the second limb of s 1(2), that is in para (*b*), is the state of mind of the accused which is directed to the consequences of the destruction of or the damage to the property.

The facts of the present case are very unusual. In most cases under s 1(2) one will not be concerned to examine whether it is the initial match or the resulting fire, or whether
d   it is the cutting of the pipe or the resulting failure of the braking system or the leakage of gas which endangers life. In the instant case, however, the distinction between the act of the defendant and the consequent damage is important.

In our view, on the true construction of s 1(2)(*b*) the intention or recklessness envisaged is directed to the possible dangers caused by the destroyed or damaged property and not the dangers inherent in the method of causing the destruction or damage.
e   For these reasons the appeal in relation to count 2 will be allowed and the conviction on that count will be quashed.

Appeal allowed.

The court refused leave to appeal to the House of Lords but certified, under s 33(2) of the Criminal
f   *Appeal Act 1968, that the following point of law of general public importance was involved in the decision: whether, on a true construction of s 1(2)(b) of the Criminal Damage Act 1971, the prosecution are required to prove that the danger to life resulted from the destruction of or damage to the property, or whether it is sufficient for the prosecution to prove that it resulted from the act of the defendant which caused the destruction or damage.*

g   *6 November. The Appeal Committee of the House of Lords granted the Crown leave to appeal.*

Solicitors: *Leslie M Bell*, Hull (for the Crown).

                                             June Meader   Barrister.

Secretary of State for Employment v Spence and others

COURT OF APPEAL, CIVIL DIVISION
STEPHEN BROWN, MUSTILL AND BALCOMBE LJJ
14, 15 MAY 1986

Employment – Continuity – Transfer of trade, business or undertaking – Transfer terminating contract of employment – Employment by transferor immediately before transfer – Employee dismissed three hours before business sold – Whether employee employed 'immediately before the transfer' of business – Whether employee entitled to redundancy payment – Transfer of Undertakings (Protection of Employment) Regulations 1981, reg 5(1)(3).

The applicants were employed by a company which went into receivership in November 1983 but continued to trade for a short time thereafter while attempts were made to find a purchaser for the business. On 25 November the receivers decided to cease trading and dismiss the work-force because there was no guarantee that there would be a successful outcome to the negotiations for sale. On 28 November at 11.00 am the work-force, including the applicants, were dismissed with immediate effect. At 2.00 pm on the same day the business was sold. The following day the work-force, including the applicants, were re-employed by the new owners and given fresh contracts of employment. The applicants applied for redundancy payments arising out of their dismissal by the receivers. Any liability for such payments fell on the Secretary of State for Employment because the company was insolvent. However, if for the purposes of reg 5[a] of the Transfer of Undertakings (Protection of Employment) Regulations 1981 the applicants had been employed by the company immediately before the transfer of the business to the new owners their contracts of employment were not terminated but were instead transferred to the new owners and they had no right to redundancy payments. The question arose whether there had been continuity in the applicants' employment, having regard to the lapse of three hours between the dismissal and the sale of the business. The industrial tribunal held that there had not been continuity in employment and that therefore the applicants were entitled to redundancy payments. On appeal by the Secretary of State the Employment Appeal Tribunal upheld the decision of the industrial tribunal. The Secretary of State appealed to the Court of Appeal, relying on reg 5(1), which provided that a 'relevant transfer [of the business] shall not operate so as to terminate the contract of employment of any person employed by the transferor', in casu the company.

Held – On its true construction reg 5(1) of the 1981 regulations only applied to contracts of employment which were subsisting at the moment of transfer of the business and therefore unless an employee was employed by the transferor of the business at the actual time of the transfer reg 5(1) could not apply, because where the termination of the contract was effected at any time before the transfer the transfer would not 'operate so as to terminate the contract of employment'. The reference in reg 5(3) to the employee having to be employed 'immediately before' the transfer merely clarified that situation. Since the applicants' contracts of employment were not in existence at the moment of transfer of the business by the receivers to the new owners, because they had been dismissed before the transfer, it followed that they were entitled to redundancy payments. The appeal would accordingly be dismissed (see p 621 e f, p 622 h j, p 623 d e and p 629 j to p 630 a, post).

Wendelboe v LJ Music ApS Case 19/83 [1986] 1 CMLR 476 and *Mikkelsen v A/S Danmols Inventar* [1986] 1 CMLR 316 applied.

Premier Motors (Medway) Ltd v Total Oil GB Ltd [1984] 1 WLR 377 and dictum of Peter Gibson J in *Bullard v Marchant* [1986] ICR at 393 approved.

---

a   Regulation 5, so far as material, is set out at p 620 h to p 621 c, post

a *Alphafield Ltd v Barratt* [1984] 3 All ER 795, *Secretary of State for Employment v Anchor Hotel (Kippford) Ltd* [1985] ICR 724 and *Fenton v Stablegold Ltd* [1986] ICR 236 overruled.

Notes

For the protection of employees in the transfer of undertakings, see Supplement to 16 Halsbury's Laws (4th edn) para 606A.

b For the transfer of Undertakings (Protection of Employment) Regulations 1981, reg 5, see 7 Halsbury's Statutory Instruments (5th reissue) 141.

Cases referred to in judgments

Alphafield Ltd v Barratt [1984] 3 All ER 795, [1984] 1 WLR 1062, EAT.
Batchelor v Premier Motors (Romford) Ltd (19 November 1982, unreported), industrial tribunal.
c *Bullard v Marchant* [1986] ICR 389, EAT.
Ellison v R & J Pullman (Retail) Ltd (28 June 1983, unreported), industrial tribunal.
Fenton v Stablegold Ltd [1986] ICR 236, EAT.
Melon v Hector Powe Ltd [1981] 1 All ER 313, HL.
Mikkelsen v A/S Danmols Inventar Case 105/84 [1986] 1 CMLR 316, CJEC.
Nokes v Doncaster Amalgamated Collieries Ltd [1940] 3 All ER 549, [1940] AC 1014, HL.
d *Premier Motors (Medway) Ltd v Total Oil GB Ltd* [1984] 1 WLR 377, EAT.
Secretary of State for Employment v Anchor Hotel (Kippford) Ltd [1985] ICR 724, EAT.
Spijkers v Gebroeders Benedik Abattoir CV Case 24/85 [1986] 2 CMLR 296, CJEC.
Wendelboe v LJ Music ApS Case 19/83 [1986] 1 CMLR 476, CJEC.

Appeal

e The Secretary of State for Employment appealed with leave against the decision of the Employment Appeal Tribunal (Sir Ralph Kilner Brown, Mr E A Webb and Mr A D Scott) ([1986] ICR 181) dated 23 September 1985 whereby it dismissed the appeal of the Secretary of State against the decision of an industrial tribunal sitting at Leicester (chairman Mr D Sneath) dated 28 September 1984 holding that the applicants, Mr G E Spence, Mr Searcy, Mr J L Such, Mr R J Soady and 17 others, were entitled to redundancy *f* payments to be paid either by their former employers, Spencer & Sons (Market Harborough) Ltd, or by the Secretary of State. The facts are set out in the judgment of Balcombe LJ.

Christopher Symons for the Secretary of State.
Jeremy McMullen for the applicants Mr Spence, Mr Searcy and Mr Such.
g

The other applicants did not appear.
Spencers were not represented.

BALCOMBE LJ (giving the first judgment at the invitation of Stephen Brown LJ).
h This is an appeal, with the leave of the Employment Appeal Tribunal, from that tribunal, which affirmed a decision of the industrial tribunal that the applicants in this case were entitled to redundancy payments. I take the facts from the decision of the industrial tribunal:

'Spencer and Sons (Market Harborough) Ltd, which employed the applicants up
j   to 28 November 1983, was put into receivership under the provisions of a debenture
in favour of the Commercial Bank of Wales. Mr Martin Iredale and Mr Hywel Jones
of Messrs Cork Gully were appointed receivers. The appointment took effect on 16
November following which a number of employees were made redundant. Mr
David Pullen was instructed by the receivers to investigate the situation. He found
that there was insufficient work to maintain the workforce, hence the original
redundancies. Following his analysis the receivers decided that there might be

enough work to keep the employees working until early February. That judgment was based on the assumption that customers should not withdraw their contracts from Spencers and in particular British Telecom for whom Spencers did approximately 80% of their work. The receivers advertised the business for sale in the Financial Times and a number of prospective purchasers came forward. In due course it was necessary for Mr Pullen to meet Mr Carew of British Telecom. This happened on Tuesday 22 November and Mr Pullen tried to convince Mr Carew that British Telecom should allow Spencers to continue to complete the contract or allow them to assign the benefit of it. Mr Carew told Mr Pullen that unless the receivers had been able to sell Spencers by Thursday 24 November, he would continue his dialogue with other suppliers, withdraw the British Telecom contract and place his business elsewhere. It was not possible to conclude an agreement with a purchaser on or before 24 November. By Friday 25 November the receivers had a clear idea to whom they wished to dispose of the business. That was the company of Econ Atkinson. Face to face negotiations with that company, however, did not start until the evening of Friday 25 November. By that time, of course, the British Telecom deadline had passed and a decision had to be made quickly in the interest of the debenture holders whether or not trading should continue. Since there was no guarantee of a successful outcome to the negotiations the receivers decided to cease trading and to dismiss the workforce. To that end Mr Pullen travelled up to Market Harborough on Monday 28 November. The workforce had reported for work that morning and they were told during the course of it to assemble at 11 am in the general office. There they were told that they were being dismissed with immediate effect ... Mr Warboys [also from Cork Gully] had been able that morning to distribute the form IP1 but was unable that morning to distribute the form IP2 and there were other papers which the employees had to collect. They were, therefore, told to return at 2 pm. It was precisely at 2 pm that an agreement between Spencer and Sons (Market Harborough) Ltd, Hywell Gwyn Jones and John Martin Iredale (receivers) and Econ Atkinson was concluded. In determining whether there was a relevant transfer, it is necessary to see what it was that was being disposed of. This is to be found in cl 2 which reads as follows: "The vendor shall sell and the purchaser shall purchase title with effect from 2 pm on the contract date: 1. The plant, the stock, the work in progress and the intangible assets. 2. Subject as is hereafter provided all the vendor's rights against third parties (including without limitation all rights in connection with such third parties' warranties and representation but excluding the benefit of claims made or notified to third parties before the contract date with respect to the assets.) 3. The goodwill of the business together with the exclusive right for the purchaser and its assignees to represent itself as carrying on the said business in succession to the vendor." The agreement contains no reference to the workforce and by the time that agreement came into existence, the workforce had ceased to exist. The time 2 pm appeared on the evidence to have been chosen because it was at about that time that Mr Taylor the Managing Director of Econ Atkinson concluded a fresh contract with British Telecom through the agency of Mr Carew. Such a contract was a condition precedent to the acquisition by Econ Atkinson of Spencers' business. Having concluded that contract, he learned for the first time that Spencers' workforce had been dismissed. That suited him because he wanted to start with a clean sheet. Econ Atkinson have their own working methods and he wanted to ensure that any of the Spencers' workforce kept on would comply with those methods. As for Spencers' business, Mr Taylor considered a number of options that afternoon. Essentially, those options were either to dispose of the assets of the business for cash, to move the operation of the business to one of their Yorkshire factories *or to maintain the business as a going concern in Market Harborough*. Those were all choices available to him under the terms of the agreement. In order to enable him to make a decision, he interviewed Mr Herrick [who was Spencers' works engineer] and probably one other member of the workforce that evening, a and decided to go for the third option. The workforce were told to report for work the following morning when they were re-employed. They were subsequently given fresh contracts of employment.' (My emphasis.)

The liability to make those payments was primarily that of Spencers, but if Spencers were insolvent it became the liability of the Secretary of State for Employment, and those liabilities are to be found in ss 81 and 106 of the Employment Protection (Consolidation) Act 1978. Spencers were in fact insolvent. The Secretary of State refused to make the b redundancy payments and so the employees went to the industrial tribunal. The hearing took place on 18 July 1984. At that hearing the Secretary of State took the point that there had been a transfer of Spencers' undertaking to Econ Atkinson and that the employees (the applicants before the tribunal) had been employed by Spencers immediately before that transfer. If he was right on both points, then he argued that the effect of reg 5 of the Transfer of Undertakings (Protection of Employment) Regulations c 1981, SI 1981/1794, was to continue the employees' contracts of employment with Econ Atkinson. Accordingly, they were not redundant and they were not entitled to redundancy payments.

So in the way that the case was argued in the industrial tribunal two questions arose: (1) was there a relevant transfer of Spencers' undertakings to Econ Atkinson; and (2) were the employees employed by Spencers immediately before the transfer? The industrial d tribunal answered both those questions in the negative in their decision given on 28 September 1984 in the following words:

'On those facts, we are quite satisfied that there was no collusion between the receivers and Econ Atkinson in the way in which events happened on Monday 28 November. They were acting independently in their own or the interests of their e clients. Applying the above facts to the law we have first had to decide whether there was a relevant transfer . . . Until the contract with British Telecom was renegotiated, there was no prospect of work for the business. That was why the receivers made their decision to dismiss the workforce on the Monday morning. Secondly, at the moment that the agreement came into effect, there was no workforce of Spencers. We cannot see how an undertaking can exist as such without f a workforce and, accordingly, we find that what was transferred was not a business or undertaking but the assets thereof. If we are wrong in our analysis of the facts and there was a relevant transfer, we find that the applicants were not employed immediately before that transfer. Three hours elapsed between their dismissal and the coming into force of the agreement . . . We . . . find that a period of 3 hours is longer than is contemplated by the expression "immediately before" . . . The g transferor dismissed its employees before the transfer. If our construction of the expression "immediately before" is wrong, then it must be very difficult for parties negotiating the transfer of an undertaking and having an eye on the regulations to know how much time has to elapse between the transferor dismissing his employees and the transfer taking effect.'

The significance of the words 'immediately before' soon becomes apparent. From that h finding, which of course allowed the employees' application for redundancy payments, the Secretary of State appealed to the Employment Appeal Tribunal, which on 23 September 1985 dismissed the appeal with some reluctance, but gave leave to appeal. I refer to the opening passage in the judgment of the Employment Appeal Tribunal, which was given by Sir Ralph Kilner Brown, who was presiding:

j 'This is an appeal by the Secretary of State for Employment against the unanimous decision of an industrial tribunal held at Leicester on 18 July 1984 to the effect that there was not a transfer of a business and that therefore there was a redundancy. We have found it a very difficult case indeed. In our respectful opinion, this is a case which might provide the Court of Appeal with an opportunity to provide guidance to industrial tribunals and the Employment Appeal Tribunal when involved with the interpretation of the [Transfer of Undertakings (Protection of Employment) Regulations 1981]'

The 1981 regulations are in fact derived from EC Council Directive 77/187. Before I go to that directive I should refer to the European Communities Act 1972, s 2(2)(a), which provides:

'Subject to Schedule 2 to this Act [which for present purposes is not material], at any time after its passing Her Majesty may by Order in Council, and any designated Minister or department may by regulations, make provision—(a) for the purpose of implementing any Community obligation of the United Kingdom, or enabling any such obligation to be implemented, or of enabling any rights enjoyed or to be enjoyed by the United Kingdom under or by virtue of the Treaties to be exercised . . .'

The effect, put shortly, of arts 100 and 117 of the EEC Treaty is that when the Council made this particular directive it became the obligation of the United Kingdom to implement it, and under that section, to which I have just referred, it could be done by Order in Council.

So I turn to consider the provisions of the directive itself. Article 1(1) of the directive provides:

'This Directive shall apply to the transfer of an undertaking, business or part of a business to another employer as a result of a legal transfer or merger.'

Article 3(1) provides:

'The transferor's rights and obligations arising from a contract of employment or from an employment relationship existing on the date of a transfer within the meaning of Article 1(1) shall, by reason of such transfer, be transferred to the transferee.'

I need read no more of that paragraph or article. Article 4(1) provides:

'The transfer of an undertaking, business or part of a business shall not in itself constitute grounds for dismissal by the transferor or the transferee. This provision shall not stand in the way of dismissals that may take place for economic, technical or organizational reasons entailing changes in the workforce.'

So I turn to consider the 1981 regulations, the preamble to which states that—

'the Secretary of State, being a Minister designated for the purposes of section 2(2) of [the European Communities Act 1972] in relation to rights and obligations relating to employers and employees on the transfer or merger of undertakings, businesses or parts of businesses, in exercise of the powers conferred by that section, hereby makes the following Regulations.'

That is, they are made to give effect to the directive. I go straight to reg 5, which is the relevant regulation in this case, and I will read the whole of it at this stage:

'(1) A relevant transfer shall not operate so as to terminate the contract of employment of any person employed by the transferor in the undertaking or part transferred but any such contract which would otherwise have been terminated by the transfer shall have effect after the transfer as if originally made between the person so employed and the transferee.

(2) Without prejudice to paragraph (1) above, on the completion of a relevant transfer—(a) all the transferor's rights, powers, duties and liabilities under or in connection with any such contract, shall be transferred by virtue of this Regulation to the transferee; and (b) anything done before the transfer is completed by or in relation to the transferor in respect of that contract or a person employed in that undertaking or part shall be deemed to have been done by or in relation to the transferee.

a   (3) Any reference in paragraph (1) or (2) above to a person employed in an undertaking or part of one transferred by a relevant transfer is a reference to a person so employed immediately before the transfer, including, where the transfer is effected by a series of two or more transactions, a person so employed immediately before any of those transactions.

(4) Paragraph (2) above shall not transfer or otherwise affect the liability of any person to be prosecuted for, convicted of and sentenced for any offence.

b   (5) Paragraph (1) above is without prejudice to any right of an employee arising apart from these Regulations to terminate his contract of employment without notice if a substantial change is made in his working conditions to his detriment; but no such right shall arise by reason only that, under that paragraph, the identity of his employer changes unless the employee shows that, in all the circumstances, the change is a significant change and is to his detriment.'

c   That regulation was clearly intended to give effect to art 3(1) of the directive. I turn to reg 8, para (1) of which reads:

'Where either before or after a relevant transfer, any employee of the transferor or transferee is dismissed, that employee shall be treated for the purposes of Part V of the 1978 Act and Articles 20 to 41 of the 1976 Order (unfair dismissal) as unfairly
d   dismissed if the transfer or a reason connected with it is the reason or principal reason for his dismissal.

(2) Where an economic, technical or organisational reason entailing changes in the workforce of either the transferor or the transferee before or after a relevant transfer is the reason or principal reason for dismissing an employee',

e   then certain other provisions take effect. Regulation 8 was clearly intended to give effect to art 4 of the directive.

With those preliminary observations, I go back to reg 5. Before I turn specifically to para (1) of reg 5, I must state the basic principle under English law, which is that a man cannot be transferred from one employer to another without his consent. Hence comes the rule that the sale or transfer of an undertaking determines the contract of employment of employees. If authority be needed for that proposition, it is to be found in the House
f   of Lords case of Nokes v Doncaster Amalgamated Collieries Ltd [1940] 3 All ER 549, [1940] AC 1014, which was concerned with the application of a section of the then Companies Act to this basic rule. I need refer only to one or two passages from the speeches.

Viscount Simon LC said ([1940] 3 All ER 549 at 552, [1940] AC 1014 at 1020):

'It will be readily conceded that the result contended for by the respondents in
g   this case would be at complete variance with a fundamental principle of our common law—namely, that a free citizen, in the exercise of his freedom, is entitled to choose the employer whom he promises to serve, so that the right to his services cannot be transferred from one employer to another without his assent.'

To the like effect Lord Atkin said ([1940] 3 All ER 549 at 556, [1940] AC 1014 at
h   1026):

'My Lords, I confess it appears to me astonishing that, apart from overriding questions of public welfare, power should be given to a court or to anyone else to transfer a man without his knowledge, and possibly against his will, from the service of one person to the service of another. I had fancied that ingrained in the personal status of a citizen under our laws was the right to choose for himself whom he
j   would serve, and that this right of choice constituted the main difference between a servant and a serf. If Parliament has so enacted, however, the result must be accepted.'

Again, without reading it, to the like effect is Lord Romer (see [1940] 3 All ER 549 at 566, [1940] AC 1014 at 1041).

Against that background, namely that without some statutory novation of the contract the transfer of an undertaking from one employer to another automatically determines contracts of service, I go back to para (1) of reg 5:

'A relevant transfer shall not operate so as to terminate the contract of employment of any person employed by the transferor in the undertaking or part transferred'

ie provided you have a relevant transfer the common law rule does not apply; the employee's contract of service is not determined. Then comes the positive aspect of the paragraph:

'but any such contract which would otherwise have been terminated by the transfer shall have effect after the transfer as if originally made between the person so employed and the transferee.'

Here one finds one of the statutory exceptions which Lord Atkin had in mind. So the paragraph has two effects: first, that a relevant transfer does not terminate a contract of employment, and the second effect, commencing with the word 'but', is that there is a statutory novation of the contract. That provision can clearly only relate to a contract of employment which is subsisting at the moment of transfer, otherwise there is nothing on which the regulation can operate.

I then turn to consider para (2) of reg 5, which starts off with the words 'Without prejudice to paragraph (1) above'; so para (2) is clearly not intended to defeat the prima facie effect of para (1). Paragraph (2)(a) says:

'... on the completion of a relevant transfer—(a) all the transferor's rights, powers, duties and liabilities under or in connection with any such contract, shall be transferred by virtue of this Regulation to the transferee...'

The words 'such contract' clearly refer back to the type of contract which is being considered in para (1). Then, under para (2)(b): 'anything done before the transfer is completed by or in relation to the transferor in respect of that contract' (and that again clearly refers back to 'such contract', namely the type of contract referred to in para (1)) 'or a person employed in that undertaking or part', and then the words 'shall be deemed to have been done by or in relation to the transferee'. The words 'or a person employed in that undertaking or part' clearly can have the effect of transferring obligations other than contractual obligations; for example, as has been put in argument, they may well embrace obligations arising in tort. I say no more about that at this stage because it may well be that the precise effect of the regulation in a tortious situation may have to be considered by another court. However, it does appear to me clearly that on the wording of the regulation the addition of the words 'or a person employed in that undertaking or part' can give rise to a transfer of obligations wider than merely contractual obligations.

Then one comes to consider para (3) of the regulation:

'Any reference in paragraph (1) or (2) above to a person employed in an undertaking or part of one transferred by a relevant transfer is a reference to a person so employed immediately before this transfer...'

Of course, on the interpretation that I have given to para (1), namely that it refers only to a contract of employment which is subsisting at the moment of transfer, the words defining the person employed as meaning a person so employed immediately before the transfer are unnecessary, but one can visualise a situation where they may clarify the position. Such a situation arose in one of the industrial tribunal cases to which we have been referred, namely *Batchelor v Premier Motors (Romford) Ltd* (19 November 1982, unreported), where an employee, a transfer being in the offing, had made it clear that he was not minded to accept the new terms of employment which the new owners were proposing for his employees, but he had never been dismissed from his existing employment with the transferor, and it might have been difficult to say at what precise moment of time, in the context of the transfer, he ceased to be employed. There was a

situation which the use of the definitive words in para (3) made it clear that that
a employee, who was employed by the transferor immediately before the relevant transfer,
had his contract carried over to the transferee, even though both parties knew that they
were not going to implement it; but the definition made it clear who was to be
responsible for dismissing him, with all the consequential effects, in those circumstances.
So, although in many cases the definition in para (3) will not be necessary in relation to
para (1), one can, as I say, visualise situations where it may be helpful. But in relation to
b the liabilities under para (2) the definition limits the liability of the transferee to
obligations arising outside contract (for example, obligations arising in tort) to those
persons employed immediately before the relevant transfer; so that in normal
circumstances they would apply only to those employees who have, putting it colloquially,
come across to the transferee.

The restrictions in para (4), that para (2) does not transfer or otherwise affect the
c liability of any person to be prosecuted for, convicted of and sentenced for any offence,
seems to me to bear out my interpretation of para (2), namely that it can include tortious
as well as contractual liability. Paragraph (5) of reg 5 is to save employees from that class
of serfdom to which Lord Atkin referred in the *Nokes* case, because it gives them a right
to say 'We are not going to be taken across'.

In my judgment this construction fits in with the scheme of the regulations as a whole.
d If a person is dismissed because of the transfer, either the impending transfer or one
which has already taken place, then he is given specific rights under reg 8. Applying that
construction of reg 5 to the facts of the present case, it is clear that the employees, the
applicants, were dismissed before the relevant transfer. Their contracts of employment
were not existing at the moment of the transfer. There was nothing on which reg 5
could bite, and accordingly the Secretary of State is liable for redundancy payments.

e Thus far I have dealt with this matter as if it were free from authority. Unfortunately
that is not the case, and so I now turn to the authorities to see if they require me to reach
any other conclusion.

First, there is some authority of the Court of Justice of the European Communities on
the directive itself. In *Wendelboe v LJ Music ApS* Case 19/83 [1986] 1 CMLR 476, I refer
first to the opinion of the Advocate General, Sir Gordon Slynn. He sets out the question
f which was being submitted to the court under art 177 of the EEC Treaty (at 478):

> 'The question asks whether the Directive requires member-States to enact
> provisions in accordance with which the transferee of an undertaking becomes liable
> in respect of obligations concerning holiday pay and compensation to [former]
> employees who are not employed in the undertaking on the date of transfer.'

g The Advocate General said (at 479):

> 'Although the question does not refer to any specific provision of the directive, it
> in fact arises under the first sub-paragraph of Article 3(1) [which he then sets out.]
> The answer turns on whether the words "existing on the date of transfer" relate to
> "rights and obligations" or to "contract of employment or ... employment
> relationship". All the parties which have lodged observations with the Court or
> *h* appeared at the hearing, namely the plaintiffs to the main case, the Danish, Dutch,
> French and the United Kingdom Governments and the Commission contend that
> the words "existing on the date of transfer" qualify "contract of employment or ...
> employment relationship" and not rights and obligations. The English language
> version could be interpreted either way though it is more natural to construe the
> *j* words "existing on the date of transfer" as applying to the words immediately
> preceding them, even in the absence of a comma before "arising" and after "(Article
> 1(1)". I understand that the same applies to the Danish version. In contrast, the
> French, Dutch, German and Italian versions make it clear beyond doubt that it is
> the contract of employment or employment relationship which must be in existence
> at the time of the transfer, and not the rights and obligations; and he sets out the

French text. I understand that the same unambiguous effect is achieved in the Dutch and German versions by means of adjectival phrases; [and he sets out those texts.] Again, the Italian version reads; [and he sets out that text.] It follows on a literal reading of the text that the rights and obligations of persons who cease to be employed in the undertaking concerned at the time of the transfer are not transferred to the transferee by virtue of the directive. This literal reading is confirmed by other factors which have been referred to by the parties. The contrary result—that a transferee is liable to former employees who had left before the transfer—would present great difficulties. It might be difficult, if not impossible, for a potential transferee to ascertain with certainty what was the extent of his liability to former employees. Both the uncertainty and the amount involved could provide a real deterrent to purchasers of the business, and in the result the business might not be sold and a large number of the workforce lose their jobs. This is contrary to the principle object of the directive, viz. to protect employees on a transfer. To limit liability to employees at the time of transfer is also wholly consistent with the scheme of the directive which is to transfer employees from one owner of the business to another on the same terms and conditions as existed prior to transfer, unless of course better terms are agreed with the transferee. Ex-employees retain rights against the transferor or pursuant to provisions adopted in accordance with Directive 80/987 of 20 October 1980 on the approximation of the laws of the member-States relating to the protection of employees in the event of the insolvency of their employer.'

Finally, from the opinion of the Advocate General (at 481):

'In my opinion, the question referred is to be answered as follows: Council Directive 77/187 must be interpreted as meaning that it does not require member-States to provide that the rights and obligations of persons who have ceased to be employed in the undertaking concerned at the time of its transfer be transferred to the transferee. However, this is subject to compliance with, and to remedies provided for member-States in implementation of, Article 4(1) of that directive.'

As I read the judgment of the court itself, it effectively agrees with the opinion of the Advocate General, because the court first notes the provisions of art 3(1) of the directive and then says (at 483):

'[13] It follows from a textual interpretation of that provision in the various language versions that it refers only to the rights and obligations of workers whose contract of employment or employment relationship is in force on the date of the transfer and not to those who have ceased to be employed by the undertaking in question at the time of the transfer. [Then there is a reference to the various different language versions of the directive.]
[14] That interpretation is confirmed by comparison of Article 3(1) with Article 3(3) . . .
[15] That interpretation of the scope of Article 3(1) is also in conformity with the scheme and the purposes of the directive, which is intended to ensure, as far as possible, that the employment relationship continues unchanged with the transferee, in particular by obliging the transferee to continue to observe the terms and conditions of any collective agreement (Article 3(2)) and by protecting workers against dismissals motivated solely by the fact of the transfer (Article 4(1)). [Then come these significant words:] Those provisions relate only to employees in the service of the undertaking on the date of the transfer, to the exclusion of those who have already left the undertaking on that date.
[16] The existence or otherwise of a contract of employment or an employment relationship on the date of the transfer within the meaning of Article 3(1) of the directive must be established on the basis of the rule of national law, subject however to observance of the mandatory provisions of the directive and, more particularly,

Article 4(1) thereof, concerning the protection of employees against dismissal by the transferor or the transferee by reason of the transfer. It is for the national court to decide, on the basis of those factors, whether or not, on the date of the transfer, the employees in question were linked to the undertaking by virtue of a contract of employment or employment relationship.'

Of course I appreciate that in the judgment of the court there are a number of references to the *date* of the transfer, but it is apparent from para [13], where the phrase is used 'at the time of the transfer', that the court in its judgment is not drawing any distinction between date and time, and is concerned with the *time* of the transfer, as indeed the Advocate General made clear.

In a subsequent case of the Court of Justice of the European Communities, *A/S Mikkelsen v Danmols Inventar* Case 105/84 [1986] 1 CMLR 316, the same Advocate General, Sir Gordon Slynn, clearly takes that view of the decision of the court in the *Wendelboe* case, because he says (at 319):

'In case 19/83 *Wendelboe v LJ Musik* it was held that only persons employed by the transferor at the moment of the transfer fall within the provision.'

In my judgment the directive has been construed by the court in the same way as I have construed the regulations which are intended to give effect to that directive. I turn, therefore, to the cases in Great Britain on the regulation itself. The first of those to which we have been referred is *Batchelor v Premier Motors (Romford) Ltd* (19 November 1982, unreported). A decision of an industrial tribunal is of course not binding on this court, but nevertheless the decision of a tribunal of which the chairman was Professor Hepple (the co-author and current editor of one of the standard text books in this field) is clearly entitled to respect. I refer to one paragraph from the finding of that industrial tribunal (para 38) which is in these terms:

'It is clear from the general scheme of the Transfer Regulations read as a harmonious code with Part VI of the 1978 Act that had Mr Batchelor [he was the applicant employee in that case] terminated his employment prior to the completion of the transfer, then he would not have been covered by Regulation 5 and his only claim, (if any), would have been against Premier [that was the transferor employer]. On the other hand, if he had reported for work as soon as Total [the transferee] took over and then resigned, Regulation 5 would clearly have applied. We are concerned with the intermediate situation in which he was in employment up to the moment of completion. In our judgment in that situation Regulation 5 also applies. If it did not, the whole purpose of the Regulations would be defeated. The transferee could simply announce that he was not intending to employ any employee of the transferor or could announce significant changes in their terms of employment offering them substantially different new contracts and thereby avoid liability under Regulation 5. So long as the employee is in the employment of the transferor at the time of completion there is an automatic transfer of his contract of employment.'

With that statement of the law I respectfully agree. There is then another case before an industrial tribunal, *Ellison v R & J Pullman (Retail) Ltd* (28 June 1983, unreported), about which I need say no more than that, on the construction which I put on the regulation, that decision was wrongly made. Then comes the decision of the Employment Appeal Tribunal in *Premier Motors (Medway) Ltd v Total Oil GB Ltd* [1984] 1 WLR 377. I do not need to recite the facts in that case, but it was a considered judgment of the Employment Appeal Tribunal presided over by the then President, Browne-Wilkinson J. I propose to read certain passages from that judgment, because in my view they correctly represent the law. Browne-Wilkinson J said (at 380):

'Before turning to the Regulations, we must say a word about the law as it stood before they were made. Under the old law, if an employer, A, transferred his business to another, B, the employees' contract of employment with A undoubtedly

came to an end. Unless B agreed to employ the employee, A was liable to pay a
redundancy payment to the employee. If B did take on the employee, A was not
liable to make a redundancy payment and the employee was treated as having
continuity of employment. Therefore under the old law it would undoubtedly have
been the vendors who were bound to make the redundancy payments to the
applicants. The new Regulations were made to implement Council Directive (77/
187/E.E.C.). The general scheme of the Regulations is directly contrary to the pre-
existing law. The general rule is that on the transfer of a business the employees of
that business are transferred with it, i.e. the employees' contract of employment
with A undergoes a statutory novation and becomes a contract of employment with
B. The Regulations seek to achieve this result without expressly amending the
existing legislation, which presumably remains in force in cases where the
Regulations do not apply.'

He then said (at 381):

'This case is of considerable importance because it is the first which has required
us to decide what is the effect of the Regulations on transactions of a kind which
occur every day, viz. the sale of a business to a purchaser who throughout indicates
that he is not going to take on some of the employees of that business. It is important
that the legal consequences of such a transaction for both employers and employees
should be clear and certain.'

He continued (at 382):

'In our judgment in the ordinary case the effect of the Regulations is that, if a
business is transferred, the employees are automatically transferred with it
irrespective of the wishes of the transferee or of the employees. The contract is
automatically continued by operation of the Regulations even if the transferee has
no wish to continue the employment. In consequence, the employees' contractual
and statutory rights become enforceable against the transferee, not the transferor.
When, as in the present case, the transferee makes it clear that he will not continue
to employ the employees, in our judgment he repudiates the continuing contract
and thereby constructively dismisses the employee. The employee is dismissed
because of redundancy and becomes entitled to a redundancy payment from the
transferee. A transferee of a business who does not wish to take over the employees
of that business will even so be liable to the employees for the redundancy payments.
To protect himself, the transferee must agree with the transferor either that the
transferor will dismiss the employee before the transfer or will indemnify the
transferee against redundancy payments and other employment liabilities.'

Finally he said (at 382–383):

'We must record that we have been much assisted in reaching this analysis by a
decision of another industrial tribunal (presided over by Professor Hepple) in
Batchelor v. Premier Motors (Romford) Ltd. which arose out of the sale of the Romford
business. The facts of that case are quite different, but the analysis by reference to
automatic transfer to the transferee and a repudiation of the contract by the
transferee is dealt with in paragraphs 38 and 39 of that decision. We are conscious
of the fact that this analysis is, in real terms, artificial: it was on the ground of
artificiality that the industrial tribunal in the present case rejected the analysis as a
possible solution. But, in our judgment, the artificiality necessarily flows from the
artificiality of the underlying concept of the Regulations, viz. the automatic
continuation between different parties but without their consent of an essentially
consensual agreement.'

I would agree with everything that Browne-Wilkinson J said in that case.
Alphafield Ltd v Barratt [1984] 3 All ER 795, [1984] 1 WLR 1062 is another decision of

the Employment Appeal Tribunal, this time with Tudor Evans J presiding. The headnote
a reads ([1984] 1 WLR 1062):

'In November 1982 the company for which the applicant worked went into
receivership. On Friday 14 January 1983 the applicant was made redundant. On
Monday 17 January the business was transferred to the employers. On the applicant's
complaint of unfair dismissal an industrial tribunal considered as a preliminary
issue whether he had been employed by the transferor of the business immediately
b before the transfer within the meaning of regulation 5(3) of the Transfer of
Undertakings (Protection of Employment) Regulations 1981, so that the Regulations
applied with the result that the employers would be liable for any compensation
resulting from the applicant's claim. The industrial tribunal found that the interval
of time between the dismissal on Friday 14 January and the transfer on the following
Monday was minimal; that the employee was employed by the transferor
c immediately before the transfer and that the Regulations applied. On the employers'
appeal:—
Held, dismissing the appeal, that it depended on the circumstances of each
particular case whether the dismissal was sufficiently proximate to the transfer for a
person to have been employed "immediately before" the transfer within the
meaning of regulation 5(3); that the industrial tribunal were entitled to find that a
d period of two days over a weekend was short enough to qualify so that under the
Regulations the employers were liable for any compensation awarded to the
applicant.'

It will of course be apparent from what I have already said that in my judgment that
case was wrongly decided. If it were correct, then it might result in reg 5(1) being ultra
e vires, because, if the regulation has to comply with the Directive, then even if the
Directive allows an element of more than a moment of time before the transfer, it is only
to the extent of the date of the transfer, and here it was held that a full weekend before
the date of the transfer was within the phrase 'immediately before'.

Then also in the Employment Appeal Tribunal, there is *Secretary of State for Employment
v Anchor Hotel (Kippford) Ltd* [1985] ICR 724. Again I read the headnote:

f 'In March 1984 the transferors agreed to sell their hotel to the transferees on 2
April 1984 and the employees were given notice that they would be dismissed on
the transfer date. The transferors made redundancy payments to the dismissed
employees but their application to the Secretary of State for Employment for a
rebate was refused on the grounds that the transferors were not the party liable to
make the redundancy payments since, as the business transfer and the employees'
g dismissals had taken place on the same day, regulation 5 of the Transfer of
Undertakings (Protection of Employment) Regulations 1981 rendered the purchasers
liable for the redundancy payments. The transferors' application to the industrial
tribunal pursuant to section 108 of the Employment Protection (Consolidation) Act
1978, for recovery of the rebate was granted on the ground that the dismissals were
operative from the date of the notice, that they were antecedent to and not
h contemporaneous with the transfer so that the regulations did not apply and the
obligation was on the transferors to make the redundancy payments. On appeal by
the Secretary of State:—
Held, allowing the appeal, that the relevant date was not the date of notice of
dismissal but the effective date of termination which in the present case was the
same as the date of the transfer; that construing the Regulations broadly, whether
j the transfer preceded, followed, or was simultaneous with a dismissal on the same
day, the effect of regulation 5 was that liability for redundancy payments passed to
the transferee and that, accordingly, the transferor was not entitled to a rebate.'

The then President of the Employment Appeal Tribunal, Waite J, said (at 729):

'Mr. Govier [who was the solicitor who appeared for the transferors] urged us, if that should be our view, to remit the claim to the industrial tribunal for a finding as to the precise order in which, on the transfer date, the expiration of the notices of dismissal on the one hand and the carrying out of the transfer on the other hand actually occurred. That would in our view involve an unnecessary waste of time and money. We accept Mr. MacLeod's submission that the order of events is irrelevant [Mr Macleod was the solicitor who appeared for the Secretary of State]. We accept, in particular, his submission that the Regulations should be construed broadly in the spirit of the Directive's declared purposes, so as to pass liability wholly to the transferee when the relevant events occur on the same day, regardless of the order of occurrence. It is an approach we have approved in other cases where the construction of the Regulations has been involved. Such an approach recognises that the construction of United Kingdom statutory instruments intended to enact the Community's directives on a national basis may require a broader and more purposive view to be taken—in the way that is already familiar to the courts of other European countries—rather than the meticulous allegiance to the draftsman's every word traditionally applied to our domestic legislation. We hold that when a dismissal notice given by the transferor expires on the same day as the transfer date, then it matters not for the purpose of the Regulations in precisely which order on that day the two events have occurred or whether they have occurred exactly simultaneously. The result will in every case be the same—a substitution of the transferee for the transferor as the party responsible for the dismissal and so liable to make a redundancy payment to the employee.'

It will again be apparent that in my judgment the industrial tribunal in that case was right; the Employment Appeal Tribunal was wrong; and indeed the approach to the construction of the directive which they adopted was peculiar because, as appears from a later passage in the judgment, they were referred to *Wendelboe v L J Music ApS*, and in the light of that decision it does seem to me that the approach which they adopted was not one which can be justified.

Fenton v Stablegold Ltd [1986] ICR 236 was another decision of a division of the Employment Appeal Tribunal with the then President, Waite J, again presiding. I refer merely, without reading it, to a passage in the judgment (at 243), where it appears that Waite J preferred the principle in *Alphafield Ltd v Barratt* to the decision in *Premier Motors (Medway) Ltd v Total Oil GB Ltd*. Again, I need say no more than that he made the wrong choice.

Finally, there is a decision of the Employment Appeal Tribunal, *Bullard v Marchant* [1986] ICR 389, Peter Gibson J presiding. The judge said (at 393):

'It is a principle of English law that an employee of an employer cannot be transferred to another employer without the employee's consent, and an employee's contract of employment with an employer automatically comes to an end on the transfer of the undertaking to another employer. It is plain that Regulation 5 (and in particular Regulation 5(1)) was designed to negate that principle. As we would have read the Regulation in the absence of any authority, the Regulation was designed to deal only with contracts of employment which are automatically terminated by a transfer which is a relevant transfer for the purpose of the Regulations; it would not apply where the termination of the contract was effected before the transfer, because in such a case the transfer would not operate to terminate the contract of employment. We would have read Regulation 5(2) as dealing with the "nuts and bolts" of Regulation 5(1) so that it only related to contracts which otherwise would have been terminated by the transfer, and not to contracts terminated before the transfer.'

After referring to the *Premier Motors* case and the approach adopted by Browne-Wilkinson J in that case, he says (at 394): 'That approach is consistent with the way in

which we would have read these Regulations in the absence of authority.' Then he says
a that the *Alphafield* and *Fenton* cases took a different view, and concludes:

> 'In those circumstances, despite the doubts which we have mentioned, we think
> it proper for us to follow the [*Alphafield*] case and therefore to hold that (as the
> industrial tribunal found) the contracts of employment of [the employees] are
> deemed to have been terminated by [the transferee in that case]. We hope that the
> true construction of regulation 5 will receive further consideration by a higher
b > court.'

Again, it will be apparent from what I have already said that the approach adopted by
Peter Gibson J and the members of the tribunal in that case was wholly correct and, if
they had felt free to decide as they thought they should, they would have reached the
right decision.

c In the present case the Employment Appeal Tribunal dismissed the appeal and so came
to the right answer, although possibly for reasons different to those which in fact they
gave. It inevitably follows from what I have said that this appeal too must be dismissed.
In the circumstances it is unnecessary to deal with the question whether the industrial
tribunal was right on the first issue, namely whether there was here a transfer of the
undertaking, but in case silence on this point should be taken as agreement with their
d decision, I must say that in my judgment they were clearly wrong. The leading case on
the question of transfer of undertakings is the House of Lords case of *Melon v Hector Powe
Ltd* [1981] 1 All ER 313, and from the headnote I need only refer to the finding (at 313–
314):

> 'The essential distinction between the transfer of a business, or part of a business,
> and a transfer of physical assets, was that in the former case the business was
e > transferred as a going concern, so that the business remained the same business but
> in different hands, whereas in the latter case the assets were transferred to the new
> owner to be used in whatever business he chose.'

A similar test was adopted by the Court of Justice of the European Communities in
considering the directive in *Spijkers v Gebroeders Benedik Abattoir CV* Case 24/85 [1986] 2
f CMLR 296. I need only refer to one other passage from *Melon v Hector Powe Ltd* [1981] 1
All ER 313 at 316, where Lord Fraser, who gave the leading speech, said:

> 'It is common ground that the appeal from the industrial tribunal to the
> Employment Appeal Tribunal and thence to the courts is open only on a question
> of law. The appellate tribunals are therefore only entitled to interfere with the
> decision of the industrial tribunal if the appellants can succeed in showing, as they
g > seek to do, that it has either misdirected itself in law or reached a decision which no
> reasonable tribunal, directing itself properly on the law, could have reached (or that
> it has gone fundamentally wrong in certain other respects, none of which is here
> alleged). The fact that the appellate tribunal would have reached a different
> conclusion of the facts is not a sufficient ground for allowing an appeal.'

h Counsel for the applicants on this issue has invited us to say that this was a decision
which on the facts the industrial tribunal was entitled to come to, and therefore this
court should not interfere. I merely refer to the industrial tribunal's own decision in this
case, particularly to the terms of the contract set out in their finding, to which I have
already referred, and to Mr Taylor's option 'to maintain the business as a going concern'.
It seems to me that it cannot be said that the existence of a workforce is vital to the
j existence of an undertaking, and so in this case the industrial tribunal reached a decision
on this issue which no reasonable tribunal, directing itself properly on the law, could
have reached. If it had been material, I would on this issue have allowed the appeal. Since
it is not material, in my judgment this appeal should be dismissed.

STEPHEN BROWN LJ. I agree with Balcombe LJ, that the appeal should be dismissed for the reasons which he has given, and I also agree with his observations on the question *a* of the transfer of the business. In my judgment the industrial tribunal were not entitled to come to the decision which they did on that matter on the facts, in particular having regard to the terms of the contract for the sale of the undertaking.

Appeal dismissed.

Solicitors: *Treasury Solicitor*; *Robin Thompson & Partners* (for the applicants Mr Spence, Mr Searey and Mr Such).

Celia Fox   Barrister.

c

Practice Note

d

COURT OF APPEAL, CIVIL DIVISION
SIR JOHN DONALDSON MR, DILLON AND CROOM-JOHNSON LJJ
22 OCTOBER 1986

Court of Appeal – Practice – Documents to be lodged by appellant – Preparation of bundles of documents – Transcripts – Notes of judgment – County court notes of evidence – Core bundles – *e* *Pagination and indexing – Binding of bundles – Legibility of documents – Time limits – RSC Ord 59, r 9.*

SIR JOHN DONALDSON MR made the following statement at the sitting of the court. The purpose of this statement is to consolidate and expand the Practice Directions issued on 18 May 1983 and 4 March 1985 (see *Practice Notes* [1983] 2 All ER 416, [1985] *f* 1 All ER 841) and at the same time to remind all concerned that it is the duty of those acting for appellants to ensure that the bundles of documents lodged for the use of the court comply with the relevant rules and directions. It is also their duty to lodge the bundles within the time limit prescribed by RSC Ord 59, r 9(1) (as amended). Neglect of these duties may lead to the appeal being struck out. Scrutiny of the bundles submitted has shown that there are certain errors and omissions which still occur very frequently. *g* For that reason, attention is drawn, in particular, to the following requirements.

Transcripts
All transcripts lodged (whether of evidence or of the judgment) must be originals. Photocopies are not permitted (see *The Supreme Court Practice 1985* vol 1, p 826, para 59/9/2).

h

Notes of judgment
In cases where there is no official transcript of the judge's judgment (eg county court cases and certain High Court hearings in chambers), either the judge's own note of his judgment must be submitted or, where there is no such note, the counsel or solicitors who appeared in the court below must prepare an agreed note of the judge's judgment *j* and submit it to him for his approval. A copy of the approved note of judgment must be included in each bundle. It should be noted, in the case of county court appeals, that concluding lines in the judge's notebook reading 'Judgment for the defendant with costs on scale 2' or the like are not 'the judge's own note of his judgment'. What is required is a note of the reasons for the decision.

a In the majority of cases the county court judge gives an extempore judgment and, pending the introduction and supply of personal dictating machines, has no full written text of it. The same applies to those cases heard in the High Court for which no official transcript of judgment is available.

In all such cases a typed version of the appellant's counsel's note of the judgment (or the solicitor's note, if he appeared for the appellant in the court below) must be prepared, agreed with the other side and submitted to the judge for his approval. Much delay has
b been caused in numerous cases by failure to put this in train promptly and expeditiously. To obviate such delays in future the following procedure must be adopted. (i) Except where the county court judge handed down his judgment in writing, or it is known *for certain* that he has a *full text* of his reasoned decision, the appellant's solicitor should make arrangements for counsel's note of judgment (or, if the solicitor appeared in the court below, his own note) to be prepared, agreed with the other side and then submitted to
c the judge, as soon as the notice of appeal has been served; he should not wait until the appeal has entered the list of forthcoming appeals. If that system is adopted, the approved note of judgment should be ready for inclusion in the bundles within the 14-day time limit for lodging documents, and no extension should be needed. (ii) Where both sides were represented by counsel in the court below, it saves time if counsel for the appellant submits his note of judgment directly to counsel for the respondent. (iii) Where the note
d of judgment has not been received back from the judge by the time the bundles are ready to be lodged, copies of the unapproved note of judgment should be lodged with the bundles; the approved note of judgment should then be substituted as soon as it is to hand. (iv) In those cases where the appellant is appearing in person, counsel or solicitors for the other side must make available their notes of judgment, whether or not the appellant has himself made any note of the reasoned judgment.

e

County court notes of evidence

In county court cases a copy of the judge's notes of evidence must be bespoken from the county court concerned and a copy of those notes must be included in each bundle. Directives (Court Business 3/85, B1351, and 4/85, B1358, para (3)) have been sent to
f county courts asking them to arrange for the notes of evidence to be transcribed as soon as the notice of appeal has been served on the county court registrar. The notes should then be ready for dispatch to the appellant or his solicitors as soon as they formally request them and make provision for the copying charges. A directive (Court Business 4/85, B1358, para (4)) has also been sent to county courts to the effect that the old practice which obtained in some county courts of refusing to make the notes of evidence available
g until counsel's agreed note of judgment has been submitted is to be discontinued.

Core bundles

In cases where the appellant seeks to place before the court bundles of documents comprising more than 100 pages, three copies of a core bundle containing the principal
h documents to which reference will be made must be lodged with the court. In such circumstances, it will not usually be necessary to lodge multiple copies of the main bundle. It will be sufficient if a single set of the full trial documents is lodged so that the court may refer to it if necessary.

j
Pagination and indexing

Bundles must be paginated clearly and there must be an index at the front of the bundle listing all the documents and giving the page references for each one. At present, many bundles are numbered merely by document. This is incorrect. Each page should be numbered individually and consecutively.

Binding of bundles

All the documents (with the exception of the transcripts) must be bound together in *a* some form (eg ring binder, plastic binder or laced through holes in the top left-hand corner). Loose documents will not be accepted.

Legibility

All documents must be legible. In particular, care must be taken to ensure that the edges of pages are not cut off by the photocopying machine. If it proves impossible to *b* produce adequate copies of individual documents, or if manuscript documents are illegible, typewritten copies of the relevant pages should also be interleaved at the appropriate place in the bundle.

Time limits

Time limits must be complied with and will be strictly enforced except where there *c* are good grounds for granting an extension. The appellant's solicitor (or the appellant, if in person) should therefore set about preparing the bundles as soon as the notice of appeal has been lodged with the Civil Appeals Office (without waiting for the appeal to enter the list of forthcoming appeals); in that way, in most cases, the bundles should be ready to be lodged within the 14-day time limit prescribed by Ord 59, r 9. An extension of time is unlikely to be obtained where the failure to lodge the bundles, transcripts, notes *d* of judgment or notes of evidence within the prescribed time limit is due to failure on the part of the appellant's solicitors (or the appellant, if in person) to start soon enough on the preparation of the bundles or the obtaining of the other documents.

Responsibility of the solicitor on the record

It seems likely that the work of documentation is often delegated to very junior *e* members of the solicitor's staff, often without referring them to the relevant rule and Practice Direction. Delegation is not, as such, objectionable, but (a) the member of staff must be instructed fully on what is required and be capable of ensuring that these requirements are met and (b) the solicitor in charge of the case must personally satisfy himself that the documentation is in order before it is delivered to the court. London agents too have a responsibility. They are not just postmen. They should be prepared to *f* answer any questions which may arise as to the sufficiency of the documentation.

Diana Procter   Barrister.

Cardiothoracic Institute v Shrewdcrest Ltd

CHANCERY DIVISION
KNOX J
6, 7, 14, 17 FEBRUARY 1986

Landlord and tenant – Business premises – Contracting out – Agreement by landlord and tenant excluding statutory provisions governing security of tenure – Order of court authorising agreement – Acceptance of rent pending application for court order – Application for order never made – Whether payment and receipt of rent creating periodic tenancy – Whether parties intending to create periodic tenancy – Landlord and Tenant Act 1954, s 38(4).

On the joint application of the landlord and the tenant under s 38(4)[a] of the Landlord and Tenant Act 1954, successive county court orders were made allowing the parties to enter into short-term tenancy agreements which excluded the provisions of ss 24 to 28 of the 1954 Act thus giving the tenant no security of tenure under the 1954 Act. In October 1983 negotiations were started for a further tenancy and between October 1983 and September 1985 a series of extensions of the existing lease were made on condition that each extension would be the subject of a tenancy agreement approved by the court excluding ss 24 to 28 of the 1954 Act. It was further agreed that until an order was made by the court there would be no legally binding agreement between the parties. The tenant remained in possession and the landlord accepted rent paid in advance in accordance with the terms of the successive extensions. In fact no application for the grant of a further tenancy under s 38(4) was made and subsequently the landlord brought an action for possession, contending that the tenant was a tenant at will and therefore unprotected under Pt II of the 1954 Act. The tenant contended that there was a concluded agreement for the grant of a tenancy on the occasion of the first two extensions made after October 1983, or alternatively that there was a periodic tenancy arising from continued possession after October 1983 coupled with the payment and acceptance of rent by the landlord thereafter.

Held – (1) A condition that a tenancy agreement negotiated between parties should be subject to the making of a court order under s 38(4) of the 1954 Act contained an implied term no legally binding grant and acceptance of a tenancy could be made that unless and until the court order had been made (see p 640 *g*, post).

(2) Where rent had been paid and accepted in the absence of a clear lease or tenancy agreement in force to explain the payment, the question whether acceptance of rent was a factor from which a new tenancy could be inferred depended on ascertaining the real intention of the parties in all the circumstances and having regard to any relevant statutory protection. Accordingly, taking into account the machinery of the 1954 Act and the parties' knowledge of its operation, it was clear that neither side had intended to create a periodic tenancy pending the grant, which both parties anticipated, of a tenancy approved by the court under s 38(4) and furthermore there was no compelling reason why any such intention should be imputed. The order for possession would accordingly be granted (see p 641 *d* to *f g* to p 642 *a f* to *h* and p 643 *g*, post); dicta of Lord Mansfield CJ in *Doe d Cheny v Batten* [1775–1802] All ER Rep at 595 and of Scarman LJ in *Longrigg Burrough & Trounson v Smith* (1979) 251 EG at 849 followed; *Strong v Stringer* (1889) 61 LT 470 distinguished.

Notes

For contracting out of Pt II of the Landlord and Tenant Act 1954, see 27 Halsbury's Laws (4th edn) paras 477–478.

---

a   Section 38(4), so far as material, provides: 'The court may—(a) on the joint application of the persons who will be the landlord and the tenant in relation to a tenancy to be granted for a term of years certain which will be a tenancy to which this Part of this Act applies, authorise an agreement excluding in relation to that tenancy the provisions of sections 24 to 28 of this Act . . .'

For the Landlord and Tenant Act 1954, Pt II (ss 24–29), s 38, see 23 Halsbury's Statutes (4th edn) 141, 163.

Cases referred to in judgment

Clarke v Grant [1949] 1 All ER 768, [1950] 1 KB 104, CA.
Doe d Cheny v Batten (1775) 1 Cowp 243, [1775–1802] All ER Rep 594, 98 ER 1066.
Doe d Bastow v Cox (1847) 11 QB 122, 116 ER 421.
Doe d Lord v Crago (1848) 6 CB 90, 136 ER 1185.
Dougal v McCarthy [1893] 1 QB 736, [1891–4] All ER Rep 1216, CA.
Hagee (London) Ltd v A B Erikson & Larson (a firm) [1975] 3 All ER 234, [1976] QB 209, [1975] 3 WLR 272, CA.
Hargreaves Transport Ltd v Lynch [1969] 1 All ER 455, [1969] 1 WLR 215, CA.
Longrigg Burrough & Trounson v Smith (1979) 251 EG 847, CA.
Strong v Stringer (1889) 61 LT 470.
Swain v Ayres (1887) 20 QBD 585; affd (1888) 21 QBD 289, CA.
Wheeler v Mercer [1956] 3 All ER 631, [1957] AC 416, [1956] 3 WLR 841, HL.

Cases also cited

Coatsworth v Johnson (1886) 55 LJQB 220, [1886–90] All ER Rep 547, CA.
Cohen v Nessdale Ltd [1982] 2 All ER 97, CA.
D'Silva v Lister House Development Ltd [1970] 1 All ER 858, [1971] Ch 17.
Heslop v Burns [1974] 3 All ER 406, [1974] 1 WLR 1241, CA.
Jackson (Francis) Developments Ltd v Hall [1951] 2 All ER 74, [1951] 2 KB 488, CA.
Law v Jones [1973] 2 All ER 437, [1974] Ch 112, CA.
Legal and General Assurance Society Ltd v General Metal Agencies Ltd (1969) 20 P & CR 953.
Maconochie Bros Ltd v Brand [1946] 2 All ER 778.
Manfield & Sons Ltd v Botchin [1970] 3 All ER 143, [1970] 2 QB 612.
Portland Managements Ltd v Harte [1976] 1 All ER 225, [1977] QB 306, CA.
Rossiter v Miller (1878) 3 App Cas 1124, [1874–80] All ER Rep 465, HL.
Sector Properties Ltd v Meah (1973) 229 EG 1097, CA.
Storer v Manchester City Council [1974] 3 All ER 824, [1974] 1 WLR 1403, CA.

Action

The plaintiff, the Cardiothoracic Institute (the landlord), which was the freehold owner of premises and buildings known as St Wilfrid's Convent, Cale Street, London SW3, brought an action for possession against the defendant, Shrewdcrest Ltd (the tenant). The facts are set out in the judgment.

Robert Pryor QC and *Paul de la Piquerie* for the landlord.
Michael Rich QC and *C J Lockhart-Mummery* for the tenant.

KNOX J. This is an action brought by the plaintiff, the Cardiothoracic Institute, against the defendant, Shrewdcrest Ltd, for possession of a freehold property known as St Wilfrid's Convent, Cale Street, London SW3 (I will call it 'the convent'). There have been changes by way of succession on both the plaintiff's and the defendant's side in the course of the history of this matter but as neither party relied on them, it will suffice to say that the plaintiff in 1982 acquired the freehold of the convent which had previously belonged to the Department of Health and Social Security, and the defendant company, Shrewdcrest Ltd, succeeded another company in the same group, Stowover Ltd, in the autumn of 1983. For the purposes of this judgment, I propose to refer to the plaintiff as the landlord and the defendant as the tenant, and ignore the changes of identity, on which it is agreed that nothing turns.

The tenant conducts a business of providing students with hostel accommodation. The landlord is, as its name indicates, a medical organisation. At all material times there was a prospect of the landlord becoming able to redevelop the convent for its own purposes at some more or less uncertain time in the future. It therefore suited both the landlord

a and the tenant for the latter to become a tenant of the convent on a short-term basis. The tenant was thereby provided with premises on which to trade, and the landlord received income and had its property occupied and protected from trespassers. But it was always important to the landlord to be able to recover possession when its redevelopment plans matured. It has not been disputed that the tenant's business was one which fell within the protection accorded to business tenancies by Pt II of the Landlord and Tenant Act

b 1954. Advantage was therefore taken of the amendments introduced to s 38 of the 1954 Act by s 5 of the Law of Property Act 1969, and on three successive occasions an order of the West London County Court was obtained on the joint application of the landlord and the tenant allowing them to enter into tenancy agreements which excluded the provisions of ss 24 to 28 of the 1954 Act, and therefore gave the tenant no security of tenure under that Act.

c Firstly, pursuant to an order dated 19 June 1980, there was an agreement dated 27 June 1980 for the grant of a lease to the tenant of the convent from 1 May 1980 till 31 October 1981 at a rent of £10,000 pa payable quarterly in advance on 1 May, August, November and February of each year. Secondly, pursuant to an order dated 31 March 1982, there was a lease dated 6 April 1982 of the convent granting the tenant a term of one year from 1 November 1981 to 31 October 1982 at a rent of £30,000 pa payable in

d advance at stated times in such a way that larger payments in July, August and September, the peak season for the tenant's business, were required than in the earlier part of the one year term. Thirdly, and finally so far as the court orders are concerned, pursuant to an order dated 9 September 1982 there was a lease dated 24 November 1982 of the convent granting the tenant a term of one year from 1 November 1982 to 31 October 1983 at a rent of £30,000, payable again in advance in the same manner weighted towards the

e summer months as was provided for by the immediately preceding lease, except that the preceding lease, being granted well after the term began, provided for an initial payment of £5,000 on execution, whereas the third lease in the chain provided for two payments of £2,500 on 1 November 1982 and 1 February 1983. Although all three of these leases were granted after the term expressed to be granted had commenced, it is common ground that even assuming that the tenant had the benefit of a protected tenancy before

f each grant, any such protection would have ceased on the grant.

By the autumn of 1983 it was clear that the landlord was not going to wish to redevelop the convent at once after 31 October 1983, and negotiations were started for a further tenancy to be granted to the tenant.

Three witnesses were called for the landlord: Brigadier Vernon, Mr Travis and Miss Carden. They were the persons who as estate managers acting for the landlord,

g successively conducted the negotiations with the tenant for extensions of the tenancy. No oral evidence at all was called by the tenant, but there was a good deal of contemporary documentary evidence, mainly in the form of correspondence, between one or other of the three persons I have named who gave evidence, and either Mr Lofts and, particularly after October 1984 when Mr Lofts severed his connection with the tenant, Mr Rivers, both of whom at the material times were directors of the tenant.

h Throughout the period between the end of October 1983 and September 1985, when a claim was advanced for the first time by the tenant to be entitled to a tenancy protected by Pt II of the 1954 Act, the landlord and tenant were in a succession of negotiations for a series of extensions of the lease granted on 24 November 1982 which determined on 31 October 1983. The tenant remained in possession of the convent throughout and paid rent in general accordance with the terms of the successive extensions under which the

j rent was altered from time to time, from the £30,000 pa reserved by the lease dated 24 November 1982, and these rent payments were made, as to the great majority, monthly in advance. In particular, almost immediately after the expiration of the last of the three tenancies the subject of the court order on 31 October 1983, that is to say on 2 November 1983, a cheque was tendered and accepted, and later cleared, for £1,000, which was the rent payable under the negotiated first extension from 1 November 1983 until 30 June

1984, and it continued to be paid in this way until April 1984 when the payments increased to £1,666·66 monthly, the rate payable from 1 November 1983 to 30 September **a** 1984 under the further extension negotiated in November 1983 from 1 July 1984 to 30 September 1984. Precisely why that increase came into force in April 1984 was not explained in evidence, but the most probable explanation is that it was demanded by the landlord's finance department on the basis of information given to it by Mr Travis. Neither the monthly £1,000 nor the monthly £1,666·66 was the same as the rent reserved by the lease which expired on 31 October 1983, which was payable quarterly, **b** subject to weighting in the summer months.

The successive extensions thus negotiated were as follows. In October 1983 an extension from 1 November 1983 to 30 June 1984 was negotiated. In November 1983, a further extension from 1 July 1984 to 30 September 1984 was negotiated. In July 1984 an extension from 1 October 1984 to 1 May 1985 was negotiated, although the precise rental and dates for payment remained undetermined until, on 29 November 1984, the **c** extension was agreed to run until 30 June 1985 and the rental and dates for payment were agreed. In April 1985 a further extension was agreed until a date in September, which was left uncertain, until in June 1985 the date was fixed by the landlord at 15 September 1985. Each of these extensions was, I find, negotiated subject to a condition that the extension should be the subject of a tenancy agreement approved by the court, excluding the operation of ss 24 to 28 of the 1954 Act, and I find that it was understood **d** and intended by both parties that until such order was obtained there would be no legally binding agreement between them, so that in principle at least both landlord and tenant were at any time free to resile from the negotiations.

I base this finding on the following considerations: until September 1985 the tenant was from time to time at pains to emphasise its lack of security of tenure, which both parties, who were fully aware of the relevant legislation, knew could only be the result of **e** a court order under s 38(4) of the 1954 Act. Late in 1982 (that is while the third lease approved by court order was still current), Mr Lofts on behalf of the tenant solicited Brigadier Vernon's help to fend off requirements from the local authority health inspector who was threatening to enforce sanitary regulations more strictly and insist on the installation of a quantity of hand basins. Mr Lofts wrote on 26 November 1982 to Brigadier Vernon as follows: **f**

'Dear Brigadier Vernon,
    Re: 76 Cale Street, SW3.
    Can you please help me? I had a meeting with Mr. Sampson of the Public Health Department of the Royal Borough of Kensington and Chelsea at this building yesterday. As our lease has been renewed for another year, the Public Health Department has to consider its position in respect of allowing us to continue without **g** providing wash hand basins in all the rooms, or not. Up until now, their attitude has been to "adopt a recommendation not to enforce the Council's standards" because of the temporary nature of our tenure, however this situation is now rolling over into the fourth year! I have explained to Mr. Sampson that in all probability this is our last period of occupation of the premises because the hospital is now ready to take the building back and in such circumstances, Mr. Sampson has indicated to me **h** that the Public Health Department will in all probability be able to adopt their previous recommendation. My application to them requesting that they do, will be greatly assisted if it can be accompanied by a letter from you indicating that we are unlikely to be able to remain for another year after it presently expires in October, 1983. I should therefore be grateful if you can write to me along such lines.' **j**

Brigadier Vernon replied on 6 December:

'This is to confirm that I have extended your Licence to occupy the Convent until 31st October, 1983. On that date your licence will be terminated as it is almost certain that the Convent will be required for use by the [landlord]. Only in the very *a*   unlikely event of funding not being available for the upgrading (and we already have well over half of it) would there be any possible chance of extending your Licence.'

That had the desired effect, since the borough environmental health officer wrote on 20 December 1982 to Mr Lofts:

b   'Dear Sir,
      I thank you for your letter dated 7th December, 1982, concerning the limited extension of your lease to 31st October, 1983. As your are aware, the Health and Housing (Environmental Health and Housing Management) Sub-Committee's decision not to enforce the Council's standards with regard to wash hand basins expired on the 31st October, 1982. This decision was based on written undertakings that hostel use would cease on the last day of October 1982. Given that your licence *c*   to occupy has been further extended, I am in this individual case only prepared to finally extend the waiver until 31st October, 1983. This decision is based on information received from my Hotels Inspector that the premises have been run in a clean and satisfactory manner.'

d   Later on, when Mr Travis had taken over from Brigadier Vernon and the first extension was de facto current, a letter was written on 26 March 1984 on behalf of Mr Lofts to Mr Travis, which reads as follows:

      'Dear Bryan . . .
      I wish to enlist your help and advice! The RBK & C Environmental Health Department have written to us informing us that in the very near future we will be issued with a Specification for works to be done for the updating of the means of *e*   escape in case of fire. A rough estimate of the works required is £20/25,000. We would obviously like confirmation that our lease will indeed end on the 30th September, 1984 or the latest news regarding any possible delay in the start of building works, and hence a possible extension. The Council have indicated that we will only be given two or three months to complete the works once they have issued their Notice. This would mean finishing the proposed works just before the end of *f*   our lease. A ridiculous situation I'm sure you will agree, and one naturally that would seriously affect our decision on whether or not we could afford to stay once the Notice has been issued. If the end of September is now definite would you be kind enough to confirm this in writing to me, and if not, let me know the latest position regarding a possible further extension.'

g   That letter is only explicable on the basis that Mr Lofts appreciated and wished, as against the local authority, to rely on the fact that the tenant's lease would be outside the protection of the 1954 Act. A renewed extension was in fact agreed on in July of that year.

      Next, there were repeated occasions when one party or the other referred to instructions to solicitors or formalities, and it was understood by both parties that what the solicitors *h*   were to be instructed to do and what the formalities were to consist of was the preparation of necessary documentation for the application, necessarily a joint one, to the court under s 38(4) of the 1954 Act. Thus, in relation to the first extension, Mr Travis wrote on 6 October 1983:

j   'I have now received official confirmation from the [landlord] that the Finance Committee has given its approval to [the tenant] having a further 8-month period as an extension of your current lease to 30th June 1984, for a total exclusive rent of £8,000 based on £1,000 per month. At the same time, consideration is being given to a further final extension to 30th September 1984, and it is hoped that the answer will be forthcoming in the next month or two. Accordingly, I shall be informing the Hospital's solicitors.'

In relation to the second extension from 1 July to 30 September 1984, a particularly valuable one from the tenant's point of view because it covered the peak tourist months, Mr Lofts wrote on 9 March 1984 to Mr Travis:

'We have still not received any documents from your solicitors in respect of the present period of lease. As time is going by (we're due to end the tenancy on the 30th September next are we not?) perhaps the formalities should be hurried along! I look forward to hearing from you.'

And he expressed himself similarly on 21 March when he wrote: 'I have written to our solicitors today asking them to hasten this matter along and so hopefully the formalities will be concluded shortly.'

In relation to the fourth extension both Miss Carden, who had taken over from Mr Travis on the landlord's side, and Mr Rivers, who had taken over from Mr Lofts on the tenant's side, referred to instructions to solicitors in the same sense. On 29 November 1984 Mr Rivers wrote to Miss Carden:

'As discussed, I am confirming our telephone conversation of today. You will be instructing your solicitors to prepare an agreement to cover the period to 30 June 1985 at our current rental of £1,666·66 per month (£20,000 per annum).'

Miss Carden's letter the next day, which crossed that letter, read, so far as material, as follows:

'Further to our telephone conversation yesterday, I confirm that, as we agreed, our solicitors will now proceed with an extension of your lease to 30th June 1985 at the current rent of £20,000 p.a. payable monthly at the rate of £1,666 per month.'

In fact, the solicitors for the parties never did finalise the intended application to the county court. This was due to the conduct on the tenant's solicitors' side which can most charitably be described as supine. No explanation was offered in evidence for their repeated failure to answer letters. In relation to the extensions after 31 October 1983, letters were written to them by the landlord's solicitors on 15 occasions asking for confirmation of the agreement made between the parties, or approval of documents for submission to the court for a joint application under s 38(4). Four replies only were elicited, and they were as follows: on 23 November 1983: 'Thank you for your letter of 16 November. I am checking my instructions and will revert to you as soon as possible'; on 19 June 1984:

'I am so sorry not to have dealt with your letters of 9 May and 1 April. [In fact the letters they had received were dated 9 April and 1 May, but nothing turns on that.] Our Client was away extensively earlier this year and I had not had a chance to get specific instructions on the proposals for the current year. I will be away until the end of next week but hope then to be able to finalise this matter.'

I regret to have to say that the statement in that second sentence is, in my judgment, untrue, in the light of the letter written by Mr Lofts on 21 March which I have already read saying that he had written to his solicitors that day asking them to hasten this matter along.

Next, on 10 April 1985, the tenant's solicitor wrote:

'Thank you for your letter of 1 April with enclosure. First, I apologise for my recent lack of communication due partly to pressure of work and partly due to the absence abroad at relevant moments of my Client. The present position is that I am instructed to finalise the matter with you, but the relevant director was away last week, and I shall be away until next Monday 15 April. Could you please bear with me and we will then try to get the matter finalised as soon as I can check the draft documents are in accordance with my Client's understanding (I have no reason to expect that they are not). I have new instructions on one point. I understand that your Clients have agreed to extend the term to a date in September. Could you please check this point and I hope to be able to finalise the matter with you next week ... P.S. I am awaiting instructions as to the significance, if any, of the planning application.'

Then finally on 5 August 1985, the tenant's solicitor wrote this:

'I apologise for my recent lack of communication. I have reminded my Clients from time to time that I am awaiting clear instructions. I myself will be away for a very short holiday, but will renew my efforts to get this matter properly under discussion on my return.'

The second sentence of that last letter was in my view disingenuous, but however that may be, there is no evidence in any of these letters of anything inconsistent with a clear appreciation by the tenant's solicitors that the agreements between the parties for extensions of the lease dated 24 November 1982 beyond 31 October 1983 were all conditional upon the grant of a court order under s 38(4) of the 1954 Act. I find that there was at all material times such a clear appreciation, and I reject any suggestion that the tenant's solicitors were unable to deal with the matter because of lack of instructions for anything more than quite short periods of time.

Finally, so far as evidence is concerned, I accept Mr Travis's evidence that when he first met Mr Lofts after taking over from Brigadier Vernon, he, Mr Travis, made it clear that his negotiations with Mr Lofts could only be on the basis of the original transaction between the landlord and the tenant, and I find that he meant thereby that any tenancy would have to be approved by the court as excluding ss 24 to 28 of the 1954 Act, and that Mr Lofts understood and accepted this.

The expression 'subject to contract' was very seldom mentioned during the negotiations regarding extensions after 31 October 1983. Mr Travis and Miss Carden accepted that they did not use those words. It was used in the landlord's solicitors' letters of 16 November 1983 and 3 December 1984 setting out their instructions as to what the parties had agreed and seeking, in vain, for confirmation or disavowal from the tenant's solicitors. I find there was no express use of those words in any oral negotiation, nor any express acceptance or indeed disavowal of the expression used in the two letters that I have mentioned. In my judgment the agreements between the parties did not have a separate 'subject to contract' term over and above the condition which I have found to exist regarding the obtaining of a court order. That condition in practice provided the same result as a 'subject to contract' stipulation in that the obtaining of an order under s 38(4) needed a joint application, and if either party had decided not to continue with the joint application it seems to me inevitable that specific performance could not have been obtained of any implied term that each party should use its best endeavours to obtain the relevant court order, because such a term would have fallen foul of s 38(1) of the 1954 Act. In this respect the position seems to me to have been different from a contract of sale subject to planning permission where a term that a party shall use its best endeavours to obtain such permission has been implied: see, for example, *Hargreaves Transport Ltd v Lynch* [1969] 1 All ER 455, [1969] 1 WLR 215.

It was argued for the tenant that the agreements for extensions were agreements for tenancies to be granted to the tenant on the terms of the earlier leases approved by the court, and that this was an agreement at most that the provisions of ss 24 to 28 of the 1954 Act should be excluded. Such an agreement, it was argued, not having itself been approved by the court, fell within the prohibition against contracting out in s 38(1) of that Act, and was therefore void. I see no reason to impute to two parties who had successfully operated the provisions of s 38(4) of the Act such a stultifying form of agreement. The conditional agreement which I have found to have been made is quite capable of achieving the result which both parties desired, and I see no reason to find that these negotiating parties, represented on both sides by persons with professional estate management experience, made an agreement which produced a result which neither of them (assuming the tenant's and its solicitors' letters to be honest) desired to achieve.

Reliance was also placed by counsel for the tenant on the argument which he put to Mr Travis in cross-examination, that security of tenure was needed by the tenant for outlay on fire precaution and other work which the tenant met, and that this was only consistent with the grant of a fixed term of some duration. In my judgment, the tenant was perfectly content to take such risk as there was in laying out moneys on fire precaution works or other improvements, notwithstanding the possibility that the landlord could withdraw before a court order could be obtained and the relevant lease executed. The tenant evaluated that risk as minimal and was proved quite right in doing so. Moreover, the tenant was, as it well knew, in a position to secure a court order on the grant of a lease in a very short space of time had it been in its interest to do so.

The issue of law which arises is what on those facts was the status of the tenant's possession after 31 October 1983. Counsel for the landlord submitted the tenant was a tenant at will and therefore unprotected by Pt II of the 1954 Act. If he is correct in this analysis of the tenant's status as that of tenant at will, the conclusion that it is outside the protection of the Act follows and is not disputed: see *Wheeler v Mercer* [1956] 3 All ER 631, [1957] AC 416, *Hagee (London) Ltd v A B Erikson & Larson (a firm)* [1975] 3 All ER 234, [1976] QB 209.

Counsel for the tenant submitted that the tenant was a tenant under a concluded agreement for the grant of a tenancy on the occasions of the agreements for the first and second extensions after 31 October 1983, and if that be rejected, then under a periodic tenancy which arose from the combination of its continued possession after 31 October 1983, coupled with the payment and acceptance by the landlord of rent thereafter. If either of these is a correct analysis, then it follows that the tenant is protected by Pt II of the 1954 Act, since there was no relevant order in fact obtained under s 38(4) of that Act.

Holding over and holding pending a negotiation were described by Scarman LJ in *Hagee (London) Ltd v A B Erikson & Larson (a firm)* [1975] 3 All ER 234 at 237, [1976] QB 209 at 217 as the classic circumstances in which a tenancy at will would exist. I have held that the landlord and the tenant were in a series of negotiations between 31 October 1983 and September 1985 and that all the extensions that were from time to time agreed during that period were agreed subject to a condition that an order under s 38(4) of the 1954 Act should be obtained. The parties were therefore, in my judgment, throughout that period in one of those classic circumstances mentioned by Scarman LJ. Indeed, had the parties not given and accepted rent during this period the case would, in my judgment, have been effectively unarguable on behalf of the tenant. The absence of a separate specific 'subject to contract' condition makes no difference to this conclusion, for there is, in my judgment, implicit in a condition that the tenancy agreement negotiated between the parties should be subject to the making of a court order under s 38(4) of the 1954 Act, a term that unless and until the court order is obtained no legally binding grant or acceptance of the tenancy should be made.

That leaves the question what was the effect of the giving and receiving of rent. The reservation of rent and its payment on a quarterly basis does not prevent there being a tenancy at will. So much was decided as long ago as 1847 in *Doe d Bastow v Cox* (1847) 11 QB 122, 116 ER 421. *Hagee (London) Ltd v A B Erikson & Larson* took this one step further. There rent was reserved quarterly in advance, and this was held not to be incompatible with the tenancy at will. Both those cases were cases of express tenancies at will. No case was cited to me of a tenancy at will being held to exist where there was a holding over after the end of the tenancy coupled with the payment and receipt of rent in advance under a proposed further tenancy under negotiation. *Wheeler v Mercer* [1956] 3 All ER 631, [1957] AC 416 was a case of holding over, but it appears from counsel's argument in the Court of Appeal that no rent was taken after the previous tenancy had expired (see [1956] 1 QB 274 at 278). The giving and receiving of rent does not of itself necessarily import the existence of a tenancy. That was decided in *Clarke v Grant* [1949] 1 All ER 768 at 768–769, [1950] 1 KB 104 at 105 where Lord Goddard CJ, after stating the facts, said:

a
'. . . the learned deputy judge . . . fell into the error of confusing an acceptance of rent after a notice to quit with an acceptance of rent after notice that an act of forfeiture has been committed. If a landlord seeks to recover possession of property on the ground that breach of covenant has entitled him to a forfeiture, it has always been held that acceptance of rent after notice waives the forfeiture, the reason being that in the case of a forfeiture the landlord has the option of saying whether or not he will treat the breach of covenant as a forfeiture. The lease is voidable, not void,

b
and if the landlord accepts rent after notice of a forfeiture it has always been held that he thereby acknowledges or recognises that the lease is continuing. With regard to the payment of rent after a notice to quit, however, that result has never followed. If a proper notice to quit has been given in respect of a periodic tenancy, such as a yearly tenancy, the effect of the notice is to bring the tenancy to an end just as effectually as if there has been a term which has expired. Therefore, the tenancy

c
having been brought to an end by a notice to quit, a payment of rent after the termination of the tenancy would only operate in favour of the tenant if it could be shown that the parties intended that there should be a new tenancy. That has been the law ever since it was laid down by the Court of King's Bench in Doe d. Cheny v. Batten ((1775) 1 Cowp 243 at 245, [1775–1802] All ER Rep 594 at 595) where Lord Mansfield said: "The question therefore is, quo animo the rent was received, and

d
what the real intention of both parties was?"'

In the typical case where the giving and receiving of rent leaves the court to infer the existence of a periodic tenancy, it is on the footing that this is the interpretation which best fills the vacuum which the parties have left. Thus, in what used to be the ordinary case of a tenancy unaffected by statutory prolongation or protection coming to an end,

e
and the parties giving and receiving rent but not expressly agreeing on the creation of a new tenancy, the preferred solution that the law has adopted is a periodic tenancy, on the footing that that is what the parties must have intended or be taken to have intended. Ultimately it is the intentions of the parties in all the circumstances that determines the result of the giving and acceptance of rent. Tenancies where there is no statutory protection of one sort or another are no longer the norm. Where statutory protection

f
does exist, that has been treated as a significant factor in evaluating the parties' intention in paying and receiving rent. The high water mark of that reasoning is to be found in Ormrod LJ's judgment in Longrigg Burrough & Trounson v Smith (1979) 251 EG 847 at 849, where he is recorded as saying:

g
'The old common law presumption of a tenancy from the payment and acceptance of a sum in the nature of rent dies very hard. But I think the authorities make it quite clear that in these days of statutory controls over the landlord's right of possession, this presumption is unsound and no longer holds. The question now is a purely open question; it is simply: is it right and proper to infer from all the circumstances of the case, including the payments, that the parties had reached an agreement for a tenancy? I think it does not now go any further than that.'

h
Counsel for the tenant submitted that this went further than was necessary for the decision. Neither of the other two judges who concurred in the result in the Court of Appeal expressed such a view, and counsel submitted it was contrary to very well-established authority, citing Doe d Lord v Crago (1848) 6 CB 90, 136 ER 1185 and Dougal v McCarthy [1893] 1 QB 736, [1891–4] All ER Rep 1216. On the other hand, he accepted that the payment and acceptance of rent did no more, even under those authorities, than

j
create a presumption, but it was, he submitted, evidence of a periodic tenancy which needed to be overcome. He also submitted that a distinction needed to be made between cases where the issue was 'Is there a tenancy at all or just a licence or trespass?' on the one hand, and cases where, as here, the issue was 'Given that there is a tenancy, what sort of tenancy is it, tenancy at will or periodic?' I reject this latter distinction as having any

practical significance, because the test enshrined in Lord Mansfield CJ's quo animo test is, in my judgment, applicable whenever one finds rent being paid and accepted without *a* there being a clear lease or tenancy agreement in force to explain the payment. The inquiry is as valid and essential whether the landlord is claiming that the occupier is a trespasser as it is if he claims that he is a tenant at will. It may be that factually it is less likely that a claimed trespasser is paying rent pursuant to a periodic tenancy, but it goes no further than that, in my judgment.

The tenant's argument in this case seems to me to fall between at least two stools. On *b* the one hand counsel for the tenant submitted that there was an agreement for letting for a term of eight months made by letter dated 6 October 1983, in which Mr Travis wrote to Mr Lofts:

'I have now received official confirmation from the [landlord] that the Finance Committee has given its approval to [the tenant] having a further 8-month period as an extension of your current lease to 30th June 1984, for a total exclusive rent of *c* £8,000 based on £1,000 per month.'

And for a further three months by a letter dated 2 December 1983, in which so far as relevant he said:

'At the same time, I am pleased to confirm that agreement has been reached whereby your lease can be extended until 30th September 1984, on a basis of a final *d* total of £20,000. Accordingly, I have today written to our Solicitors confirming this final agreement.'

On the other hand counsel submitted that the payments of rent on or shortly after 2 November 1983 created a periodic monthly tenancy. Those in my judgment are mutually exclusive possibilities.
e
Counsel for the tenant pointed to various pieces of evidence tending to show that Mr Travis, Miss Carden and Miss Oddy, the secretary to the landlord, behaved as though there was a lease in existence. This indeed they did, but in my judgment it was by way of anticipation of the grant of the projected tenancies. I do not find that conduct necessarily inconsistent with the conception of a tenancy at will pending such anticipated grant of a tenancy after the necessary court order has been obtained. *f*

The tenant's interpretation of a concluded grant of a tenancy protected by the 1954 Act seems to me less compatible with the intentions of the parties in agreeing on a tenancy subject to the approval of the court under s 38(4), and paying and accepting rent in accordance with the terms of those proposed tenancies before they came into force, than is a tenancy at will. It is clearly established that it is legitimate to have regard to relevant statutory protection in determining whether or not the acceptance of rent is a *g* factor from which a new tenancy could be created (see per Scarman LJ in *Longrigg Burrough & Trounson v Smith* 251 EG 847 at 849). Once one takes into account the machinery of the 1954 Act and the parties' knowledge of its operation it seems to me very clear that they did not intend to create a periodic tenancy pending the grant which both sides anticipated, of a tenancy approved by the court under s 38(4). Nor do I see any compelling reason why the court should impute such an intention to them if, as is *h* factually perfectly possible, they gave no serious thought to the legal repercussions of the payment and acceptance of rent.

In the circumstances I find it unnecessary to express a view either, assuming it lay within my competence to do so, on the submission of counsel for the tenant regarding what Ormrod LJ said in *Longrigg Burrough & Trounson v Smith*, or on the several cases cited by counsel for the landlord in support of the proposition that the onus of proof to *j* establish a periodic tenancy lies on the tenant.

Counsel for the tenant had another shot in his well-garnished locker, and that was the decision of Kekewich J in *Strong v Stringer* (1889) 61 LT 470. The headnote in that case reads as follows:

a
'A tenant was in possession of plots of land under an agreement for leases to be granted when he should have fulfilled certain conditions as to building. The intention of the parties was, in the view of the court, that the agreement should be regarded as a lease. The conditions were (to the landlord's knowledge) not fulfilled within the appointed time, but after that date the landlord demanded rent as under the leases, and the tenant paid it. Held, that the landlord could not, on receiving the rent, stipulate that it was received "without prejudice to any breaches of covenant
b
made up to that time in the agreement for leases".'

The remainder of the headnote I need not read.

What the headnote only partially reveals is that Kekewich J held as a matter of law that where under a building agreement which provided for leases to be granted as soon as six at least out of ten houses agreed to be built, had been covered in and drained into the main sewer, the landlord demanded and accepted rent at a time when the lessee builder
c
was in default of his covenant to build, the landlord could no longer rely as a defence to an action for specific performance with compensation on the breaches of covenant before the date when he accepted the rent. It was, however, specifically held that he could rely on any breaches of covenant later than the date of acceptance of rent as such a defence. The only authority relied on in argument and referred to in the judgment was *Swain v Ayres* (1887) 20 QBD 585; affd (1888) 21 QBD 289, CA, which was concerned with relief
d
against forfeiture under s 14 of the Conveyancing Act 1881, the predecessor of s 146 of the Law of Property Act 1925. In my judgment *Strong v Stringer* is an authority on waiver of breach of covenant by the acceptance of rent, and is not authority for the proposition that the payment of rent under a conditional agreement for the grant of a lease operates as a satisfaction of the condition. The ratio of Kekewich J's decision is to be found in two sentences. The first is where he said (61 LT 470 at 472):
e
'Therefore to my mind the right to have the leases was finally established when that cheque was paid, that is to say, on 13 Jan. 1887; from that time the plaintiff was the tenant of the defendant just as much as if all the ten parchments had been drawn up and executed.'

And the second is where he said (at 473): 'By accepting the plaintiff as tenant, however,
f
the defendant had admitted that he was entitled to the leases.' The reasoning is strongly reminiscent of the law laid down by Lord Goddard CJ concerning breaches of covenant in the passage which I read earlier from *Clarke v Grant*. The essential difference between *Strong v Stringer* and this case is that in the former the so-called condition was a term of an agreement to be performed by one of the contracting parties, whereas here the condition is a true suspensory condition not dependent on the actions or volition of one
g
party alone but on the joint action of both parties, plus the approval of the court. The point is perhaps yet another illustration of the ambiguity of the word 'condition'. I find therefore that counsel for the landlord succeeds in establishing a right to possession, and I propose so to order.

Order accordingly.

Solicitors: *Norton Rose Botterell & Roche* (for the landlord); *Wood Winfield* (for the tenant).

Evelyn M C Budd   Barrister.

Knibb and another v National Coal Board

COURT OF APPEAL, CIVIL DIVISION

SIR JOHN DONALDSON MR, NOURSE AND GLIDEWELL LJJ

30 JUNE, 11 JULY 1986

Coal mining – Subsidence – Compensation for subsidence damage – Determination of disputes – Interest – Whether Lands Tribunal having jurisdiction to award interest on award of damages – Law Reform (Miscellaneous Provisions) Act 1934, s 3 – Coal-Mining (Subsidence) Act 1957, s 13(3)(b).

A dispute between the claimants and the National Coal Board over compensation for subsidence damage caused to the claimants' property as a result of mining by the board was referred to the Lands Tribunal under the Coal-Mining (Subsidence) Act 1957. Under s 13(3)[a] of that Act the Lands Tribunal could '(a) require the Board to carry out any obligations imposed on them by [the] Act . . . (b) award damages in respect of any failure of the Board to carry out any such obligations within a reasonable time'. The damage had occurred by 31 December 1975 and on 31 July 1980 the board gave notice that it did not propose to carry out remedial works but was instead prepared to make a payment to the claimants. The tribunal determined the amount of compensation in respect of damage to the claimants' property at £2,500 and awarded that sum with interest from 31 July 1980. The board appealed, contending that the Lands Tribunal had no jurisdiction under the 1957 Act to award interest. The claimants cross-appealed, contending that interest should be awarded from 31 December 1975 because that was when the cause of action arose.

Held (Nourse LJ dissenting) – By analogy with the powers of an arbitrator appointed by agreement between the parties, the Lands Tribunal had jurisdiction under s 3[b] of the Law Reform (Miscellaneous Provisions) Act 1934 to award interest on damages awarded to the claimants under s 13(3)(b) of the 1957 Act since once the board had elected to pay compensation rather than carry out remedial work the claimants' claim was for damages under s 13(3)(b) of the 1957 Act, and the question which the 1957 Act required the Lands Tribunal to determine was wide enough to comprehend the determination and award of interest on such damages. Furthermore, interest ran from 31 December 1975, because s 1(2)[c] of the 1957 Act imposed a duty on the board to execute remedial works or make a payment 'as soon as reasonably practicable after the occurrence of any subsidence damage', ie 31 December 1975, and the board's obligation to pay compensation, with interest, arose on that date. The board's appeal would therefore be dismissed and the claimant's cross-appeal allowed (see p 648 e f h, p 649 j to p 650 b d and p 651 b to d, post).

Swift & Co v Board of Trade [1925] AC 520 and Newport BC v Monmouthshire CC [1947] 1 All ER 900 distinguished.

Notes

For reference of disputes over compensation for subsidence, see 31 Halsbury's Laws (4th edn) para 135.

For the power of an arbitrator to award interest, see 2 Halsbury's Laws (4th edn) para 580, and for cases on the subject, see 3 Digest (Reissue) 201–203, 1235–1243.

For the Law Reform (Miscellaneous Provisions) Act 1934, s 3, see 11 Halsbury's Statutes (4th edn) 580.

For the Coal-Mining (Subsidence) Act 1957, ss 1, 13, see 22 Halsbury's Statutes (3rd edn) 439, 460.

---

a   Section 13(3) is set out at p 648 d e, post

b   Section 3 is set out at p 646 d e, post

c   Section 1(2), so far as material, provides: '. . . as soon as reasonably practicable after the occurrence of any subsidence damage the [board] shall execute [remedial] works . . .'

Cases referred to in judgments

a   *A-G v BBC* [1980] 3 All ER 161, [1981] AC 303, [1980] 3 WLR 109, HL.

Chandris v Isbrandtsen Moller Co Inc [1950] 2 All ER 618, [1951] 1 KB 240, CA.

Hadley v Baxendale (1854) 9 Exch 341, [1843–60] All ER Rep 461.

Newport BC v Monmouthshire CC [1947] 1 All ER 900, [1947] AC 520, HL.

President of India v La Pintada Cia Navegacion SA [1984] 2 All ER 773, [1985] AC 104, [1984] 3 WLR 10, HL.

b   *Swift & Co v Board of Trade* [1925] AC 520, HL.

Case stated

The National Coal Board appealed by way of case stated by the Lands Tribunal against the tribunal's decision dated 16 November 1984 whereby it awarded the claimants, John Stanley Knibb and Nancy Knibb, £2,500 with interest to run from 31 July 1980. The
c   claimants also appealed by way of case stated on the ground that interest was payable from the date at which the relevant damage occurred, namely 31 December 1975, and not from 31 July 1980. The facts are set out in the judgment of Sir John Donaldson MR.

Anthony Purnell QC and *Guy Roots* for the board.
Nigel Wilkinson for the claimants.

d

Cur adv vult

11 July. The following judgments were delivered.

e   **SIR JOHN DONALDSON MR.** The primary issue raised by this appeal is whether the Lands Tribunal has jurisdiction to include a sum by way of interest when resolving a dispute as to the amount of compensation payable under the Coal-Mining (Subsidence) Act 1957. It is a matter of some general importance because, although the sum involved in the instant appeal is typically not very large, such claims are numerous and accordingly the result of this appeal will, subject to any further appeal, have a significant effect on the
f   total amount payable by the National Coal Board in respect of subsidence caused by coal mining.

The claim of Mr and Mrs Knibb (the claimants) was complicated by the fact that there were two periods during which their bungalow, at 27 Nottingham Road, Nuthall, was affected by subsidence. In 1966 they began building it on the site of a previous building. Some time between then and 1972 the bungalow, which had not yet been completed, suffered subsidence damage as a result of the mining of the Tupton seam. Arguments
g   ensued as to the extent to which the damage was caused by the mining or by a failure to build the bungalow on the foundations of the previous building. However, in 1972 this claim was settled for £2,900, which was duly paid by the board. Not all the defects were remedied and the bungalow had still not been completed when, in the period from July to December 1975, it was further affected by subsidence caused by the mining of the deeper Blackshale seam. The claimants again claimed compensation and on this occasion
h   there was the further complication that they maintained, and the board denied, that subsidence was still continuing.

The subsequent history can be briefly stated. Under s 1 of the 1957 Act the primary obligation of the board is to execute remedial works. However, it has the right to elect instead to make a payment to the claimant equal to the reasonable cost of executing remedial works or to the depreciation in the value of the dwelling house, if that be less.
j   Although it was only on 31 July 1980 that the board wrote formally to the claimants' solicitors giving notice that—

'as the reasonable cost of executing remedial works would, in the opinion of the Board, exceed the amount of the depreciation in the value of the property caused by the said damage, the Board have decided to make a payment under paragraph (a) of Section 1(4) and not to execute remedial works under Section 1(2)', the board must in fact have elected not to execute remedial works at some time before April 1979. I say that because in April 1979 the board offered to settle the claim for a payment of £6,300 plus certain costs, and in September 1979 it increased that offer to £7,000 with costs. Both these offers were, I think, on the basis of an election to pay compensation based on the reasonable cost to the claimants of executing remedial works. When, in July 1980, the board made the further and formal election to compensate on a depreciation basis, this was followed in February 1981 by a reduced offer to settle for the sum of £6,750 with costs. None of these offers were accepted by the claimants and on 5 August 1981 they referred their claim to the Lands Tribunal.

The decision of the Lands Tribunal (Mr J H Emlyn Jones FRICS) was:

'THE TRIBUNAL DETERMINED the amount of compensation payable in respect of damage to the land and premises . . . in the sum of £2,500 . . . together with interest from 31st July 1980.'

No order was made as to costs, save that the tribunal ordered a legal aid taxation. Both parties asked the tribunal to state cases for the opinion of this court, the National Coal Board on the subject of the jurisdiction to award interest and the claimants on whether interest should not have been awarded from 31 December 1975 rather than 31 July 1980 and on whether they should not have been awarded their costs.

The jurisdiction to award interest

By s 3(1) of the Law Reform (Miscellaneous Provisions) Act 1934 it is provided:

'In any proceedings tried in any court of record for the recovery of any debt or damages, the court may, if it thinks fit, order that there shall be included in the sums for which judgment is given interest at such rate as it thinks fit on the whole or any part of the debt or damages for the whole or any part of the period between the date when the cause of action arose and the date of judgment.'

Before the Lands Tribunal it was contended on behalf of the claimants that the tribunal was a court of record and the claim a claim for damages. The member held that whilst the tribunal had the characteristics of a court (see *A-G v BBC* [1980] 3 All ER 161, [1981] AC 303) he was not persuaded that it was a court of record, since it was a creature of statute and the statute creating it did not so declare. This aspect of his decision is now accepted.

The member then turned to the alternative basis on which he had been urged to assume jurisdiction to award interest, namely by analogy with the powers of arbitrators. After an exhaustive review of the authorities he held that there was no reason in logic why the Lands Tribunal should not have the same powers as an arbitrator. In reaching this decision he said that he was also influenced by the fact that smaller claims under the Act, where the rateable value of the property did not exceed £100, were referred to the county court which was a court of record and, in appropriate cases, had power to award interest. He then turned to the question of whether the proceedings were for the recovery of any debt or damages and concluded that they were properly to be regarded as for the recovery of damages.

The whole question of the power to award interest was examined exhaustively by Lord Brandon in *President of India v La Pintada Cia Navegacion SA* [1984] 2 All ER 773, [1985] AC 104 in the context of an award of interest by an arbitrator, the claim for the principal debt having been settled after the proceedings had been begun, but before the award was made. From this it emerges that there is no general common law power which entitles courts to award interest ([1984] 2 All ER 773 at 778, [1985] AC 104 at 115), but that if a claimant could bring himself within the second part of the rule in *Hadley v Baxendale* (1854) 9 Exch 341, [1843–60] All ER Rep 461 he could claim special damages, notwithstanding that the breach of contract alleged consisted of the non-payment of a debt ([1984] 2 All ER 773 at 787, [1985] AC 104 at 127). It also emerges that, so far as arbitrators are concerned—

'The true position in law is, in my opinion, not in doubt. It is this. Where parties
a   refer a dispute between them to arbitration in England, they impliedly agree that
the arbitration is to be conducted in accordance in all respects with the law of
England, unless, which seldom occurs, the agreement of reference provides
otherwise. It is on this basis that it was held by the Court of Appeal in *Chandris v
Isbrandtsen Moller Co Inc* [1950] 2 All ER 618, [1951] 1 KB 240 that, although s 3(1)
of the 1934 Act, by its terms, empowered only courts of record to include interest
in sums for which judgment was given for damages or debt, arbitrators were
b   nevertheless empowered, by the agreement of reference, to apply English law,
including so much of that law as is to be found in s 3(1) of the 1934 Act.'

(See [1984] 2 All ER 773 at 781, [1985] AC 104 at 119.)
One other decision of the House of Lords deserves mention by way of introduction,
c   namely *Newport BC v Monmouthshire CC* [1947] 1 All ER 900, [1947] AC 520, where the
award was that of a statutory, as contrasted with consensual, arbitrator, who had been
appointed under the provisions of the Local Government Act 1933 to determine the
sums to be paid by one local authority to another consequent on an alteration of
boundaries. The approach adopted by the House was to determine the mandate of the
arbitrator by reference to the terms of the statute under which he was appointed, treating
d   the statute as the equivalent of a consensual agreement to refer. It held that an arbitrator
appointed under that statute for that purpose had no power to award interest, but not
that a statutory arbitrator could not have such a power.
The mandate of the Lands Tribunal is derived from the Lands Tribunal Act 1949, the
Lands Tribunal Rules 1975, SI 1975/299, and the Coal Mining (Subsidence) Act 1957.
The 1949 Act is silent on the topic of interest, but, consistently with the fact that it is an
e   Act to amend the Acquisition of Land (Assessment of Compensation) Act 1919, under
which official arbitrators were appointed (see s 1(3) to the 1949 Act), it contains power in
s 3(6) to make rules applying to the tribunal any of the provisions of the Arbitration Acts
1889 to 1934, now, so far as material, replaced by the Arbitration Act 1950. In the
exercise of this power, r 38 of the 1975 rules applies certain sections of the 1950 Act to
all proceedings of the tribunal and certain additional sections to proceedings in which
f   the tribunal is acting as an arbitrator under a reference by consent. The sections which
apply to all proceedings are s 12 (conduct of proceedings, witnesses, etc), s 14 (interim
awards), s 17 (slip rule), s 18(5) (security for solicitors' costs), s 20 ('A sum directed to be
paid by an award shall, unless the award otherwise directs, carry interest as from the date
of the award and at the same rate as a judgment debt') qualified under the rules by the
words 'subject to any enactment which prescribed a rate of interest', and s 26 (enforcement
g   of award as a judgment of the High Court or the county court).
Section 13(1) of the 1957 Act provided that 'any question arising under this Act shall,
in default of agreement, be referred' to the county court where the rateable value of the
damaged property does not exceed £100 and in any other case to the Lands Tribunal or,
in Scotland, to the sheriff. Three features are important. The first is that the county court
is a court of record with power to include interest in the sum for which judgment is
h   given, where the claim is for the recovery of any debt or damages. The second is that the
phrase 'shall, in default of agreement, be referred' is the language of arbitration. The
third is that the phrase 'in default of agreement' is apt to cover not only agreement on
the question itself, thus obviating the necessity for any reference, but also an agreement
to resolve it by consensual arbitration.
Parliament thus seems to have approached disputes arising under the 1957 Act by
j   providing that they shall be resolved in the case of small claims by the county court, in
the case of larger claims by the Lands Tribunal as a statutory arbitrator or, in either case
if the parties so agree, by a consensual arbitrator. Two of these dispute settlers, the county
court and the consensual arbitrator, undoubtedly have power to award interest. I find it
inconceivable that the third, the Lands Tribunal, was not intended to have a similar
power, if and in so far as proceedings before the tribunal are for the recovery of a debt or

damages. The express reference to s 20 of the Arbitration Act 1950 in the tribunal's rules underlines the arbitral character of the tribunal, but does not impliedly exclude a general power to award interest, because the section does not have this effect in the context of consensual arbitration.

In the light of this conclusion, it is necessary to analyse what was the nature of the claim which the claimants referred to the tribunal. The answer is to be found in the formal notice of reference which was in the following terms:

'[the claimants] being a person claiming compensation in respect of the property described above hereby apply for the determination by the Lands Tribunal of the question of which particulars are set out below ... 3. Nature of question—dispute or case to be determined by Lands Tribunal for an Order requiring the National Coal Board to carry out their obligations under the above Act or alternatively for compensation by way of damages in respect of the failure of the National Coal Board to carry out their obligation under the above Act as a result of which [the claimants] continue to suffer damage to their property by reason of subsidence occasioned by the underground workings and operation of the National Coal Board.'

The wording of para 3 reflects that of s 13(3) of the 1957 Act, which is in the following terms:

'The tribunal, court or sheriff by whom any question is heard and determined under this Act may make such orders as may be necessary to give effect to its or his determinations and in particular may by order—(a) require the Board to carry out any obligations imposed upon them by this Act within such period as the tribunal, court or sheriff may direct; (b) award damages in respect of any failure of the Board to carry out any such obligations within a reasonable time.'

The Act does not create a civil debt owing by the board to the claimant. It creates statutory duties to execute remedial works or, at the board's election, to pay compensation. These alternatives are reflected in para (a) of s 13(3) which empowers the tribunal to make an order for specific performance within a specified time and is appropriate if the board is in breach of its duty to execute remedial works and para (b), which is appropriate if the board is in breach of its duty to make a payment. Paragraph (b) also enables the tribunal to give damages for any loss or damage consequent on any failure by the board to execute remedial works 'as soon as reasonably practicable'.

In my judgment the tribunal erred in, in effect, making a declaratory award. However, I should not like it to be thought that this conclusion involves any sort of criticism of the member. The cases which he stated are models of their kind and I doubt whether the view which I have expressed on the law was ever put to him, at least in the form which has appealed to me. It may well be that if the sole question referred had been the amount of the payment which the board should make a declaratory award would have been appropriate, but there could then have been no award of interest. But this is not what was referred. Ignoring the claim to relief under s 13(3)(a) as having been inappropriate once the board had exercised the election to pay compensation, the claimants were seeking damages. The award should have been for damages and interest at a specified rate. In fact it appears that the parties were agreed that the rate should be that applicable to judgment debts, but this should have been specified in the formal order.

I have had the advantage of reading in draft the judgment of Nourse LJ and, in the light of that judgment, I should perhaps explain why I consider that *Swift v Board of Trade* [1925] AC 520 and *Newport BC v Monmouthshire CC* [1947] 1 All ER 900 at 916, [1947] AC 520 at 556 are distinguishable.

In *Swift & Co v Board of Trade* the Food Controller had the right to requisition goods and the obligation to pay 'such compensation ... as shall, in default of agreement, be determined by the arbitration of a single arbitrator'. The arbitrator's mandate was thus to fix a figure for compensation and not to make an order for its payment or for damages for failure by the controller to pay it. If the controller failed to pay the compensation

after it had been fixed by the arbitrator, any remedy would have been by action. The
a decision on interest turned on the suggested application of the practice of the Court of
Chancery in relation to the payment of the purchase price of land. This is what Lord
Brandon in *President of India v La Pintada Cia Navegacion SA* [1984] 2 All ER 773 at 779,
[1985] AC 104 at 116 called 'the area of equity'. It is not an area with which we are
concerned and, of course, the 1934 Act had not then been passed.

In *Newport BC v Monmouthshire CC* the task of the arbitrator was again to fix a sum,
b rather than to make an award based on a failure by the authority to pay such a sum.
Failure to pay the sum so fixed would have given rise to a cause of action enforceable in
the courts and the courts could have awarded interest in respect of the period of delay in
payment after the award had fixed the amount payable (see [1947] 1 All ER 900 at 917,
[1947] AC 520 at 559 per Viscount Simon).

By contrast, the obligations of the board to pay compensation do not depend on any
c determination by an arbitrator of the amount of that compensation or, for that matter,
on his determination that particular damage is subsidence damage. The cause of action is
complete if subsidence damage occurs and the board fails to execute remedial works or
to pay compensation, in either case as soon as reasonably practicable. The mandate of the
arbitrator under s 13 of the 1957 Act is to resolve disputes as to that liability and to make
orders in the nature of specific performance or the award of damages in enforcement of
d that pre-existing liability. It is not to make a determination which will create the liability.
Thus the member's function is the same as that contemplated for the *courts* in the *Swift*
and *Monmouthshire* cases.

When interest should begin to accrue
The first case, stated at the request of the board, raised the question of whether, in
e principle, interest could be awarded for a period prior to the making of the award by the
tribunal. This I have answered in principle. The second case, stated at the request of the
claimants, challenged the decision of the member to award interest from 31 July 1980
rather than 31 December 1975 and to deny them the costs of the hearing.

The relevant part of the member's decision reads as follows:

f   'There remains the question of the date from which interest on the sum of £2,500
is to run. It seems to me that there are four possible dates:—(a) 31st August 1975,
being the date when the damage notice was served on the Board by [the claimants].
(b) 31st December 1975, being the date by which all the relevant damage had
occurred. (c) 31st July 1980, being the date when the Coal Board gave notice that
they did not propose to carry out remedial works and were therefore prepared to
make a payment as provided in section 1(4) of the Act. (d) 5th August 1981, being
g   the date of the Notice of Reference to the Lands Tribunal. I disregard the earliest
date because at that time there was no indication of the extent of the damage as
finally determined. It is true that 31st December 1975 can be taken as the date when
the cause of the action arose but at that time it was open to the Board to make good
the damage by carrying out remedial works. The date of the Notice of Reference is
the date when the proceedings in the Lands Tribunal were started, but by that time
h   damage had been suffered for a period of more than five years. In the circumstances
I consider that the proper date from which interest is to be calculated is to be the
31st July 1980 from which date the Board clearly accepted liability to pay to the
claimants a sum equal to the amount of the depreciation in the value of their
property caused by the damage.'

j   If we were to accept the member's reasoning, it would be open to the board to reduce
its liability in terms of interest by postponing its election to make payment instead of
executing remedial work and this notwithstanding that a duty to do one or the other
plainly arises 'as soon as reasonably practicable after the occasion of any subsidence
damage'. This cannot be right.

The fallacy lies in concentrating on the board's election, rather than its composite duty to execute remedial works or to pay compensation. The board does not have to do both and it has the right to elect which. The making of that election fixes the form which the duty is to be deemed to have taken ab initio. It follows that the member should have approached the matter on the footing that the board's obligation was to pay compensation 'as soon as reasonably practicable after the occurrence of the subsidence damage'. As he has held that the claimants' cause of action arose on 31 December 1975, he must have considered that this was the latest date for the performance of that duty. Accordingly, the claimants have been deprived of the use of the money, and the board has had the benefit of its use, since that date. This advantage to the board and disadvantage to the claimants falls to be redressed by an award of interest which should date from that date.

Costs of the hearing before the tribunal

There remains only the question of costs. Bearing in mind the open offers of settlement which were made, I am not persuaded that the order made by the member was other than a reasonable exercise of his discretion and accordingly I do not think that we should intervene, whether or not we should ourselves have made the same order.

Conclusion

I would answer the question raised by the case stated at the request of the board by saying that in determining under s 13(1) of the 1957 Act, the amount payable by the board to the claimants, there was no error in law in including interest in the award.

I would answer the questions raised by the case stated at the request of the claimants by saying that interest should have been awarded to run from 31 December 1975 and that there was no error of law in making no order as to costs save that there be a legal aid taxation of the claimants' costs.

NOURSE LJ. I have had the advantage of reading the judgments of Sir John Donaldson MR and Glidewell LJ in draft, but regret that I am unable to agree with them that the Lands Tribunal has power, under s 13 of the Coal-Mining (Subsidence) Act 1957, to order interest to be paid by the National Coal Board in respect of a period before the compensation is determined.

In my judgment the present case is governed by the decisions of the House of Lords in *Swift & Co v Board of Trade* [1925] AC 520 and *Newport BC v Monmouthshire CC* [1947] 1 All ER 900 at 916, [1947] AC 520 at 556. It is unfortunate that the latter decision was barely referred to in argument and the former not at all. It is possible that if they had been fully examined I could have been dissuaded from the view that there is no ground on which they can properly be distinguished in the present case. As it is, I can see no material difference between the provisions for reference to arbitration and the mandates given to the arbitrators in those cases and the provisions of s 13 of the 1957 Act. Indeed, the provisions in the *Monmouthshire* case were if anything wider, because they provided that 'the award of the arbitrator may provide for any matter for which an agreement might have provided'. In each of the three cases the task of the arbitrator was to determine a sum of money which could not be quantified beforehand. No distinction can be drawn merely because the sum to be determined in the present case is for compensation in the nature of damages or, if the correct view is that the Lands Tribunal was acting under s 13(3)(b) of the 1957 Act, actual damages.

Once the similarities between the present case and the two decisions of the House of Lords are recognised the only argument which is left is that s 13(1), in referring small claims to the county court, a court of record empowered to order the payment of interest on a debt or damages under s 3(1) of the Law Reform (Miscellaneous Provisions) Act 1934, has impliedly conferred the same power on the Lands Tribunal when dealing with large claims. However desirable that implication may be, I think that it is one which accepted principles of statutory construction do not allow us to make. You cannot, under the guise of implying something into a general enactment such as s 13, supply what are in reality the omissions of s 3(1) to extend beyond courts of record and of the Lands Tribunal Act 1949 to constitute that tribunal as such a court.

a I would therefore have allowed the appeal of the National Coal Board and answered the question raised by the case stated at their request in the contrary sense to that proposed by Sir John Donaldson MR and Glidewell LJ. But if I had shared their opinion on that question, I would also have agreed with their proposed answers to the questions raised by the case stated at the request of the claimants.

GLIDEWELL LJ. I agree with the judgment delivered by Sir John Donaldson MR.

b   I wish, however, to make clear my view that this decision is limited to the wording of this particular statute, the Coal-Mining (Subsidence) Act 1957. It should not be understood as a decision that the Lands Tribunal is entitled to award interest in every case of disputed compensation from the date on which the right to compensation arises.

As Mr Emlyn Jones observes in his admirable decision, the 1957 Act requires the Lands Tribunal to determine 'any question arising under this Act'. By analogy with the
c powers of an arbitrator appointed by agreement between the parties, the Lands Tribunal is required to apply English law, including, where appropriate, s 3 of the Law Reform (Miscellaneous Provisions) Act 1934. It is appropriate to apply that section in the present case because (a) as Sir John Donaldson MR makes clear, the claimants' claim in their reference was 'for compensation by way of damages' under s 13(3)(b) of the 1957 Act, and (b) the question which the statute requires the Lands Tribunal to determine is wide
d enough to comprehend the determination and award of interest on such damages.

An arbitrator now has the power under s 19A of the Arbitration Act 1950, inserted by the Administration of Justice Act 1982, to award simple interest 'for such period ending not later than the date of the award as he thinks fit'. If it be thought that the Lands Tribunal should have the same power to award interest for a period before the date of its award, this could be achieved by an amendment to the Lands Tribunal Rules 1975, SI
e 1975/299, to add s 19A to those sections of the Arbitration Act 1950 which already apply to proceedings in the tribunal.

Board's appeal dismissed. Claimants' appeal allowed to the extent that the first question in the case stated be answered in their favour. Board's application for leave to appeal to the House of Lords granted on terms as to costs.

f

Solicitors: *J G Tyrrell*, Eastwood (for the board); *Anderson & Co*, Nottingham (for the claimants).

Frances Rustin   Barrister.

Linnett v Coles

COURT OF APPEAL, CIVIL DIVISION
LAWTON, DILLON AND WOOLF LJJ
3, 4, 22 JULY 1986

Contempt of court – Committal – Order – Order unlawful on its face – Substitute order – Civil contempt – Defendant unlawfully committed 'until further order' for refusing to produce documents in civil litigation – Whether requirement that committal be for fixed term applying to civil contempt – Whether court having power to substitute such other order as is just – Administration of Justice Act 1960, s 13(3) – Contempt of Court Act 1981, s 14.

The defendant failed to obey orders of the court for the production of documents in the course of civil litigation and an order was made committing him to prison for contempt 'until further order'. The Official Solicitor, acting on his behalf, appealed against the committal order, contending that the order was unlawful on its face because it was for an indefinite term and therefore contrary to s 14[a] of the Contempt of Court Act 1981. On the hearing of the appeal the court accepted that argument and decided that the order was unlawful and would have to be quashed. The court indicated that it was disposed to substitute a custodial sentence of a fixed length but the Official Solicitor submitted that the court had no power or discretion to substitute any other order. The hearing was adjourned for further argument on the issues (i) whether s 14 of the 1981 Act applied to civil contempts and (ii) whether if the order was unlawful the court could exercise its appellate jurisdiction under s 13(3)[b] of the Administration of Justice Act 1960 to 'make such other order as may be just'.

Held – (1) Section 14 of the 1981 Act, which required committal orders to be for a fixed term, applied to civil contempts (see p 654 *d e*, p 657 *c* and p 658 *f*, post).

(2) Where an order committing a defendant for contempt was unlawful on its face and there had been no unfairness or material irregularity in the proceedings, the court had jurisdiction under s 13(3) of the 1960 Act to substitute such other penal order, whether a fine or imprisonment, as it thought just. However, although the court could theoretically increase the sentence it would hesitate to do so. The appeal would be allowed, the sentence quashed and, on the facts, no substitute sentence imposed (see p 654 *h*, p 655 *f g*, p 656 *g*, p 657 *a* to *c* and p 658 *c* to *f*, post).

Notes

For powers of courts on appeal in cases of contempt of court, see 9 Halsbury's Laws (4th edn) para 112, and for cases on the subject, see 16 Digest (Reissue) 115–118, 1194–1221.

For the Administration of Justice Act 1960, s 13, see 11 Halsbury's Statutes (4th edn) 176.

For the Contempt of Court Act 1981, s 14, see ibid 192.

Cases referred to in judgments

Balogh v Crown Court at St Albans [1974] 3 All ER 283, [1975] QB 73, [1974] 3 WLR 314, CA.
CBS (UK) Ltd v Manoli (1984) 135 NLJ 555, CA.
Cinderby v Cinderby (1978) 122 SJ 436, CA.

---

a   Section 14, so far as material, provides:
     '(1) In any case where the court has power to commit a person to prison for contempt of court and (apart from this provision) no limitation applies to the period of committal, the committal shall . . . be for a fixed term . . .'
b   Section 13(3), so far as material, is set out at p 654 *g*, post

Featherstone, Re (1953) 37 Cr App R 146, DC.

a *Hegarty v O'Sullivan* (1985) 135 NLJ 557, CA.

Hill Samuel & Co Ltd v Littaur (No 2) (1985) 135 NLJ 556, CA.

Hopkins, Ex p (1891) 61 LJQB 240.

McIlraith v Grady [1967] 3 All ER 625, [1968] 1 QB 468, [1967] 3 WLR 1331, CA.

O'Reilly v Mackman [1982] 3 All ER 1124, [1983] 2 AC 237, [1982] 3 WLR 1096, HL.

Peart v Stewart [1983] 1 All ER 859, [1983] 2 AC 109, [1983] 2 WLR 451, HL.

b *Wring, Re, re Cook* [1960] 1 All ER 536, [1960] 1 WLR 138, DC.

Cases also cited

Azam v Secretary of State for the Home Dept [1973] 2 All ER 765, [1974] AC 18, HL; *affg* [1973] 2 All ER 741, [1974] AC 18, CA.

Burdett v Abbot (1811) 14 East 1, 104 ER 501; *affd* (1812) 4 Taunt 401, Ex Ch; *affd* (1817)

c 5 Dow 165, [1814–23] All ER Rep 101, 3 ER 1289, HL.

Cammell Laird Shipbuilders Ltd v Trotter [1984] CA Transcript 361.

Corke, Re [1954] 2 All ER 440, [1954] 1 WLR 899, DC.

Cullen v Rose [1985] CA Transcript 804.

Danchevski v Danchevski [1974] 3 All ER 934, [1975] Fam 17, CA.

Danchevski v Danchevski (No 2) (1977) 121 SJ 796, CA.

d *Debtor, Re a* [1986] CA Transcript 231.

Fernandez, Ex p (1861) 10 CBNS 3, 142 ER 349.

Green v Secretary of State for Home Affairs [1941] 3 All ER 388, [1942] AC 284, HL.

Hinds, Ex p (No 2) [1961] 1 All ER 707, [1961] 1 WLR 325, DC.

Hunt, Re [1959] 2 All ER 252, [1959] 2 QB 69, CA; *affg* [1959] 1 All ER 73, [1959] 1 QB 378, DC.

e *Keenan, Re* [1971] 3 All ER 883, [1972] 1 QB 533, CA.

Middlesex Sheriff's Case (1840) 11 Ad & El 273, 113 ER 419.

Philpot, Re [1960] 1 All ER 165, [1960] 1 WLR 115, DC.

R v Secretary of State for the Home Dept, ex p Swati [1986] 1 All ER 717, [1986] 1 WLR 477, CA.

Smith v Smith (1983) 134 NLJ 603, CA.

f *Stockdale v Hansard* (1839) 9 Ad & El 1, 112 ER 1112.

Wellington v Wellington (1978) 122 SJ 296, CA.

Willetts v Willetts [1979] CA Transcript 142.

Appeal

The Official Solicitor, on behalf of the defendant, John William Coles, appealed pursuant

g to an extension of time for appealing and leave to appeal granted by the Court of Appeal (May, Dillon and Ralph Gibson LJJ) on 25 April 1986 against (i) an order of his Honour Judge O'Donoghue sitting as a judge of the High Court at Birmingham on 19 August 1985 whereby it was ordered that the defendant be committed for contempt of court to Her Majesty's prison at Winson Green, Birmingham 'to be there imprisoned until further order', and (ii) the direction given by his Honour Judge Micklem sitting as a judge of the

h High Court at Birmingham on or about 12 February 1986 that a warrant be issued for the defendant's arrest. The facts are set out in the judgment of Lawton LJ.

James Munby for the Official Solicitor.

John Laws as amicus curiae.

j   *Cur adv vult*

22 July. The following judgments were delivered.

LAWTON LJ. This is an appeal by the Official Solicitor, acting on behalf of the

defendant, John William Coles, against, first, an order made by his Honour Judge
O'Donoghue, sitting as a judge of the High Court at Birmingham, whereby it was   *a*
ordered that the defendant should be committed to prison for contempt of court 'until
further order' and, second, against a direction given by his Honour Judge Micklem, also
sitting as a judge of the High Court, on or about 12 February 1986 that a warrant for the
defendant's arrest should be issued. The defendant had not obeyed orders of the court for
the production of documents. The warrant was executed on 17 April 1986 and the
defendant was lodged in prison the next day.   *b*
    The appeal raises the following questions. First, was the order a lawful one having
regard to the provisions of s 14 of the Contempt of Court Act 1981? Second, if the order
was an unlawful one, has this court any jurisdiction under s 13(3) of the Administration
of Justice Act 1960 or RSC Ord 59, r 10(3) to substitute such other penal order, whether
custodial or pecuniary, as it thinks just?
    The Official Solicitor, through counsel, submitted that, as the order was unlawful on   *c*
its face, it had to be quashed and that this court had neither power nor discretion to
substitute any other order. Counsel as an amicus curiae, nominated by the Attorney
General accepted that the order on its face was unlawful but submitted that the court had
power to substitute such other order as was just.
    The defendant's failure to produce documents in the course of litigation was a civil
contempt. Doubts have been expressed whether s 14 of the 1981 Act applies to civil   *d*
contempts. In my judgment, it clearly does; first, because of its wide language and,
second, because the County Courts (Penalties for Contempt) Act 1983, which amended
s 14 of the 1981 Act, made that Act applicable to contempts in the county court. Most
contempts in that court are civil ones.
    Answering the second question calls for consideration of what led Parliament to enact
s 13 of the 1960 Act. Before then, there was no way of appealing against a finding and   *e*
sentence for criminal contempt, save when there had been a conviction on indictment
for such contempt (and there had not been one since 1902). It had been possible to appeal
to this court against a finding and sentence for civil contempt but there had been fetters
on the right of appeal. It was clearly the intention of Parliament to give a right of appeal
in criminal contempt cases and to strike off the fetters in civil contempt ones. It did so
by s 13, the relevant parts of which for the purposes of this appeal are as follows: *f*

    '(1) Subject to the provisions of this section, an appeal shall lie under this section
    from any order or decision of a court in the exercise of jurisdiction to punish for
    contempt of court (including criminal contempt); and in relation to any such order
    or decision the provisions of this section shall have effect in substitution for any
    other enactment relating to appeals in civil or criminal proceedings . . .
    (3) The court to which an appeal is brought under this section may reverse or   *g*
    vary the order or decision of the court below, and make such other order as may be
    just . . .'

If sub-s (3) is construed in the same way as any other statute is construed, namely by
considering what Parliament wanted to achieve and the words used to that end, the
appellate courts are given wide powers. If they reverse or vary the order under appeal   *h*
they may, in addition, make such other order as may be just. When this case first came
before this court (differently constituted) on 25 April 1986, it was obvious that the order
imprisoning the offender 'until further order' was unlawful and would have to be
quashed. At that date, however, there was such a long history of contumacious default
on the part of the defendant that the court was disposed to consider exercising its powers
under RSC Ord 59, r 10(3) by substituting for the unlawful order a custodial sentence of   *j*
a length which would be just. Counsel acting as amicus curiae submitted that the court
could not substitute another sentence. The appeal was adjourned for further argument.
The defendant was released on bail. The Attorney General was invited to appoint an
amicus curiae and did so.
    By the time of the resumed hearing, both counsel had done much research. The

surprising fact came to light that, although on a number of occasions since 1975 this
a court has considered whether, when there has been some irregularity in the making of a
committal order for contempt, it had power to remedy the irregularity, it does not seem
to have considered whether it could do so under s 13(3) of the 1960 Act. It has adjudged
that it had no power to do so under the 'slip rule', Ord 20, r 11 (see *Cinderby v Cinderby*
(1978) 122 SJ 436) or under the rule relating to irregularities, Ord 2 (see *Hill Samuel & Co
Ltd v Littaur (No 2)* (1985) 135 NLJ 556) or under the general powers of this court, Ord
b 59, r 10(3) (see *Hegarty v O'Sullivan* (1985) 135 NLJ 557).

   Counsel acting as amicus curiae, however, did invite our attention to s 13 of the 1960
Act. He submitted that the effect of that section was to give appellate courts jurisdiction
when, as with criminal contempts, none had existed and to extend jurisdiction when, as
with civil contempts, it had been fettered. Having given jurisdiction Parliament should
be taken to have expected appellate courts to use it which, since 1975 at least, this court
c has not done when there has been an irregularity on the face of the order. In a number
of cases this court has adjudged that, once an irregularity, however minor, is revealed in
the making or form of a committal order which has been executed, it cannot be cured: it
must be quashed; and no substitute order made. The reason why this court has acted as
it has was succinctly stated by Lord Denning MR in *Cinderby v Cinderby* (I read from the
transcript):

d   'In cases concerning the liberty of the subject, the courts have always been most
      strict to see that all the requirements of the law are complied with. On a return for
      habeas corpus, the order has always to be in proper form. I am afraid in this case
      that there was an error in the committal order. It was not in accordance with the
      prescribed form. Therefore it must be set aside and Mr Cinderby, the husband,
      must be released forthwith . . . We are so careful of the liberty of the subject that
e   everything must be done in order before a man's liberty is taken away. We cannot
      correct this order under the slip rule.'

   I accept, of course, that judges must be vigilant concerning the liberty of the subject; but,
if Parliament gives them discretionary powers, as s 13 of the 1960 Act seems to do, it is
not competent for them to refuse to exercise those powers. It would be a misuse of
f powers for a judge to say: 'I know Parliament has given me a discretion to vary orders in
contempt appeals and make just ones, but I'm never going to use them. Such is my
concern for the liberty of the subject that I am prepared to allow a contemnor who ought
to be punished for contempt to go unpunished; and that is so, notwithstanding that
Parliament envisages that I could consider imposing a just punishment.' None of the
cases in this court to which counsel for the Official Solicitor has invited our attention are
g binding on us because seemingly the court never considered what powers it had to make
a suitable order under s 13 of the 1960 Act.

   Despite what seems to be the plain meaning of s 13 counsel for the Official Solicitor
submitted that Parliament, when enacting that section, must have intended appellate
courts to apply it in a restricted way because any contemnor held in custody under a
committal order bad on its face (as the one under appeal is) could apply for and obtain a
h writ of habeas corpus ad subjiciendum whereby he would be at once released. It followed
that the power to vary and make another order could only be used in cases in which a
writ of habeas corpus would not issue. There would be few such cases because many
appeals relate to cases in which the committal order is bad on its face. This is because
courts making committal orders in civil cases have to use statutory forms which, if they
are not used, or used improperly, usually reveal irregularities in the procedure.

j   If this be right, it is surprising that, since 1960, the Official Solicitor, who appears in
most appeals against committal order for civil contempts, has not in recent years used
the habeas corpus procedure nor, as far as we know, have contemnors who have been
privately represented. It is also surprising that, if Parliament intended that this court
should only have powers limited in the way for which counsel for the Official Solicitor
contends, it gave the powers it did in wholly inappropriate language.

In order to decide whether s 13(3) should be construed narrowly, it has been necessary to consider the ambit of the writ of habeas corpus. It is a writ of right, not of course, because the party applying for it has to show some reasonable ground for being awarded it (see 3 Bl Com (1857 edn) 141). A writ of habeas corpus is probably the most cherished sacred cow in the British constitution; but the law has never allowed it to graze in all legal pastures. The proceedings of criminal courts of record seem to have forbidden it. Of the many cases drawn to our attention when error was revealed on the face of the record, only one related to a return showing detention by the order of such a court. That was the curious case of Daisy Hopkins (see *Ex p Hopkins* (1891) 61 LJQB 240), who had been convicted in the Vice-Chancellor's Court of Cambridge University of 'walking with a member of the university' and committed to the Spinning House for 14 days. Before the Indictments Act 1915 the record of a criminal conviction on indictment was a fairly complicated document. Between about 1662, when the Court of King's Bench began to exercise its supervisory jurisdiction over inferior courts, and 1915 cases must have occurred when such records were drawn up incorrectly; and since 1915 cases have occurred within my own judicial experience when the indorsement of the conviction or sentence on the indictment has been wrong. Nevertheless, writs of habeas corpus are not recorded as having issued in such cases. Before 1907, when they occurred, recourse had to be made to the writ of error; and since that year to appeals under the Criminal Appeals Acts 1907 to 1968. In *Re Featherstone* (1953) 37 Cr App R 146 at 147 Lord Goddard CJ, that master of Crown practice, said:

'The court does not grant, and cannot grant, writs of *habeas corpus* to persons who are in execution, that is to say, persons who are serving sentences passed by courts of competent jurisdiction. Probably the only case in which the court would grant *habeas corpus* would be if it were satisfied that the prisoner was being held after the terms of the sentence passed on him had expired.'

In a practice note issued in 1960 (see *Re Wring, Re Cook* [1960] 1 All ER 536 at 537, [1960] 1 WLR 138) Lord Parker CJ cited with approval what Lord Goddard CJ had said. The practice note, of course, did not say that applications for writs of habeas corpus could not be made, it discouraged them as being unlikely to succeed.

It is pertinent to remember that civil contempt of court is a common law misdemeanour which can be tried on indictment (which it never is nowadays) or summarily, either by the judge dealing with the case or on motion before the Divisional Court: see *Balogh v Crown Court at St Albans* [1974] 3 All ER 283, [1975] 1 QB 73. Having regard to what seems always to have been a limitation on the issue of the writ of habeas corpus in criminal causes or matters, it seems to me that, save in exceptional cases, it is not the appropriate remedy for appealing against committal orders. Had it been, Parliament would not have enacted s 13(3) of the 1960 Act in the terms it did. The availability of the writ of habeas corpus in exceptional circumstances, in my judgment, provides no good reason for giving this subsection any other than its ordinary meaning.

I turn now to applying the subsection to the facts of this case. After his release on bail the contemnor consulted solicitors. He then complied with the orders which he had disobeyed and apologised to the court. There would be no point in ordering him back to prison. There is the question whether justice requires that the order of imprisonment should be quashed without substituting any other order, such as a sentence of eight days which was the time he had been in custody, therefore had served, before being released on bail. Consideration of this question enables this court to indicate, as counsel for the Official Solicitor told us the Official Solicitor would like us to do, what we think are the circumstances in which the power to make a substitute order should be exercised.

Anyone accused of contempt of court is on trial for that misdemeanour and is entitled to a fair trial. If he does not get a fair trial because of the way the judge has behaved or because of material irregularities in the proceedings themselves, then there has been a mistrial, which is no trial at all. In such cases, in my judgment, an unlawful sentence cannot stand and must be quashed. It will depend on the facts of each case whether

justice requires a new one to be substituted. If there has been no unfairness or no material
a irregularity in the proceedings and nothing more than an irregularity in drawing up the
committal order has occurred, I can see no reason why the irregularity should not be put
right and the sentence varied, if necessary, so as to make it a just one.

On the wording of the subsection a just sentence could be a longer one. It is pertinent
to remember that it was enacted at a time when the Court of Criminal Appeal had power
to increase sentences. Its successor, the Criminal Division of this court, has no such
b power. In my opinion, this court should hesitate a long time before exercising its power
to increase sentences, as does nowadays the Crown Court, which has a similar power,
when hearing appeals against sentences imposed by magistrates.

I would allow the appeal and quash the sentence. On the facts of this case it is
unnecessary to substitute another sentence.

c **DILLON LJ.** I agree. I add a few words of my own since I was a member of the division
of this court which, on 25 April 1986, suspended the committal order against the
defendant, ordered his discharge from prison and invited the Attorney General to appoint
an amicus curiae to assist the court on the further hearing of his appeal.

What we were concerned about then was to see whether the court had any power to
correct the error, where a wrong sentence had been imposed by a court on a contemnor
d for contempt of court, or where it appeared on the face of the committal order that the
court officials had, in drawing up that order, failed to comply with some of the
requirements of Rules of the Supreme Court or of the County Court Rules.

The Official Solicitor is rightly charged with examining cases where there has been a
committal to prison for contempt of court, to see if there has been any unfairness or
impropriety. The practice had developed (possibly from *McIlraith v Grady* [1967] 3 All
e ER 625, [1968] 1 QB 468) that, wherever it appeared on the face of the committal order
that there had been any error, or non-compliance with the rules as to the form of the
order, the committal was almost automatically quashed by this court, at any rate if the
contemnor had been taken into custody. These applications to quash committals for
error or irregularity on the face of the order were usually made by counsel for the Official
Solicitor and very often the other party to the litigation, who had suffered from the
f contemnor's wrongful acts, was not prepared to incur the costs of instructing counsel to
oppose the Official Solicitor's application. But in this process the court had applied what
Lord Denning MR in *McIlraith v Grady* [1967] 3 All ER 625 at 627, [1968] 1 QB 468 at
477 called 'the fundamental principle that no man's liberty is to be taken away unless
every requirement of the law has been strictly complied with' so rigorously as to lead to
results, in some cases, that tend to make the court's own process appear ridiculous, results
g which, particularly in domestic violence or matrimonial cases, it is difficult to regard as
just to the other party to the litigation who has suffered from the contemnor's acts.

I would give one example, though others come easily to mind.

In *CBS (UK) Ltd v Manoli* (1984) 135 NLJ 555, a decision to which I was a party, this
court held, in relation to a committal order made in the High Court, that it is a
fundamental principle of the law relating to contempt that a person may not be
h imprisoned for contempt unless the order imprisoning him allows him to see from the
face of the order the precise contempt for which he is being imprisoned: see especially
the judgment of Griffiths LJ. This sounds well, except that in a High Court case the
contemnor will regularly be taken into custody before the committal order has been
drawn up. He will be taken into custody under the bench warrant signed by the judge,
which is not required to, and does not, specify the acts of contempt found proved. There
j is no requirement for serving the committal order, when drawn up, on the contemnor,
nor is there any occasion for doing so when the contemnor is already in custody under
the bench warrant. Yet, seemingly, if the order, when drawn up, fails, by error of the
court officials, to comply with the requirements of the rules, the detention of the
contemnor, lawful at the outset under the bench warrant, will become illegal unless this
court has power to substitute a new order to correct the error.

It was for those reasons that the other division of this court, on 25 April, invited the appointment of an amicus so that there could be full argument as to the extent of this *a* court's powers on the effective hearing of the defendant's appeal.

We have had such argument from counsel acting as amicus curiae, and he has drawn the court's attention to s 13 of the Administration of Justice Act 1960. So far as our researches have gone (and that goes also, as he has conceded, to the researches of counsel for the Official Solicitor) that section has never been drawn to the attention of this court in any of the numerous cases hitherto in which various divisions of this court have *b* quashed committal orders for irregularity appearing on the face of the order.

Section 13(1) provides that an appeal is to lie under the section from any order or decision of a court in the exercise of jurisdiction to punish for contempt of court. That must apply to orders which are bad on their face as much as to orders which are in form impeccable. Subsection (3) then provides that the court to which an appeal is brought under the section may reverse or vary the order or decision of the court below and make *c* such other order as may be just. As a matter of construction that must equally apply whether the order of the court below is good or bad on its face.

The question is then whether the fundamental principle referred to by Lord Denning MR in *McIlraith v Grady* requires that, if there is irregularity on the face of the order, the court *must* quash the committal altogether, without making any other order, however just. For the reasons given by Lawton LJ, I do not think that it does so require. Moreover, *d* I note that in *Peart v Stewart* [1983] 1 All ER 859, [1983] 2 AC 109, where a county court judge had committed a contemnor to prison for six months for civil contempt, and the House of Lords held that, under the Act as then in force, the judge had no power to impose a sentence longer than one month, the House of Lords simply reduced the sentence from the (illegal) six months to one month, and no one suggested that the sentence fell to be quashed altogether. *e*

On the special facts of this case, I agree also with the order proposed by Lawton LJ.

WOOLF LJ. I agree with both the previous judgments. Having regard to the jurisdiction of this court on an appeal as set out in those judgments, I recognise that a person, the subject of a committal order on the ground of contempt, might attempt to bypass the jurisdiction of this court by making an application for habeas corpus because he *f* appreciated that the court on an appeal would cure the defect in the order on which he would like to rely. In my view, the question would then arise whether such an application, which was designed to prevent this court making such order 'as may be just' under s 13(3) of the Administration of Justice Act 1960 amounted to an abuse of the process of the court on the basis of the reasoning of the House of Lords in *O'Reilly v Mackman* [1982] 3 All ER 1124, [1983] 2 AC 237. As was indicated in argument, the *g* court might decide that there was no reason why *O'Reilly v Mackman* should not apply in reverse. However, this point does not arise for final decision on this appeal.

Appeal allowed. Sentence quashed. No order for costs.

Solicitors: *Official Solicitor; Treasury Solicitor.* *h*

Mary Rose Plummer   Barrister.

j

Metrolands Investments Ltd v J H Dewhurst Ltd

COURT OF APPEAL, CIVIL DIVISION
SLADE, NICHOLLS LJJ AND SHELDON J
29, 30 JANUARY, 21 FEBRUARY 1986

Landlord and tenant – Rent – Review – Failure to comply with time limits – Presumption that time not of essence – Correlation between rent review clause and time limit in tenant's break clause – Both parties having option to initiate rent review – Rent review clause providing for arbitration to determine new rent on parties' failure to agree – Arbitrator's decision to be obtained within specified time limit – Landlord serving notice of rent review after expiry of time limit – Whether correlation between rent review clause and break clause making time of essence – Whether presumption that time not of the essence displaced.

The tenant was the lessee of a shop under a 21-year lease from 19 February 1968 at a rent of £1,500 for the first three years, £1,800 for the next eleven years and for the remaining seven years the open market rent at the beginning of the seven-year period (ie on 19 February 1982) as agreed by the parties or, failing agreement, as determined by an arbitrator appointed by both parties but 'not in any event [to] be less' than £1,800 per year. The lease further provided that the arbitrator's determination was to be obtained before 19 August 1981 and that the tenant was entitled, under a break clause, to terminate the lease on 18 February 1982 by serving notice on the landlord between 19 August 1981 and 18 November 1981, the object of the rent review and break clauses being that the tenant would know the new rent before deciding whether to terminate the lease under the break clause. Neither party attempted to implement the rent review clause prior to 19 August 1981 and the tenant did not attempt to implement the break clause prior to 18 November. Two weeks after that date the landlord served notice on the tenant requesting a rent review. The tenant claimed that the landlord was too late. The landlord sought a declaration that the rent payable for the last seven years was the open market rent as determined by arbitration or the court. On the trial of a preliminary issue, the judge held that the interrelation between the rent review and break clauses raised a presumption that time was of the essence of the rent review clause and that since the landlord had not complied with the time limits for initiating the rent review he was not entitled to invoke the arbitration procedure and the rent payable for the last seven years of the term was therefore £1,800 per year. The landlord appealed. At the hearing of the appeal the tenant contended that there were two indications which rebutted the normal presumption that time was not of the essence in a rent review clause, namely (i) the provision that 'in any event' the annual rent for the last seven years was to be not less than £1,800 was a default clause whereby the annual rent payable was £1,800 in default of compliance with the rent review timetable, which indicated that strict compliance with the rent review timetable was required, and (ii) the interrelation between the rent review and break clauses.

Held – (1) The provision in the lease that 'in any event' the annual rent for the last seven years was to be not less than £1,800 could not be construed as a default clause providing for the rent which was to be payable in default of compliance with the rent review timetable but was instead merely an indication that whatever might be the arbitrator's decision the rent review would not result in a drop in rent (see p 663 *e h*, post).

(2) Since the ultimate object of the court in construing a rent review clause was to ascertain the parties' intentions from the words used and since the rent review could only result in an increase in rent and was thus only for the landlord's benefit, it followed that the test to be applied was whether, from the words used, the proper intention to be imputed to the parties was that the landlord should lose his right to a rent review if the

stipulated timetable was not strictly adhered to. Having regard to the facts that (a) the landlord was likely to suffer greater detriment if he lost the right to a rent review than the tenant would suffer if the assessment of the new rent was delayed, (b) what was required by the rent review clause was the actual obtaining of the arbitrator's decision, which was an event substantially outside the landlord's control since the arbitrator might be dilatory or the tenant's submissions might delay the proceedings, and (c) the tenant had it in his own power to obviate any hardship arising from the landlord's delay by himself initiating the rent review, the interrelation between the rent review and break clauses was not sufficient to rebut the presumption that time was not of the essence in the rent review clause, and accordingly the intention properly to be attributed to the parties was that time was not of the essence. The landlord's appeal would therefore be allowed (see p 668 j to p 669 c, p 670 c to e h to p 671 a c to g, post); dictum of Lord Diplock in *United Scientific Holdings Ltd v Burnley BC* [1977] 2 All ER at 72 applied; *Coventry City Council v J Hepworth & Sons Ltd* (1982) 46 P & CR 170 distinguished.

Decision of Peter Gibson J [1985] 3 All ER 206 reversed.

Notes

For time being of the essence of a rent review clause, see 27 Halsbury's Laws (4th edn) para 216.

Cases referred to in judgment

Coventry City Council v J Hepworth & Sons Ltd (1982) 46 P & CR 170, CA; *affg* (1981) 261 EG 566.
Hill (William) (Southern) Ltd v Govier & Govier (1984) 269 EG 1168.
Richards (C) & Son Ltd v Karenita Ltd (1971) 221 EG 25.
Samuel Properties (Developments) Ltd v Hayek [1972] 3 All ER 473, [1972] 1 WLR 1296, CA.
Touche Ross & Co v Secretary of State for the Environment (1982) 46 P & CR 187, CA.
United Scientific Holdings Ltd v Burnley BC, Cheapside Land Development Co Ltd v Messells Service Co [1977] 2 All ER 62, [1978] AC 904, [1977] 2 WLR 806, HL.
Weller v Akehurst [1981] 3 All ER 411.

Cases also cited

Amalgamated Estates Ltd v Joystretch Manufacturing Ltd (1980) 257 EG 489, CA.
Bremer Vulkan Schiffbau Und Mashinenfabrik v South India Shipping Corp [1981] 1 All ER 289, [1981] AC 909, HL.
Chartered Trust plc v Maylands Green Estate Co Ltd (1984) 270 EG 845.
Knowles & Sons Ltd v Bolton Corp [1900] 2 QB 253, CA.
Lord v Lee (1868) LR 3 QB 404.
SI Pension Trustees v William Hudson Ltd (1977) 35 P & CR 54.

Appeal

The plaintiff, Metrolands Investments Ltd (Metrolands), appealed against the judgment of Peter Gibson J ([1985] 3 All ER 206) given on 21 December 1984 dismissing Metrolands' action against the defendant, J H Dewhurst Ltd (Dewhurst), for, inter alia, a declaration that the yearly rent payable by Dewhurst to Metrolands for the last seven years of a lease dated 30 January 1968 made between the parties was the yearly rent at which the demised premises might reasonably be expected to be let without premium in the open market on terms similar to those contained in the lease, and declaring instead that the yearly rent payable by Dewhurst for the last seven years of the term was £1,800. The facts are set out in the judgment of the court.

Michael Mark for Metrolands.
James Thom for Dewhurst.

Cur adv vult

21 February. The following judgment of the court was delivered.

a

SLADE LJ. This is the judgment of the court on an appeal by the plaintiff in certain landlord and tenant proceedings from an order of Peter Gibson J made on 21 December 1984 on the trial of a preliminary issue in the action. The appellant landlord is Metrolands Investments Ltd (Metrolands). The respondent tenant is J H Dewhurst Ltd (Dewhurst). The dispute between the parties concerns a rent review clause.

b   The decision of Peter Gibson J contains a very clear statement of the relevant facts and is reported in the All England Law Reports (see [1985] 3 All ER 206). The action related to a butcher's shop which was let by Metrolands to Dewhurst by a lease dated 30 January 1968 for a term of 21 years from 19 February 1968. The reddendum was in this form:

c

> 'YIELDING AND PAYING therefor during the first three years of the said term the yearly rent of [£1,500] during the next eleven years of the said term the yearly rent of [£1,800] and during the remaining seven years of the said term the yearly rent at which the demised premises might on [19 February 1982] reasonably be expected to let without premium in the open market between willing landlord and willing tenant on terms similar to those contained in this present Lease and assuming that the Lessee has observed and performed all the covenants and conditions to be observed and performed hereunder but disregarding any goodwill attaching to the demised premises by reason of the carrying on thereat of the Lessees business such yearly rent to be agreed between the Landlord and the Lessee and failing agreement to be determined by arbitration as hereinafter provided Provided always that the decision of such arbitrator shall be obtained before the expiration of the first half of the Fourteenth year of the term hereby created BUT such yearly rent shall not in any event be less than [£1,800]...'

d

e

The judge found it convenient to divide the relevant part of the reddendum relating to the last seven years of the term into four limbs: limb 1 commencing with 'during the remaining seven years' and ending with 'the lessee's business'; limb 2 commencing with 'such yearly rent' and ending with 'as hereinafter provided'; limb 3 commencing with 'provided always' and ending with 'term hereby created'; and limb 4 commencing with 'but such yearly rent' and ending with '£1,800'. I will adopt the same convenient division.

f

There are two other material provisions of the lease. Clause 4(4) provides:

> 'If any dispute question difference or controversy shall arise which under the terms of this Lease is to be referred to arbitration the same shall be referred to a single arbitrator to be agreed between the parties or failing agreement to two arbitrators (one to be appointed by each party to the reference) or their umpire pursuant to and so as with regard to the mode and consequences of any such reference and in all other respects to be in conformity with the provisions of the Arbitration Act 1950 or any statutory modification or re-enactment thereof.'

g

Clause 5 (the break clause) provides:

h

> 'PROVIDED LASTLY AND IT IS HEREBY AGREED AND DECLARED that if the Lessee shall be desirous of determining this present lease at the end of the fourteenth year of the term hereby granted and of such its desire shall deliver to the Landlord or leave for the Landlord or send by registered post to the Landlord at its registered office within the six months previous to the end of the said fourteenth year of the said term not less than three months notice in writing and shall pay all rent and perform and observe all the covenants and conditions hereinbefore contained and on the part of the Lessee to be performed and observed up to such determination then and in such case immediately after the expiration of the said period of fourteen years this present Lease shall cease and be void without prejudice to any claim by the Landlord against the Lessee in respect of any antecedent breach of any covenant or condition herein contained.'

j

The timetable envisaged by the express provisions of the reddendum and the break clause was thus as follows. (1) The date by reference to which the open market yearly *a* rent payable by Dewhurst for the last seven years of the term was to be calculated was to be 19 February 1982 (being the first day of that seven-year period). (2) The open market yearly rent payable by Dewhurst for this seven-year period was to be fixed according to the formula set out in the reddendum, either by agreement betwen the two parties or in default of agreement by arbitration. If arbitration was necessary the decision of the arbitrator was to be obtained before 19 August 1981. (3) Dewhurst would be free to *b* operate the break clause by serving written notice on Metrolands at any time between 19 August 1981 and 18 November 1981 with the effect of determining the lease on 18 February 1982.

Neither Metrolands nor Dewhurst made any attempt to agree a rent or to go to arbitration before 19 August 1981. Dewhurst did not attempt to operate the break clause before 19 November 1981. On 2 December 1981, for the first time, Metrolands by its *c* surveyors wrote to Dewhurst indicating that it wanted the rent to be reviewed, although no figure was then suggested. On 17 December 1981, Dewhurst replied to the effect that the rent review notice was invalid as being too late and pointed out that it was by then also too late for it to serve a notice under the break clause. Dewhurst, however, does not suggest that Metrolands deliberately delayed serving notice of its intention to have the rent reviewed.   *d*

On 24 October 1983 Metrolands issued proceedings against Dewhurst. By para 1 of the prayer for relief in its statement of claim it claimed a declaration, in effect, that the rent payable in the last seven years of the term is that set out in the formula embodied in limb 1 of the reddendum.

The master made a consent order that the question raised by this paragraph, and the question whether the amount of the yearly rent was to be determined by the court or by *e* arbitration or in some other way, should be tried as a preliminary issue, on the basis of an agreed statement of facts. The judge declined to grant any of the relief sought. He upheld Dewhurst's contention that time was of the essence of the rent review procedure embodied in the lease and that Metrolands' attempt to initiate that procedure in December 1981 onwards was accordingly too late.

As the judge said, the starting point for any consideration of the question whether *f* time is of the essence of rent review provisions is the decision of the House of Lords in *United Scientific Holdings Ltd v Burnley BC, Cheapside Land Development Co Ltd v Messells Service Co* [1977] 2 All ER 62 at 72, [1978] AC 904 at 930, where Lord Diplock stated the principle that—

> 'in the absence of any contra-indications in the express words of the lease or in the interrelation of the rent review clause itself and other clauses or in the surrouding *g* circumstances, the presumption is that the timetable specified in a rent review clause for completion of the various steps for determining the rent payable in respect of the period following the review date is not of the essence of the contract.'

Neither side in argument has placed any reliance on surrounding circumstances as an aid to the construction of this lease. Counsel for Dewhurst, however, has submitted to *h* us, as he submitted to Peter Gibson J, that this particular lease contains two contra-indications sufficient to rebut the normal presumption that the timetable specified in a rent review clause is not of the essence of the contract. The first suggested contra-indication is the express terms of limb 4 of the reddendum. The judge rejected this submission (see [1985] 3 All ER 206 at 210) and Dewhurst challenges this rejection in a respondent's notice. However, he accepted the sufficiency and full force of the second *j* contra-indication relied on by Dewhurst, which was the interrelation between the time limit in limb 3 of the reddendum and the break clause. This is the part of his decision which Metrolands seeks to challenge on this appeal (see [1985] 3 All ER 206 at 210–214). It has not sought to pursue certain alternative submissions which were advanced in the court below and are referred to in the report (see [1985] 3 All ER 206 at 215). The effect a   of the judge's decision was that the lease had made no express provision for the amount of the rent to be payable for the last seven years of the term if it was not ascertained by agreement or arbitration within the specified time limits; that the court itself had no power to determine a rent if those time limits were not complied with and that, in the event of non-compliance, the annual rent payable for the last seven years must continue to be the same as that payable for the preceding period, namely £1,800 (see [1985] 3 All ER 206 at 215–216, adopting the principle in *Weller v Akehurst* [1981] 3 All ER 411).

b   It will be convenient to begin by dealing with the first of the suggested contra-indications relied on by Dewhurst, since it raises a short, albeit not entirely easy, question of construction arising on the reddendum, when read in isolation.

Counsel for Dewhurst pointed out that the words 'BUT such yearly rent shall not in any event be less than [£1,800]' in limb 4 of the reddendum immediately follow the proviso at the end of limb 3, which provides, (in apparently mandatory form, in view of the use of the word 'shall'), that 'the decision of such arbitrator shall be obtained' before the stated

c   date. In his submission, the parties to the lease must have contemplated the possible contingency of a failure to obtain such a decision by the stated date. The words 'in any event', as he put it, do 'double duty' by covering the possible contingency of the arbitrator fixing an annual rent of less than £1,800 *and* the possible contingency of the failure to obtain a timeous decision from the arbitrator. Thus, in his submission, one of the two

d   purposes of limb 4, when properly construed, is to specify the rent that is to be payable in default of compliance with the time limits laid down in limb 3. The coupling of this 'in default' provision with the final time limit in limb 3 shows, in his submission, that this time limit is intended to be a strict one.

The judge rejected these submissions ([1985] 3 All ER 206 at 210):

e   'Limb 4 relates to "such yearly rent". That, as counsel for Metrolands pointed out, can only refer to the yearly rent on the hypothetical basis set out in limb 1 or on that basis and agreed or determined in limb 2. All that limb 4 does is to put a minimum figure on the yearly rent on that basis or on that basis and agreed or determined. It does not refer to the rent not ascertained by reference to limb 1 or limb 2. In my judgment, therefore, limb 4 cannot be construed as a default clause to operate on the failure to go to arbitration at all or to obtain the decision in time.'

f   The phrase 'such yearly rent' in limb 4 echoes the same phrase which is used in limb 2. In limb 2 it clearly refers to a rent to be agreed or determined according to the formula specified in limb 1. Prima facie the phrase must bear the same meaning in limb 4 as it bears in limb 2. There is, however, a further point which supports the judge's construction, to which counsel for Metrolands drew our attention. If limb 4 were

g   intended to operate as a provision fixing the rent in default of its being otherwise determined by agreement or arbitration within the specified time limits, the words 'not . . . less than' in limb 4 would be quite inappropriate.

For all these reasons, we conclude that limb 4 cannot properly be read as an 'in default' provision. We respectfully agree with the judge's conclusion on this point, and that the reddendum, read by itself, does not contain any clear indication that time is to be of the

h   essence of the rent review provisions. While the phrase 'in any event' in limb 4 is not a very clear one, we read it as meaning 'whatever may be the arbitrator's decision', so as to ensure that on any footing the rent review will be incapable of resulting in a drop in rent.

We now turn to the other suggested contra-indication relied on by Dewhurst, based on the correlation of the rent review clause with the break clause. Let it be said at once

j   that there is the clearest possible correlation of this nature. Earlier in this judgment we have set out the timetable envisaged by the express provisions of the lease. The relevant dates were clearly fixed by the draftsman in the contemplation that any necessary decision of the arbitrator would be obtained at the very latest before 19 August 1981, which was to be the start of the three months' period (19 August–18 November 1981) during which Dewhurst was to be free, if it thought fit, to serve a notice to determine the lease. The draftsman manifestly envisaged a timetable by virtue of which the lessee would know the rent which would be payable for the last seven years of the term by the time when it *a* came to make its decision whether or not to exercise its right to determine the lease.

One other important point is common ground, as it appears to have been before the judge. It is not disputed that time is of the essence for the purpose of applying the time limits specified in the break clause itself. The reasoning sufficiently appears from the following passage in the speech of Lord Diplock in the *United Scientific* case [1977] 2 All ER 62 at 72, [1978] AC 904 at 929:

b

'. . . there is a practical business reason for treating time as of the essence of such a clause, which is similar to that applicable to an option to acquire property. The exercise of this option by the tenant will have the effect of depriving the landlord of the existing source of income from his property and the evident purpose of the stipulation as to notice is to leave him free thereafter to enter into a contract with a new tenant for a tenancy commencing at the date of surrender provided for in the *c* break clause.'

It seems clear that, in referring in the *United Scientific* case [1977] 2 All ER 62 at 72, [1978] AC 904 at 930 to 'the interrelation of the rent review clause itself and other clauses', Lord Diplock himself had particularly in mind the interrelation of rent review clauses and clauses giving the tenant the right to determine the lease. In his decision in *d* *Coventry City Council v J Hepworth & Son Ltd* (1981) 261 EG 566 (upheld by this court on appeal; see (1982) 46 P & CR 170), Warner J helpfully identified and cited the following passages from the speeches in the *United Scientific* case which concerned this interrelation.

Lord Diplock said ([1977] 2 All ER 62 at 76–77, [1978] AC 904 at 935–936):

'*Samuel Properties (Developments) Ltd v Hayek* [1972] 3 All ER 473, [1972] 1 WLR 1296 may be regarded as the origin of the dichotomy between "option" on the one *e* hand and "obligation" or "machinery" on the other, the word option having been used in the lease itself to describe the landlord's right to require the rent to be reviewed. It should be treated as overruled. There was a complication in that the rent review clause was associated with a break clause which gave to the tenant the right to surrender the residue of the term on any rent review day by giving prior notice. The timetable in the rent review clause for the determination of the new *f* rent was obviously correlated with the time by which the tenant had to give notice of his intention to surrender, so as to enable him to make his decision whether or not to exercise that right in the knowledge of what the new rent would be if he continued in possession after the review date. Had that been all, as it had been in the previous and rightly decided case of *C Richards & Son Ltd v Karenita Ltd* (1971) 221 EG 25, it would, I think have been sufficient by necessary implication to make *g* time of the essence of the rent review clause because of its inter-relation with the time by which notice was to be given under the break clause—a time which, for reasons I have given earlier, I consider to be of the essence of the contract. In *Samuel Properties (Developments) Ltd v Hayek*, however, the break clause itself contained a provision under which the period during which the tenant could exercise his right to surrender would be extended in the event of the reviewed rent not having been *h* ascertained within the time stipulated in the rent review clause. So the implication that would otherwise have arisen from the association of the rent review clause with a break clause was negatived.'

Viscount Dilhorne agreed with what Lord Diplock had said about these cases (see [1977] 2 All ER 62 at 80, [1978] AC 904 at 940).

Lord Simon said ([1977] 2 All ER 62 at 85, [1978] AC 904 at 946): *j*

'However, where a rent review clause is associated with a true option (a "break" clause, for example), it is a strong indication that time is intended to be of the essence of the rent review clause—if not absolutely, at least to the extent that the tenant will reasonably expect to know what new rent he will have to pay before the

time comes for him to elect whether to terminate or renew the tenancy (cf *Samuel*
Properties (Developments) Ltd v Hayek [1972] 3 All ER 473, [1972] 1 WLR 1296). That
situation stands in significant contrast with those in the instant appeals.'

Lord Salmon said ([1977] 2 All ER 62 at 89–90, [1978] AC 904 at 951–952):

'In *Samuel Properties (Developments) Ltd v Hayek* [1972] 3 All ER 473, [1972] 1
WLR 1296 the rent revision clause which laid down the procedure for having the
open market rental value ascertained at the end of the seventh and 14th years of the
term and the rent then being raised to that level, was dressed up to look like an
option. Indeed the word "option" appeared in the clause. But, for the reasons I have
already stated, I do not think that it was a real option in the sense that any option to
renew or determine a lease is an option. The clause required the landlord to give
notice to the tenants six months prior to the expiry of the seventh year if he required
the rent to be raised to the open market rental value. If within one month of the
notice, the parties failed to agree the open market rental value this figure was to be
determined by a valuer appointed by the president of the Royal Institution of
Chartered Surveyors. But the date by which this determination was to be made was
not specified. The landlord gave his notice about one month late. The Court of
Appeal held that time was of the essence and that the landlord was precluded from
putting the rent revision clause into operation. Clause 5 of the lease so far as relevant
gave the tenant a true option to determine the lease at the end of the seventh year of
the term by giving the landlords at least one quarter's notice in writing. This break
clause was obviously inserted to protect the tenant should he not wish to pay the
increased rent during the next seven year period of the term. The proviso to the
break clause strongly suggests however that the time provisions relating to rent
revision were not of the essence of the contract. It reads: "Provided always that if
one quarter before the expiration of the first 7 . . . years of the term . . . the reviewed
rent . . . shall not have been reviewed then the right of the lessee to terminate as
herein provided shall be extended until the expiration of 1 month from the date of
the notification of the reviewed rent to the lessee." There is nothing in the proviso
nor in any other part of the lease to suggest that the new rent may not be determined
by the valuer and notification of this rent may not reach the lessee until after the
expiration of the first seven year period. In my view *Samuel Properties (Developments)*
Ltd v Hayek was wrongly decided and should be overruled.'

Lastly, Lord Fraser said ([1977] 2 All ER 62 at 98, [1978] AC 904 at 962–963):

'For these reasons I am of opinion that the equitable rule against treating time as
of the essence of a contract is applicable to rent review clauses unless there is some
special reason for excluding its application to a particular clause. The rule would of
course be excluded if the review clause expressly stated that time was to be of the
essence. It would also be excluded if the context clearly indicated that that was the
intention of the parties—as for instance where the tenant had a right to break the
lease by notice given by a specified date which was later than the last date for serving
the landlord's trigger notice. The tenant's notice to terminate the contract would be
one where the time limit was mandatory, and the necessary implication is that the
time limit for giving the landlord's notice of review must also be mandatory. An
example of such interlocked provisions is to be found in *C Richards & Son v Karenita*
Ltd (1971) 221 EG 25 where the decision that time was of the essence of the
landlord's notice could be supported on this ground, although not, as I think, on the
ground on which it was actually rested. *Samuel Properties (Developments) Ltd v Hayek*
[1972] 3 All ER 473, [1972] 1 WLR 1296 is not in this class because, although there
was a tenant's break clause, the time allowed to the tenant for giving notice was
automatically extended until one month after the notification of the reviewed rent
to the lessee.'

The relevant facts of *Samuel Properties (Developments) Ltd v Hayek* appear sufficiently

from these passages which I have cited from their Lordships' speeches. The relevant facts
of *C Richards & Son Ltd v Karenita Ltd* (1971) 221 EG 25 appear sufficiently from this   *a*
passage from the judgment of Goulding J:

> '. . . by an underlease of June 5, 1963, Nobbs (Cleaners) Ltd. demised the second
> floor of 52a Blackstock Road, London, N., to the defendants for a term of 14 years at
> a yearly rent of £700. Clause 2(11) provided that "if the landlords shall by giving
> notice in writing to the tenants at any time during the first three months of the
> seventh year of the term hereby created require a review of the rent payable   *b*
> hereunder, such rent shall be revised with effect from the expiration of the seventh
> year . . ." Clause 4(4) provided that if the tenants desired to determine the term at
> the expiration of the first seven years and gave to the landlords three months'
> previous notice in writing, then immediately on the expiration of the seven years
> the demise should cease. The period during which the landlords' notice might have
> been given began on June 6, 1969, and ended on September 5, 1969. No notice   *c*
> under clause 2(11) was given during that period, but the plaintiffs, who were now
> landlords, purported to give such a notice on February 26, 1970, when nearly nine
> months of the seventh year had elapsed. The question before the court was whether
> that late notice was effective or not.'

Coventry City Council v J Hepworth & Son Ltd (1981) 261 EG 566 likewise concerned a   *d*
rent review clause, coupled with a break clause. The rent review clause itself laid down
what Warner J described as an elaborate and precise timetable. For present purposes it
will suffice to quote the summary of the relevant provisions given in his judgment (at
568):

> 'On or before December 31 1973 the corporation might give to the tenants notice
> of its desire to increase the rent in respect of the period from April 1 1975 until the   *e*
> expiration of the term created by the lease, that is, roughly speaking, in respect of
> the second 21 years of it. I shall call that a "rent review notice". If the corporation
> gave such a notice and no agreement had been reached by February 28 1974 (that is,
> within two months), there was to be a reference to arbitration. Clearly, what was
> envisaged was that, in the two months between December 31 1973 and February 28
> 1974, there would be negotiations between the parties, which would either produce   *f*
> agreement on a new rent or be abortive. Then, if the negotiations proved to be
> abortive, the parties were given one month in which to agree upon a single
> arbitrator. If they failed to do so, each must appoint an arbitrator. The last day for
> doing that was April 30 1974. The provisions of sections 7 and 8 of the Arbitration
> Act 1950 would then apply. On or before September 30 1974 the tenants might
> give notice of their intention to determine the lease as from March 31 1975, that is   *g*
> the day before any increase of rent might take effect.'

The ultimate conclusion of Warner J and its ratio decidendi was stated by him as
follows (at 569):

> '[Counsel for the corporation (viz the city council)] submitted that it was not in
> every case where a rent review clause was associated with a tenant's option to break   *h*
> that time was of the essence of the rent review clause. That is manifestly right, as
> the House of Lords' treatment of the *Hayek* case illustrates. I do not think, however,
> that the features of the present case to which [counsel for the corporation] pointed
> are sufficient to negative the presumption that, where a rent review clause is linked
> to a tenant's option to break, time is of the essence of the rent review clause. The
> length of the term and the fact that the lease provided for only one break at 21 years   *j*
> are, I think, sufficiently explained by the circumstance that it was granted in 1953,
> at a time when inflation was at a much lower rate than now. The fact that substantial
> subletting by Hepworths was envisaged seems to me neutral. The period of nine
> months between December 31 1973 and September 30 1974 was, I think, intended,
> not to give the tenant an opportunity to serve a notice making time of the essence,

a
but to enable any necessary arbitration to have been completed by September 30 1974 or at least to be sufficiently advanced by that date to give the tenant a good idea of what the revised rent was likely to be. Lastly, I do not think that it matters that there could be no certainty that the tenant would know the precise amount of the revised rent by that date. So far as the report of *C Richards & Son Ltd v Karenita Ltd* shows, there was no such certainty in that case either.'

b
The Court of Appeal affirmed Warner J's judgment in *Coventry City Council v J Hepworth & Son Ltd* (see (1982) 46 P & CR 170). Lawton LJ, referring to the *United Scientific* decision, said (at 176):

c
'It comes to this, that their Lordships . . . were all of the opinion that, where you have a triggering off of a rent review provision started by the landlord followed by an option given to the tenant to break the lease if he so wishes, then time is to be presumed to be of the essence of the agreement unless there are contra-indications.'

He added that it made no difference, in the case of a lease which provides for triggering action followed by a break clause, and also for an interval of time between the triggering action and the date when a decision has to be made about breaking the lease, that the tenant can always serve on the landlord a notice making time of the essence of the
d
agreement. As he observed (see at 176): 'No landlord and no tenant, in my judgment, when making a lease of this kind, would have contemplated such a possibility.'

Griffiths LJ agreed, saying that he found the reasoning of Warner J so compelling that he did not wish to give any separate reasons of his own. Fox LJ also agreed without adding any further observations (see at 176).

Coventry City Council v J Hepworth & Son Ltd was followed by Mr Evans-Lombe QC,
e
sitting as a deputy judge of the High Court in the Chancery Division, in *William Hill (Southern) Ltd v Govier & Govier* (1984) 269 EG 1168. In that case, by cl 4(2) beginning 'The rent shall be reviewed at the 25th December 1982 and at the 25th December 1987', the lease provided for rent reviews at the end of the fifth and tenth years of the term. The wording of the lease thus appeared to make the reviews mandatory. If the landlord and tenant failed to agree the best rack rent, obtainable in the open market, nine months
f
before the review date, then either party might within a further period of one month refer the question of the amount of rent to a chartered surveyor nominated in default of agreement by the President of the Royal Institution of Chartered Surveyors. There was a break clause, which entitled the tenant to determine the lease at the end of the fifth or tenth year by giving the lessor three months' written notice to expire on the relevant review date.

g
The lessor, in argument, sought to distinguish the *Coventry City Council* case, particularly on the grounds that the provisions for rent review in the lease in the *William Hill* case were mandatory and took effect without any requirement of a 'trigger notice' on the lessor's part. The deputy judge rejected this suggested distinction. He described Warner J and the Court of Appeal in the *Coventry City Council* case as having held that—

h
'where such provisions are linked with provisions for rent review, *prima facie* the court will construe the provisions to make time of the essence of those relating to the review.'

(See 269 EG 1168 at 1171.) He could find nothing sufficient to lead him to a conclusion contrary to 'Warner J's *prima facie* rule.'

j
In the present case, Peter Gibson J said that the main submission put before him by counsel for Metrolands was that—

'in the *United Scientific* case itself the House of Lords had reached the conclusion that time was not of the essence, inter alia, because the tenant as well as the landlord had it in his power to initiate the rent review.'

(See [1985] 3 All ER 206 at 214.)

However, as he said, there was a major point of similarity between the case before him
and the *William Hill* case in that 'the tenant, no less than the landlord, had the right to   *a*
refer the matter to the arbitrator' (see [1985] 3 All ER 206 at 213). Nevertheless, in the
William Hill case the deputy judge clearly had considered, but rejected, the suggested
distinction drawn on that account, between a landlord's 'trigger notice' case and a case
such as that before him where the tenant, as well as the landlord, could refer the matter
to an arbitrator. Peter Gibson J, after a very careful analysis of the *William Hill* decision,
observed (at 213):
                                                                                                     b

'The decision in the *William Hill* case is of a judge, albeit a deputy, of equal
jurisdiction on a point on which there is no other direct authority by way of a
decided case; and whilst it is not binding on me I would not wish to introduce
further uncertainty into this difficult area of the law by a decision inconsistent with
his unless I was convinced that the deputy judge reached the wrong conclusion.'

                                                                                                     c
He summarised his own ultimate conclusions thus (at 214):

'In other words, in many landlord's trigger notice cases it would be open to the
tenant to find out the likely rent, just as much as in a case where he has an express
right to refer to arbitration; and yet that was not treated by Lord Diplock, Lord
Simon and Lord Fraser as relevant. The simple correlation between the rent review
clause and the break clause was enough, save where there was a specific inconsistent   *d*
provision such as the proviso in the *Samuel Properties* case. Moreover, I think that
Lord Diplock in referring, as he did, to the necessary implication as to time being of
the essence where there was an interrelation between a rent review clause and a
break clause, and Lord Simon to the like effect, were intending to lay down general
guidelines. I confess that, for the reasons so attractively advanced by counsel for
Metrolands, I do not find the simple correlation approach completely satisfying   *e*
logically. But I am unable to say that Warner J was wrong to state the applicable
presumption in the way that he did, nor am I able to say that the deputy judge in
the *William Hill* case was wrong to follow that statement. Accordingly, I shall follow
the decision in the *William Hill* case in holding that here, too, time is of the essence
of the reddendum by reason of the correlation with the break clause.'
                                                                                                     f
In the course of argument in this court, in support of the judge's judgment, counsel
for Dewhurst relied strongly on the applicable presumption as stated by Warner J in the
Coventry City Council case. He submitted that the judgments of the Court of Appeal in
that case support the existence of that presumption and that, where it is applicable, it
wholly displaces the presumption ordinarily applicable to the construction of rent review
clauses as stated by Lord Diplock in the *United Scientific* case [1977] 2 All ER 62 at 72,
[1978] AC 904 at 930. Counsel for Metrolands, on the other hand, submitted that in so   *g*
far as this court in the *Coventry City Council* case had supported the existence of any such
presumption as was referred to by Warner J, the judgment of Lawton LJ makes it clear
that the presumption only applies in a case of a lease which provides for the triggering
off of a rent review provision started by the landlord alone, followed by an option given
to the tenant to break the lease; in the present case the tenant, no less than the landlord,   *h*
has the right to initiate any review. He challenged the correctness of the principle which
Peter Gibson J derived from the speeches in the *United Scientific* case that 'the simple
correlation between the rent review clause and the break clause was enough' to make
time of the essence of the rent review clause 'save where there was a specific inconsistent
provision . . .' (see [1985] 3 All ER 206 at 214).
Throughout this debate, we think it must be borne in mind that the ultimate object   *j*
of the court in construing a rent review clause, like any other contractual provision, must
be to ascertain the parties' intentions from the particular words which they have used to
express those intentions, read, of course, in the light of any admissible evidence as to
surrounding circumstances; albeit with the assistance of the guidelines as to construction
afforded by earlier authorities. In many, perhaps most, cases, of which the present is one,

the rent review (if any) can result only in an increase, and thus is only for the landlord's
a benefit. Essentially, therefore, the question to which the court has to direct its mind is
this: is the proper intention to impute to the parties, from the words which they have
used, the intention that the landlord shall lose his right to a review if the stipulated
timetable is not strictly adhered to in the relevant respects?

In practice it is ordinarily likely that 'the detriment to the landlord of losing his review
altogether by failure to adhere strictly' to the stipulated time limit will be 'wholly
b disproportionate to the disadvantage to the tenant of a delay in the assessment of the
rent'. This, as Dillon LJ pointed out in *Touche Ross & Co v Secretary of State for the
Environment* (1982) 46 P & CR 187 at 190, appears to have been the reason why the House
of Lords in the *United Scientific* case concluded that prima facie, and in the absence of
sufficient contra-indications, it is not right to impute to the parties to a lease the intention
that time is to be of the essence for the purpose of a rent review clause. This, we think,
c should be the initial starting point on the consideration of any such clause.

However, as their Lordships recognised, in a case where a lease contains a break clause
as well as a rent review clause and the timetables of the two clauses are closely interlocked,
the interrelation of the two clauses is *likely* to suffice as a contra-indication sufficient to
rebut the ordinary presumption; though everything must depend on the wording of the
particular lease. This, we believe, was the sense in which Warner J referred to a
d 'presumption' applicable to a case of this nature.

A good example of a case where the interrelation of the two clauses did constitute a
contra-indication of this nature is *C Richards & Son Ltd v Karenita Ltd* (1971) 221 EG 25
itself. There the latest date specified for the giving of the landlord's trigger notice was 5
September 1969 and the latest date specified for the giving of the tenant's notice to
determine was six months later, namely 5 March 1970. Lord Diplock, Lord Dilhorne
e and Lord Fraser, in approving that decision in the result, did not find it necessary to spell
out in any detail the reasons why they considered the ordinary presumption to be
rebutted, but we infer that their reasoning could properly be elaborated as follows.

The intention of the parties to the lease in providing for this six-month gap must have
been to allow adequate time for the process of the review of the rent to have been
completed, or at least sufficiently advanced, by the latest date for service of the tenant's
f notice to determine, so as to give the tenant the advantages of knowing before that latest
date (a) that the lessor intended to invoke the rent review procedure, and (b) what the
revised rent was likely to be. The tenant himself must on any footing be held strictly to
the time limits laid down for the service of any notice by him to determine the lease. If
time was not regarded as being of the essence for the purpose of the lessor's trigger notice,
these potential advantages would have been subject to at least erosion and possible
g elimination by tardy service of any such notice. In these circumstances, despite the severe
potential loss which the landlord would suffer if that notice was served even one day late,
it could not reasonably be supposed that it was in the contemplation of the parties that
the tenant should be exposed to the loss of these advantages by tardy action on the part
of the landlord in initiating the rent review procedure.

Precisely the same reasoning, mutatis mutandis, was applicable in the *Coventry City
h Council* case (1981) 261 EG 566; *affd* (1982) 46 P & CR 170, CA, where the timetable
specified in the lease provided for a five months' gap between the latest date for the
giving of the landlord's trigger notice and the latest date for the giving of the tenant's
notice to determine. We respectfully agree with that decision, which in any event is
binding on us.

The lease under consideration in the *William Hill* case contained a number of features
j not present in the lease now before us and, since that decision does not bind us, we do
not find it necessary to embark on any detailed consideration of it or to express any
conclusion on the submission of counsel for Metrolands that it was wrongly decided. We
have doubts as to the usefulness of a minute comparison of the different provisions of
different leases in a case such as this. However, as the argument of counsel for Metrolands
in this court developed, it became apparent that by far his most important point (at least

to our minds) was one which, though touched on by the judge in his judgment (see [1985] 3 All ER 206 at 213), does not appear to have been placed in the forefront of *a* Metrolands' case in the court below. There is a basic difference in the provisions of the lease in the present case from those under consideration in *C Richards & Son Ltd v Karenita Ltd* and in the *Coventry City Council* case. In those two cases, the leases had one most important feature in common, that is to say *the event as to which time was held to be of the essence was one in the landlord's full control* (namely service of his trigger notice). In a case where an event included as part of the timetable in a rent review clause is one within the *b* landlord's full control, it is by no means inconceivable that he should have been willing and should have intended to commit himself to a rigid adherence to that part of the timetable, even though the consequence of a failure to do so would be that of losing the entire benefit of the relevent rent review and even though the lease does not expressly state that time is to be of the essence.

In contrast, the lease under consideration in the present case has this special and, we *c* would think, unusual feature: the event as to which time is said to be of the essence is the *actual obtaining of the arbitrator's decision*. As counsel for Metrolands pointed out, it was readily conceivable that the landlord might have acted with irreproachable promptness and diligence in setting in motion the arbitration machinery provided for by the lease, for the purpose of a rent review, but that, without any fault whatever on the landlord's part and due to events entirely beyond his control, the arbitrator's decision *d* might still not have been obtained until after 19 August 1981. The arbitrator himself, for example, might have been ill or unduly dilatory; or the final conclusion of the arbitration proceedings might have been delayed by the submission of a number of perfectly legitimate points on the part of the tenant or by other circumstances quite beyond the lessor's control. All these are matters to be taken into account when considering the intention to be imputed to the parties regarding the significance of the *e* date of the obtaining of the arbitrator's decision.

If time was to be treated as being of the essence in respect of this date, this would have meant that, subject to any powers of the court to extend time under the Arbitration Acts (as to which see below), a delay in the obtaining of the arbitrator's decision by only one day beyond 19 August 1981 would have entirely deprived the lessor of its right to a review in respect of the last seven years of this 21-year term and would have left it saddled *f* with a continuing annual rental as low as £1,800, which had been the rental payable for the preceding eleven years. In these circumstances, we think that the following observations of Viscount Dilhorne in the *United Scientific* case [1977] 2 All ER 62 at 79, [1978] AC 904 at 938–939 are apposite, spoken as they were in relation to a lease which, apart from the absence of a break clause, bore a marked similarity to that under consideration in the present case:

g

'It is most unlikely in these circumstances that the lessors, if they had been asked at the time the leases had been entered into to agree that time should be of the essence, would ever have agreed to that and I see no reason for imputing to them an intention which no reasonable landlord would have had.'

In saying this, we do not overlook the importance to the lessee of knowing before *h* 19 August 1981 what the revised rent was likely to be, so as to assist in deciding whether or not to operate the break clause. Nevertheless, as it is reasonable to assume, the parties would have been aware at the time when the lease was executed that the lessee would by no means have been left at the lessor's mercy if the lessor did not choose to set the rent review machinery in operation promptly; for the lessee itself had the same right as the lessor to set the arbitration procedure in motion. If, therefore, the lessee foresaw a risk of *j* the arbitrator's decision not being obtained by 19 August 1981 and that risk caused it concern, an obvious remedy lay in its own hands. For these reasons there can, in our judgment, be no doubt that the potential detriment to which the lessor under this particular lease would have exposed itself by agreeing that time should be of the essence as regards the stipulated date for the obtaining of the arbitrator's decision would have far *a* outweighed any potential detriment to which the lessee would have exposed itself by agreeing that it should not be.

Counsel for Dewhurst referred us to s 27 of the Arbitration Act 1950, which gives the court power to extend the time for commencing arbitration proceedings, and to s 13 of the Arbitration Act 1950, which gives it power to enlarge the time for the making of the award. He submitted that, in appropriate circumstances, it would have been open to the lessor to make an application under those sections for the purpose of avoiding the rigours

b of any strict time limit imposed by the lease in relation to the obtaining of the arbitrator's decision. With due deference to this argument, however, we would find it fanciful to attribute to the parties the intention that, on the one hand, time should be strictly of the essence as regards the latest date for the obtaining of the arbitrator's decision, but that, on the other hand, such date should be capable of extension under the Arbitration Act 1950.

This case has been very well argued on both sides. We hope we will be forgiven if we

c do not refer to all the points raised in the course of argument. It will suffice to summarise our conclusions thus. Though there is the clearest possible interrelation between the timetable embodied in the rent review clause and that embodied in the break clause, such interrelation in the context of this particular lease is not, in our judgment, a 'contra-indication' sufficient to rebut the intital presumption of construction (from which we think it right to start) that the timetable specified in the rent review clause for the

d obtaining of the arbitrator's decision is not of the essence of the contract. The principal reasons why it does not suffice for this purpose are two, which must be considered in conjunction with one another, and have not been applicable in conjunction with any previous case which has been cited to us.

First, the date of the relevant event, namely the actual obtaining of such decision, is one which is to a substantial degree outside the lessor's control. Second, any potential

e hardship to the tenant which might otherwise arise through tardy action by the landlord in initiating the rent review procedure can be eliminated or, at least, substantially mitigated, by the tenant initiating such action itself. The ultimate object of the court in construing clauses such as this, as we have already indicated, must be to ascertain the parties' intentions from the words which they have used. Weighing in the balance all the competing considerations that have been urged on us, we have come to the clear

f conclusion that the intention properly to be attributed to the parties to this particular lease is the intention that time should not be of the essence as regards the obtaining of the arbitrator's decision.

We therefore allow this appeal, but would welcome submissions as to the precise form of relief which should be granted.

g *Appeal allowed.*

Solicitors: *Willey Hargrave*, Harrogate (for Metrolands); *R A Roberts* (for Dewhurst).

Wendy Shockett   Barrister.

Practice Direction

COMPANIES COURT

Company – Compulsory winding up – Procedure – Hearing of petitions – Unopposed petitions and related applications to be heard by registrar – Other petitions to be heard by judge – Companies Act 1985, s 522.

With effect from the commencement of the Hilary Sittings 1987, the list of winding-up petitions, at present heard by the judge acting as Companies Court judge of the term on a Monday, will be heard by the Companies Court registrar on a Wednesday. The registrar will sit in court on a Wednesday each week of the term, when he will hear all unopposed petitions and related applications other than those for relief under s 522 of the Companies Act 1985 or for the restraint of advertisement of a petition. In accordance with the Practice Direction of the Lord Chief Justice of 9 May 1986 ([1986] 2 All ER 226, [1986] 1 WLR 545), solicitors, properly robed, will be permitted rights of audience before the registrar.

The Companies Court judge of the term will continue to sit on a Monday each week of the term, when he will deal with (1) petitions to confirm reductions of capital and/or share premium account, (2) petitions to sanction schemes of arrangement, (3) motions and (4) opposed winding-up petitions which have been adjourned to him by the registrar.

By direction of the Vice-Chancellor.

22 October 1986

a

Re Brightlife Ltd

CHANCERY DIVISION
HOFFMANN J
17, 18, 24 JULY 1986

b   *Company – Charge – Floating charge – Crystallisation – Debenture providing that debenture holder could serve notice converting floating charge into fixed charge – Debenture holder giving notice – Whether notice effectively converting floating charge into fixed charge – Whether debenture holder having priority over preferential creditors – Companies Act 1985, s 614(2)(b).*

c   A company executed a debenture in favour of N Ltd whereby it charged 'by way of first specific charge' the company's book debts and other debts and also created a floating charge over all other property and assets of the company. The debenture further provided that the company could not, without the permission of N Ltd, deal with its book or other debts other than in the ordinary course of collecting or realising them and that N Ltd could in specified circumstances serve notice on the company converting the floating *d*   charge into a fixed charge. In December 1984 N Ltd served such a notice on the company pursuant to the terms of the debenture converting the floating charge into a fixed charge. Subsequently, the company was voluntarily wound up owing some £200,000 to N Ltd and some £70,000 unpaid value added tax. The company's assets realised some £40,000, of which £18,000 was derived from the collection of book debts. The company also had a credit balance of £19,000 in its bank account. The questions arose whether preferential debts, such as the unpaid value added tax, took priority under s 614(2)(b)[a] of the *e*   Companies Act 1985 over the debenture holder's claim and thus whether the credit balance and the amount realised from book debts were to be applied to pay the value added tax in priority to N Ltd's claim. The Customs and Excise contended that the debenture only conferred a floating charge and that accordingly preferential debts took priority under s 614(2)(b) over N Ltd's claim. N Ltd contended that its claim took priority *f*   because the debenture created a fixed charge over the company's book debts and the credit balance in its bank account or alternatively, because the floating charge was converted into a fixed charge by the notice served on N Ltd on the company prior to the winding up.

Held – Since a balance which was normally designated as 'cash at bank' was not, as a *g*   matter of commercial practice, treated as a book debt, the charge in favour of N Ltd over the company's 'book debts and other debts' did not cover the balance in the company's bank account. Furthermore, N Ltd's charge, although expressed as being a 'first specific charge', was a floating charge, since it related to fluctuating assets, and although some restriction was placed on the company's freedom to deal with its book debts the company remained free to collect its debts and pay them into its bank account, which the company *h*   could use freely, and a right to deal with the book debts in such a manner was inconsistent with N Ltd's charge being a fixed charge. However, since there was nothing which precluded the parties from stipulating in their agreement that a floating charge would crystallise into a fixed charge on the giving of notice by the chargeholder, N Ltd had, by giving notice exercising its right to do so, effectively converted its floating charge into a fixed charge. It followed that since N Ltd's charge had become a fixed charge before the *j*   commencement of the winding up of the company, preferential creditors such as the Customs and Excise had no priority under s 614(2)(b) of the 1985 Act over N Ltd's claim (see p 676 c d f g, p 677 a b, p 680 c d h and p 681 d f, post).

---

a   Section 614(2), so far as material, is set out at p 675 *b c*, post

Notes

For the priority of debts on the winding up of a company, see 7 Halsbury's Laws (4th *a*
edn) paras 1281–1298, and for cases on the preferential debts, see 10 Digest (Reissue)
1073–1078, 6589–6617.

For the Companies Act 1985, s 614, see 8 Halsbury's Statutes (4th edn) 581.

Cases referred to in judgment

Christonette International Ltd, Re [1982] 3 All ER 225, [1982] 1 WLR 1245. *b*

Crompton & Co Ltd, Re, Player v Crompton & Co Ltd [1914] 1 Ch 954.

Governments Stock and Other Securities Investment Co Ltd v Manila Rly Co Ltd [1897] AC 81,
HL.

Griffin Hotel Co Ltd, Re, Joshua Tetley & Son Ltd v Griffin Hotel Co Ltd [1940] 4 All ER 324,
[1941] Ch 129.

Illingworth v Houldsworth [1904] AC 355, HL; *affg* sub nom *Re Yorkshire Woolcombers'* *c*
Association [1903] 2 Ch 284, CA.

Keenan Bros Ltd, Re [1986] BCLC 242, Ir SC.

Lister v Romford Ice and Cold Storage Co Ltd [1957] 1 All ER 125, [1957] AC 555, [1957] 2
WLR 158, HL.

Manurewa Transport Ltd, Re [1971] NZLR 909, NZ SC.

Nelson (Edward) & Co Ltd v Faber & Co [1903] 2 KB 367. *d*

R v Consolidated Churchill Copper Corp Ltd [1978] 5 WWR 652, BC SC.

Siebe Gorman & Co Ltd v Barclays Bank Ltd [1979] 2 Lloyd's Rep 142.

Street v Mountford [1985] 2 All ER 289, [1985] AC 809, [1985] 2 WLR 877, HL.

Woodroffes (Musical Instruments) Ltd (in liq), Re [1985] 2 All ER 908, [1986] Ch 366, [1985]
3 WLR 543.

e

Cases also cited

Armagh Shoes Ltd, Re [1984] BCLC 405.

Bond Worth Ltd, Re [1979] 3 All ER 919, [1980] Ch 228.

Davey & Co v Williamson & Sons Ltd [1898] 2 QB 194, DC.

Erven Warnink BV v Townend (J) & Sons (Hull) Ltd [1979] 2 All ER 927, [1979] AC 731, *f*
HL.

Evans v Rival Granite Quarries Ltd [1910] 2 KB 979, CA.

Evans Coleman & Evans Ltd v R A Nelson Construction Ltd (1958) 16 DLR (2d) 123, BC CA.

Horne and Hellard, Re (1895) 29 Ch D 736.

National Provincial Bank of England Ltd v United Electric Theatres Ltd [1916] 1 Ch 132.

Paul & Frank Ltd v Discount (Overseas) Ltd [1966] 2 All ER 922, [1967] Ch 348. *g*

Stein v Saywell (1969) 121 CLR 529, Aust HC.

Wallace v Universal Automatic Machines Co [1894] 2 Ch 547, [1891–4] All ER Rep 1156,
CA.

Summons

By an amended summons dated 5 August 1985 Keith David Goodman, the liquidator of *h*
Brightlife Ltd (the company), applied to the court for directions pursuant to ss 540(4) and
602 of the Companies Act 1985, for their determination of the question whether the
credit balance in the ordinary bank account of the company and the book debts should
be applied pursuant to ss 196 and 614(2)(*b*) of the 1985 Act to pay the preferential
creditors, including the Commissioners of Customs and Excise, in priority to Norandex
Inc, the holder of a debenture dated 11 April 1983. The facts are set out in the judgment. *j*

John Vallat for the liquidator.
Richard M Sheldon for Norandex.
John Mummery for the Commissioners of Customs and Excise.

Cur adv vult

24 July. The following judgment was delivered.

HOFFMANN J. Brightlife Ltd (Brightlife) is in creditors' voluntary liquidation. Its assets have realised about £40,000. It owes over £200,000 to Norandex Inc, an American company, secured by a debenture. It also owes over £70,000 to the Commissioners of Customs and Excise for value added tax. The commissioners say that Norandex's debenture conferred only a *floating* charge and therefore the claim for value added tax, being preferential, takes priority under s 614(2)(b) of the Companies Act 1985, which reads as follows:

> 'The preferential debts shall . . . so far as the assets of the company available for payment of general creditors are insufficient to meet them, have priority over the claims of holders of debentures under any floating charge created by the company, and be paid accordingly out of any property comprised in or subject to that charge.'

Norandex says that its debenture has priority because it created a *fixed* charge over most of the assets or, alternatively, because the floating charge over all the assets had become a fixed charge before the resolution for winding up.

I must first dispose of certain questions of construction. The debenture is dated 11 April 1983. It is expressed to secure all present and future indebtedness of Brightlife to Norandex. The charging clause is 3(A). Sub-clause (i) creates a 'first specific equitable charge' over freehold and leasehold property. Sub-clause (ii) charges—

> 'by way of first specific charge (a) all book debts and other debts now or at any time during the continuance of this security due or owing to Brightlife and the benefit of all securities and guarantees now or at any time held by Brightlife in relation thereto; (b) the goodwill and uncalled capital for the time being of Brightlife; and (c) the benefit of any licences for the time being in Brightlife.'

Sub-clause (iii) creates a floating charge over after-acquired freehold and leasehold property and, 'the undertaking and all other property, assets and rights whatsoever present and future of Brightlife', subject to a proviso which prohibits the creation of any other charges ranking in priority to or pari passu with the floating charge or the disposal of any assets subject to the floating charge contrary to the provisions of cl 5(ii). This important clause is quoted below.

Clause 3(B) reads:

> 'Norandex may at any time by notice to Brightlife convert the floating charge into a specific charge as regards any assets specified in the notice which Norandex shall consider to be in danger of being seized or sold under any form of distress or execution levied or threatened or to be otherwise in jeopardy and may appoint a receiver thereof.'

Clause 5 is a covenant by Brightlife that it—

> '(i) shall carry on and conduct its affairs in a proper and efficient manner; (ii) shall not without the prior consent in writing of Norandex sell transfer or otherwise dispose of the whole or, except in the ordinary course of business, any part of its undertaking property or assets (being in the aggregate substantial) or deals with its book or other debts or securities for money otherwise than in the ordinary course of getting in and realising the same which expression shall not authorise the selling, factoring or discounting by Brightlife of its book debts or other negotiable instruments held by it . . . (iv) shall furnish to Norandex . . . (c) [each quarter] a statement of the book debts owing at the end of the relevant quarter, showing their amount and from whom they are owed and any other material information in the possession of Brightlife relating thereto . . .'

Clause 13 is a covenant for further assurance in the following terms:

> 'Brightlife shall execute and do all such assurances, acts and things as Norandex may reasonably require for perfecting or protecting the security created by these

presents over the property hereby charged or any part thereof or for facilitating the realisation of such property and the exercise of all powers, authorities and discretions *a* vested in Norandex ... and shall in particular execute all transfers, conveyances, assignments and assurances of such property whether [to] Norandex or to its nominees ... which Norandex may think expedient and for the purposes of this Clause a certificate in writing by Norandex to the effect that any particular assurance, act or thing required by it is reasonably required shall be conclusive evidence of such fact.'

b

The first submission of counsel for Norandex was that cl 3(A)(ii)(a) created, according to its terms, a 'first specific charge' over 'all book debts and other debts'. Nearly £18,000 of the assets was derived from the collection of book debts. Another £19,000 was the amount which had been standing to the company's credit at the bank. This, if not a 'book debt', was a sum owing by the bank to Brightlife and therefore, in counsel's submission, an 'other debt'. The only part of the assets not derived from 'book debts or other debts' *c* was some £2,200 realised from the sale of stock. Over the rest, counsel for Norandex said that Norandex had a fixed charge and therefore priority over the commissioners.

I do not accept this submission. Firstly, I do not think that the bank balance falls within the term 'book debts or other debts' as it is used in the debenture. It is true that the relationship between banker and customer is one of debtor and creditor. It would not therefore be legally inaccurate to describe a credit balance with a banker as a debt. *d* But this would not be a natural usage for a businessman or accountant. He would ordinarily describe it as 'cash at bank' (compare the balance sheet formats in section B of Pt I of Sch 4 to the Companies Act 1985).

If cl 3(A)(ii)(a) stood alone, I might have been left in some doubt over whether 'debts' was being used in a commercial or strictly legal sense. But in my judgment the ambiguity is resolved by the use of the same words in cl 5(ii), which prohibits Brightlife from *e* dealing with its 'book or other debts' without the prior consent in writing of Norandex 'otherwise than in the ordinary course of getting in and realising the same'. A credit balance at the bank cannot sensibly be 'got in' or 'realised' and the proviso cannot therefore apply to it. If 'book debts or other debts' includes the bank balance, the consequence is that Brightlife could not have dealt with its bank account without the written consent of Norandex. It would have had to obtain such consent every time it *f* issued a cheque. The extreme commercial improbability of such an arrangement satisfies me that the parties used 'book debts and other debts' in a sense which excludes the credit balance at the bank.

Secondly, although cl 3(A)(ii)(*a*) speaks of a 'first specific charge' over the book debts and other debts, the rights over the debts created by the debenture were in my judgment such as to be categorised in law as a floating charge (compare *Street v Mountford* [1985] 2 *g* All ER 289 at 294, [1985] AC 809 at 819). In a well-known passage in *Re Yorkshire Woolcombers' Association* [1903] 2 Ch 284 at 295 Romer LJ identified three standard characteristics of a floating charge:

> '(1) If it is a charge on a class of assets of a company present and future; (2) if the class is one which, in the ordinary course of the business of the company, would be *h* changing from time to time; and (3) ... by the charge it is contemplated that, until some future step is taken by or on behalf of those interested in the charge, the company may carry on its business in the ordinary way as far as concerns the particular class of assets ...'

Counsel were agreed that the charge covered present and future debts and that such debts *j* would in the ordinary course be changing from time to time. The first two of the standard features are therefore present. But counsel for Norandex said that the charge did not allow Brightlife to deal with the debts in the ordinary way of business. Clause 5(ii) was highly restrictive of the company's power to deal with its debts.

It is true that cl 5(ii) does not allow Brightlife to sell, factor or discount debts without the written consent of Norandex. But a floating charge is consistent with some restriction

on the company's freedom to deal with its assets. For example, floating charges commonly
contain a prohibition on the creation of other charges ranking prior to or pari passu with
the floating charge. Such dealings would otherwise be open to a company in the ordinary
course of its business. In this debenture, the significant feature is that Brightlife was free
to collect its debts and pay the proceeds into its bank accounts. Once in the account, they
would be outside the charge over debts and at the free disposal of the company. In my
judgment a right to deal in this way with the charged assets for its own account is a badge
of a floating charge and is inconsistent with a fixed charge.

I was referred to *Siebe Gorman & Co Ltd v Barclays Bank Ltd* [1979] 2 Lloyd's Rep 142,
and a recent decision of the Irish Supreme Court in *Re Keenan Bros Ltd* [1986] BCLC 242,
in both of which charges over book debts were held to be fixed and not floating. In the
former case, the debenture was in favour of a bank and not only prohibited the company
from selling or charging its book debts but required that they be paid into the company's
account with that bank. Slade J decided that as a matter of construction the bank would
not have been obliged to allow the company to draw on the account at a time when it
still owed the bank money under the debenture. The company was not free to deal with
the debts or their proceeds in the ordinary course of its business. Each debt as it accrued
to the company could therefore properly be said to become subject to an equitable fixed
charge. On the other hand, the judge said ([1979] 2 Lloyd's Rep 142 at 158):

> 'If I had accepted that premise that [the company] would have had the unrestricted
> right to deal with the proceeds of any of the relevant book debts paid into its
> account, so long as that account remained in credit, I would have been inclined to
> accept the conclusion that the charge on such book debts could be no more than a
> floating charge.'

Re Keenan Bros Ltd was an even stronger case than *Siebe Gorman & Co Ltd*. Again the
debenture was in favour of a bank and this time the company was obliged to pay the
proceeds of all debts into a designated account with the bank and 'not without the prior
written consent of the bank in writing make any withdrawals or direct any payment
from the said account'. Neither case is therefore of assistance to Norandex.

I come next to the alternative submission for Norandex, namely that the floating
charge was converted into a fixed charge before the resolution for winding up. The
relevant facts are as follows. On 4 December 1984 Brightlife sent out notices of a
creditors' meeting to be held on 20 December pursuant to s 293 of the Companies Act
1948. Norandex sent Brightlife four separate notices dated 10 December. The first was a
demand for payment of £221,658. The second was a notice pursuant to cl 3(B)—

> 'of the conversion with immediate effect of the floating charge created [by the
> debenture] into a specific charge over all the assets of Brightlife Limited the subject
> of the said floating charge.'

The third was a demand pursuant to cl 13 for the execution forthwith of—

> 'a legal assignment of all book and other debts currently due to Brightlife Limited,
> specifying full details of the said debts therein.'

The fourth concerned the contractual arrangements between the parties and is now
irrelevant. The four notices were served not later than 13 December. Brightlife did not
execute the legal assignment required by the third notice and on 20 December the
winding-up resolution was passed.

Counsel for Norandex relies on the notice under cl 3(B) as having crystallised the
floating charge over all the assets before the winding up. Alternatively, he relies on the
notice under cl 13 as having done so in respect of the book debts. The uninitiated might
ask why it is important to ascertain whether the floating charge crystallised on 13
December. After all, if it did not, there can be no doubt that it would have done so when
the winding-up resolution was passed on 20 December. The importance of the dates lies
in the construction given to what is now s 614(2)(b) of the Companies Act 1985 by
Bennett J in *Re Griffin Hotel Co Ltd, Joshua Tetley & Son Ltd v Griffin Hotel Co Ltd* [1940] 4

All ER 324, [1941] Ch 129. He decided in that case that the priority given by the statute to preferential debts applied only if there was a charge still floating at the moment of the winding up and gave the preferential creditors priority in property which at that moment was comprised in the floating charge.

It follows that if the debenture holder can manage to crystallise his floating charge before the moment of winding up, s 614(2)(b) gives the preferential creditors no priority. On the other hand, in the usual case of crystallisation before winding up, namely by appointment of a receiver, they may still be entitled to priority under another section of the 1985 Act. This is s 196, which applies—

'(1) ... where either a receiver is appointed on behalf of the holders of any debentures of the company secured by a floating charge, or possession is taken by or on behalf of those debenture holders of any property comprised in or subject to the charge.'

In such a case, s 196(2) provides:

'If the company is not at the time in the course of being wound up, the [preferential debts] ... shall be paid out of assets coming to the hands of the receiver or other person taking possession, in priority to any claims for principal or interest in respect of the debentures.'

Both ss 614(2)(b) and 196 originate in the Preferential Payments in Bankruptcy Amendment Act 1897. One imagines that they were intended to ensure that in all cases preferential debts had priority over the holder of a charge originally created as a floating charge. It would be difficult to think of any reason for making distinctions according to the moment at which the charge crystallised or the event which brought this about. But *Re Griffin Hotel Co Ltd* revealed a defect in the drafting. It meant, for example, that if the floating charge crystallised before winding up, but otherwise than by the appointment of a receiver, the preferential debts would have no priority under either section. For example, if crystallisation occurred simply because the company ceased to carry on business before it was wound up, as in *Re Woodroffes (Musical Instruments) Ltd (in liq)* [1985] 2 All ER 908, [1986] Ch 366, the preferential debts would have no priority. One could construct other examples of cases which would slip through the net. Counsel for Norandex submits that this is such a case. He says that the notices under cll 3(B) and 13 caused crystallisation of the floating charge over all or part of the assets before the winding up but without the appointment of a receiver.

Since *Re Griffin Hotel Co Ltd* Parliament has made many amendments to the Companies Acts but until very recently no attempt has been made to reverse the effect of the decision. The Insolvency Act 1985 has now done so by defining a 'floating charge' as 'a charge which, as created, was a floating charge' (see s 108(3) and compare para 15 of Sch 6) but the Act had not been passed at the time of these transactions. *Re Griffin Hotel Co Ltd* has also been followed by Vinelott J in *Re Christonette International Ltd* [1982] 3 All ER 225, [1982] 1 WLR 1245. Counsel for the commissioners therefore conceded for the purpose of the hearing before me that the commissioners would have no priority in respect of any assets over which the floating charge had crystallised before the resolution for winding up. But he reserved the point for a higher court.

The argument counsel for the commissioners actually advanced before me was far more radical. He said that the events of crystallisation were fixed by law and not by the agreement of the parties. Those events were (1) winding up, (2) appointment of a receiver and (3) ceasing to carry on business. These three events and only these three would cause crystallisation notwithstanding any agreement to the contrary. Their common features were that in each case the business of the company would cease, or at any rate cease to be conducted by the directors.

Counsel for the commissioners referred to a number of cases in support of this submission. Firstly, there were cases in which it was held the crystallisation had taken place on one or other of the three events notwithstanding the absence of an express provision to that effect. For example, in *Re Crompton & Co Ltd, Player v Crompton & Co*

Ltd [1914] 1 Ch 954 Warrington J held that a floating charge crystallised on a winding
a up for the purposes of reconstruction notwithstanding that event being excluded from a
clause containing the events of default which made the loan immediately repayable. He
described winding up as an event 'which by law independently of stipulation would
make the debenture realizable' (at 964). It must be observed that Warrington J says
'independently of stipulation' and not 'notwithstanding any stipulation to the contrary'.
In a later passage he says (at 965):

b   '... the parties ... have not provided as a matter of bargaining that,
notwithstanding the general law, the other events shall not crystallize the security.'

In my judgment, when Warrington J said that crystallisation on winding up was a
matter of general law, he meant only that such a consequence was an implied term of a
floating charge in the sense described by Lord Tucker in *Lister v Romford Ice and Cold
c Storage Co Ltd* [1957] 1 All ER 125 at 143, [1957] AC 555 at 594 when he said:

'Some contractual terms may be implied by general rules of law. These general
rules, some of which are now statutory, e.g., Sale of Goods Act, 1893, Bills of
Exchange Act 1882, etc., derive in the main from the common law by which they
have become attached in the course of time to certain classes of contractual
relationships, e.g., landlord and tenant, innkeeper and guest, contracts of guarantee
d   and contracts of personal service.'

The existence of such rules of law by which terms are implied in a floating charge is not
inconsistent with the transaction being wholly consensual and the implied terms liable
to exclusion by contrary agreement.
Secondly, counsel for the commissioners relied on a number of cases in which courts
e have rejected a submission that an event of default (not being one of his three) has caused
an automatic crystallisation. The most famous of these is the decision of the House of
Lords in *Governments Stock and Other Securities Investment Co Ltd v Manila Rly Co Ltd* [1897]
AC 81. Counsel said that these cases showed that such events could not as a matter of law
cause crystallisation.
In my view, however, the speeches in the *Manila Rly* case make it clear that the House
f of Lords regarded the question as being one of construction alone. They give rise to a
plain inference that a sufficiently explicit provision for automatic crystallisation on
default would have been given effect. It is true that the commercial inconvenience of
automatic crystallisation give rise to a strong presumption that it was not intended by
the parties. Very clear language will be required. But that does not mean that it is
excluded by a rule of law.
g   The nearest any judge in this country has come to asserting such a rule of law is in
Edward Nelson & Co Ltd v Faber & Co [1903] 2 KB 367 at 376, where Joyce J, after citing
various judicial descriptions of the standard characteristics of a floating charge, said:

'It follows, I think, from these and other cases that such a debenture as this in the
present case does not cease to be a floating security ... until the company has been
wound up, or stops business, or a receiver has been appointed at the instance of the
h   debenture-holders ...'

Taken by itself, that remark may appear to lend support to counsel for the commissioners'
tripartite rule of law. But I think that a fair reading of the whole judgment shows that
Joyce J also accepted that his enumeration was subject to contrary agreement.
Thirdly, counsel for the commissioners cited several authoritative statements of the
j standard characteristics of a floating charge, particularly those of Lord Macnaghten in the
Manila Rly case and *Illingworth v Houldsworth* [1904] AC 355 at 358, and Romer LJ in the
latter case in the Court of Appeal, *Re Yorkshire Woolcombers' Association* [1903] 2 Ch 284 at
295. For example, in the *Manila Rly* case Lord Macnaghten said that it was of the essence
of a floating charge that it remained dormant 'until the undertaking charged ceases to be
a going concern, or until the person in whose favour the charge is created intervenes'.
Counsel for the commissioners said that this formulation appeared to rule out automatic

crystallisation without any act on the part of the debenture holder. To this counsel for Norandex replied that he was not asserting automatic crystallisation: both of the notices on which he relied were acts of intervention by the party entitled to the charge.

There is force in this answer but in my judgment there is a more fundamental objection to the use counsel for the commissioners seeks to make of the authorities. In *Illingworth v Houldsworth* [1904] AC 355 at 358 Lord Macnaghten was at pains to point out that he had not attempted in the *Manila Rly* case to propound a 'definition' of a floating charge. He had only offered a 'description'. In making this distinction, it seems to me that what Lord Macnaghten had in mind was that a floating charge, like many other legal concepts, was not susceptible of being defined by the enumeration of an exhaustive set of necessary and sufficient conditions. All that can be done is to enumerate its standard characteristics. It does not follow that the absence of one or more of those features or the presence of others will prevent the charge from being categorised as 'floating'. There are bound to be penumbral cases in which it may be difficult to say whether the degree of deviation from the standard case is enough to make it inappropriate to use such a term. But the rights and duties which the law may or may not categorise as a floating charge are wholly derived from the agreement of the parties, supplemented by the terms implied by law. It seems to me fallacious to argue that once the parties have agreed on some terms which are thought sufficient to identify the transaction as a floating charge, they are then precluded from agreeing to any other terms which are not present in the standard case.

Fourthly, counsel for the commissioners said that the courts should take a lead from Parliament, which in the Preferential Payments in Bankruptcy Amendment Act 1897 and subsequent company legislation apparently assumed that it need provide for only two possible events of crystallisation, namely the appointment of a receiver and a winding up. Even on counsel's own submission this means that Parliament failed to consider his third event, cessation of business. It is true that *Re Woodroffes (Musical Instruments) Ltd (in liq)* [1985] 2 All ER 908, [1986] Ch 366 was the first case in which a court expressly decided that cessation of business had crystallised a floating charge. But, as Nourse J pointed out, this had been generally assumed for about a century. Furthermore, if Parliament is to provide any guidance, it is of some interest that s 7(1)(a)(iv) of the Agricultural Credits Act 1928 creates a statutory floating charge which can be crystallised without appointment of a receiver or winding up by a notice not dissimilar from that given under cl 3(B) in this case. I therefore do not think that I can draw any inferences about the nature of a floating charge from the way in which it has been treated in legislation.

Fifthly, counsel for the commissioners said that public policy required restrictions on what the parties could stipulate as crystallising events. A winding up or the appointment of a receiver would have to be noted on the register. But a notice under cl 3(B) need not be registered and a provision for automatic crystallisation might take effect without the knowledge of either the company or the debenture holder. The result might be prejudicial to third parties who gave credit to the company. Considerations of this kind impressed Berger J in the Canadian case of *R v Consolidated Churchill Copper Corp Ltd* [1978] 5 WWR 652 where the concept of 'self-generating crystallisation' was rejected.

I do not think that it is open to the courts to restrict the contractual freedom of parties to a floating charge on such grounds. The floating charge was invented by Victorian lawyers to enable manufacturing and trading companies to raise loan capital on debentures. It could offer the security of a charge over the whole of the company's undertaking without inhibiting its ability to trade. But the mirror image of these advantages was the potential prejudice to the general body of creditors, who might know nothing of the floating charge but find that all the company's assets, including the very goods which they had just delivered on credit, had been swept up by the debenture holder. The public interest requires a balancing of the advantages to the economy of facilitating the borrowing of money against the possibility of injustice to unsecured creditors. These arguments for and against the floating charge are matters for Parliament *a* rather than the courts and have been the subject of public debate in and out of Parliament for more than a century.

Parliament has responded, first, by restricting the rights of the holder of a floating charge and, second, by requiring public notice of the existence and enforcement of the charge. For example, priority was given to preferential debts in 1897, and the Companies Act 1907 invalidated floating charges created within three months before the

b commencement of the winding up. This period has since been extended and is now one year. The registration of floating and other charges was introduced by the Companies Act 1900. The Companies Act 1907 required registration of the appointment of a receiver, and the Companies Act 1929 required notice of such appointment to be given on the company's letters and invoices.

The limited and pragmatic interventions by the legislature make it in my judgment

c wholly inappropriate for the courts to impose additional restrictive rules on grounds of public policy. It is certainly not for a judge of first instance to proclaim a new head of public policy which no appellate court has even hinted at before. I would therefore respectfully prefer the decision of the New Zealand Supreme Court in *Re Manurewa Transport Ltd* [1971] NZLR 909, recognising the validity of a provision for automatic crystallisation, to the contrary dicta in the Canadian case I have cited. For present

d purposes, however, it is not necessary to decide any questions about automatic crystallisation. The notices under cll 3(B) and 13 constitute intervention by the debenture holder and there is in my judgment no conceptual reason why they should not crystallise the floating charge if the terms of the charge on their true construction have this effect.

Counsel for the commissioners' last submission was that the actual notice under cl 3(B) was ineffective because the assets over which the charge was to be crystallised were not

e 'specified in the notice'. The notice said that it was to apply to 'all the assets of Brightlife Limited the subject of the said floating charge'. In my judgment that is sufficient specification. It is not necessary to list each separate asset. Although my decision that the notice under cl 3(B) crystallised the charge makes it unnecessary for me to decide whether the notice under cl 13 did so in respect of the book debts, I will add for the sake of completeness that in my judgment it did. The company's obligation to execute an

f assignment removed that freedom to deal with the debts which made the charge float.

I therefore declare that the debt secured by the debenture ranks in priority to the preferential debts in respect of all assets in the hands of the liquidator.

Order accordingly.

g Solicitors: *Sprecher Grier Charles* (for the liquidator); *Linklaters & Paines* (for Norandex); Solicitor for the Customs and Excise.

Evelyn M C Budd   Barrister.

Muduroglu Ltd v TC Ziraat Bankasi

COURT OF APPEAL, CIVIL DIVISION

SIR JOHN DONALDSON MR, MUSTILL AND STOCKER LJJ

9, 10, 11, 12 JUNE, 3 JULY 1986

Practice – Stay of proceedings – Foreign cause of action – Foreign court natural or appropriate forum – Factors to be considered in deciding whether stay should be granted – Dispute between Turkish company with English shareholders and Turkish bank – Whether court limited to considering only convenience and expense and plantiff's personal or juridical advantage – Whether court entitled to consider other factors – Whether court entitled to grant stay even though it would be more inconvenient and expensive for plaintiffs to bring action in Turkey.

The plaintiffs were a construction company incorporated in Northern Cyprus but controlled by shareholders and directors in England. In 1976 the plaintiffs entered into a contract with a Libyan government agency for the construction of harbour works in Libya. As part of the terms of the contract the Libyan government agency agreed to provide part payment in advance subject to the plaintiffs obtaining a guarantee to secure the repayment of the advance payment in certain circumstances. The plaintiffs accordingly obtained a guarantee from a Libyan bank backed by a counter-guarantee provided by the defendants, a Turkish bank, which although a state-owned undertaking was an autonomous legal entity which provided banking services for Turkish industry and agriculture. In particular, the defendants provided guarantees for Turkish exporters on favourable terms, and in order to take advantage of those terms the plaintiffs obtained the permission of the Turkish government to be treated as if they were incorporated in Turkey. The plaintiffs provided security for the counter-guarantee by means of an indemnity in the form of a mortgage in favour of, and cash deposits held by, the defendants. In 1979 the Libyan government agency terminated the contract and, inter alia, demanded the return of the advance payment. The Libyan bank paid under the guarantee and then called on the defendants to make payment under the counter-guarantee, which they did. Subsequently the defendants enforced the indemnity against the plaintiffs, who then commenced proceedings against the defendants in England seeking the return of the indemnity, contending that the defendants had wrongly made payment under the counter-guarantee. The defendants applied for a stay of the action on the ground that Turkey was the appropriate forum for the dispute. The plaintiffs contended that, since the controlling shareholders and directors were British subjects resident in England, the action could be tried in England with less inconvenience and expense to themselves than in Turkey, and furthermore that, in view of the political nature of the case, they would not obtain a fair trial in Turkey. The judge granted a stay of the proceedings on the grounds that Turkey was the natural forum, that the balance of convenience was in favour of the action being tried in Turkey and that there was no evidence that the plaintiffs would not obtain a fair trial there. The plaintiffs appealed to the Court of Appeal, contending that the test whether to grant a stay required the court to have regard, exclusively or primarily, to (i) convenience and expense and (ii) whether the plaintiffs would be deprived of any personal or juridical advantage by the grant of a stay, and that, applying that test, justice could be done at substantially less inconvenience and expense in England, and because of that and the risk that justice might not be done at all in the Turkish courts the stay would deprive the plaintiffs of a legitimate personal or juridical advantage. The plaintiffs further contended that the judge had been wrong to take into account what he considered to be all the relevant factors instead of restricting the exercise of his discretion to the two comparative factors of the applicable test.

Held – Although relative convenience and expense and possible deprivation of the plaintiff's personal or juridical advantage were important factors in striking a balance between the parties, they did not constitute either an exclusive test for, or a condition precedent to, the exercise of the court's discretion to grant a stay of English proceedings

where there was an alternative forum. The court would primarily consider what was the
natural forum of the dispute, taking into account such factors as where the cause of
action arose, the law applicable, the availability of witnessess and any saving of costs. In
the circumstances, the overwhelming connection between the dispute and Turkey meant
that a stay of the English proceedings ought to be granted even though there would be
relative inconvenience and possibly greater expense caused to the plaintiffs, since those
factors were not of sufficient weight to justify refusing a stay nor was there sufficient
evidence to support the plaintiffs' claim that they could not obtain a fair trial in Turkey.
It followed that the action would be stayed and the appeal dismissed (see p 695 *a b h*,
p 696 *b* to *e*, p 699 *f*, p 700 *b c*, p 709 *d* to *g j*, p 710 *c d*, p 712 *e* to *g* and p 714 *g* to p 715*c*,
post).

Dicta of Lord Reid, Lord Wilberforce and Lord Kilbrandon in *The Atlantic Star* [1973]
2 All ER at 180–181, 190, 193–194, of Lord Diplock, Lord Salmon and Lord Keith in
MacShannon v Rockware Glass Ltd [1978] 1 All ER at 629–630, 633, 644–645 and of Lord
Scarman in *Castanho v Brown & Root (UK) Ltd* [1981] 1 All ER at 151 applied.

Dictum of Robert Goff LJ in *Trendtex Trading Corp v Crédit Suisse* [1980] 3 All ER at
734 approved.

Dictum of Scott LJ in *St Pierre v South American Stores (Gath & Chaves) Ltd* [1935] All
ER Rep at 413–414 considered.

Notes

For the general principles governing stay of proceedings, see 8 Halsbury's Laws (4th edn)
paras 407, 787–788, and for cases on the subject, see 11 Digest (Reissue) 631–633, *1686–
1689*.

Cases referred to in judgments

Abidin Daver, The [1984] 1 All ER 470, [1984] AC 398, [1984] 2 WLR 196, HL.
Amin Rasheed Shipping Corp v Kuwait Insurance Co, The Al Wahab [1983] 2 All ER 884,
    [1984] AC 50, [1983] 3 WLR 241, HL.
Atlantic Star, The, Atlantic Star (owners) v Bona Spes (owners) [1973] 2 All ER 175, [1974]
    AC 436, [1973] 2 WLR 795, HL; *rvsg* [1972] 3 All ER 705, [1973] QB 364, [1972] 3
    WLR 746, CA.
Bank of Tokyo Ltd v Karoon [1986] 3 All ER 468, [1986] 3 WLR 414, CA.
Canada Malting Co Ltd v Paterson Steamships Ltd (1932) 285 US 413, US SC.
Castanho v Brown & Root (UK) Ltd [1981] 1 All ER 143, [1981] AC 557, [1980] 3 WLR
    991, HL.
Devine v Cementation Co Ltd [1963] NI 65, NI CA.
European Asian Bank AG v Punjab and Sind Bank [1982] 2 Lloyd's Rep 356, CA.
Hyman v Helm (1883) 24 Ch D 531, CA.
Logan v Bank of Scotland (No 2) [1906] 1 KB 141, [1904–7] All ER Rep 438, CA.
MacShannon v Rockware Glass Ltd, Fyfe v Redpath Dorman Long Ltd [1978] 1 All ER 625,
    [1978] AC 795, [1978] 2 WLR 362, HL; *rvsg* [1977] 2 All ER 449, [1977] 1 WLR 376,
    CA.
McHenry v Lewis (1882) 22 Ch D 397, CA.
Peruvian Guano Co v Bockwoldt (1883) 23 Ch D 225, [1881–5] All ER Rep 715, CA.
St Pierre v South American Stores (Gath & Chaves) Ltd [1936] 1 KB 382, [1935] All ER Rep
    408, CA.
Thornton v Thornton (1886) 11 PD 176, [1886–90] All ER Rep 311, CA.
Trendtex Trading Corp v Crédit Suisse [1980] 3 All ER 721; *affd* [1980] 3 All ER 721,
    [1980] QB 629, [1980] 3 WLR 367, CA; *affd* [1981] 3 All ER 520, [1982] AC 679,
    [1981] 3 WLR 766, HL.

Cases also cited

Evans Marshall & Co Ltd v Bertola SA [1973] 1 All ER 992, [1973] 1 WLR 349, CA.
Kitchens of Sara Lee (Canada) Ltd v A/S Falkefjell, The Makefjell [1975] 1 Lloyd's Rep 528,
    QBD.
Offshore International SA v Banco Central SA [1976] 3 All ER 749, [1977] 1 WLR 399.

Interlocutory appeal

The plaintiffs, Muduroglu Ltd, appealed with leave against the decision of Hobhouse J *a*
dated 26 September 1985 whereby he granted a stay of the action brought by the
plaintiffs against the defendants, TC Siraat Bankasi (a body corporate), claiming (i)
declarations that the defendants were not obliged to pay when called on to do so under a
counter-guarantee given by the defendants to Wahda Bank in respect of the plaintiffs'
performance of their obligations under a contract made with the Libyan Directorate of
Military Contracting and Procurement, and that the defendants were not entitled to *b*
debit the plaintiffs' account in respect of such payment, and (ii) repayment of the sum of
$US20m deposited by the plaintiffs with the defendants. The facts are set out in the
judgment of Mustill LJ.

Stewart Boyd QC and *Gavin Kealey* for the plaintiffs.
Sydney Kentridge QC and *Jonathan Sumption QC* for the defendants.

c

Cur adv vult

3 July. The following judgments were delivered.

MUSTILL LJ (giving the first judgment at the invitation of Sir John Donaldson MR). *d*
On 1 February 1985 Muduroglu Ltd instituted proceedings in the High Court against
TC Ziraat Bankasi. Soon afterwards the plaintiffs served the specially indorsed writ on
the defendants at their representative office in London. No objection is now taken to the
validity of this service. It was and is however contended by the defendants that the
pursuit of this action in England is an abuse of the process of the court and that the action
should be stayed so that the dispute can be carried on in Turkey, its natural forum. The *e*
matter came before Hobhouse J, who acceded to the defendants' arguments and granted
a stay. The plaintiffs now appeal.

I will begin by summarising in as uncontroversial manner as possible the origins of
this dispute and will then set out the curious history of the action and the present appeal.

The plaintiffs are a company incorporated in Nicosia, Cyprus. Their offices are a short
distance from Nicosia in that territory which, to avoid injury to political susceptibilities, *f*
I will simply call Northern Cyprus. The share capital of the plaintiffs is held, via a
Channel Islands company, by the family of Mr Efruz Sami Muduroglu, who together
with his wife and son constitute the board of directors. These three persons are British
subjects resident in England. The business of the company is in the field of construction
and civil engineering. Mr Muduroglu is also concerned with a United Kingdom company
named Muduroglu (London) Ltd which is said to have rendered ancillary services on *g*
some scale in connection with the transaction out of which the dispute has arisen.

The defendants are the largest and oldest established banking institution in Turkey.
The entire share capital is owned by the Turkish state but it is an autonomous legal entity
possessing its own board of directors. The function of the bank is to provide banking
services for Turkish industry and agriculture. One such service is the facilitation of
overseas trade by furnishing guarantees on behalf of Turkish exporters of goods and *h*
services.

During 1976 the plaintiffs entered into a contract with the Directorate of Military
Contracting and Procurement (which I will call 'the Libyan directorate') for the
construction of harbour works at the naval base at Homs. This was on a large scale. The
contract price was approximately $US220m, payable as to 75% in United States dollars
and 25% in Libyan dinars. The payment provisions were complicated but essentially (so *j*
far as concerned the US dollar portion of the price) the Libyan directorate was to provide
a letter of credit permitting an advance payment of 25% of the dollar portion plus stage
payments as the work progressed. In exchange the plaintiffs were to furnish a performance
bond for 10% of the contract value and a guarantee to secure the repayment in certain
circumstances of the 25% advance payment.

Article 22 of the contract stipulated that the Libyan directorate should have the right
a to terminate the contract in certain circumstances. In such an event the parties were to
value the works etc and in effect strike a balance. Also, the Libyan directorate were
entitled to call on the performance bond (not the advance payment guarantee)
proportionately to the value of the works left unexecuted at the date of termination.

Pursuant to the contract, during January 1977 the plaintiffs procured Wahda Bank of
Benghazi to issue a performance bond in favour of the Libyan directorate. On 27 April
b 1977 Wahda Bank also issued a guarantee in respect of the advance payment. This was
backed by a counter-guarantee given by Union Bank of Switzerland. In turn, the Swiss
bank required the plaintiffs to provide security.

During November 1977 the plaintiffs opened a branch office on the Turkish mainland
and obtained the consent of the government to be treated for the purpose of various
financial benefits as if they were incorporated in Turkey. One such benefit was the
c possibility of obtaining a guarantee from the defendants to back the Wahda advance
payment guarantee on terms (including terms as to security) much less onerous than
those required by the Swiss bank. Accordingly arrangements were made to replace the
original documents with a new set.

Thus on 27 March 1978 Wahda Bank reissued the advance payment guarantee to the
Libyan directorate. The material part read in translation as follows:

d 'Due to the request of Muduroglu Ltd. and after liquidating the counter guarantee
by Turkiye Cumhuriyeti Ziraat Bankasi who issued that counter guarantee, we
undertake to pay you upon your request and without interest the amount of
36,179,034·10 U.S. $ Thirty six million one hundred seventy nine thousand thirty
four U.S. Dollars and 10/100) as a guarantee for the Foreign Advance Payment for
Contract No. 142/126/1976 provided that the amount of the payments will be
e deducted automatically from the gross amount of the guarantee. This Letter
guarantees the Advance payment concerning the above-mentioned Tender No. 142/
126/76 and should not be used for another purpose.'

Meanwhile on 22 February 1978 a document (which I will call 'the counter-guarantee')
was issued by the defendants to Wahda Bank. This document was in the English language
f and read:

'On account and on behalf of Muduroglu Limited we give hereunder our
guarantee in replacement and in substitution of the undertaking no. 301–8096
dated 22nd April 1977 and given by the Union Bank of Switzerland.

Guarantee No 610
g In consideration of your advance payment guarantee in favour of the directorate of
military contracting and procurements Tripoli, on account of Messrs Muduroglu
Limited, as per terms annex 2a of their contract no. pro/142/126/1976 in connection
with the first and second substages of the second stage works for harbour construction
at Homs, L.A.P.S.J. for the amount of US Dollars 36,179,034·11.—(United states
Dollars Thirty six million, one hundred seventy nine thousand and thirty four
h dollar and ten cents) in all, which represents the external portion of the advance
payment referred to therein we, T.C. ZIRAAT BANKASI ANKARA BRANCH—TURKEY hereby
undertake to pay to you on first demand, irrespective of the validity and the effects
of the above-mentioned advance payment guarantee and waiving all rights and
objections and defence arising from the said advance payment guarantee any
amount up to US Dollars 36,179,034.—(Thirty six million, one hundred seventy
j nine thousand and thirty four dollar and ten cents) upon receipt of your request for
payment and your confirmation in writing or by duly encoded telex or cable that
you have requested messrs. Muduroglu Limited to repay the amount claimed by
you hereunder and that the said amount remained unpaid by Messrs Murduroglu
Limited. This guarantee is valid until 31st December 1981 (eighty-one) and expires
automatically in full should your claims, if any, not reach us on or before that date.

This guarantee is issued in accordance with current Turkish exchange control regulations. We confirm that this guarantee is unconditional and will be paid on first simple demand.'

On the same day an internal memorandum of the defendants set out the terms on which their board had agreed to take part in the transaction. We were not referred to any contemporary document showing that the plaintiffs had agreed to these terms, but they must have done, otherwise the new arrangements would not have gone ahead. In essence, the plan was for the plaintiffs to transfer to the defendants in foreign currency the sum of $36,179,034 referred to in Wahda Bank's guarantee. This was to be divided into four parts. The first $10m was to be held in an interest free foreign currency deposit account; the second $10m was to be converted into Turkish currency and deposited with the defendants; the third $10m was to be kept in a foreign currency deposit account as backing for a further guarantee to any Libyan bank so that the plaintiffs could obtain credit in Libya; the remainder was to be freely available to the plaintiffs. As security for the last two tranches the defendants were to have a mortgage over the plaintiffs' real property in Cyprus and their plant and machinery in Libya.

On 10 April 1978 the arrangements were altered by a document in the Turkish language this time addressed by the plaintiffs to the defendants. This consisted of a series of numbered paragraphs. The first dealt with the first tranche of $10m, the second with the second tranche, and the third with the security for the Wahda Bank counter-guarantee. The second paragraph stipulated that the proceeds in Turkish lire of the second tranche should be dealt with. As to one-half it was to kept in a non-interest bearing account and ultimately repaid in lire. The remainder was to be applied to the purchase of government bonds the interest being credited to the plaintiffs. The second paragraph continued:

'In the event of payment being made by your Bank to Wahda Bank in US Dollars upon a request, for any reason, by Wahda Bank for the realization of the US $36,179,034·00 counterguarantee letter given by your Bank in respect of our Firm: We undertake to pay the difference (exchange rate difference) between the buying rate current at the time of the permanent conversion of the US $10,000,000·00 sum and the selling rate at the time of payment to Wahda Bank, if at the time of payment the selling rate for the US $ is higher than at the time of the letter of guarantee transaction.'

I will call the documents which led up to and included this letter collectively 'the indemnity'.

On 17 April 1978 the sum of $20m was deposited by the plaintiffs with the defendants. Mortgages and liens were duly provided to secure the remainder of $36m.

Things went badly for the Libyan construction contract, so badly that during August 1979 it was cancelled. By this time the Libyan directorate had made the advance payment and certain progress payments. On the other hand the plaintiffs (so they assert) carried out work with a value greatly in excess of the advance payments. In these circumstances cross-claims arose between the plaintiffs and the Libyan directorate. The plaintiffs wanted reimbursement for their work and compensation for the consequences of what they regarded as a wrongful cancellation. The Libyan directorate wanted the return of the advance payment. Precisely what happened between the Libyan directorate and Wahda Bank is unknown but it is clear that the directorate demanded a partial payment under the advance payment guarantee (not, it would appear, under the performance bond).

On 2 January 1980 Wahda Bank sent to the defendants a telex in the following terms:

'Main Branch Benghazi on 2nd January, 1980 Refer to your guaranty No. 610 OUR 32/n/8/17 favour of Military Contracting and Procurement Tripoli please urgent credit out Headoffice account with Morgan Guaranty Trust Company New York USA by US $29,265,850.—as liquidation of part amount of US $36,179,034·10 according military request and urgent. Confirm us by tested cable/telex.'

On being notified the plaintiffs immediately called on the defendants not to make
a payment. In summary, they maintained that the late running of the contract was not
their fault but was due to delays by the directorate and to faulty design of the project.
The cancellation of the project was unwarranted. They went on to say that the
unconditional nature of the guarantee was restricted by the positive requirement in cl 22
of the construction contract for the finalisation of accounts between the parties. Such a
finalisation had not yet taken place and would in any event be bound to show a substantial
b balance in the plaintiffs' favour so that nothing was due from Wahda Bank to the Libyan
directorate under the guarantee. It followed that nothing could be due from the
defendants to Wahda Bank under the counter-guarantee. Moreover Wahda Bank's
demand was bad in form since it did not state, as the counter-guarantee required, that
Wahda Bank had demanded repayment by the plaintiffs and that the latter had failed to
pay; and indeed no such demand had ever been made.
c   There followed a period of intense activity. There were exchanges at a high level
between the Turkish and Libyan governments. The President of Northern Cyprus
addressed a plea to the President of Libya. The Libyan Central Bank applied pressure to
the Turkish Central Bank. Wahda Bank sent ever more urgent demands to the defendants.
       All this placed the defendants in a very difficult position. On the one hand the plaintiffs
appeared to have solid grounds for saying that the Libyan directorate was abusing the
d advance payment guarantee and that to allow Wahda Bank to take advantage of the
unconditional nature of the guarantee would be a ruinous injustice for the plaintiffs.
And if the plaintiffs were ruined the economic consequences for the Turkish community
and, particularly for that sector of society from which they drew their workforce, might
be serious. On the other hand the document issued to Wahda Bank did look like an
unconditional guarantee and for a respected state bank to decline to honour such a
e document was a grave matter which would damage the commercial reputation of the
bank and might injure the overseas trading interests of the Turkish state itself.
       In the course of considering how to escape from this dilemma the defendants' board
of directors appointed their director of commercial credits and the director of external
credits to consider and report on the problem. (This ad hoc committee has been referred
to as the 'two-man commission'.) Their report, which in translation extends to 37 pages,
f is dated 21 July 1980. Its main findings were: that the Libyan government had acted in
an arbitrary manner throughout; that there was a substantial balance of account in the
plaintiffs' favour; that accounts between the parties had never been finally adjusted as
required by the contract and that a demand under the counter-guarantee could not
properly be made until this had happened; that if anything was due under any document
it was to the performance bond, not the advance payment guarantee, that Wahda Bank
g should have looked; and that the condition precedent of a prior demand on the plaintiffs
had not been fulfilled. Substantially indorsing the plaintiffs' contentions the two-man
commission recommended that the defendants should not pay under the counter-
guarantee.
       Nevertheless on 28 August 1981 the defendants did pay Wahda Bank the sum of
$29,265,850 under the counter-guarantee. They thereupon availed themselves of the
h $20m deposit and took steps to enforce their mortgage and liens for the reimbursement
of the balance.
       Why the defendants decided to take this step has been hotly in dispute. During the
public controversy which followed the payment and the forfeiture of the security, a body
roughly equivalent to a parliamentary select committee had occasion to examine the
accounts of the defendants, and to ask for an explanation of what had happened. The
j director general of the bank stated that during the period when the defendants were
refusing to pay, the Libyan government had stated that unless they did honour this
guarantee, there was a risk that similar letters of guarantee which were being tendered
in connection with other large Turkish contracts in Libya would not be accepted. The
director general went on to say that delegates of the Turkish Central Bank, the Ministry
of Finance and Ministry of Commerce considered that the letter of guarantee should be
paid in order to facilitate a new contract of almost TL5,000m. He concluded:

'This also happened outside the means and view of Ziraat Bankasi. The delegations
led by the Central Bank President of the time as well as the Deputy Prime Minister   *a*
of the time, our present Prime Minister, stated that the payment of the guarantee
would be very expedient. Thus, in order to further our country's interests and the
development of our economy in this direction, and to prevent the acceptance of
guarantees from other banks, our Bank paid this guarantee by a decision of the
Board of Directors. This guarantee was paid at a difficult time, but for the sake of
the prospects and interests of our country.'

     b

This account of events fuelled the controversy. But the prime minister has consistently
denied that pressure was brought to bear on the defendants to pay even if they were not
liable. Officials of the defendants have deposed that the defendants received legal advice
that they were obliged to pay, although no document containing such advice has ever
been disclosed.

Finally there was a report of another committee appointed after the event to review   *c*
what had happened. The 'five-man commission' consisted of four government lawyers
and a senior official of the Ministry of Works. Opinions were divided. The majority
considered that the guarantee was unconditional and that although the Libyan directorate
had acted improperly the defendants had no choice but to make payment, unless enjoined
by order of the court: and the plaintiffs had never even tried to obtain an injunction, but
had simply left the defendants to put up the best defence it could to Wahda Bank's   *d*
demands. The report of the minority (of two) drew attention to the express statement in
the guarantee that it was subject to the conditions specified in section 2A of the appendix
of the contract, and maintained that accordingly a balance should have been struck before
Wahda Bank came down on the guarantee. They also considered that if there was liability
under any document it was the performance bond, not the advance payment guarantee.
They also pointed out the requirement of prior demand against the plaintiffs. They   *e*
accordingly disagreed with the majority.

It is neither necessary nor possible to express any opinion on the merits of this
controversy. For present purposes it is sufficient to note that there is a public and
unresolved dispute between the prime minister on the one hand and the plaintiffs and
their supporters on the other, about whether legitimate objections of the defendants to
paying Wahda Bank were overridden, at the plaintiffs' expense, by considerations of   *f*
national economic expediency. Just how far this is a live or important political issue we
are not in a position to judge but we have been shown extracts from newspapers which
tend to show that it has been brought before the public again by reports of the present
proceedings.

It is against this background that the present proceedings were launched. The only
pleading so far delivered is the special indorsement on the writ. After a recital of the   *g*
contractual relationships, this begins by setting out various matters leading to this
conclusion:

'(30) The Plaintiff contends that the Libyans' claims were in the circumstances
obviously unjustified and that such claims were not made bona fide.'

There follows a group of paragraphs in which various matters (including the report of   *h*
the two-man commission and the evidence of the director general) are relied on for the
following conclusion:

'(41) The Plaintiff contends that: (a) the Defendant was not obliged to pay the call
under the Guarantee; (b) the Defendant for a considerable period correctly refused
payment; (c) the Defendant paid the call for political reasons; (d) the Defendant was   *j*
not entitled to debit the Plaintiff with the amount of the payment or to set off the
sums deposited by the Plaintiff.'

The pleading concluded with prayers for declarations and an order for the repayment
of the $20m deposit with interest. It contains no claim relative to the other security.

a The defendants have not yet had occasion to plead to this claim so we do not know in detail what other issues they may raise. One matter did however emerge during argument. Relying on the passage in para 2 of the defendants' letter of 10 April 1978 which I have quoted the defendants are going to contend that whatever the merits of Wahda Bank's claim under the counter-guarantee, if the defendants paid on demand, they were entitled to recover from the plaintiffs under the indemnity. As one of their answers to this argument the plaintiffs are apparently intending to complain that the

b provisions embodied in the letter of 10 April 1978 were procured by commercial duress and are not binding, although it is accepted that if the defendants were indeed liable to Wahda Bank the plaintiffs are bound to indemnify them, whether there was duress or not.

In these circumstances it is quite plain that the action as initially constituted was liable to touch on every aspect of this complex transaction: the true state of accounts between

c the plaintiffs and the Libyan directorate; the right of the directorate on that state of accounts and in accordance with the law governing the document to demand payment for Wahda Bank under the advance payment guarantee; whether on the true construction of the counter-guarantee in accordance with the governing law (assumed to be Turkish) the defendants were liable to pay Wahda Bank; whether, even if they were liable, their right to an indemnity is vitiated because they paid in bad faith; whether on the true

d construction of the indemnity in accordance with the governing law (assumed to be Turkish) the defendants were entitled to recourse against the plaintiffs even if they were not liable to Wahda Bank and if so whether their prima facie right is nullified by bad faith.

This was how matters stood when the case came before Hobhouse J on the defendants' application for a stay. In preparation for the hearing a large body of evidence was

e adduced: in all, more than 800 pages of affidavits and exhibits.

Hobhouse J began his judgment by directing himself in accordance with a passage from the judgment of Robert Goff J at first instance in *Trendtex Trading Corp v Crédit Suisse* [1980] 3 All ER 721 at 734 which both parties had used as the basis for their arguments:

f '(1) "... the real test of stay depends on what the court in its discretion considers that justice demands" ... (2) The court must first consider whether there is another jurisdiction which is clearly more appropriate than England for the trial of the action. (a) Such a jurisdiction has been called the "natural or appropriate forum" ... or the "natural forum" ... The court looks for another forum which is clearly more appropriate, because the court will not lightly stay an action properly commenced in this country ... the reason being that, since the jurisdiction of the English court

g has been competently invoked, a stay should not be granted without good reason ... (b) The burden rests on the defendant to prove the existence of such other jurisdiction. (c) In considering whether there is nother jurisdiction which is clearly more appropriate the court will consider all the circumstances of the particular case, including, for example, where the cause of action arose, the connection of the parties with any particular jurisdiction, the applicable law, the availability of witnesses and

h the saving of costs. (3) If the court concludes that there is another clearly more appropriate jurisdiction, ... The burden of proof remains on the defendant. If he can show that trial in England would afford the plaintiff no real advantage, it would be unjust to refuse a stay. But, if trial in England would offer the plaintiff a real advantage, then a balance must be struck and the court must decide in its discretion whether justice demands a stay ... On either test the court will only consider

j advantages to the plaintiff which are real, i e objectively demonstrated.'

Hobhouse J went on to summarise the background of the dispute and the issues and continued:

'I now turn to the question of natural forum. It seems to me completely beyond argument that the natural forum for the dispute between the plaintiffs and the

defendants is Turkey. The relevant transactions are governed by Turkish law. The
relevant document is a Turkish document. The subject matter of the action is *a*
wholly Turkish; the action has nothing whatsoever to do with England. The parties
are either Turkish or closely connected with Turkey. I recognise that the plaintiffs
have connections with other countries as well, but there can be no denial that they
have a close cultural affinity with Turkey and they have in the past, when it suited
them, had very close connections with Turkey. Furthermore, the vast bulk of any
witnesses that may be material (it is very questionable whether there is any necessity *b*
for any witnesses at all) would be Turkish and would come from Turkey. The real
dispute in this matter is as to the effect of various documents in Turkish law. The
primary document is the letter of indemnity coupled with the indemnity obligations
that would arise under Turkish law. As regards the secondary matter of the liability
of the defendants to Wahda Bank, it seems to be the common approach of the parties
that the liability under that cross-guarantee should be considered under Turkish *c*
law. Certainly it has absolutely nothing whatsoever to do with English law. The
only other law that might be relevant would be Libyan law, and there does not seem
to be any enthusiasm to consider Libyan law as governing the liability of the
defendants; nobody has done so so far.'

Next Hobhouse J discussed the problems of Turkish law which would arise if the *d*
dispute was litigated here and repeated that in his judgment the natural forum for the
relevant dispute was the Turkish court. In the remainder of the judgment Hobhouse J
dealt with a number of issues to which I shall later return. In brief these concerned the
political aspects of the case: the question of comparative expense and convenience as
regards trial in Turkey and London; the burden of a judgment tax in Turkey where no
such tax is levied here. Hobhouse J concluded that the clear balance of convenience
remained in favour of the proceedings being conducted in Turkey. *e*
Finally Hobhouse J returned to what he described as the main point relied on by the
plaintiffs, namely that they could not get a fair trial in Turkey. He quoted Mr Muduroglu
as saying:

'The present case is not a simple civil dispute between private individuals. This is
a large claim brought against a vital state institution for a sum of dollars which a *f*
country short of dollars would be very loath to pay. Moreover, the direction of the
defendants to pay on the guarantee was made at the suggestion of Turgut Ozal, now
the prime minister ... The case might be gravely embarrassing for the present
government and it would take effective steps to prevent its being brought or heard
... Turkey, whilst having some semblance of civilian government, is still a country
largely under military rule where the freedom of speech, press and free associations *g*
are severely curtailed and arrest and torture of political opponents is widespread.
Prominent lawyers have been arrested and tortured and pressure brought on them
not to take politically sensitive cases. The judiciary is not free or independent.
Bribery and corruption are rife in Turkey ... In these circumstances it must be clear
that the plaintiffs' reasons in choosing London as the forum are that England has a
free independent judiciary not removable for political reasons and a Bar not *h*
intimidated by the threat of arrest and torture ... If the trial were held in Turkey
both lawyers and witnesses for the plaintiffs would face the possible risk of detention
and torture.'

In discussing the evidence Hobhouse J drew a distinction between political trials and
trials before the military courts, and civil trials. He concluded that there was a perfectly *j*
satisfactory and mature legal system in Turkey effective to deal with civil commercial
cases and no evidence of personal risk to the plaintiffs' directors or witnesses or lawyers.
He was satisfied that if the matter went to Turkey the plaintiffs would receive a fair trial
of their case.
Accordingly Hobhouse J held that on established principles the action must be stayed.
After studying the judgment the plaintiffs' legal advisers settled and served a notice of

appeal repeating much of the ground covered by their arguments before the judge. It appears that some time thereafter the plaintiffs and their legal advisers decided to part company and the plaintiffs began of their own accord to prepare the appeal and also to lay the ground for an application to adduce further evidence on appeal in order to reinforce the allegations of fact which the judge had rejected. To this end they prepared and caused their retiring advisers to serve a supplementary notice of appeal comprising 56 paragraphs directed to the law the merits and the various advantages and disadvantages of litigating this particular dispute in Turkey as opposed to England. In addition the plaintiffs applied initially to the Registrar of Civil Appeals and then to this court for leave to adduce further evidence extending to one thousand pages of affidavits and exhibits. The defendants strenuously objected to the adduction of this new material and this led to further exchanges of affidavit and counter affidavit, exhibit and counter-exhibit.

Accordingly it seemed that the parties were preparing to refight on the appeal the issues that had been fought before the judge albeit at even greater length if the application to adduce further evidence was allowed. At this stage there was a remarkable turn of events. The plaintiffs appointed a new team of legal advisers, led by Mr Stewart Boyd QC, who made it plain as soon as the argument was opened that with their clients' consent they proposed to jettison much of what had been said before the judge and almost all of the material comprised in the application to adduce further evidence. The reformulated case amounted to this. (a) Hobhouse J had misunderstood and therefore misapplied the statement of Robert Goff J in the *Trendtex* case. Alternatively if it had been correctly understood then even though the hearing had proceeded on the unanimous assumption that it accurately stated the law it was inconsistent with prior authority and should not be followed. (b) The plaintiffs formally abandoned as regards the English action and any future action in Turkey all the allegations of fact which they had made in relation to the merits of the claim with one possible exception. They proposed to take their stand exclusively on the construction of the counter-guarantee and the indemnity. The only exception related to the allegation that the variation in the letter of 10 April 1978 was induced by commercial duress which they might wish to raise in rebuttal if the defendants founded any proceedings on that letter. (c) The plaintiffs no longer pursued, as part of their arguments relating to the exercise of the discretion, the allegations that their lawyers and witnesses would be subject to persecution if they appeared for the defendants in a Turkish action, or that the Turkish judge might be corrupt, or might act on direct instructions from the ruling party. This forensic coup transformed an unarguable appeal into one which required the closest consideration. In my judgment even if Hobhouse J had erred in law in looking at matters other than convenience, expense and procedural advantage, an appellate court would inevitably have come to the conclusion, exercising the discretion afresh, that the issues previously summarised could not conveniently be litigated anywhere else but Turkey. The stripping-down of the issues has created an entirely new situation never addressed by the judge and I consider that it is now necessary for this court, whilst taking careful note of the views expressed by the judge, to exercise the discretion on its own account. In doing so we should in my judgment take into account those very few items of further evidence which were in fact referred to during the arguments. Whilst very far from saying that the bulk of the new documents could properly have been admitted a number of them did concern matters arising since the previous hearing (production of the two-man commission's report, evidence as to risk of prosecution, etc) and the remainder of them have caused the defendants no serious difficulty in furnishing an answer. In the unusual circumstances of this interlocutory appeal I believe that the best interests of justice would not be served by excluding material which appears germane to the issues as they now stand. That being said I should emphasise that in the end the new material has made no difference to the conclusion which I have formed.

I turn first to the law. The objection taken by counsel for the plaintiffs to the approach of the judge can best be illustrated by reference to the following passage from the speech of Lord Diplock in *MacShannon v Rockware Glass Ltd* [1978] 1 All ER 625 at 630, [1978] AC 795 at 812:

'In order to justify a stay two conditions must be satisfied, one positive and the
other negative: (a) the defendant must satisfy the court that there is another forum
to whose jurisdiction he is amenable in which justice can be done between the
parties at substantially less inconvenience or expense, and (b) the stay must not
deprive the plaintiff of a legitimate personal or juridical advantage, which would be
available to him if he invoked the jurisdiction of the English court . . .'

I will call this the *MacShannon* formula.

The primary argument of counsel for the plaintiffs is that this formula contains an
exclusive code for the exercise of the discretion to grant a stay. Only three criteria are
relevant: comparative expense, comparative convenience and the existence of a legitimate
personal or juridical advantage. There may be controversy it is admitted about the
burden of proof in relation to personal and juridical advantage. There may also be
controversy about whether the formula creates consecutive stages so that if the defendant
fails at stage (a) the court never reaches stage (b) or whether the court ascertains the
position in relation to both criteria and then proceeds to balance the one against the
other. Whichever of these is right however the court may not take into consideration
any factor other than those contained in the formula.

The alternative proposition did not form part of the main submissions of counsel for
the plaintiffs but was adopted by him in the course of argument as a position on which
he was prepared to fall back if necessary. It assumes for the purposes of argument that
the *MacShannon* formula does not create an exclusive code and that it can be appropriate
for the court to take into account criteria other than those set out in the formula.
Nevertheless, so the argument, runs compliance with those criteria is an essential prerequisite to the grant of a stay. Unless the defendant can so to speak get through the two
hoops created by parts (a) and (b) of the formula the stage of looking at the discretion in
the round will never arrive.

Counsel for the plaintiffs then develops the factual side of his arguments by asserting
that the Turkish court is not a forum in which justice can be done at substantially less
inconvenience or expense than England. Quite the reverse he says. As regards
requirement (a), there is a risk that justice cannot be done at all in the Turkish courts in
this particular case. It will also be more expensive to bring the action in those courts at
least so far as initial outlays are concerned. Whatever the position may have been when
the matter was before Hobhouse J there is nothing substantial in the way of inconvenience
to the defendants to set in the opposite side of the scale, for the dispute has now shrunk
to a series of short points of construction which can be tried in the commercial court
without the need for any witnesses of fact. As to requirement (b), much the same factors
appear again added to which is the consideration that the plaintiffs are in reality if not in
strict theory bringing the action in their own home forum.

Against this counsel for the defendants accepts that the matters cited in the *MacShannon*
formula are important elements in the inquiry but disputes that they are the only
elements or that they are conditions precedent to the exercise of what he asserts is a
general discretion. The judge approached the problem correctly and although the shape
of the action has greatly changed his answer is still correct.

In order to assess these arguments it is necessary to examine again the line of authority
which has developed the modern law on the stay of an action properly brought within
the jurisdiction. These cases have been discussed in several judgments in recent years and
it is unnecessary to rehearse their more general aspects. I will refer only to those features
which may shed light on the present point, an issue which has not hitherto arisen directly
for decision.

The first case was *St Pierre v South American Stores (Gath & Chaves) Ltd* [1936] 1 KB 382,
[1935] All ER Rep 408. The defendants in the English action were plaintiffs in an action
in Chile. The issues in both suits concerned the manner in which the plaintiffs in
England were entitled to satisfy their obligations under Chilean law to pay the rent of
premises in Chile. The defendants sought a stay under s 41 of the Supreme Court of

Judicature (Consolidation) Act 1925 on the familiar ground that the action was vexatious,
a oppressive and an abuse of the process of the court. The application failed. In the Court
of Appeal Greer LJ directed his judgment to the general question whether the litigant
applying for a stay could get justice in this country. Scott LJ agreed with the result. Since
one paragraph in his judgment formed the starting point of the later authorities I must
set this out but it is necessary to quote other passages as well. He said ([1936] 1 KB 382 at
397–398, [1935] All ER Rep 408 at 413–414):

b   '[Counsel for the appellants] as an alternative justification for an order staying the
        English action, contended, in the words of his summons, that the action is in the
        circumstances disclosed in the appellants' affidavits "vexatious, oppressive and an
        abuse of the process of the Court." I agree with the assumption that these are
        conditions to the grant of a stay, but his evidence, in my opinion, falls short of what
        is necessary. He gave, it is true, several strong reasons for contending that the
c   Chilean Court is a more convenient forum: (1.) the contract is in Spanish; (2.) the
        law of the contract is Chilean as to both interpretation and performance; (3.) the
        action is about land in Chile; (4.) the respondent companies, though registered in
        England, carry on all their business in Chile; and (5.) Chilean lawyers are so scarce
        in England that expert evidence for the Court here will be difficult to obtain. But
        these grounds go only to convenience; they do not come near to establishing the
d   allegations of the summons. He sought to rely on the considerations summed up in
        the phrase lis alibi pendens, which have in some cases led to a party, who is plaintiff
        both here and in another jurisdiction in actions against the same defendant and on
        the same disputes, being put to his election. But here the respondents are not
        plaintiffs in the Chile action; they are defendants and the appellants are the plaintiffs.
        In such a case the mere fact that the other action is pending raises no presumption
e   to the effect suggested. The true rule about a stay under s. 41, so far as relevant to
        this case, may I think be stated thus: (1.) A mere balance of convenience is not a
        sufficient ground for depriving a plaintiff of the advantages of prosecuting his action
        in an English Court if it is otherwise properly brought. The right of access to the
        King's Court must not be lightly refused. (2.) In order to justify a stay two conditions
        must be satisfied, one positive and the other negative: (a) the defendant must satisfy
f   the Court that the continuance of the action would work an injustice because it
        would be oppressive or vexatious to him or would be an abuse of the process of the
        Court in some other way; and (b) the stay must not cause an injustice to the plaintiff.
        On both the burden of proof is on the defendant. These propositions are, I think,
        consistent with and supported by the following cases: McHenry v. Lewis ((1882) 22
        Ch D 397); Peruvian Guano Co. v. Bockwoldt ((1883) 23 Ch D 225, [1881–5] All ER
g   Rep 715); Hyman v. Helm ((1883) 24 Ch D 531); Thornton v. Thornton ((1886) 11 PD
        176, [1886–90] All ER Rep 311); and Logan v. Bank of Scotland (No. 2) ([1906] 1 KB
        141, [1904–7] All ER Rep 438). I do not think that the cases upon service out of the
        jurisdiction, some of which were cited to us, are sufficiently germane to the
        principles upon which this appeal turns to call for discussion. Discretion looms
        larger in that exercise of statutory jurisdiction; under s 41 there is little, if any, room
h   for discretion; decisions on questions of degree often look like, but are not instances
        of, discretion.'

Next there was The Atlantic Star, Atlantic Star (owners) v Bona Spes (owners) [1973] 2 All ER
175, [1974] AC 436. Two members of the House of Lords dissented, attaching importance
to the fact that the right of a person possessing a maritime lien to proceed in rem
j wherever he could find the vessel was an important part of international commerce. The
majority consisted of Lord Reid, Lord Wilberforce and Lord Kilbrandon. The theme of
the three speeches was that the central paragraph from Scott LJ's judgment still
represented the stance of the English law and that the time had not yet come to assimilate
the law to the Scottish concept of forum non conveniens: a doctrine in which, as Lord
Kilbrandon pointed out, the word 'conveniens' is to be rendered as 'suitable' rather than

'convenient'. The case is however of cardinal importance in two respects. The first has received the most attention. Whilst the general shape of Scott LJ's bipartite analysis was *a* retained its content was greatly enlarged by the detachment of the words 'vexatious' and 'oppressive' from the significance which they ordinarily have in the context of an application under s 41 of the 1925 Act. There was, however, a second important feature of *The Atlantic Star*. The judgment of Scott LJ, although not that of Greer LJ, tended to make the grant or withholding of a stay into a mere fact-finding exercise. The speeches of the majority in *The Atlantic Star* are in my judgment quite inconsistent with any such *b* mechanical application of the criteria. On the contrary their Lordships are plainly speaking in terms of a general discretion.

The process of enlarging Scott LJ's formulation was taken a stage further in *MacShannon v Rockware Glass Ltd* [1978] 1 All ER 625, [1978] AC 795. The analysis still kept to the framework of the old law and repudiated any formal adoption of the Scottish principles. Once again, however, the emphasis was laid on the discretionary nature of the task to be *c* performed by the court. Lord Diplock explicitly set out to restate 'the gist' of the three majority speeches in *The Atlantic Star*, when he reworded Scott LJ's central paragraph to create 'the *MacShannon* formula'. I think it inconceivable that he could thereby have been intending to set the clock back to where it had been before *The Atlantic Star*. Quite the contrary, for, as Lord Russell pointed out, the tenor of the speeches delivered by their Lordships was to make a further and liberal dilution of the spirit of 'oppressive' and *d* 'vexatious' (see [1978] 1 All ER 625 at 640, [1978] AC 795 at 823). In four of the speeches there is reference to the 'natural forum' for the dispute and Lord Salmon, Lord Fraser and Lord Keith all relate the test to the question of injustice (see [1978] 1 All ER 625 at 635, 639, 644, [1978] 795 at 818, 822, 829). Although the formulation of Scott LJ remains the starting point of the discussion it is no longer operating as a constraint.

It was at this stage in the development of the law that Robert Goff J enunciated the test *e* from which I have already quoted. Once again the matter went to the House of Lords but I do not find anything in the judgments delivered in the higher courts to show clearly whether the views of Robert Goff J received approval on the particular aspects which are now in question.

This process of analysis then continued in *Casthanho v Brown & Root (UK) Ltd* [1981] 1 All ER 143, [1981] AC 557. The nature of the relief sought was different, namely an *f* injunction to restrain an action abroad rather than a stay of an action in England. It was however assumed that the principles to be applied were the same. Delivering the only speech Lord Scarman quoted the *MacShannon* formula but went on to say that the formula should not be construed as a statute.

In *European Asian Bank AG v Punjab and Sind Bank* [1982] 2 Lloyd's Rep 356 both parties accepted Robert Goff J's formulation of the law but Stephenson LJ did take the *g* opportunity to say that it was correct (at 365).

The latest of the authorities in the House of Lords was *The Abidin Daver* [1984] 1 All ER 470, [1984] AC 398. This was principally concerned with the effect of a lis alibi pendens but the speeches of Lord Keith and Lord Brandon again seem to me imbued with the idea of a general discretion.

Finally there was *Bank of Tokyo Ltd v Karoon* [1986] 3 All ER 468, [1986] 3 WLR 414. *h* Again there appears to have been no dispute between the parties about the principles to be applied. It may however be noted that Ackner LJ addressed himself to the question whether the English court was the natural forum. Robert Goff LJ stated that the principle adopted in the *MacShannon*'s case was now accepted to be indistinguishable from forum non conveniens. This principle, it was stated, involved—

'a policy of declining to exercise jurisdiction where there is another clearly more *j* appropriate forum; though, if in such circumstances trial in England would offer the plaintiff a real advantage, a balance must be struck and the court must decide in its discretion whether justice requires a stay.'

(See [1986] 3 All ER 468 at 484, [1984] 3 WLR 414 at 428.)

In the light of this developing line of authority it would in my judgment be impossible
a to hold that the power is to be exercised by looking at first at requirement (a) of the
MacShannon formula in isolation and then (if it is satisfied) at requirement (b) and only if
that is satisfied granting a stay. Obviously a discretion is involved. Moreover, the decided
cases seem to me to show both by way in which the principle was expressed and by the
choice of factors actually taken into account that the scope of the inquiry goes beyond
the considerations listed in the *MacShannon* formula. In *The Atlantic Star* Lord Reid spoke
b of looking to all the circumstances including the personal position of the defendant. The
list of relevant matters given by Lord Wilberforce included the fact that: 'The only
connection of any element in the action with England is that the present suit was begun
in rem against the Atlantic Star when the vessel was expected in Liverpool' (see [1973] 2
All ER 175 at 189, [1974] AC 436 at 463); and in the case of Lord Kilbrandon 'the total
absence of physical connection between England and the subject-matter of the action'
c (see [1973] 2 All ER 175 at 202, [1974] AC 436 at 477). Lord Salmon in the *MacShannon's*
case referred to the fact that the plaintiff was a Scotsman living and working in Scotland
and that the case had absolutely nothing to do with England. Lord Keith spoke of the
natural forum as being that with which the action has the most real and substantial
connection. In the *Castanho's* case the leading speech referred to England 'as the scene of
the accident' as a natural and proper forum. In the *European–Asian Bank* case Stephenson
d LJ paid regard to the nationality of the parties, the proper law and the place where the
cause of action arose. In the *Trendtex* case, as we have seen, Robert Goff J included in his
list the place where the cause of action arose, the connection of the parties with any
particular jurisdiction and the applicable law. I am satisfied that in doing so he was not
simply enumerating some of the factors which might make it more convenient or less
expensive to sue in one place rather than another. In the appellate courts where attention
e was focussed on the foreign jurisdiction clause to which the same factors were assumed
to be relevant nobody suggested that the enumeration was wrong. In *The Abidin Daver*
Lord Diplock, who knew more than anyone what the *MacShannon* formula implied,
mentioned that the parties and the subject matter had no connection with England and
later said that not only was Turkey the country with which the matter had the closest
connection but was also the natural and appropriate forum from the point of view of
f convenience and expense. Lord Keith said that by the natural forum he meant that with
which the action had the most real and substantial connection. Lord Brandon said that
the discretion involved the balancing of all relevant factors, and he included in his own
list the place of the collision and the flags of the vessels and the fact that the litigation had
no connection with England except for the arrest of one of the sister ships of the Abidin
Daver. So also in *Bank of Tokyo Ltd v Karoon* where the place where the contract was made,
g the proper law and the place of breach were all taken in to account by Ackner LJ in
deciding that in every sense the action was an American action for which New York was
the natural forum, and by Robert Goff LJ in identifying a strong connection with the
New York jurisdiction.

In these circumstances I consider that the *MacShannon* formula is not an exclusive code
for the exercise of the discretion and these factors connecting the dispute with one forum
h or another may properly be taken into account.

I thus reject the major submission of counsel for the plaintiffs. The alternative
proposition, that even if the court regards the foreign court as the natural or more
appropriate forum a stay must nevertheless be refused, is at first sight more compelling.
The crucial passage in the *St Pierre* case [1936] 1 KB 382 at 398, [1935] All ER Rep 408 at
414 begins with the words: 'In order to justify a stay two conditions must be satisfied.'
j These words survived intact the successive transmutations in *The Atlantic Star* and
MacShannon's case. When transposing the formula to suit the case of an injunction to
restrain proceedings 'must show' that the two requirements were satisfied. Thus so the
argument runs even if it must not be accepted that connective factors can be taken into
account in identifying the natural forum, the power of the court can never be exercised
unless the 'critical equation' is answered in favour of a stay.

This argument raises a problem which I have not found easy to solve. The mandatory words 'must be' cannot just be brushed aside. On the other hand the idea that compliance *a* with the *MacShannon* formula is a condition precedent seems too rigid a reflection of the broad analysis in the later judgments and certainly too rigid for a process which Lord Wilberforce described in *The Atlantic Star* as instinctive. In the end I believe that the sea change wrought by *The Atlantic Star* has extended beyond the second proposition in Scott LJ's judgment on which attention was originally focussed and has also affected the first. In my judgment the orderly exercise of this jurisdiction can best be achieved by *b* recognising that the shape of Scott LJ's formulation has now been entirely superseded and that it should be replaced by something which accords with the contemporary ideas on the subject. This is not, however, a task which this court can perform. We must acknowledge the vestigial influence of the *St Pierre* case by giving some weight to the words on which counsel for the plaintiffs relies. I believe that this can be done by giving the words 'properly brought' in the first part of the *St Pierre* formulation the flavour *c* (undoubtedly wider than they were intended to bear) of the 'natural forum'. Thus the inquiry begins with the search for the natural forum. If the answer is found to be that the foreign court is the natural forum the inquiry stops there. (This was the conclusion reached by Ackner LJ in *Bank of Tokyo Ltd v Karoon*.) But if the English court is found to be the natural forum the critical equation is brought into play.

I shall not attempt to spell out this conclusion in a new formula. It may be that my *d* own idea is not quite the same as the one expressed in the *Trendtex* case but if there is a difference it favours the plaintiffs in the present case. Certainly I see no ground for saying that by adopting the *Trendtex* formulation the judge did any injustice to the plaintiffs in the present case and I am content to proceed on the basis that his general approach was correct. I now turn to the material features of the present case. First there are the connecting factors. Here I can add nothing to what was said by the judge. The dispute *e* has everything to do with Turkey and nothing to do with England.

Second there is the national identity of the parties. Although the defendants are being sued away from their home forum this was the price which they paid for their election to establish a place of business here; and the fact that the transaction in suit was not effected through the London office does not have the same materiality as if the discretion were the very different one which falls to be exercised under RSC Ord 11, r 1. Per contra *f* the plaintiffs say that England is their home forum for those who control the company are British subjects. There is some force in this argument but I am not much impressed by it. The Northern Cypriot location of the plaintiffs is not just a corporate fiction like that of the Jersey holding company. Their real commercial base is in Northern Cyprus as witness the efforts made on their behalf by the president when they had fallen out with the Libyan directorate. Moreover the chain of transactions with which we are now *g* concerned stemmed from the preferential treatment offered by the Turkish authorities. It suited the defendants to be treated as Turkish whilst the business was being arranged. They cannot too readily claim to be treated as English now that things have gone wrong.

Next there is the relative convenience and expense of fighting the action in Turkey and England. Of course on the factual issues presented to Hobhouse J there could be only one view about this. The advantages of trying the case in Turkey was so great as to *h* swamp every other consideration. Now the position is undoubtedly different but how matters stand is not by any means clear, absent any pleadings to crystallise the issues. If I correctly understand it the present position of the defendants is as follows.

(1) As between Wahda Bank and the Libyan directorate: the plaintiffs no longer raise the issue whether there was a net balance in the Libyans' favour sufficient to justify recourse against Wahda Bank. But they do contend that the Libyans had recourse against *j* the wrong document, viz the advance payment guarantee rather than the performance bond.

(2) As between the defendants and Wahda Bank: the plaintiffs no longer contend that Wahda Bank was not liable to the Libyans and that accordingly the defendants should not have paid Wahda Bank, save only in the respect just mentioned. They do however

a maintain that it was a condition precedent to the making of a valid claim that the demand should state that a claim had been made on the plaintiffs without success. To this the defendants respond that it was sufficient if such a claim on the plaintiffs had in fact been made. The defendants contend that if the plaintiffs wished to prevent encashment they should have applied for an injunction in the Turkish court.

b (3) As between the defendants and the plaintiffs: the defendants contend and the plaintiffs deny that the passage from para 2 of the letter of 10 April 1978 has the effect of enabling the defendants to recover on simple demand irrespective of whether the defendants were liable to Wahda Bank. In addition the plaintiffs will rely, if any counterclaim is founded on the letter, on the proposition that the variations embodied in the letter were induced by duress. This raises a factual issue but not one which has any direct connection with the question whether the defendants acted in good faith in paying Wahda Bank.

c Before considering how suitable these issues are for litigation here a few comments may be made on the trial of foreign law in an English court. First many actions are brought each year in which some aspect of the relationship between the parties is governed by foreign law. This is so particularly in the Commercial Court because of the large proportion of foreign litigants who choose or are brought to appear before the court. Second so far as my one experience has shown most of these cases are decided

d solely in accordance with English law not so much because the court has applied the presumption that foreign law is the same as English law but because in so many practical respects there is insufficient difference between the commercial laws of one trading nation and another to make it worth while asserting and proving a difference. There does however remain a residue of cases where foreign law is hotly in dispute. Here it has to be fought on expert evidence with the help of written materials in the light of jurisprudential concepts and procedural systems markedly different from our own. It is part of the stock-

e in-trade of the practitioner and judge in the Commercial Court to deal with this kind of dispute and the volume of business in the court would give the lie to any suggestion that the court is seen by its users as incapable of dealing with any but characteristically English disputes. At the same time it would be unrealistic not to acknowledge that the trial of an issue of foreign law must be more complicated and expensive here than in the court to

f which the law belongs. Moreover although it does not follow that the judge at first instance here is more likely to misunderstand or misapply the law than his counterpart abroad the fact that any appeal is treated as a question of fact rather than law does make it more uncertain whether any mistake that may be made is going to be put right.

At first sight I doubted whether these considerations had much bearing on the present case. The points are mostly very short and if argued under English law in an English court would not take long to decide. (I say 'mostly' because the question whether it was a

g condition precedent to a demand under the counter-guarantee that demand should first be made on the plaintiffs is not even in English law as short as it might seem. It might be for argument under English law whether the authorities which dispense with the performance of a condition properly described as an 'idle formality' are material in a case like this.) It struck me initially that they would be just as short if decided under Turkish

h law in an English court since they are concerned principally with the interpretation of documents which are unlikely to require the marshalling of numerous statutory provisions commentaries and decided cases and the examination of principles unknown to the English law and English laywers.

On regarding the affidavits of Turkish law I am no longer so sure about this. I do not say that the Commercial Court could not cope with the issues and decide them correctly.

j But they are not entirely straightforward and I consider than the business of trial and appeal can be performed with markedly more convenience, and less expense, in Turkey than in England. This will be more than ever the case if the defendants have occasion to run their case of duress which will add new issues of fact and law.

The next factor relates to the cost of the proceedings. This has two aspects. First there is the total cost of the proceedings. The figures contained in the affidavits coupled with general knowledge of the levels of fees now prevailing in English commercial litigation suggest that the action is most unlikely to be cheaper to fight in England than in Turkey, quite apart from the additional cost of bringing expert witnesses to England. Against this is the second factor namely that of advance payments where the balance is undoubtedly the other way. Since the plaintiffs' own evidence is to the effect that the company itself is short of money they will find it hard to avoid an order for security for costs if the action is allowed to proceed and such an order has already been made for several thousands of pounds in respect of the proceedings to date. Moreover it is not to be expected that their advisers will continue very far with the action without being put in funds. It is however clear that substantially more than this will be required in Turkey because the local procedure requires the plaintiffs to furnish a sum on account of judgment tax, which is levied pro rata on the amount claimed. In the end they will get this money back from one source or another but the cost of finance will be heavy. There is a dispute about whether the initial cost can be reduced by bringing a 'pilot action' for a lesser sum to be followed in the event of success by an action for the remainder.

This does not strike me as very practical in the circumstances of the present case. There is also a dispute about whether the whole of the amount of tax has to be put up in cash or whether three-quarters can be secured in some other way. The computation of the amount claimed on which the percentage is levied is also in dispute. But even allowing for the uncertainties it seems plain that the plaintiffs would have to finance an action in Turkey to the extent of at least $250,000 and possibly greatly more, a part of which will be paid in Turkish currency and recovered at the end of the day in the same currency, with a sharp decline in value in the meantime, if the Turkish economic experience continues as it has been in the recent past. There is unquestionably a substantial procedural advantage to the plaintiffs in avoiding this burden by suing in England. The judge recognised this advantage although perhaps not to its full extent but was inclined to discount it on the ground that there was no evidence that those beneficially interested in the company would be unable to find the money. For my part I venture to differ from him in this respect: the loss is there even if the plaintiffs can afford to bear it. I should add that pending the appeal a further body of evidence was adduced to the effect that the shareholders cannot afford to bear this burden. It has not been possible to test this fully and I would prefer not to explore this issue simply treating the cost of financing the deposit as a proved and substantial disadvantage of suing in Turkey.

The most contentious topic raised by the plaintiffs' allegation is that this dispute could not receive a fair trial in a Turkish court. This no longer takes the extreme shape which it had before the judge. It is not now said that the Turkish court would have to decide the issue of fact whether (notwithstanding the denial by the present Prime Minister) the defendants had yielded to political pressure by paying under the counter-guarantee when they believed that they were not liable thus sacrificing the plaintiffs to the wider interests of the state. It is not now asserted that direct political pressure would be brought to bear on the trial judge to decide in favour of the state bank.

The revised argument is much more modest. It asserts that the propriety of the payment to Wahda Bank, and the manner in which it came to be made, is still a live political issue in Turkey, that it would be very embarrassing for the prime minister and others if it turned out that the payment need not have been made; that the trial judge would realise this, and that a Turkish judge could not be guaranteed to have the intellectual integrity and moral firmness to resist the pressures to which consciously or unconsciously he would be exposed.

An argument of this kind faces the court with a difficulty. On the one hand the court must not adopt any line of reasoning which involves a finding or assumption of impropriety or unfairness on the part of an organ of a friendly foreign state without solid evidence to support it. On the other hand the court must not be too unworldly. It must recognise that there are parts of the world where things are badly wrong and that by virtue of this very fact it may be impossible to obtain direct and complete evidence of the grounds of complaint. A balance must be struck.

Looking at the evidence adduced before us, drawn from all sources, some markedly
a more commanding of attention than others and bearing always in mind that allegations
of the present kind are much more easy to make than to rebut one does find a very real
question mark over what may be loosely termed civil rights in Turkey although there
appears to be some acknowledgment among critics that things are not now as bad as they
were. More specifically, criticisms are directed towards the military tribunals as regards
their composition and methods and as regards the treatment of the lawyers who appear
b for defendants before them. These are sufficiently substantial to have made one think
twice, or more than twice, if the question had been whether the action in England should
be stayed so that the claim should proceed before a military court in Turkey. But nobody
has suggested that this will happen. The case will be heard before a civil commercial
court. The only grounds for apprehension as to the quality of justice before such a court
suggested by the plaintiffs are that the Turkish judiciary is undermanned and that the
c terms of service are so poor that the right recruits cannot be found with many of those in
post leaving to better themselves in private practice. In addition it is said that the
pressures on the judges are increased by a recently introduced scheme for grading judges
which has been the subject of strong public expressions of concern by senior judges. for
my part I cannot find in these aspects of Turkish judicial administration any proper basis
for a finding or even a solid suspicion that the commercial judges are in general incapable
d of acting without bias or that in the particular circumstances of this case there is a risk
that the trial judge and the judges who hear any appeal will be impelled to decide these
questions of law and construction otherwise than on their merits just because a decision
inconvenient to important people would be a black mark for the future. In this
connection it is impossible to overlook the fact that when the plaintiffs were attempting
to obtain, for the purposes of the present proceedings, the report of the two-man
e commission, a document highly inconvenient to those who say that the defendants paid
Wahda Bank because they were liable to do so, they were able to extract it from the
Ministry of Trade by means of a court order. This hardly suggests that the judges are too
lacking in fibre to tackle the issues boldly. The very most that can be said in my judgment
is that if the action remains in England the possibility of unconscious pressure on the
judge could not even be raised. I take the matter into account to this extent but no
f further when considering the exercise of the discretion.

Finally, the plaintiffs rely on considerations affecting the personal safety of Mr
Muduroglu. (At one time the personal safety of witnesses and lawyers acting for the
plaintiffs was also put in question but this allegation has now been abandoned, not
surprisingly, since distinguished tribunal lawyers have felt themselves able apparently
without apprehension to swear affidavits on the plaintiffs' behalf.) The matter arises in
g this way. In an affidavit made by Mr Muduroglu at an early stage of the proceedings he
used strong language to characterise contemporary Turkey and its institutions. He said:

'Turkey, whilst having some semblance of civilian government, is still largely a
country under military rule . . . the freedom of speech, press and free association are
severely curtailed . . . arrest and torture of political opponents is widespread . . . the
judiciary is not free or independent . . . bribery and corruption are rife in Turkey.'
h
Things have now changed because although the plaintiffs do not withdraw these
allegations (in the sense of accepting that they were untrue) they no longer rely on them
in relation to the attenuated version of their case. At some time after the affidavit was
lodged it evidently struck Mr Muduroglu, or perhaps someone suggested to him, that he
might have been too outspoken. He therefore took advice from an eminent lawyer on
j the implications of these statements for his personal position in Turkey in relation to art
159 of the Turkish Code which deals with the acts against the personality of the Turkish
state. For reasons stated in his opinion and backed with citation the jurist concluded: 'I
cannot advise Mr Muduroglu that criminal proceedings under the Turkish Civil Code
would not be taken against him should he visit Turkey.' This view is contested but we
must plainly accept that Mr Muduroglu is exposed to some degree of risk if he goes to

Turkey for the trial. It is, however, to be noted that during the past year he has apparently
received no sign that the authorities would call him to account, that this is not a case in   *a*
which he or anyone else (according to the argument advanced by counsel for the
plaintiffs) will need to give evidence in Turkey, and that the root of all the trouble lies in
allegations made to support a line of argument which he no longer pursues. There
remains an undeniable advantage to Mr Muduroglu in pursuing his action in England,
where there would be no risk of his allegations attracting personal sanctions, but the
weight to be given to this consideration is in my judgment much less than if the case had   *b*
retained its original shape.

These are the factors to be taken into account. The process of balancing them against
one another cannot be rationalised at length. I will only say that although the case has
changed greatly since it was before Hobhouse J I consider that his decision not to grant a
stay was right then and remains right now. In my judgment this action properly belongs
in Turkey. I would dismiss the appeal.   *c*

STOCKER LJ. I agree. In deference to the interesting arguments which have been put
before us I venture to add some observations on the questions raised.

In directing himself on the relevant law Hobhouse J at the outset of the judgment
said:

> 'The writ was properly served and the defendants had a sufficient presence within   *d*
> the jurisdiction. Similarly, this is not a case which involves any exclusive jurisdiction
> clause. It is simply a case which involves the application of the principles of law as
> laid down in *MacShannon v Rockware Glass Ltd* [1978] 1 All ER 625, [1978] AC 795
> and it is for present purposes sufficient, and the parties likewise based their
> arguments, to refer to the summary given by Robert Goff J in *Trendtex Trading Corp
> v Crédit Suisse* [1980] 3 All ER 721 at 734.'   *e*

The judge then gave a summary of the relevant part of Robert Goff J's judgment in that
case.

The plaintiffs challenge the correctness of the summary and analysis by Robert Goff J
and submit that the proper conclusion to be drawn from the speeches of their Lordships
in *MacShannon v Rockware Glass Ltd* is that the initial test to be applied is that given by   *f*
Lord Diplock (see [1978] 1 All ER 625 at 638, [1978] AC 795 at 812) and that no inquiry
with regard to the 'natural' or 'appropriate forum' arises unless, and until, a defendant
has satisfied the onus of proving that the two conditions stated by Lord Diplock have
been met. In other words, that this passage comprises in itself a complete code to the
exclusion of other considerations at least in the initial stages so that its terms constitute a
condition precedent to consideration of any other factors. Alternatively it is contended   *g*
that this passage itself provides the test with regard to 'natural forum'. It is therefore
convenient at this stage to set out the passage in Lord Diplock's speech and the summary
in the *MacShannon* case given by Robert Goff J on which Hobhouse J relied before turning
to consider the detail of the relevant authorities. Robert Goff J summarised the effect of
the speeches of their Lordships in *MacShannon* in *Trendtex Trading Corp v Crédit Suisse*
[1980] 3 All ER 721 at 734 in the following terms: *h*

> 'It is my duty to distil from their speeches the principles which I should apply in
> the present case. As I understand it those principles are as follows: (1) "... the real
> test of stay depends on what the court in its discretion considers that justice
> demands" (see [1978] 1 All ER 625 at 636, [1978] AC 795 at 819 per Lord Salmon).
> (2) The court must first consider whether there is another jurisdiction which is   *j*
> clearly more appropriate than England for the trial of the action. (a) Such a
> jurisdiction has been called the "natural or appropriate forum" (see [1978] 1 All ER
> 625 at 631, [1978] AC 795 at 812 per Lord Diplock) or the "natural forum" (see
> [1978] 1 All ER 625 at 636, [1978] AC 795 at 818 per Lord Salmon). The court looks
> for another forum which is clearly more appropriate, because the court will not

lightly stay an action properly commenced in this country (see [1978] 1 All ER 625 at 629, 636, [1978] AC 795 at 810, 818 per Lord Diplock and Lord Salmon), the reason being that, since the jurisdiction of the English court has been competently invoked, a stay should not be granted without good reason (see [1978] 1 All ER 625 at 642, [1978] AC 795 at 826 per Lord Keith). (b) The burden rests on the defendant to prove the existence of such other jurisdiction. (c) In considering whether there is another jurisdiction which is clearly more appropriate the court will consider all the circumstances of the particular case, including, for example, where the cause of action arose, the connection of the parties with any particular jurisdiction, the applicable law, the availability of witnesses and the saving of costs. (3) If the court concludes that there is another clearly more appropriate jurisdiction, then two slightly different tests have been adumbrated. (a) A stay will be granted unless the plaintiff shows that a stay would deprive him of a legitimate personal or juridical advantage available to him in England (see [1978] 1 All ER 625 at 630, 639, [1978] AC 795 at 812, 822 per Lord Diplock, approved generally by Lord Fraser). (b) The burden of proof remains on the defendant. If he can show that trial in England would afford the plaintiff no real advantage, it would be unjust to refuse a stay. But, if trial in England would offer the plaintiff a real advantage, then a balance must be struck and the court must decide in its discretion whether justice demands a stay (see [1978] 1 All ER 625 at 636, 645, [1978] AC 795 at 819, 829 per Lord Salmon and Lord Keith). On either test the court will only consider advantages to the plaintiff which are real, ie objectively demonstrated. (It is not clear which of these two approaches enjoyed the support of Lord Russell; but from the general tenor of his speech I infer that he preferred the latter.) (4) If the court concludes that there is no other clearly more appropriate jurisdiction, then only Lord Keith appears to have considered that a stay might be granted. Such a case must be very rare.'

The passage in Lord Diplock's speech on which the plaintiffs rely is as follows ([1978] 1 All ER 625 at 630, [1978] AC 795 at 812):

'In order to justify a stay two conditions must be satisfied, one positive and the other negative: (a) the defendant must satisfy the court that there is another forum to whose jurisdiction he is amenable in which justice can be done between the parties at substantially less inconvenience or expense, and (b) the stay must not deprive the plaintiff of a legitimate personal or juridical advantage which would be available to him if he invoked the jurisdiction of the English court . . .'

omitting the reference to burden of proof which follows these words. It is perhaps relevant to observe that Lord Diplock was considering only the second and not the first limb of Scott LJ's formulation.

In order to decide whether or not the plaintiffs' submissions are well founded it is therefore necessary to consider the speeches of their Lordships in *MacShannon*'s case and the relevant cases leading up to that decision on which those speeches were founded. It seems to me that the appropriate starting point for such an analysis is *St Pierre v South American Stores (Gath & Chaves) Ltd* [1936] 1 KB 382, [1935] All ER Rep 408 since this case was declaratory of the law as it had existed for many years and stood unchallenged until 1974. The issue in that case was concerned with a dispute with regard to rents payable by one company to another in South America, jurisdiction in this country being afforded by the fact that the defendants had their head offices in London. The trial judge refused the defendants' application for a stay on the grounds that it was 'vexatious', or 'oppressive', for the actions to proceed in England. On appeal Scott LJ said ([1936] 1 KB 382 at 398, [1935] All ER Rep 408 at 414):

'The true rule about a stay under s. 41, so far as relevant to this case, may I think be stated thus: (1.) A mere balance of convenience is not a sufficient ground for depriving a plaintiff of the advantages of prosecuting his action in an English Court if it is otherwise properly brought. The right of access to the King's Court must not

be lightly refused. (2.) In order to justify a stay two conditions must be satisfied, one
positive and the other negative: (a) the defendant must satisfy the Court that the   *a*
continuance of the action would work an injustice because it would be oppressive
or vexatious to him or would be an abuse of the process of the Court in some other
way; and (b) the stay must not cause an injustice to the plaintiff. On both the burden
of proof is on the defendant. These propositions are, I think, consistent with and
supported by the following cases: *McHenry* v. *Lewis* ((1882) 22 Ch D 397); *Peruvian
Guano Co.* v. *Bockwoldt* ((1883) 23 Ch D 225, [1881–5] All ER Rep 715); *Hyman* v.   *b*
Helm ((1883) 24 Ch D 531); *Thornton* v. *Thornton* ((1886) 11 PD 176, [1886–90] All
ER Rep 311); and *Logan* v. *Bank of Scotland (No. 2)* ((1906) 1 KB 141, [1904–7] All ER
438).'

This declaration of the relevant law was considered by the House of Lords in *The
Atlantic Star* [1973] 2 All ER 175, [1974] AC 436. That action arose out of a collision
which occurred in Belgian waters between a vessel owned by Dutch shipowners and a   *c*
barge also owned by a Dutch company. Jurisdiction was afforded by the fact that the
vessel visited the port of Liverpool and was there arrested. Brandon J at first instance
refused to stay the action in England, justifying the exercise of his discretion on the
ground that to stay the action would deprive the plaintiff of an advantage which he
reasonably believed that trial in England would give him and that the defendants had
not shown that the inconvenience to them would be oppressive, despite the fact that for   *d*
five practical reasons trial in Antwerp was the appropriate forum. A preliminary step in
an action had been taken in Antwerp and thus a question of lis alibi pendens arose. On
appeal the Court of Appeal affirmed the judge's ruling but the House of Lords by a
majority reversed the decision.

In his speech Lord Reid, after stating the basis for the trial judge's decision, said ([1973]
2 All ER 175 at 180–181, [1974] AC 436 at 453–454):   *e*

'But following the trend of modern authority he felt bound to refuse to stay this
action, and this decision was upheld in the Court of Appeal ([1972] 3 All ER 705,
[1973] QB 364). The authorities are dealt with by my noble and learned friend,
Lord Wilberforce, and I shall not repeat that examination. They support the general
proposition that a foreign plaintiff, who can establish jurisdiction against a foreign   *f*
defendant by any method recognised by English law, is entitled to pursue his action
in the English courts if he genuinely thinks that that will be to his advantage and is
not acting merely vexatiously. Neither the parties nor the subject-matter of the
action need have any connection with England. There may be proceedings on the
same subject-matter in a foreign court. It may be a far more appropriate forum.
The defendant may have to suffer great expense and inconvenience in coming here.   *g*
In the end the decisions of the English and foreign courts may conflict. But
nevertheless the plaintiff has a right to obtain the decision of an English court. He
must not act vexatiously or oppressively or in abuse of the process of the English
court, but these terms have been narrowly construed . . . So I would draw some
distinction between a case where England is the natural forum for the plaintiff and
a case where the plaintiff merely comes here to serve his own ends. In the former   *h*
the plaintiff should not be "driven from the judgment seat" without very good
reason, but in the latter the plaintiff should, I think, be expected to offer some
reasonable justification for his choice of forum if the defendant seeks a stay. If both
parties are content to proceed here there is no need to object. There have been many
recent criticisms of "forum shopping" and I regard it as undesirable. I think that a
key to the solution of the problem may be found in a liberal interpretation of what   *j*
is oppressive on the part of the plaintiff. The position of the defendant must be put
in the scales. In the end it must be left to the discretion of the court in each case
where a stay is sought, and the question would be whether the defendants have
clearly shown that to allow the case to proceed in England would in a reasonable
sense be oppressive looking to all the circumstances including the personal position

a   of the defendants. That appears to me to be a proper development of the existing
law.'

Lord Wilberforce, agreeing with Lord Reid and the majority of their Lordships with
reference to the passage in the judgment of Scott LJ in the *St Pierre* case, observed ([1973]
2 All ER 175 at 190, [1974] AC 436 at 464):

b   'I now examine the English rules in this matter: the governing statement at the
present time is contained in the well-known judgment of Scott LJ in *St Pierre v South
American Stores (Gath & Chaves) Ltd* [1936] 1 KB 382 at 398, [1935] All ER Rep 408
at 414 which I shall quote later. There is a danger, as with all clear propositions, of
this receiving quasi-statutory force, and of the key words "oppressive" and "vexatious"
being too rigidly construed and applied. I do not think that these are technical
words: they can only be understood against an evolutionary background.'

c   He proceeded to consider in detail the earlier authorities and, after quoting the
ipsissima verba of Scott LJ, said ([1973] 2 All ER 175 at 193–194, [1974] AC 436 at 468):

'This clear and emphatic statement has proved its usefulness over the years. It has
been applied by judges, without difficulty to a large variety of cases. I should be
most reluctant, even if I were capable, of replacing it by some wider and more
d   general principle. But too close and rigid an application of it may defeat the spirit
which lies behind it. And this is particularly true of the words "oppressive" and
"vexatious". These words are not statutory words: as I hope to have shown from
earlier cases, they are descriptive words which illustrate but do not confine the
courts' general jurisdiction. They are pointers rather than boundary marks. They
are capable of a strict, or technical application; conversely, if this House thinks fit,
e   and as I think they should, they can in the future be interpreted more liberally. In
my opinion, the passage cited embodies the following principles—all of which have
been discussed in earlier authorities. First a plaintiff should not lightly be denied
the right to sue in an English court, if jurisdiction is properly founded. The right is
not absolute. The courts are open, even to actions between foreigners, relating to
foreign matters. But they retain a residual power to stay their proceedings. I may
f   add that, in relation, inter alia, to Admiralty suits, the existence of this power has
been explicitly affirmed in the United States of America. Mr Benedict, a writer of
acknowledged authority, says (The Law of American Admiralty (ed Kranth) (1940),
vol 1, p 260 and footnote): "Admiralty Courts have jurisdiction of Admiralty suits
entirely between foreigners when proper service can be had or property attached,
but it is discretionary with the Court whether it will accept such jurisdiction or
g   not." The judgment of Brandeis J in *Canada Malting Co Ltd v Paterson Steamships Ltd*
(1932) 285 US 413 supports this with several judicial citations. Secondly, in
considering whether a stay should be granted the court must take into account (i)
any advantage to the plaintiff; (ii) any disadvantage to the defendant: this is the
critical equation, and in some cases it will be a difficult one to establish. Generally
this is done by an instinctive process—that is what discretion, in its essence, is. But
h   there are perhaps some elements which it is possible to disengage and make explicit.
In the first place, I do not think it would be right to say that *any* advantage to the
plaintiff is sufficient to prevent a defendant from obtaining a stay. The cases say that
the advantage must not be "fanciful"—that a "substantial advantage" is enough. I
do not even think that one can say that the advantage must be substantive (ie in the
existence in English law of some more favourable substantive rules than would
j   apply elsewhere) rather than adjectival, though more weight might be given to the
former. An example given by Lord Denning MR illustrates this: a motor collision
in Italy between two Italian citizens, one of whom catches the other here and sues
him. Lord Denning MR says that this would be purely Italian and so (inferentially)
should be stayed. But if this is right, it must follow that advantage to a plaintiff is
not in itself decisive for the suit may well have been brought here because our courts

give higher damages, or damages under broader heads: so if a stay is to be granted it must be because the court can additionally consider the nature of the case, and the *a* disadvantage to the defendant. A bona fide advantage to a plaintiff is a solid weight in the scale, often a decisive weight, but not always so. Then the disadvantage to the defendant: to be taken into account at all this must be serious, more than the mere disadvantage of multiple suits; to prevail against the plaintiff's advantage, still more substantial—how much more depending how great the latter may be. The words "oppressive" or "vexatious" point this up as indicative of the degree and character of *b* the prejudice that must be shown. I think too that there must be a relative element in assessing both advantage and disadvantage—relative to the individual circumstances of the plaintiff and defendant. This was certainly a factor in the marginal case of *Devine v Cementation Co Ltd* [1963] NI 65 and without it, the case could hardly be supported.' (Lord Wilberforce's emphasis.)

Lord Kilbrandon, after citing the relevant passage from Scott LJ in the *St Pierre* case, *c* observed ([1973] 2 All ER 175 at 201–202, [1974] AC 436 at 477):

'There are plenty of earlier examples of the use of the words "oppressive" and "vexatious" in this context. But the words have, at all events today, certain shades of meaning which make it difficult to accept an uncritical construction as appropriate to all circumstances in which guidelines—and they are nothing more—may be *d* required. "Oppressive" is an adjective which ought to be, and today normally is, confined to deliberate acts of moral, though not necessarily legal, delinquency, such as an unfair abuse of power by the stronger party in order that a weaker party may be put in difficulties in obtaining his just rights. "Vexatious" today has overtones of irresponsible pursuit of litigation by someone who either knows he has no proper cause of action, or is mentally incapable of forming a rational opinion on that topic. *e* Either of these attitudes may amount to an abuse of the process of the court, but in my opinion a defendant moving for a stay cannot be compelled to bring the plaintiff's conduct within the scope of one of these grave allegations.'

It seems to me that the basis on which Lord Morris and Lord Simon dissented from the majority was based on the historical role of the High Court of Admiralty and the fact that in that jurisdiction an action in rem followed an arrest of a vessel. They were of the *f* view that those rules had been applied for so long that they should not be modified or watered down and that any such modification of these rules was in the province of Parliament and not of the courts.

The effect of this decision in my view was to relax the strict meaning of 'oppressive' and 'vexatious' to a degree which permitted consideration of such matters of the advantage or disadvantage to the parties of the choice of forum. *g*

The principles of law to be applied where a challenge is made to an action continuing in the English courts were next considered by the House of Lords in the case on which the judge's ruling in the instant case was founded, ie *MacShannon v Rockware Glass Ltd* [1978] 1 All ER 625, [1978] AC 795. The facts were that four Scotsmen injured in separate industrial accidents in Scotland brought actions for damages for personal injuries in England the cause of action being alleged in each case negligence and breach of *h* statutory duty. Jurisdiction in each case was founded on the fact that the head offices of the defendant companies were situated in England. In the first two cases Robert Goff J refused to stay the actions and his decisions were affirmed in the Court of Appeal (Lord Denning MR dissenting). In the other two cases Griffiths J felt himself bound by that decision of the Court of Appeal and granted a certificate under s 12 of the Administration of Justice Act 1968 to appeal to the House of Lords under the 'leap frog' provisions. All *j* four cases were therefore considered at the same hearing before their Lordships' House. The issues raised were (1) whether it was a reasonable justification for the choice of forum which was not the 'natural forum' that the solicitors concerned for the plaintiffs in each case instructed by trade unions were of the opinion that the scale of damages awarded in

English courts were higher than those awarded in Scottish courts for comparable injuries
and that the Scottish system of pleadings disadvantaged the plaintiffs, and (2) whether
such institution of proceedings in English courts would be 'oppressive' or 'vexatious'
within the meaning assigned to them in *The Atlantic Star* in the speeches to which
reference had already been made. After pointing out that in each case the employer was
a company who had a head office in England and that it was this fact alone that made it
possible for a High Court writ to be served on the employers in England, and that none
of the four actions had any other connections with England, and each of the employers
could have been served at their places of business in Scotland, Lord Diplock observed
([1978] 1 All ER 625 at 628, [1978] AC 795 at 809):

> 'All three members of the Court of Appeal acknowledged that Scotland was the
> natural and appropriate forum for the Fyfe and MacShannon actions. Stephenson LJ
> expressed it most emphatically in terms which I am ready to adopt, when he said
> ([1977] 2 All ER 449 at 453, [1977] 1 WLR 376 at 382): "Anyone with nothing but
> common sense to guide him would say that they ought to be tried in Scotland . . ."
> Nevertheless he considered that the decision of this House in *The Atlantic Star* [1973]
> 2 All ER 175, [1974] AC 436 compelled him to follow a course which was contrary
> to common sense and so to allow the actions to proceed in England. It thus becomes
> necessary for this House to consider whether the ratio decidendi of the majority of
> this House in *The Atlantic Star* must indeed have this lamentable consequence.'

In a later passage, after reciting the dicta of Scott LJ in the *St Pierre* case, and
commenting that the words 'oppressive' or 'vexatious' in the ordinary parlance and in
terms of art in the courts connoted an element of moral blameworthiness he continued
([1978] 1 All ER 625 at 629–630, [1978] AC 795 at 810–811):

> 'In *The Atlantic Star* [1973] 2 All ER 175, [1974] AC 436 this House was specifically
> invited to discard Scott LJ's statement as an authoritative exposition of the principles
> on which a stay of proceedings ought to be granted in English law and to substitute
> for it the Scottish legal doctrine of forum non conveniens. The House unanimously
> rejected this invitation. The minority were of opinion that this House should leave
> unchanged the English law on the topic as it had hitherto been expounded and
> applied, particularly in admiralty jurisdiction. The majority, however, were of
> opinion that the time was ripe for some further development of the common law
> which, as Lord Reid put it ([1973] 2 All ER 175 at 181, [1974] AC 436 at 453),
> would bring it more into line with the policy of Parliament and the movement of
> public opinion, and render it less reminiscent of—"the good old days, the passing of
> which many may regret, when inhabitants of this island felt an innate superiority
> over those unfortunate enough to belong to other races" . . . As a result of their re-
> examination of the statement of the law by Scott LJ in *St Pierre v South American
> Stores (Gath & Chaves) Ltd* [1936] 1 KB 382 at 398, [1935] All ER Rep 408 at 414 the
> majority were of opinion that the modification that was called for could be best
> achieved by giving to the words "oppressive" and "vexatious" what was described by
> Lord Reid and Lord Wilberforce as a more liberal interpretation. (See [1973] 2 All
> ER 175 at 181, 193, 194, [1974] AC 436 at 454, 468.) Put bluntly what this comes
> to is that if Scott LJ's judgment in *St Pierre v South American Stores (Gath & Chaves)
> Ltd* is still to be treated as the framework on which the statement of the law is built,
> the words "oppressive" and "vexatious" are no longer to be understood in their
> natural meaning but in some strained and "morally neutral meaning" (per Lord
> Kilbrandon ([1973] 2 All ER 175 at 202, [1974] AC 436 at 478)). To continue to use
> these words to express the principle to be applied in determining whether an action
> brought in England should be stayed can, in my view, lead only to confusion, as I
> believe it has in the instant cases. If these expressions are eliminated from Scott LJ's
> statement of the rule, the gist of the three speeches of Lord Reid, Lord Wilberforce
> and Lord Kilbrandon, in my opinion, enables the second part of it to be restated

thus: "In order to justify a stay two conditions must be satisfied, one positive and the other negative: (a) the defendant must satisfy the court that there is another *a* forum to whose jurisdiction he is amenable in which justice can be done between the parties at substantially less inconvenience or expense, and (b) the stay must not deprive the plaintiff of a legitimate personal or juridical advantage which would be available to him if he invoked the jurisdiction of the English court" omitting the reference to burden of proof which follows these words. If the distinction between this restatement of the English law and the Scottish doctrine of forum non *b* conveniens might on examination prove to be a fine one, I cannot think that it is any the worse for that.'

It is this reformulation of Scott LJ's dictum from the *St Pierre* case which forms the main ground of the submission on behalf of the plaintiffs in this case to which I have already made short reference. I will consider the validity of the argument hereafter, but put shortly it is submitted that this reformulation by Lord Diplock contains in itself and *c* embraces either the whole criteria to be applied or is at least a condition precedent to the consideration of other factors and thus does not permit any a priori consideration of whether or not the English courts are the 'natural' or 'appropriate' forum, and that when applied to the facts and considerations raised in the instant case the conclusion must be that the defendants have not established that a stay is justified,

Lord Diplock then related certain factors relevant to the issues such as the fact that the *d* parties, their witnesses and the doctors all resided in Scotland and observed ([1978] 1 All ER 625 at 631, [1978] AC 795 at 812):

'This it is that prima facie makes the Scottish courts the only natural or appropriate forum for each of these actions and throws on the plaintiffs the onus of showing what Lord Reid ([1973] 2 All ER 175 at 181, [1974] AC 436) called "some reasonable *e* justification" for his choice of an English court or, as I have ventured to express it, of showing that if they brought their actions in a Scottish court they would be deprived of a legitimate personal or juridical advantage which would have been available to them in the High Court in England. The advantage must be a real one. The plaintiff's own belief that there is an advantage or, what is more likely to determine where the action is to be brought, the belief of his legal advisers, however *f* genuinely it may be held, is not enough. The advantage that is relied on as a ground for diverting the action from its natural forum must be shown objectively and on the balance of probability to exist. So long as it was necessary to show "oppressive" or "vexatious" conduct by the plaintiff in the ordinary meaning of those words, the test remained subjective; an unsubstantiated but bona fide belief by the plaintiff or his legal advisers in an advantage to be obtained for him by suing in the English *g* courts might be a sufficient answer to the defendant's application for a stay. Since *The Atlantic Star* this is no longer so.'

Lord Diplock expressed the view that both the trial judge and the Court of Appeal in exercising their discretion on the basis of the belief of the respondents' solicitors with regard to the advantage to the respondents of bring the actions in England misdirected *h* themselves in law and thus vitiated the exercise of their discretion and continued ([1978] 1 All ER 625 at 633, [1978] AC 795 at 815):

'It leaves the way open to your Lordships to decide how the discretion should have been exercised. Where prima facie England is not the natural or appropriate forum in which to bring the plaintiff's action and the plaintiff relies on juridical, as *j* distinct from personal, advantages in bringing his action here instead, it is for him to prove by expert evidence the respects in which the substantive or procedural law of the natural forum differs from the corresponding English law to the disadvantage of the plaintiff. This is so as respects the law of foreign states. In the High Court and Court of Appeal in England it is also true as respects Scots law.'

Lord Salmon as a preface to his opinion at the end of the first paragraph of his speech
a observed ([1978] 1 All ER 625 at 634, [1978] AC 795 at 817):

'The case had absolutely nothing to do with England except that the plaintiff is a
member of a trade union with headquarters in England and the defendant's
registered office is also in England.'

He expressed his views with regard to the principles to be applied in the following
b terms ([1978] 1 All ER 625 at 636, [1978] AC 795 at 818):

'In an action brought in England when its natural forum is Scotland, I consider
the question as to whether it should be stayed depends on whether the defendants
can establish that to refuse a stay would produce injustice. Clearly if the trial of the
action in England would afford the Scottish plaintiff no real advantage and would
be substantially more expensive and inconvenient than if it were tried in Scotland,
c it would be unjust to refuse a stay. If, on the other hand, a trial in England would
offer the plaintiff some real personal advantage, eg if he had come to live in England,
a balance would have to be struck and the court might in its discretion consider that
justice demanded that the trial should be allowed to proceed in England (see eg
Devine v Cementation Co Ltd [1963] NI 65). To my mind, the real test of stay depends
on what the court in its discretion considers that justice demands. I prefer this test
d to the test of whether the plaintiff has behaved "vexatiously" or "oppressively" on a
so-called liberal interpretation of these words. I do not, with respect, believe that it
is possible to interpret them liberally without emasculating them and completely
destroying their true meaning. Surely if a man genuinely but wrongly believes that
it is to his advantage for his action to be tried in England rather than in Scotland,
and accepts his solicitor's advice that this will cause the defendants no unnecessary
e expense or inconvenience, he cannot properly be called vexatious or oppressive if he
opposes a stay of the action in England. Nevertheless, the court will impose a stay if,
in their discretion, they decide that the defendants have proved that it would be
unjust to refuse to do so.'

In a subsequent passage he cited with approval the passage of Lord Reid in *The Atlantic*
f *Star* [1973] 2 All ER 175 at 181, [1974] AC 536 at 454, already cited, where the distinction
is drawn between cases where England is the natural forum and cases where a plaintiff
merely comes here to serve his own ends (see [1978] 1 All ER 625 at 637, [1978] AC 795
at 820).

Lord Fraser in a short concurring speech observed ([1978] 1 All ER 625 at 639, [1978]
AC 795 at 822):
g
'I agree with my noble and learned friend, Lord Salmon, that the question for the
English court is whether the defendant, in each case considered separately, can
establish that to refuse a stay would produce injustice. I agree also with my noble
and learned friend, Lord Diplock, that the fundamental question can generally be
answered by an application of his restatement of the rule originally stated by Scott
h LJ in *St Pierre v South American Stores (Gath & Chaves) Ltd* [1936] 1 KB 382 at 398,
[1935] All ER Rep 408 at 414). I share the view of both my noble and learned
friends that, in order to clarify the law of England on this matter, the use of the
words "oppressive" and "vexatious" in this rule ought now to be discontinued; their
use in a specially broad and liberal sense seems to me to have become merely
misleading.'

j Lord Russell also concurred, observing ([1978] 1 All ER 625 at 640, [1978] AC 795 at
823):

'Your Lordships' House in *The Atlantic Star* under the guise of liberal construction
much diluted the strong spirit of "oppressive" and "vexatious", and in your
Lordships' speeches in the instant appeals I think I detect a further liberal use of the

water jug. I do not object to that, provided it be recognised, though in the result it stops not far short of balance of convenience.'

Finally, some of the observations of Lord Keith in the course of his speech appear to be very relevant to the issues in the instant case with regard to the correctness of the summary of Robert Goff J in the *Trendtex* case which formed the basis of Hobhouse J's decision in this case and with regard to the plaintiffs' submissions. After citing the passage from the speech of Lord Reid in *The Atlantic Star*, Lord Keith observed ([1978] 1 All ER 625 at 642, [1978] AC 795 at 826):

'I think Lord Reid is saying, in the second place, that where England is not the natural forum it is necessary to weigh any reasonable justification which the plaintiff may show for suing there against any disadvantages from which the defendant may show he will suffer. In certain cases these disadvantages may be inherent in the inappropriateness of the English forum and if the plaintiff can show no reasonable justification, in the shape of advantage to him, for bringing the action there, that may be sufficient for the view to be taken that the continuance of the action would, in a reasonable sense, be oppressive to the defendant. Where, on the other hand, England is the natural forum for the action, it is incumbent on the defendant, in order to secure a stay, to show that he will suffer very serious disadvantages there, and that the plaintiff will suffer no injustice in being required to resort to a different forum. In my opinion the speech of Lord Wilberforce in *The Atlantic Star* (with which Lord Kilbrandon agreed) is consistent with this view.'

He then cites a substantial passage from the speech of Lord Wilberforce and expresses his own view in the following terms ([1978] 1 All ER 625 at 644, [1978] AC 795 at 827–828):

'Lord Wilberforce, unlike Lord Reid, does not distinguish specifically between the situation where England is the natural forum and that where it is not. His words are applicable to both situations. Where England is not the natural forum, and on the evidence there is no advantage to the plaintiff in resorting there, or only a fanciful one, I do not understand Lord Wilberforce to be taking the view that it would be insufficient for the defendant to found on the general disadvantage to him of the English forum as compared with the natural forum.'

He summarises his own conclusions ([1978] 1 All ER 625 at 644–645, [1978] AC 795 at 828–829):

'My opinion therefore, in the present state of the authorities, is as follows. Where a defendant seeks a stay of proceedings on the ground that the action can and should be prosecuted elsewhere, he must show good reason why the court's discretion should be exercised in his favour. He must satisfy the court that the continuance of the action would work an injustice because it would be oppressive or vexatious to him or would be an abuse of the court in some other way, that expression being understood in a broad and reasonable sense and without any necessary moral connotations, and also that the stay would not cause an injustice to the plaintiff. Where England is the natural forum for the action, in the sense of being that with which the action has the most real and substantial connection, it is necessary for the defendant, in order to establish injustice to him and no injustice to the plaintiff, to show some very serious disadvantage to him which substantially outweighs any advantage to the plaintiff. Where however, the defendant shows that England is not the natural forum and that if the action were continued there he would be involved in substantial (ie more than de minimis) inconvenience and unnecessary expense, or in some other disadvantages, which would not affect him in the natural forum, he has made out a prima facie case for a stay, and if nothing follows it may properly be granted. The plaintiff may, however, seek to show some reasonable justification for his choice of forum in the shape of advantage to him. If he succeeds it becomes necessary to weigh against each other the advantages to the plaintiff and the disadvantages to the defendant, and a stay will not be granted unless the court concludes that to refuse it would involve injustice to the defendant and no injustice to the plaintiff. As to the nature of the advantages and disadvantages which may go into the scale on either side, I am of opinion that they must be such as are capable of being objectively demonstrated. I do not consider that mere genuine belief that an advantage or disadvantage exists, not supported by adequately established grounds, can properly affect the result. Objective matters such as I have in mind would include the place of residence of the plaintiff, as in *Devine v Cementation Co Ltd* [1963] NI 65, or solid evidence of the existence in the suggested alternative forum of a rule of law or of procedure such as to make an action there less attractive to the plaintiff than one in England. In my opinion there are no good grounds for treating as an advantage to the plaintiff the circumstances that his solicitor has advised him to bring his action in England rather than in the natural forum, nor yet the circumstance that that solicitor or another has expressed in general terms the view that the plaintiff is likely to do better in England. In the result, therefore, I find that Lord Denning MR, in his dissenting judgment in the court below ([1977] 2 All ER 449 at 451–453, [1973] 1 WLR 376 at 379–381), expressed with complete accuracy, and with greater succinctness and lucidity than I have been able to command, the effect of the decision in *The Atlantic Star* and the development in the law which is brought about.'

For my part, this passage and, in particular, the words 'where England is the natural forum for the action, in the sense of being that with which the action has the most real and substantial connection' clearly indicate that he is not limiting the consideration of the question solely to the formulation of the test as posed by Lord Diplock. It seems to me equally clear that Lord Salmon was not regarding the speech of Lord Diplock in this sense either since he expressly approved the formulation by Lord Reid in *The Atlantic Star* [1973] 2 All ER 175 at 180–181, [1974] AC 436 at 453–454 in which he draws the distinction between a case where England is the natural forum and cases where it is not. Indeed I would not for my part construe the speech of Lord Diplock, read as a whole, as indicating that the passage on which the plaintiffs rely was intended by him to be a comprehensive code excluding any consideration of the natural forum or to be a condition precedent to such consideration. In many cases including *MacShannon*'s case the 'natural forum' may be so obvious as to be beyond argument but that is in my mind no valid reason for excluding it as a relevant factor at the outset.

I have made extensive reference to the speeches of each of their Lordships in *MacShannon*'s case because it seems to be necessary to do so in order to reach a conclusion on the plaintiffs' basic submission that Hobhouse J misdirected himself in accepting the formulation by Robert Goff J of the effect of the speeches of their Lordships in *MacShannon*'s case, and thus failed to apply the correct principles to the issues before him.

I have already set out in extenso the relevant passage from Robert Goff J's judgment in the *Trendtex* case. The facts of that case itself in my view do not further the issues raised on this appeal since there was in that case an exclusive jurisdiction clause covering most of the disputed issues. Nor do I find it necessary to reach a conclusion as to whether or not the House of Lords expressly approved the dicta of Robert Goff J at first instance though for my part I would regard the approval of the basis on which he exercised his discretion to stay the proceedings as having this effect.

My conclusion from the authorities which I have cited and tried to analyse is that the passage in Lord Diplock's speech on which reliance is placed by the plaintiffs cannot be read either as a 'condition precedent to the consideration of other matters' and in particular to the question 'what is the natural or appropriate forum for the action', nor does it involve any conclusion that it forms a complete code for the determination of that issue.

My conclusion therefore is that on the issues with which Hobhouse J was concerned his decision to grant a stay was correct. Clearly England was neither the 'natural' nor the 'appropriate' forum for the reasons he specified.

I do not feel it necessary to refer to the speeches of the House of Lords in *The Abidin Daver* [1984] 1 All ER 470, [1984] AC 398, save to observe that the House concluded that the effect of *The Atlantic Star* and *MacShannon*'s case was to assimilate English law to that of Scottish law in respect of the forum nonconveniens rule.

These issues, which formed a large part of the basis of his decision, have now however largely disappeared from the case since the plaintiffs through their counsel have agreed to confine the argument before the court to the single question of the proper construction of the contractual documents.

Since Hobhouse J exercised his discretion by reference to issues which no longer arise, having regard to the limitation to which I have just referred, it is necessary to consider whether none the less that discretion in the changed circumstances was properly exercised. As I have already observed, in the light of the issues then to be argued I have no doubt whatever that Hobhouse J correctly exercised his discretion, indeed, in my view, the only possible criticism that could be made of that exercise is that he may have given less weight than it deserved to the question of the 'front-loaded' costs. None the less he carefully considered that factor.

I have had the advantage of reading the judgment of Sir John Donaldson MR with which I am wholly in agreement and I agree that with the issues limited as they now are, the proper discretion, either by the judge or, if need be, exercised by this court, fully justified the conclusion that a stay should be granted.

I too would dismiss this appeal.

SIR JOHN DONALDSON MR. The judge approached the problem posed by the application to stay the present proceedings on the basis of the law as summarised by Robert Goff J in *Trendtex Trading Corp v Crédit Suisse* [1980] 3 All ER 721 at 734. Counsel for the plaintiffs seemed somewhat hesitant in submitting that this was the wrong approach, no doubt because (a) that summary was not disapproved when the *Trendtex* case was in this court ([1980] 3 All ER 721, [1980] QB 629) or in the House of Lords ([1981] 3 All ER 520, [1982] AC 679), (b) it was expressly approved by this court in *European Asian Bank AG v Punjab and Sind Bank* [1982] 2 Lloyd's Rep 356 at 365, 368–369 and (c) it was applied by this court in *Bank of Tokyo Ltd v Karoon* [1986] 3 All ER 468, [1986] 3 WLR 414. However, he submitted that if it differed from Lord Diplock's formulation in *MacShannon v Rockware Glass Ltd* [1978] 1 All ER 625 at 630, [1978] AC 795 at 812, the latter was to be treated as authoritative, having been reaffirmed in *Castanho v Brown & Root (UK) Ltd* [1981] 1 All ER 143 at 151, [1981] AC 557 at 575 per Lord Scarman, with the agreement of Lord Wilberforce, Lord Diplock, Lord Keith and Lord Bridge (see [1981] 1 All ER 143 at 146, 152, [1981] AC 557 at 569, 577).

So stated, it may not be readily apparent why we need do more than consider whether the judge did indeed adopt the *Trendtex* approach as he purported to do but in the course of counsel for the plaintiffs' careful and persuasive argument it gradually appeared that this would be something of an over-simplification. In *Trendtex* the approach was (i) to consider whether there is 'another clearly more appropriate jurisdiction', taking account of all the circumstances of the case including where the cause of action arose the connection of the parties with any particular jurisdiction, the applicable law, the availability of witnesses and the saving of costs, and, if so, (ii) to consider whether trial in England would offer a real (ie objectively demonstrated) and legitimate personal or juridical advantage to the plaintiff (I omit problems of burden of proof), and (iii) to strike a balance between the interests of the parties and decide whether justice demanded a stay. Counsel for the plaintiffs however is really submitting that Lord Diplock's reformulation of the second paragraph of Scott LJ's statement of the law in *St Pierre v South American Stores (Gath & Chaves) Ltd* [1936] 1 KB 382 at 398, [1935] All ER Rep 408 at 414 is in the nature of a condition precedent to the imposition of a stay. However close a connection the alternative jurisdiction may have with the lis or the parties or both, a a   stay will not be imposed unless the resolution of the dispute in that jurisdiction can be achieved with substantially less inconvenience and expense to the partes *and* such a resolution would not deprive the plaintiff of a legitimate personal or juridical advantage. In other words (ii) in the above formulation should precede (i) and include a specific reference to the inconvenience and expense to both parties.

    Usually no doubt the result of the 'critical equation' between the two jurisdictions will in any event turn on relative inconvenience and expense to the parties and the legitimate
b   personal and juridical advantages claimed by the plaintiff and this point, concerning the priority to be given to these factors, will not arise. But I think that it is clear that it could arise in the present appeal, at least in the form which the lis now appears likely to take.

    Before Hobhouse J it appeared that the plaintiffs were going to maintain that the dispute had a political dimension in that the Turkish government had brought pressure on the defendant bank to pay Wahda Bank in circumstances in which there was no
c   liability to pay and that this was relevant to the issue of whether the plaintiffs were liable to the defendants. Hobhouse J expressed the view that this was an irrelevant consideration but so long as it was persisted in there were clear grounds for preferring the Turkish jurisdiction in terms of convenience and expense, since the factual witnesses would be much more easily available and if it be relevant because it is prima facie inappropriate that a foreign court should investigate the propriety of the actions of a Turkish
d   government.

    Before this court counsel for the plaintiffs has expressly abandoned any such contention and submits that the sole issue will be whether the defendant bank was liable to pay Wahda Bank and whether if it was not so liable the plaintiffs were nevertheless liable to the defendants under the counter-indemnity once the defendants had paid. This involves only the interpretation of two contracts which are governed by Turkish law. Furthermore
e   it does not appear that any statutory or other special legal provisions are applicable. The court whether Turkish or English would simply have to construe the two contracts in the light of generally applicable Turkish legal canons of construction and the general Turkish law of contract.

    Against that background, if Lord Diplock's reformulation incorporates a condition precedent, and one can therefore put on one side the natural affinity of the lis to the
f   Turkish courts, counsel for the plaintiffs is able to argue with some cogency that whilst each party can claim that resolution of the dispute in its preferred jurisdiction would be less inconvenient and less expensive for it, overall there is no substantial difference. Furthermore in so far as the judge emphasised the undoubted fact that it is easier for a court to apply its own law rather than a foreign law and this is relevant to the head of inconvenience, he can submit that such an approach would if fully accepted mean that
g   the Commercial Court should decline jurisdiction in a number of cases in which it has never done so.

    Accordingly it seems to me that it is necessary to consider whether Lord Diplock's reformulation really does incorporate a condition precedent and for this purpose to consider the authorities.

    The starting point must be *St Pierre v South American Stores (Gath & Chaves) Ltd* [1936]
h   1 KB 382 at 398, [1935] All ER Rep 408 at 414. Scott LJ in his classic statement of the law said:

    'The true rule about a stay under s. 41, so far as relevant to this case, may I think be stated thus: (1.) A mere balance of convenience is not a sufficient ground for depriving a plaintiff of the advantages of prosecuting his action in an English Court if it is otherwise properly brought. The right of access to the King's Court must not
j   be lightly refused. (2.) In order to justify a stay two conditions must be satisfied, one positive and the other negative: (*a*) the defendant must satisfy the Court that the continuance of the action would work an injustice because it would be oppressive or vexatious to him or would be an abuse of the process of the Court in some other way; and (b) the stay must not cause an injustice to the plaintiff.'

Thus stood the law until *The Atlantic Star* [1973] 2 All ER 175, [1974] AC 436. There
the House of Lords held that the words 'oppressive' and 'vexatious' should be liberalised,   *a*
or watered down, with a view to making the law less insular and chauvinistic. But I do
not understand that there was any disposition to depart from Scott LJ's approach which
by implication was that there should be a general balancing of the relevant advantages
and disadvantages of the dispute being resolved in the different jurisdictions, the critical
equation coming down in favour of a stay only if the resultant balance was against the
plaintiff to a degree which in 1936 was much greater than in 1974. Indeed the acceptance   *b*
in *The Atlantic Star* by Lord Reid that less is required to drive the plaintiff from the
English judgment seat where the plaintiff comes to England 'for his own ends', than
where it is *his* (as contrasted with the dispute's) natural forum, suggests strongly that a
general balancing process is involved and that no one factor is decisive (see [1973] 2 All
ER 175 at 181, [1974] AC 436 at 454). This was taken further by Lord Wilberforce
where, with the agreement of Lord Kilbrandon, he says that the critical equation will be   *c*
resolved 'by an instinctive process—that is what discretion, in its essence, is' (see [1973] 2
All ER 175 at 194, 198, [1974] AC 436 at 468, 473).

Next comes *MacShannon v Rockware Glass Ltd* [1978] 1 All ER 625, [1978] AC 795,
with Lord Diplock's reformulation introduced, by an acceptance that Scott LJ's judgment
in *St Pierre* is still to be treated as the framework on which the statement of the law is
built, subject to a substitution for 'oppressive' and 'vexatious' of the gist of the speeches   *d*
of Lord Reid, Lord Wilberforce and Lord Kilbrandon in *The Atlantic Star* (see [1978] 1 All
ER 625 at 630, [1978] AC 795 at 811).

Castanho v Brown & Root [1981] 1 All ER 143, [1981] AC 557 creates a further obstacle
to counsel for the plaintiffs' argument, since Lord Scarman with the agreement of his
brethren including Lord Diplock, said ([1981] 1 All ER 143 at 151, [1981] AC 557 at
575):
                                                                                            e
> 'The formula is not, however, to be construed as a statute. No time should be
> spent in speculating what is meant by legitimate. It, like the whole of the context,
> is but a guide to solving in the particular circumstances of the case the "critical
> equation" between advantage to the plaintiff and disadvantage to the defendants.'

This is not apt language to describe Lord Diplock's two conditions as conditions precedent.   *f*

Amin Rasheed Shipping Corp v Kuwait Insurance Co, The Al Wahab [1983] 2 All ER 884,
[1984] AC 50, which is the next House of Lords authority in chronological order, does
not assist on this point because it was concerned with a quite different issue, namely the
jurisdiction of the court to order service out of the jurisdiction. This leaves *The Abidin
Daver* [1984] 1 All ER 470, [1984] AC 398, in which there was a lis alibi pendens in
coincidentally the Turkish courts. Suffice it to say that again I can see no trace of   *g*
inconvenience and expense to the parties or legitimate personal or juridical advantage to
the plaintiff being treated as a condition precedent, as contrasted with an important
factor in the critical equation.

Against this background I turn to the judge's reasons for imposing a stay. Consistently
with his acceptance of the *Trendtex* case approach he began by considering what was the
natural forum for resolving the dispute. He said:
                                                                                            h
> 'I now turn to the question of natural forum. It seems to me completely beyond
> argument that the natural forum for the dispute between the plaintiffs and the
> defendants is Turkey. The relevant transactions are governed by Turkish law. The
> relevant document is a Turkish document. The subject matter of the action is
> wholly in Turkey; the action has nothing whatsoever to do with England. The
> parties are either Turkish or closely connected with Turkey. I recognise that the   *j*
> plaintiffs have connections with other countries as well, but there can be no denial
> that they have a close cultural affinity with Turkey and they have in the past, when
> it suited them, had very close connections with Turkey. Furthermore, the vast bulk
> of any witnesses that may be material, it is very questionable whether there is any

necessity for any witnesses at all, would be Turkish and would come from Turkey. The real dispute in this matter is as to the effect of various documents in Turkish law. The primary document is the letter of indemnity coupled with the indemnity obligations that would arise under Turkish law. As regards the secondary matter of the liability of the defendants to Wahda Bank, it seems to be the common approach of the parties that the liability under that cross-guarantee should be considered under Turkish law. Certainly it has absolutely nothing whatsoever to do with English law. The only other law that might be relevant would be Libyan law, and there does not seem to be any enthusiasm to consider Libyan law as governing the liability of the defendants; nobody has done so so far.'

This passage can indeed be criticised in that it may do less than justice to the plaintiffs' connections with England. The plaintiffs is a family company incorporated in the Turkish part of Cyprus, but the controlling shareholders are British subjects resident in this country. However against this must be set the fact that the plaintiffs established an office in Turkey with the express purpose of facilitating the undertaking of civil engineering work of the type which underlies the transactions which have given rise to the present dispute. In a word the plaintiffs were an English-owned Turkish-Cypriot company which wished to emphasise its Turkish character.

The judge then adverted to the fact that there were differences in the approach to questions of the construction of documents under Turkish law as compared with English law and pointed out that (a) the English court would have to deal with the matter on the basis of expert evidence possibly given through an interpreter and (b) if the dispute were to be determined by an English court the decision could not be appealed as a matter of law but would have to be appealed as a matter of fact.

Again this approach can be and, as I have already said, has been criticised on the basis that the same could have been said of many of the disputes customarily determined by the judges of the Commercial Court and that its general acceptance would involve a drastic curtailment of that court's jurisdiction. There is force in that comment, but it is a question of degree which has to be assessed on a case by case basis.

The judge then turned to what may be described as the 'Diplock factors' of inconvenience and expense to each party and the personal legal and juridical advantages of English jurisdiction from the point of view of the plaintiffs. To some extent I think that his task was made more difficult by a marked tendency on the part of Mr Muduroglu to overstate his case or to state it in extravagant language. In rejecting such overstatements and extravagance, there was a natural tendency to underestimate what remained.

The inconvenience and expense to the defendants of having to defend themselves in England is obvious but this is to some extent the same argument which they put forward with such enthusiasm in drawing attention to the fact that the plaintiffs had at the material time been in business in Ankara. It has also to be remembered that no question of alternative jurisdiction would have arisen if the defendants had not established a place of business in London and it is little to the point that they voluntarily restrict the range and nature of the business there transacted.

Against this inconvenience to the defendants has to be set the inconvenience to the plaintiffs of having to litigate in Turkey. If all that is in issue is the construction and legal effect of the guarantee given by the defendants to Wahda Bank and of the plaintiffs' counter-guarantee, the scales must come down heavily in favour of Ankara. There would then be no need for expert witnesses and there would appear to be no need for witnesses of fact to go there from England. But on behalf of the plaintiffs it is said that Mr Muduroglu would still wish to attend the hearing and give instructions to his lawyers and he would be faced not only with the cost of travelling to and staying in Turkey but would risk arrest and imprisonment. It is only this latter point which could have force and perhaps decisive force. The judge did not advert to it because it has largely arisen since the hearing before him.

Hitherto Mr Muduroglu has travelled freely to and from Turkey but in the course of resisting the stay he swore affidavits in which he asserted that the Turkish courts were not independent of the executive and that the plaintiffs could not expect to achieve a fair hearing of their complaints, since to find in their favour would involve implied criticism of the executive. He has now been advised that his conduct in this respect may have rendered him liable to arrest, trial and imprisonment. That Mr Muduroglu regards this as a very serious possibility I do not doubt but we have to assess the position objectively and on that basis I am very doubtful he is really at risk.

What was of course a primary issue before the judge was the independence of the Turkish courts. His conclusion was that whatever might be said of the military courts there was clear evidence of the independence of the civil courts. Before us counsel for the plaintiffs accepted the validity of the distinction but relied on various expressions of dissatisfaction with their lot on the part of senior members of the judiciary and in particular on complaints at the introduction of a system of grading judges which he submitted might be used to give practical effect to the executive's displeasure at a judge's decision in cases in which the executive was interested.

For my part I am not particularly surprised to find judges voicing complaints of one sort or another and do not think that this necessarily points to any lack of independence. The most congent criticism of course is that which relates to grading, but some grading is probably inherent in any system involving a career judiciary and there is no evidence of any improper use of grading. The complaint is at the introduction of grading or greater grading and not to abuse of such a system, although the possibility of abuse may well be used as an argument against the whole system.

Turning to the question of expense, there is conflicting evidence as to the extent of the court costs in Turkey, the extent to which they have to be paid in local currency and, if recoverable, will or may impose an exchange loss on the plaintiffs, the relative level of lawyers' remuneration in the two jurisdictions and the extent to which security for costs would be required. Looking at the matter broadly, I doubt whether there will be very much difference save in one important respect. This is that the Turkish system is what is known as 'front-loaded', ie a large proportion of the costs have to be paid at an early stage in the proceedings. This is without doubt a serious disadvantage for the plaintiffs.

Finally consideration must be given to the allegation that even if the Turkish civil courts enjoy judicial independence the judges would be embarrassed to have to decide this dispute in favour of the plaintiffs since this would impliedly involve criticism of the conduct of the prime minister albeit at a time when he did not hold that office. Whatever force this point might have had before the judge when it was being said that the plaintiffs wished to investigate governmental pressure on the defendants, it seems to me to be wholly lacking in any force once the issue is confined, and rightly confined, to one of the construction and legal effect of two contracts.

The case for a stay on the facts as presented to the judge seems to me to have been quite overwhelming. The defendants were a Turkish bank, the plaintiffs were a Turkish-Cypriot corporation which had deliberately set up in business in Ankara in order, for sound commercial reasons, to emphasise their Turkish character. The contracts which underlay the dispute were governed by Turkish law and they could be construed in Turkey without the aid of expert witnesses and with the benefit of a right of appeal in law. Furthermore on the plaintiffs' case an important issue was the extent and nature of the intervention of the Turkish government. Against this could only be set the need for the plaintiffs to make provision for court and legal costs at a much earlier stage of the proceedings than would be appropriate if the dispute were to be resolved in the English courts.

However, the removal or reduction in the Turkish political element as a result of counsel for the plaintiffs' concession that this is irrelevant, save to the extent that Turkish judges might feel any embarrassment in finding in favour of the plaintiffs in the realisation that this might involve some implied criticism of Turkish political policies, does not create a new situation in which the question of front-loaded costs may be said to become relatively more important. Assuming, without deciding, that this justifies or

a   requires us to exercise a fresh discretion in place of that of the judge, I would still agree with his order staying this action. The natural and appropriate forum, both for the parties and for the lis, is the Turkish courts and so great is the preponderance of factors pointing south towards Turkey that the remote possibility of Mr Muduroglu finding himself charged with an offence if he visited Turkey, a visit which while clearly desirable is not essential to the just resolution of this dispute, and the fact that the plaintiffs'
resources may well be more strained by having to fund the litigation at an earlier stage

b   in Turkey than would be the case in England, do not in my judgment, justify the English courts in retaining jurisdiction. It may be correct that the plaintiffs who have already spent a considerable amount of time and effect exploring a politico-commercial solution in Turkey may, as they assert, not seek to litigate in Turkey but I am not convinced that, whether for financial or other reasons, they could not do so if they so wished.

I would dismiss the appeal.

c
Appeal dismissed. Leave to appeal to the House of Lords refused.

5 November. The Appeal Committee of the House of Lords (Lord Keith of Kinkel, Lord Templeman and Lord Griffiths) dismissed a petition by the plaintiffs for leave to appeal.

d   Solicitors: *Allen & Overy* (for the plaintiffs); *Coward Chance* (for the defendants).

Diana Procter   Barrister.

Schofield v Church Army

e
COURT OF APPEAL, CIVIL DIVISION
DILLON AND CROOM-JOHNSON LJJ
11, 12 JUNE, 8 JULY 1986

f   *County court – Payment out of court – Money paid into court on making of garnishee order – Plaintiff having cross-claim against defendant pending in High Court – Whether special circumstances rendering it inexpedient to order payment out – RSC Ord 47, r 1(1)(a) – CCR Ord 30, r 6.*

The respondent was summarily dismissed from his employment by the appellant on the ground that he had stolen money belonging to the appellant. An industrial tribunal

g   found that he had been unfairly dismissed and ordered the appellant to pay him compensation of £8,370, subject to deductions, for unfair dismissal. The respondent obtained in the county court an ex parte order to enforce the tribunal's order and also a garnishee order nisi attaching the appellant's bank account. The appellant's bank paid £7,461·67 into court and the respondent applied under CCR Ord 30, r 6[a] for the money to be paid out to himself. Meanwhile, the appellant had commenced an action in the

h   High Court against the respondent alleging theft of 32 sums totalling £8,986 and claiming that amount and interest. The appellant accordingly opposed the county court application, contending that the money in court should not be paid out to the respondent until the High Court action had been decided. The registrar upheld the appellant's contention but on appeal the judge ordered the money in court to be paid out to the respondent, on the ground that the appellant had not adduced sufficient evidence to

j   show the strength of its case. The evidence, while showing that there were serious issues to be tried, was not sufficient to show that the appellant was likely to recover judgment against the respondent. The appellant appealed, contending that the court's discretion to

---

a   Rule 6, so far as material, is set out at p 721 j, post

order or refuse to order payment out of court under CCR Ord 30, r 6 ought to be exercised in the same way as the entry of judgment under RSC Ord 14 coupled with a stay of execution when there was no defence to the plaintiff's action but trial of a cross-claim brought by the defendant against the plaintiff was pending. The appellant also sought leave to adduce further evidence to prove its case.

Held – (1) (Per Dillon LJ) The ground asserted by the appellant for admitting further evidence, namely that it had not thought it necessary to prove its case in the High Court action to the degree or extent of proof required by the judge in the county court, was not enough to justify admitting further evidence, having regard to the fact that the evidence had been in the appellant's possession at the time of the hearing before the judge. It followed that the application to adduce further evidence on the appeal would be refused (see p 719 d e, post); *Ladd v Marshall* [1954] 3 All ER 745 applied.

(2) The scope of the court's discretion under CCR Ord 30, r 6 to order or refuse to order money paid into court by a judgment debtor to be paid out to the judgment creditor was the same as the discretion of the High Court or county court to make or refuse to make a garnishee order absolute and was also the same as the discretion of the High Court under RSC Ord 47, r 1(1)(a)[b] to stay execution of a judgment by writ of fieri facias if there were 'special circumstances' rendering it inexpedient to enforce the judgment. However, the mere fact that there was an arguable cross-claim which would support a stay of execution under RSC Ord 14 was not of itself enough to warrant a stay. On the other hand, it did not follow that what was required was more detailed and cogent proof of the strength of the appellant's case in the High Court action. On the facts, the judge had required too strict a standard of proof by the appellant and ought not to have ordered the money in court to be paid out to the respondent, because the existence of the appellant's High Court action and the evidence put forward by the appellant showing that the action raised serious issues to be tried amounted to special circumstances justifying a stay of the payment out. The appeal would therefore be allowed (see p 719 g to j, p 721 b to h and p 723 b to h, post); *Ferdinand Wagner (a firm) v Laubscher Bros & Co (a firm)* [1970] 2 All ER 174 considered.

Notes

For payment out in the county court, see 10 Halsbury's Laws (4th edn) para 341.

Cases referred to in judgments

American Cyanamid Co v Ethicon Ltd [1975] 1 All ER 504, [1975] AC 396, [1975] 2 WLR 316, HL.

Devis (W) & Sons Ltd v Atkins [1977] 3 All ER 40, [1977] AC 931, [1977] 3 WLR 214, HL.

Ladd v Marshall [1954] 3 All ER 745, [1954] 1 WLR 1489, CA.

Langdale v Danby [1982] 3 All ER 129, [1982] 1 WLR 1123, HL.

Rainbow v Moorgate Properties Ltd [1975] 2 All ER 821, [1975] 1 WLR 788, CA.

Sheppards & Co v Wilkinson & Jarvis (1889) 6 TLR 13, CA.

Wagner (Ferdinand) (a firm) v Laubscher Bros & Co (a firm) [1970] 2 All ER 174, [1970] 2 QB 313, [1970] 2 WLR 1019, CA.

Z Ltd v A [1982] 1 All ER 556, [1982] QB 558, [1982] 2 WLR 288, CA.

Interlocutory appeal

The Church Army appealed with leave granted by Dillon LJ on 17 December 1985 against the decision of his Honour Judge Christopher James given on 19 September 1985 in the Woolwich County Court whereby he allowed an appeal by the respondent, Leslie Schofield, from an order of Mr Deputy Registrar Lamdin sitting at Woolwich County Court dated 23 July 1985 ordering that the garnishee order nisi obtained by the respondent to attach the Church Army's bank account with Barclays Bank plc should not be made absolute, and ordered payment out under CCR Ord 30, r 6 to the respondent's

---

b   Rule 1(1), so far as material, is set out at p 722 d e, post

a solicitors of the sum of £7,461·67 paid in under the garnishee order, together with accrued interest and costs. The facts are set out in the judgment of Dillon LJ.

David Melville for the Church Army.
David Foskett for the respondent.

Cur adv vult

b 8 July. The following judgments were delivered.

DILLON LJ. The Church Army appeals, by leave, against a decision of his Honour Judge Christopher James given in the Woolwich County Court on 19 September 1985. The appeal raises a novel point.

c   The respondent was for a number of years the warden of a hostel run by the Church Army in Westminster to provide beds for homeless men. As warden, the respondent was responsible for the receipts of the hostel for the accommodation provided. Those receipts took the form either of cash paid by the men for their accommodation or of cheques sent by the Department of Health and Social Security (the DHSS) to the hostel in exchange for vouchers previously issued by the DHSS to the men which were handed over by the men *d* to the hostel for their accommodation. It was the duty of the respondent to keep records of all cheques and cash received, and to bank the cheques and the cash, or at any rate so much of the cash as was not required for petty cash purposes, in the Church Army's bank account.

On 26 and 27 April 1984 a routine audit at the hostel was conducted by two officials from the Church Army's headquarters. They found that a number of cheques issued to *e* the hostel by the DHSS and payable to the Church Army had not been entered in the appropriate receipts journal of the hostel. They also found, at that stage, that some half a dozen of these unrecorded cheques had been paid into the Church Army's bank account, apparently by the respondent. They concluded from their investigations that the respondent had stolen from the recorded cash receipts of the hostel amounts of cash equivalent to the amounts of the half dozen unrecorded cheques thus paid in. The *f* respondent was therefore summoned on short notice to a meeting with Mr Winch, the Director of Finance and Administration at the Church Army's headquarters. The respondent was not told the reason for the meeting. It took place on 2 May 1984 and lasted for about five minutes. At the meeting, the respondent was asked about one alleged shortfall of a sum of £350 and, as, though denying that he had stolen the money, he did not give any explanation which was satisfactory to Mr Winch, he was summarily *g* dismissed.

The respondent thereupon applied to an industrial tribunal to establish that he had been unfairly dismissed. That application was heard on 12 September 1984 by the industrial tribunal. By their decision, sent to the parties on 25 October 1984, the tribunal held that the respondent had been unfairly dismissed. In their detailed findings the tribunal found that it was not reasonable for Mr Winch to claim that the respondent had *h* stolen the money in the light of the limited investigation which the Church Army had undertaken at that time; they also found that the procedure of the Church Army in dismissing the respondent was unfair, in that the respondent did not have a proper chance to answer the allegations against him.

Having made their findings, the tribunal adjourned the question of the respondent's remedy for the parties to discuss. In the light of the findings, the respondent was prima *j* facie entitled to compensation for unfair dismissal. The amount of that compensation was agreed between the parties, and on 4 February 1985 the tribunal made a consent order ordering the Church Army to pay the respondent £8,370 compensation. That amount fell to be reduced by certain recoupment provisions. The enforcement of an order of an industrial tribunal for the payment of money is, under the relevant statute, by getting an order from the county court. Accordingly, on 1 April 1985 the respondent obtained, on an ex parte application to the Woolwich County Court, an order of that court that the Church Army pay to him the sum of £7,391·67 (being the balance of the £8,370) and £58 costs. The order provided that, if the Church Army failed to pay such sums forthwith, then the sums remaining unpaid should be recoverable as if payable under an order of the Woolwich County Court. Like any other judgment of a county court, that order is final and conclusive between the parties: see s 70 of the County Courts Act 1984.

To enforce that judgment, the respondent obtained a garnishee order nisi from the county court to attach the Church Army's bank account with Barclays Bank. As a result of that, the bank paid the sum of £7,461·67 (representing the judgment and further costs) into court in the county court on 1 July 1985. This was done under CCR Ord 30, r 4. The respondent then applied under Ord 30, r 6 for the money to be paid out to himself. This application was opposed by the Church Army, on grounds to which I shall come. The application came first before a deputy registrar on 23 July 1985. He upheld the Church Army's opposition, but the respondent appealed to the judge. That appeal came before Judge James on 19 September 1985; he set aside the registrar's order and ordered that the money in court be paid out to the respondent's solicitors. It is against that order that the Church Army now appeals; pending the hearing of the appeal the order has been stayed.

After the respondent's dismissal, the Church Army continued its investigations into his accounts. It claimed to have established, by the time of the hearing before the industrial tribunal in September 1984, that over £8,200 of cash received by the respondent was unaccounted for. It is clear law that, in considering whether an employee has been unfairly dismissed, an industrial tribunal cannot have regard to matters of which the employer was unaware at the time of the dismissal, though such matters can be taken into account in assessing the compensation for unfair dismissal even so as to reduce it to nil: see W Devis & Sons Ltd v Atkins [1977] 3 All ER 40, [1977] AC 931. In fact, the agreed figure of £8,370 compensation, the subject of the industrial tribunal's order of February 1984, did not take into account any of the alleged defalcations claimed by the Church Army (all of which are denied by the respondent). It is not suggested, however, that that order of the industrial tribunal or the subsequent order of the county court of 1 April 1985 gives rise to any form of estoppel or plea of res judicata against the Church Army.

When the sum of £8,370 was agreed as the amount of compensation, the solicitors for the Church Army made it plain in correspondence that their client proposed to bring High Court proceedings against the respondent, and did not intend to make any payment reflecting the industrial tribunal award unless and until it was found after the conclusion of the High Court proceedings that the full tribunal award or part thereof was still owing because no moneys were recoverable under the High Court proceedings or because the moneys recoverable were less than the industrial tribunal award. Accordingly, on 1 February 1985, the Church Army issued a High Court writ against the respondent, which was served on the respondent on 21 February. By the statement of claim indorsed on the writ the Church Army alleges that, from about 3 June 1981 until about 5 April 1984, the respondent stole cash sums received by him for the Church Army's use. Detailed particulars are given of 32 sums allegedly stolen, which add up to an amount of £8,986·50, and the claim is for that amount with interest.

The nature of the system of theft alleged is that the respondent, over the period referred to, failed to record 32 of the cheques received at the hostel from the DHSS in the receipts journal of the hostel, but paid those unrecorded cheques into the Church Army's bank account and, each time he did so, abstracted for his own purposes an equivalent sum in cash from his recorded cash receipts for accommodation at the hostel.

The contention of the Church Army before the deputy registrar, before Judge James and in this court has been consistently that the money paid into court by Barclays Bank should not be paid out to the respondent until the High Court action has been disposed of, because of its cross-claims against the respondent raised in the High Court action. Obviously, from the point of view of the Church Army, if it is right in its claim that the respondent has stolen £8,986·50 from it in the course of his employment, it would be

galling in the extreme and would seem unjust that it should have to pay him £7,461·62
(the sum in court) compensation for unfair dismissal before its action can come on for
trial.

At this stage I must deal with a question of evidence.

Judge James ruled against the Church Army on the ground that he did not have before
him sufficient evidence to show the strength of the Church Army's case. He said that he
thought it very possible that he would not have allowed the money to be paid to the
respondent pending the trial of the High Court action if the Church Army had brought
forward evidence to show the strength of its case. In this court, therefore, the Church
Army has sought leave to adduce further evidence, in the shape of affidavits from a
solicitor and exhibits, to show by fairly detailed analysis of the respondent's receipt and
cash books and paying in slips that, as counsel for the Church Army put it, the Church
Army has a good case against the respondent on 32 counts. Counsel for the Church Army
accepts, however, that the hearing before Judge James was a hearing on the merits, and
that further evidence can only be admitted in this court on special grounds, consistently
with *Ladd v Marshall* [1954] 3 All ER 745, [1954] 1 WLR 1489 and *Langdale v Danby*
[1982] 3 All ER 129, [1982] 1 WLR 1123. The further evidence sought to be adduced
was, however, all in the possession of the Church Army at the time of the hearing before
Judge James; it had been the basis for the statement of claim in the High Court action.
The 'special ground' asserted for admitting the evidence in this court is merely that it had
not thought it necessary, before the hearing before Judge James, to prove its case in the
High Court action to the degree or extent of proof which, as it turned out, Judge James
required of it. That is not enough, in my judgment, to justify admitting the further
evidence in this court under *Ladd v Marshall* and I would accordingly reject the
application to adduce further evidence on the appeal.

It remains to consider whether Judge James was right in the way he directed himself,
and dealt with the case, on the material which was before him.

That material included the detailed decision of the industrial tribunal after the
September 1984 hearing, the writ and statement of claim in the High Court action, the
correspondence at the time the amount of the industrial tribunal compensation was
agreed, and an affidavit of 18 July 1985 by the Church Army's solicitor which set out the
course of the High Court action down to the issue of the summons for directions, which
was then pending.

On that material, I conclude that the High Court action, which it is conceded is not
frivolous or vexatious, raises serious issues to be tried over 32 allegations of theft. But, on
that material alone, the Church Army has not shown, if it is necessary for it to show it,
that it is bound to win, or that, to adopt the words of Kerr LJ in *Z Ltd v A* [1982] 1 All ER
556 at 572, [1982] QB 558 at 585, 'it appears likely that it will recover' judgment against
the respondent in the sum claimed or a substantial part of it.

What then is the scope of the court's discretion in ordering, or refusing to order,
payment out of court under CCR Ord 30, r 6?

It must be the same as the scope of the discretion of the court, whether High Court or
county court, in deciding whether or not to make a garnishee order absolute. That would
include considering, where appropriate, the position of other creditors of the judgment
debtor and the effect on them of the making of the order (see *Rainbow v Moorgate
Properties Ltd* [1975] 2 All ER 821, [1975] 1 WLR 788); but that is not an appropriate
consideration here.

The scope of the discretion under Ord 30, r 6 would likewise, in my judgment, be the
same as the scope of the discretion of the High Court under RSC Ord 47, r 1(1)(a) to stay
execution of a judgment by writ of fieri facias where 'there are special circumstances
which render it inexpedient to enforce the judgment . . .' The reason why Ord 47, r 1
applies only to execution by writ of fieri facias would seem to be that that is the only
form of execution which can be carried through to payment by a judgment creditor
without any further order of the court; therefore, that is the case where the judgment
debtor needs power to apply to the court to stay the execution.

Counsel for the Church Army puts the case for a stay on the payment out as equivalent

to the position under RSC Ord 14 where judgment is entered for a plaintiff because there
is no defence to the action, but execution of the judgment is stayed pending the trial of
some cross-claim which the defendant has against the plaintiff. This is covered by Ord
14, r 3(2), which in terms provides:

'The Court may by order, and subject to such conditions, if any, as may be just,
stay execution of any judgment given against a defendant under this rule until after
the trial of any counterclaim made or raised by the defendant in the action.'

That has for long been the appropriate form of order under Ord 14 where the
defendant's counterclaim does not give rise to an equitable set-off which would amount
to a defence to the action: see *Sheppards & Co v Wilkinson & Jarvis* (1889) 6 TLR 13. In
that case it was stressed by Lord Esher MR that the court had no power to try the
counterclaim on an application for summary judgment under Ord 14 on the claim.
Accordingly, judgment entered on the claim under Ord 14 ought to be stayed until trial
of the counterclaim if, as it was put by Lord Esher MR, the counterclaim was 'so far
plausible that it was not unreasonably possible for it to succeed if brought to trial' or was
such that it was impossible to say that there was no prospect of it succeeding, or if, as it
was put by Lindey LJ, the counterclaim was by no means frivolous.

However, counsel for the Church Army faces difficulty in his approach by analogy to
Ord 14, in that in *Ferdinand Wagner (a firm) v Laubscher Bros & Co (a firm)* [1970] 2 All ER
174 at 178, [1970] 2 QB 313 at 319 Sachs LJ said categorically that the tests to be applied
when an application is made for a stay of execution on a judgment under Ord 47, r 1 are
quite different from those applicable to Ord 14 proceedings. Similarly, Lord Denning
MR said ([1970] 2 All ER 174 at 176, [1970] 2 QB 313 at 317):

'I am afraid that I cannot agree with the judge's approach to this matter. He
seemed to have regarded it as if there was a summons under Ord 14 in which the
question is whether there is an arguable point. But I think this procedure to enforce
a foreign judgment is quite different from Ord 14. Here is a German judgment
which is equivalent to an English judgment. If the plaintiffs had obtained an
English judgment, we should not, for one moment, grant a stay simply because the
defendants had brought a cross-claim in another action against the plaintiffs. So here
we should not stay execution in this German judgment simply because the
defendants have brought a cross-action in England against the plaintiffs.'

The fact that the judgment obtained in *Ferdinand Wagner v Laubscher Bros & Co* was a
German judgment was immaterial because it had been registered here under the Foreign
Judgments (Reciprocal Enforcement) Act 1933 and so was equivalent to an English
judgment. The facts in *Ferdinand Wagner v Laubscher Bros & Co* told strongly against the
grant of any stay of execution once it was held that the procedure under Ord 14 was not
a compelling analogy, because (a) the English action brought by the defendants raised
the selfsame issues as had been decided by the German courts in the German action and
(b) the defendants had shown a complete lack of diligence in pursuing their cross-action
in this country, until the plaintiffs sought to enforce the German judgment against them.

As I see it, the basic reason why the tests to be applied under Ord 14 are different from
the tests to be applied when a stay of execution is sought under Ord 47, r 1 is that a
judgment under Ord 14 is a summary judgment obtained at the very outset of
proceedings before the defendant has had any opportunity to litigate his cross-claims,
whatever they may be, against the plaintiff. But, if the plaintiff's case goes to trial and he
obtains judgment, it is not enough for the defendant, in order to obtain a stay of
execution, then simply (and I stress Lord Denning MR's use of the word *simply*) to show
that he has an arguable cross-claim which he has not raised as a counterclaim in the
plaintiff's action and has not got on with litigating meanwhile. Therefore, where the
judgment obtained was not under Ord 14, it is necessary for the defendant, in order to
obtain a stay, to show special circumstances which render it inexpedient to enforce the
judgment or order, and not simply an arguable cross-claim.

Counsel for the respondent submits that, in the passage in Lord Denning MR's judgment which I have cited, *Ferdinand Wagner v Laubscher Bros & Co* has laid down that a judgment of the court, otherwise than under Ord 14, stands in a specially protected position and cannot in any circumstances be stayed pending the trial of any cross-claim, however apparently strong. But, in my judgment, Lord Denning MR was not intending to go so far, his use of the word 'simply' emphasises that a stay pending trial of an arguable cross-claim is not to be well nigh automatic as under Ord 14, but, if the special circumstances of the particular case lead to the view that it is inexpedient that a judgment be enforced pending the trial of a cross-claim, then a stay may be granted. The mere fact, therefore, that the Church Army has an arguable cross-claim against the respondent which would support a stay under Ord 14, is not of itself enough to warrant a stay of execution of the judgment which the respondent has obtained in the county court by the order of 1 April 1985. More is required. But it does not follow that the more required is more detailed and cogent proof of the strength of the Church Army's case in the High Court action. The county court cannot try the High Court action on an application for payment of moneys out of court under CCR Ord 30, r 6, and it is a fruitless exercise to endeavour to balance in advance of the trial the relative strength of each party's case, since the outcome of the High Court action may well depend on the credibility of the evidence which the respondent may give at the trial as to the discrepancies alleged against him. See generally, as to the difficulty and, indeed, undesirability of attempts to weigh the strength of a case on affidavit evidence, the well-known comments of Lord Diplock in *American Cyanamid Co v Ethicon Ltd* [1975] 1 All ER 504, [1975] AC 396.

It seems to me that the 'more required' must in the present case lie in the circumstances why the claims in the High Court action have not so far been litigated, rather than in considering the strength of the evidence in support of those claims beyond the point, already reached, at which it is shown that there are serious questions to be tried.

Here, the vital point, in my judgment, is that the industrial tribunal had no jurisdiction to entertain the Church Army's claim, now raised in the High Court action, as a counterclaim to the respondent's claim for unfair dismissal. The industrial tribunal could not have awarded the Church Army judgment on its claim. It could, as I have already mentioned, have taken the Church Army's claim into account in reducing, even to nil, the compensation to be awarded to the respondent for unfair dismissal, but even in so doing it was not bound to reduce the compensation by one pound for every one pound which the Church Army could show the respondent had stolen from it.

The proceedings in the industrial tribunal were disposed of with commendable expedition by that tribunal. It has not been suggested that the Church Army has been dilatory in prosecuting the High Court action. When the amount of the compensation was agreed, the Church Army made its position plain. In these circumstances, it would, in my judgment, be wrong that the money in court should be paid out before the High Court action has come on for trial.

I would accordingly allow this appeal and discharge the order of Judge James. The money in court should remain in court in the Woolwich County Court until further order and be placed on deposit by the court.

CROOM-JOHNSON LJ. The issue before the county court judge was whether he should order the payment out to the respondent of the money which had been paid into court by the bank under the garnishee order. His power to do so was under CCR Ord 30, r 6, which reads:

'... the court may ... after hearing the judgment creditor and the judgment debtor if they appear, order the payment out of the money to the judgment creditor or make such other order in the proceedings as may be just.'

The judge's power is not fettered, and must (where appropriate) include a discretion to order a stay of the payment. In this case the judge accepted that position, but refused to order a stay.

Argument has been addressed to this court suggesting tests which ought to be applied when questions of the exercise of such a discretion arise. They have been based on the provisions of the Rules of the Supreme Court. The two rules which are relevant are RSC Ord 14, r 3(2) and Ord 47, r 1. Both of those provisions are incorporated in the County Court Rules by the County Courts Act 1984, s 76.

Order 14, r 3(2) gives power on the hearing of a summons for judgment under Ord 14, r 1 to order a stay of execution 'of any judgment given against a defendant under this rule until after the trial of any counterclaim made or raised by the defendant in the action'. The Church Army has submitted that the test to be applied in this case is the same test which would be applied on the hearing of an Ord 14 summons, and relies on *Sheppards & Co v Wilkinson & Jarvis* (1889) 6 TLR 13. In that case this court indicated that, if the plaintiff's claim must succeed but would be overtopped by a 'plausible' counterclaim, then the proper course would be to give judgment on the claim but to stay execution on it until after the hearing of the counterclaim. But the circumstances in this case did not arise under Ord 14 and it has no application.

The respondent relies on *Ferdinand Wagner (a firm) v Laubscher Bros & Co (a firm)* [1970] 2 All ER 174, [1970] 2 QB 313, a case decided under Ord 47, r 1.

Order 47, r 1 gives a power to stay execution by writ of fieri facias. So far as relevant it reads:

'(1) Where a judgment is given or an order made for the payment by any person of money, and the Court is satisfied, on an application made at the time of the judgment or order, or at any time thereafter, by the judgment debtor . . . (a) that there are special circumstances which render it inexpedient to enforce the judgment or order . . . then . . . the Court may by order stay the execution of the judgment or order by writ of *fieri facias* either absolutely or for such period and subject to such conditions as the Court thinks fit . . .'

In the present case the relevant judgment or order is the county court order of 1 April 1985 ordering the payment of the industrial tribunal's award and costs.

In *Ferdinand Wagner v Laubscher Bros & Co* the plaintiffs had obtained a judgment in Germany against the defendants. That judgment had been registered in England, where they were entitled to enforce it under the Foreign Judgments (Reciprocal Enforcement) Act 1933, s 2(2). The defendants applied for a stay of execution on the grounds that there were 'special circumstances' rendering enforcement inexpedient. The special circumstances which were alleged were that they had begun an action in England against the plaintiffs in which the points to be litigated were the identical issues as those decided in the German courts. The judge who heard the summons ordered a stay. The Court of Appeal disagreed, holding that there were no special circumstances.

Lord Denning MR (after the passage quoted by Dillon LJ) added ([1970] 2 All ER 174 at 176, [1970] 2 QB 313 at 317):

'That would be quite enough to decide the case. But I would go further. The English action raises, as far as I can see, the selfsame issues as have been determined in the courts of Germany adversely to the defendants. It would be quite wrong to grant a stay of execution so as to enable the defendants to fight the same issues all over again in England.'

Sachs LJ found against the defendants on the merits on several points. He stressed the fact that the issues in the German and English actions were identical, and that the issues could be said to be res judicata. Moreover, the contract was governed by German law. He added ([1970] 2 All ER 174 at 178, [1970] 2 QB 313 at 319):

'Accordingly whilst, of course, RSC Ord 47, r 1 may in certain circumstances be relied on when it is sought to obtain a stay on a foreign judgment in the same way as it might in certain circumstances be relied on when a stay is sought of a judgment of one of the courts of this country, that can only successfully be done when there are "special circumstances which render it inexpedient to enforce the judgment or *a* order." For my part I too, with all respect to the approach of the learned judge in chambers, consider the tests to be applied when an application is made under RSC Ord 47, r 1, quite different to those applicable to RSC Ord 14 proceedings. In the present case there are no special circumstances whatsoever that would render it inexpedient to enforce the German judgment and many that tend the other way.'

Phillimore LJ adverted to the similarity of the issues and found that there were no 'special circumstances'.

b In reliance on that case, the respondent submits that he is entitled to the fruits of his award by the industrial tribunal forthwith, and that there should be no stay of execution on it.

But, in my view, *Ferdinand Wagner v Laubscher Bros & Co* does not go as far as the respondent wants to take it. It clearly draws a distinction between the exercise of discretion under Ord 14, r 3 and Ord 47, r 1. On its facts there could have been no *c* 'special circumstances'. The discretion which had to be exercised by the judge in the present case was not for the purpose of Ord 14, r 3. It was analogous to that of Ord 47, r 1, although not actually under that rule. He was exercising it under CCR Ord 30, r 6. The issues in the Church Army's action have not been adjudicated on by the industrial tribunal. If they had been, *Ferdinand Wagner v Laubscher Bros & Co* would have been of the highest persuasive authority.

d The question in this case is whether there were circumstances which might have justified the judge in ordering a stay of the payment out, and whether the judge directed himself properly on the material which was before him. He knew from the tribunal's decision (paras 5 and 6) the nature of the allegations of theft which the Church Army is making against the respondent, and the method by which it is alleging he took its money. He had the affidavit of Mr Yonge exhibiting the statement of claim in the *e* Church Army's action, and knew the extent of the alleged thefts and therefore of the claim. He had enough material to show that there was a serious matter to be tried which, if proved, would overtop the tribunal's award. But he seems to have considered he required something tantamount to prima facie proof of all the 32 alleged thefts, or at least of the six which were mentioned to the tribunal and figured in the decision document. In that, in my opinion, he set too strict a test.

f In addition, the judge considered how far the material before him pointed to the errors in the accounts being due to dishonesty rather than to innocent mistakes. He had precise information about one discrepancy, and less precise information about five others. He thought that established a prima facie case in only one instance, and that was not enough from which to infer dishonesty.

It is true that an accumulation of inaccuracies would strengthen the inference to be *g* drawn that the explanation was dishonesty. But he had enough material to suggest that in six cases there was a sufficient indication of dishonesty.

It may well be that on a full investigation the respondent will be vindicated. But the material as it was before the judge did indicate that there is a serious issue to be tried out.

If the money is paid out and the Church Army should subsequently be successful in its action against him, there must be a risk that it will be unable to recover its money. In *h* those circumstances the judge should not have ordered the payment out of the money in court.

I would allow this appeal.

Appeal allowed.

j Solicitors: *Rubinstein Callingham* (for the Church Army); *Penelope Grant* (for the respondent).

Mary Rose Plummer   Barrister.

Practice Direction

SUPREME COURT TAXING OFFICE

Costs – Taxation – Time limit – Extension of time – Application for extension to be made on substantive hearing – Application for bill to be reduced or disallowed – Legal aid taxation – Legal Aid Act 1974, Sch 2 – RSC Ord 62, rr 28(4), 29(1)(2)(7)(c)(d) – Legal Aid (General) Regulations 1980, reg 104.

1. Parties wishing to begin proceedings for the taxation of any costs are reminded of the time limits imposed by RSC Ord 62, r 29(1) and (2).

2. A party who is unable to comply with one or more of the requirements of r 29(7)(c) and (d) should not delay beginning the proceedings for that reason but when taking the reference for taxation should apply to the taxing officer for any extension of time necessary to enable the requirements to be complied with.

3. If the proceedings are begun after the time limits have expired no formal application for extension of time need be made on taxing the reference. In such a case, unless any other party entitled to be heard on the taxation makes a prior application, the question of an extension of time may be raised as a preliminary point on the substantive hearing of the taxation.

4. In any case where the time limits have not been complied with any other party entitled to be heard on the taxation may apply either before or as a preliminary point at the substantive hearing under the provisions of Ord 62, r 28(4) for the bill to be reduced or wholly disallowed. An application under r 28(4) must be made to a taxing master or registrar.

5. Where the only taxation required is pursuant to Sch 2 to the Legal Aid Act 1974 no application is required on taking a reference out of time. In any case where he considers it appropriate so to do the taxing officer will, of his own motion, serve notice on the party entitled to the taxation under the provisions of reg 104 of the Legal Aid (General) Regulations 1980, SI 1980/1894.

6. This direction supersedes the Practice Direction dated 9 February 1984 ([1984] 1 All ER 873, [1984] 1 WLR 520), which is hereby cancelled.

27 June 1986

F T HORNE
Chief Taxing Master.

Practice Direction

a

SUPREME COURT TAXING OFFICE

Costs – Taxation – Review of taxation – Documents to be lodged by applicant – Bundles to be paginated and indexed – Time limit for lodging bundles.

b

Applicants for reviews of taxation are required to lodge with the Chief Clerk of the Supreme Court Taxing Office three bundles of documents for the use of the judge and assessors.

On receipt of the summons from the Queen's Bench or Chancery Divisions the Chief Clerk will send notice to the applicant requesting that the bundles be lodged, which should consist of copies of the following documents:

c

The summons to review
Order/judgment or other instrument providing for the taxation
Bill of costs
Objections
Respondent's answers (if any)

d

Master's answers and certificate
Affidavits filed during the course of the taxation
The legal aid certificate, any relevant amendments thereto and authority to apply for review where applicable
Any correspondence or other documents to which reference is intended to be made at the hearing of the review.

e

Bundles must be clearly paginated with an index at the front of the bundle listing all the documents and giving a page reference for each one. The bundles must be bound together. Loose documents will not be accepted.

The bundles must be lodged within 21 days from the receipt of notice from the Chief Clerk or such other time as the Chief Clerk may direct.

F T HORNE

f

16 July 1986   Chief Taxing Master.

Re Rapier (deceased)

a

QUEEN'S BENCH DIVISION

WOOLF LJ AND SIMON BROWN J

25 JUNE, 9 JULY 1986

Coroner – Inquest – Fresh inquest – New evidence – Jurisdiction to quash inquest and order fresh inquest where new evidence discovered – Circumstances in which fresh inquest will be ordered – Coroners Act 1887, s 6 – Coroners (Amendment) Act 1926, s 19.

b

The deceased, who was being held in prison in solitary confinement, was found dead in his cell, having apparently hanged himself. At the inquest into his death the jury returned an open verdict. Subsequently it came to light that there had been a prison investigation into solvent sniffing by prisoners and that on the day he died the deceased had been supplied with solvent by a fellow inmate. Inhalation of the solvent in question resulted in depression, and one of the deceased's fellow prisoners gave evidence at the prison investigation that the deceased had said that after inhaling the solvent he felt like committing suicide. The coroner applied pursuant to s 6ᵃ of the Coroners Act 1887 and s 19ᵇ of the Coroners (Amendment) Act 1926 for the inquest to be quashed and for a fresh inquest to be held to consider the new evidence.

c

d

Held – On the true construction of s 6 of the 1887 Act and s 19 of the 1926 Act, the court had power to quash an inquest and order a fresh inquest where it was necessary or desirable in the interests of justice to consider a complaint as to the conduct of the inquest or consider new evidence which might possibly have caused the coroner's jury to have come to a different conclusion, even though it could not be shown that there was a probability of a fresh inquest producing a different verdict. In the circumstances, there were compelling reasons for ordering a new inquest since (a) the coroner himself believed it to be necessary, (b) the legislation required that there be an inquest in all cases of death in prison and such an inquest should be a full and proper inquest with all material matters placed before the jury, and (c) there was a real possibility that the additional evidence could produce a different verdict. It followed that the inquest would be quashed and a fresh inquest ordered (see p 734 *b* to *f*, p 735 *c d* and p 736 *b* to *e*, post).

e

f

Re Davis (decd) [1967] 1 All ER 688 and *R v Cardiff Coroner, ex p Thomas* [1970] 3 All ER 469 considered.

Notes

For the powers of the High Court to quash a coroner's inquisition, see 9 Halsbury's Laws (4th edn) paras 1144–1146, 1150–1151, and for cases on the subject, see 13 Digest (Reissue) 184–188, 1607–1652.

g

For the Coroners Act 1887, s 6, see 11 Halsbury's Statutes (4th edn) 358.

For the Coroners (Amendment) Act 1926, s 19, see ibid 379.

Cases referred to in judgments

h

Davis (decd), Re [1967] 1 All ER 688, [1968] 1 QB 72, [1967] 2 WLR 1089, CA.

R v Cardiff Coroner, ex p Thomas [1970] 3 All ER 469, [1970] 1 WLR 1475, DC.

R v Clerk of Assize of the Oxford Circuit [1897] 1 QB 370.

R v Divine, ex p Walton [1930] 2 KB 29, [1930] All ER Rep 302, DC.

R v Great Western Rly Co (Directors) (1888) 20 QBD 410, DC.

R v Greater Manchester Coroner, ex p Tal [1984] 3 All ER 240, [1985] QB 67, [1984] 3 WLR 643, DC.

j

R v South London Coroner, ex p Thompson (1982) Times, 15 May.

---

a   Section 6, so far as material, is set out at p 727 *e g*, post

b   Section 19 is set out at p 727 *g h*, post

a   *R v Surrey Coroner, ex p Campbell* [1982] 2 All ER 545, [1982] QB 661, [1982] 2 WLR 626, DC.

Case also cited
R v Wood, ex p Atcherley (1908) 73 JP 40.

Application for judicial review
b   Francis d'Aubeville Wilson, formerly Her Majesty's Coroner for Swansea and Gower in the county of West Glamorgan, applied for an order pursuant to s 6 of the Coroners Act 1887 and s 19 of the Coroners (Amendment) Act 1926 to quash the inquisition touching the death of Philip Charles Rapier held at Gowerton near Swansea before the applicant and a jury at which an open verdict was returned on 30 May 1985 and for an order that another inquest be held touching the death of Philip Charles Rapier and that all necessary c   consequential directions be given, the authority of Her Majesty's Attorney General having been granted by the fiat of the Solicitor General dated 17 October 1985.

Peregrine Simon for the applicant.
Guy Sankey as amicus curiae.

d   *Cur adv vult*

9 July. The following judgments were delivered.

WOOLF LJ. This is an application by Francis d'Aubeville Wilson, now retired, who at the relevant times was Her Majesty's Coroner for Swansea and Gower in the county of e   West Glamorgan. The application is made under s 6 of the Coroners Act 1887 and s 19 of the Coroners (Amendment) Act 1926.
The relevant provisions of s 6 of the 1887 Act provide:

'(1.) Where Her Majesty's High Court of Justice, upon application made by or under the authority of the Attorney General, is satisfied . . . (*b.*) where an inquest has been held by a coroner that by reason of fraud, rejection of evidence, irregularity of f   proceedings, insufficiency of inquiry, or otherwise, it is necessary or desirable, in the interests of justice, that another inquest should be held, the court may order an inquest to be held touching the said death, and may, if the court think it just, order the said coroner to pay such costs of and incidental to the application as to the court may seem just, and where an inquest has been already held may quash the inquisition on that inquest . . .'

g   Section 19 of the 1926 Act provides:

'For the removal of doubts it is hereby declared, without prejudice to the generality of the provisions of section six of the Coroners Act 1887, that the powers of the High Court under that section extend to and may be exercised in any case where the Court is satisfied that by reason of the discovery of new facts or evidence h   it is necessary or desirable in the interests of justice that an inquisition on an inquest previously held concerning a death should be quashed, and that another inquest should be held.'

Authority to make this application was granted by a fiat of the Solicitor General, acting pursuant to his powers under the Law Officers Act 1944, in the absence of the Attorney j   General, dated 1 November 1985 and the application was then made in accordance with the procedure laid down in RSC Ord 53 for an application for judicial review. On 29 January 1986, having considered the papers, Nolan J gave the applicant leave, 'if this was required', to proceed with his application.
The application is not opposed but, in addition to the helpful arguments of counsel for the applicant, the court has had the benefit of the argument of counsel who appeared as amicus curiae.

The proper procedure

Counsel who appeared as amicus curiae indicated in the course of his argument that it would assist the Crown Office if the court could clarify the question whether or not it is necessary to have leave of the court to proceed with an application where an applicant has already obtained the fiat of the Attorney General pursuant to the provisions of the Coroners Act 1887. The answer to that question appears to me to depend on the nature of the application which is made. Quite apart from the statutory application to quash under the provisions to which I have made reference, the court has always had an inherent jurisdiction to exercise a supervisory role in relation to an inquest conducted by a coroner and a power if necessary to quash an inquisition. Section 35 of the 1887 Act provides:

> 'Nothing in this Act shall . . . in any manner prejudice or affect the jurisdiction of the High Court of Justice or of any judge thereof in relation to or over a coroner or his duties.'

This common law power is independent of the statutory power and is now exercised on an application for judicial review under RSC Ord 53 (see eg *R v Surrey Coroner, ex p Campbell* [1982] 2 All ER 545, [1982] QB 661 and *R v Greater Manchester Coroner, ex p Tal* [1984] 3 All ER 240, [1985] QB 67). On such an application leave must be obtained in the ordinary way.

Where an application is made under the statutory power it may be desirable, because the powers of the court are not identical, to also make an application under the common law power of the court by way of an application for judicial review. Where this is the position it is not necessary for two separate applications to be made. The applications can be and are in practice joined but they then have to be made by way of an application for judicial review and so, although the fiat of the Attorney General must already have been obtained so as to make the application under the statutory powers, it is still necessary to obtain the leave of the court because of the inclusion of an application for judicial review. In practice, the granting of leave will almost inevitably be a formality since, if the Attorney General considers that the applicant is entitled to his fiat, it is most unlikely that a court would ever refuse leave.

If, however, as in the present case, the applicant is relying solely on the statutory grounds, it is not necessary to make the application by way of an application for judicial review. The position is similar to that which exists where there is a statutory right to apply to quash a decision of a minister or government department, as, for example, under the Town and Country Planning Act 1971; on such an application there is no need to obtain leave and, equally, there is no need to obtain leave for an application to quash an inquisition which is solely made on the statutory grounds and not by way of an application for judicial review. However, in the case of an application under the 1887 Act, it is not possible to apply by notice of motion under RSC Ord 94 because the jurisdiction under that order is confined to the actions of a minister or government department. Instead, the appropriate procedure is to apply under RSC Ord 5, r 3 by originating summons. A short report in *R v South London Coroner, ex p Thompson* (1982) Times, 15 May includes a passage from a judgment of Comyn J, which states:

> 'There was a suggestion in textbooks that under the Coroners Act 1887, where the fiat of the Attorney General had been given, there was no need to seek the leave of the court. His Lordship found that the fiat did not dispense of seeking the leave of the court.'

However, that was a case where there were applications under both the common law and statutory powers and so in that case leave was required. The report is also misleading in so far as it suggests that there is a distinction between the position at common law and on judicial review, and that, therefore, there are three procedures for reviewing inquests. Historically, the procedure was by an application for the writ of certiorari (see eg *R v*

Directors of Great Western Rly Co (1888) 20 QBD 410 and *R v Clerk of Assize of the Oxford*
a *Circuit* [1897] 1 QB 370) and that is why the common law power is now exercised on an
application for judicial review. There is no separate common law procedure. As in the
majority of cases, if there is a right to relief the statutory powers will apply; if an
application for judicial review is made the court will require an explanation why, if this
is the case, no application for the fiat of the Attorney General has been made.

Although proceeding by originating summons would be technically correct and leave
b would not then be required, even where it is anticipated that there is no need to rely on
the court's powers under RSC Ord 53, in practice I would anticipate it will be felt that it
is safer to adopt the same procedure that was adopted in this case of applying by way of
judicial review, because the court will then have in reserve its other powers even though
this means that the formality of obtaining leave must be fulfilled.

Having dealt with the procedural problem, I turn to the grounds of the present
c application. These are that, since the inquest on 30 May 1985 was held into the death of
Philip Charles Rapier, new evidence has come to light which means that it is necessary
or desirable in the interests of justice that the inquisition of that inquest be quashed and
that another inquest be held at which the jury is able to consider the additional evidence.

The facts
d   At the time of his death Philip Charles Rapier was 19 years of age and was in solitary
confinement in a punishment cell in the young offenders wing of Swansea prison. He
was undergoing punishment for breach of prison rules, namely abusing a prison officer,
and he was found dead in his cell at about 9 pm, hanging by the neck from a sheet which
was tied to a bar in the cell window.

At the inquest, which was held on 30 May 1985 at Gowerton, near Swansea, the jury,
e after hearing the sworn evidence and listening to the directions given by the applicant
concerning the finding or rejecting of a verdict of suicide, returned an open verdict.

The evidence before the jury consisted of medical evidence which indicated that the
deceased had no relevant medical history, evidence of the pathologist that he was satisfied
that no third party had any hand in the deceased's death and the cause of death was
hanging, and evidence from a number of prison officers who had seen the deceased
f during the course of the day of his death. Their evidence was to the effect that the
deceased was behaving perfectly normally, he had no suicidal tendencies but he had
declined exercise on that particular day. In particular, his personal officer indicated that
he had seen the deceased after dinner on the day in question who had told him that he
would be out of punishment next day and that he would be out of the prison in six
weeks. The officer says he told the deceased, 'Keep your nose clean now and you will be
g out in six weeks' time,' and he said, 'I'll try, sir.'

Mr Bamber, the deputy governor of the prison, attended at the inquest but, apart from
asking a question, he apparently played no part in the proceedings and did not give
evidence.

Apparently, the deceased's inquest was the third inquest which had taken place in
respect of death at Swansea prison where an open verdict had been returned and this was
h a matter which troubled certain prison officers.

On the day after the inquest, two of the officers were discussing this matter, and
during discussion it was mentioned by one of the officers that there had been an
investigation between the date of the deceased's death and the inquest into possible
solvent sniffing by the deceased and another inmate. The other officer, who previously
was unaware of this investigation, because he felt the report of the investigation might
j be relevant raised the matter and eventually it became apparent that the report had not
been drawn to the attention of the coroner because those responsible felt that the contents
were irrelevant.

The result of the matter being very properly raised in this way was that there was an
investigation carried out on behalf of the Director of Public Prosecutions. On 12
September 1985 the Principal Assistant Director of Public Prosecutions wrote to the

Chief Constable of the South Wales Constabulary, stating:

> 'Although I am of the opinion that Bamber [that is the deputy governor who was *a* then acting governor], Cook [the assistant governor] and Lewis [the governor] made a grave error of judgment in not disclosing the possibility of solvent abuse by Philip Charles Rapier I do not consider that any criminal offence is disclosed against the three men. I agree that the file of evidence should be submitted to H.M. Coroner for the City of Swansea.'

b

It is right that I should interpose here that Mr Bamber had in fact been responsible for reporting the matter to higher authority after the inquest when the question of the report was raised.

Having seen the file of evidence which was submitted to him, the applicant, the coroner, says in his affidavit:

> '7. Whilst much of the evidence discovered by the police is conflicting and some *c* of it may well be untrue, it is my belief that if the Jury had had this evidence before them at the Inquest they might have agreed upon a different verdict from that expressed by them at the conclusion of the Inquest.
>
> 8. Furthermore, if the Jury had had this evidence before it, it might have felt able to have made comments on the conditions giving rise to the cause of death, for example, that the deceased was depressed or out of control due to drug taking. *d*
>
> 9. I respectfully submit that it is desirable that a July have a full view of the evidence, particularly in a case like the present where there are grounds for believing that measures could be taken which would help to prevent or render less likely the recurrence of such deaths. In such cases Juries sometimes exercise their right through the Coroner to make recommendations.'

e

It is preferable that I do not go into the evidence which was submitted after the inquest to the coroner in any more detail than is absolutely necessary. However, in order to understand the decision of the court, it is necessary to say a little about this evidence.

The evidence indicated that trichloroethane, which is a colourless volatile liquid which is marketed as Genclean and is widely used as a dry-cleaning and correcting fluid and as a degreasing agent, was available to inmates at the prison who worked in a particular *f* workshop for getting marks off clothing. The fluid was kept locked but, according to certain of the witnesses, a prisoner called Butcher, who was friends with the deceased, did keep some in a tobacco tin, and what Butcher says is that on the night in question by the use of a line he swung the tin containing the fluid from his cell to the cell of the deceased, and when the tin was returned it had been emptied. This happened approximately half an hour to just under three-quarters of an hour before the deceased *g* was found dead. There was also evidence that inmates, including Butcher and the deceased, used to sniff this solvent. Butcher indicated that he would have terrible headaches after inhaling and once or twice felt so depressed that he thought about committing suicide, and he said the deceased had also mentioned after inhaling that he felt like committing suicide.

A senior scientific officer of the Home Office Forensic Science Laboratory indicates *h* that the solvent is rapidly absorbed from the lungs and that the toxic effects of the compound include depression of the central nervous system resulting, in high concentrations, in anaesthesia and death from respiratory depression. The pathologist gave evidence at the inquest that the symptoms of inhalation usually develop in a progressing sequence:

> 'After an initial feeling of euphoria, excitation or pleasant exhilaration there is *j* enjoyment of the drowsiness and dream-like state which follows. Visual and/or auditory hallucinations can occur and these may be pleasant or terrifying. A few deep breaths produces an effect which gradually dissipates over thirty to forty-five minutes.'

a While he also indicates that sudden death can occur, I would emphasise that there is no question here of the solvent directly causing death.

I have said enough with regard to this evidence to indicate that, if it had been available to the coroner prior to the inquest, it would inevitably have been called before the jury at the inquest. In support of his contention that there should now be a fresh inquest at which this evidence should be before the jury, counsel for the applicant submits that the evidence could have a material effect on the verdict of the jury. Counsel appearing as

b amicus, however, submits it would be wrong to have a further inquest because the additional evidence could not affect the verdict since it makes it more likely, not less likely, that a jury would bring in the same open verdict. Counsel for the applicant and counsel appearing as amicus also differ in their submissions whether there would be any purpose in a fresh inquest considering the further evidence apart from the possibility of a different verdict.

c
The law

In order to evaluate these submissions, it is necessary to consider further the statutory provisions relating to inquests.

Section 3(1) of the 1887 Act requires a coroner to hold an inquest where—

d
> 'there is reasonable cause to suspect that such person has died either a violent or an unnatural death, or has died a sudden death of which the cause is unknown, or that such person has died in prison, or in such place or under such circumstances as to require an inquest . . .'

It is to be noted that solely in the case of deaths in prison there is a mandatory requirement to hold an inquest irrespective of the circumstances of the death. This appears to be a statutory recognition that, because of the nature of prison institutions, there is a special

e need for an independent investigation into deaths which occur within their walls. The same policy can be identified in the 1926 Act. Section 13(1) gives the coroner a discretion to dispense with a jury but s 13(2)(b) requires that, where the death occurred in prison or in such place or in such circumstances as require an inquest under any Act other than the 1887 Act, the coroner is required to summon a jury.

f Section 4(1) of the 1887 Act requires the coroner to examine on oath all persons who tender their evidence and 'all persons having knowledge of the facts whom he thinks it expedient to examine', so to a large extent what witnesses are called is a matter for the coroner's discretion.

Section 4(3) provides that, after hearing the evidence, the jury shall give their verdict and certify it by an inquisition in writing setting forth, so far as such particulars have been proved to them, who the deceased was and how and where and when the deceased

g came to his death.

The Coroners' Rules 1984, SI 1984/552, require that every inquest shall be held in public (r 17). Rule 36 provides:

h
> '(1) The proceedings and evidence at an inquest shall be directed solely to ascertain the following matters, namely—(a) who the deceased was; (b) how, when and where the deceased came by his death; (c) the particulars for the time being required by the Registration Acts to be registered concerning the death.
> (2) Neither the coroner nor the jury shall express any opinion on any other matters.'

Rule 42 makes it clear that verdicts of a jury should not appear to determine any

j question of criminal liability of a named person or civil liability.

Rules 36 and 42 are therefore designed to limit the scope of the inquest and to prevent the previous practice of juries adding far-reaching riders. The coroner does, however, retain the right to make a report and this is dealt with in r 43, which provides:

> 'A coroner who believes that action should be taken to prevent the recurrence of

fatalities similar to that in respect of which the inquest is being held may announce at the inquest that he is reporting the matter in writing to the person or authority who may have power to take such action and he may report the matter accordingly.' a

Apart from the coroner's ability to make a report under r 43 and apart from matters not in dispute, in the circumstances of this case, if there were to be a new inquest, the jury's and the coroner's inquiries would be confined to ascertaining whether the deceased killed himself, whether he died as a result of an accident or misadventure or whether, again, there should be an open verdict. An open verdict would only be appropriate if the b jury on the evidence could not reach one of the alternative verdicts which were available.

The question of what verdicts are open to the jury is important because counsel for the applicant rightly drew the court's attention to a note to s 6 of the 1887 Act which appears in 11 Halsbury's Statutes (4th edn) 359, which reads:

'An inquisition will not be quashed unless it is shown that there would probably c be a different verdict if a new inquest were held . . .'

In support of the note there is a reference to *Re Davis (decd)* [1967] 1 All ER 688, [1968] 1 QB 72 and *R v Cardiff Coroner, ex p Thomas* [1970] 3 All ER 469, [1970] 1 WLR 1475.

If this is a correct statement of general principle, then that could be crucial to the outcome of this application because counsel for the applicant cannot go so far as to submit that the new evidence which is now available makes it probable that a different verdict d would be reached.

I am bound to say that, before considering the authorities, my initial reaction was one of surprise in reading the note since it would seem to involve a much more restrictive approach than that which is contained in s 6 of the 1887 Act and s 19 of the 1926 Act, both of which set out the critical statutory requirement as being that it should be necessary or desirable in the interests of justice that another inquest should be held. e

Indeed, until pressed by the court, counsel appearing as amicus was not inclined to put the test as high as this. He opened his submissions by saying the test is whether the new facts and evidence would support a different verdict. On this basis, it would be sufficient if it was possible there could be a different verdict. This appears to be a much more satisfactory approach because, in many cases, and I would include this case as an example, it will be quite impossible to say what will be the effect of the new evidence. The effect f which it will have will only be known after the witnesses have given their evidence and have been questioned. They may then be believed or they may not be believed. However, whatever the outcome, it still may be in the interests of justice that their evidence should be explored in public before a jury.

With regard to the general approach to this jurisdiction, considerable help is provided by the judgment of the court given by Talbot J in *R v Divine, ex p Watson* [1930] 2 KB 29, g [1930] All ER Rep 302. In his judgment Talbot J, having referred to the fact that the desire of the coroner that there should be a new inquest had weighed with the court, went on to refer to s 6(1) and then said ([1930] 2 KB 29 at 37, [1930] All ER Rep 302 at 308):

'These are very wide words, and their generality is declared and guarded by the h Coroners (Amendment) Act, 1926, s. 19. Moreover the fact that the powers conferred by the section can be exercised only upon an application authorized by the Attorney-General indicates that they are powers beyond those which the Court already had. The same appears from s. 35 of the Act. The words "necessary or desirable in the interests of justice" are the critical words. The Court is not to attend to mere informalities, nor to criticize minutely the summing-up, or the nature of j the evidence or of the procedure. But if the inquest has been so conducted, or the circumstances attending it are such that there is real risk that justice has not been done, a real impairment of the security which right procedure provides that justice is done and is seen to be done, the Court ought not to allow the inquisition to stand.'

Turning next to *Re Davis (decd)* [1967] 1 All ER 688, [1968] 1 QB 72, it is clear that
a the headnote supports the note in Halsbury's Statutes. It is also clear that the headnote
reflects the judgments of Sellers and Russell LJJ in that case. However, the case was one
where there had already been a verdict of suicide and the court was being asked to quash
the verdict on the basis of evidence from another doctor in addition to the doctors who
had already given evidence in the case. As Sellers LJ said ([1967] 1 All ER 688 at 690,
[1968] 1 QB 72 at 82):

b
> 'The only argument ultimately relied on was that the state of the deceased's
> mental health was insufficiently investigated and that it should at least have been
> supplemented by the evidence of Dr. Raeside, who had attended the deceased
> generally since 1961 and had seen her in hospital on several occasions after the birth
> of the child, and as recently as July 20.'

c Having said that, Sellers LJ went on to say:

> 'This court could interfere, in the circumstances of this case, only if it was of
> opinion that the verdict of suicide would probably be replaced by a different verdict
> if a new inquest were to be held.'

This he considered on the evidence would not be the case.
d Russell LJ took the same view. In adopting that approach, the court was acting on the
submissions of distinguished counsel appearing on behalf of the coroner but, as far as one
can tell from the report, the precise standard to be adopted was not in dispute.
Furthermore, in that case, unlike the present case, there was no difficulty involved in
assessing the quality of the evidence. This is significant because, in the later case of *R v
Cardiff Coroner, ex p Thomas* [1970] 3 All ER 469, [1970] 1 WLR 1475 referred to in the
e note in Halsbury's Statutes, the court appears to have taken a different view from that in
Re Davis (decd) [1967] 1 All ER 688, [1968] 1 QB 72.
R v Cardiff Coroner, ex p Thomas also concerned an inquest where there had been a
verdict of suicide. The application to quash the inquisition was opposed on behalf of the
coroner, who sought to contend that, even if the evidence before the inquest did not
justify a verdict of suicide, the fresh evidence would mean that if there was a further
f inquest the verdict would still be one of suicide. Lord Parker CJ, giving a judgment with
which the other members of the court agreed, said ([1970] 3 All ER 469 at 472, [1970] 1
WLR 1475 at 1478):

> 'For my part, I cannot accept that that is the right approach to the matter. In the
> case of *Re Davis (decd)* [1967] 1 All ER 688, [1968] 1 QB 72, to which I have already
g > referred, there is no doubt that the court said that this court would only quash the
> inquisition and order a fresh inquest if it were probable that there would be a
> different verdict at the new inquest. In *Re Davis (decd)*, the applicant sought to
> adduce the evidence of a doctor, and what the court said was: "If we accept all that
> the doctor says in his affidavit, that would not enable the coroner to come to any
> different conclusion." Here the evidence is not to be adduced by the applicant but,
h > as it were, to be called by the coroner in rebuttal of the applicant's statements. No
> one can tell whether the witnesses will give the same evidence as appears on their
> affidavits. They may not go so far, they may go further. Those affidavits take the
> form largely of evidence from members of the deceased's family to the effect that
> he was in pain, that he was depressed, that he was having difficulties at home and
> that he was extremely worried and depressed at the fact that the applicant went out
j > to work and was, as he thought, neglecting the children. This court has been asked
> to rule that such evidence would not affect the matter at all. It is said that that would
> only be evidence of a background of bad health and of domestic difficulty, and
> would not be sufficient to evince any suicidal intent. That may well be so, but until
> the witnesses have given their evidence, and it is seen how far they go in that

evidence, it seems to me quite impossible for this court to rule in the matter at all. It follows, in my judgment, that an order of certiorari should go to quash this *a* inquest, and that there must be an order for a fresh inquest which, to save the coroner embarrassment, had better be heard by a different coroner.'

In relation to a case such as the one at present under consideration, this appears to me to be the correct approach. I would also adopt the approach which Lord Parker CJ adopted with regard to *Re Davis (decd)*. This means that the note in Halsbury's Statutes sets out a general test for a new inquest which is too stringent. *b*

Here, as a result of the report which has been sent to the coroner, a whole new area for inquiry, which was never investigated at the inquest, has been disclosed. It is not possible to say with any degree of confidence what will be the result of the new evidence being examined before a coroner and a jury but, contrary to the submission of counsel appearing as amicus, I consider that it would be possible for the jury to bring in a verdict of suicide as a result of the additional evidence. It is true, as counsel appearing as amicus *c* contends, that the jury might take the view that the new evidence makes the position even more uncertain. On the other hand, the jury could take the view, if they are satisfied that the deceased was under the influence of the solvent, that this caused him to become suicidal when he would not otherwise have reacted in this way. Certainly it could provide an explanation why he should commit suicide, notwithstanding the fact that his punishment was coming to an end and he was shortly to be released from prison. *d*

This case is very different from *Davis's* case. Here, it certainly would not appear that justice has been done if there were not a new inquest. The coroner responsible for the previous inquest is of this view, and it must be remembered that the inquest was dealing with a death in prison, which has to be the subject matter of an inquest even if there is nothing untoward in the circumstances of the death. While agreeing with counsel appearing as amicus that the fact that new evidence of matters of public interest is *e* discovered is not in itself sufficient to justify a new inquest, looking at the circumstances of this case as a whole it is my view that we should accede to the application of the coroner and quash the verdict, since this is necessary and desirable in the interests of justice. I therefore agree with Simon Brown J's judgment, which I have had the advantage of seeing in draft.

f

SIMON BROWN J. I agree. As Woolf LJ has pointed out, when considering whether or not to quash an inquisition and order a fresh inquest in the light of some complaint as to the conduct of the inquest or the discovery of new evidence, the legislation requires in every instance that the court should ask itself: are we satisfied that such a course is 'necessary or desirable in the interests of justice'? That is the language both of s 6(1) of the Coroners Act 1887 and of s 19 of the Coroners (Amendment) Act 1926. *g*

The important point of general application raised on this motion concerns the extent to which the Court of Appeal's decision in *Re Davis (decd)* [1967] 1 All ER 688, [1968] 1 QB 72 governs the court's approach to the exercise of this statutory power. The note to s 6 of the 1887 Act contained in 11 Halsbury's Statutes (4th edn) 359 asserts baldly:

'An inquisition will not be quashed unless it is shown that there would probably *h* be a different verdict if a new inquest were held . . .'

Reference is made to *Re Davis (decd)* and to *R v Cardiff Coroner, ex p Thomas* [1970] 3 All ER 469, [1970] 1 WLR 1475. To what extent is that an accurate statement of the law?

In my judgment, it is quite impossible to suppose that the Court of Appeal in *Re Davis* was intending to lay down any such general principle, whether in all s 6 cases or only in 'new facts or evidence' cases expressly provided for by s 19. Such a principle would clearly *j* impose a significant restriction on the apparent width of the discretion conferred by the governing provision, a restriction which I would regard as impermissible. Moreover, it postulates that the only purpose ever served by holding an inquest is that the correct verdict is arrived at, a premise which I cannot accept. True, the scope of what a coroner's a inquisition may achieve by way of a formal result has gradually been whittled down over the years. Initially, it lost its importance in the administration of the criminal law; then the Coroners Rules 1953, SI 1953/205, r 33 (as substituted by SI 1977/1881) provided:

'No verdict shall be framed in such a way as to determine any question of—(a) criminal liability on the part of a named person, or (b) civil liability.'

b Most recently the coroner's and jury's right to make recommendations was removed by r 36 of the Coroners Rules 1984, SI 1984/552. Indeed, all that remains, bar the verdict, is the coroner's limited power under r 43. But, as Woolf LJ has pointed out, there are nevertheless certain cases (of which the most pertinent is that the deceased died in prison) which by s 3(1) of the 1887 Act require that an inquest be held and indeed by s 13(2)(b) of the 1926 Act require that it be held before a jury, even though the cause of death may be clear beyond a peradventure and where the verdict could not conceivably be in doubt.

c In continuing to require coroners to summon a jury to hold a formal inquest in public in such circumstances, Parliament must be thought to attach some real value to the inquest proceedings. If then it is found that such proceedings were wholly deficient, whether by reason of irregularity or because of the subsequent discovery of important evidence, it seems to me quite wrong to suppose that the courts are precluded by the decision in Re Davis from requiring a new inquest to be held in the interests of justice.

d Although, at first blush, the judgments in Re Davis may be thought to suggest that the probability of a fresh inquest producing a different verdict is a precondition to any successful s 6 application, or at least to any which are brought on the ground of insufficient inquiry or fresh evidence, and certainly the language of probability is to be found repeatedly in the judgments, which in turn mirror the clear submission of counsel then instructed for the coroner, I have concluded that the case is not to be regarded as authority for any such general principle.

e In the first place, it is noteworthy that, in the leading judgment of the Court of Appeal, Sellers LJ expressly arrived at his conclusion 'in the circumstances of this case' and does not seek to place the judgment on any more general basis (see [1967] 1 All ER 688 at 690, [1968] 1 QB 72 at 82). Secondly, it must be appreciated that the circumstances of that case were indeed somewhat singular, not least in that the Court of Appeal then had

f before it all the relevant evidence, ie all that had been available at the original inquest and all that the applicant desired to adduce at a further inquest. This evidence, coming as all of it did from professional medical witnesses, was clear and detailed and could not be thought liable to change. In the result, the Court of Appeal was itself as well able as the coroner (who in that case was not sitting with a jury) to evaluate this evidence and arrive at a conclusion on it.

g I am confirmed in that understanding of the decision in Re Davis by reference to the subsequent decision of this court in R v Cardiff Coroner, ex p Thomas [1970] 3 All ER 469, [1970] 1 WLR 1475. In that case Lord Parker CJ commented on Re Davis as follows ([1970] 3 All ER 469 at 472, [1970] 1 WLR 1475 at 1478):

'In the case of Re Davis (decd), to which I have already referred, there is no doubt that the court said that this court would only quash the inquisition and order a fresh h inquest if it were probable that there would be a different verdict at the new inquest. In Re Davis (decd), the applicant sought to adduce the evidence of a doctor, and what the court said was: "If we accept all that the doctor says in his affidavit, that would not enable the coroner to come to any different conclusion."'

The use of the phrase 'not enable' strongly suggests that the proposed new evidence j would have failed the test not merely of *probably* producing a different verdict but also of *possibly* producing a change. Lord Parker CJ then pointed out that in R v Cardiff Coroner, ex p Thomas, in contrast to Re Davis:

'No one can tell whether the witnesses will give the same evidence as appears on their affidavits. They may not go so far, they may go further . . . This court has been

asked to rule that such evidence would not affect the matter at all . . . That may well
be so, but until the witnesses have given their evidence, and it is seen how far they *a*
go in that evidence, it seems to me quite impossible for this court to rule in the
matter at all.'

In *R v Cardiff Coroner, ex p Thomas*, of course, the verdict of suicide was in any event
open to challenge on the ground that the coroner had wrongly approached the matter;
there the new evidence was being invoked by the coroner in an attempt to save that
verdict and eliminate the need for a fresh inquest. The decision nevertheless seems to me *b*
to indicate clearly, and to my mind with manifest good sense, that, in many cases, it will
be quite impossible for the reviewing court, unlike the Court of Appeal in *Davis*'s case, to
form any sensible view on whether the new evidence creates a probability or only a
possibility that a different verdict would be arrived at on a fresh inquisition. That would
generally depend on the precise evidence eventually given and the credibility of the
witnesses who give it, not matters generally capable of final evaluation at the stage of the *c*
s 6 application. To my mind, that is the position on the instant application. This is not to
say, however, that it will not generally be of the first importance to consider so far as
possible the likelihood or otherwise of a fresh inquest arriving at a different verdict. That
will always be relevant, often critical and sometimes wholly decisive, not least in 'new
facts or evidence' cases.

So far as this case is concerned, it seems to me that there are compelling grounds for *d*
ordering a fresh inquest. In the first place, the coroner himself believes it to be necessary
and has indeed initiated the application. Secondly, the legislation requires there to be an
inquest in all cases of death in prison, and surely it should be a full and proper inquest
with all material matters placed before the jury. Thirdly, in my judgment, it may very
well be that the additional evidence here could produce a different verdict; there is, to
my mind, at least a real possibility of this. More than that one cannot say on the basis of *e*
the material before this court. That seems to me a sufficient basis, not least when coupled
with the other two considerations, for allowing this application.

Application granted. Inquest dated 30 May 1985 quashed. Order for fresh inquest.

Solicitors: *Beor Wilson & Lloyd*, Swansea (for the applicant); *Treasury Solicitor.*   *f*

Sophie Craven   Barrister.

Aden Refinery Co Ltd v Ugland Management Co
The Ugland Obo One

COURT OF APPEAL, CIVIL DIVISION
SIR JOHN DONALDSON MR, MUSTILL AND NOURSE LJJ
18, 21, 22, 31 JULY 1986

Arbitration – Award – Leave to appeal against award – Judge refusing leave to appeal to High Court on ground that arbitrators prima facie right – Applicant applying direct to Court of Appeal for leave to appeal on ground that judge failed to exercise discretion – Whether Court of Appeal having jurisdiction to entertain application – Arbitration Act 1979, s 1(3).

Arbitration – Award – Leave to appeal to Court of Appeal against grant or refusal of leave to appeal to High Court – Judge refusing leave on ground that compelled by authority to refuse leave – Applicant applying direct to Court of Appeal for leave to appeal on ground that judge failed to exercise his discretion – Whether Court of Appeal having jurisdiction to entertain application – Arbitration Act 1979, s 1(6A) – Supreme Court Act 1981, s 18(1)(f).

In the course of a demurrage dispute which was referred to arbitration the charterers were held liable to the owners. In their reasoned award the arbitrators stated that since the dispute involved an important issue on which there was a difference of opinion between London maritime arbitrators it was desirable for the question to be submitted to judicial decision. The charterers applied for leave to appeal to the High Court under s 1(3)ᵃ of the Arbitration Act 1979. The judge refused leave on the ground that there was a strong prima facie case that the arbitrators' decision was right. The charterers applied for leave to appeal against the judge's decision to the Court of Appeal. Section 1(6A)ᵇ of the 1979 Act provided that unless leave was given by the High Court no appeal lay to the Court of Appeal from a decision of the High Court to grant or refuse leave to appeal. The judge held that he was compelled by authority to refuse leave. The charterers applied direct to the Court of Appeal for leave to appeal against both refusals, contending (i) that in both instances the judge had merely applied guidelines established by authority and had failed to exercise his discretion either judicially or at all, and (ii) that accordingly, the Court of Appeal had jurisdiction to entertain a fresh application made direct to the court notwithstanding the provisions of s 1(6A) and the rule that the grant or refusal of leave was not a matter on which the court would entertain an appeal. The question arose whether the principle applicable to appeals on costs only, namely that the Court of Appeal could hear an appeal without leave of the judge notwithstanding s 18(1)(f)ᶜ of the Supreme Court Act 1981 if the appellant could show that the judge had failed to exercise his discretion judicially or at all, could be applied in the instant case.

Held – The application for leave to appeal would be refused for the following reasons—
(1) On the true construction of s 1(6A) of the 1979 Act the Court of Appeal had no jurisdiction to entertain an appeal without leave of the High Court against the grant or refusal of leave to appeal under s 1(3)(b) of the 1979 Act. The principle relating to appeals against costs only, by which the Court of Appeal could entertain an appeal on the ground that the judge had failed to exercise his discretion either judicially or at all, notwithstanding s 18(1)(f) of the 1981 Act, was limited to that particular statutory provision and could not be applied outside its own domain to other statutes. Accordingly, that principle did

---

a   Section 1(3), so far as material, provides: 'An appeal under this section may be brought by any of the parties to the reference . . . (b) . . . with leave of the court.'

b   Section 1(6A), so far as material, is set out at p 741 *a*, post

c   Section 18(1), so far as material, is set out at p 744 *g h*, post

not apply to the 1979 Act, because if such a review of a discretionary matter were permitted that would defeat the purpose for which the requirement of having to obtain leave had been introduced, namely to restrict appeals (see p 744 *j* to p 745 *a*, p 747 *d* to *j* and p 750 *g*, post); *Lane v Esdaile* [1891] AC 210 applied; *Scherer v Counting Instruments Ltd* (1977) [1986] 2 All ER 529 distinguished; *Re Racal Communications Ltd* [1980] 2 All ER 634 considered.

(2) In any event, there were no grounds for holding that the judge, although clearly aware of the guidelines laid down by authority, had reached his decision by automatic process and had failed to exercise his discretion in refusing leave on either application. It followed that the Court of Appeal had no jurisdiction to entertain the charterers' application for leave to appeal (see p 743 *g h*, p 744 *f*, p 745 *b c*, p 748 *a* and p 750 *b* to *g*, post); *Pioneer Shipping Ltd v BTP Tioxide Ltd, The Nema* [1981] 2 All ER 1030 and *Antaios Cia Naviera SA v Salen Rederierna AB, The Antaios* [1984] 3 All ER 229 considered.

Per Sir John Donaldson MR and Nourse LJ. Since the decision of an arbitrator is not binding on other arbitrators it is desirable that a judge should give favourable consideration to granting leave to appeal to the High Court if there are conflicting arbitral decisions, so that uniformity of decision by arbitrators can be achieved (see p 744 *a* to *c* and p 750 *g*, post).

Notes
For appeals to the High Court from an arbitrator, see 2 Halsbury's Laws (4th edn) para 615, and for appeals from the High Court, see ibid para 627.

For the Arbitration Act 1979, s 1, see 11 Halsbury's Statutes (4th edn) 609.

For the Supreme Court Act 1981, s 18, see ibid 774.

Cases referred to in judgments
Antaios Cia Naviera SA v Salen Rederierna AB, The Antaios [1984] 3 All ER 229, [1985] AC 191, [1984] 3 WLR 592, HL; *affg on other grounds* [1983] 3 All ER 777, [1983] 1 WLR 1362, CA.

Bew v Bew [1899] 2 Ch 467, CA.

Campbell (Donald) & Co Ltd v Pollak [1927] AC 732, [1927] All ER Rep 1, HL.

Charles v Jones (1886) 33 Ch D 80, CA.

City of Manchester, The (1880) 5 PD 221, CA.

Civil Service Co-op Society Ltd v General Steam Navigation Co Ltd [1903] 2 KB 756, CA.

Dutton v Spink & Beeching (Sales) Ltd [1977] 1 All ER 287, CA.

Edwards (Inspector of Taxes) v Bairstow [1955] 3 All ER 48, [1956] AC 14, [1955] 3 WLR 410, HL.

Jones v Curling (1884) 13 QBD 262, CA.

Kay v Briggs (1889) 22 QBD 343, CA.

Lane v Esdaile [1891] AC 210, HL.

Marsden v Lancashire and Yorkshire Rly Co (1881) 7 QBD 641, CA.

Nereide SpA di Navigazione v Bulk Oil International Ltd, The Laura Prima [1981] 3 All ER 737, HL.

Ottway v Jones [1955] 2 All ER 585, [1955] 1 WLR 706, CA.

Pioneer Shipping Ltd v BTP Tioxide Ltd, The Nema [1981] 2 All ER 1030, [1982] AC 724, [1981] 3 WLR 292, HL; *affg* [1980] 3 All ER 117, [1980] QB 547, [1980] 3 WLR 326, CA; *rvsg* [1980] 2 Lloyd's Rep 83.

Racal Communications Ltd, Re [1980] 2 All ER 634, [1981] AC 374, [1980] 3 WLR 181, HL.

Robertson v Robertson and Favagrossa (1881) 6 PD 119, [1881–5] All ER Rep 318, CA.

Scherer v Counting Instruments Ltd (1977) [1986] 2 All ER 529, [1986] 1 WLR 615, CA.

Cases also cited
Bland v Chief Supplementary Officer [1983] 1 All ER 537, [1983] 1 WLR 262, CA.

Gelberg v Miller [1961] 1 All ER 291, [1961] 1 WLR 153, DC.

Infabrics Ltd v Jaytex Ltd [1985] FSR 75, CA.

a *National Westminster Bank plc v Arthur Young McClelland Moores & Co (a firm)* [1985] 2 All ER 817, [1985] 1 WLR 1123, CA.

Applications for leave to appeal

Aden Refinery Co Ltd (the charterers) sought the leave of the Court of Appeal to appeal from (i) the refusal of Leggatt J given on 26 July 1985 to grant leave to appeal pursuant to s 1(3)(*b*) of the Arbitration Act 1979 from a majority award of the arbitrators, Mr Basil

b Eckersley, Mr Donald Davies and Mr Michael Mabbs, dated 17 May 1985 made in favour of the respondents, Ugland Management Co Ltd (the owners), and (ii) the refusal of Leggatt J given on 26 July 1985 to grant the charterers leave to appeal against the refusal of leave to appeal to the Court of Appeal. The facts are set out in the judgment of Sir John Donaldson MR.

c *Bernard Eder* for the charterers.
Dominic Kendrick for the owners.

Cur adv vult

31 July. The following judgments were delivered.

d
SIR JOHN DONALDSON MR. In July 1978 the Commercial Court Committee published the Report on Arbitration (Cmnd 7284) recommending radical reforms in the law relating to arbitration. These recommendations included the abolition of the right of appeal by way of an award in the form of a special case, which had spawned a vast number of appeals and wholly unacceptable delays in resolving commercial disputes,

e and of the power to set aside an award for error of fact or law on its face. Instead it recommended a system of judicial review based on reasoned awards, such review being subject to first obtaining the leave of the High Court and any appeal from the High Court to the Court of Appeal being subject to further restrictions. Thus the need for speed and finality, which is so essential in commerce and which arbitration is traditionally intended to provide, could be married to the equally essential continued development of

f English commercial law. Parliament approved in principle and the result is the Arbitration Act 1979.

With some prescience the committee foresaw that there would be a need for successive amendments to the law of arbitration. The rules and procedures governing arbitration are a living thing which inevitably require statutory amendment from time to time in the light of experience and changing conditions. Accordingly, the committee

g recommended the establishment of an 'Arbitration Rules Committee' with a view to relieving Parliament of the need frequently to consider detailed amendments to the current Arbitration Acts. Unfortunately this recommendation was rejected on the grounds that it was constitutionally improper for subordinate legislation to be used to amend primary legislation. If this is indeed a constitutional principle, the presence of the Hallmarking Act 1973 on the statute book is somewhat surprising. This empowers the

h Secretary of State by statutory instrument to apply the Act to metals other than gold, silver and platinum and in so doing to include provisions 'applying, extending, excluding or amending, or repealing or revoking, with or without savings, any provisions of this Act or an instrument under this Act'. An analogous power in the 1979 Act might have obviated the need for a great deal of judicial effort, regarded by some as more legislative than adjudicative, and the idea of a specialist body with legislative powers seems worth

j reviving.

The present appeal does not call for legislative effort, but it does involve a close look both at the 1979 Act, as amended by s 148(2) of the Supreme Court Act 1981, and at the guidance given by the House of Lords in *Pioneer Shipping Ltd v BTP Tioxide Ltd, The Nema* [1981] 2 All ER 1030, [1982] AC 724 and in *Antaios Cia Naviera SA v Salen Rederierna AB, The Antaios* [1984] 3 All ER 229, [1985] AC 191.

The background is concisely stated in the introductory paragraphs to a reasoned award dated 17 May 1985 by three very well-known and vastly experienced maritime arbitrators, namely Mr Basil Eckersley of counsel, Mr Donald Davies and Mr Michael Mabbs:

'1. In this case the Claimants ("Owners") claim the sum of U.S. $70,444.44 as demurrage or alternatively as damages for breach of charterparty. There is no dispute about the figure, as such, but the Respondents ("Charterers") deny that they are under any liability at all.

2. The Owners' contention is that their claim for demurrage is plainly established by the principles enunciated by the House of Lords in *The "Laura Prima"* ([1981] 3 All ER 737) Lloyd's Rep. 1 (a case decided on the Exxonvoy form which is in all material respects identical to the present Asbatankvoy form). That contention is squarely challenged by the Charterers; they say that the Owners seek to extract from the speech of Lord Roskill (which set out the unanimous view of their Lordships) a proposition of wider generality than, on a true reading, is justified.

3. In a nutshell, the issue between the parties is whether, in a case where a vessel is prevented from berthing following her arrival at the loading port as a result of adverse weather conditions, the Charterers are entitled to the benefit of the protection afforded by the last sentence of clause 6 of the charterparty, viz. ". . . where delay is caused to the vessel getting into berth after giving notice of readiness for any reason over which Charterer has no control, such delay shall not count as used laytime."

4. That issue is one of considerable practical importance and it raises a question upon which it is well-known that there is a division of view between London maritime arbitrators—a division which has manifested itself in the instant case. It is highly desirable that the question should be submitted to judicial decision and this dispute would appear to offer an ideal opportunity for the position to be resolved by such decision.'

I would add that the reasons of the majority (Messrs Eckersley and Mabbs) extended to nine pages of close reasoning and the dissenting reasons of Mr Davies to 18 pages, which were no less closely reasoned.

With this encouragement, the charterers, who had been held liable to the owners, applied to Leggatt J for leave to appeal to the High Court on the question of law arising out of the award. Such leave is required under s 1(3) of the 1979 Act and the only statutory guidance as to the circumstances in which it should be granted is to be found in s 1(4), which provides:

'The High Court shall not grant leave under subsection (3)(b) above unless it considers that, having regard to all the circumstances, the determination of the question of law concerned could substantially affect the rights of one or more of the parties to the arbitration agreement.'

This subsection is, as is apparent, intended to prevent appeals on academic questions of law, which were a feature of the old special case procedure. It is not suggested that the subsection had any application in the circumstances of the instant case. If the charterers were correct in their contentions, their rights would be affected to the tune of $US70,000, not to mention further sums in respect of interest and costs.

Leggatt J refused the application, saying:

'Despite Mr Eder's usual persuasiveness and skill in attempting to convince me that there is a strong prima facie case that the majority of the arbitrators were wrong, I am satisfied that there is a strong prima facie case that the arbitrators were right and accordingly I dismiss this application.'

The charterers wish to appeal to this court against that refusal. Section 1(6A) of the 1979 Act provides:

'Unless the High Court gives leave, no appeal shall lie to the Court of Appeal from a decision of the High Court—(a) to grant or refuse leave under subsection (3)(b) . . .'

They therefore applied for such leave but were refused, Leggatt J saying: 'In accordance with the principles laid down in *The Antaios* I feel compelled to refuse leave to appeal.' The charterers now seek to appeal to this court without leave from (a) the refusal of leave to appeal to the High Court under s 1(3), and (b) the refusal of leave to appeal to this court against that refusal.

Counsel for the charterers accepts, as he must, that prima facie s 1(6A) of the 1979 Act deprives this court of jurisdiction to entertain any appeal against the refusal of leave to appeal to the High Court under s 1(3) without the leave of that court. However, he submits that the apparent width of the ouster of our jurisdiction is subject to a concealed exception which comes into play if the judge failed to exercise his discretion judicially.

When it comes to the appeal from the judge's decision refusing leave to appeal to this court, counsel for the charterers is confronted not with a statutory ouster of jurisdiction, but with a decision of the House of Lords in *Lane v Esdaile* [1891] AC 210. There the House of Lords declined jurisdiction when Mr Lane sought in December 1888 to appeal against a decision of the Court of Appeal refusing special leave to appeal out of time against a judgment of Kay J given in July 1885. The relevant rule requiring such special leave was RSC Ord 58, r 15, which read:

'No appeal to the Court of Appeal from any interlocutory order, . . . shall, except by special leave of the Court of Appeal, be brought after the expiration of twenty-one days, and no other appeal shall, except by such leave, be brought after the expiration of one year . . .'

Lord Halsbury LC said (at 211–213):

'But when I look not only at the language used, but at the substance and meaning of the provision, it seems to me that to give an appeal in this case would defeat the whole object and purview of the order or rule itself, because it is obvious that what was there intended by the Legislature was that there should be in some form or other a power to stop an appeal—that there should not be an appeal unless some particular body pointed out by the statute (I will see in a moment what that body is), should permit that an appeal should be given. Now just let us consider what that means, that an appeal shall not be given unless some particular body consents to its being given. Surely if that is intended as a check to unnecessary or frivolous appeals it becomes absolutely illusory if you can appeal from that decision or leave, or whatever it is to be called itself. How could any Court of Review determine whether leave ought to be given or not without hearing and determining upon the hearing whether it was a fit case for an appeal? And if the intermediate Court could enter and must enter into that question, then the Court which is the ultimate Court of Appeal must do so also. The result of that would be that in construing this order, which as I have said is obviously intended to prevent frivolous and unnecessary appeals, you might in truth have two appeals in every case in which, following the ordinary course of things, there would be only one; because if there is a power to appeal when the order has been refused, it would seem to follow as a necessary consequence that you must have a right to appeal when leave has been granted, the result of which is that the person against whom the leave has been granted might appeal from that, and inasmuch as this is no stay of proceeding the Court of Appeal might be entertaining an appeal upon the very same question when this House was entertaining the question whether the Court of Appeal ought ever to have granted the appeal. My Lords, it seems to me that that would reduce the provision to such an absurdity that even if the language were more clear than is contended on the other side one really ought to give it a reasonable construction. My Lords, I confess that when I look both at the subject-matter with which the order deals and at the language of the order itself it seems to me obvious that it was intended that the decision should be final (whether that is said in terms or not seems to me to be immaterial), unless the Court of Appeal, the body there prescribed, in the exercise of that jurisdiction should give leave to appeal. As no leave has been given in this case, and as no appeal can be brought unless leave has been given, I am of opinion that this preliminary objection ought to prevail, and that this appeal should be dismissed, and I so move your Lordships.'

Lord Herschell said (at 214–215):

'I think that the matter was intrusted, and intended to be intrusted, to their discretion; and that the exercise of a discretion of that sort intrusted to them is not, within the true meaning of the Appellate Jurisdiction Act, an order or judgment from which there can be an appeal. My noble and learned friend on the Woolsack has pointed out the inconveniences which would arise from a contrary decision; and I am certainly fortified in that conclusion by the view which was taken by the Court of Appeal with reference to a very similar provision. In sect. 45 of the Judicature Act 1873 (36 & 37 Vict. c. 66), which provides for appeals to a Divisional Court from an inferior Court, it is provided that "the determination of such appeals respectively by such Divisional Courts shall be final unless special leave to appeal from the same to the Court of Appeal shall be given by the Divisional Court by which any such appeal from an inferior Court shall have been heard." In that case the discretion is entrusted to the Divisional Court. In the case of *Kay* v. *Briggs* ((1889) 22 QBD 343) the Divisional Court had refused leave to appeal. Thereupon it was attempted in the Court of Appeal to review their determination in that respect. The Court of Appeal took the view that they were unable to entertain the question and could not review the decision of the Divisional Court; and the Master of the Rolls uses language which appears to me to be quite appropriate to the present question. He says: "If this Court could overrule the discretion given by that section to Divisional Courts the practical effect would be to allow an appeal here in every case, because the facts of each case would be brought before us in order to enable us to decide whether or not we ought to overrule that discretion. I think that the real meaning of sect. 45 is to confine the power to give leave to appeal absolutely to the Divisional Courts." Now if you substitute for "the Divisional Courts" "the Court of Appeal," every word of that is strictly applicable to the present case; and indeed if the contention of the appellants were well founded I think it would follow that under this sect. 45 there could be an appeal to the Court of Appeal from a refusal by the Divisional Court, and an appeal again from the Court of Appeal to this House; so that every County Court case might be brought up to this House upon the question whether an appeal should be allowed or not.'

Lord Bramwell, Lord Macnaghten, Lord Field and Lord Hannen made concurring speeches.

Counsel for the charterers submits that the principle affirmed in *Lane v Esdaile* is again subject to a limitation, in that it applies only where the court or judge to whom the discretion to grant or refuse leave to appeal is entrusted exercises that discretion judicially and he draws attention in particular to the phraseology of Lord Herschell: 'the matter was intrusted, and intended to be intrusted, to their discretion.'

There are thus two issues. First, what discretion did Leggatt J exercise and how did he exercise it? Second, are s 1(6A) of the 1979 Act and the *Lane v Esdaile* decision subject to the qualification urged on us by counsel for the charterers?

It is clear from the judge's reasons, and I would in any event have assumed, that he had the House of Lords' decisions in *The Nema* and *The Antaios* well in mind.

Under *The Nema* guidelines in the case of a 'one-off' contractual clause, judges are advised to refuse leave to appeal if they consider that the arbitrator might have been right. In the case of standard terms, of which the present is an example, they are advised to apply rather less strict criteria, taking account of whether or not a decision on the question or questions of law would add significantly to the clarity and certainty of

English commercial law. But even then the advice is that leave to appeal should be
refused, unless the judge considers that a strong prima facie case has been made out that
the arbitrator has been wrong in his construction. If there was ever any doubt about the
purely advisory, limited and mutable status of these guidelines, it was removed by Lord
Diplock's speech in *The Antaios* [1984] 3 All ER 229 at 232, [1985] AC 191 at 200 where
he said:

> 'Like all guidelines how judicial discretion should be exercised they are not
> intended to be all-embracing or immutable, but subject to adaptation to match
> changes in practices when these occur or to refinement to meet problems of kinds
> that were not foreseen, and are not covered by, what was said by this House in *The
> Nema* [1981] 2 All ER 1030, [1982] AC 724.'

The Antaios itself was concerned with both the grant or refusal of leave to appeal to the
High Court and with the grant or refusal of leave to appeal to the Court of Appeal against
such a grant or refusal (the 's 1(6A) question'), leave to appeal to this court having been
given by Staughton J. Lord Diplock said ([1984] 3 All ER 229 at 236–237, [1985] AC 191
at 205):

> 'This brings me to "the s 1(6A) question" canvassed in Staughton J's second
> judgment of 19 November 1982: when should a judge give leave to appeal to the
> Court of Appeal from his own grant or refusal of leave to appeal to the High Court
> from an arbitral award? I agree with him that leave to appeal to the Court of Appeal
> should be granted by the judge under s 1(6A) only in cases where a decision whether
> to grant or to refuse leave to appeal to the High Court under s 1(3)(b) in the particular
> case in his view called for some amplification, elucidation or adaptation to changing
> practices of existing guidelines laid down by appellate courts, and that leave to
> appeal under s 1(6A) should *not* be granted in any other type of case. Judges should
> have the courage of their own convictions and decide for themselves whether,
> applying existing guidelines, leave to appeal to the High Court under s 1(3)(b) ought
> to be granted or not. In the sole type of case in which leave to appeal to the Court of
> Appeal under s 1(6A) may properly be given the judge ought to give reasons for his
> decision to grant such leave so that the Court of Appeal may be informed of the
> lacuna, uncertainty or unsuitability in the light of changing practices that the judge
> has perceived in the existing guidelines; moreover, since the grant of leave entails
> also the necessity for the application of *Edwards (Inspector of Taxes) v Bairstow* [1955]
> 3 All ER 48, [1956] AC 14 principles by the Court of Appeal in order to examine
> whether the judge had acted within the limits of his discretion, the judge should
> also give the reasons for the way in which he had exercised his discretion.' (Lord
> Diplock's emphasis.)

Against this background I have not the slightest doubt that Leggatt J knew that he had
a discretion in relation both to leave to appeal to the High Court and to leave to appeal to
this court against his decision on that question and that he was intending to exercise that
discretion. The use of the phrase 'I am compelled to refuse leave to appeal [to the Court
of Appeal]' in context meant no more than that if he had done so, he would have been
treating this case as an exception to the general approach advised in *The Antaios*.

The next question which therefore arises is whether Leggatt J exercised his discretion
judicially. So far as concerns his refusal of leave to appeal to this court, the contrary is
scarcely arguable, since it is clear that Leggatt J saw no lacuna, uncertainty or unsuitability
in *The Nema/Antaios* guidelines. In the case of his refusal to grant leave to appeal to the
High Court, I am unable to give quite so succinct an answer.

In *The Antaios* [1983] 3 All ER 777 at 782, [1983] 1 WLR 1362 at 1369–1370 in this
court I expressed the view that leave to appeal should be granted where it is known that
there are differing schools of thought about a question of law of general interest, each of
which could claim adherents amongst the judiciary. My reason for expressing this view
was, of course, that the whole purpose of allowing judicial review of commercial awards
is to remove doubts about such questions in the general interests of the trades concerned.

Lord Diplock commented that 'decisions are one thing; dicta are quite another' (see
[1984] 3 All ER 229 at 235, [1985] AC 191 at 204) and to this extent disagreed with me. *a*
I, of course, accept the correction, but, giving full effect to it, I would like to reaffirm my
view that where there are conflicting decisions at first instance, a judge should give
favourable consideration, in an appropriate case, to giving leave to appeal if, but only if,
he is of the view that it was a proper case for the High Court not only to add another
judicial decision, but, having done so, to grant a certificate and leave to appeal to this
court under s 1(7) of the 1979 Act. It is not in the interests of arbitrators or the *b*
commercial community that a situation should be allowed to continue in which there
are conflicting decisions, each of which binds all commercial arbitrators.

What was not considered in *The Antaios* was a situation in which there are no judicial
decisions at first instance, but there are conflicting decisions by arbitrators. Since no
arbitrator's decision binds any other arbitrator, the same reasoning would apply mutatis
mutandis and in my judgment a judge should in such a case give favourable consideration *c*
to granting leave to appeal to the High Court, but not necessarily beyond that court, in
order that there might be a decision binding all arbitrators and producing uniformity of
decision by all arbitrators.

In the instant case it is not entirely clear whether there have been conflicting arbitral
decisions, although I would myself have construed the statement by the arbitrators that
the award 'raises a question on which it is well known that there is a division of view' *d*
between London maritime arbitrators', coupled with the plea that it be resolved, as
indicating that there had been. I might therefore myself have granted leave to appeal.
Indeed, I think that I would probably have done so, because I firmly believe that the
Commercial Court exists to serve the interests of its customers *as those customers see them*,
and I should have been extremely reluctant to reject a plea from so well informed a
source as these three arbitrators.
                                                                                        e
That said, the question still remains: did the judge fail to exercise his discretion
judicially? The answer must be that there are no reasons for suspecting, and still less for
finding, that he did. All that I can say is that I would probably have reached a different
decision, but the possibility of differences of opinion is inherent in the exercise of
discretionary powers. Even if, therefore, counsel for the charterers were right in his
submission that he could escape the obstacles raised by s 1(6A) of the 1979 Act and by *f*
Lane v Esdaile, if he could show a failure by the judge to exercise his discretion judicially,
I would have dismissed any appeal. But in fact I do not think that these escape routes
exist.

Counsel for the charterers' whole argument is based on the curious, but well-
established, view of the law which binds this court to hold that s 18(1)(*f*) of the Supreme
Court Act 1981, which provides:
                                                                                        g
'No appeal shall lie to the Court of Appeal . . . (*f*) without the leave of the court
or tribunal in question, from any order of the High Court or any other court or
tribunal . . . relating only to costs which are by law left to the discretion of the court
or tribunal . . .'

has no application, if this court is able to say that the judge in the court below did not *h*
really exercise his discretion at all or based the exercise of his discretion on an inadmissible
reason. This is referred to by the cognoscenti as 'the *Scherer* principle', after *Scherer v
Counting Instruments Ltd* (1977) [1986] 2 All ER 529, [1986] 1 WLR 615.

In *Re Racal Communications Ltd* [1980] 2 All ER 634, [1981] AC 374 an attempt was
made to apply the same principle to s 441 of the Companies Act 1948 and it was rejected
by the House of Lords, the relevant statutory provision being 'The decision of the High *j*
Court . . . on an application under this section shall not be appealable'. The ratio of the
decision was that the *Scherer* principle was explicable only on the basis that whereas the
ouster of jurisdiction contained in s 18(1)(*f*) of the Supreme Court Act 1981 was on its
face limited and the limitation had been construed restrictively, that in s 441 was plainly
unlimited. The same reasoning would apply to the ouster of jurisdiction contained in

s 1(6A) of the 1979 Act. This provides an alternative ground for rejecting jurisdiction to
a hear an appeal from the refusal of Leggatt J to grant leave to appeal to the High Court.
There remains the plea that we hear, and allow, an appeal from the judge's refusal to
grant leave to appeal to this court. If granted, this would of course enable us to vary the
judge's order to one granting leave and this in turn would have removed the s 1(6A)
obstacle to our hearing an appeal from the refusal of leave to appeal to the High Court.
Although *Lane v Esdaile* was undoubtedly concerned with a discretionary refusal of special
b leave to appeal, and for this reason did not consider a case in which it could be argued
that no discretion had been exercised or that it had been exercised for an inadmissible
reason, I have no doubt that it should be applied without qualification for the reasons set
out in the speech of Lord Halsbury LC, from which I have already quoted.
For those reasons I would decline to entertain the appeals.

c **MUSTILL LJ.** I agree. Section 1(6A) of the Arbitration Act 1979, as inserted by s 148(2)
of the Supreme Court Act 1981, provides:

'Unless the High Court gives leave, no appeal shall lie to the Court of Appeal from
a decision of the High Court—(a) to grant or refuse leave under subsection 3(b) . . .'

These words could not be plainer, nor can there be any doubt that Parliament intended
d when amending the 1979 Act to eliminate a potential source of delay, which might
frustrate the primary purpose of the Act. The essence of the applications now before the
court is that the amendment missed its mark, and indeed that there was no way in which
Parliament could have achieved its object, for however hard the legislature tried to
prevent an appeal, there was no form of words which could exclude an overriding
discretion to intervene when the circumstances are such that the judge either failed in
e any true sense to exercise a discretion, or based his exercise on flawed foundations. The
charterers go on to assert that the decision of Leggatt J to refuse leave to appeal from
the arbitrators to the High Court, and from the High Court to this court, were subject to one
or other of these fatal defects.
These submissions, very cogently presented by counsel for the charterers, proceeded
by way of analogy with the long-established exercise by this court of a power to set aside
f the decision of the High Court on matters of costs alone, notwithstanding that by statute
no appeal may be brought on such matters except with the leave of the judge. This
practice was reasserted in 1977 by this court in *Scherer v Counting Instruments Ltd* (1977)
[1986] 2 All ER 529 at 536, [1986] 1 WLR 615 at 621. Buckley LJ summarised the
position as follows:

g '(1) The normal rule is that costs follow the event. That party who turns out to
have unjustifiably either brought another party before the court or given another
party cause to have recourse to the court to obtain his rights is required to
recompense that other party in costs. But, (2) the judge has under s 50 of the 1925
Act an unlimited discretion to make what order as to costs he considers that the
justice of the case requires. (3) Consequently, a successful party has a reasonable
expectation of obtaining an order for his costs to be paid by the opposing party but
h has no right to such an order, for it depends on the exercise of the court's discretion.
(4) This discretion is not one to be exercised arbitrarily: it must be exercised
judicially, that is to say in accordance with established principles and in relation to
the facts of the case. (5) The discretion cannot be well exercised unless there are
relevant grounds for its exercise, for its exercise without grounds cannot be a proper
j exercise of the judge's function. (6) The grounds must be connected with the case.
This may extend to any matter relating to the litigation and the parties' conduct in
it, and also to the circumstances leading to the litigation, but no further. (7) If no
such ground exists for departing from the normal rule, or if, although such grounds
exist, the judge is known to have acted not on any such ground but on some
extraneous ground, there has effectively been no exercise of the discretion. (8) If a

party invokes the jurisdiction of the court to grant him some discretionary relief and establishes the basic grounds therefor but the relief sought is denied in the exercise of discretion, as in *Dutton v Spink & Beeching (Sales) Ltd* [1977] 1 All ER 287 and *Ottway v Jones* [1955] 2 All ER 585, [1955] 1 WLR 706, the opposing party may properly be ordered to pay his costs. But where the party who invokes the court's jurisdiction wholly fails to establish one or more of the ingredients necessary to entitle him to the relief claimed, whether discretionary or not, it is difficult to envisage a ground on which the opposing party could properly be ordered to pay his costs. Indeed, in *Ottway v Jones* [1955] 2 All ER 585 at 591, [1955] 1 WLR 706 at 715 Parker LJ said that such an order would be judicially impossible, and Evershed MR said that such an order would not be a proper judicial exercise of the discretion, although later he expressed himself in more qualified language (see [1955] 2 All ER 585 at 587, 588–589, [1955] 1 WLR 706 at 708, 711). (9) If a judge, having relevant grounds on which to do so, has on those grounds, or some of them, made an order as to costs in the exercise of his discretion, his decision is final unless he gives leave to a dissatisfied party to appeal. (10) If, however, he has made his order having no relevant grounds available or having in fact acted on extraneous grounds, this court can entertain an appeal without leave and can make what order it thinks fit.'

In order to decide whether the rules of practice exemplified by *Scherer* in the case of costs can and should be transferred to appeals of the type now in issue, it is first necessary to identify the principle on which the practice is founded. This has proved a difficult task, and it is unfortunate that the present case has come forward for decision not long before the House of Lords is due to hear an appeal in which the doctrine is directly in issue. Subject to any authoritative guidance which is given hereafter, I would offer the following explanation.

The problem arose from two statutory provisions. Section 49 of the Supreme Court of Judicature Act 1873 laid down:

'No order made by the High Court of Justice or any Judge thereof, by the consent of the parties, or as to costs only, which by law are left to the discretion of the Court, shall be subject to any appeal, except by leave of the Court or Judge making such order.'

The rules of court contained in the schedule to that Act provided (by r 47) that except as regards the right of trustees and mortgagees and other persons to costs out of an estate, the costs of and incidental to all proceedings in the High Court should be in the discretion of the court. This provision was, however, altered by the Supreme Court of Judicature Act (1873) Amendment Act 1875, so that the old rule (which now became r 55) was made subject to a proviso:

'Provided, that where any action or issue is tried by a jury, the costs shall follow the event, unless upon application made at the trial for good cause shown the Judge before whom such action or issue is tried or the Court shall otherwise order.'

These provisions appear to have fathered two lines of authority. In *Jones v Curling* (1884) 13 QBD 262 it was held, resolving a question left open in *Marsden v Lancashire and Yorkshire Rly Co* (1881) 7 QBD 641, that since the judge in a jury trial had no jurisdiction to deprive the successful party of his costs except 'for good cause shown', the Court of Appeal had the right to inquire into whether good cause had really been shown, for this was an objective question, not within the discretion of the judge. This line of reasoning became obsolete when s 5 of the Supreme Court of Judicature Act 1890 removed the proviso and re-opened the discretion. It is, however, possible that the influence of *Jones v Curling* lingers on.

The second strand of authority arose from a conflict between *Charles v Jones* (1886) 33 Ch D 80 and *The City of Manchester* (1880) 5 PD 221. In *Charles v Jones* the Court of Appeal read s 49 in its literal sense. If the case was one where the judge had a discretion as to costs, his decision was final. In *The City of Manchester*, however, the court took a different view in a case allowing an appeal where the judge had a discretion but exercised it in a particular way in the mistaken belief that he was bound to do so by a rule of general application. See also *Robertson v Robertson and Favagrossa* (1881) 6 PD 119 at 123, [1881–5] All ER Rep 318 at 319. In *Bew v Bew* [1899] 2 Ch 467 the matter came before the Court of Appeal once again, when (after consultation with the judges of the other division of the court) the court decided in favour of the view expressed in *The City of Manchester*. Specific reference was made to the language of s 49.

Only a few years later, in *Civil Service Co-op Society Ltd v General Steam Navigation Co Ltd* [1903] 2 KB 756, the Court of Appeal was able to take for granted a right to intervene in certain cases. As Lord Halsbury LC said (at 765):

'No doubt, where a judge has exercised his discretion upon certain materials which are before him, it may not be, and I think is not, within the power of the Court of Appeal to overrule that exercise of discretion. But the necessary hypothesis of the existence of materials upon which the discretion can be exercised must be satisfied.'

Thereafter, notwithstanding doubts expressed by Viscount Dunedin and Viscount Sumner in *Donald Campbell & Co Ltd v Pollak* [1927] AC 732 at 755, 760, [1927] All ER Rep 1 at 13, 15–16 about the juristic basis of the doctrine, the rule as enunciated in *Scherer* appears never to have been questioned.

Is there anything in the *Scherer* cases which compels s 1(6A)(a) to be read in accordance with anything other than its plain meaning and their plain intent? I think not. It seems to me that these cases have their origin in the terms of the statutory provisions with which they were concerned. I acknowledge that there are difficulties in construing a statute which grants a right of appeal in situations where the judge has no discretion as enabling the appellate court to assume jurisdiction where the judge does have a discretion but behaves as if he does not. There may also be problems arising from the fact that the test for deciding whether the appellate court can entertain an appeal is stated in terms very close to the test for deciding whether an appellate court, having once entertained the appeal, ought to interfere with the judge's discretion and allow the appeal: for this might be said to deprive s 18(1)(f) of the Supreme Court Act 1981 of almost all its effect. These are objections which may cast doubt on whether the *Scherer* principle can really be reconciled with the statutes and rules relating to costs. But that it was so founded does seem to me tolerably clear. The words of the 1981 Act are significantly different. Although s 1(3)(b) does of course create a discretion, the word is not used, and in particular is not used in any way to draw a line between the cases where the court may and may not entertain an appeal.

Thus, I do not find that the principles governing appeals on costs can properly be transferred to the present context. I should only add this, that if the rationale of the *Scherer* doctrine is not as suggested above, I am unable (with proper deference to the very learned judges who created it) to see what it might be: and in such a circumstance, I believe that the best course, when dealing with legislation so differently conceived, is to read the statute as meaning what it says.

I should have reached this conclusion independently of *Re Racal Communications Ltd* [1980] 2 All ER 634, [1981] AC 374, but the reasoning in that case lends support to the conclusion that the *Scherer* doctrine cannot safely be applied outside its own immediate domain.

Accordingly I hold that the court has no jurisdiction to entertain the present appeal. I say the present appeal, because I can envisage that if a judge had in truth never reached 'a decision' at all on the grant or refusal of leave, but had reached his conclusion, not by any intellectual process, but through bias, chance, whimsy, or personal interest, an appellate or other court might find a way to intervene. Of course, nothing of this kind was suggested here. Leggatt J did arrive at a decision. I prefer to leave the case of impropriety to be dealt with later, if ever it is alleged.

There is another ground on which I would dismiss the application in relation to the 'first-tier' appeal, namely that even if the *Scherer* principle were to apply in this field, it is not shown that in deciding as he did Leggatt J failed to exercise any discretion at all. Some observations on the guidelines provided in *Pioneer Shipping Ltd v BTP Tioxide Ltd, The Nema* [1981] 2 All ER 1030, [1982] AC 724 and *Antaios Cia Naviera SA v Salen Rederierna AB, The Antaios* [1984] 3 All ER 229, [1985] AC 191 may be made by way of background.

Since the Common Law Procedure Act 1854, and indeed (by means of a different procedure) for some decades before, an arbitrator had the power to state a case for the decision of the court on a question of law arising in the course of the reference. By 1970 a series of statutes and decisions had created a situation in which the court was maintaining a tight grip on the legal content of arbitrators' awards. In practice, an alert party had a virtually unrestricted right of appeal on any question of law which could be spelt out of the issues in the arbitration, save for those which were academic, trifling or incapable of serious argument. This state of affairs came under serious attack both here and abroad, and a debate developed in which it was generally accepted that there were arguments both for and against the abolition of the right of appeal on questions of law.

In favour of the abolition, there were two principal factors. First, it was held in many quarters that the right of appeal was objectionable in principle. True, some measure of judicial control is inevitable, but it should be kept to a minimum. The right of appeal, so the argument ran, was an unacceptable infringement of the parties' right to submit their dispute to a final decision by the tribunal of their choice. Second, the possibility of an appeal was a source of delay, especially in a case where the matter went to the Court of Appeal, or even beyond, even where the appeal was brought in good faith. Experience showed that some unscrupulous respondents exploited the appeal procedure in order to postpone the moment when an adverse award would have to be honoured. Third, whatever the merits of these two objections, there was no doubt that they found favour with a substantial proportion of potential users of the English arbitral system, and deterred them from bringing to this country disputes which would otherwise have come here, to the detriment of English arbitration and the country's financial health.

Against this, there were arguments in favour of retaining a right of appeal. In the first place, such a right enables a party who has contracted to have his disputes decided according to English law, to put the matter right if the arbitrator, whether by choice or mistake, decides it in some other way. Second, the existence of judicial control enables the court to ensure that parties to commercial contracts can be confident that the law will be correctly applied, thus promoting certainty and facilitating the settlement of disputes. Third, the interests of English commercial law, and hence of the commercial community, require that the law should continue to develop through the means of precedents, stemming from disputes reaching the court on appeal from arbitrators.

I believe that most of those who engaged in the debate preceding the 1979 Act were willing to accept that there was substance in all of these submissions. The controversy concerned the relative weight which they should be given. In the event, the Act produced a compromise. It was a compromise which leaned markedly in favour of finality, in three respects: (i) the parties are given, except in the specially reserved cases, the right to contract out of the right of appeal; (ii) in all cases the appeal cannot be brought without the leave of the court; (iii) the right of onward appeal has been greatly attenuated.

Although the general tenor of the legislation was clear, there was for a time some uncertainty as to the principles on which the new discretion should be exercised. These were largely laid to rest by *The Nema* [1981] 2 All ER 1030 at 1037, [1982] AC 724 at 739, where the House emphasised—

'a parliamentary intention to give effect to the turn of the tide in favour of finality in arbitral awards (particularly in non-domestic arbitrations . . .), at any rate where this does not involve exposing arbitrators to a temptation to depart from "settled principles of law".'

Similarly, in *The Antaios* [1984] 3 All ER 229 at 232, [1985] AC 191 at 199, Lord Diplock
a spoke of the parliamentary intention—

> 'to promote speedy finality in arbitral awards rather than that insistence on
> meticulous semantic and syntactical analysis of the words in which businessmen
> happen to have chosen to express the bargain made between them, the meaning of
> which is technically, though hardly commonsensically, classified in English
> jurisprudence as a pure question of law'.

b
In my judgment a distinction is to be drawn between, on the one hand, these and
similar passages from the speeches in the two leading cases and, on the other, the
'guidelines' which are contained in those speeches. The former contain authoritative
pronouncements on the spirit in which the judge should approach the exercise of his
discretion under s 3(1)(*b*). They set the tone for the appeal procedure. The judge must
c honour them, and there is no reason to doubt that all judges do honour them. The status
of the guidelines is different. They were, as it seems to me, intended simply to guide the
judge by furnishing him with illustrations of the way in which the spirit of the legislation
can be given practical effect in certain situations commonly encountered.
I believe that the distinction between these two aspects of *The Nema* and *The Antaios* is
sometimes overlooked, and that the guidelines are from time to time treated as if they
d constituted a complete and immutable code, converting the exercise of the discretion
conferred on the judge by statute into a mechanical process yielding an answer which
follows inexorably, once a dispute and the resulting award have been assigned to one of
various categories. To employ the guidelines in this way would in my opinion be a
mistake. It is understandable that counsel should wish to latch onto any words in the
speeches which appear to favour the grant or refusal of leave in the individual case, and
e it is natural that the judges also should pay close regard to the precise wording of the
guidelines: for, after all, their Lordships' House has twice had occasion to correct
misapprehensions as to the correct use of the discretion, and no judge would care to seem
indifferent to what is said in the speeches, the more so after the stern rebuke delivered in
The Antaios to Bench and Bar alike. Understandable or not, however, I believe that this is
not the way to use the help which the guidelines have provided.
f In my judgment the discretion conferred by s 1(3)(*b*) remains a discretion. The tension
between the conflicting factors to which I have referred persists, although the weight to
be given to each of them has been authoritatively prescribed by the House of Lords. The
speeches could not legislate for every situation which the judge might face. Disputes
vary infinitely in complexity and intellectual difficulty, in the prominence which issues
of law play in the overall resolution of the dispute; in their size, and in their significance
g for the commercial futures of the parties. Questions of law vary from those which are of
general importance to the community at large, those which are important to the
international trading community, those which are important to the members of a
particular trade, those which are important to some members of that trade, faced with
similar problems, down to those which are of no importance to anyone except the parties.
The answer to the question of law may be obvious or delicately balanced. Awards may
h be long or short, lucid or opaque. They may reveal unanimity of opinion, or sharp
divisions. Every application for leave to appeal is different. No judicial pronouncement,
however elaborate, could legislate for them all. It seems to me plain that in stating the
guidelines their Lordships did not set out to do so. It involves no disrespect at all to note
that experience has cast up problems which the guidelines (as distinct from the statements
of general principle) do not cover, and practical difficulties which in some instances make
j it impossible to put into effect the procedures which they envisage. This situation is
precisely what was foreseen when the guidelines were pronounced: see *The Antaios* [1984]
3 All ER 229 at 232, [1985] AC 191 at 200 per Lord Diplock.
Thus, if Leggatt J had taken the view that the guidelines formally bound him to arrive
at a particular conclusion, without regard to the individual circumstances of the

application before him, he would in my judgment have misunderstood the law. If he had left out of account the importance of appeals on questions of general significance to *a* the continued development of English commercial law, or if he had ignored the service which the courts can perform to mediate where conflicting arbitral decisions are in circulation at the same time, he would have exercised the discretion on an unsound basis; and if the *Scherer* principle had been applicable in this field, there would have been grounds for an appellate court to intervene. In fact, however, I can draw no such inference. The argument of counsel for the charterers is founded on the word 'accordingly' *b* in the terse account of the judge's reasons which Sir John Donaldson MR has already quoted. For my part, I do not understand this word as an indication that, having matched the facts against the guidelines, the judge proceeded directly to a decision, without exercising an independent judgment about whether this was a suitable case for an appeal. The judge's finding of a strong prima facie case that the majority were right was plainly an important element which the judge evidently treated as tipping the scale. But it does *c* not follow that he regarded it as conclusive in itself, and neglected all the other relevant factors. No doubt there are judges who would have reached a different conclusion, in the light of the arbitrators' own expressed opinion on the value of a ruling from the High Court. But the discretion was for the judge, not the arbitrators, to exercise, and it is in the nature of a discretion that judges may differ in their opinion.

Thus, I consider that there would be no ground on which the court would be entitled *d* to set aside the refusal of leave to appeal to the High Court, even if this court had jurisdiction to take such a step. The question of leave to appeal to this court from the decision of Leggatt J refusing such leave need not be examined at length. Counsel for the charterers rightly accepted that the court can have no jurisdiction to reverse the decision of the judge unless the *Scherer* principle can be applied. For the same reasons as previously stated in relation to the application under s 1(3)(b), I consider that this principle is not *e* germane to the system of arbitration appeals, and in any event I do not read the judge's reasons as demonstrating that he reached his decision by any automatic process. Instead, they seem to me simply to indicate that having been reminded of what was said in *The Antaios*, and taking note of the constraints imposed by the legislature and emphasised by the House on an onward appeal, he thought it proper (possibly against what would otherwise have been his own personal inclination) to bring the dispute to finality. Again, *f* I believe that other judges might have taken a different view, but this is no ground for us to interfere.

NOURSE LJ. I agree. I do not wish to add anything to the judgments which have been delivered by Sir John Donaldson MR and Mustill LJ.

Applications dismissed. Leave to appeal to the House of Lords refused. *g*

Solicitors: *Holman Fenwick & Willan* (for the charterers); *Sinclair Roche & Temperley* (for the owners).

Diana Procter   Barrister.

a
Bank of Baroda v Panessar and others

CHANCERY DIVISION
WALTON J
9, 10, 11, 12, 13, 16 JUNE, 7 JULY 1986

b
Company – Debenture – Demand made under debenture – Money payable on demand – Whether notice demanding repayment required to specify amount due – Whether debtor company entitled to reasonable time to repay amount owing.

On 22 September 1981 two associated companies executed a debenture in favour of a bank in respect of moneys owed. The debenture provided for the repayment 'on demand' of all moneys thereby secured and, in default of compliance, for the bank to be entitled
c
to appoint a receiver. The following day the three shareholders in the companies and their wives executed guarantees to the bank in support of the debenture. In November 1983 the bank decided to act under the debenture and served on the companies a notice stating 'We hereby demand all monies due to us . . .' About an hour later the bank appointed a receiver who took control of the companies. Subsequently the bank brought an action against the shareholders and their wives under the guarantees for the amount
d
outstanding owed by the companies. The shareholders contended, inter alia (i) that the appointment of the receiver was invalid because the demand for repayment did not specify the amount due, and therefore proper notice requiring repayment had not been given, and (ii) that the companies had not been given sufficient time to pay the amount outstanding and in particular had not been given time to arrange finance from an alternative source of which the bank was aware.

e
Held – (1) A notice demanding repayment of moneys secured by a debenture did not have to specify the amount due. The demand made by the bank was accordingly valid (see p 758 j to p 759 c, post); *Bunbury Foods Pty Ltd v National Bank of Australia Ltd* (1984) 51 ALR 609 followed.
(2) If money due under a debenture was payable on demand the debtor company was
f
entitled, once demand was made, to reasonable time to implement the mechanics of payment, eg to deliver a cheque by return or to transfer the necessary funds from one bank account to another, but it was not entitled to any time to raise the money if it was not at hand. On the facts, the companies had had sufficient time to make repayment if the money to do so had been at hand. The bank was accordingly entitled to judgment under the guarantees (see p 759 h to 760 e and p 764 g, post); *Cripps (Pharmaceutical) Ltd v*
g
Wickenden [1973] 2 All ER 606 applied; *Massey v Sladen* (1869) LR 4 Exch 13 considered; *ANZ Banking Group (NZ) Ltd v Gibson* [1981] 2 NZLR 513, *Ronald Elwyn Lister Ltd v Dunlop Canada Ltd* (1982) 135 DLR (3d) 1, *Mister Broadloom Corp* (1968) *Ltd v Bank of Montreal* (1984) 4 DLR (4th) 74 and *Bunbury Foods Pty Ltd v National Bank of Australasia Ltd* (1984) 51 ALR 609 not followed.

h
Notes
For appointment of a receiver, see 7 Halsbury's Laws (4th edn) para 879.

Cases referred to in judgment
ANZ Banking Group (NZ) Ltd v Gibson [1981] 2 NZLR 513, NZ HC.
Bradford Old Bank Ltd v Sutcliffe [1918] 2 KB 833, CA.
j
Brighty v Norton (1862) 3 B & S 305, 122 ER 116.
Bunbury Foods Pty Ltd v National Bank of Australasia Ltd (1984) 51 ALR 609, Aust HC.
Campbell v Commercial Banking Co of Sydney (1879) 40 LT 137, PC.
Clyde Properties Ltd v Tasker [1970] NZLR 754, NZ SC.
Cripps (Pharmaceutical) Ltd v Wickenden, R A Cripps & Sons Ltd v Wickenden [1973] 2 All ER 606, [1973] 1 WLR 994.

de Bussche v Alt (1878) 8 Ch D 286, [1874–80] All ER Rep 1247, CA.
Habib Bank Ltd v Habib Bank AG Zurich [1981] 2 All ER 650, [1981] 1 WLR 1265, CA.
Hawtin & Partners Ltd v Pugh (25 June 1975, unreported), Ch D.
Humphrey v Roberts (1866) 5 SCR (NSW) 376, NSW SC.
Lister (Ronald Elwyn) Ltd v Dunlop Canada Ltd (1982) 135 DLR (3d) 1 Can SC.
Mir Bros Projects Pty Ltd v 1924 Pty Ltd [1980] 2 NSWLR 907, NSW SC.
Massey v Sladen (1868) LR 4 Exch 13.
Mister Broadloom Corp (1968) Ltd v Bank of Montreal (1984) 4 DLR (4th) 74, Ont CA.
Moore v Shelley (1883) 8 App Cas 285, PC.
National Westminster Bank plc v Morgan [1985] 1 All ER 821, [1985] AC 686, [1985] 2
　　WLR 588, HL.
Save (Acoustics) Ltd v Pimms Furnishing Ltd (11 January 1985, unreported), Ch D.
*Taylor Fashions Ltd v Liverpool Victoria Trustees Ltd, Old & Campbell Ltd v Liverpool Victoria
　　Trustees Co Ltd* [1981] 1 All ER 897, [1982] QB 133, [1981] 2 WLR 576.
Toms v Wilson (1863) 4 B & S 442, 122 ER 524.

Cases also cited

Pledge v Buss (1860) 6 Jur NS 695, 70 ER 585.
Tucker v Laing (1856) 12 K & J 745, 69 ER 982.
Wheatley v Bastow, Re Collins (1855) 7 De G M & G 558, 44 ER 218.

Action and counterclaim

By a writ issued on 11 July 1984 the plaintiff, Bank of Baroda, brought an action against
six defendants, Avtar Singh Panessar, Kewal Singh Panessar and Kulwant Singh Panessar
(the husbands) and Karuna Devi Panessar, Balvinder Panessar and Kamaljit Panessar (the
wives), claiming £832,035·18 under two guarantees executed by the defendants on 23
September 1981, together with interest. By a counterclaim served on 18 March 1985 the
defendants claimed against the bank and Surjit Kumar Singla (the receiver appointed by
the bank to manage two companies, Lowcroft Ltd and Glimtone Ltd, in which the
husbands were the shareholders) a declaration that the invalid appointment of the
receiver released them from liability under the guarantees and damages for negligence
in failing to preserve the assets of the companies or to realise them to the best advantage.
The facts are set out in the judgment.

Michael Crystal QC and *John Higham* for the bank.
John Moncaster for the husbands.
Cenydd Howells for the wives.
Peter Cresswell QC and *Gregory Mitchell* for the receiver.

Cur adv vult

7 July. The following judgment was delivered.

WALTON J. Lowcroft Ltd and Glimtone Ltd were two companies both engaged in the
fashion trade, which were owned in roughly equal shares by Mr Avtar Singh Panessar
(the first defendant), Mr Kewal Singh Panessar (the third defendant) and Mr Kulwant
Singh Panessar (the fifth defendant), who I will collectively refer to as 'the husbands'. The
second defendant is the wife of the first defendant, the fourth defendant is the wife of
the third defendant, the sixth defendant is the wife of the fifth defendant. I will
collectively refer to the second, fourth and sixth defendants as 'the wives'.

Lowcroft Ltd and Glimtone Ltd banked with the plaintiffs, Bank of Baroda, at their
Whitechapel branch. On 22 September 1981 those two companies joined together in
giving an all-moneys debenture in respect of the moneys owed by both companies to the
bank. As is usual and common form, the debenture provided for the repayment of all
moneys thereby secured on demand and, in default of compliance with such demand,

the bank became entitled to appoint a receiver thereunder. Nothing turns on the
a execution of that debenture. On the following day, 23 September 1981, a guarantee in
respect of each company to the bank was given on behalf of, on its face, each of the
defendants. The guarantees apparently bear, on each effective page thereof, the signatures
of each of the defendants.

There is a direct conflict of evidence between a certain Mr Mistry, who on the
completed guarantees indorsed each with a statement that each of the signatures was put
b on in his presence, and the defendants. The story of the defendants is to the effect that
the bank required the guarantees to be signed and the husbands took them to the
premises of Lowcroft, where each of them duly signed and, having rung up on the
telephone his wife, obtained her express authority to sign the guarantee in her name,
which he then did, but not (at any rate according to the first defendant), intending
thereby to imitate her own signature.

c The story of Mr Mistry, who was a teller at the bank, was to a very different effect. He
said that the husbands put their signatures to the guarantees in the office of the then
bank manager on the morning of 23 September 1981, and that the fifth defendant, later
on the evening of that day, drove him round first of all to the fifth defendant's house,
where the sixth defendant signed the guarantees in the presence of Mr Mistry. After the
guarantees had been so signed, the fifth defendant drove Mr Mistry to the house of his
d brother, the third defendant, and exactly the same thing happened. Mr Mistry handed
the forms to the third defendant and he asked his wife to sign the forms and she did sign
them in Mr Mistry's presence. And then that was repeated once again in the case of the
second defendant, the wife of the first defendant.

The story of the husbands and their wives being quite different, it becomes necessary,
first of all, to look at the documents themselves to see how they bear out the stories of
e either parties, and then to consider the witnesses themselves. So far as the documents go,
there is one circumstance which tells against Mr Mistry's version of events. Mr Mistry
was quite clear that the dating of the forms took place after the husbands had signed in
the manager's office, and that by the time the wives came to sign that dating was
therefore on the form. There were produced during the course of the trial what were
obviously photostats of the two guarantees in question, bearing the signatures of all six
f guarantors, but without the date being on the form at all, nor indeed the indorsement of
Mr Mistry to the effect that he had witnessed the signatures, although, of course, this is
of no particular significance for this point. Therefore Mr Mistry must be mistaken as to
one point, namely, assuming of course his story to be otherwise right, the time when the
dating of the forms took place.

When one turns to the story of the husbands and their wives, the most obvious and
g crucial fact is that the signature of the third defendant's wife, made by him (according to
his and his wife's story), is in a totally different ink to the signature in which he himself
signed. Now that appears unlikely in the extreme. When asked if he could explain this,
his only reply was to the effect that, oh well, perhaps there was a telephone conversation
before he had finished writing his wife's name, or something of that nature. But it seems
to me that that is hardly a good explanation. However, the point is, taken by itself,
h probably not conclusive. Nor again, by itself, is the fact that the signature of the second
defendant thereon bears a very close relationship to a signature which was undoubtedly
hers. So I now turn to an examination of the witnesses.

Mr Mistry was an extremely good witness. He was, of necessity, severely cross-
examined and remained completely unshaken. It is a very odd story for him to have
made up on behalf of the bank, if he was making up a story, and he certainly gave no
j sign of it when cross-examined.

So far as the husbands were concerned, none of them struck me as being a particularly
good witness. In particular, there is the astonishing case, of which Mr Sherlock Holmes
would doubtless have desired to have been seised, of the invisible brokers' men. So far as
Lowcroft is concerned, which was indeed the main concern of the fifth defendant and
their brother Surjit, there appears to have been a considerable number of brokers' men

taking possession under executions without having been observed by anybody doing so. And, indeed, although only walking possession was taken, presumably forms must have been signed by somebody on behalf of Lowcroft, and yet not one of the husbands would admit to the slightest knowledge of the circumstance that there had been any such executions. In the case of Glimtone it was not a sheriff's execution but a distress levied by a landlord. Here, once again, the third defendant (who was basically the brother concerned with this company) professed complete and utter ignorance of this having taken place at all. I am therefore left in the case of the husbands with this situation, that they are incapable of recollecting accurately what, at the time I am convinced, must have been the most extraordinary series of shocks to them. On that basis, I find it very difficult to believe that they can accurately remember what happened in relation to the signing of the guarantees, which were mere documents required by the bank and which did not, of themselves, have any adverse effect on their business. But even apart from this specific inability to remember matters which must have been of the greatest possible importance to them at the time they happened, the impression made by each one of them in the witness box was not a very happy one at all.

I now turn to the three wives. The first wife (the second defendant) attempted in the witness box a squalid piece of deception on the court, which was so childish as to be almost unbelievable, but was doubtless intended to persuade the court that the signature which appeared on the guarantee and which bore every mark of similarity to an undoubtedly admitted signature of hers on another document witnessed by a solicitor was not hers. Counsel for the wives asked her to give me a specimen of her signature, which she then did and which was passed up to me. But on my pointing out to her that in fact this was a completely different signature to that which was appended to the document to which I have referred, she replied that, oh well, this was the signature which she now used, having used a completely different signature in 1981. That episode only served to confirm the general opinion I had previously formed of her truthfulness.

So far as the fourth defendant was concerned, although she had sworn an affidavit in these proceedings in English, and was examined in English, it turned out that the only grasp of our language to which she would admit was minimal, and finally she retreated to the position where she did not understand anything at all, save to continually repeat that, in fact, she had not signed the document as alleged by Mr Mistry, but had simply given her husband permission to sign her name. Having regard to her refusal to acknowledge that she knew any English (which for all I know may be perfectly accurate) it was quite impossible to form any view as to her reliability. Nor was the matter of the sixth defendant any better. She knew slightly more English, but once again, under cross-examination, did not understand any of the questions put to her. So, all in all, I am afraid this presented, on the part of the defendants, a very unsatisfactory picture. In the circumstances I think that I should be quite safe in accepting the evidence of Mr Mistry in preference to the evidence of any of the defendants. And I would finally point out that in the defence of these defendants, when sued on the guarantee, what was alleged was that the husbands were authorised to sign documents on their wives' behalves in case of urgency, and that the defendants' husbands signed, or had signed, the said guarantees without these defendants being aware of them in any way whatsoever. And the second application by counsel for the wives to amend the defence, made after the case was well under way (and which, of course, I rejected), contained the allegation that, 'None of such Defendants knows who signed such guarantees in her name', whereas the evidence put forward on their behalf was, as we have seen, of an entirely different nature. It seems to me that, if, as alleged by the wives, there were these conversations over the telephone in which they authorised their husbands specifically to sign the guarantees, they could not conceivably, at any stage, have given the instructions which led to the kind of defence to which I have just referred. So that is another straw in the wind which I think indicates clearly that the approach that I have made to this is the correct one. Of course, had the original defence stood, it would have been a complete defence so far as the wives were concerned, because there was no question of urgency in the sense in which I think it was

intended to be understood in that defence, so that they would rightly be able to plead
a that their husbands had no authority to bind them by signing on their behalf. I will not
comment on the reasons which may have led to the wives changing their story
completely, but, having done so, it does not appear to me that at the end of the day it
would make really any difference whether I accepted, as I have done unhesitatingly, Mr
Mistry's evidence, or whether I accepted, on this point, the evidence of the wives and
their husbands, because the wives did in fact give authority, according to each of them,
b to her husband to sign on her behalf. It would, under the circumstances, have been better
had the husbands signed per pro, but in fact they did not. But that is of no materiality
whatsoever. The situation is that the wives are bound by signatures so affixed by their
authority in any event.

Now at the opening of the trial counsel for the wives applied to me twice for leave to
amend the defence so as to plead undue influence. It seems to me that this is not
c something to which I could possibly, at that stage of the case, give effect. The plea of
undue influence would only have been a valid one if counsel for the wives could have
made out that there was undue influence as between the husbands and the wives, and, of
course, above and beyond that, that that undue influence was exercised by the husbands
on behalf of the bank and for the purposes of the bank. At the very least, from the bank's
point of view, that would have meant that they would have had to trace the former
d manager of the bank, because the present manager of the bank was not the person who
was there in 1981, and take a proof from him and possibly other witnesses. Under the
circumstances, to allow such an amendment would have entailed a lengthy adjournment.
The bank was in a position to go ahead and, indeed, the application was only made after
counsel for the bank had commenced his opening. Therefore, it seems to me that any
such application was made far too late. Counsel for the wives did then press on me that
e in all the circumstances of the case the bank owed a duty to the wives of explanation of
what was, undoubtedly, a very serious undertaking by the wives. But it does not seem to
me that this is so in the slightest. There is here no relationship of any description between
the bank and the wives. The wives were not customers of the bank; the bank never at
any stage took it on itself to offer any advice to the wives as to the course that they should
adopt; it never pressed the wives to sign the guarantees, in any way whatsoever. And it
f seems to me that following on the recent case in the House of Lords, *National Westminster
Bank plc v Morgan* [1985] 1 All ER 821, [1985] AC 686, there is no ground for saying that
the bank, in any way whatsoever, owed any duty to the wives. Accordingly, the claim of
the wives, based on equitable considerations, appears to me to fall completely.

But now one must move on to 25 November 1983. What had happened, so far as the
affairs of Lowcroft and Glimtone were concerned, was that, repeatedly, both those
g companies had exceeded overdraft limits set by the bank, and the bank had, and I think,
perhaps here, Mr Almeida, the bank's manager at the bank's Whitechapel branch, may
have had some influence with the bank's head office, overlooked the violations of the
limit, and was, from time to time, content to allow the two companies to operate on
limits in excess of those to which they were entitled.

And so it came about that the head office of the bank finally lost patience with the
h companies and decided to demand its money and appoint a receiver. I do not know
precisely how much the bank at this date knew of the situation of the companies, but
that the companies were technically insolvent is beyond all question. The first defendant,
who was the leading brother in all matters, acknowledged in the witness box that neither
company was in a position to pay its debts as and when they fell due. He, nevertheless,
stoutly maintained that neither company was insolvent; but, by that, what he meant was
j that had the assets of the companies been liquidated, there should have been enough to
pay off the creditors in full and leave a surplus. That, on anything known to me, seems
to be an entire misconception of the position. By this date, Lowcroft was suffering
executions in respect of unpaid judgment debts, and Glimtone had suffered a distress by
the landlord for non-payment of rent, which was not paid out on the distress being
effected.

However, there appears to be some dispute as to the amount of stock which was held by the companies at this particular time. When the receiver of the companies, who was appointed by the bank, brought an action against the husbands in the name of the companies, alleging that large lines of stock had been wrongfully shifted by the husbands to another company of theirs, affidavits were sworn on behalf of the husbands pointing out that, owing to the financial difficulties of Lowcroft and Glimtone, they had not been able to acquire the necessary amount of stock that they should have had there at that time, it being of course in the run-up to Christmas. Now, of course, those answers do not suit them and they seek to deny them and allege that, on the contrary, the shop of each company was bursting with stock. In fact, I do not accept this evidence on their behalf and I believe the original affidavits that they swore, which coincided with the position on the ground, namely that there was not any stock of much materiality in either of the shops.

Mr Almeida, the manager of the Whitechapel branch of the bank, had been told to get in early on 25 November 1983 at 9 am, by Mr Satta of head office, and I have no doubt whatsoever that that is precisely what happened. That is what Mr Almeida says. Mr Almeida was a good and compelling witness and I am prepared to believe him as distinct from believing any of the three defendant husbands, or their fourth brother, Surjit, who was also involved with the affairs of Lowcroft. It so happened that Mr Almeida garaged his car at Lowcroft's premises and from time to time accepted their hospitality to the extent of a cup of coffee in the morning before walking to the bank's Whitechapel branch. On the morning in question he cannot have done so, in spite of evidence to the effect that he did, because he had to be, and was, at the office of the bank at 9 am. Shortly afterwards, Mr Satta dictated forms of demand note, and so on and so forth, over the telephone, and these were duly typed by Mr Almeida's typist. They were very short. They were then signed by Mr Almeida and the two notes were, I am quite satisfied, dispatched. One was taken by Mr Almeida himself, who carried it round to the registered offices and shop of Lowcroft and deposited the same on the counter, where there did not appear to be anyone about, by at the latest 9.45 am. The other demand could not be served quite so easily because the premises (but not the registered office) of Glimtone Ltd, was situate at Mortimer Street, which was some considerable distance from the bank. The messenger was a Mr Trevedi. He left the Whitechapel branch of the bank at approximately 9.30 am, and then took a taxi, which he found in about five minutes, which took him to Glimtone's premises at Mortimer Street, and he thinks he reached it at some time between 10.00 am and 10.15 am. And, once again, what he did was to leave the sealed envelope containing the demand on the counter of the ground floor. A question arises, with which I shall have to deal later, as to the validity of those notices, because they did not mention any fixed sum, but merely demanded repayment of the moneys due under the debenture in general terms and, in the case of Glimtone, because the demand was not left at its registered office.

Meanwhile, the intended receiver, Mr Singla, who had been alerted by the bank's head office that his services might be required, turned up at Mr Almeida's office at the Whitechapel branch where, I believe, shortly after 11 am he was handed by Mr Almeida two notices of appointment, one in respect of each company. Mr Almeida and Mr Singla then went round to the premises of Lowcroft. Mr Singla dispatched one of his staff to the premises of Glimtone.

It was sought to be said by the husbands that the notices demanding repayment did not, in fact, come in the manner I have just described, but were brought in the one case by Mr Singla, and in the other case were brought by Mr Singla's assistant. I am quite positive, having heard the evidence of Mr Singla, that that is completely untrue and that they had had the notices since the times I have already mentioned. Of course, it may very well be, having regard to the completely casual attitude, which we have already noted, which the husbands displayed to notices, even of the most serious type, that, having had the notices, they disregarded them completely and paid no attention to them whatsoever until Mr Singla himself did in fact appear, or, in the case of Glimtone, his *a* assistant appeared, when the gravity of the situation may very well have struck home to them for the first time. There is some dispute as to what happened to a customer who was being served at Lowcroft at the time, but on Mr Singla discovering the notices of execution, whereunder all the stock had been seized by way of walking possession, he decided that it was expedient to close the businesses down, and did, in fact, do so in both cases.

b It is now alleged by the defendants that the appointment of Mr Singla as receiver was not justified under the terms of the debenture, in that, first of all, no proper notice requiring repayment of the moneys thereby secured was given and, second, that no sufficient opportunity was given to the companies to pay off the moneys thereby demanded, before the receiver was in fact appointed. And in fact it is pleaded in the defence of the male defendants, and adopted by the female defendants, that Lowcroft and Glimtone had, as the bank knew, an available alternative source of finance from *c* Trade and Industry Acceptance Corp, and a reasonable time for compliance with the demand for repayment was a time which would have enabled Lowcroft and Glimtone to be refinanced by Trade and Industry Acceptance Corp. There is no conceivable justification in law for the last part of that plea, but so far as the actual factual situation is concerned, on cross-examination of the witness from Trade and Industry Acceptance Corp (produced on behalf of the defendants to prove this very point), he was forced to *d* admit that one of the many things that Trade and Industry Acceptance Corp could not have done was to have paid over money to pay out the bank under its debenture. This is, I am afraid, yet another example, although not a particularly striking one, of the non-correspondence between the ideas of the defendants and what the factual situation at any particular time, indeed, was. And, of course, it is then said that the effect of the bank's purportingly appointing Mr Singla as receiver, had the effect of discharging the liability *e* of the guarantors under the guarantees, or indeed, short of that, that it would give the two companies a good claim against Mr Singla in respect of trespass, which claim could be set-off against the indebtedness of those companies to the bank. Accordingly, I now turn to the questions of law involved.

The demand in each case took the form of a letter directed to the directors of the relevant company and, of course, was dated 25 November 1983, under the hand of the *f* manager of the Whitechapel branch. It reads:

'Dear Sir,
   We hereby demand all monies due to us under the powers contained in the debenture mortgage dated 22nd September 1981.'

g It will be observed that no reference whatsoever is made in that demand to the amount of money actually secured by the debenture which the company was being called on to pay. Counsel for the husbands took the point that the demand should have specified the amount of money due. He pointed out that the bank was in a far better position than either of the companies to know the precise amount of money due and owing to it. And he instanced the fact that cheques might very well have been drawn by the company on *h* its account, but the company would have no means of knowing whether those cheques had, in fact, been presented, nor, if they had been presented, whether they had been honoured or not. On the other side of the coin, it is quite clear that in many such cases, and probably in this particular case, where a considerable slice of international trade was being carried on, certainly by Glimtone, it would be an extremely difficult matter for the bank to know precisely the amount of money due to it. Counsel for the husbands *j* again suggested that this might be cured by making a demand for £x up to the end of business on a particular day, together with all moneys subsequently accrued. This would be a most clumsy and peculiar form of notice, the like of which I must say I have never, in all my experience, seen. It is very curious that there does not appear to be any particular English authority dealing with the point. If there is any, none of the counsel involved in this case have been able to point to it.

However, counsel for the receiver was able to refer me to a persuasive case in the High Court of Australia, *Bunbury Foods Pty Ltd v National Bank of Australasia Ltd* (1984) 51 ALR 609. In that case, under a debenture given by a company to a bank to secure moneys lent, the company undertook—

> 'to pay to the bank on demand all moneys which are now or may from time to time hereafter be owing or remain unpaid to the bank.'

When the bank demanded payment of the loan moneys, it did not, in its notice, specify the amount then owing by the company. It was held by the whole court that that notice was nevertheless valid.

The court reviewed the earlier English authorities, including *Massey v Sladen* (1868) LR 4 Exch 13, where Cleasby B quite clearly thought that in the case of such a stringent clause as that now under discussion, the creditor ought to make a demand which was specific, letting the debtor know what is the sum he insists on the payment of. But the High Court of Australia dealt with that case, and others, as follows (51 ALR 609 at 619–620):

> 'Upon the making of a demand the debtor has a reasonable time to obtain the money. True it is, that in the absence of a specific statement of the debt, he may lack precise knowledge of the amount which he must pay in order to avoid enforcement or realization of the security. On the other hand, to require the creditor in all cases to specify the amount of the debt may operate to impose an onerous burden upon him. Some accounts may be so complex and so constantly changing that it is difficult at any given time to ascertain or to assert the precise amount that is due and payable. Indeed, the ascertainment of the amount may in some instances require the resolution over time of complex issues of fact and law. Yet, in order to preserve the value to the creditor of his security, he may need to call up the debt as a matter or urgency. It is of some materiality to note that it is not essential to the validity of a notice calling up a debt that it correctly states the amount of the debt. Even a notice given to the mortgagor by the mortgagee as a condition precedent of a power of sale is not rendered invalid because it demands payment of more than is due (*Humphrey v Roberts* ((1866) 5 SCR (NSW) 376 at 385–387); *Campbell v Commercial Banking Co of Sydney* ((1879) 40 LT 137 at 140); *Clyde Properties Ltd v Tasker* ([1970] NZLR 754 at 757–758); *Mir Bros Projects Pty Ltd v 1924 Pty Ltd* ([1980] 2 NSWLR 907 at 926)). It may be thought that this provides sufficient reason for insisting that the creditor should specify the amount of the debt in his notice demanding payment for the validity of the notice will not be imperilled by an error in the statement of the amount. However, there is little point in requiring that the notice should state the amount if the correctness of the amount is not essential to the validity of the notice. In this situation insistence on the requirement may result in creditors taking insufficient care in stating the amount of the debt, thereby contributing to confusion on the part of debtors. The foregoing examination supports the view that the interests of the parties will be more adequately protected by the principle that the debtor must be allowed a reasonable opportunity to comply with the demand before the creditor can enforce or realize the security than by the adoption of the suggested proposition that the notice of demand must specify the amount of the debt. In determining whether the debtor has had such an opportunity it will be relevant to take account of the debtor's knowledge, lack of knowledge and means of knowledge of the amount due and of the information which the creditor has provided in that respect, including the response which he has made to any inquiry by the debtor.'

Although, as will be seen shortly, I do not think that the English law as to the period of time available to the debtor is quite as there presented by the High Court of Australia, it appears to me that the reasoning, in relation to the content of the notice of demand, is very persuasive. I cannot see any reason why the creditor should not do precisely what he is, by the terms of his security, entitled to do, that is to say to demand repayment of

all moneys secured by the debenture. As the High Court points out, it would seem stupid
a that the creditor could put in, without imperilling the validity of the notice, an entirely
wrong sum, and that is much more likely to give rise to confusion and difficulty than is
the form of the notice adopted in that and the present case. Indeed, it is quite clear that
knowledge of the precise amount of the sums outstanding is only required in the
exceptional case, because in most cases (as in the present case) the debtor has no real
means whatsoever of paying off the sum which is due, and it would seem to be idle to
b put the creditor to what might be very considerable expense in ascertaining the precise
amount due when there is no likelihood that the sum will represent a realistic target at
which the debtor can aim. If, on the contrary, the debtor is in a position to pay off the
sum demanded and wishes to know the exact and precise sum, he can communicate with
the creditor and ask the creditor what sum he is expecting to be paid. And, under those
circumstances, one imagines that the creditor would say: 'Well, the last accounts, which
c are not complete, show in fact a sum of £x owing from you. If you can pay that sum at
once, then we need not worry too much about the additional sum; we can settle that
later', or something along those lines. At any rate, on this point, I propose to follow the
Australian case, which seems to me to be redolent of good common sense.

The next question which arises is, then, had sufficient time for compliance with that
demand been allowed before the receiver was appointed? I take as my starting point that
d well-known dictum of Blackburn J in *Brighty v Norton* (1862) 3 B & S 305 at 312, 122 ER
116 at 118:

> 'I agree that a debtor who is required to pay money on demand, or at a stated
> time, must have it ready, and is not entitled to further time in order to look for it.'

This extremely strict view of the matter was refined by Lord Cockburn CJ in *Toms v*
e *Wilson* (1863) 4 B & S 442 at 453, 122 ER 524 at 529, where he said:

> 'We are all of the opinion that . . . By the terms of the bill of sale, the plaintiff was
> under an obligation to pay immediately upon demand in writing, and if he did not
> then the defendants were entitled to take possession of and sell the goods. Here such
> a demand was made. The deed must receive a reasonable construction, and it could
> not have meant that the plaintiff was bound to pay the money in the very next
f instance of time after the demand, but that he must have reasonable time to get it
> from some convenient place. For instance, he might require time to get it from his
> desk, or to go across the street, or to his bankers for it.'

That quotation was indorsed by Sir Barnes Peacock in the Privy Council in *Moore v Shelley*
(1883) 8 App Cas 285 at 293. These passages were cited, approved and applied by Goff J
g in *Cripps (Pharmaceutical) Ltd v Wickenden, R A Cripps & Sons Ltd v Wickenden* [1973] 2 All
ER 606, [1973] 1 WLR 944. The interval of time in that case was approximately one
hour, and the judge said that the plaintiffs could not object on the ground that they were
not given time to find the money, or that the interval was too short. I have myself already
followed *Cripps (Pharmaceutical) Ltd v Wickenden* in my judgment in *Hawtin & Partners*
Ltd v Pugh (25 June 1975, unreported). Precisely the same points as are in issue in the
h present case were in issue in that case, and I followed *Cripps (Pharmaceutical) Ltd v*
Wickenden. The summary of the matter as I then saw it, and as I still see it, is as follows:

> 'The third point raises very fundamental issues as to money payable "on demand"
> indeed. I will first of all state my view of the law and then turn to the authorities
> which Mr Hames cited to me to see how they accord with it. Money payable "on
j demand" is repayable immediately on demand being made. Indeed, so much is this
> so that there is no doubt that the periods of time mentioned in the Limitation Act
> 1939 commence running from the date of the demand and not from any later time
> (see *Bradford Old Bank Ltd v Sutcliffe* [1918] 2 KB 833). Nevertheless, it is physically
> impossible in most cases for a person to keep the money required to discharge the
> debt about his person. He may in a simple case keep it in a box under his bed; it

may be at the bank or with a bailee. The debtor is therefore not in default in making the payment demanded unless and until he has had a reasonable opportunity of *a* implementing whatever reasonable mechanics of payment he may need to employ to discharge the debt. Of course, this is limited to the time necessary for the mechanics of payment. It does not extend to any time to raise the money if it is not there to be paid.'

In practice, in 99 cases out of 100, all this is completely academic, because the debtor has not got the money available anyway and the demand is only a step towards some *b* other end, eg bringing an action, appointing a receiver in the case of a company, and so forth. In this case the debtor cannot possibly claim any additional time as, there being no payment that he can make, there can be no pretence that he requires any additional time to implement the mechanics of payment.

English law therefore, in my judgment, has definitely adopted the mechanics of payment test. In order to see why this should be so, one has only to consider the case of a *c* debtor who, perhaps for very legitimate reasons, keeps the money available to pay off his creditor, both he and the creditor being situate in London, in a bank in Scotland. It cannot possibly be the law that the debtor would have the right to the space of time necessary to journey to Scotland and back again before he was in default in complying with a demand for payment. There is no reason why he should not keep the money in Scotland but, if he does, he must then arrange for such mechanics of payment as are, *d* under modern conditions, available for the transfer of the money to his creditor, and, as is well known in these days of telex, fax and other methods of communication and transfer of money, the time required for that is exceptionally short. Therefore, it appears to me that in a case such as the present, where no question as to the authenticity of the actual demand itself, which might require another telephone call, comes into question, the time allowed by the bank to the companies was, in both cases, amply sufficient. *e*

It appears that a slightly different approach has been adopted by a number of Commonwealth authorities. In these, the amount of time to be allowed for the debtor to comply with the demand, has been stated in a number of cases to be a 'reasonable time'. The difficulty inherent in this formulation is that the test of reasonableness is left wholly imprecise: reasonable for doing what? This has never been directly stated in any of these cases, but on the other hand it has been said that what is a reasonable time depends on all *f* the circumstances of the case. In practice there does not seem to have been much difference in the actual application of the two tests, but as a commercial matter (and a debenture is very much a commercial matter), it appears to me that a time limited to the implementation of the mechanics of payment, a short but adequate period, is to be preferred to the test of a 'reasonable time depending on all the circumstances of the case', as this would appear to be wholly imprecise, and the danger of underestimating the *g* period from the creditor's point of view would be considerable. Moreover, it would appear to be wholly unfair to the creditor that the period should depend on all the circumstances of the case, since he may very well not know, and have no means of knowing, all such circumstances. If this test does prove to be the one ultimately adopted, it must surely depend on all such circumstances as are known to the creditor.

Having made this general critique of the Commonwealth cases, I will start a short *h* review thereof by reference to an English case to which some of them refer, and on which counsel for the husbands, indeed, sought to rely (though of course principally on the content of notice point) in the present case. It is *Massey v Sladen* (1869) LR 4 Exch 13. In this case money was payable instantly on demand. However, on the construction of the deed, it was held by Kelly CB (at 17):

j
'. . . if a personal demand could not be made by reason of the plaintiff's absence from his place of business, then that notice should be left or given in such a way that, if reasonable diligence were used, it might without substantial delay come to his knowledge. [But] if he is on the premises he must make some answer to the demand, either offering to pay at once, or, if he were unable to do so, admitting his

inability, in which latter case the defendants would have been entitled to seize at
a once.'

In fact what happened was that a demand was made in the debtor's absence from the
premises and the seisure took place immediately after the demand had been made. It is
hardly surprising that the court held the seisure to have been wrongful.

Now it is perfectly true that Kelly CB also said that what was contemplated was a
demand with a reasonable time for complying with it (at 18), but from his remarks
b already quoted, it is quite clear that this time was only intended by the Chief Baron as
the time required for payment, ie the mechanics of payment test, although not put in so
many words. And it is to be observed that all the other members of the court agreed
with him.

In *ANZ Banking Group (NZ) Ltd v Gibson* [1981] 2 NZLR 513 Holland J in the High
Court undoubtedly adopted the 'reasonable time' test, although *Cripps (Pharmaceutical)*
c *Ltd v Wickenden* was one of the cases cited to him. This resulted in his listing some ten
factors, including, in particular, one of which the creditor would have been ignorant,
namely, that there was no evidence that the demand for payment had actually come to
the attention of any officer of the company. And another of the factors he took into
account was that there was no indication at any stage ever given to the bank that the
demand could or would be met. In the event, he held a time gap of approximately two
d hours sufficient.

There follows *Lister (Ronald Elwyn) v Dunlop Canada Ltd* (1982) 135 DLR (3d) 1 in the
Supreme Court of Canada. In that case, unfortunately, *Cripps (Pharmaceutical) Ltd v*
Wickenden was not cited. The Supreme Court picked up from *Massey v Sladen* the
expression that 'the debtor must be given some notice on which he might reasonably
expect to be able to act' and translated that into 'reasonable notice'. In fact, in that case,
e no time at all was given, whereas it appeared from the evidence that the funds could have
been obtained 'in fairly short order', whatever that might have meant. But, with all
respect to the Supreme Court, it does not appear to have considered the context in which
the observations in *Massey v Sladen* were made.

In *Mister Broadloom Corp (1968) Ltd v Bank of Montreal* (1984) 4 DLR (4th) 74 in the
Ontario Court of Appeal, a case again in which *Cripps (Pharmaceutical) Ltd v Wickenden*
f was not cited, it was held that a debtor who owed money payable on demand was entitled
to a reasonable time to meet a demand. And it was stated by Blair JA that 'what
constitutes a reasonable time is a question of fact to be determined on the facts of every
case' (at 75).

The ratio decidendi of the court was put by him as follows (at 80):

g   '... the question [is] whether the period of 40 to 50 minutes was a reasonable
time to meet an unexpected demand for immediate payment of the large sum of
$1,500,000. Merely to ask the question is to invite the obvious response that it could
not be a reasonable time unless there plainly were no resources available to meet the
debt or unless it were certain that the debtors would abscond with their assets'.

h With that the other members of the court concurred. It is, I think, quite clear that the
Justice of Appeal was not considering anything approaching the 'mechanics of payment'
test, but some other, unspecified test. However, the court was of the opinion that in
pursuance of the test they considered applicable, if 'plainly there were no resources
available to meet the debt' the time would have been sufficient. It seems to me that to
make the length of notice required to be given depend on this circumstance is to create
j confusion, principally because (as I have indicated already) this is a circumstance which,
in many cases, may not be known to the creditor at all. In the event, in the light of *Cripps*
(Pharmaceutical) Ltd v Wickenden it is I think clear that this is not the law of England.

I have already noticed *Bunbury Foods Pty Ltd v National Bank of Australasia Ltd* (1984) 51
ALR 609, again a case in which *Cripps (Pharmaceutical) Ltd v Wickenden* was not cited. I
do not think it adds anything to the discussion.

However, as it appears that under the doctrine of 'reasonable time', almost anything can be taken into consideration, in particular the fact that there were plainly no resources to meet the debt, in the present case, if it were necessary so to hold, I would unhesitatingly come to the conclusion that there plainly were no resources available to meet the debt, and that that had in fact, whether or not known to the bank, been very plain indeed for some considerable time. Accordingly, even if the 'reasonable time' did apply, the end result would, in this particular case, be no different.

As I have already indicated, counsel for the husbands took the point that the notice served on Glimtone was not properly served since the service did not take place at its registered office, but at its principal, indeed its only, place of business. The provisions of the debenture of 22 September 1981, in relation to service of notices thereunder, are contained in cl 10 thereof and read as follows:

'A demand or notice hereunder shall be made in writing signed by an officer of the bank and may be served on the mortgagors or either of them either personally or by telex. A demand or notice by the post may be addressed to a mortgagor at its address or place of business last known to the bank or to its registered office and a demand or notice so addressed and posted shall be effective notwithstanding that it be returned undelivered.'

From this it is apparent that service of notices was contemplated as being made (i) either personally or by post and (ii) either at its place of business last known to the bank, or at its registered office. I agree that the clause does not, in terms, deal with the combination of (i) personal service and (ii) this being effected at its place of business, but since no such special provision as is included in the last sentence of cl 10 will be required in this case, the absence of any such special reference is quite unremarkable. The debenture is a commercial document intended to have commercial validity. I cannot imagine a better place at which to serve a notice intended to reach those in control of the company's affairs than at its one and only place of business, being the sole address for the company given on its notepaper. Accordingly, I do not think that there is anything in this point.

I now turn to an entirely different matter which, in view of the foregoing, does not arise, but which, in case this matter were to go to a higher court, might well arise. It is simply this, that if I had come to the conclusion that Mr Singla had not been validly appointed as receiver of either of the two companies, I would have come to the conclusion that this was a matter of which neither company could complain, being estopped from so doing.

If Mr Singla was not validly appointed, then it followed that from 25 November 1983 until July 1984, when he completed his receivership, Mr Singla was consistently infringing the rights of both companies. It is, perhaps, worth recording the fact that when he announced his presence, or his appointment was announced by his employee, nobody on the defendants' behalf said, and this would really have been the only effective objection that could have been made, 'The bank has not allowed us enough time to collect the money to pay it before making your appointment.' As we know, such an objection could not have been properly made.

But it is not, of course, the mere absence of objection which has created an estoppel. Thus, as early as the same day as he was appointed the first defendant wrote to Mr Singla giving him notice that 'we will obtain you whatever open market offer you get on the lease of' 46 Mortimer Street (Glimtone's premises) and stating that, if he ignored the offer, he would be held responsible for the consequences. On 30 November 1983 the first defendant wrote again to the receiver stating that he had requested several people to contact him regarding the sale of the leases of 8–10 Whitechurch Lane, the property of Lowcroft. The first defendant caused his solicitors to write to the receiver on 14 December 1983, seeking his assistance, as such, in relation to a claim against a third party. In December 1983 the receiver caused Lowcroft and Glimtone to commence proceedings against the husbands and another of their companies. No objection was ever taken to the effect that this action was incompetent.

a   Again, on 12 January 1984, the receiver and the first defendant met and entered into a conditional agreement for the purchase by the defendants of the stock and premises of both companies. The first defendant again caused his solicitors to write on 18 January 1984 confirming the broad principles of those proposals, and he again himself wrote on 24 January 1984 stating that he was going to reconsider his offer. And so on, right down to the issue of the writ in the present action, by which time, for practical purposes, the receivership had been fully completed. The defendant companies were, by the brother

b   who throughout was the leading member of the family, dealing with the receiver on the footing that he was validly appointed. It seems to me that, under these circumstances, there can be no real doubt but that the companies are themselves estopped from denying that, indeed, the receiver was validly appointed. The principle of estoppel applicable can be taken from *Habib Bank Ltd v Habib Bank AG Zurich* [1981] 2 All ER 650 at 666, [1981] 1 WLR 1265 at 1285, where Oliver LJ applied the test which he had previously himself

c   formulated in *Taylor Fashions Ltd v Liverpool Victoria Trustees Ltd* [1981] 1 All ER 897 at 915, [1982] QB 133 at 151–152 in these terms:

> '... whether ... it would be unconscionable for a party to be permitted to deny that which, knowingly or unknowingly, he has allowed or encouraged another to assume to his detriment ...'

d   Basing himself on the same line of reasoning, Mr Andrew Morritt QC, sitting as a deputy judge of the High Court in *Save (Acoustics) Ltd v Pimms Furnishing Ltd* (11 January 1985, unreported) came, under similar circumstances, to precisely the same conclusion. If it were necessary to reach this conclusion, I would also come unhesitatingly to the conclusion that the estoppel would separately lie in favour of the bank. True it is, of course, that the appointment of the receiver by the bank, as distinct from the individual

e   actions of the receiver in disposing of the assets of the company, each one of them, if his appointment was invalid, being a separate trespass, took place once and for all when the appointment was made. Therefore, bearing in mind the distinction drawn by the Court of Appeal in *de Bussche v Alt* (1878) 8 Ch D 286 at 314, [1874–80] All ER Rep 1247 at 1253 between acquiescence during the commission of the infringement of a legal right and acquiescence thereafter, it might be said that there was no possibility of the bank

f   being able to take advantage of an estoppel. But the crucial point here is that, although that is undoubtedly true, the bank could have mitigated the consequences of the action which it had taken if at any time it had been brought home to it that that action had been invalid. At no time would there have been the slightest difficulty in the bank serving a valid notice under the debenture, giving the companies sufficient time to pay, and then reappointing Mr Singla or some other receiver. Accordingly, it appears to me

g   that, if necessary, the bank would have its own right of estoppel to assert. But the situation being that the companies are not able, under any circumstances, to complain of the appointment, then I do not think that anybody who has guaranteed the liabilities of the company to the bank is in a position to assert the invalidity of the appointment which the companies themselves cannot. It was indeed suggested by counsel for the wives that the effect of an invalid appointment of a receiver by the bank would, under the normal

h   rules relating to guarantees, vitiate them on the principle that the relationship between the parties would thereby have been disturbed. The most attractive way in which he put his submission was that the appointment of the receiver effected a loss of the securities held by the creditor (the bank) so that on paying the sums due under their guarantee, the guarantors would not be entitled to all the securities which originally were held by the creditor. But I think that this misses the point completely. It misses it for the reason that

j   the guarantors on payment off, in the kind of situation with which we are dealing, are quite clearly not entitled to any securities which have been properly realised by the creditor. But, above and beyond that, there being, of course, in the case imagined no proper disposal, what the security of the creditor is, is the totality of the assets of the company under its debenture, whatever those assets may be, and those assets are continually changing. If a trespasser comes in and destroys assets, then the assets of the

company change. The assets change because instead of having the physical assets which
have been so destroyed, it now has a claim against the trespasser. But the mere fact that   *a*
the nature of the assets has been changed in this way discharges nothing. And the
situation therefore is that if Mr Singla had been a trespasser, the assets of the company
would have been rather different from those which were there when he commenced his
operations, but nevertheless they would be the assets over which the bank had a charge;
and so, to the extent that they were not properly realised, they would have to be handed
over to the guarantors in due course.   *b*

One of the points that counsel for the wives sought to make was to treat Mr Singla as
an invalidly appointed receiver as being the agent of the bank by whom he was appointed.
This seems to me not to be the case at all. The proposition can be put in this way: can an
invalid exercise of a power to appoint X as the agent of Y have the effect of making X the
agent of the appointor? And I can see no conceivable reason why it should do so. The
person making the appointment is definitely not appointing an agent of his own, he is   *c*
giving no authority to the receiver to bind him in any way whatsoever. It is perfectly
true, of course, that there are cases to this effect, that if, having made the appointment as
agent of the company, the debenture holder then controls the receiver and what the
receiver does, it may be concluded that in fact the receiver is his agent. But nothing of
the kind has been suggested in the present case. Mr Singla went his own sweet way,
conducting the affairs of the companies as he thought best, but in purported status as   *d*
agent of the companies. And I see nothing at all which would render the bank liable for
any acts of Mr Singla as receiver if he was invalidly appointed. I think that this view of
the law coincides with the view taken by Parliament under the Insolvency Act 1985,
because s 47 thereof provides:

> 'Where the appointment of a person as the receiver or manager of a company's
> property under powers contained in an instrument is discovered to be invalid . . .   *e*
> the court may order the person by whom or on whose behalf the appointment was
> made to indemnify the person appointed against any liability which arises solely by
> reason of the invalidity of the appointment.'

If, in fact, the person so appointed was the agent of the appointor anyway, then it must
follow, as night follows day, that, as such agent, he would in any event be entitled to an   *f*
indemnity from his principal. And a section which provides that a court may, but is not
bound to, order such an indemnity is totally contrary to that view of the law.

Having now dealt with all the points of principle which arise, I can deal with the
action and counterclaim very simply. The claim in the action by the bank is for payment
by the defendants of the sums due to it under the two guarantees, together with interest,
and it is entitled to judgment in respect thereof accordingly. There is a counterclaim by   *g*
the husbands against the bank and Mr Singla. The counterclaim against the bank was
expressed to be if Mr Singla's appointment as receiver was invalid. It therefore falls to be
dismissed, but remains on foot to the extent that it has not been abandoned, and if a
higher court were to take a different view as to the validity of Mr Singla's appointment,
then it would be open to these defendants to press their claim that the bank owed these
defendants, as guarantors, a duty of care to preserve and realise to the best advantage, the   *h*
bank's security for the liabilities guaranteed, which they would then argue had failed as
a result of making such appointment, or purported appointment, to do. So far as Mr
Singla himself is concerned, the counterclaim against him for wrongful administration
of the assets of the companies whilst acting as receiver has been abandoned.

The wives simply counterclaimed a declaration that the invalid appointment of Mr
Singla, as receiver, released them from liability under the two guarantees. Having regard   *j*
to the fact that his appointment was valid, the counterclaim does not arise; but equally,
in my judgment, had it not been, no different result would have followed. This
counterclaim therefore stands dismissed.

Judgment for the bank. Counterclaim dismissed.

The court then heard argument on costs.

a

WALTON J. I now have to deal with the costs of the case and, first of all, there is the question of the bank's costs as against the guarantors. Now, this is, so far as I am aware, a new point. I certainly have never met it before myself. But the terms of the guarantee are that—

b
> 'the guarantors will pay you ['you' being the bank] on demand [among other things] all costs charges and expenses which you may incur in enforcing or obtaining payment of the sums of money due to you from his principal, either alone or in conjunction, as aforesaid, or attempting so to do.'

Now, junior counsel for the bank submits to me that those words mean exactly what they say, and all costs which the bank might incur in enforcing or obtaining payment of
c the sums of money due to it from the defendants in the case are covered by those words. Certainly, it is difficult to see what they refer to, if they do not refer to costs on an indemnity basis, all costs which you may incur in enforcing payment or obtaining payment; and that, most naturally, applies to litigation. Indeed, I do not know of any other way, certainly on the facts of the present case, in which the bank might have enforced or obtained payment of the sums of money otherwise than by litigation.
d Counsel for the husbands took the point that, in fact if that was right, that ousted the discretion which normally resides in the court, as to whether to grant costs on an indemnity or standard basis, and he said that very much clearer words were required to do that than we have here, even if it could be done.

Well, treating this as an entirely novel point, it seems to me that it is not possible for a person in the position of the bank to exclude the discretion of the court, but one
e nevertheless starts from the position that the contractual position between the parties is that the costs will be paid on an indemnity basis. I cannot think that the words 'all costs' mean anything other than that.

So one starts from the position that that is the contractual position but not (as I venture to think) binding on the court. The court might very well take the view that, in the circumstances of any particular case, that was a contractual provision which it ought to
f overlook and it ought not to give effect to. However, when one comes to consider whether this is such a case, I think the circumstances are all one way. Counsel for the bank has pointed out to me that, in this case, the defences of the defendants raise the point that guarantees, the guarantees on which the bank sued, were not signed properly by all parties, that no demand for payment was ever made and also that alternative finance was available. And, really, those were persisted in to an extent which was totally
g and utterly unreasonable.

The one which was persisted in most unreasonably was the question of alternative financing. In order to meet that point, the bank had to trace (as they did) and find a witness, Mr Gonzales, from the supposed financiers, Trade and Industry Acceptance Corp, who in fact attended at the court and gave evidence to the fact that this was a lot of poppycock and there was no question of Trade and Industry Acceptance Corp being
h prepared to bale out the bank in this way; and the defendants were not deterred by that in the slightest. They called a witness who, at the conclusion of his cross-examination (and one can see why it was at the conclusion), had to admit that the one thing Trade and Industry Acceptance Corp could not do, or, rather, one of the many things Trade and Industry Acceptance Corp could not do, was to bale out the bank.

Now, under those circumstances it appears to me that this is very far from being an
j ordinary case. This is a case where large parts of the defence have been totally unrealistic from the start. I cannot imagine that, if Mr Gonzales had been asked the right question, as he should have been, when the first statement from him was taken, he would not have given as honest an answer to it as he did when he was asked the question finally in the witness box, and that would have saved quite a considerable amount of time in itself.

We have had all the palaver about the signature of the guarantees, that again required an enormous amount of evidence, whereas the final version (and it was only the final version) put forward on behalf of the wives would have led to precisely exactly the same situation, without the necessity of a large attendance of witnesses.

So far as the demands not being served, I do not think for one moment that the husbands were being dishonest: They were simply incapable of realising what was really going on in the business. Anybody who can overlook distress by a landlord and executions levied on behalf of judgment creditors must be living in cloud-cuckoo-land, and I do not think that anybody who is living in cloud-cuckoo-land is entitled to increase the length of the trial by an exploration of that somewhat mythical country and then claim that the court should not give full effect to a clear provision in the guarantee itself.

Therefore, so far as the bank is concerned, I have no hesitation whatsoever at the end of the day in saying that I think, basing myself first on the exact terms of the guarantee, but also (if it were necessary) on the way in which the action has been conducted on behalf of the defendants, and I must make it perfectly clear that I am not making the slightest criticism of counsel, but the way the matter has been conducted on behalf of the defendants makes it just and proper that this is a case where the award of costs should be on an indemnity basis.

Now, the other matter relates to the claim against the receiver. This is a claim in negligence against Mr Singla. It is a very serious claim indeed, with which a professional man is faced. That has ultimately been abandoned. Now, if it had been abandoned at the beginning of the case, and I can see no reason why it should not have been because there was, in fact, no shadow of a suggestion (so far as I could see) that Mr Singla had done anything in the slightest wrong, assuming his appointment was valid, if that had been abandoned at that stage, then, although I think it would have been very rough on Mr Singla to have had to prepare for an attack of this nature, requiring, as it must do in all cases where a professional man's competence is in question, the most meticulous preparation, I think the proper order would have been merely an order for costs on the standard basis. But it was not. It was kept hanging over his head right until the last moment, and was kept hanging over his head without the slightest, faintest, justification for it that I can see and, under those circumstances, and here purely as a matter of discretion, I think that the receiver also should have his costs on an indemnity basis.

Now, it was pointed out to me this morning, for the first time, that the wives have been legally aided since 6 June 1986; therefore I am afraid the order for costs against them has, very unfortunately, to be split into two parts: one down to the end of 5 June 1986, on the same basis as applicable to the husbands, but as from 6 June 1986, again an order for costs on the same basis, but such costs not to be enforced without an order of this court.

Bank and receiver awarded costs on indemnity basis.

Solicitors: *Isadore Goldman & Son* (for the bank); *Thompson & Co* (for the husbands); *David Goble & Co* (for the wives); *Barlow Lyde & Gilbert* (for the receiver).

Hazel Hartman   Barrister.

a
Netherlands Insurance Co Est 1845 Ltd v Karl Ljungberg & Co AB
The Mammoth Pine

PRIVY COUNCIL

b LORD BRIDGE OF HARWICH, LORD BRIGHTMAN, LORD GRIFFITHS, LORD OLIVER OF AYLMERTON AND LORD GOFF OF CHIEVELEY

5 MARCH, 23 APRIL 1986

Marine insurance – Measure of indemnity – Bailee clause – Expenses incurred by assured in bringing action against carriers to preserve time-bar – Clause providing that assured under duty *c* *to ensure that all rights against carriers were properly preserved and exercised – No express provision in contract entitling assured to recover expenses of preserving rights against carriers – Whether term could be implied – Whether expenses recoverable from insurers – Institute Cargo Clauses (All Risks) 1 January 1963 edn, cl 9.*

The respondents were the consignees of goods which were insured with the appellants
d under a policy of marine insurance for a voyage from Singapore to Denmark. The policy (i) contained a sue and labour clause empowering the respondents to bring an action to safeguard and recover the goods if there was any loss and entitling them to be reimbursed by the appellants for their expenses in doing so, and (ii) incorporated cl 9 of the Institute Cargo Clauses (All Risks) 1 January 1963 edition which imposed on the respondents a duty to take reasonable measures to avert or minimise a loss and to ensure that all rights against the carriers, bailees or other third parties were properly preserved and exercised.
e On arrival in Denmark part of the cargo was found to be missing or damaged and the respondents claimed against the appellants under the policy. The appellants denied liability and in addition asserted that the respondents were bound by cl 9 to preserve any claim against the carriers before it was time-barred. The respondents instituted proceedings both in Japan against the carriers to preserve the claim and in Singapore
f against the appellants claiming losses under the policy. In the Singapore proceedings the respondents obtained judgment against the appellants for part of their claim and compromised the remainder and then claimed from the appellants the costs incurred in commencing proceedings against the carriers in Japan. The appellants denied liability for those costs, contending that cl 9 imposed on the respondents an obligation to preserve, at their own expense, the claim against the carriers for the benefit of the appellants. The
g judge dismissed the respondents' claim and they appealed to the Court of Appeal of Singapore, which allowed their appeal, holding that since the appellants had required the respondents to institute the proceedings against the carriers in Japan they were bound to indemnify the respondents against the expenses incurred to the extent that the appellants had thereby benefited. The appellants appealed to the Privy Council.

h **Held** – (1) Clause 9 of the policy did not, either expressly or impliedly, restrict the obligation of the assured to preserve rights against the carriers to cases where the insurers had requested the assured to do so, and therefore the fact that the respondents had commenced proceedings in Japan against the carrier at the appellants' unequivocal insistence did of itself give rise to any duty by the appellants to indemnify the respondents, since the appellants were merely requesting, as they were justified in doing, that the
j respondents perform their duty under the contract (see p 770 c to f, post).

(2) However, in order to give business efficacy to the contract, a term was to be implied entitling the respondents to recover from the appellants the costs incurred under cl 9 in ensuring that all rights against the carriers were properly preserved, because (a) cl 9 was to be construed in the context of the contract as a whole, (b) the obligation imposed on the respondents was for the appellants' benefit and (c) since the obligation

could require the respondents not merely to commence proceedings but to pursue them, the appellants would have a positive incentive to delay a settlement if they were not *a* liable to reimburse the respondents' costs. The appeal would therefore be dismissed (see p 770 *g* to p 771 *c f* to *j*, post).

Notes
For the assured's duties under a sue and labour clause, see 25 Halsbury's Laws (4th edn) para 264.   *b*

Cases referred to in judgment
Barnett (Arthur) Ltd v National Insurance Co of New Zealand Ltd [1965] NZLR 874, NZ CA.
Duus Brown & Co v Binning (1906) 11 Com Cas 190.

Appeal   *c*
Netherlands Insurance Co Est 1845 Ltd appealed, pursuant to leave granted by the Court of Appeal of the Republic of Singapore (Wee Chong Jin CJ, Kulasekaram and Rajah JJ) on 18 April 1983, against the decision of that court (Kulasekaram, Chua and Rajah JJ) on 26 November 1982 allowing an appeal by the respondents, Karl Ljunberg & Co AB, the consignees of goods insured with the appellants under a policy of marine insurance, from the order of Wee Chong Jin CJ in the High Court in chambers dated 12 February 1982 *d* whereby he dismissed the respondents' application for an order that the appellants indemnify them in respect of the legal costs of two actions brought by the respondents in Japan against (1) Sanko Steamship Co Ltd, the owners of the vessel Mammoth Pine, and (2) Mammoth Bulk Carriers Ltd, the charterers of the vessel, being the carriers of goods which on discharge were found to be missing or damaged. The facts are set out in the judgment of the Board.   *e*

Anthony Clarke QC and Niru K Pillai (of the Singapore Bar) for the appellants.
Simon Tuckey QC and John Rowland for the respondents.

23 April. The following judgment of the Board was delivered.
                                                                                       f
LORD GOFF OF CHIEVELEY. There is before their Lordships an appeal from a judgment of the Court of Appeal of the Republic of Singapore. The subject of the appeal is a claim by the respondents, Karl Ljungberg & Co AB, against the appellants, Netherlands Insurance Co Est 1845 Ltd, under a policy of marine insurance. Under that policy, a consignment of plywood was insured by the appellants for a voyage from Singapore to Esbjerg in Denmark. The policy incorporated the Institute Cargo Clauses (All Risks) in the edition dated 1 January 1963. On discharge of the goods at Esbjerg, *g* some were found to be missing and others to be damaged. The respondents, as consignees of the goods and assignees of the policy, claimed against the appellants in respect of both the shortage and the damage, but the appellants denied liability.

The goods had been discharged at Esbjerg in March 1980. Any claim against the carriers would become time-barred in March 1981. The respondents' claim against the *h* appellants under the policy was made in January 1981, and liability was denied by them shortly afterwards. If the claim against the carriers was to be preserved, it was plain that proceedings must be commenced against them without delay. Following correspondence between the parties, in the course of which the appellants through their solicitors asserted that the respondents were bound by the terms of the bailee clause in the policy (the terms of which their Lordships will set out in a moment) to preserve the claim against the *j* carriers, the respondents commenced proceedings against the carriers in Japan in order to preserve the time-bar.

The respondents also commenced proceedings in Singapore against the appellants, claiming their losses under the policy. They obtained summary judgment in respect of the short delivery. Thereafter their claim in respect of the cargo damage was compromised. But there remained outstanding the question of the costs incurred by the *a* respondents in commencing proceedings against the carriers in Japan. For these, the respondents claimed that the appellants were responsible; the appellants denied liability, asserting that the bailee clause in the policy imposed on the respondents the obligation to preserve the claim against the carriers for the benefit of the appellants but at the respondents' expense. The matter came before Wee Chong Jin CJ, who dismissed the respondents' claim for these expenses, but without giving any reasons. The respondents then appealed to the Court of Appeal (Kulasekaram, Chua and Rajah JJA), which allowed

b the appeal, on the ground that, in the correspondence which had passed between the parties, the appellants had required the respondents to commence the proceedings against the carriers and that, on that basis, the appellants were bound to indemnify the respondents against the expense incurred by them, to the extent that the appellants had thereby benefited, i e in the proportion that the appellants had been held, or had agreed, to be liable to the respondents for the insured loss. From that decision the appellants now

c appeal, with the leave of the Court of Appeal.

It is at this stage desirable to set out the relevant provisions of the policy. The policy incorporates the hallowed wording of Lloyd's standard form, including the sue and labour clause which is in the following terms:

d '. . . and in case of any Loss or Misfortune, it shall be lawful to the Assured, their Factors, Servants and Assigns, to sue, labour and travel for, in and about the Defence, Safeguard and Recovery of the said Goods and Merchandises or any Part thereof without Prejudice to this Assurance and to be reimbursed the Charges whereof by the Assurers.'

The policy is expressed to be subject to certain clauses, including the Institute Cargo Clauses (All Risks). As already stated the relevant Institute clauses are in the edition dated

e 1 January 1963, and these include cl 9 (the bailee clause), which is in the following terms:

'It is the duty of the Assured and their Agents, in all cases, to take such measures as may be reasonable for the purpose of averting or minimising a loss and to ensure that all rights against carriers, bailees or other third parties are properly preserved and exercised.'

f It is right to record that there is, on the face of the policy, under the heading 'IMPORTANT PROCEDURE IN THE EVENT OF LOSS OR DAMAGE FOR WHICH ASSURERS MAY BE LIABLE', a series of provisions which include one in terms identical to the bailee clause in the Institute clauses.

The appeal before their Lordships raises two separate issues. The first is whether, as the

g Court of Appeal held, the expense of starting the proceedings in Japan was incurred by the respondents at the request of the appellants, thereby imposing on the appellants a duty to indemnify the respondents. The second is whether, if that conclusion cannot be accepted, it is implicit in the terms of the policy that the appellants are bound to indemnify the respondents against their expenditure.

Their Lordships have found themselves unable to agree with the reasoning of the

h Court of Appeal; but, since they accept the argument of the respondents on the second issue, they trust that it will not be thought discourteous to the Court of Appeal if they deal with the first issue comparatively briefly.

The matter was referred to by the respondents' solicitors in a letter to the appellants' solicitors dated 15 January 1981, in which they asserted that the duty on the respondents under the policy to preserve claims by the commencement of proceedings against the

j carriers only arose when, on payment of the claim, the appellants became subrogated to the respondents' rights against the carriers. In reply on 16 January, the appellants' solicitors stated that the respondents' duty under the policy to preserve their rights was in no way affected by the appellants' decision to admit or deny liability under the policy. Further correspondence followed in which the parties' solicitors reiterated their clients' positions, culminating in a letter from the appellants' solicitors dated 28 January 1981 which contained the following passage (on which the respondents particularly rely):

'Our clients put your clients to notice that should your clients not preserve our clients' rights and interests in any event, on an entirely "without prejudice" basis, this would be an additional ground for our clients to deny liability under the policy.'

This correspondence of course took place with reference to the bailee clause. The Court of Appeal expressed the opinion that—

'the clause does not place any obligation on the insured to take proceedings against third parties unless the insurer has called upon the insured to perform its obligation thereunder.'

They then concluded that—

'upon a reading of the correspondence which had passed between [the parties] the proper inference to be drawn was that the [appellants] had required the [respondents] to commence the actions against the third parties.'

The respondents did not seek to support that reasoning before their Lordships; and, with all respect to the Court of Appeal, their Lordships consider that the respondents were right to adopt that course. The clause did not in terms restrict the obligation of the assured to preserve rights to cases where the insurers had requested the assured to do so; and there is no basis on which any such term can be implied. The respondents, however, founding their argument in particular on the passage in the appellants' solicitors' letter dated 28 January 1981 quoted above, submitted that the appellants' insistence that the respondents preserve the appellants' rights and interests 'in any event', coupled with the threat to deny liability if such rights were not preserved and, in particular, their insistence that the respondents were under a duty to preserve rights against the carriers, was a clear and unequivocal direction to the respondents to commence proceedings in Japan before the right of action was lost by expiry of time, which would give rise to a duty on the appellants to indemnify the respondents against the costs incurred by them in consequence of such direction. This submission their Lordships are unable to accept. The position was that the appellants were simply asserting that the respondents were under an obligation, under the bailee clause, to preserve their rights as against the carriers. They were justified in so doing; and a request by them to the respondents to perform their duty under the relevant contract could not give rise to any duty to indemnify the respondents, unless the contract expressly or impliedly imposed such a duty on them.

Their Lordships therefore turn to the second issue on the appeal, which, in their opinion, is the crucial issue in the case. Before their Lordships, the appellants submitted first that, under the bailee clause, the respondents were under a duty to commence the Japanese proceedings in order to ensure that all rights against the carriers were properly preserved, and further that, under the clause, there was no express obligation on the appellants to indemnify the respondents against any expenditure thereby incurred. With those submissions, their Lordships agree. The crucial question is whether any term should be implied in the policy. As to that, the appellants submitted that such a term could only be implied if business efficacy required it, and that their Lordships should not yield to the temptation to imply such a term merely because they thought it reasonable to do so. Again, their Lordships accept the submission. They turn therefore to the question whether a term should be implied to give efficacy to the contract.

In considering that question, their Lordships do not think it right to consider the words 'to ensure that all rights against carriers, bailees or other third parties are properly preserved and exercised' in isolation. It is first of all desirable to have regard to their setting in the contract of insurance. In this connection, it is to be remembered that, in the event of the insurers paying a claim of an assured for cargo damage under the policy, they would become subrogated to the rights of the assured against the carriers in respect of the relevant damage. If the insurers then wished to enforce such rights against the carriers in legal proceedings, they would be entitled to do so and, although in England they must proceed in the name of the assured, they can do so as dominus litis though only on the basis that they indemnify the assured against costs. From this it follows that,

on the appellants' submission before the Board, the assured would be responsible for the
a costs of litigation commenced under the bailee clause up till the time of payment of the
claim by the insurers, but thereafter the cost of litigation would fall on the insurers. This
is in itself a somewhat surprising result; and it is not be forgotten that, under the bailee
clause, the obligation on the assured is not merely to commence proceedings but to
ensure that all the specified rights are 'properly preserved and exercised'. Costs may,
therefore, be incurred by the assured, in performing their obligations under the clause,
b not merely in commencing litigation to preserve a time-bar but in pursuing litigation so
commenced in order to prevent it from lapsing or being otherwise prejudiced by delay;
and it is notorious that such costs can, in certain jurisdictions, be by no means
insignificant. On the appellants' approach, therefore, it follows that the insurers might
have a positive incentive to delay a settlement, thus throwing a greater burden of costs
on the assured; and this would be by virtue of an obligation imposed under the policy
c which requires the assured to take a course of action which is plainly intended to be for
the benefit of the insurers.

The appellants' argument has also to be considered in relation to the fact that the policy
contains a sue and labour clause under which it shall be lawful to the assured—

'to sue labour and travel for, in and about the Defence, Safeguard and Recovery
of the said Goods . . . and to be reimbursed the Charges whereof by the Assurers.'
d
It can of course be said, as indeed it was said on behalf of the appellants, that the fact that
the sue and labour clause makes express provision for reimbursement of the assured by
the insurers, whereas the bailee clause does not do so, militates against the implication of
a term in the bailee clause to the same effect. But it is not to be forgotten that a marine
insurance policy consists of a number of provisions, some of which (often the most
e important) are provisions contained in one or more documents which are incorporated
by reference; and their Lordships doubt if the terms of the sue and labour clause in the
standard form have much impact on the construction of the bailee clause included in the
Institute Cargo Clauses. They consider it to be of more significance that the bailee clause
itself commences by imposing an obligation on the assured 'to take such means as may
be reasonable for the purpose of averting or minimising a loss' without expressly stating
f whether costs so incurred by the assured shall be reimbursed by the insurers; and yet it
was accepted in the course of argument that the assurers must be under a duty to make
such reimbursement. The conjunction of the two obligations in the bailee clause, one of
which admittedly carries a duty of reimbursement by the insurers, reinforces the
respondents' argument that an implied duty of reimbursement applies to both obligations
under the clause.

g The respondents placed in the forefront of their submissions the proposition that the
obligation on the assured under the bailee clause properly to preserve and exercise all
rights against carriers was an obligation imposed on them for the benefit of the insurers.
Their Lordships do not feel able to accept that, as a general proposition, the mere fact
that an obligation is imposed on one party to a contract for the benefit of the other carries
with it an implied term that the latter shall reimburse the former for his costs incurred
h in performance of the obligation. But the fact that, in the present case, the relevant
obligation is indeed for the benefit of the insurers is, their Lordships consider, a material
factor which may be taken into account; and when that factor is considered together
with all the other factors which their Lordships have set out, they consider that a term
must be implied in the contract, in order to give business efficacy to it, that expenses
incurred by an assured in performing his obligations under the second limb of the bailee
j clause (in the form now under consideration) shall be recoverable by him from the
insurers in so far as they relate to the preservation or exercise of rights in respect of loss
or damage for which the insurers are liable under the policy.

In conclusion, their Lordships wish to refer to certain matters which were drawn to
their attention in the course of argument.

First, they were referred by counsel for the appellants to *Arnould on Marine Insurance*
(16th edn, 1981) para 1320, n 28, in which the editors expressed the opinion that the

bailee clause, in the form now under consideration, cannot be construed as entitling the assured to recover from the insurers the costs of proceedings against third parties. As *a* against that, however, the editors of *MacGillivray and Parkington on Insurance Law* (7th edn, 1981) para 1185 suggest that it is arguable that such costs are recoverable. For the reasons they have given their Lordships prefer the more tentative opinion expressed in the latter work.

Second, attention was drawn to the fact that, in earlier and later editions of the Institute Cargo Clauses, express provision was made for the recovery of such costs; and it was *b* submitted for the appellants that this pointed to the conclusion that the omission of such an express right of recovery from the bailee clause in the edition of 1 January 1963 must be read as intended deliberately to deprive the assured of his right to costs. However, even on the assumption that their Lordships are entitled to look at an earlier edition of the clauses for the purpose of construction of a later edition, the form which the clause took in the earlier edition is too different to provide any helpful guidance to the *c* construction of the clause in its later form.

Finally, their Lordships were properly referred to a number of authorities, in particular to *Duus Brown & Co v Binning* (1906) 11 Com Cas 190 and decision of the Court of Appeal of New Zealand in *Arthur Barnett Ltd v National Insurance Co of New Zealand Ltd* [1965] NZLR 874; but, on examination, neither of these authorities proved to be sufficiently in point to be of assistance in the construction of the bailee clause which it fell to their *d* Lordships to consider in the present case.

For the reasons they have given, their Lordships dismiss the appeal with costs.

Appeal dismissed.

Solicitors: *Holman Fenwick & Willan* (for the appellant); *Mackenzie Mills* (for the *e* respondents).

Mary Rose Plummer   Barrister.

Films Rover International Ltd and others v *f*
Cannon Film Sales Ltd

CHANCERY DIVISION
HOFFMANN J
19, 20, 21, 22, 26, 27, 28 AUGUST 1986

g

Injunction – Interlocutory – Mandatory injunction – Circumstances in which mandatory injunction may be granted in interlocutory proceedings – Test of whether injustice to defendant if plaintiff granted injunction but failing at trial outweighing injustice to plaintiff if injunction refused but plaintiff succeeding at trial.

The defendant was an English company engaged in film distribution by means of *h* financing and acquiring rights in films which it then distributed worldwide through sub-distributors in different countries. In order to effect distribution in Italy the defendant entered into a contract with R, acting on behalf of the plaintiff, a company which R later incorporated in Guernsey for the purpose of the contract. Some time later, following a change in the defendant's management, the defendant wished to renegotiate the contract with the plaintiff with a view to splitting the distribution proceeds between the defendant and plaintiff on terms much less favourable to the plaintiff than previously. The new *j* terms caused a dispute to arise between the parties, and the defendant, claiming that the plaintiff was in breach of the contract, refused to send to the plaintiff dubbing material for certain films with the result that the plaintiff was unable to distribute them for exhibiting in Italy. The plaintiff accordingly issued a summons seeking, inter alia, an interlocutory mandatory injunction requiring the films to be delivered to the plaintiff.

a At the hearing of the application for the injunction the defendant contended that the court should not grant the application because the plaintiff had not established a high probability that it would succeed in establishing its legal right at trial.

Held – In determining whether to grant an interlocutory injunction the question for the court was not whether the injunction sought was mandatory or prohibitory but whether the injustice that would be caused to the defendant if the plaintiff was granted
b an injunction and later failed at trial outweighed the injustice that would be caused to the plaintiff if an injunction was refused and he succeeded at trial. Where the injunction was indisputably 'mandatory' that same test applied to determine whether the case was normal (in which case the court was required to feel a high degree of assurance that the plaintiff would succeed at trial before an injunction would be granted) or exceptional in that because withholding an injunction carried with it a greater risk of injustice than
c granting it the injunction should be granted even though the court did not feel a high degree of assurance that the plaintiff would succeed at trial. Since (a) there was no difficulty about the formulation of the order in an enforceable form, (b) it was difficult to see how delivery of the films to the plaintiff would cause uncompensatable loss to the defendant, (c) failure to deliver the films would cause loss to the plaintiff which might be very difficult to quantify and might also force the plaintiff to renegotiate the contract
d because of commercial pressure, and (d) in terms of preserving the status quo the process of distribution which had been set in motion ought not to be interrupted, there was in the circumstances a much greater risk of injustice being caused if the injunction was withheld and the plaintiff was right than if the injunction was granted and the plaintiff did not succeed at trial. Therefore it would be right to grant the injunction (see p 780 *j* to p 781 *e*, p 782 *h*, p 783 *b* and p 785 *a c* to *g*, post).
e   *Shepherd Homes Ltd v Sandham* [1970] 3 All ER 402 and *Locabail International Finance Ltd v Agroexport* [1986] 1 All ER 901 considered.

Notes
For mandatory injunctions generally, see 24 Halsbury's Laws (4th edn) paras 946–952, and for cases on the subject, see 28(2) Digest (Reissue) 998–1000, 284–306.
f

Cases referred to in judgment
American Cyanamid Co v Ethicon Ltd [1975] 1 All ER 504, [1975] AC 396, [1975] 2 WLR 316, HL.
Associated Portland Cement Manufacturers Ltd v Teigland Shipping A/S, The Oakworth [1975] 1 Lloyd's Rep 581, CA.
g *Cayne v Global Natural Resources plc* [1984] 1 All ER 225, CA.
Continental Grain Co v Islamic Republic of Iran Shipping Lines and Government Trading Corp of Iran, The Iran Bohonar [1983] 2 Lloyd's Rep 620, CA.
Evans Marshall & Co Ltd v Bertola SA [1973] 1 All ER 992, [1973] 1 WLR 349, CA.
Locabail International Finance Ltd v Agroexport, The Sea Hawk [1986] 1 All ER 901, [1986] 1 WLR 657, CA.
h *Shepherd Homes Ltd v Sandham* [1970] 3 All ER 402, [1971] Ch 340, [1970] 3 WLR 348.

Motion
The plaintiffs, (1) Films Rover International Ltd, (2) Monitor TV and Merchandising Srl, (3) Proper Films Ltd and (4) Luigi de Rossi, sought (i) an injunction restraining the defendants, Cannon Film Sales Ltd (formerly Thorn-EMI Film Distributors Ltd) (Thorn-
j EMI), whether by themselves their servants or agents or otherwise howsoever from causing or permitting the distribution, exhibition or other use of three feature films the subject matter of an agreement dated 5 December 1985 made between the first plaintiffs and the defendants in Italy and/or in any manner inconsistent with the terms of the agreement and/or other than in proper compliance with the agreement, and (ii) an order that the defendants forthwith deliver to the plaintiffs the films. The facts are set out in the judgment.

Roderick Cordara and *David Joseph* for the plaintiffs.
Alan Pardoe for Thorn-EMI.

a

HOFFMANN J. This is a motion for an interlocutory mandatory injunction ordering the defendant to deliver up to the plaintiffs or their order certain materials required for producing the master prints of the Italian versions of three feature films. In my judgment the motion succeeds.

Cannon Film Sales Ltd, the present name of the defendant, is an English company *b* which under various successive names has been engaged for many years in film production and distribution. When the material events in this action began, it was known as Thorn-EMI Film Distributors Ltd and I shall call it 'Thorn-EMI'. It does not nowadays produce films itself but finances and acquires rights in films made by others. These are then distributed all over the world through sub-distributors in different countries.

c

In Italy film distribution to cinemas (known in the trade as 'theatrical' distribution) is largely in the hands of a company called SpA Consorzio Italiano Distributori Indipendenti Film (CIDIF) which, as its name might suggest, is a consortium of independent distributors and exhibitors. It has been engaged in film distribution for about 30 years and has very considerable expertise. Thorn-EMI has had a number of films distributed through CIDIF in the past and when, in June 1985, it had a package of 17 films made or *d* to be made which it wished to be distributed in Italy over the next two or three years, it entered into negotiations with CIDIF.

It appears however that Thorn-EMI was unable to negotiate acceptable financial terms with CIDIF. It therefore decided to contract with an intermediary who would be willing to make the advance and other payments Thorn-EMI required but would use CIDIF as agent to effect the actual distribution. The chosen intermediary was the fourth plaintiff, *e* Mr Luigi de Rossi. He and his brother Angelo are well established in the business of distributing films in Italy for television and he also has close links with CIDIF.

The de Rossi brothers operate through a number of companies. Angelo is managing director of the second plaintiff, Monitor TV and Merchandising Srl, which is engaged in film distribution for television and has a separate contract for the distribution of the same 17 films after they have been shown in the cinemas. For the purposes of this motion I *f* am not concerned with this contract; it stands in the background as a contract dependent on the contract for theatrical distribution. For this latter purpose, another company called Monitor Srl has been formed with Mr Luigi de Rossi as managing director. It is this company which acts as Italian intermediary between Thorn-EMI and CIDIF.

A further complication was introduced into the contractual structure by Italian exchange control. The advances were payable in US dollars. It seems that consent could *g* not be obtained to the payment of advances in foreign currency by an Italian company except against delivery of the films. The arrangements with Mr de Rossi contemplated delivery of the films at various times over two years but payment of advances from the commencement of the contract. It was therefore necessary to introduce a non-Italian company as the party contracting with Thorn-EMI and to finance its payment of advances from outside Italy. There was a similar problem over the television contract and for this *h* purpose the de Rossi brothers had introduced the third plaintiff, a Guernsey company called Proper Films Ltd. Its arrangements are solely concerned with television rights and again are not in the forefront of this motion. For the purpose of contracting for theatrical distribution, Mr Luigi de Rossi decided to incorporate a new Guernsey company, the first plaintiff, Films Rover International Ltd. I shall call this company 'Films Rover'.

This is how Mr Victor Bateman, who negotiated the agreement on behalf of Thorn- *j* EMI, explained the structure of the transaction in an affidavit sworn on 31 July 1986, during the hearing of this motion:

'Mr. Luigi de Rossi is very well known to us and trusted by us. He is a man who operates through a variety of corporate vehicles, to suit his own purpose, but as long as Mr. Luigi de Rossi is in the driving seat the Defendants have normally been

a
happy to do business with his companies . . . My concern was that C.I.D.I.F. should be the actual physical distributors of the films: if we were unable to deal with them directly, and had to deal with them indirectly then so be it: the object was, one way or the other, to secure their services . . . If Mr. Luigi de Rossi wanted to do the deal through [Films Rover] . . . I felt that was entirely up to him.'

The Films Rover agreement

b
The detailed terms of the contract between Thorn-EMI and the de Rossi interests were negotiated in Milan and London in October and November 1985. Mr Luigi de Rossi was assisted by Mrs Penny Karlin, who is a freelance negotiator with considerable experience in dealing with theatrical film rights. She has also negotiated on behalf of CIDIF. Thorn-EMI was represented by Mr Bateman, who had been dealing with Mrs Karlin and CIDIF for many years. The commercial terms were agreed in mid-November and a contract expressed to be between Thorn-EMI and Films Rover was prepared. This is the contract

c
in issue in this action. The date has not been filled in at the commencement but someone at Thorn-EMI has typed at the foot of the first page the words 'Films Rover International 05/12/85'. It has therefore been called the contract dated 5 December 1985. Mr Luigi de Rossi signed it on behalf of Films Rover on 6 January 1986. I shall call it 'the Films Rover agreement'.

d
I must now say something about the terms of the Films Rover agreement. The body of the agreement contained Thorn-EMI's standard form of distributorship agreement. Thorn-EMI was defined as 'Licensor' and Films Rover as 'Distributor'. There was then a schedule which contained all the terms which had been specially negotiated. Paragraph 15 of the schedule said that:

e
'The present Agreement has been made with the Distributor because of its distribution operation as it presently exists. The Distributor acknowledges that this is essential for Licensor and undertakes to maintain the organisation and quality of its operation at the same level during the Term; in particular any change in key management of the Distributor during the Term shall entitle Licensor at its absolute discretion to terminate this Agreement.'

f
In the context of the background known to the parties, I think it is clear that this clause meant that Films Rover had been chosen because it was controlled by Luigi de Rossi and enjoyed the services of Mrs Karlin and that they had connections with CIDIF. Formally, Films Rover had nothing which could be described as a 'distribution operation'. It was a company with Guernsey directors taking instructions from Luigi de Rossi's Swiss lawyers. On 15 November 1985 Luigi de Rossi signed a sub-distribution agreement between Films Rover and Monitor Srl which contained a clause in very similar terms.

g
The schedule to the Films Rover agreement provided for the grant by Thorn-EMI to Films Rover of the Italian theatrical distribution rights in 17 named films to be delivered over a period of two years. The financial terms were that Thorn-EMI was to be paid an advance of $US1·5m by 24 monthly instalments commencing in January 1986. These advances were apportioned among those 11 of the 17 films which were thought more

h
likely to succeed at the box office. The contract then provided for different methods of allocating first, the receipts from films with advances and second, receipts from films to which no advances had been apportioned.

In the case of films with advances, the gross receipts (ie the moneys received by Films Rover or its sub-distributors from cinema owners in respect of any particular film) were to be divided in the following way. Until takings at Italian box offices from showing a

j
film reached 4bn lire, 65% of the gross receipts were to be applied towards recoupment of distribution expenses and repayment of the advance. The remaining 35% was to be retained by the distributor. After the 4bn lire takings mark had been passed, Thorn-EMI was to receive 70% of the gross receipts and the distributor 30%. There was also a proviso for retrospectively reducing the amount of the advance payable in respect of any film to whatever sum (if any) had been obtained by way of gross receipts after recoupment of distribution expenses in the six months after first release. Thus if a film failed to cover its

distribution expenses, the distributor was entitled to repayment of the whole advance and could deduct a proportionate part from future instalments of the total $1·5m advance payment. On the other hand, a shortfall in distribution expenses was for the account of the distributor.

The accounting for the gross receipts of films without advances was much simpler. They were first to be applied to recoup distribution expenses and then divided between licensor and distributor in the proportion of 65% to 35%.

The standard form part of the agreement contains fairly elaborate terms covering the mechanics of supplying the films for distribution, the actual arrangements for distribution and the accounting for the proceeds. I shall return to some of these in more detail later. For the moment I notice only that the agreement contemplates the distributor ordering a copy or copies of the film from the licensor and submitting it for censorship approval. In the case of an English language film, this generally involves the distributor in preparing at his own expense a version dubbed into Italian.

Operation of the Films Rover agreement

During the period from January to April the Films Rover agreement was operated by both parties. The instalments of the $1·5m advance were paid as they fell due. Three of the 17 films were dubbed into Italian, passed through the censor and released pursuant to sub-distributorship agreements between Films Rover and Monitor Srl and between Monitor Srl and CIDIF. None of these three was successful; in fact the distributors were left about $500,000 out of pocket, but there is no suggestion that this was caused by any failure on the part of Films Rover or its sub-distributors to comply with their obligations.

The three films with which this motion is concerned are called 'Highlander', 'Hitcher' and 'Link'. I shall call them 'the three films'. Films Rover appears to have ordered one copy of each during January; on 20 January Thorn-EMI sent Monitor SRL an invoice for copies. These were 'work prints', suitable for showing to the trade but inferior in quality to the prints which would eventually be used for dubbing. They were screened at a meeting of potential exhibitors organised by Luigi de Rossi and Mrs Karlin in Rome on 28 January. On 11 February Mrs Karlin wrote Mr Bateman an enthusiastic letter. The attendance of CIDIF-related exhibitors had been excellent. Although the films were shown in English versions and the exhibitors had little English, the showing of 'Highlander' was followed by sustained applause and the other two were also well received. Mrs Karlin said that they planned to release 'Hitcher' and 'Link' at the commencement of the film-going season after Italians had returned from their summer holidays in September or October. 'Highlander' would be given 'the prestigious Xmas release date'. Some 50 initial prints of 'Hitcher' and 'Link' would be required and 100 to 150 of 'Highlander', the latter being, as Mrs Karlin explained, probably a record number for any film release in Italy. She planned early distribution of trailers from May onwards as part of a 'sustained launching campaign'. All three films were to be dubbed in June in the hope that one could be shown at the annual congress of Italian film distributors in Rome on 25 and 26 June, described as a 'showcase event'. Mrs Karlin says that she discussed these proposals over the telephone with Mr Bateman and Mr Simenon of Thorn-EMI on numerous occasions and that they were delighted and enthusiastic. This is not contradicted in either of the affidavits Mr Bateman has sworn in these proceedings. In March 'Highlander' was released in France (through other distributors) and enjoyed enormous success. Towards the end of April Mr Bateman invited the de Rossi brothers and Mrs Karlin to a grand dinner party to be held at the forthcoming Cannes Festival for the purpose, among other things, of promoting 'Hitcher' and 'Highlander'.

The Cannon take-over

On 1 May 1986 Thorn-EMI was taken over by the Cannon Group, a group of companies controlled by Mr Yoram Globus and Mr Menahem Golan. They were dissatisfied with Thorn-EMI's distribution contracts, which they considered to be on terms unduly favourable to the distributors. In an interview to a journalist at the Cannes Festival in early May, Mr Golan said:

a
'We will not live by the old contracts. Anyone who wants a relationship with us must renegotiate. Otherwise they can sue us. We must deal aggressively now to change the situation. Within one year we will bring this company to huge profits.'

There has been no disavowal of this pronouncement.

b
In late April and early May Mrs Karlin was anxious to obtain the necessary materials (the 'internegatives', 'music and effects tracks' and so forth) for dubbing the three films. Actors, engineers and studio had been booked for 19 May with a view to having the films ready for the exhibitors' congress at the end of June. She spoke on the telephone to Thorn-EMI employees, but nothing arrived. On 8 May Thorn-EMI sent a telex saying that the 'Highlander' and 'Link' materials would be ready around 16 May and that the availability of 'Hitcher' would be advised.

c
At Cannes in mid-May Mr Luigi de Rossi met a Mr Moraskie, executive vice-president of Cannon International, who had taken charge of Thorn-EMI's film distribution business. There is some dispute about what precisely was said and how Mr Moraskie said it, but there is no doubt that he tried to persuade Mr de Rossi to renegotiate the Films Rover agreement. Mr de Rossi stood his ground.

The course of the dispute

d
No materials for dubbing were delivered during May. Having made their arrangements, Mr de Rossi and Mrs Karlin went ahead as best they could with the work prints of 'Highlander' and 'Hitcher' which had been in their possession since January. This enabled them to record the Italian voices but not to prepare the complete print, for which the internegative and music and effects tracks were still needed. At the end of May they also commenced the advertising campaign for 'Highlander'. Trailers were shown on television and prepared for the distributors' congress, advertisements placed in

e
trade magazines and newspapers and posters printed from materials already supplied by Thorn-EMI.

On 3 June Mrs Karlin sent a lengthy telex of complaint to Thorn-EMI. She said that despite frequent requests for the dubbing materials for the three films she had received no reply. The distributors' congress was due to be held at the end of the month and dubbing would have to be completed as soon as possible if the films were to be ready.

f
Thorn-EMI replied two days later saying that Mr Moraskie would deal with the matter when he returned from Japan around 12 June. On 10 June Mrs Karlin telexed again. Why did Thorn-EMI offer no reasons for failing to deliver? On 13 June she telexed again, saying that she had been promised a reply by midday that day. The mixing session to complete the dubbed version of 'Highlander' was due to commence on 17 June. This time she threatened legal action unless the materials were sent at once.

g
On 16 June Mr Moraskie replied. After saying that Thorn-EMI was continuing to trade, he said:

'2. No materials have ever been specifically withheld from [Films Rover].
3. There is no default under the agreement for Italy.'

h
Paragraph 5 threatened proceedings for defamation and para 6 said:

'Further in reference to our contract we expect by return that you fulfil your obligations under clause 3 concerning the initial print order and the initial release requirements as well as the release obligations under clause 9 for all of which you have proper forms in your possession.'

j
Paragraph 6 of this telex was the first suggestion since Mrs Karlin had begun pressing for the films that Films Rover was in breach of its obligations under the agreement. The 'initial print order' was a reference to what the contract calls the 'Minimum Initial Print Order', defined in the appendix as one 35mm print. In respect of the three films, these had been ordered and sent in January. The 'initial release requirements' were, it seems, originally intended to be defined in the schedule as the release of a certain number of prints in cities defined as 'the Key Cities' within a certain number of weeks of delivery.

But the parties had not agreed on the number of prints, the identities of the key cities or the number of weeks within which release should take place. Instead, blanks were left in the schedule and the words 'Subject to Licensor's Approval' written there instead. It therefore seems clear that there was no 'initial release requirement' with which the distributor could have failed to comply. All that the contract said was that the licensor should at some unspecified stage have the right to approve these aspects of the distribution. The release obligations under cl 9 also gave the licensor a right of prior approval of 'all major aspects of the distribution of the film' but there had been no previous suggestion that Thorn-EMI were objecting to anything which Films Rover (which in practice meant its sub-sub-distributor CIDIF) were proposing to do. On the contrary, as Mr Bateman has sworn, Thorn-EMI trusted Mr de Rossi and had full confidence in CIDIF.

Mrs Karlin replied on 17 June. She denied any breaches of the agreement, saying that it would not be possible to supply better information about the proposed distribution arrangements until the films were actually available. For example, Italian exhibitors were prepared to make provisional bookings but would not enter into firm agreements until they were sure that they would get the films. This has more or less been the position of the parties ever since, Mr Moraskie claiming that he was entitled to more details about distribution to enable him to exercise Thorn-EMI's rights of approval and Films Rover saying it could not provide better information until it was in a position to tell CIDIF, the exhibitors, advertisers and so forth that the films were definitely available.

On 20 June Mr Moraskie sent Mr Luigi de Rossi a telex containing his proposals for renegotiated terms. These were cancellation of the rights in 10 of the 17 films, retention of rights in the three already released and, in order to obtain the remaining four (including the three films) a further non-returnable advances of $862,500 payable against delivery. Gross receipts for each film after recoupment of distribution costs were to be split 50% to each party until the advance had been recouped and then 60% to licensor and 40% to distributor. These proposals were rejected by Mr de Rossi.

The dispute then shifted into a higher gear. Thorn-EMI instructed solicitors, who went through the agreement to find any provisions which they could allege Films Rover had breached. On 22 June they sent Mr de Rossi an aggressive telex. It began with an assertion that Films Rover, though 'purportedly a Jersey [sic] resident company' was in fact controlled from Italy and an innuendo that Mr de Rossi was evading Italian taxes ('Would you please confirm that the Italian fiscal authorities are aware of the trading profits of Rover and other companies.') They repeated that no materials had been withheld: 'Cannon is not in a position to effect delivery . . . until performance by Rover of its obligations under the agreement'. The alleged obligations which Films Rover had 'quite categorically not fulfilled' were the initial release requirement, the minimum initial print order and the 'advertising commitment'. I have already dealt with the allegations about the initial release requirement and the minimum initial print order, which had appeared in Mr Moraskie's telex. The complaint about the 'advertising commitment' has since been abandoned.

The telex went on to say that any arrangements to screen films to Italian distributors at the congress on 25 June 'were made by Rover without the consent of Thorn or Cannon who cannot therefore be bound by these arrangements'. This assertion can be contrasted with the uncontradicted evidence of Mrs Karlin that Mr Bateman and other Thorn-EMI employees had been notified well before the Cannon takeover of the proposal to screen one of the films at the Congress and had received the proposal with enthusiasm. The telex continued as follows:

'As to the unauthorised advertising by Rover of the availability of the films in breach of its requirements to obtain the licensor's approval, if Rover has been foolhardy enough to advertise the availability of the films before it has performed its own obligations and obtained approval from Thorn/Cannon of the initial release requirements, the key cities, the advertising commitment and before making the

a

minimum initial print order, then these problems are clearly of Rover's own making and neither Cannon nor Thorn can be liable for Rover's losses.'

A final paragraph read as follows:

b

'Your telex [of 17 June] contains clear admissions that Rover is in breach of the agreement and has no intention of rectifying its breach. Unless this situation is rectified immediately Cannon will have no alternative but to commence proceedings against Rover pursuant to which Cannon will seek punitive damages.'

c

After protest from Mr de Rossi's Italian lawyer, Thorn-EMI's solicitors returned to their theme in a lengthy telex dated 30 June. Now it was alleged that by appointing Monitor Srl and CIDIF as sub-distributors, Films Rover had wrongfully assigned or sub-let its rights under the agreement and that the Films Rover arrangements were 'a flagrant violation' of Italian exchange control. ('Please confirm that you have reported these irregular activities to the Italian customs and excise and other fiscal authorities.') The only reason why Thorn-EMI had not delivered the dubbing materials, it was said, was because of Films Rover's own default. Mr de Rossi was said to have accepted the proposals in Mr Moraskie's telex of 20 June and then 'reneged on [the] agreement'; an allegation which is now admitted to have been completely without substance. This was followed by an even more unpleasant allegation:

d

'Your clients have made suggestions which cause our clients concern because they imply that there are material irregularities in business operations within Italy. Our clients cannot expose themselves to criminal sanctions for conspiracy to avoid tax or evade exchange control regulations and we suggest that your clients put their own house in order before they make groundless allegations against third parties.'

e

No evidence has been offered in support of this allegation. On 4 July the monthly instalment of $62,500 was paid and accepted.

Films Rover then instructed solicitors and after some further correspondence Thorn-EMI's solicitors on 8 July purported to terminate the Films Rover agreement on the grounds of the alleged breaches. Besides the ones already mentioned, it was alleged that Films Rover had wrongfully entered 'Link' for a minor film festival. This allegation has

f

also since been abandoned. Nevertheless, in spite of all these breaches, Thorn-EMI said that it was still willing to enter into a new agreement on the terms of its telex of 20 June. This proposal was still unacceptable to Mr de Rossi and the writ in this action was issued on 11 July.

I have described the correspondence before action at some length despite the fact that it contains a good deal of material which is no longer in issue. I have done so because I

g

think that it throws much light on the true motives of Thorn-EMI in refusing to deliver the material for the three films and I do not conceal that, in a way in which I shall later explain, I have taken this into account in the exercise of my discretion.

The litigation

h

The action was commenced in the Commercial Court. On 15 July the plaintiffs issued a summons claiming an order that Thorn-EMI 'do forthwith deliver to the Plaintiffs' solicitors or otherwise to the Plaintiffs' order the Scheduled materials'. The schedule listed the materials required for preparing prints of the three films. In the alternative, the plaintiffs asked for injunctions in two different forms which amount to no more than semantic variations on the one I have quoted. I shall return later to the significance, if any, of these distinctions. Thorn-EMI has offered an undertaking pending trial that it

j

will not distribute the films otherwise than through Films Rover, but the plaintiffs say that is not enough. They must have the films.

The summons was first heard by Webster J on Thursday 24 July and then adjourned part heard to the Monday. On the Friday there was a dramatic development. A company search by Thorn-EMI's solicitors in Guernsey to discover the identity of the directors of

Films Rover revealed that the company had not been incorporated until 6 February 1986, some two months after Luigi de Rossi had purported to contract on its behalf. On this point the action very nearly foundered. Webster J ceased hearing the summons and it was transferred to the Chancery Division and heard as a motion by order by his Honour Judge Paul Baker QC sitting as a judge of the High Court. On 5 August Judge Baker dismissed the motion on the ground that the plaintiffs had no arguable case for asserting the existence of any contract between Films Rover and Thorn-EMI. There was an appeal and on 15 August Lloyd and Stocker LJJ said that there was an arguable issue, which could only be resolved at the trial, as to whether a contract existed on one of three grounds: first, that a new contract had been made by the agreement of what the parties thought was a variation to the original contract made after Films Rover had been incorporated; second, that the parties, having acted on the assumption that there was a binding contract in dealing with each other and with third parties were estopped by convention from denying its validity; and third that by virtue of s 36(4) of the Companies Act 1985 the contract took effect as if made between Thorn-EMI and the fourth plaintiff, Mr Luigi de Rossi.

The Court of Appeal has held that these are matters to be decided by the trial judge and not at this interlocutory stage. I will therefore say no more about them except to comment that I think it would be a blot on English jurisprudence if this contract, acted on by both sides, had now to be held null and void. The issues concerning the alleged breaches, so far as they have not already been abandoned, can also be resolved only by the judge at trial. I therefore approach the claim for a mandatory interlocutory injunction on basis that the plaintiffs' legal rights remain to be determined at the trial and that they are at least as likely to fail as to succeed.

The mandatory injunction

In the forefront of his argument counsel for Thorn-EMI submitted that the court should not grant an interlocutory mandatory injunction, amounting to specific performance of one of Thorn-EMI's alleged contractual obligations, unless there appeared a high probability that Films Rover would succeed in establishing its legal right at the trial. In this case the Court of Appeal has gone no further than to say that Films Rover has an arguable case and, as I have already said, I propose to treat that as meaning that Films Rover is at least as likely to fail as to succeed. Counsel said that fell well short of the standard of persuasion necessary for the grant of an interlocutory mandatory injunction.

In support of this proposition, counsel for Thorn-EMI relied in particular on the recent decision of the Court of Appeal in *Locabail International Finance Ltd v Agroexport, The Sea Hawk* [1986] 1 All ER 901 at 906, [1986] 1 WLR 657 at 664 in which Mustill LJ (with whom Balcombe LJ agreed) approved the following passage from the judgment of Megarry J in *Shepherd Homes Ltd v Sandham* [1970] 3 All ER 402 at 412, [1971] Ch 340 at 351:

> 'Third, on motion, as contrasted with the trial, the court is far more reluctant to grant a mandatory injunction than it would be to grant a comparable prohibitory injunction. In a normal case the court must, inter alia, feel a high degree of assurance that at the trial it will appear that the injunction was rightly granted; and this is a higher standard than is required for a prohibitory injunction.'

Mustill LJ went on to say that although this judgment pre-dated *American Cyanamid Co v Ethicon Ltd* [1975] 1 All ER 504, [1975] AC 396 the statement of principle 'in relation to the very special case of the mandatory injunction' was not affected by what had been said in the House of Lords in that case.

I would respectfully agree that there is no inconsistency between the passage from Megarry J and what was said in the *Cyanamid* case. But I think it is important in this area to distinguish between fundamental principles and what are sometimes described as 'guidelines', ie useful generalisations about the way to deal with the normal run of cases falling within a particular category. The principal dilemma about the grant of

interlocutory injunctions, whether prohibitory or mandatory, is that there is by definition
a risk that the court may make the 'wrong' decision, in the sense of granting an injunction
to a party who fails to establish his right at the trial (or would fail if there was a trial) or
alternatively, in failing to grant an injunction to a party who succeeds (or would succeed)
at trial. A fundamental principle is therefore that the court should take whichever course
appears to carry the lower risk of injustice if it should turn out to have been 'wrong' in
the sense I have described. The guidelines for the grant of both kinds of interlocutory
injunctions are derived from this principle.

   The passage quoted from Megarry J in *Shepherd Homes Ltd v Sandham* [1970] 3 All ER
402 at 412, [1971] Ch 340 at 351 qualified as it was by the words 'in a normal case', was
plainly intended as a guideline rather than an independent principle. It is another way of
saying that the features which justify describing an injunction as 'mandatory' will usually
also have the consequence of creating a greater risk of injustice if it is granted rather than
withheld at the interlocutory stage unless the court feels a 'high degree of assurance' that
the plaintiff would be able to establish his right at a trial. I have taken the liberty of
reformulating the proposition in this way in order to bring out two points. The first is to
show that semantic arguments over whether the injunction as formulated can properly
be classified as mandatory or prohibitory are barren. The question of substance is whether
the granting of the injunction would carry that higher risk of injustice which is normally
associated with the grant of a mandatory injunction. The second point is that in cases in
which there can be no dispute about the use of the term 'mandatory' to describe the
injunction, the same question of substance will determine whether the case is 'normal'
and therefore within the guideline or 'exceptional' and therefore requiring special
treatment. If it appears to the court that, exceptionally, the case is one in which
withholding a mandatory interlocutory injunction would in fact carry a greater risk of
injustice than granting it even though the court does not feel a 'high degree of assurance'
about the plaintiff's chances of establishing his right, there cannot be any rational basis
for withholding the injunction.

   In *Shepherd Homes Ltd v Sandham* Megarry J spelled out some of the reasons why
mandatory injunctions generally carry a higher risk of injustice if granted at the
interlocutory stage: they usually go further than the preservation of the status quo by
requiring a party to take some new positive step or undo what he has done in the past;
an order requiring a party to take positive steps usually causes more waste of time and
money if it turns out to have been wrongly granted than an order which merely causes
delay by restraining him from doing something which it appears at the trial he was
entitled to do; a mandatory order usually gives a party the whole of the relief which he
claims in the writ and makes it unlikely that there will be a trial. One could add other
reasons, such as that mandatory injunctions (whether interlocutory or final) are often
difficult to formulate with sufficient precision to be enforceable. In addition to all these
practical considerations, there is also what might be loosely called a 'due process' question.
An order requiring someone to do something is usually perceived as a more intrusive
exercise of the coercive power of the state than an order requiring him temporarily to
refrain from action. The court is therefore more reluctant to make such an order against
a party who has not had the protection of a full hearing at trial.

   Megarry J recognised, however, that none of these was a necessary concomitant of a
mandatory injunction. For example, there is sometimes a sense in which a mandatory
injunction is needed to preserve the status quo. In charterparty withdrawal cases the
Commercial Court has frequently granted interlocutory injunctions restraining an owner
from using the ship otherwise than in accordance with the terms of the charter (see per
Lord Denning MR in *Associated Portland Cement Manufacturers Ltd v Teigland Shipping
A/S, The Oakworth* [1975] 1 Lloyd's Rep 581). Although negative in form, these are (in
the case of a time or voyage charter) mandatory in effect because they require the owner
to continue to provide the ship. In these cases there is what might (at some risk of
oxymoron) be called a 'dynamic status quo' which consists in the continuing use of the
vessel on the charterer's business. Counsel for the plaintiffs also referred me to *Continental*

Grain Co v Islamic Republic of Iran Shipping Lines and Government Trading Corp of Iran, The Iran Bohonar [1983] 2 Lloyd's Rep 620, in which the Court of Appeal made a mandatory order requiring owners to direct their vessel to deviate to a safe port and discharge cargo to which the plaintiff claimed title. The order was made because the court considered that there was a serious question to be tried as to whether on the true construction of the Hague Rules the owners were under a contractual obligation to do so. Neither of the Lords Justices (nor for that matter counsel) seem to have suggested that such an order should not be made unless the court felt a high degree of assurance that the plaintiff's construction was right. On the contrary, Ackner LJ said ([1983] 2 Lloyd's Rep 620 at 623):

> 'Whether that argument will succeed or not is another matter. We have had the advantage of [the] submissions [of counsel for the defendants] and it would be churlish to say that they lack force, but speaking for myself I am satisfied that there is a serious question to be argued on this subject.'

I would venture to suggest that *The Iran Bohonar* was plainly a case in which, despite the mandatory character of the injunction, the risk of the injustice which would be caused by 'wrongly' withholding it was far greater than the risk of injustice if it turned out to have been wrongly granted. It is easy to construct other counterexamples by way of exception to the proposition that mandatory injunctions are more drastic and irreversible in effect and involve greater expense and inconvenience if wrongly granted than prohibitory injunctions.

These considerations lead me to conclude that the Court of Appeal in *Locabail International Finance Ltd v Agroexport* [1986] 1 All ER 901 at 906, [1986] 1 WLR 657 at 664 was not intending to 'fetter the court's discretion by laying down any rules which would have the effect of limiting the flexibility of the remedy', to quote Lord Diplock in the *Cyanamid* case [1975] 1 All ER 504 at 510, [1975] AC 396 at 407. Just as the *Cyanamid* guidelines for prohibitory injunctions which require a plaintiff to show no more than an arguable case recognise the existence of exceptions in which more is required (compare *Cayne v Global Natural Resources plc* [1984] 1 All ER 225), so the guideline approved for mandatory injunctions in *Locabail* recognises that there may be cases in which less is sufficient. It is significant that both Mustill and Balcombe LJJ did not merely rely on the mandatory nature of the injunction. They went on to explain why in the particular circumstances of the case, the granting of the injunction would give rise to an unacceptable risk of injustice. Mustill LJ said that the injunction would put the defendant 'in an irretrievable difficulty', that the defendants appeared unable to comply and would therefore 'inevitably be in breach' and that if they failed to comply, they had no officers or assets within the jurisdiction and there was no way in which the injunction could be enforced.

The exercise of discretion

I can now say why in my judgment this is a case in which there is a much greater risk of causing injustice by withholding an injunction (if the plaintiffs are right) than by granting it (if the plaintiffs are wrong) and why I think it would in all the circumstances be right to make such an order.

First, there is no difficulty about the formulation of the order in an enforceable form. The defendant will be required only to perform one relatively simple operation, namely to put together certain materials specified in the schedule to the summons and admitted to be in its possession and send them to the order of Films Rover in Italy. It is not suggested that Thorn-EMI would not know precisely what has to be done. Counsel for Thorn-EMI relied on the decision of the Court of Appeal in *Evans Marshall & Co Ltd v Bertola SA* [1973] 1 All ER 992 at 1007, [1973] 1 WLR 349 at 382, in which Sachs LJ said of an exclusive distribution agreement (for sherry):

> 'It is true to say that specific performance of such an agreement will not be ordered . . .'

The plaintiffs in that case do not appear to have claimed specific performance and in my

a judgment the reason why Sachs LJ made that remark was not because it would have been unjust to require the defendants to perform the contract but in recognition of the familiar practical problems of enforcing by order a contract running for a lengthy term and involving mutual obligations of trust and confidence. If the Lord Justice had thought that apart from such practical difficulties it would be unjust to enforce the agreement at an interlocutory stage, he would not have granted a negative injunction to 'encourage'

b the defendant to perform the contract. No practical problems arise in this case.

Second, it is difficult to see how delivery of the films to Films Rover could cause uncompensatable loss to the defendant. The defendant through Mr Bateman has in the course of these proceedings reasserted its confidence in Mr de Rossi and CIDIF as distributors. It would have no hesitation in allowing Films Rover to have the films if the latter was willing to agree to more favourable terms and it has significantly made no

c attempt to arrange any alternative form of distribution. This at any rate suggests that it expects Films Rover to return to the negotiating table and agree to pay more. The distribution of the films will create a sum of money in Italy over which the parties can litigate at their leisure. Indeed it seems to me that an order which permits the distribution of the films by the plaintiff has some analogy (although there are obvious differences) with the sale of a perishable produce while its ownership is in dispute. Mr Moraskie, in a

d lyric passage in his affidavit, describes films as 'mercurial, finite and wasting assets'. In later evidence he disputes the need for hurry in releasing the films in Italy but I doubt whether they improve with age.

The point most powerfully developed by counsel for Thorn-EMI was that Films Rover had not complied and did not intend to comply with its obligations under the contract to provide information about and seek approvals for its distribution plans. This, he said,

e had two consequences: first, that Films Rover, which was seeking specific performance of one of Thorn-EMI's obligations under the contract, could not show that it had performed and was ready willing and able to perform its own contractual obligations, and second, that it would be inequitable to make an interlocutory order requiring Thorn-EMI to perform its obligation to deliver the films when it had no assurance that Films Rover would comply with its obligations and (on past history) grounds to doubt its

f intention to do so.

This argument makes it necessary for me to examine the contractual provisions about approvals and provision of information. The main relevant provisions are as follows. By cl 9(a) the licensor has—

'a right of approval on an on-going basis with respect to all major aspects of the distribution of the Film in the Territory, including, without limitation, the initial

g release campaign, distribution policy, exhibition contract terms, the total amount and specific items of the advertising budget, the advertising campaign, release dates, release patterns, theatres in Key Cities, marketing strategy and any modifications or amendments to them.'

I have already mentioned the financial provisions, which give the distributor the right

h (in the case of films with allocated advances) to apply 65% of the gross receipts to the recoupment of distribution expenses. By cl 6(E)(iv) of the schedule, all such distribution expenses must be first approved by the licensor in writing and by cl 16(x) the failure of the distributor to obtain the licensor's prior approval of any matter as to which it has a right of approval is an event of default which entitled the licensor to terminate the agreement and, under a cross-default provision, any other agreements with the

j distributor.

The provision concerning information is cl 15(k), which says that:

'The Distributor shall promptly complete and return to Licensor such forms as the Licensor shall provide to the Distributor relating to but not limited to the matters contained in Clauses 3(a) [material requirements] 3(c) [supply of further prints] . . . 8(1)(c) [advertising and publicity campaign] . . . 9(a) [distribution plans] . . . etc].'

For the purposes of cl 15(k), Thorn-EMI has devised various forms to be completed by distributors. It is agreed that Films Rover did not submit some of these forms for the first three films already distributed. Thorn-EMI says that this was a gross breach of the agreement. Mrs Karlin says that she provided the same information in letters, telexes and telephone calls and explained to Mr Bateman why she did not think that the forms were suited to reporting the Italian market. Mr Bateman, she says, accepted her point of view. In particular, she says that when a new employee of Thorn-EMI wrote to her on 5 March 1986 asking her to submit the forms, she had a number of discussions with Mr Bateman and he said that he had taken the employee to task for writing such a letter. None of this is contradicted by Mr Bateman. There is therefore at lowest a triable issue as to whether Thorn-EMI did not waive its right to submission of the forms.

As to the future, there can be no doubt that Thorn-EMI is entitled under the contract to insist on the completion of its forms. Mrs Karlin thinks that the information on the forms is less helpful to Thorn-EMI than information she has provided in other ways but Films Rover recognise that that is a matter for Thorn-EMI. There is no particular difficulty about supplying the information required by the forms except that of timing. In the case of the three films, Films Rover has not yet made firm bookings and advertising plans and the information is therefore not yet available. But the information will obviously become available before distribution and Films Rover says through its counsel that it understands the position and has no intention of failing to supply the necessary forms. It has every incentive to do so because failure to obtain approval would not only result in the expenses being disallowed for deduction from gross receipts but would afford a ground for termination to a licensor which has shown every inclination to rely on any ground available and many which are not.

The contract says nothing about when the forms have to be supplied but I think it is a reasonable inference that those which contain information relevant to proposals which Thorn-EMI have a right to approve should be submitted in time to enable such approval to be given or withheld before the proposals are carried into effect. Thus the notes supplied with form SR 2 dealing with the advertising publicity budget says that the purpose of the form is—

'to enable you to submit a budget for approval prior to the release of the picture so that major expenditure can be authorised BEFORE any sums have been irrevocably committed.'

There is however nothing in the contract which says that the provision of such information and delivery of the film are concurrent obligations in the sense that Thorn-EMI is entitled to hold up delivery of the film until the information has been received. In the present case Films Rover says, as it seems to be with some plausibility, that such a requirement would be wholly impracticable. Until it is certain of having the film, it is in no position to approach exhibitors for firm dates or plan an advertising campaign. At the beginning of May it was planning such a campaign and says that it had kept Mr Bateman in close touch with what it was doing, but since then Thorn-EMI's refusal to co-operate has prevented any progress. Mr Moraskie says that he is unwilling to let Films Rover have the films until he has been given sufficient information in sufficient detail to enable him to exercise Thorn-EMI's contractual rights to approve the advertising budget, distribution arrangements and so forth. I would have been more impressed by this claim if Thorn-EMI had shown any interest in these details before Films Rover refused to renegotiate.

It seems to me that there is no evidence to suggest that Films Rover, if supplied with the films, will fail to comply with its obligations under the contract to provide information and seek approvals. Counsel for Thorn-EMI accepts (although he did not necessarily put it in quite the same way) that to give commercial efficacy to the contract there must be an implied term that approvals will not be unreasonably withheld. I therefore think that once Thorn-EMI have provided the films, the contract will be properly and sensibly operated. If Thorn-EMI have any complaints about distribution expenses, they can be dealt with on the taking of the account.

Third, failure to deliver the films will cause loss to Films Rover which may be very
difficult to quantify. It planned to release them in September and (with Thorn-EMI's
approval) notified this to distributors, secured provisional bookings and incurred
advertising expenditure. If films are not successful after a delayed release, it will be
impossible to prove that the failure was caused by the delay. Furthermore, Films Rover's
cash flow will suffer from the delay in exploiting the films and their goodwill with
exhibitors will be damaged.

Fourth, there is the question of the status quo. I have seldom known an application for
interlocutory relief in which both sides have not claimed that they were seeking to
uphold the status quo. Counsel for Thorn-EMI says that the films are in England and the
status quo is that they should stay here. The negative undertaking which Thorn-EMI
have offered would preserve the position. Counsel for the plaintiffs says that Films Rover
is embarked on the process of distributing the three films in Italy and the status quo is to
allow that process to continue. In this case I think that what I have called the dynamic
status quo is commercially the more important and that the process of distribution which
was set in motion in January 1986 should not be interrupted.

Finally, I return to the significance of the correspondence which I earlier examined in
some detail. It strongly suggests that Thorn-EMI under its new management regards
breach of contract and litigation as (to adapt the well-known aphorism of von Clausewitz)
the continuation of commercial negotiations by other means. It has been trying to
persuade Mr de Rossi to renegotiate and the withholding of the three films may be an
attempt to bring pressure on him and his companies to achieve this aim. I see no reason
to suppose that if the injunction is not granted, Thorn-EMI may not succeed. The
plaintiffs say that unless they are assured of receiving the films fairly soon, the commercial
pressure which they are under will force them to renegotiate. In that case, a refusal of
the injunction will mean that although Films Rover may have had a good case, it will
have been unable to bring it to trial. In this respect the case is the converse of *Cayne v
Global Natural Resources plc* [1984] 1 All ER 225, in which the plaintiffs were seeking an
interlocutory injunction (as it happens, prohibitory in nature) which would in practice
have deprived the defendants of the right to a trial.

This seems to me to involve a substantial risk of a special kind of injustice. Denial of
the injunction may enable a party to achieve a commercial objective by a calculated
disregard of the basic principle of a civil society that 'men perform their covenants made'.
The film world is tough and ruthless but not a state of nature. In weighing the risks of
injustice which granting or refusing the injunction would entail, I have taken this
qualitative consideration into account.

For the reasons I have already given, there appears to me no difference in substance
between the various forms of injunction claimed in the summons. Paragraph 2 says in
the clearest terms what Thorn-EMI are required to do and I shall therefore make the
order in those words.

Order accordingly.

Solicitors: *Denton Hall & Burgin* (for the plaintiffs); *Jeffrey Green & Russell* (for Thorn-
EMI).

Jacqueline Metcalfe   Barrister.

R v Slater

COURT OF APPEAL, CRIMINAL DIVISION
MAY LJ, MICHAEL DAVIES AND ALLIOTT JJ
16 JUNE 1986

Sentence – Forfeiture order – Forfeiture of property – Property – Property used for committing any offence – Defendant convicted of conspiracy to supply drugs – Court making forfeiture order in respect of money in defendant's possession – Money provided by purchasers of drugs – Purchasers committing offence when buying drugs from defendant – Whether money used for purpose of committing any offence – Whether money used for commission of offence by defendant – Powers of Criminal Courts Act 1973, s 43(1).

The police searched the appellant's premises and found £1,136 in cash and a large quantity of cannabis resin. The appellant was convicted of conspiracy to supply a controlled drug and sentenced to a term of imprisonment. The recorder purported also to make a forfeiture order under s 43(1)[a] of the Powers of Criminal Courts Act 1973 in respect of the money, on the ground that it was likely to be the proceeds of a dishonest action and accordingly had been 'used for the purpose of committing, or facilitating the commission of, any offence'. The appellant appealed against the forfeiture order. The Crown contended that the court had power to make an order under s 43(1) where property had been used for the purpose of the commission of any offence by anyone and that therefore the court had had power to make the order in the circumstances because the money had been provided by purchasers of the drugs, who had themselves been using it to commit an offence when buying the drugs.

Held – On the true construction of s 43(1) of the 1973 Act the power to make a forfeiture order was confined to property which was used for or facilitated, or was intended to be used for, the commission of an offence by the person convicted of the offence. It followed therefore that a forfeiture order could not be made in respect of money which had been used by others to purchase drugs from the appellant. Accordingly, the recorder had had no power to make the order and the appeal would therefore be allowed (see p 788 c to f, post).

Notes

For forfeiture in respect of controlled drug offences, see 30 Halsbury's Laws (4th edn) para 779.

For the Powers of Criminal Courts Act 1973, s 43, see 12 Halsbury's Statutes (4th edn) 649.

Case referred to in judgment

R v Cuthbertson [1980] 2 All ER 401, [1981] AC 470, [1980] 3 WLR 89, HL.

Appeal against sentence

On 3 January 1986 in the Crown Court at Snaresbrook before Mr L L Rose sitting as an assistant recorder, the appellant, John Kingston Slater, pleaded guilty to one count of conspiracy to supply a controlled drug and two counts of handling and was sentenced to a total of 33 months' imprisonment. The court also made a forfeiture order under s 43 of the Powers of the Criminal Courts Act 1973 in respect of £1,136 found at the appellant's home and an order for the destruction of the drugs. The appellant appealed with leave of Leonard J against the sentence in respect of the forefeiture order only. The facts are set out in the judgment of the court.

---

a   Section 43(1) is set out at p 787 *g h*, post

John Hilton (assigned by the Registrar of Criminal Appeals) for the appellant.
Graeme Ford for the Crown.

a

MAY LJ. On 3 January 1986 in the Crown Court at Snaresbrook the appellant pleaded guilty to one count of conspiracy to supply a controlled drug and was sentenced to 18 months' imprisonment, and also to two counts of handling on which he was sentenced to 9 months' imprisonment concurrent on each but consecutive to the 18 months' on the conspiracy count.

b

He admitted being in breach of a two-year suspended sentence imposed in July 1983 in the Crown Court at Lewes. Six months of that was activated to run consecutively. In the result the appellant was made subject to a total of 33 months' imprisonment.

In addition the assistant recorder made a forfeiture order in respect of £1,136 under the power which he thought was given to him by virtue of s 43 of the Powers of Criminal Courts Act 1973, as well as an order for destruction of the drugs.

c

The appellant now appeals against sentence solely in respect of the forfeiture order by leave of the single judge.

The facts of the case are these. On 7 June 1985 in the early morning the police searched the appellant's premises. They found some £700 in cash on the mantelpiece and a total of over 4,500 grams of cannabis resin with a street value of nearly £11,000. He said that

d

the cannabis was there because he was minding it for someone. He claimed that the money was, and I quote, 'Just a bit of readies,' and denied there being any more. However, a search of his person produced a further £436 which he claimed to have won on the horses. That, with the £700 previously found, made up the £1,136 which was the subject matter of the forfeiture order. Plastic cash bags and elastic bands were also found. So much for the drugs offence.

e

A Barclaycard and six traveller's cheques were also found, and they formed the subject of the two handling counts. The appellant claimed and confirmed in interview that someone had given them to him to sell.

In so far as the drugs offence and the foreeiture order were concerned, it was and is common ground that, as the offence charged was a conspiracy to supply a controlled drug, there was no power to forfeit the relevant drugs under s 27 of the Misuse of Drugs

f

Act 1971. That is the usual provision under which drugs are forfeited in these cases, but the decision of their Lordships' House in *R v Cuthbertson* [1980] 2 All ER 401, [1981] AC 470 makes it quite clear that the parties were correct in taking the view that it could not be said that the offence was one under the 1971 Act and that therefore the s 27 powers did not apply.

However, the Crown contended before the recorder below that a forfeiture order could

g

be made by virtue of the provisions of s 43(1) of the 1973 Act. Those are as follows:

> 'Where a person is convicted of an offence punishable on indictment with imprisonment for a term of two years or more and the court by or before which he is convicted is satisfied that any property which was in his possession or under his control at the time of his apprehension—(a) has been used for the purpose of committing, or facilitating the commission of, any offence; or (b) was intended by

h

> him to be used for that purpose; the court may make an order under this section in respect of that property.'

The way the matter went in the court below is this. When the question of the money arose, the recorder said:

> 'I must take it, on what I have heard, that that £1,136 is likely to be the proceeds

j

> of a dishonest action and, therefore, I would have to make the order for forfeiture, however sorry I may feel for his "common law" wife. I do, accordingly, make that order for forfeiture.'

However, counsel then appearing on behalf of the Crown intervened, rightly, and pointed out that, by virtue of the precise wording of s 27 of the 1971 Act, there was no power thereunder to make the order as the recorder seemed to be doing. But he nevertheless asked the recorder to make the order under s 43 and, after there had been certain argument on the point, the recorder said: 'I am going to make an order for forfeiture under the Powers of the Criminal Courts Act 1973, s 43. If I am wrong about it, of course you will no doubt be able to put me right.'

The argument for the appellant before us has been very much the same as the argument was before the recorder below. It has been to the effect that, on the proper construction of s 43, the finding of the recorder that, the money is likely to be the proceeds of a dishonest action, or proceeds of sale of the drugs, is not within the section.

In reply to that contention, counsel for the Crown has pointed to the width of the subsection, and he urges that the proper construction of, for instance, para (a) of s 43(1) of the 1973 Act is so that it reads: '. . . has been used for the purpose of committing any offence by anyone.' He then argues from that standpoint that the purchasers who bought the drugs and provided the proceeds which were found and made up the £1,136 had themselves been using it for the purpose of committing offences by them. Thus on that wide construction of the relevant subsection there was power in the recorder to make the forfeiture order that he did make.

With all respect to that argument, it is one which we cannot accept. It places, we think, far too wide a construction on s 43. In our judgment that subsection is confined to property said to come within its scope used for facilitating the commission of, or intended to be used for the commission of, an offence by the person convicted of the offence, and who is referred to in the first few words of the subsection. In other words, instead of construing para (a) as contended for by the Crown 'has been used for the purpose of committing any offence by anyone', in our view the proper construction of that particular passage is 'has been used for the purpose of committing any offence by him', which necessarily refers back to the person convicted of an offence in the opening part of the section.

That being so, it follows that in our judgment there was no power in the recorder to make the forfeiture order which he did make in the instant case. Thus to that extent this appeal must be allowed and the forfeiture order set aside.

The remaining part of the sentence of course remains.

Appeal allowed. Forfeiture order set aside.

Solicitors: *D M O'Shea* (for the Crown).

Dilys Tausz   Barrister.

a   R v Bury Magistrates, ex parte N (a minor)

QUEEN'S BENCH DIVISION
WATKINS LJ AND OTTON J
23, 26 JUNE, 30 JULY 1986

b   *Legal aid – Criminal cases – Refusal of legal aid – Review of decision to refuse legal aid – When application for review to be made – Application required to be made no later than 21 days before 'date fixed for ... trial ... or ... inquiry' – Offence triable either way – Magistrates refusing legal aid – Magistrates refusing to allow review of refusal because application made within 21 days of defendant's first appearance in court – Whether first appearance in court is 'date fixed for ... trial ... or ... inquiry' – Legal Aid in Criminal Proceedings (General) Regulations 1968, reg*
c   *6E(2)(c).*

On 6 May 1986 the applicant was arrested and charged with the offence of obtaining property by deception, which was an offence triable either on indictment or summarily. He was released on bail until 3 June, when he was to appear before the magistrates' court. On 14 May the magistrates refused his application for legal aid and informed him that d   he was not entitled to apply to a criminal legal aid committee for a review of the refusal of his application. The magistrates took the view that, notwithstanding that it would be the date of his first appearance before the court, 3 June was 'the date fixed for the trial of an information or the inquiry into an offence as examining justices' and that therefore the applicant had not made his application for legal aid at least 21 days before that date, as required by reg 6E(2)(c)ᵃ of the Legal Aid in Criminal Proceedings (General) Regulations 1968. The applicant applied for an order of certiorari to quash the magistrates' decision e   that he was not entitled to apply for a review of the decision to refuse legal aid.

Held – On the true construction of reg 6E(2)(c) of the 1968 regulations, if a person was charged with an offence triable either way 'the date fixed for the trial of [the] information or the inquiry into [the] offence as examining justices' was not the date of the applicant's f   first appearance in court after being charged, because it was only then that the court had power to fix the date for trial or inquiry. It followed that the 21-day period for appealing against the refusal of legal aid was not to be computed by reference to the date of a person's first appearance in court after being charged but by reference to the date fixed for the trial or inquiry. An order of certiorari would therefore be granted quashing the decision of the magistrates that the applicant was not entitled to apply for a review of g   their decision to refuse legal aid (see p 792 *b* to *j* and p 793 *h*, post).

Notes
For legal aid in magistrates' courts, see 11 Halsbury's Laws (4th edn) paras 754, 757, and 29 ibid para 357.

h   **Cases cited**
R v City of Cambridge, ex p Leader (1980) 144 JP 208, DC.
R v Haslemere (Inhabitants) (1863) 32 LJMC 30.
Wozniak v Wozniak [1953] 1 All ER 1192, [1953] P 179, CA.

Application for judicial review
j   N, a minor suing by his father and next friend, applied, with leave of Gatehouse J granted on 9 June 1986, for judicial review by way of (i) an order of certiorari to remove to the Divisional Court of the Queen's Bench and quash the decision of the justices at Bury Magistrates' Court dated 14 May 1986 that the applicant was not entitled to apply to a criminal legal aid committee for a review of the decision of the justices that the applicant's

---

a   Regulation 6E(2), so far as material, is set out at p 791 *b c*, post

application for legal aid be refused, and (ii) an order of mandamus directed to the justices
requiring them to discharge their duty under the Legal Aid in Criminal Proceedings   *a*
(General) Regulations 1968, SI 1968/1231, by informing the applicant of the relevant
provisions under which he could apply to the criminal legal aid committee for review of ·
the justices' refusal of legal aid and supplying him with copies of Forms 14A and 14B to
enable him to apply for legal aid after the refusal. The facts are set out in the judgment
of Otton J.

b

John Lyons for the applicant.
Caroline J Swift for the justices.

Cur adv vult

c

30 July. The following judgments were delivered.

OTTON J (giving the first judgment at the invitation of Watkins LJ). In this matter the
applicant seeks judicial review of the decision of the justices at the Bury Magistrates'
Court on 14 May 1986—

d

    'that the Applicant be not entitled to apply to a Criminal Legal Aid Committee
    for a review of the decision of the said Justices that the Applicant's application for
    legal aid be refused.'

Leave to move was granted by the single judge.
    The facts can be stated briefly. On 6 May 1986 the applicant was arrested and charged
with one offence of obtaining property by deception contrary to s 15(1) of the Theft Act *e*
1968. He was released on bail until 3 June on which date he was to make his appearance
before the justices. On 7 May the applicant instructed his solicitors to act on his behalf in
relation to these criminal proceedings. The solicitors submitted a written application for
legal aid to the justices. On 14 May one of the justices refused the application on the
ground that it did 'not appear to the court desirable to make an order, in the interests of
justice', and informed the applicant that he was—   *f*

    'not entitled to apply by way of a review of the said decision to refuse the
    Applicant's application for legal aid to a Criminal Legal Aid Committee . . .'

Thus when the applicant appeared before the justices on 3 June he did not have the
benefit of legal aid. Furthermore, by virtue of the relevant regulations he did not have
any right or opportunity to apply to the criminal legal aid committee for a review of the *g*
magistrates' refusal of legal aid.
    The applicant seeks the following relief: (i) an order for certiorari quashing the decision
of the justices; and (ii) an order of mandamus requiring the justices to discharge their
duty under the Legal Aid in Criminal Proceedings (General) Regulations 1968, SI 1968/
1231.
    Regulation 6c(1) of the 1968 regulations provides: *h*

    'Where an application for a legal aid order is refused, the court or the proper
    officer of the court shall notify the applicant or, where the application was made by
    his parent or guardian, the parent or guardian, stating that the application has been
    refused on one or both of the following grounds, that—(*a*) it does not appear to the
    court or the proper officer of the court desirable to make an order in the interests of *j*
    justice; or (*b*) it does not appear to the court or the proper officer of the court that
    the applicant's disposable income and disposable capital are such that he requires
    assistance in meeting the costs he may incur, and shall inform him of the provisions,
    if any, of these Regulations which relate to the circumstances in which he may
    apply to a criminal legal aid committee for the decision to be reviewed.'

a
By reg 6E(1) of the regulations, where an application for a legal aid order has been refused after being considered for the first time by a magistrates' court, the applicant may apply for a review to the appropriate criminal legal aid committee. By reg 6E(2) an application for review shall only lie to the committee where (a) the applicant is charged with an indictable offence or an offence triable either way, and (b) the application for a legal aid order has been refused on the grounds specified in reg 6C(1)(a), to which I have referred, and—

b
'(c) the application for a legal aid order was made no later than 21 days [according to para 3.2.d of Lord Chancellor's Department circular LCD (84)1 dated 3 January 1984, '21 days' means 21 clear calendar days] before the date fixed for the trial of an information or the inquiry into an offence as examining justices, where such a date had been fixed at the time that the application was made.'

c
There is no dispute that the applicant was charged with an offence which was triable 'either way', and that his application for a legal aid order had been refused on the grounds specified in reg 6C(1)(a). The question this court has to consider was whether the proceedings on 3 June was 'the date fixed for the trial of an information or the inquiry into an offence as examining justices' within reg 6E(2)(c).

When the matter first came before this court the justices were not represented. An affidavit by the clerk to the justices for the petty sesssional division at Bury was placed before the court. Paragraph 9 states:

d

e
'I have the following comments to make regarding the matters appertaining to the Legal Aid application by the Applicant which I crave the Court to consider when deciding upon this case:—a. a copy of the Applicant's charge sheet was delivered to the court office by the Greater Manchester Police. The said charge sheet was dated the 6th day of May 1986 and indicated that the Applicant had been granted bail to appear before Bury Magistrates' Court on the 3rd day of June 1986 ... b. No indication was given to the Court by the Greater Manchester Police, the Crown Prosecution Service, the Applicant or the Applicant's solicitor that the 3rd day of June 1986 would not be the date of trial.'

f
The matter was adjourned to enable counsel to represent the justices. Counsel for the justices told us that there was an agreement or arrangement between the local law society and the justices in Greater Manchester that the words 'date fixed' referred to the date when it is understood that the hearing of the information or the inquiry as examining justices will actually take place.

g
Some magistrates' courts in the area, including Bury, although they are aware of the agreement, still regard the first appearance as the 'date fixed', unless the court is informed that it is the intention of the accused to plead not guilty (if by summary trial) or that the matter is to proceed by way of trial on indictment. About 50% of defendants in the area on their first appearance elected summary trial and pleaded guilty.

h
If an application is made when there is less than 21 days before that date and refused by the magistrates, the relevant part of the form is deleted, as there is insufficient time for a refusal to be reviewed by the committee before the set date. Thus it became clear to this court that the proper construction of these regulations was a matter of considerable importance to the Greater Manchester area and possibly of national importance.

j
Counsel for the applicant submits that, where a person is charged with an offence which is triable either way, the first appearance at court after being charged can never be in practice 'the date fixed for the trial of an information or the inquiry into an offence as examining justices'. The first appearance is only the first step in the procedure and four alternative courses are open to the magistrates. (1) The justices may merely remand the accused in custody or on bail. (2) If the accused elects trial on indictment then the justices may 'inquire' as examining justices. (3) If summary trial is chosen, the justices consider and decide whether to accept jurisdiction. If the justices consent to hearing the trial summarily, then in practice the prosecution witnesses are not present and the prosecution

is not in a position to proceed. Thus the hearing will be adjourned to a date fixed for the trial of the information. (4) The only circumstances in which there could be a final *a* determination of the case on the first appearance is if the magistrates agree to accept jurisdiction, the accused pleads guilty, and he wishes the case to be disposed of on that date without any further adjournment for the purpose of social inquiry reports or to call witnesses on his behalf.

Consequently, counsel for the applicant submits that on a proper construction of the regulations, where an application for legal aid is made less than 21 days before the first *b* appearance, an applicant is not to be deprived of his right of appeal to the criminal legal aid committee.

In my judgment, the date of the first appearance is not and can never be the 'date fixed for trial' within the regulations. The charge sheet merely requires the accused to attend the court on a particular date in order to answer to the charge. The top copy of the charge sheet is handed to the accused and it states in terms: *c*

'On your first appearance before the magistrates' court no witnesses will be required to attend. If you propose to plead not guilty a convenient date for the hearing of the case will be arranged by the court . . .'

Thus, on its face, the charge sheet not only indicates that the first appearance date is not the date fixed for trial, but it implies that the date of the trial or inquiry will be a *d* subsequent date. There is no power in the police to fix the date for trial or inquiry into an offence. Only the court can do so on the occasion of the first appearance.

In order to do so the court must first consider the case as it then stands. If the accused elects summary trial, the magistrates will then decide whether to accept or decline jurisdiction. If they decline jurisdiction they then become 'examining justices' and they decide on the mode, place and date of the committal proceedings. Even if it were decided *e* to proceed there and then, it is only at that moment when the date becomes 'fixed'. In practice this is unlikely, if ever, to be on the same day.

If the justices accept jurisdiction and the plea is taken, two situations arise. (1) If the plea is not guilty then the prosecution will in practice, because the witnesses have not been required to attend, ask for an adjournment and a date to be fixed. The date is then fixed. If, by chance, the prosecution is in a position to proceed there and then, the defence *f* agrees, and the court agrees to hear the case on the same day, the date then becomes fixed. If the defence opposes and asks for an adjournment and is refused, and the court orders the case to proceed immediately, the date is again then fixed. (2) If the accused pleads guilty, the same procedural consequences follow. The fact that he may have indicated that he intends to ask the court to deal with the matter summarily and to plead guilty on the date shown in the charge sheet does not fix this date for trial. This occurs when the *g* court agrees to proceed on that basis. It is thus inaccurate for the clerk to state:

'No indication was given to the Court by the Greater Manchester Police, the Crown Prosecution Service, the Applicant or the Applicant's solicitor that the 3rd day of June 1986 would not be the date of trial.'

None of these has the power to indicate that it is the date fixed for trial. *h*

It follows that I would grant an order for certiorari quashing the decision or purported decision of the justices that the applicant was not entitled to apply to the criminal legal aid committee for a review of the decision to refuse legal aid.

WATKINS LJ. I agree. The point is issue here is undoubtedly of importance generally. Our determination of it is likely to affect justices and their clerks in many parts of *j* England and Wales. The right of a person who has been refused legal aid by a justice or justices to apply for a review of the decision to a criminal legal aid committee must be carefully safeguarded by a proper construction and application of reg 6E of the Legal Aid in Criminal Proceedings (General) Regulations 1968, SI 1968/1231.

In 1984 the Law Society acknowledged that the matter of construction of the relevant
a parts of the regulation to put it in their words, 'has been causing problems in several
parts of the country'. I quote from a notice which appeared in the Law Society's Gazette,
the concluding passage of which is as follows ([1984] LS Gaz 2267):

> 'It is understood that some courts have interpreted the words "date fixed for the
> trial of an information" to mean the next date when the case comes before the court.
> It was agreed at a joint committee of The Law Society and the Justices' Clerks'
b > Society on 11 July 1984 that this is an incorrect interpretation and that the words
> "date fixed for the trial of an information or the inquiry into the offence as
> examining justices . . ." referred to the date when it is understood *the trial of the
> committal will actually take place.*'

This praiseworthy attempt to solve the problems has not, to say the least, been wholly
c successful as the facts of the present case make clear. There are a number of similar
applications to this court to that made by the applicant involving an identical issue
arising from decisions of justices at Manchester City and Warrington which await our
decision. We are told that they are but a few of the many instances in which an
unsuccessful applicant for legal aid has been improperly deprived of the opportunity of a
review of refusal by a criminal legal aid committee. If that is right, then obviously a most
d regrettable situation obtains in some if not more magistrates' courts, and the need for
uniformity of practice based on a proper construciton of the regulation is apparent.

Some indication of the vast incidence of applications for legal aid to justices will serve
to highlight even further the importance of putting right what is obviously wrong.
Counsel for the justices told us that in the Bury Magistrates' Court alone in one recent
year there were in approximate figures 1,500 applications, 360 of which were refused.
e When one thinks of the very large number of magistrates' courts there are, it is not
difficult to envisage how onerous the task of justices, likewise members of review
committees, is, in the exercise of discretion to grant or refuse legal aid. They must on the
one hand do their best to ensure that they do not withhold legal aid unjustly and on the
other, with similar regard for the public interest, deny this assistance when it is not
warranted. In the present context, of course, justices must permit or refuse review of
f refusal on a proper legal basis.

Nothing we say should in any sense be taken as critical of justices in discharging their
functions as to legal aid generally. Our anxiety is to assist them into uniformity of
approach on the troublesome question of 'date fixed for . . . trial' so that all complaints
on this score may be laid to rest.

Lastly, I wish to emphasise that we quash the decision of the justices in the present
g case to refuse legal aid, not by doubting the propriety of the exercise of their discretion
in that regard, but solely because we must of necessity do so, seeing that we are driven to
quash their decision as to review. I should add that the justices' discretion has not been
challenged before us. On the facts as we know them we do not see how it could have
been. Nevertheless, a justice will have to consider afresh the applicant's application and
if needs be ensure that a proper opportunity is provided for review of the decision.
h The orders of certiorari and mandamus applied for will be granted.

Orders of certiorari and mandamus granted.

Solicitors: *Graham Leigh Pfeffer & Co*, Prestwich (for the applicant); *Ian C Webb*, clerk to
the justices, Bury (for the justices).

j
                                                            Dilys Tausz   Barrister.

Bankers Trust Co v Galadari and another (Chase Manhattan Bank NA intervening)

COURT OF APPEAL, CIVIL DIVISION

KERR, PARKER AND BALCOMBE LJJ

6 AUGUST, 14 OCTOBER 1986

Execution – Writ of fi fa – Priority between competing writs – Effect of erroneous court order – Judgment creditor delivering writ to sheriff for execution – Sheriff obtaining walking possession of goods – Judgment subsequently set aside and sheriff instructed not to proceed with execution – Second writ issued by another judgment creditor – Original judgment restored by Court of Appeal – Effect of restoration of judgment on priority of original writ – Whether original writ retaining priority over subsequent writ.

The plaintiffs issued a writ of fieri facias against the first defendant's goods pursuant to a judgment which they had obtained against him for over $US6·5m. The sheriff obtained walking possession of goods at the first defendant's residence under the writ. Thereafter the first defendant's wife gave notice of claim to the goods, but before the sheriff could issue an interpleader summons a bank issued a writ of fieri facias against the first defendant's goods pursuant to a judgment for over $US11m which it had obtained against him. The bank did not deliver its writ to the sheriff for execution because it was unlikely that there would be any surplus after the plaintiffs' writ, which had priority, had been executed. The plaintiffs' judgment was later set aside and the plaintiffs instructed the sheriff to lift walking possession and not to issue the interpleader summons. The bank then delivered its writ to the sheriff for execution but he was unable to execute it and instead he issued an interpleader summons because the wife continued to maintain her claim to the goods. The Court of Appeal subsequently restored the plaintiffs' judgment and the plaintiffs requested the sheriff to retake possession of the goods forthwith in priority over the bank. The sheriff refused and required the plaintiffs to issue a new writ. The plaintiffs applied to the Court of Appeal for directions as to the effect of the restoration of their judgment on the priority of their writ over the bank's writ.

Held – The effect of the withdrawal of the sheriff from possession due to an erroneous court order was to be dealt with by the court as a matter of practice rather than law and the court would ensure that a party did not suffer by reason of the erroneous order, with the result that the judgment creditor for whom the sheriff had taken possession would not be made to start again and issue a fresh writ when the erroneous order was set aside. Furthermore, the priority of a writ was not necessarily lost by its temporary invalidity, since priority was a matter of equity and accordingly, if the temporary invalidity of the writ was not caused by any fault or voluntary action or inaction on the part of the creditor but by an erroneous decision of a lower court, the court would ensure that when the matter was put right the creditor did not lose the benefit of action taken under what was subsequently held to have been throughout a valid judgment. Since the plaintiffs had countermanded their instructions to the sheriff to proceed with execution solely because of the erroneous order of the court it would be inequitable to deprive them of their priority unless some special reason was shown for removing it, and since no special reason had been shown the plaintiffs were entitled to priority over the bank (see p 797 g to p 798 c h to p 799 b g to p 800 d, post).

P B J Davis Manufacturing Co Ltd v Fahn [1967] 2 All ER 1274 applied.

Hunt v Hooper (1844) 12 M & W 664 considered.

Per curiam. Where a judgment pursuant to which a writ of fieri facias has been issued is set aside, it is the creditor's duty to inform the sheriff of that fact. Once he is so informed the sheriff cannot proceed with execution unless and until the judgment is restored and he has been notified of that fact. However, if in the interim period the a sheriff has had any dealings with the goods or their proceeds which would have been wrongful as against the creditor had the judgment not been set aside, he is not liable to the creditor in respect of such dealings. If a creditor whose judgment has been set aside gives notice to the sheriff that the order to set aside is under appeal and thereafter the sheriff receives for execution another writ in respect of the same goods, the sheriff should not proceed beyond possession without applying to the court for directions and giving notice to both creditors of that application (see p 799 c to e and p 800 d, post).

b
Notes
For priority of writs of fieri facias, see 17 Halsbury's Laws (4th edn) para 439, and for cases on the subject, see 21 Digest (Reissue) 358–360, 2467–2485.

Cases referred to in judgments
c Davis (P B J) Manufacturing Co Ltd v Fahn (Fahn, claimant) [1967] 2 All ER 1274, [1967] 1 WLR 1059, CA.
Hunt v Hooper (1844) 12 M & W 664, 152 ER 1365.

Case also cited
Hutchinson v Johnston (1787) 1 Term Rep 729, 99 ER 1346.

d
Application for directions
The plaintiffs, Bankers Trust Co, applied for directions consequent on the decision of the Court of Appeal (Kerr, Parker and Balcombe LJJ) on 7 July 1986 whereby that court allowed an appeal by the plaintiffs against the judgment of Webster J dated 6 June 1986 setting aside a judgment in default of defence obtained by the plaintiffs against the first e defendant, Abdul Latif Ebraham Galadari, on 4 April 1986 in an action brought by the plaintiffs against the first defendant and the second defendant, Abdul Rahim Ebraham Galadari, on a promissory note, and ordered that the judgment of 4 April 1986 be restored. The directions sought were as to the effect of the restored judgment on the priority between a writ of fieri facias issued by the plaintiffs against the first defendant's goods pursuant to the original judgment of 4 April 1986 and a writ of fieri facias issued f on 22 May 1986 by Chase Manhattan Bank NA pursuant to a judgment dated 18 May 1986. The Sheriff of Greater London had required the plaintiffs to issue a new writ. Chase Manhattan Bank NA were given leave to intervene in the proceedings. The facts are set out in the judgment of Parker LJ.

Timothy Charlton for the plaintiffs.
g Peter Irvin for the Chase Manhattan Bank.
Thomas Shields for the Sheriff of Greater London.
The defendants did not appear.

Cur adv vult

14 October. The following judgments were delivered.

h
PARKER LJ (giving the first judgment at the invitation of Kerr LJ). On 7 July 1986 this court, constituted as it is at present, allowed an appeal by the plaintiffs from a judgment of Webster J given on 6 June by which he ordered that default judgment obtained by the plaintiffs against the first defendant on 4 April should be set aside. The order of this court was that the judgment of Webster J be set aside and that the judgment j of 4 April, which was for over $US6·5m, be restored.
    What this court is now to determine is the effect of, or what directions should be given pursuant to, its own order of 7 July in respect of a writ of fieri facias which had been issued by the plaintiffs pursuant to the judgment of 4 April. To that writ I shall hereafter refer as 'the plaintiffs' writ'.
    The relevant facts may be shortly stated. The plaintiffs' writ was issued on 9 April and was delivered to the sheriff to be executed at 4.30 pm on the same day. Section 138 of

the Supreme Court Act 1981 provides that a writ of fieri facias against goods issued from the High Court shall bind the property in the goods of the execution debtor as from the time when the writ is delivered to the sheriff for execution.

a

It should be noted that the property in the goods is bound from the time of delivery of the writ and not from the time when the sheriff obtains possession under the writ.

On 9 May the sheriff obtained walking possession of the goods at the first defendant's residence at 2 Courtenay Avenue, Hampstead, London N6 and made an inventory of the goods there found.

b

Thereafter notice of claim to the goods was given by the first defendant's wife and in the ordinary course the next step would have been the issue of a sheriff's interpleader summons. Before any such summons had been issued, however, further events occurred. On 19 May Chase Manhattan Bank NA (Chase Manhattan) obtained judgment against the first defendant for a sum in excess of $US11m. Pursuant to that judgment Chase Manhattan, on 22 May, obtained the issue of a writ of fieri facias against the goods of the first defendant. I shall hereafter refer to that writ as 'the Chase Manhattan writ'. That writ was not, however, then delivered to the sheriff for execution, since Chase Manhattan were aware that the plaintiffs had obtained judgment against the first defendant and had delivered their writ to the sheriff for execution. They were accordingly advised that it was unlikely that there would be any surplus after the execution of the plaintiffs' writ which would have priority.

c

On 6 June, however, the situation was changed by the order of Webster J that the plaintiffs' judgment be set aside and by a letter from the plaintiffs' solicitors to the sheriff's office in the terms following:

d

> 'We refer to our letter of 16th May and write to inform you that the Defendant's application to set aside Judgment was today granted by the Commercial Court. Accordingly, we would be obliged if you would instruct the Sheriff to lift the Walking Possession Order and not to issue the Interpleader Summons.'

e

In the light of the judgment of Webster J it was clearly the duty of the plaintiffs' solicitors to write in some such terms.

On 10 June Chase Manhattan, having learned of the order of Webster J, delivered the Chase Manhattan writ to the sheriff for execution. Thereafter the sheriff attempted unsuccessfully to execute that writ and on 25 June, the first defendant's wife having intimated that she maintained her claim to the goods at 2 Courtenay Avenue, he issued an interpleader summons in respect of the goods intended to be seized by him at that address.

f

There matters stood when, on 7 July, this court ordered that the order of Webster J be set aside and the plaintiffs' judgment of 4 April be restored. On 8 July the plaintiffs notified the sheriff's office of the order and requested the sheriff to retake possession forthwith and to give the plaintiffs priority over Chase Manhattan. This request the sheriff declined, contending that the plaintiffs would have to issue a fresh writ and that their priority would date from the time when such writ was delivered to him for execution.

g

As a result, the plaintiffs now apply to this court seeking to regain or maintain the priority which they would admittedly have had had their judgment not been erroneously set aside. Their application is resisted by Chase Manhattan. The sheriff, whilst supporting Chase Manhattan's view of the law, seeks principally to ensure that, if this court should take a different view of the law, it should make clear what his position will be.

h

The plaintiffs' contention that their writ should have priority has the merit of simplicity. They say: 'Our writ was obtained pursuant to the judgment of 4 April. It was delivered to the sheriff on 9 April and it thereby gained priority over all writs subsequently so delivered. True the judgment pursuant to which it was issued was erroneously set aside on 6 June, but that judgment was restored on 7 July. The issue and delivery of our writ were, therefore, both effected pursuant to a valid judgment and cannot or should not be affected either by the erroneous order of 6 June or the letter which our solicitors wrote on the same day.'

j

In support of this contention they rely on the decision of this court in *P B J Davis*
a Manufacturing Co Ltd v Fahn (Fahn, claimant) [1967] 2 All ER 1274, [1967] 1 WLR 1059.
In that case the judgment creditor issued a writ of fieri facias and delivered it to the
sheriff for execution. The sheriff duly took possession under the writ but the debtor's
wife claimed that the property seized belonged to her. The sheriff took out an interpleader
summons and served the judgment creditor. On the return of the summons the creditor
sought a special appointment for the hearing of the wife's disputed claim but the master
b refused the request for such an appointment and dealt with the matter on the material
then before him. He ordered that 'the [wife's] claim be allowed and the sheriff withdraw
from possession of the goods seized by him under the writ of fi. fa.' (see [1967] 2 All ER
1274 at 1276, [1967] 1 WLR 1059 at 1061). The sheriff duly withdrew pursuant to such
order. On an appeal by the creditor the appeal was allowed and the order of the master
set aside.
c   In the course of his judgment Lord Denning MR said ([1967] 2 All ER 1274 at 1276,
[1967] 1 WLR 1059 at 1061):

> '. . . counsel for the sheriff has raised a point of practice. The master ordered the
> sheriff to withdraw, and he has withdrawn. What is to happen when this court
> reverses the master's order? Does it mean there is to be a new writ of fi. fa., a new
> summons for interpleader, a new claim, and all the procedure to be gone through
d > again? I do not think so. When this court reverses the order of the master, we
> should restore, as near as may be, the position as it was before. We will direct that
> the sheriff retake possession now and that his possession be deemed to have
> continued in the interval since the master's order; but we ought to protect the sheriff
> by holding that he is not to be liable in respect of any dealings with the goods in the
> meantime. He can now go into possession once again as he did originally.'

e
In a short concurring judgment Danckwerts LJ said:

> 'I agree. I certainly think that if the judgment creditor obtains a writ of execution
> and then is met by a claim by the debtor's wife that all the property in the
> matrimonial home either belongs to her or is subject to hire-purchase agreements
> in her name, the creditor is entitled to have the matter properly investigated, and
f > also that in the meantime he should not lose the benefit of the possession by the
> sheriff. I agree with LORD DENNING, M.R., that the appeal should be allowed.'

That case is different from the present in that the judgment pursuant to which the
writ of fieri facias was issued was never set aside but remained valid throughout. The
case is, however, of considerable assistance. It shows this court dealing with the effect of
g the withdrawal from possession pursuant to an erroneous order as a matter of practice,
not law. It recognises that this court should ensure that a party does not suffer by reason
of an erroneous decision of a lower court. It establishes that where a sheriff withdraws
from possession pursuant to an erroneous order of the court there is no need, when the
order is set aside, for the judgment creditor to start again and issue a fresh writ.
     The fact that the question raised is one of practice, not law, is, in my view, confirmed
h by the terms of RSC Ord 46, r 8. Rule 8(1) provides that writ of execution is valid in the
first instance for 12 months beginning with the date of issue. Rule 8(2), however,
provides that the validity of a writ which has not been wholly executed may be extended
from time to time for a period of 12 months at any time if an application for an extension
is made to the court 'before the day next following that on which the writ would
otherwise expire or such later day, if any, as the Court may allow'. An application for an
j extension may thus be made and allowed after a writ has expired. The matter is one for
the discretion of the court. Thus far no direct assistance on the question of priorities is
afforded, but r 8(4) provides:

> 'The priority of a writ, the validity of which has been extended under this rule,
> shall be determined by reference to the date on which it was originally delivered to
> the sheriff.'

Hence, if a writ has expired and a competing writ is delivered to the sheriff after such expiry but the original writ is subsequently extended, it will retain its priority notwithstanding that it had for a period no validity and that during such period a competing writ had been delivered to the sheriff.

In such a situation a court dealing with an application for extension would no doubt consider whether it was just that a creditor who had allowed his writ to expire without application should be permitted to retain his priority, for it is necessary to remember that priorities are a matter of equity. That priority is not necessarily lost by a temporary invalidity of a writ is, however, clear.

Where, as here, temporary invalidity is in no way due to the fault or volunary action or inaction of the creditor but to the erroneous decision of the court, I have no doubt that this court should, if it can, ensure that, when the matter is put right, the creditor should not lose the benefit of what he has done under what has been held to be, throughout, a valid judgment.

Chase Manhattan, however, contend that this court cannot, or at least in all the circumstances should not, allow the plaintiffs the priority which they seek. They rely in support of their contention on *Hunt v Hooper* (1844) 12 M & W 664, 152 ER 1365. In that case one Bird had obtained a writ of fieri facias against the goods of Ward and delivered it to the sheriff for execution. On the next day, however, Ward offered Bird £50 to stay execution. Bird, as a result, first verbally requested the sheriff to suspend execution and then gave him written notice not to execute until further order. Five days later the plaintiff also delivered to the sheriff for execution a writ of fieri facias against the goods of Ward and the sheriff seized the goods pursuant to that writ. The next day, however, Ward having failed to pay the £50, Bird instructed the sheriff to proceed with execution under his writ.

The goods seized were then sold by the sheriff and the proceeds paid to Bird, a return of nulla bona being made to the plaintiff's writ. The plaintiff then sued the sheriff for the proceeds and succeeded. He raised two contentions. The first was that Bird's writ had never been delivered for execution at all. This contention was negatived by the jury. The second was that, even if the writ had originally been delivered for execution, the orders not to execute had the effect of depriving Bird of the priority gained by the original delivery for execution. This contention succeeded. Parke B, giving the judgment of the court, said (12 M & W 664 at 673, 152 ER 1365 at 1369):

'We are, therefore, of opinion, that in this case the countermand of the execution of the writ was equivalent to its withdrawal at the time, and Bird's writ could not be considered as having been delivered to the sheriff to be executed until the order to proceed after the delivery of the plaintiff's, and consequently the rule must be absolute to enter a verdict for 27*l*. 5*s*. 11*d*., the amount realized. Rule absolute.'

In my view that case does not materially assist Chase Manhattan. There, before anything had been done under this writ, Bird had voluntarily instructed the sheriff not to proceed. Here, on the other hand, the sheriff had acted under the writ and obtained walking possession. The plaintiffs' solicitors' letter of 6 June was in no sense a voluntary countermanding of the delivery of the writ for execution but a letter which they were in duty bound to write as a result of the judgment of Webster J. There is a vast difference between an instruction given as a necessary consequence of an order of the court and an instruction given pursuant to a voluntary bargain between the creditor and the judgment debtor. In the latter case it would clearly be inequitable to allow the creditor to maintain his priority against subsequent creditors. In the former, in the absence of very special circumstances, it would, in my view, equally clearly be inequitable to deprive him of his priority if the order is subsequently reversed. The plaintiffs' writ was issued pursuant to the judgment of 4 April. That judgment has been restored. The issue of the writ was therefore entirely valid. There can be no need for the issue of a second writ and in my view the priority originally acquired by the delivery of the writ must survive or be restored unless some special reason is shown for removing it.

a Chase Manhattan submitted that there were here good reasons for doing so if, contrary to the primary contention, the court had power to maintain or restore such priority. I find it unnecessary to set out the details of such submission. It is sufficient to say that I can see no good reason for doing other than restoring the plaintiffs to the position in which they were before the erroneous judgment of Webster J. I would therefore direct that the plaintiffs are entitled to priority over Chase Manhattan and that the sheriff is at liberty to proceed under the walking possession originally obtained, subject always, of

b course, to the wife establishing her claim to the goods in interpleader proceedings. Whether any further directions are required for the protection of the sheriff is a matter on which submissions on his behalf can be made.

It only remains to consider the sheriff's position consequent on the fact that the practice of requiring a new writ in circumstances such as the present is in my view wrong. I cannot, for my part, see that more is required than to say that, where the

c judgment pursuant to which a writ of fieri facias has been issued is set aside, it is the duty of the creditor so to inform the sheriff, that once so informed the sheriff cannot proceed with the execution unless and until the judgment is restored and he has been notified of the fact and that, if in the interim period he has had any dealings with the goods or their proceeds which would have been wrongful as against the creditor had the judgment not been set aside, he is not to be liable to the creditor in respect of such dealings.

d If a creditor whose judgment has been set aside gives notice to the sheriff that the order to set aside is under appeal and thereafter the sheriff receives for execution another writ in respect of the same goods, he should not, in my view, proceed beyond possession without applying to the court for directions and giving notice to both creditors of such application.

e **KERR LJ.** I had considerable doubts during the argument whether the decision of this issue in favour of the plaintiffs would conflict with the judgment of the Court of Exchequer in *Hunt v Hooper* (1844) 12 M & W 664, 152 ER 1365 delivered by Parke B. The facts of that case have already been summarised in the judgment of Parker LJ and are clearly quite different from those of the present one. In particular, as pointed out by him, execution of the writ was there suspended at the voluntary request of the first

f judgment creditor (Bird) to the sheriff (Hooper) because Bird had made a bargain with the judgment debtor (Ward). In these circumstances the first judgment creditor clearly had no merits whatever as against the second judgment creditor (Hunt), whereas in the present situation the merits appear to me to rest clearly on the side of the plaintiffs. Their solicitors' instructions to the sheriff to suspend execution were forced on them by the error of the trial judge in having set aside a regular judgment obtained by them in

g circumstances which this court decided to have been wholly objectionable. It follows that in law this judgment should have remained in force throughout, and that, as a matter of justice, this judicial error should equally not cause any loss of priority for a writ of fieri facias based on that judgment once it had been restored.

The point of concern which I felt about *Hunt v Hooper* was that the judgment could be read as laying down two general propositions, viz (i) that a writ of fieri facias is only valid,

h in the sense of having to be treated as delivered to the sheriff, during any period when he has instructions to execute it and not during any period when such instructions are suspended, and (ii) that any further writ of fieri facias delivered for execution during such period of invalidity of the earlier writ must have priority over it. Thus the submission which Parke B accepted was as follows (12 M & W 664 at 672, 152 ER 1365 at 1368):

j '. . . Bird's writ ought to have no preference, because, though it was first delivered to be executed, such execution was afterwards countermanded, and, whilst such countermand continued, the writ must be considered as not delivered at all *to be executed*, because the sheriff could not act upon it, and that the second order to execute could give no priority.' (My emphasis.)

However, on further consideration I think that *Hunt v Hooper* is only authority for point
(i), not point (ii) as well. Instructions to the sheriff to suspend execution of a writ
undoubtedly suspends its validity so long as such instructions are in force, whatever may
have occasioned them to be given. Thus, if the sheriff executes a subsequent writ during
this period, his dealings with the debtor's goods in favour of another judgment creditor
cannot be called in question. The same applies, for instance, during the period after the
expiry of a writ of fieri facias and before any order renewing it under RSC Ord 46, r 8, to
which Parker LJ has referred. During this period the writ is obviously not in force at all.

    But these considerations only support proposition (i) above; they are not determinative
of (ii). On the contrary, as pointed out by Parker LJ, the effect of Ord 46, r 8(4) is that
priority is not lost as the result of a period of invalidity after a writ has expired if it is
subsequently 'extended', ie in effect revived. Similarly, I do not think that *Hunt v Hooper*
lays down any general proposition on the lines of (ii) above. Thus, in the passage which I
have cited from the judgment of Parke B he merely says in this regard that 'the second
order to execute could give no priority'. In the circumstances this conclusion was
inevitable, and, in so far as priorities raise issues of equity, the contrary could not then
have been argued before that court, even if the merits had permitted any such argument
on the facts, as they do here.

    In the result I consider that *Hunt v Hooper* is not an authority which inhibits us from
deciding the issue as to priority in favour of the plaintiffs and I agree with the judgment
of Parker LJ.

BALCOMBE LJ. I agree with the judgments of both Kerr and Parker LJJ.

Declaration that plaintiffs have priority over Chase Manhattan.

Solicitors: *Rowe & Maw* (for the plaintiffs); *Allen & Overy* (for Chase Manhattan); *Burchell
& Ruston* (for the Sheriff of Greater London).

                                                            Mary Rose Plummer   Barrister.

Wilsher v Essex Area Health Authority

COURT OF APPEAL, CIVIL DIVISION

SIR NICOLAS BROWNE-WILKINSON V-C, MUSTILL AND GLIDEWELL LJJ

13, 14 JANUARY, 28, 29, 30 APRIL, 1, 2, 6, 7 MAY, 24 JULY 1986

Medical practitioner – Negligence – Duty of care – Standard of care – Specialist hospital unit – Duty and standard of care required of specialist unit – Junior doctor in unit inserting catheter into baby's vein instead of artery – Junior doctor consulting senior registrar who failed to notice error – Senior registrar subsequently making same error – Baby given excess oxygen as result of error – Whether health authority could be directly liable for failure to provide proper staff for unit – Whether any concept of team negligence – Whether inexperience of doctor a defence.

Medical practitioner – Negligence – Burden of proof – Failure to take step in treatment designed to avert or minimise risk – Whether onus of proof on doctor to prove plaintiff's injuries not caused by failure to take step.

Medical practitioner – Negligence – Causation – Breach of duty causing or materially contributing to damage – Enhancement of existing risk – Doctor's negligence merely one of several factors which could have caused injury – Existence and extent to which doctor's negligence contributed to plaintiff's injury not able to be ascertained – Whether doctor liable for breach of duty.

The plaintiff was an infant child who was born prematurely suffering from various illnesses, including oxygen deficiency. His prospects of survival were considered to be poor and he was placed in the 24-hour special care baby unit at the hospital where he was born. The unit was staffed by a medical team, consisting of two consultants, a senior registrar, several junior doctors and trained nurses. While the plaintiff was in the unit a junior and inexperienced doctor monitoring the oxygen in the plaintiff's bloodstream mistakenly inserted a catheter into a vein rather than an artery but then asked the senior registrar to check what he had done. The registrar failed to see the mistake and some hours later, when replacing the catheter, did exactly the same thing himself. In both instances the catheter monitor failed to register correctly the amount of oxygen in the plaintiff's blood, with the result that the plaintiff was given excess oxygen. The plaintiff subsequently brought an action against the health authority claiming damages and alleging that the excess oxygen in his bloodstream had caused an incurable condition of the retina resulting in near blindness. At the trial of the action the judge awarded the plaintiff £116,199. The health authority appealed to the Court of Appeal, contending, inter alia, (i) that there had been no breach of the duty of care owed to the plaintiff because the standard of care required of the doctors in the unit was only that reasonably required of doctors having the same formal qualifications and practical experience as the doctors in the unit, and (ii) that the plaintiff had failed to show that the health authority's actions had caused or contributed to the plaintiff's condition since excess oxygen was merely one of several different factors any one of which could have caused or contributed to the eye condition from which the plaintiff suffered.

Held – (1) Where hospital treatment was provided by a specialist unit or team of doctors, the existence of a duty of care and the standard of care required of the unit and its members were to be determined on the basis that—

(a) (per Sir Nicolas Browne-Wilkinson V-C and Glidewell LJ) there was no reason why, in certain circumstances, a health authority could not be directly liable to a plaintiff if it failed to provide sufficient or properly qualified and competent medical staff for the unit (see p 831 g and p 833 h j, post);

(b) there was no concept of 'team negligence', in the sense that each individual member of the team was required to observe the standards demanded of the unit as a whole, because it could not be right, for example, to expose a student nurse to an action for negligence for her failure to possess the experience of a consultant (see p 812 *j* to p 813 *b*, p 831 *h* and p 832 *h*, post);

(c) (Sir Nicolas Browne-Wilkinson V-C dissenting) the standard of care required of members of the unit was that of the ordinary skilled person exercising and professing to have that special skill, but that standard was to be determined in the context of the particular posts in the unit rather than according to the general rank or status of the people filling the posts, since the duty ought to be tailored to the acts which the doctor had elected to perform rather than to the doctor himself. It followed that inexperience was no defence to an action for medical negligence. However (per Glidewell LJ), an inexperienced doctor who was called on to exercise a specialist skill and who made a mistake nevertheless satisfied the necessary standard of care if he had sought the advice and help of his superior when necessary (see p 813 *b* to *d g* to *j* and p 830 *j* to p 831 *d h*, post); *Bolam v Friern Hospital Management Committee* [1957] 2 All ER 118 applied;

(d) a plaintiff could not shift the burden of proof onto a defendant doctor or the doctor's employer merely by showing that a step in the treatment which was designed to avert or minimise a risk had not been taken in the particular circumstances (see p 814 *c* to *e g*, p 815 *f g*, p 816 *f* and p 832 *h*, post); dictum of Peter Pain J in *Clark v MacLennan* [1983] 1 All ER at 427 disapproved.

(2) Although the junior doctor had not been negligent and had satisfied the relevant standard of care by consulting his superior, the registrar had been negligent in failing to notice that the catheter had been mistakenly inserted in a vein rather than an artery and accordingly the health authority was vicariously liable for the registrar's negligence (see p 817 *f*, p 818 *f* to *h*, p 831 *d e* and p 834 *d* to *f*, post).

(3) (Sir Nicolas Browne-Wilkinson V-C dissenting) On the issue of causation, a defendant was liable to a plaintiff in an action for medical negligence where his conduct enhanced an existing risk that injury would ensue, notwithstanding either that the conduct in question was merely one of several possible risk factors, any one of which could have caused the injury, or that the existence and extent of the contribution made by the defendant's breach of duty to the plaintiff's injury could not be ascertained. On the facts, the plaintiff had established a sufficient connection between the excessive exposure to oxygen and the development of his eye condition for the defendants to be liable to the plaintiff in negligence on the basis that their breach of duty was the cause of the plaintiff's injury. The appeal would therefore be dismissed (see p 828 *j* to p 829 *d f* and p 832 *e f*, post); *McGhee v National Coal Board* [1972] 3 All ER 1008 applied.

Per curiam. The sooner that pre-trial disclosure of the respective contentions or expert evidence becomes the norm rather than the exception in medical negligence suits the better will justice be served and (per Sir Nicolas Browne-Wilkinson V-C) the Supreme Court Rule Committee should, as a matter of urgency, look again at the question of exchange of medical reports before trial (see p 830 *f g*, p 832 *g h*, p 835 *j* to p 836 *a*, post).

Notes

For the duty and the standard of care required of the medical profession, see 34 Halsbury's Laws (4th edn) para 12, and for cases on the subject, see 33 Digest (Reissue) 262–268, 2162–2330.

For the burden of proof of causation of injury in an action for damages, see 12 Halsbury's Laws (4th edn) para 1141 and 34 ibid paras 54–56, and for cases on the subject, see 36(1) Digest (Reissue) 57–65, 190–237.

Cases referred to in judgments

A/S Rendal v Arcos Ltd [1937] 3 All ER 577, HL.
Bolam v Friern Hospital Management Committee [1957] 2 All ER 118, [1957] 1 WLR 582.
Bonnington Castings Ltd v Wardlaw [1956] 1 All ER 615, [1956] AC 613, [1956] 2 WLR 707, HL.
Clark v MacLennan [1983] 1 All ER 416.

a   *Gardiner v Motherwell Machinery and Scrap Co Ltd* [1961] 3 All ER 831, [1961] 1 WLR
       1424, 1961 SC (HL) 1, HL.
   McDermid v Nash Dredging and Reclamation Co Ltd [1986] 2 All ER 676, [1986] QB 965,
       [1986] 3 WLR 45, CA.
   McGhee v National Coal Board [1972] 3 All ER 1008, [1973] 1 WLR 1, HL.
   Murray (a minor) v Kensington and Chelsea and Westminster Health Authority (1 May 1980,
       unreported), QBD; *affd* [1981] CA Transcript 339.

b   *Nicholson v Atlas Steel Foundry and Engineering Co Ltd* [1957] 1 All ER 776, [1957] 1 WLR
       613, HL.
   Rahman v Kirklees Area Health Authority [1980] 3 All ER 610, [1980] 1 WLR 1244, CA.
   Thompson v Smiths Shiprepairers (North Shields) Ltd [1984] 1 All ER 881, [1984] QB 405,
       [1984] 2 WLR 522.
   Whitehouse v Jordan [1980] 1 All ER 650, CA; *affd* [1981] 1 All ER 267, [1981] 1 WLR

c   246, HL.

Cases also cited

   Barnett v Chelsea and Kensington Hospital Management Committee [1968] 1 All ER 1068,
       [1969] 1 QB 428.
   Brown v Rolls Royce Ltd [1960] 1 All ER 577, [1960] 1 WLR 210, HL.

d   *Hucks v Cole* (1968) 112 SJ 483, CA.
   Junor v McNicol (1959) Times, 26 March, HL.

Appeal

By a notice of appeal dated 31 January 1985 the defendants, Essex Area Health Authority,
appealed against the judgment of Peter Pain J given on 21 December 1984 whereby he
e adjudged that the defendants, their servants or agents were guilty of negligence and that
such negligence had caused injury loss and damage to the infant plaintiff, Martin Graham
Wilsher, suing by his mother and next friend Heather Marjorie Wilsher. The facts are
set out in the judgment of Mustill LJ.

Ian Kennedy QC and *Stephen Miller* for the defendants.
f *Stuart McKinnon QC* and *James Badenoch* for the plaintiff.

Cur adv vult

24 July. The following judgments were delivered.

g **MUSTILL LJ** (giving the first judgment at the invitation of Sir Nicolas Browne-
Wilkinson V-C). Martin Wilsher was born on 14 December 1978. He was a tiny baby,
and his birth was nearly three months early. His prospects of survival were very poor:
according to one estimate they were as low as one chance in five. He could not breathe
effectively, and for more than eleven weeks he needed extra oxygen. Repeatedly, the
oxygen, carbon dioxide and acid balances of his blood went awry. From time to time he
h ceased to breathe. An early extra-ventricular haemorrhage led to hydrocephalus, for
which he required surgery. On one occasion he was believed to have pneumonia.
Undoubtedly, he lingered close to death, and there was always present the spectre of
brain damage. Yet Martin is alive and well today with his intellect unimpaired. Beyond
doubt this is due to the treatment which he received during his long days and night in
the special care baby unit at the Princess Alexandra Hospital, Harlow.

j   Sadly, Martin is nearly blind. He suffers from retrolental fibroplasia, an incurable
condition of the retina. On his behalf it is said that this condition was caused by an exess
of oxygen tension in his bloodstream during the early weeks, attributable to a want of
proper skill and care in the management of his oxygen supply. A claim was put forward
on his behalf against the Essex Area Health Authority which is still before the courts
more than seven years after the event. After a trial which was made more difficult than

it need have been, by circumstances which I shall later describe, Peter Pain J held the defendants liable in the sum of £116,199·14. Against the judgment the defendants now appeal.   *a*

This action, and the resulting appeal, give rise to three groups of questions.

1. Were there occasions during Martin's stay in the special baby care unit when the oxygen tension of his blood was allowed to attain and remain at an unacceptably high level? For this purpose, it is necessary to distinguish between a related series of incidents occurring in the first two days after the baby's birth, and a number of isolated occasions   *b* during the succeeding weeks. I will call these 'the first episodes' and 'later episodes' respectively.

2. Did any of the episodes of which complaint is made take place through any breach of duty for which the defendants are liable?

3. If so, was any breach of duty the proximate cause of the physical affliction, and the financial loss, of which the plaintiff now complains?   *c*

At the trial there were other issues, relating to the aetiology of the plaintiff's current problems with his right eye, and to the proper quantification of his financial loss. The findings of the judge on these issues are not now disputed.

Narrative

Before addressing the difficult issues of fact and law to which these questions give rise,   *d* it is convenient first to summarise the physiological and clinical background to the dispute, and then to set out in outline those aspects of the story which are not in dispute. First, as to the bloodstream. Blood is the medium by which substances are carried from one part of the body to another. To each living cell are conveyed the materials which it needs in order to live and perform its own particular task; one of these materials is oxygen. The bloodstream also removes from the cells those waste products whose   *e* presence inhibits their functions; amongst these products is carbon dioxide. The blood is enabled to act as an efficient carrier of oxygen and carbon dioxide by the special properties of haemoglobin, the principal component of the red blood cells, which has the capacity to enter into reversible reaction with oxygen and carbon dioxide. The amount of these gases taken up by the haemoglobin is dependent on the partial pressure (or tension) of the gas in the blood. The reaction is rapidly reversible. Thus, the haemoglobin takes up   *f* oxygen under the high partial pressures encountered at the alveoli in the lungs and releases it rapidly, when the partial pressure falls, at the tissues. Haemoglobin does not absorb oxygen indefinitely. There comes a point at which all the available haemoglobin has been converted to oxyhaemoglobin. This is reached at a partial pressure (P_{O_2}) of about 12 kilopascals (kPa). Beyond this point, a very small proportion of gas enters directly into solution in the blood fluids. As partial pressures are increased, the amount   *g* of oxygen thus transported by the blood is increased, but not in an efficient manner, so that there is no point in increasing the P_{O_2} indefinitely.

The transportation of carbon dioxide proceeds in a similar manner, but in the reverse direction. The partial pressure of carbon dioxide (P_{CO_2}) and the P_{O_2} are related in a manner which it is unnecessary to describe. Another related variable is the pH value of the blood, a measure of the acidity or alkalinity of the fluid.   *h*

The blood is moved from one part of the body to another through the circulatory system. The motive agent is the heart. The right-hand portion of the heart is responsible for the circulation of venous blood. In the fully-formed human it receives into the right atrium the oxygen-depleted blood, via the inferior and superior vena cava. The blood passes to the right ventricle through a valve and is forced into the lungs via the pulmonary artery. Thence the oxygenated blood returns to the left atrium, enters the left ventricle   *j* and is pumped into the arterial system through the aorta and other vessels.

In the fetal child the mechanism is different. The baby depends entirely on the placental blood of the mother, which is already oxygenated. The infant lungs have no part to play. Accordingly, most of the blood flow across the lungs is short-circuited by two routes. First, the ductus arteriosus connects the pulmonary artery, which in the self-a   sufficient human conveys venous blood to the lungs, to the aorta which conveys arterial blood away from the heart. Second, a valve between the right and left atria, named the foramen ovale, admits blood from the right (venous) side of the heart to the left atrium, and thence to the left ventricle and the arterial side of the system. In the full-term infant, which can and must breathe through its own lungs, these short circuits are useless. The ductus arteriosus becomes vestigial, and the foramen ovale is soon tightly sealed.

b   The premature child is in a quite different situation. Mechanically and biochemically its system is not yet fully formed. It cannot breathe properly, or cannot breathe at all. Formerly, premature babies would die, or if they survived would suffer brain damage for want of sufficient oxygen. During the first half of this century medical science began to put this right. Premature babies were helped to breathe by artificial means, and were enabled to live in environments which were much richer in oxygen than ordinary atmospheric air. The result was a precipitous decline in the perinatal mortality of

c   premature babies. Various methods are currently used to ameliorate the respiratory problems of premature babies. First, there is ventilation, called intermittent mandatory ventilation (IMV) in the case papers, which employs electromechanical means to make the baby breathe. Second, there is continuous positive air pressure (CPAP), which maintains a pressure sufficient to prevent the lungs from entirely closing, and hence facilitates the opening of the lungs on the in-breath. Third, there is the provision of an

d   oxygen-enriched atmosphere, by a headbox or other device, in which the baby can breathe spontaneously, with its respiratory deficiencies compensated by higher oxygen content of the air in the lungs. The records report the degree of enrichment in terms of percentages; sometimes the baby is breathing 100% oxygen. The higher the percentage of oxygen when the baby is breathing, the higher the Po_2 is likely to be, but the units in which the figures are expressed are different, and the two are only loosely connected.

e   The success of these developments in the neonatal care of premature babies has been dramatic. There are untold numbers of people alive today who would have perished, if born more than 50 years ago; or who, if they had survived, would have suffered from irreversible brain damage. But after a while it began to seem that there might be a price to pay. In the early 1940s a quite new affliction was noticed. It was found that some premature babies were suffering from a formation of fibrous tissue behind the lens of

f   the eye. For this novel complaint the term retrolental fibroplasia (hereafter RLF) was coined. For a while, it was regarded simply as a disease of prematurity, ie as a disease to which premature babies were subject, but which had not previously been observed, because most premature babies died. In the 1950s, however, it was observed that there appeared to be an association, if not a correlation in strictly statistical terms, between the use of enriched oxygen to save premature babies from death or brain damage and the

g   incidence of RLF. This led to a reaction, whereby the use of enriched oxygen environments was abated. The consequence was expressed graphically in an article by K W Cross 'Cost of preventing retrolental fibroplasia' Lancet 1973;**ii**:954–6:

h   'It is suggested that while the policy of restricting the amount of oxygen in incubators has diminished the number of cases of retrolental fibroplasia (R.L.F.) in the U.K., it has concurrently increased the number of deaths in the first 24 hours of life. A rough estimate suggests that for each case of blindness prevented, there is an excess of 16 deaths. It is further suggested that the proper cost of preventing R.L.F. would be the supply of adequate equipment and staff in all premature-baby units.'

j   Once again there was a reaction. The assumption that excess oxygen was likely to be a prime cause of RLF continued to exercise an important influence; perhaps, as we shall later see, more important in the past than it is today. At the same time, the price in death and brain damage of avoiding blindness in the premature child was too high to be uncritically accepted. A balance must be struck. The baby should have a high enough Po_2 to keep it alive and well, but not so high as to risk damage to its sight. Since the question is one of balancing risks, there can be no clear cut-off point at which the Po_2 level passes from the wholly acceptable to the wholly unacceptable. There was, however, a broad consensus in the evidence led at the trial that if the Po_2 level rose above 15 kPa of blood measured in the abdominal aorta (which would have a Po_2 less than the blood at the retina (see post), steps should promptly be taken to reduce it. Some witnesses would have preferred to put the level rather lower than this. A level at or rather above 5 kPa would reflect a measurement of pure venous blood, and would of course be much too low. Again, there are no absolute requirements for the carbon dioxide tension, but a reading of 10·0 kPa or above would be markedly too high. For a good acid balance, the pH of the blood should be about 7·42.

At the time in question, the means of maintaining this balance were threefold. First, there was informed observation of the child's appearance. A child suffering from oxygen deficiency would become cyanosed: it would seem 'dusky'. A child with sufficient oxygen would have a healthy appearance: it would be 'ruddy'. Crude as they might seem, these criteria were valuable. Skilful neonatal nurses knew their babies. But the test operated only in one direction. A dusky baby could be assumed to have too little oxygen. But a ruddy baby might have either enough or too much.

Second, there were measurements of arterial blood samples. These could show the partial pressures of oxygen and carbon dioxide and also the pH of the blood. They were performed on a machine operated by a technician. The samples could be obtained ab extra by an arterial stab. The problem with arterial samples was that in 1977 the sample had to be as large as 0·5 ml, whereas the entire blood supply of a baby of Martin Wilsher's size was not more than about 100 ml. There was no scope for continuous sampling. Moreover, an arterial stab was unpleasant for the baby; it became increasingly difficult to find a correct site; and like any form of handling it tended to depress the Po_2, and hence falsify the reading.

Third, the Po_2 could be directly measured by means of an indwelling probe. These were of various kinds. The one employed at the neonatal unit in Harlow was the Searle Oxygen Monitoring System. This consisted of a hollow catheter, at the tip of which was an electronic sensor. An electrical conductor ran down the catheter and was connected to a monitor outside the patient's body, where the Po_2 level was registered on a dial. A small aperture was located about 1 cm behind the sensor, through which samples of blood could be obtained, for the purpose of conventional blood gas analysis. It was recognised that the electrical monitor could not be relied on to give a consistently accurate reading, and if a significant discrepancy (which the makers of the instrument said was usually regarded as greater than 10%) was noted between the reading on the dial and the results of blood gas analysis on samples drawn down the catheter, it was necessary to recalibrate the monitor. This was effected by means of a calibrating knob, which was turned so as to bring the reading on the dial into conformity with the results of the blood gas analysis. If any appreciable time had elapsed between the taking of the sample and the return of the analysis from the laboratory, a proportionate calculation would have to be made so as to ensure that the calibration was not based on a blood gas figure which was out of date. The operating instructions of the Searle device had this to say about calibration:

'The main purpose of this system of continuous monitoring is to provide an indication of trends in oxygen tension between the times when blood samples are taken regularly for analysis of blood gas parameters. As with conventional umbilical catheters, blood samples should be taken to confirm the calibration at least every six to eight hours.'

In the case of a newly-born baby there is ready access for the catheter to the blood vessels, in the shape of one vein and two arteries, previously circulating the fetal blood to the placenta, the severed ends of which are presented at the stump of the umbilical cord. If the arterial route is taken, the catheter is inserted into one of the arteries. Its route is at first downwards towards the femoral artery, where it turns upwards in a loop and passes into the abdominal aorta. Care has to be taken not to situate the tip of the catheter at a level where it may occlude the entrance to one of the blood vessels supplying the abdominal organs. This danger was well recognised at the material time, and it was the practice to verify the position of the tip by means of an X-ray.

At first sight, it might be assumed that a reading of oxygen tension taken by a probe
situated in the lower abdominal aorta would give a reasonably accurate reflection of the
partial pressure in the blood vessels which supply the retina. This is not, however,
necessarily the case, since there may be right to left shunting through the ductus
arteriosus, causing some admixture of venous blood into the arterial blood in the aorta.
The ophthalmic artery is, however, 'upstream' of the shunt, and is fed by pure arterial
blood, so that a reading from an arterial catheter will understate the Po_2 at the retina. A
radial arterial stab will, by contrast, give a more accurate picture, since the radial artery is
also upstream of the shunt. Account has to be taken of this factor when assessing the
results of blood gas readings.

Against this background, I turn to the events which led up to the present dispute.

The special care baby unit at the Princess Alexandra Hospital was the creation of Dr
J D Hardy, a consultant paediatrician with the Essex Area Health Authority. When he
took over the post he had to decide whether to build up a new unit, with little in the way
of equipment or staff, or to refer all sick neonates elsewhere, with all the risk of mortality
which that involved. He decided to build up his own unit, and from 1976 onwards he
was able to accumulate equipment, raising half of the cost from charity, by great personal
efforts. He also succeeded in finding the necessary staff. At the time in question, the staff
of the unit included Dr Hardy and another consultant, together with one of his registrars,
Dr Z I Kawa. This doctor had qualified abroad in 1970, and possessed six years' experience
in paediatric medicine, which included one year of intensive baby care. Although Dr
Kawa was primarily concerned with the paediatric wards, he was also responsible, on
those nights or weekends when he was on call, for covering the duties of the medical
registrar with whom he alternated. Below Dr Kawa in the hierarchy were two senior
house officers. These changed from time to time. They included a Dr Stamboulis and
also Dr A R Wiles, who remained in the unit until 5 January 1979. The latter had
qualified in New Zealand during 1974. Dr Stamboulis was involved during the daytime
with the maternity area and special care baby unit, whilst Dr Wiles dealt with another
ward. At night-time the two house officers rotated cover, with whoever was on duty
being responsible for all paediatrics, including the special care unit, the obstetrics unit,
one ward and the paediatric casualty department. Each had every other weekend and
every other night off duty. Otherwise they were continuously working or on call.

The nursing officer in charge of the special care baby unit was Miss J K Pearson. She
had 15 years' experience as a qualified nurse, much of it in neonatal nursing. The unit
comprised three neonatal nursing sisters by day and two by night. There were also two
or three staff midwives or neonatal nurses as well as subordinate nursing staff. In 1978
the unit housed on an average some 15 children, of whom a maximum of two would be
on ventilators or in incubators.

Martin Wilsher was born at the Harlow Hospital at 2325 hrs on the night of Friday,
15 December 1978. Although it was the weekend, Dr Wiles was standing by, because
the baby was so much premature. Martin was as ill as could be expected. Dr Wiles said
that he was a very floppy blue baby. There were problems getting him to breathe, and
he was intubated. After eight minutes the tube was out and he was taken down to the
special care baby unit. His colour improved when an oxygen mask was applied.

Dr Wiles promptly began the usual procedures for a baby so premature. In particular,
he set out to pass an arterial catheter for connection to the Searle device. This happened
some time after 0100 hours on Saturday, 16 December. Dr Wiles made a mistake. The
severed ends of the blood vessels presented at the umbilical stump are very fine-bored. It
is hard to tell which is which. Dr Wiles inserted the catheter into a vein instead of an
artery. Nobody has suggested that this amounted to actionable negligence, for it was an
error which competent doctors could and from time to time did commit. The catheter
did not pursue a downward course and turn up again, as it would have done if inserted
into an artery. Instead, it went almost straight up along the line of the baby's trunk,
entering the right atrium of the heart through the vena cava. Thence it passed transversely
across the heart, through the foramen ovale, and lodged in the left atrium.

The monitor was then connected. The first electronic readings were taken, and a blood

The monitor was then connected. The first electronic readings were taken, and a blood sample was drawn through the catheter. Dr Wiles telephoned the technician at home to *a* come in to analyse the sample. The chance event that the catheter had entered the venous system but had penetrated the arterial side of the heart made the readings doubly deceptive. If the sensor and the sampling hole had remained on the venous side, the Po_2 readings would have been so low that the faulty location might at once have been recognised. Instead, the fluid being sampled contained arterial blood. But it was also admixed (to a degree unknown) with venous blood passing through the foramen ovale. *b* The partial pressure of the oxygen in the sample thus bore no relation to the pressure of the oxygen in the blood which was reaching the retina.

For the whole of the next 24 hours the doctors were afflicted by two quite different problems in their efforts to keep the oxygen partial pressure under control. The first problem was one which they recognised: namely that there was something wrong with the monitor. The electronic messages from the sensor did not correspond with the results *c* of analysing the samples drawn down the catheter. It is pointless to speculate about the reasons. The sampling hole was 1 cm to the right side of the sensor, and may have been drawing blood richer in oxygen. Perhaps the electronics were not working well.

The second problem was one which the doctors did not recognise: namely that both the electronic sensor tip and the blood sampler just behind it were investigating the wrong blood.
d

Having inserted the catheter, Dr Wiles arranged for an X-ray, which he inspected. He then called for Dr Kawa to come and check what he had done. Dr Kawa looked at the X-ray and decided that the tip of the catheter was too high, so he directed that it should be withdrawn by 2 cm. Neither doctor realised that the configuration of the catheter disclosed by the X-ray meant that it must be following the line of a vein, not an artery; nor indeed did the consultant radiologist when she made a routine examination of the *e* plates some time after this episode was over.

At about 1000 hrs Dr Kawa decided to change the catheter, probably because of the discrepancies in the readings. Dr Wiles withdrew the old catheter and Dr Kawa inserted the new one. Again the instrument was inserted in a vein. A further X-ray was taken and inspected, but again the error in placing the catheter was not recognised. The new catheter appeared to perform no better than the old. Entries in the clinical notes suggest *f* that attempts to calibrate the monitor from 1345 hrs onwards were given up, and at 2200 hrs the monitor was abandoned as 'useless on this catheter'. It is reasonable to assume that, throughout this later period, the medical staff were controlling the oxygen supply by reference partly to the baby's colour and partly to the results of the blood gas analyses. These had been consistently disturbing: the Po_2 and pH were too low, the Pco_2 was too high. Accordingly, the baby was put on the ventilator and the oxygen content of *g* the administered air was raised progressively until by 2200 hrs the figure stood at 100%, where it evidently remained throughout the night of 16–17 December 1978.

The following table summarises the blood gas readings of the first thirty hours:

Date	Time	Monitor	BLOOD GASES EX CATHETER				
			Po_2	Pco_2	pH	Oxygen %	Comments
16 Dec	0200	5	5·8	8·9	7·15	70	
	1000	13	7·7	9·3	7·08	60	After catheter pulled down
	1315		5·4	9·0	7·14	80	On CPAP after second catheter inserted
	1620	11	5·9	6·2	7·26	80–90	
	2200		8·6	6·4	7·29	95–100	on IMV
17 Dec	0730		10·1	6·0	7·28	100	on CPAP/IMV

26·0　(ex arterial stab)

So matters stood when Dr Wiles returned to duty at 0700 hrs on 17 December. He

was puzzled by what he saw. The baby's colour seemed better than it should be having
regard to the blood gas figures. He decided to check everything, including the second
X-ray. He must have become suspicious about the position of the catheter, for he wrote
in the clinical notes: 'umbilical catheter seems arterial on X-ray—check with arterial
stab.' He then obtained a sample by arterial stab, and took this together with a sample
drawn by the catheter to the laboratory, carrying them himself in the interests of speed
and safety. The analyses showed a Po_2 of 10·1 kPa for the catheter sample and 26 kPa for
the stab sample. In his own words, after receiving the figure of 26 kPa, he jumped off
the couch and ran back to the unit. He turned the controls from ventilation to CPAP,
and then began to reduce the oxygen supply. As a first reaction he wrote: 'Baby has
probably been supersaturated with O_2 for about 28 hours.' However, after a telephone
conversation with Dr Hardy, and looking back over the records, he added: 'Probably less
than 12 hours.' Subsequently, the catheter was changed again. This time it was in an
artery and the blood gas samples thenceforth became a reliable guide. This marked the
conclusion of the first episode.

It is convenient to pause here, because the negligence alleged in relation to the first
episode, and the consequences said to flow from the negligence, are of a quite different
character from those asserted in relation to later stages of the baby's case. It can be seen
that the first episode fell into two parts.

(a) Whilst the first catheter was in place: as originally sited, and then retracted. During
this period, which lasted for 8 of the baby's first 11 hours, both the monitor and the gas
samples were unreliable. The former may have been due to deficiencies in the electronics;
the latter was undoubtedly caused by the wrong positioning of the sampling orifice of
the catheter. The consequences of the mistake in positioning the catheter are impossible
to ascertain without knowing what the baby actually received by way of oxygen and
what consideration led the medical staff to decide what levels of oxygen to supply. All
one can say is that the baby appears to have been on CPAP with concentrations of 60–
80%. Whether this was too much, and what the true Po_2 levels were, is impossible to
determine.

(b) Between the insertion of the second catheter and the recognition of the mistake.
This period lasted for about 24 hours. The electronic side of the monitor is irrelevant for
almost all of this period, since it was soon recognised as unreliable (see above). The crucial
factor was that the blood gas samples were giving readings which were too low because
the sampling orifice of the catheter was in the wrong place. The progressive increase to
pure oxygen must have been an attempt to remedy the situation apparently disclosed by
these false figures.

In these circumstances, I believe that the plaintiff's advisers were right to accept (in
conformity with Dr Wiles's revised opinion) that the adverse consequences of the
misplacement cannot be shown to have manifested themselves in terms of excessive Po_2
until some time between 1620 hours and 2200 hours, when the concentrations of
administered oxygen were reaching really high levels; and I also believe that the
defendants' advisers were right to accept that the levels probably did become unacceptably
high at about the time when the baby started to receive pure oxygen. This gives a bracket
of about 8 to 12 hours as the duration of the period during which the baby's Po_2 levels
became excessive because of the mistake in siting the second catheter. What those levels
actually were cannot, of course, be deduced.

When one turns to the remainder of the exposures about which the plaintiff complains,
the position is quite different. Here, there is no complaint about the accuracy of the
blood gas samples. On the contrary, they are relied on as the only safe guide to the baby's
oxygen tension, drawn as they were from the correctly placed third catheter. The
allegation is directed to the monitor which, it is said, was relied on by the nursing staff
when controlling the oxygen concentration, which was in fact giving inaccurate readings
and which ought to have been restored to accuracy by more frequent calibration against
blood samples.

The exposures originally criticised are said to have taken place on 19–20 December, on
28–29 December, on 8 January, on 11 January, on 17 January and on 22–23 January. On

each occasion the figures for Po_2, derived either from blood gas analyses or from the monitor, showed an excess over 15 kPa. The plaintiff's argument was that this excess continued for substantial periods, and that it was negligent to allow the figure to remain so high for so long. By way of elaboration, it was argued for the plaintiff that on these occasions the intervals between the taking of blood gas analyses were too long, so that the nurses were controlling the baby's oxygen supply by reference to the readings on a monitor which, for lack of calibration, might well have been reading too low, thus leading to the administration of excess oxygen. In essence, the judge has held that, with the exception of the last episode, the defendants gave no adequate reason for not taking more frequent readings, and have failed to displace the inference that, in the absence of additional analyses, the baby must be taken to have suffered high oxygen tensions for excessive periods. On the hearing of the appeal, it was accepted on behalf of the plaintiff that the finding of the judge in relation to the penultimate exposure could not be sustained. The argument therefore centred on the three remaining exposures. I return to these in more detail at a later stage.

Breach of duty
The law
   This appeal raises three questions of law relating to the allegation that the defendants are liable for breach of duty. (1) What is the nature of the cause of action on which the plaintiff relies? (2) What standard of care was demanded of those members of the medical and nursing staff who are said to have been negligent? (3) On whom rests the burden of proof in relation to the allegation of negligence?
   Before addressing these questions, we must face up to a problem which must oppress many of those who have to deal with cases of this kind. Expressed in terms of the present case, it is this. Here we have a medical unit which would never have existed but for the energy and public spirit of Dr Hardy. If the unit had not been there, the plaintiff would probably have died. The doctors and nurses worked all kinds of hours to look after the baby. They safely brought it through the perilous shoals of its early life. For all that we know, they far surpassed on numerous occasions the standard of reasonable care. Yet it is said that for one lapse they (and not just their employers) are to be found to have committed a breach of duty. Nobody could criticise the mother for doing her best to secure her son's financial future. But has not the law taken a wrong turning if an action of this kind is to succeed?
   I must say at once that no rhetorical question of this kind formed part of any argument advanced by counsel for the defendants, and rightly so in my opinion. It could not be acceptable crudely to say that the plaintiff should count himself fortunate to be alive, or that he must take the rough with the smooth. Nor can I envisage any practicable system of liability which would enable a professional man to say that, so long as he had provided an adequate service on average, he should not be held liable for occasions when his performance fell below the norm. The risks which actions for professional negligence bring to the public as a whole, in the shape of an instinct on the part of a professional man to play for safety, are serious and are now well recognised. Nevertheless, the proper response cannot be to temper the wind to the professional man. If he assumes to perform a task, he must bring to it the appropriate care and skill. What the courts can do, however, is to bear constantly in mind that, in those situations which call for the exercise of judgment, the fact that in retrospect the choice actually made can be shown to have turned out badly is not in itself a proof of negligence, and to remember that the duty of care is not a warranty of a perfect result.
   Returning to the first of the questions stated above, it appears that the nature of the plaintiff's cause of action was never explored in the course of the trial. The result has been to create problems, both with the judgment itself and with the arguments addressed on the duty of care. This may be illustrated by the claims based on the first episode. One

a way to formulate the claim would be to assert negligence on the part of one or more individuals, and then hold the employer vicariously liable for the acts of these individuals. Here, the attention would be focused on Dr Kawa and Dr Wiles. If either of these fell short of the standard of care required of him as an individual, then that person would be liable (although not sued) and so also would be the defendants. Conversely, if each of the two men did all that could properly be expected of him, neither the doctors nor the defendants would be liable.

b There is, however, a quite different proposition which might have been advanced, namely that the defendants are directly liable for any adverse consequences of the episode. For example, it might have been said that the defendants owed a duty to ensure that the special baby care unit functioned according to the standard reasonably to be expected of such a unit. This approach would not require any consideration of the extent to which the individual doctors measured up to the standards demanded of them as individuals, c but would focus attention on the performance of the unit as a whole. A rather different form of the argument might have been advanced on the following lines. Although the catheter, with its monitor and sampling facility, is a valuable instrument, it will yield misleading and potentially·dangerous results if the head is in the wrong place. The defendants therefore owed a duty, if they were to use the catheter on patients entrusted to their care, to ensure that those who were to operate the device knew how to detect d when it was wrongly placed, and on their own evidence the junior doctors did not know this. Finally, it might have been said that, if the junior doctors did not have sufficient skill or experience to provide the special care demanded by such a premature baby, the defendants were at fault in appointing them to the posts which they held.

If the nature of the plaintiff's cause of action had been a live issue on this appeal, it would have been necessary to look with care at the developing line of authority on e liability for medical negligence. For counsel for the defendants asserted roundly that no health authority ever had been, or in principle ever could be, under any such direct liability as suggested, except perhaps in the case of a person being appointed to a post for which he is not qualified. In the event, however, counsel for the plaintiff explicitly disclaimed on the plaintiff's behalf any intention to put forward a case of direct liability. The trial had been conducted throughout, he made clear, exclusively on the basis of f vicarious liability. It is therefore unnecessary to express any opinion on the validity in law of a claim on the alternative basis. Unfortunately, this does not deprive the point of all practical significance in the present context. Possibly because the statement of claim could be read as raising a direct claim and possibly also because the circumstances of the trial precluded a systematic analysis of the plaintiff's real complaints, Peter Pain J approached the question of negligence on a basis different from the one which was g common ground before this court. Thus, in the course of discussing the authorities, he said:

'It was contended by [junior counsel] for the defendants that in establishing the standard of care owed by the defendants I should bear in mind that the mistake as to where the catheter was originally inserted was made by Dr Wiles, who was then a fairly junior doctor of limited experience. I cannot accept this. The action is h brought against the defendants and not against Dr Wiles. I must follow the standard of care propounded by May J in *Murray (a minor) v Kensington and Chelsea and Westminster Health Authority* (1 May 1980, unreported): "But as a matter of law I think that Robert was entitled to expect from the defendants, it so happens in the person of Dr Marfitt, that standard of care to be expected of a hospital holding itself out as capable of taking care of premature babies."'

j Later, when rounding off his views on the facts, Peter Pain J said:

'I hold that the failure to interpret the X-ray correctly was negligent in the defendants. They fell short of the proper standard of care for a special care baby unit, partly through Dr Wiles's difficulty through inexperience in reading the X-ray and partly through Dr Kawa's carelessness in not checking the X-ray properly.'

The judge, therefore, never had occasion to express an opinion on the individual standards of care demanded of Dr Kawa and Dr Wiles, standards which, as both parties agreed on the argument of the appeal, were not the same. Nor did he perform a similar task in relation to those who might be alleged to be negligent in relation to the later episodes; I say 'might be alleged' because, in relation to the later episodes, the plaintiff has never identified even the categories of persons, let alone the individuals, for whom the defendants are to be held vicariously liable. The problem must therefore be approached de novo.

It is convenient to begin by mentioning a number of considerations which, in my judgment, have no bearing on the present appeal.

In the first place, there is the situation where the doctor embarks on a form of treatment which is still comparatively untried, with techniques and safeguards which are still in the course of development, or where the treatment is of particular technical difficulty. In such a case, if the decision to embark on the treatment at all was justifiable and was taken with the informed consent of the patient, the court should, in my judgment, be particularly careful not to impute negligence simply because something has gone wrong. For my part, however, I do not accept that any such consideration is relevant here. So far as concerns the first episode, there was nothing novel about the use of an umbilical catheter, nor was there any technical difficulty in examining the X-ray to verify that the catheter was in the right place. Again, although the management of this baby was plainly a difficult matter for several weeks, the techniques to be adopted were not of a novel or recondite kind, and there is no suggestion that, if it had been appropriate to take more frequent blood gas samples at the time of the later episodes, the persons concerned would not have had the means and opportunity to do so. This does not appear to me a case where the staff of the baby unit were operating on the frontiers of medical science.

Again, I accept that full allowance must be made for the fact that certain aspects of treatment may have to be carried out in what one witness (dealing with the use of a machine to analyse the sample) called 'battle conditions'. An emergency may overburden the available resources, and, if an individual is forced by circumstances to do too many things at once, the fact that he does one of them incorrectly should not lightly be taken as negligence. Here again, however, the present case is in a different category, for none of those accused of negligence who were called to give evidence on their own behalf suggested that, if mistakes were made, this happened because their attention was distracted by having to do something else at the same time, or because they had to take a difficult decision on the spur of the moment.

Next, there is the established body of authority, of which *Bolam v Friern Hospital Management Committee* [1957] 2 All ER 118 at 121–122, [1957] 1 WLR 582 at 586–587 is a conspicuous example, to the effect that a doctor who adopts a practice accepted as proper by a responsible body of medical men skilled in the relevant branch of medicine is not to be taken as negligent merely because there is a contrary view. Although this principle may have some bearing on the later episodes, it can have nothing to do with the first episode, for, although there were witnesses who regarded it as excusable in a young doctor not to know about the significance of the loop and its absence, there was no body of medical opinion which could regard it as appropriate to overlook the indications given by the X-rays as to the position of the catheter. The doctors made a mistake, although not necessarily a culpable one.

I now turn to the real content of the standard of care. Three propositions were advanced, the first by junior counsel for the plaintiff. It may, I think, be fairly described as setting a 'team' standard of care, whereby each of the persons who formed the staff of the unit held themselves out as capable of undertaking the specialised procedures which that unit set out to perform.

I acknowledge the force of this submission, so far as it calls for recognition of the position which the person said to be negligent held within this specialised unit. But, in so far as the proposition differs from the last of those referred to below, I must dissent,

for it is faced with a dilemma. If it seeks to attribute to each individual members of the
a team a duty to live up to the standards demanded of the unit as a whole, it cannot be
right, for it would expose a student nurse to an action in negligence for a failure to possess
the skill and experience of a consultant. If, on the other hand, it seeks to fix a standard
for the performance of the unit as a whole, this is simply a reformulation of the direct
theory of liability which leading counsel for the plaintiff has explicitly disclaimed.

The second proposition (advanced on behalf of the defendants) directs attention to the
b personal position of the individual member of the staff about whom the complaint is
made. What is expected of him is as much as, but no more than, can reasonably be
required of a person having his formal qualifications and practical experience. If correct,
this proposition entails that the standard of care which the patient is entitled to demand
will vary according to the chance of recruitment and rostering. The patient's right to
complain of faulty treatment will be more limited if he has been entrusted to the care of
c a doctor who is a complete novice in the particular field (unless perhaps he can point to
some fault of supervision in a person further up the hierarchy) than if he has been in the
hands of a doctor who has already spent months on the same ward, and his prospects of
holding the health authority vicariously liable for the consequences of any mistreatment
will be correspondingly reduced.

To my mind, this notion of a duty tailored to the actor, rather than to the act which he
d elects to perform, has no place in the law of tort. Indeed, the defendants did not contend
that it could be justified by any reported authority on the general law of tort. Instead, it
was suggested that the medical profession is a special case. Public hospital medicine has
always been organised so that young doctors and nurses learn on the job. If the hospitals
abstained from using inexperienced people, they could not staff their wards and theatres,
and the junior staff could never learn. The longer-term interests of patients as a whole
e are best served by maintaining the present system, even if this may diminish the legal
rights of the individual patient, for, after all, medicine is about curing, not litigation.

I acknowledge the appeal of this argument, and recognise that a young hospital doctor
who must get onto the wards in order to qualify without necessarily being able to decide
what kind of patient he is going to meet is not in the same position as another professional
man who has a real choice whether or not to practice in a particular field. Nevertheless, I
f cannot accept that there should be a special rule for doctors in public hospitals; I
emphasise *public*, since presumably those employed in private hospitals would be in a
different category. Doctors are not the only people who gain their experience, not only
from lectures or from watching others perform, but from tackling live clients or
customers, and no case was cited to us which suggested that any such variable duty of
care was imposed on others in a similar position. To my mind, it would be a false step to
g subordinate the legitimate expectation of the patient that he will receive from each
person concerned with his care a degree of skill appropriate to the task which he
undertakes to an understandable wish to minimise the psychological and financial
pressures on hard-pressed young doctors.

For my part, I prefer the third of the propositions which have been canvassed. This
relates the duty of care, not to the individual, but to the post which he occupies. I would
h differentiate 'post' from 'rank' or 'status'. In a case such as the present, the standard is not
just that of the averagely competent and well-informed junior houseman (or whatever
the position of the doctor) but of such a person who fills a post in a unit offering a highly
specialised service. But, even so, it must be recognised that different posts make different
demands. If it is borne in mind that the structure of hospital medicine envisages that the
lower ranks will be occupied by those of whom it would be wrong to expect too much,
j the risk of abuse by litigious patients can be mitigated, if not entirely eliminated.

I now turn to the third question, which relates to the burden of proof. It is most
readily illustrated by a citation from an earlier judgment of the same judge, Peter Pain J,
in *Clark v MacLennan* [1983] 1 All ER 416 at 427, in which, after discussing the decision
of the House of Lords in *McGhee v National Coal Board* [1972] 3 All ER 1008, [1973] 1
WLR 1, he said:

'On the basis of this authority, counsel for the plaintiff contended that, if the plaintiff could show (1) that there was a general practice not to perform an anterior colporrhaphy until at least three months after birth, (2) that one of the reasons for this practice was to protect the patient from the risk of haemorrhage and a breakdown of the repair, (3) that an operation was performed within four weeks and (4) that haemorrhage occurred and the repair broke down, then the burden of showing that he was not in breach of duty shifted to the defendants. It must be correct on the basis of *McGhee* to say that the burden shifts so far as damages are concerned. But does the burden shift so far as the duty is concerned? Must the medical practitioner justify his departure from the usual practice? It is very difficult to draw a distinction between the damage and the duty where the duty arises only because of a need to guard against the damage. In *McGhee's* case it was accepted that there was a breach of duty. In the present case the question of whether there was a breach remains in issue. It seems to me that it follows from *McGhee* that where there is a situation in which a general duty of care arises and there is a failure to take a precaution, and that very damage occurs against which the precaution is designed to be a protection, then the burden lies on the defendant to show that he was not in breach of duty as well as to show that the damage did not result from his breach of duty.'

The judge then went on the apply the principle which he had stated in *Clark v MacLennan* to the later episodes of the present case, although not to the first episode, in respect of which he made an affirmative finding of negligence. His conclusion on the later episodes was:

'I therefore cannot find that the defendants have established that the high readings that occurred prior to 11 January 1979 occurred without negligence on their part.'

With respect, I must dissent from this approach, although I acknowledge the problems which this entails. If, as *McGhee v National Coal Board* certainly decides, there are special rules governing standard or burden of proof in those cases where the current state of knowledge does not permit the proof or disproof of a causal connection between breach and loss, the maintenance of a different rule for proving the breach itself will not always be easy to achieve in practice, since in some instances breach and causation will be closely linked. This is illustrated by the present case, where the issue whether there were long periods of excessive oxygenation might be assigned either to the part of the case concerned with breach of duty or to the group of questions concerned with the consequences of the breach of duty. I prefer the former view, but the question is not easy. None the less, I would find it impossible, unless impelled by binding authority, to hold that proof of the primary facts constituting negligence is in some way dispensed with merely by showing that some step, which is designed to avert or minimise a risk, has not in the particular circumstances been taken. I now turn to the decided cases.

Turning to the authorities cited, the first is *McGhee v National Coal Board* itself. Here, the pursuer was exposed to the effects of brick dust during his working day, in circumstances which did not constitute a breach of duty by his employers. His exposure was, however, prolonged by the failure of the employers to provide washing facilities, so that he had to cycle home still covered in dust and sweat. The lower courts held that this failure did constitute a breach of duty. The pursuer contracted dermatitis. There was no doubt that the complaint was brought about by contact with dust, but it was impossible on the current state of medical knowledge to prove whether or not the additional period of exposure tipped the scale to cause the pursuer to contract the disease when otherwise he would not have done so. The pursuer was, however, able to show that the failure to provide showers materially increased the risk that dermatitis would set in. The House of Lords held that this was sufficient to connect the breach of duty with the pursuer's loss.

Plainly, the decision in *McGhee* has no direct bearing on the issues in the present case concerning the alleged breach of duty, for such a breach had already been established

before the case reached the House of Lords. Indeed, in certain of the speeches there
a appears to be implicit the idea that, in a sense, the proof of breach is equivalent to proof
of causation, if the damage which the required standard of care is designed to forestall
has in fact materialised. Nor do I see how the fiction (for such Lord Wilberforce
acknowledged it to be) whereby proof of an enhancement of risk was equated to proof of
a contribution to the injury can be transferred to a situation where negligence, rather
than causation, is in dispute. Is it to be held that, once the defendant is shown to have
b done an act which involves an element of risk to another, the court must always presume
that his act is a breach of a duty of care unless he proves the contrary? Surely this cannot
be right, for there are many instances (notably in the practice of medicine) where one
person may properly take risks in the best interests of another, and there is no reason or
principle in holding that it is for the defendant to justify his conduct. Nor, to my mind,
is it legitimate to fasten on the feature of *McGhee* that the effect of the breach was
c unknown, and to say by analogy that, where a plaintiff suffers damage through the acts
or omissions of someone and where the nature and quality of the acts cannot be
ascertained, a presumption must be made in favour of the plaintiff. Certainly, there are
situations where a plaintiff can win where the circumstances of the damage are unknown.
But, in cases of res ipsa loquitur the plaintiff succeeds in spite, not because, of the
uncertainty as to the precise course of events. The injurious acts speaks for itself, and
d there is no need for any presumption.

The next authority relied on is *Clark v MacLennan* [1983] 1 All ER 416. The plaintiff,
who had recently given birth, suffered from a not uncommon postnatal complaint. In
order to give the plaintiff relief, the defendant performed an operation one month after
birth. It was the usual practice not to perform this operation until three months after
birth, the purpose of the delay being to avoid certain consequences. Unfortunately,
e precisely those consequences did occur, and the plaintiff's disability became permanent.
Peter Pain J held that the defendants were liable in negligence.

If I may say so, the summary of the evidence contained in the judgment in *Clark v
MacLennan* has certainly persuaded me that, as a decision on the facts, the case is
unimpeachable. Moreover, although the judge indicated that he proposed to decide the
case on burden of proof (at 425), this could be understood as an example of the forensic
f commonplace that, where one party has, in the course of the trial, hit the ball into the
other's court, it is for that other to return it. But the prominence given in the judgment
to *McGhee* and the citation from *Clark* in the present case suggest that the judge may have
set out to assert a wider proposition, to the effect that in certain kinds of case of which
Clark and the present action form examples, there is a general burden of proof on the
defendant. If this is so, then I must respectfully say that I find nothing in *McGhee* or in
g general principle to support it.

Finally, there was *Thompson v Smiths Shiprepairers (North Shields) Ltd* [1984] 1 All ER
881, [1984] QB 405. The plaintiffs had for many years been employed in the yards of
shipbuilders and shiprepairers. In the course of time they became progressively more
hard of hearing because of industrial noise. It was held at the trial that, after a certain
date, the employers should have taken steps to prevent the hearing loss, but that before
h that date they were not in breach of duty. Thus, as in *McGhee*, there were consecutive
periods of excusable and inexcusable exposure to risk. It was therefore argued that the
whole of the hearing loss should be attributed to the defendants' fault. This argument
failed, because the evidence showed conclusively that most of the hearing loss had taken
place during the earlier period; an apportionment between the losses taking place during
the two periods was possible, although not with any precision; and it would be wrong to
j hold the defendants liable for a contribution to the plaintiffs' hearing losses which was
known not to be the result of the defendants' breach. This aspect of the case had nothing
to do with breach of duty, which had already been dealt with at a stage of the judgment
before apportionment came to be considered. Nor, in relation to causation, did the
judgment do more than attempt a summary of *McGhee* and an explanation of why it did
not apply to the case in hand. It does not, to my mind, offer any help in regard to the
problem now under discussion.

Accordingly, I would hold that, so far as concerns the issue of negligence, the facts of the present case must be approached on the footing that the burden of proof rests on the plaintiff.

The facts: first episode

It will be recalled that two catheters were inserted into the plaintiff's umbilical vein. The first insertion was performed by Dr Wiles alone, at about 0100 hrs on 16 December 1978. An X-ray was taken, which was studied by both doctors. Neither observed that it was misplaced, although Dr Kawa did conclude that the tip was too high, and asked for it to be pulled back. The second insertion was performed by Dr Kawa, with Dr Wiles in attendance, at about 1000 hrs on the same day. Another X-ray was taken. The evidence suggests that the plate was seen by both doctors. Neither observed that the catheter was misplaced.

The mistakes made on these two occasions, for mistakes they undeniably were, were of a rather unusual kind. To recognise the misplacements did not call for the kind of meticulous study of the X-ray plates for which there might be insufficient time during the busy life on the ward. Nor did it require any profound skill or learning. Once furnished with the necessary elementary knowledge of the circulatory system, and told how to apply it, even a layman can recognise when the instrument is not in an artery. In that sense, the misplacement was obvious. But in another sense it was not obvious, and this was because the doctors did not apply their anatomical knowledge to what they saw on the plates. In the words of Dr Kawa, 'It just did not click.' The question is whether it should have done.

The first step is to see what explanation the doctors gave for this omission. Dr Wiles knew that it was possible for a catheter to be accidentally inserted in a vein, for he himself had diagnosed just such an occurrence about a month previously. Two locum doctors had put a catheter in a vien. When Dr Wiles saw the X-ray he recognised that the catheter had gone into the portal vein towards the liver. This was obvious to him because the catheter took a sharp bend to the right. When he looked at Martin Wilsher's first X-ray, he thought it showed an arterial line that was placed too high. He possibly did know that there would be a loop if the catheter was in an artery, but that was not what he was looking for on the X-ray. He would have been looking for a deflection to a different line such as he had seen before, and would also be looking at the position of the tip. He thought that the tip was in the knuckle of the aorta, and did not realise the significance of the fact that the tip was aimed towards the baby's left (through the two atria) rather than to the right (at the aortic knuckle).

Dr Wiles was asked very few questions about the crucial second catheter. He simply said that what he saw on the X-ray was the same as before; if anything, appearing slightly more to the left, but that was probably just twisting of the baby's body. Finally, when he checked the X-ray again on the Sunday morning, he thought, and noted down, that it still looked like an arterial catheter. He was not asked to explain his thought processes on these two occasions when he looked at the second catheter, but presumably they were the same as on the first occasion.

Turning to Dr Kawa, he had considerable experience of inserting umbilical catheters, on average at the rate of about one per week since he had joined the special care unit. He did not say in evidence whether he knew of the risk of accidental insertion in a vein, but it seems safe to assume that he did. In relation to the first catheter, he said that the purpose of the X-ray was to ascertain the condition of the lungs as well as the position of the tip. He knew that the artery had a downward loop, but had never come across the point before (ie that the catheter must have been inserted into a vein since otherwise the X-ray would show up a loop), and it just did not click. Later, he said:

'Q. On this occasion, as we know, looking at the first two X-rays, you did not make sure that you had put the catheter into an artery. Is that not right? A. I did make sure. I mean, looking at the X-ray I was sure that it was arterial to start with.

It would have helped me more if I would have inserted the catheter myself. Looking at the X-ray after somebody else has, I mean half of the, shall we say, advantage here of judging about the position of the catheter is not there. You would be in a better position to judge about the correctness, shall we say, of the position of the catheter if you had inserted it yourself.

Q. You came along to check somebody else's work? A. Correct . . .

Q. Why did you not spot that? A. I do not know. Now in retrospect it seems much easier to observe. Maybe I just had a look at it, did not have any second thoughts in my mind that it was arterial; a quick glance, "OK, it is too high," pull it down, and that is it, as simple as that. Then perhaps turned your attention to some other concomitant [?] condition of the lungs, the [?] etc. Once you have satisfied yourself that you have got the catheter, shall we say, in an artery, the right place, you do not waste another second to think more about it, give it any more thought.'

Dr Kawa had nothing to say about his inspection of the second X-ray. This is a pity, because one of the reasons which he gave for failing to detect the misplacement of the first catheter, namely that he assumed that a catheter inserted by someone else was in the right place, did not apply to the second catheter, which he had inserted himself. Perhaps if asked he would have said that he inserted the catheter in the same blood-vessel as had been used on the previous occasion, and assumed that Dr Wiles had got it right. We do not know.

The position is therefore that the two doctors accounted for the mistake in quite different ways. Dr Wiles knew that the X-ray could be used to verify the route of the catheter through the vascular tree, and looked at it with that specific purpose in mind. He did not, however, realise the significance not only of the absence of a deflection but also of the absence of a loop. By contrast, Dr Kawa did not use the X-ray to verify that the instrument was in an artery.

The judge plainly found these explanations insufficient. As previously mentioned, however, he was measuring both doctors' performance against the standard expected of a special care baby unit. For my part, I believe that the yardstick should be the standard expected of the individual doctor holding the particular post which he did hold in the unit. In relation to Dr Kawa, this distinction is immaterial, since the judge described his error as 'carelessness', which must be a finding of negligence whatever test is applied. But with Dr Wiles it was ascribed to inexperience. I am not confident that the judge would have found this doctor to have been negligent, applying the test which I prefer.

With this in mind I turn to the expert evidence. On this part of the case, the evidence of the experts, distinguished and fair-minded as they were, must be approached with some reserve. In the first place, the unhappy history of the proceedings (to which I shall later refer) had the consequence that Dr Harvey, Professor Hull and Dr Roberton gave evidence before either of the Harlow doctors; Dr Chiswick gave evidence before Dr Kawa; and, although Professor Campbell gave evidence after both Harlow doctors, it appears from the transcript that he may not have been fully aware of what they had said. In consequence, a substantial amount of their evidence on this topic amounted to speculation about the two doctors' thought processes, rather than a commentary on what those processes actually were. Thus, for example, Professor Hull took it to be clear from the notes that Dr Wiles had looked at the X-ray to see where the tip was, and went on to express the view that young doctors were being misled into not using radiography to verify that the catheter was arterial by the fact that almost all the works of reference spoke exclusively of using it to check the position of the tip. In fact, we know that Dr Wiles was not so misled, but did look at the X-rays for the purpose (amongst others) of ensuring that the catheter was not in a vein.

Second, the attention of the expert witnesses tended to be focused on the knowledge and capability of the young and inexperienced house officer. There was little separate consideration of the standard to be expected of the registrar.

Third, on a number of occasions the witnesses were asked, or volunteered, opinions on whether the mistakes were 'understandable'. In company with the judge, I do not find these helpful. Any sound professional will recognise that he himself had committed errors in the past, and can understand that other competent men may do the same. But an understandable mistake may still be negligent (see *Whitehouse v Jordan* [1980] 1 All ER 650 at 666 per Donaldson LJ; [1981] 1 All ER 267, [1981] 1 WLR 246, HL). A similar comment may be made, to some extent, on the use of the word 'blameworthy'.

I do not intend to set out the expert evidence at length. On the one side, Professor Hull in his first report stated that any doctor who passes an umbilical catheter into a new-born baby must be able to assess where the tip of the catheter is sited and that means that he must be able to read the X-ray. If the X-ray is misread then it is a serious mistake. Dr Harvey said that anyone concerned in administering treatment in a unit such as this should be able to read an X-ray like this correctly. He would not accept the suggestion that the mistake was not blameworthy. Dr Roberton also considered that anyone putting in an umbilical arterial catheter should have the necessary skill to interpret the X-ray. A competent house officer should be able to identify exactly the position of the catheter. Dr Chiswick said that it was not conventional practice to take note of the route, but nevertheless considered that either the doctor who put the catheter in or a doctor working with him, responsible for the unit at that time, should know whether the catheter has gone into a vein or an artery. He thought that this was a mistake which a doctor in the position that these doctors were in, in a baby care unit, ought not to have made; but he added that he could hardly call it blameworthy.

On the other side, Professor Hull in his oral evidence withdrew the opinion contained in his report, because subsequent inquiries had shown him that there was virtually nothing about the loop in the literature, and the junior doctors whom he had asked did not know about it. The defendants also relied on the notation placed on the X-ray by the consultant radiographer after a routine inspection of the plates three days after the event. If a person experienced in the study of X-rays could believe the catheter to be in the aortic knuckle, how could it be negligent for the other doctors to make the same mistake? For myself, I am not disposed to attach much weight to this. The radiographer was not called, so we know nothing about her thought processes, or what she was looking for, or whether she was even aware that umbilical catheters might be accidentally misplaced. The standard of care must, it seems to me, be different in respect of the task which this lady was performing from the one to be demanded of the doctors on the baby care unit.

In the light of all this evidence I have come to the clear conclusion that the judge was right to find that Dr Kawa was negligent. He was in charge of the unit; he was called in expressly to verify the work of Dr Wiles on the first occasion, and himself inserted the catheter on the second. I fully recognise the danger of hindsight, and acknowledge that something which is obvious, once isolated and pointed out, is not necessarily obvious when it is encountered in the course of the day's work. Even so, I consider that somebody in the position of Dr Kawa should have recognised the implications of what he saw; and whether his failure resulted from an absence of the necessary knowledge about the clue which the absence of a loop would provide, or (as seems more likely) he never applied his mind at all to the route taken by the catheter, the conclusion is the same. He fell short of the required standard of care and the defendants are vicariously liable for any proved consequences of his negligence.

If this is right, the position of Dr Wiles is of no practical importance (except of course to the doctor himself), since it is not suggested that his acts caused any damage additional to any which flowed from the acts of Dr Kawa. The problem is not easy. The judge formed a good impression of Dr Wiles. His evidence reads well in the transcript. He was plainly an energetic and caring man, to whom the baby owed a great deal. Moreover, he did three important things right: he looked at the X-ray to see whether the catheter was arterial; he called Dr Kawa to check his work; and he was alert enough to see that the baby's appearance did not match the recorded figures. At the same time, the weight of the expert evidence favoured the view that he should have detected the error, and I find it disturbing to think that a doctor could be regarded as measuring up to the standards of a his post in the baby care unit if he is incapable of recognising that the instrument on which he relies is so positioned as to give dangerously misleading information. If the judge had clearly found, applying the test previously stated, that Dr Wiles had been personally negligent, I would, with the same reluctance as expressed by the judge, have concluded that this court should not interfere. But I do not think that he did find this, and in the circumstances I do not think it appropriate to add a new finding adverse to this doctor's skill and care which has no bearing on the outcome of the action.

b

The facts: later episodes

The shape of this part of the case is harder to make out. On a number of occasions the Po_2, as measured by samples taken either from a correctly-positioned catheter or by an arterial stab, exceeded 15 kPa. At one time the plaintiff appears to have been asserting c that this should not have happened. This is no longer the case. It is not now contended that the occurrence of transient elevations above that figure, what were called 'spikes', was a matter for blame. It is quite clear that this concession was rightly made. The baby's Po_2 was volatile. He was very ill on many occasions. An improvement in (for example) Pco_2 had to be bought by measures which would push up his Po_2. The best management could not prevent the level from rising too high. What had to be done was to ensure d that, other clinical factors permitting, it remained there for the shortest possible time.

The case now presented is that the defendants failed in this regard. It is said that, because the medical staff did not take sufficient blood gas samples to calibrate the monitor, the nurses relied on the monitor at times when it was not giving accurate readings, so that they did not take steps to reduce what in reality were excessive partial pressures of oxygen.

e On this matter the judge has found (i) that the defendants have not proved that they were free from fault in allowing such long periods to elapse, (ii) that there were excessive periods when the oxygen tension was too high. For the reasons already stated, I consider that the first finding erroneously places the burden of proof on the defendants. The judge has not found affirmatively whether or not they were negligent. Is it legitimate for this court to make its own finding? Eight years after the event, I believe that we must try. A f retrial must be avoided, unless all else fails.

For this purpose I will consider in relation to each episode not only the allegation that the intervals between sampling were excessive, but also the assumption (or perhaps positive finding) that the Po_2 remained excessive for 'lengthy periods'.

By way of introduction it must be noted that Dr Hardy regarded a range of about 7 to 13 kPa as acceptable for Po_2. Dr Stamboulis, who was the houseman at the relevant time, g prescribed a range of 10 to 15 kPa, but Miss Pearson did not agree, and aimed to keep the reading between 10 and 12 kPa. The alarms on the monitor were set at 5 and 15 kPa. It was not suggested on behalf of the plaintiff that Miss Pearson's policy was wrong, or that the nurses did not carefully try to put it into practice. Rather the reverse, since it was the plaintiff's case that reliance on the monitor readings had led the nurses to think that the level of oxygen supply was safe when it was not.

h At the trial, complaint was made about five later episodes. The complaint which was related to events on 22–23 January 1979 was rejected by the judge. Another, concerned with 17–20 January, appears to have been inferentially accepted, but was abandoned on the argument of the appeal, there being no evidence that the Po_2 ever did exceed the equivalent of 15 kPa for a sample taken in the aorta. (At this stage, the catheter had been removed, and samples were taken by stab.) The circumstances of those remaining were j as follows.

(a) *20 December 1978*

Late on 19 December 1978 the baby had an incident of apnoea. At 2230 hrs a blood gas sample revealed the following:

Po_2	Monitor	Pco_2	pH
12·5	11	13·4	6·92

The figures for Pco_2 and pH were very poor. The baby was put on ventilation to flush
out the CO_2; the notes indicate half-hourly CPAP and ventilation, with oxygen   *a*
concentrations of 65–70 and 80–90% respectively. The ventilation would tend to increase
the Po_2. This treatment, which was ordered by Dr Wiles, produced the following results,
obtained at 1030 hrs on 20 December:

Po_2	Monitor	Pco_2	pH	Calibrated monitor
17·5		6·6	7·20	15

b

According to the notes, the proportional calibration exercise performed when the analysis
result came back resulted in a resetting at 15 kPa when the needle had been reading
13·5 kPa. The Po_2 had thus fallen. (The proportional calculation suggests that the
monitor needle must have been reading rather more than 15 kPa when the sample was
taken.)

At 2115 hrs on the same day there was another gas analysis yielding the following   *c*
figures:

Po_2	Monitor	Pco_2	pH
10·6	11	11	7·14

The Po_2 level was thus back in control, although the Pco_2 was now high again. By this
time the concentrations of administered oxygen has been reduced. That concluded
episode (a), as identified by the argument for the plaintiff.   *d*

(b) *28–29 December 1978*

The relevant figures are as follows:

Date	Time	Po_2	Monitor	Pco_2	pH	Calibrated monitor
27 Dec	1000			9·7	7·18	13·4
27 Dec	1400		13·0			
28 Dec	1100	17·4		6·5	7·27	14·2
29 Dec	1345	18·8	15	5·7	7·25	18·3 (at 1600 hrs)
29 Dec	2300	6·4	10	7·0		

e

f

The clinical and nursing notes indicate that the baby was alternatively on IMV and
CPAP during 28–29 December. The PO_2 of 17·4 kPa was based on a sample taken whilst
the baby was on IMV at 35–45% oxygen. The readings made later on the same day were
taken when the baby was on IMV.

(c) *6–8 January 1979*

On 6 January the baby had a severe cyanotic attack lasting for ten minutes, but
responded when oxygen was applied by face mask. At 1130 hours on 7 January the figure
was: *g*

Po_2	Pco_2	pH
10·6	8·1	7·22

At 1315 hrs on 7 January an accident occurred, resulting in the baby receiving no oxygen
supply. The monitor reading fell to 5 kPa and the baby became very cyanotic. He was
put on a face mask. His colour improved, and the monitor reading went to more than
15 kPa. There was no further blood gas analysis until 1115 hrs on 8 January, which
yielded: *h*

Po_2	Pco_2	pH
13·5	8·4	7·17

I now turn to the evidence. So far as concerned the general practice, Dr Harvey said   *j*
that, in the initial stages, his custom was to perform checks three or four times daily
during the first two days after insertion, and then, if it seemed satisfactory, to reduce the
figures to once or twice each day. He thought that the manufacturers' instructions were
very cautious. Also, he preferred not to exhaust too much of the baby's blood supply by

taking samples. Dr Wiles said that in the first two days they would sample much more

a often than daily, unless they had reason for more frequent checks. It was not something that was suggested to be done whilst he was on call at night. Miss Pearson did not discuss the policy of sampling, and Dr Stamboulis, who had the care of the baby for most of this time, was not called. It appears from the records, however, that Dr Hardy's practice was followed in this case. The new catheter was checked three times in ten hours on 17 December, and thereafter twice a day for several days.

b   Of the other witnesses, Dr Roberton said that, in the early days of the baby's illness, the blood gases should be sampled, where there was an indwelling catheter, three, four or five times a day. Dr Chiswick considered that when the monitor had settled down one could do blood gas tests once or twice a day. If the Po_2 was high, one might want to do two blood gases a day. To miss a whole day might be bad practice, but it would depend on the prevailing circumstances. The quantity of blood loss by sampling would not as a

c single factor be a realistic limitation on the frequency of sampling.

Turning to the individual episodes, with regard to the episode of 19–20 December 1978 Dr Roberton thought that, after the reading of 12·5 kPa on the night of 19 December, readings should have been more frequent. The Pco_2 was much too high, and the pH was exceptionally low, and he would have liked to check that they were improving. Also, the Po_2 control was not good, so they should have checked the

d calibration of the catheter. They should undoubtedly have been checked before the blood gas at 1030 hrs on 20 December.

Dr Chiswick pointed out that, with the baby alternating between IMV and CPAP, the Po_2 would oscillate, making the results of any additional blood gas samples hard to use.

Dr Campbell thought that the staff were probably busy getting the baby ventilated and did not have time to do a sample, particularly as the laboratory technician was off

e duty during the night. It would have been helpful to have additional blood gases, but he could understand the doctors asking the nurses to keep an eye on the monitor.

In my judgment, if the judge had found that the defendants were at fault in not taking an additional reading overnight, the finding would have been hard to assail, in the light of the evidence of Dr Roberton. But he did not do so, given his opinion on burden of proof, and I believe that the position is not so clear-cut as to justify this court in making

f a finding against the defendants on its own account. The same conclusion applies a fortiori to the 11-hour gap after the reading at 1030 hrs on 20 January. The position had been unsatisfactory, but the levels were falling sharply during the period between the sampling and the return of the samples from the laboratory, and the staff could well have been justified in concluding that the situation was in hand.

I should add a few words about the duration of any time when the Po_2 was excessive.

g The judge has not found explicitly that this particular episode was one which involved 'lengthy periods' of exposure. If he has done so by implication, I must respectfully disagree. I accept that there must have been some period before 1030 hrs on 20 January when the monitor was not reading truly and when the staff were unaware that the true partial pressure was above the 15 kPa mark. But there is no means of knowing, as Dr Roberton accepted, how long this had lasted. The increase cannot be assumed to have

h been on a straight-line basis, particularly in view of the alternation between IMV and CPAP. As regards the position after 1030 hrs on 20 January, the Po_2 was falling rapidly, and there is no reason to suppose that it remained above 15 kPa for much longer than it takes to get the blood gas results back from the laboratory.

I now turn to the episode of 28–29 December. Periods of 25 hours and $26\frac{3}{4}$ hours elapsed between the first and second and the second and third critical blood gas analyses.

j Dr Wiles explained that normally Dr Stamboulis did the blood gas samples when he arrived at about 9 or 10 o'clock in the morning. He did not know why the reading on 29 December had been postponed until the afternoon. Dr Roberton described this as a particularly dangerous period, but did not deal explicitly with the intervals between readings, although the tenor of his evidence as a whole is plainly to the effect that they were too long. Dr Chiswick said that it would have been helpful to have had a blood gas sample in the intervening period. He went on to say, however, that this was in an ideal *a* world, and that he honestly felt that the doctors' course of action was reasonable. Professor Campbell accepted that further blood gas samples should have been taken between the three crucial sets of readings.

On this evidence, is it legitimate for this court to make a finding of negligence which the trial judge has not made? After much hesitation, I have come to the conclusion that it is not. The witnesses did not squarely address the question whether the decision to *b* allow intervals of a day to elapse was one which no house doctor occupying the post which he did occupy, and faced with the clinical situation which he did face, could properly have made. I do not think that on such scanty materials we can properly hold that the doctors were negligent, striking although the facts undoubtedly were.

I should add a few words on what the position would have been if I had reached the opposite conclusion, and hence had been called on to decide whether there were lengthy *c* periods of hyperoxygenation which could have been avoided by more frequent tests. We have no firm data on this, apart from the knowledge (from the calibrations) that the meter readings fell while the samples were being analysed on 28 December, and that they remained nearly constant on 29 December. Dr Roberton in his report spoke of a likelihood that the baby was exposed to sustained hyperoxaemia. In evidence, however, he acknowledged that one could only speculate about the position in the 24-hour period *d* after the calibration of 14·2 kPa. Dr Chiswick was of the view that, during the periods of CPAP at least, it would be very unlikely that the Po_2 levels would be in the region of 17 to 18 kPa. (The baby was on IMV at the times of the sampling.) Professor Campbell agreed that there would have been periods of high Po_2 but thought that a sustained period was unlikely in view of the fluctuating ambient oxygen and the use of IMV and CPAP. It was difficult to interpret the position from the documents alone, without *e* getting a feel for the fluctuating course of the baby.

On this material I would hold that the judge was not justified in finding that there were lengthy periods of excessive Po_2. That there were some periods of excess is indisputable, for there cannot just have been spikes, coinciding by chance with the moments when the samples were taken. But there is no means of knowing how long the periods lasted. Moreover, and this is just as important, it is impossible to tell whether, if *f* extra samples had been taken, they would have made any difference. It is recognised that the error on the monitor varies, and that the baby's Po_2 varies. For all that anyone can tell, any extra sample might have been taken at a time when the monitor was performing within tolerance (as it was at 1345 hrs on 29 December) and when the Po_2 level happened to be acceptable. In such a situation the nurses would be reassured, not warned.

Finally, there is the incident of 7–8 January. I can deal with this briefly. It happened *g* at a time when the monitor was not being calibrated daily, a practice of which Dr Chiswick and, no doubt, the other doctors disapproved. But there is no evidence to show that the episode was other than transient. Indeed, there is no evidence to show that the Po_2 ever exceeded 15 kPa, since the reading was taken from the monitor, not a blood gas analysis. Plainly, there had been an accident which called for the immediate application of oxygen. There may have been an overshoot. The staff were watching the monitor. No *h* doubt, they reduced the oxygen supply as soon as they thought it safe to do so. I can see no reason to suppose that taking a sample later on the same day would have made any difference.

Causation   *j*

The primary case for the plaintiff at the trial was that, even if the breach of duty was not the sole cause of his developing RLF, nevertheless it made a significant contribution, and accordingly is to be treated as the proximate cause for the purpose of an award of damages: see *Bonnington Castings Ltd v Wardlaw* [1956] 1 All ER 615, [1956] AC 613.

a Evidence to this effect was given by Dr Harvey and Dr Roberton, and the first report of Professor Hull might also be read in this sense. In the event, however, the judge did not take this line for, although there are passages in his judgment which might be understood as findings of a proved proximate cause, this can hardly have been the effect intended, given the prominence of the argument based on *McGhee v National Coal Board* [1972] 3 All ER 1008, [1973] 1 WLR 1. Moreover, although if the judge had expressed a preference for the evidence of the plaintiff's experts on this point, we might have been

b justified in making our own finding in favour of the plaintiff, he did not do so, and the division of opinion is too sharp to make such a step permissible on the basis of the transcripts and literature alone.

Thus, we must consider the correctness of the route which Peter Pain J preferred to take. This was as follows. (1) It is common ground that exposure to excessive Po_2 involves an increased risk of RLF. (2) Therefore, the plaintiff was subjected to an increased risk of RLF by the episode or episodes for which the defendants were to blame. (3) Accordingly,

c the burden was on the defendants to show that the exposures did not cause harm: see *McGhee*. (4) The defendants have not discharged this burden, and accordingly the plaintiff's disability is to be treated as caused by their breach.

Before considering the difficult problems of law raised at the third stage of this argument, I must consider the facts, since we have been assured (and the transcript bears

d this out) that the connection between high exposure to oxygen and risk of RLF was not common ground at the trial. This is important, because counsel for the plaintiff have accepted that *McGhee* will not help their case, unless a connection of this kind is demonstrated.

A considerable volume of written material was formally put in at the trial. Because of the way the evidence came forward, very little of this was explored before the judge, and

e still less was discussed on the appeal. It would, therefore, be quite inappropriate for this court to base any conclusions on these documents. Still, it is useful to refer to some of them, as part of the historical perspective of the oral evidence. As already stated, the idea of a connection between RLF and prematurity was developed in the early 1950s. Writing many lears later, W A Silverman in an article entitled 'The Lesson of Retrolental Fibroplasia' *Scientific American* 1977;**236**(6):100–7 was able to say that:

f 'By now [ie by 1954] it was apparent that the reason for the sudden appearance of the disease was related to the general acceptance of a hypothesis (put forward in the early 1940's) that the high toll of brain damage in premature infants was caused by a lack of oxygen that up to then had not been recognized. This view provided the rationale for the continuous administration of a high concentration of oxygen, even to babies who showed no abnormal symptoms ... Oxygen at high concentrations

g can be toxic, as it proved to be to the developing blood vessels of the retina of the premature infant.'

Already, it had been shown that, of the infants born during a two-year period with birth weights of less than 1600 gm in the United States, 30% were afflicted by RLF. J D Baum and J P M Tizard had written in 1970, in an article entitled 'Retrolental Fibroplasia:

h Management of Oxygen Therapy' *Br Med Bull* 1970;**26**(2):171–4, that the link between RLF and oxygen therapy 'is certain', and they had suggested a pathogenesis involving the constriction of retinal blood vessels. One year later, Dr Alec Garner and Professor Norman Ashton had written that it was 'now common knowledge' that RLF is due to the toxic effects of oxygen (see *Proc R Soc Med* 1971;**64**:774–7). However, even as these words were in the press, a project was being carried out under the direction of V E Kinsey et al,

j involving the prospective study at five important teaching hospitals in the United States of 719 surviving premature babies, of whom 76 developed RLF. Elaborate statistical exercises were performed on this quite small sample. Ultimately, amidst many conclusions to the effect that various correlations were not proven, there emerged the opinion that the most important risk factors were low birth weight and the duration (not the concentration) of the oxygen treatment. We have, however, been shown sharp criticisms in learned journals of the methodological basis of this study.

Later, another study by M Shohat, S H Reisner, R Krikler et al entitled 'Retinopathy of Prematurity: Incidence and Risk Factors' *Pediatrics* 1983;**72**:159–63, suggested a number of significant factors, including apnoea and the number of transfusions. Duration of oxygen exposure and the number of episodes of Po_2 levels greater than 70 mmHg were not significantly higher in the RLF groups. The writer concluded that:

> 'In spite of the more careful attention to the monitoring of oxygen therapy, the incidence of ROP [ie retinopathy of prematurity] is high . . . It is possible that other risk factors still need to be determined.'

Finally, a thorough review of the literature was made by J F Lucey and B Dangman in a special article entitled 'A Reexamination of the Role of Oxygen in Retrolental Fibroplasia' *Pediatrics* 1984;**73**: 82–96, which the authors described as—

> 'a review of the evidence indicating that "excessive" oxygen administration is but one cause of RLF. In the present "epidemic" it may not even be the major cause.'

(It may be noted that this article was clearly written in the context of malpractice claims asserting that RLF was an iatrogenic disease.) The writers cited the results of studies on very small samples. They pointed out that some babies with low oxygen administration (and, as other studies showed, some babies with no extra oxygen) developed RLF; other babies with high oxygen did not develop the disease. The article went on to enumerate various conditions (in one case affecting only two infants) which might be associated with RLF. Of these, the authors draw particular attention to hypoxia. Relationships with apnoea and intraventricular haemorrhage (IVH) are also material. The authors concluded:

> 'A critical review of the literature of retrolental fibroplasia indicates that the cause of this disease is not yet known. Oxygen is certainly a critical factor but it is still not possible to make precise recommendations as to the amount or the duration of therapy that is safe . . . A study of the present epidemic indicates that excessive oxygen administration probably plays a minor role, in contrast to the first epidemic in which prolonged oxygen administration was clearly a major factor.'

The evidence given by the expert witnesses at the trial reflects the differences of opinion to be found in the literature; and indeed the present uncertainties to which this branch of medical science is subject are shown by the existence of contradictions within the evidence of more than one of the witnesses. I think it amounts to this. (1) Nobody is now sure of the mechanism which brings about RLF. Experiments involving babies are impermissible, and those performed on very young animals are not necessarily to be relied on. (2) The meagre data indicate correlations between RLF and a number of factors. (3) Because the mechanism is unknown, it is impossible at present to be sure of the extent to which the associations with RLF demonstrate a causal connection between a particular factor and the onset of the disease. For example, there is evidence of an association between the incidence of intraventricular haemorrhage (IVH) and RLF. But this does not mean that IVH causes RLF. It is just as consistent with the opinion that premature babies with a low birth weight are prone to suffer IVH, and also prone to suffer RLF, or are prone to suffer conditions the remedy of which causes RLF. To say that RLF is a disease of prematurity, which it undoubtedly is, does not mean that factors such as the inadvertent administration of oxygen to a premature baby in an attempt to keep it alive have no part in the causation of the disease. (4) The evidence does implicate exposure to oxygen as a causative factor, particularly in the very early days of the baby's life. What is no longer so clear as it was is that the concentration rather than the duration of the exposure is crucial. Moreover, the evidence from the 'first epidemic' of the 1940s related to long exposures at high concentrations. It cannot be uncritically transferred to a situation where the indiscriminate use of oxygen has ceased. The findings thus made can, I believe, be made with the appropriate degree of confidence even by a court which

has not seen or heard the evidence. What has caused me much anxiety is whether, by
a making a further finding on an issue where there was a sharp conflict between the expert
witnesses, we are not going too far in the effort to avoid a retrial. This issue related to the
possibility that the first episode could have caused RLF. Dr Harvey and Dr Roberton
considered that it could. The evidence of Dr Hardy was equivocal. Dr Hall in his oral
evidence (but not his report) and Dr Chiswick were of the opinion that it could not.
Nevertheless, although conscious of the need not to overstep the functions of an appellate
b court, I believe it legitimate, after reading and rereading the evidence, to add one further
finding, namely (5) The weight of the expert evidence was that high Po_2 levels of the
kind experienced in the first episode can, particularly at an early stage of the baby's life,
lead to RLF, although nobody can say that in this particular instance the first episode,
rather than some other unknown factor, was definitely the cause, or one of the causes, of
the injury.
c   With these findings in mind I turn to *McGhee v National Coal Board* [1972] 3 All ER
1008, [1973] 1 WLR 1. Because this case is so central to the present appeal, I must quote
the judgments at length, but will first recapitulate the findings of fact. The pursuer
sweated profusely, so that the outer level of his skin was softened and easily injured. The
particles of dust clung to him and injured the outer layer, exposing to injury or infection
the tender cells below. This led to dermatitis. The exertion of cycling home while still
d caked with sweat and grime made him liable to further injury until he could wash. The
effect of such abrasion of the skin is cumulative in the sense that the longer a subject is
exposed to injury the greater the chance of his developing dermatitis.
      In the Court of Session it was held that the pursuer had to prove that his additional
exposure to injury caused by his having to cycle home unwashed caused the disease in
the sense that it was more probable than not that this additional exposure to injury was
e the cause of it, or at least materially contributed to it. This he failed to do. The House of
Lords disagreed. Lord Reid's conclusion on the medical evidence was that the fact that
the man had to cycle home caked with grime and sweat added materially to the risk that
this disease might develop. He continued ([1972] 3 All ER 1008 at 1011, [1973] 1 WLR
1 at 4–5):

f   'I cannot accept the view expressed in the Inner House that once the man left the
      brick kiln he left behind the causes which made him liable to develop dermatitis.
      That seems to me quite inconsistent with a proper interpretation of the medical
      evidence. Nor can I accept the distinction drawn by the Lord Ordinary between
      materially increasing the risk that the disease will occur and making a material
      contribution to its occurrence. There may be some logical ground for such a
      distinction where our knowledge of all the material factors is complete. But it has
g   often been said that the legal concept of causation is not based on logic or philosophy.
      It is based on the practical way in which the ordinary man's mind works in the
      everyday affairs of life. From a broad and practical viewpoint I can see no substantial
      difference between saying that what the defender did materially increased the risk
      of injury to the pursuer and saying that what the defender did made a material
h   contribution to his injury.'

      Lord Wilberforce said that there could be little doubt that the pursuer's dermatitis
resulted from a combination, or accumulation, of two causes: exposure to dust while
working in hot conditions in the kiln and the subsequent omission to wash thoroughly
before leaving the place of work; the second of these, but not the first, was, on the
findings, attributable to the fault of the respondents. He continued ([1972] 3 All ER
j 1008 at 1012, [1973] 1 WLR 1 at 6):

      'My Lords, I agree with the judge below to the extent that merely to show that a
      breach of duty increases the risk of harm is not, in abstracto, enough to enable the
      pursuer to succeed. He might, on this basis, still be met by successful defences.
      Thus, it was open to the respondents, while admitting, or being unable to contest

that their failure had increased the risk, to prove, if they could, as they tried to do, that the appellant's dermatitis was "non-occupational". But the question remains *a* whether a pursuer must necessarily fail if, after he has shown a breach of duty, involving an increase of risk of disease, he cannot positively prove that this increase of risk caused or materially contributed to the disease while his employers cannot positively prove the contrary. In this intermediate case there is an appearance of logic in the view that the pursuer, on whom the onus lies, should fail—a logic which dictated the judgments below. The question is whether we should be satisfied *b* in factual situations like the present, with this logical approach. In my opinion, there are further considerations of importance. First, it is a sound principle that where a person has, by breach of duty of care, created a risk, and injury occurs within the area of that risk, the loss should be borne by him unless he shows that it had some other cause. Secondly, from the evidential point of view, one may ask, why should a man who is able to show that his employer should have taken certain *c* precautions, because without them there is a risk, or an added risk, of injury or disease, and who in fact sustains exactly that injury or disease, have to assume the burden of proving more: namely, that it was the addition to the risk, caused by the breach of duty, which caused or materially contributed to the injury? In many cases of which the present is typical, this is impossible to prove, just because honest medical opinion cannot segregate the causes of an illness between compound causes. *d* And if one asks which of the parties, the workman or the employers should suffer from this inherent evidential difficulty, the answer as a matter in policy or justice should be that it is the creator of the risk who, ex hypothesi, must be taken to have foreseen the possibility of damage, who should bear its consequences.'

After quoting from the speech of Lord Keith in *Bonnington Castings Ltd v Wardlaw* [1956] 1 All ER 615 at 622, [1956] AC 613 at 626, Lord Wilberforce went on to say ([1972] 3 All *e* ER 1008 at 1013, [1973] 1 WLR 1 at 7):

'The evidential gap which undoubtedly existed there (ie the absence of proof that but for the addition of the "guilty" dust the disease would not have been contracted) is similar to that in the present case and is expressed to be overcome by inference . . . The present factual situation has its differences: the default here consisted not in *f* adding a material quantity to the accumulation of injurious particles but by failure to take a step which materially increased the risk that the dust already present would cause injury. And I must say that, at least in the present case, to bridge the evidential gap by inference seems to me something of a fiction, since it was precisely this inference which the medical expert declined to make. But I find in the cases quoted an analogy which suggests the conclusion that, in the absence of proof that the *g* culpable condition had, in the result, no effect, the employers should be liable for an injury, squarely within the risk which they created and that they, not the pursuer, should suffer the consequence of the impossibility, foreseeably inherent in the nature of his injury, of segregating the precise consequence of their default.'

The analysis by Lord Simon was in the following terms ([1972] 3 All ER 1008 at 1014–1015, [1973] 1 WLR 1 at 8–9):   *h*

'The question, then, is whether on the evidence the appellant brought himself within this rule. In my view, a failure to take steps which would bring about a material reduction of the risk involves, in this type of case, a substantial contribution to the injury. In this type of case a stark distinction between breach of duty and causation is unreal. If the provision of shower baths was (as the evidence showed) a *j* precaution which any reasonable employer in the respondents' position would take, it means that such employer should have foreseen that failure to take the precaution would, more probably than not, substantially contribute towards injury; this is sufficient prima facie evidence. That "material reduction of the risk" and "substantial contribution to the injury" are mirror concepts in this type of case appears also from a Viscount Simond's speech in *Nicholson v Atlas Steel Foundry & Engineering Co Ltd* [1957] 1 All ER 776 at 779–781, [1957] 1 WLR 613 at 618–620, where he was applying the concept of "substantial contribution" laid down in *Bonnington Castings Ltd v Wardlaw* [1956] 1 All ER 615, [1956] AC 613: ". . . it was practicable for the respondents to have reduced the risk . . . It follows that owing to the default of the respondents, the deceased was exposed to a greater degree of risk than he should have been, and, though it is impossible even approximately to quantify the particles

b which he must in any event have inhaled and those which he inhaled but need not have, I cannot regard the excess as something so negligible that the maxim 'de minimis' is applicable." See also the Lord Ordinary (Lord Kilbrandon) in *Gardiner v Motherwell Machinery and Scrap Co Ltd* 1961 SC (HL) 1 at 3, a dermatitis case, where he rehearsed the pursuer's argument, which he accepted, as follows: ". . . that the washing facilities which were provided were inadequate and primitive, and that, if

c they had been up to standard, the risk of dermatitis would have been very much reduced." His judgment was upheld in your Lordships' House ([1961] 3 All ER 831, [1961] 1 WLR 1424), the headnote stating (1961 SC (HL) 1): ". . . where a workman who had not previously suffered from a disease, contracted that disease after being subjected to conditions likely to cause it, and showed that it started in a way typical of disease caused by such conditions, he established a *prima facie* presumption that

d his disease was caused by those conditions; and that, since, in the present case, the employers had failed to displace the presumption, they were liable to the workman in damages at common law." To hold otherwise would mean that the respondents were under a legal duty which they could, in the present state of medical knowledge, with impunity ignore.'

e Next, Lord Kilbrandon said ([1972] 3 All ER 1008 at 1015–1016, [1973] 1 WLR 1 at 9–10):

'It would have been possible to state the argument in this way: "The appellant cannot show that it is more probable than not that, if a shower had been provided, he as an individual would not have contracted dermatitis. Therefore it is impossible to say that the respondents were under a duty to him as an individual to supply a

f shower; A cannot have owed to B a duty to take a precaution the absence of which B fails to show probably caused him injury." The duty can only be examined in relation to the individual who complains of the breach of it; it is not owed to him as a mere potential victim of dermatitis; and this is unaffected by the fact that other men, for reasons we do not understand, would not have required the benefit of the precaution. But once the breach of duty to the appellant has been accepted, this

g argument seems to me to become untenable. It depends on drawing a distinction between the possibility and the probability of the efficacy of the precautions. I do not find it easy to say in the abstract where one shades into the other; it seems to me to depend very much on the nature of the case. This a a case in which the actual chain of events in the man's body leading up to the injury is not clearly known. But there are effective precautions which ought to be taken in order to prevent it. When

h you find it proved (a) that the defenders knew that to take the precaution reduces the risk, chance, possibility or probability of the contracting of a disease, (b) that the precaution has not been taken, and (c) that the disease has supervened, it is difficult to see how those defenders can demand more by way of proof of the probability that the failure caused or contributed to the physical breakdown.'

j Finally, Lord Salmon said ([1972] 3 All ER 1008 at 1018, [1973] 1 WLR 1 at 12–13):

'My Lords, I would suggest that the true view is that, as a rule, when it is proved, on a balance of probabilities, that an employer has been negligent and that his negligence has materially increased the risk of his employee contracting an industrial disease, then he is liable in damages to that employee if he contracts the disease notwithstanding that the employer is not responsible for other factors which have

materially contributed to the disease: *Bonnington Castings Ltd v Wardlaw* [1956] 1 All
ER 615, [1956] AC 613 and *Nicholson v Atlas Steel Foundry & Engineering Co Ltd*
[1957] 1 All ER 776, [1957] 1 WLR 613. I do not find the attempts to distinguish
those authorities from the present case at all convincing. In the circumstances of the
present case, the possibility of a distinction existing between (a) having materially
increased the risk of contracting the disease, and (b) having materially contributed
to causing the disease may no doubt be a fruitful source of interesting academic
discussions between students of philosophy. Such a distinction is, however, far too
unreal to be recognised by the common law. I would accordingly allow the appeal.'

These speeches raise problems. In the first place, Lord Wilberforce conceived that the
doctrine expounded went to burden of proof. It left the defendants with the task of
proving that the breach of duty did not cause the loss. The other members of the House,
by contrast, seem to have concluded that, once it was proved that the breach of duty
increased the risk, this ipso facto proved a connection between the breach and the injury.

Fortunately, it is not necessary to examine this apparent difference in reasoning,
because the judge has found that in the present case the defendants have failed to
discharge the burden of which Lord Wilberforce spoke. The defendants did not, as I
understand it, challenge this conclusion and, if they had done so, I would have held that
the conclusion was plainly right.

Equally, there is another question which we do not have to solve. In the speeches of
Lord Simon and Lord Kilbrandon, and perhaps of others, there is the idea that duty and
causation are opposite sides of the same coin. Once the plaintiff has established a breach
of duty, comprising a failure to take measures to forestall a known or knowable risk, the
necessary causation proves itself. This analysis is not so easily applied to the present case,
where the risk may be of two different kinds: the first exists if it is known that excess
oxygen can cause RLF. Here, anyone who allows excess oxygen to be administered runs
the risk of causing injury, even though the injury is not certain to materialise. But there
is also a risk even if it is not known, but merely suspected, that excess oxygen can cause
RLF. Once again, a person who allows excess oxygen to be administered runs the risk of
causing injury; but here, the contingency is double, not single. A prudent doctor,
familiar with current medical opinion, will not run either of these risks unless the
circumstances force him to do so. Yet there is a difference in kind as well as degree
between the two. Can a causal connection be presumed in the second case, as well as the
first?

In the end I have not found it necessary to solve this troublesome problem, because on
the evidence I find it proved that excess oxygen can cause or contribute to RLF, so that
the case falls into the first category. But for this, I would have inclined to the view that
McGhee v National Coal Board could not be applied, and I believe that ultimately counsel
for the plaintiff did not press the argument to the contrary.

There is, however, one problem which must be tackled. I had at one time believed
that the present case is on all fours with *McGhee*, and that any apparent difference between
the two simply stemmed from the way in which the problem happened to be expressed.
I am now persuaded that this is not so, and that the two situations really are different. In
McGhee there was only one risk operating, namely that contact of a sweaty skin with
brick dust would lead to dermatitis. The fact that such contact did cause the injury was
not in dispute. Just as in *Bonnington Castings Ltd v Wardlaw* the defenders' fault lay in not
in taking proper steps to reduce that single risk. The uncertainty was whether the fault
had tipped the scale. In the present case there is a greater uncertainty. Instead of a single
risk factor known to have caused the injury there is a list of factors, which cannot be fully
enumerated in the current state of medical science, any one of which might have caused
the injury. What the defendants did was not to enhance the risk that the known factors
would lead to injury, but to add to the list of factors which might do so. I acknowledge
that this is much further from the facts of *Bonnington Castings Ltd v Wardlaw*, which was
the springboard for *McGhee*, than were the facts of *McGhee* itself.

a   The question is whether this makes a crucial difference. The root of the problem lies in the fact that, for reasons of policy, the House of Lords mitigated the rigour of the rule that the plaintiff must prove that the breach caused the loss in the interests of achieving a result which was considered to be just. Given that this was a decision based on policy, rather than a chain of direct reasoning, the difficulty is to know whether a similar approach can properly be adopted in the different circumstances of the present case. After much hesitation I have come to the conclusion that it can. Reading all the speeches

b   together, the principle applied by the House of Lords seems to me to amount to this. If it is an established fact that conduct of a particular kind creates a risk that injury will be caused to another or increases an existing risk that injury will ensue, and if the two parties stand in such a relationship that the one party owes a duty not to conduct himself in that way, and if one party does conduct himself in that way, and if the other party does suffer injury of the kind to which the injury related, then the first party is taken to

c   have caused the injury by his breach of duty, even though the existence and extent of the contribution made by the breach cannot be ascertained. If this is the right analysis, it seems to me that the shape taken by the enhancement of the risk ought not to be of crucial significance. In *McGhee* the conduct of the employers made it more likely that the pursuer would contract dermatitis, and he did contract dermatitis. Here, the conduct of those for whom the defendants are liable made it more likely that Martin would contract

d   RLF, and he did contract RLF. If considerations of justice demanded that the pursuer succeed in the one case, I can see no reason why the plaintiff should not succeed in the other.

Finally, I should mention certain observations of Lord Wright (with whose speech the other members of the House of Lords agreed) in *A/S Rendal v Arcos Ltd* [1937] 3 All ER 577 at 586–588 which have come to the attention of the court since the conclusion of the

e   argument. Since we have not had the benefit of submissions on them, and since they were uttered in a context very different from the present, it would not be appropriate to found any conclusions on them. It does, however, appear that they are consistent with the views on causation which I have endeavoured to express.

Accordingly, I would hold that the plaintiff has established both a breach of duty by the defendants and a sufficient connection with the loss which he has suffered. This is

f   sufficient to establish liability, and I would dismiss the appeal.

Although this is a long judgment I cannot part from the appeal without saying something about the history of the action. I do so, not to criticise the practitioners who conducted the case, but to draw attention to certain features of medical negligence litigation as currently conducted in England and Wales.

The first features speaks for itself: it is delay. The events in question happened in the

g   first two months of Martin Wilsher's life. He is now aged $7\frac{1}{2}$ years. Surely this will not do. Quite plainly, the parties cannot be expected to join battle straight away. Time is needed for diagnosis, advice, reflection and possibly negotiation. But it is unfair to expect witnesses at a trial of this kind (or indeed of any kind) to remember what happened six years before. It is also unfair to the parties. These cases are of great importance to both sides: to the parent who has to plan her child's future and to the doctors who are accused

h   of a breach of duty. They should not have to wait so long.

Secondly, the procedures adopted before trial were such as to make the trial quite unnecessarily difficult to conduct, and to create a real risk of injustice. What happened was this. During April 1981 a statement of claim was served, the material part of which read:

j   'The Defendants by their servants or agents the medical and/or nursing staff at the said hospital, were negligent in their care management and treatment of the Plaintiff as below set forth.'

There followed seven allegations, of which two were abandoned, and one was not pursued. The remainder included:

'(iv) They failed accurately and safely to monitor the arterial blood oxygen;
(v) They administered too high a concentration of oxygen to the Plaintiff,
whereby the arterial oxygen was raised to a dangerous level.'

No particulars were ever given of the persons said to have been negligent, or of when or
how they were negligent. The defence was served during May 1981. It said nothing. It
did not even admit the plaintiff's allegation that the catheter had been put into the vein
rather than the artery. No request for particulars, notice to admit or interrogatory was
served by either side.

On 30 September 1981 Master Creightmore made an order by consent. It dealt with
discovery and inspection, but also provided: 'A medical report be agreed, if possible, and
that if not the medical evidence be unlimited.' In consequence, there was no full
exchange of experts' reports before the trial. We are told that one or two reports were in
fact served, but this seems to have made matters worse, not better. The fact that Dr
Harvey's first report dealt only with the catheter led the defendants to think that,
whatever the statement of claim might say, the case was about the catheter and nothing
else. The plaintiff's advisers, on the other hand, could not have anticipated that Professor
Hull would at the trial disavow certain opinions expressed in his report, which appeared
to favour the plaintiff on both breach and causation.

In the result, the parties realised, soon after the case began, that they had misunderstood
what the case was about. As was stated before us, it was fought 'in the dark'. It lasted four
weeks instead of the allotted five days, which not only imposed great pressure of time on
all concerned, but meant that the scheduling of the expert witnesses was put quite out of
joint. The judge had nothing to read beforehand except some pleadings which told him
nothing. The evidence of the plaintiff's and defendants' witnesses came forward in no
sort of order, sometimes by instalments. Nearly 150 pages of medical literature were put
in, without prior exchange, or any opportunity for proper scrutiny.

All this could have been avoided if there had been adequate clarification of the issues
before the trial. The master is not to be criticised for making a consent order, in the light
of *Rahman v Kirklees Area Health Authority* [1980] 3 All ER 610, [1980] 1 WLR 1244. But
I believe that practitioners do their clients and the interests of justice no service by
continuing to pursue this policy of concealment. Certainly, as the very experienced
members of the court pointed out in *Rahman v Kirklees Area Health Authority*, there can be
problems in making a defendant disclose his experts' reports. Nevertheless, these and
similar problems are faced and solved all the time in cases before the Commercial Court
and the official referees, where it is now axiomatic on technical issues that all the cards
must be on the table before the trial begins. Those cases are concerned with money.
Here, there are also human issues of great importance. To me it seems wrong that in this
area of the law, more than in any other, this kind of forensic blind-man's buff should
continue to be the norm.

For the reasons previously stated, I would dismiss this appeal.

GLIDEWELL LJ. I have had the great advantage of reading in draft the judgments of
Sir Nicolas Browne-Wilkinson V-C and Mustill LJ. I shall comment only about two
subjects on which they do not agree.

Firstly, what is the proper test to be applied to decide whether a doctor, engaged as
were the doctors in this case in a special unit caring for premature babies, has been
negligent? The test usually applied is that adopted in his judgment by Peter Pain J from
the charge to a jury by McNair J in *Bolam v Friern Hospital Management Committee* [1957]
2 All ER 118 at 121, [1957] 1 WLR 582 at 586:

'The test is the standard of the ordinary skilled man exercising and professing to
have that special skill. A man need not possess the highest expert skill at the risk of

being found negligent. It is well-established law that it is sufficient if he exercises
the ordinary skill of an ordinary competent man exercising that particular art.'

I agree with the judge that this is the correct test by which to weigh the conduct of all
the doctors in the present case.

If I understand him correctly, Sir Nicolas Browne-Wilkinson V-C would apply a less
stringent test to a newly-qualified practitioner, who has accepted an appointment in
order to gain experience. The suggested test would only hold such a doctor liable 'for acts
or omissions which a careful doctor with his qualifications and experience would not
have done or omitted'. With great respect, I do not believe this is the correct test. In my
view, the law requires the trainee or learner to be judged by the same standard as his
more experienced colleagues. If it did not, inexperience would frequently be urged as a
defence to an action for professional negligence.

If this test appears unduly harsh in relation to the inexperienced, I should add that, in
my view, the inexperienced doctor called on to exercise a specialist skill will, as part of
that skill, seek the advice and help of his superiors when he does or may need it. If he
does seek such help, he will often have satisfied the test, even though he may himself
have made a mistake. It is for this reason that I agree that Dr Wiles was not negligent.
He made a mistake in inserting the catheter into a vein, and a second mistake in not
recognising the signs that he had done so on the X-ray. But, having done what he thought
right, he asked Dr Kawa, the senior registrar, to check what he had done, and Dr Kawa
did so. Dr Kawa failed to recognise the indication on the X-ray that the catheter was in
the vein, and some hours later himself inserted a replacement catheter, again in the vein,
and again failed to recognise that it was in the vein. Whichever of the suggested tests of
negligence should be applied to Dr Wiles, we are all agreed that Dr Kawa was negligent,
and that the defendants must therefore be liable for any damage to the plaintiff proved
to have been caused by that negligence.

So far, I have considered negligence in relation only to the first 36 hours of Martin's
life, to the time early in the morning of 17 December 1978 when Dr Wiles realised that
the catheter was in the vein. I can express my views about the proof of negligence in
relation to the later episode shortly. I agree with Mustill LJ that the judge was wrong to
hold that the burden was on the defendants to show that they were not in breach of duty
on the later occasions on which it is alleged that Martin was subjected to excessive blood
oxygen pressure. I also agree that, the burden of proof being on the plaintiff, the evidence
before us does not establish that the defendants were negligent on the later occasions.
When one turns to causation, therefore, the only relevant negligence is that of Dr Kawa
during the first episode.

There are, however, two other comments I should make in relation to negligence.
Firstly, I agree with Sir Nicolas Browne-Wilkinson V-C that there seems to be no reason
in principle why, in a suitable case different on its facts from this, a hospital management
committee should not be held directly liable in negligence for failing to provide sufficient
qualified and competent medical staff. Secondly, I agree with and adopt the rejection by
Mustill LJ of the suggested concept of 'team negligence'.

I now turn to consider the second point of disagreement between Sir Nicolas Browne-
Wilkinson V-C and Mustill LJ, that relating to causation. I too have found this a most
difficult question to decide, but in the end I am in agreement with Mustill LJ that the
plaintiff has proved sufficient facts to come within the principle of *McGhee v National
Coal Board* [1972] 3 All ER 1008, [1973] 1 WLR 1; and thus to succeed.

I gratefully adopt Mustill LJ's summary of the effect of the medical evidence. I
emphasise his fifth conclusion that—

'The weight of the expert evidence was that high Po_2 levels of the kind experienced
in the first episode can, particularly at an early stage of the baby's life, lead to RLF,
although nobody can say that in this particular instance the first episode, rather than
some other unknown factor, was definitely the cause, or one of the causes, of the
injury.'

Although the judge said that it was common ground that excessive blood oxygen pressure increases the risk of RLF, we were told that this was not accepted, and the medical *a* evidence bears this out. Nevertheless, I agree with Mustill LJ that the evidence does, on balance, prove that excess blood oxygen pressure can cause or contribute to RLF, and thus that the negligent administration of an excess of oxygen increases the risk of RLF.

There are, however, a number of other disabilities or diseases from which premature babies are liable to suffer which, singly or in combination, can or may cause RLF. Thus, in Martin's case, the evidence goes no further than establishing the following range of *b* possible causes of his RLF: (i) the excess Po_2 during the first episode; (ii) the excess Po_2 during the first episode plus possible excess Po_2 during one or more of the later episodes for which the defendants are not liable; (iii) the excess Po_2 during the first episode, plus one or more of the other disabilities and diseases of prematurity; (iv) one or more of the other disabilities and diseases of prematurity, excessive Po_2 not being a causative factor. Neither plaintiff nor defendants can prove which of these possibilities is correct. *c*

How, then, does the decision in *McGhee v National Coal Board* assist the plaintiff in such a state of uncertainty? I think it essential to note that, in that case, the original exposure to brick dust and the failure to provide adequate washing facilities were treated as separate causes. It is, of course, true that the lack of washing facilities resulted in Mr McGhee continuing to be exposed to the brick dust, but, as a matter of analysis, the failure for which the defendants were responsible was itself a separate cause. The plaintiff *d* could not prove that, if he had been able to wash before he left his workplace, he would not have contracted dermatitis. All he could prove was the increase of risk. The dermatitis was thus caused either by the original exposure to brick dust alone or by that exposure plus the failure to provide washing facilities. Proof of a possible causative factor for which the defendants were not liable and of a factor which increased the risk of contracting the disease for which they were liable was, the House of Lords held, sufficient *e* to establish liability.

Of course, the factual situation in this case is more complex than that in *McGhee v National Coal Board*, but, in my view, the principle is the same. Indeed, one difference is in the plaintiff's favour here, since it is possible in this case that the excess Po_2 in the first episode alone caused Martin's RLF, whereas nobody suggested that the exposure to brick dust after leaving work could alone have caused Mr McGhee's dermatitis. So, in the *f* present case, the plaintiff has proved that his RLF was either (a) caused or contributed to by the negligence for which the defendants are responsible or (b) caused or contributed to by one or more of the other disabilities or diseases, with the excess Po_2 in the first episode increasing the risk of him contracting RLF.

For these reasons, albeit on narrower and different grounds from those adopted by the judge, I also would dismiss the appeal. *g*

I conclude by indorsing what Mustill LJ has said about the difficulties created for the judge, and for the parties themselves, by the lack of any material pre-trial disclosure of their respective contentions or expert evidence. The sooner that such disclosure becomes the norm rather than the exception in medical negligence suits, the better will justice in this field be served.

h

SIR NICOLAS BROWNE-WILKINSON V-C. I gratefully adopt the statement of the facts and the findings made by Mustill LJ in his judgment. Save as to the two points with which I will deal hereafter, I am also in complete agreement with his conclusions and reasoning on the issues of law which arise. *j*

The first point on which I differ from Mustill LJ relates to the question of negligence. On this issue I disagree, not with his decision, but with the process whereby he reaches his conclusion. I enter into this field with hesitation since it is one in which I have virtually no experience. But I cannot accept that the standard of care required of an

individual doctor holding a post in a hospital is an objective standard to be determined
irrespective of his experience or the reason why he is occupying the post in question.

In English law, liability for personal injury requires a finding of personal fault (e g
negligence) against someone. In cases of vicarious liability such as this, there must have
been personal fault by the employee or agent of the defendant for whom the defendant
is held vicariously liable. Therefore, even though no claim is made against the individual
doctor, the liability of the defendant health authority is dependent on a finding of
personal fault by one or more of the individual doctors. The general standard of care
required of a doctor is that he would exercise the skill of a skilled doctor in the treatment
which he has taken on himself to offer.

Such being the general standard of care required of a doctor, it is normally no answer
for him to say the treatment he gave was of a specialist or technical nature in which he
was inexperienced. In such a case, the fault of the doctor lies in embarking on giving
treatment which he could not skilfully offer: he should not have undertaken the
treatment but should have referred the patient to someone possessing the necessary skills.

But the position of the houseman in his first year after qualifying or of someone (like
Dr Wiles in this case) who has just started in a specialist field in order to gain the necessary
skill in that field is not capable of such analysis. The houseman has to take up his post in
order to gain full professional qualification; anyone who, like Dr Wiles, wishes to obtain
specialist skills has to learn those skills by taking a post in a specialist unit. In my
judgment, such doctors cannot in fairness be said to be at fault if, at the start of their
time, they lack the very skills which they are seeking to acquire.

In my judgment, if the standard of care required of such a doctor is that he should
have the skill required of the post he occupies, the young houseman or the doctor seeking
to obtain specialist skill in a special unit would be held liable for shortcomings in the
treatment without any personal fault on his part at all. Of course, such a doctor would be
negligent if he undertook treatment for which he knows he lacks the necessary experience
and skill. But one of the chief hazards of inexperience is that one does not always know
the risks which exist. In my judgment, so long as the English law rests liability on
personal fault, a doctor who has properly accepted a post in a hospital in order to gain
necessary experience should only be held liable for acts or omissions which a careful
doctor with his qualifications and experience would not have done or omitted. It follows
that, in my view, the health authority could not be held vicariously liable (and I stress
the word *vicariously*) for the acts of such a learner who has come up to those standards,
notwithstanding that the post he held required greater experience than he in fact
possessed.

The only argument to the contrary (and it is a formidable one) is that such a standard
of care would mean that the rights of a patient entering hospital will depend on the
experience of the doctor who treats him. This, I agree, would be wholly unsatisfactory.
But, in my judgment, it is not the law. I agree with the comments of Mustill LJ as to the
confusion which as been caused in this case both by the pleading and by the argument
below which blurred the distinction between the vicarious liability of the health
authority for the negligence of its doctors and the direct liability of the health authority
for negligently failing to provide skilled treatment of the kind that it was offering to the
public. In my judgment, a health authority which so conducts its hospital that it fails to
provide doctors of sufficient skill and experience to give the treatment offered at the
hospital may be directly liable in negligence to the patient. Although we were told in
argument that no case has ever been decided on this ground and that it is not the practice
to formulate claims in this way, I can see no reason why, in principle, the health authority
should not be so liable if its organisation is at fault: see *McDermid v Nash Dredging and
Reclamation Co Ltd* [1986] 2 All ER 676 esp at 684–685, [1986] QB 965 esp at 978–979
(reported since the conclusion of the argument).

Claims against a health authority that it has itself been directly negligent, as opposed
to vicariously liable for the negligence of its doctors, will, of course, raise awkward

questions. To what extent should the authority be held liable if (eg in the use of junior housemen) it is only adopting a practice hallowed by tradition? Should the authority be **a** liable if it demonstrates that, due to the financial stringency under which it operates, it cannot afford to fill the posts with those possessing the necessary experience? But, in my judgment, the law should not be distorted by making findings of personal fault against individual doctors who are, in truth, not at fault in order to avoid such questions. To do so would be to cloud the real issues which arise. In the modern world with its technological refinements, is it sensible to persist in making compensation for those who **b** suffer from shortcomings in technologically advanced treatment depend on proof of fault, a process which the present case illustrates can consume years in time and huge sums of money in costs? Given limited resources, what balance is to be struck in the allocation of such resources between compensating those whose treatment is not wholly successful and the provision of required treatment for the world at large? These are questions for Parliament, not the courts. But I do not think the courts will do society a **c** favour by distorting the existing law so as to conceal the real social questions which arise.

I have dealt at such length with this issue because the standard of care applicable is of general importance. But, in the event, I reach the same conclusion on this issue as Mustill LJ. In my view, Dr Wiles was not negligent. He failed to identify the wrongly inserted catheter, despite the absence of the 'loop' disclosed on the X-rays, because he lacked the experience to look for such loop. Professor Hull's evidence shows that junior doctors of **d** Dr Wiles's experience in special care baby units were in general unaware of the significance of such loop. In the circumstances, I do not think Dr Wiles was negligent in failing, through lack of experience, to appreciate the significance of the X-ray showing no loop in the course which the catheter took. Moreover, Dr Wiles called in his superior, Dr Kawa, to check what he had done.

However, the case of Dr Kawa is quite different. He was an experienced registrar with **e** six years' paediatric experience, including one year of intensive baby care. His shortcomings in failing to spot the absence of the 'loop' cannot be put down to inexperience and I agree with the judge that his evidence discloses a negligent failure to apply his mind properly to the question whether the catheter had been properly inserted. I therefore agree that Dr Kawa was negligent and that the health authority is vicariously liable for such negligence. **f**

The second matter on which I differ from Mustill LJ is the causation question. I find this a very difficult point and am in real doubt as to the correct answer. To apply the principle in *McGhee v National Coal Board* [1972] 3 All ER 1008, [1973] 1 WLR 1 to the present case would constitute an extension of that principle. In *McGhee* there was no doubt that the pursuer's dermatitis was physically caused by brick dust; the only question was whether the continued presence of such brick dust on the pursuer's skin after the **g** time when he sould have been provided with a shower caused or materially contributed to the dermatitis which he contracted. There was only one possible agent which could have caused the dermatitis, viz brick dust, and there was no doubt that the dermatitis from which he suffered was caused by that brick dust.

In the present case the question is different. There are a number of different agents which could have caused the RLF. Excess oxygen was one of them. The defendants failed **h** to take reasonable precautions to prevent one of the possible causative agents (eg excess oxygen) from causing RLF. But no one can tell in this case whether excess oxygen did or did not cause or contribute to the RLF suffered by the plaintiff. The plaintiff's RLF may have been caused by some completely different agent or agents, eg hypercarbia, intraventricular haemorrhage, apnoea or patent ductus arteriosus. In addition to oxygen, each of those conditions has been implicated as a possible cause of RLF. This baby **j** suffered from each of those conditions at various times in the first two months of his life. There is no satisfactory evidence that excess oxygen is more likely than any of those other four candidates to have caused RLF in this baby. To my mind, the occurrence of RLF following a failure to take a necessary precaution to prevent excess oxygen causing RLF provides no evidence and raises no presumption that it was excess oxygen rather than

a one or more of the four other possible agents which caused or contributed to RLF in this case.

The position, to my mind, is wholly different from that in *McGhee*, where there was only one candidate (brick dust) which could have caused the dermatitis, and the failure to take a precaution against brick dust causing dermatitis was followed by dermatitis caused by brick dust. In such a case, I can see the common sense, if not the logic, of

b holding that, in the absence of any other evidence, the failure to take the precaution caused or contributed to the dermatitis. To the extent that certain members of the House of Lords decided the question on inferences from evidence or presumptions, I do not consider that the present case falls within their reasoning. A failure to take preventive measures against one out of five possible causes is no evidence as to which of those five caused the injury.

c My difficulty is that in *McGhee* two members of the House (Lord Reid and Lord Wilberforce) accepted that the decision in that case was based not on logic but on common sense or public policy. The difficulty is to know whether, as Mustill and Glidewell LJJ think, it is right to extend further an illogical decision taken on grounds of policy to cover the present case, ie does this case fall within the rationale of the principle applied in *McGhee*? With the greatest hesitation, I have come to the conclusion that this

d case does not fall within the rationale. In my view, it was fundamental to the decision in *McGhee* that the dermatitis was undoubtedly physicially caused by brick dust. Thus, when Lord Reid said ([1972] 3 All ER 1008 at 1011, [1973] 1 WLR 1 at 5):

'From a broad and practical viewpoint I can see no substantial difference between saying that what the respondents did materially increased the risk of injury to the appellant and saying that what the respondents did made a material contribution to

e his injury'

he made those remarks against the background that the precautions should have been taken against brick dust, that the risk which was increased was injury by brick dust and that the actual physical cause of the dermatitis was brick dust. As Lord Reid said, manifestly there is common sense in the view that, in such a case, there is sufficient to

f prove causation from the failure to take the precaution against dermatitis caused by brick dust. So, again, when Lord Wilberforce said ([1972] 3 All ER 1008 at 1013, [1973] 1 WLR 1 at 7):

'... the employers should be liable for an injury, squarely within the risk which they created and ... they, not the pursuer, should suffer the consequence of the impossibility, foreseeably inherent in the nature of his injury, of segregating the

g precise consequence of their default'

the public policy which he was applying stems from the fact that the defendants created the risk (ie the continued presence of brick dust), and the injury (ie dermatitis caused by brick dust) fell 'squarely' within that risk. That formulation of the principle cannot be applied in this case. The risk created by the plaintiffs was RLF caused by excess oxygen;

h unless and until you can say that the plaintiff's RLF was caused by oxygen, it is impossible to say that the injury falls 'squarely within the risk'. In my view, there is no ground of public policy which requires the defendants to be held liable for an injury which they may well not have caused and which the steps they ought to have taken would not have avoided if, in fact, the cause of the plaintiff's RLF was not excess oxygen but one of the four other candidates.

j For these reasons, and with considerable diffidence, I differ from Mustill LJ on the causation question. For myself, I would have allowed the appeal because the plaintiff has failed to establish that the defendants' negligence caused his RLF.

Finally, I would like expressly to indorse the remarks made by Mustill LJ at the end of his judgment concerning the delay that has occurred in this case and the procedures

adopted before the trial. The judge in his judgment commented on the difficulties with
which he was faced arising from those procedures. In my view, the Rule Committee
should, as a matter of urgency, look again at the question of exchange of medical reports
before trial.

*Appeal dismissed. Leave to appeal to the House of Lords granted on terms. Stay refused. Direction
for payment into court of whole sum, with indication that defendants ought to give serious
consideration to an ex gratia release of some money to enable plaintiff's mother to meet necessary
immediate expenditure.*

Solicitors: *Hempsons* (for the defendants); *Attwater & Liell*, Harlow (for the plaintiff).

Vivian Horvath   Barrister.

Holden v Chief Constable of Lancashire

COURT OF APPEAL, CIVIL DIVISION
SIR JOHN ARNOLD P AND PURCHAS LJ
28 NOVEMBER 1985

*Damages – Exemplary damages – Oppressive, arbitrary or unconstitutional conduct by Crown
servant – Unconstitutional action – Wrongful arrest – Whether unconstitutional action required
to be oppressive or aggravating before exemplary damages can be awarded.*

The plaintiff, who was thought by the police to be acting suspiciously, was arrested and
detained in a holding cell at a police station for 20 minutes. Subsequently the plaintiff
brought an action for damages for wrongful arrest. At the hearing of the trial it was
conceded that the plaintiff had been unlawfully arrested. In his summing up the judge
ruled that the question whether to award exemplary damages would be withdrawn from
the jury because the arrest and subsequent imprisonment was only for 20 minutes and
there was no evidence of oppressive behaviour, and accordingly the only issue for the
jury was the amount of compensatory damages. The jury awarded the plaintiff £5. The
plaintiff appealed, contending that the judge had been wrong to withdraw from the jury
the issue of exemplary damages.

Held – A plaintiff could recover exemplary damages for unconstitutional action, such as
an unlawful arrest, by a servant of the Crown even though there had been no oppressive
behaviour or other aggravating circumstances present. Accordingly, the question whether
to award exemplary damages should have been left to the jury with an appropriate
direction as to the special features of the case, such as the absence of any aggravating
circumstances, which they could in their discretion have taken into account in deciding
whether to award such damages and, if so, the amount. Since the judge had applied the
wrong test the appeal would be allowed (see p 841 *b* to *d f g* and p 842 *a* to *c*, post).

Dictum of Lord Devlin in *Rookes v Barnard* [1964] 1 All ER at 410 explained.

Per curiam. A police officer does not necessarily commit an unconstitutional act which
calls for exemplary damages the moment he acts without authority (see p 840 *j* to p 841
a g, post).

Notes

For the award of exemplary damages, see 12 Halsbury's Laws (4th edn) para 1190, and
for cases on the subject, see 17 Digest (Reissue) 80–83, 11–17.

Cases referred to in judgments

a   *Benson v Frederick* (1766) 3 Burr 1845, 97 ER 1130.
    Cassell & Co Ltd v Broome [1972] 1 All ER 801, [1972] AC 1027, [1972] 2 WLR 645, HL.
    Huckle v Money (1763) 2 Wils 205, 95 ER 768.
    Rookes v Barnard [1964] 1 All ER 367, [1964] AC 1129, [1964] 2 WLR 269, HL.
    Wilkes v Woods (1763) Lofft 1, 98 ER 489.

Appeal

b   The plaintiff, Gary Holden, appealed against the judgment of his Honour Judge Morris-Jones QC given on 19 February 1985 in the Blackpool County Court whereby he ordered that judgment be entered for the plaintiff in the sum of £5 in an action for wrongful arrest brought by the plaintiff against the defendant, the Chief Constable of Lancashire. The facts are set out in the judgment of Purchas LJ.

c   *Nigel J Ley* for the plaintiff.
    Elizabeth Rylands for the defendant.

PURCHAS LJ (giving the first judgment at the invitation of Sir John Arnold P). This is an appeal from an order made by his Honour Judge Morris-Jones QC in the Blackpool County Court on 19 February 1985, when he entered judgment for the sum of £5 d damages, a figure that had been assessed by the jury by way of compensatory damages for wrongful arrest.

The circumstances out of which the action was brought can be shortly stated. In the early hours of the morning of 5 September 1983 the plaintiff was one of a number of youths who had been travelling in a motor car which had been stopped by a member of the police force. Their conduct during the course of the event was such as would and did e lead the police officer to think that there was something wrong and that possibly a crime either had been or was about to be committed. There was a dispute on the facts. The case of the plaintiff and his witnesses was that, far from running away from the car and drawing suspicion to themselves, they had walked quietly away to the sea front nearby.

On the other hand the evidence for the defendant was to the effect that the plaintiff and the others, when the car stopped, ran away from the car. It was further established f that the plaintiff and at least one of his friends had criminal records. In his directions to the jury the judge referred to the fact that the plaintiff had twice before been concerned in cases involving wrongful arrest and invited the jury to consider whether on the night in question the plaintiff and his friends were 'trailing their coats'.

The police officer himself had made some inquiries about the registration of the car, but it is right to say that there was nothing illegal or criminal about the use of the car or g anything wrong established against the plaintiff and his friends. So it was that the judge rightly ruled, and there is no challenge, that there was a wrongful arrest and a wrongful detention for something like 20 minutes. The only method of the arrest was that the police officer held the arm of the plaintiff in a perfectly proper manner, apart from the fact that the arrest was not lawful, and no complaint has been made about the way he conducted himself in that short interlude.

h   The two matters which arise on this appeal, however, are, first, it is said that, on a submission made by counsel, the judge ruled that in the circumstances of this case it was not open to the jury to consider exemplary damages and so the matter was not left to them. It has been submitted by counsel for the plaintiff that that was an error in law and that the judge should, in this case, have left the question of exemplary damages to the jury, albeit with such guidance and direction as was proper, but that he should not have j wholly excluded the consideration of exemplary damages (even if the jury were eventually to reject an award of that kind) from them. Counsel for the plaintiff has relied on the classic case of *Rookes v Barnard* [1964] 1 All ER 367, [1964] AC 1129, to which I shall shortly return.

The second complaint made by counsel for the plaintiff related to the judge's directions on compensatory damages. Whereas at the beginning of his directions the judge gave a perfectly proper direction in these terms:

'We call the compensation given to a plaintiff whose rights have been infringed, damages. Members of the jury, the wrong is false imprisonment. The word "false" *a* is used in the same sense as a false step, that is, an erroneous imprisonment is an infringement of the liberty of the subject, and of course, the law does not look lightly on that. You will bear that in mind. I do not detract from what I have just told you when I go on to say that the juries in cases of this type are told, as I tell you now, moderation in all things, particularly in this. I am sure you won't, but don't for one moment, because you heard talk of policemen and liberty of the subject, go *b* wild; moderation, I tell you, should be your guide. Now members of the jury, the compensation has got to be for the harm done to him. He was without his liberty for 20 minutes or so. He was in a police station, he was in a holding cell. You must compensate him for that loss of liberty for that period. You are entitled to take into account the motives and conduct of the police officer and whether insult and injured feeling are proper subjects for compensation. Anxiety. Yes, that is a proper subject *c* for compensation. Thus, under those headings really, I will remind you what the plaintiff said and what the police constable said.'

Thereafter, the judge faithfully rehearsed the evidence and directed the jury's attention to the various aspects which they should consider, if they thought it relevant, in coming to the figure for compensatory damages.

However, the judge returned to the conduct of the police officer, and he said: *d*

'There is not a suggestion of any violence on the part of the police officer, is there? You see, so often in cases such as this sometimes that factor comes into it and if that factor is established to a jury's satisfaction, that unlawful and unreasonable force has been used, well, up go the damages, but here there is no suggestion of that. All the officer did was to hold him by the arm, nothing more. So, no suggestion of physical *e* violence on the part of the police.'

Then later, the judge came to the part of his directions about which complaint is made by counsel for the plaintiff. The judge said:

'So, did this policeman make a mistake? A mistake which the law properly says is an infringement of a man's rights, but in circumstances such that it certainly does *f* not call for ample compensation. It is a matter for you.'

That passage, counsel for the plaintiff submits, as understood by the members of the jury in its ordinary English, might well have indicated to them that because the wrongful arrest in respect of which compensation was to be awarded arose out of a simple mistake made by the police officer, then in some way they should award something less than *g* 'ample compensation'.

Bearing in mind that the judge had already excluded exemplary damages, it is difficult to see what can be meant and what could be understood by the jury from that phrase 'ample compensation', other than that it means full or complete compensation or 'quite enough'. I have used some of the definitions to be found in the *Shorter Oxford Dictionary.* Whatever it may truly have been intended to mean there was a danger of indicating to *h* the jury that in some way they should reduce the compensation, which they otherwise would have awarded, because the arrest arose out of a mistake on the part of the police.

In my judgment, that is a confusing if not misleading direction and, notwithstanding the very full and accurate treatment of the problem in the earlier parts of the directions, that statement coming just towards the end, might well have influenced the jury. It was one of the matters probably most fresh in the minds of the jury, although there was an *j* adjournment overnight between the giving of that part of the direction and their retirement. It would not be safe, in my judgment, to allow the verdict to stand as it may well be that, in coming to the admittedly low figure of £5, the jury may well have been influenced by the direction of the judge that they did not have to give full compensation because the policeman made a mistake.

So on that aspect of the case, I think counsel for the plaintiff has established one of the
grounds of his appeal and would be entitled to a retrial, unless there was some agreement
between the parties which would permit us to make our own assessment of damages.
Unfortunately, counsel has not been able to obtain instructions so our hands are tied,
subject only to the provisions of RSC Ord 59, r 11(1).

I cannot, in view of what I have said, find it within myself to say that there is not a
possibility of a substantial wrong or miscarriage in the shape of the very low award being
made in the circumstances and I would myself feel unable to refuse a new trial within
the ambit of Ord 59, r 11.

I now return to the first ground on which counsel for the plaintiff seeks an order for a
retrial, on the grounds of the ruling by the judge on the question of exemplary damages.
I confess to some hesitation on this part of the case. It seems an overbroad and simplistic
approach to say, as counsel says, that every case of unconstitutional action by a servant of
the government necessarily falls within an area where exemplary damages may be
awarded.

The authority on which counsel for the plaintiff relies is one to which I have already
referred: *Rookes v Barnard*. The speech of Lord Devlin deals in particular detail with the
question of exemplary damages. It is necessary for me only to consider in this judgment
what is called the first of the two categories to which Lord Devlin referred in his speech,
a part of his speech with which all the other Lords of Appeal agreed.

Lord Devlin said ([1964] 1 All ER 367 at 410, [1964] AC 1129 at 1225–1226):

'These authorities convince me of two things. [Lord Devlin had been reviewing
some of the older cases.] First, that your lordships could not without a complete
disregard of precedent, and indeed of statute, now arrive at a determination that
refused altogether to recognise the exemplary principle. Secondly, that there are
certain categories of cases in which an award of exemplary damages can serve a
useful purpose in vindicating the strength of the law, and thus affording a practical
justification for admitting into the civil law a principle which ought logically to
belong to the criminal. I propose to state what these two categories are; and I propose
also to state three general considerations which, in my opinion, should always be
borne in mind when awards of exemplary damages are being made. I am well aware
that what I am about to say will, if accepted, impose limits not hitherto expressed
on such awards and that there is powerful, though not compelling, authority for
allowing them a wider range. I shall not therefore conclude what I have to say on
the general principles of law without returning to the authorities and making it
clear to what extent I have rejected the guidance which they may be said to afford.
The first category is oppressive, arbitrary or unconstitutional action by the servants
of the government. I should not extend this category,—I say this with particular
reference to the facts of this case,—to oppressive action by private corporations or
individuals. Where one man is more powerful than another, it is inevitable that he
will try to use his power to gain his ends; and if his power is much greater than the
other's, he might perhaps be said to be using it oppressively. If he uses his power
illegally, he must of course pay for his illegality in the ordinary way; but he is not
to be punished simply because he is the more powerful. In the case of the
government it is different, for the servants of the government are also the servants
of the people and the use of their power must always be subordinate to their duty of
service. It is true that there is something repugnant about a big man bullying a
small man and very likely the bullying will be a source of humiliation that makes
the case one for aggravated damages, but it is not in my opinion punishable by
damages.'

Then Lord Devlin continues to the second category which is not relevant to
considerations of this appeal, namely where the defendant's conduct has been calculated
to make a profit for him which might well extend beyond the powers of compensation
by ordinary awards for damages.

The judge ruled in these words:

> 'In *Rookes v Barnard* Lord Devlin stated three categories of arrest which were *a*
> appropriate for an award of exemplary damages. It is conceded that the actions of a
> police officer are to be regarded as the action of the government and fall within
> category one, but that, of course, is not sufficient of itself to justify an award of
> exemplary damages. There must be conduct over and above that. Examples are: a
> malicious arrest, cruelty in the mode of arrest, insolence, assault or prolonged
> imprisonment unnecessarily. In my view none of those factors are present in this *b*
> case. The arrest and consequent imprisonment covered a period of about 20 minutes.
> There is no suggestion of assault. There is no suggestion of oppressive behaviour,
> and therefore, my view is that it is not open to the jury in this case to make an award
> of exemplary damages, so the only issue left for the jury is: what is the proper figure
> in respect of those headings of damages sometimes labelled compensatory and
> aggravated?' *c*

There is certainly an area of academic discussion as to the full significance of the speech
of Lord Devlin in *Rookes v Barnard*, and I quote only from *McGregor on Damages* (14th
edn, 1980) para 318, dealing with the passage of Lord Devlin's speech which I have just
cited relating to government servants. It reads:

> 'Accordingly, the facts of *Rookes* itself, which concerned trade unions and trade *d*
> disputes, fell outside this category. It may be a matter for speculation how far the
> House, in selecting this category, was really impressed by the difference in the
> context of damages between the public and private sector and how far it was
> motivated by the need to retain some scope for exemplary damages in order not to
> appear to be acting too cavalierly with the adoption of precedent.'

The author is there referring to three cases, one of which has been relied on by counsel *e*
for the plaintiff, namely *Huckle v Money* (1763) 2 Wils 205, 95 ER 768, and the others
being *Wilkes v Woods* (1763) Lofft 1, 98 ER 489 and *Benson v Frederick* (1766) 3 Burr 1845,
97 ER 1130.

I continue citing from *McGregor*:

> 'In such a search, what better authorities to leave standing than those in which *f*
> exemplary damages had originated? In *Broome v Cassell & Co Ltd* ([1972] 1 All ER
> 801, [1972] AC 1027) Lord Diplock doubted whether today it was still necessary to
> retain this category, but in any event it seems unlikely that in practice there will be
> many cases which will fall within it. The tort books and the court lists are hardly
> full of cases of actions arising out of oppressive conduct of public servants. Indeed it
> is probably true to say that the first three cases of the opening salvo in the campaign *g*
> for exemplary damages are the only decisions of the past two centuries which
> survive, after *Rookes*, by virtue of falling within this category.'

The burden of the submission of counsel for the plaintiff is that the first sentence in
the description of the first category, which I have already cited, lists three types of action
by servants of government: (1) oppressive, (2) arbitrary and (3) unconstitutional. Counsel *h*
draws our attention to the use of the word 'or' in that class.

It has been pointed out in the passage from *McGregor* that *Rookes v Barnard* itself was
not concerned with servants of the government. Therefore, to that extent, Lord Devlin's
first category, and particularly the unconstitutional acts by servants of the government
were not directly in point. However, it is clear that Lord Devlin was defining a limited
number of classes to which awards of exemplary damages could be restricted rather than *j*
considering the possibility of further restrictions within these classes.

I find surprising the proposition in its broadest sense proposed by counsel for the
plaintiff, if I have understood his submission correctly. This was to the effect that the
moment a police officer acts without authority he acts unconstitutionally and that his
behaviour, therefore, falls within Lord Devlin's first category. In making an arrest

unlawfully, it is submitted, the officer acted in contravention of Magna Carta as was
a pointed out by the Pratt CJ in *Huckle v Money* and clearly was acting unconstitutionally.

I would wish to reserve the full ambit of this approach. It may well be that the
unconstitutional actions of a servant of the government would fall within this category
if there was some element not oppressive or arbitrary, because those are two different
categories, but in some way in which there was an improper use of constitutional or
executive power. It is difficult, I admit, to see where the line should be drawn and it may
b be that, at some future occasion, that line will have to be reconsidered.

For the purposes of this appeal, *Rookes v Barnard* shows those categories within which
Lord Devlin said that exemplary damages may serve or can serve a useful purpose. In my
judgment, the judge applied the wrong test when he said, in effect, that either there
must be evidence of oppressive behaviour or, in the other examples he gave, malicious
arrest, cruelty in the mode of arrest, insolence, assault or prolonged imprisonment. If
c full effect is to be given to the word 'or' in the category 'oppressive, arbitrary or
unconstitutional action by government servants' wrongful arrest falls within the category
without any of the added qualifications suggested by the judge, in which case the
question whether or not to award exemplary damages should have been left to the jury
with appropriate directions as to what special features of the case they might in their
discretion take into account in deciding whether or not to award such damages, and, if
d so, how much. Amongst such features which the jury in this case might well be asked to
consider would be the absence of those aggravating circumstances on which the judge
based his ruling and also the fact, if the jury accepted that it happened, that the plaintiff
induced the commission of the wrongful arrest by 'trailing his coat'.

For those reasons, with regret, I cannot uphold the judge's ruling and again on that
ground, if no other course is open, as there will be a retrial as a result of the appellant
e succeeding on the misdirection point, the question of exemplary damages should also be
considered by the jury.

I would add only this, that had there not been the misdirection with which I dealt in
the first part of this judgment and the jury had still returned, in the light of a proper
direction, a sum as low as £5 I would, on the sole point of law in the ruling, have been
minded to exercise the right given to this court to withhold a new trial under Ord 59,
f r 11, but, as there is the other ground on which I would allow this appeal, that question
does not arise.

For those reasons, I would allow this appeal and, with a degree of reluctance, order a
new trial.

SIR JOHN ARNOLD P. I agree as regards, first of all, the matter to which Purchas LJ
g has referred first, the direction that the circumstances of the case are not such as to call
for ample compensation and I agree also in relation to the matter founded on the speech
of Lord Devlin in *Rookes v Barnard* [1964] 1 All ER 367, [1964] AC 1129. I share to the
full the misgivings which Purchas LJ has expressed of the extent to which, in the case of
a tort committed by a Crown servant or a policeman in the course of his duty, and the
implications which the ruling has in relation to the application of exemplary damages,
h but I derive some comfort from the conclusion that a careful reading of Lord Devlin's
speech does not, as I think, disclose that in every case coming within a relevant category
there must be an award of exemplary damages.

In the passage to which Purchas LJ referred, Lord Devlin says ([1964] 1 All ER 367 at
410, [1964] AC 1129 at 1226): '. . . there are certain categories of cases in which an award
of exemplary damages can serve a useful purpose . . .' In my judgment, the circumstance
j that a case comes within a category does not make it follow as the night the day that
exemplary damages will be awarded. It merely leaves it open to the jury to award
exemplary damages in such cases.

I also derive assistance from the circumstance where Lord Devlin draws attention to
the circumstance that it is part of the function of the judge to ensure that the weapon of
the jury of awarding exemplary damages is used with restraint and it seems to be

inescapable that it is perfectly proper, in summing up to a jury, to draw the jury's attention to their power to give or to withhold exemplary damages while drawing their attention also to the circumstance of the judge's view that the case comes within the relevant category and pointing out to them the facts which it is proper for them to take into account in deciding whether to award exemplary damages or not (see [1964] 1 All ER 367 at 411, [1964] AC 1129 at 1227).

In this particular case, in my judgment, it would be entirely proper for the judge, when summing up to the jury, to point out to them the matters which he has dealt with in his ruling to which Purchas LJ has already drawn attention, the factors proper to operate on the minds of the jury in deciding whether or not this is a case in which they should award any exemplary damages. By so doing he would be performing the function designated by Lord Devlin as to seeing that the weapon is used with restraint (see [1964] 1 All ER 367 at 411, [1964] AC 1129 at 1227).

I agree that, in the result, there will have to be a new trial and the case will, therefore, be remitted to Blackpool County Court, to be heard wherever is convenient, for that to be effected.

Order accordingly.

Solicitors: *J S Siergant & Co*, Chorley (for the plaintiff); *Brian Hill*, Preston (for the defendant).

Bebe Chua   Barrister.

Spiliada Maritime Corp v Cansulex Ltd
The Spiliada

HOUSE OF LORDS

LORD KEITH OF KINKEL, LORD TEMPLEMAN, LORD GRIFFITHS, LORD MACKAY OF CLASHFERN AND LORD GOFF OF CHIEVELEY

7, 8, 9 JULY, 19 NOVEMBER 1986

Practice – Service out of the jurisdiction – Alternative forum available – Appropriate forum – Forum in which case can be tried more suitably for parties' interests and ends of justice – Burden of proof – Forum with which action has most real and substantial connection – Effect of deprivation of legitimate personal or juridical advantage – Effect of prior litigation involving similar parties and same issues, experts and lawyers – Principles to be applied – Factors to be considered – RSC Ord 11, r 1(1).

Practice – Stay of proceedings – Foreign defendant – Appropriate forum – Forum in which case can be tried more suitably for parties' interests and ends of justice – Burden of proof – Forum with which action has most real and substantial connection – Effect of deprivation of legitimate personal or juridical advantage – Effect of prior litigation involving similar parties and same issues, experts and lawyers – Principles to be applied – Factors to be considered.

The respondents were sulphur exporters in British Columbia. In November and December 1980 they loaded two cargoes of sulphur, one aboard the appellants' vessel Spiliada for shipment to India and the other aboard the Cambridgeshire, a vessel owned by an English company for shipment to South Africa and Mozambique. The charterparties relating to both cargoes contained an English arbitration clause. The appellants were a Liberian corporation and the Spiliada, which flew the Liberian flag, was managed partly in Greece and partly in England. Both the appellants and the respondents had English insurers. The cargoes loaded aboard both the Spiliada and the Cambridgeshire were wet when loaded and as a result caused severe corrosion to the holds of both vessels. The owners of the Cambridgeshire commenced proceedings in England claiming damages against the respondents. In the course of the trial of that action the appellants, who were supported by the same insurers as the owners of the Cambridgeshire, briefed the same solicitors as the owners of the Cambridgeshire and commenced an action claiming damages against the respondents. The appellants obtained leave ex parte to issue and serve a writ on the respondents out of the jurisdiction pursuant to RSC Ord 11, r 1(1)[a]. The respondents applied to discharge the order giving leave but the judge dismissed the application and held that it was a proper case for service out of the jurisdiction, principally because the teams of lawyers and experts on both sides had already acquired detailed knowledge of the facts and issues in the course of the Cambridgeshire action and therefore it was in the interests of efficiency, expedition and economy that the appellants' action proceed in England rather than British Columbia, and more particularly because if the action proceeded in England the parties would probably settle on the basis of the outcome of the Cambridgeshire action. The respondents appealed against the judge's refusal to discharge the leave. At the hearing of the appeal the appellants contended, inter alia, that since the relevant limitation period for bringing an action had expired in British Columbia but not in England they would be deprived of a legitimate juridical advantage if they were forced to bring their action in British Columbia.

---

a   Rule 1(1), so far as material, provides: '. . . service of a writ out of the jurisdiction is permissible with the leave of the Court in the following cases, that is to say . . . (*f*) if the action begun by the writ is brought against a defendant . . . to enforce, rescind, dissolve, annul or otherwise affect a contract, or to recover damages or obtain other relief in respect of the breach of a contract, being (in either case) a contract which . . . (iii) is by its terms, or by implication, governed by English law . . .'

Held – (1) The fundamental principle applicable to both the stay of English proceedings on the ground that some other forum was the appropriate forum and also the grant of *a* leave to serve proceedings out of the jurisdiction was that the court would choose that forum in which the case could be tried more suitably for the interests of all the parties and for the ends of justice (see p 846 *c d*, p 847 *a* to *c*, p 853 *d e* and p 854 *j*, post); dictum of Lord Kinnear in *Sim v Robinow* (1892) 19 R (Ct of Sess) 665 applied; *Société du Gaz de Paris v SA de Navigation 'Les Armateurs Français'* 1926 SC (HL) 13 considered.

(2) In the case of an application for a stay of English proceedings the burden of proof *b* lay on the defendant to show that the court should exercise its discretion to grant a stay. Moreover, the defendant was required to show not merely that England was not the natural or appropriate forum for the trial but that there was another available forum which was clearly or distinctly more appropriate than the English forum. In considering whether there was another forum which was more appropriate the court would look for that forum with which the action had the most real and substantial connection, eg in *c* terms of convenience or expense, availability of witnesses, the law governing the relevant transaction, and the places where the parties resided or carried on business. If the court concluded that there was no other available forum which was more appropriate than the English court it would normally refuse a stay. If, however, the court concluded that there was another forum which was prima facie more appropriate the court would normally grant a stay unless there were circumstances militating against a stay, eg if the plaintiff *d* would not obtain justice in the foreign jurisdiction (see p 846 *c d*, p 847 *a* to *c*, p 854 *j*, p 855 *h j* and p 856 *a* to *e*, post); *Société du Gaz de Paris v SA de Navigation 'Les Armateurs Français'* 1926 SC (HL) 13, *The Atlantic Star* [1973] 2 All ER 175, *MacShannon v Rockware Glass Ltd* [1978] 1 All ER 625 and *The Abidin Daver* [1984] 1 All ER 470 considered.

(3) Applications under RSC Ord 11, r 1(1) for leave to serve proceedings out of the jurisdiction were to be determined according to the same principles applicable to the stay *e* of English proceedings subject, however, to the burden being on the plaintiff to show that leave should be granted and to the court being required to consider both the residence or place of business of the defendant and the relevant ground invoked by the plaintiff when deciding whether to exercise the discretion to grant leave. Accordingly, the plaintiff was required to show not merely that England was the appropriate forum for the trial of the action but that it was clearly the appropriate forum. However, in *f* discharging the burden lying on him the plaintiff was not confined to showing that justice could not be obtained in an alternative forum or if so, only at excessive cost, delay or inconvenience, but was entitled to rely on the nature of the dispute, the legal and practical issues involved and such questions as local knowledge, availability of witnesses and their evidence and expense (see p 846 *c d*, p 847 *a* to *c*, p 857 *d* to *g j*, p 858 *c* to *f h j* and p 859 *b d*, post); dicta of Lord Diplock and Lord Wilberforce in *Amin Rasheed Shipping* *g* *Corp v Kuwait Insurance Co* [1983] 2 All ER at 891, 893, 896 considered.

(4) The fact that the granting of a stay of English proceedings or the refusal of leave under RSC Ord 11, r 1(1) to serve proceedings out of the jurisdiction might deprive the plaintiff of a legitimate personal or juridical advantage available to him under the English jurisdiction would not, as a general rule, deter the court from granting a stay or refusing leave if it was satisfied that substantial justice would be done to all the parties in the *h* available appropriate forum. Accordingly, the fact that a foreign forum had a more limited system of discovery or lower awards of damages would not necessarily deter the court from granting a stay or refusing leave. On the other hand, where the plaintiff's claim was time-barred in the appropriate forum but he had not acted unreasonably in failing to commence proceedings within the limitation period applicable there, practical justice required the court not to deprive him of the benefit of having complied with the *j* time-bar in England (see p 846 *c d*, p 847 *a* to *c*, p 859 *c f* to *h* and p 860 *b f* to *h*, post); dictum of Lord Diplock in *MacShannon v Rockware Glass Ltd* [1978] 1 All ER 625 at 630 considered.

(5) On the facts, the preparation for the Cambridgeshire action required of the teams of lawyers and experts appearing or assisting both the appellants and the respondents, the fact that the solicitors for the owners in both actions were instructed by the same insurers,

a who were managed in England and were dominus litis, and the fact that the dispute concerned a contract the proper law of which was English law, meant that England was the appropriate forum in which the case could be more suitably tried. The judge had therefore been justified in holding that the case was suitable for service of the writ out of the jurisdiction. The appeal would accordingly be allowed (see p 846 c d, p 847 a to c, p 861 b c, p 861 j to p 862 h and p 863 g, post).

b **Notes**
For service of writ out of the jurisdiction with leave, see 37 Halsbury's Laws (4th edn) paras 172, 178.

For stay of proceedings on ground of forum non conveniens, see ibid para 444.

As from a day to be appointed RSC Ord 11, r 1 is to be substituted by RSC (Amendment No 2) 1983, SI 1983/1181, r 7.

c **Cases referred to in opinions**
Abidin Daver, The [1984] 1 All ER 470, [1984] AC 398, [1984] 2 WLR 196, HL.
Amin Rasheed Shipping Corp v Kuwait Insurance Co, The Al Wahab [1983] 2 All ER 884, [1984] AC 50, [1983] 3 WLR 241, HL.
Aratra Potato Co Ltd v Egyptian Navigation Co, The El Amria [1981] 2 Lloyd's Rep 119, CA.
Athanasia Comninos, The [1981] Com LR 132.
d *Atlantic Star, The, Atlantic Star (owners) v Bona Spes (owners)* [1973] 2 All ER 175, [1974] AC 436, [1973] 2 WLR 795, HL.
BP Exploration Co (Libya) Ltd v Hunt [1976] 3 All ER 879, [1976] 1 WLR 788.
Bibby Bulk Carriers Ltd v Cobelfret NV, The Cambridgeshire (6 October 1982, unreported), QBD.
Blue Wave, The [1982] 1 Lloyd's Rep 151.
e *Britannia Steamship Insurance Association Ltd v Ausonia Assicurazioni SpA* [1984] 2 Lloyd's Rep 98, CA.
Clements v Macaulay (1866) 4 Macph (Ct of Sess) 583.
Crédit Chimique v James Scott Engineering Group Ltd 1982 SLT 131.
European Asian Bank AG v Punjab and Sind Bank [1982] 2 Lloyd's Rep 356, CA.
Hadmor Productions Ltd v Hamilton [1982] 1 All ER 1042, [1983] 1 AC 191, [1982] 2 WLR f 322, HL.
Hagen, The [1908] P 189, [1908–10] All ER Rep 21, CA.
Ilyssia Cia Naviera SA v Bamaodah, The Elli 2 [1985] 1 Lloyd's Rep 107, CA.
Longworth v Hope (1865) 3 Macph (Ct of Sess) 1049.
MacShannon v Rockware Glass Ltd [1978] 1 All ER 625, [1978] AC 795, [1978] 2 WLR 362, HL.
g *Sim v Robinow* (1892) 19 R (Ct of Sess) 665.
Société du Gaz de Paris v SA de Navigation 'Les Armateurs Français' 1926 SC (HL) 13.
Société Générale de Paris v Dreyfus Bros (1885) 29 Ch D 239; affd (1887) 37 Ch D 215, [1886–90] All ER Rep 206, CA.
Trendtex Trading Corp v Crédit Suisse [1981] 3 All ER 520, [1982] AC 679, [1981] 3 WLR 766, HL; affg [1980] 3 All ER 721, [1980] QB 629, [1980] 3 WLR 367, CA; [1980] 3 h All ER 721, QBD.
Tyne Improvement Comrs v Armement Anversois SA, The Brabo [1949] 1 All ER 294, [1949] AC 326, HL.
Union Carbide Corp, Re (12 May 1986), US DC (NY).
Union Industrielle et Maritime v Petrosul International Ltd, The Roseline (23 March 1984, unreported), Can Fed Ct.

j **Interlocutory appeal**
Spiliada Maritime Corp, the owners of the ship Spiliada, appealed with leave of the Appeal Committee of the House of Lords granted on 9 May 1985 against the decision of the Court of Appeal (Oliver and Neill LJJ) ([1985] 2 Lloyd's Rep 116) on 7 March 1985 allowing an appeal by the respondents, Cansulex Ltd, from the order of Staughton J in chambers on 16 November 1984 whereby he dismissed the application of Cansulex

under RSC Ord 12, r 8 to set aside the order of Neill J granted ex parte on 10 October 1983 giving leave to the shipowners to serve a writ of summons on Cansulex in Vancouver, British Columbia or elsewhere in Canada pursuant to RSC Ord 11, r 1(1)(f)(iii) in an action brought to recover damages for breach of a contract of affreightment. The facts are set out in the opinion of Lord Goff.

Kenneth Rokison QC and *Nicholas Legh-Jones* for the shipowners.
Robert Alexander QC and *Peter Goldsmith* for Cansulex.

Their Lordships took time for consideration.

19 November. The following opinions were delivered.

LORD KEITH OF KINKEL. My Lords, I have had the benefit of reading in draft the speech to be delivered by my noble and learned friend Lord Goff. I agree with it and for the reasons he gives would allow the appeal and restore the order of Staughton J.

LORD TEMPLEMAN. My Lords, in these proceedings parties to a dispute have chosen to litigate in order to determine where they shall litigate. The principles which the courts of this country should apply are comprehensibly reviewed and closely analysed in the speech of my noble and learned friend Lord Goff. Where the plaintiff is entitled to commence his action in this country, the court, applying the doctrine of forum non conveniens will only stay the action if the defendant satisfies the court that some other forum is more appropriate. Where the plaintiff can only commence his action with leave, the court, applying the doctrine of forum conveniens will only grant leave if the plaintiff satisfies the court that England is the most appropriate forum to try the action. But whatever reasons may be advanced in favour of a foreign forum, the plaintiff will be allowed to pursue an action which the English court has jurisdiction to entertain if it would be unjust to the plaintiff to confine him to remedies elsewhere.

In the present case, a vessel managed partly in Greece and partly in England, flying the flag of Liberia and owned by a Liberian corporation is said to have been damaged by a cargo loaded by a British Columbian shipper and carried from Vancouver to India. Both sets of insurers are English. Similar litigation took place in Canada concerning the vessel Roseline. Similar litigation took place in England over another vessel, the Cambridgeshire, after Staughton J had refused to stay the action. If Staughton J had good reason to try *The Cambridgeshire*, it is difficult to see that he had bad reason for trying *The Spiliada*.

The factors which the court is entitled to take into account in considering whether one forum is more appropriate are legion. The authorities do not, perhaps cannot, give any clear guidance as to how these factors are to be weighed in any particular case. Any dispute over the appropriate forum is complicated by the fact that each party is seeking an advantage and may be influenced by considerations which are not apparent to the judge or considerations which are not relevant for his purpose. In the present case, for example, it is reasonably clear that the respondents, Cansulex Ltd, prefer the outcome of the *Roseline* proceedings in Canada to the outcome of the *Cambridgeshire* proceedings in England and prefer the limitation period in British Columbia to the limitation period in England. The appellants, Spiliada Maritime Corp (the shipowners), and their insurers hold other views. There may be other matters which naturally and inevitably help to produce in a good many cases conflicting evidence and optimistic and gloomy assessments of expense, delay and inconvenience. Domicile and residence and place of incident are not always decisive.

In the result, it seems to me that the solution of disputes about the relative merits of trial in England and trial abroad is pre-eminently a matter for the trial judge. Commercial court judges are very experienced in these matters. In nearly every case evidence is on affidavit by witnesses of acknowledged probity. I hope that in future the judge will be allowed to study the evidence and refresh his memory of the speech of my noble and a learned friend Lord Goff in this case in the quiet of his room without expense to the parties; that he will not be referred to other decisions on other facts; and that submissions will be measured in hours and not days. An appeal should be rare and the appellate court should be slow to interfere. I agree with my noble and learned friend Lord Goff that there were no grounds for interference in the present case and that the appeal should be allowed.

b **LORD GRIFFITHS.** My Lords, I have had the advantage of reading in draft the speeches prepared by my noble and learned friends Lord Templeman and Lord Goff. For the reasons they give I would allow the appeal.

LORD MACKAY OF CLASHFERN. My Lords, I have had the advantage of reading in draft the speeches prepared by my noble and learned friends Lord Templeman and c Lord Goff. I agree with them and for the reasons which they give I would allow the appeal.

LORD GOFF OF CHIEVELEY. My Lords, there is before your Lordships an appeal, brought by leave of your Lordships' House, against a decision of the Court of Appeal (Oliver and Neill LJJ) ([1985] 2 Lloyd's Rep 116) whereby they reversed a decision of d Staughton J in which he refused an application by the respondents, Cansulex Ltd, to set aside leave granted ex parte to the appellants, Spiliada Maritime Corp, to serve proceedings on the respondents outside the jurisdiction. The effect of the decision of the Court of Appeal was, therefore, to set aside the leave so granted and the proceedings served on the respondents pursuant to that leave.

e (1) *The facts of the case*
    As this appeal is concerned with an interlocutory application, I must, like the courts below, take the facts from the affidavit evidence filed on behalf of the parties. The appellants (whom I shall refer to as 'the shipowners') claim to be (and can, for the purposes of this appeal, be accepted as being) the owners of a bulk carrier, of about 20,000 tonnes deadweight, called the Spiliada. The shipowners are a Liberian corporation, and their f vessel flies the Liberian flag; but their managers are in Greece, though some part of the management takes place in England. The respondents (whom I shall refer to as 'Cansulex') carry on business in British Columbia as exporters of sulphur. The shipowners chartered their vessel to an Indian company called Minerals and Metals Trading Corp of India Ltd (whom I shall refer to as 'MMTC') under a voyage charter dated 6 November 1980, for the carriage of a cargo of sulphur from Vancouver to Indian ports. The charterparty g contained a London arbitration clause. Pursuant to that charterparty, the vessel proceeded to Vancouver and there loaded a cargo of sulphur between 18 and 25 November 1980. The sulphur was loaded on board the vessel by order of Cansulex, who were fob sellers of the sulphur to MMTC. Bills of lading were then issued to, and accepted by, Cansulex. The bills were shipped bills, Cansulex being named as shippers in the bills. Clause 21 on the reverse of the bills of lading provided that, subject to certain clauses which are for h present purposes immaterial, the bills of lading 'no matter where issued, shall be construed and governed by English law, and as if the vessel sailed under the British Flag'. The bills were signed by agents for and by authority of the master. The cargo was discharged at ports in India between 29 December 1980 and 6 February 1981.
    It has been alleged by the shipowners that the cargo of sulphur so loaded on the vessel was wet when loaded and as a result caused severe corrosion and pitting to the holds and j tank tops of the vessel. The shipowners have claimed damages from Cansulex in respect of the damage so caused. The shipowners rely on the age of the ship at the time of the voyage (she was then three years old) and the condition of the holds before and after the voyage. The shipowners have advanced their claim against Cansulex as shippers under the contract of carriage contained in or evidenced by the bills of lading to which I have already referred, basing their claim on art 4, r 6 of the Hague Rules incorporated into the

bills, and on a warranty implied by English law that dangerous cargo will not be shipped
without warning. Arbitration proceedings have also been commenced by the shipowners
against MMTC in London under the arbitration clause in the voyage charter. It is open
to MMTC to bring arbitration proceedings in London against Cansulex under the sale
contract between them, by virtue of the London arbitration clause in that contract. Leave
was obtained by the shipowners to issue and serve a writ on Cansulex outside the
jurisdiction on a ground contained in RSC Ord 11, r 1(1)(ƒ)(iii), viz that the action was
brought to recover damages in respect of the breach of a contract which was by its terms
governed by English law.

Cansulex then applied for an order to set aside such leave and all subsequent
proceedings. The application came before Staughton J on 26 October 1984. The hearing
of the application took place while there was proceeding before Staughton J a very similar
action, in which Cansulex were also defendants. That action concerned a ship called the
Cambridgeshire, owned by an English company, Bibby Bulk Carriers Ltd. In it, the
owners claimed damages for damage alleged to have been caused to their vessel by a
cargo of sulphur loaded on her at Vancouver in November and December 1980, for
carriage to South Africa and Mozambique. The defendants in the action were the
charterers of the ship, Cobelfret NV, and three shippers: Cansulex, Petrosul International
Ltd and Canadian Superior Oil Ltd. In that action, Cansulex (supported by Petrosul
International Ltd, another Canadian company) who had been served with proceedings
outside the jurisdiction on the same ground as in the present case, applied in September
1982 for the leave to serve proceedings on them outside the jurisdiction, and all
subsequent proceedings, to be set aside. Staughton J heard that application and dismissed
it, holding that there was a good arguable case that the Canadian companies were parties
to a contract governed by English law, and that the case was a proper one for service out
of the jurisdiction (see *Bibby Bulk Carriers Ltd v Cobelfret NV, The Cambridgeshire* (6 October
1982, unreported)). There was no appeal from that decision. The trial of the *Cambridgeshire*
action started on 15 October 1984, again before Staughton J. He recorded in his judgment
in the present case that there were no less than 15 counsel engaged in the *Cambridgeshire*
action; that each was equipped with 75 files; and that the then estimate for the length of
the trial was six months.

There has been another set of proceedings concerning damage to a vessel alleged to
have been caused by a wet sulphur cargo shipped at Vancouver. This concerned a ship
called the Roseline. The matter came before the Federal Court of Canada in March 1984,
the defendant being Petrosul International Ltd (see *Union Industrielle et Maritime v Petrosul
International Ltd, The Roseline* (23 March 1984, unreported)). The owners of the Roseline
claimed a declaration that a contract existed between them and Petrosul under which
disputes were to be referred to arbitration in Paris. The contract was said to have been
contained in or evidenced by a bill of lading, in which Petrosul were named as shippers.
Reed J upheld a contention by Petrosul that they were not a party to any contract with
the owners, or at least not a party to any contract containing an arbitration clause; the
judge's conclusion was reached on the basis that the bill of lading, in the hands of
Petrosul, 'partook of the nature of a receipt or a document of title', and that use for this
purpose did not make the document a contractual one so far as Petrosul were concerned.
There is doubt whether a similar conclusion would be reached in English law; Staughton
J was told that there was an unreported decision of Mustill J to the contrary effect (see *The
Athanasia Comninos* [1981] Com LR 132). However, Staughton J held, and it is now
accepted by Cansulex, that in the present case there is a good arguable case that Cansulex
were parties to the bill of lading contract, and so parties to a contract governed by English
law.

It is right that I should record that the judge was told that there were other disputes
concerning similar damage to ships alleged to have been caused by sulphur loaded at
Vancouver; but he knew no more about them.

(2) *The decision of Staughton J*

The judge approached the application of Cansulex in the present case as follows.

a   Having concluded that there was a good arguable case that the shipowners and Cansulex were parties to a contract governed by English law, he then proceeded to consider whether the case had been shown to be, as a matter of discretion, a proper case for service out of the jurisdiction. He referred first to the decision of this House in *Amin Rasheed Shipping Corp v Kuwait Insurance Co, The Al Wahab* [1983] 2 All ER 884, [1984] AC 50, and in particular to certain passages (which I will quote later) from the speeches in that case of Lord Diplock and Lord Wilberforce (see [1983] 2 All ER 884 at 891, 896, [1984]

b   AC 50 at 65, 72), and to a suggested conflict between those two passages; but, following a decision of the Court of Appeal in *Ilyssia Cia Naviera SA v Bamaodah, The Elli 2* [1985] 1 Lloyd's Rep 107, he concluded that the suggested conflict was more apparent than real, and that the appropriate test for him to apply was that if the English court is shown to be distinctly more suitable for the ends of justice, then the case is a proper one for service out of the jurisdiction. He then said:

c
'In considering the exercise of discretion I must, of course, assume that the *Spiliada* action will come to trial eventually, either in England or in Canada. In fact, that seems to me improbable. After the *Cambridgeshire* proceedings have reached a final conclusion, with vast expenditure of money, time and effort, I think it very likely that the parties to the *Spiliada* dispute will have little appetite for litigation, and will

d   reach a compromise. Cansulex feature as defendants in both actions, and are presently represented by the same solicitors and counsel in both. The plaintiff shipowners are, of course, different in the two actions, but they too are represented by the same solicitors and counsel, and it may be that they are supported by the same insurers. So I suspect that what I am in fact deciding is not where the *Spiliada* action will ultimately be tried, but whether a settlement will be reached against the

e   background of litigation pending in England or of litigation pending in Canada. Nevertheless, it is the prospect of a trial which provides the sanction to induce a settlement, and in my judgment I must decide this application on the assumption that a trial there will be.'

f   This was, so far as the *Cambridgeshire* action was concerned, a prescient observation. For, on 18 January 1985 the parties to that action settled their differences. Furthermore, his thought that 'it may be that they [the shipowners] are supported by the same insurers' was one which would certainly have occurred to other experienced commercial practitioners, and the judge's tentative inference that both the Cambridgeshire and the Spiliada were entered in the same P & I club was confirmed before your Lordships; indeed, the solicitors acting for the owners in both cases have commenced proceedings

g   against a number of Canadian sulphur exporters, including Cansulex, on behalf of various shipowners all entered in the same P & I club.
The judge then turned to consider the various factors which were said to influence the choice between an English and Canadian court. I need not list them all. The most important were (1) availability of witnesses, (2) multiplicity of proceedings and (3) a matter which was regarded as crucial by the judge, which I will call the *Cambridgeshire*

h   factor and which relates to preparation for very substantial proceedings.
On availability of witnesses, the judge had this to say:

'Apart from those matters, I now have, after listening to the opening speech in the *Cambridgeshire* trial for 15 days, a somewhat clearer picture of what the relative

j   importance of the issues is likely to be. The principal or most important events in the case occurred in Vancouver, but many events of significance occurred in many other places. The most important witnesses of fact will be from Cansulex and various other concerns in Vancouver, and the ship's officers. But there are likely to be a great many witnesses from other places. In the *Cambridgeshire* applications I concluded that, in terms of witness/hours, events in Vancouver were likely to loom largest at the trial. I am no longer convinced that that was right, even leaving out of account the expert evidence. Certainly, there will be a very substantial body of evidence dealing with events which did not take place in Vancouver. As to the expert witnesses, I am told that all but one of them in the *Cambridgeshire* action are English. But, as I then said, experts can travel, or be replaced by other experts. It is true that the *Cambridgeshire* plaintiffs are an English company and the ship is British, whereas the *Spiliada* plaintiffs are Liberian; so is their ship; and their managers are in Greece, although some part of the management takes place in England. That means that the *Spiliada* action has much less connection with England, but it does not give it any greater connection with Vancouver. It is also true that two witnesses in the *Cambridgeshire* action decline to come to England to give evidence, so that their evidence will have to be taken on commission in North America. Nevertheless, I reach the clear conclusion that Vancouver is not overall a more suitable place for trial than England in terms of the convenience of witnesses. Indeed, if one assumes that the parties will wish to have the same experts as in the *Cambridgeshire* action, I would say that England is shown to be more suitable.'

I should interpolate that the judge was not right in thinking that all but one of the experts in the *Cambridgeshire* action were English; in fact, two of Cansulex's experts came from England and four from elsewhere (one from Canada, one from the United States, and two from Europe: from Scandinavia and Greece). This was drawn to the judge's attention at the end of his judgment. The judge then stated that he did not however regard this difference as significant; no doubt he had it in mind that all the owners' experts were from England.

Next, turning to the question of multiplicity of proceedings, he referred to the facts that Cansulex wished to join their insurers and possibly others as third parties, which they could only do in Canada, and that the shipowners wished to join MMTC as co-defendants with Cansulex, which would obviously be a sensible course if it could be achieved. As to the former, he gave the same weight to it as he did in the *Cambridgeshire* application; as to the latter, he gave less, because, whereas the relevant charterers were joined as co-defendants in the *Cambridgeshire* action, in the present case (following, it appears, lobbying by both sides) he felt that he should regard the shipowners' objective of joining MMTC as problematical.

Turning to the *Cambridgeshire* factor, which he regarded as crucial, the judge had this to say:

'But at the end of the day what seems to me important is this. [Counsel for Cansulex] submits that Cansulex, having been put to the trouble and expense of bringing their witnesses and senior executives here once, should not have to bear the same burden again. [Counsel for the plaintiff shipowners] replies that litigation is not like a football or cricket season, with one fixture at home and the other away. The trouble with such an attractive analogy or metaphor is that it tends to take one's eye off the ball, so to speak. Indeed, if all other things were equal, I should be inclined to hold that even-handed justice *would* be served best if one action were tried here and the other in Canada. But all other things are far from equal. The plaintiffs' solicitors have made all the dispositions and incurred all the expense for the trial of one action in England; they have engaged English counsel and educated them in the various topics on which expert evidence will be called; they have engaged English expert witnesses; and they have assembled vast numbers of documents. They have also, no doubt, educated themselves on the issues in the action. All that has been done on behalf of Cansulex as well, save that one of their expert witnesses is Canadian. If they now wish to start the process again in Canada, that is their choice. But it seems to me that the additional inconvenience and expense which would be thrust on the plaintiffs if this action were tried in Canada far outweighs the burden which would fall on Cansulex if they had to bring their witnesses and senior executives here a second time. There might have been an appeal from my decision on the *Cambridgeshire* applications, but there was not. I a appreciate that there are a number of significant points of distinction between the two cases, including the principal ones that I have mentioned. It may then in a sense be hard on Cansulex if the decision reached on the *Cambridgeshire* applications should have the effect of determining their application in this case. But in my judgment it does, in the circumstances and for the reasons that I have mentioned. Overall it would be wasteful in the extreme of talent, effort and money if the parties to this case were to have to start again in Canada. The case is a proper one for service

b out of the jurisdiction.' (Staughton J's emphasis).

On that basis, the judge decided not to accede to Cansulex's application. After he had prepared his judgment, evidence was placed before him on behalf of the shipowners with regard to the relevant limitation period applicable in British Columbia. It transpired that that period was two years, and had expired by November 1982, long before the hearing of Cansulex's application before the judge. The shipowners sought to rely on this

c point, apparently on the basis that to send the case back to British Columbia would deprive them of a legitimate juridical advantage in this country. However, the judge, having already concluded that the action should be tried here, irrespective of the time-bar point, did not think it necessary to consider that matter.

d ### (3) The decision of the Court of Appeal

In the Court of Appeal Neill LJ (who delivered the first judgment) referred to the speech of Lord Diplock in *Hadmor Productions Ltd v Hamilton* [1982] 1 All ER 1042 at 1046, [1983] 1 AC 191 at 220 and both he and Oliver LJ referred to the speech of Lord Brandon in *The Abidin Daver* [1984] 1 All ER 470 at 482, [1984] AC 398 at 420, which state the limited grounds on which an appellate court may interfere with the exercise of a trial judge's discretion. They also, like the judge, regarded themselves bound by the

e decision of the Court of Appeal in the *Ilyssia* case [1985] 1 Lloyd's Rep 107 to regard the difference between the speeches of Lord Diplock and Lord Wilberforce in the *Amin Rasheed* case [1983] 2 All ER 884, [1984] AC 50 as more apparent than real. Neill LJ reviewed the judge's assessment of the various factors as follows. With regard to the availability of witnesses, he felt that even on the judge's own analysis of the facts the convenience of the parties and the witnesses probably tilted the scales towards British

f Columbia as the forum, but certainly did not show that an English court was 'distinctly more suitable for the ends of justice'. On multiplicity of proceedings, he saw force in the criticism of counsel for Cansulex that this was at most a neutral factor, and certainly did not bring the scales down heavily on the side of England. On the relevance of the *Cambridgeshire* factor, while rejecting the primary submission of counsel for Cansulex that the *Cambridgeshire* litigation was wholly irrelevant, he considered that the judge

g attached far too much importance to it. He said ([1985] 2 Lloyd's Rep 116 at 124):

'The fact that the London solicitors who are presently acting are firms of great eminence and the further fact that members of these firms have acquired detailed knowledge about the shipment of sulphur cargoes from Vancouver are pointers to trial in England but should not be regarded as of decisive importance if other factors

h tilt the balance the other way.'

He held that it was impossible to conclude that the relevant factors, when taken together, showed that the English court was distinctly more suitable for the ends of justice. On this view of the case, it became necessary for him to consider the impact of the time-bar in British Columbia. On that he adopted the view of Oliver LJ that the existence of a

j time-bar was a neutral factor. He therefore decided to allow the appeal.

Oliver LJ, like Neill LJ, accepted that they were bound to follow the decision of the Court of Appeal in the *Ilyssia* case, on the basis of which he thought it right to follow the view of Lord Wilberforce in the *Amin Rasheed* case, and he did not therefore accept the submission of counsel for Cansulex that the judge had propounded the wrong test. He then considered the exercise of the judge's discretion. He reviewed the judge's assessment

of the availability of witnesses in considerable detail and pointed out that the judge had
proceeded on an erroneous assumption that all the experts in the *Cambridgeshire* action
were English. He went on to express the opinion that the supposed advantages of
England as a forum were, in this respect, far less clear-cut than the judge had appeared to
have imagined. In his opinion, the highest that it could be put on the shipowners' side
was that the factor of convenience of witnesses was neutral. He then considered the point
of multiplicity of proceedings, and rejected criticism of the judge's approach because the
point seemed to him to have played a neutral role in the judge's decision. Turning to the
Cambridgeshire factor, he was very critical of the judge's approach. He summarised the
principal criticism of counsel for Cansulex as follows ([1985] 2 Lloyd's Rep 116 at 133):

> 'But what, [counsel for Cansulex] asked forensically, does all that amount to
> beyond this, that the plaintiffs say, in effect, "we wish, for the purposes of our own
> and because it is convenient to do so, to retain the services of particular legal advisers
> and experts who happen to be resident and practising in England. Therefore, our
> desire to retain English legal advisers makes England a more appropriate forum for
> the hearing of the dispute".'

Oliver LJ accepted that criticism as well founded. He concluded that, in giving to the
Cambridgeshire action the decisive and conclusive weight that he did, the judge erred in
principle.

Finally, Oliver LJ considered the impact of the time-bar in British Columbia. He came
to the conclusion that the time-bar was not of itself a factor which ought to carry the day.
The difficulty in the way of the shipowners' argument that, by sending the case to be
tried in British Columbia, they would be deprived of a legitimate juridical advantage in
that the action was not time-barred in England, was that what was one side's advantage
must be another's disadvantage. This pointed, of course, to a time-bar being regarded as
a neutral factor. Even if, following the decision of Sheen J in *The Blue Wave* [1982] 1
Lloyd's Rep 151, it was to be treated as a factor on which the shipowners as plaintiffs
could rely unless they had acted unreasonably in allowing the time-bar to elapse in the
relevant foreign jurisdiction, that could be of no benefit to the shipowners in the present
case, because there was no evidence tendered on their behalf providing any satisfactory
explanation why no steps were taken to ascertain what the law of British Columbia was.
Furthermore, the factor of the time-bar in British Columbia could not in any event be
conclusive; because the evidence showed that it was open to the shipowners to sue
Cansulex in the federal court in any province in Canada. Accordingly, in agreement with
Neill LJ, he decided that the appeal of Cansulex should be allowed.

(4) Submissions of counsel

Before your Lordships, the shipowners submitted that the Court of Appeal, having
accepted that the judge applied the correct test, went beyond its limited power of review
of the exercise of the judge's discretion. The real reason for its intervention was that it
disagreed with the weight attached by the judge to the *Cambridgeshire* factor and was
then, it was submitted, over-astute to discover an error which would enable it to
substitute its own discretion for his. For Cansulex, on the other hand, it was submitted
that the Court of Appeal was fully entitled to interfere with the judge's exercise of his
discretion, substantially for the reasons given by it; but it was further submitted that, in
any event, both the judge and the Court of Appeal should have applied the more
stringent test set out in the passage from Lord Diplock's speech in the *Amin Rasheed* case
[1983] 2 All ER 884 at 893, [1984] AC 50 at 68 which, if correctly applied, should
certainly have led to the same order as that made by the Court of Appeal.

In considering the submissions of counsel, for whose assistance I am most grateful, it
is necessary to review the applicable principles. I say this for two particular reasons. First,
since the courts below have been troubled by apparent differences between observations
of Lord Diplock and Lord Wilberforce in the *Amin Rasheed* case, it is, I think, desirable
that this House should now resolve those differences. Second, since the question of the

a
relevance of a time-bar has now arisen in a number of cases, including the present, it is desirable that this House should give further consideration to the relevance of what has been called a 'legitimate personal or juridical advantage', with special reference to time-bars. But, in any event, the law on this subject is still in a state of development; and it is perhaps opportune to review the position at this stage, and in particular to give further consideration to the relationship between cases where jurisdiction has been founded as of right by service of proceedings on the defendant within the jurisdiction, but the

b
defendant seeks a stay of the proceedings on the ground of forum non conveniens, and cases where the court is invited to exercise its discretion, under RSC Ord 11, to give leave for service on the defendant out of the jurisdiction.

(5) *The fundamental principle*
In cases where jurisdiction has been founded as of right, ie where in this country the

c
defendant has been served with proceedings within the jurisdiction, the defendant may now apply to the court to exercise its discretion to stay the proceedings on the ground which is usually called forum non conveniens. That principle has for long been recognised in Scots law; but it has only been recognised comparatively recently in this country. In *The Abidin Daver* [1984] 1 All ER 470 at 476, [1984] AC 398 at 411 Lord Diplock stated that, on this point, English law and Scots law may now be regarded as indistinguishable.

d
It is proper therefore to regard the classic statement of Lord Kinnear in *Sim v Robinow* (1892) 19 R (Ct of Sess) 665 at 668 as expressing the principle now applicable in both jurisdictions. He said:

'. . . the plea can never be sustained unless the Court is satisfied that there is some other tribunal, having competent jurisdiction, in which the case may be tried more

e
suitably for the interests of all the parties and for the ends of justice.'

For earlier statements of the principle, in similar terms, see *Longworth v Hope* (1865) 3 Macph (Ct of Sess) 1049 at 1053 per the Lord President (McNeill) and *Clements v Macaulay* (1866) 4 Macph (Ct of Sess) 583 at 592 per the Lord Justice-Clerk (Inglis), and for a later statement, also in similar terms, see *Société du Gaz de Paris v SA de Navigation 'Les Armateurs Français'* 1926 SC (HL) 13 at 22 per Lord Sumner.

f
I feel bound to say that I doubt whether the Latin tag 'forum non conveniens' is apt to describe this principle. For the question is not one of convenience, but of the suitability or appropriateness of the relevant jurisdiction. However, the Latin tag (sometimes expressed as forum non conveniens and sometimes as forum conveniens) is so widely used to describe the principle, not only in England and Scotland, but in other Commonwealth jurisdictions and in the United States, that it is probably sensible to

g
retain it. But it is most important not to allow it to mislead us into thinking that the question at issue is one of 'mere practical convenience'. Such a suggestion was emphatically rejected by Lord Kinnear in *Sim v Robinow* (1892) 19 R (Ct of Sess) 665 at 668 and by Lord Dunedin, Lord Shaw and Lord Sumner in the *Société du Gaz* case 1926 SC (HL) 13 at 18, 19, and 22 respectively. Lord Dunedin said, with reference to the expressions forum non competens and forum non conveniens:

h
'In my view, "competent" is just as bad a translation for "*competens*" as "convenient" is for "*conveniens*". The proper translation for these Latin words, so far as this plea is concerned, is "appropriate".'

Lord Sumner referred to a phrase used by Lord Cowan in *Clements v Macaulay* (1866) 4 Macph (Ct of Sess) 583 at 594, viz 'more convenient and preferable for securing the ends

j
of justice', and said:

'. . . one cannot think of convenience apart from the convenience of the pursuer or the defender or the Court, and the convenience of all these three, as the cases show, is of little, if any, importance. If you read it as "more convenient, that is to say, preferable, for securing the ends of justice," I think the true meaning of the doctrine is arrived at. The object, under the words *"forum non conveniens"* is to find that *forum* which is the more suitable for the ends of justice, and is preferable *a* because pursuit of the litigation in that *forum* is more likely to secure those ends.'

In the light of these authoritative statements of the Scottish doctrine, I cannot help thinking that it is wiser to avoid use of the word 'convenience' and to refer rather, as Lord Dunedin did, to the *appropriate* forum.

b

(6) *How the principle is applied in cases of stay of proceedings*
    When the principle was first recognised in England, as it was (after a breakthrough in *The Atlantic Star, Atlantic Star (owners) v Bona Spes (owners)* [1973] 2 All ER 175, [1974] AC 436) in *MacShannon v Rockware Glass Ltd* [1978] 1 All ER 625, [1978] AC 795, it cannot be said that the members of this House spoke with one voice. This is not surprising; because the law on this topic was then in an early stage of a still continuing *c* development. The leading speech was delivered by Lord Diplock. He put the matter as follows ([1978] 1 All ER 625 at 630, [1978] AC 795 at 812):

> 'In order to justify a stay two conditions must be satisfied, one positive and the other negative: (a) the defendant must satisfy the court that there is another forum to whose jurisdiction he is amenable in which justice can be done between the *d* parties at substantially less inconvenience or expense, and (b) the stay must not deprive the plaintiff of a legitimate personal or juridical advantage which would be available to him if he invoked the jurisdiction of the English court.'

This passage has been quoted on a number of occasions in later cases in your Lordships' House. Even so, I do not think that Lord Diplock himself would have regarded this *e* passage as constituting an immutable statement of the law, but rather as a tentative statement at an early stage of a period of development. I say this for three reasons. First, Lord Diplock himself subsequently recognised that the mere existence of 'a legitimate personal or juridical advantage' of the plaintiff in the English jurisdiction would not be decisive: see *The Abidin Daver* [1984] 1 All ER 470 at 475, [1984] AC 398 at 410, where he recognised that a balance must be struck. Second, Lord Diplock also subsequently *f* recognised that no distinction is now to be drawn between Scottish and English law on this topic, and that it can now be said that English law has adopted the Scottish principle of forum non conveniens: see *The Abidin Daver* [1984] 1 All ER 470 at 476, [1984] AC 398 at 411. It is necessary therefore now to have regard to the Scottish authorities; and in this connection I refer in particular not only to statements of the fundamental principle, but also to the decision of your Lordships' House in the *Société du Gaz* case 1926 SC (HL) *g* 13. Third, it is necessary to strike a note of caution regarding the prominence given to 'a legitimate personal or juridical advantage' of the plaintiff, having regard to the decision of your Lordships' House in *Trendtex Trading Corp v Crédit Suisse* [1981] 3 All ER 520, [1982] AC 679, in which your Lordships unanimously approved the decision of the trial judge ([1980] 3 All ER 721) to exercise his discretion to stay an action brought in this country where there existed another appropriate forum, ie Switzerland, for the trial of *h* the action, even though by so doing he deprived the plaintiffs of an important advantage, viz the more generous English procedure of discovery, in an action involving allegations of fraud against the defendants.

    In my opinion, having regard to the authorities (including in particular the Scottish authorities), the law can at present be summarised as follows.

    (a) The basic principle is that a stay will only be granted on the ground of forum non *j* conveniens where the court is satisfied that there is some other available forum, having competent jurisdiction, which is the appropriate forum for the trial of the action, ie in which the case may be tried more suitably for the interests of all the parties and the ends of justice.

    (b) As Lord Kinnear's formulation of the principle indicates, in general the burden of proof rests on the defendant to persuade the court to exercise its discretion to grant a stay (see, e g, the *Société du Gaz* case 1926 SC (HL) 13 at 21 per Lord Sumner and Anton *Private International Law* (1967) p 150). It is, however, of importance to remember that each party will seek to establish the existence of certain matters which will assist him in persuading the court to exercise its discretion in his favour, and that in respect of any such matter the evidential burden will rest on the party who asserts its existence. Furthermore, if the court is satisfied that there is another available forum which is prima facie the appropriate forum for the trial of the action, the burden will then shift to the plaintiff to show that there are special circumstances by reason of which justice requires that the trial should nevertheless take place in this country (see para (f) below).

(c) The question being whether there is some other forum which is the appropriate forum for the trial of the action, it is pertinent to ask whether the fact that the plaintiff has, ex hypothesi, founded jurisdiction as of right in accordance with the law of this country, of itself gives the plaintiff an advantage in the sense that the English court will not lightly disturb jurisdiction so established. Such indeed appears to be the law in the United States, where 'the court hesitates to disturb the plaintiff's choice of forum and will not do so unless the balance of factors is strongly in favor of the defendant' (see Scoles and Hay *Conflict of Laws* (1982) p 366, and cases there cited); and also in Canada, where it has been stated that 'unless the balance is strongly in favor of the defendant, the plaintiff's choice of forum should rarely be disturbed' (see Castel *Conflict of Laws* (3rd edn, 1974) p 282). This is strong language. However, the United States and Canada are both federal states; and, where the choice is between competing jurisdictions within a federal state, it is readily understandable that a strong preference should be given to the forum chosen by the plaintiff on which jurisdiction has been conferred by the constitution of the country which includes both alternative jurisdictions.

A more neutral position was adopted by Lord Sumner in the *Société du Gaz* case 1926 SC (HL) 13 at 21, where he said:

'All that has been arrived at so far is that the burden of proof is upon the defender to maintain that plea. I cannot see that there is any presumption in favour of the pursuer.'

However, I think it right to comment that that observation was made in the context of a case where jurisdiction had been founded by the pursuer by invoking the Scottish principle that, in actions in personam, exceptionally jurisdiction may be founded by arrest of the defender's goods within the Scottish jurisdiction. Furthermore, there are cases where no particular forum can be described as the natural forum for the trial of the action. Such cases are particularly likely to occur in commercial disputes, where there can be pointers to a number of different jurisdictions (see, e g, *European Asian Bank AG v Punjab and Sind Bank* [1982] 2 Lloyd's Rep 356), or in Admiralty, in the case of collisions on the high seas. I can see no reason why the English court should not refuse to grant a stay in such a case, where jurisdiction has been founded as of right. It is significant that in all the leading English cases where a stay has been granted there has been another clearly more appropriate forum: in *The Atlantic Star* [1973] 2 All ER 175, [1974] AC 436 (Belgium), in *MacShannon's* case [1978] 1 All ER 625, [1978] AC 795 (Scotland), in *Trendtex Trading Corp v Crédit Suisse* [1981] 3 All ER 520, [1982] AC 679 (Switzerland) and in *The Abidin Daver* [1984] 1 All ER 470, [1984] AC 398 (Turkey). In my opinion, the burden resting on the defendant is not just to show that England is not the natural or appropriate forum for the trial, but to establish that there is another available forum which is clearly or distinctly more appropriate than the English forum. In this way, proper regard is paid to the fact that jurisdiction has been founded in England as of right (see *MacShannon's* case [1978] 1 All ER 625 at 636–637, [1978] AC 795 at 819–820 per Lord Salmon); and there is the further advantage that on a subject where comity is of importance it appears that there will be a broad consensus among major common law jurisdictions. I may add that if, in any case, the connection of the defendant with the English forum is a fragile one (for example if he is served with proceedings during a short visit to this country), it should be all the easier for him to prove that there is another clearly more appropriate forum for the trial overseas.

(d) Since the question is whether there exists some other forum which is clearly more appropriate for the trial of the action, the court will look first to see what factors there are which point in the direction of another forum. These are the factors which Lord Diplock described, in *MacShannon's* case [1978] 1 All ER 625 at 630, [1978] AC 795 at 812, as indicating that justice can be done in the other forum at 'substantially less inconvenience or expense'. Having regard to the anxiety expressed in your Lordships' House in the *Société du Gaz* case 1926 SC (HL) 13 concerning the use of the word 'convenience' in this context, I respectfully consider that it may be more desirable, now that the English and Scottish principles are regarded as being the same, to adopt the expression used by Lord Keith in *The Abidin Daver* [1984] 1 All ER 470 at 479, [1984] AC 398 at 415 when he referred to the 'natural forum' as being 'that with which the action has the most real and substantial connection'. So it is for connecting factors in this sense that the court must first look; and these will include not only factors affecting convenience or expense (such as availability of witnesses), but also other factors such as the law governing the relevant transaction (as to which see *Crédit Chimique v James Scott Engineering Group Ltd* 1982 SLT 131), and the places where the parties respectively reside or carry on business.

(e) If the court concludes at that stage that there is no other available forum which is clearly more appropriate for the trial of the action, it will ordinarily refuse a stay: see, e g, the decision of the Court of Appeal in *European Asian Bank AG v Punjab and Sind Bank* [1982] 2 Lloyd's Rep 356. It is difficult to imagine circumstances when, in such a case, a stay may be granted.

(f) If, however, the court concludes at that stage that there is some other available forum which prima facie is clearly more appropriate for the trial of the action, it will ordinarily grant a stay unless there are circumstances by reason of which justice requires that a stay should nevertheless not be granted. In this inquiry, the court will consider all the circumstances of the case, including circumstances which go beyond those taken into account when considering connecting factors with other jurisdictions. One such factor can be the fact, if established objectively by cogent evidence, that the plaintiff will not obtain justice in the foreign jurisdiction: see *The Abidin Daver* [1984] 1 All ER 470 at 476, [1984] AC 398 at 411 per Lord Diplock, a passage which now makes plain that, on this inquiry, the burden of proof shifts to the plaintiff. How far other advantages to the plaintiff in proceeding in this country may be relevant in this connection, I shall have to consider at a later stage.

(7) *How the principle is applied in cases where the court exercises its discretionary power under RSC Ord 11*

As I have already indicated, an apparent difference of view is to be found in the speeches of Lord Diplock and Lord Wilberforce in the *Amin Rasheed* case [1983] 2 All ER 884 at 891, 893, 896, [1984] AC 50 at 65–66, 68, 72. In that case Lord Diplock said:

'. . . the jurisdiction exercised by an English court over a foreign corporation which has no place of business in this country, as a result of granting leave under Ord 11, r 1(1)(*f*) for service out of the jurisdiction of a writ on that corporation, is an exorbitant jurisdiction, ie it is one which, under general English conflict rules, an English court would not recognise as possessed by any foreign court in the absence of some treaty providing for such recognition. Comity thus dictates that the judicial discretion to grant leave under this paragraph of Ord 11, r 1(1) should be exercised with circumspection in cases where there exists an alternative forum, viz the courts of the foreign country where the proposed defendant does carry on business, and whose jurisdiction would be recognised under the English conflict rules.'

Again, he said:

'. . . the onus under Ord 11, r 4(2) of making it "sufficiently appear to the Court that the case is a proper one for service out of the jurisdiction under this Order" lies

on the would-be plaintiff. Refusal to grant leave in a case falling within r $1(1)(f)$
does not deprive him of the opportunity of obtaining justice, because ex hypothesi
there exists an alternative forum, the courts of the country where the proposed
defendant has its place of business where the contract was made, which would be
recognised by the English courts as having jurisdiction over the matter in dispute
and whose judgment would be enforceable in England. The exorbitance of the
jurisdiction sought to be invoked where reliance is based exclusively on r $1(1)(f)(iii)$
is an important factor to be placed in the balance against granting leave. It is a factor
that is capable of being outweighed if the would-be plaintiff can satisfy the English
court that justice either could not be obtained by him in the alternative forum; or
could only be obtained at excessive cost, delay or inconvenience.'

In contrast, Lord Wilberforce said:

'RSC Ord 11, r 1(1) merely states that, given one of the stated conditions, such
service is permissible, and it is still necessary for the plaintiff (in this case the assured)
to make it "sufficiently appear to the Court that the case is a proper one for service
out of the jurisdiction under this Order" (RSC Ord 11, r 4(2)). The rule does not
state the considerations by which the court is to decide whether the case is a proper
one, and I do not think we can get much assistance from cases where it is sought to
stay an action started in this country, or to enjoin the bringing of proceedings
abroad. The situations are different (compare the observations of Stephenson LJ in
Aratra Potato Co Ltd v Egyptian Navigation Co, The El Amria [1981] 2 Lloyd's Rep 119
at 129). The intention must be to impose on the plaintiff the burden of showing
good reasons why service of a writ, calling for appearance before an English court,
should, in the circumstances, be permitted on a foreign defendant. In considering
this question the court must take into account the nature of the dispute, the legal
and practical issues involved, such questions as local knowledge, availability of
witnesses and their evidence and expense.'

In *Ilyssia Cia Naviera SA v Bamaodah* [1985] 1 Lloyd's Rep 107, the Court of Appeal had
to consider the apparent difference between the two approaches expressed by Lord
Diplock and Lord Wilberforce. Ackner LJ resolved the difference as follows (at 113):

'[Counsel for the defendant] submits that Lord Diplock's statement was intended
to be an exhaustive one. When reliance is based exclusively upon r. $1(1)(f)(iii)$, it is
only capable of being outweighed if the would-be plaintiff can satisfy the English
court that either justice cannot be obtained by him in the alternative forum or could
only be obtained at excessive cost, delay or inconvenience. Like Mr. Justice
Staughton, I do not accept that submission. As I read the speech in the context of
that case as a whole Lord Diplock was emphasizing that where exclusive reliance is
placed upon r. $1(1)(f)(iii)$ then the burden of showing good reasons justifying
service out of the jurisdiction is a particularly heavy one, and he illustrated this by
the examples which he gave of the situations which were capable of tipping the
balance in favour of the granting of leave. Thus construed, as the learned Judge
points out, there is no conflict between Lord Diplock's statement and that of Lord
Wilberforce . . . Lord Wilberforce there states that in order to decide whether the
case is a proper one the Court must take into account the nature of the dispute, the
legal and practical issues involved, such questions as local knowledge, availability of
witnesses and their evidence and expense.'

May LJ spoke in similar terms (at 118). The practical effect was, however, as is reflected
in the judgment of Oliver LJ in the present case, that the statement of principle of Lord
Wilberforce was accepted as being the applicable principle.

With that conclusion, I respectfully agree; but I wish to add some observations of my
own. The first is this. Lord Wilberforce said that he did not think that we can get much
assistance from cases where it is sought to stay an action started in this country, or to

enjoin the bringing of proceedings abroad; in this connection he referred to certain observations of Stephenson LJ in *Aratra Potato Co Ltd v Egyptian Navigation Co, The El Amria* [1981] 2 Lloyd's Rep 119 at 129. It is right to point out that, in the relevant passage in his judgment in that case, Stephenson LJ was only expressing caution with regard to assimilating cases of a stay to enforce a foreign jurisdiction clause with cases of a stay on the principle of forum non conveniens under *MacShannon*'s case. He was not addressing himself to the question of the applicable principles under RSC Ord 11, and, while sharing Lord Wilberforce's concern about help to be derived, in Ord 11 cases, from cases where an injunction is sought to restrain proceedings abroad, I respectfully doubt whether similar concern should be expressed about help to be derived from cases of forum non conveniens. I cannot help remarking on the fact that when Lord Wilberforce came, at the end of the passage from his speech which I have quoted, to state the applicable principle, his statement of principle bears a marked resemblance to the principles applicable in forum non conveniens cases. It seems to me inevitable that the question in both groups of cases must be, at bottom, that expressed by Lord Kinnear in *Sim v Robinow* (1892) 19 R (Ct of Sess) 665 at 668, viz to identify the forum in which the case can be suitably tried for the interests of all the parties and for the ends of justice. That being said, it is desirable to identify the distinctions between the two groups of cases. These, as I see it, are threefold. The first is that, as Lord Wilberforce indicated, in the Ord 11 cases the burden of proof rests on the plaintiff, whereas in the forum non conveniens cases that burden rests on the defendant. A second, and more fundamental, point of distinction (from which the first point of distinction in fact flows) is that in the Ord 11 cases the plaintiff is seeking to persuade the court to exercise its discretionary power to permit service on the defendant outside the jurisdiction. Statutory authority has specified the particular circumstances in which that power *may be* exercised, but leaves it to the court to decide whether to exercise its discretionary power in a particular case, while providing that leave shall not be granted 'unless it shall be made sufficiently to appear to the Court that the case is a proper one for service out of the jurisdiction' (see RSC Ord 11, r 4(2)).

Third, it is at this point that special regard must be had for the fact stressed by Lord Diplock in the *Amin Rasheed* case [1983] 2 All ER 884 at 891, [1984] AC 50 at 65 that the jurisdiction exercised under Ord 11 may be 'exorbitant'. This has long been the law. In *Société Générale de Paris v Dreyfus Bros* (1885) 29 Ch D 239 at 242–243 Pearson J said:

> '. . . it becomes a very serious question . . . whether this Court ought to put a foreigner, who owes no allegiance here, to the inconvenience and annoyance of being brought to contest his rights in this country, and I for one say, most distinctly, that I think this Court ought to be exceedingly careful before it allows a writ to be served out of the jurisdiction.'

That statement was subsequently approved on many occasions, notably by Farwell LJ in *The Hagen* [1908] P 189 at 201, [1908–10] All ER Rep 21 at 26 and by Lord Simonds in your Lordships' House in *Tyne Improvement Comrs v Armement Anversois SA, The Brabo* [1949] 1 All ER 294 at 305, [1949] AC 326 at 350. The effect is, not merely that the burden of proof rests on the plaintiff to persuade the court that England is the appropriate forum for the trial of the action, but that he has to show that this is clearly so. In other words, the burden is, quite simply, the obverse of that applicable where a stay is sought of proceedings started in this country as of right.

Even so, a word of caution is necessary. I myself feel that the word 'exorbitant' is, as used in the present context, an old-fashioned word which perhaps carries unfortunate overtones; it means no more than that the exercise of the jurisdiction is extraordinary in the sense explained by Lord Diplock in the *Amin Rasheed* case [1983] 2 All ER 884 at 891, [1984] AC 50 at 65. Furthermore, in Ord 11 cases, the defendant's place of residence may be no more than a tax haven to which no great importance should be attached. It is also significant to observe that the circumstances specified in Ord 11, r 1(1), as those in which the court may exercise its discretion to grant leave to serve proceedings on the defendant outside the jurisdiction, are of great variety, ranging from cases where, one would have

thought, the discretion would normally be exercised in favour of granting leave (eg
a where the relief sought is an injunction ordering the defendant to do or refrain from
doing something within the jurisdiction) to cases where the grant of leave is far more
problematical. In addition, the importance to be attached to any particular ground
invoked by the plaintiff may vary from case to case. For example, the fact that English
law is the putative proper law of the contract may be of very great importance (as in *BP
Exploration Co (Libya) Ltd v Hunt* [1976] 3 All ER 879, [1976] 1 WLR 788, where, in my
b opinion, Kerr J rightly granted leave to serve proceedings on Mr Hunt out of the
jurisdiction); or it may be of little importance as seen in the context of the whole case. In
these circumstances, it is, in my judgment, necessary to include both the residence or
place of business of the defendant and the relevant ground invoked by the plaintiff as
factors to be considered by the court when deciding whether to exercise its discretion to
grant leave; but, in so doing, the court should give to such factors the weight which, in
c all the circumstances of the case, it considers to be appropriate.

(8) *Treatment of 'a legitimate personal or juridical advantage'*
     Clearly, the mere fact that the plaintiff has a legitimate personal or juridical advantage
in proceedings in England cannot be decisive. As Lord Sumner said of the parties in the
Société du Gaz case 1926 SC (HL) 13 at 22:

d   'I do not see how one can guide oneself profitably by endeavouring to conciliate
     and promote the interests of both these antagonists, except in that ironical sense, in
     which one says that it is in the interests of both that the case should be tried in the
     best way and in the best tribunal, and that the best man should win.'

Indeed, as Oliver LJ pointed out in his judgment in the present case, an advantage to the
e plaintiff will ordinarily give rise to a comparable disadvantage to the defendant; and
simply to give the plaintiff his advantage at the expense of the defendant is not consistent
with the objective approach inherent in Lord Kinnear's statement of principle in *Sim v
Robinow* (1892) 19 R (Ct of Sess) 665 at 668.
     The key to the solution of this problem lies, in my judgment, in the underlying
fundamental principle. We have to consider where the case may be tried 'suitably for the
f interests of all the parties and for the ends of justice'. Let me consider the application of
that principle in relation to advantages which the plaintiff may derive from invoking the
English jurisdiction. Typical examples are: damages awarded on a higher scale; a more
complete procedure of discovery; a power to award interest; a more generous limitation
period. Now, as a general rule, I do not think that the court should be deterred from
granting a stay of proceedings, or from exercising its discretion against granting leave
g under RSC Ord 11, simply because the plaintiff will be deprived of such an advantage,
provided that the court is satisfied that substantial justice will be done in the available
appropriate forum. Take, for example, discovery. We know that there is a spectrum of
systems of discovery applicable in various jurisdictions, ranging from limited discovery
available in civil law countries on the continent of Europe to the very generous pre-trial
oral discovery procedure applicable in the United States of America. Our procedure lies
h somewhere in the middle of this spectrum. No doubt each of these systems has its virtues
and vices; but, generally speaking, I cannot see that, objectively, injustice can be said to
have been done if a party is, in effect, compelled to accept one of these well-recognised
systems applicable in the appropriate forum overseas. In this, I recognise that we appear
to be differing from the approach presently prevailing in the United States: see, eg, the
recent opinion of Judge Keenan in *Re Union Carbide Corp* (12 May 1986) in the District
j Court for the Southern District of New York, where a stay of proceedings in New York,
commenced on behalf of Indian plaintiffs against Union Carbide arising out of the tragic
disaster in Bhopal, India in December 1984, was stayed subject to, inter alia, the condition
that Union Carbide was subject to discovery under the model of the United States Federal
Rules of Civil Procedure after appropriate demand by the plaintiff. But in the *Trendtex*
case [1981] 3 All ER 520, [1982] AC 679 this House thought it right that a stay of

proceedings in this country should be granted where the appropriate forum was Switzerland, even though the plaintiffs were thereby deprived of the advantage of the more extensive English procedure of discovery of documents in a case of fraud. Then take the scale on which damages are awarded. Suppose that two parties have been involved in a road accident in a foreign country, where both were resident, and where damages are awarded on a scale substantially lower than those awarded in this country. I do not think that an English court would, in ordinary circumstances, hesitate to stay proceedings brought by one of them against the other in this country merely because he would be deprived of a higher award of damages here.

But the underlying principle requires that regard must be had to the interests of all the parties and the ends of justice; and these considerations may lead to a different conclusion in other cases. For example, it would not, I think, normally be wrong to allow a plaintiff to keep the benefit of security obtained by commencing proceedings here, while at the same time granting a stay of proceedings in this country to enable the action to proceed in the appropriate forum. Such a conclusion is, I understand, consistent with the manner in which the process of saisie conservatoire is applied in civil law countries; and cf s 26 of the Civil Jurisdiction and Judgments Act 1982, now happily in force. Again, take the example of cases concerned with time-bars. Here a special problem arises from the fact that, in English law, limitation is classified as a procedural rather than as a substantive matter. Let me consider how the principle of forum non conveniens should be applied in a case in which the plaintiff has started proceedings in England where his claim was not time-barred, but there is some other jurisdiction which, in the opinion of the court, is clearly more appropriate for the trial of the action, but where the plaintiff has not commenced proceedings and where his claim is now time-barred. Now, to take some extreme examples, suppose that the plaintiff allowed the limitation period to elapse in the appropriate jurisdiction, and came here simply because he wanted to take advantage of a more generous time-bar applicable in this country; or suppose that it was obvious that the plaintiff should have commenced proceedings in the appropriate jurisdiction, and yet he did not trouble to issue a protective writ there; in cases such as these, I cannot see that the court should hesitate to stay the proceedings in this country, even though the effect would be that the plaintiff's claim would inevitably be defeated by a plea of the time-bar in the appropriate jurisdiction. Indeed, a strong theoretical argument can be advanced for the proposition that, if there is another clearly more appropriate forum for the trial of action, a stay should generally be granted even though the plaintiff's action would be time-barred there. But, in my opinion, this is a case where practical justice should be done. And practical justice demands that, if the court considers that the plaintiff acted reasonably in commencing proceedings in this country, and that, although it appears that (putting on one side the time-bar point) the appropriate forum for the trial of the action is elsewhere than England, the plaintiff did not act unreasonably in failing to commence proceedings (for example by issuing a protective writ) in that jurisdiction within the limitation period applicable there, it would not, I think, be just to deprive the plaintiff of the benefit of having started proceedings within the limitation period applicable in this country. This approach is consistent with that of Sheen J in The Blue Wave [1982] 1 Lloyd's Rep 151. It is not to be forgotten that, by making its jurisdiction available to the plaintiff, even the discretionary jurisdiction under RSC Ord 11, the courts of this country have provided the plaintiff with an opportunity to start proceedings here; accordingly, if justice demands, the court should not deprive the plaintiff of the benefit of having complied with the time-bar in this country. Furthermore, as the applicable principles become more clearly established and better known, it will, I suspect, become increasingly difficult for plaintiffs to prove lack of negligence in this respect. The fact that the court has been asked to exercise its discretion under RSC Ord 11, rather than that the plaintiff has served proceedings on the defendant in this country as of right, is, I consider, only relevant to consideration of the plaintiff's conduct in failing to save the time-bar in the other relevant alternative jurisdiction. The appropriate order,

where the application of the time-bar in the foreign jurisdiction is dependent on its
a   invocation by the defendant, may well be to make it a condition of the grant of a stay or
the exercise of discretion against giving leave to serve out of the jurisdiction, that the
defendant should waive the time-bar in the foreign jurisdiction; this is apparently the
practice in the United States of America.

(9) *Application of the principles to the facts of the present case*
b   The judge proceeded on the basis that the relevant test was that 'if the English court is
shown to be distinctly more suitable for the ends of justice, then the case is a proper one
for service out of the jurisdiction'. The applicable principles are, I believe, as I have stated
them to be; and the judge's approach was in accordance with those principles. I am
therefore unable to accept the submission made on behalf of Cansulex that there was any
material error of principle on the part of the judge.
c   I turn then to the question whether the Court of Appeal was entitled to interfere with
the judge's exercise of his discretion. First, I take the criticism of the judge's assessment
of the factor of availability of witnesses. It was said that he erred in thinking that all
Cansulex's expert witnesses in the *Cambridgeshire* action were from England, whereas in
fact two were from England, and four were from elsewhere. However, as I have recorded,
this was drawn to his attention at the end of his judgment: he then took into account the
d   true position, and said that this difference was not of significance. No doubt, in making
that observation, he had it in mind that all the owners' expert witnesses in the
Cambridgeshire action were from England. Next, Neill LJ commented ([1985] 2 Lloyd's
Rep 116 at 123):

'. . . even on [the judge's] own analysis of the facts the convenience of the parties
and the witnesses probably tilted the scales towards British Columbia as the forum,
e   but certainly did not show that an English court would be "distinctly more suitable
for the ends of justice".'

Similar observations were made by Oliver LJ. For my part, I consider, with all respect,
that these comments were not justified. At this stage, the judge did not have to apply the
overall test, but merely to assess the merits of the particular factor under consideration;
f   and I cannot help but think that the judge, with all his experience derived from hearing
a substantial part of the *Cambridgeshire* action, was better placed to make an assessment of
this factor than the Court of Appeal.
Turning to the factor of multiplicity of proceedings, the judge referred to the
possibility of MMTC being joined as co-defendants in the English proceedings as
problematical. Before the Court of Appeal counsel submitted on behalf of Cansulex that
g   the other proceedings were at most a neutral factor and certainly did not bring the scales
down on the side of England. Neill LJ saw force in this criticism. But, once again, the
judge did not have to decide, and did not decide, that this particular factor was decisive
of the case. Moreover, if (as I think) the judge gave weight to this factor, he was, in my
judgment, entitled to do so. There is much to be said, in the interests of justice, in favour
of the shipowners' claims against both Cansulex and MMTC being tried in the same
h   proceedings; and, having regard to the advice given to MMTC by their solicitors, there
was a prospect that, if it was decided that the case should be heard in England, MMTC
would, acting in their own interests, accept their own solicitors' advice. Indeed, if this
were to happen, it might also be agreed that a claim over by MMTC against Cansulex
should be included in the same proceedings, rather than be arbitrated in London under
an arbitration clause in the sale contract.
j   But the crucial point, in the judge's view, was the *Cambridgeshire* factor. This was
regarded, certainly by Neill LJ, as relevant; and in this I find myself to be in agreement.
The criticism of the judge's view of this factor goes, therefore, to its weight, as Neill LJ
indicated when he said that it seemed to him that the judge attached far too much
importance to this factor. With all respect, however, when I read the judgments of both

Oliver and Neill LJJ, I consider that they underrated it. I believe that anyone who has been involved, as counsel, in very heavy litigation of this kind, with a number of experts *a* on both sides and difficult scientific questions involved, knows only too well what the learning curve is like: how much information and knowledge has to be, and is, absorbed, not only by the lawyers but really by the whole team, including both lawyers and experts, as they learn about the interrelation of law, fact and scientific knowledge, having regard to the contentions advanced by both sides in the case, and identify in their minds the crucial matters on which attention has to be focused, why these are the crucial matters, *b* and how they are to be assessed. The judge in the present case has considerable experience of litigation of this kind, and is well aware of what is involved. He was, in my judgment, entitled to take the view (as he did) that this matter was not merely of advantage to the shipowners, but also constituted an advantage which was not balanced by a countervailing equal disadvantage to Cansulex, and (more pertinently) further to take the view that having experienced teams of lawyers and experts available on both sides of the litigation, *c* who had prepared for and fought a substantial part of the *Cambridgeshire* action for Cansulex (among others) on one side and the relevant owners on the other, would contribute to efficiency, expedition and economy, and he could have added, in my opinion, both to assisting the court to reach a just resolution, and to promoting a possibility of settlement, in the present case. This is not simply a matter, as Oliver LJ suggested, of financial advantage to the shipowners: it is a matter which can, and should, *d* properly be taken into account, in a case of this kind, in the objective interests of justice.

For these reasons alone, I am of the opinion that this is a classic example of a case where the appellate court has simply formed a different view of the weight to be given to the various factors, and that this was not, therefore, an appropriate case for interfering with the exercise of the judge's discretion. But, in addition, there are two other factors which the judge could, but did not, take into account, in support of the conclusion which he in *e* fact reached. First, he was, in my judgment, entitled to take into account, in assessing the *Cambridgeshire* factor, the fact that, although the owners in the two cases were different, the solicitors for the owners were in both cases instructed by the same insurers; and he was also entitled to take into account that the insurers of the shipowners in the present case are managed in England. Usually this is a matter of no concern in English litigation; because, in subrogation claims, the action is in this country (unlike other countries) *f* brought in the name of the assured, and the rights being enforced are the rights of the assured. But in the case of an application such as that in the present case, it is shutting one's eyes to reality to ignore the fact that it is the insurers who are financing the litigation and are dominus litis; and this is, in my view, a relevant factor to be taken into account (see the *Société du Gaz* case 1926 SC (HL) 13 at 20 per Lord Sumner). Second, it was a relevant factor that this litigation was being fought under a contract of which the *g* putative governing law was English law, and that this was by no means an insignificant factor in the present case, since there was not only a dispute as to the effect of the bill of lading contract (as to which, as I have already recorded, there appears to be some difference of opinion between English and Canadian judges), but also, it appears, as to the nature of the obligations under the contract in respect of what is usually called dangerous cargo. However, had the judge taken these matters into account, they would *h* only have reinforced the conclusion which he in fact reached.

(10) *The effect of the time-bar in British Columbia*

On the view of the case which I have formed, it is not strictly necessary to consider the effect of the time-bar in British Columbia; but, since the point has been fully argued *j* before us, I propose briefly to express my views on it.

First, I cannot think that the fact (if it be the case) that the shipowners' claim was not time-barred if brought in the federal courts of Canada in provinces other than British Columbia (one suggestion was the federal court sitting in the neighbouring Province of

Alberta) was of any relevance. On this, I accept the submission of the shipowners that it
_a_   cannot be in the interest of the parties or in the interests of justice that the action should
effectively be remitted to a forum which cannot be described as appropriate for the trial
of the action.

Second, I do not think that the discretionary power which is, I understand, vested in
the courts of British Columbia to waive the time-bar, is relevant in this case. The point is
simply that the shipowners' claim is not time-barred in England but may be treated as
_b_   time-barred in British Columbia. In these circumstances, the question inevitably arises
whether the English court, if it were minded to set aside the leave to serve proceedings
on Cansulex out of the jurisdiction, should do so on the condition that Cansulex should
waive any right to rely on the time-bar applicable in British Columbia.

So it is necessary to consider whether justice required the imposition of such a term.
The evidence before the Court of Appeal showed that neither the shipowners nor their
_c_   legal advisers were aware of the two-year limitation period applicable in British Columbia.
Cansulex did not draw the matter to their attention in their affidavit evidence; the
shipowners' solicitors simply stumbled on it when investigating the availability of
suitable lawyers in Vancouver. Next, although Cansulex had applied to the English court
to set aside the proceedings in the _Cambridgeshire_ action, they had not appealed from the
judge's adverse decision on the point and the _Cambridgeshire_ action had proceeded to trial. ·
_d_   Furthermore, had the shipowner's solicitors considered the matter, experience would
have indicated that, having regard to the law as generally understood to prevail before
the decision of this House in the _Amin Rasheed_ case [1983] 2 All ER 884, [1984] AC 50, in
which the speeches were delivered in July 1983, and to the prominence hitherto given to
legitimate personal and juridical advantages in the English jurisdiction (see, in particular,
the decisions of the Court of Appeal in _Britannia Steamship Insurance Association Ltd v_
_e_   _Ausonia Assicurazioni SpA_ [1984] 2 Lloyd's Rep 98 and the _Ilyssia_ case [1985] 1 Lloyd's Rep
107), it was improbable that any different conclusion would be reached on an application
to set aside the leave granted in the present case. In this connection, it is to be observed
that the shipowners' cause of action against Cansulex in the present case must have
accrued in November 1980 (when the loading of the cargo on board the Spiliada in
Vancouver was completed) and so was prima facie time-barred in British Columbia by
_f_   November 1982, nine months before the decision of this House in the _Amin Rasheed_ case.
In my judgment, had the point arisen, I would have been minded to hold that, in all the
circumstances of the case, the shipowners had acted reasonably in commencing
proceedings in this country, and that they had not acted unreasonably in failing to
commence proceedings in British Columbia before the expiry of the limitation period
there. In these circumstances, had I agreed with the Court of Appeal that the judge erred
_g_   in the exercise of his discretion, I would nevertheless only have set aside the proceedings,
to enable proceedings to be brought in British Columbia, on the condition that Cansulex
should waive its right to rely on the time-bar in British Columbia.

However, for the reasons I have given I would allow the appeal with costs here and
below, and restore the order of Staughton J.

_h_

(11) _Postscipt_

I feel that I cannot conclude without paying tribute to the writings of jurists which
have assisted me in the preparation of this opinion. Although it may be invidious to do
so, I wish to single out for special mention articles by Mr Adrian Briggs 'Forum non
conveniens—now we are ten' (1983) 3 LS 74 and 'The Staying of Actions on the Ground
_j_   of "Forum Non Conveniens" in England Today' [1984] Lloyd's MCLQ 227, and the
article by Miss Rhona Schuz 'Controlling Forum-Shopping: The Impact of _MacShannon v_
Rockware Glass Ltd' (1986) 35 ICLQ 374. They will observe that I have not agreed with
them on all points; but even when I have disagreed with them, I have found their work
to be of assistance. For jurists are pilgrims with us on the endless road to unattainable

perfection; and we have it on the excellent authority of Geoffrey Chaucer that conversations among pilgrims can be most rewarding.

Appeal allowed.

Solicitors: *Holman Fenwick & Willan* (for the shipowners); *Linklaters & Paines* (for Cansulex).

Mary Rose Plummer   Barrister.

Practice Direction

CHANCERY DIVISION

Bankruptcy – Practice – Proof of continuing debt – Certificate – Bankruptcy Act 1914, s 5(2) – Insolvency Act 1986, s 271(1)(a) – Bankruptcy Rules 1952, r 167 – Insolvency Rules 1986, r 6.25(1).

On the hearing of a petition for a bankruptcy order, to satisfy the court that the debt on which the petition is founded has not been paid or secured or compounded for, the court will normally accept as sufficient a certificate signed by the person representing the petitioning creditor in the following form:

'I certify that I have/my firm has made inquiries of the petitioning creditor(s) within the last business day prior to the hearing/adjourned hearing and to the best of my knowledge and belief the debt on which the petition is founded is still due and owing and has not been paid or secured or compounded for (save as to   )

Signed.................... Dated............'

For the convenience of practitioners this certificate will be printed on the attendance slips. It will be filed after the hearing. A fresh certificate will be required on each adjourned hearing.

This practice note will take effect on 29 December 1986, when the Act and rules come into effect, in respect of all petitions heard on or after that date whether or not presented and filed earlier.

JOHN BRADBURN
25 November 1986   Chief Bankruptcy Registrar.